THE
ALL ENGLAND
LAW REPORTS

2002

Volume 2

Editor
CRAIG ROSE   Barrister

Butterworths
LexisNexis™

Members of the LexisNexis Group worldwide

United Kingdom	Butterworths Tolley, a Division of Reed Elsevier (UK) Ltd, Halsbury House, 35 Chancery Lane, LONDON, WC2A 1EL, and 4 Hill Street, EDINBURGH EH2 3JZ
Argentina	Abeledo Perrot, Jurisprudencia Argentina and Depalma, BUENOS AIRES
Australia	Butterworths, a Division of Reed International Books Australia Pty Ltd, CHATSWOOD, New South Wales
Austria	ARD Betriebsdienst and Verlag Orac, VIENNA
Canada	Butterworths Canada Ltd, MARKHAM, Ontario
Chile	Publitecsa and Conosur Ltda, SANTIAGO DE CHILE
Czech Republic	Orac sro, PRAGUE
France	Editions du Juris-Classeur SA, PARIS
Hong Kong	Butterworths Asia (Hong Kong), HONG KONG
Hungary	Hvg Orac, BUDAPEST
India	Butterworths India, NEW DELHI
Ireland	Butterworths (Ireland) Ltd, DUBLIN
Italy	Giuffré, MILAN
Malaysia	Malayan Law Journal Sdn Bhd, KUALA LUMPUR
New Zealand	LexisNexis Butterworths, WELLINGTON
Poland	Wydawnictwa Prawnicze PWN, WARSAW
Singapore	Butterworths Asia, SINGAPORE
South Africa	Butterworths Publishers (Pty) Ltd, DURBAN
Switzerland	Stämpfli Verlag AG, BERNE
USA	LexisNexis, DAYTON, Ohio

A CIP Catalogue record for this book is available from the British Library.

Printed and bound in Great Britain by William Clowes Ltd, Beccles and London

ISBN for the complete set of volumes: 0 406 85159 X
for this volume:

ISBN 0-406-95248-5

9 780406 952486

Visit Butterworths LexisNexis *direct* at www.butterworths.com

House of Lords

The Lord High Chancellor of Great Britain: Lord Irvine of Lairg

Lords of Appeal in Ordinary

Lord Bingham of Cornhill
Lord Slynn of Hadley
Lord Nicholls of Birkenhead
Lord Steyn
Lord Hoffmann
Lord Hope of Craighead

Lord Hutton
Lord Saville of Newdigate
Lord Hobhouse of Woodborough
Lord Millett
Lord Scott of Foscote
Lord Rodger of Earlsferry

Court of Appeal

The Lord High Chancellor of Great Britain

The Lord Chief Justice of England: Lord Woolf
(President of the Criminal Division)

The Master of the Rolls: Lord Phillips of Worth Matravers
(President of the Civil Division)

The President of the Family Division: Dame Elizabeth Butler-Sloss

The Vice-Chancellor: Sir Robert Andrew Morritt

Lords Justices of Appeal

Sir Paul Joseph Morrow Kennedy
Sir Simon Denis Brown (Vice-President of the
    Civil Division)
Sir Christopher Dudley Roger Rose
    (Vice-President of the Criminal Division)
Sir Peter Leslie Gibson
Sir Robin Ernest Auld
Sir Malcolm Thomas Pill
Sir William Aldous
Sir Alan Hylton Ward
Sir Konrad Hermann Theodor Schiemann
Sir Mathew Alexander Thorpe
Sir Mark Howard Potter
Sir Henry Brooke
Sir Igor Judge (Senior Presiding Judge for England
    and Wales)
Sir George Mark Waller
Sir John Frank Mummery
Sir Charles Barrie Knight Mantell
Sir John Murray Chadwick

Sir Robert Walker
Sir Richard Joseph Buxton
Sir Anthony Tristram Kenneth May
    (Vice-President of the Queen's
    Bench Division)
Sir Simon Lane Tuckey
Sir Anthony Peter Clarke
Sir John Grant McKenzie Laws
Sir Stephen John Sedley
Sir Jonathan Hugh Mance
Dame Brenda Marjorie Hale
Sir David Nicholas Ramsey Latham
Sir John William Kay
Sir Bernard Anthony Rix
Sir Jonathan Frederic Parker
Dame Mary Howarth Arden
Sir David Wolfe Keene
Sir John Anthony Dyson
Sir Andrew Centlivres Longmore
Sir Robert John Anderson Carnwath

High Court of Justice

The Lord High Chancellor of Great Britain
The Lord Chief Justice of England
The President of the Family Division
The Vice-Chancellor
The Senior Presiding Judge for England and Wales
The puisne judges of the High Court

Chancery Division

The Lord High Chancellor of Great Britain
The Vice-Chancellor

Sir Francis Mursell Ferris
Sir John Edmund Frederic Lindsay
Sir Edward Christopher Evans-Lombe
Sir Robin Raphael Hayim Jacob
Sir William Anthony Blackburne
Sir Gavin Anthony Lightman
Sir Colin Percy Farquharson Rimer
Sir Hugh Ian Lang Laddie
Sir Timothy Andrew Wigram Lloyd

Sir David Edmund Neuberger
Sir Andrew Edward Wilson Park
Sir Nicholas Richard Pumfrey
Sir Michael Christopher Campbell Hart
Sir Lawrence Anthony Collins
Sir Nicholas John Patten
Sir Terrence Michael Elkan Barnet Etherton
Sir Peter Winston Smith (appointed 15 April 2002)

Queen's Bench Division

The Lord Chief Justice of England

Sir Patrick Neville Garland
Sir Michael John Turner
Sir Richard George Rougier
Sir Stuart Neil McKinnon
Sir Thomas Scott Gillespie Baker
Sir Douglas Dunlop Brown
Sir Michael Morland
Sir Roger John Buckley
Sir Anthony Brian Hidden
Sir John Michael Wright
Sir Peter John Cresswell
Sir Christopher John Holland
Sir Richard Herbert Curtis
Dame Janet Hilary Smith
Sir Anthony David Colman
Sir John Thayne Forbes
Sir Michael Alexander Geddes Sachs
Sir Stephen George Mitchell
Sir Rodger Bell
Sir Michael Guy Vicat Harrison

Sir William Marcus Gage
Sir Thomas Richard Atkin Morison
Sir Andrew David Collins
Sir Maurice Ralph Kay
Sir Anthony Hooper
Sir Alexander Neil Logie Butterfield
Sir George Michael Newman
Sir David Anthony Poole
Sir Martin James Moore-Bick
Sir Gordon Julian Hugh Langley
Sir Roger John Laugharne Thomas
Sir Robert Franklyn Nelson
Sir Roger Grenfell Toulson
Sir Michael John Astill
Sir Alan George Moses
Sir Timothy Edward Walker
Sir David Eady
Sir Jeremy Mirth Sullivan
Sir David Herbert Penry-Davey
Sir Stephen Price Richards

[*continued on next page*]

Sir David William Steel
Sir Charles Antony St John Gray
Sir Nicolas Dusan Bratza
Sir Michael John Burton
Sir Rupert Matthew Jackson
Dame Heather Carol Hallett
Sir Patrick Elias
Sir Richard John Pearson Aikens
Sir Stephen Robert Silber
Sir John Bernard Goldring
Sir Peter Francis Crane
Dame Anne Judith Rafferty
Sir Geoffery Douglas Grigson
Sir Richard John Hedley Gibbs
Sir Richard Henry Quixano Henriques
Sir Stephen Miles Tomlinson
Sir Andrew Charles Smith

Sir Stanley Jeffrey Burnton
Sir Patrick James Hunt
Sir Christopher John Pitchford
Sir Brian Henry Leveson
Sir Duncan Brian Walter Ouseley
Sir Richard George Bramwell McCombe
Sir Raymond Evan Jack
Sir Robert Michael Owen
Sir Colin Crichton Mackay
Sir John Edward Mitting
Sir David Roderick Evans
Sir Nigel Anthony Lamert Davis
Sir Peter Henry Gross
Sir Brian Richard Keith
Sir Jeremy Lionel Cooke
Sir Richard Alan Field
Sir Christopher John Pitchers

Family Division

The President of the Family Division

Sir Robert Lionel Johnson
Dame Joyanne Winifred Bracewell
Sir Jan Peter Singer
Sir Nicholas Allan Roy Wilson
Sir Nicholas Peter Rathbone Wall
Sir Andrew Tristram Hammett Kirkwood
Sir Hugh Peter Derwyn Bennett
Sir Edward James Holman
Dame Mary Claire Hogg

Sir Christopher John Sumner
Sir Anthony Philip Gilson Hughes
Sir Arthur William Hessin Charles
Sir David Roderick Lessiter Bodey
Dame Jill Margaret Black
Sir James Lawrence Munby
Sir Paul James Duke Coleridge
Sir Mark Hedley

Official Judgment Numbers
and
Paragraph References

Since 11 January 2001, official judgment numbers have been given to all judgments delivered in the House of Lords, Privy Council, both divisions of the Court of Appeal and the Administrative Court. All such judgments have fixed paragraph numbering, as do judgments delivered on or after 11 January 2001 in those parts of the High Court which did not then adopt the system of official judgment numbers (see Practice Note (judgments: neutral citation) [2001] 1 All ER 193 for the Court of Appeal and the High Court). On 14 January 2002 the system of judgment numbers was extended to all parts of the High Court (see Practice Direction (High Court judgments: neutral citation) [2002] 1 All ER 351). We have adopted the following practice in respect of judgments with official judgment numbers and official paragraph numbering:

- The official judgment number is inserted immediately beneath the case name;
- Official paragraph numbers are in bold in square brackets;
- Holding references in the headnotes, and any other cross-references, are to an official paragraph number, not to a page of the report;
- When such a judgment is subsequently cited in another report,

(i) the official judgment number is inserted before the usual report citations in the case lists and on the first occasion when the case is cited in the text. Thereafter, only the report citations are given;

(ii) All 'at' references are to the official paragraph number rather than to a page of a report, with the paragraph number in square brackets but not in bold;

(iii) The 'at' reference is only given in conjunction with the first report cited; eg [2001] 4 All ER 159 at [16], [2001] AC 61. If an 'at' reference is included on the first occasion when the case is cited, it also appears alongside the official judgment number.

For the avoidance of doubt, these changes do not apply to reports of judgments delivered before 11 January 2001 or to the citation of such cases in other reports.

CITATION

These reports are cited thus:

[2002] 2 All ER

REFERENCES

These reports contain references to the following major works of legal reference described in the manner indicated below.

Halsbury's Laws of England

The reference 14 *Halsbury's Laws* (4th edn) para 185 refers to paragraph 185 on page 90 of volume 14 of the fourth edition of *Halsbury's Laws of England*.

The reference 15 *Halsbury's Laws* (4th edn reissue) para 355 refers to paragraph 355 on page 283 of reissue volume 15 of the fourth edition of *Halsbury's Laws of England*.

The reference 7(1) *Halsbury's Laws* (4th edn) (1996 reissue) para 9 refers to paragraph 9 on page 24 of the 1996 reissue of volume 7(1) of the fourth edition of *Halsbury's Laws of England*.

Halsbury's Statutes of England and Wales

The reference 26 *Halsbury's Statutes* (4th edn) 734 refers to page 734 of volume 26 of the fourth edition of *Halsbury's Statutes of England and Wales*.

The reference 40 *Halsbury's Statutes* (4th edn) (2001 reissue) 269 refers to page 269 of the 2001 reissue of volume 40 of the fourth edition of *Halsbury's Statutes of England and Wales*.

Halsbury's Statutory Instruments

The reference 14 *Halsbury's Statutory Instruments* (2001 issue) 201 refers to page 201 of the 2001 issue of volume 14 of the grey volumes series of *Halsbury's Statutory Instruments*.

Cases reported in volume 2

Page

Digest of cases reported in volume 2

xv

House of Lords petitions

This list, which covers the period 28 November 2001 to 30 May 2002, sets out all cases which have formed the subject of a report in the All England Law Reports in which an Appeal Committee of the House of Lords has, subsequent to the publication of that report, refused leave to appeal. Where the result of a petition for leave to appeal was known prior to the publication of the relevant report a note of that result appears at the end of the report.

Middlesborough BC v Safeer [2001] 4 All ER 630. Leave to appeal refused 6 February 2002 (Lord Nicholls of Birkenhead, Lord Hope of Craighead and Lord Rodger of Earlsferry).

Burman v Mount Cook Land Ltd [2002] 1 All ER 144. Leave to appeal refused 25 March 2002 (Lord Bingham of Cornhill, Lord Hope of Craighead and Lord Scott of Foscote).

Bank of China v NBM LLC [2001] 4 All ER 954. Leave to appeal refused 26 Mach 2002 (Lord Steyn of Hadley, Lord Hutton and Lord Millett).

R v Criminal Injuries Compensation Appeals Panel, ex p August [2001] 2 All ER 874. Leave to appeal refused 26 March 2002 (Lord Steyn of Hadley, Lord Hutton and Lord Millett).

BHP Petroleum Great Britain Ltd v Chesterfield Properties Ltd [2001] 2 All ER 914. Leave to appeal refused 22 April 2002 (Lord Steyn of Hadley, Lord Hutton and Lord Rodger of Earlsferry).

Loutchansky v Times Newspapers Ltd (No 2) [2002] 1 All ER 652. Leave to appeal refused 30 April 2002 (Lord Nicholls of Birkenhead, Lord Hoffman and Lord Hobhouse of Woodborough).

Loutchansky v Times Newspapers Ltd [2001] 4 All ER 115. Leave to appeal refused 16 May 2002 (Lord Hutton, Lord Mackay of Clashfern).

A v B (a company) [2002] 2 All ER 545. Leave to appeal refused 30 May 2002 (Lord Bingham of Cornhill, Lord Hope of Craighead and Lord Scott of Foscote).

Hatton v Sutherland
Barber v Somerset County Council
Jones v Sandwell Metropolitan Borough Council
Bishop v Baker Refractories Ltd
[2002] EWCA Civ 76

COURT OF APPEAL, CIVIL DIVISION
BROOKE, HALE AND KAY LJJ
27–30 NOVEMBER 2001, 5 FEBRUARY 2002

e

Negligence – Duty to take care – Employer – Duty to protect employee from foreseeable risk of danger to health – Liability for employee's psychiatric illness caused by stress at work – Guidance.

f In each of four conjoined appeals, the defendant employer appealed against a finding of liability for an employee's psychiatric illness caused by stress at work. Two of the claimants were teachers in public sector comprehensive schools; the third was an administrative assistant at a local authority training centre; while the fourth was a raw material operative in a factory. In the first two appeals, the claimants had not told their employers that their health was suffering due to overwork. In contrast, the claimant in the third appeal, J, had twice formally

g complained to her employer that her health was being harmed by problems at work, but no extra help had been provided even though the employer had acknowledged that such help should have been provided. In the fourth appeal, the claimant had been unable to cope with a reorganisation at work, but had not informed his employer that his doctor had advised him to change his job. On the

h appeals, the Court of Appeal considered the principles that governed such claims. In particular, it considered whether they were subject to any special control mechanisms or whether the ordinary principles of employer's liability applied; the factors to be taken into account by the court in determining whether the harm was reasonably foreseeable; whether any occupations were to be regarded

j as so inherently stressful that resulting physical or psychological harm was always foreseeable; the circumstances in which the employer would be in breach of his duty; causation; and the apportionment of damages in cases where the harm suffered had more than one cause.

Held – (1) There were no special control mechanisms applying to claims for psychiatric (or physical) illness or injury arising from the stress of doing the work

that the employee was required to do. The ordinary principles of employer's
liability applied. The threshold question was whether the particular kind of harm—   *a*
an injury to health (as distinct from occupational stress) which was attributable
to stress at work (as distinct from other factors)—to the particular employee was
reasonably foreseeable. Foreseeability depended upon what the employer knew
or ought reasonably to have known about the individual employee. Because of
the nature of mental disorder, it was harder to foresee than physical injury, but   *b*
might be easier to foresee in a known individual than in the population at large.
An employer was usually entitled to assume that the employee could withstand
the normal pressures of his job unless he knew of some particular problem or
vulnerability. The test was the same whatever the employment: there were no
occupations which should be regarded as intrinsically dangerous to mental health
(see [20], [22]–[25], [29], [43], below).   *c*

(2) Factors likely to be relevant in answering the threshold question included
the nature and extent of the work done by the employee, and signs from the
employee of impending harm to health. The employer was generally entitled to
take what he was told by his employee at face value, unless he had good reason
to think the contrary. He did not generally have to make searching inquiries of   *d*
the employee or seek permission to make further inquiries of his medical
advisors. To trigger a duty to take steps, the indications of impending harm to
health arising from stress at work had to be plain enough for any reasonable
employer to realise that he should do something about it. The employer would
only be in breach of duty if he had failed to take the steps which were reasonable   *e*
in the circumstances, bearing in mind the magnitude of the risk of harm
occurring, the gravity of the harm which might occur, the costs and practicability
of preventing it and the justifications for running the risk. The size and scope of
the employer's operation, its resources, and the demands it faced were relevant
in deciding what was reasonable: those included the interests of other employees
and the need to treat them fairly, for example, in any redistribution of duties. An   *f*
employer could only reasonably be expected to take steps which were likely to
do some good, and the court was likely to need expert evidence on that. An
employer who offered a confidential advice service, with referral to appropriate
counselling or treatment services, was unlikely to be found in breach of duty. If
the only reasonable and effective step would have been to dismiss or demote the   *g*
employee, the employer would not be in breach of duty in allowing a willing
employee to continue in the job. In all cases, therefore, it was necessary to
identify the steps which the employer both could and should have taken before
finding him in breach of his duty of care. The claimant had to show that the
breach of duty had caused or materially contributed to the harm suffered. It was   *h*
not enough to show that occupational stress had caused the harm. Where the
harm suffered had more than one cause, the employer should only pay for that
proportion of the harm suffered which was attributable to his wrongdoing, unless
the harm was truly indivisible. It was for the defendant to raise the question of
apportionment. The assessment of damages would take account of any
pre-existing disorder or vulnerability and of the chance that the claimant would   *j*
have succumbed to a stress-related disorder in any event (see [17], [26]–[29],
[31]–[36], [39], [42], [43], below).

(3) Applying those principles in the instant cases, the appeal in J's case would
be dismissed, but the remaining appeals would be allowed (see [48]–[50],
[57]–[59], [66], [67], [72]–[74], below).

Notes

a For an employer's duty at common law to take reasonable care for his employees' safety, see 16 *Halsbury's Laws* (4th edn) (2000 reissue) para 32.

Cases referred to in judgment

Alcock v Chief Constable of South Yorkshire Police [1991] 4 All ER 907, [1992] 1 AC
b   310, [1991] 3 WLR 1057, HL.
Allied Maples Group Ltd v Simmons & Simmons (a firm) [1995] 4 All ER 907, [1995] 1 WLR 1602, CA.
Bonnington Castings Ltd v Wardlaw [1956] 1 All ER 615, [1956] AC 613, [1956] 2 WLR 707, HL.
Calascione v Dixon (1993) 19 BMLR 97, CA.
c *Cook v S* [1967] 1 All ER 299, sub nom *Cook v Swinfen* [1967] 1 WLR 457, CA.
Davies v Taylor [1972] 3 All ER 836, [1974] AC 207, [1972] 3 WLR 801, HL.
Doyle v Wallace [1998] PIQR Q146, CA.
Garrett v Camden London BC [2001] EWCA Civ 395, [2001] All ER (D) 202 (Mar).
Holtby v Brigham & Cowan (Hull) Ltd [2000] 3 All ER 421, CA.
d *McGhee v National Coal Board* [1972] 3 All ER 1008, [1973] 1 WLR 1, HL.
McIntyre v Filtrona Ltd [1996] CA Transcript 1310.
McLoughlin v Grovers (a firm) [2001] EWCA Civ 1743, [2001] All ER (D) 335 (Nov).
Page v Smith [1995] 2 All ER 736, [1996] AC 155, [1995] 2 WLR 644, HL; *rvsg* [1994] 4 All ER 522, CA; *rvsg* [1993] PIQR Q55.
Page v Smith (No 2) [1996] 3 All ER 272, [1996] 1 WLR 855, CA.
e *Paris v Stepney BC* [1951] 1 All ER 42, [1951] AC 367, HL.
Petch v Comrs of Customs and Excise [1993] ICR 789, CA.
Rahman v Arearose Ltd [2001] QB 351, [2000] 3 WLR 1184, CA.
Stokes v Guest, Keen and Nettlefold (Bolts and Nuts) Ltd [1968] 1 WLR 1776.
Thompson v Smiths Shiprepairers (North Shields) Ltd [1984] 1 All ER 881, [1984] QB
f   405, [1984] 2 WLR 522.
Vernon v Bosley (No 1) [1997] 1 All ER 577, CA.
Walker v Northumberland CC [1995] 1 All ER 737.
Waters v Comr of Police of the Metropolis [2000] 4 All ER 934, [2000] 1 WLR 1607, HL.
White v Chief Constable of the South Yorkshire Police [1999] 1 All ER 1, [1999] 2 AC
g   455, [1998] 3 WLR 1509, HL.
Wilsher v Essex Area Health Authority [1988] 1 All ER 871, [1988] AC 1074, [1988] 2 WLR 557, HL.
Wilsons and Clyde Coal Co Ltd v English [1937] 3 All ER 628, [1938] AC 57, HL.
Withers v Perry Chain Co Ltd [1961] 3 All ER 676, [1961] 1 WLR 1314, CA.

h
Cases also cited or referred to in skeleton arguments

Bailey v Rolls Royce (1971) Ltd [1984] ICR 688, CA.
Ball v Post Office [1995] PIQR 5.
Barrett v Enfield London BC [1999] 3 All ER 193, [1999] 3 WLR 79, HL.
j *Bolton v Stone* [1951] 1 All ER 1078, [1951] AC 850, HL.
Bourhill v Young [1942] 2 All ER 396, [1943] AC 92, HL.
Cross v Highlands and Islands Enterprise [2001] IRLR 336, Ct of Sess (OH).
General Cleaning Contractors Ltd v Christmas [1952] 2 All ER 1110, [1953] AC 180, HL.
Gillespie v Commonwealth of Australia (1991) 104 ACTR 1, ACT SC.
Glasgow Corp v Muir [1943] 2 All ER 44, [1943] AC 448, HL.

Henderson v Wakefield Shirt Co Ltd [1997] PIQR P413, CA.

Kossinski v Chrysler UK Ltd (1973) 15 KIR 225, CA.

McLoughlin v Grovers (a firm) [2001] EWCA Civ 1743, [2001] All ER (D) 335 (Nov).

Morris v West Hartlepool Steam Navigation Co Ltd [1956] 1 All ER 385, [1956] AC 552, HL.

Rorrison v West Lothian College 2000 SCLR 245, Ct of Sess (OH).

Wagon Mound, The (No 2), Overseas Tankship (UK) Ltd v Miller Steamship Co Pty Ltd [1966] 2 All ER 709, [1967] 1 AC 617, PC.

Appeals

Hatton v Sutherland

The defendant, Terence Sutherland, as chairman of the governors of St Thomas Becket RC High School, appealed with the permission of Judge Trigger from his decision at Liverpool County Court on 7 August 2000 awarding the claimant, Penelope Hatton, £90,756·83 in damages and interest on her claim against the governors for psychiatric illness caused by stress at work. The facts are set out in the judgment of the court.

Barber v Somerset CC

The defendant, Somerset County Council, appealed with the permission of Hale LJ granted on 12 March 2001 from the order of Judge Roach at Exeter County Court on 8 March 2001 awarding the claimant, Leon Alan Barber, £101,041·59 in damages and interest on his claim against the council for psychiatric illness caused by stress at work. The facts are set out in the judgment of the court.

Jones v Sandwell Metropolitan BC

The defendant, Sandwell Metropolitan Borough Council, appealed with the permission of Hale LJ granted on 14 February 2001 from the order of Judge Nicholl at Birmingham County Court on 31 October 2000 awarding the claimant, Olwen Jones, £157,541 in damages and interest on her claim against the council for psychiatric illness caused by stress at work. The facts are set out in the judgment of the court.

Bishop v Baker Refractories Ltd

The defendant, Baker Refractories Ltd, appealed with the permission of Hale LJ granted on 12 March 2001 from the order of Judge Kent-Jones at Leeds County Court on 26 January 2001 awarding the claimant, Melvyn Edward Bishop, £7,000 in general damages on his claim against the company for psychiatric illness caused by stress at work. The facts are set out in the judgment of the court.

Andrew Collender QC and *Stephen Archer* (instructed by *Rollingsons*) for the defendant school governors in Mrs Hatton's case.

Peter Atherton (instructed by *Silverbeck Rymer*, Manchester) for Mrs Hatton.

Andrew Hogarth (instructed by *Veitch Penny*, Exeter) for the defendant council in Mr Barber's case.

Robert P Glancy QC and *Christopher Goddard* (instructed by *Graham Clayton*, Exeter) for Mr Barber.

Ralph Lewis QC (instructed by *Simpson & Co*, Birmingham) for the defendant council in Mrs Jones' case.

a *Mark Anderson* (instructed by *Martineau Johnson*, Birmingham) for Mrs Jones.
Robert F Owen QC (instructed by *Whitfield Hallam Goodall*, Batley) for the defendant company in Mr Bishop's case.
Howard Elgot (instructed by *Morrish & Co*, Leeds) for Mr Bishop.

Cur adv vult

b 5 February 2002. The following judgment of the court, to which all members contributed, was delivered.

INDEX

APPENDIX

e

HALE LJ.

1. INTRODUCTION

[1] These four appeals are related only by their subject matter. In each a defendant employer appeals against a finding of liability for an employee's psychiatric illness caused by stress at work. Two of the respondent claimants were *f* teachers in public sector comprehensive schools; another was an administrative assistant at a local authority training centre; the fourth was a raw materials operative in a factory. There is broad agreement as to the applicable principles of law. But there are difficulties in applying the principles developed in the context of industrial accidents to these very different circumstances. Hearing four very different cases together has also cast valuable light upon how those difficulties *g* might be resolved in individual cases.

[2] This judgment of the court, to which we have all contributed, is arranged as follows. First we consider some relevant background considerations; then the legal principles and how these are to be applied in this class of case; and we conclude with a summary of the questions to be asked in determining individual *h* cases. Then we summarise the facts and our conclusions in each of the four cases under appeal. The details of each of these cases are contained in the appendix, which also contains an analysis of issues relating to damages which arose in two of the appeals.

j

2. BACKGROUND CONSIDERATIONS

[3] This type of case has been described as the 'next growth area' in claims for psychiatric illness: see N J Mullany, 'Fear for the Future: Liability for Infliction of Psychiatric Disorder' in N J Mullany (ed), *Torts in the Nineties* (1997) p 107. This growth is due to developing understanding in two distinct but interrelated areas of knowledge.

Psychiatric ill-health

a

[4] The first is of psychiatric illness generally. The Law Commission, in their consultation paper on *Liability for Psychiatric Illness* (1995) (Law Com no 137), commented at para 1.9 (pp 5–6):

b

c

'We are aware from our preliminary consultations that there are strongly-held views on this topic. On the one hand, there are those who are sceptical about the award of damages for psychiatric illness. They argue that such illness can easily be faked; that, in any event, those who are suffering should be able "to pull themselves together"; and that, even if they cannot do so, there is no good reason why defendants and, through them, those who pay insurance premiums should pay for their inability to do so ... On the other hand, medical and legal experts working in the field, who are the people who most commonly encounter those complaining of psychiatric illness, have impressed upon us how life-shattering psychiatric illness can be and how, in many instances, it can be more debilitating than physical injuries.'

d

[5] The latter we entirely accept. But although there have been great advances in understanding of the nature and causes of psychiatric ill-health, there are still important differences between physical and mental disorders. (1) The dividing line between a normal but unpleasant state of mind or emotion and a recognised psychiatric illness or disorder is not easy to draw. Psychiatric textbooks tell us

e

that with a physical disease or disability, the doctor can presuppose a perfect or 'normal' state of bodily health and then point to the ways in which his patient's condition falls short of this. There is probably no such thing as a state of perfect mental health. The doctor has instead to presuppose some average standard of functioning and then assess whether his patient's condition falls far enough short of that to be considered a disorder. However, there is now a considerable degree

f

of international agreement on the classification of mental disorders and their diagnostic criteria, the two most commonly used tools being the most recent *American Diagnostic and Statistical Manual of Mental Disorder*, published by the American Psychiatric Association (4th edn, 1994) (DSM-IV) and the World Health Organisation's *ICD-10 Classification of Mental and Behavioural Disorders: Clinical Descriptions and Diagnostic Guidelines* (1992). (2) While some of the major

g

mental illnesses have a known or strongly suspected organic origin, this is not the case with many of the most common disorders. Their causes will often be complex and depend upon the interaction between the patient's personality and a number of factors in the patient's life. It is not easy to predict who will fall victim, how, why or when. (3) For the same reason, treatment is often not

h

straightforward or its outcome predictable: while some conditions may respond comparatively quickly and easily to appropriate medication others may only respond, if at all, to prolonged and complicated 'talking treatments' or behavioural therapy. There are strong divergences of views amongst psychiatrists on these issues.

j

[6] In their report on *Liability for Psychiatric Illness* (1998) (Law Com no 249) at para 1.2 (p 2) the Law Commission referred to the divergence of academic views on the approach the law should take:

'At one end of the scale are those who argue that the same principles that apply to liability for physical injury should be applied to liability for psychiatric illness, and there is no legitimate reason to impose special restrictions in respect of claims for the latter [most forcefully by N J Mullany and P R Handford in *Tort Liability for Psychiatric Damage* (1993)]. At the other extreme are those who argue that liability for psychiatric illness should be abandoned altogether. They say that the arbitrary rules which are required to control potential liability are so artificial that they bring the law into disrepute [cogently expressed by Dr J Stapleton "In Restraint of Tort", in P Birks (ed) *The Frontiers of Liability* (1994) vol 2, pp 94–96].'

Both the law and the Law Commission have followed a middle course, in some cases treating a recognised psychiatric illness as no different in principle from a physical injury or illness, while in others imposing additional 'control mechanisms' so that liability does not extend too far.

Occupational stress

[7] The second area of developing understanding is of the nature and extent of occupational stress. We have been referred to three particularly helpful documents. The first is the report of a working party of the Health Education Authority, *Stress in the public sector—Nurses, police, social workers and teachers* (1988). This discusses the 'Meaning of Stress' in app 1:

'... as with many words in a living language, the word "stress" has acquired a vague, catch-all meaning, used by different people to mean different things. It is used to describe both physical and mental conditions, and the pressures which cause those conditions. It is also used to describe stress which is beneficial and harmful both in its sources and in its effects.'

Hence the definition of stress adopted in that report was 'an excess of demands upon an individual in excess of their ability to cope'. The report confirmed that the four occupations discussed had much in common in this respect.

[8] Second is the report of the Education Service Advisory Committee of the Health and Safety Commission, *Managing occupational stress: a guide for managers and teachers in the schools sector* (1990). This adopted a similar definition: '... stress is a process that can occur when there is an unresolved mismatch between the perceived pressures of the work situation and an individual's ability to cope.' It confirmed, if confirmation were needed, that teaching can be a stressful profession. It is also a profession which has undergone profound changes in recent years.

[9] The third is a general booklet of guidance from the Health and Safety Executive, *Stress at Work* (1995). This is particularly helpful in distinguishing clearly between *pressure, stress,* and *the physical or psychiatric consequences* (p 2):

'There is no such thing as a pressure free job. Every job brings its own set of tasks, responsibilities and day-to-day problems, and the pressures and demands these place on us are an unavoidable part of working life. We are, after all, paid to work and to work hard, and to accept the reasonable pressures which go with that. Some pressures can, in fact, be a good thing. It is often the tasks and challenges we face at work that provide the structure to our working days, keep us motivated and are the key to a sense of achievement and job satisfaction. But people's ability to deal with pressure is not limitless. Excessive workplace pressure and the stress to which it can lead can be harmful. They can damage your business's performance and undermine the health of your workforce.'

a   Stress is defined (p 4) as 'the reaction people have to excessive pressures or other types of demand placed upon them. It arises when they worry that they can't cope'. It can involve both physical and behavioural effects, but these 'are usually short-lived and cause no lasting harm. When the pressures recede, there is a quick return to normal'.

b   'Stress is not therefore the same as ill-health. But in some cases, particularly where pressures are intense and continue for some time, the effect of stress can be more sustained and far more damaging, leading to longer-term psychological problems and physical ill-health.'

c   [10] Two other important messages emerge from these documents. First, and perhaps contrary to popular belief, harmful levels of stress are most likely to occur in situations where people feel powerless or trapped. These are more likely to affect people on the shop floor or at the more junior levels than those who are in a position to shape what they do. Second, stress—in the sense of a perceived mismatch between the pressures of the job and the individual's ability to meet them—is a psychological phenomenon but it can lead to either physical or mental *d*   ill-health or both. When considering the issues raised by these four cases, in which the claimants all suffered psychiatric illnesses, it may therefore be important to bear in mind that the same issues might arise had they instead suffered some stress-related physical disorder, such as ulcers, heart disease or hypertension.

e   *Differences from other work-related harm*
      [11] Mr Hogarth, on behalf of the appellant defendant in *Barber's* case, has pointed to several differences between this and other kinds of work-related harm, such as injuries suffered in accidents at work or illnesses caused by exposure to deleterious physical conditions at work. These are in addition to the general *f*   differences between physical and psychiatric disorders discussed earlier. (1) The most significant relates to who knows what. The employer is or should be aware of what is going on in his own factory, school or office. He is much less aware of what is going on in his employees' minds or in their lives outside work. There are many other people, such as family, friends and colleagues, who are likely to know far more about this than the employer. Indeed, the employee may very *g*   well wish to minimise or conceal the true state of affairs from his employer: no one wants to be thought unable to cope. (2) The employer is or should be largely in control of the workplace, equipment and physical conditions in which the work is done. He is much less in control of the way in which many of his employees, especially professionals or those who are expected to prioritise their *h*   own tasks, choose to do their work and balance the demands of their work and life outside the workplace. (3) The employer can be expected to take responsibility for keeping the physical risks presented by the workplace to a minimum. But responsibility both for causing and for doing something about its psychological risks may be shared between many people, family, friends and the *j*   individual himself, as well as the employer. An individual who recognises that he is experiencing levels of stress which may be harmful to him has to make some decisions about how to respond to this. The employer's room for manoeuvre may in some cases be limited. At the extreme, his only option may be to dismiss the employee who cannot cope with the job.
      [12] There are some jobs which are intrinsically physically dangerous: the most obvious examples are the armed forces, fire-fighting and the police. The

employee agrees to run the inevitable risks of the job, although not those which
are the result of his employers' negligence. Psychological *pressures* are inevitable
in all jobs, although greater in some than in others. But it is, as the documents
quoted show, rather more difficult to identify which jobs are intrinsically so
stressful that physical or psychological *harm* is to be expected more often than in
other jobs. Some people thrive on pressure and are so confident of their abilities
to cope that they rarely if ever experience stress even in jobs which many would
find extremely stressful. Others experience harmful levels of stress in jobs which
many would not regard as stressful at all.

[13] When imposing duties and setting standards, the law tries to strike a
balance which is reasonable to both sides. Here there are weighty considerations
on each side. It is in everyone's interests that management should be encouraged
to recognise the existence and causes of occupational stress and take sensible
steps to minimise it within their organisation. It is in the interest of the individual
employees who may suffer harm if their employers do not. It is in the interest of
the particular enterprise which may lose efficiency and workers if it does not. It
is in the public interest that public services should not suffer or public money be
wasted. Concern about this issue arose during a period of great upheaval in the
workforce, and in many large organisations, bringing changes in management
ethos, instability and insecurity. The documents we have seen all aim to
encourage management to take the issue of occupational stress seriously.

[14] The law of tort has an important function in setting standards for
employers as well as for drivers, manufacturers, health care professionals and
many others whose carelessness may cause harm. But if the standard of care
expected of employers is set too high, or the threshold of liability too low, there
may also be unforeseen and unwelcome effects upon the employment market. In
particular, employers may be even more reluctant than they already are to take
on people with a significant psychiatric history or an acknowledged vulnerability
to stress-related disorders. If employers are expected to make searching inquiries
of employees who have been off sick, then more employees may be vulnerable
to dismissal or demotion on ill-health grounds. If particular employments are
singled out as ones in which special care is needed, then other benefits which are
available to everyone in those employments, such as longer holidays, better
pensions or earlier retirement, may be under threat.

[15] Some things are no one's fault. No one can blame an employee who tries
to soldier on despite his own desperate fears that he cannot cope, perhaps
especially where those fears are groundless. No one can blame an employee for
being reluctant to give clear warnings to his employer of the stress he is feeling.
His very job, let alone his credibility or hopes of promotion, may be at risk. Few
would blame an employee for continuing or returning to work despite the
warnings of his doctor that he should give it up. There are many reasons why the
job may be precious to him. On the other hand it may be difficult in those
circumstances to blame the employer for failing to recognise the problem and
what might be done to solve it.

[16] There is an argument that stress is so prevalent in some employments, of
which teaching is one, and employees so reluctant to disclose it, that all
employers should have in place systems to detect it and prevent its developing
into actual harm. As the above discussion shows, this raises some difficult issues
of policy and practice which are unsuitable for resolution in individual cases
before the courts. If knowledge advances to such an extent as to justify the
imposition of obligations upon some or all employers to take particular steps to

a protect their employees from stress-related harm, this is better done by way of regulations imposing specific statutory duties. In the meantime the ordinary law of negligence governs the matter.

[17] However, we do know of schemes now being developed and encouraged which recognise and respond to the peculiar problems presented both to employees and employers. The key is to offer help on a completely confidential *b* basis. The employee can then be encouraged to recognise the signs and seek that help without fearing its effects upon his job or prospects; the employer need not make intrusive inquiries or overreact to such problems as he does detect; responsibility for accessing the service can be left with the people who are best equipped to know what the problems are, the employee, his family and friends; and if reasonable help is offered either directly or through referral to other *c* services, then all that reasonably could be done has been done. Obviously, not all employers have the resources to put such systems in place, but an employer who does have a system along those lines is unlikely to be found in breach of his duty of care towards his employees.

d 3. THE LAW

[18] Several times while hearing these appeals we were invited to go back to first principles. Liability in negligence depends upon three interrelated requirements: the existence of a duty to take care; a failure to take the care which can reasonably be expected in the circumstances; and damage suffered as a result of that failure. These elements do not exist in separate compartments: the *e* existence of the duty, for example, depends upon the type of harm suffered. Foreseeability of what might happen if care is not taken is relevant at each stage of the inquiry. Nevertheless, the traditional elements are always a useful tool of analysis, both in general and in particular cases.

f *Duty*

[19] The existence of a duty of care can be taken for granted. All employers have a duty to take reasonable care for the safety of their employees: to see that reasonable care is taken to provide them with a safe place of work, safe tools and equipment, and a safe system of working (see *Wilsons and Clyde Coal Co Ltd v English* [1937] 3 All ER 628, [1938] AC 57). However, where psychiatric harm is *g* suffered, the law distinguishes between 'primary' and 'secondary' victims. A primary victim is usually someone within the zone of foreseeable physical harm should the defendant fail to take reasonable care (see *Page v Smith* [1995] 2 All ER 736, [1996] AC 155). A secondary victim is usually someone outside that zone: typically such a victim foreseeably suffers psychiatric harm through seeing, *h* hearing or learning of physical harm tortiously inflicted upon others. There are additional control mechanisms to keep liability towards such people strictly within bounds (see *Alcock v Chief Constable of South Yorkshire Police* [1991] 4 All ER 907, [1992] 1 AC 310). In *White v Chief Constable of the South Yorkshire Police* [1999] 1 All ER 1, [1999] 2 AC 455, the House of Lords applied that distinction to police officers (and others) who were not themselves within the zone of physical danger *j* caused by the defendant's negligence, but had to deal with the consequences of catastrophic harm to others in the course of their duties. Lord Steyn observed that:

'The rules to be applied when an employee brings an action against his employer for harm suffered at his workplace are the rules of tort. One is therefore thrown back to the ordinary rules of the law of tort which contain

restrictions on the recovery of compensation for psychiatric harm ... The
duty of an employer to safeguard his employees from harm could also be *a*
formulated in contract ... But such a term could not be wider in scope than
the duty imposed by the law of tort.' (See [1999] 1 All ER 1 at 36, [1999] 2 AC
455 at 497–498.)

Taken to its logical conclusion this would apply the same distinction between *b*
those inside and those outside the zone of foreseeable risk of physical harm to the
employer's general duty of care to his employees.

[20] We have not been invited to go down that road, no doubt because it is
not open to us. In *Petch v Comrs of Customs and Excise* [1993] ICR 789 it was
accepted that the ordinary principles of employers' liability applied to a claim for
psychiatric illness arising from employment, although the claim failed. In the *c*
landmark case of *Walker v Northumberland CC* [1995] 1 All ER 737, Colman J
applied those same principles in upholding the claim. Both have recently been
cited with approval in this court in *Garrett v Camden London BC* [2001] EWCA Civ
395, [2001] All ER (D) 202 (Mar). Also in *White's* case, Lord Hoffmann stated:

> 'The control mechanisms were plainly never intended to apply to all cases *d*
> of psychiatric injury. They contemplate that the injury has been caused in
> consequence of death or injury suffered (or apprehended to have been
> suffered or as likely to be suffered) by someone else.' (See [1999] 1 All ER 1
> at 43, [1999] 2 AC 455 at 504.)

e
As to *Walker's* case, he commented: 'The employee ... was in no sense a
secondary victim. His mental breakdown was caused by the strain of doing the
work which his employer had required him to do.' (See [1999] 1 All ER 1 at 44,
[1999] 2 AC 455 at 506.)

[21] In summary, therefore, claims for psychiatric injury fall into four different
categories. (1) Tortious claims by primary victims: usually those within the *f*
foreseeable scope of physical injury, for example, the road accident victim in *Page
v Smith*; some primary victims may not be at risk of physical harm, but at risk of
foreseeable psychiatric harm because the circumstances are akin to those of
primary victims in contract (see (3) below). (2) Tortious claims by secondary
victims: those outside that zone who suffer as a result of harm to others, for *g*
example, the witnesses of the Hillsborough disaster in *Alcock's* case. (3) Contractual
claims by primary victims: where the harm is the reasonably foreseeable product
of specific breaches of a contractual duty of care towards a victim whose identity
is known in advance, for example, the solicitors' clients in *Cook v S* [1967] 1 All ER
299, [1967] 1 WLR 457, *McLoughlin v Grovers (a firm)* [2001] EWCA Civ 1743, *h*
[2001] All ER (D) 335 (Nov), or the employees in the cases of *Petch*, *Walker* and
Garrett, and in all the cases before us. (4) Contractual claims by secondary
victims: where the harm is suffered as a result of harm to others, in the same way
as secondary victims in tort, but there is also a contractual relationship with the
defendant, as with the police officers in *White's* case.

[22] There are, therefore, no special control mechanisms applying to claims *j*
for psychiatric (or physical) injury or illness arising from the stress of doing the
work which the employee is required to do. But these claims do require
particular care in determination, because they give rise to some difficult issues of
foreseeability and causation and, we would add, identifying a relevant breach of
duty. As Simon Brown LJ pithily put it in *Garrett's* case:

a

'Many, alas, suffer breakdowns and depressive illnesses and a significant proportion could doubtless ascribe some at least of their problems to the strains and stresses of their work situation: be it simply overworking, the tensions of difficult relationships, career prospect worries, fears or feelings of discrimination or harassment, to take just some examples. *Unless, however, there was a real risk of breakdown which the claimant's employers ought reasonably*

b

to have foreseen and which they ought properly to have averted, there can be no liability.' (See [2001] All ER (D) 202 (Mar) at [63]; my emphasis.)

Foreseeability

[**23**] To say that the employer has a duty of care to his employee does not tell us what he has to do (or refrain from doing) in any particular case. The issue in

c

most if not all of these cases is whether the employer should have taken positive steps to safeguard the employee from harm: his sins are those of omission rather than commission. Mr Robert Owen QC, for the appellant defendant in *Bishop's* case, saw this as a question of defining the duty; Mr Ralph Lewis QC, for the appellant defendant in *Jones'* case, saw it as a question of setting the standard of care in order to decide whether it had been broken. Whichever is the correct

d

analysis, *the threshold question is whether this kind of harm to this particular employee was reasonably foreseeable.* The question is not whether psychiatric injury is foreseeable in a person of 'ordinary fortitude'. The employer's duty is owed to each individual employee, not to some as yet unidentified outsider (see *Paris v Stepney BC* [1951] 1 All ER 42, [1951] AC 367). The employer knows who his

e

employee is. It may be that he knows, as in *Paris'* case, or ought to know, of a particular vulnerability; but he may not. *Because of the very nature of psychiatric disorder, as a sufficiently serious departure from normal or average psychological functioning to be labelled a disorder, it is bound to be harder to foresee than is physical injury.* Shylock could not say of a mental disorder, 'If you prick us, do we not

f

bleed?' *But it may be easier to foresee in a known individual than it is in the population at large.* The principle is the same as in other cases where there is a contractual duty of care, such as solicitors' negligence (see *Cook v S, McLoughlin v Grovers*).

[**24**] However, are there some occupations which are so intrinsically stressful that resulting physical or psychological harm is always foreseeable? Mr Lewis appeared to accept that this was so: he gave the examples of traffic police officers

g

who regularly deal with gruesome accidents or child protection officers who regularly investigate unthinkable allegations of child abuse. Some warrant for this might be drawn from the way in which Dillon LJ formulated the foreseeability test in *Petch's* case [1993] ICR 789 at 796–797:

h

'... unless senior management in the defendants' department were aware or ought to have been aware that the plaintiff was showing signs of impending breakdown, or were aware or ought to have been aware that his workload carried a real risk that he would have a breakdown, then the defendants were not negligent in failing to avert the breakdown ...'

j

Later (at 798) he referred to the same two-pronged test: '... but Mr. Bamfield had no knowledge of any sign whatever of impending danger, nor was he bound to regard the plaintiff's workload, so eagerly accepted, as per se dangerous.' These observations were made in the context of a particular employee in a particular high grade civil service post. They were not made in the context of such posts as a whole. The notion that some occupations are in themselves dangerous to mental health is not borne out by the literature to which we have already

referred: it is not the job but the interaction between the individual and the job
which causes the harm. Stress is a subjective concept: the individual's perception   *a*
that the pressures placed upon him are greater than he may be able to meet.
Adverse reactions to stress are equally individual, ranging from minor physical
symptoms to major mental illness.

[25] All of this points to there being a single test: *whether a harmful reaction to
the pressures of the workplace is reasonably foreseeable in the individual employee*   *b*
concerned. *Such a reaction will have two components:* (1) *an injury to health; which*
(2) *is attributable to stress at work*. The answer to the foreseeability question will
therefore depend upon the interrelationship between the particular characteristics
of the employee concerned and the particular demands which the employer casts
upon him. As was said in *McLoughlin v Grovers*, expert evidence may be helpful
although it can never be determinative of what a reasonable employer should   *c*
have foreseen. A number of factors are likely to be relevant.

[26] These include the *nature and extent of the work being done by the employee*.
Employers should be more alert to picking up signs from an employee who is
being overworked in an intellectually or emotionally demanding job than from
an employee whose workload is no more than normal for the job or whose job is   *d*
not particularly demanding for him or her. It will be easier to conclude that harm
is foreseeable if the employer is putting pressure upon the individual employee
which is in all the circumstances of the case unreasonable. Also relevant is
whether there are signs that others doing the same work are under harmful levels
of stress. There may be others who have already suffered injury to their health
arising from their work. Or there may be an abnormal level of sickness and   *e*
absence amongst others at the same grade or in the same department. But if
there is no evidence of this, then the focus must turn to the individual, as
Colman J put it in *Walker*'s case [1995] 1 All ER 737 at 752:

> 'Accordingly, the question is whether it ought to have been foreseen that
> Mr Walker was exposed to a risk of mental illness materially higher than that   *f*
> which would ordinarily affect a social services middle manager in his
> position with a really heavy workload.'

[27] More important are the *signs from the employee himself*. Here again, it is
important to distinguish between signs of stress and signs of impending harm to
health. Stress is merely the mechanism which may but usually does not lead to   *g*
damage to health. *Walker*'s case is an obvious illustration: Mr Walker was a
highly conscientious and seriously overworked manager of a social work area
office with a heavy and emotionally demanding case load of child abuse cases.
Yet although he complained and asked for help and for extra leave, the judge held
that his first mental breakdown was not foreseeable. There was, however,   *h*
liability when he returned to work with a promise of extra help which did not
materialise and experienced a second breakdown only a few months later. If the
employee or his doctor makes it plain that unless something is done to help there
is a clear risk of a breakdown in mental or physical health, then the employer will
have to think what can be done about it.   *j*

[28] Harm to health may sometimes be foreseeable without such an express
warning. Factors to take into account would be frequent or prolonged absences
from work which are uncharacteristic for the person concerned; these could be
for physical or psychological complaints; but there must also be good reason to
think that the underlying cause is occupational stress rather than other factors;
this could arise from the nature of the employee's work or from complaints made

a about it by the employee or from warnings given by the employee or others
around him.

[29] But when considering what the reasonable employer should make of the
information which is available to him, from whatever source, what assumptions
is he entitled to make about his employee and to what extent he is bound to probe
further into what he is told? *Unless he knows of some particular problem or*
b *vulnerability, an employer is usually entitled to assume that his employee is up to the*
normal pressures of the job. It is only if there is something specific about the job or
the employee or the combination of the two that he has to think harder. But
thinking harder does not necessarily mean that he has to make searching or
intrusive inquiries. *Generally he is entitled to take what he is told by or on behalf of the*
employee at face value. If he is concerned he may suggest that the employee
c consults his own doctor or an occupational health service. But he should not
without a very good reason seek the employee's permission to obtain further
information from his medical advisors. Otherwise he would risk unacceptable
invasions of his employee's privacy.

[30] It was argued that the employer is entitled to take the expiry of a GP's
d certificate as implicitly suggesting that the employee is now fit to return to work
and even that he is no longer at risk of suffering the same sort of problem again.
This cannot be right. A GP's certificate is limited in time but many disorders are
not self-limiting and may linger on for some considerable time. Yet an employee
who is anxious to return to work, for whatever reason, may not go back to his GP
for a further certificate when the current one runs out. Even if the employee is
e currently fit for work, the earlier time-limited certificate carries no implication
that the same or a similar condition will not recur. The point is a rather different
one: *an employee who returns to work after a period of sickness without making further*
disclosure or explanation to his employer is usually implying that he believes himself fit to
return to the work which he was doing before. The employer is usually entitled to
f take that at face value unless he has other good reasons to think to the contrary
(see *McIntyre v Filtrona Ltd* [1996] CA Transcript 1310).

[31] These then are the questions and the possible indications that harm was
foreseeable in a particular case. But how strong should those indications be
before the employer has a duty to act? Mr Hogarth argued that only 'clear and
unequivocal' signs of an impending breakdown should suffice. That may be
g putting it too high. But *in view of the many difficulties of knowing when and why a*
particular person will go over the edge from pressure to stress and from stress to injury to
health, the indications must be plain enough for any reasonable employer to realise that
he should do something about it.

h *Breach of duty*

[32] What then is it reasonable to expect the employer to do? His duty is to
take reasonable care. What is reasonable depends, as we all know, upon the
foreseeability of harm, the magnitude of the risk of that harm occurring, the
gravity of the harm which may take place, the cost and practicability of
j preventing it, and the justifications for running the risk (see the oft-quoted
summary of Swanwick J in *Stokes v Guest, Keen and Nettlefold (Bolts and Nuts) Ltd*
[1968] 1 WLR 1776 at 1783).

[33] It is essential, therefore, once the risk of harm to health from stresses in
the workplace is foreseeable, to consider whether and in what respect the
employer has broken that duty. There may be a temptation, having concluded
that some harm was foreseeable and that harm of that kind has taken place, to go

on to conclude that the employer was in breach of his duty of care in failing to
prevent that harm (and that that breach of duty caused the harm). But *in every* *a*
case it is necessary to consider what the employer not only could but should have done.
We are not here concerned with such comparatively simple things as gloves,
goggles, earmuffs or non-slip flooring. Many steps might be suggested: giving the
employee a sabbatical; transferring him to other work; redistributing the work;
giving him some extra help for a while; arranging treatment or counselling; *b*
providing buddying or mentoring schemes to encourage confidence; and much
more. But in all of these suggestions it will be necessary to consider how
reasonable it is to expect the employer to do this, either in general or in particular:
the size and scope of its operation will be relevant to this, as will its resources, whether in
the public or private sector, and the other demands placed upon it. Among those other
demands are the interests of other employees in the workplace. It may not be reasonable *c*
to expect the employer to rearrange the work for the sake of one employee in a
way which prejudices the others. As we have already said, an employer who tries
to balance all these interests by offering confidential help to employees who fear
that they may be suffering harmful levels of stress is unlikely to be found in
breach of duty: except where he has been placing totally unreasonable demands *d*
upon an individual in circumstances where the risk of harm was clear.

[34] Moreover, *the employer can only reasonably be expected to take steps which are*
likely to do some good. This is a matter on which the court is likely to require expert
evidence. In many of these cases it will be very hard to know what would have
done some let alone enough good. In some cases the only effective way of
safeguarding the employee would be to dismiss or demote him. There may be *e*
no other work at the same level of pay which it is reasonable to expect the
employer to offer him. *In principle the law should not be saying to an employer that it*
is his duty to sack an employee who wants to go on working for him for the employer's
own good. As Devlin LJ put it in *Withers v Perry Chain Co Ltd* [1961] 3 All ER 676 at
680, [1961] 1 WLR 1314 at 1320: *f*

'The relationship between employer and employee is not that of
schoolmaster and pupil ... The employee is free to decide for herself what
risks she will run ... if the common law were to be otherwise it would be
oppressive to the employee by limiting his ability to find work, rather than
beneficial to him.' *g*

Taken to its logical conclusion, of course, this would justify employers in
perpetuating the most unsafe practices (not alleged in that case) on the basis that
the employee can always leave. But we are not here concerned with physical
dangers: we have already rejected the concept of an unsafe occupation for this
purpose. If there is no alternative solution, it has to be for the employee to decide *h*
whether or not to carry on in the same employment and take the risk of a
breakdown in his health or whether to leave that employment and look for work
elsewhere before he becomes unemployable.

Causation *j*
[35] Having shown a breach of duty, *it is still necessary to show that the particular*
breach of duty found caused the harm. It is not enough to show that occupational
stress caused the harm. Where there are several different possible causes, as will
often be the case with stress related illness of any kind, the claimant may have
difficulty proving that the employer's fault was one of them (see *Wilsher v Essex*
Area Health Authority [1988] 1 All ER 871, [1988] AC 1074). This will be a particular

a problem if, as in *Garrett v Camden London BC* [2001] All ER (D) 202 (Mar), the main cause was a vulnerable personality which the employer knew nothing about. However, *the employee does not have to show that the breach of duty was the whole cause of his ill-health: it is enough to show that it made a material contribution* (see *Bonnington Castings Ltd v Wardlaw* [1956] 1 All ER 615, [1956] AC 613).

b *Apportionment and quantification*

[36] Many stress-related illnesses are likely to have a complex aetiology with several different causes. In principle a wrongdoer should pay only for that proportion of the harm suffered for which he by his wrongdoing is responsible (see e g *Thompson v Smiths Shiprepairers (North Shields) Ltd* [1984] 1 All ER 881, [1984] QB 405, *Holtby v Brigham & Cowan (Hull) Ltd* [2000] PIQR Q293 and *Rahman v Arearose Ltd* [2001]
c QB 351, [2000] 3 WLR 1184). *Thompson's* case and *Holtby's* case concerned respectively deafness and asbestosis developed over a long period of exposure; not only were different employers involved but in *Thompson's* case some of the exposure by the same employer was tortious and some was not. Apportionment was possible because the deterioration over particular periods of time could be
d measured, albeit in a somewhat rough and ready fashion.

[37] *It is different if the harm is truly indivisible*: a tortfeasor who has made a material contribution is liable for the whole, although he may be able to seek contribution from other joint or concurrent tortfeasors who have also contributed to the injury. In *Rahman's* case, Laws LJ quoted the following illuminating discussion from *Prosser and Keeton on Torts* (5th edn, 1984) pp 345–346:
e

'If two defendants, struggling for a single gun, succeed in shooting the plaintiff, there is no reasonable basis for dividing the injury between them, and each will be liable for all of it. If they shoot the plaintiff independently, with separate guns, and the plaintiff dies from the effect of both wounds,
f there can still be no division, for death cannot be divided or apportioned except by an arbitrary rule ... If they merely inflict separate wounds, and the plaintiff survives, a basis for division exists, because it is possible to regard the two wounds as separate injuries ... There will be obvious difficulties of proof as to the apportionment of certain elements of damages, such as physical and mental suffering and medical expenses, but such difficulties are not
g insuperable, and it is better to attempt some rough division than to hold one defendant [liable] for the wound inflicted by the other. Upon the same basis, if two defendants each pollute a stream with oil, in some instances it may be possible to say that each has interfered to a separate extent with the plaintiff's rights in the water, and to make some division of the damages. It is not
h possible if the oil is ignited, and burns the plaintiff's barn.'

[38] In *Bonnington Castings Ltd v Wardlaw* [1956] 1 All ER 615, [1956] AC 613, the employee was exposed to harmful dust, all of it at work, but some of it in breach of duty and some not: the employer was held liable for the whole of the damage caused by the combination of the 'guilty' and 'innocent' dust. The
j question of apportionment was not argued. The problem there, as in *McGhee v National Coal Board* [1972] 3 All ER 1008, [1973] 1 WLR 1, was whether the claimant could prove causation at all, given the possible contribution of both 'guilty' and 'innocent' dust to his illness.

[39] As Stuart-Smith LJ commented in *Holtby's* case [2000] 3 All ER 421 at 428 (para 20):

'[The claimant] will be entitled to succeed if he can prove that the defendants' tortious conduct made a material contribution to his disability. But strictly speaking the defendant is liable only to the extent of that contribution. However, if the point is never raised or argued by the defendant, the claimant will succeed in full as in the *Bonnington* case and *McGhee*'s case.'

Clarke LJ went further and placed at least the evidential burden of establishing the case for apportionment upon the defendant (at 433 (para 35)):

'It seems to me that once the claimant has shown that the defendants' breach of duty has made a material contribution to his disease, justice requires that he should be entitled to recover in full from those defendants unless they show the extent to which some other factor, whether it be "innocent" dust or tortious dust caused by others, also contributed.'

But he acknowledged that these cases should not be determined by the burden of proof: assessments of this kind are 'essentially jury questions which have to be determined on a broad basis'.

[40] Hence the learned editors of *Clerk and Lindsell on Torts* (18th edn, 2000) at para 2-21, state that 'Where it is possible to identify the extent of the contribution that the defendant's wrong made to the claimant's damage then the defendant is liable only to that extent, and no more'. This may raise some difficult factual questions. *Calascione v Dixon* (1993) 19 BMLR 97 is an example of apportionment between different causes, one the fault of the defendant, the other not: the claimant suffered post traumatic stress disorder as a result of seeing the aftermath of the accident in which her son was killed, but her normal grief reaction had become abnormal as a result of later events. In *Vernon v Bosley (No 1)* [1997] 1 All ER 577, the majority in this court held that the whole of the claimant's psychiatric injury was the result of the accident in which his two daughters died, although Stuart-Smith LJ dissented on the ground that it had not been shown that it was caused by his witnessing the unsuccessful attempts to rescue them, that is by the breach of the defendant's duty towards him. These were both, of course, secondary victims. *Rahman*'s case is an example of apportionment of the psychiatric injury suffered by a primary victim between different tortfeasors. Neither tort caused the whole injury, some was caused mainly by one, some mainly by the other, and some by their combined effect. Neither tortfeasor would have been held liable for the whole.

[41] Hence if it is established that the constellation of symptoms suffered by the claimant stems from a number of different extrinsic causes then in our view a sensible attempt should be made to apportion liability accordingly. There is no reason to distinguish these conditions from the chronological development of industrial diseases or disabilities. The analogy with the polluted stream is closer than the analogy with the single fire. Nor is there anything in the *Bonnington* case or *McGhee*'s case requiring a different approach.

[42] Where the tortfeasor's breach of duty has exacerbated a pre-existing disorder or accelerated the effect of pre-existing vulnerability, the award of general damages for pain, suffering and loss of amenity will reflect only the exacerbation or acceleration. Further, the quantification of damages for financial losses must take some account of contingencies. In this context, one of those contingencies may well be the chance that the claimant would have succumbed to a stress-related disorder in any event. As it happens, all of these principles are

a exemplified by the decision of Otton J at first instance in *Page v Smith* [1993] PIQR Q55 (and not appealed by the claimant: see *Page v Smith (No 2)* [1996] 3 All ER 272, [1996] 1 WLR 855). He reduced the multiplier for future loss of earnings (as it happens as a teacher) from ten to six to reflect the many factors making it probable that the claimant would not have had a full and unbroken period of employment in any event and the real possibility that his employers would have
b terminated his employment because of his absences from work.

4. SUMMARY

[**43**] From the above discussion, the following practical propositions emerge. (1) There are no special control mechanisms applying to claims for psychiatric (or physical) illness or injury arising from the stress of doing the work the
c employee is required to do (see [22], above). The ordinary principles of employer's liability apply (see [20], above). (2) The threshold question is whether this kind of harm to this particular employee was reasonably foreseeable (see [23], above): this has two components (a) an injury to health (as distinct from occupational stress) which (b) is attributable to stress at work (as distinct from
d other factors) (see [25], above). (3) Foreseeability depends upon what the employer knows (or ought reasonably to know) about the individual employee. Because of the nature of mental disorder, it is harder to foresee than physical injury, but may be easier to foresee in a known individual than in the population at large (see [23], above). An employer is usually entitled to assume that the employee can withstand the normal pressures of the job unless he knows of some
e particular problem or vulnerability (see [29], above). (4) The test is the same whatever the employment: there are no occupations which should be regarded as intrinsically dangerous to mental health (see [24], above). (5) Factors likely to be relevant in answering the threshold question include: (a) The nature and extent of the work done by the employee (see [26], above). Is the workload much
f more than is normal for the particular job? Is the work particularly intellectually or emotionally demanding for this employee? Are demands being made of this employee unreasonable when compared with the demands made of others in the same or comparable jobs? Or are there signs that others doing this job are suffering harmful levels of stress? Is there an abnormal level of sickness or absenteeism in the same job or the same department? (b) Signs from the employee of impending
g harm to health (see [27], [28], above). Has he a particular problem or vulnerability? Has he already suffered from illness attributable to stress at work? Have there recently been frequent or prolonged absences which are uncharacteristic of him? Is there reason to think that these are attributable to stress at work, for example because of complaints or warnings from him or
h others? (6) The employer is generally entitled to take what he is told by his employee at face value, unless he has good reason to think to the contrary. He does not generally have to make searching inquiries of the employee or seek permission to make further inquiries of his medical advisers (see [29], above). (7) To trigger a duty to take steps, the indications of impending harm to health
j arising from stress at work must be plain enough for any reasonable employer to realise that he should do something about it (see [31], above). (8) The employer is only in breach of duty if he has failed to take the steps which are reasonable in the circumstances, bearing in mind the magnitude of the risk of harm occurring, the gravity of the harm which may occur, the costs and practicability of preventing it, and the justifications for running the risk (see [32], above). (9) The size and scope of the employer's operation, its resources and the demands it faces

are relevant in deciding what is reasonable; these include the interests of other
employees and the need to treat them fairly, for example, in any redistribution of
duties (see [33], above). (10) An employer can only reasonably be expected to
take steps which are likely to do some good: the court is likely to need expert
evidence on this (see [34], above). (11) An employer who offers a confidential
advice service, with referral to appropriate counselling or treatment services, is
unlikely to be found in breach of duty (see [17], [33], above). (12) If the only
reasonable and effective step would have been to dismiss or demote the employee,
the employer will not be in breach of duty in allowing a willing employee to
continue in the job (see [34], above). (13) In all cases, therefore, it is necessary to
identify the steps which the employer both could and should have taken before
finding him in breach of his duty of care (see [33], above). (14) The claimant must
show that that breach of duty has caused or materially contributed to the harm
suffered. It is not enough to show that occupational stress has caused the harm (see
[35], above). (15) Where the harm suffered has more than one cause, the employer
should only pay for that proportion of the harm suffered which is attributable to his
wrongdoing, unless the harm is truly indivisible. It is for the defendant to raise the
question of apportionment (see [36], [39], above). (16) The assessment of damages
will take account of any pre-existing disorder or vulnerability and of the chance that
the claimant would have succumbed to a stress-related disorder in any event (see
[42], above). We will now apply these principles to the facts of the four cases before
us. For convenience we are including only a brief summary of the individual cases
in the main body of this judgment. They are given more extensive treatment in
the appendix.

5. MRS HATTON

[44] Mrs Hatton began teaching in 1976. From 1980 to 1995 she taught French
at a comprehensive school in Huyton, Liverpool. In October 1995 she was signed
off from work because of depression and debility and never returned. She retired
on ill-health grounds in August 1996. The defendant school governors appeal
against the order of Judge Trigger in the Liverpool County Court on 7 August
2000 awarding her a total of £90,765·83 in damages and interest. His findings and
the evidence are discussed at [75]–[127] of the appendix.

[45] She had two months off work suffering from depression in 1989,
following the break-up of her marriage. Her two sons, born in about 1983 and
1988, lived with her. But she continued to enjoy her work and was coping with
the workload until September 1992.

[46] Mrs Hatton's workload was no greater or more burdensome than that of
any other teacher in a similar school. Nor had she complained to anyone about
it. Certain changes had taken place in the school years 1992–1993 and 1993–1994
but their effect had been absorbed by September 1994. In 1992 the school went
over to a modular GCSE French course. No other teacher found that this course
involved more preparation and marking after the first few weeks. Mrs Hatton did
not complain. The head of her department was absent from January 1993 and
retired in May 1993 and supply teachers were used for a while. No one knew that
this was involving her in much more work outside school. In September 1993 it
was decided to use English rather than supply teachers to help out with French.
Mrs Hatton was off work for a considerable part of 1993 to 1994 but did not tell
anyone at the school that she attributed her absences to overwork. In September
1994 a new head of department was appointed and the use of English teachers
stopped. Her work regime this year was entirely normal compared with other

a French teachers. The only difference in the year from September 1995 was a re-timing and reduction by one in her free periods, about which she did complain to the deputy head.

[47] Mrs Hatton's pattern of absence and illness was on the face of it readily attributable to causes other than stress at work. In January 1994 she was off work for a month following an attack in the street. In April 1994 one of her sons had *b* to go into hospital for a considerable period. A deputy head sent her home. She remained away for the rest of the term, certified with depression and debility. She saw a stress counsellor in August 1994 but did not tell the school about this. When she returned in September 1994 she attributed her absence to her son's illness. During the school year 1994–1995 she had no absences due to depression or debility, but she did have a number of absences for minor physical ailments, *c* including 19 days for sinusitis. She was a smoker who had suffered from this before.

[48] Her workload and her pattern of absence taken together could not amount to a sufficiently clear indication that she was likely to suffer from psychiatric injury as a result of stress at work such as to trigger a duty to do more *d* than was in fact done. The school could not reasonably be expected to probe further into the causes of her absence in the summer term 1994 when she herself had attributed it to problems at home which the school knew to be real. Hence the claim must fail at the first threshold of foreseeability.

[49] Even if the breakdown had been foreseeable, the judge would have had *e* to resolve the conflict in the expert evidence as to its causes and what if anything the school might have done to prevent it. The judge was entitled to find that her own perception of stress at work was at least a contributory factor. But he should have had difficulty in concluding that it was the only factor, given the evidence of the defendants' expert witness, Dr Wood. He should also have identified a *f* specific breach of duty which had contributed to the illness: an omission to do something without which it would in all probability not have happened. If there was no breach of duty in not probing further into her account of the summer of 1994, the only possible candidates are a failure to probe further into her pattern of physical illness in 1994–1995 or to react to her complaint about the 1995 timetable. It would, however, be difficult to conclude that anything the school *g* could have done by that stage would have made a difference.

[50] This is a classic case where no one can be blamed for the sad events which brought Mrs Hatton's teaching career to an end. It was sought to meet some of the obvious difficulties in her case by the argument that teaching is such a stressful profession that by 1995 all employers should have had in place systems *h* which would overcome the reluctance of people like Mrs Hatton to reveal their difficulties and seek help. We have already explained why we take the view that, although an employer who does have such a system is unlikely to be found in breach of duty, it is not for this court to impose such a duty upon all employers, or even upon all employers in a particular profession.

j
6. MR BARBER

[51] Mr Barber was also an experienced secondary school teacher. He was appointed head of maths at East Bridgwater Community School in 1984 and remained there until 12 November 1996 when he ceased work on medical advice. He accepted early retirement on 31 March 1997. The defendant local education authority appeal against the order of Judge Roach in the Exeter County Court on

8 March 2001 awarding him a total of £101,041·59 in damages and interest. His findings and the evidence are discussed in paras [139] to [163] of the appendix.   *a*

[52] The school was under particular pressure in the year 1995–1996. It was a comprehensive school in a deprived area of Bridgwater. Its roll had more than halved between the mid-1980s and the mid-1990s and resources had fallen accordingly. Restructuring became essential. However, there was comparatively little effect upon the maths department, as opposed to others. In September 1995   *b* Mr Barber, in common with other heads of department, became the 'area of experience co-ordinator' in maths. There was still the same number of maths teachers but the two former deputy heads of his department were given pastoral rather than management roles. To keep his former salary level Mr Barber took on another responsibility, as project manager in charge of publicity and media relations. He was working long hours.   *c*

[53] The evidence was that all the area of experience co-ordinators, and the senior management team, were suffering from work overload at this time. In addition to the restructuring and worries over falling rolls, the school was due for an OFSTED inspection in autumn 1996. While everyone was in the same boat, the evidence did not support the suggestion that Mr Barber was more   *d* overworked than any of his peers in these difficult circumstances. The judge found that his workload was not so extreme as to put his employers on notice.

[54] Mr Gill, one of the two deputy heads, was in charge of the timetable and curriculum and saw all the co-ordinators periodically. In October 1995 Mr Barber told him that the loss of his deputies was resulting in more work, and in February 1996 that work overload was affecting both him and the maths department.   *e* Mr Gill did not appreciate that Mr Barber was by then finding things too much; he advised Mr Barber to prioritise and delegate more.

[55] Mr Barber had developed depressive symptoms during the autumn 1995 term but told no one at school about these. He felt worse during the spring 1996 term but again told no one at school. He explored the possibility of other jobs or   *f* taking early retirement. In May 1996 he had three weeks off work with depression: he was surprised to be told the diagnosis as he had never thought of himself in that way. When he came back he had an informal meeting with the head, Mrs Hayward, and raised his concerns that he was finding things difficult. On 16 July 1996, he saw Mrs Newton, the other deputy head, and told her that he could not cope and that the situation was becoming detrimental to his health.   *g* She referred him to Mr Gill, who was more sympathetic. This was very shortly before the end of the summer term. He did not tell either of them about the symptoms of weight loss, lack of sleep and out-of-body experiences which he described in his evidence.

[56] Mrs Hayward retired unexpectedly at the end of term and Mr Gill   *h* became acting headmaster. On return for the autumn term he expressed some concern about Mr Barber and asked a colleague to keep an eye on him. Mr Barber had continued to suffer symptoms of stress over the summer holidays but had not been able to discuss these with his doctor. He first raised them with the doctor in October. In November he lost control in the classroom and was   *j* advised to stop work immediately.

[57] This was a classic case in which it is essential to consider at what point the school's duty to take some action was triggered, what that action should have been, and whether it would have done some good. Instead, the judge first considered whether the illness was caused by stress at work and reached the conclusion that it was. No doubt this was because the school had argued that

a Mr Barber's breakdown was caused by other things, and the judge had to resolve that issue. There was certainly evidence entitling him to hold that stress at work had made a material contribution. But that in itself was not enough to lead to the conclusion that the school was in breach of duty or that its breach caused the harm.

[58] Mr Barber did not think of himself as a candidate for psychiatric illness

b until it was diagnosed in May 1996. The first the school knew of any possible adverse effects upon his health of the difficulties at work which they were all experiencing was after his return. He simply told Mrs Hayward that he was not coping very well. He made a more explicit reference to his health to Mrs Newton and Mr Gill, but did not explain the symptoms from which he was suffering. This was just before the summer holidays, which are usually a source of relaxation and

c recuperation for hard-pressed teachers. Indeed he was unable to tell his own doctor about his symptoms until the month before the crisis arose. He told no one at school of any problems during that term.

[59] In those circumstances it is difficult indeed to identify a point at which the school had a duty to take the positive steps identified by the judge. It might have

d been different if Mr Barber had gone to Mr Gill at the beginning of the autumn term and told him that things had not improved over the holidays. But it is expecting far too much to expect the school authorities to pick up the fact that the problems were continuing without some such indication. Given the speed with which matters came to a head that term it might be difficult to sustain the judge's finding that temporary help would have averted the crisis. But in our view the

e evidence, taken at its highest, does not sustain a finding that they were in breach of their duty of care towards him.

7. MRS JONES

[60] Mrs Jones was employed as an administrative assistant at Trainwell, a

f local authority training centre, from August 1992 until 20 January 1995 when she went off sick with anxiety and depression. She never returned and was made redundant when the centre closed at the end of 1996. The defendant local authority appeal against the order of Judge Nicholl in the Birmingham County Court on 31 October 2000 awarding her a total of £157,541 damages and interest. The judge's findings and the evidence are discussed at [176]–[199] of the

g appendix.

[61] Mrs Jones' job was unique, a new post resulting from the consolidation of training activities in one site. The tasks were varied and the deadlines tight. They included submitting monthly claims to the local Training and Enterprise Council on which the whole operation depended. The judge found that she was having

h to work grossly excessive hours over the 37 per week required by her contract of employment. There was unchallenged evidence that her personnel officer, Mr King, had acknowledged in February 1993 that they knew it was a gamble to expect one person to do the work of two to three.

[62] She complained of overwork to her immediate managers, Mr Papworth

j and his deputy, from an early stage. She complained to Mr King at head office in February 1993. She also complained to him of unfair treatment and that she had been threatened with non-renewal of her temporary post if she persisted in her complaints of overwork. He said that he would try to get her extra help. Extra help was earmarked for her by Mr Papworth's superior but diverted by Mr Papworth to other tasks. In July 1994, Mrs Jones complained to Mrs York, who had taken over as her personnel officer, in a five-page document listing the

problems under 'health', 'excessive workload', 'equal opportunities', and
'managerial disagreements'. Once again it was noted that extra help should be
provided but none was forthcoming. In November 1994, Mrs Jones invoked the
formal grievance procedure, complaining of discrimination in her unsuccessful
application for an instructor's job at Trainwell and harassment during her time
there which had affected her health. The grievance hearing did not take place
until January 1995 when it was adjourned. She went off sick shortly afterwards.

[63] The judge also found that she had been 'harassed' by Mr Papworth. He
meant that she had been treated unreasonably in such matters as his reaction to
her complaints of overwork, dismissing these with the unfounded suggestion
that she had more than enough time to do what was required of her, threatening
her with loss of her job if she complained, failing to allocate the extra help
provided to her, and completely inappropriate behaviour around the grievance
hearing. This was not a case like Mr Barber's where everyone was overworked
and under pressure, but one where the job itself made unreasonable demands
upon an employee in a comparatively junior grade, and the management
response to her complaints was itself unreasonable.

[64] Mrs Jones did not go off work sick during any of this time. She did not
even consult her GP until March 1994, when she consulted him about abdominal
problems which he noted might be psychosomatic. Thereafter she suffered from
headaches which were not eased by multiple analgesics, although he diagnosed
migraine rather than psychiatric illness. There was therefore no specific medical
event which might have alerted her employers to the risk of the breakdown
which occurred in January 1995.

[65] However, the employers did know that excessive demands were being
placed upon Mrs Jones. They also knew that she was complaining of unreasonable
behaviour by her immediate manager. These were taken sufficiently seriously
for extra help to be arranged, not once but twice, but it was not actually provided.
She made two written formal complaints, one in July and one in November 1994,
that problems at work were causing harm to her health. It was not disputed that
they did in fact cause her breakdown in January 1995.

[66] The question, therefore, is not whether they had in fact caused harm to
her health before January 1995, but whether it was sufficiently foreseeable that
they would do so for it to be a breach of duty for the employers to carry on
placing unreasonable demands upon her and not to follow through their own
decision that something should be done about it. We have concluded, not
without some hesitation, that the evidence before the judge was sufficient to
entitle him to reach the conclusion that it was. We are conscious that the council
relied mainly on the evidence of Mr Papworth, which the judge did not find
impressive. They did not call either Mr King or Mrs York to explain what they
had made of Mrs Jones' complaints, and in particular her complaints in 1994 of
the adverse effect that these problems were having on her health. Unlike the
other cases before us, this was one such as was envisaged by Lord Slynn of Hadley
in *Waters v Comr of Police of the Metropolis* [2000] 4 All ER 934 at 938, [2000] 1 WLR
1607 at 1611, where the employer knew that the employee was being badly
treated by another employee and could have done something to prevent it.

[67] Once it is concluded that the combination of the way in which she was
being treated and her formal complaints about it made injury to her health
foreseeable, it is not difficult to identify what might have been done to prevent
the injury which in fact occurred. The judge was entitled to conclude that failure
to do this caused her breakdown. There was no challenge to the quantification

a of damages in this case. We have not therefore been able to consider whether any of the matters discussed earlier in this judgment might have led to any modification of the award. Our conclusion on liability should not be taken as any indication of our view on the appropriate measure of damages in this or any other such case.

b 8. MR BISHOP

[68] Mr Bishop worked for the defendant company from 1979 until February 1997 when he had a mental breakdown and attempted suicide. He never returned to work and was dismissed in 1998. The defendant appeals against the order of Judge Kent-Jones in the Leeds County Court on 26 January 2001 awarding him general damages of £7,000 and adjourning his claim for loss of earnings. The
c judge's findings and the evidence are discussed in the appendix at [211]–[223].

[69] The defendant was taken over by an American company in 1992 and reorganisation began. New shift patterns were introduced in 1994. Work was reorganised so that employees were expected to do a greater variety of tasks. Mr Bishop was at that time employed on mixer cleaning and graphite blowing.
d But in 1995 the mixer cleaning tasks were spread among other employees for health and safety reasons. Mr Bishop was employed mainly in receiving and distributing raw materials. Most employees welcomed the new shifts and coped well with the reorganisation. Mr Bishop did not. He was a meticulous worker, set in his ways, who found it hard to adjust and to make the very limited decisions now expected of him.

e [70] He complained about this to his manager, Mr Fairhurst, and asked to go back to his old work. His opposite number on the alternating shift also mentioned to Mr Fairhurst, and less formally to the foreman, his concern that Mr Bishop was not coping. Mr Fairhurst explained to Mr Bishop that there was nothing he could do: his old job was no longer available and he could not rearrange the work so as
f to give Mr Bishop what he wanted. He tried to reassure Mr Bishop that he was doing a good job and had nothing to worry about.

[71] Nevertheless, Mr Bishop did worry. He went to see his GP in November 1996. He was advised to change his job. He did not tell his employers about this. He was away from work between 24 January and 16 February 1997. Some of this time he would have been off shift. For the other times he submitted two sick
g notes referring to 'neurasthenia'. He returned to work for two days, after which there was a holiday and then the usual four days off. He returned on 24 February and his breakdown took place the following day.

[72] There was nothing unusual, excessive or unreasonable about the demands which were being placed upon Mr Bishop by his work. The sad fact was
h that he was unable to cope with the changes. His employers knew that he was unhappy and wanted to go back to the old ways, but they were not told of the advice given to him by his doctor. The two sick notes were not in themselves such clear signs of a risk to his mental health that a reasonable employer should have realised that something should be done.

j [73] Even if they had been, there was nothing that the employer could reasonably be expected to do. The job that he wanted was no longer available. The work which was available could not be reorganised to suit one employee. The reality was that the GP's advice was correct: the only solution would have been to dismiss him. The employer could not be in breach of duty for failing to dismiss an employee who wanted to continue and master the job despite the advice given to him by his own doctor.

9. CONCLUSION

[74] We therefore allow the defendants' appeals in the cases of Mrs Hatton, Mr Barber and Mr Bishop. Not without some hesitation, we dismiss the appeal in the case of Mrs Jones.

APPENDIX

A. MRS HATTON

1. *Introduction*

[75] Mrs Penelope Hatton taught French at the school which became known as St Thomas a Becket, Huyton between January 1980 and October 1995. She then had a breakdown in her health. She retired on health grounds in August 1996. Judgment was entered in her favour for £90,765·83 on the grounds that the school authorities had failed to take reasonable steps to protect her from suffering her stress-related psychiatric illness. They appeal to this court on liability and on issues relating to damage and mitigation. By a respondent's notice Mrs Hatton seeks to uphold the judgment on liability on grounds not relied on by the judge.

[76] One feature of this case was that Mrs Hatton never complained to anyone at the school that she was being overworked. Indeed, when the school's head teacher asked her when she returned to the school in September 1994 after spending nearly a whole term at home with a depressive illness whether there was anything the school could do to help, she said that there was not, and that her problems lay at home. Another was the fact that although the judge heard oral evidence over three-and-a-half days, and also received a large amount of documentary evidence, in his short judgment he did not refer to a number of significant parts of the evidence, or explain why he preferred the evidence given by Mrs Hatton to the evidence given by others. So far as the evidence of the three expert witnesses was concerned, he mentioned one of them once and the others not at all. It has therefore been necessary for this court to examine all the evidence in some detail.

[77] The history can conveniently be divided into the following periods of time: (i) prior to September 1992; (ii) September 1992–July 1993; (iii) September 1993–July 1994; (iv) September 1994–July 1995; (v) September–October 1995.

2. *The history prior to September 1992*

(i) The judge's findings

[78] Mrs Hatton got her first teaching post at a different school in September 1976. She moved to the defendants' school in January 1980 as second-in-command of the modern languages department. The head of the department was Mr Treanor. Between 1980 and 1985 she was allowed up to five 80-minute free periods each week. She could prepare much of her teaching work and do other tasks like marking during school hours. She would also spend one or two hours each evening on tasks like these. She taught French up to A-level standard, and found the work of teaching students of that aptitude satisfying and fulfilling. By the mid-1980s, however, when the school amalgamated with another school, there were no children taking A-level French. She continued to have four free periods each week following the amalgamation, and her workload generally did not increase. Indeed, the pupil-teacher ratio in the department did not alter materially between 1985 and 1996.

a

(ii) Other matters not recorded by the judge

[79] Mrs Hatton was married to a policeman, by whom she had two sons. Her marriage broke up in 1989, and thereafter she lived by herself with the two boys. She was off work for two months that year, suffering from depression. She told the judge that until the start of the 1991–1992 academic year she enjoyed her job and was able to cope with the workload. The French department was then

b staffed by Mr Treanor, Mrs Hatton and one other teacher. She said that she thought she had started teaching children with special educational needs in Years 10 and 11 that year, but in her witness statement she had said she began teaching these children six years earlier. It was common ground on the appeal that she was still coping with her workload until September 1992.

c

3. *September 1992–July 1993*

(i) The judge's findings

[80] In September 1992 Mr Treanor decided that GCSE French should now be taught in a modular form. The judge said that Mrs Hatton, along with many

d other teachers, found that this involved far more preparation and far more marking. An added complication was caused by the fact that Mr Treanor became unwell in January 1993, suffering from stress and anxiety. He retired on grounds of ill-health in May 1993. Miss Hampson, the head of English, was put in charge of the French department, and arrangements were made to engage supply

e teachers to support Mrs Hatton and the other French teacher.

[81] The judge found that these two teachers had to do extra work to help the supply teachers prepare their lessons, and that from 1993 onwards Mrs Hatton found that her out of classroom work was increasing to rather more than one or two hours an evening. He also said that the teaching of French to children with

f special educational needs created difficulties for the teachers.

(ii) Other matters not recorded by the judge

[82] There was a conflict of evidence about the extra demands made by modular teaching which the judge did not identify, much less resolve. Mrs Hatton said that it was agreed with Mr Treanor that she would teach

g modular French to the less able pupils in Years 10 and 11, while the other teacher would continue teaching the traditional GCSE course to the abler pupils. She accepted that the burden that modular French imposed on a teacher varied with the ability of the children being taught. The tests for pupils of lower ability (whom she was teaching, at any rate during this initial year) were generally

h multiple choice tests requiring one-word answers, and the marking was quick and easy. The only administrative task imposed on her, except for a period immediately following Mr Treanor's departure, was to select the best result for each child in each skills area at the end of term and pass it to the head of department. She told the judge that parts of the modular course were more

j demanding than conventional GCSE and parts were less demanding.

[83] Mrs Hatton complained that because the modular course had no set coursework, she had to dip into textbooks and prepare her own worksheets. She said it was a totally different type of syllabus. Sometimes there would be two tests in one week, one in another, and three in another, so that it was an ongoing process of testing which had to be recorded and marked and set in an exam situation.

[84] The judge received unchallenged evidence from two other French
teachers who told him that after the first two or three weeks modular   a
French involved no extra work. Mrs Parry, who joined the school as head of
the French department in September 1994, said that it was only during the first
two or three weeks that she spent as much time as Mrs Hatton said was needed
for preparation and marking. Teachers were provided with the syllabus, and the
teaching demands were not significantly different from conventional GCSE   b
teaching. Mrs Sansbury, who came to the school as a 23-year-old newly qualified
supply teacher the following year, and who took over Mrs Hatton's classes after
she left, gave evidence to similar effect. It was common ground that there was,
in fact, no evidence to support the judge's finding that any other teacher, let alone
many other teachers, found that modular teaching involved far more preparation
and far more marking. There was also no evidence that Mrs Hatton had   c
complained to anyone that she found modular teaching burdensome.

[85] In these circumstances Mr Collender QC, who appeared for the school,
contended that the judge should have found that the school authorities neither
knew nor ought to have known that the move to modular French would impose
a materially different teaching burden on Mrs Hatton, and that it did not in fact   d
impose such a burden. Mr Atherton, who appeared for Mrs Hatton, maintained
that there was no evidence that the school gave any consideration, in terms of
additional hours, to the effect of introducing modular French, or to the effect on
Mrs Hatton when she had to take over the administration of modular French
immediately after Mr Treanor's departure. He said that it was axiomatic that
teachers will vary in their responses to changes at work, and that the judge was   e
entitled to accept the gist of Mrs Hatton's evidence about the burden it imposed
on her. It appears to us that the judge ought to have made findings about these
matters.

[86] So far as supply teaching is concerned, the only evidence about the extra
work this created during school hours was that from time to time Mrs Hatton   f
had to leave her class and help a supply teacher set the work. Extra marking and
printing extra work sheets took up about two hours a week while the supply
teachers were there. It was common ground that nobody at the school knew
how many hours Mrs Hatton was working out of school hours. Mr Atherton
maintained that an attentive head teacher would have realised the extra work she
would have to do out of school as a result of the various changes and disruptions   g
in 1992–1993.

4. *September 1993–July 1994*

(i) The judge's findings   h
[87] Mr Wood became head teacher in September 1993. By now it had been
decided to use teachers from the English department to teach French instead of
supply teachers. Between 5 and 24 November 1993 Mrs Hatton was off work
with a viral infection. In January 1994 she was attacked in the street and stayed
off work for a month. She then returned to work for the rest of the term, apart   j
from the odd day's absence. From 18 April 1994 she was off work for 62 days.
Her GP certified that her absence was due to depression and debility. The judge
said that during that absence her eldest son was sufficiently ill to warrant
detention in hospital for a considerable period.

[88] The judge found as a fact that one of the major precipitating factors which
caused her long absence from work was the stress she was suffering consequent

a on the increased duties and pressures being applied on her at the school. The school knew that she was a single mother and that one of her children was in hospital and, from the sick notes, that she was suffering from fairly large-scale depression and debility. The school did not, however, know that she went to see a stress counsellor during the summer holidays of 1994.

b (ii) Other matters not recorded by the judge

[89] The judge got the sequence of events wrong in April 1994. Mr MacNamara, one of the deputy head teachers, gave unchallenged evidence that he saw Mrs Hatton looking dreadful one day at school. When he asked her the reason, she said she had been up all night with her son who was seriously ill at the hospital. Mr MacNamara sent her home, and this was the start of her long
c absence from work.

[90] There was a lot of evidence about the events of this year which the judge did not mention. The number of special needs classes Mrs Hatton taught had now been reduced from five to two. She conceded that she was now used to teaching modular French. The use of supply teachers had ceased. She conceded
d that she was now doing normal teaching, although she complained of the administrative work connected with modular French. She was away from school in any event (including school holidays) for 11 of the 25 weeks between the start of the winter term and 18 April 1994, when her prolonged absence began. She suffered anxiety, as well as physical injuries, as a result of the assault, which took some time to settle.

e [91] Mr Collender complains that the judge did not mention, much less give any reasons for rejecting, the evidence given by Dr Wood, his client's medical expert, about the likely cause of Mrs Hatton's long absence in April–July 1994. Since this long absence, and the school's reaction to it, marks the high water mark of Mrs Hatton's case, it is necessary to consider the expert evidence about it in
f some detail.

(iii) The expert evidence

[92] Dr Wood is a consultant forensic psychiatrist who has been concerned with the treatment and assessment of people with stress-related illnesses for many years. He said that the causes of stress are cumulative. Since the end of the
g 1993 summer term Mrs Hatton had not been at school all that much. Running a house with two small children as a single mother is stressful in itself, and he believed that if it had not been for the assault and her son's serious illness she would not have become ill in the April–July 1994 period.

[93] He said that Mrs Hatton was recognisable as an obsessional individual
h who was prone to anxiety and depression when under pressure. Such a person is likely to spend more and more time trying to get things right as a function of her illness rather than as a function of the amount of work she has to do. It is quite common for such people on different occasions to lay the blame on a single cause because this is more comfortable for them, although other things are causing or
j contributing to the pressure. Thus Mrs Hatton attributed her illness to the work overload when speaking to a stress counsellor in August, and to her son's illness when speaking to her head teacher in September.

[94] Dr Baker, the claimant's expert, is a neuropsychologist, who specialises in dealing with people with brain injuries. He felt unable to comment on the situation at the school. He felt that overwork, the assault and the boy's illness all contributed to Mrs Hatton's illness at this time. He accepted that there was no

objective evidence of a work overload, but he pointed to the fact that Mrs Hatton
thought subjectively that this was a stressful factor. He was certainly willing to *a*
accept that her long absence had to be attributed to more than just stress alone.

[95] Mr Atherton suggested that the judge might have accepted Mrs Hatton's
evidence that she did not consider the effect of the assault to be still a problem in
April 1994, and that the judge might have been influenced by what she had said
to her GP in May and her stress counsellor in August about the cause of her *b*
troubles being a stressful job. In our judgment the judge ought to have
considered the effect of all the evidence more carefully before making his findings
in relation to this period.

5. *September 1994–July 1995*

c

(i) The judge's findings

[96] The judge found that in spite of Mrs Parry's arrival as head of the French
department, Mrs Hatton had a similar workload as in the previous academic year.
Indeed, the introduction of the national curriculum involved extra duties and
responsibilities, particularly in relation to children with special educational needs. *d*
It was particularly difficult to interest these children in French.

[97] The judge referred to a brief meeting in September 1994 between
Mrs Hatton and Mr Wood. She attributed her lengthy absence to the illness of
her son, and did not indicate to Mr Wood that anything specific was troubling
her. The judge found that she was fearful of being seen to be making unnecessary
complaints because of the pressures she was under. Mr Wood, on the other *e*
hand, appeared to the judge to be a man who perhaps did not have the ability to
comprehend that depression in one of his teachers was something which required
detailed and sensitive handling.

[98] The judge found that during this year Mrs Hatton had no specific
absences due to debility or depression. He recorded, however, a number of *f*
absences: three days for influenza, five days for the same cause, 19 days due to
sinusitis, two days due to a sore throat, and two other very short absences due to
a virus and an upset stomach respectively. He commented, however, that even
a casual look at her health record should have made it apparent to the school
authorities that these absences were becoming increasingly frequent. He said it
was now clear that by September 1995 Mrs Hatton was teetering on the brink of *g*
a serious illness which was stress-induced.

(ii) Other matters not recorded by the judge

[99] It was common ground that for the academic year 1994–1995 the use of
supply teachers had ceased, the use of English teachers in the French department *h*
had ceased, the ratio of teachers to pupils remained unaltered, and Mrs Hatton's
free time had increased by one hour per fortnight. Mrs Parry said that
Mrs Hatton never complained to her about her workload. Mrs Hatton, for her
part, said that apart from teaching modular French there was nothing different,
difficult or unusual about her teaching regime for this academic year. *j*
Dr Dunham, the chartered psychologist and stress management consultant who
gave evidence on her behalf, accepted that her work regime this year was entirely
normal compared with other French teachers. Mr Atherton, however,
maintained that the judge had been entitled to rely on a passage in Mrs Hatton's
witness statement in which she said that the requirement to teach National
Curriculum French to special needs children caused a massive strain. In our

a judgment the judge ought to have taken into consideration the unchallenged evidence that there was nothing unusual about Mrs Hatton's workload during this academic year.

6. September–October 1995

b (i) The judge's findings
[**100**] The judge described how the timetable for this year gave her two free periods in the first week and three in the second week of each two-week rota. This represented a slight diminution in the number of free periods available for preparation and marking. In the first week of the rota one of these free periods was early on the Monday morning and the other towards the end of the Friday, *c* which made these periods less useful to her. He found that she did her best to tell Mr MacNamara that she took a very dim view of this further reduction in her free periods and the alteration of their timing, and that she left him in no reasonable doubt that she was finding it increasingly difficult to manage her teaching tasks. Mr MacNamara could not alter the timetable for that year, but he promised to *d* look into the problem for the following year which gave Mrs Hatton, the judge found, very little, if any, solace.

[**101**] He said that by October 1995 she was suffering badly from her stress-induced condition. From 16 October she was signed off work by her GP, suffering from depression and debility, and she was never able to return. She retired on grounds of ill-health with effect from 31 August 1996.
e

(ii) Other matters not recorded by the judge
[**102**] Mrs Sansbury told the judge that when she took over Mrs Hatton's classes, she found the modular French teaching quite straightforward. She was given a guide, and it took her two to three weeks to become familiar with it. After *f* that it was quite easy to follow. She would spend one to two hours each week preparing work, and two to three hours each week marking.

[**103**] Mr Wood said that there was nothing unusual about Mrs Hatton's workload or the amount of free time she was given. The school's aim was to allow teachers 10% of their time off in a 50-period fortnight, and this was what the new timetable allowed for. In the two previous years she had been allowed *g* slightly more than 10%. The immediate cause of Mrs Hatton's breakdown had come when she had attended a day organised by the Knowsley Careers Service. Mr Wood said that it was a friendly, enjoyable day, but Mrs Hatton was afraid that it meant that more burdens would be placed on her, and her resistance completely broke down.
h

7. The employers' obligations

(i) The judge's findings
[**104**] The judge said that stress connoted a process of behavioural, emotional, *j* mental and physical reactions caused by prolonged, increasing or new pressures which were significantly greater than a person's coping resources. He referred to the increasing volume of pre-1994 literature which documented the effect of such stress on professional persons (such as teachers) in particular. He said that the effects of increasing pressures in the professional workplace were or ought to be as well-recognised as the dangers for pedestrians of seriously defective paving stones in a busy thoroughfare. Extra demands were undoubtedly being placed on

professional people, and the fact that one person might be able to absorb such a degree of stress did not in itself absolve an employer from being liable when another person performing similar work succumbed to stress.

[105] The judge referred to the 1990 guide for managers and teachers in the schools sector to which we have referred in [8], above. The judge referred to the way in which this guide encouraged every education authority to devise its own statement on managing stress at work, and to emphasise the importance of senior management commitment to the practical implementation of its policy. He said that there were many similar publications warning of the dangers of stress-induced illness.

[106] He was critical of the school for having done nothing before September 1995 to implement any of these recommendations. He said that by the summer of 1995, at the very latest, the school authorities ought to have realised that Mrs Hatton was on the brink of suffering a bad psychological reaction as a consequence of the mounting pressure in her job over the previous years. They ought to have heeded the long period of absence in 1994 due to depression and debility and her other frequent illnesses, and linked these absences with her increased workload and increased responsibilities. He said that their response to these absences and to the increased workload was minimal.

[107] The judge felt that Mr Wood lacked any empathy or understanding of the effects of stress on persons for whom he was responsible. He was critical of the very short meeting which represented Mr Wood's only response to her long absence in 1994, when he had made no attempt to analyse the causes of her absences or to press delicately with her the root causes of her travails. He had recognised that something was wrong but he did not do enough to get to the bottom of what was wrong.

[108] The judge said that Mrs Hatton's nervous and psychological illness, which came on in October 1995, was both foreseeable and avoidable. He said that if by 1994 there had been a system of checks and balances at the school to pick up the early warning signs of stress, it was highly probable that her breakdown could have and would have been avoided. These measures would have involved the provision at time of extra teaching staff and the provision of more free periods (or free periods at a better time in the timetable). The judge said they would have been comparatively minimal.

[109] He added that the provision of a culture at the school of caring, a culture of sensitivity, and the setting aside of time by persons such as the head teacher, or by someone such as a deputy head teacher, to enable regular one-to-one meetings to take place with members of staff, would have generated such a degree of trust between Mrs Hatton and her superior teachers that her problems would have been identified and redressed. The judge said that in this context he accepted the evidence of Dr Baker, who said that more attention should have been provided for Mrs Hatton after her return to work in September 1994. If extra support had been provided for her, it was highly probable that her illness would not have occurred.

(ii) Other evidence not recorded or analysed by the judge

[110] Mr Wood described to the judge the support mechanisms for teachers at the school. If a member of staff had a concern, they would go to their head of department or head of faculty. If it was a pastoral matter, they would go to the head of year. At the time there was also a structure of four senior teachers, two deputy head teachers and himself as head teacher. If a member of staff wanted to

a come straight to him, he would listen, and people came every day. The school chaplain was also available.

[111] The school was previously a voluntary-aided school, but between 1993 and 1999 it became a grant-maintained school, so that its former links with the Knowsley Local Education Authority were severed. Mr Wood did not think that there was any published stress policy prior to 1995, but Mrs Hatton, as an
b experienced teacher, would have been aware of the support structures. He also described the external counselling services that were available to teachers.

[112] He said that the support mechanisms would either be triggered by a teacher saying that he/she was in trouble, or there would be obvious signs that all was not well: noise from the classroom, or time off, or a teacher not looking
c as bright and cheerful as usual. He said that the old culture was gone, and that if a teacher had a problem at school he/she would be expected to share it.

[113] He said that in September 1994 he had gone to see Mrs Hatton. He was conscious that she had been off work for a considerable time, and he felt he should meet her and ask if there was anything the school could do. She told him that the problem was not in the school and that there was nothing the school
d could do for her. She thanked him for offering to help. He said that there were a number of courses of action he had in mind, but he had to respect her decision that she did not want to receive any help from him. She wanted to keep her problems to herself, and he felt that he should not pry.

[114] He told the judge that the school knew all about the assault and her son's
e illness and that he knew the contents of her sick notes. He said that he never knew how great her problems were because she did not wish to discuss them with him. She had had time off school for reasons he understood to be not related to the school, and with which he could not help. He had wanted to open up a dialogue with her about her problems, but she did not want to engage in such a dialogue. When she was at the school she did a good job.
f [115] He told the judge the different techniques the school used when a teacher complained of a work overload. They might move a lesson to another member of staff, or bring in an unqualified teaching assistant to help, or advise a stressed teacher to have a few days off here and there. Even though there was no written policy, the school certainly had established practices and procedures to
g help people who were having difficulty in the classroom.

[116] Dr Wood, the psychiatrist, was asked for his views on the literature on which Mr Atherton relied. He agreed that stress management was a helpful process in any work situation. He was sceptical, however, about the value of stress audits. He said that they represented a way of managing change. Staff
h would be canvassed about their views on what was going on at the school, in a kind of opinion poll. The difficulty about this approach was that very often this kind of audit leads to disappointment in the long run. The resources may not be there to meet the staff's wishes, and it can be very demoralising when it all comes to nothing. The cynics tend to lead the grumbling, and people may feel worse in
j the long run. He added that a stress audit is a fairly dodgy process if it is not seen through to the end. The factors that prevent this are usually beyond the control of school managers.

[117] When asked about Mr Wood's conduct in September 1994 Dr Wood said that managers are in a very difficult position if they try and get behind what their staff tell them. The margin between appropriate concern and prying into a teacher's personal affairs is a very narrow one. Dr Wood provided a confidential

counselling service to members of the West Yorkshire Fire Brigade, and he said
that 80% of their referrals turned out to relate to domestic stress.   *a*

[118] He said that there might have been a range of causes for Mrs Hatton's
breakdown in October 1995. Sometimes a previous episode of depression reduces
a person's resilience and makes a further episode more likely, and Mrs Hatton
had endured two such episodes, in 1989 and 1994. Her single parent status with
two young children to care for and the lack of a close confidant to share her   *b*
worries was another possible factor. Another was that the majority of depressive
illnesses came out of the blue without any particular cause. There was some
evidence in her medical notes of anxiety about the health of a member of her
family which led to anxiety about her own health in July 1995. She had had
antibiotics twice in 1995 for different types of infection, and this may have
undermined her. All in all, it took very little to tip her over. If she had been   *c*
involved in work other than teaching it would have taken very little extra stress
in her situation at work to tip the balance against her. There were pressures
inherent in her job, and in September 1995 she was no longer able to tackle it with
the resilience of an ordinary individual.

[119] Dr Wood recognised that an employer had a duty of care to provide a   *d*
safe workplace, and that good management was desirable in all organisations. He
said that, in general, management in schools did not yet seem to be very
sophisticated. When he was asked about the contents of some of the literature
on stress management, he said that a great deal of what was being put to him was
well up the scale towards counsels of perfection. His experience of managers in
this sort of situation is that they apply common sense which serves reasonably   *e*
well in many respects. The Health and Safety Commission (HSC) advice
represented an alternative school of thought, but there were costs as well as gains
in stress management programmes. They were extremely time-consuming and
expensive, and he and others had never found any organisation which implemented
all the HSC's recommendations.   *f*

[120] Although he did not mention him by name, it is clear that the judge was
heavily influenced by the evidence given by Mr Dunham. He is a stress
management consultant who has been writing books and articles about stress in
the teaching profession for over 25 years. His original witness statement was
coloured by a view of the facts which was not supported by the evidence the
judge received at the trial.   *g*

[121] There were two features of Mr Dunham's evidence which need special
mention. The first was his reliance on reg 3 of the Management of Health and
Safety at Work Regulations 1992, SI 1992/2051, which obliges every employer to
make a suitable and sufficient assessment of the risks to the health and safety of
his employees to which they are exposed whilst they were at work. He did not   *h*
suggest that his client had a claim for damages for breach of statutory duty, but
he said that a stress audit would have represented a fulfilment of that duty, so far
as risks of psychological injury to school staff were concerned. He cited a 1998
article of his which suggested that such an audit would attempt to identify what
levels of stress existed within the school, and whether job satisfaction and   *j*
physical and mental health were better in some parts of the school than in others.
He felt that the fact that Mr Treanor had retired because of stress-related
ill-health indicated that all was not well.

[122] He also emphasised the importance of leadership from the top.
According to European Commission recommendations for reducing work stress,
published in 1997, employers, such as the authorities at this school, needed to

a take action to raise awareness of the issue of work-related stress, and to acknowledge that it was not a personal problem nor a weakness but an issue that the organisation as a whole could address. People should be encouraged to come forward when problems seemed to be emerging, and stress awareness should be made part of the school's management systems.

[123] In his oral evidence Mr Dunham said that the failure to assess the risks
b of work overload on Mrs Hatton and her colleague in the French department following Mr Treanor's departure was perhaps more important than the lack of a formal stress audit. He conceded that a number of the allegations of negligence he made in the witness box were not mentioned in his report, and he accepted that the school authorities might have more experience than he had in managing such a school. He had not been inside a comprehensive school since 1990. He
c had no experience of modular French.

[124] He said that Mrs Hatton ought to have received much closer support from September 1994 onwards. At the start of that term the school ought to have prolonged the discussion about what had happened the previous term, in order to try and assess whether the issue of stigma was a factor in the answers
d Mrs Hatton gave to Mr Wood. It was superficial for Mr Wood to accept her answer. His reaction did not recognise the possible existence in this school of a barrier which would prevent teachers expressing their true feelings, particularly to people in authority. If he had been in Mr Wood's position he thought he would have said 'Can we meet again?' He accepted, however, that other people
e with a different character might reasonably have taken a different view and accepted Mrs Hatton's reply at its face value, although he added that he thought they might have been misled.

[125] He accepted that it was reasonable for the school to expect her to teach a small number of special needs children. He thought every teacher ought to be
f capable of coping with the change to modular teaching, although he queried the manner of its introduction. He said it was reasonable for the school to employ supply teachers when Mr Treanor left. He accepted that if there was over-capacity in the English department, it was reasonable to use English teachers able to teach French for the lower ability range. He criticised Mrs Hatton for not bringing her true feelings to Mr Wood's notice in September 1994. He accepted that her
g programme of work for that academic year was completely normal. Apart possibly for the sinusitis, he accepted that there were no incidents that year referable to stress at work. He said that if he had been at the school he would have needed to know how she was coping, because some people will go on working when they ought to stop. He accepted, however, that it was reasonable
h for the defendants to assume that she had recovered from her earlier problems.

[126] Dr Baker accepted that when he had written his report he had known nothing about Mrs Hatton's son's illness. Nor had he known that Mrs Hatton had told Mr Wood that her absence had been due to problems at home and not to problems at work. Even though he accepted that the assault and the son's
j illness would have been factors contributing to her depressive illness in 1994, he felt that more care and attention should have been paid to her on her return. If he had been in Mr Wood's shoes he would have wanted to monitor the situation for six months. He accepted that as the doctor's certificates had stopped, it was reasonable for the school to assume that she was fit to return to work. He also accepted that if the position had been monitored for six months after September 1994 no absences due to depressive ill-health would have been noticed.

[127] He knew that sinusitis could be associated with heavy smoking, and as *a* Mrs Hatton was a heavy smoker this would have been a reasonable explanation for that illness. He felt that when she queried the timetable in September 1995 some effort should have been made to monitor her progress, because she was then at risk of developing a further period of anxiety and depression.

8. *The respondent's notice*

[128] The main point raised in the respondent's notice was that the judge should have found that it was not necessary for Mrs Hatton to prove that the defendants knew or should have known that the particular requirements of her work were likely to cause her to develop stress-related psychiatric illness. This argument was founded on the contention that the risk that teachers might *c* develop mental illness due to the stressful nature of their work was well documented in the literature available to the court. The judge should have found the defendants to have been in breach of a duty to take action to assess and reduce such a risk by providing appropriate instruction and counselling services, and by encouraging the use of such services. If this had been done, Mrs Hatton would have used these services and avoided the illness which terminated her teaching *d* career. It was argued that because teaching had been identified in the literature as work which was likely to cause teachers to develop stress-related illness, the case was distinguishable from *Walker v Northumberland CC* [1995] 1 All ER 737.

[129] In his submissions both to the judge and to this court Mr Atherton relied heavily on his contention that teachers as a class were particularly vulnerable to *e* stress. He said that the literature demonstrated that there were many teachers in need of protection which was not yet available to them. He told the judge that this was an opportunity for a judgment to be delivered which would change social attitudes. If teachers were being required to work longer and longer hours, there was a corresponding obligation on their employers to ensure that a safety *f* net was provided (in the form of advice and training and stress strategies) to those who ran into difficulties, as they surely would.

9. *Our conclusion on liability*

[130] We consider that this judgment cannot stand. At the very least the *g* action should be retried in order that findings of fact might be made which properly reflected the evidence and proper reasons were given why one side's evidence should be preferred to the other side's. There was, as our analysis has shown, overwhelming evidence which tended to show that except during the two terms following Mr Treanor's departure Mrs Hatton was not given any *h* more work than was reasonable for a French teacher of her experience to undertake. The judge did not explain why, despite all this evidence, he was disposed to find that she was subjected to an increased workload.

[131] It is, however, possible to go one step further. For the reasons set out in our main judgment at [48]–[50], the judge approached the question of the *j* school's legal duty to Mrs Hatton in the wrong way. We are satisfied that even on Mrs Hatton's own evidence her breakdown in health was not reasonably foreseeable by the school. The judge should also have identified the specific breach of duty which contributed to her illness and explained why anything the school could have done at the time she complained about the 1995 timetable could have made any difference.

a

10. *Damages*

[132] The issue as to damages arises in this way. There is no dispute about the award of £6,000 for general damages or the award for lost earnings between 31 August 1996 and 1 December 1998. The defendants, however, challenge the way in which the judge approached the question of compensating her for loss of earnings, or earning capacity after that date.

b

[133] The judge accepted Dr Baker's evidence that she would have been well enough to seek employment as a teacher again by about June 1998. He said that given the economic problems on Merseyside and the difficulties of obtaining part-time teaching work in private schools in the area, it would be reasonable to expect her to have obtained such employment by December 1998. After that date he deducted from the net salary she would have received at the school a notional net earning capacity which gradually increased from £600 per month to £625 per month by the date of the trial. So far as the future was concerned he applied a multiplier of six to a net loss of £8,760 p a. In the result, the award was made up as follows:

c

d

General damages	£6,000
Past loss of earnings (gross of CRU)	£46,876·14
Future loss of earnings	£53,560
	£106,436·14
CRU	£18,866·31
	£87,569·83
Interest	£3,106
	£90,675·83

e

[134] The defendants complained that the basis for the monthly figure of £600 was not explained. Moreover Mrs Hatton did not seek to adduce any evidence of her earning capacity. In the absence of such evidence the judge should have made a modest lump sum award for disadvantage on the labour market.

f

[135] The defendants were not arguing that she should give credit for her ill-health retirement pension of £500 a month. They maintained, however, as an alternative argument, that the evidence suggested that she had a significantly greater earning capacity than that suggested by the judge. She had told the judge that she had checked with the Teachers' Pension Agency as to what she could and could not do, so as to avoid impinging on her pension, and that she had found out that she was not allowed to teach at a school run by a local education authority if she wished to continue to receive her pension. In any event, she said that she did not think she would want to go back into a situation like the one she left before.

g

[136] The defendants argued that it was not just to have no regard to her pension payment when calculating her losses, while allowing her to take into account the possibility of losing her pension as a reason for limiting her job search. She had said that she was searching for work at an annual salary of £12,000 gross (£9,575 net). This figure should have been taken as the best indicator of her residual earning capacity.

h

[137] Mr Atherton showed us how the judge had intervened during his final submissions at the trial to indicate that he was thinking of finding that Mrs Hatton had an earning capacity which he would draw from his knowledge of the world in the absence of evidence. He said that the judge's approach was reasonable, given Mrs Hatton's disadvantage in the labour market due to her age, medical history and lack of transferable skills. He showed us that even Dr Wood had considered that his client would not be able to cope with the pressures of teaching

j

in the public sector. She had not in fact said that she had made no effort to resume
public sector teaching because she might lose her pension, and Mr Atherton said *a*
that no inference to that effect could fairly be made. Her lack of success in
applying for jobs suggested that the salary figures suggested by the defendants
were unrealistically high.

[138] If we had upheld this judgment on liability, we would have awarded her
a sum of £10,000 in respect of her loss of earning capacity for the period from *b*
1 December 1998 onwards. The idea that she might have been able to go on
teaching at any comprehensive school and avoided stress-related illness appears
to us to be a little far-fetched, and Mrs Hatton clearly made no attempt to find any
public sector teaching, part-time or otherwise, for fear of losing her pension. We
consider that there is considerable force in the defendant's contentions, and that
justice demands that we should approach the question of compensation for the *c*
period in the broad-brush way we have indicated.

B. MR BARBER

1. *Introduction*   *d*

[139] Mr Barber was an experienced maths teacher. He was appointed head
of maths at East Bridgwater Community School in January 1984 when he was
nearly 40 years old. He remained at the school until 12 November 1996 when he
succumbed to a serious depressive disorder. He has not taught since, and he
accepted early retirement on 31 March 1997. Judgment was entered in his favour *e*
for £101,041·59, inclusive of interest. Judge Roach held that the defendants, who
were the local education authority, had demonstrated a want of care for
Mr Barber's health. He had been exposed to a materially higher risk of injury to
his mental health than a teacher working in a similar position with a similar heavy
workload. The defendants appeal on liability and on the amount of the damages
award.   *f*

2. *The judge's findings*

[140] The judge found that Mr Barber was a dedicated and conscientious
teacher. The school was a comprehensive school, situated in a deprived area of
Bridgwater. Its roll had fallen from about 1,000 in the mid-1980s to about 450 ten *g*
years later. This drop in numbers had had a significant effect on the school
budget.

[141] It was therefore decided to restructure the staffing arrangements. In
future the academic departments would be headed by 'area of experience
co-ordinators'. The former posts of deputy head of department were abolished *h*
or drastically reduced in number, and in smaller departments junior staff were
re-assigned to other posts of responsibility. In general the academic departments
were downsized and streamlined to reflect the lower number of pupils now being
attracted to the school.

[142] The judge said that as a result of these changes Mr Barber became the *j*
maths area of experience co-ordinator in March 1995. He found that he
effectively continued to be head of the maths department, but with fewer staff,
and he was paid a reduced salary commensurate with his reduced position. His
two former deputies were assigned to other duties. As a result of all this, the
judge said that he was left heading a smaller department without any significant
assistance or support from deputies.

a [143] In order that he could keep his former salary level he was allowed to apply for another area of responsibility, and in May 1995 he was appointed project manager in charge of publicity and media relations. The judge said that this was seen as an important post. The school needed successful publicity and good community ties in order to halt the decline in pupil numbers and reverse the falling annual budgets.

b [144] The subsequent history, as recounted by the judge, can be briefly summarised. He said that Mr Barber had a full teaching timetable together with his new media job. He was working 61 to 70 hours a week, and the pressures took their toll. He had never suffered from psychiatric illness before, but he developed depressive symptoms during 1995, and in May 1996 his doctor signed him off work because of depression brought about by his workload. He returned c three weeks later and re-assumed his responsibilities in full. Although he complained to the headmistress and her two deputies about the work pressures, nothing was done to ease them, and on 12 November 1996 he went down with his serious illness.

[145] Mrs Hayward was the head teacher, and the judge found that she had an d autocratic and bullying leadership style. She had two deputies, Mrs Newton and Mr Gill. Mr Gill was in charge of the timetable. On 31 October 1995 Mr Gill noted that Mr Barber had told him that the loss of his deputies had resulted in more work for him. On 20 February 1996 Mr Gill noted that work overload was affecting both Mr Barber and the maths department. Mr Gill told the judge that he was urging Mr Barber to prioritise his work. The judge said that Mr Gill did e not at that stage appreciate that Mr Barber was finding the work now too heavy for him to cope with. He formed the impression that Mr Gill sympathised with Mr Barber but felt impotent about remedying the situation.

[146] When Mr Barber returned from his three-week sick leave in May 1996, he had an informal meeting with Mrs Hayward. The judge found that he raised f with her his concerns that he was finding things difficult and that he was not coping very well with the workload. Mrs Hayward was not sympathetic. She said that all her staff were under stress, and she gave Mr Barber no help in alleviating his workload. On 16 July he saw Mrs Newton. He told her he could not cope with his workload and that the situation was becoming detrimental to his health. He said he had already had to take time off work for stress and g depression, and that he could not see himself in his post in the immediate future if the work content remained the same. Mrs Newton simply referred him to Mr Gill without taking any steps to investigate or remedy the situation herself. Mr Barber found Mr Gill to be more sympathetic, but apart from telling him again to prioritise Mr Gill took no steps to improve his situation or consider what h might be done.

[147] The judge found that Mr Barber's meeting with Mrs Hayward in June represented a clear warning to the school's senior management that he needed help to carry out his duties, even if that help would have had to be limited in time on account of budgetary constraints. He said that Mrs Hayward's response to his j difficulties was inadequate. At the very least Mr Barber's position needed investigating. He said that the responses of Mrs Newton and Mr Gill were similarly inadequate.

[148] In the judge's view, a prudent employer, faced with the knowledge of a work overload dating back to the autumn of 1995, and increasing in 1996 to the extent that the employee had to take time off work, would have investigated the employee's situation to see how his difficulties might be alleviated. Mr Barber

had told the head teacher and the two deputy heads that he was having difficulty
in coping, and that his health was declining. The judge said that it must have been *a*
apparent, given his time off work for stress in May 1996, that the risk to injury to
his mental health was significant, and higher than that which would have related
to a teacher in a similar position with a heavy workload. The failure to
investigate or provide at the least temporary assistance led to Mr Barber's
attempting to cope, and in the result inevitably failing in the attempt.   *b*

[149] The judge was also critical of the fact that the defendant education
authority had no policy in place as to the effect of stress on teachers in
Mr Barber's position. The HSC guide (see [8], above) had been published in 1990,
and this guide highlighted the need to be sensitive about the possibility of
teaching staff suffering from stress. It also spoke of a complementary need to
develop a supportive culture for teachers. The judge considered that if the senior *c*
management team at the school had been aware of the guide, and had followed
its advice, the crisis that affected Mr Barber would have been averted.

[150] Although other reasons for Mr Barber's illness were canvassed in
evidence, the judge rejected them as the precipitate cause or causes of the illness.
He found on the balance of probabilities that it was the stress prompted by *d*
Mr Barber's work which was the 'spur' to his depressive illness.

3. The respondent's notice

[151] In a respondent's notice reference was made to certain items of evidence
not mentioned by the judge. One witness, Alistair Johnston, told the judge that
before the end of the summer term of 1996 Mrs Hayward was heard to say *e*
something about Mr Barber's health. In the following term Mr Gill, who was
now the acting head following Mrs Hayward's sudden retirement, had expressed
concern to him about Mr Barber. Mrs Newton had also given evidence to the
effect that Mr Barber's sister had told her how concerned his family was about
him. He never seemed to stop working. Mr Glancy QC, who appeared for *f*
Mr Barber, encouraged us to read large parts of the evidence. In response to his
suggestion, we have read it all.

4. Other background evidence

[152] The evidence given by Mr Gill filled out the picture painted by the
judge. Although the school was still maintained by the local education authority *g*
the new arrangements for local management of schools gave it control over its
budget for the first time. With a cascading school roll and a reduced income, the
school had to do the best it could with the resources it had, both monetary and
human.

[153] This was one of the reasons why the school had shifted to the system of *h*
co-ordinating areas of experience, which came into effect in September 1995.
This change in itself made little difference to the maths department, which simply
became the maths area of experience. On the creative arts and science sides, on
the other hand, there were more major upheavals, in the former instance because
a number of autonomous teaching units were now being co-ordinated for the *j*
first time, and in the latter because science teachers had to contend with split
sites. Mr Barber's two former deputies did not stop teaching maths. The change
which Mr Barber resented was that their management skills were now required
for pastoral roles, because it had been decided that the small size of the maths area
of experience did not warrant one deputy head, let alone two. The number of
staff teaching maths remained constant. It appears to us that the judge

a misunderstood the changes that came into effect in September (not March) 1995 when he made a finding that Mr Barber now had fewer staff.

[154] Mr Gill had encouraged Mr Barber to develop his areas of responsibility more clearly, to prioritise and to be willing to delegate when he conducted a confidential review of his performance as a teacher in 1992. He had then been relieved of that role, and it was a review conducted by Mrs Newton in July 1996

b which led to Mr Barber being referred to him, since he was now in charge of the curriculum. When he had taken over that responsibility in September 1995 he had spoken to all the new co-ordinators, and it was at his meetings with Mr Barber in this capacity that he made the notes which the judge quoted in his judgment.

[155] His evidence to the judge was that he had told Mr Barber how he ought

c to prioritise his work better. He should rank things in order of importance. He should go and see the person who organised the daily staffing, if he felt he was being obliged to cover for absent staff. If this did not achieve results, he would expect Mr Barber to come back to him. He would fix the date for their next meeting at the end of each meeting. When Mr Barber complained of work

d overload in February 1996, Mr Gill encouraged him to identify the jobs he really did not need to do. He should ask himself what other people might be able to do to help him: support staff or staff from outside the school. He should identify what it was that was really causing his problems. In para 42 of his second witness statement Mr Gill said that Mr Barber's media link responsibilities required him simply to act as a funnel, and that if he really spent as much time on this task as

e he now claimed, this illustrated his lack of ability to delegate relatively simple tasks to other people.

[156] The school was under particular pressure in the academic year 1995–1996 because in addition to the structural changes and worries over the falling numbers of pupils and the prospect of an OFSTED inspection in autumn

f 1996, one senior member of staff had died and Mrs Newton, one of the deputy heads, was away from school for some time for a hip replacement. Mr Gill told the judge that he considered that every area of experience co-ordinator, and indeed the whole of the school's senior management team, were suffering from work overload at this time. He did not consider that Mr Barber's job involved working any longer hours than the jobs performed by the six other co-ordinators.

g

5. *The evidence about Mr Barber's health*

[157] It is against this background that Mr Hogarth, who appeared for Somerset County Council, invited us to consider whether there was evidence that the school authorities should have reasonably foreseen that Mr Barber was

h likely to suffer from stress-induced psychiatric illness. In this context he invited us to consider carefully the relevant paragraphs of Mr Barber's very long witness statement, and the oral evidence he gave to the judge about them. We were invited to note the difference between what Mr Barber described as happening to him from time to time and what he told the people at the school about them.

j [158] His first description of adverse effects on his health related to the last two months of 1995. He said that he found that he was losing weight. He thought that he looked drawn and would wake up regularly in the night. It felt as if he was having out-of-body experiences. He believed he had completed tasks which he hadn't completed and he became confused. He did not suggest he told anybody at the school about any of this, although members of his family became concerned during the Christmas holidays.

[159] During the following term he said he continued to feel terrible at school, and was feeling even worse than he had done at the end of the Christmas term. He lost the sense of fun in teaching. He explored the possibility of finding another teaching post, and he also investigated what would happen if he were to retire due to ill-health, because at that time a teacher was permitted to retire and to undertake other teaching in retirement. He did not suggest he told anybody at the school about his concerns over his health that term.

[160] He said that the pressures continued in the summer term until his GP signed him off work for three weeks in May. He said he was astounded when the doctor told him he was suffering from depression because he had never thought of himself in that way. He went to the coast for a while on his doctor's advice. When he returned the doctor advised him to take longer off work, but he felt guilty about burdening his colleagues as a result of his absence. He therefore returned to work on 24 May 1996. In his witness statement he did not say that he spoke to anybody at the school on his return about his concerns over his health. He merely expressed surprise that nobody had inquired about it, given that his sick notes had recorded that he was suffering from stress and depression.

[161] He spoke of an asthma attack during the summer holiday in 1996, which his family believed to be stress-related, although the expert witnesses later discounted any connection. He said he tried unsuccessfully to discuss his rising stress problems with his doctor at the end of the summer holidays, and that he continued to suffer from stress and depression in the autumn term. He went to see his doctor in October, and wrote to him on 25 October 1996, following that meeting. In this letter he described how he now felt fear and fright, an inability to settle and a sapping of energy so that any task took a vastly disproportionate amount of time to get achieved. He felt sleepy and drained in the classroom, and he knew that at school and at home things were spiralling out of control. He did not send the school a copy of this letter, or tell anyone at the school how he was feeling. Although his doctor replied on 30 October 1996 to suggest another meeting, Mr Barber did not do anything about this suggestion until 12 November, when an incident in class led him to see his doctor that evening. He was told to stop work immediately.

[162] In his witness statement Mr Barber said that his complaints to senior members of staff initially related only to his workload, and that he did not discuss the effect that the workload was having on his health. It was when he returned to the school after his absence in May 1996 that he first raised the concerns about his health which the judge found established on the evidence. In his written account of his meeting with Mrs Hayward in his witness statement he said he explained to her that his workload was getting too much and that he felt that he was not coping very well. He said that he told Mrs Newton forcefully that he was unable to cope with his workload, and that it was becoming impossible and was detrimental to his health. He also told her that if the workload continued and his health continued to decline he could not see himself being in the post in a year's time. In his meeting with Mr Gill at the end of the summer term he referred to the fact that his health had recently suffered due to his excessive workload.

[163] In his oral evidence he told the judge that between his return to school in May and the end of the summer term on 20 July, he thought he continued to suffer from weight loss and loss of sleep and what he called out-of-body experiences. He did not tell anybody at the school about these symptoms. Nor did he mention them to his union's regional officer, although he was a union representative at the school. Nor did any member of his family write to the

a school. He said that on the three occasions when he spoke to senior members of the management team about his health during the summer term of 1996 he told them that his health was declining, that he was becoming ill, that he had been off ill, and that he was looking for some way forward to reduce the pressures on him. He did not describe his symptoms in more specific terms.

b 6. *Liability: our conclusions*

[164] Mr Hogarth criticised the judge for failing to link causation with breach of duty. The judge had so structured his judgment that he had concluded that Mr Barber's depressive illness was caused by the stress he suffered at work following the restructuring before he considered the nature of the duty the defendants owed him, the circumstances in which they were in breach of that
c duty, and whether it was reasonably foreseeable to them that Mr Barber would suffer a psychiatric illness as a consequence of that breach.

[165] It appears to us that these criticisms were well founded. We have set out our reasons for holding that the judge's findings on liability cannot stand in our main judgment at [57]–[59], and we need not repeat them here.

d
7. *Damages*

[166] There is no appeal against the judge's award of £10,000 by way of general damages for a moderately severe psychiatric illness. The judge went on to find that Mr Barber was fit to return to work on 1 April 1998. He expressed the view that there should be no reduction for the possibility of any future psychiatric
e difficulty in the event that Mr Barber had not suffered his depressive illness in 1996, and had continued to work for the defendant. The judge said that Mr Barber had never suffered from mental illness before, and had seldom visited his GP, and that there was nothing in the experts' reports to justify such a finding.

[167] The judge also took the view on the balance of probability that
f Mr Barber would have continued in his chosen profession until retirement age but for his illness, provided that he had received assistance to alleviate the work overload and the pressures to which he had been subjected during 1996.

[168] The parties had agreed that a multiplier of four from the date of the trial was appropriate by way of a compromise of any dispute there might otherwise have been about Mr Barber's likely retirement age, and the judge computed his
g award of damages on this basis.

[169] Mr Hogarth submitted that the judge was wrong to approach his assessment of what might happen in the future by making a finding on the balance of probability that Mr Barber would otherwise have continued working until his normal retirement age, and by extrapolating from that assessment a
h conclusion that this would have happened, making no discount from his award for the chance that things might not have turned out that way. He relied in this context on the judgment of Otton LJ in *Doyle v Wallace* [1998] PIQR Q146 at 148–150, where reference is made to a passage in the speech of Lord Reid in *Davies v Taylor* [1972] 3 All ER 836 at 838, [1974] AC 207 at 213, and to the
j judgment of Stuart-Smith LJ in *Allied Maples Group Ltd v Simmons & Simmons (a firm)* [1995] 4 All ER 907 at 914–916, [1995] 1 WLR 1602 at 1609–1611.

[170] Mr Glancy invited us to approach Mr Barber's case as if it fell into the second of the three classes of case discussed by Stuart-Smith LJ in the *Allied Maples* case [1995] 4 All ER 907 at 915, [1995] 1 WLR 1602 at 1610–1611. This is the type of case in which a defendant employer has negligently failed to provide earmuffs or breathing apparatus or a safety-belt, and a question arises whether the injured

employee would have used this equipment if it had been provided. In these
circumstances, once it is decided on the balance of probability that the employee   *a*
would have taken advantage of these facilities if they had been available, the
court will find that he would have done so, and makes its further findings on this
basis.

[171] This type of case, however, which focuses on what would probably have
happened in the past, is entirely different from a case where a court has to make   *b*
an estimate of what may happen in the future. If there is a chance that an event
may occur which would mean that an injured plaintiff would not have gone on
working until retirement age in any event, then a familiar way of taking that
chance into account is to reduce the multiplier used for calculating future loss.
The first instance decision of Otton J in *Page v Smith* [1993] PIQR Q55 at 75–76
provides a good example of this technique at work.   *c*

[172] Mr Glancy argued, in the alternative, that an appropriate adjustment to
the multiplier had already been made when the multiplier of four was agreed.
While we have no doubt that ordinary contingencies were taken into account,
like the chance of death or some other kind of serious incapacitating injury or
illness befalling Mr Barber before retirement age, when the multiplier was   *d*
agreed, we can see no evidence of any further discount being made for the chance
to which Mr Hogarth referred.

[173] In our judgment the judge was wrong not to reduce the multiplier for
future loss to cover the chance that if Mr Barber had continued with a similar
teaching job, his health might nevertheless have broken down in the same way.
He was a man, after all, who had showed himself on the evidence unable to adopt   *e*
the alleviating measures that were necessary if he was to manage his not
unreasonable workload successfully. There was evidence that he had disliked the
changes the school had felt obliged to introduce, and on the hypothesis (which
the judge adopted) that he would have opted to soldier on as a teacher until his
normal retirement age, we consider that there was a significant chance, which the   *f*
judge should have taken into account when computing damages, that he would
have found it altogether too much for him, to the extent that his health would
have been detrimentally affected in the same way.

[174] Given that on this hypothesis we are to imagine that he would have
continued to work uninterruptedly from November 1996 onwards, we consider
that an annual multiplier of one (not four) would have been more appropriate for   *g*
computing future loss if proper account were taken of the chance to which we
have referred. In the event we have decided to allow the defendants' appeal on
liability, so that this part of our decision will only become relevant if another
court were to hold that we were wrong on the liability issue.

h

C. MRS JONES

[175] Mrs Jones was employed as an administrative assistant at Trainwell, a
local authority training centre, from August 1992. On 20 January 1995 she went
off sick with anxiety and depression and never returned. She was made redundant
on 31 December 1996 when Trainwell was closed. Judgment was entered in her   *j*
favour for £157,541, made up of £22,500 general damages, together with interest
of £1,300, past loss of earnings, medical expenses and travelling expense totalling
£32,499, together with interest of £6,422, and future loss of earnings, pension and
medical and prescription costs totalling £94,820. The defendants appeal against
the judge's factual findings and conclusions that they were in breach of duty
towards her; there is no appeal on causation or the quantum of damage.

1. Facts

[176] The claimant was born in 1953. She returned to work aged 35 in 1988. She was employed by Sandwell Metropolitan Borough Council. At first she worked for Sandwell College doing desk-top publishing in the mornings and teaching typing, word processing and computing to YTS and unemployed people in the afternoons. In 1991 she had a period of absence from work. She reported to her doctor feeling low and depressed with early morning waking for two months. Her doctor prescribed amitryptilene, an antidepressant. This was acknowledged by the claimant's psychiatric expert at trial to be a significant depressive episode. The claimant sought to deny that there was anything wrong with her at the time but the judge did not accept that. He concluded that it fitted the pattern which both the psychiatrist and psychologist had discerned from her earlier history, that she had a vulnerable personality.

[177] In 1992 the council decided to amalgamate its youth training activities in one establishment, Trainwell. Mrs Jones applied for an instructor's job there but narrowly missed it. So she then applied successfully for the job of administrative assistant there, hoping to move on to an instructor's post in due course. She began work on 10 August 1992.

[178] The job description describes her role as 'to support the co-ordinator/manager in maintaining financial and administrative systems for the operation of Trainwell'. Working hours were 8.30 am to 5.00 pm Mondays to Thursdays and 8.30 am to 1.30 pm Fridays. The grade was between 3 and 4. (This meant that her starting salary was around £9,500 increasing to around £11,100.) Fifteen specific responsibilities were listed:

'1. Responsible for the provision of administrative support to the Manager in the day to day operation of Trainwell.

2. To maintain the purchase and sales ledgers for Trainwell and to prepare monthly statements on these ledgers.

3. To prepare claims for grants from the Training and Enterprise Council.

4. To arrange payments for work placement providers.

5. To assist trainees in opening Building Society/Bank Accounts.

6. To provide work experience for trainees in established office procedures.

7. To complete recruitment and termination documentation for trainees.

8. To maintain trainee's records, including holiday and sickness.

9. To check and collate trainee's weekly time sheets.

10. Financial administration including:
—invoice work placement providers
—preparing sales invoices
—processing petty cash income and expenditure.

11. Collation of statistical information on trainees.

12. To attend in-service training sessions and courses as required.

13. To be informed of, observe and actively promote, the Equal Opportunity Policies and practises [sic] of the Council in general and Trainwell in particular.

14. Use of new technology as required.

15. Such other duties as may be appropriate to achieve the objectives of Trainwell's Youth Training Workshop commensurate with the postholder's salary grade, abilities and aptitudes.'

[179] The judge found that this was a highly-responsible job. She had to do effectively the whole administration for Trainwell. The most important part was the collation of information and submission of monthly claims for funding to the local Training and Enterprise Council (TEC). This was vital to the continued existence of Trainwell and deadlines were strict. The rest of her work was also responsible and had to be done on time. There is no challenge to those findings.

[180] It was also a new job. Trainwell had previously operated from two sites with a full-time administrative assistant at each and a senior person responsible to them for the TEC bids and budgets. All three jobs were now being covered by one person. Mrs Bell, who had stayed on for a few weeks to train Mrs Jones in the work, acknowledged that the tasks were varied and the deadlines tight. The post holder would be kept busy but Mrs Bell thought that Mrs Jones could cope with good time management. However when Mrs Jones saw Mr King, her personnel officer, on 5 February 1993 she recorded him as saying that it was a 'calculated gamble to give one person the job of two to three'. Mr King provided a witness statement for the proceedings, together with two sets of notes of the meeting. Mrs Jones, whose husband had accompanied her, also provided a set of notes. Mr King was not however called to give evidence. Hence the judge treated Mrs Jones' evidence of the meeting as unchallenged. There was also no dispute that the work increased in April 1993 with a change to a new computer database.

[181] There was a dispute about how much time Mrs Jones did in fact spend on the job. In para 3 of the particulars of claim it was put at rarely less than 48 hours a week, and often as many as 60. In a schedule to the further information it had gone up to more than 81 hours a week, with additional help from her husband. This was challenged as incredible and also inconsistent with Mrs Jones' taking on a time consuming college course at the same time. The judge thought it impossible to say precisely what hours she worked; they probably varied from week to week; on some occasions she probably did work the sort of hours suggested; this was not happening all the time but for a sufficient amount of the time to be grossly excessive.

[182] There was no dispute that she complained of being overworked from an early date. The response of her immediate superiors, Trainwell's manager Mr Papworth and his deputy Mrs Sheldon, was unsympathetic. Early in 1993, they did a rough calculation of the time needed for the work, which showed that she only needed 32 hours a week. When she went with her husband to see Mr King in February 1993, he noted her saying that she took work home virtually every night and at weekends and once worked until 1.30 am. Mrs Jones noted that she had said that she was greatly offended by suggestions that she only needed to prioritise, 'as I worked in excess of 13 hours per day and on a regular basis worked Saturdays and Sunday'.

[183] Mr King also noted that she complained of constant 'chipping away' about her performance, telling her off for arriving four minutes late after she had worked until 1.30 am, and making 'veiled threats' not to renew her temporary appointment at the end of March 1993. She was also concerned that if her contract were not renewed she would not get a fair reference. She did not feel that she could complain to her line manager, Mr Papworth, as he and his deputy were causing the stress. Mr Papworth had made recent threats concluding that if she ever repeated the contents of their conversation he would deny that it took place. Mrs Jones' notes describe the same incident thus:

'Mr Papworth advised me when Mrs Sheldon left the office that he had discussed the situation with Mr Watts [his superior] and they had decided that a reorganisation would take place and two jobs would be created one at scale one and another at scale two and was told that with my work record do you think you would get one of these jobs if you applied. This I took to be a threat to try and silence my opposition to the excessive workload within the admin dept. Mr Papworth stated that if I told anybody about this conversation the he would deny it.'

Mr King's conclusion was that 'she is not objecting to her grade or the volume of work, just the "knocks" that she keeps on taking'. She did not want him to do anything at the moment, merely to realise the problems. Mrs Jones' note records that Mr King stated that he would try to get further help. She said that she would like to continue to do the job, would see if help was forthcoming and would not seek further action 'to see if the situation got better'.

[184] Towards the end of that year Mr Watts did try to provide her with some extra help. Claudette Henry was asked to spend a day a week at Trainwell to help her and learn how to do the job. Most of her first day was taken up with Mrs Jones explaining the work. When she returned the next week she was told that she was no longer to assist Mrs Jones but was to do the typing instead.

[185] In June 1994, Mrs Jones asked Mrs York, who had taken over from Mr King as her personnel officer, for a transfer. She prepared a five-page document headed 'strictly private and confidential' which she took with her for a discussion with Mrs York on 27 July 1994. This listed the problems under four headings: health, excessive workload, equal opportunities and managerial disagreements. Under 'health', she stated: 'The situation is that I am under continual pressure for which I am now suffering stress related health problems. Many of these problems were related to Dave King in a meeting some 12 months ago.' In fact, the notes of her meeting with Mr King do not record that she made any complaint about her health, although she certainly made complaints about her workload and the other pressures she was under.

[186] Under 'excessive workload', she stated:

'Excessive and complex workload with only myself knowing the rules, regulations and technical details of the TEC claim ... I have on many occasions worked after midnight to formulate claims also on one occasion working with the assistant manager at Trainwell until 7.30 pm on Friday evening, all day Saturday until 7.00 pm and all day Sunday until 5.00 pm Also on numerous occasions working Friday afternoons, all this without remuneration or time off in lieu.'

She also complained that she had been told by Mrs Sheldon that the additional help arranged the previous year was still allocated for that purpose but Mr Papworth had denied it. Under 'equal opportunities' she complained that she thought it unlikely that she would be given an equal opportunity to apply for any forthcoming vacant positions even though she was qualified for an instructor's post. Under 'managerial disagreements' she complained that it was hard to discuss these matters within Trainwell because of a 'power struggle' between managers. She was also frequently called upon to mediate between managers and skill instructors. There were 'a lot of tensions and problems' at Trainwell.

[187] Like Mr King, Mrs York did not give evidence, nor was there any witness statement or (it would appear) note from her about the meeting. The

outcome was that Mrs York would speak to Mr Watts but without mentioning
Mrs Jones by name. On 16 August Mr Watts issued a 'note for further action' *a*
which provided for further administrative help for Mrs Jones. That again does
not seem to have been forthcoming. Meanwhile Mrs Jones applied for three
other jobs which she did not get.

[188] Mrs Jones had not by then consulted her doctor about any work-related
problems. Her only visit since starting work at Trainwell was in March 1994 for *b*
abdominal problems. She did not mention problems at work, but the doctor did
note '?psychosomatic'. She next consulted him on 16 August complaining of
headaches not eased by multiple analgesics. Again she did not mention work
problems. He diagnosed migraine. She went back to her doctor for further
medication on 2 September. He prescribed ibuprofen.

[189] In September she applied for the job of skills instructor at Trainwell. She *c*
was interviewed on 2 November by Mr Papworth, Mrs York and Mrs Pearson.
She did not get it. She felt that the odds had been stacked against her. She found
out later that Mr Papworth had told one of the instructors that she was not going
to get the job because of her accent. (She learned much later that his interview
notes recorded the word 'liar' against her denial of being late on occasions.) She *d*
also felt at a disadvantage because she had just come back from holiday and was
nervous. The judge found that the others also got that impression.

[190] On 23 November 1994 Mrs Jones invoked the formal grievance
procedure, complaining that she had been discriminated against when she
applied for this position, and also of 'harassment encountered during my
28 months of employment at Trainwell' which had affected her health. There *e*
was no complaint about overwork. Mr Papworth went to see her about the
grievance and said that he could understand her complaining about the excessive
hours but 'what's this about harassment?'.

[191] The hearing of her complaint did not take place until 17 January 1995.
Mr Papworth insisted that she took a holiday both to see her union representative *f*
to prepare for it and for the hearing itself. At the hearing it became apparent that
she was complaining of long hours and overwork and Mr Watts disappeared; so
the matter was adjourned. Mr Papworth later upbraided her for talking to a
sympathetic colleague about what had happened.

[192] On 20 January 1995 Mrs Jones went off sick and never returned. In
February 1996 her treating psychiatrist diagnosed— *g*

'an acute anxiety state 12 months ago which has developed into a
generalised anxiety state with agoraphobia accompanied by mild depression
and obsessive compulsive symptoms of which the anxiety symptoms seem
the most troublesome.' *h*

She was made redundant from the end of 1996 when the council closed Trainwell
down.

[193] The importance of the job she had been doing there was demonstrated
by the 'chaos' which ensued after her departure. The documentation went
downhill to such an extent that the TEC threatened to claim back amounts they *j*
had paid. Mr Papworth's managerial shortcomings eventually resulted in a
disciplinary hearing in July and September 1996. Among the findings were a
failure to ensure sufficient managerial control of the administrative and financial
procedures resulting in the submission of inaccurate claims; and various
management deficiencies, including a failure to respond adequately to concerns
expressed by staff, resulting in 'an atmosphere of general disquiet, no teamwork,

a a lack of respect and a demotivated workforce with poor morale': an echo of what Mrs Jones had told Mrs York back in 1994.

2. The judge's findings

[194] The judge found that Mrs Jones was being overworked and that the allegation of harassment against Mr Papworth was made out. He found that the
b major causes of her breakdown were the excessive hours of work and the harassment she was subjected to. He then considered whether this was foreseeable: specifically he asked himself, 'what would a reasonable employer have foreseen as likely to result from the factors I have described?'.

[195] The council argued that she had taken no time off for depression; her
c own GP did not diagnose it in August or September 1994; she made no visits to the occupational health department; she made out she was fine when colleagues asked; the council had no knowledge of her vulnerability; and even her husband did not realise that she was heading for a breakdown.

[196] The judge thought that the reason for that was that she was the type of person who bottled up her feelings, put a brave face on her situation, was
d determined to cope and not let anyone see that it was getting her down. But the question was not whether they did foresee it but whether they should have done so.

[197] Several factors led him to conclude that they should have done so. First was the importance of the job she was doing, the 'lynchpin on which Trainwell's continued existence hinged'. Second, there was the stress which Mr Papworth
e and to a lesser extent Mrs Sheldon were imposing upon her. Third, she had alerted Mr King to both of these but could not complain of the excessive hours in case her appointment was not continued. Mr King should have realised that there was a risk of injury to her mental health if things continued as they were. But nothing was done. She then complained to Mrs York, who could have asked
f her about her health problems or advised her to consult the occupational health department. This was a 'compelling cry for help' and the second clear indication of risk to her health posed by overwork and harassment. This was followed by Mrs Jones' performance at the instructor interview: it should have been obvious to Mrs York that all was not well with Mrs Jones at that time. Finally there were the events surrounding the grievance hearing: she should not have been required
g to return to work after the hearing had been adjourned, when she was subjected to just the sort of unreasonable behaviour from Mr Papworth which she feared.

[198] It is clear from this summary that the judge was eliding the question of whether injury to her mental health was foreseeable with the question of what a reasonable employer would have done about it. He never expressly asked
h himself the second question.

[199] He next discussed the medical evidence in more detail. Mr Willmott, the psychologist instructed on behalf of Mrs Jones, considered that there was evidence of stress and depression from at least August 1994 and that stress at work was a major contributory factor in the development of her depressive
j illness and anxiety. Dr Bond, the psychiatrist instructed on behalf of the council, believed that her condition developed in January 1995, and eventually agreed that there were work-related factors influencing the development of her depression. The judge concluded that the trouble started in 1994 and that if steps had been taken in July 1994, let alone in February 1993, to deal with the causes of her overwork and to stop the harassment, she might well have recovered. Those steps were not taken and she did not recover: the chaotic grievance hearing, after

which she was required to return to work, and the further mistreatment she then
suffered were 'the straw which broke the back of an extremely willing camel'.
a

3. *The arguments on appeal*

[**200**] The appellant council takes issue with the judge's finding that the
claimant's mental illness was foreseeable. They rely upon all the points relied
upon before the trial judge, outlined at [195], above. But they also take issue with *b*
his findings of fact as to the hours worked by the claimant and the 'harassment'
suffered from Mr Papworth.

[**201**] As to the volume of work, the judge was well aware of the discrepancies
in the claimant's case. He was also well aware of the need to treat her evidence
with some caution, because he had rejected her account of the earlier episode in
1991. But he noted that the claimant's present account was consistent with the *c*
account she said that she had given to Mr King in February 1993. Mr King had
acknowledged that it was a gamble to expect one person to do the work of two
to three. The judge also noted that no one had done a proper time and motion
study of what the job required. Mrs Bell thought that it was manageable but she
was a highflier. All the other observations were that it was too much for one *d*
person. Both Mr King and Mrs York had proposed extra help. Mr Papworth
himself had acknowledged that he could see what she meant about the excessive
hours. Perhaps the best indication was the chaos which ensued when Mrs Jones
left.

[**202**] The issue is not exactly how many hours Mrs Jones actually worked.
The judge was entitled to find that she regularly worked way beyond the 37 hours *e*
for which she was paid. She was a dedicated and ambitious employee who was
anxious to show that she could do the work required even if it took more than
the allotted hours. The issue is whether the demands placed upon her were
reasonable in all the circumstances. It is not necessarily reasonable to expect so
much of an administrative assistant whose pay and status are not those of a *f*
professional with an open-ended commitment to getting the job done. The judge
was amply justified in reaching the conclusion that Mrs Jones was overworked.

[**203**] This is allied to the question of harassment. The judge based his findings
on Mr Papworth's general and specific shortcomings as a manager. Again,
whether those collectively amount to 'harassment' as it is understood in other
contexts is not the point. The point is whether the behaviour towards Mrs Jones *g*
was reasonable in all the circumstances. An employee in her position should not
be placed in a dilemma where she feels unable to complain about her workload
because of threats, not only to her future employment, but also to her future
employability. The combination of unreasonable demands and an unreasonable
reaction to complaints about those demands justifies a finding of *h*
unreasonable conduct even if the epithet 'harassment' is not appropriate.

[**204**] But that finding does not answer the questions which had to be
answered in this case. The judge had first to consider the issue of foreseeability.
The defendant had some powerful points to make: in particular, there was no
sickness absence during the period in question; there was no complaint of injury *j*
to health to Mr King in 1993; the complaint of injury to health in July 1994 was
unspecific; had it been further investigated, it would have elicited nothing of any
value because the claimant's own doctor had not yet been consulted about, let
alone detected any work-related illness; and the claimant's own husband, who
was exceptionally involved and supportive, had not anticipated it. It is also
argued that the council had no knowledge of the earlier episode in 1991; but that

a is less powerful, because she was also working for the council at the time, albeit in a different post.

[205] The judge did not clearly separate the issues of foreseeability, breach of duty and causation as he should have done. It is impermissible to reason that because a defendant has behaved unreasonably the risk of psychiatric injury should have been foreseen. Equally it is impermissible to reason that because an b injury has resulted from stress at work it has resulted from an employer's breach of duty.

[206] However, Mr Anderson is right to argue on behalf of Mrs Jones that unreasonable demands are relevant to the question of foreseeability. Placing unreasonable demands upon an employee and then responding in an unreasonable way to the employee's complaints about those demands are among c the factors to be taken into account in deciding whether the employer knew or ought to have known that the pressures of the job were causing occupational stress. Mrs York clearly did know that much. This knowledge was coupled with two express warnings from the employee that this occupational stress was indeed damaging her health. On balance, therefore, and bearing in mind that neither d Mr King nor Mrs York gave evidence, the judge was entitled to find that actual damage to her health was foreseeable.

[207] Once that hurdle is crossed, Mr Anderson is also right to argue that it was easy to identify a relevant breach of duty. Senior management knew that there were complaints of overwork which were likely to have some substance but that line management was making it impossible to make an effective e complaint. They actually offered help. But because of line management's attitude that help was never effective. If psychiatric harm was the foreseeable result of doing nothing when there were obvious steps which could have been taken it is easier to conclude that there had been a breach of duty. Although the judge does not in terms address the risk/benefit question he was entitled to f conclude that there was a breach of duty when it was the employer's own unreasonable demands which were producing a foreseeable risk of harm to the employee's health.

[208] Unlike the others before us, this is the sort of case described by Lord Slynn in *Waters v Comr of Police of the Metropolis* [2000] 4 All ER 934 at 938, [2000] 1 WLR 1607 at 1611:
g
'If an employer knows that acts being done by employees during their employment may cause physical or mental harm to a particular fellow employee and he does nothing to supervise or prevent such acts, when it is in his power to do so, it is clearly arguable that he may be in breach of his h duty to that employee. It seems to me that he may also be in breach of that duty if he can foresee that such acts may happen and if they do, that physical or mental harm may be caused to an individual.'

[209] The question still arises of whether that breach of duty caused the harm which was suffered. Was the judge entitled to conclude that if something had j been done to lighten the claimant's workload and acknowledge the validity of her complaints her eventual breakdown could have been avoided? The underlying vulnerability would still have been there, as would the claimant's basic ambition to become an instructor rather than an administrator. But the judge gave sound reasons for preferring the view of the expert psychologist instructed on behalf of the claimant to that of the expert instructed for the defence, who had not been supplied with all the relevant material.

4. *Conclusion*

[210] It must be acknowledged that although the judge gave a long and detailed judgment, it did not address each of the issues in turn in a systematic manner. This was not an easy case and would have benefited from such an approach. Nevertheless, there was evidence before the judge which entitled him to reach the factual conclusions he did, and from those to conclude that the indications of risk to mental health were strong enough for a reasonable employer to think that he should do something about it, not least because senior management *did* think that there was something they should do. That something was to cease placing unreasonable demands upon the claimant. There was also expert evidence from which the judge was entitled to conclude that it was the failure to take those steps which caused, or at least materially contributed to, the claimant's mental illness. There is no challenge to his assessment of the damages resulting. It was for these reasons, which are set out more succinctly in our main judgment at [66], [67], that we are dismissing the employers' appeal in Mrs Jones' case.

D. MR BISHOP

[211] Mr Bishop left school at the age of 15 without any formal qualifications. He worked at an abattoir for ten years, and he then worked for the defendant company between April 1979 and February 1997. In the early hours of the morning of 25 February 1997 he suffered a mental breakdown, associated with a suicide attempt (which was interpreted as a cry for help). He has not worked since then. He was awarded £7,000 by way of general damages because the defendants had failed to take appropriate steps to protect him from the real risk of an impending mental breakdown. The defendants appeal against the judge's ruling on liability.

[212] Mr Bishop's difficulties surfaced in the following way. In 1992 an American company had taken over the defendant company, and in 1995–1996 they introduced changes in their employees' work patterns, designed to achieve more modern and efficient working methods. Employees were now required to undertake a wider range of jobs, some of which involved a greater mental input than had previously been the case. There is a helpful list of the jobs Mr Bishop was now required to do at the beginning of his particulars of claim.

[213] The judge said that these changes had been agreed with the trade unions and that on the whole the workmen preferred the changes. Although the shifts were longer, and the series of shifts were longer, there were longer breaks between shifts. Mr Wilson, who gave evidence at the trial, did the same work as Mr Bishop on the other shift and he coped with the changes. Mr Bishop did not.

[214] Mr Bishop was now in his mid-40s. He had coped with his previous more limited tasks, but the new tasks got him down. He was meticulous by nature, perhaps a bit set in the jobs he had done, and rather slow. He could not cope with the new, more efficient ways of doing things, and he worried that he could not do his job properly.

[215] It was common ground that he told his manager, Mr Fairhurst, about the stresses he felt. He told the judge that he spoke to him about 12 times in the three months which led up to the collapse. Mr Fairhurst accepted that Mr Bishop had discussed his problems with him on three to six occasions. He also mentioned his difficulties to Mr Wilson when they changed shifts. Mr Wilson was sufficiently concerned on one occasion that he went and told Mr Fairhurst that there was something wrong with Mr Bishop, and that he was not coping. He

a also told Mr Fairhurst about Mr Bishop's wish for a change in his job, because he was not happy with the many duties now being imposed on him. Mr Wilson also mentioned this less formally to Mr Turner, the foreman.

[216] Mr Bishop was away from work between 24 January and 16 February 1997. For some of this time he would have been absent anyway. For the rest of the time he was sick, and he submitted two sick notes from his GP which referred
b to neurasthenia. The judge said that this history should have set alarm bells ringing. The defendants ought to have investigated the situation immediately. Even if there was no alternative work available for Mr Bishop they ought to have taken him off his job immediately. They knew that there was no alternative source for his stress other than his work, and that he had no personal problems.
c They were not allowed to say that because they had nothing else for him to do, he had to continue at the job which was causing him injury and was likely to cause him even more serious injury if he continued to do it.

[217] This was in effect what they did, the judge said, and within a short time Mr Bishop suffered a complete mental breakdown due to the stress of his job. This, the judge held, was entirely foreseeable. The defendants could have given
d him counselling, or training, or a period of rest. If in the end they had discovered that he could not do the work, they should either have found him a job which he could do, or terminated his employment. This would have been preferable and more reasonable than to adopt a course which would give him a mental breakdown.

e [218] The judge accepted that the defendants had no duty to provide him with an alternative job. This did not mean that they could simply insist on his continuing to do a job when it was reasonably foreseeable that he would suffer injury to his health if he did continue with it.

[219] The judge was critical of the fact that Mr Fairhurst had received no
f training about possible problems concerned with stress at work and that he was not aware of the possible causes of such stress. He did not think that this was a topic which had ever been raised at management level. Mr Fairhurst had never seen the Health and Safety Executive's (HSE) guidance on Stress at Work (see [9], above), which had been published a year or two before Mr Bishop's final breakdown. The judge said that in the 1990s properly responsible companies
g ought to have been aware of the factors leading to cause stress.

[220] In these circumstances he held that the defendants should have taken appropriate steps to avoid the consequences of sending Mr Bishop back to a job where there was a real risk of his suffering a mental breakdown. The only reason why they did not take such steps was that they did not realise the risk. He
h therefore found the defendants liable to Mr Bishop for the breakdown and its results. He then made the award of general damages which is not under challenge. He adjourned the trial of other issues relating to damages because of the existence of an unresolved dispute as to whether Mr Bishop's supervening back condition would in any event have prevented him from continuing to work
j for the defendants or to do any other work which involved lifting.

[221] The judge did not mention the fact that Mr Bishop's doctor had told him on 1 November 1996 that he ought to have a career change. He had told the doctor that he wanted to do his job and master it, and he never told the defendants about his doctor's advice. Mr Bishop said that Mr Fairhurst had explained to him that the sheltered kind of job he wished to do was simply not available.

[**222**] For his part, Mr Fairhurst told the judge that although Mr Bishop had asked for a move, there was nothing to indicate that his performance was suffering. The jobs were being done, the quality assurance procedures were being followed and the paperwork was being completed. Although he had not seen the HSE publication *Stress at Work* he said that as somebody responsible for managing people he knew that stress might cause anxiety and depression. He agreed that harmful levels of stress were most likely to occur where pressures piled up on top of each other, but he had not previously thought that it was more likely that people might feel trapped, unable to exert control over the demands placed on them if they were at more junior levels in a business. He accepted as a matter of common sense that it was best so far as possible to match a job with the abilities and motivations of the person employed to do the job.

[**223**] The most striking feature of Mr Bishop's case was that his employers had no notice that he was likely to suffer a psychiatric illness if he continued in his job. Mr Bishop had concealed from his employers the advice that his doctor had given him the previous November, and two sick notes referring to neurasthenia are a shallow foundation for the finding the judge made with the benefit of hindsight. Mr Bishop knew that his employers had no other work for him, and that his doctor had advised him to change jobs. He chose to go back to work, as he was entitled to do, but there is in our judgment no evidential basis for a finding that the breakdown in his health was reasonably foreseeable, and in any event there was nothing the employers could have done to continue Mr Bishop's employment, if he could not cope with it, because work of the kind he wanted to do was not now available.

[**224**] We have set out in our main judgment at [72], [73] our reasons for allowing this appeal.

Appeal in Mrs Jones' case dismissed. Other appeals allowed. Permission to appeal refused.

Kate O'Hanlon Barrister.

a
Marcic v Thames Water Utilities Ltd
[2002] EWCA Civ 64

COURT OF APPEAL, CIVIL DIVISION
LORD PHILLIPS OF WORTH MATRAVERS MR, ALDOUS AND WARD LJJ
b
3, 4 DECEMBER 2001, 7 FEBRUARY 2002

Nuisance – Sewer – Overflow – Flooding of neighbouring premises – Overloading of sewer resulting in repeated flooding of claimant's property – Statutory sewerage undertaker failing to take steps to prevent flooding – Whether sewerage undertaker c *liable at common law for failure to prevent flooding – Whether failure infringing claimant's right to respect for home and right to peaceful enjoyment of possessions under human rights convention – Human Rights Act 1998, Sch 1, Pt I, art 8, Pt II, art 1.*

d The defendant company was a statutory sewerage undertaker, responsible under the Water Industry Act 1991 for providing sewers for the removal of sewage and surface water in the area in which the claimant's house was situated. When constructed, those sewers had been sufficient to meet the foreseeable needs of removing surface and foul water from the area, but they had become inadequate because of the increase of water and sewage discharged into them. As a result, e since June 1992 the sewers had, on occasion, discharged both surface water and foul water into the claimant's front garden and thence into his back garden, damaging the fabric of his house. It was reasonably practicable for the company to prevent the flooding of the claimant's property, but, under the company's system of priorities, there was no prospect of the necessary work being carried out in the future. The claimant commenced proceedings against the company, f seeking damages in respect of the damage sustained. He relied, inter alia, on various common law causes of action, including nuisance, and on two provisions of the European Convention for the Protection of Human Rights and Fundamental Freedoms 1950 (as set out in Sch 1 to the Human Rights Act 1998), namely the right to respect for a person's home under art 8(1)[a] and the right to peaceful g enjoyment of possessions under art 1[b] of the First Protocol to the convention. The judge concluded that the company had infringed those rights since the implementation of the 1998 Act on 2 October 2000, and that it was therefore in breach of s 6(1) of the 1998 Act which rendered it unlawful for a public authority to act in a manner that was incompatible with convention rights. However, he h rejected the common law claims, and accordingly concluded that the claimant was entitled to damages only in respect of the period after the implementation of the 1998 Act. The company appealed against the judge's conclusion that it was liable under the 1998 Act, while the claimant cross-appealed against the rejection of his common law claims.

j a Article 8, so far as material, provides: '1. Everyone has the right to respect for his ... home ...
   2. There shall be no interference by a public authority with the exercise of this right except as is in accordance with the law and is necessary in a democratic society ... for the protection of the rights ... of others.'
   b Article 1, so far as material, provides: 'Every natural or legal person is entitled to the peaceful enjoyment of his possessions ...'

Held – The claimant had a valid claim in nuisance against the company under the
clearly-established principle that ownership of land carried with it a duty to do *a*
whatever was reasonable, in all the circumstances, to prevent hazards on the
land, however they might arise, from causing damage to a neighbour. The
company was the owner of, and in control of, the sewers from which the foul and
surface water had escaped onto the claimant's land, and of the system to which
those sewers were connected. It was operating that system as a commercial *b*
venture in order to make profits for its shareholders, and was in no more
favourable a position than a landowner on whose property a hazard had
accumulated by the act of a trespasser or of nature. At all material times, the
company had, or should have had, knowledge of the hazard. It was therefore
under a duty to the claimant to take such steps as, in all the circumstances, were
reasonable to prevent the discharge of surface and foul water onto his property, *c*
and the reasonableness of its conduct had to be judged having regard to all the
steps that were open to it to abate the nuisance, whether under statutory powers
or otherwise. The company had failed to demonstrate that it was not reasonably
practicable for it to prevent the nuisance. The claimant's entitlement to damages
at common law for that nuisance displaced any right that he would otherwise *d*
have had under the 1998 Act. However, the company had failed to establish that
the judge had been wrong to hold that it had infringed the claimant's convention
rights. Accordingly, the appeal would be dismissed and the cross-appeal allowed
(see [55], [82], [83], [87], [94]–[96], [103], [104], [120], below).

    Goldman v Hargrave [1966] 2 All ER 989 and *Leakey v National Trust for Places of
Historic Interest or Natural Beauty* [1980] 1 All ER 17 applied. *e*

    Glossop v Heston and Isleworth Local Board [1874–80] All ER Rep 836 criticised
and distinguished.

    Decision of Judge Richard Havery QC [2001] 3 All ER 698 reversed in part.

Notes *f*

For the right to respect for home and the right to property, see 8(2) *Halsbury's
Laws* (4th edn reissue) paras 152, 165, and for the liability of an occupier of land
for a nuisance that he has not created, see 34 *Halsbury's Laws* (4th edn reissue)
para 56.

    For the Human Rights Act 1998, Sch 1, Pt I, art 8, Pt II, art 1, see 7 *Halsbury's
Statutes* (4th edn) (1997 reissue) 524, 525. *g*

Cases referred to in judgment

A-G v Guardians of the Poor of Union of Dorking (1881) 20 Ch D 595, [1881–5] All ER
    Rep 320, CA.
Allen v Gulf Oil Refining Ltd [1981] 1 All ER 353, [1981] AC 1001, [1981] 2 WLR 188, *h*
    HL.
British Road Services v Slater [1964] 1 All ER 816, [1964] 1 WLR 498.
British Waterways Board v Severn Trent Water Ltd [2001] EWCA Civ 276, [2001] 3
    All ER 673, [2001] Ch 32, [2001] WLR 613.
Bybrook Barn Centre v Kent CC [2001] BLR 55, CA.
Charing Cross Electricity Supply Co v Hydraulic Power Co [1914] 3 KB 772, [1914–15] *j*
    All ER Rep 85, CA.
Dear v Thames Water (1992) 33 Con LR 43.
Delaware Mansions Ltd v Westminster City Council [2001] UKHL 55, [2001] 4 All ER
    737, [2001] 3 WLR 1007.

a *Department of Transport v North West Water Authority* [1983] 3 All ER 273, [1984] AC
     336, [1983] 3 WLR 707, HL; *rvsg* [1983] 1 All ER 892, [1984] AC 336, [1983] 3
     WLR 105, DC.
   Dunne v North Western Gas Board [1963] 3 All ER 916, [1964] 2 QB 806, [1964] 2
     WLR 164, CA.
   Geddis v Proprietors of Bann Reservoir (1878) 3 App Cas 430, HL.
b *Glossop v Heston and Isleworth Local Board* (1879) 12 Ch D 102, [1874–80] All ER Rep
     836, CA.
   Goldman v Hargrave [1966] 2 All ER 989, [1967] 1 AC 645, [1966] 3 WLR 513, PC.
   Guerra v Italy (1998) 4 BHRC 63, ECt HR.
   Hammersmith and City Rly Co v Brand (1869) LR 4 HL 171, [1861–73] All ER Rep
     600, HL.
c *Hammond v Vestry of St Pancras* (1874) LR 9 CP 316.
   Hesketh v Birmingham Corp [1924] 1 KB 260, [1922] All ER Rep 243, CA.
   Holbeck Hall Hotel Ltd v Scarborough BC [2000] 2 All ER 705, [2000] QB 836, [2000]
     2 WLR 1396, CA.
   Job Edwards Ltd v Company of Proprietors of the Birmingham Navigations [1924] 1 KB
d   341, CA.
   Jones v Llanrwst UDC [1911] 1 Ch 393, [1908–10] All ER Rep 922.
   Leakey v National Trust for Places of Historic Interest or Natural Beauty [1980] 1 All ER
     17, [1980] QB 485, [1980] 2 WLR 65, CA.
   Longhurst v Metropolitan Water Board [1948] 2 All ER 834, HL.
   Metropolitan Asylum District v Hill (1881) 6 App Cas 193, [1881–5] All ER Rep 536,
e   HL.
   Midwood & Co Ltd v Mayor, Aldermen and Citizens of Manchester Corp [1905] 2 KB
     597, [1904–7] All ER Rep 1364, CA.
   Powell v UK (1990) 12 EHRR 355, ECt HR.
   Pride of Derby and Derbyshire Angling Association Ltd v British Celanese Ltd [1953] 1
f   All ER 179, [1953] Ch 149, [1953] 2 WLR 58, CA; *affd* [1952] 1 All ER 1362.
   Read v J Lyons & Co Ltd [1946] 2 All ER 471, [1947] AC 156, HL.
   Rickards v Lothian [1913] AC 263, [1911–13] All ER Rep 71, PC.
   Robinson v Mayor and Corp of the Borough of Workington [1897] 1 QB 619, CA.
   Rylands v Fletcher (1868) LR 3 HL 330, [1861–73] All ER Rep 1, HL.
   S v France (1990) 65 DR 250, E Com HR.
g *Sedleigh-Denfield v O'Callaghan (Trustees for St Joseph's Society for Foreign Missions)*
     [1940] 3 All ER 349, [1940] AC 880, HL.
   Smeaton v Ilford Corp [1954] 1 All ER 923, [1954] Ch 450, [1954] 2 WLR 668.
   Southport Corp v Esso Petroleum Co Ltd [1954] 2 All ER 561, [1954] 2 QB 182, [1954]
     3 WLR 200, CA; *affd* [1955] 3 All ER 864, [1956] AC 218, [1956] 2 WLR 81, HL.
h *Stovin v Wise (Norfolk CC, third party)* [1996] 3 All ER 801, [1996] AC 923, [1996] 3
     WLR 388, HL.
   Stretton's Derby Brewery Co v Mayor of Derby [1894] 1 Ch 431, [1891–4] All ER Rep
     731.

   Cases also cited or referred to in skeleton arguments
j *Baron v Portslade UDC* [1900] 2 QB 588, CA.
   Haigh v Deudraeth RDC [1945] 2 All ER 661.
   Hatton v UK App No 36022/97 (2 October 2001, unreported), ECt HR.
   Hobart v Southend-on-Sea Corp (1906) 4 LGR 757; *on appeal* (1906) 22 TLR 530, CA.
   Howard v UK (1987) 9 EHRR 116, E Com HR.

Queally v London Borough of Brent (6 December 1996, unreported), QBD.

R (on the application of Mahmood) v Secretary of State for the Home Dept [2001] 1 WLR 840, CA.

Radstock Co-op and Industrial Society v Norton-Radstock UDC [1968] 2 All ER 59, [1968] Ch 605, CA.

Slater v Worthington's Cash Stores (1930) Ltd [1941] 3 All ER 28, [1941] 1 KB 488, CA.

Sporrong v Sweden (1982) 5 EHRR 35, ECt HR.

Appeal and cross-appeal

The defendant, Thames Water Utilities Ltd (Thames), appealed with permission of Judge Richard Havery QC (i) from that part of his order, made in the Technology and Construction Court on 14 May 2001 ([2001] 3 All ER 698), whereby he held, on the determination of preliminary issues, that the failure of Thames to execute works necessary to prevent flooding to the property of the claimant, Peter Marcic, at 92 Old Church Lane, Stanmore, Middlesex, was in breach of s 6(1) of the Human Rights Act 1998, and (ii) from the judge's order of 10 July 2001 ([2001] 4 All ER 326) that Mr Marcic would be awarded damages for that breach assessed on the basis set out in the order. Mr Marcic cross-appealed from those parts of the judge's order on 14 May 2001 effectively dismissing, inter alia, his claims against Thames for nuisance, negligence and breach of statutory duty. The facts are set out in the judgment of the court.

David Pannick QC and *Michael Daiches* (instructed by *Simon Byrne*) for Thames.
Stephen Hockman QC and *Peter Harrison* (instructed by *South & Co*) for Mr Marcic.

Cur adv vult

7 February 2002. The following judgment of the court was delivered.

LORD PHILLIPS OF WORTH MATRAVERS MR.

Introduction

[1] Mr Peter Marcic lives in Stanmore, Middlesex. His house is situated within the extensive area within which Thames Water Utilities Ltd (Thames) provide sewers for the removal of sewage and surface water. Since June 1992 these sewers have, on occasion, discharged both surface water and foul water into Mr Marcic's front garden and thence into his back garden. This has damaged the fabric of his house, though he has successfully taken steps to prevent it getting inside his home. In these proceedings Mr Marcic claims damages from Thames for the damage that he has sustained.

[2] Mr Marcic is not alone in his plight. In Thames' area there are many thousands of households facing the risk of internal or external flooding as a consequence of discharge from overburdened sewers. Thames has fought this case as an important test case because of the implications that it has for their liability to these households.

[3] This is not the first claim that has been brought against a sewerage undertaker in respect of damage caused by discharge from overcharged sewers. The law reports disclose a series of actions where such claims have been advanced, spanning well over a century. A few have succeeded but most have failed.

a [4] In this action Judge Havery QC, has resolved a number of issues of liability and measure of damage (see [2001] 3 All ER 698). He held that he was bound by authority to dismiss claims by Mr Marcic founded in *Rylands v Fletcher* (1868) LR 3 HL 330, [1861–73] All ER Rep 1, nuisance and negligence. He considered whether a claim could be founded upon breach by Thames of duties owed under statute, or upon a negligent failure to exercise statutory powers and concluded b that it could not.

[5] Judge Havery then turned to consider a claim by Mr Marcic founded on an alleged breach by Thames of the Human Rights Act 1998. He held that Thames had, since the Act came into force, infringed Mr Marcic's right to respect for his home under art 8 of the European Convention for the Protection of Human Rights and Fundamental Freedoms 1950 (as set out in Sch 1 to the 1998 Act) and c his right to the peaceful enjoyment of his possessions under art 1 of the First Protocol to the convention. It followed that Thames were in breach of s 6(1) of the 1998 Act. The judge held that damages for this breach should be assessed by reference to its effect on the value of Mr Marcic's home on the premise that Thames would be taking no steps to prevent the flooding in the foreseeable d future.

[6] Both parties have appealed against Judge Havery's decision. Thames have challenged his finding that they have contravened the 1998 Act. Mr Marcic has contended that the judge erred in rejecting his claims based on common law and statute, thereby depriving him of his entitlement to damages in respect of the period before 2 October 2000, when the 1998 Act came into force.

e [7] Before summarising the rival contentions of law and exploring the issues that they raise, we propose to set out the material facts relating to both Mr Marcic and Thames and the relevant provisions of the Water Industry Act 1991, under which Thames derive their powers and duties. We are assisted in our task by the careful analysis of the facts made by Judge Havery. This has not been challenged f by either party and we shall incorporate some of the judge's findings in our judgment.

The flooding experienced by Mr Marcic

[8] Mr Peter Marcic, who is now in his early 60s, lives at number 92, Old Church Lane, Stanmore, Middlesex. That property is a substantial family house g with a front garden and a large rear garden. It lies within a residential area in a street of individually-built houses. It dates from the inter-war period. Mr Marcic bought the property in the mid-1970s. He began to live in the property in 1980 and has lived there ever since. The property is frequently flooded. It lies at or near the lowest point in Old Church Lane. It was first significantly affected by h flooding on 9 June 1992. Since then it has been regularly and seriously affected by flooding and back flow of foul water from the defendant's sewer system.

[9] Under the road there is a foul water sewer and a surface water sewer. Mr Marcic's property has a dual, or combined, drainage system. That is to say, the surface water from the roof and the ground flows into the same drain as the sewage. The combined effluent flows into the foul water sewer under the road.

j [10] At times of heavy rain, the footpath between the road and Mr Marcic's property becomes flooded with surface water, sometimes emerging from the overcharged surface water sewer. The foul water sewer can also become overcharged by reason of widespread local use of combined drainage systems. The parties' drainage experts agreed that it is also possible that householders,

concerned about surface water flooding at times of heavy rainfall, lift the covers
of the inspection chambers within their properties, thereby allowing accumulated   *a*
surface water to enter the foul sewer.

[11] Water on the ground in Mr Marcic's front garden is collected from the
patio through metal grilles overlying gullies which run beside the house and
debouch into his foul drainage. When the foul water sewer is overcharged, the
foul water backs up and can force open the manhole cover in Mr Marcic's front   *b*
garden, thereby escaping into the garden. If the flood water in his front garden is
sufficiently deep, however, the manhole does not open. In that case the foul
water backs up through the grilles into the overlying surface water.

[12] Mr Marcic has made some boards to put at the front of his property as a
defence against flooding. They are not entirely satisfactory since water can pass
both underneath and over the top. He cannot keep them in position permanently   *c*
since they impede access to the premises. It takes him about 15 mins to set them
up in the evening or when he considers a flood to be imminent, and five minutes
to take them down in the morning or after a flood has subsided.

[13] In 1992, it took half an hour of heavy rainfall to cause flooding incidents
at Mr Marcic's property. The problem remained roughly the same until 1996.   *d*
Since 1996 the position has progressively deteriorated. Only 15 minutes of heavy
rainfall or some hours of steady drizzle are now sufficient to cause flooding.

[14] When the front garden is flooded, the water reaches the brickwork of the
walls of the house both below and above the level of the damp course. The water
often rises to about three-quarter inch below the level of the front door threshold.
Before carrying out some works on his property, Mr Marcic had to open his side   *e*
gate and garage doors to let the water run through to the back garden, bypassing
the house. That caused the back garden to be immersed. Water lay there for a
few days. When it subsided it left deposits of sludge and debris. Mr Marcic has
had built a manhole connected to pipes so that some flood water is carried back
from his front garden underneath the garage and to the bottom of his back   *f*
garden. That has to some extent alleviated the damage to the back garden. He
considers that it is only by having carried out those works that he has prevented
floodwater from entering his house. He has spent some £16,000 on that system.

[15] The principal incidents of flooding were two in number in 1992; one in
each of the years 1993, 1994, 1995 and 1996; two in 1997; none in 1998; four in
1999 and four or five in 2000.   *g*

[16] Mr Marcic described the effect of the flooding in a witness statement.
That description has not been challenged. It was as follows:

> 'My house has been badly affected. Damp and a musty smell are present
> in my front dining room for months after each flooding. Cracks are visible   *h*
> all over the walls and ceiling, some quite large, showing signs of subsidence.
> My house is a detached property where I have spent a good part of my life
> trying to do it up and make it into a home. I now cannot so easily part with
> it, yet I find it very difficult to live with the mess. Any measures to remove
> the damp and its effects, such as the subsidence, are pointless until the   *j*
> regular flooding is prevented. The garden is also affected. On most
> occasions the floodwater contains levels of organic (oily) contaminants that
> run off streets and tarmac which poison the plants. At one time after heavy
> flooding I tried to use a garden hose to wash off the oily sheen from the
> surface but I only managed to disperse it. Some fully-grown conifers and

a

shrubs have died. The soil has become contaminated and consolidated through persistent flooding, resulting in poor drainage. The vegetation has become poorly as water-logging deprives the roots of oxygen and drowns them. Those plants that do thrive are moss and weeds which are in abundance.'

b

[17] The judge accepted the following evidence of a structural engineer, jointly instructed by the parties, of the damage caused by the flooding to Mr Marcic's home:

'There has been no subsidence or heave of the external walls of the house … There has been subsidence of parts of the concrete ground floor slab resulting in cracking in the internal partition walls supported on the slab and in internal walls and ceilings in the first floor storey. This has been caused, or at least greatly contributed to … by floodwater entering already formed voids beneath the ground floor slab and softening the clay subsoil still in contact with the slab. It is probable that had the floodwater not been present the slab would have continued to support the internal walls without subsidence movement leading to cracking. It is also probable that had the voids not been present the floodwater would not have caused subsidence of the slab … Cracking in the second floor storey walls has been caused by spread of the roof, most likely as a result of the slight dropping of internal vertical support to the roof structure because of the subsidence of the ground floor slab … A full remedial work scheme could be carried out using grout injection below the ground floor slab. This would probably require detailed prior investigation beneath the slab, for example using radar survey equipment to trace the voids and help to plan grout injection positions.'

c

d

e

[18] The judge annexed to his judgment a joint statement by drainage experts dealing with the cause of the flooding experienced by Mr Marcic and possible schemes to alleviate this. That statement refers to two causes of flooding: (1) flooding caused by an accumulation of surface water at times of heavy rainfall which the sewers are unable to remove because they have become full to overflowing; (2) flooding caused by overflow from the surcharged surface and foul water sewers. The former type of flooding would occur if there were no sewerage system in place at all. The latter type of flooding is directly attributable to the existence of the sewers, which transmit surface and foul water from other areas served by the system and discharge this onto Mr Marcic's property.

f

g

[19] Different legal principles govern Thames' liability in relation to the two types of flooding. The judgment below has not sought to differentiate between the two. Judge Havery has proceeded on the basis that the cause of the nuisance resulting from the flooding and the damage caused to Mr Marcic's property has been surface and foul water discharged from the surface water and foul water sewers. Thus, for instance, in his judgment, he states (at [38]):

h

'Here, the nuisance is the backing up and overflowing of foul water from the foul water sewer and the overflowing of surface water from the surface water sewer. The nuisance is caused by the overcharging of those sewers.'

j

As we said earlier, the judge's analysis of the facts has not been challenged. We shall, accordingly, proceed on the basis that the only relevant flooding was that attributable to discharge from the foul water and surface sewers.

[20] Mr Marcic first complained about the flooding that he was experiencing in 1992. Initially he approached his local authority. They were unable to procure any assistance for him. In 1995 they referred him to Thames. His approaches to Thames at first elicited no more by way of response than bare acknowledgments. A letter to the managing director resulted in his being sent a cheque for £40, which he returned.

[21] In October 1997 Mr Marcic's solicitors wrote to the Secretary of State for the Environment about the problem. Three months later they received a reply from the Department of the Environment referring them to the Customer Services Committee of the Office of Water Services. In the letter it was explained that sewerage undertakers' duties under s 94 of the 1991 Act were enforceable under s 18 of the Act by the Director General of Water Services, who was the independent economic regulator for the water industry. The letter went on to explain that Customer Service Committees had been set up by the Director General to assist him in his role of protecting customers' interests and investigating complaints.

[22] No approach was made to the Office of Water Services by or on behalf of Mr Marcic. Thames contend that such an approach was the appropriate remedy—indeed the only remedy—open to Mr Marcic. Whether they are correct in this contention is the fundamental issue raised on this appeal. Before exploring that issue it is necessary to draw attention to some aspects of the statutory regime under which Thames provide their services.

The statutory regime

[23] The 1991 Act is a consolidation Act which sets out the powers and duties of both water undertakers and sewerage undertakers. This appeal is solely concerned with the role of Thames as a sewerage undertaker. The relevant provisions of the Act are as follows:

[24] A 'general duty' to provide a sewerage system is placed on a sewerage undertaking by s 94. That section reads, so far as material, as follows:

'(1) It shall be the duty of every sewerage undertaker—(a) to provide, improve and extend such a system of public sewers (whether inside its area or elsewhere) and so to cleanse and maintain those sewers as to ensure that that area is and continues to be effectually drained; and (b) to make provision for the emptying of those sewers and such further provision (whether inside its area or elsewhere) as is necessary from time to time for effectually dealing, by means of sewage disposal works or otherwise, with the contents of those sewers ...
(3) The duty of a sewerage undertaker under subsection (1) above shall be enforceable under section 18 above—(a) by the Secretary of State; or (b) with the consent of or in accordance with a general authorisation given by the Secretary of State, by the Director.'

[25] Section 18 provides, so far as material, as follows:

'(1) Subject to subsection (2) and sections 19 and 20 below, where in the case of any company holding an appointment under Chapter I of this Part the Secretary of State or the Director is satisfied—(a) that that company is contravening—(i) any condition of the company's appointment in relation to which he is the enforcement authority; or (ii) any statutory or other requirement which is enforceable under this section and in relation to which he is the enforcement authority; or (b) that that company has contravened any such condition or requirement and is likely to do so again, he shall by a final enforcement order make such provision as is requisite for the purpose of securing compliance with that condition or requirement.

(2) Subject to section 19 below, where in the case of any company holding an appointment under Chapter I of this Part—(a) it appears to the Secretary of State or the Director as mentioned in paragraph (a) or (b) of subsection (1) above; and (b) it appears to him that it is requisite that a provisional enforcement order be made, he may (instead of taking steps towards the making of a final order) by a provisional enforcement order make such provision as appears to him requisite for the purpose of securing compliance with the condition or requirement in question.

(3) In determining for the purposes of subsection (2)(b) above whether it is requisite that a provisional enforcement order be made, the Secretary of State or, as the case may be, the Director shall have regard, in particular, to the extent to which any person is likely to sustain loss or damage in consequence of anything which, in contravention of any condition or of any statutory or other requirement enforceable under this section, is likely to be done, or omitted to be done, before a final enforcement order may be made
…

(8) Where any act or omission constitutes a contravention of a condition of an appointment under Chapter I of this Part or of a statutory or other requirement enforceable under this section, the only remedies for that contravention, apart from those available by virtue of this section, shall be those for which express provision is made by or under any enactment and those that are available in respect of that act or omission otherwise than by virtue of its constituting such a contravention.'

[26] Section 22, sub-ss (1) and (2) provide as follows:

'(1) The obligation to comply with an enforcement order shall be a duty owed to any person who may be affected by a contravention of the order.

(2) Where a duty is owed by virtue of subsection (1) above to any person, any breach of the duty which causes that person to sustain loss or damage shall be actionable at the suit of that person.'

[27] Section 106 gives a right to communicate with public sewers, in the following terms:

'(1) Subject to the provisions of this section—(a) the owner or occupier of any premises in the area of a sewerage undertaker; or (b) the owner of any private sewer draining premises in the area of any such undertaker, shall be entitled to have his drains or sewer communicate with the public sewers of that undertaker and thereby to discharge foul water and surface water from those premises or that private sewer.'

[28] Chapter 1 of Pt VI of the 1991 Act gives a sewerage undertaker a wide variety of powers to enable it to carry out its functions, including the power of compulsory purchase of land (s 155), powers to lay pipes in streets (s 158), powers to lay pipes in other land (s 159) and power to carry out works to deal with foul water and pollution (s 161).

[29] Section 179 vests all pipes laid and sewage works constructed by the sewerage undertaker in the undertaker.

[30] Part V of the Act empowers a sewerage undertaker to charge for the services provided. Section 2(2)(b) of the Act requires the Secretary of State and the Director to carry out their duties in such a way as to secure that undertakers 'are able (in particular, by securing reasonable returns on their capital) to finance the proper carrying out of the functions of such undertakers'.

Some facts about Thames and their policy in relation to flooding

[31] Thames are one of the Thames Water plc group of companies. Thames are a statutory water and sewerage undertaker for the purposes of the Water Act 1989 and the 1991 Act. As statutory sewerage undertaker, Thames are responsible for an area stretching from Cirencester to Brentwood and from Banbury to Crawley. Within that area, Thames are responsible for some 80,000 km of public sewers ranging in size from 100 mm to over 6 m in diameter. There are 361 sewage treatment works and over 2,000 sewage pumping stations which serve some 5,400,000 connected properties and a population of some 12m.

[32] The revenue of Thames comes from water and sewerage charges. Those charges are fixed from time to time by the Director General of Water Services (the DG). In fixing the charges, the DG includes allowance for the cost of works necessary to remove properties from the risk of internal flooding. In more detail, the procedure is as follows. Every five years Thames submit a strategic business plan to the DG. That plan includes a statement of the capital funding needed to achieve what Thames believe to be a reasonable level of alleviation of flooding. Thames keep a database of flooding history identifying flooding incidents and the properties concerned. The DG reviews the submissions and sets the number of properties he requires to be removed from the flooding history database. He includes allowance for the cost of that in his assessment of the level of charges to be permitted. He issues directives setting out targets for performance by sewerage undertakers, one of which includes the alleviation of the risk of flooding of properties at risk. The category of property at risk of flooding for which allowance is made by the DG in the charges is properties at risk of internal flooding by foul or surface water. There is no allowance for properties at risk only of external flooding. Thus, in particular, Mr Marcic's property, which has not suffered internal flooding, is not allowed for.

[33] The flooding history database, which Thames maintain with the approval of the DG, includes all properties in Thames' area which are assessed to be at risk of flooding. There are three categories of risk. Risk A applies to properties statistically categorised as being at risk of internal flooding twice or more in ten years. Risk B applies to properties at risk of internal flooding once or more, but less than twice, in ten years. Risk X applies to all other properties with a history of flooding, including properties subject only to external flooding.

[34] For the period 1990 to 1995, the DG required 3,910 risk A properties to be removed from the risk of internal flooding. In fact, 3,943 properties were so removed. For the period from 1995 to 2000, the target was 3,700 risk A properties. The achieved figure was 4,397 properties and the cost £132m. For the period 2000 to 2005, Thames is required to remove 1,500 risk A or risk B properties. The cost allowed is £46m.

[35] Between 1990 and 1997, Thames have carried out in the London Borough of Harrow 19 flooding projects, affecting 243 properties, at a cost of £9,433,300.

a **[36]** The way in which Thames determine priorities for spending moneys to alleviate flooding is by way of a points system. A customer impact score is attached to a given flooding incident. Points are awarded for various factors, eg whether the flooding is of foul water or of surface water, whether it is internal or external, whether the property is a school, hospital or nursing home, and whether the customer has been forced to vacate the property temporarily. In the

b case of external flooding, additional points are attached by reference to the frequency of such events, provided that the frequency is at least three events in five years. In the case of internal flooding, weightings are attached to the total by reference to the number of such incidents in a ten-year period, provided that it exceeds one, and to the time elapsed since the most recent event, provided that it is not more than ten years. The score is compared with the estimated cost of

c the necessary engineering project. The threshold for what Thames regard as the viability of an engineering project to alleviate the risk of flooding is 100 points per million pounds. Cases where the figure falls below 100 points per million pounds can be referred to a review group of Thames who can consider any additional factors. Examples of such factors are specific vulnerabilities of the customer, (eg

d old age, sickness or disablement), whether the matter has received press coverage and whether a member of Parliament or a local councillor is involved in the matter.

[37] Statistical evidence was given in respect of houses in Thames' area at risk of flooding. Some 18,000 properties suffered or were at risk of internal flooding. Thames' policy gave priority to these. Their evidence was that if they diverted

e funding to all who were in a similar position to Mr Marcic, this would compromise their ability to perform their statutory functions.

[38] The judge found that, applying Thames' system of priorities, there was no prospect of any work being carried out in the foreseeable future to prevent the flooding of Mr Marcic's property. Thames accepted that it would be possible to

f remedy Mr Marcic's flooding problem without diverting resources from the 18,000 properties at risk of internal flooding and the judge held, on the basis of this evidence, that it was reasonably practicable for Thames to prevent Mr Marcic's flooding. He concluded, however, that it would cost Thames a sum in the order of £1,000m to alleviate the flooding problems of all its customers who were in a similar position to Mr Marcic or whose properties were at risk of

g internal flooding once every ten years. In the financial year 1999–2000 profits of the Thames group after tax were £344m. The judge concluded that it would take several, if not many, years, to alleviate the problems of all these customers in the absence of an increase in sewerage charges.

h *The claim based on common law*

[39] In dismissing Mr Marcic's claim in *Rylands v Fletcher* (1868) LR 3 HL 330, [1861–73] All ER Rep 1, nuisance, negligence and breach of statutory duty, the judge felt himself bound by a line of authority beginning with the case of *Glossop v Heston and Isleworth Local Board* (1879) 12 Ch D 102, [1874–80] All ER Rep 836.

j He concluded:

'The effect of the above authorities is that a statutory drainage undertaker is not liable to a person in its area who suffers damage by flooding where the claim is based on failure on the part of the undertaker to undertake works to fulfil its statutory duty of drainage of the area. That is so whether the cause

of action is nuisance, the principle in *Rylands v Fletcher* or breach of statutory
duty. It is clear that those authorities also cover the case of negligent
non-feasance.' (See [2001] 3 All ER 698 at [29].)

[40] The judge held that Mr Marcic's claim was a claim for non-feasance. It
was a claim for failure to perform Thames' statutory duty. He held (at [41]):

'However the argument is put, it reduces to the question whether the
defendant is liable for failing, negligently or otherwise, to fulfil its statutory
duty by carrying out the works necessary to prevent repetition of the
nuisance.'

[41] The judge went on to consider whether a claim lay for breach of statutory
duty. After referring to ss 18 and 22 of the 1991 Act he concluded (at [45]) that
their effect was that—

'an action for breach of statutory duty to enforce the defendant's duty
under s 94 effectually to drain the area does not lie at the suit of an injured
person unless an enforcement order has been made. No such order has been
made in this case.'

[42] Finally the judge considered whether, despite the fact that no action lay
for breach of statutory duty simpliciter, a claim could be made against Thames
for negligently failing to carry out their statutory duty under the principles laid
down in *Stovin v Wise (Norfolk CC, third party)* [1996] 3 All ER 801, [1996] AC 923.
He concluded that the policy of the Act was clear. There was no statutory
liability to pay compensation and the policy excluded the existence of a common
law duty of care to perform the statutory duty.

The issues
[43] On behalf of Mr Marcic, Mr Hockman QC submitted that the judge erred
in holding that the *Glossop* line of authority gave Thames immunity for
non-feasance, having particular regard to (i) the fact that Thames was an
enormously profitable commercial enterprise which had chosen to operate a
sewerage undertaking under the statutory scheme as a business and (ii) the need
to develop the common law in accordance with the convention.

[44] On behalf of Thames, Mr Daiches accepted that the judge had gone too
far in holding that Thames could not be liable at common law for non-feasance.
He submitted, however, that on the facts of this case Thames were under no
liability for non-feasance. The strict liability under *Rylands'* case had no
application. So far as nuisance and negligence were concerned, the only action
that Thames could take to prevent the flooding of Mr Marcic's property would
require the purchase of land and the exercise of statutory powers. The law of
nuisance did not impose a duty to purchase someone else's land in order to abate
a nuisance, nor did it impose a duty to take action where this could only be done
by exercising statutory powers. To base an action in negligence upon a failure to
exercise statutory powers, it was necessary for Mr Marcic to satisfy the
requirements identified in *Stovin's* case, and this he could not do.

Rylands v Fletcher
[45] In *Pride of Derby and Derbyshire Angling Association Ltd v British Celanese Ltd*
[1953] 1 All ER 179 at 202–203, [1953] Ch 149 at 189 Denning LJ observed:

a

'... I doubt whether the doctrine of *Rylands v. Fletcher* ((1868) LR 3 HL 330, [1861–73] All ER Rep 1) applies in all its strictness to cases where a local authority, acting under statutory authority, build sewers which afterwards overflow, or sewage disposal works which later pour out a polluting effluent, for the simple reason that the use of land for drainage purposes by the local authority is "such a use as is proper for the general benefit of the

b

community", and is on that ground exempt from the rule in *Rylands v. Fletcher*: see *Rickards v. Lothian* ([1913] AC 263 at 280, [1911–13] All ER Rep 71 at 80), per LORD MOULTON ... approved by the House of Lords in *Read v. J. Lyons & Co., Ltd.* ([1946] 2 All ER 471 at 475, [1947] AC 156 at 169) per VISCOUNT SIMON ... and per LORD UTHWATT ([1946] 2 All ER 471 at 484, [1947] AC 156 at 187); and also on the ground of statutory authority: see *Hammond*

c

v. St. Pancras Vestry ((1894) LR 9 CP 316 at 322) per BRETT, J ...'

[46] We share the doubts expressed by Denning LJ for the reasons that he gave. For reasons that will become apparent, however, it is not necessary for us to express a concluded view on whether a claim lies under *Rylands'* case and we shall not do so.

d

Nuisance

[47] Counsel for Mr Marcic submitted to Judge Havery that the line of authority that begins with *Glossop v Heston and Isleworth Local Board* (1879) 12 Ch D 102, [1874–80] All ER Rep 836 cannot stand with the more recent development

e

of the law of nuisance. The judge was not persuaded that there had been any relevant change in the law. We propose to address the law of nuisance in three stages. First we shall consider the manner in which the common law has developed up to the present day. Then we shall consider the impact on liability in nuisance of statutory authority. Finally we shall consider the line of authority

f

that specifically addresses the liability in nuisance of sewerage undertakings.

The common law of nuisance

[48] The origin of the action for nuisance was identified by Lord Wright in *Sedleigh-Denfield v O'Callaghan (Trustees for St Joseph's Society for Foreign Missions)* [1940] 3 All ER 349 at 364, [1940] AC 880 at 902 as the assize of nuisance, a real

g

action supplementary to the assize of novel disseisin. The assize was superseded by the action on the case for nuisance which sounded in damages. In 1940 Lord Wright approved the succinct definition of private nuisances as—

h

'interferences by owners or occupiers of property with the use or enjoyment of neighbouring property ... The ground of responsibility is the possession and control of the land from which the nuisance proceeds ... A balance has to be maintained between the right of the occupier to do what he likes with his own and the right of his neighbour not to be interfered with. It is impossible to give any precise or universal formula, but it may broadly be said that a useful test is perhaps what is reasonable according to the

j

ordinary usages of mankind living in society, or, more correctly, in a particular society. The forms which nuisance may take are protean.' (See [1940] 3 All ER 349 at 364, [1940] AC 880 at 903.)

[49] Prior to 1940, liability in nuisance had generally resulted from activities carried on by the occupier of land. In *Sedleigh-Denfield's* case the issue was

whether the occupiers of land were liable for flooding to a neighbour's land that
was caused by an obstruction to a culvert on the occupiers' land that had been   *a*
placed there by a trespasser. The House of Lords held that liability was
established because the occupiers, through their agents, had become aware of
their obstruction and permitted it to continue. The following passage in Salmond
Law of Torts (5th edn, 1920) p 260, approved in a dissenting judgment of Scrutton
LJ in *Job Edwards Ltd v Company of Proprietors of the Birmingham Navigations* [1924]   *b*
1 KB 341, was held to be good law:

> 'When a nuisance has been created by the act of a trespasser, or otherwise
> without the act, authority, or permission of the occupier, the occupier is not
> responsible for that nuisance unless, with knowledge or means of knowledge
> of its existence, he suffers it to continue without taking reasonably prompt   *c*
> and efficient means for its abatement.'

[50] Viscount Maugham put the test of liability as follows:

> 'The statement that an occupier of land is liable for the continuance of a
> nuisance created by others, e.g., by trespassers, if he continues or adopts   *d*
> it—which seems to be agreed—throws little light on the matter, unless the
> words "continues or adopts" are defined. In my opinion, an occupier of land
> "continues" a nuisance if, with knowledge or presumed knowledge of its
> existence, he fails to take any reasonable means to bring it to an end, though
> with ample time to do so. He "adopts" it if he makes any use of the erection,
> building, bank or artificial contrivance which constitutes the nuisance. In   *e*
> these sentences, I am not attempting exclusive definitions.' (See [1940] 3 All
> ER 349 at 358, [1940] AC 880 at 894.)

[51] *Goldman v Hargrave* [1966] 2 All ER 989, [1967] 1 AC 645 was a case which
came to the Privy Council from the High Court of Australia. The issue was
whether the occupier of land on which a fire had started by natural causes was   *f*
under a duty to take reasonable steps to prevent the fire spreading to the land of
his neighbour. The Board held that he was. Early in the judgment of the Board,
Lord Wilberforce addressed the question of the legal classification of the duty
owed by the occupier. He said:

> '... the case is not one where a person has brought a source of danger onto   *g*
> his land, nor one where an occupier has so used his property as to cause a
> danger to his neighbour. It is one where an occupier, faced with a hazard
> accidentally arising on his land, fails to act with reasonable prudence so as to
> remove the hazard. The issue is therefore whether in such a case the
> occupier is guilty of legal negligence, which involves the issue whether he is   *h*
> under a duty of care, and, if so, what is the scope of that duty. Their
> Lordships propose to deal with these issues as stated, without attempting to
> answer the disputable question whether if responsibility is established it
> should be brought under the heading of nuisance or placed in a separate
> category ... the tort of nuisance, uncertain in its boundary, may comprise a   *j*
> wide variety of situations, in some of which negligence plays no part, in
> others of which it is decisive. The present case is one where liability, if it
> exists, rests upon negligence and nothing else; whether it falls within or
> overlaps the boundaries of nuisance is a question of classification which need
> not here be resolved. What then is the scope of an occupier's duty, with

a regard to his neighbours, as to hazards arising on his land? With the possible exception of hazard of fire, to which their Lordships will shortly revert, it is only in comparatively recent times that the law has recognised an occupier's duty as one of a more positive character than merely to abstain from creating, or adding to, a source of danger or annoyance. It was for long satisfied with the conception of separate or autonomous proprietors, each of *b* which was entitled to exploit his territory in a "natural" manner and none of whom was obliged to restrain or direct the operations of nature in the interest of avoiding harm to his neighbours.' (See [1966] 2 All ER 989 at 991–992, [1967] 1 AC 645 at 656–657.)

c [52] Lord Wilberforce went on to reject the occupier's contention that a distinction was to be drawn between a hazard created by the act of a trespasser, as in *Sedleigh-Denfield v O'Callaghan (Trustees for St Joseph's Society for Foreign Missions)* [1940] 3 All ER 349, [1940] AC 880 and a hazard created by act of nature. The occupier came under a duty of care in either case. He dealt with the scope of the duty:

d 'How far does it go? What is the standard of the effort required? What is the position as regards expenditure? It is not enough to say merely that these must be "reasonable," since what is reasonable to one man may be very unreasonable, and indeed ruinous, to another: the law must take account of the fact that the occupier on whom the duty is cast has, ex hypothesi, had this hazard thrust upon him through no seeking or fault of his own. His interest, *e* and his resources, whether physical or material, may be of a very modest character either in relation to the magnitude of the hazard, or as compared with those of his threatened neighbour. A rule which required of him in such unsought circumstances in his neighbour's interest a physical effort of which he is not capable, or an excessive expenditure of money, would be *f* unenforceable or unjust. One may say in general terms that the existence of a duty must be based upon knowledge of the hazard, ability to foresee the consequences of not checking or removing it, and the ability to abate it … the standard ought to be to require of the occupier what it is reasonable to expect of him in his individual circumstances. Thus, less must be expected of the infirm than of the able-bodied: the owner of a small property where a *g* hazard arises which threatens a neighbour with substantial interests should not have to do so much as one with larger interests of his own at stake and greater resources to protect them: if the small owner does what he can and promptly calls on his neighbour to provide additional resources, he may be held to have done his duty: he should not be liable unless it is clearly proved *h* that he could, and reasonably in his individual circumstance should, have done more.' (See [1966] 2 All ER 989 at 996, [1967] 1 AC 645 at 663.)

[53] *Goldman's* case was a controversial decision and, in *Leakey v National Trust for Places of Historic Interest or Natural Beauty* [1980] 1 All ER 17, [1980] QB 485, where damages were claimed for a collapse of soil onto the plaintiffs' land, *j* counsel for the defendant occupiers contended that it did not represent the law of England. Alternatively they contended that any duty in respect of a hazard arising naturally on land lay in negligence and not in nuisance. The Court of Appeal rejected both contentions. In the leading judgment, Megaw LJ dealt with the second point:

'It is convenient at this stage to deal with the second proposition put
forward by the defendants in the present appeal. The plaintiffs' claim is *a*
expressed in the pleadings to be founded in nuisance. There is no express
reference to negligence in the statement of claim. But there is an allegation
of a breach of duty, and the duty asserted is, in effect, a duty to take
reasonable care to prevent part of the defendants' land from falling onto the
plaintiffs' property. I should, for myself, regard that as being properly *b*
described as a claim in nuisance [we believe that this should read
"negligence"]. But even if that were, technically, wrong, I do not think that
the point could or should avail the defendants in this case. If it were to do so,
it would be a regrettable modern instance of the forms of action successfully
clanking their spectral chains; for there would be no conceivable prejudice to
the defendants in this case that the word "negligence" had not been expressly *c*
set out in the statement of claim.' (See [1980] 1 All ER 17 at 25–26, [1980] 1
QB 485 at 514.)

[54] In ruling that the duty of care identified in *Goldman's* case was one that
arose under English law, Megaw LJ considered the scope of the duty at some
length in a passage which included the following statement: *d*

'The criteria of reasonableness include, in respect of a duty of this nature,
the factor of what the particular man, not the average man, can be expected
to do, having regard, amongst other things, where a serious expenditure of
money is required to eliminate or reduce the danger, to his means. Just as, *e*
where physical effort is required to avert an immediate danger, the
defendant's age and physical condition may be relevant in deciding what is
reasonable, so also logic and good sense require that, where the expenditure
of money is required, the defendant's capacity to find the money is relevant.
But this can only be in the way of a broad, and not a detailed, assessment;
and, in arriving at a judgment on reasonableness, a similar broad assessment *f*
may be relevant in some cases as to the neighbour's capacity to protect
himself from damage, whether by way of some from of barrier on his own
land or by way of providing funds for expenditure on agreed works on the
land of the defendant.' (See [1980] 1 All ER 17 at 37, [1980] 1 QB 485 at 526.)

[55] In *British Road Services v Slater* [1964] 1 All ER 816 at 820, [1964] 1 WLR *g*
498 at 504 Lord Parker CJ remarked upon the tendency of the law 'more and
more to assimilate nuisance and negligence'. This is more true than ever today.
Where a claim is based on damage caused by the act of an occupier of land, he is
likely to be held to have used his land unreasonably if it was reasonably
foreseeable that his act would harm his neighbour's land. In such circumstances, *h*
the test of liability in nuisance and negligence overlaps to the extent that the two
can become indistinguishable. Where, however, the claim is for a failure to take
action, the position is not the same. It is only in exceptional circumstances that
the law of negligence imposes a duty to act to prevent harm rather than a duty
not to act in a way that will cause harm. If cases such as *Goldman* and *Leakey* are
to be categorised as cases in negligence, then this must reflect the fact that *j*
ownership or control of realty is one of the exceptional circumstances that give
rise to a duty of care to take action. At the end of the day the question of
categorisation is academic. As Megaw LJ observed, the forms of action no longer
rule us. The two cases clearly establish that ownership of land carries with it a

a duty to do whatever is reasonable in all the circumstances to prevent hazards on the land, however they may arise, from causing damage to a neighbour.

[56] The approach of the Court of Appeal in *Leakey*'s case has been applied so as to impose on the owner or occupier of land a measured duty of care to prevent damage to a neighbour's land from lack of support due to natural causes (see *Holbeck Hall Hotel Ltd v Scarborough BC* [2000] 2 All ER 705, [2000] QB 836). It has

b also been applied by the House of Lords to the duty of a landowner not to permit tree roots to cause damage by encroaching on a neighbour's land (see *Delaware Mansions Ltd v Westminster City Council* [2001] UKHL 55, [2001] 4 All ER 737, [2001] 3 WLR 1007).

Statutory authority

c [57] Thames carry out their functions as sewerage authority in the performance of the duties and the exercise of the powers conferred on them by the 1991 Act. The question arises of how, if at all, this affects their common law duties in nuisance and negligence.

[58] In *Allen v Gulf Oil Refining Ltd* [1981] 1 All ER 353, [1981] AC 1001 Gulf Oil

d had built an oil refinery pursuant to powers conferred on them by statute. The plaintiff, who lived near the factory, brought an action in nuisance in respect of noise, smell and vibrations caused by the refinery. Gulf Oil contended that they had a defence in that they had statutory authority to build and operate the refinery. The case came to the House of Lords on a preliminary issue of whether this defence was sound in law. In the leading speech Lord Wilberforce ruled as

e follows:

'We are here in the well-charted field of statutory authority. It is now well settled that where Parliament by express direction or by necessary implication has authorised the construction and use of an undertaking or

f works, that carries with it an authority to do what is authorised with immunity from any action based on nuisance. The right of action is taken away (see *Hammersmith and City Railway Co v Brand* (1869) LR 4 HL 171 at 215, [1861–73] All ER Rep 60 at 72 per Lord Cairns). To this there is made the qualification, or condition, that the statutory powers are exercised without "negligence", that word here being used in a special sense so as to

g require the undertaker, as a condition of obtaining immunity from action, to carry out the work and conduct the operation with all reasonable regard and care for the interests of other persons (see *Geddis v Proprietors of Bann Reservoir* (1878) 3 App Cas 430 at 455 per Lord Blackburn). It is within the same principle that immunity from action is withheld where the terms of the

h statute are permissive only, in which case the powers conferred must be exercised in strict conformity with private rights (see *Metropolitan Asylum District v Hill* (1881) 6 App Cas 193, [1881–5] All ER Rep 536).' (See [1981] 1 All ER 353 at 356, [1981] AC 1001 at 1011.)

[59] Lord Wilberforce expanded on the meaning of 'negligence' in this

j context:

'If I am right upon this point, the position as regards the action would be as follows. The respondent alleges a nuisance, by smell, noise, vibration etc. The facts regarding these matters are for her to prove. It is then for the appellants to show, if they can, that it was impossible to construct and

operate a refinery on the site, conforming with Parliament's intention, without creating the nuisance alleged, or at least a nuisance ... the statutory *a* authority extends beyond merely authorising a change in the environment and an alteration of standard. It confers immunity against proceedings for any nuisance which can be shown (the burden of so showing being on the appellants) to be the inevitable result of erecting a refinery on the site, not, I repeat, the existing refinery, but any refinery, however carefully and with *b* however great a regard for the interest of adjoining occupiers it is sited, constructed and operated. To the extent and only to the extent that the actual nuisance (if any) caused by the actual refinery and its operation exceeds that for which immunity is conferred, the plaintiff has a remedy.' (See [1981] 1 All ER 353 at 357–358, [1981] AC 1001 at 1013–1014.)
c

[60] In *Department of Transport v North West Water Authority* [1983] 1 All ER 892, [1984] AC 336 statutory authority was invoked by way of defence by a water undertaker in answer to a claim in nuisance in respect of damage caused by a burst water main. Webster J ([1983] 1 All ER 892 at 895, [1984] AC 336 at 344) set out the following propositions, which were subsequently approved by the House of Lords ([1983] 3 All ER 273, [1984] AC 336):
d

'1. In the absence of negligence, a body is not liable for a nuisance which is attributable to the exercise by it of a duty imposed on it by statute: see *Hammond v Vestry of St Pancras* (1874) LR 9 CP 316. 2. It is not liable in those circumstances even if by statute it is expressly made liable, or not exempted from liability, for nuisance: see [*Stretton's Derby Brewery Co v Mayor of Derby*] *e* [1894] 1 Ch 431, [1891–4] All ER Rep 731, and *Smeaton v Ilford Corp* [1954] 1 All ER 923, [1954] Ch 450. 3. In the absence of negligence, a body is not liable for a nuisance which is attributable to the exercise by it of a power conferred by statute if, by statue, it is not expressly either made liable, or not exempted from liability, for nuisance: see *Midwood & Co Ltd v Manchester Corp* [1905] 2 *f* KB 597, *Longhurst v Metropolitan Water Board* [1948] 2 All ER 834, and *Dunne v North Western Gas Board* [1963] 3 All ER 916, [1964] 2 QB 806. 4. A body is liable for a nuisance by it attributable to the exercise of a power conferred by statute, even without negligence, if by statute it is expressly either made liable, or not exempted from liability, for nuisance: see *Charing Cross Electricity Supply Co v Hydraulic Power Co* [1914] 3 KB 772, [1914–15] All ER *g* Rep 85. In these rules, references to absence of negligence are references to—"the qualification, or condition, that the statutory powers are exercised without 'negligence', that word being used in a special sense so as to require the undertaker, as a condition of obtaining immunity from action, to carry out the work and conduct the operation with all reasonable regard and care *h* for the interests of other persons ..." (See *Allen v Gulf Oil Refining Ltd* [1981] 1 All ER 353 at 356, [1981] AC 1001 at 1011 per Lord Wilberforce.)'

[61] In the present case Mr Marcic's case is pleaded in breach of statutory duty, negligence and nuisance. The statutory duty alleged is that arising under s 94(1) of the Water Industry Act 1991. The effect of s 18(8) coupled with s 22 is that *j* Mr Marcic cannot found a claim that relies on an allegation of breach of s 94. Thus no action lies for breach of statutory duty. The judge correctly so held.

[62] Under the concluding words of s 18(8) any common law claim will lie which does not involve the averment of violation of the Act. Thames have not

a sought to establish that the flooding of Mr Marcic's property was the inevitable consequence of the exercise of their statutory duties or powers so that they have not been negligent in the special meaning of that word in *Allen*'s case. As that case makes plain, the burden of establishing this defence falls on Thames. In the event the judge held that Thames had the resources and the powers necessary to remedy the nuisance. It follows that no defence of statutory authority has been

b made out in relation to the claims founded in negligence and nuisance. The issue is whether such claims lie at common law. It is time to look at the line of authority which led the judge to conclude that they do not.

Liability in nuisance of sewerage undertakers

[63] In *Glossop v Heston and Isleworth Local Board* (1879) 12 Ch D 102, [1874–80]

c All ER Rep 836 a landowner brought an action in nuisance against the local board for failing to prevent sewers, which had recently been transferred by statute to the board, from polluting the River Crane which flowed through his land. The Court of Appeal held that the board was not liable. The precise reasoning of the court has not been found easy to analyse. It is generally agreed that James LJ

d approached the claim as if it was for an injunction requiring the board to perform its statutory duty of installing a sewerage system. Thus he held:

> 'If the sewer, being in the state in which it was transferred to them, would, independently of the Act of Parliament, give to any landowner or any riparian proprietor a right to an injunction to restrain the use of that sewer,
e or the abuse of that sewer, it appears to me they would be in the same position as any other owner of a sewer would be. But the case here is not based upon any common law nuisance, or any nuisance existing, or any damage existing irrespective of the neglect of the Act, but upon the alleged neglect to comply with the provisions of the Act of Parliament.' (See (1879) 12 Ch D 102 at 110, [1874–80] All ER Rep 836 at 838.)

f
[64] James LJ went on to hold that the alleged breach of statutory duty did not give rise to a private law entitlement to relief, but that the appropriate remedy would be to seek a mandamus.

[65] Brett LJ's judgment was to similar effect. He said:

g
> 'Under those circumstances what is their position with regard to the law? They have done no act. It is suggested it might have been proved they had done some act, and it was said the Plaintiff was taken by surprise. I cannot accede to that argument. It seems to me that the statement of claim is founded upon an allegation that the Defendants have merely neglected to carry out the purposes of the Act, and the very statement of claim, which
h must have been made before any act of the Defendants that could mislead the course of the litigation had occurred, assumes that the Plaintiff could not state any act done by the Defendants which was a wrongful act, but that the claim of the Plaintiff was founded solely upon a neglect by the Defendants to perform their duty under the Act ...' (See (1879) 12 Ch D 102 at 119–120,
j [1874–80] All ER Rep 836 at 843.)

[66] Cotton LJ first said that an injunction should not be granted unless the court was satisfied that there was a particular mode by which they could implement a scheme of drainage, which it was not. He went on to draw a distinction between the case before the court and cases in which plaintiffs had

successfully brought proceedings in relation to nuisances caused by sewage   a
undertakings. Thus he said:

> 'Here it is not that the Defendants have done a wrongful act, and that they
> are seeking to protect that wrongful act by saying that unless they do it they
> cannot do something else, but the Plaintiff asks that they may be called upon
> to exercise the powers of this Act, because that will relieve him from   b
> nuisance and injury—an injury not done by the act of the Defendants, but
> which existed before the Defendants came into existence. Those cases are
> not at all authorities for the suggestion that we should make a mandatory
> decree without seeing that there is a practical mode of carrying into effect the
> powers given by this Act of Parliament.' (See (1879) 12 Ch D 102 at 128,
> [1874–80] All ER Rep 836 at 847.)   c

[67] *Glossop's* case was followed by the Court of Appeal in *A-G v Guardians of
the Poor of Union of Dorking* (1881) 20 Ch D 595, [1881–5] All ER Rep 320. So far as
a claim in common law for nuisance was concerned, Jessel MR held that no claim
lay because there was no way that the defendants could prevent third parties   d
from discharging into the sewers vested in them. Turning to the question of
breach of statutory duty he held that the defendants were doing the best that they
could to introduce a scheme of drainage. An injunction should not be granted
when there was no way that it could be complied with.

[68] Cotton LJ said:
                                                                            e
> '… the Act does not give authority to use or do anything so as to commit
> a nuisance; and, as was pointed out by Lord Justice *James*, and I think also by
> myself in our judgment in the *Glossop Case*, it means simply this, if you want,
> for the purpose of doing anything, to rely upon authority given by the Act,
> you must do that thing so as not to commit a nuisance. Here they are doing   f
> nothing, they are not constructing a new system of sewers. It was said that
> they are in fact using this sewer by allowing it to be used as part of the
> existing system of drainage which is vested in them. That is, they are not
> substituting a new system of sewerage, and in my opinion the mere fact that
> they have not substituted a new system of sewerage cannot make this the
> using of the sewer by them when it is used without any leave granted by   g
> them under the rights which are granted by the Act to householders. That
> being so, in my opinion they are doing no act, and the injunction ought not
> to be granted.' (See (1881) 20 Ch D 595 at 609, [1881–5] All ER Rep 320 at
> 326-327.)
                                                                            h
[69] *Robinson v Mayor and Corp of the Borough of Workington* [1897] 1 QB 619 was
a case that more closely resembled that before us. The plaintiff suffered damage
as a result of sewage baying back and overflowing into his houses. The sewers,
when built, had been adequate, but they had become overcharged as a result of
additional buildings which had exercised their statutory right to connect to the   j
sewer. The claim does not appear to have been founded in nuisance, but simply
in breach of statutory duty in failing to provide an effectual sewerage system.
The Court of Appeal dismissed the claim, following *Glossop's* case. In the course
of his judgment, Lopes LJ remarked (at 622):

a 'It was admitted at the trial that the plaintiff's case was one of non-feasance. There would be no duty on the part of the defendants unless it had been created by the statute, and the duty so created is to the public ...'

[70] In *Jones v Llanrwst UDC* [1911] 1 Ch 393, [1908–10] All ER Rep 922 Parker J distinguished *Glossop's* case in holding a local authority responsible for discharging sewage into a stream. He held that the plaintiff was complaining of *b* a private wrong and that the defendants had inherited the common law obligations of their predecessors, who had constructed the sewerage system. He added that the defendants had not confined themselves to leaving things as they found them, but had laid new sewers connected with the system and enlarged a very considerable part of the system that they had inherited. This alone took the *c* case outside *Glossop's* case.

[71] In *Hesketh v Birmingham Corp* [1924] 1 KB 260, [1922] All ER Rep 243 the Court of Appeal held that the defendants were not liable for discharging a sewer into a stream, for they had statutory authority to do so and had exercised their right without negligence. In the course of his judgment, Scrutton LJ remarked that 'the general rule is that a local authority is liable for misfeasance but not for *d* non-feasance' (see [1924] 1 KB 260 at 271, [1922] All ER Rep 243 at 248).

[72] In *Pride of Derby and Derbyshire Angling Association Ltd v British Celanese Ltd* [1953] 1 All ER 179, [1953] Ch 149 the plaintiffs sued Derby Corp, the sewerage undertaker, in nuisance for discharging sewage into the River Derwent. The corporation argued that the sewerage works were adequate when constructed, *e* but had become inadequate because of the growth of the population of Derby. The case was one of non-feasance. *Glossop's* case demonstrated that there was no liability in such circumstances.

[73] Evershed MR gave the leading judgment. He started by analysing the reasoning in *Glossop's* case and *A-G v Guardians of the Poor of Union of Dorking* (1881) 20 Ch D 595, [1881–5] All ER Rep 320, which he did not find easy. He said *f* this of them:

'But, whatever may be the true ratio decidendi of the judgments in [*Glossop v Heston and Isleworth Local Board* (1879) 12 Ch D 102, [1874–80] All ER Rep 836] and the *Dorking* case which followed, they must, I think, clearly be taken as deciding that, where a local authority has inherited drains or sewers under *g* the Public Health Act [1875], and those drains or sewers constitute a nuisance by reason only that they have ceased to deal adequately with the sewage of the authority's district, then the local authority, not having themselves been at fault save that they have not used the powers vested in them to enlarge the sewerage system, are not liable to be sued in the courts, *h* for such an action would be, in effect, an action to compel them to exercise their statutory powers or perform their statutory duty ... But the [*Glossop* and *Dorking* decisions] are themselves limited to cases where the local authority have, to use the word which I have already used, "inherited" the drains and sewers from some predecessor. They do not in terms cover the *j* case where the local authority have themselves constructed the sewerage system. Indeed, some of the language of BRETT, L.J., and COTTON, L.J., seems to indicate a distinction in that respect vital to the question of liability.' (See [1953] 1 All ER 179 at 194, [1953] Ch 149 at 174–175.)

[74] Evershed MR distinguished *Glossop's* case, holding the corporation liable:

'It seems to me, therefore, that the question whether the principle of the
[*Glossop* case] is applicable only where the authority sued has not itself *a*
constructed the sewers complained of as creating a nuisance by pollution has
not yet been actually decided. For my part, I see great force in the argument
of counsel for the corporation that there is no logical or valid distinction
between the case where a local authority have inherited, say, half a century
ago, sewers and drains made (and at the time of their construction *b*
adequately made) by some predecessor, and a case in which a local authority
themselves made, half a century ago, some sewers and drains which, when
they were made, were similarly adequate properly to drain the city or town
without causing pollution. But I think that it is unnecessary that I should
express a concluded view on the point, because, on the facts, I think that the
present case is clearly distinguishable from the type of case considered in the *c*
earlier authorities. We are here concerned, not with a drain or a sewer down
which local inhabitants (having the right so to do) send sewage matter which
passes, accordingly, into a river, but with sewage disposal works built on the
Derby Corporation's own land ... what the corporation are doing, as I follow
it, is pumping or otherwise diverting into the river, by such mechanical or *d*
other means as may be there, the effluent after treatment in the beds and
tanks of the disposal works ...' (See [1953] 1 All ER 179 at 196–197, [1953] Ch
149 at 179–180.)

[75] He went on to observe that the plaintiffs' case was not obliquely directed
to commanding a local authority to perform a public duty: *e*

'The point is one which the judge noted (and I think that it was a legitimate
consideration on his part), where he said ([1952] 1 All ER 1326 at 1337): "The
plaintiffs' claim here is not that the corporation have neglected to provide
further sewers, although it may be that the remedy for that of which they
complain will be the construction of further sewers. They are not ratepayers *f*
of Derby who complain of the insufficiency of the drainage of the city. Their
complaint is the converse, namely, that the city is so drained that their
property outside it is damaged." It follows that many of the observations
which JAMES, L.J., directed to the plaintiff in the [*Glossop*] case would, on any
view, be quite inapplicable to the present case.' (See [1953] 1 All ER 179 at
197, [1953] Ch 149 at 180.) *g*

[76] Denning LJ started his judgment by observing that 'Homer nodded'
when, in *Hesketh v Birmingham Corp* [1924] 1 KB 260, [1922] All ER Rep 243
Scrutton LJ stated that the general rule was that local authorities were liable for
misfeasance, but not for non-feasance. He went on to analyse the *Glossop* line of
authorities in the following manner: *h*

'... it must be remembered that a person may "continue" a nuisance by
adopting it, or in some circumstances by omitting to remedy it: see
Sedleigh-Denfield v. O'Callaghan ([1940] 3 All ER 349, [1940] AC 880) ... When
a local authority take over or construct a sewage and drainage system which
is adequate at the time to dispose of the sewage and surface water for their *j*
district, but which subsequently becomes inadequate owing to increased
building which they cannot control, and for which they have no
responsibility, they are not guilty of the ensuing nuisance. They obviously
do not create it, nor do they continue it merely by doing nothing to enlarge

a or improve the system. The only remedy of the injured party is to complain to the Minister ...' (See [1953] 1 All ER 179 at 203, [1953] Ch 149 at 190.)

[77] Denning LJ distinguished these cases, holding that the corporation was liable to the plaintiffs on the following basis:

b 'When the increased sewage came into their sewage disposal works at Spondon, they took it under their charge, treated it in their works, and poured the effluent into the river Derwent, but their treatment of it was not successful in rendering it harmless. It was still noxious. Their act in pouring a polluting effluent into the river makes them guilty of nuisance. Even if they did not create the nuisance, they clearly adopted it within the principles *c* laid down in *Sedleigh-Denfield v. O'Callaghan,* and they are liable for it at common law unless they can defend themselves by some statutory authority.' (See [1953] 1 All ER 179 at 203–204, [1953] Ch 149 at 191.)

[78] Romer LJ concurred, holding that once it was conceded that the corporation had created a nuisance by discharging noxious material from their *d* sewage treatment works they could only escape liability by showing that this was the inevitable result of doing that which the statute had authorised them to do (see [1953] 1 All ER 179 at 205, [1953] Ch 149 at 193). This they could not do.

[79] In *Smeaton v Ilford Corp* [1954] 1 All ER 923, [1954] Ch 450 overflow from the defendants' sewer had damaged the plaintiff's property. The defendants had *e* constructed the sewer, but it had originally been adequate for its purpose and no negligence was alleged. It had become inadequate because of the growth of housing that discharged into it. Upjohn J held that there was no action that the defendants could take to prevent the overflow. In these circumstances he dismissed the plaintiff's claim in nuisance, *Rylands v Fletcher* and trespass. One reason that he gave for his decision ([1954] 1 All ER 923 at 927–928, [1954] Ch 450 *f* at 463) was that no claim in nuisance could be based on the fact that the sewer had become inadequate for its purpose, citing the passage in the judgment of Denning LJ in *Pride of Derby and Derbyshire Angling Association Ltd v British Celanese Ltd* [1953] 1 All ER 179, [1953] Ch 149, which we have quoted above.

[80] In *Dear v Thames Water* (1992) 33 Con LR 43 the plaintiff sued Thames *g* Water in respect of flooding from storm water which was caused by backing up from a culvert over which Thames Water had no control. Judge Bowsher held that in these circumstances Thames Water was under no liability in nuisance. He relied on *Glossop v Heston and Isleworth Local Board* (1879) 12 Ch D 102, [1874–80] All ER Rep 836 in so holding. The plaintiff sought to rely on *Leakey v National Trust for Places of Historic Interest or Natural Beauty* [1980] 1 All ER 17, *h* [1980] QB 485 but the judge held (at 69) that this had not affected the *Glossop* line of authority. He added:

j 'Leakey's case was a case which dealt with the common law duty of a private landowner. It has no application to the situation of a public authority, whose responsibilities must be considered in the light of the specific statutes governing the situation, even where, as here, breach of statutory duty is not alleged. *Glossop's* case is still binding on me, and it can be reconciled with *Leakey's* case, if it is necessary to reconcile the two, within the application of the reasonableness test, which still has to be worked out in detail.'

Are Thames liable in nuisance?

[81] We now turn to apply the authorities that we have considered above to the facts of this case. We propose first to consider Thames' position under the general principles of the common law, before turning to see whether the *Glossop* line of authority affects the position. We proceed upon the basis, that appears to be common ground, that: (1) The flooding is caused by the inadequacy of a section of the sewerage system which Thames inherited. (2) That section, when constructed, was adequate to meet the foreseeable needs of removing surface water and foul water from the area that it served. (3) The section has become inadequate because of the increase of water and sewage discharged into it which has been effected by third parties as of right under s 106 of the 1991 Act, or predecessors of that section to like effect.

The general principles of the law of nuisance

[82] Thames are the owners of and in control of the sewers from which the foul and surface water has escaped, and of the system to which those sewers are connected. The judge ([2001] 3 All ER 698 at [38]) held in his judgment that, on the premise that the sewers constituted the nuisance, Thames, by passively using the sewers in order to carry out its statutory duty of draining its area, passively permitted the nuisance to continue and thereby adopted the nuisance.

[83] We agree with this part of the judge's analysis. Indeed we think that the matter can be put higher against Thames. The sewers form part of a system which Thames are operating as a commercial venture in order to make profits for their shareholders. Thames are in no more favourable position than a landowner on whose property a hazard accumulates by the act of a trespasser or of nature. At all material times Thames have had, or should have had, knowledge of the hazard. If the principles identified in *Goldman v Hargrave* [1966] 2 All ER 989, [1967] 1 AC 645 and *Leakey's* case are applied, these facts placed Thames under a duty to Mr Marcic to take such steps as, in all the circumstances, were reasonable to prevent the discharge of surface and foul water onto Mr Marcic's property.

[84] This raises a question of burden of proof. Does Mr Marcic have to prove that Thames have not done all that was reasonable, or does Thames have to prove that they have done all that was reasonable? In *Southport Corp v Esso Petroleum Co Ltd* [1954] 2 All ER 561 at 571, [1954] 2 QB 182 at 197 Lord Denning MR said:

'One of the principal differences between an action for a public nuisance and an action for negligence is the burden of proof. In an action for a public nuisance, once the nuisance is proved and the defendant is shown to have caused it, then the legal burden is shifted on to the defendant to justify or excuse himself. If he fails to do so, he is held liable, whereas, in an action for negligence, the legal burden in most cases remains throughout on the plaintiff. In negligence the plaintiff may gain much help from provisional presumptions like the doctrine of res ipsa loquitur, but, nevertheless, at the end of the case the judge must ask himself whether the legal burden is discharged. If the matter is left evenly in the balance, the plaintiff fails. But in public nuisance, as in trespass, the legal burden shifts to the defendant, and it is not sufficient for him to leave the matter in doubt. He must plead and prove a sufficient justification or excuse.'

a [85] The editors of *Clerk & Lindsell on Torts* (17th edn, 1995) after quoting from this passage, remark (p 904 (para 18–28)):

'... in relation to private nuisance there seems no reason why the maxim *res ipsa loquitur* should not apply in appropriate cases to require the defendant to show that he was not at fault and was not negligent.'

b [86] We agree with this comment. In *Allen v Gulf Oil Refining Ltd* [1981] 1 All ER 353 at 357, 358, 359, [1981] AC 1001 at 1013, 1014, 1015 the House of Lords held that it was for the plaintiff to prove the nuisance, but then for the defendant to prove absence of negligence, giving that word the special meaning accorded to it. Once a claimant has proved that a nuisance has emanated from land in the possession or control of the defendant, the onus shifts to the defendant to show c that he has a defence to the claim, whether this be absence of 'negligence' in a statutory authority case or that he took all reasonable steps to prevent the nuisance, if it is a *Leakey* situation.

[87] In the present case Thames did not set out to prove that they had taken all reasonable steps to prevent causing a nuisance to Mr Marcic. They did, d however, seek to show that their system of priorities was a fair way of devoting limited resources to the widespread problem of nuisances emanating from their sewers. Arguably, had they established this, they might have established also that they had done everything that was reasonable within the *Leakey* test. We say 'arguably' because we cannot readily accept that a body with the actual and potential resources of Thames is in a position to rely on lack of resources to justify e not merely taking no immediate steps, but taking no steps at all to abate a nuisance such as that suffered by Mr Marcic. In the event, however, Thames failed to persuade the judge that their system of priorities was a fair one. We agree with the judge's conclusion, and thus a *Leakey* defence cannot be made out on this basis.

f [88] Mr Daiches submitted none the less that Thames could not be held liable under the *Leakey* principle. He did so on two grounds: (i) In order to abate the nuisance Thames would have to acquire land in order to construct the necessary works. The *Leakey* duty of care could not extend that far. (ii) In order to abate the nuisance Thames would have to make use of their statutory powers. The *Leakey* duty could not be invoked so as to require this.

g [89] In support of his first ground, Mr Daiches referred us to an observation of Scrutton LJ in his seminal judgment in *Job Edwards Ltd v Company of Proprietors of the Birmingham Navigations* [1924] 1 KB 341 at 360: 'surely a landowner cannot be required to execute permanent works on another person's land, if he could not then stop the fire on his own land'.

h [90] We do not read this statement as one of principle that a defendant can never be obliged to purchase land in order to abate a nuisance emanating from land that he already owns. It may be that the *Leakey* test will seldom involve such a duty, but where a massive corporation, such as Thames, is carrying on business as a sewerage undertaker, we consider that the common law duty to take reasonable steps not to permit a nuisance to continue will often involve the j requirement to add to the substantial land areas that it already owns.

[91] In advancing his submission, Mr Daiches very properly drew our attention to the facts of the case of *Bybrook Barn Centre v Kent CC* [2001] BLR 55. In that case the Court of Appeal held that the owners of land downstream of the claimants' land were liable in nuisance for failure to enlarge a culvert, which was

causing a stream to back up and flood the claimants' land. Mr Daiches informed us that, although this is not apparent from the report, the only way of enlarging the culvert was by the purchase of land adjacent to the defendants' own property. As the point now taken by Mr Daiches was not taken in the *Bybrook Barn* case, we do not consider that the *Bybrook Barn* case is fatal to his case. We do, however, consider that it exemplifies the fact that the *Leakey* duty is not subject to the limitation for which he contends.

[92] We turn to Mr Daiches' contention that, when considering what Thames can reasonably be required to do under the *Leakey* principle to abate the nuisance, no regard can be had to their statutory powers. His reasoning appears from the following passage in his skeleton argument:

> '37. In the absence of express statutory authority, a public body (or it is submitted a private body exercising public functions) is in principle liable for torts in the same way as a private person—see *Stovin v Wise* [1996] 3 All ER 801 at 821, [1996] AC 923 at 946 per Lord Hoffmann ... It is submitted that, by the same token, a public body cannot be under a *greater* liability at common law than a private person would be, merely because of the existence of its statutory powers.
>
> 38. The question whether a public body comes under a duty to exercise its statutory duties and statutory powers depends on *entirely different principles*, namely the principles laid down by Lord Hoffmann in *Stovin v Wise* [1996] 3 All ER 801 at 822–823, [1996] AC 923 at 947–958.'

[93] We do not consider that Mr Daiches' reasoning is correct. The foundation of a claim in nuisance is the fact that the defendant has caused or permitted the nuisance to occur. It is the emanation of the nuisance from land within the control of the defendant that is the foundation of the claim to relief. The existence of the statutory power may become relevant when considering what the defendant could reasonably have done to prevent the nuisance. The duty to take reasonable steps to abate the nuisance is not, however, founded on the fact that the statutory power exists. This position is in contrast to a case such as *Stovin v Wise (Norfolk CC, third party)* [1996] 3 All ER 801, [1996] AC 923 where the defendant would have been under no duty at all but for the statute, whose provisions were the foundation of the claim.

[94] We are in no doubt that, when applying the *Leakey* test of duty to a sewerage undertaking such as Thames, the reasonableness of Thames' conduct must be judged having regard to all the steps that it is open to Thames to take to abate the nuisance, whether under statutory powers or otherwise. In this context we would draw attention to an observation of Chadwick LJ in *British Waterways Board v Severn Trent Water Ltd* [2001] EWCA Civ 276 at [74], [2001] 3 All ER 673 at [74], [2001] Ch 32. In that case it had been argued that the defendant sewerage undertaker had an implied power to discharge sewage into canals and watercourses implicit in its statutory power to lay and maintain pipes under the Water Industry Act 1991. Chadwick LJ said (at [74]):

> '... for my part, I would not expect an implied power of that nature to follow from the fact that a company limited by shares (which, it may be assumed, are to pass out of public ownership in due course, if the objective of privatisation is to be achieved) has been appointed as a sewerage undertaker to carry out the duties imposed by s 94 of the Water Industry Act.

a   What I would expect to find (and do find) in the legislation is a power to acquire by compulsory purchase, with the authority of the Secretary of State and upon payment of compensation, the rights which the undertaker needs to carry out its functions.'

b   [95] It would be an unrealistic, indeed an absurd, exercise to consider whether Thames had taken reasonable steps, having regard to their individual circumstances, to abate the nuisance, without including their statutory powers in those circumstances.

     [96] For these reasons, unless the *Glossop* line of authority alters the position, we have concluded that Thames are liable to Mr Marcic for the nuisance that he has suffered for the entire period covered by his claim.

c

The Glossop line of authority

     [97] If *Glossop*'s case and the cases that followed it are to be treated as cases dealing with claims in nuisance, we consider that they cannot survive the development of that law in *Goldman v Hargrave* [1966] 2 All ER 989, [1967] 1 AC
d   645 and *Leakey v National Trust for Places of Historic Interest or Natural Beauty* [1980] 1 All ER 17, [1980] QB 485. *Glossop*'s case was decided at a time when the law of nuisance drew a clear distinction between misfeasance and non-feasance. Having regard to the finding in *Glossop*'s case (1879) 12 Ch D 102, [1874–80] All ER Rep 836 that the defendants had not been guilty of any wrongful act, it is not surprising that there was no finding of liability in nuisance. Judge Havery held
e   ([2001] 3 All ER 698 at [37]) that *Leakey*'s case introduced no new principle into the law of nuisance, accepting a submission that it applied a principle going back to the end of the nineteenth century. We do not agree. *Goldman*'s and *Leakey*'s cases saw a significant extension of the law of nuisance, which had already been radically extended by the decision in *Sedleigh-Denfield v O'Callaghan* (*Trustees for St*
f   *Joseph's Society for Foreign Missions*) [1940] 3 All ER 349, [1940] AC 880.

     [98] The Court of Appeal in *Glossop*'s case dismissed the suggestion that an action would lie in nuisance almost out of hand. They treated the defendants on the same basis as a landowner through whose land a stream flowed into which others, over whom he had no control, discharged sewage. They held that the gist of the action was a claim for failure to perform a statutory duty. Such a claim
g   could only be brought in public law. This reasoning was thrown into question once the law of negligence recognised that a person who owns or controls land cannot remain passive in the face of a hazard arising on his land, even if he is in no way responsible for the creation of that hazard. The Court of Appeal could not have approached the facts in *Glossop*'s case in the way that they did, had they
h   been considering those facts today. The same is true of *A-G v Guardians of the Poor of Union of Dorking* (1881) 20 Ch D 595, [1881–5] All ER Rep 320 and *Robinson v Mayor and Corp of the Borough of Workington* [1897] 1 QB 619. There are, however, other bases for distinguishing *Glossop*'s case and the cases which followed it.

     [99] The Court of Appeal in *Glossop*'s case treated the claim as if it were a claim
j   for failure to perform a statutory duty. Thus, at the start of his judgment, James LJ observed:

     'If this action could be maintained, I do not see why it could not in a similar manner be maintained by every owner of land in that district who could allege that if there had been a proper system of sewage his property would be very much improved.' (See (1879) 12 Ch D 102 at 109, [1874–80] All ER Rep 836 at 837.)

[100] In *Pride of Derby and Derbyshire Angling Association Ltd v British Celanese Ltd* [1953] 1 All ER 179, [1953] Ch 149 the Master of the Rolls commented, by way of contrast with *Glossop*'s case, that the plaintiffs' case was not obliquely directed to commanding a local authority to perform a public duty. The complaint was not of failure to drain the city, but of draining the city in such a way that the plaintiffs' property was damaged. The same is true of Mr Marcic's case. He is not complaining of failure on the part of Thames to drain his property. He is complaining of the fact that their drainage of the property of others is resulting in discharge from Thames' system which is damaging his property.

[101] In *Bybrook Barn Centre v Kent CC* [2001] BLR 55 at 61 Waller LJ put forward the following analysis of the sewerage cases:

'... the main distinction between the situations in *Glossop, Smeaton,* and [*Dear v Thames Water* (1992) 33 Con LR 43] as compared to *Pride of Derby* would appear to me to be as follows. First, in cases such as *Glossop, Smeaton* and *Dear*, the plaintiffs were members of the public for whose benefit the sewers or sewerage system had been installed, and what the plaintiffs were in effect doing was seeking an order to compel the local authority to carry out their statutory duty to provide an adequate system. That was found to be seeking a public law remedy and provided one reason why the plaintiffs' actions in private nuisance could not succeed, (see Evershed MR ([1953] 1 All ER 179 at 194, [1953] Ch 149 at 174–175) and Denning LJ ([1953] 1 All ER 179 at 203, [1953] Ch 149 at 190) in *Pride of Derby*; Upjohn J in *Smeaton* ([1954] 1 All ER 923 at 927, [1954] Ch 450 at 463) and Judge Bowsher in *Dear* (1992) 33 Con LR 43 at 58–59). Second, the statutory provisions imposing duties, providing powers, and granting exemptions, were important in those cases. In *Pride of Derby* the statutory provision on which the council was relying as protecting them from liability, was found by the court in fact to confirm that there was liability. In *Smeaton* the statutory provision was "generously" construed to relieve the statutory authority from liability under the rule in *Rylands v Fletcher* albeit I accept that was not the basis for relief from the liability in nuisance. In *Dear* the case really turned on whether there was liability in relation to the exercise of statutory powers. Third, as Upjohn J's judgment in *Smeaton* showed, it will be a relevant consideration as to whether a defendant should be liable for "continuing" a nuisance created by forces for which that defendant is not responsible, whether it is reasonably practicable for that person to prevent the nuisance continuing. In *Smeaton* the finding was that it was not reasonably practicable to do so. In *Pride of Derby* it is difficult to discern this point being considered in any detail, but, since an injunction was granted, albeit suspended for a reasonable period, the implication is that it must have been contemplated that prevention was reasonably practicable. In *Dear* the finding of the judge was that the defendants did not have immediate physical control of the thing causing the nuisance. On that basis for example he distinguished *Goldman* and *Leakey* (see ((1992) 33 Con LR 43 at 70)).'

[102] Mr Daiches submitted that the crucial element in this analysis was the question of whether or not it was reasonably practicable to prevent the

a continuance of the nuisance. He submitted that in the present case it was not, but this was on the basis that the purchase of land and the exercise of statutory powers had to be disregarded when considering what was practicable. We have ruled against him on this point.

[103] In summary, our conclusion is that Mr Marcic has a valid claim in nuisance under the common law. That claim is not a concealed attempt to make *b* Thames perform a statutory duty. The *Glossop* line of authority is no bar to it. Thames have failed to demonstrate by way of defence that it was not reasonably practicable for them to prevent the nuisance. Mr Marcic's cross-appeal succeeds.

[104] What are the consequences of this? We have been dealing with matters that Judge Havery dealt with as preliminary points, and no argument has been addressed to us as to the measure of damages to be applied to his claim in *c* nuisance. It is reasonable to assume, however, that the damages to which Mr Marcic is entitled will afford him 'just satisfaction' for the wrong that he has suffered. On that premise, and having regard to the provisions of s 8(3) of the Human Rights Act 1988, Mr Marcic's right to damages at common law displaces any right that he would otherwise have had to damages under the Act. Thames' *d* appeal against the judge's finding that they were in breach of s 6 of that Act and art 8 of the convention thus becomes academic. Accordingly, we propose to deal with it very shortly.

The claim under the 1998 Act

e [105], [106] Judge Havery found that Thames' failure to carry out works to bring to an end the repeated flooding of Mr Marcic's property constituted an interference with his right to respect for his home under art 8 of the convention and of his entitlement to peaceful enjoyment of his possessions under art 1 of the First Protocol. He held that the interference resulted not from active interference but from a failure to act, for which Thames could none the less be liable (see *f Guerra v Italy* (1998) 4 BHRC 63 at 76 (para 58).

[107] The judge went on to hold that the rights interfered with were not unqualified. Under art 8(2) interference could be justified where 'necessary in a democratic society in the interests of … the economic well-being of the country … or for the protection of the rights and freedoms of others'. He held that in *g* deciding what was justified it was appropriate to apply the following passage of the judgment of the Strasbourg Court in *Powell v UK* (1990) 12 EHRR 355 at 368 (para 41):

'Whether the present case be analysed in terms of a positive duty on the State to take reasonable and appropriate measures to secure the applicants' *h* rights under paragraph (1) of Article 8 or in terms of an "interference by a public authority" to be justified in accordance with paragraph (2), the applicable principles are broadly similar. In both contexts regard must be had to the fair balance that has to be struck between the competing interests of the individual and of the community as a whole; and in both contexts the *j* State enjoys a certain margin of appreciation in determining the steps to be taken to ensure compliance with the Convention.'

[108] The judge held that on the facts of the present case, it was necessary to decide whether Thames' scheme of priorities had struck a fair balance between the competing interests of Mr Marcic and of their other customers. It was

common ground that the onus was on Thames to establish this. Thames had
failed to do so. It followed that Mr Marcic's claim under the 1998 Act succeeded.   *a*

[109] Mr Marcic has not challenged the judge's approach, but it has been
attacked by Thames. Mr Pannick QC's starting point was that the judge had
correctly identified that a fair balance had to be struck between protection of
Mr Marcic's fundamental rights and the general interest of the community. He
argued that Parliament enjoyed a wide area of discretion of judgment when   *b*
deciding how to secure a fair balance. The statutory scheme, currently embodied
in the 1991 Act but with a lengthy pedigree, incorporated an internal mechanism
to achieve that balance. A complaint had to be made to the delegated authority
that the undertaker had not properly performed its statutory duty. If the
authority concluded that the case was made out, an enforcement order would be
made. Anyone affected by breach of the enforcement order could claim   *c*
compensation. The decision of the authority was subject to judicial review. This
scheme satisfied the requirements of the convention.

[110] We did not find these submissions in point. Had Mr Marcic's claim been
solely for breach of Thames' statutory duty, Mr Pannick's submissions would
have been pertinent in addressing any suggestion that the provisions of s 18(8)   *d*
were in conflict with art 6 of the convention. But Mr Marcic's claim is not just for
breach of statutory duty—it is for interference with his human rights as an
incident of the performance by Thames of their statutory duty. The statutory
scheme does not purport to cater for such an eventuality—indeed the statute
confers no right to compensation for acts or omissions which predate an
enforcement notice, even if these constitute a breach of statutory duty.   *e*
Mr Pannick suggested that this might be a respect in which the statute was
incompatible with the convention. The reality is that the provisions of s 18
provide a procedure for striking the necessary balance in the case of those who
claim that they are being denied the benefits that Thames is required to provide
to them under the statute. They provide no answer to a claim such as   *f*
Mr Marcic's.

[111] For these reasons Mr Pannick has failed to persuade us that the judge
was wrong to hold that Thames had infringed Mr Marcic's convention rights.

Unanswered questions   *g*

[112] Mr Marcic's case in nuisance has been advanced on the basis that
Thames were in breach of the duty to take reasonable steps to abate the nuisance,
adopting the test in *Leakey's* case. Mr Marcic has succeeded on that basis. That
principle applies where the cause of a nuisance has arisen on the defendant's land
without any involvement on his part. In those circumstances the duty on the   *h*
defendant is no more than to do what is in all the circumstances reasonable to
abate the nuisance. In considering what is reasonable, the resources of the
defendant are a material factor. If more is required to abate the nuisance than can
reasonably be expected from him, he will not be responsible for the consequences
of the nuisance.

[113] Where a sewerage undertaker in performance of its statutory duty and   *j*
in the exercise of its statutory powers constructs a new system it will be liable if
this results in a foreseeable nuisance unless this was inevitable (see *Allen v Gulf Oil
Refining Ltd* [1981] 1 All ER 353, [1981] AC 1001). It will be no answer to show
that disproportionate expenditure would have been needed to avoid the

a nuisance. That may, however, be a reason for the court to award damages in respect of the nuisance rather than a mandatory injunction to abate it.

[114] Where a nuisance results because an existing system becomes surcharged as a consequence of increased user, it does not seem to us just that the liability of the undertaker should depend upon whether in all the circumstances there are steps which the undertaker should reasonably have taken to abate the *b* nuisance. If a single house is at risk of flooding by sewerage discharge once every five years, this may not justify the investment that would be needed to remove that risk. It does not follow, however, that it is just that the householder should receive no compensation for the damage done. The flooding is a consequence of the benefit that is provided to those making use of the system. It seems to us at least arguable that to strike a fair balance between the individual and the general *c* community, those who pay to make use of a sewerage system should be charged sufficient to cover the cost of paying compensation to the minority who suffer damage as a consequence of the operation of the system.

[115] This result would be achieved if the principle in *Rylands v Fletcher* (1868) LR 3 HL 330, [1861–73] All ER Rep 1 were to be applied to sewage, although, as *d* we have indicated above, it is questionable whether this could be achieved without a degree of modification of legal principle. Such modification may, however, be necessary if our common law is to march in step with the requirements of the convention.

[116] When considering Mr Marcic's claim under the 1998 Act, the judge proceeded on the premise that this required a fair balance to be struck between *e* the competing interests of Mr Marcic and Thames' other customers. In this context he was prepared to contemplate that the system of priorities used by Thames might be 'entirely fair', notwithstanding that this would result in nothing being done to remedy Mr Marcic's flooding in the foreseeable future. We doubt whether such a situation would be compatible with Mr Marcic's rights under art *f* 8. The decision of the Strasbourg Commission in *S v France* (1990) 65 DR 250 suggests to the contrary.

[117] In that case the claimant complained that her rights under art 8 and s 1 of the First Protocol were interfered with as a result of the nuisance caused to her home by a nearby power station. The Commission held that, although noise and *g* other types of nuisance might be the unavoidable consequence of measures not directed against the claimant, they none the less interfered with her human rights, but that payment to her of compensation had had the result that the interference did not go beyond what was necessary in a democratic society. The Commission observed (at 263):

h   'It is not in dispute that the nuclear power station was lawfully built and brought into service by Electricité de France. Nor can there be any doubt that the construction of a nuclear power station serves the interest of the economic well-being of the country. In order to determine whether the interference in this case can be regarded as "necessary in a democratic *j* society", it must first be decided whether it was proportionate in relation to the legitimate interest the works were intended to serve. When a State is authorised to restrict rights or freedoms guaranteed by the Convention, the proportionality rule may well require it to ensure that these restrictions do not oblige the person concerned to bear an unreasonable burden.'

[118] This suggests that where an authority carries on an undertaking in the
interest of the community as a whole it may have to pay compensation to a
individuals whose rights are infringed by that undertaking in order to achieve a
fair balance between the interests of the individual and the community.

[119] We have referred to these matters, which have not been explored in the
present action, lest sewerage undertakers assume from our judgment that their
liability to pay compensation for damage done by discharge from an overcharged b
sewer is dependent upon whether or not there are measures which they should
reasonably have taken to prevent the discharge. That does not necessarily follow
from our judgment.

[120] For the reasons that we have given Thames' appeal is dismissed and
Mr Marcic's cross-appeal is allowed. We shall hear counsel on the appropriate
order.

Appeal dismissed. Cross-appeal allowed. Permission to appeal refused.

Kate O'Hanlon   Barrister.

a

Fuller v Strum
[2001] EWCA Civ 1879

COURT OF APPEAL, CIVIL DIVISION
PETER GIBSON, CHADWICK AND LONGMORE LJJ

b 1, 2 NOVEMBER, 7 DECEMBER 2001

Probate – Will – Validity – Knowledge and approval – Burden on propounder to establish 'righteousness of the transaction' – Judge finding testator having known and approved of part of will only – Whether judge misapplying doctrine of 'righteousness of
c *the transaction'.*

In 1989 the testator was preparing to emigrate. He entered into a written agreement with F, the son of old friends, whereby he undertook to invest a sum of money for F in the country in which he was planning to settle. The agreement, which had been written by F but contained certain idiosyncratic phrasing inserted
d by the testator, was signed at the testator's house in the presence of two other friends. The testator, who was of full testamentary capacity and had not been subjected to any undue influence, then told F that he wanted to prepare a will. They went to another room by themselves. When they returned to their companions some 45 to 60 minutes later, the testator was holding the will. That document, which contained the same idiosyncratic phrasing as the investment
e agreement, had been written legibly by F on a will form provided by the testator and, according to F, in terms dictated to him by the testator. The execution of the will was properly witnessed by their companions, with the testator covering up the will's contents. The will named F as executor, and the dispositions included pecuniary legacies, totalling just under 30% of the testator's disposable assets, to
f F, his sister and her daughters, with all of whom the testator had long been on affectionate terms. There was a further pecuniary legacy to another old friend, G, while the residuary estate was left to the testator's adopted son, S, 'albeit very grudgingly' according to the terms of the will. The testator asked F and the witnesses not to reveal to S the existence of the will which referred to the latter in highly derogatory terms. The testator left a metal deed box with F for safekeeping,
g and made him swear not to open it until the testator's death. After emigrating, the testator always went to the room containing the box on his visits to England. When the testator died in 1998, F found the will in the deed box. On learning of its existence, S entered a caveat against the will. F responded by bringing proceedings for probate of the will, naming S, who would have taken on intestacy, as sole
h defendant. At trial, S alleged, inter alia, that the testator had not known and approved the contents of the will. The judge concluded that the case was one in which the suspicion of the court should be aroused, that F had failed to remove that suspicion and that the testator had known and approved of only two things, namely that he was making a will and that he was making the bequest to G. He
j therefore pronounced against F's appointment as executor and all the dispositive contents of the will other than the legacy to G. On F's appeal, the Court of Appeal considered whether the judge had been correct to affirm the validity of only part of the will and, in particular, whether he had properly applied the doctrine of 'the righteousness of the transaction', which placed on the propounder of a will, in circumstances arousing the court's suspicion, the burden of proving affirmatively that the deceased had known and approved of the will that he was executing.

Held – Where a will had been duly executed by a deceased of testamentary
capacity who knew that he was making a will and was shown to have known and   *a*
approved of a specific part of that will, the court had to consider how real was the
possibility that the deceased had not known and approved of the remainder of
the will. That required a careful examination of all the circumstances, including the
directions and dispositions of the will, but the circumstances in which it would be
proper to find such a curate's egg of a will were likely to be rare. It would   *b*
certainly not be proper for the court to pronounce against part of a will as a means
of expressing its disapproval of the propounder. Although the doctrine of 'the
righteousness of the transaction' was a salutary one, the phrase itself, redolent of
morality, was unfortunate. It was not to be taken by the court as a licence to
refuse probate to a document of which it disapproved, whether the disapproval
stemmed from the circumstances in which the document had been executed or   *c*
from its contents. There was no overriding requirement of morality. What was
involved was simply the satisfaction of the test of knowledge and approval, but
the court insisted that, given the suspicion aroused, it had to be the more clearly
shown that the deceased knew and approved the contents of the will so that the
suspicion was dispelled. Suspicion could be aroused in varying degrees, depending   *d*
on the circumstances, and what was needed to dispel the suspicion would vary
accordingly. The standard of proof, however, was always the normal civil
standard, ie satisfaction on the preponderance or balance of probability. In the
instant case, the level of suspicion aroused was at the lower end of the scale, and
it was simply incredible that the testator had never at any time read the will or
understood its contents. It followed that F had discharged the burden of dispelling   *e*
the suspicion aroused in the court, and accordingly his appeal would be allowed
(see [32], [33], [36], [41], [54], [55], [64], [65], [70]–[72], [75], [76], [79], below).

   Barry v Butlin (1838) 2 Moo PC 480, *Fulton v Andrew* [1874–80] All ER Rep 1240
and *Wintle v Nye* [1959] 1 All ER 552 considered.

                                                                              f
Notes
For the exclusion of part of a will and for the onus of establishing the righteousness
of the transaction, see 17(2) *Halsbury's Laws* (4th edn reissue) paras 301, 318.

Cases referred to in judgments
Atter v Atkinson (1869) LR 1 P & D 665.   *g*
Austin, Re (1929) 73 SJ 545.
Barry v Butlin (1838) 2 Moo PC 480, 12 ER 1089, PC.
Benmax v Austin Motor Co Ltd [1955] 1 All ER 326, [1955] AC 370, [1955] 2 WLR
   418, HL.
Dabbs (dec'd), Re, Hart v Dabbs [2001] WTLR 527.   *h*
Fuld (dec'd), Re, (No 3), Hartley v Fuld (Fuld intervening) [1965] 3 All ER 776, [1968]
   P 675, [1966] 2 WLR 717.
Fulton v Andrew (1875) LR 7 HL 448, [1874–80] All ER Rep 1240, HL.
H (minors) (sexual abuse: standard of proof), Re [1996] 1 All ER 1, [1996] AC 563,
   [1996] 2 WLR 8, HL.   *j*
Watt (or Thomas) v Thomas [1947] 1 All ER 582, [1947] AC 484, HL.
Wintle v Nye [1959] 1 All ER 552, [1959] 1 WLR 284, HL.

Appeal
The claimant, Michael Fuller, the executor named in the will of Max Moses Strum
(deceased), appealed with permission of Robert Walker LJ from the decision of

a Jules Sher QC, sitting as a deputy judge of the High Court, on 20 December 2000
([2001] WTLR 677), whereby he pronounced only for the validity of part of the
will and granted letters of administration to the defendant, Geoffrey Strum, the
deceased's adopted son. The facts are set out in the judgment of Peter Gibson LJ.

Michael Fuller appeared in person.

b *Jack Mitchell* (instructed by *Embertons*, Enfield) for Geoffrey Strum.

Cur adv vult

7 December 2001. The following judgments were delivered.

c **PETER GIBSON LJ.**
   [1] The claimant, Michael Fuller (Michael), appeals against the order of Mr Jules
Sher QC, sitting as a deputy judge of the High Court, on 20 December 2000 in a
probate action (see [2001] WTLR 677). The judge pronounced for the force and
validity of a will only in respect of certain standard directions and one of five
d pecuniary legacies. In respect of all the other terms of the will, including the
appointment of Michael as executor, the judge was not satisfied of the
righteousness of the transaction. The judge refused permission to appeal, but this
appeal is brought with the permission of Robert Walker LJ.
   [2] The judge's highly unusual order arises out of highly unusual circumstances.
The late Max Moses Strum (the testator) was born in 1920 in Halberstadt in
e Germany. He was Jewish. At the beginning of the 1939–1945 war he came to
England as a refugee from Nazi Germany. In 1940 he married another Jewish
refugee, Gertrude Levinson. He became a British citizen in 1948. In 1955 he and
his wife a adopted a ten-day-old boy, the defendant, Geoffrey Strum (Geoffrey).
Geoffrey was born out of wedlock to an Irish mother. The testator worked as a
f waiter at the well-known London restaurant, Bloom's, during his working life.
He was a Zionist and keen to go to Israel, but his wife was not, and during her
life emigration to Israel was out of the question. His wife had a stroke in 1975 and
was confined to a wheelchair. Eventually she became bedridden. She died on 27
January 1985.
   [3] The testator owned the home where he lived, 162 Glengall Road, Woodford
g Green. Geoffrey, who has not married, lived in the house too. By the end of 1988
the testator had decided to sell the house and emigrate to Israel.
   [4] The testator was a sociable and friendly man and was liked by all who
knew him. There was a society of Jewish refugees from Europe who used to meet
in restaurants in the East End. The testator and his wife used to meet Michael's
h parents, whom the judge found to be their close friends, and Michael and his
sister Vivienne knew the testator well enough to call him 'Uncle Max'. Michael
at one time worked in Bloom's, the testator having got Michael the job, and later
the testator used to go with Michael, who ran a weekend car boot sale business,
to help him run his car boot sales. Michael is about 11 years older than Geoffrey.
j Vivienne has two daughters.
   [5] The trusting relationship between the testator and Michael can be seen
from the circumstances of the sale by the testator of his house. Michael was
selling his own house at that time with a view to moving to a smaller house. The
testator agreed to sell his house to Michael for about £95,000, a price which
represented an undervalue of some £10,000 or so. For three months before
completion on 31 March 1989 the testator allowed considerable work to be done

to the house to make it suitable for Michael and to create two separate flats, one
for Vivienne and her daughters, and one for Michael's and Vivienne's aunt,   *a*
Clara. Even before 31 March, Clara and Vivienne had moved into their flats.
Throughout this period whilst the work was being done the testator and Geoffrey
continued to live in the house. As the judge found (at 680):

> '... this was a source of irritation and anxiety to [Geoffrey] who was   *b*
> concerned as to what would happen and who would be responsible for all
> these works if the intended purchase went off for any reason. Moreover,
> [Geoffrey] was not pleased about the undervalue.'

In fact Michael paid for all the conversion works, which indeed was Geoffrey's
belief, as he himself said in evidence. March 31 was an eventful day. In addition   *c*
to the completion of the sale of the house to Michael, the testator executed two
documents, one called 'Receipt and Undertaking' and the other the 'Testator's
Will' which would appear to be the only will he ever executed.

[6] The execution of the first document came about in the following way,
according to Michael's evidence to the judge. Michael had spare money to invest   *d*
from the sale of his house for £270,000, even after the purchase and conversion of
the testator's house, and the testator was concerned that Michael should invest
wisely to safeguard his future, as he felt that Michael's income from car boot sales
was 'built on straw'. The testator repeatedly asked Michael to give him £25,000
to invest for Michael in Israel at what were said to be the very high rates of
interest obtainable there, and he said that he could guarantee Michael 10% p a   *e*
simple interest and that in ten years' time he would guarantee to double
Michael's money. Michael decided to give the testator £15,000 to invest for him.
Clara spoke to the testator about his financial affairs in Michael's presence and
suggested that he really ought to make a will before going to Israel. The testator
said that it was a good idea and would seek advice on the wording from a retired   *f*
solicitor whom he knew. A few days later in a discussion between Clara, Michael
and the testator one of them suggested that if the testator was to take £15,000
from Michael, they should record it in writing and have the transaction witnessed
by a third party to protect both Michael and the testator. They therefore arranged
to meet on 31 March 1989 for tea and Michael agreed to bring Isaac Aghajanoff
who was known to the testator, Clara and Michael.   *g*

[7] Michael on 31 March brought Mr Aghajanoff to 162 Glengall Road, where,
in the sitting room, the testator and Clara were having tea. Michael produced
£15,000 in cash in 15 bundles of notes, each of £1,000. Michael asked the testator
if he wanted to count the money but the testator said that he trusted Michael.
Mr Aghajanoff and Clara heard the conversation and saw Michael give the   *h*
testator the money. Vivienne popped in and saw the money, and Michael
commented that he was giving £15,000 to the testator to invest in Israel.

[8] Michael had already drafted a rough form of words to evidence the
transaction. He gave that to the testator to look at. The testator spent some time
reading the document through and asked Michael to insert some words (the   *j*
words 'God Forbid' twice and a reference to executors and administrators which
he had been advised to insert). Michael then wrote out the full form of the
document which the testator signed. Michael offered to go out and get
photocopies for everyone present, but Clara at her suggestion typed up the final
form on her own typewriter in her bedroom and the testator signed the typed
version. Michael then procured photocopies and when he returned he gave a

a copy to each of the testator, Mr Aghajanoff and Clara. He kept the original manuscript document and the testator kept the original typed version.

[9] The document which the testator signed was in the following form:

'RECEIPT AND UNDERTAKING

b I, MAX STRUM, of 162 Glengall Road, Woodford Green, Essex, hereby confirm that I have on this 31st day of March 1989 received from Mr. Michael Fuller, also of 162 Glengall Road, Woodford Green, the sum of £15,000 (Fifteen thousand pounds) in cash, and I hereby undertake to use and/or invest that money on his behalf, and promise to repay that money (plus simple interest of 10% per annum, whether or not interest rates or property values rise or fall) on the 31st day of March 1999, i.e. a guaranteed

c total sum of £30,000 (Thirty thousand pounds). If, God Forbid, Michael should die before 31/3/99, his wish is that the principal of £15,000 (plus accrued simple interest at 10% per annum, calculated from the date hereof up to and including the date of his death) is to be paid to, and shared equally between, his sister, Mrs. Vivienne Cummings, and her two daughters (Miss Sarah Cummings and Miss Michelle Cummings), all of 162 Glengall

d Road, Woodford Green. In, God Forbid, the event of my death before 31/3/99, then I hereby request the Executors or Administrators of my Estate to repay the principal of £15,000 (plus accrued simple interest at 10% per annum, calculated from the date hereof up to and including the date of my death) to Mr. Michael Fuller at the earliest possible time.

e Copies with:—
MAX STRUM
CLARA TEITLER
ISAAC AGHAJANOFF'

f [10] By the time of the trial Clara had died, but Mr Aghajanoff gave evidence confirmatory of what Michael said had occurred in relation to the receipt and undertaking and Vivienne also gave evidence that she had seen a large pile of currency and had been told by Michael that he was giving the testator £15,000 to invest in Israel because of the far higher rate of interest there and that it was intended that the testator would repay Michael in ten years' time.

g [11] The making and execution of the will then followed in these circumstances, according to Michael. At that point the testator suddenly said 'Before you take Isaac home, let's go and write up my will' and he asked Mr Aghajanoff if he would mind witnessing the testator's will. At the testator's request Michael went with the testator into Clara's bedroom. Again Mr Aghajanoff's evidence was to the

h same effect. Mr Aghajanoff could not, of course, say what went on in the bedroom while he and Clara stayed in the sitting room.

[12] Michael's evidence was that the testator had two blank will forms with him. They both sat on the bed while the testator dictated the terms which he wanted in the will. Michael wrote them out on a pad. The testator had some

j notes to which he referred and which the testator had prepared in advance. The testator said to Michael that he had been told of some legal terms such as 'testamentary expenses' and had been advised of the need for full names and addresses of the beneficiaries by the retired solicitor whom he had consulted. The testator read and altered what Michael was writing. The testator wanted to put in a few kind words about each legatee and Michael was embarrassed when the testator referred to him. When the testator said what he had previously

mentioned to Michael and Clara, that he was minded to leave the residue to the
state of Israel, Michael reminded the testator that Clara and Michael had tried to
persuade him that it was not right to leave nothing to Geoffrey and that Clara had
pointed out that Geoffrey, who had been a great disappointment to the testator,
was still young enough to change and might turn out to be a 'mensch' (a decent
human being). The testator after reflecting said that he would leave the residue
to Geoffrey, though with grave misgivings. The testator said that he wanted
Michael to be his executor because he really did not like his son. Michael wrote
the terms out onto one of the will forms in pencil. When he got to the bequest
to Geoffrey, the testator suddenly burst out with a tirade against him and insisted
on putting in words very critical of him. Michael said that it was very strong stuff
but was told by the testator very firmly to 'just put it in'; so he did. Michael
complied with the testator's request to write out the will in ink on the second will
form in capital letters and to try to get it all on one page. Michael then gave the
will to the testator who read it through carefully. When satisfied with the final
draft, the testator tore up the notes and earlier drafts. The whole process took 45
to 60 minutes. The testator then came back into the sitting room with the will in
hand.

[13] Michael's evidence then continued that the testator went to the breakfast
bar, laid the will on the surface, placed a sheet of paper over the text leaving space
at the bottom for signatures. The testator called Clara and Mr Aghajanoff over to
witness his will, Michael standing out of the way. The testator signed the will
followed by Clara and Mr Aghajanoff. The testator thanked them, telling
Mr Aghajanoff 'You should live to be 120' (a Jewish blessing), folded the will up
(it is of double A4 size), put it in his pocket and swore Michael, Clara and
Mr Aghajanoff to secrecy because, he said: 'Geoffrey will kill me if he finds out
what I have done.' Throughout the afternoon he had been on edge in case
Geoffrey appeared. Michael then took Mr Aghajanoff home. Mr Aghajanoff's
evidence was again confirmatory of Michael's evidence. He said that he could
not read any writing in the will save for the words 'This is the Last Will &
Testament of me MAX MOSES STRUM'.

[14] The testator then went up to Vivienne's flat to have a cup of coffee with
her. He tapped his chest over his inside jacket pocket and told her that he had just
signed his will and he made her swear not to tell Geoffrey.

[15] The will, signed that day by the testator and witnessed by Mr Aghajanoff
and Clara, was in the following form:

'This is The Last Will & Testament
of me MAX MOSES STRUM
of 162 GLENGALL ROAD, WOODFORD GREEN,
in the County of ESSEX made this 31ST (THIRTY-FIRST)
day of MARCH one thousand nine hundred
and EIGHTY-NINE.
I hereby revoke all Wills and Codicils made by me at any time heretofore.
I appoint
                    MICHAEL FULLER
to be my Executor, and direct that all my Debts and Funeral Expenses shall
be paid as soon as conveniently may be after my decease.

I give and bequeath unto BETTY GRIFFIN OF 144, HIGHAM HILL ROAD, E.17, MY
VERY LOYAL, LOVING FRIEND AND COMPANION FOR MANY YEARS THE SUM OF £6,000
(SIX THOUSAND POUNDS) FREE OF TAX. I GIVE AND BEQUEATH UNTO VIVIENNE

CUMMINGS THE SUM OF £6,000 (SIX THOUSAND POUNDS) FREE OF TAX. I GIVE AND
BEQUEATH UNTO SARAH CUMMINGS THE SUM OF £6,000 (SIX THOUSAND POUNDS)
FREE OF TAX. I GIVE AND BEQUEATH UNTO MICHELLE CUMMINGS THE SUM OF
£6,000 (SIX THOUSAND POUNDS) FREE OF TAX. VIVIENNE AND HER DAUGHTERS
HAVE ALWAYS WELCOMED ME INTO THEIR HOME, GIVEN ME MEALS AND OFTEN
TAKEN ME OUT. I KNOW THEY WILL REMEMBER "UNCLE MAX" WITH AFFECTION. I
GIVE AND BEQUEATH UNTO MICHAEL FULLER THE SUM OF £10,000 (TEN THOUSAND
POUNDS) FREE OF TAX. (THE FOUR LAST NAMED BENEFICIARIES ALL RESIDE AT 162
GLENGALL ROAD, WOODFORD GREEN.) I HAVE KNOWN MICHAEL, AND OUR
FAMILIES HAVE BEEN FRIENDS, FOR OVER 40 YEARS. HE HAS BEEN A LOYAL AND
TRUSTED ALLY AND CONFIDANTE OF MINE AND I WILL NEVER FORGET HIM
TELLING ME THAT SHOULD I, GOD FORBID, EVER NEED A KIDNEY TRANSPLANT, HE
WOULD NOT HESITATE IN DONATING ONE OF HIS TO ME. THOSE WERE THE
KINDEST WORDS ANYONE HAS EVER SAID TO ME. MICHAEL WAS ALMOST LIKE A
SON TO ME AND I KNOW HE WILL REMEMBER ME WITH GREAT AFFECTION. THE
£15,000 (FIFTEEN THOUSAND POUNDS) OF MICHAEL'S MONEY THAT I AM HOLDING IS
THE SUBJECT OF AN EARLIER DOCUMENT. I HAVE BEEN THINKING OF LEAVING THE
RESIDUE OF MY ESTATE TO CHARITY, AND NOT TO MY ADOPTED SON GEOFFREY. IN
ALL THE YEARS I NURSED MY WIFE, HIS MOTHER, HE NEVER ONCE RAISED A FINGER
TO HELP ME. I WILL NEVER FORGET OR FORGIVE THAT ON LEAVING THE HOSPITAL
WHERE HIS MOTHER HAD JUST DIED, HE SAID TO ME, "MUM SAID YOU SHOULD SELL
THE HOUSE AND GIVE ME HALF THE MONEY." I HATE HIM LIKE POISON, THAT IRISH
BASTARD. HOWEVER, ON REFLECTION I DO GIVE AND BEQUEATH, AFTER PAYMENT
OF ALL TESTAMENTARY EXPENSES AND ALL TAXES, THE RESIDUE OF MY ESTATE
UNTO GEOFFREY STRUM, ALBEIT VERY GRUDGINGLY.'

(The words in lower case are words printed in the will form. The words in
capitals are in manuscript.)

[16] The first-named legatee, Mrs Griffin, was a dear friend of the testator who
had seen her virtually daily for the previous five years and who went to stay with
her on 31 March until he left for Israel some ten days later. Her evidence was that
just before he left, he told her that he had made a will and left her something in it.

[17] Also on or shortly after 31 March, the testator made two gifts, one of
£16,000 to Geoffrey and another of £3,000 to £4,000 to Mrs Griffin. Geoffrey
was asked, but could give no explanation of, why the particular sum of £16,000 was
chosen.

[18] Two other significant events occurred before the testator left for Israel.
One is that the testator made a photocopy of the will which he gave to Michael.
The other is that he left a locked metal deed box with Michael for safekeeping.
Subsequently on a visit from Israel he gave Michael a key to the deed box but
made Michael swear not to open it unless he asked Michael to do so or died.

[19] After moving to Israel the testator visited England twice a year in the
early years and on every occasion went to the room containing the deed box.
The testator died in Israel on 24 December 1998. Geoffrey telephoned Michael
the next day to tell him of the death. Michael telephoned Geoffrey a few days
later to ask if Geoffrey had found the testator's will. Geoffrey refused to believe
that the testator had made a will. The will was found by Michael in the deed box.

[20] Geoffrey insisted that the signature on the will was not that of the testator
and he caused a caveat to be entered on 25 February 1999. On 6 August 1999
Michael commenced these proceedings, seeking probate of the will in solemn
form. Geoffrey is the only person who would take on intestacy and he was named

as the sole defendant. By his defence he alleged that the testator did not know and approve the contents of the will, that the testator's signature was a forgery and, by amendment, that the signature was obtained by undue influence. He counterclaimed for the grant to him of letters of administration.

[21] The case came before the judge for five days in October 2000, both sides being represented by counsel. The judge heard evidence from Michael, Mr Aghajanoff, Vivienne, Mrs Griffin and another old friend of the testator, Zena Starr. Geoffrey gave evidence on his own behalf, and his partner since 1992, Lynne Collins, gave evidence but she could not speak to the events of 31 March 1989. Sidney Aaronberg also gave evidence of the testator's ignorance of financial matters. The judge described him as 'a long term friend' of the testator, but on Mr Aaronberg's own oral evidence, though he met the testator when Mr Aaronberg was a customer at Bloom's, he was not really a friend of the testator before he emigrated to Israel.

[22] Each side had obtained a handwriting expert's report relating to the allegation of forgery, but a single joint expert, Dr Audrey Giles, was appointed by the court. She gave a written report, but in the interests of saving costs was not asked by either of the parties or the judge to give oral evidence. Her conclusion was that the signature of the testator on the receipt and undertaking was genuine but that there was 'very strong positive evidence' that the signature on the will was a forgery.

[23] The main issue at the trial was the alleged forgery. The judge, in his detailed and painstaking reserved judgment, dealt at some length with that issue. He pointed out that if Dr Giles was correct, not only would Michael but also Mr Aghajanoff (and possibly Vivienne) have been guilty of fraud. Having seen them give evidence, the judge was not prepared so to conclude. He held that the will was duly executed by the testator.

[24] Apart from forgery the only defence of Geoffrey which was maintained at the trial was want of knowledge and approval. The judge rejected Michael's account of what occurred when he and the testator went into Clara's bedroom on 31 March 1989. This was for two central reasons. One was that the judge had been able to build up a picture of the testator and his relationship with his son and the judge thought it inconsistent with that picture that the testator would himself have created the sentence 'I hate him like poison, that Irish bastard', or subscribe to it if someone else had created it. The judge did not believe that the testator knew or approved of those words when he signed the will. He concluded ([2001] WTLR 677 at 687): 'I cannot accept that the will, prepared in the hand of the claimant, was read over to Max Strum or by him in the way the claimant has told me that it was.' That conclusion of the judge is expressed in a noticeably limited way. The second central reason was that the judge did not believe that he had been told the whole truth about the monetary transaction which took place on 31 March 1989 in relation to the £15,000.

[25] The judge described the evidence in the case as presenting a classic case in which the suspicion of the court ought to be aroused, and counsel for Michael did not dispute that. The judge explained why his suspicion had been aroused. First he referred to the major role played by Michael in the preparation of a will that 'diverted' a third to a half of the testator's estate away from his next of kin and in favour of Michael and his family. Second the judge said it was particularly unfortunate that having played so major a role in the preparation of the will, the alleged reading over of the will by or to the testator was done in the secrecy of Clara's bedroom and he said that Michael had only himself to blame for the fact

a that the judge was not prepared to accept Michael's word for it. The judge said (at 697):

> 'I find that the language of the will is so out of character with the picture of Max Strum that I have gleaned from the evidence, and so inconsistent with the gift of £16,000 to the defendant and with the other evidence of the relationship between father and son, that I have serious doubts as to whether
b Max Strum knew and approved of anything in the will signed by him on 31 March 1989 other than the gift of a legacy of £6,000 to Betty Griffin.'

The judge found that he knew and approved of only two things, namely that he was making a will and was leaving Mrs Griffin £6,000. The judge said that Michael had failed to remove the suspicion which had been aroused in the court and so he
c pronounced against Michael's appointment as executor and all the dispositive contents of the will other than Mrs Griffin's legacy.

[26] The order made by the judge leaves intact the opening part of the will stating that this was the last will of the testator, that he was revoking all previous wills and codicils and directing the payment of his debts and funeral expenses.
d It also leaves the gift to Mrs Griffin, with the laudatory description of her. But the appointment of Michael as executor prior to that gift is deleted as are all the other parts of the will up to the signature and attestation. Geoffrey was granted letters of administration by the judge.

[27] When giving permission to appeal, Robert Walker LJ suggested that further evidence of the size of the estate might be admitted. Michael then sought to
e obtain an order requiring Geoffrey to provide full details of the estate of the testator. But the order of the judge granting Geoffrey letters of administration had been stayed by Robert Walker LJ, and Geoffrey's application was refused on 11 October 2001 by Chadwick LJ, who, however, directed Geoffrey to verify on oath the list of assets in the estate on 7 September 2001, to which his solicitor had
f already deposed, and indicated that Geoffrey should include any additional information known to him. In his judgment Chadwick LJ had pointed out that what was of most relevance to the court was the value of the estate at 31 March 1989. Geoffrey has sworn a witness statement in which, in addition to that verification, he has stated that the value of the estate at 31 March 1989 was £96,452·60 and that after transfers of some £70,000 to an account with Barclays Overseas and the gift
g of £16,000 there was a balance of just over £10,000. I note that, rightly, the £15,000 cash delivered by Michael to the testator has been left out of account. I also note that the gift to Mrs Griffin is not referred to, perhaps because it may have occurred a day or two later than the gift to Geoffrey.

[28] For this appeal Mr Fuller sought permission to adduce further evidence
h not put before the judge. This included statements from six persons who had known the testator. Most of them wanted to give evidence of what they say were the numerous occasions on which the testator had spoken disapprovingly of Geoffrey and had used the term 'that bastard' or 'that Irish bastard' of Geoffrey and to testify to the good relations the testator had had with Michael and
j Vivienne and her daughters. The further evidence also included evidence of the high rates of interest obtainable in Israel before and after 31 March 1989. It further included an affidavit by Edward Zeid, who describes himself as an accountant, in which he said that some time after the death of the testator's wife, the testator came to see Mr Zeid, said he was selling his house and emigrating to Israel and informed him of having £212,000 to invest or transfer prior to emigration. We indicated early in the appeal hearing that save for two affidavits, on which we

deferred our ruling until we gave judgment on the appeal, we would not admit
the further evidence, which could have been put before the judge. The two *a*
affidavits were made by deponents who, arguably, were persons reasonably not
known at the time of the trial to have material evidence. One is Tony Reading,
who worked as a caterer at Michael's car boot sales for about ten years from 1985
but had not seen Michael since 1996 until meeting him by chance this summer
and Michael has told us that he had not previously been aware that the testator *b*
had spoken to Mr Reading on material matters. Mr Reading's evidence was of
many conversations with the testator before and after he went to Israel (the
testator attended Michael's car boot sales when on visits from Israel), of the
affection between Michael and the testator, of the testator telling Mr Reading on
at least two occasions that he had left Michael, Vivienne and her daughters
money in his will, that 'Whenever Max referred to his son it was to call him a *c*
bastard', and that he had invested some of Michael's money in Israel. The other
affidavit was that of Mr Zeid. Again Michael has told us that he was unaware of
his evidence until volunteered by Mr Zeid to Michael after the trial.

[29] Mr Mitchell, appearing before us as he did before the judge for Geoffrey,
argued against the admission of this evidence which, he submitted, was not *d*
important in the light of the other evidence heard by the judge and, in the case of
Mr Zeid's evidence, was unsubstantiated by documentary or other evidence. He
asked to cross-examine the deponents if the evidence was admitted.

[30] In the event it is unnecessary to rule on that further evidence. It is
sufficient to determine this appeal on the evidence before the judge plus the
uncontroversial details of what is known about the testator's estate at 31 March *e*
1989 which are now put before the court by Geoffrey. I therefore wholly
disregard all the further evidence which Michael sought to put in.

[31] In considering this appeal I am acutely conscious that the judge had the
advantage, which an appellate court does not have, of having seen and heard the
witnesses and observed their demeanour. So long as a trial judge cannot clearly *f*
be seen to have misused that advantage the appellate court must accept the
findings of primary fact, evidence of which the trial judge received from witnesses
in a position to give that evidence (see, for example, *Watt (or Thomas) v Thomas*
[1947] 1 All ER 582, [1947] AC 484). But where direct evidence is lacking and the
trial judge makes inferences from primary facts, it is easier for an appellate court
to interfere with those inferences if in its view they are not justified, though even *g*
then the appellate court will give weight to the trial judge's opinion (see, for
example, *Benmax v Austin Motor Co Ltd* [1955] 1 All ER 326, [1955] AC 370).

[32] Probate proceedings peculiarly pose problems for the court because the
protagonist, the testator, is dead and those who wish to challenge the will are
often not able to give evidence of the circumstances of the will. The doctrine of *h*
'the righteousness of the transaction' whereby the law places a burden on the
propounder of the will, in circumstances where the suspicion of the court is
aroused, to prove affirmatively that the deceased knew and approved of the will
which he was executing, is a salutary one which enables the court in an
appropriate case properly to hold that the burden has not been discharged. *j*

[33] But 'the righteousness of the transaction' is perhaps an unfortunate term,
suggestive as it is that some moral judgment by the court is required. What is
involved is simply the satisfaction of the test of knowledge and approval, but the
court insists that, given that suspicion, it must be the more clearly shown that the
deceased knew and approved the contents of the will so that the suspicion is
dispelled. Suspicion may be aroused in varying degrees, depending on the

a circumstances, and what is needed to dispel the suspicion will vary accordingly. In the ordinary probate case knowledge and approval are established by the propounder of the will proving the testamentary capacity of the deceased and the due execution of the will, from which the court will infer that knowledge and approval. But in a case where the circumstances are such as to arouse the suspicion of the court the propounder must prove affirmatively that knowledge b and approval so as to satisfy the court that the will represents the wishes of the deceased. All the relevant circumstances will be scrutinised by the court which will be 'vigilant and jealous' in examining the evidence in support of the will (*Barry v Butlin* (1838) 2 Moo PC 480 at 483, 12 ER 1089 at 1090 per Parke B).

[34] However, it is instructive to consider the recent decision of Lloyd J in *Re Dabbs (dec'd), Hart v Dabbs* [2001] WTLR 527, as illustrating the properly c objective approach of the court in a case where the suspicion of the court has been aroused. In that case the propounder of the will made by a wealthy 74-year-old man was a person who was alleged to have killed the deceased unlawfully. The propounder was an executor under the will, was named as a specific legatee and the sole residuary legatee, had played an active part in the preparation of the d will and organised the process of the signing of the will by the deceased and the witnesses. There was no professional assistance or involvement of any kind in the will-making process, no evidence that the deceased prepared the will himself or gave instructions for its preparation, no evidence that the deceased read the will or had it read to him before or after it had been made or that he retained a copy or, apart from what can be inferred from evidence that he told one legatee e of what he intended to do by his will (and that was partly inaccurate), that he knew about its terms. The propounder did not give evidence. Nevertheless Lloyd J was satisfied that the will should be admitted to probate. This was because knowledge and approval could be inferred in all the circumstances. Lloyd J heard evidence from the attesting witnesses that the will and certain other f documents executed at the same time were duly executed, that there was reference during the signing ceremony to the fact that the purpose of the attendance of the witnesses was to witness the deceased's signature of his will and that the deceased covered up some of the documents. Lloyd J commented that that evidence showed that the deceased was not being deceived as to the nature of the document he was signing and that he had at least had the opportunity of g seeing the documents before they were covered up. Lloyd J also noted that the provisions of the will were neither complex nor difficult to grasp. He said (at 551): 'So long as he read the document he would have had no difficulty in taking in its provisions, even if someone else had prepared it.' Lloyd J said that apart from the gift of residue to the propounder there was not much in the will to provoke h suspicion in itself as being different from what one might expect the deceased to do. Lloyd J found that the evidence showed the deceased to have been alert and not likely to allow himself to be persuaded to do what he did not want to do. On that evidence the will was admitted to probate. We are told that the judgment in *Re Dabbs* was provided to Mr Sher QC after he had reserved, but before he had j delivered, judgment. But the judge makes no reference to it in his judgment.

[35] Two other cases were referred to by the judge at the end of his judgment as supporting the propriety of upholding part of a will and pronouncing against the remainder of the will. One was *Re Austin* (1929) 73 SJ 545, a decision of Swift J. In that case a former solicitor, who had been struck off the roll for professional misconduct, propounded a will under which he was named as an executor and the residuary legatee. The will which the former solicitor had prepared contained

an unusual attestation clause stating that the will had the deceased's knowledge
and approval. Swift J said that he did not think the deceased understood what he   *a*
was doing with regard to the next of kin, that the circumstances in which the will
was prepared and signed excited the greatest suspicion and that the onus on the
propounder had not been discharged. He pronounced in favour of certain
legacies and against the remainder. This case is too briefly reported to be of much
assistance. The other case was *Fulton v Andrew* (1875) LR 7 HL 448, [1874–80] All ER   *b*
Rep 1240. In that case the propounders of a will, which had been professionally
drawn through their agency, were named as executors, specific legatees and
residuary legatees. The Court of Probate directed the case to be tried at the
assizes where the judge asked the opinion of the jury on a number of questions
including whether the deceased knew and approved of the residuary clause
giving the residue to the propounders. The jury answered that question in the   *c*
negative and the House of Lords held that it was open to the jury so to decide,
having regard to the circumstances, which included instructions to the draftsman
of the will which left open to question whether the executors were to be given
the residue as trustees for certain children. The reasons for the decision of the
jury are of course not known, so that again the case is not of great help.   *d*

[36] I do not doubt that it is possible for a court to find that part of a will did
have the knowledge and approval of the deceased and that another part did not.
An example would be if a solicitor, who has been instructed to draft a will, obtains
the deceased's approval of the draft but subsequently before execution adds a
clause without drawing it to the attention of the testator and keeps the executed
will. But the circumstances in which it will be proper to find such a curate's egg   *e*
of a will are likely to be rare. In my judgment it would not be proper for the court
to pronounce against part of a will as a means of expressing the court's
disapproval of the propounder. Where a will has been duly executed by a
deceased of testamentary capacity who knew that he was making a will and is
shown to have known and approved of a specific part of the will, the court must   *f*
consider how real is the possibility that the deceased did not know and approve
of the remainder of the will and that requires a careful examination of all the
circumstances including the directions and dispositions of the will.

[37] In the present case there is now no question but that the will was duly
executed by the testator who (a) was fully of testamentary capacity, (b) was not
said to be unable to read or to have poor eyesight, (c) was not subjected to undue   *g*
influence, (d) initiated the will-making process by himself suggesting that he
make a will to be witnessed by Mr Aghajanoff and Clara, (e) immediately before
the will was prepared and executed, had executed a legal document containing
terms the language of which he had caused to be modified by the insertion of
idiosyncratic language ('God Forbid') and which he was content to sign in a   *h*
manuscript form written out by Michael, (f) having spent 45 to 60 minutes in
Clara's bedroom over the will, emerged with the will (written out by Michael) in
hand, (g) covered up the contents of the will when signing it in the presence of
witnesses who signed the attestation clause, (h) took away the executed will,
(i) subsequently made or caused to be made a copy of the will for Michael, and   *j*
(j) left the original will in the locked deed box to which he had access when in
England.

[38] To those facts I would add one other to which Michael testified, but
which, although noted by the judge, was not the subject of an express finding.
That was that the testator himself provided the will forms which were used in the
preparation of the will. Mr Mitchell put to Michael in cross-examination that he

a had purchased the will forms. That was denied by Michael and no evidence was produced by Geoffrey to support what Mr Mitchell had alleged. Mr Mitchell did not pursue this point in his closing submissions. Given that the testator on 31 March 1989 himself suggested the making of the will, I can see no reason to doubt Michael's evidence that the testator provided the will forms, and I note that the judge himself referred to Michael's evidence on this before he described that

b part of Michael's evidence, which he specifically rejected, of what occurred in the bedroom.

[39] In the circumstances there are only three possibilities, as Chadwick LJ pointed out in the course of the argument before us: (1) Michael told the truth and the will was made with the knowledge and approval of the testator; (2) Michael deceived the testator as to the contents of the will save for the legacy to Mrs Griffin; (3) the

c testator did not care what Michael put in the will, save for the legacy to Mrs Griffin.

[40] The judge rejected the first possibility and Mr Mitchell readily accepted that the third could not be right in view of the fact that the testator covered up the contents when the will was being signed and his signature attested and that

d the testator was very anxious that Geoffrey should not know about the will. The judge did not expressly consider the second possibility but he could only have concluded that the testator's knowledge and approval had not been established on the basis that the second possibility was a real possibility. The judge of course did not have direct evidence on the point other than from Michael.

e [41] There are very considerable difficulties in regarding the deception of the testator by Michael as a real possibility. This is not the common case, where the suspicion of the court is aroused, of a propounder of a will who has been instrumental in procuring the will and is the major beneficiary under it, and of a testator who has been denied a proper opportunity to read and understand the will or, having executed it, to check its contents. If one leaves wholly out of

f account Michael's evidence of what happened in Clara's bedroom, the picture that emerges from the evidence before the judge is this. Here was an elderly man who had just realised his only major asset (his house), was about to emigrate to Israel and wanted to make a will; moreover he wanted to do it with Michael's assistance. Further, he had made preparations for it at least to the extent of obtaining the will forms. He spent at least three-quarters of an hour in the

g preparation of the will. He must have had the opportunity to see the simple provisions which had been written, very legibly in capital letters, on a single page, because the will was in his hands when he came out of the bedroom and he appeared to know enough of its contents to want to cover up the dispositive parts of the will and to be anxious lest Geoffrey learnt of the will. Moreover, he took

h away the executed will and had ample opportunities to read the will then or when making a copy of the will or before placing the will in the deed box or when going back to the room where the deed box was kept on subsequent visits. It is simply incredible that the testator did not at any time read the contents of the will, and, if he read them, it is impossible to believe that he did not understand the contents.

j The style of the will and in particular the idiosyncratic comments on the beneficiaries grab the attention of the reader and make it even more unlikely that the testator did not know and approve the contents.

[42] I turn next to a consideration of the provisions of the will other than Mrs Griffin's legacy to see if in reality they give rise to a possibility that the testator did not know and approve of them. The first provision struck out by the judge is the appointment of Michael as executor. The testator must be taken to

have known that he needed to appoint an executor because the printed part of the
form told him so. Michael was the person to whom alone the testator looked to *a*
go with him into the privacy of Clara's bedroom to draft the will and whom he
trusted to write out the provisions of the will, the contents of which he did not
want the attesting witnesses to know. The deed box in which the will was found
by Michael was entrusted to Michael's care and, significantly, so eventually was
the key to that box, as I have already recounted. The testator could hardly have *b*
intended Geoffrey to be his executor: he did not even want Geoffrey to know that
he had made a will. Further it is plain from evidence before the judge other than
from Michael alone that the testator's relations with Michael at the time the will
was made were good. On the judge's own finding, Michael was the son of close
friends of the testator, he knew the testator well enough to call him 'Uncle Max',
he had had a job at Bloom's thanks to the testator, he was allowed to buy the *c*
testator's house at a 10% discount and he was trusted enough by the testator to
carry out considerable building works on the house months before completion.
Geoffrey, in cross-examination, accepted that the testator used to go to help
Michael run his car boot sales. When Michael's evidence, that the testator after
the death of his wife used to go to Michael's house two or three times a week, *d*
because they enjoyed each other's company, was put to Geoffrey in cross-
examination, he acknowledged that that could have been the case. Geoffrey said
that he thought the testator was lonely. But it is plain that it was Michael to
whom he turned to ease that loneliness. In my judgment in the light of all this
evidence it is impossible to hold that there was a real possibility that the testator
did not have knowledge and approval of the provision appointing Michael as *e*
executor.

[43] The provisions immediately following the gift to Mrs Griffin are the
legacies of £6,000 to each of Vivienne and her two daughters, accompanied as
those gifts are by the comments that they had always welcomed the testator into
their house, given him meals and often taken him out, and that the testator knew *f*
that they would remember 'Uncle Max' with affection. I did not understand that
anything in those comments was challenged by Geoffrey as being inaccurate. He
was not in a position to gainsay those comments. The judge found that Vivienne,
the daughter of the testator's close friends, did call him 'Uncle Max'. We know
that as soon as the will had been executed, the testator went to have a coffee with
Vivienne and confided in her that he had made a will. In the circumstances there *g*
is nothing, as it seems to me, inherently improbable in the testator giving legacies
to Vivienne and her daughters and in making kindly comments in the will about
them, as he had about Mrs Griffin, unless it be that the 'diversion', to use the
judge's word, of £18,000 from Geoffrey as next of kin is a significant point. I will
return to this later. *h*

[44] The next disposition in the will is the gift of £10,000 to Michael, with the
comments about him. That there should be such comments is again consistent
with the style adopted by the testator in his gift to Mrs Griffin. The first comment,
that the testator had known Michael, and their families had been friends, for over
40 years, is factually correct. The first part of the second comment, that Michael *j*
had been a loyal and trusted ally and confidante, again seems to me factually
unchallengeable. But the testator goes on to refer to the incident of the offer of a
kidney transplant. That such a statement was made by Michael to the testator is
confirmed by Geoffrey who had been told of it by the testator. However,
whereas what is contained in the will is appreciative of the generous thought
behind what Michael said, Geoffrey's evidence was that the testator did not

a understand why Michael had said it as the testator was then not ill. Mr Mitchell drew attention to the blanket assessment made by the judge in his judgment that wherever there was a conflict (and the judge accepted that there were not many occasions when there was) between Geoffrey on the one hand and Michael, Vivienne or the other witnesses in support of Michael's case on the other, the judge preferred the evidence of Geoffrey whom he found to be a reliable witness.

b Mr Mitchell suggested that there was a conflict or an inconsistency between the sentiment said by Michael to be that of the testator in his will and what Geoffrey said was the testator's comment on the offer by Michael. This point is not mentioned by the judge as a reason for finding knowledge and approval of the will not proved, and I doubt if there is a conflict or inconsistency. Even if one accepts that the testator made so churlish a comment to Geoffrey about the generous

c offer by Michael at the time it was made, it does not follow that the testator by the time of the will did not hold the view expressed in the will, which seems much more in character. The insertion of the words 'God Forbid' in the reference to the kidney offer is characteristic of the testator, as can be seen from the evidence of the drafting of the receipt and undertaking, to which I have referred in [9],

d above. The final comment that Michael was almost like a son to the testator and would remember the testator with great affection accords with what we know of their relationship. Again, I will come back to whether the amount of the legacy is significant later.

[45] The next provision in the will is the reference to the £15,000 transaction. It will be recalled that one of the two central reasons why the judge rejected

e Michael's evidence of what occurred in Clara's bedroom was the judge's belief that he had not been told the whole truth about that transaction. The judge accepted the evidence of Mr Aaronberg, that the testator knew practically nothing about elementary financial matters. The judge thought it most unlikely that Michael committed £15,000 of his own money to the testator to invest for him

f and pointed to the unfavourable nature of the transaction for the testator, guaranteeing as it did a 10% return each year over ten years. The judge's view that he had not been told the whole truth about the transaction cannot be challenged on the evidence before the judge. But in my judgment what equally cannot be challenged is that a transaction took place on 31 March 1989 whereby £15,000 in cash passed from Michael to the testator and the receipt and undertaking

g relating thereto was executed by the testator after perusal and modification by him. Mr Aghajanoff's evidence supports Michael's on this and Vivienne saw the money and was told the purpose of the transaction. Moreover the judge omits to mention that the one witness for Michael whose evidence the judge was prepared to accept without qualification, Mrs Griffin, gave evidence that before

h the testator went to Israel he told her that he was holding money for Michael and that several times while the testator was living in Israel he commented to her about the money which he was holding for Michael. That evidence in her witness statement was adhered to in her oral evidence. In these circumstances the reference to the £15,000 in the will cannot be said to be one which the testator

j could not have intended.

[46] The final provisions of the will relate to the gift of residue to Geoffrey. Strangely the judge has held that even that gift had not been shown to have the testator's knowledge and approval. The will states that the testator had been thinking of leaving the residue to charity and not to Geoffrey, that Geoffrey never helped while the testator nursed his wife, and it then refers to an incident, described as unforgettable and unforgivable, when Geoffrey had stated just after

his mother's death that the mother had said that the testator should sell the house
and give him half the money. Geoffrey was cross-examined on that incident, and
did not deny that it had occurred but said it was at a different time:

> 'The conversation you're referring to occurred when, in round about
> January 1989, I just said that Mum promised me, you know, she said that she
> wanted to protect me, there's half the house, that's what she said. But that
> was the sum, the whole sum, and then he said he wanted to give me some
> money, that's all.'

The judge accepted Geoffrey's evidence on this. He also accepted that the
conversation was in the testator's mind in March 1989 and was mentioned to
Michael and that that is how it found expression in the will but with the distortion
that it happened on the very night of the death of the testator's wife. The judge
said that he could not decide how the distortion came about, but he did not
accept that the testator knew and approved of it.

[47] The comment in the will on Geoffrey, 'I hate him like poison, that Irish
bastard', is the language which the judge found to be quite uncharacteristic of the
testator as a description of Geoffrey. Although Mr Aghajanoff had given evidence
that on 31 March 1989 the testator had, on emerging from Clara's bedroom with
the will, referred to Geoffrey as 'that bastard', the judge rejected that. The judge
said that he had heard evidence 'from a number of sources from which I have
been able to build up a picture of Max Strum and his relationship with his son'.
The judge went on to say that it was simply not consistent with that picture that
the testator would himself have created that sentence or subscribe to it if someone
else had created it.

[48] Although the judge referred to evidence from a number of sources, so far
as the evidence of witnesses was concerned, of the witnesses in support of Geoffrey's
case Geoffrey alone could give evidence of the relationship between him and
the testator and himself at the only material time, that is to say at the time of the
making of the will. The fact that there was evidence from several witnesses, such
as Lynne Collins, of a good relationship between the testator and Geoffrey in the
testator's later years in Israel is irrelevant. I have already referred, in [5], above,
to the judge's finding that the sale of the house to Michael was a source of
irritation and anxiety to Geoffrey who was not pleased about the undervalue.
Geoffrey himself in cross-examination said it was 'a cause of friction'. The judge
found that the testator and Geoffrey had arguments over it.

[49] That there were other causes of friction is plain from Geoffrey's own
evidence and from the judge's findings. When it was put to Geoffrey that the
testator was concerned with his inability to hold down a job, he said:

> 'I've shown that I worked all those years, although I wasn't working in a
> nine to five job. He was only concerned that I'd—he wanted a traditional
> route, which I wasn't that type of person to hold down a traditional job. I
> wasn't of that mentality, being more of an artistic persuasion than he was, so
> he didn't understand where I was coming from that's all I can say.'

The judge had no doubt that the testator wanted Geoffrey to achieve more than
he did achieve, and found that the testator did not like Geoffrey pursuing a
singing career and did not respect Geoffrey's interests in singing and drama. The
judge said: 'This was the background to what plainly was not an easy relationship
at the best of times.'

a [50] The judge referred to Geoffrey's evidence that he was short of money from time to time and asked the testator for money. The judge accepted that the testator complained from time to time about this to his friends and acquaintances. The judge also referred to the fact that the relationship between the testator and Geoffrey had been put under considerable strain because of the illness of the testator's wife. The judge thought it plain that the relationship between the testator

b and Geoffrey had its ups and downs. It seems to me no less plain that the will was made at a time when that relationship was having a down, because of the sale of the house to Michael at an undervalue.

[51] The poor view the testator took of Geoffrey before the testator went to Israel is even clearer if the evidence of those who testified for Michael is taken into account, all of whom spoke of the difficult relationship between the testator and

c Geoffrey. It is sufficient to refer only to the evidence of two witnesses. Mrs Griffin was found to be a straightforward witness and the judge accepted her evidence. It will be recalled that the testator saw her every day about the time of the making of the will. In her witness statement she said that the testator used to get very irate about Geoffrey, whom the testator felt to be lazy and never to have held a

d proper job, that the testator moaned to her that Geoffrey got on his nerves and made him sick and that they had a very volatile relationship. In cross-examination she said that the testator and Geoffrey 'weren't all that close', that they often had disagreements, and that the testator was sometimes frightened of Geoffrey and she repeated that the testator was scared of him. The other witness to whose evidence I shall refer is Mrs Starr. This is because the judge said that he broadly

e accepted that the things which the testator was alleged by her to have said concerning Geoffrey were indeed said, though the judge suspected that they had grown in the telling. Mrs Starr in her witness statement said of the testator:

f > '… on countless occasions he would pour his heart out to me about the terrible relationship he had with his adopted son Geoffrey and that they had suffered terribly through his selfish and uncaring ways. All he wanted was money without ever helping Max care for his disabled wife.'

She said that the testator told her how rude Geoffrey was to him and his wife and said that he thought Geoffrey was 'mershugar' (mad) because of his screaming at both of them and that he hardly ever worked and only wanted to become a rock

g star. The testator told her that to try to escape from Geoffrey he was moving to Israel. She repeated in cross-examination that the testator described Geoffrey as selfish and uncaring, and had given as examples that when the testator's wife was very ill, Geoffrey was never any help, he was never there and didn't want to know. Even allowing for the degree of exaggeration which the judge suggested

h was present in Mrs Starr's evidence, it is quite clear that the testator did not think well of Geoffrey, at any rate in the period when the will was made.

[52] A matter of particular significance to the judge as being inconsistent with the language of the will was the gift of £16,000 to Geoffrey. The judge appears to have thought it impossible that the testator would use such abusive language in

j relation to Geoffrey and yet give him £16,000. I think that the judge has omitted to take proper account of two things. The first is that under the will itself the condemnation of Geoffrey did not stop the testator from making a gift of the bulk of the estate by way of residue to Geoffrey. The second is that, as is apparent from the conversation between the testator and Geoffrey which the judge held to have occurred in January 1989, Geoffrey had been promised by his mother that he should have half the house, and so he was asking the testator for half the proceeds on the sale to honour that promise. But instead of letting him have nearly £50,000, the testator was giving him only £16,000 immediately plus the residue under the will. Viewed in that light, there is no inconsistency between the language of the will and the gift of £16,000.

[53] That leads me to consider whether the size of the legacies to Michael, Vivienne and her daughters was so great a 'diversion' of the estate from Geoffrey as next of kin as to lend support to the judge's conclusion that the only disposition of which the testator had knowledge and approval was the legacy to Mrs Griffin. The notion that, when a testator makes a will which does not simply mirror what would happen on intestacy, there is a diversion from the next of kin seems to me a strange one, but, leaving that aside, I cannot see that the size of those legacies is in any way surprising. It seems to me that this matter should be looked at in the light of all the assets available for disposal by the testator on 31 March 1989. The testator had some £96,000 of such assets. If all his testamentary dispositions were valid, he was giving to Mrs Griffin £3,000–£4,000 immediately and £6,000 by the will, £18,000 to Vivienne and her children by the will, £10,000 to Michael by the will, and to Geoffrey £16,000 immediately and £42,000–£43,000 by the will. Thus if one lumps together the legacies to Vivienne and her daughters and Michael, they were receiving a little under 30% of the testator's disposable assets, somewhat less than the one-half or the one-third to one-half which the judge thought.

[54] After that, I fear, overlengthy review of the material circumstances I can now express my views on the judge's conclusions. First, the picture which the judge had built up of the relationship between the testator and Geoffrey seems to me, with all respect to the judge, a distorted one not justified by the evidence, if that picture is viewed, as it should be, at the date of the will. At that date the relationship was poor. No less unjustified is the inference drawn by the judge that the testator would never refer to Geoffrey in terms like 'I hate him like poison, that Irish bastard'. When Geoffrey was asked by Mr Mitchell if the testator would 'often use the term bastard', he replied 'No', not 'Never'. Nor could Geoffrey speak to what the testator said of him in his absence. Whilst the judge made one finding of primary fact on the date of the conversation between the testator and Geoffrey about the promise to Geoffrey of half the house with which the date suggested in the will is inconsistent, the judge expressly made no finding of how that came about. That single inconsistency, in a comment about Geoffrey as distinct from a disposition, seems to me to be altogether too slight a discrepancy to enable the conclusion to be drawn that the testator did not know and approve of the dispositions in the will (other than that to Mrs Griffin). Moreover consideration of the contents of the will does not enable the objective observer to conclude that there is a real possibility that Michael deceived the testator as to those contents. In particular the difficulties to which I have drawn attention in [41], above remain unanswerable. I am satisfied that the judge's conclusions were wrong.

[55] I have considered whether in the circumstances the appropriate course would be to order a new trial. But I have concluded that there would be no point in so ordering. It seems to me that the suspicion roused in the court by Michael participating in the will-making process and by him and his family taking a relatively modest benefit thereunder must in all the circumstances rank at the lower end of the scale, and that Michael has discharged the burden on him of dispelling that suspicion. I would therefore allow the appeal, set aside the judge's order and pronounce for the force and validity of the entire will.

CHADWICK LJ.

[56] The claimant, Mr Michael Fuller, is named as executor in a document dated 31 March 1989. The document is written in Mr Fuller's own hand on a stationers' will form. It purports to be the last will and testament of Mr Max Strum. Mr Max Strum died on 24 December 1998. These proceedings were commenced by Mr Fuller on 6 August 1999. He asked the court to pronounce in solemn form in favour of the document as the true will of the testator.

[57] The proceedings came for trial before Mr Jules Sher QC, sitting as a deputy judge of the High Court in the Chancery Division ([2001] WTLR 677). The judge held that the document was executed by the testator in the presence of two witnesses who themselves attested the execution in accordance with s 9 of the Wills Act 1837. He pronounced in favour of so much of the document as is not struck out in the copy annexed to his order dated 20 December 2000; and he pronounced against so much of the document as is struck out in that copy. The effect of that order is that the document to be admitted to probate contains, in addition to the name and address of the testator, the date and the attestation clause, only three operative provisions: (i) a revocation of all previous wills and codicils (of which, so far as is known, there were none); (ii) a direction that debts and funeral expenses should be paid as soon as conveniently may be after his death; and (iii) a pecuniary legacy of £6,000 to Mrs Betty Griffin—described as his very loyal, loving friend and companion for many years. The whole of the rest of the document—including (i) the appointment of Mr Fuller as executor, (ii) four other pecuniary legacies (amounting together £28,000) and (iii) the gift of the residue of the estate to his adopted son Geoffrey—was held to be of no testamentary effect.

[58] The basis upon which the judge made the order that he did was his conclusion that he could not be satisfied that the testator knew and approved of any part of his will other than the legacy to Mrs Griffin. As he put it (at 697):

'... I find that the inspiration to leave something to [Mrs Griffin] must have come from Max Strum himself and that he knew and approved of two very simple things on 31 March 1989, namely, that he was making a will and was leaving Betty Griffin £6,000 in it. I do not know what else he knew and approved of on that day. I cannot help but seriously doubt whether the remainder of the contents of the will received his approval.'

That conclusion may, I think, fairly be described as surprising. The judge accepted that the testator knew that he was making a will. He accepted that the testator knew that the will contained a legacy to Mrs Griffin; and that the testator not only approved of that legacy but was the inspiration for it. But he did not accept that the testator knew and approved of the other contents of the home-made document which he believed to be his will.

[59] It is not, and cannot be, in dispute that, before admitting the document to probate, the judge needed to be satisfied that it did truly represent the testator's testamentary intentions; or, to use the traditional phrase, that the testator 'knew and approved' its contents. Nor is it in dispute that, if satisfied that the testator knew and approved of part only of the contents of the document, the judge was bound, before admitting the document to probate, to require that those parts with respect to which he was not so satisfied be struck out. If he were right to take the view that there was serious doubt whether parts of the document did truly represent the testator's testamentary intentions, then he cannot be criticised for taking the course that he did. But the judge's finding that there was serious

doubt whether the whole of a home-made document—executed by a testator who (as the judge found) knew and believed that, by executing that document, he was making his will—did truly represent the testator's testamentary intentions raises a number of questions.

[60] First, did the judge think that there was a serious doubt that the testator knew that the document which he executed contained more than just the legacy to Mrs Griffin? For my part, I think it impossible to hold that the testator did not know that the document contained more than the single legacy. The legacy to Mrs Griffin is comprised in the first two lines of the manuscript text. There are, in all, 23 lines of manuscript text. It must have been obvious to the testator, if he looked at the document at all, that the manuscript text was far more extensive than would have been needed to name one pecuniary legatee. And there was evidence that the testator had, at the least, looked at the document—even if he had not read it. The judge accepted that the testator had covered up the manuscript text before he and the attesting witnesses signed the document. There is nothing in the judgment to suggest that the judge was not satisfied that the testator knew that the document contained more than just the single legacy. The question whether the testator knew that the document contained much more manuscript text than would be needed to bequeath a single legacy cannot have been the subject of the serious doubt to which the judge referred.

[61] Second, if the judge accepted that the testator knew that there were another 19 lines of manuscript text, did the judge think that that there was a serious doubt that the testator, himself, believed that he knew what was in the document which he intended to execute as his will? In other words, did the judge think that there was a real possibility that this testator was prepared to execute a will without, himself, believing that he knew what the will contained? There is nothing in the judgment which suggests that the judge thought that this was a testator who was so careless of his affairs that he might be prepared to execute a document as his will in the knowledge that he did not know what it contained. As Peter Gibson LJ has pointed out in his judgment, if one leaves wholly out of account Mr Fuller's evidence of what happened in his Aunt Clara's bedroom, the picture remains that of an elderly man who had just realised his only major asset; who was about to emigrate to Israel; who wanted to make a will; and who had obtained law stationers' will forms for that purpose. In my view it was not open to the judge to reach to the conclusion, on the evidence which he did accept, that there was any real possibility that this was a testator who would execute a document as his will if he did not, himself, believe that he knew what the document contained. I do not think that the judge did reach that conclusion. The question whether the testator, himself, believed that he knew what the document contained cannot have been the question about which the judge had serious doubt.

[62] Once it is accepted—as, in my view, it must be accepted—(i) that the testator knew that the document which he executed as his will contained much more manuscript text than would be needed to bequeath the single legacy to Mrs Griffin and (ii) that the testator, himself, believed that he knew what the document contained, the only basis remaining for the doubt which the judge expressed is that there was a real possibility that the testator was deceived by Mr Fuller. In order to hold that there was a real possibility that the testator was deceived by Mr Fuller as to the contents of the document it is necessary to be satisfied not only (i) that there was a real possibility that Mr Fuller misrepresented to the testator the content of what he (Mr Fuller) had written in the document—

a that is to say, that the words actually written were not the words which Mr Fuller had told the testator (or otherwise led the testator to believe) had been written—but also (ii) that there was a real possibility that the testator did not at any time—that is to say, either at the time that the document was executed or, thereafter, when going to the room in which the deed box contained the document was kept—take the opportunity to read the document. I agree with Peter Gibson LJ
b that, if the testator did read the document, he must have understood the contents. This is not a case in which the effect of what had been written would, or might, not have been readily intelligible. Indeed, as Peter Gibson LJ has put it: 'The style of the will and in particular the idiosyncratic comments on the beneficiaries grab the attention of the reader …'

[63] I am driven, therefore, to the conclusion that the judge did think that
c there was a real possibility that the testator never took the opportunity to read the document—either before or after he had executed it as his will. Although the judge does not say, in terms, that he reached that conclusion, that conclusion is a necessary step in the reasoning which he must have adopted in order to reach the conclusion which he did express—that there was serious doubt whether the
d manuscript contents of the document (other than the legacy to Mrs Griffin) were known and approved by the testator. I, like Peter Gibson LJ, find it incredible that the testator never took the opportunity to read the document which he believed to be his will. But the judge had the great advantage of seeing and hearing the witnesses give their evidence. This court does not have that advantage; and it is important, in my view, not to fall into the trap of thinking that listening to
e Mr Fuller address us in person in support of his appeal is any substitute for listening to his evidence at a trial. We cannot properly reverse the judge on what is, on analysis, a question of fact, unless satisfied that it was not open to him to find that there was a real possibility (i) that the testator was deceived by Mr Fuller because he never took the opportunity to read the document at the time that he
f executed it as his will and (ii) that the deception never came to light because the testator never took the opportunity to read the document thereafter.

[64] I am satisfied that the judge fell into error. I think that he did so because he failed to keep in mind that the task in which he was engaged was that of assessing evidence and reaching conclusions as to fact on the balance of probability. I suspect that he may have been misled by the phrase used by Lord
g Hatherley, in *Fulton v Andrew* (1875) LR 7 HL 448 at 471, to describe the evidential burden which the law imposes on one who has been instrumental in procuring a will under which he takes a benefit. Lord Hatherley (at 472) described that burden as 'the onus of shewing the righteousness of the transaction'.

[65] It is important to appreciate that Lord Hatherley's phrase—redolent of
h morality as it now seems to be—is not to be taken by the court as a licence to refuse probate to a document of which it disapproves; whether that disapproval stems from the circumstances in which the document was executed as a will or whether it stems from the contents of the document. The question is not whether the court approves of the circumstances in which the document was
j executed or of its contents. The question is whether the court is satisfied that the contents do truly represent the testator's testamentary intentions. That is not, of course, to suggest that the circumstances of execution or the contents may not, in the particular case, be of the greatest materiality in reaching a conclusion whether or not the testator did know and approve of the contents of the document—and did intend that they should have testamentary effect. But their importance is evidential. There is no overriding requirement of morality. If Lord

Hatherley's reference to 'the righteousness of the transaction' in a speech
delivered in the late nineteenth century leads to misunderstanding at the   *a*
beginning of the twenty-first century, then the time has come to consider
whether that phrase is still helpful. For my part, I think it is better to avoid it.

[66] The starting point is the seminal passage in the opinion of the Privy
Council delivered by Parke B in *Barry v Butlin* (1838) 2 Moo PC 480 at 482–483, 12
ER 1089 at 1090:   *b*

> 'The rules of law according to which cases of this nature are to be decided,
> do not admit of any dispute, so far as they are necessary to the determination
> of the present Appeal: and they have been acquiesced in on both sides. These
> rules are two; the first that the *onus probandi* lies in every case upon the party
> propounding a Will; and he must satisfy the conscience of the Court that the *c*
> instrument so propounded is the last Will of a free and capable Testator. The
> second is, that if a party writes or prepares a Will, under which he takes a
> benefit, that is a circumstance that ought generally to excite the suspicion of
> the Court, and calls upon it to be vigilant and jealous in examining the
> evidence in support of the instrument, in favour of which it ought not to   *d*
> pronounce unless the suspicion is removed, and it is judicially satisfied that
> the paper propounded does express the true Will of the deceased.'

[67] Parke B went on to explain what is meant by the onus probandi in that
context. He said:

>   *e*
> 'The strict meaning of the term *onus probandi* is this, that if no evidence is
> given by the party on whom the burthen is cast, the issue must be found
> against him. In all cases the *onus* is imposed on the party propounding a Will,
> it is in general discharged by proof of capacity, and the fact of execution, from
> which the knowledge of and assent to the contents of the instrument are
> assumed, and it cannot be that the simple fact of the party who prepared the *f*
> Will being himself a Legatee, is in every case, and under all circumstances, to
> create a contrary presumption, and to call upon the Court to pronounce
> against the Will, unless additional evidence is produced to prove the
> knowledge of its contents by the deceased. A single instance, of not
> unfrequent occurrence, will test the truth of this proposition. A man of
> acknowledged competence and habits of business, worth £100,000, leaves   *g*
> the bulk of his property to his family, and a Legacy of £50 to his confidential
> attorney, who prepared the Will: would this fact throw the burthen of proof
> of actual cognizance by the Testator, of the contents of the Will, on the party
> propounding it, so that if such proof were not supplied, the Will would be
> pronounced against? The answer is obvious, it would not. All that can truly *h*
> be said is, that if a person, whether attorney or not, prepares a Will with a
> Legacy to himself, it is, at most, a suspicious circumstance, of more or less
> weight, according to the facts of each particular case; in some of no weight
> at all, as in the case suggested, varying according to circumstances; for
> instance the *quantum* of the Legacy, and the proportion it bears to the *j*
> property disposed of, and numerous other contingencies: but in no case
> amounting to more than a circumstance of suspicion, demanding the vigilant
> care and circumspection of the Court in investigating the case, and calling
> upon it not to grant probate without full and entire satisfaction that the
> instrument did express the real intentions of the deceased. Nor can it be
> necessary, that *in all such cases*, even if the Testator's capacity is doubtful, the

a precise species of evidence of the deceased's knowledge of the Will is to be in the shape of instructions for, or reading over the instrument. They form, no doubt, the *most* satisfactory, but they are not the *only* satisfactory description of proof, by which the cognizance of the contents of the Will may be brought home to the deceased. The Court would naturally look for such evidence; in some cases it might be impossible to establish a Will

b without it, but it has no right in every case to require it.' (See (1838) 2 Moo PC 480 at 484–486, 12 ER 1089 at 1091.)

[68] Those passages were approved by the House of Lords in *Fulton v Andrew*— see the speech of Lord Cairns LC ((1875) LR 7 HL 448 at 461, [1874–80] All ER Rep 1240 at 1244) (with whom the other members of the House agreed)—and,

c again, in *Wintle v Nye* [1959] 1 All ER 552 at 557–558, 561, [1959] 1 WLR 284 at 291, 295—see the speeches of Viscount Simonds and Lord Reid, respectively.

[69] Confirmation that what has come to be known as the rule in *Barry v Butlin* is an evidential rule can be found in the judgment of Scarman J in *Re Fuld (dec'd) (No 3), Hartley v Fuld (Fuld intervening)* [1965] 3 All ER 776, [1968] P 675. It was

d necessary, in that case, for the judge to decide whether the English requirements as to proof of knowledge and approval were a part of substantive law—in which case they would be irrelevant in the circumstances that the testator died domiciled in Germany; or whether they were rules of evidence—in which case they fell to applied as part of the lex fori. After referring to the reaffirmation, in *Wintle v Nye*, of the rule in *Barry v Butlin*, Scarman J said:

e 'In my opinion, the whole point of the rule is evidential; it is concerned with the approach required of the court to the evidence submitted for its consideration. In the ordinary case proof of testamentary capacity and due execution suffices to establish knowledge and approval, but in certain circumstances the court is to require further affirmative evidence. The

f character of the rule as evidential emerges clearly from the speeches of Viscount Simonds and of Lord Reid.' (See [1965] 3 All ER 776 at 781, [1968] P 675 at 697.)

[70] If the first limb of the rule identifies the person propounding the will as the person on whom the burden of proof lies, it is the second limb which informs

g the court as to the nature of the inquiry which it is to make. What, then, is the standard of proof which the court must require in that inquiry? There is, to my mind, nothing in the statement the law by the Privy Council in *Barry v Butlin* which suggests that the standard of proof required in relation to knowledge and approval in a probate case is other than the civil standard—that is to say, that the

h court must be satisfied, on the balance of probability, that the contents of the will do truly represent the testator's intentions. Indeed, it seems to me that it is to that standard that Parke B was referring when he spoke of the court being 'judicially satisfied'. Nor do I think that there is anything in *Fulton v Andrew* to suggest that the standard is other than the civil standard. I can see no reason why probate

j proceedings in general, or the issue of knowledge and approval in probate proceedings in particular, should treated as an exception to the general rule—recognised by Lord Nicholls of Birkenhead in *Re H (minors) (sexual abuse: standard of proof)* [1996] 1 All ER 1 at 16, [1996] AC 563 at 586—that 'Where matters in issue are facts the standard of proof required in non-criminal proceedings is the preponderance of probability, usually referred to as the balance of probability'. But, as Lord Nicholls went on to point out there was '[b]uilt into the preponderance of probability standard … a generous degree of flexibility in respect of the seriousness of the allegation'. Lord Nicholls said:

'This approach also provides a means by which the balance of probability standard can accommodate one's instinctive feeling that even in civil proceedings a court should be more sure before finding serious allegations proved than when deciding less serious or trivial matters.' (See [1996] 1 All ER 1 at 17, [1996] AC 563 at 586–587.)

[71] It is, I think, this flexibility of approach within the civil standard of proof which lies behind the observations of Viscount Simonds in *Wintle v Nye* [1959] 1 All ER 552 at 557, [1959] 1 WLR 284 at 291:

'In all cases the court must be vigilant and jealous. The degree of suspicion will vary with the circumstances of the case. It may be slight and easily dispelled. It may, on the other hand, be so grave that it can hardly be removed. In the present case, the circumstances were such as to impose on the respondent as heavy a burden as can well be imagined.'

I think, also, that Lord Reid had the same approach in mind when, in the context of very special facts in *Wintle v Nye*, and after referring to the direction to the jury in *Atter v Atkinson* (1869) LR 1 P & D 665 at 668, that 'you ought to be well satisfied, from evidence calculated to exclude all doubt, that the testator not only signed it, but knew and approved of its contents', he said:

'To my mind, the direction of the learned judge was not at all calculated to make the jury realise that they must be "satisfied from evidence calculated to exclude all doubt" or even all reasonable doubt that the respondent had not only shown to the testatrix the relevant information and discussed the will with her but had brought home to her mind the effect of her will …' (See [1959] 1 All ER 552 at 561, [1959] 1 WLR 284 at 296.)

[72] I am satisfied that there is no basis for an approach that requires, in all cases, that a person propounding a will which he has prepared, and under which he takes a benefit, must satisfy the court by evidence which excludes all doubt—or by evidence which excludes all reasonable doubt (the standard of proof required in criminal proceedings)—that the testator knew and approved the contents of the will. The standard of proof required in probate proceedings (as in other non-criminal proceedings) is satisfaction on the preponderance (or balance) of probability. But the circumstances of the particular case may raise in the mind of the court a suspicion that the testator did not know and approve the contents of the document which he has executed which is so grave that, as Viscount Simonds observed in *Wintle v Nye*, it can hardly be removed.

[73] I return, therefore, to the finding of the judge in the present case: that, after hearing the evidence, he remained in serious doubt whether the contents of the document executed on 31 March 1989 (other than the pecuniary legacy to Mrs Griffin) were approved by the testator. I gratefully adopt the statement and analysis of the facts contained in the judgment of Peter Gibson LJ. Like him, I take the view that the dispositions made by the testator in the document executed as his will do not, of themselves, excite any great suspicion. They seem to me to be explicable by the warm relationship between the testator and Mr Fuller's parents; a relationship which had extended to Mr Fuller, his sister and her children. Nor do I find any cause for grave suspicion in the circumstances in which the document was executed. The document was executed at a time when it was

a natural and obvious that the testator, who had made no earlier will, should wish to put his affairs in order. And, as it seems to me, it was natural and obvious that he should turn to Mr Fuller for assistance.

[74] The circumstances in which that assistance was given require Mr Fuller to satisfy the court—by evidence which goes beyond proof of testamentary capacity and due execution—that the contents of the document do truly *b* represent the testator's testamentary intentions. Mr Fuller could not do that by his own direct evidence of the writing out of the document in his Aunt Clara's bedroom—because the judge did not accept his evidence. But, after rejecting Mr Fuller's evidence of what had happened in the bedroom, the judge still had to give weight to the evidence, from Mr Fuller and the other witnesses, which he did not reject. And, in the light of that evidence as a whole, the judge had to ask *c* himself whether there was a real possibility that the testator had never taken the opportunity to read the document which he believed to be his will.

[75] In my view, in the light of the evidence which the judge had accepted, the possibility that this testator had not taken the opportunity to read the document which he believed to be his will was so unlikely—indeed, I would say, so incredible— *d* that it could not be accepted as a real possibility unless the grounds for suspicion that the document did not truly represent the testator's intentions were so strong as to be insurmountable. But, as I have said, this is not a case in which the suspicion aroused by the circumstances in which the document was executed, and its contents, comes anywhere near to being insurmountable. The judge, having correctly identified the need for vigilance, ought to have concluded that *e* any proper suspicion was dispelled.

[76] For those reasons, as well as for the reasons given in the other judgments in this court which I have the advantage of reading in draft, I would allow this appeal. I, too, would make the order which Peter Gibson LJ has proposed.

f **LONGMORE LJ.**

[77] Any person who puts forward a document as being the last will of the deceased must establish that the testator knew and approved the contents of the will when he executed it. Normally, so long as there is no problem of lack of testamentary capacity, the testator's knowledge and approval of the contents of his will will be assumed from the fact that he has signed the document and had it *g* attested in proper form. There is, however, a class of case where this will not be assumed and that is where the person, who writes or prepares a will, himself takes a benefit under it. In such cases, even if no undue influence is alleged, the court needs to be satisfied that the testator did know and approve the contents of his will before executing it and the court will not rely on the signature of the testator *h* alone for that purpose. Viscount Simonds stated the law briefly in *Wintle v Nye* [1959] 1 All ER 552 at 557, [1959] 1 WLR 284 at 291:

'It is not the law that in no circumstances can a solicitor or other person who has prepared a will for a testator take a benefit under it. But that fact creates a suspicion that must be removed by the person propounding the *j* will. In all cases the court must be vigilant and jealous. The degree of suspicion will vary with the circumstances of the case. It may be slight and easily dispelled. It may, on the other hand, be so grave that it can hardly be removed.'

The suspicion is that the testator may not have known or not have approved the contents of the document.

[78] Some of the older cases say that the onus on a person who takes a benefit under a will which he has been instrumental in preparing or obtaining is 'the onus of shewing the righteousness of the transaction', see e g *Fulton v Andrew* (1875) LR 7 HL 448 at 472 per Lord Hatherley. This is not, to my mind, a separate onus from that of dispelling the suspicion the testator may not have known or may not have approved the contents of the will; it is merely a more grandiloquent way of expressing exactly the same concept. The vigilance and jealousy of the court is directed to being satisfied that the testator did know and approve the contents of his will; no less but also no more. The question in the present case is, therefore, whether Mr Fuller, as the propounder of the will, has removed the suspicion that the testator did not know or did not approve its contents. The deputy judge held that he had not removed that suspicion (see [2001] WTLR 677).

[79] I agree with my Lords that the only right answer to the question on the evidence before the court is that Mr Fuller has discharged that onus. For the judge not to have been so satisfied, he must have concluded that there was a real possibility that, although the testator knew that Mr Fuller had prepared a will at his (the testator's) request over the course of about three-quarters of an hour, although he appointed Mr Fuller as his executor and although he covered up the contents of the will when he asked the attestors to witness his signature, he did not know or approve what was in the document. The only possible scenario that fits is that the testator dictated something to Mr Fuller but Mr Fuller wrote something else on the paper which, shortly thereafter, the testator signed. There was no basis for this conclusion in the evidence and nowhere in the judgment does the judge state that he does consider this as a real possibility. He merely states that he does not accept Mr Fuller's evidence in certain important respects and he then concludes that the onus of showing that the testator knew and approved the contents of the will has not been discharged. But the one does not follow from the other unless the above scenario was a real possibility. To my mind it was not a real possibility on the facts of the case and the appeal must, therefore, be allowed.

Appeal allowed.

Kate O'Hanlon   Barrister.

a

R v Jones
[2002] UKHL 5

HOUSE OF LORDS

LORD BINGHAM OF CORNHILL, LORD NOLAN, LORD HOFFMANN, LORD HUTTON AND
b LORD RODGER OF EARLSFERRY

21, 22 NOVEMBER 2001, 20 FEBRUARY 2002

*Criminal law – Trial – Commencement of trial – Defendant absconding before
commencement of trial – Whether court having discretion to commence trial in*
c *defendant's absence.*

In January 1998 the defendant was arraigned on a charge of conspiracy to rob and
pleaded not guilty. He was bailed to appear for his trial which was fixed for 1 June
1998, but did not surrender to the Crown Court for trial and warrants were issued
for his arrest. The defendant's legal representatives withdrew from the
d proceedings in the light of his failure to attend. The trial was relisted to
commence on 5 October. By that date, the defendant had not been arrested and
had not surrendered. The case was adjourned to the following day, when he had
still not been arrested and had not surrendered. The judge took the view that the
defendant had deliberately frustrated the attempt of the prosecuting authorities
to have the case finally concluded, and ruled that the trial should begin in his
e absence. He was convicted and sentenced to imprisonment. The defendant was
arrested at the end of December 1999, and subsequently appealed against his
conviction. The Court of Appeal dismissed the appeal, holding that the
defendant's trial was not unfair and that, by his conduct, he had clearly and
expressly waived his right to be present and legally represented at the trial. The
f court nevertheless certified that a question of general public importance was
involved in its decision, namely whether the Crown Court could conduct a trial
in the absence, from its commencement, of the defendant. On his appeal to the
House of Lords, the defendant contended that to begin a trial in the defendant's
absence was inconsistent with the jurisprudence of the European Court of
g Human Rights, or was contrary to principle, or was apt, in practice, to work
injustice.

Held – Where a criminal defendant of full age and sound mind, with full
knowledge of a forthcoming trial, voluntarily absented himself, there was no
reason in principle why his decision to violate his obligation to appear and not to
h exercise his right to appear should have the automatic effect of suspending the
criminal proceedings against him until such time, if ever, as he chose to surrender
himself or was apprehended. If he voluntarily chose not to exercise his right to
appear, he could not impugn the fairness of the trial on the ground that it had
followed a course different from that which it would have followed had he been
j present and represented. Moreover, there was nothing in the jurisprudence of
the European Court of Human Rights to suggest that a trial of a criminal
defendant held in his absence was inconsistent with the European Convention for
the Protection of Human Rights and Fundamental Freedoms 1950 (as set out in
Sch 1 to the Human Rights Act 1998). Accordingly, the Crown Court did have a
discretion to conduct a trial in the absence, from its commencement, of the

defendant. That discretion should, however, be exercised with the utmost care and caution. If the absence of a defendant were attributable to involuntary illness *a* or incapacity, it would very rarely, if ever, be right to exercise the discretion in favour of commencing the trial, at any rate unless the defendant was represented and had asked that the trial should begin. The seriousness of the offence was not a matter which was relevant to the exercise of the discretion. The judge's overriding concern was to ensure that the trial, if conducted in the absence of the *b* defendant, would be as fair as circumstances permitted, and lead to a just outcome. Those objects were equally important whether the offence charged was serious or relatively minor. Furthermore, it was generally desirable that a defendant should be represented even if he had voluntarily absconded, since that would provide a valuable safeguard against the possibility of error and oversight. For that reason, trial judges routinely asked counsel to represent a defendant who *c* had absconded during the trial, and counsel in practice acceded to such an invitation. Such a practice was to be encouraged when the defendant absconded before the trial began. The failure to follow that practice in the instant case did not, however, give ground for complaint by the defendant since (Lord Hoffmann and Lord Rodger dissenting) his decision to abscond in flagrant breach of his bail *d* conditions could reasonably be thought to have shown such complete indifference to what might happen in his absence as to support the Court of Appeal's finding of waiver. In any event, the defendant had enjoyed his convention right to a fair trial. Accordingly, the appeal would be dismissed (see [9]–[11], [13]–[20], [23], [32], [35], [36], [38]–[42], [77], below).

R v Jones, Planter and Pengelly [1991] Crim LR 856 approved.   *e*

Notes

For a trial in the absence of the accused, see 11(1) *Halsbury's Laws* (4th edn reissue) para 945.   *f*

Cases referred to in opinions

Brown v Stott (Procurator Fiscal, Dunfermline) [2001] 2 All ER 97, [2001] 2 WLR 817, PC.

Brozicek v Italy (1989) 12 EHRR 371, ECt HR.

Caborn-Waterfield, Re [1960] 2 All ER 178, [1960] 2 QB 498, [1960] 1 WLR 792, DC. *g*

Colozza v Italy (1985) 7 EHRR 516, ECt HR.

Condron v UK (2001) 31 EHRR 1, ECt HR.

Crosby v US (1993) 506 US 255, US Sup Ct; rvsg (1990) 917 F 2d 362, US CA (8th Circuit).

Delcourt v Belgium (1970) 1 EHRR 355, ECt HR.   *h*

Doorson v Netherlands (1996) 22 EHRR 330, ECt HR.

Ekbatani v Sweden (1988) 13 EHRR 504, ECt HR.

Ensslin v Germany (1978) 14 DR 64, E Com HR.

Gregory v UK (1997) 25 EHRR 577, ECt HR.

HM Advocate v Monson (1893) 1 Adam 114, Ct of Justiciary.   *j*

Krombach v Bamberski Case C-7/98, [2001] All ER (EC) 584, [2001] QB 709, [2001] 3 WLR 488, [2001] ECR I-1935, ECJ.

Lala v Netherlands (1994) 18 EHRR 586, ECt HR.

Millar v Dickson 2002 SC (PC) 30, PC.

a *Montgomery v HM Advocate, Coulter v HM Advocate* [2001] 2 WLR 779, PC.
Omar v France (1998) 29 EHRR 210, ECt HR.
Pelladoah v Netherlands (1994) 19 EHRR 81, ECt HR.
Pfeifer v Austria (1992) 14 EHRR 692, ECt HR.
Poitrimol v France (1993) 18 EHRR 130, ECt HR.
Pullar v UK (1996) 22 EHRR 391, ECt HR.
b *R v Abrahams* (1895) 21 VLR 343, Vic Full Ct.
R v Berry (1897) LT Jo 110.
R v Bertrand (1867) LR 1 PC 520, PC.
R v Browne (1906) 70 JP 472.
R v Donnelly (12 June 1997, unreported), CA.
R v Howson (1981) 74 Cr App R 172, CA.
c *R v Jones (REW) (No 2)* [1972] 2 All ER 731, [1972] 1 WLR 887, CA.
R v Jones, Planter and Pengelly [1991] Crim LR 856, CA.
R v Pendleton [2001] UKHL 66, [2002] 1 All ER 524, [2002] 1 WLR 72.
R v Shaw (Elvis) [1980] 2 All ER 433, [1980] 1 WLR 1526, CA.
R v Tonner [1985] 1 All ER 807, [1985] 1 WLR 344, CA.
d *Stanford v UK* (1994) Times, 8 March, ECt HR.
Sweeney v HM Advocate (1893) 21 R (J) 44, Ct of Justiciary.
Taylor v US (1973) 414 US 19, US Sup Ct.
Van Geyseghem v Belgium App No 26103/95 (21 January 1999, unreported), ECt
HR.
e *Virgin Islands v Brown* (1975) 507 F 2d 186, US CA (3rd Circuit).

Appeal
Anthony William Jones appealed with leave of the Appeal Committee of the
House of Lords given on 27 June 2001 from the order of the Court of Appeal
(Rose LJ, Hooper and Goldring JJ) on 31 January 2001 ([2001] EWCA Crim 168,
f [2001] 3 WLR 125, [2001] All ER (D) 256) dismissing his appeal against his
conviction in the Crown Court at Liverpool on 9 October 1998 of conspiracy to
rob, after a trial in his absence, before Judge Holloway and a jury. The Court of
Appeal certified that a point of law of general public importance, set out at [1],
below, was involved in its decision. The facts are set out in the opinion of Lord
Bingham of Cornhill.

g

Stephen Solley QC and *Graham Brodie* (instructed by *Sharpe Pritchard* as agents for
Quinn Melville, Liverpool) for the appellant.
David Perry and *Duncan Penny* (instructed by the *Crown Prosecution Service*) for the
Crown.

h

Their Lordships took time for consideration.

20 February 2002. The following opinions were delivered.

j **LORD BINGHAM OF CORNHILL.**
[1] My Lords, the question before the House, rightly certified by the Court of
Appeal (Criminal Division) ([2002] EWCA Crim 168, [2001] 3 WLR 125, [2001] All
ER (D) 256 (Jan)) as one of general public importance, is: 'Can the Crown Court
conduct a trial in the absence, from its commencement, of the defendant?' To
that question the Court of Appeal gave an affirmative answer, while emphasising

that the discretion to proceed with a trial in the absence, from the beginning, of
the defendant is one to be exercised with extreme care and only in the rare case
where, after full consideration of all relevant matters, including in particular the
fairness of a trial, the judge concludes (at [22][a]) that the trial should proceed.

[2] The agreed facts are brief. On 18 August 1997 a robbery took place at a
post office in Liverpool in the course of which some £87,000 was stolen. The
appellant (Mr Jones) was arrested nearby shortly afterwards and was charged.
On 3 December 1997 he and a co-defendant, Mr Roberts, were committed on bail
for trial at the Crown Court in Liverpool. In January 1998 both defendants were
arraigned and pleaded not guilty. A trial date of 9 March 1998 was fixed but
vacated and replaced with a trial date of 1 June 1998. On 1 June 1998, neither the
appellant nor his co-defendant surrendered to the Crown Court for trial and
warrants were issued for their arrest. The trial was relisted to commence on 5
October 1998. Neither the appellant nor his co-defendant had been arrested by
that date, and neither had surrendered. The case was adjourned to the following
day, when it was listed for trial before Judge Holloway. The appellant and his
co-defendant had still not been arrested and they had still not surrendered. The
legal representatives acting for the appellant had previously withdrawn from the
proceedings in light of his failure to attend on 1 June 1998, and at the hearing on
6 October those representing the co-defendant also withdrew from the
proceedings.

[3] The transcript of the hearing on 6 October shows that the initial reaction
of the judge, based on instinct and long experience, was that a trial could not
begin in the absence of a defendant, whatever the reason for his absence. The
judge showed obvious reluctance to embark on the trial in those circumstances.
It was however urged upon him that further delay would be very unfair to a large
body of witnesses, some of whom had undergone a very traumatic experience,
and after reference to the decided cases he ruled that the trial should begin, taking
the view that the defendants had deliberately frustrated the attempt of the
prosecuting authorities to have the case finally concluded. He indicated that
anything of advantage to the defendants would be highlighted during the
evidence and that any material of assistance to the defendants would be put
before the jury. The trial accordingly proceeded and the judge in his summing
up warned the jury not to hold the absence of the defendants against them.

[4] On 9 October 1998 both the appellant and his co-defendant were convicted
on unanimous verdicts of conspiracy to rob, and on the same day the judge
sentenced each of them to 13 years' imprisonment. It was not until 14 months
later, at the end of December 1999, that the appellant was arrested. He was
brought before the court and admitted his failure to surrender to custody. At a
hearing before Judge Holloway on 4 January 2000, the appellant was sentenced
to serve 12 months' imprisonment for his failure to surrender to custody,
concurrently with the sentence already imposed upon him for conspiracy to rob.
The appellant sought leave to appeal against conviction and, on refusal by the
single judge, renewed his application to the full court. The renewed application
was listed to be heard on 16 January 2001, with other appeals raising a similar
issue. The appellant was represented by leading and two junior counsel at that

_____

a   Editor's note: Paragraph [22] of the Court of Appeal's judgment is not fully set out in their
     Lordships' opinions. For ease of reference, we have set it out in full as an appendix at the end of the
     opinions.

a hearing when leave to appeal was granted and his appeal heard. It was however dismissed on 31 January 2001. Having ruled on the issue of principle, the Court of Appeal considered the appellant's case and (at [41]) said:

'As the judge made clear to the jury in summing up, the only possible explanations of the forensic evidence were either guilt or that there had been a massive police conspiracy to contaminate the defendant's clothing before
b it was examined by the forensic science laboratory. Although the defendant, now in custody, has been present at his appeal and able to instruct the solicitors and leading counsel who now represent him, no submission in support of the second explanation has been advanced to this court. Nor is it suggested that, if he had attended his trial, he could or would have provided
c an innocent explanation for the contamination of his clothing, his presence in the vicinity of the robbery or fleeing from the police, or that he was unconnected with the walkie-talkie found near the scene. In our judgment there is no reason, in all these circumstances, to regard his conviction as unsafe or his trial as unfair and accordingly his appeal against conviction is dismissed.'
d

No application to call fresh evidence was made to the Court of Appeal. At the hearing on 4 January 2000 it was acknowledged by counsel representing the appellant that his failure to appear on the date fixed for trial had been deliberate. It was not suggested either at that hearing or in the Court of Appeal that he had
e been unaware of his obligation to appear on the date fixed for the trial or that he had been unaware of that date or that he had been unaware of the likely consequences if he did not appear.

[5] The certified question raises a question of principle, but it falls to be answered in the factual context of this case. It is particularly important to note that the appellant was arraigned and pleaded not guilty in January 1998, but that
f his trial did not then commence (see R v Tonner [1985] 1 All ER 807, [1985] 1 WLR 344). He was bailed to appear at his trial on 1 June 1998. He had the benefit of legal aid to instruct, and did instruct, solicitors and counsel to represent him at his trial. He knew the date of the trial and of his obligation to attend and deliberately decided to absent himself for reasons of his own. He had no reason to believe that
g the trial would not proceed in his absence or that his legal representatives would be able to represent him if he did not appear.

[6] For very many years the law of England and Wales has recognised the right of a defendant to attend his trial and, in trials on indictment, has imposed an obligation on him to do so. The presence of the defendant has been treated as a very important feature of an effective jury trial. But for many years problems
h have arisen in cases where, although the defendant is present at the beginning of the trial, it cannot (or cannot conveniently or respectably) be continued to the end in his presence. This may be because of genuine but intermittent illness of the defendant (as in R v Abrahams (1895) 21 VLR 343 and R v Howson (1981) 74 Cr App R 172); or misbehaviour (as in R v Berry (1897) LT Jo 110 and R v Browne
j (1906) 70 JP 472); or because the defendant has voluntarily absconded (as in R v Jones (REW) (No 2) [1972] 2 All ER 731, [1972] 1 WLR 887 and R v Shaw (Elvis) [1980] 2 All ER 433, [1980] 1 WLR 1526). In all these cases the court has been recognised as having a discretion, to be exercised in all the particular circumstances of the case, whether to continue the trial or to order that the jury be discharged with a view to a further trial being held at a later date. The

existence of such a discretion is well-established, and is not challenged on behalf of the appellant in this appeal. But it is of course a discretion to be exercised with great caution and with close regard to the overall fairness of the proceedings; a defendant afflicted by involuntary illness or incapacity will have much stronger grounds for resisting the continuance of the trial than one who has voluntarily chosen to abscond.

[7] In *R v Abrahams* (1895) 21 VLR 343 at 347 Williams J opined that if an accused person failed to appear at trial and was found, when the trial came on, to have absconded, he had clearly waived his right to be present and the prosecution might elect to go on with the trial in his absence; in such event, the judge would exercise his discretion whether to allow the trial to continue, paying particular attention to whether the defendant was represented. But those were not the facts of that case, and these observations must be treated as obiter. It was not until 1991 that the lawfulness of commencing a trial on indictment in the absence of the defendant came before the court as a matter for decision. It may well be that the more restrictive approach taken in earlier days towards the bailing of defendants charged with serious offences helped to ensure that such defendants did appear at their trials. The mandatory terms of the Bail Act 1976 have led to the grant of bail even to defendants, such as the appellant, who might well be thought suitable subjects for custodial restraint pending trial. Be that as it may, the issue fell to be decided in *R v Jones, Planter and Pengelly* [1991] Crim LR 856. In that case three defendants stood trial charged with a number of offences, but after some days, two of the defendants, who were on bail, absconded and the recorder aborted the trial against all three defendants and discharged the jury. When the case was listed to be tried on a second occasion, one defendant appeared and the other two did not. The trial judge ordered that the trial should begin against the absent defendants as well as the defendant who was present, and on appeal it was argued that he should not have begun the trial against the absent defendants. That contention was rejected. As appears from the transcript of the judgment of Lord Lane CJ, giving the judgment of the court, it was held to be quite plain in principle that there was a discretion in the judge to order a trial to continue, or indeed to start, not only where a person had voluntarily absented himself but also, as Griffiths LJ had held in *R v Howson* (1981) 74 Cr App R 172, where he had been involuntarily absent. A similar ground of appeal was advanced, unsuccessfully, in *R v Donnelly* (12 June 1997, unreported). The House must now decide whether it should overrule this authority as being inconsistent with Strasbourg jurisprudence, or contrary to principle, or apt in practice to work injustice. Counsel for the appellant submits that the authority should be overruled on all those grounds.

[8] The European Court of Human Rights and the Commission have repeatedly made clear that it regards the appearance of a criminal defendant at his trial as a matter of capital importance (see, for example *Poitrimol v France* (1993) 18 EHRR 130 at 146 (para 35); *Pelladoah v Netherlands* (1994) 19 EHRR 81 at 94 (para 40); *Lala v Netherlands* (1994) 18 EHRR 586 at 597 (para 33)). That court has also laid down (1) that a fair hearing requires a defendant to be notified of the proceedings against him (see *Colozza v Italy* (1985) 7 EHRR 516 at 523–524 (para 28); *Brozicek v Italy* (1989) 12 EHRR 371); (2) that a person should as a general principle be entitled to be present at his trial (see *Ekbatani v Sweden* (1988) 13 EHRR 504 at 509 (para 25)); (3) that a defendant in a criminal trial should have the opportunity to present his arguments adequately and participate effectively (see

a   *Ensslin v Germany* (1978) 14 DR 64 at 115; *Stanford v UK* (1994) Times, 8 March);
(4) that a defendant should be entitled to be represented by counsel at trial and on
appeal, whether or not he is present or has previously absconded (see *Delcourt v
Belgium* (1970) 1 EHRR 355 at 366–367 (para 25); *Poitrimol*'s case (at 146, 147
(paras 34, 38)); *Pelladoah*'s case (at 94 (para 40)); *Lala*'s case (at 597–598 (paras
33–34)); *Van Geyseghem v Belgium* App No 26103/95 (21 January 1999, unreported)
b   (para 34); *Omar v France* (1998) 29 EHRR 210 at 233 (paras 41–42)). The right to
be defended has also been described by the European Court of Justice of the
European Communities as a fundamental right deriving from the constitutional
traditions common to the member states of the European Union (see *Krombach v
Bamberski* Case C-7/98, [2001] All ER (EC) 584, [2001] ECR I-1935).

c   [9] All these principles may be very readily accepted. They are given full effect
by the law of the United Kingdom. But the European Court of Human Rights has
never found a breach of the European Convention for the Protection of Human
Rights and Fundamental Freedoms 1950 (as set out in Sch 1 to the Human Rights
Act 1998) where a defendant, fully informed of a forthcoming trial, has
voluntarily chosen not to attend and the trial has continued. In *Ensslin*'s case
d   (1978) 14 DR 64, in which proceedings were continued during the absence of the
defendants caused in large measure by self-induced illness, the proceedings were
held to have been properly continued. In *Poitrimol*'s case (1993) 18 EHRR 130 at
145 (para 31) the court questioned whether a full hearing on appeal could be
required by a defendant who had waived his right to appear and defend himself
e   at trial. In *Van Geyseghem*'s case (para 28) the court was not concerned that the
applicant had not wished to avail herself of her right to attend an appeal hearing.
In a concurring opinion in that case Judge Bonello held that the presence of a
defendant during his trial was basically his right, not his obligation. There is
nothing in the Strasbourg jurisprudence to suggest that a trial of a criminal
f   defendant held in his absence is inconsistent with the convention.

[10] In turning to general principle, I find it hard to discern any principled
distinction between continuing a trial in the absence, for whatever reason, of a
defendant and beginning a trial which has not in law commenced. If, as is
accepted, the court may properly exercise its discretion to permit the one, why
should it not permit the other? It is of course true that if a trial has begun and run
g   for some time, the inconvenience to witnesses of attending to testify again on a
later occasion, and the waste of time and money, are likely to be greater if the trial
is stopped than in the case of a trial that has never begun. But these are matters
which, however relevant to the exercise of discretion, provide no ground for
holding that a discretion exists in the one case and not in the other. The common
h   law of Scotland, as I understand, provided, and s 92(1) of the Criminal Procedure
(Scotland) Act 1995 now stipulates, that no part of a trial on indictment may take
place outwith the presence of the accused. The law of England and Wales, while
conferring a right and imposing an obligation on the defendant to be present at a
trial on indictment, has never been held to include any comparable rule. If a
j   criminal defendant of full age and sound mind, with full knowledge of a
forthcoming trial, voluntarily absents himself, there is no reason in principle why
his decision to violate his obligation to appear and not to exercise his right to
appear should have the automatic effect of suspending the criminal proceedings
against him until such time, if ever, as he chooses to surrender himself or is
apprehended.

[11] Counsel for the appellant laid great stress on what he submitted was the inevitable unfairness to the defendant if a trial were to begin in his absence after *a* he had absconded. His legal representatives would be likely to regard their retainer as terminated by his conduct in absconding, as happened in this case. Thus there would be no cross-examination of prosecution witnesses, no evidence from defence witnesses, and no speech to the jury on behalf of the defendant. The judge and prosecuting counsel, however well-intentioned, could not know *b* all the points which might be open to the defendant. The trial would be no more than a paper exercise (as Judge Holloway at one point described it) almost inevitably leading to conviction. The answer to this contention is, in my opinion, that one who voluntarily chooses not to exercise a right cannot be heard to complain that he has lost the benefits which he might have expected to enjoy had *c* he exercised it. If a defendant rejects an offer of legal aid and insists on defending himself, he cannot impugn the fairness of his trial on the ground that he was defended with less skill than a professional lawyer would have shown. If, after full professional advice, he chooses not to exercise his right to give sworn evidence at the trial, he cannot impugn the fairness of his trial on the ground that the jury never heard his account of the facts. If he voluntarily chooses not to *d* exercise his right to appear, he cannot impugn the fairness of the trial on the ground that it followed a course different from that which it would have followed had he been present and represented.

[12] Considerations of practical justice in my opinion support the existence of the discretion which the Court of Appeal held to exist. To appreciate this, it is *e* only necessary to consider the hypothesis of a multi-defendant prosecution in which the return of a just verdict in relation to any and all defendants is dependent on their being jointly indicted and jointly tried. On the eve of the commencement of the trial, one defendant absconds. If the court has no discretion to begin the trial against that defendant in his absence, it faces an acute dilemma: either the whole trial must be delayed until the absent defendant is *f* apprehended, an event which may cause real anguish to witnesses and victims; or the trial must be commenced against the defendants who appear and not the defendant who has absconded. This may confer a wholly unjustified advantage on that defendant. Happily, cases of this kind are very rare. But a system of criminal justice should not be open to manipulation in such a way. *g*

[13] I would accordingly answer Yes to the certified question and dismiss this appeal. In doing so I would stress, as the Court of Appeal did in that the discretion to commence a trial in the absence of a defendant should be exercised with the utmost care and caution (see [2001] 3 WLR 125 at [22]). If the absence of the defendant is attributable to involuntary illness or incapacity it would very rarely, *h* if ever, be right to exercise the discretion in favour of commencing the trial, at any rate unless the defendant is represented and asks that the trial should begin. The Court of Appeal's checklist of matters relevant to exercise of the discretion (at [22](5)) is not of course intended to be comprehensive or exhaustive but provides an invaluable guide. I would add two observations only. *j*

[14] First, I do not think that 'the seriousness of the offence, which affects defendant, victim and public', listed in [22](5)(viii) as a matter relevant to the exercise of discretion, is a matter which should be considered. The judge's overriding concern will be to ensure that the trial, if conducted in the absence of the defendant, will be as fair as circumstances permit and lead to a just outcome.

a These objects are equally important, whether the offence charged be serious or relatively minor.

[15] Secondly, it is generally desirable that a defendant be represented even if he has voluntarily absconded. The task of representing at trial a defendant who is not present, and who may well be out of touch, is of course rendered much more difficult and unsatisfactory, and there is no possible ground for criticising

b the legal representatives who withdrew from representing the appellant at trial in this case. But the presence throughout the trial of legal representatives, in receipt of instructions from the client at some earlier stage, and with no object other than to protect the interests of that client, does provide a valuable safeguard against the possibility of error and oversight. For this reason trial judges routinely ask counsel to continue to represent a defendant who has absconded during the trial,

c and counsel in practice accede to such an invitation and defend their absent client as best they properly can in the circumstances. The current legal aid regulations provide for that contingency (see the Criminal Defence Service (General) (No 2) Regulations 2001, SI 1437/2001). It is in my opinion a practice to be encouraged when the defendant absconds before the trial begins. But the failure to follow it

d here gives no ground for complaint by the appellant. The Court of Appeal said in their judgment (at [41]): 'This defendant, as it seems to us, had, clearly and expressly by his conduct, waived his right to be present and to be legally represented.' That conclusion has not been challenged on behalf of the appellant and is in my opinion a tenable conclusion. While there is no direct evidence to show that the appellant knew what the consequences of his absconding would

e be, there is nothing to suggest a belief on his part that the trial would not go ahead in his absence or that, although absent, he would continue to be represented. His decision to abscond in flagrant breach of his bail conditions could reasonably be thought to show such complete indifference to what might happen in his absence as to support the finding of waiver. I note, however, the reservations expressed

f by my noble and learned friends concerning the finding of waiver, and recognise the force of their reasoning. If, contrary to my opinion, the Court of Appeal were wrong to make the finding of waiver, and I am wrong to accept it, I would none the less hold that the appellant enjoyed his convention right to a fair trial, for all the reasons given by my noble and learned friend Lord Rodger of Earlsferry.

g **LORD NOLAN.**

[16] My Lords, I have had the advantage of reading a draft of the speech of my noble and learned friend Lord Bingham of Cornhill. For the reasons he gives, I too would dismiss this appeal. In view of the importance of the case, however, I would wish to add a few words of my own on two aspects of the matter.

h [17] First, in common, I believe, with all of your Lordships, I would hold that under English law the discretion of the trial judge to proceed with the trial in the absence of the defendant exists in principle (subject to the satisfaction of all the appropriate safeguards) not only after but before the trial has begun, though naturally it will have to be exercised with even greater care in the latter case. The

j decision on this point of the Court of Appeal in *R v Jones, Planter and Pengelly* [1991] Crim LR 856 was in my judgment correct and should be upheld.

[18] Secondly, I would not for my part criticise the conclusion of the Court of Appeal ([2001] EWCA Crim 168 at [41], [2001] 3 WLR 125 at [41], [2001] All ER (D) 256 (Jan)) in their judgment, that 'this defendant ... had, clearly and expressly by his conduct, waived his right to be present and to be legally represented.' In

the case of an absconding defendant the critical question for the judge, as it seems
to me, is whether the defendant has deliberately and consciously chosen to absent   *a*
himself from the court. If so, then normally, no doubt, the judge would make an
express finding to that effect, and would summarise his reasons for the finding.
In the present case the judge made no such express finding but clearly drew an
equivalent inference. The point need not, however, detain us, because no
objection has been taken to the inference drawn by the judge. That being so, it   *b*
would seem to me that, where, as in the present case, a defendant has had the
advantage of legal advice and representation at all stages prior to the
commencement of the trial, his deliberate and conscious choice to take no further
part in the proceedings could permissibly be described as a waiver of his rights of
attendance and of legal representation at his trial, both at common law and under   *c*
art 6 of the European Convention for the Protection of Human Rights and
Fundamental Freedoms 1950 (as set out in Sch 1 to the Human Rights Act 1998).
But acknowledging the force of the views expressed by my noble and learned
friends Lord Hoffmann and Lord Rodger of Earlsferry, and bearing in mind the
near impossibility of the trial judge's task, if he had to be satisfied of the   *d*
defendant's knowledge of the full extent of his rights before deciding whether
those rights had been waived, I would prefer to express my conclusion in this
appeal in agreement with my noble and learned friend Lord Bingham on this
broader basis that, even if there were no waiver, the appellant none the less
enjoyed the convention right to a fair trial.

e

LORD HOFFMANN.
   [19] My Lords, I have had the advantage of reading in draft the speeches of my
noble and learned friends Lord Bingham of Cornhill and Lord Rodger of
Earlsferry. I agree with both of them. Like Lord Rodger, I am not comfortable   *f*
with the notion that the defendants waived their rights under art 6 of the
European Convention for the Protection of Human Rights and Fundamental
Freedoms 1950 (as set out in Sch 1 to the Human Rights Act 1998). Waiver
requires consciousness of the rights which have been waived. I agree that there
is nothing to show that the defendants must have known that if they did not turn   *g*
up on the date set for trial, it would proceed in their absence and without
representation on their behalf. I would prefer to say that they deliberately chose
not to exercise their right to be present or to give adequate instructions to enable
lawyers to represent them.
   [20] But I do not read the European cases as laying down that a trial may   *h*
proceed in the absence of the accused only if there has been a waiver of the right
to a fair trial. The question in my opinion is not whether the defendants waived
the right to a fair trial but whether in all the circumstances they got one. It is
whether on the particular facts of the case the proceedings, taken as a whole and
including the appellate process, satisfied the requirements of the convention.   *j*
That, as I understand it, is the question which the European jurisprudence
requires to be answered. For the reasons given by my noble and learned friends,
with which I entirely agree, I think that the Court of Appeal ([2001] EWCA Crim
168, [2001] 3 WLR 125, [2001] All ER (D) 256 (Jan)) was right to hold that there
had been no infringement of art 6. I would therefore dismiss the appeal.

LORD HUTTON.

a

[21] My Lords, a person charged with a criminal offence has a right to be present at his trial and to defend himself in person or by instructing counsel to represent him. This right is recognised by the common law and by the European Convention for the Protection of Human Rights and Fundamental Freedoms 1950 (as set out in Sch 1 to the Human Rights Act 1998).

b

[22] In the present case the appellant was granted bail and, with full knowledge of the date on which his trial for the offence of robbery was due to commence, absconded before that date so that he was not present in court on that date and on subsequent dates on which his trial was relisted to commence. The judge decided to proceed with the trial and the appellant was convicted by the jury. The issue which arises on this appeal is whether in such circumstances the Crown Court can conduct a trial in the absence of the defendant.

c

[23] I consider that the authorities make it clear that a court has power to proceed with a trial when the defendant has deliberately absconded before the commencement of the proceedings to avoid trial, although it is clear that the power to proceed in such circumstances should be exercised by the trial judge with great care.

d

[24] The authorities also show that there are two stages in the approach to be taken to the matter. The first stage is that although the defendant has a right to be present at his trial and to put forward his defence, he may waive that right. The second stage is that where the right is waived by the defendant the judge must then exercise his discretion as to whether the trial should proceed in the absence of the defendant.

e

[25] The matter was discussed in the judgments of the court in Victoria in *R v Abrahams* (1895) 21 VLR 343 where the defendants were present at the commencement of the trial but were absent at a later stage due to illness. Williams J said (at 346):

f

'The primary and governing principle is, I think, that in all criminal trials the prisoner has a right, as long as he conducts himself decently, to be present, and ought to be present, whether he is represented by counsel or not. He may waive this right if he so pleases, and may do this even in a case where he is not represented by counsel. But then a further and most important principle comes in, and that is, that the presiding Judge has a discretion in either case to proceed or not to proceed with the trial in the accused's absence.'

g

[26] Hood J stated (at 353):

h

'All that we are here deciding, in my opinion, is that the presiding Judge *may* in misdemeanours proceed without the presence of the prisoner, where the absence is voluntary. He has in law a discretion, but that discretion should be exercised with great reluctance, and with a view rather to the due administration of justice than to the convenience or comfort of anyone.'

j

[27] In *R v Jones (REW) (No 2)* [1972] 2 All ER 731, [1972] 1 WLR 887 the defendant absconded during his trial which the judge ordered should continue in his absence. He was convicted and eight months after his conviction applied for an extension of time for leave to appeal, and his application was refused by the Court of Appeal. The Court of Appeal held that the judge had exercised his

discretion properly and cited with approval the judgments in *R v Abrahams*. Roskill LJ stated:

'This court respectfully adopts that language as correctly stating the position. The only question this court has to decide is whether Judge Gillis exercised his discretion properly. In the view of this court he plainly did so exercise it ... To grant this application at this stage would, in the view of this court, be to put a premium on prisoners jumping bail; it may even have the effect of encouraging others to do so. It may also have as a side-effect, increasing the reluctance of a court in a very long trial to grant bail lest the applicant's conduct be repeated by others. To put a premium on jumping bail is something which this court is not for one moment prepared to countenance. This application is entirely without merit, notwithstanding the skill with which it has been advanced. There is no ground whatever for granting this extension of time. The applicant has brought this entirely on his own head, and he must now take the consequences. The application therefore is refused.' (See [1972] 2 All ER 731 at 736, [1972] 1 WLR 887 at 892.)

[28] In *R v Jones, Planter and Pengelly* [1971] Crim LR 856, where the defendants were absent from the commencement of the trial, Lord Lane CJ stated:

'It is quite plain in principle that there is a discretion in the judge to order a trial to continue or indeed to start in these circumstances, not only where a person voluntarily absents himself, but also, as the judgment of Griffiths LJ in *R v Howson* (1981) 74 Cr App R 172 indicates, where he has involuntarily been absent.'

[29] Mr Solley QC, for the appellant, relied on the decision of the United States Supreme Court in *Crosby v US* (1993) 506 US 255. In that case the defendant did not appear at the commencement of his trial and the trial proceeded in his absence and he was convicted. The Supreme Court allowed his appeal. However I do not consider that that decision supports the appellant's case because it was based on r 43 of the Federal Rules of Criminal Procedure which provided:

'(a) PRESENCE REQUIRED. The defendant shall be present at the arraignment, at the time of the plea, at every stage of the trial including the impaneling of the jury and the return of the verdict, and at the imposition of sentence, except as otherwise provided by this rule.
(b) CONTINUED PRESENCE NOT REQUIRED. The further progress of the trial to and including the return of the verdict shall not be prevented and the defendant shall be considered to have waived the right to be present whenever a defendant, initially present,
(1) is voluntarily absent after the trial has commenced ...'

Blackmun J stated (at 262):

'The language, history, and logic of Rule 43 support a straightforward interpretation that prohibits the trial *in absentia* of a defendant who is not present at the beginning of trial. Because we find Rule 43 dispositive, we do not reach Crosby's claim that his trial *in absentia* was also prohibited by the Constitution.'

a [30] Moreover, there are other statements by United States appellate courts cited in the judgment of the Supreme Court which give support to the view that, in the absence of a provision such as r 43, there is no reason of substance for distinguishing between the absence of a defendant at the commencement of a trial and his absence at a later stage. Thus in *Crosby's* case itself the intermediate appellate court stated:

b   'It would be anomalous to attach more significance to a defendant's absence at commencement than to absence during more important substantive portions of the trial.' (See (1990) 917 F 2d 362 at 365.)

And in *Virgin Islands v Brown* (1975) 507 F 2d 186 at 189 another appellate court stated that there are no 'talismanic properties which differentiate the *c* commencement of a trial from later stages'.

[31] Mr Solley also sought to rely on the jurisprudence of the European Court of Human Rights. Article 6 of the convention provides that in the determination of any legal charge against him a person is entitled to a fair trial and art 6(3)(c) provides that a person has the right 'to defend himself in person or through legal *d* assistance of his own choosing'.

[32] In my opinion the jurisprudence of the Court of Human Rights does not assist the appellant. There is no decision of that court relating to a case where a defendant, with full knowledge of the date on which it was to commence, deliberately absconded before his trial at which, if he had been present, he would have been able to exercise the right given by art 6(3)(c).

e [33] In *Colozza v Italy* (1985) 7 EHRR 516 where the applicant was declared by a judge to be untraceable and it was not established that the notice of the criminal proceedings had been personally served on him and he was convicted in his absence, the court stated (at 524–525):

f   '28 … In conclusion, the material before the Court does not disclose that Mr. Colozza waived exercise of his right to appear and to defend himself or that he was seeking to evade justice. It is therefore not necessary to decide whether a person accused of a criminal offence who does actually abscond thereby forfeits the benefit of the rights in question …

    29 … It is not the Court's function to elaborate a general theory in this area. *g* As was pointed out by the Government, the impossibility of holding a trial by default may paralyse the conduct of criminal proceedings, in that it may lead, for example, to dispersal of the evidence, expiry of the time limit for prosecution or a miscarriage of justice. However, in the circumstances of the case, this fact does not appear to the Court to be of such a nature as to justify *h* a complete and irreparable loss of the entitlement to take part in the hearing.'

[34] In *Poitrimol v France* (1993) 18 EHRR 130 at 145 (para 31) the court stated:

    'Proceedings held in an accused's absence are not in principle incompatible with the Convention if the person concerned can subsequently obtain from a court which has heard him a fresh determination of the merits of the *j* charge, in respect of both law and fact. It is open to question whether this latter requirement applies when the accused has waived his right to appear and to defend himself, but at all events such a waiver must, if it is to be effective for Convention purposes, be established in an unequivocal manner and be attended by minimum safeguards commensurate to its importance.'

[35] In the present case I consider that the deliberate decision of the defendant to abscond in breach of his bail conditions to avoid his forthcoming trial on a serious charge justifies the inference that he had no intention of putting forward a defence at that trial and that therefore he did waive his right to defend himself in an unequivocal manner. Accordingly I am of opinion that the Court of Appeal ([2001] EWCA Crim 168, [2001] 3 WLR 125, [2001] All ER (D) 256 (Jan)) was entitled to hold that there had been such a waiver. I further consider that the position of the appellant was adequately safeguarded in two ways. First, it was safeguarded by the fair and careful way in which the judge, and also prosecuting counsel, conducted the trial. As the Court of Appeal stated in its judgment:

> 'This defendant, as it seems to us, had, clearly and expressly by his conduct, waived his right to be present and to be legally represented. Thereafter the course of the trial was, as it seems to us, as fair as it could be, the defendant having waived those rights. Prosecuting counsel (whose duty under paragraph 11.1 of the Bar Council's Code of Conduct was not to attempt to obtain a conviction by all means at his command and not to regard himself as appearing for a party, but to lay before the court fairly and impartially the whole of the facts which comprised the case for the prosecution) and the judge did all they reasonably could to ensure that the trial was fair, in the unusual circumstances prevailing.' (See [2001] 3 WLR 125 at [41].)

Secondly, the position of the defendant was safeguarded by his right to appeal against his conviction to the Court of Appeal. He exercised this right and the Court of Appeal conducted a careful review of the evidence against him and concluded at [41] of its judgment that 'the case against the defendant was in our view overwhelming'.

[36] My noble and learned friends Lord Hoffmann and Lord Rodger of Earlsferry have expressed reservations about the finding of the Court of Appeal as to waiver. As I have stated I consider, with respect, that the Court of Appeal was entitled to make this finding. But I would add that it is self-evident that the right given by art 6(3)(c) of the convention to the defendant to defend himself in person or to instruct counsel to defend him is a right to be exercised by the defendant himself—it cannot be exercised on his behalf by someone else. Therefore even if the finding could not be made in the present case that there was an unequivocal waiver by the defendant, I consider that where no defence was put forward at the trial in consequence of the defendant's deliberate decision not to be present, there was no violation of the right given to him by art 6(3)(c)—rather the defendant chose not to exercise that right. As Salmon J stated in delivering the judgment of the Divisional Court (constituted by himself, Lord Parker CJ and Ashworth J) in *Re Caborn-Waterfield* [1960] 2 All ER 178 at 181, [1960] 2 QB 498 at 508–509:

> 'The applicant was treated with complete fairness and indeed was shown every consideration by the French court. He was fully apprised of the very strong case that he had to meet, and repeatedly given the fullest opportunity of meeting it. He elected not to do so and on three separate occasions, without any excuse, he failed to appear in person before the French court. Accordingly, it certainly does not lie in his mouth to complain that the case was dealt with in his absence.'

a Whilst this observation was not made with reference to art 6(3)(c) I consider that it is equally applicable to it.

[37] Mr Solley further relied on the principle stated in *R v Bertrand* (1867) LR 1 PC 520 at 534 (which was referred to in the judgments in *R v Abrahams* (1895) 21 VLR 343):

b 'It is a mistake, moreover, to consider the question only with reference to the Prisoner. The object of a trial is the administration of justice in a course as free from doubt or chance of miscarriage as merely human administration of it can be—not the interests of either party. This remark very much lessens the importance of a Prisoner's consent, even when he is advised by Counsel, and substantially, not, of course, literally, affirms the wisdom of the common
c understanding in the profession, that a Prisoner can consent to nothing.'

Mr Solley submitted that the public interest in the proper administration of justice free from doubt or chance of miscarriage required a defendant to be present at his trial at its commencement or at any rate for some part of it, to ensure that the case of the prosecution was properly challenged and tested, and
d that there could not be public confidence in the reliability of a conviction if the defendant had not been present at his trial.

[38] The discretion of a judge to proceed with a trial in the absence of the defendant is one to be exercised with great care, but in my opinion there can be circumstances where in the interests of justice a judge is entitled to decide to proceed, particularly when the defendant has deliberately absconded to avoid
e trial. Some of the circumstances in the present case were described as follows by the trial judge, Judge Holloway, in his careful ruling:

'There are 35 live witnesses due to give evidence today, some of whom are civilians who must have experienced a quite terrifying event when they were held up by armed, masked men and this robbery took place. Some of the
f civilian witnesses have already indicated that they are less than happy to attend on a future occasion. Some of the prosecution witnesses have already been dispensed with because of the concern that they have about continual delay ... In normal circumstances I am bound to say that my reaction initially to the proposition was that it would seem wrong to pursue any criminal trial, and particularly one as serious as this, in the absence of either a defendant or
g indeed in the absence of any assistance from counsel or solicitors on their behalf. But on the other hand there is another competing interest which seems to me to take precedence over that particular one and that is that there are 35 witnesses outside court who have come here for the second time today and who are anxiously awaiting the prospect of having to give
h evidence and in view of the defendants' deliberate absenting of themselves the trauma that some of them have experienced during the course of this incident is unlikely to go away until such time as they actually have had this case finally dealt with either with the defendants pleading guilty, which is obviously not their intention, or indeed the trial taking place and a jury
j coming to a decision ... this is a strong case for the prosecution where clearly the defendants have frustrated and deliberately frustrated the authorities in trying to have this case finally concluded ... I cannot in all conscience feel it is appropriate that those witnesses should be made to wait for what could be 6, 12, 18 months, two years or some other period of time well into the future by which time some may not be willing to give evidence, some may have

passed on, some may have gone to another part of the world, emigrated; all sorts of problems can arise which would then be to the advantage of these absent defendants.'

In these circumstances I consider that the judge was entitled to come to the conclusion that the trial should proceed and, in my opinion, as I have stated, the public interest in a just result was safeguarded by the fair and careful way in which the judge and prosecuting counsel conducted the trial and by the right of the defendant to challenge his conviction in the Court of Appeal.

[39] I am in respectful agreement with my noble and learned friend Lord Bingham that the matters relevant to the exercise of the discretion set out by the Court of Appeal in para [22](5) of its judgment constitute a most valuable guide, and I further agree with the observations which he makes in respect of that list in his speech at [14], [15].

[40] For the reasons which I have given I would answer the certified question in the affirmative and would dismiss this appeal.

LORD RODGER OF EARLSFERRY.

[41] My Lords, I have had the advantage of reading the speech of my noble and learned friend, Lord Bingham of Cornhill, in draft. I agree with him that the appeal should be dismissed, but on the matter of the European Convention for the Protection of Human Rights and Fundamental Freedoms 1950 (as set out in Sch 1 to the Human Rights Act 1998) I would reach that result by another route.

[42] As Lord Bingham has explained, there is a tract of authority showing that for many years English courts have had the power to continue a criminal trial in the absence of the defendant. Understandably, counsel for the appellant did not seek to challenge these cases. While there may be pragmatic arguments to suggest that there is a difference between a trial that begins in the absence of the defendant and a trial that begins with the defendant present but has to continue in his absence, I can identify no difference of principle between the two situations. That being so, as a matter of principle, there must indeed be power for the English courts to start a trial when the defendant absconds. That power does not appear to have been explicitly recognised in the cases until the decision of the Court of Appeal (Criminal Division) in *R v Jones, Planter and Pengelly* [1991] Crim LR 856. In the present case the Court of Appeal ([2002] EWCA Crim 168 at [22](3), [2001] 3 WLR 125 at [22](3), [2001] All ER (D) 256 (Jan)) (Rose LJ) reviewed the authorities and concluded that in English law 'the trial judge has a discretion as to whether a trial should take place or continue in the absence of a defendant and/or his legal representatives'. Having had the advantage of considering the analysis of the English authorities in Lord Bingham's speech, I would respectfully agree with it and with Rose LJ's conclusion as to the effect of those authorities.

[43] In arguing that there was no power to allow a trial to begin in the absence of the defendant, counsel for the appellant drew attention to the position in Scotland where, subject to one exception, under solemn procedure the accused must be present throughout his trial. Under that system it is indeed impossible for the court to begin or continue a trial when the accused absconds. The controlling philosophy of Scots law on this matter is the same today as 200 years ago when, in his *Commentaries on the Law of Scotland, Respecting Crimes* (1844), Vol II, pp 269–270, Baron Hume wrote:

a   'Let us now suppose, that the accused is absent at calling the libel, but the prosecutor appears and insists. With one exception, which was introduced in evil times, in cases of treason, it has been our invariable custom, that on no sort of proceeding can here take place, as for trial of the crime libelled. It is considered, that unless the accused is present to take charge of his own interest, there can be no security for doing full justice to his case; for pleading

b   all his defences, bringing forward all his evidence, stating all objections to the evidence on the other part, and still less for taking advantage of all those pleas and grounds of challenge, which may arise in the course of the proceedings in the trial. Besides, (though this is certainly an inferior consideration,) the Judges ought not to be called on to apply or declare the law, except in circumstances which afford the means of carrying their

c   sentence into effect. On these grounds, the peremptory rule has long been settled, of requiring the personal presence of the pannel in every step, from first to last, of the trial, with the exception only of continuations of the diet; so that if he even withdraw at the last stage of all, after a verdict of guilty has been returned against him, still the court cannot proceed to apply the

d   sentence of the law.'

I refer also to *Alison's Practice of the Criminal Law of Scotland* (1833), p 349. Although not mentioned by Hume, there was in fact some statutory support for the rule in s 10 of the Criminal Justice Act 1587, providing, inter alia, that all the witnesses and proof were to be 'allegit, ressonit and deducit to the assyse in

e   presence of the pairtie accusit in face of iudgement and na utheris wayes'. This provision was, somewhat prosaically, consolidated in s 145(1) of the Criminal Procedure (Scotland) Act 1975 as 'no part of a trial shall take place outwith the presence of the accused' and is now to be found in s 153(1) of the Criminal Procedure (Scotland) Act 1995. If, for instance, an accused falls ill during the trial and cannot attend, the trial must be adjourned until he is fit or, if that is not

f   practicable, the diet must be deserted pro loco et tempore, authority being given to the Crown to start fresh proceedings when the accused recovers. So the requirement for the accused to be present at his trial is applied consistently.

[44] The only significant change to the Scottish system since Baron Hume's time is that statute now confers a specific power on the trial judge to order the

g   accused to be removed if he misconducts himself so as to make it impossible for a proper trial to take place. In the case of an unrepresented accused, the court must appoint counsel or a solicitor to represent his interests during his absence (see s 153(2)). This exception was enacted in 1980 after doubts had arisen as to whether the judge had any such power at common law to allow a trial to proceed in the accused's absence even where he was disrupting it. The contrast with the

h   flexible approach of English law could not be more stark.

[45] Hume was, of course, well aware of the risk that accused persons would abscond and so make a trial impossible. He explains (Vol II, pp 270–271) how in his day the courts tackled the problem by pronouncing a sentence of fugitation or outlawry in order either to compel 'those wicked and dangerous persons, who

j   abscond owing to consciousness of their guilt' to appear in court or else to drive them 'out of the country'. *Alison's Practice*, (pp 349–354) is to the same effect. The system of fugitation was still being operated at least as late as the end of the nineteenth century (see *HM Advocate v Monson* (1893) 1 Adam 114 at 116 and *Sweeney v HM Advocate* (1893) 21 R (J) 44). It was eventually abolished by s 15(2) of the Criminal Justice (Scotland) Act 1949. Nowadays the penalty for failing to appear for trial is somewhat less drastic. If on bail, the accused who fails to appear can be prosecuted for breach of the relevant condition of his bail. In solemn proceedings, the maximum sentence is imprisonment for two years. Alternatively, proceedings may be taken for contempt of court, again with a maximum sentence of two years' imprisonment. It would be idle to pretend that these sanctions are so effective that accused persons never fail to attend for trial and never abscond during their trial.

[46] Under the Scottish system, if an accused absconds before or during the trial or is taken ill during the trial and cannot attend, jurors and witnesses may well be inconvenienced. There is also a risk that recollections may fade before the accused is traced and brought back for trial. Sometimes, it is true, a trial has to proceed against only some of the accused when, ideally, all should have been tried together. Depending on the circumstances, that may be thought to affect the presentation of their case either by the Crown or by the other accused. But Scots law has always struck the balance in this way between the rights of the accused and these wider interests of justice. So courts and prosecutors accept the position—especially, perhaps, because dock identification of the accused is the norm and trials, which are structured accordingly, really require his presence. In any event in 1975, and again in 1995, Parliament endorsed the balance as previously struck by the law of Scotland. The significant point is that, for whatever reason, Parliament has never legislated in the same way for England and Wales to require the trial to take place in the presence of the defendant. More particularly, Parliament has refrained from doing so, even though the English courts have for many years been exercising a discretion to allow trials to be completed when the defendant is not present. The inference which I draw is that, for England and Wales, Parliament remains content for these matters to be regulated by the exercise of a judicial discretion, weighing the relevant factors, including, where appropriate, a defendant's flagrant decision to abscond.

[47] In describing the approach which courts should adopt in the light of the authorities on English law and on the convention, the first two principles which the Court of Appeal laid down were these:

'(1) A defendant has, in general, a right to be present at his trial and a right to be legally represented. (2) Those rights can be waived, separately or together, wholly or in part, by the defendant himself. They may be wholly waived if, knowing, or having the means of knowledge as to, when and where his trial is to take place, he deliberately and voluntarily absents himself and/or withdraws instructions from those representing him. They may be waived in part if, being present and represented at the outset, the defendant, during the course of the trial, behaves in such a way as to obstruct the proper course of the proceedings and/or withdraws his instructions from those representing him.' (See [2001] 3 WLR 125 at [22].)

Applying those principles to the appellant's case, the Court of Appeal held (at [41]): 'This defendant, as it seems to us, had, clearly and expressly by his conduct, waived his right to be present and to be legally represented.' The attractions of that robust approach are obvious. For my part, however, I am not satisfied that in the circumstances of this case the appellant can be said to have waived these rights under art 6 of the convention.

a [48] The European Court of Human Rights has held in *Poitrimol v France* (1993) 18 EHRR 130 at 145 (para 31) that any waiver of a defendant's right to appear and to be represented at his trial—

'must, if it is to be effective for Convention purposes, be established in an unequivocal manner and be attended by minimum safeguards b commensurate to its importance.'

The court was there applying its previous decisions to the same effect in *Pfeifer v Austria* (1992) 14 EHRR 692 at 712 (para 37) and earlier cases. The Privy Council adopted that approach to waiver of a right to a fair hearing before an independent and impartial tribunal in *Millar v Dickson* 2002 SC (PC) 30. Lord Bingham of c Cornhill held (at [31]) that for these purposes 'unequivocal' meant 'clear and unqualified'. A defendant could not waive a right if he was unaware that he could make the claim in question. I refer also to the opinion of Lord Hope of Craighead (see paras [54], [55]).

[49] In this case I am unable to find anything in the actings of the appellant that would amount to a clear and unqualified election not to claim his rights under d art 6 to be present or to be represented. Nor, of course, was there anything which could have acted as a safeguard attending any waiver of such important rights. Lord Bingham has pointed out that the appellant did not formally challenge the finding of the Court of Appeal that, by his conduct, he had waived these rights. None the less, the matter was aired in the course of the hearing before your e Lordships. Moreover, it concerns the application of the appellant's convention rights and it is accordingly a matter about which the House must itself be satisfied.

[50] The appellant and his co-defendant certainly knew that a trial was to take place in their case. It had originally been fixed for 9 March 1998 but that date was vacated at the instance of the defence. The defendants last attended the police f station in accordance with the terms of their bail in March 1998. Neither appeared for trial on 1 June of that year. Nor did they attend for trial on 5 or 6 October, by which time it had become clear that they had both absconded in order to avoid standing trial. The appellant was not represented at the hearings in October.

g [51] These facts certainly justify the inference that the appellant knew that he would not be present when his trial was due to take place. That does not, in itself, justify the conclusion that he had waived his right to be present or to be represented at any trial of the charges against him. Such an inference could be drawn only if one could be satisfied that the appellant not only knew that the trial was due to take place when he would be absent, but also knew that it could take h place even though he was not there and even though he was not represented. In *Taylor v US* (1973) 414 US 19 the United States Supreme Court felt able indeed to draw such an inference in a case where the defendant had absconded during his trial, leaving behind a judge, jury and witnesses ready to continue. In the circumstances of this case, however, neither inference can readily be drawn.

j [52] So far as the first is concerned, it is sufficient perhaps to notice that the initial reaction of the very experienced judge, Judge Holloway, was that no trial could take place in the absence of the defendants. He had never heard of such a thing and neither had the colleagues whom he consulted. An official at the Criminal Appeals Office thought that it might be possible—but he could not put his finger on a case. It would, I believe, be rash to attribute to the appellant

greater knowledge of the arcana of English criminal procedure than Judge
Holloway and his colleagues actually possessed. Doubtless, the appellant would
have been aware that, if eventually brought to justice, he would be punished for
absconding to avoid trial. But I see no proper basis for going further and
assuming that he would actually have known that he was liable to be tried and
sentenced in his absence. I am accordingly unable to draw the conclusion that the
appellant had unequivocally waived his right to be present at any trial.

[53] The inference that he had waived his right to representation at any trial
of the charge against him is even more difficult. One would have to infer that the
appellant knew that, if the court decided to proceed to try him in his absence, it
would do so in a situation where no counsel or solicitor was there to represent
him on the very serious charge of armed robbery. In fact, at the hearing on 6
October 1998, the appellant was unrepresented from the outset, while the
counsel and solicitor for his co-defendant withdrew from acting at the hearing.
We were told that, in certain other cases, when a trial has proceeded in the
absence of the defendant counsel have agreed to remain in court and to act, even
in a limited way, on behalf of the defendant. The Court of Appeal ([2001] 3 WLR
125 at [22](5)(iv)) indeed envisaged that this might happen in future cases and that
the presence or absence of representation would be a factor to be considered by
the judge in deciding whether the trial should proceed in the absence of the
defendant. There is nothing in the Court of Appeal's narrative of the facts to
show whether the appellant knew that no counsel or solicitor would appear on
his behalf at the hearing on 6 October or that the trial judge was likely to exercise
his discretion by going on with the trial without the appellant being represented.
In these circumstances I am again unable to conclude that, merely by deliberately
absconding, the appellant had unequivocally waived his right under art 6(3)(c) of
the convention to be represented by counsel at any trial of the charges against
him.

[54] For these reasons I prefer to deal with the case on the basis that the
appellant had not unequivocally waived his right to be present or to be
represented under art 6(3)(c). His absence simply meant that he was not in a
position to exercise either of these rights when the judge decided to proceed with
the trial. The question then comes to be whether there has been a breach of the
appellant's rights under art 6. As Mr Perry submitted, that question falls to be
determined on a consideration of the whole of the proceedings, including those
in the Court of Appeal.

[55] In arguing that the proceedings did not meet the requirements of art 6,
Mr Solley referred to a number of decisions of the European Court of Human
Rights. Lord Bingham has analysed them and I accordingly need not do so.
While they provide useful guidance on particular points, the court has been at
pains to emphasise that '[i]t is not the Court's function to elaborate a general
theory in this area' (see *Colozza v Italy* (1985) 7 EHRR 516 at 524 (para 29)). In
saying this, the court was recognising that the contracting states have many
different systems of procedure. The means by which they secure a fair trial in the
absence of the defendant are correspondingly various. Here the issue has to be
determined by looking at the way in which the courts handled the problem under
English criminal procedure and by deciding whether, in the result, the appellant
can be said to have had a fair hearing. In that regard the decisions of the Court of
Human Rights relating to very different procedures can be of only limited
assistance.

a [56] The most striking feature of the trial in this case was, of course, that the defendants were not in court and there was no one to represent them. Mr Solley suggested that the significance of this could be gauged from Judge Holloway's assessment that, for this very reason, the defendants were likely to be found guilty by the jury. By contrast, at the next stage, in the Court of Appeal, the appellant was present at the hearing. He was also represented by senior and

b junior counsel, just as he was represented by senior and junior counsel before your Lordships' House. For these hearings he enjoyed the benefit of legal aid from public funds. The courts and legal system thus made no attempt to prevent him from being represented. In this respect his predicament is quite different, for instance, from that of the defendant in the proceedings before the appeal court at Aix-en-Provence in *Poitrimol v France* (1993) 18 EHRR 130. Here, in the Court of

c Appeal ([2002] EWCA Crim 168, [2001] 3 WLR 125, [2001] All ER (D) 256 (Jan)) the appellant had every opportunity to exercise his rights to be present and to be represented. Mr Solley argued that this was too little, too late. But it is a matter to which your Lordships are entitled to attach considerable importance since it is plain that the representation was effective and that the Court of Appeal paid

d careful attention to the arguments advanced on behalf of the appellant. This is conclusively demonstrated not only by their meticulous judgment considering the points made by counsel, but also by the fact that, while the appellant's appeal against conviction was refused, his appeal against sentence resulted in the sentence being reduced from 13 to 11 years' imprisonment.

e [57] The question must therefore be whether the hearing in the Court of Appeal, with the appellant fully and effectively represented, was such that, when the proceedings in this case are considered as a whole, one can say that the appellant has had a fair hearing in terms of art 6 even though he was not represented before the jury.

f [58] In the course of summarising the principles to be applied by courts in relation to the trial of a defendant in his absence, Rose LJ indicated (at [22](4)) that the discretion to allow a trial to take place or continue in the absence of the defendant—

> 'must be exercised with great care and it is only in rare and exceptional cases that it should be exercised in favour of a trial taking place or continuing,
g particularly if the defendant is unrepresented.'

Lord Bingham has stressed this caution and I would do so too. I should also wish to associate myself with his comments as to the desirability of a defendant being represented even if he has voluntarily absconded. The decision of Judge
h Holloway to proceed with the trial in the absence of the defendants and in the absence of any representative was therefore exceptional. In taking it, he had regard to a number of factors. One, of course, was the fact that the defendants' absence was not due to illness or some other misfortune but to a deliberate decision on their part to abscond. The judge also took into account the fact that there were 35 witnesses who had come to court for the second time and who
j were anxiously awaiting the prospect of giving evidence. Their trauma following the robbery would be unlikely to go away until the defendants' guilt or innocence was determined in one way or another. If the trial did not proceed they would have to wait for an indefinite period, at the end of which some might not be willing to give evidence, some might have died and others might have emigrated. All kinds of problems could arise which would then be to the advantage of the

defendants. In having regard in this way to the potential interests of the victims, jurors and wider public as well as to the rights of the accused, the judge was acting consistently with the established jurisprudence on art 6. The Court of Human Rights has recognised that in an appropriate case the interests of the defence are balanced against those of witnesses or victims called upon to testify (see *Doorson v Netherlands* (1996) 22 EHRR 330 at 358 (para 70)). The wider public interest is always a factor to be kept in mind in applying art 6 (see *Brown v Stott (Procurator Fiscal, Dunfermline)* [2001] 2 All ER 97, [2001] 2 WLR 817). The judge's decision to proceed with the trial in this case was, of course, one of the matters which the Court of Appeal examined. They considered various criticisms which counsel for the appellant had made of the judge's decision but they concluded (at [41]):

'In our judgment, the judge's exercise of discretion is not susceptible to effective challenge. He directed himself correctly in accordance with the law. He had very clearly in mind the possible prejudice to the defence if the trial proceeded without the defendant being present or represented. He did not have regard to any irrelevant factor. He reached a conclusion to continue with the trial which, in the light of his inevitable finding that the defendant had deliberately absented himself from court and from contact with his lawyers many months before trial, was well within the ambit of his discretion.'

[59] The first thing to notice is, therefore, that in deciding to go ahead with the trial, the judge exercised a discretion which under English law will only rarely result in proceedings being taken in the absence of a defendant. The Court of Appeal examined the judge's exercise of that discretion in the circumstances of this case and held that his decision to proceed was sound, being well within the ambit of what he could properly do, having regard to the various factors which he mentioned. The fact that a judge has to make a positive decision to allow a trial to proceed in the absence of a defendant and the fact that only in exceptional cases will it be proper to do so are fundamental elements of the scheme for ensuring that any such proceedings will be fair. The reasoned decision of the Court of Appeal that the judge was justified in proceeding with the trial in the particular circumstances of this case is therefore an initial pointer towards the fairness of these proceedings.

[60] In turning to examine the course of the trial, it is necessary to bear in mind the broad outline of the case against the appellant. The evidence is described by Rose LJ (at [37]). I therefore need mention only the salient points.

[61] The armed robbery happened at Euston Street Post Office in Liverpool. A police officer, PC Mangan, chased the appellant and arrested him in a yard about 500m away from the locus. The prosecution case was based not just on the evidence of the victims, bystanders and police officers but also on scientific evidence relating both to a jacket found near the yard and to the appellant's clothes. Moreover, there was evidence that the robbers had been talking to one another by radio. A walkie-talkie, like one which the appellant had bought some time before, was found near him. He was the holder of a licence for such a radio.

[62] In the face of this powerful body of evidence connecting him with the robbery there were only two possible ways in which the jury could have concluded that the appellant was not guilty. First, they might have concluded that he had been the victim of one or more dishonest policemen who had falsified the evidence, in particular by contaminating the clothing, to make it look as if the

a   appellant had been involved. Alternatively, by some coincidence, the appellant and his co-defendant had happened to be in the wrong place at the wrong time, wearing the wrong clothes, with the result that they had been confused with the real robbers. These were the only possibilities that occurred to the judge. There were indeed no others. Before the Court of Appeal, with the appellant present, his counsel made no submission in support of the conspiracy line of defence.

b   Nor, as Rose LJ explains (at [41]) did counsel suggest that, if the appellant had attended the trial, he could or would have provided an innocent explanation for the contamination of his clothing, his presence in the vicinity of the robbery or his flight from the police. He could not have shown that he was unconnected with the walkie-talkie. I should record that in the proceedings before the House counsel did not challenge this passage in the judgment of the Court of Appeal nor

c   did he seek to put forward any innocent explanation at this stage.

[63] In the absence of any innocent or more compelling explanation to account for the prosecution evidence, the chances of the appellant and his fellow defendant being convicted were obviously great. That is what the judge was recognising when, in considering whether to proceed with the trial, he expressed

d   the view that the defendants would inevitably be convicted if the trial went ahead in their absence and without them being represented. But the Court of Appeal proceedings show that neither the presence at the trial of the appellant himself nor the presence of any representative would have led to any alternative theory being advanced to account for the prosecution evidence or to any additional evidence being led to contradict it.

e   [64] The jury were well aware of the two possible ways of accounting for the prosecution evidence against the appellant. In his summing-up the judge was careful to draw the jury's attention to them, not only when giving an overview at the end but at various points during his account of the evidence. In this way the judge did all that he could to ensure that, when they considered their verdict,

f   the members of the jury had these possible lines of defence in mind and were able to give them whatever weight they considered to be appropriate.

[65] Prosecuting counsel was conscious that he was dealing with defendants who were neither present nor represented. He took this matter into account in the way that he led his evidence. As he acknowledged when the judge was considering whether to allow the trial to proceed, there could be no question of

g   cutting corners. The judge records that prosecuting counsel did indeed adopt a slightly more challenging approach to his own witnesses than would have been normal in a case where the defendants were represented. In particular, he looked to see whether there were any areas that ought to be highlighted in view of the fact that the defendants were not present or represented. While it is not

h   suggested that, in itself, what prosecuting counsel did made up for the lack of representation for the appellant, it is nevertheless a matter to be considered when deciding whether the proceedings can be regarded as fair. It should also not be forgotten that, if prosecuting counsel had acted unfairly by taking advantage of the absence of representation to cut corners, misrepresent the evidence or

j   blacken the defendants, the judge could have stopped the trial. Indeed he could have done so if he had detected unfairness in the proceedings, whatever its source. In fact, of course, prosecuting counsel acted with propriety and the judge saw no reason to intervene.

[66] The judge's summing up was obviously of even greater importance than usual. In it he gave the jury a number of directions specifically tailored to the

situation where the defendants were neither present nor represented. The
members of the jury were directed that they had to reach their verdict on the
evidence which they had heard and on nothing else. They were not to speculate.
These directions are of a familiar kind, but the judge stressed that, where the
defendants were unrepresented, it was particularly important for the jury not to
speculate. They were also told, specifically, that they must not speculate as to the
reasons for the defendants' absence and that they should not assume that the
defendants' failure to attend court in any way at all established that either or both
of them were guilty. The jury should carefully assess the evidence as they would
have done if the defendants had been present and had been represented by
counsel. The judge also told the jury not to assume that the fact that the
defendants had not been there to give evidence in any way at all helped the
prosecution to prove their case. It was vitally important for the jury to remember
that there was no burden placed on a defendant to prove that he was not guilty.

[67] These directions, carefully designed to deal with the particular situation
that had arisen, were no mere formality. On the contrary, given the experience
of judges and practitioners over many years and in various jurisdictions, it is
proper to proceed on the basis that the jury, having taken an oath to do justice,
will in fact have duly applied the directions when considering their verdicts.
Indeed the system of trial by jury depends upon this assumption. I refer to the
observations of Lord Hope in *Montgomery v HM Advocate, Coulter v HM Advocate*
[2001] 2 WLR 779 at 810 and to the authorities which he cites. As he notes, the
Court of Human Rights attaches importance to directions to a jury which are
specifically designed to deal with a difficulty that has arisen in the proceedings.
Pullar v UK (1996) 22 EHRR 391 at 404–405 (paras 37–41) and *Gregory v UK* (1997)
25 EHRR 577 at 594–595 (paras 46–48) may serve as examples. It is appropriate
for this House also to attach importance to these directions.

[68] At this stage the various strands relating to the trial can be drawn
together. The judge carefully considered whether to allow the trial to go ahead
in the particular circumstances. The Court of Appeal reviewed his decision and
supported it. At the actual trial various steps were taken to make due allowance
for the fact that the appellant was neither present nor represented. Prosecuting
counsel took care to lead the evidence fully and in a way that did not conceal any
weaknesses. The possible lines of defence were put before the jury. Although no
evidence was led to support those lines, the appellant can point to none that could
have been led. The jury, who had taken the appropriate oath, were given specific
directions that they were not to speculate as to the reasons for the defendants'
absence and that the burden of establishing their guilt rested on the prosecution,
just as if the defendants had been present. All these are important factors to be
taken into account when considering the fairness of the proceedings as a whole.

[69] When the appellant was eventually apprehended, he appealed against his
conviction and sentence. The nature of that appeal and the powers of the Court
of Appeal are of relevance for the purposes of art 6 of the convention. In
considering the appeal against conviction, the Court of Appeal were applying the
test in s 2(1) of the Criminal Appeal Act 1968 under which they had to allow the
appellant's appeal if they thought his conviction was unsafe. In *Condron v UK*
(2001) 31 EHRR 1 at 24 (para 65) the Court of Human Rights emphasised that,
where the issue was raised, the Court of Appeal required to consider whether the
appellant's rights under art 6 had been secured:

a
'... the question whether or not the rights of the defence guaranteed to an accused under Article 6 were secured in any given case cannot be assimilated to a finding that his conviction was safe in the absence of any enquiry into the issue of fairness.'

Here the Court of Appeal ([2001] 3 WLR 125, [2001] All ER (D) 256 (Jan)) followed that approach. Rose LJ expressed (at [41]) his conclusion on the appellant's appeal against conviction in these words:

b

'In our judgment there is no reason, in all these circumstances, to regard his conviction as unsafe *or his trial as unfair* and accordingly his appeal against conviction is dismissed.' (My emphasis.)

c
[70] So the proceedings in the Court of Appeal allowed the appellant to advance arguments not merely on the substantive merits of his conviction but also on the fairness of the trial. The Court of Appeal had power to consider both aspects and, as their judgment and their conclusion show, they were conscious of the need to examine both aspects and they did so.

d
[71] Mr Solley argued that, even though the Court of Appeal could and did review the merits of the conviction and the fairness of the proceedings in this way, the appeal process was insufficient to ensure the fairness of the proceedings under art 6. What was required, he said, was that the appeal should be conducted before a court which could rehear the evidence. In this connection he relied on the observation of the European Court in *Poitrimol v France* (1993) 18 EHRR 130 at 145 (para 31):

e

'Proceedings held in an accused's absence are not in principle incompatible with the Convention if the person concerned can subsequently obtain from a court which has heard him a fresh determination of the merits of the charge, in respect of both law and fact.'

f
Here, he said, the appellant had been unable to obtain a fresh determination from a jury in a trial in which he had been present and represented. It is true, of course, that there has been no new trial of that kind. But, as it explained in *Colozza v Italy* (1985) 7 EHRR 516, the court is not concerned to lay down general doctrines in this area. The passage in *Poitrimol*'s case has to be read in the context of that case, involving a particular form of French proceedings.

g
[72] M Poitrimol had been tried in the tribunal correctionnel in Marseilles where, though absent, he had been represented. While he appealed against his conviction, he made no complaint about the fairness of those proceedings. His complaint was that the subsequent proceedings before the cour d'appel at Aix-en-Provence had been unfair. There is nothing to suggest that those proceedings would have involved anything more than pleadings on behalf of M Poitrimol. The appeal court refused his request to be tried inter partes in his absence because there was an outstanding warrant for his arrest. It therefore tried the case without M Poitrimol being present or being represented by his counsel, but under art 410 of the Code of Criminal Procedure the proceedings were conducted 'as if he [had been] present'. The appeal court eventually ruled that the pleadings on his behalf were inadmissible and upheld the judgment of the lower court in its entirety. The significance of the proceedings being conducted as if M Poitrimol had been present was that he thereby lost the right of a defendant in proceedings in absentia to use the art 489 procedure to render the

h

j

judgment null and void by simply applying to the court to set it aside and to
rehear the case. His only possible recourse against the judgment was an appeal
to the cour de cassation, but that route was blocked by a (separate) rule that no
such appeal lay where there was an outstanding warrant for his arrest. In these
circumstances the Strasbourg court held that there had been a breach of art 6 of
the convention.

[73] It is apparent, therefore, that the observation on which Mr Solley relied
was made in a very particular context where the appeal court at Aix had refused
to consider the submissions of M Poitrimol's lawyer and had also effectively cut
off any further redress, whether by a rehearing before the appeal court or by an
application to the cour de cassation. In effect, he had no means of having his case
heard at all.

[74] Here, by contrast, the appellant has been able to appeal, with the benefit
of legal aid, not only to the Court of Appeal but indeed to your Lordships' House.
The Court of Appeal would not, of course, ever rehear a case in the sense of
having all the witnesses led before them. That is not part of the English system,
for in that system justice can be done without it. But the Court of Appeal have
full powers to consider any legal issue, to consider the transcript of the relevant
parts of the evidence and to receive additional evidence if they consider it
necessary or expedient to do so in the interests of justice (see s 23(1)(c) and (2) of
the 1968 Act). Having considered any additional evidence, the Court of Appeal
may, of course, decide to refuse the appeal. But, equally, they may decide to
allow the appeal outright or they can allow it and, if they consider that the
interests of justice so require, order a retrial—at which the defendant would, of
course, be represented. The House has recently given guidance on the exercise
of these powers in *R v Pendleton* [2001] UKHL 66, [2002] 1 All ER 524, [2002] 1
WLR 72 and has stressed that the Court of Appeal should consider a conviction
to be unsafe if the additional evidence, if given at the trial, might reasonably have
affected the decision of the trial jury to convict. In my view, under the English
system, these wide powers of the Court of Appeal are sufficient, even in the case
of a trial in absence, to allow the court to monitor and secure the fairness of the
proceedings.

[75] For present purposes, the mere existence of the power to receive
additional evidence is significant. The appellant could have invoked it if his
absence or lack of representation had actually meant that the jury reached their
verdict in ignorance of potentially exculpatory evidence. Of course, he could not
in fact suggest this and therefore he could not invoke this particular power. But
it was available: that is one of the guarantees of the fairness of the proceedings.

[76] In the event, the Court of Appeal, having these extensive powers and
being conscious of them, reviewed both the safety of the appellant's conviction
on the merits and the fairness of the proceedings as a whole. Not surprisingly, in
view of the evidence against him, counsel for the appellant appears to have
mounted no real challenge to the merits of his conviction. The Court of Appeal
were satisfied that, on the merits, the conviction was safe. Applying their great
experience, for the reasons which they gave in considerable detail, they also came
to the view that the proceedings, albeit unusual, had indeed been fair. It would
be impertinent to say more than that this was a view which they were entitled to
reach and which should be accorded great respect.

a [77] When the whole of the proceedings, before the trial court and in the Court of Appeal, are taken into account in this way, it can be seen that the appellant's rights under art 6 have not been infringed. The other challenges to the proceedings must also be rejected for the reasons given by Lord Bingham. I would accordingly dismiss the appeal.

b *Appeal dismissed.*

Kate O'Hanlon   Barrister.

APPENDIX

c '[22] In our judgment, in the light of the submissions which we have heard and the English and European authorities to which we have referred, the principles which should guide the English courts in relation to the trial of a defendant in his absence are these: (1) A defendant has, in general, a right to be present at his trial and a right to be legally represented. (2) Those rights d can be waived, separately or together, wholly or in part, by the defendant himself. They may be wholly waived if, knowing, or having the means of knowledge as to, when and where his trial is to take place, he deliberately and voluntarily absents himself and/or withdraws instructions from those representing him. They may be waived in part if, being present and e represented at the outset, the defendant, during the course of the trial, behaves in such a way as to obstruct the proper course of the proceedings and/or withdraws his instructions from those representing him. (3) The trial judge has a discretion as to whether a trial should take place or continue in the absence of a defendant and/or his legal representatives. (4) That discretion must be exercised with great care and it is only in rare and f exceptional cases that it should be exercised in favour of a trial taking place or continuing, particularly if the defendant is unrepresented. (5) In exercising that discretion, fairness to the defence is of prime importance but fairness to the prosecution must also be taken into account. The judge must have regard to all the circumstances of the case including, in particular: (i) the nature and circumstances of the defendant's behaviour in absenting himself from the g trial or disrupting it, as the case may be and, in particular, whether his behaviour was deliberate, voluntary and such as plainly waived his right to appear; (ii) whether an adjournment might result in the defendant being caught or attending voluntarily and/or not disrupting the proceedings; (iii) the likely length of such an adjournment; (iv) whether the defendant, though h absent, is, or wishes to be, legally represented at the trial or has, by his conduct, waived his right to representation; (v) whether an absent defendant's legal representatives are able to receive instructions from him during the trial and the extent to which they are able to present his defence; (vi) the extent of the disadvantage to the defendant in not being able to give j his account of events, having regard to the nature of the evidence against him; (vii) the risk of the jury reaching an improper conclusion about the absence of the defendant; (viii) the seriousness of the offence, which affects defendant, victim and public; (ix) the general public interest and the particular interest of victims and witnesses that a trial should take place within a reasonable time of the events to which it relates; (x) the effect of delay on the memories of witnesses; (xi) where there is more than one defendant and not all have absconded, the undesirability of separate trials, and the prospects of a fair trial for the defendants who are present. (6) If the judge decides that a trial should take place or continue in the absence of an unrepresented defendant, he must ensure that the trial is as fair as the circumstances permit. He must, in particular, take reasonable steps, both during the giving of evidence and in the summing up, to expose weaknesses in the prosecution case and to make such points on behalf of the defendant as the evidence permits. In summing up he must warn the jury that absence is not an admission of guilt and adds nothing to the prosecution case.'

Terry v East Sussex Coroner
[2001] EWCA Civ 1094

COURT OF APPEAL, CIVIL DIVISION
SIMON BROWN, MAY AND DYSON LJJ
19 JUNE, 12 JULY 2001

Coroner – Inquest – Duty to hold inquest – Post-mortem examination – Coroner declining to hold inquest into deceased's death following receipt of post-mortem examination report – Deceased's widow making statutory challenge to coroner's decision – Whether coroner functus officio after deciding not to hold inquest as a result of post-mortem examination report – Whether court to apply judicial review test in statutory challenge to decision not to hold inquest – Coroners Act 1988, ss 13(1)(a), 19(3).

T died in 1994, aged 71. For many years, his work had exposed him to asbestos dust. His family regarded his death as asbestos-related and wanted an inquest to be held into it since death from industrial illness was a well-recognised category of unnatural death. Under s 8 of the Coroners Act 1988, the coroner was required to hold an inquest if he had reasonable cause to believe that the deceased had died such a death. Where, however, the coroner had reasonable cause to suspect that a person had died a sudden death of which the cause was unknown, s 19(1)[a] of the 1988 Act empowered the coroner to direct a post-mortem examination if he were of the opinion that such an examination might prove an inquest to be unnecessary. Section 19(3) required the coroner to send the registrar of deaths a certificate stating the cause of death as disclosed by the post-mortem examination report where he was satisfied, as a result of the examination, that an inquest was unnecessary. On the day following T's death, the coroner obtained, pursuant to s 19, a post-mortem examination report which stated that the primary cause of death was respiratory failure and chronic obstructive airway disease, not asbestosis. He therefore declined to hold an inquest into T's death, and his successor as coroner subsequently refused to hold an inquest for the same reason. In 1999 T's widow obtained the Attorney General's fiat to make an application to the High Court pursuant to s 13[b] of the 1988 Act for an order that an inquest be held. Under s 13(1)(a), the court could make such an order where it was satisfied that the coroner had refused or neglected to hold an inquest which ought to be held. On the application, the Divisional Court held that, once a coroner had decided under s 19(3) that an inquest was unnecessary, a presumption arose against holding such an inquest thereafter, which was rebuttable only by a change of circumstances of some significance or by powerful evidence. It further held that there was no evidence which indicated that an inquest could arrive at a verdict different from that of the coroner and that, in any event, he had posed the correct questions and his decisions were therefore unimpeachable. Accordingly, the court concluded that it was not entitled to order the holding of an inquest. On the appeal by T's widow, the coroner contended that he had become functus officio once he had decided, under s 19(3), not to hold an inquest since such a decision took the place of an inquest. T's widow contended that, whether or not

---

a   Section 19 is set out at [7], below
b   Section 13, so far as material, is set out at [18], below

the coroner was functus, the court should accede to her application under s 13. In particular, she contended that the court had a wide jurisdiction under that provision and could decide that an inquest ought to be held even if it was impossible to stigmatise as irrational the coroner's conclusion that there was no reasonable cause to suspect that the death was unnatural and even if the verdict on any inquest would almost certainly be that of death by natural causes.

Held – (1) A coroner did not become functus officio once he had decided, under s 19(3) of the 1988 Act, not to hold an inquest. The s 19 procedure did not take the place of an inquest. Although the registration of the death on the basis of an ascertained and certified cause following a statutorily bespoke post-mortem examination provided a firmer foundation for the decision not to hold an inquest than a mere decision to that effect taken under s 8, it did not follow that in the former case the coroner was functus officio when in the latter he plainly was not. That conclusion did not in any way undermine the obvious value of the s 19 procedure which in many cases would continue to eliminate the need for an inquest. As regards the receipt of fresh evidence, the question for the coroner, as it remained throughout, was whether he thought that there was reasonable cause to suspect that the death was unnatural. A s 19 post-mortem report clearly concluding that the death was from natural causes would provide a firm foundation for a negative answer, but it was not necessary in that connection to adopt the concept of a rebuttable presumption or the language of significant change of circumstances or powerful evidence (see [14]–[16], [28], [29], below); *R v Greater Manchester North District Coroner, ex p Worch* [1987] 3 All ER 661 considered.

(2) On an application under s 13(1)(a) of the 1988 Act, the court should apply the same test as on a judicial review challenge, and accordingly it could not conclude that an inquest 'ought to be held' unless the coroner had misdirected himself in law or his factual conclusion was irrational. Not only would it be most unfortunate if a different test were to be applied to the two forms of application, but it would also offend the language of the statute. A coroner could not properly be said to have refused or neglected to hold an inquest unless he was at fault, and that would not be the case unless the common law test were satisfied. In the instant case, the decision of the coroner was obviously reasonable, and the Divisional Court had been correct in rejecting the s 13 application. Accordingly, the appeal would be dismissed (see [21], [26]–[28], below).

Notes
For inquests and post-mortem examinations and for the High Court's statutory power to order an inquest, see 9(2) *Halsbury's Laws* (4th edn reissue) paras 837, 969.

For the Coroners Act 1988, ss 13, 19, see 11 *Halsbury's Statutes* (4th edn) (2000 reissue) 669, 676.

Cases referred to in judgments
Associated Provincial Picture Houses Ltd v Wednesbury Corp [1947] 2 All ER 680, [1948] 1 KB 223, CA.
R v Greater Manchester North District Coroner, ex p Worch [1987] 3 All ER 661, [1988] 1 QB 513, [1987] 3 WLR 997, CA.
R v Inner London North Coroner, ex p Touche [2001] EWCA Civ 383, [2001] 2 All ER 752, [2001] QB 1206, [2001] 3 WLR 148.

a   *R v Poplar Coroner, ex p Thomas* [1993] 2 All ER 381, [1993] QB 610, [1993] 2 WLR 547, CA.

Rapier (decd), Re [1986] 3 All ER 726, [1988] QB 26, [1986] 3 WLR 830.

Appeal

b   Margaret Terry, the widow of Albert Edward Hayes Terry, appealed with permission of Lord Phillips of Worth Matravers MR granted on 5 February 2001 from the decision of the Divisional Court (Lord Woolf CJ and Rafferty J) on 29 November 2000 ([2001] QB 559) dismissing her application for an order under s 13(1)(a) of the Coroners Act 1988 requiring the respondent, the Coroner for East Sussex (Alan Craze), to hold an inquest into her husband's death. The facts are set out in the judgment of Simon Brown LJ.

c

Anthony Allston (instructed by *Dean Wilson & Laing,* Brighton) for the appellant.
Jonathan Hough (instructed by *Angela Reid,* Lewes) for the coroner.

Cur adv vult

d   12 July 2001. The following judgments were delivered.

SIMON BROWN LJ.

[1] Albert Edward Hayes Terry died at Hove on 26 May 1994. He was 71. For many years his work had exposed him to asbestos dust. Since he died, his family
e   have come to regard his death as asbestos-related and they want an inquest to be held into it: death from industrial illness is a well-recognised category of unnatural death (see *R v Poplar Coroner, ex p Thomas* [1993] 2 All ER 381 at 385, [1993] QB 610 at 627). Her Majesty's coroners for East Sussex, Dr Gooding at the time of the deceased's death and subsequently Mr Craze, have consistently
f   declined to hold such an inquest. On the day following the death, Dr Gooding, pursuant to s 19 of the Coroners Act 1988, had obtained from a forensic pathologist, Dr Elspeth Morrison, a post-mortem examination report stating the primary cause of death as respiratory failure and chronic obstructive airway disease (not asbestosis).

[2] The appellant, the deceased's widow, in September 1999 obtained the
g   Attorney General's fiat to make an application to the High Court under s 13 of the 1988 Act for an order that an inquest be held into the deceased's death. The Divisional Court on 29 November 2000 dismissed the application (see [2001] QB 559). The appellant now appeals to this court with the permission of Lord Phillips of Worth Matravers MR. The main issue upon which he gave permission,
h   although not in fact determinative of the appeal, was an issue raised by the coroner himself as to whether, once he had decided not to hold an inquest under s 19(3) of the 1988 Act, he became functus officio. This is said to have been a matter of doubt and difficulty amongst coroners for many years.

[3] The second issue on the appeal is whether in any event—irrespective,
j   therefore, of whether or not the coroner was functus once he had decided not to hold an inquest—the court should accede to this s 13 application by the deceased's widow. The Divisional Court held not.

Issue 1—functus officio

[4] When does a coroner become functus officio? Certainly he does so once an inquest has been held. Even if important new evidence then comes to light,

there cannot be another inquest into the death unless and until the High Court
so orders under s 13 of the 1988 Act. *Re Rapier (decd)* [1986] 3 All ER 726, [1988]   *a*
QB 26 illustrates the point, the s 13 application there having been initiated by the
coroner himself. Equally certainly the coroner does not become functus officio
merely because he decides that he has no duty (and, therefore, no power) to hold
an inquest under s 8 of the 1988 Act, and notifies the registrar of deaths of his
decision by what is colloquially called Pink Form A (see this court's decision in   *b*
R v Inner London North Coroner, ex p Touche [2001] EWCA Civ 383, [2001] 2 All ER
752, [2001] QB 1206 as a recent case in point). What is for decision on this appeal
is whether a coroner becomes functus officio if, following a post-mortem
examination ordered by him under s 19 of the 1988 Act, he decides that an inquest
is unnecessary and sends the registrar of deaths a certificate in what is known as
Pink Form B showing the cause of death as that disclosed by the post-mortem   *c*
examination report.

[5] The Divisional Court (Lord Woolf CJ and Rafferty J) in reserved
judgments given on 29 November 2000 concluded ([2001] QB 559 at 563) that
once a coroner has made his decision not to hold an inquest under s 19(3)—

> 'At that stage his coronial function is complete. However, it must be in the   *d*
> interests of justice that he could in certain circumstances proceed to review
> his procedure and/or conclusion if appropriate. He must, in my judgment,
> be able to do so, but only if assured of a change of circumstances of some
> significance. Putting it a different way, the *rebuttable* presumption must be
> that once he has been informed, has investigated and has made a decision, he   *e*
> has performed his statutory duty. It follows, therefore, that only upon the
> provision to the coroner of powerful evidence is he required to take further
> action. Where there is such evidence produced it would be contrary to the
> spirit of the statute to require him to seek an order of this court before
> ordering an inquest. Section 19(4) expressly preserves a residual jurisdiction
> which enables him to hold an inquest in the two sets of circumstances there   *f*
> specified and the powers of the High Court under section 13 suggest that the
> residual jurisdiction is of a general nature.' (See para 14 of Rafferty J's leading
> judgment with which Lord Woolf CJ simply agreed.)

[6] In granting permission to appeal to this court Lord Phillips MR concluded   *g*
that that judgment 'does not wholly resolve [the] difficulty'.

[7] The relevant statutory provisions are these:

> '**8.**—(1) Where a coroner is informed that the body of a person ("the
> deceased") is lying within his district and there is reasonable cause to suspect
> that the deceased—(a) has died a violent or an unnatural death; (b) has died   *h*
> a sudden death of which the cause is unknown; or (c) has died in prison or in
> such a place or in such circumstances as to require an inquest under any
> other Act, then, whether the cause of death arose within his district or not,
> the coroner shall as soon as practicable hold an inquest into the death of the
> deceased …   *j*
> **19.**—(1) Where a coroner is informed that the body of a person is lying
> within his district and there is reasonable cause to suspect that the person has
> died a sudden death of which the cause is unknown, the coroner may, if he
> is of opinion that a post-mortem examination may prove an inquest to be
> unnecessary—(a) direct a legally qualified medical practitioner whom, if an
> inquest were held, he would be entitled to summon as a medical witness

a under section 21 below; or (b) request any other legally qualified medical practitioner, to make a post-mortem examination of the body and to report the result of the examination to the coroner in writing.

(2) For the purposes of a post-mortem examination under this section, the coroner and any person directed or requested by him to make the examination shall have the like powers, authorities and immunities as if

b the examination were a post-mortem examination directed by the coroner at an inquest into the death of the deceased.

(3) Where a post-mortem examination is made under this section and the coroner is satisfied as a result of it that an inquest is unnecessary, he shall send to the registrar of deaths a certificate under his hand stating the cause of death as disclosed by the report of the person making the examination.

c (4) Nothing in this section shall be construed as authorising the coroner to dispense with an inquest in any case where there is reasonable cause to suspect that the deceased—(a) has died a violent or an unnatural death; or (b) has died in prison or in such a place or in such circumstances as to require an inquest under any other Act.'

d
[8] The effect of s 19 (earlier enacted as s 21 of the Coroners (Amendment) Act 1926) was considered by this court in *R v Greater Manchester North District Coroner, ex p Worch* [1987] 3 All ER 661, [1988] 1 QB 513. I need cite only the following passages from Slade LJ's leading judgment:

e '... there can be no doubt that s 21(1) of the 1926 Act [now s 19] was intended to confer an entirely new power on coroners to order a post-mortem before an inquest, provided that the three conditions specified in the subsection are satisfied, namely: (1) the coroner "is informed that the dead body of a person is lying within his jurisdiction"; (2) "there is reasonable cause to suspect that the person has died a sudden death of which the cause

f is unknown"; and (3) "the coroner is of opinion that a post-mortem examination may prove an inquest to be unnecessary ..." ...

First, the coroner has to consider whether the three conditions specified in s 21(1) are satisfied. If, but only if, he is so satisfied, he is under no *immediate* obligation to arrange an inquest "as soon as practicable" as he would

g otherwise have to do under s 3(1) of [the Coroners Act 1887] [now s 8(1)], but may instead order a post-mortem. However, s 21(1) itself confers no power whatever to dispense with an inquest.

The second stage of the process arises when the result of the post-mortem is known. If, but only if, the case is not [within what is now s 8(1)(c)], and the

h post-mortem shows that the death was due to natural causes, the coroner may be satisfied that an inquest is unnecessary. If that is so, he can accordingly dispense with an inquest. However, s 21(3) [now s 19(4)] is there as a reminder so as to make it clear that, after the result of the post-mortem is known, the coroner will still be obliged to order an inquest if the case [falls within what are now paras (a) or (c) of s 8(1)].' (See [1987] 3 All ER 661 at

j 667, 668, [1988] 1 QB 513 at 527, 528.)

[9] In short, if the coroner is satisfied that the three pre-conditions are satisfied, he is under no immediate obligation to hold an inquest as soon as practicable (as otherwise he would be bound to do under s 8(1)(b) since by definition he must have reasonable cause to suspect that the deceased died a sudden death of which the cause is unknown) and can order a post mortem. If then the post-mortem

examination shows that death was due to natural causes, an inquest will be
unnecessary since the case will fall neither within para (a) nor para (b) of s 8(1),   *a*
nor could it fall within para (c) since the third pre-condition would not then in any
event have been satisfied.

[10] Given that plain scope and rationale of s 19, I have difficulty in
understanding why the coroner's position at the end of stage 2—assuming he
decides that an inquest is unnecessary—should be any different from his position   *b*
in an ordinary s 8 case when he simply decides at the outset that there is no
reasonable cause to suspect that the case falls within any of the paragraphs of
s 8(1).

[11] What, then, do the legal commentators say? *Jervis on Coroners* (11th edn,
1993), pp 326–327, reads:
                                                                                         c
'18–05 There is a question mark as to when exactly a coroner becomes
functus officio. Before 1927, there was no power to dispense with an inquest
where the statutory criteria were satisfied. Nowadays, however, there is a
procedure whereby in the case of a sudden death the cause of which is not
known, the coroner may order a post-mortem examination to be made and   *d*
may thereafter dispense with an inquest (the so-called "Pink Form B"
procedure). It is not clear whether utilising that procedure renders the
coroner thereafter *functus officio* in relation to that particular death or
whether if he thereafter discovered further evidence bringing the case within
the other criteria for holding an inquest he could so do without an
application to the court having to be made.   *e*

18–06 The Attorney-General has in the past refused his *fiat* to an
application to the High Court to set aside a "Pink Form B" on the ground
that it was unnecessary, as the coroner was not *functus officio*. This does not
sit easily with the fact that, by statute, the post-mortem examination and the
coroner's decision taken upon the report thereof take the place of the inquest   *f*
which (if held) would have made the coroner *functus officio*.

18–07 On the other hand, a coroner who signs "Pink Form A" to inform
the Registrar of Deaths that he does not propose to hold an inquest, so as to
permit registration of the death, does not in any event become *functus officio*,
because no inquiry equivalent to an inquest has taken place. Consequently,
if information subsequently comes to light and the coroner considers he   *g*
would otherwise have jurisdiction, he is not prevented from acting merely
because of his earlier decision not to hold an inquest. "Pink Form A" is an
administrative convenience for the Registrar of Deaths, and not a substitute
for a coronial inquiry.'

                                                                                         h
[12] Volume 9(2) *Halsbury's Laws* (4th edn reissue) para 948 reads:

'Where a coroner has ordered a post-mortem examination and decided
that an inquest is unnecessary, the issue of the appropriate certificate to the
registrar of deaths does not constitute an inquest; and the Attorney General
may thus refuse a coroner's request for a fiat to apply to the court for an   *j*
order to hold an inquest on the grounds that, as no inquest had been held,
the coroner is not functus officio.'

[13] It is Mr Hough's submission on behalf of the coroner, founded to some
extent on para 18–06 of *Jervis on Coroners*, that the s 19 procedure where it leads
to a decision that an inquest is unnecessary and results therefore in the coroner's

a certificate to the registrar of deaths, takes the place of an inquest. Mr Hough argues:

'Like an inquest, this procedure is based upon a medical investigation and a coronial decision. Like an inquest, it results in the death being registered on the basis of an ascertained and certified cause.'

b [14] I would reject this argument. I cannot accept that the s 19 procedure takes the place of an inquest. No doubt the registration of the death on the basis of an ascertained and certified cause following a statutorily bespoken post-mortem examination provides a firmer foundation for the decision not to hold an inquest than a mere decision to that effect taken under s 8. It does not, however, follow c that in the former case the coroner is functus officio when in the latter he plainly is not. Nor to my mind does this conclusion in any way undermine the obvious value of the s 19 procedure which in many cases will continue to eliminate the need for an inquest. In short, I prefer the view expressed by Dr Burton as the editor of Halsbury's Laws to that expressed in Jervis.

d [15] Having then concluded that the coroner is not functus officio in a s 19 case, what should be his approach to the receipt of fresh evidence? Was the Divisional Court right in its view that, once the coroner has decided under s 19(3) that an inquest is unnecessary, a presumption arises against thereafter holding such an inquest which is rebuttable only by what Rafferty J ([2001] QB 559 at 563 (para 14)) referred to variously as 'a change of circumstances of some significance' e and 'powerful evidence'.

[16] To my mind, the difficulty with this approach is that it appears to conflict with the plain language of s 8 which requires an inquest to be held whenever 'there is reasonable cause to suspect that the deceased ... died ... an unnatural death'. As was explained in Ex p Touche [2001] 2 All ER 752 at [16], it is, of course, f for the coroner to decide whether there is reasonable cause to suspect that a particular death is unnatural, and his decision will not be challengeable unless it is Wednesbury unreasonable (see Associated Provincial Picture Houses Ltd v Wednesbury Corp [1947] 2 All ER 680, [1948] 1 KB 223) or involves a self-misdirection in law. That said, however, the question for the coroner remains the same throughout: does he think there is reasonable cause to suspect that the death was unnatural? g No doubt, as I observed earlier, a s 19 post-mortem report clearly concluding that the death was from natural causes will provide a firm foundation for the answer No. But I would not myself in this connection adopt the concept of a rebuttable presumption nor the language of significant change of circumstance or powerful evidence.

h *Issue 2—should the court accede to this s 13 application?*

[17] Whereas issue 1 was a pure issue of law, issue 2 involves questions of both law and fact.

[18] Section 13 of the 1988 Act provides as follows:

j '(1) This section applies where, on an application by or under the authority of the Attorney-General, the High Court is satisfied as respects a coroner ("the coroner concerned") either—(a) that he refuses or neglects to hold an inquest which ought to be held; or (b) where an inquest has been held by him, that (whether by reason of fraud, rejection of evidence, irregularity of proceedings, insufficiency of inquiry, the discovery of new

facts or evidence or otherwise) it is necessary or desirable in the interests of
justice that another inquest should be held.

(2) The High Court may—(a) order an inquest or, as the case may be,
another inquest to be held into the death ...'

[19] The present application, of course, is made under s 13(1)(a) and gives rise
to a discretion in the court to order an inquest if, but only if, the court is satisfied
that the coroner 'refuses or neglects to hold an inquest which ought to be held'.

[20] Mr Allston's contention on behalf of the appellant is that the Divisional
Court gave no real consideration to the ambit of this power as to which there is
no previous authority. It is his submission that the court has a wide jurisdiction
under this section and that it can decide that 'an inquest ... ought to be held' even
if the coroner's own conclusion that there is no reasonable cause to suspect that
the death was unnatural cannot be stigmatised as irrational—even, indeed, if the
verdict on any inquest would almost certainly be that of death by natural causes.
Mr Allston criticises in particular Rafferty J's conclusion (at 570):

'I do not consider that there is evidence which indicates that an inquest
could arrive at a verdict different from that of the coroner. In any event,
since he posed himself the proper questions, and the decisions he thereafter
reached are unimpeachable, this court is not entitled to order an inquest to
be held.'

[21] I would reject this argument. Rather it seems to me that the self-same test
should apply under s 13(1)(a) as applies on a judicial review challenge. The court
cannot conclude that 'an inquest ... ought to be held' unless the coroner has
misdirected himself in law or his factual conclusion is irrational. *Ex p Touche* itself
had been brought before the court as a s 13 application as well as a judicial review
challenge (see [2001] 2 All ER 752 at [57]) yet no one suggested that the court's
powers of intervention there were wider under the statute than at common
law—indeed, the s 13 application was simply sidelined. Not only would it be
most unfortunate if a different test were to be applied to the two forms of
application, but to my mind it would also offend the language of the statute: I do
not think that a coroner could properly be said to have 'refuse[d] or neglect[ed]'
to hold an inquest' unless he was at fault and this would not be the case unless the
common law test were satisfied.

[22] What, then, of the coroner's conclusion here on the facts, his continuing
view that there is no reasonable cause to suspect that the deceased died of
asbestosis? Mr Allston maintains his criticisms of this conclusion although to my
mind entirely unconvincingly. The facts are very fully and fairly set out over
several pages of the judgment below and, since that is now reported, I think it
unnecessary to repeat them here.

[23] The point which Mr Allston naturally stresses beyond all else is that on
3 April 1998, nearly four years after the death, the medical appeal tribunal
allowed an appeal by the deceased's son from the earlier decision of the
adjudicating medical authority, Dr Ward, of 1 September 1993, and concluded
that from 1 January 1992 the deceased had suffered impaired lung function due to
pneumoconiosis (asbestosis).

[24] Given, however, that that conclusion was so exiguously reasoned, and
that it was contrary to the views expressed by all the other doctors in the
case—Dr Ward, Dr Morrison who had conducted the post mortem, Professor
Corrin, the 'internationally renowned pathologist' at the Royal Brompton

a   Hospital, and Dr Hartley, the deceased's own treating physician who reported to the appellant's solicitors even after the medical appeal tribunal's decision that 'there seems no evidence to support the change of mind' and that, putting the case at its highest, the diagnosis of asbestosis is not 'absolutely excluded' ('not completely rule[d] out')—it is surely not surprising that the coroner maintained his stance and that the Divisional Court considered ([2001] QB 559 at 570

b   (para 35)) 'there is [no] evidence which indicates that an inquest could arrive at a verdict different from that of the coroner'.

[25] Mr Allston drew our attention to a passage in a 1980 Home Office circular (18/1980), quoted in para 15–27 of *Jervis on Coroners* (p 298):

c   '... the Home Office expresses the view that as far as possible no differing conclusions should be reached by coroners (and their pathologists) on the one hand and medical boarding centres (respiratory diseases) on the other, and therefore encourages discussions between them in cases of possible disagreement, or even postponement by the coroner of the conclusion of his inquest until the conclusions of the medical boarding centre are available.'

d   [26] I recognise, of course, the general undesirability of having 'differing conclusions' such as that reached in this case. Since, however, the coroner's conclusion is not merely obviously reasonable but one which the Divisional Court, having before it, as was conceded, all the evidence which would be put before any inquest, clearly regarded as the only proper one, the Home Office circular cannot provide a basis for allowing this application.

e   [27] In my judgment the Divisional Court were correct in their decision on the determinative second issue. I would dismiss this appeal.

MAY LJ.
[28] I agree.

f   **DYSON LJ.**
[29] I also agree.

Appeal dismissed.

Dilys Tausz   Barrister.

Reid Minty (a firm) v Taylor   *a*

[2001] EWCA Civ 1723

COURT OF APPEAL, CIVIL DIVISION
WARD, MAY AND KAY LJJ
29 OCTOBER 2001   *b*

*Costs – Order for costs – Indemnity costs – Whether court having power to award
indemnity costs under its general discretion only where party guilty of moral lack of
probity or conduct deserving of moral condemnation – CPR 44.3.*

The claimant brought proceedings for libel against the defendant. In September   *c*
1999 the defendant's solicitors wrote to the claimant, inviting it to discontinue the
proceedings on terms that it would pay the defendant's costs on the standard
basis. The letter also stated that, in the event of that offer not being accepted, the
defendant would draw it to the court's attention and seek indemnity costs.
The claimant did not accept the defendant's invitation to settle. Further   *d*
correspondence aimed at settling the litigation then passed between the parties,
including a letter from the defendant's solicitors in December 1999 stating that
their client's costs to date were £100,000 but offering to settle his claim for costs
at £50,000. No settlement was reached and the case went to trial in December
2000. Judgment was given for the defendant after the jury upheld his defence of
justification. The defendant then applied for an order for indemnity costs against   *e*
the claimant. The judge held that the application fell within CPR Pt 44, that the
court could only make an order for indemnity costs under that Part if a party
had been guilty of a moral lack of probity or conduct deserving of moral
condemnation and that there had been no such conduct on the claimant's part.
Accordingly, the judge dismissed the application. On the defendant's appeal, the   *f*
issue arose whether the court's power to award indemnity costs under its general
discretion on costs in CPR 44.3[a] was confined to the circumstances specified by
the judge. Rule 44.3 provided that, in deciding what order to make about costs,
the court had to have regard to all the circumstances including, inter alia, the
conduct of all the parties and any admissible offer to settle that was drawn to the
court's attention.   *g*

Held – A party could be made subject to an order for indemnity costs under
CPR 44.3 even though there had been no moral lack of probity or conduct
deserving of moral condemnation on its part. The discretion under r 44.3 was to
be exercised judicially, in all the circumstances, having regard to the matters   *h*
referred to in that provision. It included a discretion to decide whether some or
all of the costs awarded should be on a standard or indemnity basis. If costs were
awarded on an indemnity basis, in many cases there would be some implicit
expression of disapproval of the way in which the litigation had been conducted,
but that would not necessarily be so in every case. Litigation could be conducted   *j*
in a way that was unreasonable and which justified an award of costs on an
indemnity basis, but which could not properly be regarded as lacking moral
probity or deserving moral condemnation. It could not be right, however, that
every defendant in every case could put themselves in the way of claiming costs

---

a   Rule 44.3, so far as material, is set out at [16], below *a* on an indemnity basis simply by inviting the claimant at an early stage to give up, discontinue and pay the defendant's costs on a standard basis. It might be different if a defendant offered to move some way towards a claimant's position and the result was more favourable to the defendant than that. In the instant case, the letter of September 1999, though relevant, might not by itself take the case for indemnity costs very far. It was very close to an invitation by the *b* defendant to the claimant to throw its hand in, and made little real concession. The letter of December 1999 might be more persuasive, although all the relevant circumstances had to be taken into account. The judge had proceeded on a mistaken view of the law, and his decision would therefore be set aside. Accordingly, the appeal would be allowed, and the matter remitted to the judge for further determination (see [27]–[31], [33], [35], [36]–[40], below).

c   *Petrotrade Inc v Texaco Ltd* [2001] 4 All ER 853 and *McPhilemy v Times Newspapers Ltd (No 2)* [2001] 4 All ER 861 considered.

Cases referred to in judgments
Baron v Lovell [1999] CPLR 630, CA.
d *McPhilemy v Times Newspapers Ltd (No 2)* [2001] EWCA Civ 933, [2001] 4 All ER 861.
Petrotrade Inc v Texaco Ltd [2001] 4 All ER 853, CA.
Raja v Rubin [1999] 3 All ER 73, [2000] Ch 274, [1999] 3 WLR 606, CA.

Appeal
e The defendant, Gordon Taylor, appealed with permission of Gray J from his decision on 19 December 2000 dismissing his application for an order requiring the claimant firm of solicitors, Reid Minty, to pay costs on the indemnity basis in respect of an unsuccessful action for libel brought by it against the defendant. The facts are set out in the judgment of May LJ.

f
Thomas Shields QC, Harvey Starte and *Jeremy Morgan* (instructed by *Gouldens*) for the defendant.
Andrew Monson and *Nicholas Bacon* (instructed by *Reid Minty*) for the claimant.

WARD LJ.
g   [1] May LJ will give the first judgment.

MAY LJ.
    [2] This is an appeal by successful defendants from a costs judgment and order of Gray J on 19 December 2000. The judge himself gave permission to appeal.
h   [3] The judgment and the appeal concern costs in a libel action in which the jury, after a 12-day trial, found in favour of the defendant's defence of justification. The publication in issue was on 6 November 1996 in an interview broadcast on Radio 5 Live. The protagonists in the litigation were both concerned with professional football and professional footballers. The occasion was the House of *j* Commons, in advance of a meeting with a member of Parliament. I do not think it necessary to say any more about the substance of the proceedings.
    [4] The brief relevant chronology—relevant that is to this appeal—is as follows. The broadcast, as I say, was a radio broadcast on 6 November 1996 and the writ was issued on 8 January 1997. There was exchange of pleadings and amended pleadings, disclosure and so forth and the time came, in 1999, when, on 22 July, the defendant's application to strike the claim out for want of prosecution

or as an abuse of process was dismissed by Master Foster. He made an order for claimant's costs in cause of the application. Questions then aired about further specific discovery were adjourned to the judge in charge of the jury list.

[5] It was then that on 1 September 1999 the solicitors acting for the defendant wrote a letter headed 'without prejudice, save as to costs' in which they referred to a letter of the same date concerning a proposed amendment to their client's defence. The proposed amendment which was subsequently allowed was strengthening and widening the defence of justification, bringing into it serious allegations against the claimant, including allegations of dishonesty. The letter of 1 September ended in these terms:

'We would also emphasise to you that the Defendant has every intention of resisting this claim as strenuously as possible for as long as necessary. In these circumstances we are instructed to invite the Claimant to discontinue its claim on the following terms as to costs, namely the Claimant will pay the Defendant's costs of the action on the standard basis up to the date of service of the notice of discontinuance pursuant to CPR Part 38.3, including all costs not already provided for by Orders of the Court, to be taxed if not agreed. Should this offer of terms for the disposal of these proceedings not be accepted, the Defendant will draw its terms to the attention of the Court on his succeeding at trial and seek all costs incurred after seven days from the date of this letter on an indemnity basis.'

[6] That suggestion was not acceded to. The action continued. Gray J gave permission to amend the defence. There was an amended reply which reinforced allegations by the claimant that the defendant was malicious. There was a request for further information regarding the amended reply. On 1 December 1999, the claimant made what they referred to as a CPR Pt 36 offer to accept £1 and their costs in full and final settlement of the proceedings.

[7] In response to that, two days later, on 3 December 1999, the defendant's solicitors on instructions wrote to say that he would accept £50,000 in full and final settlement of his claim for costs in the proceedings if the action was settled within the next seven days. That was a letter which asserted that the defendant's estimated costs to date were in the order of £100,000. Those proposals did not produce a settlement.

[8] On 3 May 2000 the claimant wrote saying that they had received an offer of insurance in relation to the proceedings and that the premium they were going to be paying was £157,500 and that they would accept this proposal unless the defendant responded with a view to settlement within five days. Subsequently, on 8 November 2000, the claimant gave notice of entering into a conditional fee agreement with itself (the claimant being a firm of solicitors) and gave notice of a policy of insurance having been entered into.

[9] Accordingly, these offers and counter-offers having been made and turned down, in a trial in which each side was alleging that the other was dishonest and where the judge had ruled that the publication was on an occasion of qualified privilege, the jury found in favour of the defendant on the issue of justification. So there was judgment for the defendant. The judge was invited to make an indemnity costs order in favour of the defendant. He declined to do so, saying:

'I am by no means unsympathetic with the application that is made on behalf of the defendant that the claimant should be ordered to pay the costs of the action on an indemnity basis. But I have to say that it appears to me a   that Mr Shields is unable to bring himself within CPR Pt 36 and, in particular, r 21 of Pt 36. That rule is concerned with the position where the claimant does better than his Pt 36 offer. There is, in the CPR, no, as it were, converse provision which governs the position that arises where a defendant has made a proposal as to the way in which an action may be compromised. In those circumstances, it appears to me that I am driven back, when considering an

b   application for indemnity costs, to the more general basis on which costs can be ordered on an indemnity footing. The relevant rule is r 44.4, the note to which I think accurately summarises what I understand to be the effect of the authorities on this topic by saying that indemnity costs should only be awarded on an indemnity basis if there has been some sort of moral lack of probity or conduct deserving of moral condemnation on the part of the

c   paying party. I do not think that I can go so far as to say that applies in this case. Accordingly, I order that the defendant should have his costs on a standard basis, not an indemnity basis.'

[10] The essence of the main ground of appeal is that the judge misdirected himself in saying that costs should only be awarded on an indemnity basis if there

d   has been some sort of moral lack of probity or conduct deserving of moral condemnation on the part of the paying party.

[11] Mr Shields opened his submissions today by saying that the letter of 1 September 1999 was pivotal. But he developed submissions in the circumstances of the pleaded case, its result and the various offers and counter-offers that have

e   been made, to say not only that the judge applied the wrong principle but that this court should in substitution award indemnity costs to the defendant.

[12] It is axiomatic, I think, to start with CPR 1.1, which (as everybody knows) says: 'These Rules are a new procedural code with the overriding objective of enabling the court to deal with cases justly.'

f   [13] Being a new procedural code, the CPR are not to be taken as embodying or taking on board the baggage of the old Rules of the Supreme Court (RSC); and generally speaking, although there are exceptions, most of the procedural cases decided under the RSC (or indeed the County Court Rules) are not of relevance—or certainly not of central relevance—to an interpretation of these new rules.

g   [14] It is necessary to see what r 36.21 says. It says:

'(1) This rule applies where at trial—(a) a defendant is held liable for more; or (b) the judgment against a defendant is more advantageous to the claimant, than the proposals contained in a claimant's Part 36 offer.

h   (2) The court may order interest on the whole or part of any sum of money (excluded interest) awarded to the claimant at a rate not exceeding 10% above base rate for some or all of the period starting with the latest date on which the defendant could have accepted the offer without needing the permission of the court.

j   (3) The court may also order that the claimant is entitled to—(a) his costs on the indemnity basis from the latest date when the defendant could have accepted the offer without needing the permission of the court; and (b) interest on those costs at a rate not exceeding 10% above base rate.'

[15] That of course applies, as Gray J observed, to a claimant's Pt 36 offer. There is no equivalent provision in Pt 36 for a defendant's Pt 36 offer. Mr Shields submits that it should be applied by analogy so that where an offer such as was

made on 1 September 1999 is not accepted a defendant should be entitled to
indemnity costs if the defence succeeds.

[16] As Gray J observed, the court has to look to CPR Pt 44 for provisions relevant
to this matter. They are r 44.3 and parts of r 44.4. Dealing with r 44.3 first, we find
this:

'**44.3** (1) The court has discretion as to—(a) whether costs are payable by
one party to another; (b) the amount of those costs; and (c) when they are to
be paid ...

(4) In deciding what order (if any) to make about costs, the court must
have regard to all the circumstances, including—(a) the conduct of all the
parties; (b) whether a party has succeeded on part of his case, even if he has
not been wholly successful; and (c) any payment into court or admissible
offer to settle made by a party which is drawn to the court's attention
(whether or not made in accordance with Part 36) ...

(5) The conduct of the parties includes—(a) conduct before, as well as
during, the proceedings, and in particular the extent to which the parties
followed any relevant pre-action protocol; (b) whether it was reasonable for
a party to raise, pursue or contest a particular allegation or issue; (c) the
manner in which a party has pursued or defended his case or a particular
allegation or issue; and (d) whether a claimant who has succeeded in his
claim, in whole or in part, exaggerated his claim.'

[17] Rule 44.4 provides, under the heading 'Basis of assessment':

'(1) Where the court is to assess the amounts of costs (whether by
summary or detailed assessment) it will assess those costs—(a) on the
standard basis; or (b) on the indemnity basis, but the court will not in either
case allow costs which have been unreasonably incurred or are unreasonable
in amount.'

[18] The rule then goes on to indicate what costs on a standard basis and on
the indemnity basis involve.

[19] Mr Shields has referred us to two post-CPR authorities on the subject of
costs. The first of these was the case of *Petrotrade Inc v Texaco Ltd* [2001] 4 All ER 853,
a Court of Appeal decision in a constitution presided over by Lord Woolf MR, on
23 May 2000. That was a case where the court was considering costs in consequence
of r 36.21. Lord Woolf MR said (at 856):

'62. However, it would be wrong to regard the rule [36.21] as producing
penal consequences. An order for indemnity costs does not enable a claimant
to receive more costs than he has incurred. Its practical effect is to avoid his
costs being assessed at a lesser figure. When assessing costs on the standard
basis the court will only allow costs "which are proportionate to the matters
in issue" and "resolve any doubt which it may have as to whether costs were
reasonably incurred or reasonable and proportionate in amount in favour of
the paying party". On the other hand, where the costs are assessed on an
indemnity basis, the issue of proportionality does not have to be considered.
The court only considers whether the costs were unreasonably incurred or
for an unreasonable amount. The court will then resolve any doubt in favour
of the receiving party. Even on an indemnity basis, however, the receiving
party is restricted to recovering only the amount of costs which have been
incurred (see CPR 44.3 and 44.5).

a

63. The ability of the court to award costs on an indemnity basis and interest at an enhanced rate should not be regarded as penal because orders for costs, even when made on an indemnity basis, never actually compensate a claimant for having to come to court to bring proceedings ...

64. The power to order indemnity costs or higher rate interest is a means of achieving a fairer result for a claimant. If a defendant involves a claimant

b

in proceedings after an offer has been made, and in the event, the result is no more favourable to the defendant than that which would have been achieved if the claimant's offer had been accepted without the need for those proceedings, the message of r 36.21 is that, prima facie, it is just to make an indemnity order for costs and for interest at an enhanced rate to be awarded. However, the indemnity order need not be for the entire proceedings nor, as

c

I have already indicated, need the award of interest be for a particular period or at a particular rate. It must not however exceed the figure of 10% referred to in Pt 36.'

[20] So there we find that an award of costs on an indemnity basis is not intended to be penal and that regard must be had to what in the circumstances is

d

fair and reasonable.

[21] That message also appears in a short passage from the judgment of Brooke LJ in a case called *Baron v Lovell* [1999] CPLR 630, a Court of Appeal decision on 27 July 1999 in a court presided over by Lord Woolf MR. It concerned the question of sending an appropriately-authorised legal representative to attend

e

a pre-trial review. Of that Brooke LJ said (at 640):

'If a defendant's lawyers choose not to send a representative with appropriate authority to attend a pre-trial review and choose not to ensure that the client (who in this case should be equated with the defendant's insurer) attends the review, the judge, who is likely to be the trial judge, is

f

likely to note their absence. If he considers that that party has acted unreasonably in this way in connection with the litigation in breach of a direction of the court, there may come a time when he decides that it is appropriate to make an order for indemnity costs against that party, or to exercise his power to award interest on damages at a much higher rate than what is usual, if those powers are available to him. The whole thrust of the

g

CPR regime is to require the parties to behave reasonably towards each other in the conduct of the litigation. The old antagonistic point scoring, which used to drag personal injuries cases out and run up the costs, should now be at an end.'

h

[22] So there again the emphasis is on what is reasonable.

[23] Mr Shields submits that the judge was wrong to fetter his discretion in the way that he did. Mr Bacon emphasises that the *Petrotrade* case was concerned only with indemnity costs under r 36.21. He submits that there is a distinction between the court's discretion under that rule and under r 44.4. He refers to the case of *McPhilemy v Times Newspapers Ltd (No 2)* [2001] EWCA Civ 933 at [29],

j

[2001] 4 All ER 861 at [29], a libel case in which questions of costs arose, where Simon Brown LJ said (at 874):

'When dismissing the principal appeal, we left over for decision whether Times Newspapers Ltd should pay the claimant's costs of that appeal on a standard or an indemnity basis. Clearly rather more of a stigma attaches to an indemnity costs order made in this context than in the context of a r 36.21

offer, although even then no moral condemnation of the defendant's lawyers
is necessarily implied ...' *a*

[24] That suggests in itself that Gray J may have misdirected himself.

[25] Mr Bacon submits, contrary to what Lord Woolf MR said in the *Petrotrade*
case, that the stigma referred to by Simon Brown LJ imports some sort of
punitive effect. But, as I have indicated, Simon Brown LJ said that no moral *b*
condemnation was implied. Mr Bacon submits that there is no real difference
between an expression of disapproval and moral condemnation. He also referred
us to *Raja v Rubin* [1999] 3 All ER 73, [2000] Ch 274, a decision of 19 March 1999,
but that was a decision before the new procedural code of the CPR was in
operation. Mr Bacon came close to submitting that r 44.3 is not concerned with
matters going to indemnity costs, which was to be found in r 44.4. *c*

[26] Mr Monson, who dealt with the merits of the matter, submitted that
Gray J applied the correct test and that he correctly extracted it from the notes to
r 44.4 in the White Book which relied on pre-CPR cases. He submitted that there
is no real difference between conduct deserving moral condemnation and
unreasonable conduct of litigation in any manifestation. The respondent's *d*
written submissions in this court referred to numerous pre-CPR authorities and
submitted that their principles survived into the CPR.

[27] In my judgment, the judge here was wrong to constrain himself in the
way that he did. He was, I think, implicitly guided by pre-CPR authorities which
are no longer apt for the new procedural code in this respect. Under the CPR, it
is not, in my view, correct that costs are only awarded on an indemnity basis if *e*
there has been some sort of moral lack of probity or conduct deserving moral
condemnation on the part of the paying party. The court has a wide discretion
under r 44.3 which is not constrained, in my judgment, by authorities decided
under the rules which preceded the introduction of the CPR. The discretion has
to be exercised judicially, in all the circumstances, having regard to the matters *f*
referred to in r 44.3(4) and 44.3(5). The discretion as to the amount of costs
referred to in r 44.3(1)(b) includes a discretion to decide whether some or all of
the costs awarded should be on a standard or indemnity basis. Rule 44.4 describes
the way in which an assessment on each basis is to operate, but does not prescribe
the circumstances in which orders on one or the other of the bases is to be made.

[28] As the very word 'standard' implies, this will be the normal basis of *g*
assessment where the circumstances do not justify an award on an indemnity
basis. If costs are awarded on an indemnity basis, in many cases there will be
some implicit expression of disapproval of the way in which the litigation has
been conducted. But I do not think that this will necessarily be so in every case.
What is, however, relevant to the present appeal is that litigation can readily be *h*
conducted in a way which is unreasonable and which justifies an award of costs
on an indemnity basis, where the conduct could not properly be regarded as
lacking moral probity or deserving moral condemnation.

[29] The circumstances referred to in r 44.3(4) include any payment into court
or admissible offer to settle which each of the parties may have made. But it *j*
seems to me that in the present appeal the letter of 1 September 1999 by itself,
although relevant, may not take the case for indemnity costs very far. I do not
see that there is much to be made of an analogy for defendants with r 36.21. That
rule applies to claimants. There is no equivalent rule for defendants who must,
in my view, look elsewhere for means of putting themselves in the strongest
possible position as to costs.

a [30] The letter of 1 September 1999 was very close to an invitation by a defendant to the claimant to throw his hand in, and it made little real concession. I appreciate that it might be said that the offer gave away the possibility of costs on a more favourable basis than the standard basis for some or all of the case so far. But it cannot be right that every defendant in every case can put themselves in the way of claiming costs on an indemnity basis simply by inviting the claimant

b at an early stage to give up, discontinue and pay the defendant's costs on a standard basis. It might be different if a defendant offers to move some way towards a claimant's position and the result is more favourable to the defendant than that.

[31] Thus, in my view, the letter of 3 December 1999 may be rather more persuasive than the letter of 1 September 1999—although I emphasise that the

c court has to take all relevant circumstances into account.

[32] There will be many cases in which, although the defendant asserts a strong case throughout and eventually wins, the court will not regard the claimant's conduct of the litigation as unreasonable and will not be persuaded to award the defendant indemnity costs. There may be others where the conduct

d of a losing claimant will be regarded in all the circumstances as meriting an order in favour of the defendant of indemnity costs. Offers to settle and their terms will be relevant and, if they come within Pt 36, may, subject to the court's discretion, be determinative.

[33] Since, in my view, the judge proceeded on a mistaken view of the law, his decision should I think be set aside. The question then arises whether this court

e should proceed to exercise its discretion and make the decision anew. The court has power to do this, and Mr Shields invites us to do it. So does Mr Monson, who has made extensive submissions on the merits; although, of course, he argues for a different result from that for which Mr Shields contends.

[34] I am not persuaded that we should do this. We have a very small view of

f the conduct of the parties in this litigation. It is limited to the nature of the case to be derived from the pleadings, its result, a few letters, and quite abbreviated submissions by counsel. The judge heard the case over 12 days and heard all the evidence. He was well versed in the long previous preparatory history. I appreciate that the judge expressed sympathy with the application for indemnity costs, but I do not personally consider that I have a secure feel for this litigation

g in the round, so as to be able to judge fairly what the costs order should be. I have, for instance, no means of judging whether at trial the claimant's case was throughout obviously going to fail; or whether, although the jury's verdict was in favour of the defendant, it was a close-run thing. Nor is it clear to me whether the claimant's letter of 1 December 1999 was a genuine offer or the manifestation

h of a libel action with no substance. I am sure that there will have been many other aspects of each party's conduct which need to be considered and taken into account.

[35] For these reasons I would allow the appeal, order the judge's costs order to be set aside and remit the matter to him for further determination.

j
KAY LJ.

[36] I agree.

[37] I only want to add one other matter. The approach of the CPR is a relatively simple one: namely, if one party has made a real effort to find a reasonable solution to the proceedings and the other party has resisted that sensible approach, then the latter puts himself at risk that the order for costs may

be on an indemnity basis. What would be a reasonable solution will depend on all the circumstances of the case, and might, in a case which is clearly of no merit, *a* include pointing out, in such detail as is appropriate, the fundamental weaknesses of the case being presented by the other side and inviting consideration of abandonment. That was not the circumstances of the letter of 1 September 1999, which was simply an expression that the case was of no merit at all and inviting abandonment. If there had been more detail and more explanation, then it might *b* have carried greater weight in the general consideration of the circumstances.

[38] But for the reasons given by May LJ, I agree that this appeal should be allowed and the matter remitted to the judge for further consideration.

WARD LJ.

[39] I can have some sympathy for the judge who based himself largely on the *c* notes to the CPR 44.4, as they then appeared in the White Book to the effect that some disgraceful conduct deserving of moral condemnation was necessary to justify costs being awarded on an indemnity basis. That approach is erroneous for the reasons given by my Lords, with which I agree.

[40] Although I was tempted to seize upon the judge's introductory remark *d* that he was 'by no means unsympathetic with the application' for costs to be paid on an indemnity basis, and so robustly exercise my discretion to give effect to what may be read between the lines, I am persuaded by my Lords that we do not have the full feel of the case. So I too would allow the appeal, but send it back to the judge.

Appeal allowed.

Kate O'Hanlon   Barrister.

a # Capital Trust Investments Ltd v Radio Design TJ AB and others
[2002] EWCA Civ 135

b COURT OF APPEAL, CIVIL DIVISION
SCHIEMANN, CLARKE AND ARDEN LJJ
13 DECEMBER 2001, 15 FEBRUARY 2002

c *Arbitration – Stay of court proceedings – Conditional application – Application for summary judgment in event that application for stay unsuccessful – Whether step in proceedings – Whether agreement that 'any dispute' be settled by arbitrators providing for arbitration of claims which could not have been in contemplation of parties – Arbitration Act 1996, s 9(3).*

d The claimant company commenced proceedings against the defendant, a Swedish company, claiming damages for deceit or negligent misrepresentation or both in connection with an allotment of preference shares in the defendant for which the claimant had paid SEK 1,200 per share and which it alleged was actually worth no more than about SEK 200 per share. The alleged misrepresentations related essentially to the state of readiness of the defendant's mobile telecommunications product for commercial production and to the use to which *e* the proceeds of the allotment of shares would be put. The application form for the preference shares provided that 'any dispute arising out of this application … shall be settled exclusively by arbitrators …'. The master granted a stay of the proceedings under s 9(4) of the Arbitration Act 1996 on the ground that the parties had agreed that the claim should be submitted to arbitration. The *f* claimant's appeal against the master's order was dismissed. The claimant further appealed and the questions arose, inter alia, (i) whether, on the true construction of the agreement, the parties had agreed to submit some or all of the claims to arbitration and (ii) whether the defendant had taken a 'step in the proceedings' within the terms of s 9(3)[a] of the 1996 Act by making an application, subsequent to its application for a stay, for summary judgment in the event that the *g* application for a stay was unsuccessful.

Held – (1) A party might, at any rate in a compromise agreement supported by consideration, agree to release claims or rights of which he was unaware, even claims which could not on the facts known to the parties have been imagined, if *h* appropriate language was used to make plain that intention. However, in the absence of clear language, the court would be very slow to infer that a party intended to surrender rights and claims of which he was unaware and could not have been aware. Nevertheless, the submission in the instant case that a similar approach led to the conclusion that the claimant's claims for damages for *j* negligent and fraudulent misrepresentation were not intended by the parties to be referred to arbitration, on the ground that, when the contract was made, the parties could not have contemplated that the claimant might be able to advance a claim for damages of that kind, would be rejected: although it was true that the claimant was unaware of facts giving rise to the possibility of a claim for

---

a Section 9, so far as material, is set out at [54], below

negligence or fraudulent misrepresentation, it had also been unaware of facts
which might have given rise in the future to a claim for damages for breach of a
contract, and that would almost always be the case when a contract was made.
An arbitration or jurisdiction clause, such as that at issue, was very different from
a general release; its purpose was to provide a machinery for the resolution of
disputes which might arise in the future. The purpose of the phrase 'arising out
of' in the clause was to ensure that all claims which could fairly be said to arise b
out of the application were included: the parties would likely have had in mind
the possibility of claims for negligent misrepresentation, not because the claimant
was aware of such a claim at the time, but because such claims did sometimes
arise out of prospectuses where the investment proved less advantageous than
had been hoped. It was also not unknown for claims based on alleged fraudulent
misrepresentation to be made in such circumstances. It followed that the parties c
would have been likely to have wanted one tribunal to determine all such claims,
and it was far more likely than not that the parties had intended that claims for
damages for deceit or negligent misrepresentation and claims for damages for
breach of contract should all be determined by one tribunal. There was no
sensible basis upon which it could be held that, although the parties had used d
language which it was conceded was wide enough to include such claims, they
had to be taken to have intended to exclude them. It followed that the claims
advanced in the action all fell within the arbitration clause (see [46], [48]–[51],
[53], [66], below); *Bank of Credit and Commerce International SA (in liq) v Ali* [2001]
1 All ER 961 applied.

(2) The defendant's application for summary judgment was not a 'step in the e
proceedings' within the terms of s 9(3) of the 1996 Act. In order to constitute a
'step in the proceedings', the conduct of the party applying for a stay had to be
such as to demonstrate an election to abandon his right to a stay, in favour of
allowing the action to proceed, and to have the effect of invoking the jurisdiction
of the court. Moreover, an act which would otherwise be regarded as a step in f
the proceedings would not be treated as such if the applicant had specifically
stated that he intended to seek a stay. The application made by the defendant had
not expressed the defendant's willingness to go along with a determination of the
courts instead of arbitration. On the contrary, it made it clear that the application
for summary judgment was only advanced in the event that its application for a
stay was unsuccessful. It followed that the action would be stayed under s 9(4) of g
the 1996 Act so that it could be arbitrated and accordingly, the appeal would be
dismissed (see [56]–[60], [65], [66], below); *Patel v Patel* [1999] 1 All ER (Comm)
923 considered.

Decision of Jacob J [2001] 3 All ER 756 affirmed.

h

Notes

For acknowledgment of service and step in the proceedings, see 2 *Halsbury's Laws*
(4th edn reissue) para 627.

For the Arbitration Act 1996, s 9, see 2 *Halsbury's Statutes* (4th edn) (1999
reissue) 573. j

Cases referred to in judgment

Ashville Investments Ltd v Elmer Contractors Ltd [1988] 2 All ER 577, [1989] QB 488,
[1988] 3 WLR 867, CA.

Bank of Credit and Commerce International SA (in liq) v Ali [2001] UKHL 8, [2001] 1
All ER 961, [2001] 2 WLR 735.

a *Eagle Star Insurance Co Ltd v Yuval Insurance Co Ltd* [1978] 1 Lloyd's Rep 357, CA.

Harbour Assurance Co (UK) Ltd v Kansa General International Assurance Co Ltd [1993] 3 All ER 897, [1993] QB 701, [1993] 3 WLR 42, CA.

Houldsworth v City of Glasgow Bank (1880) 5 App Cas 317, HL.

Investors Compensation Scheme Ltd v West Bromwich Building Society, Investors Compensation Scheme Ltd v Hopkin & Sons (a firm), Alford v West Bromwich
b *Building Society, Armitage v West Bromwich Building Society* [1998] 1 All ER 98, [1998] 1 WLR 896, HL.

Kuwait Airways Corp v Iraq Airways Corp [1994] 1 Lloyd's Rep 276, CA.

Malik v Bank of Credit and Commerce International SA (in liq), Mahmud v Bank of Credit and Commerce International SA (in liq) [1997] 3 All ER 1, [1998] AC 20, [1997] 3 WLR 95, HL.
c *Patel v Patel* [1999] 1 All ER (Comm) 923, [2000] QB 551, [1999] 3 WLR 322, CA.

Pearson (S) & Son Ltd v Dublin Corp [1907] AC 351, [1904–7] All ER Rep 255, HL.

Pitchers Ltd v Plaza (Queensbury) Ltd [1940] 1 All ER 151, CA.

Appeal
d The claimant, Capital Trust Investments Ltd (CTIL), appealed with permission of Chadwick LJ granted on 23 March 2001 against the order of Jacob J on 16 February 2001 ([2001] 3 All ER 756) whereby he dismissed the claimant's appeal against the order of Master Bowman, on 27 June 2000, ordering a stay of the proceedings against the first defendant, Radio Design TJ AB. The second to
e seventh defendants, Tor Bjorn Johnson, Erik Miteregger, Arnfinn Roste, Chris Bataillard, JP Morgan International Capital Corp and Brummer & Partner Kapitalförvaltning AB, did not appear. The facts are set out in the judgment of the court.

Stephen Smith QC (instructed by *Gouldens*) for CTIL.
f *Alan Steinfeld QC* (instructed by *Reynolds Porter Chamberlain*) for Radio Design.

Cur adv vult

15 February 2002. The following judgment of the court was delivered.

g **CLARKE LJ** (giving the judgment of the court at the invitation of Schiemann LJ).

Introduction
[1] This is an appeal brought by permission of Chadwick LJ against an order of Jacob J dated 16 February 2001 ([2001] 3 All ER 756) dismissing the appeal of
h the claimant (CTIL) against an order of Master Bowman dated 27 June 2000 ordering a stay of the proceedings against the first respondent (Radio Design) under s 9(4) of the Arbitration Act 1996. The stay was granted on the ground that the parties had agreed that Radio Design's claim should be submitted to arbitration in Sweden.

j [2] Three issues arise for determination on this appeal. The first is whether Radio Design was a party to an agreement with CTIL containing an arbitration clause. This issue was determined in favour of Radio Design by both the master and the judge. Chadwick LJ said that, if it had stood alone, he would not have granted permission for a second appeal. The second issue is whether, if the answer to the first question is yes, the parties agreed, on the true construction of the agreement, to submit all or some of the claims in this action to arbitration in

Sweden. This point was not taken before the master or the judge, but has been *a* advanced because of the terms in which Chadwick LJ granted permission to appeal. The third point is whether, if the parties agreed to submit some or all of these claims to arbitration, CTIL has taken a step in the proceedings such as to deprive it of its right to seek a stay by reason of s 9(3) of the 1996 Act. This point was taken before the judge, but not before the master. Chadwick LJ expressed the view that it was a point of principle of sufficient general importance to merit *b* the consideration of this court on a second appeal.

[3] The action is brought in order to advance claims for damages for deceit and/or negligent misrepresentation in connection with an allotment of 33,333 B3 preference shares in Radio Design for which CTIL paid SEK 1,200 a share, and thus a total of SEK 40m (about £2·6m), in August 1998. CTIL says that the shares were worth no more than about SEK 200 per share. The alleged *c* misrepresentations related essentially to the state of readiness of Radio Design's mobile telecommunications product for commercial production and to the use to which the proceeds of the allotment of the shares would be put. As the judge colourfully put it, CTIL's case is that the picture painted to it was knowingly and deliberately false since the system was 'no more than an inchoate heap of junk *d* and the company and its directors knew that'.

[4] This appeal is concerned only with CTIL's claim against Radio Design, but CTIL also sues a number of other defendants, namely four individual directors and two corporate investors. As far as we are aware, none of those defendants seeks a stay of the proceedings. None of them could do so under the agreement relied upon by Radio Design. *e*

The amended particulars of claim

[5] In the amended particulars of claim CTIL relies upon a number of oral representations made at various meetings in London in February to July 1998 and upon written representations contained in various financial projections, but in *f* particular upon written representations contained in a document entitled Confidential Information Memorandum. The representations are said to have been made fraudulently and/or negligently and to have induced CTIL to buy the shares.

Confidential information memorandum *g*

[6] The memorandum (CIM) is dated 27 May 1998 and is in effect a prospectus. It is a substantial document of some 83 pages in length. It was sent to individual potential named investors including CTIL. On the first page, under the headings 'Radio Design AB Excellence in Radio System Concepts' and 'Private Placement of Series B3 Preferred Shares' the placement agent is named *h* as Enskilda Securities, which is or was a division of a Swedish bank and which we shall call 'Enskilda'. The CIM begins by saying that it does not constitute an offer to sell, or a solicitation of an offer to buy, any securities or any of the businesses or assets described in it.

[7] Thereafter, the first section of the CIM is entitled 'Notices to Investors'. It *j* begins by stating that Radio Design is furnishing the CIM solely for the consideration of institutional and sophisticated investors who have sufficient knowledge and experience to evaluate the merits and risks of such an investment and who have no need of liquidity in their investment and can afford to lose the whole investment. It makes clear that it is not intended that there should be a public placing and includes the following:

a 'Radio Design and its directors (being …) accept responsibility for the information contained in this Memorandum, including the information contained in this Memorandum that relates to Radio Design. To the best of the knowledge, information and belief of Radio Design and its directors (who have taken reasonable care to ensure that such is the case), the information contained in this Memorandum is in accordance with the facts

b and does not omit anything likely to affect the import of such information.

No person has been authorised to provide any information or to make any representation with respect to the company or the Placing Shares which is not contained in this Memorandum and, if given or made, such information or representation may not be relied upon as having been authorised by the company. Prospective investors may not rely on any information not

c contained in this Memorandum …

Radio Design has engaged the Placement Agent to act as placement agent and financial advisor with respect to the Placing Shares. The Placement Agent is not advising any person other than Radio Design with respect to the Placing, and will not be responsible to any subscriber of the Placing Shares

d for the protections afforded to customers of the Placement Agent or otherwise. The Placement Agent holds warrants to subscribe for 10,000 new common B shares at SEK 650 per share before 31 December 2000.

Any prospective investor will be required to acknowledge in the purchase contract that it has itself been and continues to be solely responsible for making its own independent investigation and appraisal of the business,

e operations, financial conditions, prospects, creditworthiness and affairs of the Company and the Placing Shares, and has not relied on and is not relying on any person to provide it with any information relating to such matters or to check or enquire into the adequacy, accuracy or reasonableness of any representation, warranty or statement, projection, assumption or

f information provided by or on behalf of the Company, including any contained in this Memorandum.

No representation or warranty, express or implied, is made by the Placement Agent or any of its affiliates or any of its or their directors, officers or employees as to the accuracy or completeness of the information

g contained herein …'

[8] The 'Notices to Investors' part of the CIM also makes it clear that Radio Design and Enskilda as placement agent reserved the right to reject any offer to subscribe for the shares for any reason. The body of the CIM sets out what it describes as risk factors and specifies the use which Radio Design intended to

h make of the proceeds of the subscription. It then sets out a considerable amount of detail about Radio Design. The CIM was signed by the directors of Radio Design.

[9] It is we think plain (and not in dispute) that both parties will wish to rely upon the contents of the CIM at any trial of the merits. CTIL will rely upon the

j representations contained in it, whereas Radio Design (and the directors) will rely upon the qualifications or exemptions. Examples both of the kind of representation likely to be relied upon by CTIL and of the kind of qualification and exemption likely to be relied upon by Radio Design can be seen in the extracts from the CIM quoted above.

[10] It is clear from the terms of the CIM, and indeed from other documents which were put before the court, that as placing agent Enskilda was acting as the

agent for Radio Design in connection with the placement or proposed placement
of the shares. In that capacity it prepared an application form and sent it to
interested investors including CTIL. We now turn to the application form
because, for present purposes, it is the most important document in the case.

The application form

[11] The copy of the application form which we have was signed by CTIL on
29 July 1998. It is described as an application form for subscription of shares in
Radio Design, to be submitted by 22 July to Enskilda. It then states: 'With
reference to the CIM ... we hereby subscribe for 33,333 Shares, issued at a price
of SEK 1,200 per share.' On its face that is a curious statement because it is plain
that the form is itself an application form and not (without more) a contractual
document as between CTIL and Radio Design.

[12] The form continues, so far as relevant:

'CTIL acknowledges and accepts that:

—This application for shares is binding and irrevocable;

—By submitting this application for shares we irrevocably authorise
Enskilda ... to subscribe for the above indicated number of Shares on our
behalf;

—We have read and understood the information included in the CIM,
dated 27 May 1998 and the letter entitled "Revisions to the intended
placement", dated 16 July 1998;

—The Articles of Incorporation, Section 3, of Radio Design, are to be
amended in respect of the amount payable on liquidation of the Shares, from
SEK 950 to SEK 1,200 (the "Amendment") and that the Amendment must be
resolved upon by an extraordinary general meeting of shareholders of Radio
Design (the "EGM") ...

—Due to the Amendment, the issuance of shares (the "New Issue") is
subject to the approval of the EGM;

—Radio Design has further confirmed that it will take the necessary steps
to execute the Amendment and the New Issue, immediately after (i) we have
deposited SEK 40 million into an escrow account of Enskilda ... held with
Skandinavska Enskilda Banken (the "Escrow Account"), the details of which
are set forth below), and (ii) Brummer ... Pictet Global ... Telecom Partners
... and Global Equity ... have together deposited an amount equal to or in
excess of SEK 88 million into the Escrow Account ...'

[13] The matters stated to be expressly acknowledged and accepted by CTIL
continue with a number of particular points, including the steps to be taken by
Radio Design to effect an EGM and the steps to be taken by Enskilda to refund
the SEK 40m deposit in the event, for example, that approval by an EGM was not
registered by the Swedish authorities. They also include an express authorisation
to Enskilda to subscribe for shares on CTIL's behalf subject to two conditions,
namely the EGM approving the amendment and the new issue and Enskilda
obtaining a valid certificate from Skandinavska Enskilda Banken (SEB)
confirming that the investors had together deposited an amount equal to or in
excess of SEK 128m into the escrow account.

[14] After the matters expressly acknowledged and accepted by CTIL, the
form continues:

a 'In connection with the submission of this application form we agree to arrange for an amount of SEK 40 million to be deposited in the Escrow Account, on a date yet to be determined but not later than 29 July 1998, in order that Enskilda .... can, on our behalf, subscribe for the Shares as agreed above.'

b [15] There follows the provision which formed the basis of Radio Design's application to the master, as follows:

'Applicable Law, Arbitration
This application for subscription of shares in Radio Design ... shall be governed by and construed in accordance with the laws of the country of Sweden with regard to the conflict of laws. Any dispute arising out of this
c application for shares in Radio Design ... shall be settled exclusively by arbitrators in accordance with the Swedish Arbitration Act ... The arbitration proceedings shall take place in Stockholm.'

[16] The application form then sets out details of the escrow account and
d provides a box in which appear the date, namely 29 July 1998 and the signature of CTIL. Finally the following appears above the date and two signatures on behalf of Enskilda:

'Confirmation by escrow account manager
We, Enskilda ... hereby agree to abide by the terms and conditions set
e forth above and to perform in accordance therewith.'

The subscription
[17] The EGM contemplated in the application form was held on 10 August 1998. It carried the 'Amendment' and approved an increase in capital by
f subscription to new B3 shares on the following conditions:

'1. The right to subscribe for the new shares—deviating from the shareholders' preferential right—shall be exclusive to legal entities that have given Enskilda ... power of attorney to subscribe for the new shares.
There shall be no over-subscription.
g 2. The new shares shall be issued at a price of SEK 1,200 per share, when the issue price has been fixed on the basis of the estimated market value of the new share ...'

[18] A document entitled 'Subscription List' was then issued which recited the
h resolutions passed at the EGM on 10 August and added: 'The board of directors of Radio Design ... may hereby invite to subscribe for shares in accordance with the resolution.' The following appears at the foot of the document:

'Enskilda ... hereby, by proxy, subscribe for 106,666 shares of series Preference B3.
j Stockholm 11 August 1998.
Enskilda ...'

The document was signed on behalf of Enskilda.
[19] During the hearing of the appeal it was not clear what happened then. It was agreed that the parties should be permitted to put further limited information before the court in that regard. As a result we received a letter from

Reynolds Porter Chamberlain on behalf of Radio Design dated 14 December
explaining the position as follows: a

> 'We have now ascertained that the allotment of shares took place
> electronically and there is no physical document recording the registration
> of shares following the allotment ... We understand that, as a matter of
> practice in Sweden, it is not possible for a company to hold its own issued but
> unallotted shares. We are informed by Osa Kjellander, in house counsel for   b
> Enskilda, that on the 19th August 1998 (4.43 pm) an account was opened
> with SEB (of which Enskilda was at that time a part) in which the issued
> shares were notionally "created". At 4.50 pm the shares were "allotted" into
> the names of companies and individuals. This was, in effect, a book keeping
> exercise. Ms Kjellander informs us that Enskilda is unable, due to issues of   c
> confidentiality, to confirm the identity of those companies and individuals
> but she was able to confirm that the shares were not registered to Enskilda.'

We subsequently received a letter from Gouldens on behalf of CTIL accepting
that account as accurate. It thus appears that, of the total of 106,666 shares
referred to in the subscription list, CTIL received 33,333 shares in the manner   d
described.

Was Radio Design party to an arbitration agreement?

[20] Both the master and the judge held that Radio Design was a party to an
agreement on the terms of the application form and that it was a party to the
arbitration clause contained in it. Mr Smith submits that they were wrong so to   e
hold. In a compelling argument he submits that the purpose of the application
form was to give Enskilda authority on behalf of CTIL to subscribe for the shares
at SEK 1,200 per share and to set up the terms upon which Enskilda were to
operate the escrow account, but that there is nothing in the form to suggest that
Radio Design was or was to be a party to a contract based upon it. Mr Steinfeld   f
accepts that the form did indeed have the two purposes relied upon by Mr Smith,
but submits that it had a further purpose, namely to apply to Radio Design for
33,333 of the new shares at SEK 1,200 per share.

[21] At one stage during the course of the argument it was thought that the
form might evidence an agreement between CTIL and Radio Design from the
time it was signed by CTIL, on the basis that the form was proposed to CTIL by   g
Enskilda as placing agent for Radio Design and that it contains or evidences
obligations on the part of Radio Design, as for example to hold an EGM.
However, we are persuaded that that is not correct, especially since neither
counsel espoused such an analysis.

[22] Mr Steinfeld's submissions, which were in essence accepted by the judge,   h
may be summarised in this way: (i) the application form was drawn up by
Enskilda as Radio Design's placement agent as the form which had to be used by
any person or entity who or which wanted to subscribe for the shares; (ii) the
form contained an irrevocable offer to Radio Design to subscribe for the shares at
SEK 1,200 per share subject to certain conditions being satisfied. Some of those   j
conditions had to be satisfied by Radio Design, but failure to do so would not be
a breach of contract but would simply deprive Enskilda of authority to subscribe
for the shares on CTIL's behalf; and (iii) the offer was accepted when the shares
were duly allotted, which was when Radio Design accepted Enskilda's offer
contained in the subscription list to subscribe for 106,666 shares on behalf of
those, including CTIL, who had given it authority to do so. It now appears that

a that occurred on or before 19 August when the 33,333 shares were, as it were, created and allotted to CTIL.

[23] As stated above, it is common ground that the application form, which was signed by CTIL and Enskilda both had the effect of creating Enskilda CTIL's agents by giving Enskilda irrevocable authority to subscribe for the shares on CTIL's behalf and had the effect that Enskilda bound itself as a principal to set up b and operate the escrow account in accordance with the terms of the application form. Moreover, we entirely accept Mr Smith's submission that those agreements came into effect on 29 July 1998 when the form was signed on behalf of CTIL. It does not, however, follow that the form was not also an offer to Radio Design. It is agreed that Enskilda was wearing two hats when signing the form. The question is whether it was also wearing a third hat, as agent of Radio Design, c and, if so whether a contract came into existence between Radio Design and CTIL on the terms of the form as found by the master and the judge.

[24] Mr Smith submits that the form was not an offer to Radio Design to do anything and that Radio Design was not interested in the rights and obligations to which the form gave rise, which (he says) no doubt explains why there is no d evidence that Radio Design ever saw the form or asked to see it. He submits that the subscription relationship between CTIL and Radio Design commenced on 11 August 1998 when Enskilda signed the subscription list on CTIL's behalf. Mr Smith further submits that the judge paid too much attention to the form of the document and insufficient regard to its substance.

[25] There is, in our judgment, considerable force in Mr Smith's submissions e and we would not reject them as emphatically as the judge did when he said that the answer to the question whether the arbitration clause was part of a contract between Radio Design and CTIL was 'obviously so'. The form must be construed as a whole and set against the surrounding circumstances. Approaching the matter in that way, we have reached the conclusion that the f master and the judge were correct and that Mr Steinfeld's submissions are to be preferred to those of Mr Smith. Our reasons are shortly as follows.

[26] The form is described as an application form for subscription of shares in Radio Design. It was prepared by Enskilda as Radio Design's placing agent. We do not think that there can be any doubt that Radio Design was aware that investors were being asked to apply for shares on a form designed by Enskilda as g its agent. The form was to be submitted to Enskilda. It seems to us that the natural meaning of the form in these circumstances is that it was what it was stated to be, namely an application for shares to Radio Design and that the application was to be made by submitting the form to Enskilda as Radio Design's agent. Thus the expression 'this application for shares' in the form was an h application to Radio Design for shares in Radio Design made by submitting the form to Enskilda as Radio Design's agent. At the same time, by its signature on the form, CTIL created Enskilda its agent for the purposes of subscribing for the shares. We accept Mr Steinfeld's submission that that was essentially a matter of mechanics, which was a sensible arrangement, given that Swedish company law j requires a subscriber to sign a subscription list, so that Enskilda was authorised to sign the subscription list on behalf of the investors. It is plain that Radio Design was aware what was happening because, as set out above, it was resolved at the EGM that the right to subscribe to the new shares should be exclusive to the legal entities which had given Enskilda power of attorney to subscribe for the new shares. That power of attorney or authority was conferred on Enskilda by the application form.

[27] The escrow arrangement was also essentially a matter of mechanics to ensure, on the one hand, that the investors provided the money which would be available to Radio Design if it accepted the offer and, on the other hand, that the money would be repaid to the investors if for any reason the offer became ineffective because of failure of a condition precedent or because Radio Design did not accept the offer. The escrow arrangement thus protected the company and the investors and it was natural that Enskilda should act as principals with regard to it.

[28] It seems to us that it is important to have in mind the underlying purpose of the application form, namely to apply to Radio Design for its shares. As the judge said, significantly it was for Radio Design to accept or refuse the offer. He added that once one appreciates that the document is an offer document there is really only one answer to the question 'to whom is the offer made?'. Mr Smith submits that that is an entirely inappropriate question. He submits that a perusal of the form as a whole shows that the form did not contain an offer to Radio Design and that Enskilda was not acting as the agent of Radio Design but only in the two capacities to which we have already referred. However, we do not agree.

[29] As we see it, Mr Smith's argument disregards the underlying, and indeed express, purpose of the form, namely as an application form for the shares. That application could only be made to Radio Design or, in this case, to its placing agent Enskilda. The application could not be being made to Enskilda as agent for CTIL. Nor could it be being made to Enskilda as principal. If it was an application at all, it must have been made to Enskilda as agent of Radio Design. It was an integral part of the whole subscription process, as evidenced by the condition that other investors should contribute SEK 88m to the escrow account.

[30] We have set out above some of the matters expressly acknowledged and accepted by CTIL by signing the form. It is we think plain that those provisions were intended to have contractual effect. If that is correct, it seems to us to be a pointer to the conclusion that it was intended that Radio Design should be a party to the contract to be evidenced by the form if it accepted CTIL's offer to subscribe to the shares. For example, the express statement that CTIL had read and understood the information contained in the CIM would not be relevant if the purpose of the form were simply to appoint Enskilda as CTIL's agent and to create the escrow. It only makes sense as a term in a contract with Radio Design upon which Radio Design could, if necessary, rely if it accepted CTIL's irrevocable offer to subscribe for the shares and a dispute subsequently arose.

[31] Finally, we should say a word about what Mr Smith described as CTIL's timing point to which we have already referred. It is that a contract came into existence between CTIL and Enskilda when the form was signed by CTIL and that the arbitration agreement thus came into effect at that time. Mr Smith submits that it is a strained and unrealistic approach to the form to conclude that a contract on the terms of the form also came into existence between CTIL and Radio Design much later, namely on allotment of the shares. He submits that such an approach overlooks the fact that there is no evidence that Radio Design was informed of the terms of the form, and in particular of the arbitration clause, and that it appears to proceed on the assumption that at one and the same moment Enskilda could be making an offer on behalf of one principal and accepting an offer on behalf of another.

[32] However, we do not think that there is any difficulty about such an analysis once it is appreciated that the underlying purpose of CTIL in filling in the form was, as the form says, to apply for subscription of shares in Radio Design

a because the only way in which the form could itself be an application for such subscription would be on the basis that it was an application to Radio Design, either directly, or, as in this case, to its placing agent Enskilda.

[33] This analysis seems to us to be supported by the terms of the applicable law and arbitration clause itself, which is quoted above. The clause expressly provides for 'this application for subscription for shares' to be governed by

b Swedish law 'with regard to the conflict of laws' and that 'any dispute arising out of this application for shares in Radio Design ... shall be settled exclusively by arbitrators' in Sweden. Since the application for shares is being made to Radio Design, those words naturally cover disputes between the applicant, CTIL, and the company, Radio Design. Indeed they are more apt to cover such a dispute than a dispute as to the terms of the agency agreement between CTIL and

c Enskilda or as to the terms upon which Enskilda was agreeing to operate the escrow account. They are no doubt sufficiently wide to cover all three classes of dispute, but they most naturally cover a dispute between CTIL and Radio Design.

[34] In his skeleton argument, Mr Smith submits that the judge's conclusion

d renders meaningless the formal assumption of responsibility by Radio Design in the CIM for the information provided in it. That is because of the immunity from suit for misrepresentations inducing a subscription for shares which (as we understand it) Swedish law confers on Swedish companies. That immunity is similar (if not identical) to the rule which previously applied here, as established by *Houldsworth v City of Glasgow Bank* (1880) 5 App Cas 317. Mr Smith points to

e the facts that the CIM was prepared by Linklaters & Paines and that it was given to CTIL in London, considered by CTIL in London and acted on by CTIL in London.

[35] However, we see no reason not to accept Mr Steinfeld's submission that it will be open to CTIL to argue before the Swedish arbitrators that the clause

f only applies the principles of Swedish conflicts of law and that, by the application of those principles, the misrepresentations complained of should be determined according to English law. However, whether that is so or not, the terms of the agreement seem to us to be reasonably clear.

[36] In all the circumstances we have reached the conclusion that the judge was right and would only add a word on the material sent to us after the

g argument was concluded. Reynolds Porter Chamberlain enclosed a page of the shareholders agreement asserting that it was plain from it that the identities of CTIL and the other proposed investors referred to in the application form were well known to Radio Design. In response Gouldens took issue with that conclusion, enclosed a complete copy of the shareholders' agreement and drew

h attention to the jurisdiction clause in it, which provided that any matter arising out of or in connection with the agreement should be brought before the Swedish courts, which should have exclusive jurisdiction. Gouldens submitted that it was strange indeed that a dispute between the parties to the agreement (of which Radio Design was one) should be the subject of litigation whereas, on Radio

j Design's case, a dispute between each individual subscriber and Radio Design arising out of the allotment must proceed to arbitration.

[37] We agree that there are some oddities in the position, but these considerations do not seem to us to alter the conclusion that Radio Design became a party to a contract on the terms of the application form, including the arbitration clause, when it allotted shares in acceptance of the offer. We have not seen a copy of the shareholders' agreement signed by CTIL, but the draft, which

names CTIL and the other investors as a party, expressly refers to 'an Application
Form of even date herewith' and thus supports the conclusion that Radio Design,   *a*
which signed the copy of the agreement which we have seen, was, as we would
have expected, but contrary to Mr Smith's submission, aware of the application
form.

[38] We do not know why the jurisdiction clause in the shareholders'
agreement was in different terms from the jurisdiction clause in the application   *b*
form, but no one has suggested that its effect is that CTIL and Radio Design
agreed that the claims being advanced by CTIL in this action should be submitted
to the exclusive jurisdiction of the courts of Sweden.

[39] For the reasons which we have given, our conclusion is that the judge was
right to hold that the application form was an offer to Radio Design to subscribe   *c*
for shares on certain terms, which had contractual effect when the offer was
subsequently accepted by allotment of the shares to CTIL. Since the form
included the arbitration clause, the next question is whether, on the true
construction of the clause, the parties agreed to submit to arbitration all or some
of the claims which CTIL seeks to make in this action.

d

True construction of arbitration clause

[40] As we indicated above, this point was not taken either before the master
or before the judge. Nor was it contained in CTIL's appellant's notice or in its
skeleton argument in support of its application for permission to appeal. It has
now been raised because, in giving permission to appeal, Chadwick LJ said that   *e*
the question whether CTIL's claim that it was induced to subscribe for shares in
Radio Design by fraudulent and/or negligent misrepresentation falls within the
arbitration agreement was at least arguable. Radio Design raised no objection to
the point being taken for the first time on appeal to this court and, accordingly,
we have decided to permit it to be raised. It has been treated as a question of   *f*
English law.

[41] After receiving Chadwick LJ's reasons, there followed some speculation
on the part of Radio Design as to how the point might be put. One possibility
suggested was that it might be said that a claim for rescission would be outside
the clause, but, whether that is so or not, as Mr Steinfeld observed in his skeleton
argument, it is not relevant here because CTIL does not seek rescission of the   *g*
agreement but claims damages for negligent or fraudulent misrepresentation. In
any event Mr Smith does not espouse it, very fairly observing that it would be a
difficult point to argue in the light of s 7 of the 1996 Act.

[42] A second possibility might have been an argument that a claim for
damages for negligent or fraudulent misrepresentation inducing a contract does   *h*
not give rise to a 'dispute arising out of this application for shares' within the
meaning of the clause. However, as we understand it, Mr Smith does not
advance a submission along these lines. He is, in our opinion, right to adopt this
stance. He fairly draws attention to evidence of Swedish law that the words
'arising out of' are in principle wide enough to encompass a claim based on   *j*
pre-contractual representations. We would simply add that it seems to us that, if
the matter were to be determined under English law, such a claim would, as a
matter of language, be held to arise out of the application for shares since CTIL's
case is that it was induced to make that very application by the misrepresentations
alleged. It is not necessary to discuss this point further given the concession made
by Mr Smith.

a [43] The question as formulated by Mr Smith can be stated in this way: whether (1) assuming that CTIL and Radio Design were parties to the arbitration agreement and (2) even though the words of the agreement are so wide that, read literally, they would encompass pre-contractual misrepresentations, (3) the parties are therefore to be taken to have intended that the agreement should extend so far, (4) even though the innocent party could not possibly have been **b** aware at the time that it might have a claim in deceit and/or for negligent misrepresentation. Mr Smith submits that the answer to that question is No.

[44] Mr Smith concedes that he can point to no case which is directly in point. However, he refers to two. The first is *S Pearson & Son Ltd v Dublin Corp* [1907] AC 351, [1904–7] All ER Rep 255, which is authority for the proposition that it is not possible to exclude liability for one's own fraud. However, as we think Mr **c** Smith recognises, that principle has no direct application here because the clause relied upon by CTIL does not exclude liability for fraud but simply refers the dispute to arbitration in Sweden for determination in accordance with the principles of Swedish conflicts of law. It does not, in our opinion, assist CTIL.

[45] More importantly, Mr Smith relies upon the approach recently adopted **d** by the House of Lords in *Bank of Credit and Commerce International SA (in liq) v Ali* [2001] UKHL 8, [2001] 1 All ER 961, where the question was one of construction of a settlement agreement which released BCCI from—

e 'all or any claims whether under statute, common law or in equity of whatsoever nature that exist or may exist and, in particular, all or any claims rights or applications of whatsoever nature that the applicant has or may have or has made or could make in or to the industrial tribunal, except the applicant's rights under [the bank's] pension scheme.'

The question for decision was whether the employee was prevented by that **f** agreement from advancing a claim for what have become known as stigma damages, that is damages caused by his association with BCCI as a bank of ill-repute. The claim was put both as a claim for the breach of an implied term of his contract of employment under which BCCI owed him a duty not to carry on a dishonest or corrupt business and as a claim in deceit on the basis that he had been induced to work for the bank by the false representation that it was an **g** honest and creditworthy financial institution: see [2001] 1 All ER 961 at [4] per Lord Bingham of Cornhill.

[46] The correct approach to the construction of the release can we think be clearly seen from the following passages from the speech of Lord Bingham:

h '[8] I consider first the proper construction of this release. In construing this provision, as any other contractual provision, the object of the court is to give effect to what the contracting parties intended. To ascertain the intention of the parties the court reads the terms of the contract as a whole, giving the words used their natural and ordinary meaning in the context of **j** the agreement, the parties' relationship and all the relevant facts surrounding the transaction so far as known to the parties. To ascertain the parties' intentions the court does not of course inquire into the parties' subjective states of mind but makes an objective judgment based on the materials already identified. The general principles summarised by Lord Hoffmann in *Investors Compensation Scheme Ltd v West Bromwich Building Society, Investors Compensation Scheme Ltd v Hopkin & Sons (a firm), Alford v West Bromwich*

Building Society, Armitage v West Bromwich Building Society [1998] 1 All ER 98
at 114–115, [1998] 1 WLR 896 at 912–913 apply in a case such as this.

[9] A party may, at any rate in a compromise agreement supported by
valuable consideration, agree to release claims or rights of which he is
unaware and of which he could not be aware, even claims which could not
on the facts known to the parties have been imagined, if appropriate
language is used to make plain that that is his intention ...

[10] But a long and in my view salutary line of authority shows that, in the
absence of clear language, the court will be very slow to infer that a party
intended to surrender rights and claims of which he was unaware and could
not have been aware.'

Lord Bingham then considered a number of the decided cases in that line of
authority and concluded:

'[17] ... I think these authorities justify the proposition advanced in para 10
above and provide not a rule of law but a cautionary principle which should
inform the approach of the court to the construction of an instrument such
as this ... the judges I have quoted expressed themselves in terms more
general than was necessary for decision of the instant case, and I share their
reluctance to infer that a party intended to give up something which neither
he, nor the other party, knew or could know that he had.'

[47] The majority of the House of Lords (Lord Hoffmann dissenting) held that
the employees' claims were not precluded by the release. Lord Browne-Wilkinson
simply agreed with Lord Bingham. Lord Nicholls and Lord Clyde made speeches
in which, as we read them, they adopted what was essentially the same approach
as that adopted by Lord Bingham. It is perhaps of note that Lord Nicholls was
struck by the fact that neither party could have been aware of the possibility of a
claim for stigma damages when they agreed the release because the possibility of
such a claim only arose when, as Lord Nicholls put it (at [33]), the House of Lords
changed the law in *Malik v Bank of Credit and Commerce International SA (in liq)*,
Mahmud v Bank of Credit and Commerce International SA (in liq) [1997] 3 All ER 1,
[1998] AC 20.

[48] Mr Smith submits that a similar approach leads to the conclusion that
CTIL's claims for damages for negligent and fraudulent misrepresentation were
not intended by the parties to be submitted to arbitration. He recognises that this
is a very different case from *Ali*'s case, but he submits that when the contract was
made the parties (and in particular CTIL) could not have contemplated that CTIL
might be able to advance a claim for damages of this kind. In this regard he relies
upon this passage in the speech of Lord Clyde ([2001] 1 All ER 961 at [86]):

'Even without formulating any definition of the precise scope of the
agreement, it seems to me that if the parties had intended to cut out a claim
of whose existence they could have no knowledge they would have
expressed that intention in words more precise than the generalities which
they in fact used. In so far as Mr Naeem may also seek to present a claim in
tort for fraudulent misrepresentation inducing him to start the employment
in the first place or to continue in it thereafter, while the legal basis for such
a claim may not be particularly novel, the idea of such a claim at the time
when the parties made the agreement at the termination of the employment

seems to me correspondingly remote from what the parties might reasonably be taken in the circumstances to have contemplated.'

[49] Mr Smith submits that much the same can be said here, but we are unable to accept that submission. This seems to us to be a very different situation from that being considered by the House of Lords in *Ali*'s case. It is true that CTIL was unaware of facts giving rise to the possibility of a claim for negligent or fraudulent misrepresentation. However, it was also unaware of facts which might give rise in the future to a claim for damages for breach of contract. That will almost always be the case at the time the contract is made.

[50] An arbitration or jurisdiction clause is very different from a general release. The purpose of such a clause is to provide a machinery for the resolution of disputes which might arise in the future. It is not, we think, suggested that the clause would not be wide enough to include claims for breach of contract, whether committed negligently or fraudulently or otherwise. In any event, the clause is in our judgment plainly wide enough to include such claims. As we see it, the purpose of using the wide words 'arising out of' is to ensure that all claims which can fairly be said to arise out of the application are included. The parties would be likely to have in mind the possibility of claims for negligent misrepresentation arising out of the CIM, not because CTIL was aware of such a claim at the time it signed the form or at the time the contract was made but because experience suggests that such claims do sometimes arise out of prospectuses where the investment proves less advantageous than the investor had hoped. It is also not unknown for claims based on alleged fraudulent misrepresentation to be made in such circumstances.

[51] In our judgment the parties would be likely to have wanted one tribunal to determine all such claims. It seems to us to be far more likely than not that the parties intended that claims for damages for deceit or negligent misrepresentation and claims for damages for breach of contract should all be determined by one tribunal. In these circumstances we see no sensible basis upon which it could be held that, although the parties used language which it is conceded is wide enough to include such claims, they must be taken to have intended to exclude them.

[52] In *Ashville Investments Ltd v Elmer Contractors Ltd* [1988] 2 All ER 577, [1989] QB 488 and *Harbour Assurance Co (UK) Ltd v Kansa General International Assurance Co Ltd* [1993] 3 All ER 897, [1993] QB 701, claims for rectification of a contract and claims for a declaration of non-liability under a contract on the ground of illegality were respectively held to be within arbitration clauses using similar language to that used in the instant case. In both those cases the court emphasised the likelihood that the parties would have wanted one-stop adjudication. Thus Bingham LJ said in the *Ashville Investments* case:

'I would be very slow to attribute to reasonable parties an intention that there should in any foreseeable eventuality be two sets of proceedings.' (See [1988] 2 All ER 577 at 599, [1989] QB 488 at 517.)

See also to the same effect per Hoffmann LJ in the *Harbour Assurance* case, quoting that passage ([1993] 3 All ER 897 at 917, [1993] QB 701 at 726).

[53] In all these circumstances we reject Mr Smith's submission and hold that the claims advanced in this action are all within the arbitration clause, when construed in accordance with the principles summarised by Lord Bingham in para [8] of his speech in *Ali*'s case quoted above.

Step in the proceedings

[54] As indicated above, CTIL asserted before the judge, but not before the master, that Radio Design was not entitled to apply for a stay of this action because it took a 'step in the proceedings' within the meaning of s 9(3) of the 1996 Act. Section 9(3) and (4) provides as follows:

'(3) An application may not be made by a person before taking the appropriate procedural step (if any) to acknowledge the legal proceedings against him or after he has taken any step in those proceedings to answer the substantive claim.

(4) On an application under this section the court shall grant a stay unless satisfied that the arbitration agreement is null and void, inoperative, or incapable of being performed.'

[55] It is common ground that, on the assumption that these claims are within the arbitration agreement to which both Radio Design and CTIL are parties, Radio Design is entitled to a stay unless it took a step in the proceedings within the meaning of s 9(3). Section 9(3) is for present purposes in similar terms to s 1(1) of the Arbitration Act 1975 and s 4 of the Arbitration Act 1950. The question what amounts to a step in the proceedings has been considered a number of times under those sections and their predecessors: see eg *Pitchers Ltd v Plaza (Queensbury) Ltd* [1940] 1 All ER 151, *Eagle Star Insurance Co Ltd v Yuval Insurance Co Ltd* [1978] 1 Lloyd's Rep 357, *Kuwait Airways Corp v Iraq Airways Corp* [1994] 1 Lloyd's Rep 276 and *Patel v Patel* [1999] 1 All ER (Comm) 923, [2000] QB 551.

[56] In the *Eagle Star* case, in a passage which was subsequently followed in the *Kuwait Airways* case, Lord Denning MR ([1978] 1 Lloyd's Rep 357 at 361) put the underlying principle in this way:

'On those authorities, it seems to me that in order to deprive a defendant of his recourse to arbitration a "step in the proceedings" must be one which impliedly affirms the correctness of the proceedings and the willingness of the defendant to go along with a determination by the Courts of law instead of arbitration'.

[57] More recently, this court considered s 9(3) of the 1996 Act in *Patel v Patel*. Lord Woolf MR said ([1999] 1 All ER (Comm) 923 at 925, [2000] QB 551 at 555) that the old law was conveniently summarised in *Mustill & Boyd: Commercial Arbitration* (2nd edn, 1989) p 472, where the editors said:

'The reported cases are difficult to reconcile, and they give no clear guidance on the nature of a step in the proceedings. It appears, however, that two requirements must be satisfied. First, the conduct of the applicant must be such as to demonstrate an election to abandon his right to stay, in favour of allowing the action to proceed. Second, the act in question must have the effect of invoking the jurisdiction of the court.'

As we read Lord Woolf MR's judgment, a similar approach should be adopted under the 1996 Act. In the same case ([1999] 1 All ER (Comm) 923 at 927–928, [2000] QB 551 at 558) Otton LJ approved the following statement at para 6.19 of Merkin *Arbitration Law* (1991):

'The old authorities, which remain good law under the 1996 Act, established the following propositions ... (e) An act which would otherwise a be regarded as a step in the proceedings will not be treated as such if the applicant has specifically stated that he intends to seek a stay.'

[58] Applying those principles, the judge held that Radio Design had not taken a step in the proceedings within the meaning of s 9(3) of the 1996 Act. We entirely agree. The facts are shortly these. Radio Design issued an application for b a stay on 6 December 1999. On 22 February 2000 the application was amended to refer expressly to s 9 of the 1996 Act and to make the assertion that Radio Design had filed an acknowledgment of service but that it had 'not taken any step in the action (such as filing a defence) to answer the substantial claim'. Both parties served evidence including evidence of Swedish law, although by the time the matter came before the judge it was agreed that there was no difference c between English and Swedish law as to the principles applicable to the questions who were parties to the agreement and what the agreement meant.

[59] Before the application was heard by the master, on 2 May 2000, Radio Design issued a further application notice in which it recited the fact that an application for a stay had been made and continued:

d
'In the event that its application for a stay is unsuccessful, the first defendant [ie Radio Design] applies for summary judgment against the claimant ...'

The ground was that under Swedish law the claim had no real prospect of e succeeding because under Swedish law a company is not liable for misrepresentations made on its behalf in connection with an issue of shares.

[60] It appears to us that that application was not a 'step in the proceedings' on the basis of the principles set out above. Thus, it did not (in the words of Lord Denning) express the willingness of Radio Design to go along with a f determination of the courts instead of arbitration. On the contrary, it made it clear that the application for summary judgment was only advanced 'in the event that its application for a stay is unsuccessful'. In Merkin's words, approved by Otton LJ, the application made it clear that it was specifically seeking a stay, with the result that a step which would otherwise be a step in the proceedings, namely an application for summary judgment, is not so treated.

g [61] Thereafter the master heard evidence of Swedish law which covered the issues raised in both summonses, which were heard at the same time. It was no doubt thought by both parties and the court that that was a sensible step because there was a considerable overlap between the issues. No one objected and CTIL did not assert that Radio Design could not now make its application for a stay h because it had taken a step in the proceedings within the meaning of s 9(3) of the 1996 Act. Radio Design's skeleton argument before the master made it clear that the application for summary judgment was only being made 'in the event of the court refusing such stay'.

[62] The hearing took place before the master on 14 and 15 June 2000 and he j reserved judgment. He gave judgment on the stay on 27 June and asked the parties whether in view of that judgment either party wanted him to deliver judgment on the summary judgment application. Both parties invited him to do so in case his judgment on the stay was set aside on appeal. He handed down his judgment on that question on 31 July 2000. He made an order dismissing the action, but it is now agreed that that order should not have been made because the action had been stayed.

[63] The judge heard the appeal against the stay on 18 and 19 January 2001.
He handed down his judgment on 16 February and refused to hear an appeal *a*
against the master's second order. He did, however, expressly discharge the
order, no doubt in the light of his decision that CTIL's claim must be heard by
arbitration in Sweden.

[64] We have already expressed our view, in agreement with the judge, that
Radio Design did not take a step in the proceedings when it made its application *b*
for summary judgment on 2 May. Nor, in our judgment, did it do so thereafter.
The hearing before the master was conducted on the same basis as set out in the
summons, namely that Radio Design's application for summary judgment was
being made only if a stay was refused. We do not think it can fairly be held that
that position changed when the parties asked the master to deliver a judgment on
the summary judgment application because they only did so in case an appeal *c*
against the stay failed. There was equally no change before the judge.

[65] In short, Radio Design has at no stage indicated a willingness that the
courts should determine CTIL's claims instead of arbitrators. On the contrary, it
has asserted throughout that the action should be stayed under s 9(4) of the 1996
Act. We would therefore dismiss the appeal on this ground. *d*

Conclusions

[66] For the reasons set out above we dismiss CTIL's appeal on all three
grounds and uphold the order of the master and the judge that the action be
stayed under s 9(4) of the 1996 Act so that it can be arbitrated in Sweden.

Appeal dismissed.

Kate O'Hanlon   Barrister.

Rees v Darlington Memorial Hospital NHS Trust

a

[2002] EWCA Civ 88

b COURT OF APPEAL, CIVIL DIVISION
WALLER, ROBERT WALKER AND HALE LJJ
19 DECEMBER 2001, 14 FEBRUARY 2002

c *Damages – Unwanted pregnancy – Negligence – Disabled woman wishing to be sterilised because of her disability – Surgeon aware of reason for sterilisation but performing operation negligently – Woman becoming pregnant and giving birth to healthy child – Whether disabled woman entitled to recover costs of bringing up healthy child attributable to her disability where child conceived as a result of negligently-performed sterilisation.*

d The claimant, a woman with a genetic condition which left her severely visually disabled, wished to be sterilised. The consultant who carried out the operation had been informed of her disability, and knew that her reasons for wanting the operation included her belief that her eyesight would bar her from looking after a child. The sterilisation operation was performed negligently, and the claimant *e* subsequently gave birth to a son. Although there was a risk that he had inherited his mother's genetic condition, that risk was low. In proceedings for negligence against the defendant hospital trust, the claimant sought damages for the full costs of bringing up her child. The judge ruled against the claimant on the determination of a preliminary issue, and she appealed. On the appeal, the Court of Appeal considered whether recovery was precluded by a House of Lords *f* authority that established that able-bodied parents could not recover damages for the costs of bringing up a healthy child born as a result of medical negligence or whether an analogy could be drawn with a Court of Appeal authority which established that able-bodied parents of a disabled child, born as a result of such negligence, could recover those costs of rearing the child that were attributed to his disabilities.

g

Held – (Waller LJ dissenting) Where, to the knowledge of the surgeon, a disabled woman wished to be sterilised because of her disabilities but subsequently gave birth to a healthy child as a result of the sterilisation being negligently performed, she was entitled to recover as damages those extra costs of bringing up the child *h* that were attributable to her disability. There was a crucial difference between such a parent and an able-bodied parent of a healthy child. Although able-bodied parents would benefit from a nanny or other help in looking after the child, they did not need such help in order to be able to discharge the basic parental responsibility of looking after the child properly and safely, and to avoid the risk *j* that the child might have to be taken away to be looked after by social services or others, to the detriment of the child as well as the parent. In contrast, a disabled parent might need help if she were to be able to discharge the most ordinary tasks involved in the parental responsibility which had been placed upon her as a result of the defendant's negligence. Accordingly, just as the extra costs involved in discharging that responsibility towards a disabled child could be recovered, so too could the extra costs involved in a disabled parent discharging that responsibility towards a healthy child. There was nothing unfair, unjust, unreasonable, unacceptable or morally repugnant in permitting such recovery, at least where the surgeon knew of the woman's disability and was aware that it was the reason why she wished to avoid having a child. It followed in the instant case that the appeal would be allowed to the extent of setting aside the judge's ruling, and substituting a ruling that the claimant might claim those extra costs, if any, of bringing up her child as were attributable to her disability (see [22]–[24], [26], [34], [37], [41], [42], below).

Parkinson v St James and Seacroft University Hospital NHS Trust [2001] 3 All ER 97 applied.

McFarlane v Tayside Health Board [1999] 4 All ER 961 distinguished.

Notes

For damages recoverable for a negligently-performed sterilisation, see 12(1) Halsbury's Laws (4th edn reissue) para 896.

Cases referred to in judgments

Bank of Credit and Commerce International (Overseas) Ltd (in liq) v Price Waterhouse (No 2) [1998] PNLR 564, CA.

Caparo Industries plc v Dickman [1990] 1 All ER 568, [1990] 2 AC 605, [1990] 2 WLR 358, HL.

Groom v Selby [2001] EWCA 1522, [2001] All ER (D) 250.

McFarlane v Tayside Health Board [1999] 4 All ER 961, [2000] 2 AC 59, [1999] 3 WLR 1301, HL.

Parkinson v St James and Seacroft University Hospital NHS Trust [2001] EWCA Civ 530, [2001] 3 All ER 97, [2002] QB 266, [2001] 3 WLR 376.

Thake v Maurice [1986] 1 All ER 497, [1986] QB 644, [1986] 2 WLR 337, CA

Udale v Bloomsbury Area Health Authority [1983] 2 All ER 522, [1983] 1 WLR 1098.

White v Chief Constable of the South Yorkshire Police [1999] 1 All ER 1, [1999] 2 AC 455, [1998] 3 WLR 1509, HL.

Cases also cited or referred to in skeleton arguments

Barrett v Enfield LBC [1999] 3 All ER 193, [2001] 2 AC 550, HL.

Emeh v Kensington and Chelsea and Westminster Area Health Authority [1984] 3 All ER 1044, [1985] 1 QB 1012, CA.

Fassoulas v Ramey (1984) 450 So 2d 822, Florida SC.

Lim Poh Choo v Camden and Islington Area Health Authority [1979] 2 All ER 910, [1980] AC 174, HL.

Livingstone v Rawyards Coal Co (1880) 5 App Cas 25, HL.

McKay v Essex Area Health Authority [1982] 2 All ER 771, [1982] QB 1166, CA.

Miller v United States Steel Co (1990) 902 F 2d 573, US CA (7th Circuit).

Perrett v Collins [1998] 2 Lloyd's Rep 255, CA.

Roberts v Bro Taf Health Authority [2001] All ER (D) 353.

Williams v Natural Life Health Foods Ltd [1998] 2 All ER 577, [1998] 1 WLR 830, HL.

X v Bedfordshire CC, M (a minor) v Newham London BC, E (a minor) v Dorset CC [1995] 3 All ER 353, [1995] 2 AC 633, HL.

Appeal

The claimant, Karina Rees, appealed with permission of Stuart Brown QC from his decision, sitting as a deputy judge of the High Court on 16 May 2001, whereby, on the determination of a preliminary issue, he held that she was not

a entitled to recover as damages any of the costs of bringing up her son who was
born as a result of the negligence of the defendant, Darlington Memorial Hospital
NHS Trust. The facts are set out in the judgment of Hale LJ.

Robin de Wilde QC and *Joseph O'Brien* (instructed by *Blackett Hart & Pratt*,
Newcastle) for the claimant.
b *Jeremy Stuart-Smith QC* (instructed by *Eversheds*, Newcastle) for the defendant.

Cur adv vult

14 February 2002. The following judgments were delivered.

c **HALE LJ** (delivering the first judgment at the invitation of Waller LJ).
   [1] This is an appeal from the ruling of Mr Stuart Brown QC, sitting as a
deputy judge of the High Court, on a preliminary issue. The claimant seeks
damages for a sterilisation operation which was negligently performed, following
which she gave birth to a son. The issue is whether she is entitled to recover any,
d and if so which, of the costs of bringing him up. The point raised is novel and
important: this is the first, and so far as the researches of counsel have revealed,
the only such case involving a disabled mother whose reason for not wanting a
child was that her disability would make it difficult for her to look after and bring
him up properly.

e *The agreed facts*
   [2] The material parts of the agreed statement of facts may be summarised as
follows: (a) The claimant suffers from a genetic condition known as retinitis
pigmentosa. Since the age of two she has been blind in one eye and has only
limited vision in the other. She is severely visually handicapped. (b) The referral
f letter from her GP to the consultant who carried out the operation informed him
that she was registered partially sighted, her vision had deteriorated over
previous years and she had recently given up work, she had great difficulty in
finding a suitable method of contraception, she was adamant that she did not
want and would never want children, she felt that her eyesight would bar her
from looking after children, she was anxious about health matters and scared at
g the thought of labour and delivery. (c) When she saw the consultant, she
remained adamant, and told him that her very poor eyesight made it very difficult
for her to look after a baby. (d) The sterilisation was performed on 18 July 1995.
The right fallopian tube was not adequately occluded. (e) Her son Anthony was
conceived in July 1996 and born on 28 April 1997. His father has no desire to be
h involved with him. There is a risk that he has inherited retinitis pigmentosa but
it is low.
   [3] Unfortunately the agreed facts go no further. We know that the claimant
is bringing up Anthony herself with the help of her mother and other relatives
who live nearby. We have been told that she does not cook because she feels it
j to be too dangerous but she does try to dress him. We can only imagine the sort
of difficulties facing them both. We have no evidence as to how, if at all, it is
more costly for the claimant to look after Anthony than it would be for a mother
who does not have her disability.
   [4] Proceedings were begun in September 1999. Negligence was admitted.
The House of Lords gave judgment in *McFarlane v Tayside Health Board* [1999] 4
All ER 961, [2000] 2 AC 59 in November 1999. They held that the parents could

not claim the costs of bringing up a healthy child born as a result of a failed
sterilisation. This case was transferred to the High Court for determination of the   *a*
preliminary issue in November 2000. This court decided the case of *Parkinson v
St James and Seacroft University Hospital NHS Trust* [2001] EWCA Civ 530, [2001] 3
All ER 97, [2002] QB 266 in April 2001. It held that such a parent could claim the
extra costs of bringing up a disabled child. The deputy judge decided the
preliminary issue against the claimant on 16 May 2001. It is understandable that   *b*
the parties felt at the time that the matter could be dealt with by way of a
preliminary issue. In retrospect, and given that liability was admitted, it might
have been easier to determine the legal issues in the context of concrete evidence
of what might be involved.

The issue and arguments   *c*

[5] The issue is very simple to state but difficult to resolve: does the House of
Lords' decision in *McFarlane*'s case mean that none of the costs of bringing up a
healthy child can ever be claimed whatever the circumstances or can it be
distinguished in the particular circumstances of this case? We have not been
presented with any statistics but it is safe to assume that these circumstances are   *d*
unusual. The experience of the 15 years in which these claims were recognised
in both English (and then Scottish) law does not suggest that negligent
sterilisations are common. The novelty of the present claim suggests that the
proportion of those where the parent has sought sterilisation because of a
disability which is likely to hamper her ability to bring up a child will be small.

[6] Mr de Wilde QC, for the mother, was, as the judge put it, 'somewhat coy'   *e*
about precisely what he sought to recover. His primary case before the judge was
that he should have the full costs of bringing up Anthony, on the basis that
McFarlane's case had no application at all to this case. It was only his secondary
case that, by analogy with *Parkinson*'s case, he should have the extra costs
attributable to the mother's disability. This is perhaps unsurprising, as the   *f*
decision in *Parkinson*'s case was handed down only shortly before the hearing
before the judge. But it meant that no great thought had been given to what
those extra costs might be and how they might or might not be different from
those incurred by any parent faced with having to look after a child she never
meant to have. This problem featured heavily in the reasoning of the judge and
in the arguments of Mr Stuart-Smith QC for the defendant before him and again   *g*
before us. Mr de Wilde did eventually concede before us that he was seeking
only those extra costs, but again without precise definition or particulars.

[7] The argument for the mother was put in two ways, relying respectively
upon the reasoning of Brooke LJ and myself in *Parkinson*'s case. Brooke LJ
identified five techniques derived from recent decisions of the House of Lords for   *h*
determining whether to uphold a claim for financial loss in situations 'outside the
normal run of cases involving physical injury or physical damage' (see [2001] 3 All
ER 97 at [16]). He pointed out that there was no longer a single correct test. As
Sir Brian Neill had said in *Bank of Credit and Commerce International (Overseas) Ltd
(in liq) v Price Waterhouse (No 2)* [1998] PNLR 564 at 586, 'if the facts are properly   *j*
analysed and the policy considerations are correctly evaluated the several
approaches will yield the same result'. Brooke LJ summarised (at [26]) the five
techniques thus: (i) whether the defendant had assumed responsibility for the
services rendered so as to be liable for the economic consequences if he
performed them negligently; (ii) what the purpose of the services was; (iii)
whether it was legitimate to take the law forward one further step by analogy

a with established categories of liability; (iv) whether, given foreseeability and sufficient proximity, it was fair, just and reasonable to hold the defendant responsible for the losses in question; and (v) whether the principles of distributive justice would provide a more just solution to the problem than an approach founded solely upon principles of corrective justice.

b [8] Applying those techniques to the facts of *Parkinson's* case [2001] 3 All ER 97, he concluded (at [50]) that they permitted recovery of the special costs of rearing a disabled child by the following route: the birth of a disabled child was a foreseeable consequence of negligently performing the operation; there was a very limited group of people who might be affected by the negligence; there was no difficulty in principle in accepting the proposition that the surgeon should be deemed to have assumed responsibility for these foreseeable and disastrous *c* consequences; the purpose of the operation was, among other things, to prevent these; this was not a radical step into the unknown, given the experience of the 15 years before *McFarlane's* case [1999] 4 All ER 961, [2000] 2 AC 59; foreseeability and proximity were therefore established and given the financial and emotional drain associated with the extraordinary care required by a disabled child, the *d* award of the special upbringing costs involved would be fair, just and reasonable; and ordinary people would believe that an award limited to those extra costs would be just. He could find nothing in the majority reasoning in *McFarlane's* case to preclude that result.

[9] Mr de Wilde therefore argues that each of those propositions, applied by Brooke LJ in *Parkinson's* case, can be applied to this case. Indeed, in some respects *e* they might be thought to apply even more strongly: the birth of any child is an even more foreseeable consequence of the negligence than is the birth of a disabled child; the only person who could be affected, if the claim is limited to the extra costs occasioned by the disability, is the mother herself; the main purpose of the operation was to prevent jus. that; the surgeon knew all about it; hence *f* their proximity is particularly close; he assumed responsibility for preventing this particular woman from having a child and could easily be taken to assume responsibility for the particular financial consequences to her of having the child; it is surely fair, just and reasonable that a surgeon should be held responsible for these costs and any ordinary person would think it so.

g [10] In addition to the reasons given by Brooke LJ in *Parkinson's* case I took the view that the underlying reason why their Lordships had concluded that the costs of bringing up a healthy child were not recoverable was that the law, if not the parents, had to conclude that a child brings benefits as well as costs. As the latter might be calculated but the former could not, they had to be assumed to cancel one another out, whether or not they did so in fact. I called this a 'deemed *h* equilibrium'. By this metaphor I meant simply that the benefits brought by the child were deemed sufficient to negative the claim brought in *McFarlane's* case, which was for the ordinary costs of bringing up a healthy child. Understandably, however, Mr de Wilde argues that, if the disability of the child can upset that equilibrium, so too can the disability of the parent.

j [11] The contrary argument advanced by Mr Stuart-Smith is this. Everyone who seeks a sterilisation has, it can be assumed, a good reason for wanting to avoid having a child: the obvious examples are a risk to the health of the mother or of any prospective child, having enough children already, wanting to go back to work to improve the family's finances, feeling unable to cope either physically or financially with another mouth to feed. Indeed, at least three of these applied to the Parkinson family. Yet these parents can claim nothing for having to look

after a healthy child they did not, at least initially, want to have. Why should a
mother whose reason is her own disability be treated any differently?   *a*

[12] This is a powerful argument which impressed the judge. He regarded her
losses as no different in kind from those suffered by a high-flying career woman
who would have to give up her job or engage expensive child care or by a
struggling single mother whose whole life (and that of her other children) might
be ruined by the extra burden of care. Hence the analogy with the handicapped   *b*
child was less than complete. To single out this one type of case as an exception
to the general rule, or as upsetting the 'deemed equilibrium', would be 'to
re-embark on the slippery slope of trying to evaluate benefit and burden'.

McFarlane's case

[13] It must be remembered that the rule laid down by the House of Lords in   *c*
McFarlane v Tayside Health Board [1999] 4 All ER 961, [2000] 2 AC 59 is itself an
exception to what would otherwise be the normal rule. Their Lordships gave
different reasons for making it. There is no need here to repeat the masterly
analysis of their reasoning in Brooke LJ's judgment in *Parkinson v St James and
Seacroft University Hospital NHS Trust* [2001] 3 All ER 97, [2002] QB 266. They   *d*
were united in their reluctance to ascribe these to public or social policy. By this
I take it they meant such utilitarian arguments as were debated at first instance in
Thake v Maurice [1986] 1 All ER 497, [1986] QB 644 and *Udale v Bloomsbury Area
Health Authority* [1983] 2 All ER 522, [1983] 1 WLR 1098. Rather, they appealed
to legal policy. By this I take it they meant the values implicit in such legal
concepts as what is 'fair, just and reasonable', or 'restitution', or simply 'justice'.   *e*

[14] Thus, Lord Slynn of Hadley stated that the question was not simply one
of quantification but of liability, 'of the extent of the duty of care which is owed
to the husband and wife' (see [1999] 4 All ER 961 at 971, [2000] 2 AC 59 at 75).
The doctor had a duty of care but it did not follow that it included the costs of
rearing the child. It was not fair, just and reasonable to impose upon him liability   *f*
for the consequential responsibilities, imposed on or accepted by the parents to
bring up a child. But it is difficult to discern why he thought that this was not fair,
just and reasonable. He had already rejected the direct application of the 'benefits
rule':

> 'To reduce the costs by anything resembling a realistic or reliable figure for   *g*
> the benefit to the parents is well nigh impossible unless it is assumed that the
> benefit of a child must always outweigh the cost which, like many judges …
> I am not prepared to assume.' (See [1999] 4 All ER 961 at 971, [2000] 2 AC 59
> at 75.)

He concluded simply that '[t]he doctor does not assume responsibility for those   *h*
economic losses' (see [1999] 4 All ER 961 at 972, [2000] 2 AC 59 at 76).

[15] Lord Steyn relied upon the Aristotelian distinction between corrective
justice and distributive justice, although he also said that '[i]f it were necessary to
do so, I would say that the claim does not satisfy the requirement of being fair,
just and reasonable' (see [1999] 4 All ER 961 at 978, [2000] 2 AC 59 at 83). His   *j*
reasons were much clearer. Although he did not regard the 'set-off' of benefits
against detriments as the correct legal analysis, the 'many and undisputed
benefits' which the parents had derived and would derive from the child were
'relevant in an assessment of the justice of the parents' claim' (see [1999] 4 All ER
961 at 977, [2000] 2 AC 59 at 81–82). The ordinary person, embodied in the
traveller on the Underground, would—

a 'have in mind that many couples cannot have children and others have the sorrow and burden of looking after a disabled child. The realisation that compensation for financial loss in respect of the upbringing of a child would necessarily have to discriminate between rich and poor would surely appear unseemly to them. It would also worry them that parents may be put in the position of arguing in court that the unwanted child, which they accepted

b and care for, is more trouble than it is worth. Instinctively, the traveller on the Underground would consider that the law of tort has no business to provide legal remedies consequent upon the birth of a healthy child, which all of us regard as a valuable and good thing.' (See [1999] 4 All ER 961 at 977, [2000] 2 AC 59 at 82.)

c [16] Lord Hope of Craighead relied upon the benefits of bringing the child up within the family, both in the short and the longer term. He concluded:

'... it would not be fair just or reasonable, in any assessment of the loss caused by the birth of the child, to leave those benefits out of account. Otherwise the pursuers would be paid far too much. They would be relieved
d of the cost of rearing the child. They would not be giving anything back to the wrongdoer for the benefits. But the value which is to be attached to those benefits is incalculable. The costs can be calculated, but the benefits, which in fairness must be set against them, cannot. The logical conclusion, as a matter of law, is that the costs to the pursuers of meeting their
e obligations to the child during her childhood are not recoverable as damages. It cannot be established that overall and in the long run, those costs will exceed the value of the benefits. This is economic loss of a kind which must be held to fall outside the ambit of the duty of care which was owed to the pursuers ...' (See [1999] 4 All ER 961 at 990–991, [2000] 2 AC 59 at 97.)

f [17] Lord Clyde, on the other hand, hesitated to adopt the approach formulated in terms of the existence of a duty to avoid causing damage of a particular kind. He found it difficult to analyse the claim for maintenance as a separate obligation. He too rejected the direct application of the offsetting principle, because the losses and benefits were of 'quite a different character' (see [1999] 4 All ER 961 at 996, [2000] 2 AC 59 at 103). The answer for him lay in the
g 'basic idea which lies behind a claim for damages in delict, that is the idea of restitution' (see [1999] 4 All ER 961 at 997, [2000] 2 AC 59 at 104). Having the enjoyment of a child free of any cost to themselves did not accord with the idea of restitution or an award of damages which did justice between the parties.

[18] Lord Millett also rejected the direct offsetting the costs against the
h benefits in the individual case. The choice was between allowing no recovery on the basis that the benefits must be taken as outweighing any loss or allowing full recovery on the basis that the benefits, being incalculable and incommensurable, must be left out of account. He opted for the former. Society had to regard the balance as beneficial. It was morally offensive to regard a normal, healthy baby
j as more trouble and expense than it is worth. The advantages and disadvantages of parenthood were inextricably bound together: 'Nature herself does not permit parents to enjoy the advantages and dispense with the disadvantages.' (See [1999] 4 All ER 961 at 1005, [2000] 2 AC 59 at 114).

[19] Hence, all their Lordships rejected the application of the rule that any benefits should offset the costs in an individual case. But with the possible exception of Lord Slynn, they all relied upon the benefits of having a healthy child

as an important element in arriving at a just result. At least three of them
concluded that the law should always assume that the benefits outweighed the   *a*
sort of costs which were claimed in that case.

Conclusions

[20] All of their Lordships' discussion was on the basis that the child was
healthy, and therefore that the costs were those of bringing up a healthy child. It   *b*
did no violence to their reasoning to conclude in *Parkinson's* case that the extra
costs of bringing up a disabled child altered the justice of the case. In *McFarlane's*
case [1999] 4 All ER 961, [2000] 2 AC 59 the parents were no different from any
others in their ability actually to look after the child. They may not have wanted
to do so initially. It may have been a financial struggle for them to do so. But in
terms of the actual care required by the child, they were as well able to provide   *c*
this as any other parent. Their Lordships did not consider the position of a parent
who might be different.

[21] For the reasons that I explained at considerable length in *Parkinson's* case
[2001] 3 All ER 97, [2002] QB 266, the principal detriment suffered by anyone who
becomes a parent against their will is the legal and factual responsibility to look   *d*
after and bring up the child. The out-of-pocket expenditure on food, clothes,
travel, education, pocket money, and much more, is only the consequence of that
responsibility. I would be the first to recognise and acknowledge that that
responsibility brings with it great joys and great compensations. As their
Lordships said, the task of carrying out any real balancing exercise in any
individual case is both impossible and invidious. The parents who spend the   *e*
most on their child may in fact get much less pleasure, let alone much less
long-term benefit, from that investment. The parents who have little money to
spend but a great deal of love and attention to give may get much more. But who
can say? That is why they must be assumed to cancel one another out. That is
why the high-flying career woman whose sterilisation fails is in no better position   *f*
than the hard-pressed single parent.

[22] It is probably safe to assume that the ordinary person would be more
sympathetic to the hard-pressed single parent than to the high-flying career
woman. But they differ from one another only in their financial circumstances
and the law does not usually regard this as relevant. There is, however, a crucial
difference between them and a seriously disabled parent. These able-bodied   *g*
parents are both of them able to look after and bring up their child. No doubt
they would both benefit from a nanny or other help in doing so. But they do not
need it in order to be able to discharge the basic parental responsibility of looking
after the child properly and safely, performing those myriad essential but
mundane tasks such as feeding, bathing, clothing, training, supervising, playing   *h*
with, reading to and taking to school which every child needs. They do not need
it in order to avoid the risk that the child may have to be taken away to be looked
after by the local social services authority or others, to the detriment of the child
as well as the parent. That is the distinction between an able-bodied parent and
a disabled parent who needs help if she is to be able to discharge the most   *j*
ordinary tasks involved in the parental responsibility which has been placed upon
her as a result of the defendant's negligence.

[23] Hence I would conclude that, just as the extra costs involved in
discharging that responsibility towards a disabled child can be recovered, so too
can the extra costs involved in a disabled parent discharging that responsibility
towards a healthy child. Of course we can assume that such a parent benefits, and

a benefits greatly, from having a child she never thought she would have. We can and must assume that those benefits negative the claim for the ordinary costs of looking after and bringing him up. But we do not have to assume that it goes further than that. She is not being over-compensated by being given recompense for the extra costs of childcare occasioned by her disability. She is being put in the same position as her able-bodied fellows.

b [24] In real life it is impossible to separate the doctor's assumption of responsibility for preventing pregnancy from the assumption of responsibility for preventing parenthood and the parental responsibility it brings. The two go hand in hand just as pregnancy and childbirth go hand in hand. The law has limited the doctor's responsibility because of the incalculable benefit the child must be presumed to bring. But if that incalculable benefit is put at risk by the very fact *c* which led the parent to ask for the sterilisation, there is nothing unfair, unjust or unreasonable in holding that the surgeon assumes a more extensive responsibility for the consequences, at least where he knew of the disability and that this was the reason why she wished to avoid having a child.

[25] All this is predicated on the assumption that there will be some extra costs *d* which are attributable not to the fact of having a child to bring up but to the fact that the mother is severely visually handicapped. We do not have any evidence of that. They are bound to vary with the nature of the disability and what the individual mother can and cannot do. But assessing these does not take us down the slippery slope of comparing benefit and burden, because the ordinary benefits and burdens have already been taken out of the account. Just as there is *e* considerable experience and expertise in assessing the special needs of disabled children, there is also considerable experience and expertise in assessing the special needs of disabled adults, including disabled parents. Some special equipment and adaptations to the home may be needed, as may some assistance with necessary tasks which the mother cannot do. That is very far from shifting *f* the burden of child care onto someone else: the object is to compensate for those things for which compensation will be needed if both mother and child are to enjoy the benefits of living together as a family. It would be ironic indeed if a rule based upon the assumed benefits to a parent (let alone a child) of having a child to bring up were applied in such a way as to preclude them enjoying that benefit at all.

g [26] Thus I would allow the appeal and substitute a ruling that the mother may claim those extra costs, if any, of bringing up her child as are attributable to her disability.

ROBERT WALKER LJ.

h [27] I have had the advantage of reading in draft the judgments of Hale LJ and Waller LJ. I would say at the outset that I agree with Hale LJ's observations (in [3], [4], above) that the direction for the trial of a preliminary issue can be seen, with hindsight, as regrettable. It would have been better to consider the legal issues with the benefit of findings of fact as to the circumstances in which *j* Anthony Rees is being cared for and brought up.

[28] I agree with Waller LJ that this is obviously a difficult area. But this court is not short of authoritative guidance. There is the decision of the House of Lords in *McFarlane v Tayside Health Board* [1999] 4 All ER 961, [2000] 2 AC 59, which is binding on this court. We are also bound by this court's decision in *Parkinson v St James and Seacroft University Hospital NHS Trust* [2001] EWCA Civ 530, [2001] 3 All ER 97, [2002] QB 266. *Parkinson's* case was followed (by a similarly but not

identically constituted court) in *Groom v Selby* [2001] EWCA 1522, [2001] All ER
(D) 250. On this appeal counsel for the NHS Trust did not submit that *Parkinson's*
case was inconsistent with the House of Lords' decision in *McFarlane's* case or
that it ought not to be followed.

[29] In their judgments in *Parkinson's* case Brooke LJ and Hale LJ very closely
analysed the five speeches delivered in *McFarlane's* case. It is unnecessary to
repeat their analysis but I draw attention to some salient points. Although their
Lordships disavowed any intention of deciding the case on the grounds of public
(or social) policy, there is a strong moral element in the basis of the decision. This
appears most clearly in the speeches of Lord Steyn and Lord Millett, in passages
which have often been cited but which bear repetition.

[30] Lord Steyn said:

'My Lords, to explain decisions denying a remedy for the cost of bringing
up an unwanted child by saying that there is no loss, no foreseeable loss, no
causative link or no ground for reasonable restitution is to resort to
unrealistic and formalistic propositions which mask the real reasons for the
decisions. And judges ought to strive to give the real reasons for their
decision. It is my firm conviction that where courts of law have denied a
remedy for the cost of bringing up an unwanted child the real reasons have
been grounds of distributive justice. That is, of course, a moral theory. It
may be objected that the House must act like a court of law and not like a
court of morals. That would only be partly right. The court must apply
positive law. But judges' sense of the moral answer to a question, or the
justice of the case, has been one of the great shaping forces of the common
law.' (See [1999] 4 All ER 961 at 977, [2000] 2 AC 59 at 82.)

[31] Lord Millett said:

'In my opinion the law must take the birth of a normal, healthy baby to be
a blessing, not a detriment. In truth it is a mixed blessing. It brings joy and
sorrow, blessing and responsibility. The advantages and the disadvantages
are inseparable. Individuals may choose to regard the balance as
unfavourable and take steps to forego the pleasures as well as the
responsibilities of parenthood. They are entitled to decide for themselves
where their own interests lie. But society itself must regard the balance as
beneficial. It would be repugnant to its own sense of values to do otherwise.
It is morally offensive to regard a normal, healthy baby as more trouble and
expense that it is worth.' (See [1999] 4 All ER 961 at 1005, [2000] 2 AC 59 at
113–114.)

[32] Lord Millett's emphatic reference to a 'normal, healthy baby' is echoed in
most of the other speeches. All or most of the references are set out in the
judgments in *Parkinson's* case and I need not repeat them. The point is summed
up in Hale LJ's judgment in *Parkinson's* case [2001] 3 All ER 97 at [87]: 'At the heart
of it all is the feeling that to compensate for the financial costs of bringing up a
healthy child is a step too far.'

[33] There is not the same intuitive feeling that it would be exorbitant
compensation to award damages for financial burdens which are the direct
consequence of the disability of a child who is born disabled after a failed
sterilisation, and which would not be incurred in consequence of the birth of a
normal, healthy child. The court's moral intuition to refuse recovery in the case
of a healthy child is given legal substance and effect either by applying the

a three-stage *Caparo* test (see *Caparo Industries plc v Dickman* [1990] 1 All ER 568, [1990] 2 AC 605) or by an approach which inquires into the surgeon's assumption of responsibility (see the analysis in Brooke LJ's judgment in *Parkinson*'s case, especially at [26], [33]–[42]). By contrast it does not offend the *Caparo* test to hold a surgeon responsible for financial burdens uniquely referable to the disability of a disabled child whose birth was a foreseeable consequence of the surgeon's

b negligence.

[34] After reading Hale LJ's draft judgment in this appeal I formed the view, largely in agreement with the reasoning in her judgment, that there would also be no offence to the *Caparo* test in permitting recovery of damages for the financial burdens of bringing up a child uniquely referable to the disability of a woman who, because of her disability, has decided that she should not have a

c child, and has explained that reason to her consultant. (On this point I do respectfully question Lord Millett's view, in *McFarlane*'s case [1999] 4 All ER 961 at 1002, [2000] 2 AC 59 at 109–110, that the parents' reasons for wishing to avoid childbirth are immaterial and that medical advisors would not normally inquire about them. If, as in this case, the reasons are communicated to the

d consultant—and presumably passed on to the surgeon if different—they may be relevant to the issue of the surgeon's assumption of responsibility.)

[35] I cannot however accept the 'deemed equilibrium' theory set out in Hale LJ's judgment in *Parkinson*'s case [2001] 3 All ER 97 at [87]–[91] (and mentioned in her judgment in this case at [10]). It is an attractive and convenient theory in the sense that it enables expenses uniquely referable to disablement

e (whether of mother or child) to be seen as economic loss unrelieved by any countervailing benefit or advantage. If costs and benefits (in the absence of disablement) are assumed to be equal, costs uniquely referable to disablement are economic loss which ought to be recoverable in full.

[36] In *Parkinson*'s case Hale LJ said (at [90]) that the solution of deemed

f equilibrium, as well as having attractions, was binding on this court. I respectfully doubt whether it is binding. Lord Slynn of Hadley went no further than to say ([1999] 4 All ER 961 at 971, [2000] 2 AC 59 at 75) that he was not prepared to assume that the benefit of a child must always outweigh the cost. Lord Steyn referred to the question of benefits and burdens several times in his discussion of the authorities, but ultimately based his decision on distributive justice. Lord

g Hope of Craighead recognised ([1999] 4 All ER 961 at 990, [2000] 2 AC 59 at 97) that a child brings benefits as well as costs, but used the impossibility of calculating the benefits as part of the basis for his conclusion on the *Caparo* test. Lord Clyde was against any set-off:

h   'It may be that the benefit which a child represents to his or her parent is open to quantification, but there is no principle under which the law recognises such a set off. A parent's claim for the death of a child is not offset by the saving in maintenance costs which the parent will enjoy. Nor, as was noted by the discussion in the present case, is the loss sustained by a mineworker who is rendered no longer fit for work underground offset by

j   the pleasure and benefit which he may enjoy in the open air of a public park.' (See [1999] 4 All ER 961 at 996, [2000] 2 AC 59 at 103.)

Lord Millett saw the choice as being—

'between allowing no recovery on the basis that the benefits must be regarded as outweighing any loss, and allowing full recovery on the basis

that the benefits, being incalculable and incommensurable, must be left out
of account.' (See [1999] 4 All ER 961 at 1003, [2000] 2 AC 59 at 111.)   *a*

[37] In my view this appeal can and should be allowed, to the limited extent
indicated in the judgment of Hale LJ, without the need to rely on a principle of
deemed equilibrium. Subject to the points raised in the judgment of Waller LJ,
to which I must turn, I would base my decision on there being nothing unfair,   *b*
unjust, unreasonable, unacceptable or morally repugnant in permitting recovery
of compensation for a limited range of expenses which (when specified and
proved) will be found to have a very close connection with the mother's severe
visual impairment, and nothing to do with the blessings which the birth of her
healthy son may have brought her.

[38] Waller LJ has expressed doubts about the equilibrium theory and it will   *c*
be apparent that I share those doubts. Apart from that Waller LJ is concerned
about the making of exceptions to the principle established in *McFarlane*'s case
and of transgressing the boundaries which the House of Lords set in that case. I
share those concerns, and I recognise that wherever the boundary is set, there
will always be cases close to one or other side of the boundary illustrating 'the   *d*
imperfect reality of the way the law of torts actually works' (see Lord Hoffmann
in *White v Chief Constable of the South Yorkshire Police* [1999] 1 All ER 1 at 42, [1999]
2 AC 455 at 504).

[39] In *McFarlane*'s case the House of Lords was concerned (on the main claim
for damages) with a claim for the total cost of bringing up a normal, healthy child.
Lord Steyn made clear both at the beginning of his speech ([1999] 4 All ER 961 at   *e*
973, [2000] 2 AC 59 at 77) and at the end ([1999] 4 All ER 961 at 979, [2000] 2 AC
59 at 84) that his speech was addressed to that pleaded claim, and the other
speeches (with the possible exception of that of Lord Slynn) were to similar effect.
They do not address the special problem of a disabled child or that of a disabled
mother.   *f*

[40] Waller LJ draws attention to the case of a woman with several children
who is not disabled but whose physical and mental health and family
circumstances may be so fragile that the birth of another child (even though
healthy) would be a disaster for her. It is hard to see how, consistently with
McFarlane's case, she could claim substantial damages for childcare costs
following negligent sterilisation, and it hardly makes the position more   *g*
satisfactory to say (by way of explanation) that she could not prove any such costs
which were uniquely referable to the fact that she was physically exhausted and
emotionally depressed. (If she was the parent who had undergone the
sterilisation operation, and her health was shown to have deteriorated in
consequence of pregnancy and childbirth, she might have a remedy for personal   *h*
injuries.)

[41] But these difficulties should not in my view deter this court from allowing
the possibility of recovery (which is all it is, on the preliminary issue) in
circumstances which, as I see it, are not covered by *McFarlane*'s case and are a
legitimate extension of *Parkinson*'s case. Disabled persons are a category of the   *j*
public whom the law increasingly recognises as requiring special consideration
(the Disability Discrimination Act 1995 is an important landmark) and the
developing law as to disability should (as Hale LJ explained in *Parkinson*'s case
[2001] 3 All ER 97 at [91]) avoid the sort of definitional problems which Lord
Hoffmann referred to in *White v Chief Constable of the South Yorkshire Police* [1999]
1 All ER 1 at 47, [1999] 2 AC 455 at 510.

a [42] For these reasons I agree with Hale LJ that the appeal should be allowed to the limited extent which she proposes.

WALLER LJ.

[43] I have read the judgment of Hale LJ in draft. I can gratefully accept the statement of facts and her identification of the issue. I am however unable to
b agree with her conclusion.

[44] That the court is in a difficult area needs no emphasis. The area is peculiarly difficult because, as was recognised by a majority in *McFarlane v Tayside Health Board* [1999] 4 All ER 961, [2000] 2 AC 59, on normal principles the claim there for damages for bringing up a healthy child born as a result of the negligence of a surgeon, would succeed (see Hale LJ's judgment in *Parkinson v St*
c *James and Seacroft University Hospital NHS Trust* [2001] EWCA Civ 530 at [76], [2001] 3 All ER 97 at [76], [2002] QB 266 with which I respectfully agree). This to my mind is emphasised by the fact that if one follows the route advocated by Brooke LJ for reaching the conclusion he did, as to why the extra costs of bringing up a disabled child should be recoverable, at para [50] of his judgment,
d sub-paras (i)– (v) would, (adapted to deal with the position of a healthy child) point to a conclusion of liability. It is only when the court has to consider whether it is 'fair, just or reasonable' under his sub-para (vi) and/or whether applying the principles of distributive justice under his sub-para (vii), whether it is 'fair for the law to make an award' of the extra expenses, that any distinction can be drawn. So on his route the position comes down simply to this. Liability
e in both situations would by normal principles be established, but the court is entitled to take the view that it is fair to allow the recovery of the extra costs of looking after a disabled child, even though it takes the view that it is not fair to allow the recovery of the costs of looking after a healthy child.

[45] Once the court begins to disallow recovery, although normal principles would allow recovery, and once the court starts to consider the making of
f exceptions to that decision—we are, as I see it, truly in the area of distributive justice as identified in *White v Chief Constable of the South Yorkshire Police* [1999] 1 All ER 1, [1999] 2 AC 455. The costs of recovering the expenses of looking after a healthy child born through the negligence of a surgeon, are costs which the court has said should not be recovered, and if that is the boundary that a court has
g set, it is important that the court does not make exceptions to that rule, which would seem to be unjust to the persons unable to recover as a result of that rule.

[46] Hale LJ in *Parkinson's* case came to the view that a mother could recover the extra costs of bringing up a disabled child by a route different from that adopted by Brooke LJ, as well as agreeing with the reasons of Brooke LJ. Sir
h Martin Nourse agreed with both judgments, and thus, I accept, also adopted the additional route which my Lady used. It is this route which forms a part of her judgment in this case.

[47] She suggested in *Parkinson's* case (at [87]) that at the heart of the House of Lords' decision in *McFarlane's* case was the concept:

j   'A healthy child brings benefits as well as costs; it is impossible accurately
         to calculate those benefits so as to give a proper discount; the only sensible
         course is to assume that they balance one another out.'

She pointed out that some would challenge the assumption that the benefits did cancel out the costs, and she was not happy with the notion that a child was being treated as a commodity of benefit to parents, but she concluded (at [90]):

'The solution of deemed equilibrium also has its attractions and is in any
event binding upon us. Indeed, it provides the answer to many of the
questions arising in this case.'

[48] Adopting this concept her conclusion in *Parkinson*'s case was that since
such equilibrium related to the benefits of having a healthy child being weighed
against the costs of bringing up a healthy child, that left room for the recovery of
damages for the extra costs of bringing up a disabled child. (See Hale LJ's
judgment in *Parkinson*'s case [2001] 3 All ER 97 at [90].)

[49] In her judgment in this case, once again Hale LJ (at [23]) would seek to
use the concept of deemed equilibrium. This time she would suggest that the
extra costs of a disabled mother in bringing up her child was not in the calculation
that their Lordships in *McFarlane*'s case [1999] 4 All ER 961, [2000] 2 AC 59 were
carrying out.

[50] My difficulty is that I do not find it easy to extract from the speeches of a
majority of their Lordships in *McFarlane*'s case that they necessarily thought in
terms of an 'equilibrium' with precise quantities on either side of the balance.
Indeed, it seems to me that Lord Slynn is saying ([1999] 4 All ER 961 at 970, [2000]
2 AC 59 at 74) that one cannot do that exercise, and one sees in the speech of Lord
Hope of Craighead a description of the benefits of having a healthy child; and
then him saying that the 'value which is to be attached to these benefits is
incalculable' (see [1999] 4 All ER 961 at 990, [2000] 2 AC 59 at 97). That does not
suggest to me that he is saying there is an equilibrium. It seems to me that it is
the concept of incalculability of the benefits which leads to the conclusion that
costs of care should not be recoverable. If anything it is because in some cases the
benefit might be such as to provide a substantial balance in favour of benefits
when weighed against the costs of care that leads to the result that the costs of
care should not be recoverable.

[51] I stress that it does not follow that I am disagreeing with the decision in
Parkinson's case (by which of course in any event we are bound). What in
McFarlane's case their Lordships were concerned with was a healthy child and not
a disabled child. There was thus, I accept, room to reach the conclusion that was
reached that it was fair, just, and reasonable to award the extra costs.

[52] Where the court is concerned with the birth of a healthy child, it seems
to me that before contemplating the making of an exception to the general rule
established by *McFarlane*'s case one must examine with even greater care (if that
is possible) whether any exception is justified, because (as I have stressed) the
House of Lords were concerned with the award of damages in relation to the
birth of a healthy child. In that context one must take into consideration how
such an exception would be perceived by others who, as already stated, would
have recovered damages on normal principles but will not recover because of the
McFarlane decision, or, perhaps more accurately, one must take into account how
the ordinary person would perceive the fairness of the exception.

[53] Let me address some examples, I hope not too extreme. If one takes the
facts to be that a woman already has four children and wishes not to have a fifth;
and if one assumes that having the fifth will create a crisis in health terms, unless
help in caring for the child was available. She cannot recover the costs of caring
for the child which might alleviate the crisis, as I understand *McFarlane*'s case. I
would have thought that her need to avoid a breakdown in her health was no
different from the need of someone already with a disability, and indeed her need
might be greater depending on the degree of disability. Does she, or ordinary

a   people, look favourably on the law not allowing her to recover but allowing someone who is disabled to recover?

[54] If one were to add that the lady with four children was poor, but the lady with a disability was rich—what then? It would simply emphasise the perception that the rule was not operating fairly. One can add to the example by making comparisons between possible family circumstances of the different mothers.

b   Assume the mother with four children had no support from husband, mother or siblings, and then compare her with the person who is disabled, but who has a husband, siblings and a mother all willing to help. I think ordinary people would feel uncomfortable about the thought that it was simply the disability which made a difference.

[55] If a disabled person has a healthy child, and finds that she can, contrary to

c   her anxieties, cope with that child with the help of family and others, I would have thought that in Lord Hope's words the benefits of having that child would be incalculable. It is the fact that such benefits of having that healthy child are incalculable which it seems to me leads to the result that the court simply should not give damages for the birth of that child. It is because the court is simply not

d   prepared to go into a calculation which involves weighing one aspect against the other which in my view should bring about the conclusion that it is not fair, just, and reasonable that a disabled person should recover when other mothers in as great a need cannot. On the basis of distributive justice I believe that ordinary people would think that it was not fair that a disabled person should recover when mothers who may in effect become disabled by ill-health through having a healthy child would not.

[56] I would thus be in favour of dismissing the appeal.

Appeal allowed.

Kate O'Hanlon   Barrister.

Re S (children: care plan)
Re W (children: care plan)

[2002] UKHL 10

HOUSE OF LORDS

LORD NICHOLLS OF BIRKENHEAD, LORD MACKAY OF CLASHFERN, LORD BROWNE-WILKINSON, LORD MUSTILL AND LORD HUTTON

12–15 NOVEMBER 2001, 14 MARCH 2002

Family proceedings – Orders in family proceedings – Care order – Interim care order – Whether court having supervisory role over local authority's discharge of parental responsibilities under care order – Whether making of care orders incompatible with right to fair trial and right to respect for family life – Guidance on exercise of discretion to grant interim care order – Children Act 1989, s 38 – Human Rights Act 1998, ss 3, 7, 8, Sch 1, Pt I, arts 6, 8.

In two conjoined appeals arising out of care proceedings, the Court of Appeal made two major adjustments and innovations in the construction and application of the Children Act 1989. First, the court enunciated guidelines intended to give trial judges a wider discretion to make an interim care order, under s 38[a] of the 1989 Act, rather than a final care order, where the care plan seemed inchoate or where the passage of a relatively brief period seemed bound to see the fulfilment of some event or process vital to planning and deciding the future. Secondly, the court propounded a new procedure by which, at the trial, the essential milestones of a care plan would be identified and elevated to 'starred' status. If a starred milestone was not achieved within a reasonable time after the date set at trial, the local authority would be obliged to reactivate the interdisciplinary process that contributed to the creation of the care plan. The local authority had at least to inform the child's guardian of the position, and either the guardian or the local authority would then have the right to apply to the court for further directions. In introducing the starred milestone procedure, the Court of Appeal relied on s 3[b] of the Human Rights Act 1998 which required the court, so far as it was possible to do so, to read and give effect to legislation in a way that was compatible with rights under the European Convention for the Protection of Human Rights and Fundamental Freedoms 1950 (as set out in Sch 1 to the 1998 Act). In particular, the court held that where elements of the care plan were so fundamental that there was a real risk of a breach of convention rights if they were not fulfilled, and there was some reason to fear that they might not be fulfilled, it was justifiable to read into the 1989 Act a power in the court to require a report on progress. The

---

a   Section 38, so far as material, provides: '(1) Where—(a) in any proceedings on an application for a care order ... the proceedings are adjourned ... the court may make an interim care order ... with respect to the child concerned ...
    (4) An interim order made under or by virtue of this section shall have effect for such period as may be specified in the order, but shall in any event cease to have effect on whichever of the following events first occurs—(a) the expiry of the period of eight weeks beginning with the date on which the order is made ... '

b   Section 3, so far as material, is set out at [37], below

a court also appeared to place reliance on ss 7[c] and 8[d] of the 1998 Act which extended the court's powers to grant relief in cases where a public authority was acting unlawfully by acting in a way incompatible with a convention right. On appeals to the House of Lords by, in one of the cases, the mother of children who had been made subject to a final care order, the local authority in the other case and the Secretary of State in both cases, the principal issue was the soundness of

b the Court of Appeal's initiative, both in respect of the introduction of the starring system and the extended use of interim care orders. A further issue arose as to whether, if it did not permit the introduction of the starring system, the 1989 Act was compatible with two provisions of the convention—the right to a fair hearing under art 6(1)[e] and the right to respect for family life under art 8[f]. The alleged incompatibility with art 8 was the absence from the 1989 Act of an

c adequate remedy if a local authority failed properly to discharge its parental responsibilities.

Held – (1) The introduction of a 'starring' system could not be justified as a legitimate exercise in interpreting the 1989 Act in accordance with s 3 of the 1998

d Act. It was a cardinal principle of the 1989 Act that courts were not empowered to intervene in the way local authorities discharged their parental responsibilities under final care orders. Parliament had entrusted to local authorities, not the courts, the responsibility for looking after children who were the subject of care orders, and the new starring system would depart substantially from that principle. It constituted amendment of the 1989 Act, not its interpretation, and

e accordingly the Court of Appeal had exceeded the bounds of its judicial jurisdiction under s 3 of the 1998 Act. Moreover, the starring system went much further than providing a judicial remedy to the victims of actual or proposed unlawful conduct by local authorities entrusted with the care of children, and accordingly ss 7 and 8 of the 1998 Act did not provide a legal basis for the

f introduction of the new system (see [36], [42]–[44], [48], [50], [107], [114]–[116], below); dictum of Lord Steyn in *R v A* [2001] 3 All ER 1 at [44] explained.

(2) The failure by the state to provide an effective remedy for a violation of art 8 was not itself a violation of that provision, and accordingly even if the 1989 Act failed to provide an adequate remedy, it was not for that reason incompatible with art 8. Moreover, the making of a care order pursuant to the 1989 Act, and a

g decision whether a care order should be continued or discharged, accorded with the requirements of art 6(1). A care order was made by the court in proceedings to which the parents were parties. The position regarding decisions by the local authority on the care of a child while a care order was in force was not quite so straightforward, but it was not easy to think of an instance where the civil rights

h of parents or children, protected by art 6(1), were more extensive than their art 8 rights, which had the protection accorded in domestic law by ss 7 and 8 of the

---

c   Section 7, so far as material, provides: '(1) A person who claims that a public authority has acted (or proposes to act) in a way which is made unlawful by section 6(1) may—(a) bring proceedings against the authority under this Act in the appropriate court or tribunal, or (b) rely on the

j   Convention right or rights concerned in any legal proceedings, but only if he is (or would be) a victim of the unlawful act … '

d   Section 8, so far as material, provides: '(1) In relation to any act (or proposed act) of a public authority which the court finds is (or would be) unlawful, it may grant such relief or remedy, or make such order, within its powers as it considers just and appropriate … '

e   Article 6, so far as material, is set out [65], below

f   Article 8 is set out at [52], below

1998 Act. Any shortcoming was, therefore, likely to be more theoretical than real. In so far as a failure to comply with art 6(1) lay in the absence of effective machinery for protecting the civil rights of young children who had no parent or guardian able and willing to act for them, there was a statutory lacuna, not a statutory incompatibility (see [59], [64], [75]–[77], [81], [86], [107], [114]–[116], below).

(3) From a reading of s 38 of the 1989 Act as a whole, it was abundantly clear that the purpose of an interim care order, so far as presently material, was to enable the court to safeguard the welfare of a child until such time as the court was in a position to decide whether or not it was in the best interests of the child to make a care order. When that time arrived depended on the circumstances of the case and was a matter for the judgment of the trial judge. That was the general, guiding, principle. The corollary to that principle was that an interim care order was not intended to be used as a means by which the court might continue to exercise a supervisory role over the local authority in cases where it was in the best interests of a child that a care order should be made. An interim care order was, thus, a temporary 'holding' measure. Inevitably, time was needed before an application for a care order was ready for decision. When a local authority formulated a care plan in connection with an application for a care order, there were bound to be uncertainties. Despite all those inevitable uncertainties, when deciding whether to make a care order the court should normally have before it a care plan which was sufficiently firm and particularised for all concerned to have a reasonably clear picture of the likely way ahead for the child for the foreseeable future. Cases varied so widely that it was impossible to be precise about the test to be applied by a court when deciding whether to continue interim relief rather than to proceed to make a care order. The court had always to maintain a proper balance between the need to satisfy itself about the appropriateness of the care plan and the avoidance of over-zealous investigation into matters which were properly within the administrative discretion of the local authority (see [90]–[92], [99], [100], [102], [107], [114]–[116], below).

(4) In the instant cases, the mother's appeal would be dismissed, while the appeals of the Secretary of State and the local authority would be allowed so far as they had challenged the Court of Appeal's introduction of the starring system (see [103], [105], [107], [114]–[116], below).

Notes

For care orders and interim orders, see 5(3) *Halsbury's Laws* (4th edn reissue) paras 418–419, and for the right to a fair trial and the right to respect for family life, see 8(2) *Halsbury's Laws* (4th edn reissue) paras 134, 149, 151.

For the Children Act 1989, s 38, see 6 *Halsbury's Statutes* (4th edn) (1999 reissue) 426.

For the Human Rights Act 1998, ss 3, 7, 8, Sch 1, Pt I, arts 6, 8, see 7 *Halsbury's Statutes* (4th edn) (1999 reissue) 502, 505, 507, 523, 524.

Cases referred to in opinions

A (a minor) (care proceedings), Re [1993] 1 FCR 164, [1993] 1 WLR 291.

A v Liverpool City Council [1981] 2 All ER 385, [1982] AC 363, [1981] 2 WLR 948, HL.

Airey v Ireland (1979) 2 EHRR 305, [1979] ECHR 6289/73, ECt HR.

a *C v Solihull Metropolitan BC* [1992] 2 FCR 341.
CH (a minor) (care or interim order), Re [1998] 2 FCR 347, CA.
F v Lambeth London BC [2001] 3 FCR 738.
Hokkanen v Finland (1994) 19 EHRR 139, [1994] ECHR 19823/92, ECt HR.
KDT (a minor) (care order: conditions), Re [1994] 2 FCR 721, CA.
Kent CC v C [1993] 1 All ER 719, [1993] Fam 57, [1992] 3 WLR 808.
b *L (minors) (care proceedings: appeal), Re* [1996] 2 FCR 352, CA.
M, Re (29 June 2001, unreported), Fam D.
Marckx v Belgium (1979) 2 EHRR 330, [1979] ECHR 6833/74, ECt HR.
McMichael v UK [1995] 2 FCR 718, ECt HR.
Nielsen v Denmark (1988) 11 EHRR 175, [1988] ECHR 10929/84, ECt HR.
c *Poplar Housing and Regeneration Community Association Ltd v Donoghue* [2001]
    EWCA Civ 595, [2001] 4 All ER 604, [2001] 3 WLR 183.
R (care proceedings: adjournment), Re [1998] 3 FCR 654, CA.
R (minors) (care proceedings: care plan), Re [1994] 2 FCR 136.
R (on the application of Alconbury Developments Ltd) v Secretary of State for the
d   *Environment, Transport and the Regions* [2001] UKHL 23, [2001] 2 All ER 929,
    [2001] 2 WLR 1389.
R v A [2001] UKHL 25, [2001] 3 All ER 1, [2002] 1 AC 45, [2001] 2 WLR 1546.
R v Lambert [2001] UKHL 37, [2001] 3 All ER 577, [2001] 3 WLR 206.
R v Secretary of State for the Home Dept, ex p Daly [2001] UKHL 26, [2001] 3 All ER
    433, [2001] 2 WLR 1622.
e *R v Stack* [1986] 1 NZLR 257, NZ CA.
Ringeisen v Austria (No 1) (1971) 1 EHRR 455, [1971] ECHR 2614/65, ECt HR.
S and D (child case: powers of court), Re [1995] 1 FCR 626, CA.
TP v UK [2001] 2 FCR 289, ECt HR.
W v Hertfordshire CC [1985] 2 All ER 301, [1985] AC 791, [1985] 2 WLR 892, HL.
f *W v UK* (1987) 10 EHRR 29, [1987] ECHR 9749/82, ECt HR.

Appeals

Re S (children: care plan)

g The appellant mother appealed with permission of the Appeal Committee of the
House of Lords given on 2 October 2001 from the order of the Court of Appeal
(Thorpe, Sedley and Hale LJJ) on 23 May 2001 ([2001] EWCA Civ 757, [2001] 2
FCR 450) dismissing her appeal from the decision of Judge Sander at Plymouth
County Court on 1 November 2000 granting the respondent, Torbay Council,
care orders in respect of two of the mother's children. The Secretary of State for
h Health appealed with permission of the Appeal Committee of the House of Lords
given on 2 October 2001 from that part of the Court of Appeal's decision which
introduced a system of 'starred' milestones in respect of care plans. The facts are
set out in the opinion of Lord Nicholls of Birkenhead.

Re W (children: care plan)

j The Secretary of State for Health and Bedfordshire County Council appealed
with permission of the Appeal Committee of the House of Lords given on 2
October 2001 from the order of the Court of Appeal (Thorpe, Sedley and
Hale LJJ) on 23 May 2001 ([2001] EWCA Civ 757, [2001] 2 FCR 450) allowing an
appeal by the respondent parents from care orders granted by Judge Hamilton at

Luton County Court on 11 December 2000 in respect of their two children. The facts are set out in the opinion of Lord Nicholls of Birkenhead.   a

Allan Levy QC and *Catriona Duthie* (instructed by *Blake Lapthorn*, agents for *Hooper & Woolen*, Torquay) for the mother in the Torbay case.
Anna Pauffley QC and *Claire Roswell* (instructed by *Head of Legal Services*, Torbay Council) for Torbay.   b
Robin Tolson QC and *Keir Starmer* (instructed by *Woollcombe Beer Watts*, Newton Abbot) for the guardian ad litem in the Torbay case.
Philip Sales and *Deborah Eaton* (instructed by the *Solicitor for the Department of Health*) for the Secretary of State in both cases.
Cherie Booth QC, Lee Arnot, Stefano Nuvoloni and *Conor Gearty* (instructed by *Sharpe Pritchard*, agents for *Head of Legal Services*, Bedfordshire County Council) for Bedfordshire.   c
Ian Peddie QC, Sarah Forster, Nicholas Khan and *Rebecca Mitchell* (instructed by *Thomas Eggar Church Adams*, agents for *Motley & Hope*, Biggleswade) for the parents in the Bedfordshire case.
Robin Tolson QC and *Simon Tattersall* (instructed by *Borneo Linnells*, Bedford) for the guardian ad litem in the Bedfordshire case.   d

Their Lordships took time for consideration.

14 March 2002. The following opinions were delivered.   e

LORD NICHOLLS OF BIRKENHEAD.
[1] My Lords, these appeals concern the impact of the Human Rights Act 1998 on Pts III and IV of the Children Act 1989. The Court of Appeal (Thorpe, Sedley and Hale LJJ, [2001] EWCA Civ 757, [2001] 2 FCR 450) made, in the words of f
Thorpe LJ, two major adjustments and innovations in the construction and application of the 1989 Act. The principal issue before your Lordships' House concerns the soundness of this judicial initiative.

The Torbay case   g
[2] The appeals concern four children, two in the Torbay case and two in the Bedfordshire case. The cases are factually unrelated. In the Torbay case the mother had three children: P, who is a boy born in August 1987, M, a boy born in January 1991, and J, a girl born in January 1992. The children are now 14, 11 and ten years old. The appeal concerns the two younger children. The father of P, the eldest child, played no part in these proceedings. The mother met the father h
of M and J in 1987. They started to cohabit in 1989.
[3] Serious problems emerged in May 1999 when P ran away from home and refused to return. He said that his stepfather, namely, the father of M and J, had repeatedly beaten him and that he was afraid of him. Torbay Council arranged a foster placement. The father denied the charge and the mother supported him. j
They united to reject and isolate P. At a case conference held in November 1999 the father behaved appallingly. He was arrested for threatening behaviour, charged and subsequently sentenced to community service. This prompted Torbay to issue an application for a care order in respect of P and supervision orders in respect of M and J.

a [4] In May 2000 P told a fuller story. He described how the father had buggered him on several occasions. A child protection investigation followed. Again the father denied the allegations. Again the mother supported him. M and J were then taken into care, pursuant to an emergency protection order of 7 June 2000, and placed in foster care. In July 2000 the mother and the father separated, apparently in order to strengthen the mother's case for the return of M and J. The

b paediatric examinations of the children were inconclusive. But an acknowledged expert in this field reported that the father presented an unacceptable risk to the children and that the mother was incapable of protecting them. He recommended therapy for her. At this stage the separation of the mother and father became permanent. The mother was then aged 36. The father was 31 years old.

c [5] Torbay, the local authority, sought care orders in respect of all three children. Its care plan for P was that he should remain in foster care. The care plan for M and J was that an attempt should be made to rehabilitate them with their mother. After hearing much evidence, Judge Sander, sitting at Plymouth County Court, made findings of fact on 1 November 2000. The father was found

d to have sexually abused P and beaten the children with a slipper. The mother had failed to protect the children. Both parents had emotionally abused the children, particularly by rejecting P.

[6] Everyone agreed there should be a care order in respect of P. There was contention over what order should be made regarding the two younger children.

e Discussions took place regarding the care plan for them. The mother and the children's guardian elicited assurances from Torbay on the package of support and treatment available to the family which was needed to make rehabilitation viable. Counsel for the mother, Miss Duthie, sought some guarantee of performance, or a safeguard in the event of breach. She submitted that a care

f order should not be made on the footing that all power and responsibility would pass to Torbay. This, she submitted, would constitute a breach of the human rights of the mother and the children. Such an order was neither necessary nor proportionate to the end to be achieved. Based on previous experience, of which evidence was given, the mother was very sceptical about whether Torbay would carry out the care plan for M and J. The mother contended that interim care

g orders should be made. Torbay and the children's guardian sought final care orders.

[7] The judge made final care orders in respect of all three children on 1 November 2000. She expressed confidence that Torbay would implement the care plan.

h [8] Unhappily, this confidence proved to be misplaced. There was, as the Court of Appeal accepted, a 'striking and fundamental' failure to implement the care plan regarding M and J. Most of the assurances given by the social workers, and accepted by the children's guardian and the judge, proved vain. The mother's principal complaints were as follows. The care plan envisaged

j reunification within six to nine months. But in the four-and-a-half months which had elapsed between the making of the care orders and the hearing of the appeal nothing had happened. The planned family therapy work had not taken place. A social worker was not provided to assist the mother. The Hillside Family Centre programme was not started until early in March. The therapy proposed for the mother was not under way.

[9] The Court of Appeal observed that this 'sad history of potentially disastrous failure' fully vindicated the line taken by Miss Duthie at the trial. The Court of Appeal acquitted Torbay of bad faith. The most that could be said against the council was that at the trial it had too readily promised support for which the mother later proved to be ineligible. The principal cause of 'these serious failings' was a financial crisis within the unitary authority leading to substantial cuts in the social services budget.

[10] The mother's primary contention in the Court of Appeal was that the judge had erred in rejecting her contention that interim care orders, as distinct from final care orders, were the appropriate relief regarding M and J. Torbay and the children's guardian opposed this contention. They submitted that the mother's appeal should be dismissed. The children's guardian also sought directions for trial under s 7 of the 1998 Act by a High Court judge to establish the nature and extent of Torbay's breaches, if any, of its duty to the children under s 6 of that Act.

The Bedfordshire case

[11] The Bedfordshire case concerns two boys: J, born in May 1989, and A, born in August 1991. They are now 12 and ten years old. Their mother, now aged 38, is American. Their father, aged 46, is British. The parents met in the United States and married in this country. Their children were born here. They have had a volatile relationship, separating and being reconciled on a number of occasions. They have spent significant periods living apart. Throughout their lives the children have had contact with their father. Until 6 September 1999 the children lived with their mother.

[12] At times, during much of the children's lives, there has been concern about their parents' ability to meet the children's needs. This has centred on the parents' relationship and the mother's mental health. In 1999 this anxiety deepened. The mother made allegations against the father. These were not substantiated. The mother's conduct deteriorated. There was concern about the children's emotional development, and the failure of the parents to acknowledge the extent of the problem.

[13] On 2 September 1999 Bedfordshire County Council applied for care orders. Pursuant to an emergency protection order and interim care orders, periodically renewed, the children were placed with foster parents. Bedfordshire's final care plan was that the children should be placed with the maternal grandparents, with continuing direct contact with both parents. The grandparents lived in the United States. They agreed to move to England to care for the children. The children were to remain in foster care until the grandparents moved here.

[14] The children's guardian also supported placement with the maternal grandparents. The final report of the guardian concluded that the parents had not made sufficient changes for the children to be returned safely to their care for the foreseeable future.

[15] The applications for care orders came before Judge Hamilton, sitting in Luton County Court, on 20 November 2000. He heard evidence over nine days, and gave judgment on 11 December. The judge concluded that the children were unable to return safely to the joint care of their parents: 'possibly, or even probably, it may be appropriate in 12 to 18 months, but not now'. All the parties agreed that the maternal grandparents would be suitable carers, although the

a evidence that they would be able to come here was 'exiguous in the extreme'. The judge described the care plan as inchoate, because of all the uncertainties involved. In addition to uncertainty about the grandparents' position, the uncertainties included the outcome of further assessment and therapy for the boys, the final outcome of marital work for the parents, and the possibility of improvements with the mother's personality trait. The judge made care orders
b for both children.

The outcome in the Court of Appeal

[16] The Court of Appeal ([2001] 2 FCR 450) heard appeals in both cases together. The parties' arguments were wide-ranging as, indeed, they were before your Lordships' House. The Secretary of State for Health was joined as a party
c because of claims for a declaration that ss 31, 33(3), 38 and 100 of the 1989 Act are incompatible with the European Convention for the Protection of Human Rights and Fundamental Freedoms 1950 (as set out in Sch 1 to the 1998 Act).

[17] Stated shortly, the two innovations fashioned by the Court of Appeal were these. First, the court enunciated guidelines intended to give trial judges a
d wider discretion to make an interim care order, rather than a final care order. The second innovation was more radical. It concerns the position after the court has made a care order. The Court of Appeal propounded a new procedure, by which at the trial the essential milestones of a care plan would be identified and elevated to a 'starred status'. If a starred milestone was not achieved within a reasonable time after the date set at trial, the local authority was obliged to
e 'reactivate the interdisciplinary process that contributed to the creation of the care plan'. At the least the local authority must inform the child's guardian of the position. Either the guardian or the local authority would then have the right to apply to the court for further directions: see the judgment of Thorpe LJ ([2001] 2 FCR 450 at [29], [30]).

f [18] The Court of Appeal regarded the outcome of the appeal in the Torbay case as finely balanced. The court declined to disturb the judge's order. The court also dismissed the application by the children's guardian for directions for trial under s 7 of the 1998 Act. Progress had been sufficient to make referral to the High Court an unnecessary distraction from the main business of getting on with the care plan. An application for 'starring' of the care plan was referred to
g the judge.

[19] On 2 July 2001 Judge Sander starred various items in the final care plan. She directed that Torbay was to provide a progress report to the children's guardian or, in the absence of the guardian, the court if a starred element was not achieved within 14 days of the specified dates. The House was told that the
h starred plan is working well and that the children's interests are now being met.

[20] As to the Bedfordshire case, the Court of Appeal held it was clear that the care plan was insufficiently mature and that Judge Hamilton had wanted more time to await developments. He had been constrained by the case law to make the full care order. The judge should have insisted on more information before
j making the order, or on a report back if things did not turn out as expected. The court allowed the appeal in this case, replacing the care order with an interim care order and remitting the case to Judge Hamilton for his further consideration.

[21] Later developments in the Bedfordshire case should be mentioned briefly. Setting aside the care order had the unfortunate consequence of augmenting the uncertainty about the children's home for the near future. The

maternal grandparents were reluctant to come to this country to care for the
children unless a final care order was made. On 24 October 2001 Judge Hamilton
made a final care order with the consent of the children's guardian, and without
any opposition from the parents. This care order was not starred. The parents
stated they will apply for the care order to be discharged if the children have not
been reunited with them by October 2003.

[22] Before your Lordships' House the Secretary of State for Health and
Bedfordshire Council appealed against the reasoning of the Court of Appeal on
its two innovations, not against the substantive orders made. In the Torbay case
the mother of the children appealed against the order made by the Court of
Appeal. Torbay Council supported the appeal of the Secretary of State and
Bedfordshire Council.

Starred milestones

[23] Two preliminary points can be made at the outset. First, a cardinal
principle of the 1989 Act is that when the court makes a care order it becomes the
duty of the local authority designated by the order to receive the child into its care
while the order remains in force. So long as the care order is in force the authority
has parental responsibility for the child. The authority also has power to decide
the extent to which a parent of the child may meet his responsibility for him: s 33.
An authority might, for instance, not permit parents to change the school of a
child living at home. While a care order is in force the court's powers, under its
inherent jurisdiction, are expressly excluded: s 100(2)(c) and (d). Further, the
court may not make a contact order, a prohibited steps order or a specific issue
order: s 9(1).

[24] There are limited exceptions to this principle of non-intervention by the
court in the authority's discharge of its parental responsibility for a child in its care
under a care order. The court retains jurisdiction to decide disputes about
contact with children in care: s 34. The court may discharge a care order, either
on an application made for the purpose under s 39 or as a consequence of making
a residence order (ss 9(1) and 91(1)). The High Court's judicial review jurisdiction
also remains available.

[25] These exceptions do not detract significantly from the basic principle.
The 1989 Act delineated the boundary of responsibility with complete clarity.
Where a care order is made the responsibility for the child's care is with the
authority rather than the court. The court retains no supervisory role, monitoring
the authority's discharge of its responsibilities. That was the intention of
Parliament.

[26] Consistently with this, in *Kent CC v C* [1993] 1 All ER 719, [1993] Fam 57
Ewbank J decided that the court has no power to add to a care order a direction
to the authority that the child's guardian ad litem should be allowed to have a
continuing involvement, with a view to his applying to the court in due course if
thought appropriate. In *Re KDT (a minor) (care order: conditions)* [1994] 2 FCR 721
the Court of Appeal rightly approved this decision and held that the court has no
power to impose conditions in a care order. There the condition sought by the
child's guardian was that the child should reside at home.

[27] This cardinal principle of the 1989 Act represented a change in the law.
Before the 1989 Act came into operation the court, in exercise of its wardship
jurisdiction, retained power in limited circumstances to give directions to a local
authority regarding children in its care. The limits of this jurisdiction were

a considered by your Lordships' House in *A v Liverpool City Council* [1981] 2 All ER 385, [1982] AC 363 and *W v Hertfordshire CC* [1985] 2 All ER 301, [1985] AC 791. The change brought about by the 1989 Act gave effect to a policy decision on the appropriate division of responsibilities between the courts and local authorities. This was one of the matters widely discussed at the time. A report made to ministers by an inter-departmental working party 'Review of Child Care Law' b (September 1985) drew attention to some of the policy considerations. The particular strength of the courts lies in the resolution of disputes: its ability to hear all sides of a case, to decide issues of fact and law, and to make a firm decision on a particular issue at a particular time. But a court cannot have day-to-day responsibility for a child. The court cannot deliver the services which may best serve a child's needs. Unlike a local authority, a court does not have close, c personal and continuing knowledge of the child. The court cannot respond with immediacy and informality to practical problems and changed circumstances as they arise. Supervision by the court would encourage 'drift' in decision making, a perennial problem in children cases. Nor does a court have the task of managing the financial and human resources available to a local authority for d dealing with all children in need in its area. The authority must manage these resources in the best interests of all the children for whom it is responsible.

[28] The 1989 Act, embodying what I have described as a cardinal principle, represents the assessment made by Parliament of the division of responsibility which would best promote the interests of children within the overall care system. The court operates as the gateway into care, and makes the necessary e care order when the threshold conditions are satisfied and the court considers a care order would be in the best interests of the child. That is the responsibility of the court. Thereafter the court has no continuing role in relation to the care order. Then it is the responsibility of the local authority to decide how the child should be cared for.

f [29] My second preliminary point is this. The 1989 Act has now been in operation for ten years. Over the last six years there has been a steady increase in the number of children looked after by local authorities in England and Wales. At present there are 36,400 children accommodated under care orders, compared with 28,500 in 1995, an increase of 27 per cent. In addition local authorities provide accommodation for nearly 20,000 children under s 20 orders (children in g need of accommodation). A decade's experience in the operation of the Act, at a time of increasing demands on local authorities, has shown that there are occasions when, with the best will in the world, local authorities' discharge of their parental responsibilities has not been satisfactory. The system does not always work well. Shortages of money, of suitable trained staff and of suitable h foster carers and prospective adopters for difficult children are among the reasons. There have been delays in placing children in accordance with their care plans, unsatisfactory breakdown rates and delays in finding substitute placements.

[30] But the problems are more deep-seated than shortage of resources. In November 1997 the government published Sir William Utting's review of j safeguards for children living away from home. Mr Frank Dobson, then Secretary of State for Health, summarised his reaction to the report:

'It covers the lives of children whose home circumstances were so bad that those in authority, to use the jargon, took them into care. The report reveals that in far too many cases not enough care was taken. Elementary safeguards were not in place or not enforced. Many children were harmed

rather than helped. The review reveals that these failings were not just the
fault of individuals—though individuals were at fault. It reveals the failure
of a whole system.'

[31] In autumn 1998 the government published its *Response to the Children's
Safeguards Review* (Cm 4105) and launched its 'Quality Protects' programme,
aimed at improving the public care system for children. Conferences have also
been held, and many research studies undertaken, both private and public, on
particular aspects of the problems. Some of the problems were discussed at the
bi-annual President's Interdisciplinary Conference on Family Law 1997, attended
by judges, child psychiatrists, social workers, social services personnel and other
experts. The proceedings of the conference were subsequently published in book
form, *Divided Duties* (1998). The sharpness of the divide between the court's
powers before and after the making of a care order attracted criticism. The
matters discussed included the need for a care plan to be open to review by the
court in exceptional cases. One suggestion was that a court review could be
triggered by failure to implement 'starred' key factors in the care plan within
specified time-scales. The guardian ad litem would be the appropriate person to
intervene.

[32] This was the source of the innovation which found expression in the
judgments of the Court of Appeal in the present appeals. The House was
informed by counsel that the starred milestones guidance given by the Court of
Appeal was not canvassed in argument before the court. This guidance appeared
for the first time in the judgments of the court.

[33] The jurisprudential route by which the Court of Appeal found itself able
to bring about this development was primarily by recourse to s 3 of the 1998 Act.
Hale LJ said ([2001] 2 FCR 450 at [79]–[80]):

'Where elements of the care plan are so fundamental that there is a real risk
of a breach of Convention rights if they are not fulfilled, and where there is
some reason to fear that they may not be fulfilled, it must be justifiable *to read
into the 1989 Act* a power in the court to require a report on progress ... the
court would require a report, either to the court or to [CAFCASS] ... who
could then decide whether it was appropriate to return the case to court ...
[W]hen making a care order, the court is being asked to interfere in family
life. If it perceives that the consequence of doing so will be to put at risk the
Convention rights of either the parents or the child, the court *should be able*
to impose this very limited requirement as a condition of its own
interference.' (My emphasis.)

Section 3 of the 1998 Act

[34] The judgments in the Court of Appeal are a clear and forceful statement
of the continuing existence of serious problems in this field. In the nature of
things, courts are likely to see more of the cases which go wrong. But the view,
widespread among family judges, is that all too often local authorities' discharge
of their parental responsibilities falls short of an acceptable standard. A disturbing
instance can be found in the recent case of *F v Lambeth London BC* [2001] 3 FCR
738. Munby J said (at [38]) that the 'blunt truth is that in this case the state has
failed these parents and these boys'.

[35] It is entirely understandable that the Court of Appeal should seek some
means to alleviate these problems: some means by which the courts may assist

a children where care orders have been made but subsequently, for whatever reason, care plans have not been implemented as envisaged and, as a result, the welfare of the children is being prejudiced. This is entirely understandable. The courts, notably through their wardship jurisdiction, have long discharged an invaluable role in safeguarding the interests of children. But the question before the House is much more confined. The question is whether the courts have
b power to introduce into the working of the 1989 Act a range of rights and liabilities not sanctioned by Parliament.

[36] On this I have to say at once, respectfully but emphatically, that I part company with the Court of Appeal. I am unable to agree that the court's introduction of a 'starring system' can be justified as a legitimate exercise in interpretation of the 1989 Act in accordance with s 3 of the 1998 Act. Even if the
c 1989 Act is inconsistent with arts 6 or 8 of the convention, which is a question I will consider later, s 3 does not in this case have the effect suggested by the Court of Appeal.

[37] Section 3(1) provides: 'So far as it is possible to do so, primary legislation … must be read and given effect in a way which is compatible with the
d Convention rights.' This is a powerful tool whose use is obligatory. It is not an optional canon of construction. Nor is its use dependent on the existence of ambiguity. Further, the section applies retrospectively. So far as it is possible to do so, primary legislation 'must be read and given effect' to in a way which is compatible with convention rights. This is forthright, uncompromising language.

[38] But the reach of this tool is not unlimited. Section 3 is concerned with
e interpretation. This is apparent from the opening words of s 3(1) 'so far as it is possible to do so'. The side heading of the section is 'Interpretation of legislation'. Section 4 (power to make a declaration of incompatibility) and, indeed, s 3(2)(b) presuppose that not all provisions in primary legislation can be rendered convention compliant by the application of s 3(1). The existence of this limit on
f the scope of s 3(1) has already been the subject of judicial confirmation, more than once: see, for instance, Lord Woolf CJ in *Poplar Housing and Regeneration Community Association Ltd v Donoghue* [2001] EWCA Civ 595 at [75], [2001] 4 All ER 604 at [75], [2001] 3 WLR 183 and Lord Hope of Craighead in *R v Lambert* [2001] UKHL 37 at [79]–[81], [2001] 3 All ER 577 at [79]–[81], [2001] 3 WLR 206.

g [39] In applying s 3 courts must be ever mindful of this outer limit. The 1998 Act reserves the amendment of primary legislation to Parliament. By this means the 1998 Act seeks to preserve Parliamentary sovereignty. The 1998 Act maintains the constitutional boundary. Interpretation of statutes is a matter for the courts; the enactment of statutes, and the amendment of statutes, are matters for Parliament.

h [40] Up to this point there is no difficulty. The area of real difficulty lies in identifying the limits of interpretation in a particular case. This is not a novel problem. If anything, the problem is more acute today than in past times. Nowadays courts are more 'liberal' in the interpretation of all manner of documents. The greater the latitude with which courts construe documents, the
j less readily defined is the boundary. What one person regards as sensible, if robust, interpretation, another regards as impermissibly creative. For present purposes it is sufficient to say that a meaning which departs substantially from a fundamental feature of an Act of Parliament is likely to have crossed the boundary between interpretation and amendment. This is especially so where the departure has important practical repercussions which the court is not

equipped to evaluate. In such a case the overall contextual setting may leave no
scope for rendering the statutory provision convention compliant by legitimate a
use of the process of interpretation. The boundary line may be crossed even
though a limitation on convention rights is not stated in express terms. Lord
Steyn's observations in R v A [2001] UKHL 25 at [44], [2001] 3 All ER 1 at [44],
[2002] 1 AC 45 are not to be read as meaning that a clear limitation on convention
rights in terms is the only circumstance in which an interpretation incompatible b
with convention rights may arise.

[41] I should add a further general observation in the light of what happened
in the present case. Section 3 directs courts on how legislation shall, as far as
possible, be interpreted. When a court, called upon to construe legislation,
ascribes a meaning and effect to the legislation pursuant to its obligation under s c
3, it is important the court should identify clearly the particular statutory
provision or provisions whose interpretation leads to that result. Apart from all
else, this should assist in ensuring the court does not inadvertently stray outside
its interpretation jurisdiction.

[42] I return to the 1989 Act. I have already noted, as a cardinal principle of d
the 1989 Act, that the courts are not empowered to intervene in the way local
authorities discharge their parental responsibilities under final care orders.
Parliament entrusted to local authorities, not the courts, the responsibility for
looking after children who are the subject of care orders. To my mind the new
starring system would depart substantially from this principle. Under the new
system the court, when making a care order, is empowered to impose an e
obligation on an authority concerning the future care of the child. In future, the
authority must submit a progress report, in circumstances identified by the court,
either to the court or to the Children and Family Court Advisory and Support
Service (CAFCASS). This is only the first step. The next step is that the court,
when seised of what has happened after the care order was made, may then call f
for action. If it considers this necessary in the best interests of the child, the court
may intervene and correct matters which are going wrong. In short, under the
starring system the court will exercise a newly-created supervisory function.

[43] In his judgment Thorpe LJ noted that the starring system 'seems to
breach the fundamental boundary between the functions and responsibilities of
the court and the local authority' (see [2001] 2 FCR 450 at [31]). I agree. I consider g
this judicial innovation passes well beyond the boundary of interpretation. I can
see no provision in the 1989 Act which lends itself to the interpretation that
Parliament was thereby conferring this supervisory function on the court. No
such provision was identified by the Court of Appeal. On the contrary, the
starring system is inconsistent in an important respect with the scheme of the h
1989 Act. It would constitute amendment of the 1989 Act, not its interpretation.
It would have far-reaching practical ramifications for local authorities and their
care of children. The starring system would not come free from additional
administrative work and expense. It would be likely to have a material effect on
authorities' allocation of scarce financial and other resources. This in turn would j
affect authorities' discharge of their responsibilities to other children. Moreover,
the need to produce a formal report whenever a care plan is significantly departed
from, and then await the outcome of any subsequent court proceedings, would
affect the whole manner in which authorities discharge, and are able to discharge,
their parental responsibilities.

a [44] These are matters for decision by Parliament, not the courts. It is impossible for a court to attempt to evaluate these ramifications or assess what would be the views of Parliament if changes are needed. I echo the wise words of Cooke P in the New Zealand case of *R v Stack* [1986] 1 NZLR 257 at 261–262:

b 'It would amount to amending the Act by judicial legislation. In a sensitive and controversial field which the New Zealand Parliament may be said to have taken to itself, we do not consider that this court would be justified in such a course. If the Act is to be amended it should be done by Parliament after full consideration of the arguments of policy.'

c In my view, in the present case the Court of Appeal exceeded the bounds of its judicial jurisdiction under s 3 in introducing this new scheme.

Sections 7 and 8 of the 1998 Act

[45] Sections 7 and 8 of the 1998 Act have conferred extended powers on the courts. Section 6 makes it unlawful for a public authority to act in a way which is incompatible with a convention right. Section 7 enables victims of conduct d made unlawful by s 6 to bring court proceedings against the public authority in question. Section 8 spells out, in wide terms, the relief a court may grant in those proceedings. The court may grant such relief or remedy, or make such order, within its powers as it considers just and appropriate. Thus, if a local authority conducts itself in a manner which infringes the art 8 rights of a parent or child, the e court may grant appropriate relief on the application of a victim of the unlawful act.

[46] This new statutory power has already been exercised. In *Re M* (29 June 2001, unreported) a local authority reviewed its care plan for a child in its care. The authority finally ruled out any further prospect of the child returning to live f with her mother or of ever going to live with her father. In proceedings brought by the parents Holman J set aside the decision. The decision making process was unfair by not involving the parents to a degree sufficient to provide their interests with the requisite protection. In so ordering Holman J was proceeding squarely within the extended jurisdiction conferred by ss 7 and 8. The court applied the provisions of the 1998 Act in the manner Parliament intended, there in respect of g a breach of art 8.

[47] In the present case the Court of Appeal seems to have placed some reliance on ss 7 and 8 for the extension of the court's powers envisaged by the starring system. Thorpe LJ said ([2001] 2 FCR 450 at [32]):

h 'The responsibility on the courts in the exercise of extended or additional powers is of course to ensure that they are used only to avoid or prevent the breach of an art 6 or art 8 right of one of the parties. If no actual or prospective breach of right is demonstrated the power does not arise.'

[48] I do not think ss 7 and 8 can be pressed as far as would be necessary if they j were to bring the introduction of the starring system within their embrace. Sections 7 and 8 are to be given a generous interpretation, as befits their human rights purpose. But, despite the cautionary words of both Thorpe and Hale LJJ, the starring system goes much further than provide a judicial remedy to victims of actual or proposed unlawful conduct by local authorities entrusted with the care of children.

[49] Section 7 envisages proceedings, brought by a person who is or would be a victim, against a public authority which has acted or is proposing to act unlawfully. The question whether the authority has acted unlawfully, or is proposing to do so, is a matter to be decided in the proceedings. Relief can be given against the authority only in respect of an act, or a proposed act, of the authority which the court finds is or would be unlawful. For this purpose an act includes a failure to act. But the starring system would impose obligations on local authorities in circumstances when there has been no such finding and when, indeed, the authority has committed no breach of a convention right and is not proposing to do so. Unless an authority is acting in bad faith, the possibility or prospect of non-fulfilment, for example, of a placement for a child cannot by itself be evidence that the authority is 'proposing' to act unlawfully contrary to s 6. Nor can the non-fulfilment of a starred event, when the obligation to report arises, necessarily be equated with a breach or threatened breach of a convention right. Failure to adhere to a care plan may be due to a change in circumstances which, in the best interests of the child, calls for a variation from the care plan which was approved by the court.

Statutory incompatibility

[50] Thus far I have concluded that, even if there is incompatibility between the 1989 Act and arts 6 or 8 of the convention, the introduction of the starring system is beyond the powers of the court under s 3 of the 1998 Act. Moreover, ss 7 and 8 of the 1998 Act do not provide a legal basis for the introduction of this new system.

[51] The mother of the children in the Torbay case contended that if the 1989 Act does not permit the introduction of the starring system, the Act is incompatible with arts 6 and 8. She claims to be a victim of an infringement of her rights under these two articles. Save for the intervention of the Court of Appeal matters might well have gone even more seriously wrong. She seeks a declaration of incompatibility pursuant to s 4 of the 1998 Act. I now turn to consider whether the 1989 Act is incompatible with either of these articles of the convention. I start with art 8.

Compatibility and art 8

[52] Article 8 of the convention provides:

'1. Everyone has the right to respect for his private and family life, his home and his correspondence.

2. There shall be no interference by a public authority with the exercise of this right except such as is in accordance with the law and is necessary in a democratic society in the interests of national security, public safety or the economic well-being of the country, for the prevention of disorder or crime, for the protection of health or morals, or for the protection of the rights and freedoms of others.'

[53] The essential purpose of this article is to protect individuals against arbitrary interference by public authorities. In addition to this negative obligation there are positive obligations inherent in an effective concept of 'respect' for family life: see *Marckx v Belgium* (1979) 2 EHRR 330 at 342 (para 31). In both contexts a fair balance has to be struck between the competing interests

a of the individual and the community as a whole: see *Hokkanen v Finland* (1994) 19 EHRR 139 at 168–169 (para 55).

[54] Clearly, if matters go seriously awry, the manner in which a local authority discharges its parental responsibilities to a child in its care may violate the rights of the child or his parents under this article. The local authority's intervention in the life of the child, justified at the outset when the care order was

b made, may cease to be justifiable under art 8(2). Sedley LJ pointed out that a care order from which no good is coming cannot sensibly be said to be pursuing a legitimate aim. A care order which keeps a child away from his family for purposes which, as time goes by, are not being realised will sooner or later become a disproportionate interference with the child's primary art 8 rights (see

c [2001] 2 FCR 450 at [45]).

[55] Further, the local authority's decision making process must be conducted fairly and so as to afford due respect to the interests protected by art 8. For instance, the parents should be involved to a degree which is sufficient to provide adequate protection for their interests: *W v UK* (1987) 10 EHRR 29 at 49–50 (paras 62–64).

d [56] However, the possibility that something may go wrong with the local authority's discharge of its parental responsibilities or its decision-making processes, and that this would be a violation of art 8 so far as the child or parent is concerned, does not mean that the legislation itself is incompatible, or inconsistent, with art 8. The 1989 Act imposes on a local authority looking after

e a child the duty to safeguard and promote the child's welfare. Before making any decision with respect to such a child the authority must, so far as reasonably practicable, ascertain the wishes and feelings of the child and his parents: s 22. Section 26 provides for periodic case reviews by the authority, including obtaining the views of parents and children. One of the required reviews is that

f every six months the local authority must actively consider whether it should apply to the court for a discharge of the care order: see the Review of Children's Cases Regulations 1991, SI 1991/895. Every local authority must also establish a procedure for considering representations, including complaints, made to it by any child who is being looked after by it, or by his parents, about the discharge by the authority of its parental responsibilities for the child.

g [57] If an authority duly carries out these statutory duties, in the ordinary course there should be no question of infringement by the local authority of the art 8 rights of the child or his parents. Questions of infringement are only likely to arise if a local authority fails properly to discharge its statutory responsibilities. Infringement which then occurs is not brought about, in any meaningful sense,

h by the 1989 Act. Quite the reverse. Far from the infringement being compelled, or even countenanced, by the provisions of the 1989 Act, the infringement flows from the local authority's failure to comply with its obligations under the Act. True, it is the 1989 Act which entrusts responsibility for the child's care to the local authority. But that is not inconsistent with art 8. Local authorities are

j responsible public authorities, with considerable experience in this field. Entrusting a local authority with the sole responsibility for a child's care, once the 'significant harm' threshold has been established, is not of itself an infringement of art 8. There is no suggestion in the Strasbourg jurisprudence that absence of court supervision of a local authority's discharge of its parental responsibilities is itself an infringement of art 8.

[58] Where, then, is the inconsistency which is alleged to exist? As I
understand it, the principal contention is that the incompatibility lies in the
absence from the 1989 Act of an adequate remedy if a local authority fails to
discharge its parental responsibilities properly and, as a direct result, the rights of
the child or his parents under art 8 are violated. The 1989 Act authorises the state
to interfere with family life. The Act empowers courts to make care orders
whose effect is to entrust the care of children to a public authority. But the
selfsame Act, while conferring these wide powers of interference in family life,
omits to provide any sufficient remedy, by way of a mechanism for controlling
an erring local authority's conduct, if things go seriously wrong with the
authority's care of the child. It is only to be expected, the submission runs, that
there will be occasions when the conduct of a local authority falls short of the
appropriate standards. An Act which authorises state interference but makes no
provision for external control when the body entrusted with parental
responsibility fails in its responsibilities is not compatible with art 8. The
extensive supervisory functions and responsibilities conferred on the Secretary of
State in Pt XI of the Act, including his default powers under s 84, are not sufficient
in practice to provide an adequate and timely remedy in individual cases.

[59] In my view this line of argument is misconceived. Failure by the state to
provide an effective remedy for a violation of art 8 is not itself a violation of art 8.
This is self-evident. So, even if the 1989 Act does fail to provide an adequate
remedy, the Act is not for that reason incompatible with art 8. This is the short
and conclusive answer to this point.

[60] However, I should elaborate a little further. In convention terms, failure
to provide an effective remedy for infringement of a right set out in the
convention is an infringement of art 13. But art 13 is not a convention right as
defined in s 1(1) of the 1998 Act. So legislation which fails to provide an effective
remedy for infringement of art 8 is not, for that reason, incompatible with a
convention right within the meaning of the 1998 Act.

[61] Where, then, does that leave the matter so far as English law is
concerned? The domestic counterpart to art 13 is ss 7 and 8 of the 1998 Act, read
in conjunction with s 6. This domestic counterpart to art 13 takes a different form
from art 13 itself. Unlike art 13, which declares a right ('Everyone whose rights
... are violated shall have an effective remedy'), ss 7 and 8 provide a remedy.
Article 13 guarantees the availability at the national level of an effective remedy
to enforce the substance of convention rights. Sections 7 and 8 seek to provide
that remedy in this country. The object of these sections is to provide in English
law the very remedy art 13 declares is the entitlement of everyone whose rights
are violated.

[62] Thus, if a local authority fails to discharge its parental responsibilities
properly, and in consequence the rights of the parents under art 8 are violated,
the parents may, as a longstop, bring proceedings against the authority under s 7.
I have already drawn attention to a case where this has happened. I say 'as a
longstop', because other remedies, both of an administrative nature and by way
of court proceedings, may also be available in the particular case. For instance,
Bedfordshire council has an independent visitor, a children's complaints officer
and a children's rights officer. Sometimes court proceedings by way of judicial
review of a decision of a local authority may be the appropriate way to proceed.
In a suitable case an application for discharge of the care order is available. One

a would not expect proceedings to be launched under s 7 until any other appropriate remedial routes have first been explored.

[63] In the ordinary course a parent ought to be able to obtain effective relief, by one or other of these means, against an authority whose mishandling of a child in its care has violated a parent's art 8 rights. More difficult is the case, to which Thorpe LJ drew attention ([2001] 2 FCR 450 at [34]), where there is no parent able *b* and willing to become involved. In this type of case the art 8 rights of a young child may be violated by a local authority without anyone outside the local authority becoming aware of the violation. In practice, such a child may not always have an effective remedy.

[64] I shall return to this problem at a later stage. For present purposes it is sufficient to say that, for the reason I have given, the failure to provide a young *c* child with an effective remedy in this situation does not mean that the 1989 Act is incompatible with art 8: failure to provide a remedy for a breach of art 8 is not itself a breach of art 8.

Compatibility and art 6

d [65] The position regarding art 6(1) is more complicated. Article 6(1) provides:

> 'In the determination of his civil rights and obligations ... everyone is entitled to a fair and public hearing within a reasonable time by an independent and impartial tribunal established by law.'

e [66] The starting point here is to note that art 6(1) applies only to disputes (contestations) over (civil) rights and obligations which, at least arguably, are recognised under domestic law. Article 6(1) does not itself guarantee any particular content for civil rights and obligations in the substantive law of contracting states: see *W v UK* (1987) 10 EHRR 29 at 54 (para 73). The European *f* Court of Human Rights has recently reiterated this interpretation of art 6(1), in *TP v UK* [2001] 2 FCR 289 at 316 (para 92).

[67] The case of *McMichael v UK* [1995] 2 FCR 718 illustrates this limitation on the scope of art 6(1). Under Scots law the natural father of a child born outside marriage did not automatically have parental rights in respect of the child. Since Mr McMichael had not taken steps to obtain legal recognition of his status as a *g* father, art 6(1) had no application to his complaint that he had not been allowed to see the confidential reports submitted in the care proceedings.

[68] On the other side of the line is the well known case of *W v UK*, concerning parental rights of access. This case pre-dated the 1989 Act. The European Court of Human Rights considered that a parental rights resolution did not extinguish *h* all parental rights regarding access to a child in care. The court held that when a parent claimed access to his child the determination of a parental right was just as much in issue as when a parent applied for the discharge of a parental rights resolution or a care order. Accordingly, a substantial dispute over access fell within art 6(1).

j [69] Thus, when considering the application of art 6(1) to children in care, the European Court of Human Rights focuses on the rights under domestic law which are then enjoyed by the parents or the child. If the impugned decision significantly affects rights retained by the parents or the child after the child has been taken into care, art 6(1) may well be relevant. It is otherwise if the decision has no such effect.

[70] I pause to note one consequence of this limitation on the scope of art 6(1). Since art 6(1) is concerned only with the protection of rights found in domestic law, a right conferred by the convention itself does not as such qualify. Under the convention, art 13 is the guarantee of an effective remedy for breach of a convention right, not art 6(1). Article 6(1) is concerned with the protection of other rights of individuals. Thus, a right guaranteed by art 8 is not in itself a civil right within the meaning of art 6(1).

[71] Although a right guaranteed by art 8 is not *in itself* a civil right within the meaning of art 6(1), the 1998 Act has now transformed the position in this country. By virtue of the 1998 Act art 8 rights are now part of the civil rights of parents and children for the purposes of art 6(1). This is because now, under s 6 of the 1998 Act, it is unlawful for a public authority to act inconsistently with art 8.

[72] I have already noted that, apart from the difficulty concerning young children, the court remedies provided by ss 7 and 8 should ordinarily provide effective relief for an infringement of art 8 rights. I need therefore say nothing further on this aspect of the application of art 6(1). I can confine my attention to the application of art 6(1) to *other* civil rights and obligations of parents and children.

[73] In this regard a further aspect of the phrase 'civil rights' should be noted. The Strasbourg case law interprets this expression as directed essentially at rights which English law characterises as private law rights. This does not mean that administrative decisions by public authorities, characterised by English law as matters regulated by public law, are outside the scope of art 6(1). The Strasbourg jurisprudence has brought such decisions within art 6(1), on the basis that such decisions can determine or affect rights in private law: see, for instance, *Ringeisen v Austria (No 1)* (1971) 1 EHRR 455 at 489–490 (para 94).

[74] In taking this step the jurisprudence of the European Court of Human Rights has drawn back from holding that art 6(1) requires that all administrative decisions should be susceptible of, in effect, substantive appeal to a court, with the court substituting its views for the decision made by the administrator. Article 6(1) is not so crude or, I might add, so unrealistic. Article 6(1) is more discerning in its requirements. The extent of judicial control required depends on the subject matter of the decision and the extent to which this lends itself to judicial decision. This area of the law has recently been discussed by Lord Hoffmann in *R (on the application of Alconbury Developments Ltd) v Secretary of State for the Environment, Transport and the Regions* [2001] UKHL 23 at [77]–[122], [2001] 2 All ER 929 at [77]–[122], [2001] 2 WLR 1389.

[75] This principle, that the required degree of judicial control varies according to the subject matter of the impugned decision, is important in the context of the 1989 Act, to which I can now turn. There is no difficulty about the making of a care order. The effect of a care order is to endow a local authority with parental responsibility for a child. Accordingly, the making of a care order affects the 'civil rights' of the parents. The making of a care order affects their rights as parents, and art 6(1) applies. In this regard English law, expressed in the 1989 Act, accords with the requirements of art 6(1). A care order is made by the court, in proceedings to which the parents are parties.

[76] Likewise, the question whether a care order should be continued or discharged affects the parents' civil rights. Here also, the 1989 Act is in harmony with art 6(1). Under the Act the parents may apply to the court for the discharge of the care order.

a [77] The position regarding decisions taken by the local authority on the care of a child while a care order is in force is not quite so straightforward. By law a parent has rights, duties, powers and responsibilities in relation to a child. This is recognised in the definition of parental responsibility in the 1989 Act, s 3(1). Under the 1989 Act the parental responsibility of a parent does not cease when a care order is made. The subject matter of decisions made by a local authority

b acting under its statutory powers while a care order is in force range widely, from the trivial to matters of fundamental importance to parents and children. Hence the extent to which decisions by an authority affect the private law rights of parents and children also varies widely. Some affect the continuing parental responsibility of a parent, others do not.

c [78] Decisions on the day-to-day care of a child are towards the latter edge of this range. In the ordinary course disputes about such decisions attract the requirements of art 6(1), if at all, only to an attenuated extent. The *parents'* rights in respect of the control of the day to day care of the child were decided by the making of the care order and the grant of parental responsibility to the local authority. Nor do such decisions involve the determination of the civil rights of

d the *child*. The upbringing of a child normally and inevitably requires that those with parental responsibility for the child exercise care and control over the child and make decisions regarding where the child shall live and how the child's life shall be regulated: see *Nielsen v Denmark* (1988) 11 EHRR 175 at 191 (para 61). I see no reason to doubt that, in so far as art 6(1) requires judicial control of such decisions, this requirement is satisfied in this country by the availability of judicial

e review.

[79] Other decisions made by a local authority may vitally affect the parent-child relationship. Decisions about access are an example, for which the 1989 Act makes provision for the involvement of the court. But there are other important decisions for which the 1989 Act makes no provision for court

f intervention. A decision by a local authority under s 33(3)(b) that a parent shall not meet certain of his parental responsibilities for the child may, depending on the facts, be an instance. More generally, it is notable that when a care order is made questions of a most fundamental nature regarding the child's future may remain still to be decided by the local authority; for example, whether rehabilitation is still a realistic possibility. Consistently with the Strasbourg

g jurisprudence such decisions attract a high degree of judicial control. It must be doubtful whether judicial review will always meet this standard, even if the review is conducted with the heightened scrutiny discussed in *R v Secretary of State for the Home Dept, ex p Daly* [2001] UKHL 26, [2001] 3 All ER 433, [2001] 2 WLR 1622.

h [80] Any shortcoming here is not, strictly, made good by ss 7 and 8 of the 1998 Act. As already noted, s 8 enables the court to grant relief only in respect of conduct of a public authority made unlawful by s 6. For the present purpose the relevant public authority is the court itself. In failing to provide a hearing as guaranteed by art 6(1) the court is not acting unlawfully for the purposes of s 6.

j The court is simply giving effect to the 1989 Act: see s 6(2)(a) of the 1998 Act. The court has no power to act otherwise. Section 6 is not the source of any such power. Section 6 is prohibitory, not enabling.

[81] I hasten to add an important practical qualification. Although any shortcoming here is not strictly made good by ss 7 and 8, it is difficult to visualise a shortcoming which would have any substantial practical content. It is not easy

to think of an instance in this particular field where the civil rights of parents or
children, protected by art 6(1), are more extensive than their art 8 rights. Their
art 8 rights have the protection accorded in domestic law by ss 7 and 8. In practice
this art 8 protection would, in the present context, seem to cover much the same
ground as art 6(1). So any shortcoming is likely to be more theoretical than real.

[82] I must note also a difficulty of another type. This concerns the position
of young children who have no parent or guardian able and willing to become
involved in questioning a care decision made by a local authority. This is an
instance of a perennial problem affecting children. A parent may abuse a child.
The law may provide a panoply of remedies. But this avails nothing if the
problem remains hidden. Depending on the facts, situations of this type may give
rise to difficulties with convention rights. The convention is intended to
guarantee rights which are practical and effective. This is particularly so with the
right of access to the courts, in view of the prominent place held in a democratic
society by the right to a fair trial: see *Airey v Ireland* (1979) 2 EHRR 305 at 314 (para
24). The guarantee provided by art 6(1) can hardly be said to be satisfied in the
case of a young child who, in practice, has no way of initiating judicial review
proceedings to challenge a local authority's decision affecting his civil rights. (In
such a case, as already noted, the young child would also lack means of initiating
s 7 proceedings to protect his art 8 rights.)

[83] My conclusion is that in these respects circumstances might perhaps arise
when English law would not satisfy the requirements of art 6(1) regarding some
child care decisions made by local authorities. In one or other of the
circumstances mentioned above the art 6 rights of a child or parent are capable of
being infringed.

[84] I come to the next and final step. This is to consider whether the
existence of possible infringements in these circumstances means that the 1989
Act is incompatible with art 6(1).

[85] Here again, the position is not straightforward. The convention violation
now under consideration consists of a failure to provide access to a court as
guaranteed by art 6(1). The absence of such provision means that English law
may be incompatible with art 6(1). The United Kingdom may be in breach of its
treaty obligations regarding this article. But the absence of such provision from
a particular statute does not, in itself, mean that the statute is incompatible with
art 6(1). Rather, this signifies at most the existence of a lacuna in the statute.

[86] This is the position so far as the failure to comply with art 6(1) lies in the
absence of effective machinery for protecting the civil rights of young children
who have no parent or guardian able and willing to act for them. In such cases
there is a statutory lacuna, not a statutory incompatibility.

[87] The matter may stand differently regarding the inability, of parents and
children alike, to challenge in court care decisions, however fundamental, made
by a local authority while a care order is in force. This matter may stand
differently because, judicial review apart, the opportunity to challenge such
decisions in court would be in conflict with the scheme of the 1989 Act. This
gives rise to yet another issue: whether inconsistency with a basic principle of a
statute, as distinct from inconsistency with express provisions within the statute,
gives rise to incompatibility for the purpose of s 4.

[88] This issue does not call for decision on these appeals. I prefer to leave it
open, for two reasons. As already noted, this problem is theoretical rather than
real, given the court remedies available for breach of art 8 rights. Secondly, the

a issue does not need to be decided in the present case, for this reason. Even if
conflict with the scheme of the Act constitutes incompatibility, the present case
is not one where the House should make a declaration of incompatibility.
Ordinarily the court will grant such relief only to a person who is a victim of an
actual or proposed breach of a convention right. In the Torbay case the essential
problem was 'drift' in the local authority's implementation of the care plan. But
b in practice the mother did not lack a court forum in which to express her deep
concern at the lack of progress. Her appeal enabled her to raise these matters in
the Court of Appeal. The intervention of that court appears to have galvanised
the local authority into taking the necessary action, if belatedly. I do not think
there has been a violation of the mother's rights under art 6(1).

c
Interim care orders

[89] I turn to the other 'revisionary application' of the 1989 Act adumbrated
by the Court of Appeal. This concerns the extended use of interim care orders.
The source of the court's power to make an interim care order is s 38. The power
exists when an application for a care order or a supervision order is adjourned (s
d 38(1)(a)) or the court has given a direction to a local authority under s 37 to
undertake an investigation of a child's circumstances (s 38(1)(b)). Section 38
contains tight limits on the period for which an interim care order has effect: eight
weeks initially, thereafter four weeks. The circumstances in which an interim
care order ceases to have effect include also the disposal of the application for a
e care order or a supervision order, in both s 38(1)(a) and s 38(1)(b) cases.

[90] From a reading of s 38 as a whole it is abundantly clear that the purpose
of an interim care order, so far as presently material, is to enable the court to
safeguard the welfare of a child until such time as the court is in a position to
decide whether or not it is in the best interests of the child to make a care order.
f When that time arrives depends on the circumstances of the case and is a matter
for the judgment of the trial judge. That is the general, guiding principle. The
corollary to this principle is that an interim care order is not intended to be used
as a means by which the court may continue to exercise a supervisory role over
the local authority in cases where it is in the best interests of a child that a care
order should be made.

g
[91] An interim care order, thus, is a temporary 'holding' measure. Inevitably,
time is needed before an application for a care order is ready for decision. Several
parties are usually involved: parents, the child's guardian, the local authority,
perhaps others.   Evidence has to be prepared, parents and other people
interviewed, investigations may be required, assessments made, and the local
h authority must produce its care plan for the child in accordance with the guidance
contained in Local Authority Circular LAC (99) 29 *Care Plans and Care Proceedings
Under the Children Act 1989.* Although the 1989 Act itself makes no mention of a
care plan, in practice this is a document of key importance. It enables the court
and everyone else to know, and consider, the local authority's plans for the future
j of the child if a care order is made.

[92] When a local authority formulates a care plan in connection with an
application for a care order, there are bound to be uncertainties. Even the basic
shape of the future life of the child may be far from clear. Over the last ten years
problems have arisen about how far courts should go in attempting to resolve
these uncertainties before making a care order and passing responsibility to the

local authority. Once a final care order is made, the resolution of the uncertainties *a* will be a matter for the authority, not the court.

[93] In terms of legal principle one type of uncertainty is straightforward. This is the case where the uncertainty needs to be resolved before the court can decide whether it is in the best interests of the child to make a care order at all. In *C v Solihull Metropolitan BC* [1992] 2 FCR 341 the court could not decide whether a care order was in the best interests of a child, there a 'battered baby', without *b* knowing the result of a parental assessment. Ward J made an appropriate interim order. In such a case the court should finally dispose of the matter only when the material facts are as clearly known as can be hoped. Booth J adopted a similar approach, for a similar reason, in *Re A (a minor) (care proceedings)* [1993] 1 FCR 164, [1993] 1 WLR 291.

[94] More difficult, as a matter of legal principle, are cases where it is obvious *c* that a care order is in the best interests of the child but the immediate way ahead thereafter is unsatisfactorily obscure. These cases exemplify a problem, or a 'tension', inherent in the scheme of the 1989 Act. What should the judge do when a care order is clearly in the best interests of the child but the judge does not approve of the care plan? This judicial dilemma was described by Balcombe *d* LJ in *Re S and D (child case: powers of court)* [1995] 1 FCR 626 at 635 perhaps rather too bleakly, as the judge having to choose between 'the lesser of two evils'.

[95] In this context there are sometimes uncertainties whose nature is such that they are suitable for immediate resolution, in whole or in part, by the court in the course of disposing of the care order application. The uncertainty may be of such a character that it can, and should, be resolved so far as possible before the *e* court proceeds to make the care order. Then, a limited period of 'planned and purposeful' delay can readily be justified as the sensible and practical way to deal with an existing problem.

[96] An instance of this occurred in *Re CH (a minor) (care or interim order)* [1998] 2 FCR 347. In that case the mother had pleaded guilty to causing grievous bodily *f* harm to the child. The judge was intensely worried by the sharp divergence of professional view on placement. The local authority cautiously favoured rehabilitation. The child's guardian ad litem believed adoption was the realistic way to promote the child's future welfare. The judge made the care order without hearing any expert evidence on the disputed issue. The local authority would itself obtain expert advice, and then reconsider the question of placement. *g* The Court of Appeal (Kennedy and Thorpe LJJ) held that the fact that a care order was the inevitable outcome should not have deflected the judge from hearing expert evidence on this issue. Even if the issue could not be finally resolved before a care order was made, it was obviously sensible and desirable that, in the circumstances of the case, the local authority should have the benefit of the *h* judge's observations on the point.

[97] Frequently the case is on the other side of this somewhat imprecise line. Frequently the uncertainties involved in a care plan will have to be worked out after a care order has been made and while the plan is being implemented. This was so in the case which is the locus classicus on this subject: *Re R (minors) (care proceedings: care plan)* [1994] 2 FCR 136. There the care plan envisaged placing the *j* children in short-term foster placements for up to a year. Then a final decision would be made on whether to place the children permanently away from the mother. Rehabilitation was not ruled out if the mother showed herself amenable to treatment. Wall J said (at 149):

a   '... there are cases (of which this is one) in which the action which requires
to be taken in the interests of children necessarily involves steps into the
unknown ... provided the court is satisfied that the local authority is alert to
the difficulties which may arise in the execution of the care plan, the function
of the court is not to seek to oversee the plan but to entrust its execution to
the local authority.'

b
In that case the uncertain outcome of the treatment was a matter to be worked
out after a care order was made, not before. The Court of Appeal decision in *Re
L (minors) (care proceedings: appeal)* [1996] 2 FCR 352 was another case of this type:
see Butler-Sloss LJ (at 362). So also was the decision of the Court of Appeal in *Re
R (care proceedings: adjournment)* [1998] 3 FCR 654.

c   [98] These are all instances of cases where important issues of uncertainty
were known to exist before a care order was made. Quite apart from known
uncertainties, an element of future uncertainty is necessarily inherent in the very
nature of a care plan. The best laid plans 'gang aft a-gley'. These are matters for
decision by the local authority, if and when they arise. A local authority must
d   always respond appropriately to changes, of varying degrees of predictability,
which from time to time are bound to occur after a care order has been made and
while the care plan is being implemented. No care plan can ever be regarded as
set in stone.

[99] Despite all the inevitable uncertainties, when deciding whether to make
a care order the court should normally have before it a care plan which is
e   sufficiently firm and particularised for all concerned to have a reasonably clear
picture of the likely way ahead for the child for the foreseeable future. The
degree of firmness to be expected, as well as the amount of detail in the plan, will
vary from case to case depending on how far the local authority can foresee what
will be best for the child at that time. This is necessarily so. But making a care
f   order is always a serious interference in the lives of the child and his parents.
Although art 8 contains no explicit procedural requirements, the decision making
process leading to a care order must be fair and such as to afford due respect to
the interests safeguarded by art 8: see *TP v UK* [2001] 2 FCR 289 at 311 (para 72).
If the parents and the child's guardian are to have a fair and adequate opportunity
to make representations to the court on whether a care order should be made,
g   the care plan must be appropriately specific.

[100] Cases vary so widely that it is impossible to be more precise about the
test to be applied by a court when deciding whether to continue interim relief
rather than proceed to make a care order. It would be foolish to attempt to be
more precise. One further general point may be noted. When postponing a
h   decision on whether to make a care order a court will need to have in mind the
general statutory principle that any delay in determining issues relating to a
child's upbringing is likely to prejudice the child's welfare: s 1(2) of the 1989 Act.

[101] In the Court of Appeal Thorpe LJ ([2001] 2 FCR 450 at [29]) expressed
the view that in certain circumstances the judge at the trial should have a 'wider
j   discretion' to make an interim care order 'where the care plan seems inchoate or
where the passage of a relatively brief period seems bound to see the fulfilment
of some event or process vital to planning and deciding the future'. In an
appropriate case, a judge must be free to defer making a care order until he is
satisfied that the way ahead 'is no longer obscured by an uncertainty that is
neither inevitable nor chronic'.

[102] As I see it, the analysis I have set out above adheres faithfully to the scheme of the 1989 Act and conforms to the procedural requirements of art 8 of the Convention. At the same time it affords trial judges the degree of flexibility Thorpe LJ is rightly concerned they should have. Whether this represents a small shift in emphasis from the existing case law may be a moot point. What is more important is that, in the words of Wall J in *Re R (minors)*, the court must always maintain a proper balance between the need to satisfy itself about the appropriateness of the care plan and the avoidance of 'over-zealous investigation into matters which are properly within the administrative discretion of the local authority'. This balance is a matter for the good sense of the tribunal, assisted by the advocates appearing before it (see [1994] 2 FCR 136 at 146).

The outcome of the appeals

[103] I would dismiss the appeal of the mother in the Torbay case. When rejecting the mother's submission that the appropriate order was an interim order, Judge Sander regarded the care plan as clear. The work and therapy would take months. The outcome was neither known nor certain, but the children needed the security of not having further court proceedings hanging over them. I can see no basis for faulting the judge's decision to proceed to make a full care order at once.

[104] Nor do later events provide good reason for now discharging the care order and substituting an interim care order. That would be simply a means of enabling the courts to monitor Torbay's discharge of its parental responsibilities. Happily, however egregious the past failings of Torbay, the current position is that all seems to be going well.

[105] I would allow the appeals of the Secretary of State for Health and Bedfordshire so far as they have challenged the Court of Appeal's introduction of the starring system. Judge Sander's 'starring' order dated 2 July 2001 should be set aside.

[106] I must finally make an observation of a general character. In this speech I have sought to explain my reasons for rejecting the Court of Appeal's initiative over starred milestones. I cannot stress too strongly that the rejection of this innovation on legal grounds must not obscure the pressing need for the government to attend to the serious practical and legal problems identified by the Court of Appeal or mentioned by me. One of the questions needing urgent consideration is whether some degree of court supervision of local authorities' discharge of their parental responsibilities would bring about an overall improvement in the quality of child care provided by local authorities. Answering this question calls for a wider examination than can be undertaken by a court. The judgments of the Court of Appeal in the present case have performed a valuable service in highlighting the need for such an examination to be conducted without delay.

LORD MACKAY OF CLASHFERN.

[107] My Lords, I have had the advantage of reading in draft the speech of my noble and learned friend Lord Nicholls of Birkenhead. I agree that these appeals should be allowed to the extent that he has proposed and with the reasons he has given.

[108] Since I had a part in the process of enacting the Children Act 1989 and in a public lecture I had suggested that the idea of starring stages of a care plan

a should be considered so that the court might have an opportunity of considering whether to intervene if the plan was not being carried out, I feel it appropriate to add some observations. At the start of the hearing I invited counsel to say whether any party had any objection to my sitting and I was glad to be told on behalf of all parties they had no such objection.

[109] When the 1989 Act was enacted the United Kingdom was a party to the
b European Convention for the Protection of Human Rights and Fundamental Freedoms 1950 (as set out in Sch 1 to the Human Rights Act 1998) although at that time the convention was not incorporated into our domestic law. Accordingly the 1989 Act was framed in a way which took account of the terms of the convention as then understood. For example, s 34 is a reflection of the requirement that a dispute relating to access is for decision by the court. In my
c opinion, the fundamental change brought about by the 1989 Act placing the responsibility for looking after children who are the subject of care orders squarely on the local authorities is not in any way incompatible with the convention. In discharging its responsibility the local authority has the duty of respecting the convention rights of the child and of each member of the child's
d family. If a dispute arises whether this duty has been breached in any particular case the person aggrieved can now invoke the court's jurisdiction to determine it, under s 7 of the 1998 Act, if no other route is available. I agree that in so far as there are rights conferred in our domestic law which are not convention rights, there may be a lacuna but I doubt whether this involves any substantial content. If the duty is breached in respect of a child who has no person to raise the matter
e on his behalf, for example an orphan, an important question arises, to which I must now turn.

[110] Over the years since the 1989 Act took effect there have been far too many cases in which the system has failed children in care. Lord Nicholls has referred to the then Secretary of State's response to Sir William Utting's report in
f November 1997 and the subsequent Quality Protects Programme. That there are still serious problems in this field is evident from the powerful statements in the Court of Appeal in the present case and the decision in *F v Lambeth London BC* [2001] 3 FCR 738 to which my Lord has referred. It was strongly submitted by the guardians that the measures taken for example by Bedfordshire County Council though welcome were not sufficient to eliminate these problems.

g [111] When I suggested that a starring system should be considered it was in order to address these problems generally rather than problems with human rights that I had in mind. Having had the benefit of the very clear and cogent arguments which have been advanced to your Lordships I consider that there is no guarantee that the system would identify only the cases with genuine
h problems or that all the cases with such problems would be identified. There is no necessary correlation between failure to meet dates predetermined as important at the time the care order is made and serious deficiency in the care provided to the child. The system would require resources and to the extent that it did not meet its aims these would be wasted.

j [112] In agreeing that the appeal should succeed against the starring I would strongly urge that the government and Parliament give urgent attention to the problems clearly described by the Court of Appeal and by my noble and learned friend so that we do not continue failing some of our most vulnerable children.

[113] As a practical matter I do not see how a child who has no person to raise the matter on his behalf can be protected from violation of his or her human

rights or the rights conferred on him or her by our domestic law, other than by reliance on an effective means by which others bring the violation to notice.

LORD BROWNE-WILKINSON.

[114] My Lords, for the reasons given by my noble and learned friend, Lord Nicholls of Birkenhead with which I agree. I too would allow these appeals to the extent which he proposes.

LORD MUSTILL.

[115] My Lords, for the reasons given by my noble and learned friend, Lord Nicholls of Birkenhead with which I agree. I too would allow these appeals to the extent, which he proposes.

LORD HUTTON.

[116] My Lords, I have had the advantage of reading in draft the speech of my noble and learned friend Lord Nicholls of Birkenhead. I agree with it and for the reasons which he gives I would make the orders which he proposes.

Mother's appeal in the Torbay case dismissed. Other appeals allowed.

Kate O'Hanlon   Barrister.

a
Kiam v MGN Ltd
[2002] EWCA Civ 43

COURT OF APPEAL, CIVIL DIVISION
SIMON BROWN, WALLER AND SEDLEY LJJ
b   10, 11 DECEMBER 2001, 28 JANUARY 2002

Libel and slander – Damages – Appeal – Excessive award – Power of Court of Appeal to substitute own award on ground that jury's award excessive – Circumstances in which power to be exercised – Courts and Legal Services Act 1990, s 8.

c
The claimant brought proceedings for libel against the defendant newspaper publisher in respect of an article which had been published maliciously and was untrue in every material respect. There were also various aggravating features in the way the publisher had conducted the litigation and the trial. The judge instructed the jury that they could award aggravated compensatory damages, *d* pointed out that no personal injury claim was likely to attract a general damages award of more than £150,000 and emphasised that the decision on damages was the jury's alone. He suggested, however, that an award of less than £40,000 would not properly reflect the seriousness of the slur on the claimant and the subsequent aggravation of the injury to his feelings, while an award of more than £75,000 to £80,000 might be considered excessive, given the scale of damages *e* generally. The jury awarded the claimant £105,000. The publisher appealed against the jury's award, contending that it was excessive. It therefore invoked s 8[a] of the Courts and Legal Services Act 1990 which, through rules of court made under that provision, empowered the Court of Appeal, in cases where it had power to authorise a new trial on the ground that damages awarded by the jury were excessive, to substitute for the sum awarded by the jury such sum as *f* appeared to it to be proper. At the hearing of the appeal, by which time the maximum award of general damages in personal injury cases had been increased to £200,000, the Court of Appeal considered the circumstances in which it could interfere with a jury's award of damages.

g
Held – (Sedley LJ dissenting) The Court of Appeal should not interfere with a jury's award of damages unless it regarded it as substantially exceeding the most that any jury could reasonably have thought appropriate. The question for the court under s 8 of the 1990 Act was whether a reasonable jury could have thought the award necessary to compensate the claimant and to re-establish his *h* reputation. If the answer was No, the award was to be regarded as excessive and the court would substitute for it a proper award. That award would be the highest which the jury could reasonably have thought necessary, not whatever sum the court thought appropriate, wholly uninfluenced by the jury's view. That was so because the Court of Appeal should take as much account as it properly *j* could of the jury's attitude to the case. In the instant case, the judge's bracket was entirely reasonable, but the jury's award should not be condemned as 'unreasonable' unless it was out of all proportion to what could have been sensibly awarded. It was not excessive having regard to the great deference that was to be shown to jury awards in defamation cases, the large percentage

---

a   Section 8 is set out at [16], below

differences between the juries' awards and those substituted for them in the few
s 8 cases in which the Court of Appeal had been prepared to intervene, and the
fact that increase in the maximum award of general damages in personal injury
cases had had the effect of raising the ceiling for juries' libel awards to almost
twice the sum under appeal. Accordingly, the appeal would be dismissed (see
[48], [49], [53], [57], [58], [60], below); *John v MGN Ltd* [1996] 2 All ER 35 and *Kiam
v Neil (No 2)* [1996] EMLR 493 considered.

Per Simon Brown LJ. If a judge intends to suggest a bracket for damages, it is
preferable for the bracket to be formally discussed with the parties before it is
fixed, giving each side a proper opportunity to argue the matter after having
exchanged authorities and brief skeleton submissions indicating how they propose
to argue the matter. If either side suggests that there is a close comparable in
point, consideration should be given to handing to the jury a note identifying the
particular points which each side wishes to emphasise. Otherwise, counsel should
not generally refer to comparables and, if they do, the judge should be alert to
explain to the jury how those are properly taken into account in his own bracket
(see [56], below).

Notes

For appeals from awards of damages by juries, see 12(1) *Halsbury's Laws* (4th edn
reissue) para 1162.

For the Courts and Legal Services Act 1990, s 8, see 11 *Halsbury's Statutes* (4th
edn) (2000 reissue) 1298.

Cases referred to in judgments

A-G v Guardian Newspapers Ltd (No 2) [1988] 3 All ER 545, [1990] 1 AC 109, [1988]
2 WLR 805, CA.
Ford v Blurton, Ford v Sauber (1922) 38 TLR 801, CA.
Gorman v Mudd [1992] CA Transcript 1076.
Heil v Rankin [2000] 3 All ER 138, [2001] QB 272, [2000] 2 WLR 1173, CA.
Houston v Smith [1993] CA Transcript 1544.
John v MGN Ltd [1996] 2 All ER 35, [1997] QB 586, [1996] 3 WLR 593, CA.
Jones v Pollard [1997] EMLR 233, CA.
Khodaparast v Shad [2000] 1 All ER 545, [2000] 1 WLR 618, CA.
Kiam v Neil (No 2) [1996] EMLR 493, CA.
Pickett v British Rail Engineering Ltd, British Rail Engineering Ltd v Pickett [1979] 1 All
ER 774, [1980] AC 136, [1978] 3 WLR 955, HL.
Rantzen v Mirror Group Newspapers (1986) Ltd [1993] 4 All ER 975, [1994] QB 670,
[1993] 3 WLR 953, CA.
Sutcliffe v Pressdram Ltd [1990] 1 All ER 269, [1991] 1 QB 153, [1990] 2 WLR 271, CA.
Tolstoy Miloslavsky v UK (1995) 20 EHRR 442, [1995] ECHR 181/91, ECt HR.
Ward v James [1965] 1 All ER 563, [1966] 1 QB 273, [1965] 2 WLR 455, CA.
Youssoupoff v Metro-Goldwyn-Mayer Pictures Ltd (1934) 50 TLR 581, CA.

Cases also cited or referred to in skeleton arguments

Blackshaw v Lord [1983] 2 All ER 311, [1984] QB 1, CA.
Cassell & Co Ltd v Broome [1972] 1 All ER 801, [1972] AC 1027, HL.
Clark v Chief Constable of Cleveland Constabulary [1999] TLR 363, CA.
Hayward v Thompson [1981] 3 All ER 450, [1982] QB 47, CA.
Joyce v Sengupta [1993] 1 All ER 897, [1993] 1 WLR 337, CA.
Manson v Associated Newspapers Ltd [1965] 2 All ER 954, [1965] 1 WLR 1038, DC.

a

Reynolds v Times Newspapers Ltd [1999] 4 All ER 609, [2001] 2 AC 127, HL.
Riches v News Group Newspapers Ltd [1985] 2 All ER 845, [1986] QB 256, CA.
Rookes v Barnard [1964] 1 All ER 367, [1964] AC 1129, HL.
Thompson v Comr of Police of the Metropolis, Hsu v Comr of Police of the Metropolis
[1997] 2 All ER 762, [1998] QB 498, CA.

b

Appeal

The appellants, MGN Ltd, appealed with permission of the Court of Appeal granted on 11 October 2000 from the award of damages of £105,000 made against it by a jury on 10 March 2000 after the trial before it and Moore-Bick J of an action for libel brought against the appellants by the respondent, Victor Kermit Kiam II.

c The facts are set out in the judgment of Simon Brown LJ.

Victoria Sharp QC (instructed by *Olswang*) for the appellants.
Desmond Browne QC and *Lucy Moorman* (instructed by *Peter Carter-Ruck*) for the respondent.

d

Cur adv vult

28 January 2002. The following judgments were delivered.

e **SIMON BROWN LJ.**

INTRODUCTION

[1] On 10 March 2000, at the end of a five day libel trial before Moore-Bick J and a jury, judgment was entered for the claimant, Mr Victor Kiam II, for £105,000 damages. Although Mr Kiam died on 27 May 2001 it is not suggested

f that his death affects the outcome of this appeal and I shall call him simply the respondent. The jury made plain that their award was for aggravated compensatory damages. MGN Ltd (the appellants), the publishers of the libel, now appeal against the quantum of the award by leave of this court granted on 11 October 2000. Although other grounds were earlier canvassed, the sole question remaining for decision is whether the award of £105,000 was excessive and, if so, what is the

g proper sum to substitute for it.

THE LIBEL

[2] The libel sued upon was the lead article published prominently in colour in the 'City Slickers' column of The Mirror on 6 January 1999. The author was

h Mr Hipwell. Under the banner headline 'MY COMPANY HAS BOUGHT IT' and alongside a large photograph of the respondent, the text read:

'<u>Victor's profits go up in smoke</u>

j He liked the Remington shaver so much that he bought the company. But unfortunately for 72-year-old American entrepreneur Victor Kiam, he also liked the cigarette lighter company so much, he bought that too. And according to sources at the Crawley-based company, he could put it into receivership "any time now". Kiam, who runs the business from his sun-drenched Florida home as executive chairman, is so fed up with the firm into which he has ploughed more than £10 million, that he is thinking of closing it down.

Debt   *a*

After a succession of dismal trading results, bad debt provisions, escalating losses and a share price that has fallen off a cliff during the past year, Kiam has finally had enough. Company sources confirm he could easily put the shutters up on Ronson within the next few weeks. The latest problem centres on the departure of finance director Laurie Todd, who bailed out just before Christmas. Todd appeared to leave the company on amicable terms   *b* to join bigger firm Staveley Industries, but friends say he had faced some major problems with Ronson's £8 million refinancing programme, put together by Kiam. Shares in the cigarette lighter maker first arrived on the stock market in the mid 1980s at 60p. But they were suspended last June at 4·5p and resumed trading in September at just 1·5p. Yesterday Kiam, who also invented the Cross Your Heart bra in the 1950s, must have watched in   *c* horror as he saw another 10 per cent wiped off the value of his substantial shareholding. Critics of the company say that Kiam has failed to unlock the value of the Ronson brand. One advertising industry expert told **Slicker**: "Ronson lighters and pens are very upmarket and have a whiff of James Bond about them, but Kiam hasn't managed to capitalise on this at all. This is   *d* puzzling as he's a charismatic guy who clearly understands brand marketing." **Slicker** says: Never mind, Vic. Your place in history is secure thanks to that great "I bought the company" catchphrase. Perhaps now is the time to hang up your boots and concentrate on getting a tan.'

A further caption next to the photograph read: 'BLAZING AWAY: Victor Kiam has   *e* finally lost patience with the cigarette maker Ronson, into which he has poured £10 million.'

THE DEFAMATORY MEANINGS

[3] The respondent relied on both the natural and ordinary meaning of the   *f* words and also an innuendo. The article suggested, he contended, first, that his entrepreneurial ability, on which he had based his business success and reputation in the past, had wholly deserted him so that he was now fit only for retirement; secondly, that he was prepared to give up on Ronson and close it down with obviously devastating consequences for staff who would lose their jobs, shareholders their money and customers their contracts; and thirdly, that   *g* Ronson's imminent financial collapse was attributable to his own professional failures, first in having put together a refinancing programme so flawed that it caused Ronson's finance director (Mr Todd) to resign, and secondly in failing to exploit the value of the Ronson brand name, the so-called 'whiff of James Bond', thereby indicating that he had lost his marketing and entrepreneurial ability.   *h*

[4] As to the innuendo, a number of those reading the article would have read too the respondent's interview in the July/August 1998 edition of Brands, a magazine for retailers, expressing his confidence in Ronson's survival and making a five year commitment to the company, and/or his circular letter dated 18 September 1998 to Ronson's customers reassuring them about the company's   *j* financial stability and future. The article would have suggested by way of innuendo that the respondent had lied or misled the public about his commitment to Ronson and the company's financial viability.

[5] Given the narrow basis of this appeal, the jury must be assumed to have accepted the respondent's contention that the article bore all those meanings. Similarly they must be assumed to have accepted the respondent's case on all the

a many aggravating features of the case upon which the respondent relied and which the judge left for their consideration. These I must now summarise.

THE AGGRAVATING FACTS

[6] The article was untrue in every material respect and had been published maliciously. The respondent had become executive chairman and chief marketing
b officer of Ronson in July 1998, a month after the London Stock Exchange suspended its share listing. He had invested not £10m but £1m. He was intent on saving the company and had committed himself wholeheartedly to doing so, remaining in England and away from his family for the purpose. There was no question of him having 'had enough' and 'thinking of closing it down'. The refinancing programme had been a complete success and, when the article was
c published, the company's losses were no longer 'escalating' but rather were diminishing. Mr Todd left Ronson solely because he had been headhunted by a bigger company. The story could easily have been checked with Ronson, Mr Todd, or the respondent himself. None of them, however, had been contacted. Although, moreover, the reader was led to believe that the story was based on numerous
d sources, disclosure of Mr Hipwell's notebook indicated a single unidentified source who in any event had suggested that Mr Hipwell speak to Mr Todd (which, of course, he did not do). Discovery further revealed that Mr Hipwell had made use of a Sunday Telegraph article of 1 March 1998 (before the respondent joined Ronson) which itself had referred to 'bad debt provisions, escalating losses, a share price that has fallen off a cliff over the last two years'. Mr Hipwell could
e therefore be seen to have applied to Ronson's position in January 1999 the Sunday Telegraph description of its position some ten months earlier before the refinancing of the company under Mr Kiam's leadership. Other earlier statements had been similarly distorted. In short, Mr Hipwell's complete indifference to the truth was amply demonstrated. By the time of trial he had been dismissed for (unrelated)
f gross misconduct. He was not in those circumstances called as a witness to explain his conduct. Neither did Mr Piers Morgan, the editor, give evidence.

[7] When invited by the respondent's solicitors on 8 January 1999 to publish an article correcting the errors and apologising to Mr Kiam, the editor denied that the article was materially inaccurate save only as to the extent of the respondent's investment in the company. That alone he offered to correct and he refused to
g apologise. Even after June 1999 when the appellants served their defence pleading neither justification nor fair comment, no apology was made. The absence of apology was the more serious since the respondent had told his acquaintances that he would shortly be getting one. He had, indeed, attached his solicitor's letter of 8 January to a circular letter sent on 12 January 1999 to his many friends
h and customers with a view to reassuring them as to the true position.

[8] Shortly before trial the appellants published in the City Slickers column three further short articles about the respondent and Ronson respectively on 7 December 1999, 13 January 2000, and 14 January 2000. Put briefly, these suggested that the respondent was deceiving the stock market by concealing plans to merge Ronson
j with an Internet company; they said that Ronson's shares were 'ready to roll big time'. The respondent was naturally concerned, fearing that readers would be drawn into a false market in the shares and then blame him for their predicament. Again, no one checked the truth of those articles with the respondent or anyone else at Ronson and again they were accepted at trial to be factually incorrect.

[9] Another major aggravating feature of the case was the appellants' conduct at trial and not least suggestions made in counsel's closing speech to the jury that

'Mr Kiam is simply impossible to satisfy', that 'no amount of money will satisfy Mr Kiam', and that in both this case and an earlier case against The Sunday Times in 1994 (*Kiam v Neil (No 2)* [1996] EMLR 493 to which I shall return) the respondent had wanted 'his day in court' and nothing the appellants did could have prevented it. None of these allegations had been put to the respondent in cross-examination; rather his evidence that he was not a quitter had been turned against him and used as a stick for criticism. Furthermore, although the appellants' only witness, their legal manager, had accepted in cross-examination that the article was obviously damaging to the respondent, counsel continued to submit to the jury that it was not defamatory at all, thereby adding to the imputation that the respondent had acted wholly unreasonably in ever bringing the claim.

[10] The article had been published to some 6·37m readers. No apology for it had ever been given. True, by open letter dated 1 March 1999 (five days before the trial began) the appellants had offered £50,000, costs and an apology. That, however, was regarded by the respondent as too little, too late, and in the event no apology was published. The appellants' case to the end was that no damages should be payable since the article, though untrue, was simply not defamatory. The respondent gave evidence of distress, upset, annoyance and frustration. All this was undisputed; so too was strong supporting evidence from his wife, his son, and fellow Ronson directors.

[11] All these matters notwithstanding, it is the appellants' case that £105,000 was quite simply excessive so that this court should intervene and substitute for it some lesser award. Before, however, turning to consider the court's powers and the authorities governing the proper approach to its exercise, there are other important features of this case to which I must refer.

OTHER FEATURES OF THE CASE

[12] First is this. The respondent had claimed not only aggravated damages but also exemplary damages. A ruling as to that was not made until the final morning of the trial, just before counsel's speeches. The judge ruled that whilst there was evidence which enabled the jury to find malice, there was insufficient evidence from which to infer that the appellants had 'carried out a calculation' that publication of this article 'would give it a commercial advantage which would outweigh any liability it might incur to Mr Kiam'. The exemplary damages claim was accordingly withdrawn. The issue of malice nevertheless remained before the jury for two reasons: first because in any event it went to the question of aggravated damages; secondly because, lest the jury were to accept the appellants' case that the article was simply not defamatory of the respondent, there remained an alternative claim for damages for malicious falsehood. In the event, having found for the respondent on his claim for libel, no verdict was called for regarding malicious falsehood.

[13] The next point to note is the care with which the judge warned the jury about matters which might wrongly have inflated their award. Having given his ruling on exemplary damages, he instructed the jury (before counsels' speeches) to put that aspect of the case completely out of their minds and said there would be 'no question of awarding exemplary or punitive damages'. Twice in his summing up he reminded the jury of this direction: first, when explaining why they might award aggravated damages: 'not, I emphasise, to punish the defendants, but in order to award him fair and reasonable compensation for the injury which he has received, aggravated by the defendants' conduct'; secondly, just before the

a jury retired, when he expressly reiterated that they must put exemplary damages
'entirely out of your mind'.

[14] Similarly he warned the jury to ignore completely the effect of the articles
on Ronson itself and to bear in mind that the three later articles went only to
aggravation; the respondent was not claiming further damage to his reputation
arising from them.

b [15] The final matter of importance to mention is the guidance given by the
judge as to the appropriate level of damages in the case. Having pointed out that
no personal injury claim was likely to attract a general damage award of more
than £150,000, and having instanced awards of some £100,000 for the loss of both
arms and some £45,000 for the loss of a hand, the judge referred briefly to the
Elton John case (*John v MGN Ltd* [1996] 2 All ER 35, [1997] QB 586) and to the
c respondent's earlier action (*Kiam v Neil (No 2)*) and continued:

'Now although, as I seek to emphasise, the decision on damages is yours
and yours alone, much may depend on the meanings which you find this
article bore. But I would suggest that, if you find that the article bears the
more serious defamatory meanings of the kind suggested by Mr Kiam, you
d may think that an award of much less than £40,000 would not properly
reflect the seriousness of the slur on him, and the subsequent aggravation of
the injury to his feelings. You might also think that an award of more than
£75,000–£80,000 might be considered excessive, given the scale of damages
generally. I have to stress that the decision is yours and yours alone.'

e
THE COURT'S POWERS
[16] Section 8 of the Courts and Legal Services Act 1990 provides:

'(1) In this section "case" means any case where the Court of Appeal has
power to order a new trial on the ground that damages awarded by a jury are
f excessive or inadequate.

(2) Rules of court may provide for the Court of Appeal, in such classes of
case as may be specified in the rules, to have power, in place of ordering a
new trial, to substitute for the sum awarded by the jury such sum as appears
to the court to be proper.'

g [17] The first relevant rule of court was RSC Ord 59, r 11(4) which applied to
appeals set down after 31 January 1991 and provided:

'In any case where the Court of Appeal has power to order a new trial on
the ground that damages awarded by a jury are excessive or inadequate, the
h Court may, in lieu of ordering a new trial ... substitute for the sum awarded
by the jury such sum as appears to the Court to be proper ...'

[18] The rule presently in force is CPR 52.10(3): 'In an appeal from a claim
tried with a jury the Court of Appeal may, instead of ordering a new trial ... (b)
vary an award of damages made by the jury.'

j
THE AUTHORITIES
[19] The early authorities, in particular *Sutcliffe v Pressdram Ltd* [1990] 1 All ER
269, [1991] 1 QB 153, *Rantzen v Mirror Group Newspapers (1986) Ltd* [1993] 4 All ER
975, [1994] QB 670 and *John v MGN Ltd* [1996] 2 All ER 35, [1997] QB 586, have
been rehearsed many times in subsequent decisions and I shall content myself,
therefore, with a relatively brief summary of their effect.

[20] In *Sutcliffe*'s case a £600,000 compensatory award was set aside by the
Court of Appeal on the grounds that it must have been made on the wrong basis,   *a*
almost certainly so as to punish Private Eye. It was the court's inability to reassess
the damages itself that led to the enactment of s 8 of the 1990 Act.

[21] Shortly after *Sutcliffe*'s case the barrier against intervention was lowered.
This was not, however, the consequence of s 8—how could it be? The power to
reassess only arises where the Court of Appeal already 'has power to order a new   *b*
trial'. Rather it was the effect of art 10 of of the European Convention for the
Protection of Human Rights and Fundamental Freedoms 1950 (as set out in Sch 1
to the Human Rights Act 1998) and Lord Goff of Chieveley's speech in *A-G v
Guardian Newspapers Ltd (No 2)* [1988] 3 All ER 545 at 660, [1990] 1 AC 109 at
283–284, which together caused Neill LJ, giving the judgment of the court in
Rantzen's case, to say: *c*

> '... it seems to us that the grant of an almost limitless discretion to a jury
> fails to provide a satisfactory measurement for deciding what is "necessary in
> a democratic society" or "justified by a pressing social need". We consider
> therefore that the common law if properly understood requires the courts to
> subject large awards of damages to a more searching scrutiny than has been   *d*
> customary in the past. It follows that what has been regarded as the barrier
> against intervention should be lowered. The question becomes: could a
> reasonable jury have thought that this award was necessary to compensate
> the plaintiff and to re-establish his reputation?' (See [1993] 4 All ER 975 at
> 994, [1994] QB 670 at 692.)   *e*

[22] At the same time as the Court of Appeal was lowering the threshold of
intervention it was also considering how best to assist the jury in its task of
assessing damages. Lord Donaldson of Lymington MR in *Sutcliffe*'s case suggested,
that a jury could be guided—

> 'in terms which will assist them to appreciate the real value of large sums
> ... the judge could, I think, properly invite them to consider what the result
> would be in terms of weekly, monthly or annual income if the money were
> invested in a building society deposit account without touching the capital
> sum awarded or, if they have in mind smaller sums, to consider what they
> could buy with it.' (See [1990] 1 All ER 269 at 284, [1991] 1 QB 153 at 179.)   *g*

[23] This was carried further in *Rantzen*'s case when the court suggested:

> '... that over a period of time the awards made by the Court of Appeal
> [under s 8 of the 1990 Act] would provide a corpus to which reference could
> be made in subsequent cases. Any risk of overcitation would have to be   *h*
> controlled by the trial judge, but to prevent reference to such awards would
> seem to us to conflict with the principle that restrictions on freedom of
> expression should be "prescribed by law." The decisions of the Court of
> Appeal could be relied upon as establishing the prescribed norm.' (See [1993]
> 4 All ER 975 at 995–996, [1994] QB 670 at 694.)   *j*

[24] The court, however, continued to rule out any reference to awards in
personal injury cases and concluded:

> 'It is to be hoped that in the course of time a series of decisions of the Court
> of Appeal will establish some standards as to what are, in the terms of s 8 of
> the 1990 Act, "proper" awards. In the meantime the jury should be invited

a to consider the purchasing power of any award which they may make. In addition they should be asked to ensure that any award they make is proportionate to the damage which the plaintiff has suffered and is a sum which it is necessary to award him to provide adequate compensation and to re-establish his reputation.' (See [1993] 4 All ER 975 at 997, [1994] QB 670 at 695–696.)

b [25] The matter of guidance was taken still further in *John*'s case. Bingham MR, giving the judgment of the court (consisting also of Neill and Hirst LJJ), said:

c 'We agree with the ruling in (*Rantzen v Mirror Group Newspapers (1986) Ltd* [1993] 4 All ER 975, [1994] QB 670) that reference may be made to awards approved or made by the Court of Appeal. [*Rantzen*'s case had in fact referred only to "awards made by the Court of Appeal".] As and when a framework of awards is established this will provide a valuable pointer to the appropriate level of award in the particular case. But it is plain that such a framework will not be established quickly: it is now five years since s 8(2) of d the 1990 Act and Ord 59, r 11(4) came into force, and there is no case other than (*Gorman v Mudd* [1992] CA Transcript 1076), *Rantzen* and (*Houston v Smith* [1993] CA Transcript 1544) in which the court has itself fixed the appropriate level of award. It is true that awards in this category are subject to the same objection that time can be spent by the parties on pointing to similarities and differences. But, if used with discretion, awards which have e been subjected to scrutiny in the Court of Appeal should be able to provide *some* guidance to a jury called upon to fix an award in a later case.' (See [1996] 2 All ER 35 at 52, [1997] QB 586 at 612.)

[26] Additionally, and importantly, the court in *John*'s case also concluded that the time had come when judges and counsel should be free to draw the jury's f attention to the conventional compensatory scales of award in personal injury cases, the ceiling for such awards being at that date some £125,000. The court said that 'juries may properly be asked to consider whether the injury to his reputation of which the plaintiff complains should fairly justify any greater compensation', and expressed the view that it is 'offensive to public opinion, and g rightly so, that a defamation plaintiff should recover damages for injury to reputation greater, perhaps by a significant factor, than if that same plaintiff had been rendered a helpless cripple or an insensate vegetable' (see [1996] 2 All ER 35 at 54, [1997] QB 586 at 614).

[27] As to 'the process of mentioning figures', the court said:

h 'We can for our part see no reason why the parties' respective counsel in a libel action should not indicate to the jury the level of award which they respectively contend to be appropriate, nor why the judge in directing the jury should not give a similar indication. The plaintiff will not wish the jury to think that his main object is to make money rather than clear his name. j The defendant will not wish to add insult to injury by underrating the seriousness of the libel. So we think the figures suggested by responsible counsel are likely to reflect the upper and lower bounds of a realistic bracket. The jury must, of course, make up their own mind and must be directed to do so. They will not be bound by the submission of counsel or the indication of the judge. If the jury make an award outside the upper or lower bounds of any bracket indicated and such award is the subject of appeal, real weight must be given to the possibility that their judgment is to be preferred to that of the judge. The modest but important changes of practice described above would not in our view undermine the enduring constitutional position of the libel jury. Historically, the significance of the libel jury has lain not in their role of assessing damages, but in their role of deciding whether the publication complained of is a libel or no. The changes which we favour will, in our opinion, buttress the constitutional role of the libel jury by rendering their proceedings more rational and so more acceptable to public opinion.' (See [1996] 2 All ER 35 at 55, [1997] QB 586 at 615–616.)

[28] The final authority requiring detailed consideration is *Kiam v Neil (No 2)* [1996] EMLR 493, important both for its general statements on the correct approach to quantum appeals in libel cases and also as an obviously relevant comparable for the purposes of the present case. At this stage, however, I am concerned only with the general approach.

[29] Having quoted the court's judgment in *John*'s case (part of the passage set out in [27], above), Beldam LJ said (at 507–508):

'It is, I think, necessary to bear in mind that Parliament has repeatedly declined to attenuate the right of a plaintiff who claims trial by jury in a libel action ... Whilst it is tempting to think that the greater the guidance given by judges, the more rational the jury's conclusion is likely to be, it seems to me that if the failure of the jury to keep its award within bounds indicated by a judge gives rise merely to the possibility that their judgment is to be preferred to that of the judge, the court may appear to preserve only the semblance of a right which Parliament has repeatedly affirmed. At present it remains the plaintiff's constitutional right ... I would therefore approach the question suggested by Neill LJ [in *Rantzen v Mirror Group Newspapers (1986) Ltd* [1993] 4 All ER 975 at 994, [1994] QB 670 at 692]: "Could a reasonable jury have thought that this award was necessary to compensate the plaintiff and to re-establish his reputation?" by allowing an appropriate degree of flexibility to a jury of twelve to tailor its award to the injury done to Mr Kiam's reputation. Unless the Times establishes that the award so judged is out of proportion, this court would not be entitled to substitute its own assessment ...'

[30] Evans LJ, in a passage much relied upon by Mr Browne QC for the respondent, said (at 513):

'If this [The Sunday Times' submission that the Court of Appeal now has to form its own estimate of whether the damages awarded were excessive] means that the Court has to assess what it regards as a "reasonable" figure without regard to the jury's award then I cannot accept this submission. If correct, it would mean that the measure of compensation and liability would depend upon the views of three (or five) judges rather than of the jury. This would be to usurp the traditional and statutory function of the jury, and whether it would lead to greater certainty in predicting the amount of the eventual award (a factor which has been regarded as important under the European Convention) must be a matter for debate. If on the other hand the appellants' submission is that the court should consider whether the figure is one which "a reasonable jury" (see the conclusion in *Rantzen* quoted above) could properly award then it seems to me that this is entirely in line not only with *Rantzen* but also with the common law authorities to which Lord a   Donaldson MR referred in (*Sutcliffe v Pressdram Ltd* [1990] 1 All ER 269, [1991] 1 QB 153) ... The significance of the judgments in *Rantzen* and (*John v MGN Ltd* [1996] 2 All ER 35, [1997] QB 586), in my view, is that the legal requirements of a valid award have been re-defined in the light of recent developments in the law, including recognition as part of the common law of the principles expressed in the European Convention. In considering

b   whether the jury's figure is excessive, or inadequate, therefore, the court has to define the legal limits and decide whether the award is outside them, or not. The limits include the court's own assessment of what a reasonable jury could properly decide, because that is the only way in which the courts can combine the requirements of the law with the jury's freedom of decision. But this does not mean, in my judgment, that within those limits the court is

c   permitted to give effect to its own view as to the reasonableness or otherwise of the jury's award.'

[31] Pill LJ said (at 516–517):

'... I agree that awards which in the words of the Master of the Rolls in *John*

d   ([1996] 2 All ER 35 at 48, [1997] QB 586 at 608) are "in sums wildly disproportionate to any damage conceivably suffered by the plaintiff" constitute a mischief and there is need to seek means, as the Courts have been doing, by which to eliminate that mischief and also to ensure that the Court of Appeal can be, as Lord Lester described it, a safety net. The danger I foresee in inviting juries to make comparisons with other cases,

e   comparisons which would inevitably become elaborate as each party emphasises particular but different features of those other cases, is that the jury will be distracted from their central duty to consider the circumstances of the case in hand and make an award based on their conscientious assessment of what is involved. I agree with the Master of the Rolls' call for

f   discretion in citing awards. In this context, a "battle of comparables" in front of a jury may produce its own injustice, as well as being time consuming and costly. In (*Tolstoy Miloslavsky v UK* (1995) 20 EHRR 442), the European Court of Human Rights acknowledged that "the absence of specific guidelines in the legal rules covering the assessment of damages must be seen as an inherent feature of the law of damages in this area". Inherent in jury trial is

g   a degree of respect for the jury's sense of values.'

[32] There is, to my mind, a certain tension apparent within these various citations. On the one hand the court manifests its concern that libel damages are unhealthily high: '... a road to untaxed riches ... [the] legal process fail[ing] to

h   command the respect of lawyer and layman alike', as Bingham MR put it in *John v MGN Ltd* [1996] 2 All ER 35 at 51, [1997] QB 586 at 611, and in particular disproportionately high in comparison to personal injury awards. This, of course, was why *John*'s case introduced the right to refer to personal injury damages and suggested that juries be guided by reference to brackets, the proposed ceiling for

j   any libel award being the maximum recoverable for the gravest personal injuries. On the other hand the court continues to place emphasis on the importance of the jury's role in assessing damages.

[33] The statement in *John*'s case [1996] 2 All ER 35 at 55, [1997] QB 586 at 616 that 'Historically, the significance of the libel jury has lain not in their role of assessing damages, but in their role of deciding whether the publication complained of is a libel or no' is, perhaps, difficult to reconcile with the judgments

in *Kiam v Neil (No 2)*; and still more so with Nourse LJ's judgment in *Sutcliffe v Pressdram Ltd* [1990] 1 All ER 269 at 287, [1991] 1 QB 153 at 182:

'When one turns to the matter of damages the primacy of the jury is seen to be even more firmly established. I do not know that it was ever doubted that the amount of the damages should be left to the jury. The rule received the unqualified support of Scrutton LJ in *Youssoupoff v Metro-Goldwyn-Mayer Pictures Ltd* (1934) 50 TLR 581 at 584: "The constitution has thought, and I think there is great advantage in it, that the damages to be paid by a person who says false things about his neighbour are best decided by a jury representing the public ..."'

[34] True it is that in *John's* case the court suggested that the changes they were introducing would 'buttress the constitutional role of the libel jury by rendering their proceedings more rational and so more acceptable to public opinion'. But this, of course, will be so only if the jury substantially accepts the bracket which the judge suggests to them and does not take too literally the comment (as here) that 'the decision is yours and yours alone'—in line with the court's judgment in *John's* case (see [27], above) that juries must be directed 'to make up their own mind' as to the appropriate award.

COMPARABLES

[35] It is time now to summarise those few defamation cases in which the Court of Appeal has itself had to consider juries' awards of damages in the exercise of its s 8 power. There are six in all. In five the damages were reassessed. In the sixth, *Kiam v Neil (No 2)*, the court refused to interfere with the award. I shall mention a seventh case also, one of malicious falsehood. Chronologically they are as follows.

(1) *Gorman v Mudd* [1992] CA Transcript 1076

[36] The plaintiff, the Conservative MP for Billericay, complained of a 'mock press release' written and circulated by the defendant, Mudd, a prominent member of the local community and chairman of the Billericay Conservative Businessman's Association, to 91 people most of whom knew something of the underlying quarrel between the parties. The publication suggested that the plaintiff had sought to destroy the association and to humiliate the defendant out of personal spite. The tone of the release was unpleasant (suggesting for example, that the plaintiff's female charms were inadequate despite a hormone implant). Although a plea of qualified privilege was upheld, the jury found express malice. There was no apology. Rather Mrs Gorman had been subjected to unpleasant cross-examination which had increased her sense of humiliation. The Court of Appeal reduced the jury's award of £150,000 to £50,000 (worth £63,000 in January 2001).

(2) *Rantzen v Mirror Group Newspapers (1986) Ltd* [1993] 4 All ER 975, [1994] QB 670

[37] The action concerned four articles in the same issue of The People including one on the front page and a leading article, all covering the same story about Esther Rantzen's organisation, Childline. The articles suggested that the plaintiff had protected a teacher who had revealed to Childline abuses of children occurring at a school where he taught, by keeping secret that he himself was a pervert, unfit to have any child in his care. The suggestion was that Miss Rantzen

a had protected the teacher as a reward for his help. In so doing she had abandoned her own moral standards; her public statements of concern for abused children were insincere and hypocritical. Finally it was suggested that she had lied when informing the newspaper that publication of the story would hamper the police investigation when the truth was that she wished to avoid exposure of her own misconduct and omissions. The defendant pleaded justification and lost. The

b allegations were very grave, going to the heart of the core attributes of Miss Rantzen's character. The Court of Appeal reduced the jury's award of £250,000 to £110,000 (£133,000 today).

(3) Houston v Smith [1993] CA Transcript 1544

c [38] The parties were doctors (respectively male and female), operating separate practices within the same building. The defendant falsely accused the plaintiff of harassing her and her staff, groping them and fondling them sexually. The allegation was made in the hearing of several of the plaintiff's patients in the doctors' joint waiting room. The defendant denied having suggested impropriety with her staff but sought to justify her allegation of personal harassment, alleging

d that the plaintiff had brushed up against her deliberately. The allegation of sexual harassment was plainly a matter of the utmost gravity for a general practitioner. There were furthermore a number of aggravating features of the case and there had been no apology. The publication, however, had been only to a very small number of people. The Court of Appeal reduced the jury's award of £150,000 to

e £50,000 (£62,000 today).

(4) John v MGN Ltd [1996] 2 All ER 35, [1997] QB 586

[39] The action concerned an article in The Sunday Mirror which covered two inside pages and was introduced on the front page by a headline 'Elton's diet of death' and a photograph of the plaintiff, stating that he had suffered from bulimia

f and was now hooked on a bizarre new diet that could kill him. It described his behaviour at a party in California where he was seen to put food in his mouth, chew it and then spit it out. The plaintiff had never been at the party and was 'incensed' by the article because he had had eating and drug and alcohol addiction problems but had cured himself, publicising the facts on television. The newspaper

g had offered an apology but, its terms not being agreed, none was published. The claim was defended on the grounds that the words were not defamatory. Bingham MR observed that 'though the article was false, offensive and distressing, it did not attack [the plaintiff's] personal integrity or damage his reputation as an artist'. The Court of Appeal reduced the jury's award of compensatory damages from £75,000 to £25,000 (£28,000 today) and the award of exemplary damages

h from £275,000 to £50,000.

(5) Kiam v Neil (No 2) [1996] EMLR 493

[40] The libel was published in The Sunday Times business section to a readership of some three million. It consists of the following short paragraph in a long article

j criticising the National Westminster Bank:

'Another high profile NatWest customer is Victor Kiam, owner of the Remington razor company. He is being sued by NatWest after defaulting on a £13·5 million loan he used to buy New England Patriots, the American football team. Kiam has also filed for bankruptcy protection.'

[41] The article also carried the innuendo to members of the public who had bought Remington shavers relying on a money refund promise if they were not satisfied, that Mr Kiam had induced them to buy when he was in no position to fulfil the promise.

[42] Mr Kiam was horrified to read the article. He protested vigorously and demanded an apology. Three weeks later the newspaper admitted that the report was untrue and published an apology in agreed terms. The jury awarded £45,000 compensatory damages (£51,000 today). In dismissing the defendant's appeal the court characterised the libel as follows:

'It would be hard to imagine a more damaging allegation against a successful entrepreneur ... [The libel] struck at the core of his life's achievement and personality and ... had had a prolonged and significant effect on him personally ... [It was] a widespread, grave and irresponsible assertion of insolvency against a prominent entrepreneur ...' (See [1996] EMLR 493 at 498, 510 per Beldam LJ.)

'To describe the damaging and untrue assertion which the article made about the plaintiff's management of his financial affairs, with or without the innuendo, which he also alleged, as a "not very serious" libel upon a successful international businessman and entrepeneur, as the plaintiff is, seems to me to be wholly unreal ... Here, the libel was potentially as serious for the plaintiff as any which did not impute dishonesty could be; the circulation of the newspaper was enormous, and the libel appeared in the section which sets out to be read widely in business and financial circles ...' (See [1996] EMLR 493 at 515 per Evans LJ.)

(6) *Jones v Pollard* [1997] EMLR 233

[43] The plaintiff complained of two articles in consecutive issues of The Sunday Mirror which accused him of pimping for the KGB by organising sex with Russian prostitutes for British businessmen visiting Russia who could then be blackmailed. The defendants pleaded justification. The plaintiff conceded in evidence that he was a persistent womaniser, but denied procuring prostitutes, though a tape of a conversation with a journalist in which the plaintiff was apparently arranging an assignment between the journalist and a prostitute was introduced in evidence (the plaintiff's explanation being that he was either drunk or fantasising). The defendants called no evidence and the judge withdrew from the jury such parts of the plea of justification as suggested contact with the KGB. The Court of Appeal reduced the jury's award of £100,000 to £40,000 (£44,000 today). In doing so they held that the jury must have concluded that the charge of procuring prostitutes was made out in part and that there were other matters which went to reduce the damages. Hirst LJ, giving the only reasoned judgment, said (at 259):

'... I ask the same question as that asked by Neill L.J. in (*Rantzen v Mirror Group Newspapers (1986) Ltd* [1993] 4 All ER 975, [1994] QB 670), namely could a reasonable jury have thought that this award was necessary to compensate the plaintiff and to re-establish his reputation? In my judgment, grave though the libel is, and grave though the aggravation has been, the answer to that question is decisively no. First, I can see no justification for an award which is comparable with *Rantzen*, approximately double the awards either approved or substituted by the Court of Appeal in (*Houston v*

Smith [1993] CA Transcript 1544) and (*Kiam v Neil (No 2)* [1996] EMLR 493), and no less than four times the award substituted in (*John v MGN Ltd* [1996] 2 All ER 35, [1997] QB 586). Secondly, it is in my judgment out of all proportion to personal injury awards of a comparable amount, which embrace such very serious injuries as paraplegia and total blindness; these personal injuries awards ... do not of course establish a scale in the libel field, but I feel sure that, had that comparison been available to the jury in the present case (as it would be today in the post-*John* era), they would not have awarded anything like £100,000, even if the plaintiff had enjoyed an unblemished reputation. Thirdly, when the material in reduction of damages is also taken into account (as of course it must be) the award seems to me still more gravely disproportionate to the injury caused'.

(7) Khodaparast v Shad [2000] 1 All ER 545, [2000] 1 WLR 618
[44] The claimant in this malicious falsehood case was an Iranian woman who worked as a teacher at an Iranian religious school in London. The defendant was her former lover. He created a set of mock-up documents using photographs of the claimant superimposed on pornographic pictures from a magazine and inserting words which suggested that the claimant was advertising sexual services. These were sent to the daughter of a newspaper editor. The newspaper did not publish but the documents were circulated widely in the Iranian community in London. The judge awarded £20,000 as general damages for malicious falsehood but said that, had the claim been brought in defamation, he would have awarded £50,000. The Court of Appeal described this as an 'eminently reasonable' figure.

INCREASE IN PERSONAL INJURY DAMAGES
[45] The one other important consideration to be noted before finally coming to the central question raised by this appeal is that in 2000, by the Court of Appeal's decision in *Heil v Rankin* [2000] 3 All ER 138, [2001] QB 272, the maximum general damage award available in personal injury cases has been increased from £150,000 to £200,000—see the Judicial Studies Board's *Guidelines for the Assessment of General Damages in Personal Injury Cases* (5th edn, 2000).

THE RIVAL ARGUMENTS
[46] Miss Victoria Sharp QC (junior counsel rather than leading counsel instructed below) submits that the award here was plainly excessive, some 30% higher than the upper limit of the judge's bracket which itself she contends was too high and the whole of which in any event postulated the jury finding 'the more serious defamatory meanings ... suggested by Mr Kiam'. Miss Sharp furthermore suggests that this libel could not possibly be regarded as worth double the award approved in Mr Kiam's first case, *Kiam v Neil (No 2)*. That, she submits, was an unusually close comparable; both The Sunday Times' defamation and its apology were included in the jury's bundle in the present case. This award, she argues, is also clearly too high in comparison both with the much graver libel in *Rantzen*'s case and with general damage awards in personal injury cases, the ceiling for which was only £150,000 at the time of this award and is even now only £200,000. Justification, Miss Sharp points out, was never pleaded; rather the only defence was that the article was not libellous, so that there was less than the usual need for vindication. Furthermore, although late in the day, there was both the offer of an apology and a substantial offer of damages (£50,000). Finally, the most serious of the pleaded meanings, the innuendo,

would have been understood only by a small proportion of the overall
readership.   *a*

[47] Mr Browne QC submits that particular respect must be paid to a jury's verdict
where, as here, the issues have been presented to it accurately and dispassionately
in an unimpeachable summing up. He reminds us of Bingham MR's dictum in
John v MGN Ltd [1996] 2 All ER 35 at 48, [1997] QB 586 at 607 that 'the more closely
[the libel] touches the plaintiff's personal integrity, professional reputation,   *b*
honour, courage, loyalty and the core attributes of his personality, the more
serious it is likely to be', and submits that this libel by its natural and ordinary
meanings damaged the respondent's professional reputation, and by innuendo
attacked his personal integrity (not least, for example, in the eyes of the 1,500 staff
at Ronson whose jobs were at stake). He argues that this was a graver libel than
in *Kiam v Neil (No 2)* and that it was attended by altogether more serious   *c*
aggravating features, not least the appellants' refusal until the very eve of trial to
offer any form of apology, their publication of further untruthful articles and
finally their counsel's inflammatory closing speech. Above all, Mr Browne
reminds us that the jury (and, indeed, the judge who decided what bracket to
suggest to the jury) were present throughout this five-day hearing, listening to all   *d*
the witnesses and speeches and observing their effect on the respondent, whereas
we, of course, were not. The judge himself, moreover, refused permission to
appeal, observing that 'this was an award by the jury which, although higher than
I suggested would be appropriate, was not clearly extravagant'.

THE CORRECT APPROACH   *e*

[48] This court can only interfere with a jury's award if it is 'excessive'. (We
are not here concerned with the other limb of the power, to vary an 'inadequate'
award.) The question for the court is whether a reasonable jury could have
thought the award necessary to compensate the claimant and to re-establish his
reputation. If the answer is No, the award is to be regarded as excessive and the   *f*
court will substitute for it a 'proper' award. But what *is* a 'proper' award? Is it
whatever sum the court thinks appropriate, wholly uninfluenced by the jury's
view? Or is it rather the highest award which the jury could reasonably have
thought necessary? I take it to be the latter. In *Gorman v Mudd* [1992] CA
Transcript 1076, for example, where the court substituted an award of £50,000 for
the jury's award of £150,000, Neill LJ concluded that 'on no possible view could   *g*
the award of damages exceed £50,000', Rose LJ agreeing 'that a proper award
cannot exceed £50,000'. The Court of Appeal should surely take as much account
as it properly can of the jury's attitude to the case and only on this approach
would it be doing so.

[49] To my mind, therefore, this court should not interfere with the jury's   *h*
award unless it regards it as substantially exceeding the most that any jury could
reasonably have thought appropriate.

[50] When one comes to consider the seven 'comparables' summarised above
and stands back from their detailed facts, the following points stand out. Only
four of the seven cases concerned national newspapers: *Rantzen v Mirror Group*   *j*
Newspapers (1986) Ltd [1993] 4 All ER 975, [1994] QB 670, *John v MGN Ltd* [1996] 2
All ER 35, [1997] QB 586, *Kiam v Neil (No 2)* [1996] EMLR 493 and *Jones v Pollard*
[1997] EMLR 233. Of those four libels, that in *John's* case did not go to the 'core
attributes' of the claimant's personality and that in *Jones'* case was to a substantial
extent justified. The substituted award in *Rantzen's* case (updated to today's value)
exceeded the award in the present case by £28,000. The award in *Kiam v Neil (No 2)*

a was approved but so too might have been a larger award and in any event the aggravating features in the present case were substantially more serious. Yet more striking is this: in three of the five cases in which this court interfered— Gorman's case, Houston v Smith [1993] CA Transcript 1544 and John's case—the sums substituted were only *one third* of those awarded by the jury. In the other two cases the jury's awards were reduced by *more than half*—in Rantzen's case b from £250,000 to £110,000, in Jones' case from £100,000 to £40,000.

[51] In the present case Miss Sharp submits that the most that any reasonable jury could have awarded would have been £50,000. If that was so, of course, then here too the damages would be reduced by more than half. But that would mean that the jury had been seriously misled by the judge's suggested bracket and that c he is open to criticism no less than they are.

[52] This, so far as counsel's experience goes, is the first s 8 case to be considered by this court in which the judge has suggested to the jury a bracket for damages. Plainly the bracket itself is not sacrosanct. But it can hardly be thought irrelevant. For one thing it must inevitably have influenced the jury. For another, it reflects the judge's own view of the gravity of the libel—and he like d the jury was present at the trial.

[53] With these thoughts in mind let me finally state my own conclusions on the appeal. I can now do so comparatively briefly. (i) The judge's bracket seems to me entirely reasonable. Certainly, having regard to his advantages over us, I am not prepared to fault it. (ii) Given that the premise of this bracket was the e jury's acceptance of the more serious suggested defamatory meanings, I take the judge's own view to be that an appropriate award here would have been some £60,000 (the middle of his bracket). (iii) That, however, is not to say that £60,000 is the correct (or 'proper') award here. Rather, as already stated, the proper sum is for this purpose the most that any reasonable jury could have awarded. If, as I f would hold, the bracket of £40,000–£80,000 was reasonable, so too on any view would have been an award of £80,000. One must then bear in mind 'the possibility that [the jury's] judgment is to be preferred to that of the judge' (see the passage cited in John's case at [27], above), a very real possibility given this court's emphasis in Kiam v Neil (No 2) upon the continuing pre-eminence of the jury's role in assessing libel damages. In short the jury's award should not be g condemned as 'unreasonable' unless it is out of all proportion to what could sensibly have been thought appropriate. (iv) Although I have not found this an easy case and confess to having initially thought the award 'excessive', I have finally reached the opposite conclusion. I am influenced most particularly by three considerations. First, the practice of showing deference to damages awards h even when made by judges and even when assessed in the more standardised field of personal injuries—see for example Pickett v British Rail Engineering Ltd, British Rail Engineering Ltd v Pickett [1979] 1 All ER 774 at 782, 799, [1980] AC 136 at 151, 172; manifestly a far greater deference must be shown to jury awards in defamation cases. Secondly, I am struck by the large percentage differences j between the juries' awards and those substituted for them in the few s 8 cases in which this court has been prepared to intervene. Thirdly, and, as I recognise, to a degree fortuitously, the effect of Heil v Rankin has been to raise the ceiling for juries' libel awards to almost twice that now under appeal in this case; leaving therefore a very substantial margin to accommodate the yet graver libels which have to be slotted into the overall bracket. (v) None of this is to say that the present award should itself henceforth be regarded as a true comparable; only

that it is not so far removed from my own (or evidently, the trial judge's) view of the true value of the claim as to justify the exercise of the s 8 power.   *a*

POSTSCRIPT

[54] Given that this is the first bracket to have been considered by the Court of Appeal I would venture these further reflections on the use of brackets and, indeed, the use of comparables generally.   *b*

[55] Although the court in *John's* case (in the passage cited at [27], above) saw no reason why counsel should not indicate to the jury the level of award they respectively contended to be appropriate, Pill LJ in *Kiam v Neil (No 2)* (in the passage cited at [31], above) foresaw 'The danger I foresee in inviting juries to make comparisons with other cases, comparisons which would inevitably become elaborate as each party emphasises particular but different features of   *c*
those other cases' so that 'a "battle of comparables" in front of a jury may produce its own injustice, as well as being time consuming and costly'. In practice, we are told, counsel in libel cases do not ordinarily address the jury on libel comparables or, indeed, mention figures at all save that counsel for the defendant for obvious reasons sometimes refers to personal injury awards. This seems to me entirely   *d*
sensible and, indeed, commendable and for my part I think that generally speaking the only detailed guidance on figures should come from the judge.

[56] In the present case, it appears, the judge indicated to counsel before their closing speeches his own proposed bracket without at that stage having invited or received any assistance on the matter. His initial bracket was £45,000–£80,000 (marginally higher, therefore, than the final bracket suggested to the jury).   *e*
Counsel then reacted, counsel for the defendants with 'extreme alarm' to the figure of £45,000 as the bottom of the bracket; Mr Browne for the claimant by indicating that he intended to suggest to the jury that the claim was worth at least double the £45,000 award made in *Kiam v Neil (No 2)*. It would seem to me preferable for the bracket to have been more formally discussed before it was   *f*
fixed, with each side being given a proper opportunity to argue the matter after having exchanged authorities and brief skeleton submissions indicating how they proposed to argue the matter. If, as in the present case, either side suggests that there is a close comparable in point, consideration should be given to handing to the jury an agreed note identifying the particular points which each side wishes to emphasise. Otherwise, counsel should not generally refer to comparables and,   *g*
if they do, the judge should be alert to explain to the jury how these are being properly taken into account in his own bracket.

RESULT

[57] I would dismiss this appeal.   *h*

WALLER LJ.

[58] I agree that for the reasons given by Simon Brown LJ that this appeal should be dismissed.

[59] Naturally a comparison between the general damages awarded for   *j*
serious personal injuries with those awarded in libel actions gives cause for anxiety. Furthermore at first sight the award seems a very high one. But what weighs with me on the critical question whether this court should interfere are the following factors. (i) The jury in this case were made aware (as is now the practice) of the sort of damages that would be awarded in personal injury cases. (ii) In an impeccable summing up they were given a bracket of £40,000 to

a £75,000–£80,000, but told 'I have to stress that the decision is yours and yours alone'. (iii) 'If the jury make an award outside any bracket indicated real weight must be given to the possibility that their judgment is to be preferred to that of the judge.' (See the passage quoted from the judgment of Bingham MR in *John v MGN Ltd* [1996] 2 All ER 35, [1997] QB 586 quoted at [27], above.) (iv) For the Court of Appeal to interfere, the award must be one which no jury properly
b directed could have arrived at or as the notes in the former annual practice continued and without citing the authorities there referred to:

> 'The matter may be otherwise expressed by saying that the verdict must be an "impossible" verdict ... or represent an entirely erroneous estimate ... or show no reasonable proportion between the amount awarded and the
c   amount sustained ...'

(v) The judge who had provided the bracket and presided over the five-day trial with the opportunity of getting a full 'feel' of the case which this court is simply not in a position to do, in refusing permission to appeal said: '... this was an award by the jury which, although higher than I suggested would be appropriate, was
d not clearly extravagant.'

[60] I have read the draft judgment of Sedley LJ and although I understand the strength of his views, it seems to me that whilst it remains the tradition for damages in defamation to be assessed by the jury, one must be careful in assuming that there should be the close analogy with personal injury awards which he assumes. We simply do not know precisely what views juries hold on
e such things. The verdict of a jury properly directed should not lightly be overturned in the court of appeal. For reasons which I do not understand to differ from Simon Brown LJ in my view this court should not interfere with the jury's award in this case.

f **SEDLEY LJ.**

[61] The law governing general damages depends upon the fiction that suffering can be translated into money. Because it is a fiction, damages as a whole are arbitrary. But as between damages for one kind of injury and another, both legal certainty and elementary justice require careful regard to be had to relativities.
g [62] It was because of the vagaries of jury verdicts and awards in personal injury cases that the courts were given power, initially in 1854 (see *Ford v Blurton, Ford v Sauber* (1922) 38 TLR 801); then by s 6 of the Administration of Justice (Miscellaneous Provisions) Act 1933, and presently by s 69(3) of the Supreme Court Act 1981, to grant or refuse jury trial in such actions. In the exercise of this
h power the courts have since the decision of this court in *Ward v James* [1965] 1 All ER 563, [1966] 1 QB 273 adopted a uniform policy of having both liability and quantum tried by judge alone.

[63] One intended consequence of this development has been a reasonably coherent tariff of awards for personal injuries, which since 1992 has enabled the
j Judicial Studies Board to publish a booklet, *Guidelines for the Assessment of General Damages in Personal Injury Cases*, now in its fifth edition (2000). A second consequence has been that the traditional inhibition on the citation of comparables to trial courts has gone.

[64] It was the repeated contrast between the elevated sums awarded by juries in libel actions and the modest sums awarded by judges for personal injuries which led first to adverse public comment (though its main source, the media,

could not be said to have been disinterested) and then to judicial intervention. The critical decision was *John v MGN Ltd* [1996] 2 All ER 35, [1997] QB 586. There *a* a jury had awarded a popular singer-songwriter £75,000 compensatory damages and £275,000 exemplary damages for a newspaper story which untruthfully asserted that he was following a bizarre and probably harmful diet. In 1993, when the jury made this award, a claimant reduced by brain injury to a vegetative state might at highest have recovered general damages of £125,000; for a spinal injury *b* causing permanent spastic quadriparesis or unremitting headaches, at most £50,000; for the loss of both arms or both legs, £100,000.

[65] It was plain that the law was coming into disrepute and that something needed to be done. No doubt a freeing-up of damages awards generally was one possibility; but the policy adopted by this court to the same end in *John's* case was to level libel awards towards comparability with personal injury awards. These, *c* while open to criticism for being ungenerous, are intended to be sensitive to inflation (see *Heil v Rankin* [2000] 3 All ER 138, [2001] QB 272). The wide latitude given to juries before *John's* case was decided in December 1995 was held by the European Court of Human Rights in *Tolstoy Miloslavsky v UK* (1995) 20 EHRR 442 not to offend against the requirement of art 10 of the European Convention for *d* the Protection of Human Rights and Fundamental Freedoms 1950 (as set out in Sch 1 to the Human Rights Act 1998) that any restraint on free expression must be prescribed by law. The methodology of damages introduced by *John's* case is therefore certainly convention-compliant.

[66] But it is apparent that the decision in *John's* case has not succeeded in its avowed purpose. Counsel have helpfully prepared for us a table of recent *e* indications given by trial judges to juries of suggested upper limits to any awards they make for defamation. In three recent high-profile cases the figure has been £150,000. For a disabled claimant that is a sum which represents both grave trauma and lifelong suffering. In others, indicating an upper end of £50,000 or £75,000, judges have told libel juries that in personal injury terms this represents *f* the loss of a limb or paraplegia. Generally, though not always, jury awards have stayed within the figures suggested by the judge. But looking at these figures, it seems to me that the train has left the station again and is now accelerating.

[67] It may be that the re-escalation of libel damages is due in part to the fact that it began from a high base. This court replaced the enormous award in *John's* case with a sum of £25,000 general damages and £50,000 exemplary damages. *g* Since I am dissenting, it will not be disruptive of precedent if I respectfully remark that in 1993, £25,000 was more than a claimant would get for the loss of sight in one eye, or for any but the gravest facial scarring. It was the sort of sum awarded to a person so psychiatrically traumatised as to face many years, possibly a lifetime, of inability to cope with relationships and of vulnerability to further *h* trauma. In a case in which, as the court pointed out, the libel had neither attacked the plaintiff's personal integrity nor damaged his artistic reputation, how a figure of £25,000 articulated with the personal injury tariff is not immediately apparent and is not explained in the judgment of the court.

[68] Restarting from this already generous base, there has been a perceptible *j* process of what Americans might call compensation creep, pushing up not only the brackets given by judges to juries but the base from which this court is now invited to start its reconsideration of arguably excessive awards.

[69] Even in this inflationary situation I do not consider that the award of £105,000 to Mr Kiam can be regarded as anything but excessive. It is some 30% above the top of the bracket proposed by the judge, a bracket which in itself—for

a the reasons I have been considering—is unrealistically high, and no less so for being commensurate with other recent judicial directions. Even if one takes the jury award of £45,000 upheld by this court in *Kiam v Neil (No 2)* [1996] EMLR 493 as a starting point, I do not consider that any award of general damages exceeding £60,000 can be sustained in the present case.

b [70] To be sure, this was a spiteful, insolent and damaging story, based on slapdash research, published without any justification and without even asking the claimant about it. It was repeated more than once and was defended in one way or another until the end of the trial. All of this I accept and so, clearly, did the jury. It was their verdict in his favour which vindicated Mr Kiam's good name. There was no ongoing damage that anybody could point to, except no doubt that some of the mud would have stuck in some people's minds. But c substantially it was all over within 14 months of the original publication. To put this, by an award of £105,000, on a compensatory par with the wreckage of a human life by brain damage or the loss of both legs below the knee is, in my opinion, indecent. Even a sum of £60,000 represents considerably more than, for example, a young woman would get for severely disfiguring facial scarring.

d [71] In this situation, it is relevant to ask what has gone so fundamentally wrong. The answer is not very far to seek. A fair analogy with personal injury damages would require judges to point out to juries that the compensation for the sometimes unspeakable grief of a bereavement is set at present by law at £7,500 (see s 1A(3), (5) of the Fatal Accidents Act 1976), and that the humiliation and wretchedness of being traduced in public with no chance to reply, bad as that e is, is unlikely to be worse than this. The judge might then turn to the judgment of Hirst LJ in *Jones v Pollard* [1997] EMLR 233 at 243, where a checklist of compensable factors advanced by Mr Andrew Caldecott QC and accepted by counsel both in that case and in this is cited with approval:

f '1. The objective features of the libel itself, such its gravity, its prominence, the circulation of the medium in which it is published, and any repetition.

2. The subjective effect on the plaintiff's feelings (usually categorized as aggravating features) not only from the publication itself, but also from the defendant's conduct thereafter both up to and including the trial itself.

g 3. Matters tending to mitigate damages, such as the publication of an apology.

4. Matters tending to reduce damages …

5. Special damages.

6. Vindication of the plaintiff's reputation past and future.'

h [72] This list, it should be remembered, is not a cash register on which a series of sums of money accumulates. Most of what it contains is subsumed in the hurt for which the basic award compensates. Special damage is separately quantifiable, so that a person who has, for example, lost his job as a result of a lie published about him is entitled to full but separate compensation. Mr Kiam suffered no j such loss. The vindication of the claimant's reputation is the principal function of the verdict itself: it will be double counting if any but a modest element of the general damages goes to this.

[73] Perhaps most important is the question of wilful or reckless behaviour on the defendant's part in publishing the libel. As Mr Caldecott's list makes clear, this feeds into general compensatory damages only to the extent that it has made the wound to the claimant worse. It is, of course, humiliating to be lied about in

the press without even having been asked about the truth of the story; but at least on one view it is more, not less, humiliating to be lied about after having told the authors of the libel that it is completely untrue. Where the deliberate or reckless publication of untruths properly counts in libel is in opening the door to an award of exemplary damages. But in the present case, and without cross-appeal, exemplary damages were withdrawn by the judge from the jury.

[74] What I strongly suspect has happened in this case is understandable, but it is also appealable. Mr Browne QC legitimately opened his pleaded case for exemplary damages in full to the jury. Significant passages of his speech denounce the newspaper's cavalier conduct in powerful and resonant terms. What is more, even when at the end of the trial the judge withdrew the issue of exemplary damages, there remained for the jury the charge of malicious falsehood as an alternative to libel. In order to deal with this the judge had to explain to the jury the ingredients of malice—publishing a false statement without knowing or caring whether it is true or false or, worse, knowing it to be untrue—and the description may well have rung fresh bells with the jury, supported as it was by Mr Browne's closing submissions. That is probably one reason for the high award. Secondly, juries in these cases probably consider that they are dealing with wealthy media organisations for whom a four or five-figure sum is little more than petty cash. They ask themselves, and judges and lawyers too ask themselves, what is the use of setting damages at a level which makes libel cheap at the price.

[75] The law's answer, which has its own anomalies, is that in a case where the evidence reaches a sufficiently cogent level to attract an award of exemplary damages such a defendant can be taught that libel does not pay. The principal anomaly is that the penalty goes into the claimant's pocket as a pure windfall. But in a great many cases proof of a cold-blooded cost-benefit calculation that it was worth publishing a known libel is not there, and the ineffectiveness of a moderate award in deterring future libels is painfully apparent. It is this, I believe, that is leading both judges and juries once more to lift the level of general damages for libel into a different league from personal injury damages, at least in cases like the present where the newspaper has not simply got its facts wrong but has behaved outrageously from start to finish. Although this was a predictable by-product of any serious restriction of compensatory damages for libel, it is strangely enough a factor which, so far as counsel have been able to show us, is not addressed in any of the appellate decisions on the limitation of libel damages. Judges, juries and the public face the conundrum that compensation proportioned to personal injury damages is insufficient to deter, and that deterrent awards make a mockery of the principle of compensation.

[76] I do not, even so, believe that there is any necessary incompatibility between the moderation of compensatory awards for libel and the punitive and deterrent purposes which exemplary damages serve. Punishment in a modern society is not the business of private individuals: it is a matter for the state. If a motorist drives recklessly he will have to compensate any victim for the injury he inflicts, but it is to the state that he answers by way of punishment for his abuse of the right to drive a vehicle. Where it is appropriate that the victim should be fully compensated for his injury and loss, it is inappropriate that he should pocket the proceeds of punishment. If, comparably, the enormous power of the news media to misinform and to injure is to be matched with legal responsibility going beyond simple compensation and involving punitive measures, it is likewise to the state that the media ought to answer. A defendant who so conducts himself as to deserve punishment by law can and should be tried with the full safeguards

a   of due process and proof beyond reasonable doubt. He should also be prepared
to face the consequences of being convicted.

[77] It is Parliament who alone can decide whether this should happen. What
needs unravelling is the single proceeding in which compensation and punishment
have for centuries have been rolled together, and which is not appropriately
adapted, either in its process or in its outcome, to the increasingly fundamental
b   distinctions between the two. No doubt, as Lord Denning MR said in *Ward v
James* [1965] 1 All ER 563, [1966] 1 QB 273, jury trial has no equal when honour
or integrity are at stake. But when it comes to damages, the three virtues which
he went on to enumerate—assessability, uniformity and predictability—also
matter a great deal. Something needs to be done about the conflict between the
need for fair but balanced compensation for victims of libel and the equal and
c   opposite need to prevent libel from paying. It is possible within the present law
for damages to be assessed by judges; but the underlying tension between
compensation and deterrence is something, as it seems to me, that Parliament
alone can resolve. So far as the courts are concerned it is now apparent that
attempting to reduce the bracket produces an understandable but impermissible
d   reaction against the effects of making libel cheap to commit.

[78] For my part, therefore, I would allow this appeal on the narrow ground
that even by comparison with other libel awards, but especially by comparison
with personal injury awards, the figure awarded by the jury as compensatory
damages is wholly excessive. Although I have given £60,000 as the highest figure
which I believe to be defensible in the present state of law and practice, the
e   general level of compensatory libel damages which it represents is also in my
view indefensible.

Appeal dismissed. Permission to appeal refused.

Dilys Tausz   Barrister.

Kiam v MGN Ltd (No 2)

[2002] EWCA Civ 66

COURT OF APPEAL, CIVIL DIVISION

SIMON BROWN, WALLER AND SEDLEY LJJ

28 JANUARY, 6 FEBRUARY 2002

Costs – Order for costs – Indemnity costs – Circumstances in which refusal of offer to settle would attract indemnity costs under court's general discretion on costs – CPR 44.3(4).

The defendant appealed unsuccessfully against an award of damages of £105,000 by a jury in a libel case. On the dismissal of the appeal, the successful claimant applied for the costs of the appeal on an indemnity rather than standard basis. The essential ground of the application was that the claimant's solicitors, by letter headed 'Without Prejudice Save as to Costs', had made a pre-appeal offer to accept £75,000 and to return to the defendant £30,000 plus appropriate interest, an offer which the defendant had simply ignored. The claimant relied on a Court of Appeal decision which held that indemnity costs could be awarded, under the court's general discretion on costs in CPR Pt 44, where litigation was conducted in a way that was unreasonable, even though the conduct could not properly be regarded as lacking moral probity or deserving moral condemnation. CPR 44.3(4)[a] required the court, when deciding what order to make about costs, to have regard to all the circumstances including any admissible offer to settle made by a party which was drawn to the court's attention, whether or not made in accordance with CPR Pt 36. Under CPR 36.21[b], the court was required, where that provision applied, to make an order for indemnity costs against a defendant unless it considered it unjust to do so. The purpose of that provision was to encourage claimants to make offers, but there was no counterpart to that rationale with regard to defendants. On the application, the Court of Appeal considered the circumstances in which it was appropriate to award indemnity costs under Pt 44 in respect of the refusal of a settlement offer.

Held – It would be a rare case where the refusal of a settlement offer would attract, under CPR Pt 44, not merely an adverse order for costs, but an order on an indemnity rather than on a standard basis. Although conduct, falling short of misconduct deserving of moral condemnation, could be so unreasonable as to justify an order for indemnity costs, such conduct would need to be unreasonable to a high degree, not merely wrong or misguided in hindsight. An indemnity costs order made under Pt 44, unlike one made under Pt 36, did carry at least some stigma. It was of its nature penal rather than exhortatory. It should not be

---

a   Rule 44.3, so far as material, is set out at [3], below

b   Rule 36.21, so far as material, provides: '(1) This rule applies where at trial—(a) a defendant is held liable for more; or (b) the judgment against a defendant is more advantageous to the claimant, than the proposals contained in a claimant's Pt 36 offer ...

(3) The court may ... order that the claimant is entitled to (a) his costs on an indemnity basis from the latest date when the defendant could have accepted the offer without needing the permission of the court ...

(4) Where this rule applies, the court will make the orders referred to in [paragraph] (3) unless it considers it unjust to do so ...'

a understood that under the CPR it was now generally appropriate to condemn in indemnity costs those who declined reasonable settlement offers. In the instant case, it was quite impossible to regard the defendant's refusal of the claimant's offer as unreasonable, let alone unreasonable to so pronounced a degree as to merit an award of indemnity costs. Accordingly, the application would be refused, and the claimant would instead be awarded his costs of the appeal on a

b standard basis (see [12], [13], [16]–[18], below).

Reid Minty (a firm) v Taylor [2002] 2 All ER 150 explained.
McPhilemy v Times Newspapers Ltd (No 2) [2001] 4 All ER 861 considered.

Cases referred to in judgments
McPhilemy v Times Newspapers Ltd (No 2) [2001] EWCA Civ 933, [2001] 4 All ER
c   861, [2002] 1 WLR 934.
Petrotrade Inc v Texaco Ltd [2001] 4 All ER 853, [2002] 1 WLR 947, CA.
Reid Minty (a firm) v Taylor [2001] EWCA Civ 1723, [2002] 2 All ER 150.

Cases also cited or referred to in skeleton arguments
d John v MGN Ltd [1996] 2 All ER 35, [1997] QB 586, CA.
Kiam v Neil (No 2) [1996] EMLR 493, CA.

Application for costs
The respondent, Victor Kermit Kiam II, applied for an order under CPR Pt 44 requiring the appellants, MGN Ltd, to pay on an indemnity basis his costs of an
e appeal brought by the appellants from the jury's award of damages of £105,000 in an action for libel brought by the respondent against the appellants, such appeal having been dismissed by the Court of Appeal on 28 January 2002 ([2002] 2 All ER 219). The facts are set out in the judgment of Simon Brown LJ.

f   Desmond Browne QC and Lucy Moorman (instructed by Peter Carter-Ruck & Partners)
     for the respondent.
Andrew Caldecott QC (instructed by Olswang) for the appellants.

Cur adv vult

g 6 February 2002. The following judgments were delivered.

SIMON BROWN LJ.
     [1] Upon the handing down of our judgments on 28 January 2002 ([2002] EWCA Civ 43, [2002] 2 All ER 219), dismissing by a majority MGN Ltd's appeal against the jury's award of £105,000 damages to the late Mr Kiam (the appeal
h ultimately being argued on the sole ground that the award was excessive), Mr Browne QC for the successful respondent applied for the costs of the appeal on an indemnity rather than standard basis. The essential basis for the application was that on 27 June 2001 Mr Kiam's solicitors, by letter headed 'Without Prejudice Save as to Costs', had offered to accept £75,000 and to return to the
j appellants £30,000 plus appropriate interest, an offer which the appellants simply ignored.
     [2] The application seemed to me to raise an important point of principle and we had the advantage of both written and oral submissions upon it.
     [3] The question of indemnity costs orders following upon offers of settlement has recently been explored in a trilogy of Court of Appeal decisions: Petrotrade Inc v Texaco Ltd [2001] 4 All ER 853, [2002] 1 WLR 947, McPhilemy v

Times Newspapers Ltd (No 2) [2001] EWCA Civ 933, [2001] 4 All ER 861, [2002] 1
WLR 934, and *Reid Minty (a firm) v Taylor* [2001] EWCA Civ 1723, [2002] 2 All ER
150. The first two of these cases dealt specifically with the claimant's position
under CPR Pt 36 and decided that an order for indemnity costs under r 36.21(3)
was not penal and carried no stigma or implied disapproval of the defendant's
conduct and so ought generally to be made where a claimant recovers in court
more than he has previously offered to take. The two cases are fully reported and
I need not further summarise them. The *Reid Minty* case, however, has broken
new ground. To some extent it appears to suggest that the Pt 36 approach may
allow defendants too, by way of CPR 44.3, to claim indemnity costs when they
defeat a claim having previously made a settlement offer which the claimant has
declined. The most directly relevant part of r 44.3 is para 4 which reads:

> 'In deciding what order (if any) to make about costs, the court must have
> regard to all the circumstances, including—(a) the conduct of all the parties;
> (b) whether a party has succeeded on part of his case, even if he has not been
> wholly successful; and (c) any payment into court or admissible offer to
> settle made by a party which is drawn to the court's attention (whether or
> not made in accordance with Part 36).'

[4] The leading judgment in the Court of Appeal was given by May LJ (and to
this I shall return) but Kay LJ pithily added:

> 'The approach of the CPR is a relatively simply one: namely, if one party
> has made a real effort to find a reasonable solution to the proceedings and the
> other party has resisted that sensible approach, then the latter puts himself at
> risk that the order for costs may be on an indemnity basis. What would be a
> reasonable solution will depend on all the circumstances of the case ...' (See
> [2002] 2 All ER 150 at [37].)

[5] It is principally upon the *Reid Minty* case that Mr Browne relies in
submitting that the unsuccessful appellants here, having refused the 'reasonable
solution' and 'sensible approach' represented by Mr Kiam's offer (to take reduced
damages of £75,000), should accordingly pay the costs of the appeal on an
indemnity basis. Mr Browne does not go so far as to suggest that the respondent
is in the same position as a first instance claimant who beats his own Pt 36 offer.
He submits, however, and with this I agree, that he is in a comparable position to
that of a first instance defendant whose position was explored in the *Reid Minty*
case.

[6] The reason why I regard this application as raising an important point of
principle is this: the underlying rationale of r 36.21—to encourage claimants to
make offers—has simply no counterpart with regard to defendants. As
Chadwick LJ pointed out in *McPhilemy's* case, the provision in Pt 36 that, where
it applies, the court will order indemnity costs 'unless it considers it unjust to do
so' is—

> 'intended to provide an incentive to a claimant to make a Pt 36 offer. The
> incentive is that a claimant who has made a Pt 36 offer (which is not
> accepted) and who succeeds at trial in beating his own offer stands to receive
> more than he would have received if he had not made the offer.' (See [2001]
> 4 All ER 861 at [19].)

[7] I myself put it thus:

a   'The judge below, without the benefit of this court's judgment in
Petrotrade Inc v Texaco Ltd [2001] 4 All ER 853, wrongly directed himself that
an indemnity costs order under CPR 36.21 is of a penal nature and implies
condemnation of the defendant's conduct and so would be unjust unless the
defendants had behaved unreasonably in continuing the litigation after the
offer. That misunderstands the rationale of the rule. It is not designed to
b   punish unreasonable conduct but rather as an incentive to encourage
claimants to make, and defendants to accept, appropriate offers of
settlement. That incentive plainly cannot work unless the non-acceptance of
what ultimately proves to have been a sufficient offer ordinarily advantages
the claimant in the respects set out in the rules.' (See [2001] 4 All ER 861 at
[28].)

c
[8] If the claimant thought that, even if he were to make and then beat an
offer, he was going to get no more than his costs on the standard basis, why
would he make it? It would afford him no advantage at all. He would do better
simply to claim at large and recover his costs whatever measure of success he
gained. His position is, in short, quite different from that of the defendant who
d   plainly has every incentive to make a settlement offer, generally by way of
payment into court, irrespective of the basis on which any costs order will be
made. Take any ordinary damages claim. A defendant wishing to protect himself
will pay money into court. The incentive to do so is self-evident. The incentive
does not need to be created or stimulated by raising the defendant's expectation
e   as to the level of costs he will recover. And, consistently with this, where
payments in are not beaten, defendants routinely recover their costs on the
standard basis; I know of no rule or practice in such cases for making indemnity
costs orders.
[9] With these thoughts in mind, I return to the *Reid Minty* case in which the
central issue arising was whether the trial judge had been right to direct himself
f   'that indemnity costs should only be awarded on an indemnity basis if there has
been some sort of moral lack of probity or conduct deserving of moral
condemnation on the part of the paying party' (see [2002] 2 All ER 150 at [9]).
[10] In holding that to be a misdirection, May LJ referred to the following
passage in my judgment in *McPhilemy*'s case [2001] 4 All ER 861 at [29]:

g   'When dismissing the principal appeal, we left over for decision whether
Times Newspapers Ltd should pay the claimant's costs of that appeal on a
standard or an indemnity basis. Clearly rather more of a stigma attaches to
an indemnity costs order made in this context than in the context of a r 36.21
offer, although even then no moral condemnation of the appellant's lawyers
h   is necessarily implied ...'

[11] May LJ's essential approach to the question of indemnity costs for
unreasonable conduct appears from the following two paragraphs:

'[28] As the very word "standard" implies, this will be the normal basis of
j   assessment where the circumstances do not justify an award on an
indemnity basis. If costs are awarded on an indemnity basis, in many cases
there will be some implicit expression of disapproval of the way in which the
litigation has been conducted. But I do not think that this will necessarily be
so in every case. What is, however, relevant to the present appeal is that
litigation can readily be conducted in a way which is unreasonable and which
justifies an award of costs on an indemnity basis, where the conduct could

not properly be regarded as lacking moral probity or deserving moral condemnation ...

[32] There will be many cases in which, although the defendant asserts a strong case throughout and eventually wins, the court will not regard the claimant's conduct of the litigation as unreasonable and will not be persuaded to award the defendant indemnity costs. There may be others where the conduct of a losing claimant will be regarded in all the circumstances as meriting an order in favour of the defendant of indemnity costs. Offers to settle and their terms will be relevant and, if they come within Pt 36, may, subject to the court's discretion, be determinative.'

[12] I for my part, understand the court there to have been deciding no more than that conduct, albeit falling short of misconduct deserving of moral condemnation, *can* be so unreasonable as to justify an order for indemnity costs. With that I respectfully agree. To my mind, however, such conduct would need to be unreasonable to a high degree; unreasonable in this context certainly does not mean merely wrong or misguided in hindsight. An indemnity costs order made under Pt 44 (unlike one made under Pt 36) does, I think, carry at least some stigma. It is of its nature penal rather than exhortatory. The indemnity costs order made on the principal appeal in *McPhilemy's* case was certainly of that character. We held ([2001] 4 All ER 361 at [29]) that the appeal involved an abuse of process on the footing that 'to have permitted the defendants to argue their case on perversity must inevitably have brought the administration of justice into disrepute among right thinking people'.

[13] It follows from all this that in my judgment it will be a rare case indeed where the refusal of a settlement offer will attract under Pt 44 not merely an adverse order for costs, but an order on an indemnity rather than standard basis. Take this very case. No encouragement in the way of an expectation of indemnity costs was required for him to make his offer to accept £75,000: its object was to protect the respondent against a standard costs order were the court, say, to reduce the damages to that level. Where, as here, one member of the court considered the jury's award 'wholly excessive', and thought that £60,000 would have been the highest sustainable award, it seems to me quite impossible to regard the appellant's refusal to accept the £75,000 offer as unreasonable, let alone unreasonable to so pronounced a degree as to merit an award of indemnity costs. It is very important that the *Reid Minty* case should not be understood and applied for all the world as if under the CPR it is now generally appropriate to condemn in indemnity costs those who decline reasonable settlement offers.

[14] I recognise, of course, that under an indemnity costs order the receiving party only recovers the amount of costs actually incurred. But those costs may well be disproportionate (proportionality not being an issue under an indemnity order). In any event, the greater the disparity between the settlement figure offered and that achieved (and prima facie, therefore, the more 'unreasonable' the rejection of the offer) the more the receiving party will be in pocket as against what he was prepared to accept/pay so as to be in a position to meet any costs shortfall.

[15] I add only this. Mr Browne sought to bolster his application by reference to a second submission, namely that time and costs were wasted in preparing both written and oral arguments upon two other grounds of appeal which in the event were abandoned at the outset of the hearing. I think it unnecessary to deal with this in detail. Suffice it to say that it would be generally undesirable to

a penalise by indemnity costs a decision not to press particular points in the interests of the expeditious disposal of the appeal. I can see no good reason for departing from that policy here.

[16] I would accordingly refuse this application and award the respondent his costs of the appeal on the standard basis.

b **WALLER LJ.**
[17] I agree.

SEDLEY LJ.
[18] I also agree.

Order accordingly.

Dilys Tausz   Barrister.

Paragon Finance plc v Staunton
Paragon Finance plc v Nash

[2001] EWCA Civ 1466

a

COURT OF APPEAL, CIVIL DIVISION

b

THORPE, DYSON LJJ AND ASTILL J

24, 25 JULY, 15 OCTOBER 2001

Consumer credit – Extortionate credit bargain – Mortgage – Variable interest rate clause – Mortgagee failing to adjust charging rates in line with Bank of England or prevailing market rates – Whether extortionate credit bargain – Consumer Credit Act 1974, ss 137, 138.

c

Contract – Implied term – Mortgage – Variable interest clause – Whether term to be implied that discretion to vary interest be exercised fairly as between the parties and not arbitrarily, capriciously or unreasonably.

d

Contract – Unfair terms – Mortgage – Variable interest clause – Discretion of lender to set interest rate – Whether setting of interest rate constituting 'contractual performance' – Unfair Contract Terms Act 1977, s 3(2)(b)(i).

e

The claimant mortgage company claimed possession as mortgagee from the defendants in two actions on the ground that the defendants were in arrears with their mortgage interest repayments. Both mortgage agreements contained variable interest clauses. The defendants admitted the arrears of interest, but asserted that, by reason of the rates of interest that they were required to pay, the mortgage agreements were extortionate credit bargains within the meaning of s 138[a] of the Consumer Credit Act 1974. The defendants did not complain that the agreements were extortionate credit bargains at the outset, but rather that the agreements had become extortionate at a later date when, by reason of the claimant's failure to adjust the charging rates in line with Bank of England or prevailing market rates, the interest payable so far exceeded those rates as to be exorbitant. The defendants accordingly sought, by counterclaims, orders that the loan agreements be reopened under s 139[b] of the 1974 Act. The claimant's applications for orders that the defences and counterclaims be struck out on the ground that they had no real prospect of succeeding at trial were granted and applications by the defendants to amend their pleadings were refused. The defendants appealed, and the following issues, inter alia, fell to be determined: (i) whether the discretion given to the claimant in the mortgage agreements to vary the interest rate was subject to an implied term that it was bound to exercise that discretion 'fairly as between both parties to the contract, and not arbitrarily, capriciously or unreasonably'; (ii) whether the mortgage agreements were extortionate credit bargains within the meaning of s 138 of the 1974 Act; and (iii) whether the claimant's reliance on discretion to vary interest rates was contrary to s 3(2)(b)(i)[c] of the Unfair Contract Terms Act 1977.

f

g

h

j

---

a   Section 138, so far as material, is set out at [10], below
b   Section 139, so far as material, is set out at [10], below
c   Section 3, so far as material, is set out at [71], below

a
Held – The appeals would be dismissed for the following reasons—

(1) The power given to the claimant by the mortgage agreements to set interest rates from time to time was not completely unfettered. A construction to the contrary would mean that the claimant would be completely free, in theory at least, to specify interest rates at the most exorbitant level. Neither the existence of the regulatory powers of the Director General of Fair Trading nor **b** the fact that borrowers could redeem their mortgages and seek loans from another source were good reasons for holding that the power to set rates of interest was completely unfettered. Furthermore, commercial considerations were not sufficient to exclude an implied term that the discretion to vary interest rates should not be exercised dishonestly, for an improper purpose, capriciously or arbitrarily. It followed that it was necessary to give effect to the reasonable **c** expectations of the parties that there be implied into both agreements a term that the rates of interest not be set dishonestly, for an improper purpose, capriciously or arbitrarily. Moreover, there was a implied term of both agreements that the claimant would not set rates of interest unreasonably in a *Wednesbury* sense, but that was not to imply a term that the lender would not set unreasonable rates (see **d** [30], [32], [34], [35], [41], [42], [82], below); dicta of the Court of Appeal in *Lombard Tricity Finance Ltd v Paton* [1989] 1 All ER 918 at 923 disapproved.

(2) Subsequent changes in rates of interest were irrelevant to the question whether the credit bargains were extortionate. The effect of the section of the 1974 Act dealing with the calculation of the total charge for credit and the regulations made thereunder was that subsequent variations of the rate of **e** interest were excluded from the calculation of the total charge of credit and therefore from being part of the 'credit bargain' to be assessed as extortionate or otherwise under s 137. Moreover, s 138 provided that the factors relevant to that question were not only the credit agreement and other transactions which were to be taken into account in computing the total charge for credit, but also factors **f** present at the time the credit bargain was made, such as prevailing interest rates. On a natural reading of s 138, the matters to be considered, such as the level of prevailing interest rates, were to be considered as at the date when the credit bargain was made and at no other time (see [63]–[66], [82], below).

(3) The setting of interest rates under a discretion given by the contract was not 'contractual performance' within the meaning of s 3(2)(b) of the 1977 Act. **g** There was no relevant obligation on the claimant and therefore nothing that could qualify as 'contractual performance' for the purpose of the section. Even if that was wrong, by fixing the rate of interest at a particular level, the claimant was not altering any performance of any obligation assumed by it under the contract: rather, it was altering the performance required of the borrower. For s 3(2)(b) to **h** apply, a contract term had to be one which had a substantial effect on the contractual performance reasonably expected of the party relying on the term, which was not so in the instant case (see [75]–[77], [82], below); *Timeload Ltd v British Telecommunications plc* [1995] EMLR 459 and *Zockoll Group Ltd v Mercury Communications* [1999] EMLR 383 distinguished.

j
Notes

For variation of consumer credit agreements, extortionate credit bargains, and liability arising in domestic contracts, see respectively 9(1) *Halsbury's Laws* (4th edn reissue) paras 243, 269, 823.

For the Consumer Credit Act 1974, ss 137, 138, see 11 *Halsbury's Statutes* (4th edn) (2000 reissue) 114.

For the Unfair Contract Terms Act 1977, s 3, see 11 *Halsbury's Statutes* (4th edn) (2000 reissue) 232.

Cases referred to in judgments

Abu Dhabi National Tanker Co v Product Star Shipping Ltd, The Product Star (No 2) [1993] 1 Lloyd's Rep 397, CA.

Associated Provincial Picture Houses Ltd v Wednesbury Corp [1947] 2 All ER 680, [1948] 1 KB 223, CA.

Equitable Life Assurance Society v Hyman [2000] 3 All ER 961,[2000] 3 WLR 529, HL.

Gan Insurance Co Ltd v Tai Ping Insurance Co Ltd (No 2) [2001] EWCA Civ 1047, [2001] 2 All ER (Comm) 299.

J & J Securities Ltd v Khan and Khan (18 August 1999, unreported), Bradford Cty Ct.

Lombard Tricity Finance Ltd v Paton [1989] 1 All ER 918, CA.

Rahman v Sterling Credit Ltd [2001] 1 WLR 496, CA.

Timeload Ltd v British Telecommunications plc [1995] EMLR 459, CA.

Wills v Wood [1984] CCLR 7, CA.

Zockoll Group Ltd v Mercury Communications Ltd [1999] EMLR 385, CA.

Appeals

Paragon Finance plc v Nash

Geoffrey Nash and Jennifer Valerie Nash appealed from the order of Mr Recorder Havelock-Allan QC on 4 September 2000 whereby he struck out their defence and counterclaims to a claim brought by the claimant, Paragon Finance plc, for possession as mortgagee of 75 Clifton Road, London SE25 on the grounds that they had no real prospects of succeeding at trial and refused their application for permission to amend. The facts are set out in the judgment of Dyson LJ.

Paragon Finance plc v Staunton

William Staunton and Mary Staunton appealed from the order of Mr Recorder Havelock-Allan QC on 4 September 2000 whereby he struck out their defence and counterclaims to a claim brought by the claimant, Paragon Finance plc, for possession as mortgagee of 12 Valentines Road, Ilford, Essex on the grounds that they had no real prospects of succeeding at trial and refused their application for permission to amend. The facts are set out in the judgment of Dyson LJ.

Mr Nash appeared in person.

Edward Bannister QC and *Donald Broatch* (instructed by *Joseph Aaron & Co*, Ilford) for Mrs Nash.

Damian Falkowski (instructed by *Joseph Aaron & Co*, Ilford) for Mr and Mrs Staunton.

Ali Malek QC and *Peter Wulwik* (instructed by *Wragge and Co*, Birmingham) for the claimant in both appeals.

Cur adv vult

15 October 2001. The following judgments were delivered.

a **DYSON LJ** (giving the first judgment at the invitation of Thorpe LJ).

INTRODUCTION

[1] These appeals raise a number of points of general importance in relation to ss 137–139 of the Consumer Credit Act 1974. Paragon Finance plc (the claimant) claims possession as mortgagee from Mr and Mrs Nash in the first action and b from Mr and Mrs Staunton in the second action on the grounds that they are in arrears with their mortgage interest repayments. Both mortgages contain variable interest clauses. The mortgagors admit the arrears of interest, but assert that, by reason of the rates of interest that they were required to pay, the loan agreements are extortionate credit bargains within the meaning of s 138 of the 1974 Act. No complaint is made that the loan agreements were extortionate credit c bargains at the outset. The mortgagors say, however, that the loan agreements became extortionate at a later date when, by reason of the claimant's failure to adjust the charging rates in line with Bank of England or prevailing market rates, the interest payable so far exceeded those rates as to be exorbitant. By their counterclaims, the mortgagors seek orders that the loan agreements be reopened d under s 139 of the 1974 Act. The claimant applied for an order that the defence and counterclaims be struck out on the grounds that they had no real prospects of succeeding at trial. In a careful and comprehensive judgment handed down on 4 September 2000, Mr Recorder Havelock-Allan QC struck out the mortgagors' pleadings in both actions, and refused applications for permission to amend to which I shall come in due course. The mortgagors appeal against the Recorder's e decisions. Before I identify the issues that have been raised in these appeals, I need to set out the relevant facts.

THE FACTS

[2] Until April 1997, the claimant was called 'The National Home Loans f Corporation plc'. It first entered the mortgage market in the mid-1970s. The attraction of the claimant to would-be borrowers was that it was willing to make self-certification loans, i e loans to borrowers who vouched for their income. The company was badly affected by rising interest rates in the late 1980s, and got into serious financial difficulties. It was forced to withdraw from further lending in 1991. It was refinanced by a consortium of banks in 1992, and re-entered the g market in 1994 via a new subsidiary company, Home Loans Direct Ltd, which in 1997 changed its name to Paragon Mortgages Ltd (Paragon). At the heart of both actions is the complaint that the claimant has consistently charged interest rates which are significantly higher than those of other mortgage lenders, and has done so in order to cover the cost of its refinancing or to retrieve its financial position.

h [3] Mr and Mrs Nash live at 75 Clifton Road, South Norwood, London SE25. On 5 February 1987, they received an offer of loan from the claimant in a sum of £45,000 by way of remortgage of their property. The offer specified that the loan was to be for 25 years. The capital was to be secured by an endowment policy. The interest was to be payable monthly at a variable rate. The starting rate was stated to be 12·75%. The offer of loan incorporated certain special conditions as j well as the printed general conditions of the claimant then current. These latter incorporated the claimant's mortgage conditions (1986 edition).

[4] On 30 March 1987, Mr and Mrs Nash entered into a loan agreement on the terms of the offer and the loan was secured by a legal charge on their property. They paid the interest as required. In December 1992, they surrendered the endowment policy. They paid the surrender value to the claimant, and converted

the loan to a repayment basis, so that each monthly payment covered both interest and capital. Their financial circumstances took a turn for the worse, and they fell into arrears. By March 1999, the arrears exceeded £5,000. The claimant started proceedings on 5 May 1999.

[5] Mr and Mrs Staunton live at 12 Valentines Road, Ilford, Essex. The claimant made an offer of loan to them on 11 October 1990. The proposed loan was for £70,145 for a period of 25 years, with interest payable monthly at a variable rate, and repayment of capital secured by an endowment policy. The offer also included a fee for incorporating into the loan agreement the provisions of the claimant's stabilised rate facility. By this facility, the borrower was able to cap the amount of interest payable each month. Payment of interest at the variable rate (the charging rate) in excess of the cap (the stabilised rate) would be deferred by converting the excess into part of the capital amount of the loan. When, in any month, the charging rate exceeded the stabilised rate, the difference would be credited to the borrower's mortgage account as a 'monthly credit' up to a maximum figure specified in the offer of loan. In the case of Mr and Mrs Staunton, this figure (the maximum deferred interest to be capitalised) was £10,500. The offer of loan made to them described the maximum approved loan as being £80,645 (£70,145 plus 10,500), and provided that the stabilised rate of interest was to be 10·49%.

[6] On 21 December 1990, Mr and Mrs Staunton entered into a loan agreement on the terms of the offer of loan from the claimant, including the stabilised rate facility. The loan was secured by a legal charge on the property. The loan agreement incorporated a set of printed general conditions and the claimant's mortgage conditions (1990 edition). In September 1996, they repaid some capital, and thereafter the repayments included both interest and capital. Mr and Mrs Staunton discharged all their interest liabilities under the loan agreement until August 1998 when the monthly instalments due increased from £548·13 to £928·75. The Recorder said that there was no evidence as to the reason for this sudden jump, but he inferred that it was due, at least in part, to the fact that the maximum deferred interest had been exceeded, so that the stabilised rate period had come to an end. Mr and Mrs Staunton fell into arrears. The claimant started proceedings on 15 June 1999 asserting that by now the arrears amounted to approximately £6,700.

THE CLAIMANT'S STANDARD CONDITIONS

[7] General conditions (1986) edition:

'6. INTEREST

Interest will be charged from the date on which the loan is completed. The rate current at the date of this Offer of Loan is as specified in the Offer of Loan. If the rate of interest should change before the Loan is completed, the Company may give the Applicant notice of the change by any method permitted under the Company's Mortgage Conditions for the giving of notice of such change to existing Borrowers ...

7. MONTHLY PAYMENTS

The Monthly Payment specified in the Offer of Loan is calculated on the applicable rate of interest current at the date of this offer... However, the rate of interest may change before (as well as after) the loan is completed and other factors such as insurance premiums or tax rates may affect the amount of the Monthly Payment.'

a   [8] Mortgage conditions (1986 edition):

'1. DEFINITIONS

1.5 "Interest" means interest at the rate applicable to the Mortgage from time to time ...

1.12 "Payment" means the monthly payment notified to the Borrower as constituting the Payment for the time being by notice given by the Company

b   whether by any offer of loan or revision thereof prior to or at the time of the Mortgage or under these Conditions thereafter.

2. PAYMENTS

2.1 The Borrower covenants that he will pay to the Company

2.1.2 The Payment ...

c   2.2 The Payment may be calculated so as to include all or any part of capital, interest and such costs, expenses, liabilities and moneys recoverable or payable and premiums, sums expended and costs and expenses incurred as aforesaid and may be varied to take account from time to time of any increase or decrease in any of the same or any change in the rate or incidence of any tax.

d   3. INTEREST

3.3 Interest shall be charged at such rate as the Company shall from time to time apply to the category of business to which the Company shall consider the Mortgage belongs and may accordingly be increased or decreased by the Company at any time and with effect from such date or

e   dates as the Company shall determine provided that the Company will take such steps as it considers to be reasonable and appropriate to bring any such increase or decrease to the attention of the Borrower and further provided that without prejudice to the generality of the foregoing either written notice given in accordance with the provisions in that behalf hereinafter

f   contained or publication of such notice in at least two national daily newspapers shall constitute reasonable and appropriate notice for the purposes of this clause ...

7. COMPANY'S REMEDIES

7.3 If the Borrower

7.3.1 is in default of the payment of any two Payments in whole or in part or for two Months in the payment of any sums ... then in any such case all

g   moneys secured by the Mortgage including Interest shall become immediately due and payable and all mortgagees' powers by statute as hereby applied shall immediately become exercisable by the Company and the Company may at any time thereafter and without previous notice to the Borrower and

h   without the Borrower's agreement exercise all or any of such powers.'

[9] General conditions (1990 edition):

'8. INTEREST AND MONTHLY PAYMENTS

8.1 The rate of interest applicable to the Loan and the monthly payment will be as specified in the Offer of Loan as varied from time to time in

j   accordance with the applicable Mortgage Condition indicated in the Offer of Loan.'

THE CONSUMER CREDIT ACT 1974

[10] The principal conditions with which these appeals are concerned are contained in ss 137–139, which provide:

'**137. Extortionate credit bargains.**—(1) If the court finds a credit bargain
extortionate it may re-open the credit agreement so as to do justice between the
parties. *a*

(2) In this section and sections 138–140—(a) "credit agreement" means any
agreement between an individual (the "debtor") and any other person (the
"creditor") by which the creditor provides the debtor with credit of any amount,
and (b) "credit bargain"—(i) where no transaction other than the credit *b*
agreement is to be taken into account in computing the total charge for credit,
means the credit agreement, or (ii) where one or more other transactions are to
be so taken into account, means the credit agreement and those other
transactions, taken together.

138. When bargains are extortionate.—(1) A credit bargain is extortionate if *c*
it—(a) requires the debtor or a relative of his to make payments (whether
unconditionally, or on certain contingencies) which are grossly exorbitant, or
(b) otherwise grossly contravenes ordinary principles of fair trading.

(2) In determining whether a credit bargain is extortionate, regard shall be had
to such evidence as is adduced concerning—(a) interest rates prevailing at the *d*
time it was made, (b) the factors mentioned in subsections (3) to (5), and (c) any
other relevant considerations.

(3) Factors applicable under subsection (2) in relation to the debtor
include—(a) his age, experience, business capacity and state of health; and (b) the
degree to which, at the time of making the credit bargain, he was under financial *e*
pressure, and the nature of that pressure.

(4) Factors applicable under subsection (2) in relation to the creditor
include—(a) the degree of risk accepted by him, having regard to the value of any
security provided; (b) his relationship to the debtor; and (c) whether or not a
colourable cash price was quoted for any goods or services included in the credit *f*
bargain …

139. Reopening of extortionate agreements.—(1) A credit agreement may, if the
court thinks just, be reopened on the ground that the credit bargain is
extortionate—(a) on an application for the purpose made by the debtor or any
surety to the High Court, county court or sheriff court; or (b) at the instance of *g*
the debtor or a surety in any proceedings to which the debtor and creditor are
parties, being proceedings to enforce the credit agreement, any security relating
to it, or any linked transaction; or (c) at the instance of the debtor or a surety in
other proceedings in any court where the amount paid or payable under the
credit agreement is relevant. *h*

(2) In reopening the agreement, the court may, for the purpose of relieving
the debtor or a surety from payment of any sum in excess of that fairly due and
reasonable, by order—(a) direct accounts to be taken … between any persons;
(b) set aside the whole or part of any obligation imposed on the debtor or a surety
by the credit bargain or any related agreement, (c) require the creditor to repay *j*
the whole or part of any sum paid under the credit bargain or any related
agreement by the debtor or a surety, whether paid to the creditor or any other
person, (d) direct the return to the surety of any property provided for the
purposes of the security, or (e) alter the terms of the credit agreement or any
security instrument.'

THE ISSUES

a

Mr and Mrs Nash

[11] (i) Was there a breach of the express term contained in cl 3.3 of the general conditions (1986 edition)?

b
Mr and Mrs Nash and Mr and Mrs Staunton

(ii) Was there an implied term that, in exercising its discretion to vary interest rates, the claimant was bound to make its judgment fairly, honestly and in good faith, and not arbitrarily, capriciously or unreasonably? (iii) If there was such an implied term, was the claimant in breach of it? (iv) Was the loan agreement an extortionate credit bargain within the meaning of s 138 of the 1974 Act? (v) Is the

c   counterclaim for relief under s 139 of the 1974 Act time-barred by the Limitation Act 1980? (vi) Is the claimant's reliance on discretion to vary interest rates contrary to s 3(2)(b)(i) of the Unfair Contract Terms Act 1977?

Mr and Mrs Staunton

d   (vii) Did the credit bargain grossly contravene ordinary principles of fair dealing (and was the credit bargain therefore extortionate within the meaning of s 138(1)(b) of the 1974 Act) on the grounds that the claimant did not sufficiently explain the effect of the stabilised rate facility?

[12] Both appeals concern applications to strike out under CPR 3.4 and under the inherent jurisdiction of the court. The grounds relied on by the claimant are

e   that the amended defences and counterclaims disclose no reasonable grounds of defence or are an abuse of the process of the court. The Recorder adopted the test of asking in each case whether the defence and counterclaim had any real prospect of success. It is common ground that the Recorder adopted the correct test.

f
Breach of the express term in cl 3.3 of the general conditions (1986 edition)
applicable to the Nash mortgage

[13] This is a new point not taken in the court below. The proposed substitute amended defence and counterclaim alleges that there was a breach of cl 3.3 in that—

g
'the claimants applied different rates of interest to the defendants' loan from those which were applied to later borrowers falling within the same category of business as did the defendants, without having any or any sufficient grounds for discriminating in this way against the defendants.'

h   [14] The particulars relied on are contained in two schedules to the draft pleading. The first is a schedule of interest rates from 1 March 1986 to 1 April 1998: it compares the claimant's 'standard' mortgage interest rates on house purchase and remortgage (payable by mortgagors such as Mr and Mrs Nash) with its 'Blue Chip' remortgage interest rates. This shows that from 1986 until early

j   1997, the 'standard' rates were about 2–3% higher than the Blue Chip rates. In 1997 and 1998, the differential rose to about 4%. The second schedule is Table 3 in the expert's report of Mr R Rosenberg dated 14 April 2000. Mr Rosenberg was the expert instructed on behalf of Mr and Mrs Nash in these proceedings. This table compares the rates of interest payable between April 1997 and May 1999 (a) by borrowers (such as the appellants) who took out mortgages with the claimant in the late 1980s and early 1990s with (b) later borrowers who obtained

mortgages from Paragon from the mid-1990s and who have benefited from the
highly competitive rates then being offered by Paragon. This table shows a *a*
differential of a little above 4%. Mr Bannister QC submits that the relevant
'category of business' within the meaning of cl 3.3 is 'first legal charges over
residential property'.

[15] In answer to this new case, Mr Ali Malek QC makes the following points.
First, the pleading does not attempt to define the 'category of business' to which *b*
Mr and Mrs Nash belong. Secondly, the first schedule does not show a breach. It
compares two different products marketed by the claimant, namely its standard
loans and its 'Blue Chip Home Loans'. The claimant's Blue Chip loans differed
from its standard loans in that they were subject to different terms, and set a rate
of interest based on LIBOR (London Inter-Bank Offered Rate). Thirdly, as
regards the table in Mr Rosenberg's report, the position is that the business *c*
written by Paragon differed from that written by the claimant: it was lower risk,
and therefore not the same category of business with that of Mr and Mrs Nash.

[16] I am in no doubt that there was no breach of cl 3.3 of the Nash loan
agreement. The phrase 'category of business' is not a term of art and it is not
defined. The clause referred to the 'category of business to which the Company *d*
shall consider the Mortgage belongs' (my emphasis). It is clear that the claimant
considered that its standard borrowers did not belong to the same category of
business as its Blue Chip borrowers, or the subsequent Paragon borrowers. It is
true that the evidence is somewhat exiguous. This may be because the allegation
of breach of cl 3.3 was not made in the court below. It is also true that the
evidence as to the circumstances in which the claimant withdrew from the *e*
lending market in 1991 and re-emerged in 1994 are not explained in the witness
statements before the court. But there is material in the documents that are
before the court from which it is possible to say with some confidence what
happened. By 1991, the claimant was in financial trouble. One result of this was
that the money markets were charging higher rates for lending to the claimant *f*
because it was perceived as a greater risk than other mortgage lenders. Not
surprisingly, these higher charges were passed on to borrowers (who were about
70,000 in number). The claimant, therefore, decided to withdraw from the
lending market. In 1994, it decided to re-enter the market through a different
entity, Paragon. According to the claimant's chief executive, the plan was to
'undertake relatively low risk business which will be suitable for securitisation'. *g*

[17] I cannot accept that cl 3.3 obliged the claimant to charge the same rate of
interest to all mortgagors who had borrowed money to secure first legal charges
on residential property. And yet that is the effect of Mr Bannister's submission.
It is a submission which ignores the fact that the clause defines the category of
business by reference to the opinion of the claimant. But it also involves the *h*
proposition that the claimant would have agreed to charge the same rate of
interest to all borrowers who had granted first charges on residential property
regardless of the other terms of the loan, the credit rating of the borrower and
matters of that kind. That is a most unlikely commercial arrangement which I
would not impute to the claimant without clear express words. For these *j*
reasons, I consider that the allegation of breach of cl 3.3 has no real prospect of
success, and should not be permitted by way of amendment.

Implied term

[18] The amended defences and counterclaims that were before the Recorder
both pleaded that the discretion given to the lender to vary the interest rate was

a subject to an implied term. Two alternative formulations were put forward in the pleadings, viz (a) the claimant would determine the rate 'in line with interest rates being charged from time to time by mortgage lenders within England and Wales to status borrowers'; or (b) 'the interest rate would only vary in accordance with the changes in the interest rate of the Bank of England from time to time'. The Recorder rejected each of these formulations, saying that they

b stood no real prospect of success (para 127). There is no appeal from that part of his judgment.

[19] It was also pleaded that upon the true construction of the variation of rate clause, the claimant was bound to exercise its discretion to vary the interest rate 'fairly as between both parties to the contract, and not arbitrarily, capriciously or unreasonably'. The Recorder rejected this construction of the contract, but said

c (para 121) that his decision would be different if the defendants had sought to achieve the same result by way of an implied term. Encouraged by this remark, the defendants in both proceedings applied to the Recorder for permission to amend their defences and counterclaims. The implied term was formulated in accordance with the Recorder's suggestion. Permission was, however, refused on the grounds

d that the pleadings gave insufficient particulars of breach.

[20] All the appellants appeal against the Recorder's refusal to grant permission to amend their defences to plead breach of an implied term. The implied term that it is sought to plead in the substitute amended pleadings is at para 6 of the amended defences, and is in these terms:

e   'It was an (or a further) implied term of the contract, to be implied into the clause conferring the discretion to vary interest rates referred to at paragraph 3 above being an obvious qualification or to give business efficacy to or to give effect to the reasonable expectation of the parties that that discretion was a discretion which the claimants were bound to exercise fairly honestly

f   and in good faith as between both parties to the contract, and not arbitrarily, capriciously or unreasonably; and that in making a decision or decisions under the said power the claimants would give proper consideration to the matter, taking into account all relevant matters and ignoring irrelevant matters.'

g [21] The breaches are alleged at para 7 of the proposed pleadings. It alleges that the claimant has exercised its discretion in a manner which is unfair and/or arbitrary and/or unreasonable by increasing the appellants' loan repayment interest rates and/or failing to decrease them (a) without reference to prevailing market rates, and/or (b) taking into account an irrelevant matter, namely its own

h financial difficulties. Particulars are then given comparing the claimant's rates with the standard rates from time to time of the Halifax Building Society, these being taken as representative of the prevailing market.

[22] Mr Malek submits that the appellants would have no real prospect of establishing the implied term at a trial, and in any event the Recorder exercised

j his discretion correctly in refusing permission to amend the pleadings on the grounds that the alleged breaches were not sufficiently particularised. Mr Bannister and Mr Falkowski submit that (a) the term for which they contend is to be implied, or at least that it has not been shown that there would be no real prospect of establishing such an implied term at a trial, and (b) the Recorder should have granted permission to amend to plead the implied term and the allegations of breach of it.

Was there an implied term in the terms pleaded?

[23] The decision of this court in *Lombard Tricity Finance Ltd v Paton* [1989] 1 All ER 918 has loomed large in the debate on this issue. In that case, the defendant borrower entered into a credit agreement with the plaintiff credit company to finance the purchase of a computer. The agreement provided that interest would be 'subject to variations by the creditor from time to time on notification as required by law'. The borrower fell into arrears with his monthly payments. The lender started proceedings claiming the amount due. The judge dismissed the claim on the grounds that the agreement did not comply with the statutory requirements as to notification of variations in the rate of interest. The lender's appeal was allowed by this court. Staughton LJ gave the judgment of the court. It was common ground that the lender could vary the interest rate in its absolute discretion. If the exercise of the discretion had been subject to some fetter, that would potentially have had a bearing on the issues raised on the appeal. No doubt aware of the wider significance of the concession, the court went to some trouble to explain why in its opinion the concession had been rightly made. The court said (at 923):

'On two potential issues there has been no dispute before us. The first is whether the contract does, as a matter of construction, provide that Lombard may vary the interest rate in their absolute discretion, subject only to due notice. The second, whether such a contract, if made, is lawful. Counsel for Mr Paton concedes that the answer is Yes to both questions. But as the case is of some general importance, and as his concessions mean that he is, to some extent at any rate, unable to support the reasoning of Judge Heald in the county court, we think it right to explain why in our view they were rightly made. In general it is no doubt unusual for a contract to provide that its terms may be varied unilaterally by one party, in his absolute discretion, to the detriment of the other; in general one would require clear words to achieve that result. But in this particular case it is, we think, part of the background, matrix or surrounding circumstances that market rates of interest are known to vary from time to time and that some variation was very likely to occur during the lifetime of this agreement. There is also provision that the borrower may bring it to an end at any time by repaying the amount outstanding. In theory he could thus avoid the effect of an increase in the interest rate, if he found it unattractive. But we recognise that in practice this remedy is unlikely to be available, since he is unlikely to have the money, or to be able to borrow it from some other lender at less than the prevailing market rate. Counsel for Lombard observed that the provision of credit is a competitive industry, and that the effect of competition is likely to restrain Lombard from a capricious increase in their interest rate. That is no doubt true if they increase rates by the same amount and at the same time for both new and old borrowers, as he tells us they do. Indeed if a provider of credit capriciously treated old borrowers unfavourably, one would hope that the Director General of Fair Trading would consider whether he should still have a licence under the 1974 Act. It was also suggested that the provisions of the Act relating to extortionate credit bargains might provide protection for the borrower. But counsel for Mr Paton suggested that ss 137 and 138 may apply only to the original credit agreement, and not to how it is subsequently operated. It is unnecessary to express any view on that point. Bearing all those considerations in mind, we consider that on a fair reading

a

of the agreement it does provide, as counsel for Mr Paton accepts, that Lombard may increase the interest rate at their absolute discretion subject only to notice. A power to vary the rate is conferred in plain terms, there is no other express restriction on it and we can see no sufficient basis for any implied restriction.'

b

[24] The Recorder relied on the *Lombard* case in arriving at his decision that the implied terms alleged in the amended defences that were before him when he delivered his judgment on the main issues had no real prospect of success. At para 126 of his judgment, he said:

c

'These points were well made by Mr Falkowski: but I do not consider that they are sufficient to justify placing the *Lombard* decision on one side. The fact is that most of the matters to which the Court of Appeal had regard as being "factual matrix" in the *Lombard* case pply equally here. The residential mortgage market is highly competitive. Not only do rates vary up and down during the currency of a mortgage loan but the competition between lenders and the variety of risk means that rates may not all vary at the same time or by the same amount. I recognise that it is not easy for a borrower with negative equity in his property to switch mortgage lender and re-mortgage elsewhere: but if negative equity is not a problem it is quite possible for a borrower to move from one lender to another. There is mobility in the residential mortgage market, and has been for the best part of the last decade. On the evidence I have seen, I am unable to find that either Mr and Mrs Nash or Mr and Mrs Staunton were at any time "locked in" to their loan agreements with the claimant by reason of negative equity. Certainly they have no problem of negative equity now and are most unlikely to have done in the past five years. Furthermore, as I have already noted, neither loan agreement appears to have contained any early redemption penalty after the first two years. It therefore seems to me that the only factor which could have seriously inhibited the defendants' ability to re-mortgage elsewhere was their personal creditworthiness. The problem is that this factor is precisely the factor which may justify an enhanced rate of interest being charged by the lender, when compared with market rates generally.'

d

e

f

g

[25] At paras 127–130, he explained why he thought that an implied term such as that for which the defendants sought permission to amend at the hearing on 4 September 2000 had a real prospect of success. He relied in particular on *Abu Dhabi National Tanker Co v Product Star Shipping Ltd, The Product Star (No 2)* [1993] 1 Lloyd's Rep 397. That case concerned a charterparty under which the master and the owners had a discretion in determining whether any port to which the vessel was ordered was dangerous. In the express terms of the charter, the discretion was unqualified. The question was whether any restriction on the exercise of the discretion was to be implied. In giving the leading judgment of the court, Leggatt LJ said (at 404):

h

j

'Where A and B contract with each other to confer a discretion on A, that does not render B subject to A's uninhibited whim. In my judgment, the authorities show that not only must the discretion be exercised honestly and in good faith, but, having regard to the provisions of the contract by which it is conferred, it must not be exercised arbitrarily, capriciously or unreasonably'.

[26] It will be seen at once that the formulation of the implied term for which the appellants now contend is closely based on this passage in the judgment of

Leggatt LJ. The authorities to which Leggatt LJ was referring were charterparty cases. The Recorder said that in his view there was nothing special about charter contracts which sets them apart from other kinds of contract such as contracts of loan. As he put it 'a contract where one party truly found himself subject to the whim of the other would be a commercial and practical absurdity'.

[27] Mr Bannister submits that the *Lombard* case is not authority against the implication of the term for which he contends. It was concerned with a question of construction. No argument had been addressed to the court on the question whether any term should be implied, and it is misconceived to treat the passage ([1989] 1 All ER 918 at 923) as holding that as a matter of law a variation clause *could not* be subject to an implied term. In short, he submits that this passage is both obiter and wrong.

[28] Mr Malek submits that in a case such as this, a term will only be implied if the strict test of necessity has been satisfied: see, for example, per Lord Steyn in *Equitable Life Assurance Society v Hyman* [2000] 3 All ER 961 at 970, [2000] 3 WLR 529 at 539. He submits that this test is not satisfied in this case for a number of reasons. First, commercial considerations require a lender to behave sensibly when fixing interest rates. Market forces dictate that the interest rate must be competitive and comparable with other available interest rates, since if it is not, the borrowers will simply go elsewhere. Secondly, the regulatory framework is relevant. The Director General of Fair Trading has considerable regulatory powers, including the power to grant or withhold licences under s 25 of the 1974 Act. Thirdly, neither the Nash nor the Staunton agreements prevented the borrowers from redeeming their mortgages and remortgaging elsewhere, although they did contain certain penalty provisions in the event of early redemption.

[29] Fourthly, Mr Malek submits that it is inherently unlikely that at the date of the making of a variable interest loan agreement, a lender would agree to restrict the rates to 'reasonable' rates. There are problems of determining the yardstick by reference to which reasonableness is to be judged. There are different types of loans and mortgages suitable for different kinds of borrowers. Moreover, there are different types of lending institution ranging from high street banks and building societies to so-called 'tertiary' or 'non-status' lenders. The latter carry out the most limited checks of the proposed borrower's financial circumstances, and they often deal with borrowers who have a poor credit rating. Mr Malek also makes the point that if the lender were precluded from demanding 'unreasonable' interest rates, there would be endless disputes as to what was payable, and it is most unlikely that the lender would have agreed to a term which had that consequence.

[30] I cannot accept the submission of Mr Malek that the power given to the claimant by these loan agreements to set the interest rates from time to time is completely unfettered. If that were so, it would mean that the claimant would be completely free, in theory at least, to specify interest rates at the most exorbitant level. It is true that in the case of the Nash agreement, cl 3.3 provides that the rate charged is that which applies to the category of business to which the claimant considers the mortgage belongs. That prevents the claimant from treating the Nashes differently from other borrowers in the same category. But it does not protect borrowers in that category from being treated in a capricious manner, or, for example, being subjected to very high rates of interest in order to force them into arrears with a view to obtaining possession of their properties.

[31] The Stauntons do not even have the limited protection that is afforded by cl 3.3 of the Nash agreement. In the absence of an implied term, there would be

a nothing to prevent the claimant from raising the rate demanded of the Stauntons to exorbitant levels, or raising the rate to a level higher than that required of other similar borrowers for some improper purpose or capricious reason. An example of an improper purpose would be where the lender decided that the borrower was a nuisance (but had not been in breach of the terms of the agreement) and, wishing to get rid of him, raised the rate of interest to a level that it knew he could *b* not afford to pay. An example of a capricious reason would be where the lender decided to raise the rate of interest because its manager did not like the colour of the borrower's hair.

[32] It seems to me that the commercial considerations relied on by Mr Malek are not sufficient to exclude an implied term that the discretion to vary interest rates should not be exercised dishonestly, for an improper purpose, capriciously *c* or arbitrarily. I shall come shortly to the question whether the discretion should also not be exercised unreasonably. But before doing so, I should explain in a little more detail why I would reject Mr Malek's submission that there is no need for an implied term at all.

[33] Of course, I accept as a general proposition that a lender must have an eye *d* to the market when it sets its rates of interest. To do otherwise is bound ultimately to lead to commercial disaster. But commercial considerations of that kind will not necessarily deter a lender from acting improperly in all situations. They may not deter a lender from unfair discrimination against an individual borrower. They may not even avail a class of borrowers. Take the present cases. *e* The appellants borrowed from the claimant which withdrew from the lending business in 1991. The rates of interest offered by Paragon are highly competitive. But the history of the interest rates demanded by the claimant in the late 1990s demonstrates how limited the deterrent argument is. The proof of the pudding is in the eating. Between 1989 and 1992, the difference between the claimant's standard rate and the rate demanded by the Halifax Building Society was *f* approximately two percentage points. By 1997, the gap was in excess of four points. In March 1999 it rose to 5·14%, when the claimant's rate was 12·09% and the Halifax rate was 6·95%.

[34] The argument based on the existence of the regulatory powers of the Director General of Fair Trading is in my view not sufficient to deny the implied *g* term. I note that in the *Lombard* case, the court said that if a lender capriciously treated old borrowers unfavourably 'one would *hope* that the Director General of Fair Trading would consider whether he should still have a licence under the 1974 Act' (my emphasis). One would indeed have such a hope, but that does not seem to me to be a secure basis on which to decide that there is no need for an implied *h* term that a lender will not exercise the discretion to set rates of interest capriciously. There are two strands to the argument that found favour with the court in the *Lombard* case: (a) it is implicitly accepted that the lender should not act capriciously; but (b) there is no need to impose an obligation on the lender not to act capriciously, because there is no realistic possibility that he will do so. I can *j* see that there may be no need to impose such an obligation on a lender where it would be impossible for him to act in breach of it. But it is, inter alia, for the very reason that lenders can act unfairly and improperly that the Director General has the power to withdraw licences from those who provide credit to consumers. In my judgment, the existence of the Director General and the fact that he has certain regulatory powers is not a good reason for holding that the power to set rates of interest is absolutely unfettered.

[35] Finally, I must consider whether the fact that the borrowers can redeem their mortgages and seek loans from another source if the rates are set *a* capriciously etc is a sufficient reason for acceding to Mr Malek's argument. In my view, it is not. As with the last point, this is not so much an argument against the need to imply a term as an argument that it is unlikely to be broken because the lender will be aware that it is open to the borrower to go elsewhere. But it seems to me to be obvious that there may be circumstances in which the lender will act *b* capriciously towards an individual borrower knowing that it might compel the borrower to redeem the mortgage and go elsewhere. Indeed, the lender may have decided to increase the rate of interest for that very reason. But why should the lender be able capriciously to compel the borrower to find another lender with impunity? The borrower may find it difficult to find another lender, especially if he has fallen into arrears with the first lender as a result of that *c* lender's interest rate policy. His employment status may have changed adversely since he entered into the first loan agreement. The process of remortgaging is costly. The new lender will probably require a survey. There will be lawyers' fees. And there may be a penalty for early redemption.

[36] It follows that I do not agree with the obiter dicta expressed by this court *d* in the *Lombard* case in the passage that I have cited. I would hold that there were terms to be implied in both agreements that the rates of interest would not be set dishonestly, for an improper purpose, capriciously or arbitrarily. I have no doubt that such an implied term is necessary in order to give effect to the reasonable expectations of the parties. I am equally in no doubt that such an implied term is one of which it could be said that 'it goes without saying'. If asked at the time of *e* the making of the agreements whether it accepted that the discretion to fix rates of interest could be exercised dishonestly, for an improper purpose, capriciously or arbitrarily, I have no doubt that the claimant would have said 'of course not'.

[37] I come, therefore, to the question whether the implied term should also extend to 'unreasonably'. The first difficulty is to define what one means by *f* 'unreasonably'. Mr Bannister was at pains to emphasise that he was not saying that the rates of interest had to be reasonable rates in the sense of closely and consistently tracking LIBOR or the rates charged by the Halifax Building Society. He said that what he meant by the unreasonable exercise of the discretionary power to set the rate of interest was something very close to the capricious or arbitrary exercise of that power. *g*

[38] As we have seen, in *The Product Star* Leggatt LJ said that where A and B contract with each other to confer a discretion on A, the discretion must be exercised honestly and in good faith, and not 'arbitrarily, capriciously or unreasonably'. In that case, the judge held the owner acted unreasonably in the sense that there was no material on which a reasonable owner could reasonably *h* have exercised the discretion in the way that he did. Leggatt LJ (with whom the other two members of the court agreed) found that various factors called into question the owners' good faith and strongly suggested that their decision was arbitrary. He also upheld the judge's approach to the question of reasonableness. Thus the word 'unreasonably' in the passage at [1993] 1 Lloyd's Rep 397 at 404 *j* must be understood in a sense analogous to 'unreasonably' in the *Wednesbury* sense: *Associated Provincial Picture Houses Ltd v Wednesbury Corp* [1947] 2 All ER 680, [1948] 1 KB 223.

[39] This question whether an apparently unfettered discretion is subject to an implied limitation that it must be exercised reasonably has been considered in other contexts. They were helpfully reviewed by Mance LJ in *Gan Insurance Co*

a *Ltd v Tai Ping Insurance Co Ltd (No 2)* [2001] EWCA Civ 1047, [2001] 2 All ER (Comm) 299. That case concerned a reinsurance contract which contained a clause which provided that no settlement or compromise of a claim could be made or liability admitted by the insured without the prior approval of the reinsurers. One of the questions that arose was whether the right to withhold approval was subject to any (and if so what) restriction. The judge held that the *b* reinsurers could not withhold approval unless there were reasonable grounds for doing so. Mance LJ (with whom Latham LJ agreed) decided that the right to withhold consent was less restricted. Having reviewed a number of previous authorities, Mance LJ said ([2001] 2 All ER (Comm) 299 at [64]) that what was proscribed in all of them was 'unreasonableness in the sense of conduct or a decision to which no reasonable person having the relevant discretion could have *c* subscribed'. He said:

d 'I would therefore accept, as a general qualification, that any withholding of approval by reinsurers should take place in good faith after consideration of and on the basis of the facts giving rise to the particular claim and not with reference to considerations wholly extraneous to the subject matter of the particular reinsurance' (See [2001] 2 All ER (Comm) 299 at [67].)

[40] After a detailed consideration of what considerations could properly be take into account, he said:

e 'If there is any further implication, it is along the lines that the reinsurer will not withhold approval arbitrarily, or (to use what I see as no more than an expanded expression of the same concept) will not do so in circumstances so extreme that no reasonable company in its position could possibly withhold approval. This will not ordinarily add materially to the requirement that the reinsurer should form a genuine view as to the appropriateness of settlement *f* or compromise without taking into account considerations extraneous to the subject matter of the reinsurance.' (See [2001] 2 All ER (Comm) 299 at [73].)

[41] So here too, we find a somewhat reluctant extension of the implied term to include unreasonableness that is analogous to *Wednesbury* unreasonableness. I *g* entirely accept that the scope of an implied term will depend on the circumstances of the particular contract. But I find the analogy of *Gan Insurance* and the cases considered in the judgment of Mance LJ helpful. It is one thing to imply a term that a lender will not exercise his discretion in a way that no reasonable lender, acting reasonably, would do. It is unlikely that a lender who was acting in that way would *h* not also be acting either dishonestly, for an improper purpose, capriciously or arbitrarily. It is quite another matter to imply a term that the lender would not impose unreasonable rates. It could be said that as soon as the difference between the claimant's standard rates and the Halifax rates started to exceed about two percentage points, the claimant was charging unreasonable rates. From the *j* appellants' point of view, that was undoubtedly true. But from the claimant's point of view, it charged these rates because it was commercially necessary, and therefore reasonable, for it to do so.

[42] I conclude therefore that there was an implied term of both agreements that the claimant would not set rates of interest unreasonably in the limited sense that I have described. Such an implied term is necessary in order to give effect to the reasonable expectations of the parties.

Should the Recorder have granted permission to amend?

[43] The issue here is whether on the basis of the draft pleadings in their present *a* form, the appellants have a real prospect of successfully establishing breaches of the implied term. Mr Bannister relies on para 106 of the Recorder's judgment. In that paragraph, the Recorder held 'not without considerable hesitation' that there was a real prospect of success for the argument that the claimant had contravened the 'ordinary principles of fair dealing' in fixing its interest rates. At para 131, he said *b* 'not without misgivings' that for much the same reasons as he had concluded at para 106 that there was an arguable case that the credit bargains were extortionate that 'if the correct implied term were to be pleaded, the allegation of breach is not so improbable that it stands no real prospect of success and it ought to be struck out'. The 'correct implied term' was that to which I have referred at paras 36 and 42 above.   *c*

[44] What were the factors that led the Recorder to conclude at para 106 that the allegation of breach of the 'correct' implied term had a real prospect of success? They were:

'(i) whether the claimants' witness and the defendants' witnesses are comparing like with like when they are comparing rates of interest, and what the *d* correct comparisons should be, (ii) the suggestion, implicit in the defendants' criticism of the claimants' failure to reduce rates in line with the market, that the reason why the claimant's rates were kept high had nothing to do with the lending risk and everything to do with NHL's financial difficulties, and (iii) the statement made by Mr Rosenberg that the rate of interest charged by *e* Paragon to new lenders is lower than that charged to customers of NHL, such as Mr and Mrs Nash and Mr and Mrs Staunton. If the difference is not explicable in terms of risk, there is at least room for an argument (I say no more) that the claimant is not treating all of its customers fairly (see Staughton LJ in *Lombard Tricity Finance Ltd v Paton* [1989] 1 All ER 918, quoted in para 61 above.)'   *f*

[45] But at para 7 of the draft pleading that is now relied on by the appellants, the breaches alleged are that the claimant fixed the rates of interest (a) without reference to prevailing market rates, and/or (b) taking into account an irrelevant consideration, namely its own financial difficulties. The particulars of breach that are given are based on a comparison of the claimant's rates of interest and those *g* of the Halifax, especially between 1995 and 2000, and a comparison of the claimant's rates and those of Paragon after April 1997. The rates charged by the Halifax are taken as the paradigm of 'prevailing market rates'.

[46] In my judgment, the mere fact that the rates charged were made 'without reference to the prevailing rates' is not evidence from which it can be inferred *h* that, in fixing them, the claimant acted in breach of the implied term. It is not said by Mr Bannister that the rates set by the claimant had to match those of the Halifax. As Mr Rosenberg points out in his report (para 4.3.7), the claimant was not regarded as a sub-prime lender; it was a centralised lender with no branch network; and relied on self-certification by borrowers. It was not in the same *j* category of lenders as the Halifax. The real complaint is that the gap between the claimant's rates and those charged by the Halifax widened from 1995 onwards. It widened from about two percentage points to four to five points. One of the reasons for this according to counsel for the claimant (if not the only reason) was that the claimant was in serious financial difficulties because many of its borrowers had defaulted, the money markets charged higher rates for lending to

a the claimant because it was perceived to be a greater risk than other mortgage lenders, and these higher costs had been passed on to borrowers. It is the fact that the claimant took this into account in deciding at what level to fix its rates that forms the basis of the second way in which the case of breach of the implied term is put. In my view, if it was the case that the rates were increased because the claimant was in financial difficulties for reasons of that kind, that would not be a

b breach of the implied term. If a lender is in financial difficulty, for example, because it is obliged to pay higher rates on interest to the money market, then it is likely to have to pass those increased costs on to its borrowers. If in such circumstances the rate of interest charged to a borrower is increased, it is impossible to say that the discretion to set the rate of interest is being exercised for an improper purpose, capriciously, arbitrarily or in a way in which no

c reasonable lender would reasonably do.

[47] On the material placed before this court, there is no evidence to suggest that the decision to widen the gap between the rates of interest charged by the claimant to the appellants and the standard rates charged by the Halifax Building Society to its borrowers was motivated by other than purely commercial

d considerations. The claimant is not a charitable institution. Its aim is to make a profit by lending money. It follows that if it encounters financial difficulties, it may feel obliged to raise the interest rates paid by its borrowers. In deciding whether to raise interest rates, it will have to make fine commercial judgments. But if it decides to take that course in order to overcome financial difficulties, it is not acting dishonestly, capriciously or in an arbitrary manner. It is not taking into

e account an irrelevant consideration. Nor is it acting in a way which is so unreasonable that it can be said of it that no reasonable lender would take that course if placed in that situation.

[48] It follows that in my view, there is no real prospect that the appellants would be able to prove at trial that the claimant acted in breach of the implied

f term in relation to either of these appellants. Accordingly, I would uphold the decision of the Recorder to refuse permission to amend.

EXTORTIONATE CREDIT BARGAIN?

Can variations in rates of interest be taken into account at all?

g [49] In summary, the Recorder held as follows. The notice of interest rate increases or decreases could not fairly be described as 'transactions' so as to form part of a 'credit bargain' within the meaning of s 137(2) of the 1974 Act (paras 38–39 of the judgment); nor were they relevant considerations within the meaning of s 138(2)(c) in assessing whether the credit bargain was one which, after its inception, became extortionate (paras 40–64); so that the appellants' causes of

h action (if any) accrued when they entered into the loan agreements (para 64).

[50] Mr Bannister accepts that the notices of changes in interest rates are not 'transactions' so as to form part of a 'credit bargain' within the meaning of s 137(2). But he submits that the question whether subsequent transactions are to be taken into account in determining whether a credit bargain is extortionate

j is a 'red herring'. The only inquiry required by the 1974 Act is whether a credit bargain requires the borrower to make payments which are grossly exorbitant (s 138(1)(a)) or otherwise grossly contravenes ordinary principles of fair dealing (s 138(1)(b)).

[51] As regards s 138(1)(a), the appellants are plainly required by the terms of the loan agreements and mortgages (ie the credit bargains) to pay interest at the rates that have been demanded. The agreements, therefore, fall within s 138(1)(a)

unless the claimant discharges the burden on it of showing that the payments so required to be made were not 'grossly exorbitant': see s 171(7) of the 1974 Act.   *a*

[52] Mr Bannister submits that, quite apart from the burden of proof, there was ample evidence to support the view that the rates demanded of borrowers since the early to mid-1990s were grossly exorbitant. At paras 106–107, the Recorder examined the evidence and concluded 'not without considerable hesitation' that, if (contrary to his view) post-contract events were relevant, then   *b* he would not have struck out the appellants' argument that the credit bargains were extortionate.

[53] Mr Malek submits that a variation in interest rates after a credit bargain is entered into does not come within ss 137–139 of the 1974 Act. The relevant inquiry should be limited to facts existing at the time of entering into the bargain.   *c* In support of this submission, Mr Malek makes the following points. First, if subsequent events were relevant to the question whether the credit bargain is extortionate, the issue would become unacceptably uncertain. Secondly, the language of ss 137–139 is all directed to the circumstances that exist at the date of the making of the credit bargain. The present tense is used in ss 137(1), 138(1) and 139(1). The time at which the factors listed in s 138(2)–(5) are to be applied in   *d* determining whether a credit bargain is extortionate is the time of the making of the agreement.

[54] Thirdly, s 189(1) of the 1974 Act provides that 'total charge for credit' is defined as meaning a sum calculated in accordance with regulations under s 20(1). The relevant regulations are the Consumer Credit (Total Charge for   *e* Credit) Regulations 1980, SI 1980/51. Regulation 2 provides that:

'(1) Any calculation under these Regulations shall be made on the following assumptions ... (d) in the case of a transaction which provides for variation of the rate or amount of any item included in the total charge for credit in consequence of the occurrence after the relevant date of any event,   *f* the assumption that the event will not occur; and, in this sub-paragraph, "event" means an act or omission of the debtor or of the creditor or any other event (including where the transaction makes provision for variation upon the continuation of any circumstance, the continuation of that circumstance) but does not include an event which is certain to occur and of which the date of occurrence, or the earliest date of occurrence, can be   *g* ascertained at the date of the making of the agreement ...'

[55] Regulation 3 provides:

'**3** *Total charge for credit* For the purposes of the Act, the total charge for   *h* the credit which may be provided under an actual or prospective agreement shall be the total of the amounts determined as at the date of the making of the agreement of such of the charges specified in regulation 4 below as apply in relation to the agreement but excluding the amount of the charges specified in regulation 5 below.'

j

[56] Regulation 4 provides:

'**4** *Items included in total charge for credit* Except as provided in regulation 5 below, the amounts of the following charges are included in the total charge for credit in relation to an agreement:—(a) the total of the interest on the credit which may be provided under the agreement ...'

a **[57]** It follows that, as the Recorder said at paras 38 and 63 of his judgment, variations in the rate of interest charged in consequence of unpredictable future occurrences are to be excluded from the calculation of the total charge for credit and are excluded from being part of the credit bargain under the definition contained in s 137(2)(b).

b **[58]** The question whether a subsequent interest rate change may be relevant in determining whether a credit bargain is extortionate has been considered on a number of occasions in the county court, but never at any higher level. It is clearly a matter of very considerable importance, since credit bargains commonly provide that the rate of interest shall be at the discretion of the lender. In every case but one, the county court judge held that subsequent changes in interest rates are irrelevant to the question whether the credit bargain is extortionate.

c The exception is *J & J Securities Ltd v Khan and Khan* (18 August 1999, unreported), a decision of Judge Altman at Bradford County Court.

[59] The point has been the subject of academic comment. Goode *Consumer Credit Law and Practice* (1999) vol 1, para 47.27 says:

d 'The time as at which the bargain is to be tested. The question is whether the credit bargain is extortionate, not whether it has become unprofitable through a drop in the level of interest rates, nor whether the creditor has acted unconscionably in enforcing it. The Court has adequate powers to grant relief to the debtor from the consequences of unconscionable enforcement. Whether the credit bargain is extortionate has to be determined

e as at the date of the credit agreement, not in the light of subsequent events.'

[60] Professor Goode cites two cases in support of this last sentence: *Harris v Clarson* [1910] 27 TLR 30 and *Harrison v Gremlin Holdings Property Ltd* [1962] NSWR 112. The first is a decision under the Moneylenders Act 1900, and the second a decision under the Moneylenders and Infants Loan Act 1941 of New

f South Wales. With respect to Professor Goode, like the Recorder, I do not derive any support from these decisions, based as they are on a consideration of different statutes which contain language that is significantly different from that of the 1974 Act.

[61] But in his commentary on s 138 of the 1974 Act in vol 2, para 5.268, Professor Goode says:

g '*Is extortionate*. The time at which the factors listed in the section are to be applied is the time of the agreement. This is explicit in sub-ss (2)(a) and (3)(b), and it would be neither sensible nor a natural reading of the language of the section to construe the remaining provisions otherwise'.

h In this passage, Professor Goode does not cite the two earlier authorities and bases his view on the language of s 138 alone.

[62] Guest and Lloyd *The Encyclopaedia of Consumer Credit Law* (1975), vol 1, para 2-139 states that 'it is possible that under sub-s (2)(c) [of s 138] factors arising during the agreement may be relevant'. But a little later in the same paragraph

j the authors record that in the *Lombard* case the Court of Appeal left open the question whether ss 137 and 138 might apply to the unfair operation of a clause which empowered the creditor to vary the rate of interest unilaterally at his discretion, and state 'but it is submitted that, in principle, these sections apply only to the original credit bargain'.

[63] In my judgment, the Recorder was right to hold that the subsequent changes in rates of interest were irrelevant to the question whether the credit

bargains were extortionate. The submission advanced by Mr Bannister is
seductively simple. It is that the interest payments that the appellants were
required to make were payments required to be made by the credit agreements.
Accordingly, they were payments to which s 138(1) applies, and if they were
grossly exorbitant, that would be sufficient to render the credit bargains
extortionate. It is to be noted that Mr Bannister does not submit that changes in
interest rates are capable of being 'other relevant considerations' within the
meaning of s 138(2)(c).

[64] But I cannot accept his argument. My principal reason is that variations
in rates of interest are excluded from the calculation of the 'total charge for credit'
and therefore excluded from being part of the credit bargain. Section 137(1)
provides that a credit agreement may be reopened if the credit bargain is
extortionate. Section 137(2)(b) defines 'credit bargain' by reference to the
transaction or transactions that are to be taken into account in computing the
'total charge for credit'. It is not in dispute that the effect of s 20 of the 1974 Act
and the 1980 regulations is that (with exceptions that are immaterial for present
purposes) subsequent variations of the rate of interest are not taken into account in
determining the total charge for credit. This is the clear effect of regs 2(1)(d), 3 and 4
of the 1980 regulations and s 20(1) of the 1974 Act which provides:

'(1) The Secretary of State shall make regulations containing such
provisions as appear to him appropriate for determining the true cost to the
debtor of the credit provided or to be provided under an actual or
prospective consumer credit agreement (the "total charge for credit"), and
regulations so made shall prescribe—(a) what items are to be treated as
entering into the total charge for credit, and how their amount is to be
ascertained; (b) the method of calculating the rate of the total charge for
credit.'

[65] Thus the purpose of the 1980 regulations is to determine the 'true cost to
the debtor of the credit provided', and it does this by defining the total charge for
credit. The definition of 'credit bargain' in s 137(2)(b) is based on the transaction
or transactions which are taken into account in determining the total charge for
credit. The total charge for credit is central to a consideration of whether a credit
bargain is extortionate. It would be extraordinary if the rules for computing the
total charge for credit were to be ignored in deciding whether a credit bargain is
extortionate, and yet that is the effect of Mr Bannister's submission. He submits
that s 137(2)(b) serves no other purpose than that of defining the credit bargain,
and ensuring that all transactions that are taken into account in computing the
total charge for credit, and not merely the credit agreement, are taken into
account. I agree that s 137(2)(b) does serve that purpose. But it does not follow
that the rules for computing the total charge for credit can be ignored when
deciding whether a credit bargain is extortionate. An important purpose of the
regulations which define the total charge for credit is to provide a measure by
reference to which it can be determined whether a credit bargain is extortionate.
Regulation 2 contains detailed provisions as to the assumptions that should be
made in carrying out the calculation.

[66] Quite apart from the argument based on the 1980 regulations, I derive
support from the language of s 138 itself. The factors that are relevant to the
question whether a credit bargain is extortionate are not only the credit
agreement and other transactions that are to be taken into account in computing
the 'total charge for credit', but also other factors present at the time when the

a credit bargain was made. Thus it is expressly provided in s 138(2)(a) (interest rates prevailing) and s 138(3)(b) (financial pressure) that the relevant time for considering these matters is the time of the making of the credit bargain. It is also the natural reading of s 138(3)(a) (age, experience, business capacity and state of health), s 138(4)(a) (degree of risk), s 138(4)(b) (relationship to the debtor), s 138(4)(c) (quote of a colourable cash price for goods or services included in the b credit bargain) that all of these matters are to be considered as at the date when the credit bargain is made, and at no other time.

[67] It might be said that, if variations in rates of interest are not to be taken into account in deciding whether a credit bargain is extortionate, then there is a glaring lacuna in the protection provided by the 1974 Act. Mr Malek was unable to suggest any policy reason why the protection should be limited in this way. c But if I am right in holding that the discretion to set variable interest rates is subject to an implied restriction that it will be exercised in the way that I have described, then the lacuna is less considerable than it might appear. Moreover, the measure of the protection that is undoubtedly afforded by the 1974 Act should not be overstated. At para 47.26 of *Consumer Credit Law and Practice*, d Professor Goode says:

'Nevertheless, it seems clear that the concepts of extortion and unconscionability are very similar. "Extortionate", like "harsh and unconscionable", signifies not merely that the terms of the bargain are stiff, or even unreasonable, but that they are so unfair as to be oppressive. This carries with it the notion of e morally reprehensible conduct on the part of the creditor in taking grossly unfair advantage of the debtor's circumstances. This element of moral culpability, in the form of abuse of power or bargaining position, is well brought out in the judgment of Sir John Donaldson MR in *Wills v Wood* ([1984] CCLR 7):

f "It is, of course, clear that the Consumer Credit Act 1974 gives and is intended to give the widest possible control over credit bargains which, for a variety of reasons, might be considered 'extortionate'. But the word is 'extortionate', not 'unwise'. The jurisdiction seems to me to contemplate at least a substantial imbalance in bargaining power of which one party has taken advantage".'

g [68] In practice, there are unlikely to be many situations in which an allegation of breach of the term that I have held should be implied would fail where the same allegation, expressed as a complaint that the rate of interest is 'grossly exorbitant' so as to render the transaction 'extortionate', would succeed.

h *Were the rates of interest grossly exorbitant?*

[69] In view of my conclusion that the subsequent rates of interest are irrelevant to the question whether a credit bargain is extortionate, I shall deal with this issue very shortly. The particulars relied on by the appellants are precisely the same as those relied on as particulars of breach of the implied term j for which they contend. For substantially the same reasons as I have rejected their case on breach of the implied term, I would hold that the allegation that the rates of interest were grossly exorbitant has no real prospect of success. The rates are not merely required to be exorbitant. The appellants must show that they are grossly exorbitant. In my judgment, if one looks at the rates alone, the disparity between the rates that the claimant was charging the appellants from about 1995 onwards and those charged during this period either by the Halifax or by Paragon

was not such as to make the claimant's rates grossly exorbitant. It may be said that they were high, even unreasonably high, but that is insufficient. Thus, even if the subsequent rates could be taken into account in deciding whether the credit bargains were extortionate, I am not persuaded that the appellants would have real prospects of success on this issue at trial.

THE LIMITATION ISSUES

[70] A number of arguments were addressed to us as to when the cause of action under s 139 of the 1974 Act first arose, and indeed as to whether the Limitation Act 1980 applies at all to such a cause of action. I mention in passing that in *Rahman v Sterling Credit Ltd* [2001] 1 WLR 496, it was held by this court that a claim to reopen an agreement under s 139 is 'an action upon a specialty' for which the relevant limitation period under s 8 of the 1980 Act is 12 years. Mr Bannister submits that this decision proceeded on the basis of a concession by counsel for the borrower that a claim to relief under s 139 is an action upon a specialty, and that it is wrong. Since I have reached the clear conclusion that the appellants have no real prospect of succeeding in their claim under s 139, it is unnecessary for me to decide the limitation point, and I do not propose to do so.

SECTION 3(2)(B)(I) OF THE UNFAIR CONTRACT TERMS ACT 1977

[71] Section 3 of the 1977 Act provides so far as material:

'(1) This section applies as between contracting parties where one of them deals as consumer or on the other's written standard terms of business.

(2) As against that party, the other cannot by reference to any contract term … (b) claim to be entitled—(i) to render a contractual performance substantially different from that which was reasonably expected of him, or (ii) in respect of the whole or any part of his contractual obligation, to render no performance at all, except in so far as (in any of the cases mentioned above in this subsection) the contract term satisfies the requirement of reasonableness.'

[72] It is submitted on behalf of the appellants that they were reasonably entitled to expect that, in performing their side of the bargain, the claimant would not apply rates which were substantially out of line with rates applied by comparable lenders to borrowers in comparable situations to the appellants. It is contended that the setting of interest rates is 'contractual performance' within the meaning of s 3(2)(b) of the 1977 Act, and that the claimant set interest rates that defeated that expectation.

[73] The first question is whether the fixing of rates of interest under a discretion given by the contract was 'contractual performance' within the meaning of s 3(2)(b). Mr Broatch submits that it is. He relies on two authorities. The first is *Timeload Ltd v British Telecommunications plc* [1995] EMLR 459. In that case, the plaintiff set up a free telephone inquiry service, and entered into a contract with BT whereby BT provided the plaintiff with the use of a certain telephone number. There was a clause in the contract which authorised BT to terminate apparently without reason. BT gave one month's notice of termination, and the plaintiff sought an injunction to restrain BT from terminating. It was held by the Court of Appeal that it was at least arguable that a clause purporting to authorise BT to terminate without reason purported to permit partial or different performance from that which the plaintiff was entitled to expect, and that s 3(2) of the 1977 Act applied. But the licence agreement imposed clear performance obligations on BT. Thus, cl 1.1 obliged BT to provide the various services there set out. In these

a circumstances, it is not difficult to see why the court thought that it was at least arguable that a clause authorising termination of the obligation to provide those services for no good reason purported to permit a contractual performance different from that which the customer might reasonably expect.

[74] The second authority is *Zockoll Group Ltd v Mercury Communications Ltd* [1999] EMLR 385. This was another telecommunications case. The plaintiff planned
b to set up a network of franchisees to provide goods and services to the public in response to telephone inquiries. It entered into a contract with Mercury under which it obtained a number of telephone numbers. Mercury wished to withdraw one number from the plaintiff and asserted that it was entitled to do so at its sole discretion. The plaintiff brought proceedings and relied on s 3(2)(b)(i) of the 1977 Act. The court held that the withdrawal of the disputed number did not
c render the contractual performance substantially different from what was expected. Mr Broatch points out that it is implicit in the decision of the court that it was accepted that the withdrawal of the disputed number was *capable of being* contractual performance substantially different from that which it was reasonable to expect.

d [75] In my judgment, neither of these authorities assists Mr Broatch's submission. In both cases, the defendant telecommunications provider was contractually bound to provide a service. The question was whether the withdrawal of the service in the particular circumstances of the case was such as to render the contract performance (ie the provision of that service) substantially different from that which it was reasonable for the other contracting party to expect. The present cases are quite
e different. Here, there is no relevant obligation on the claimant, and therefore nothing that can qualify as 'contractual performance' for the purposes of s 3(2)(b)(i). Even if that is wrong, by fixing the rate of interest at a particular level the claimant is not altering the performance of any obligation assumed by it under the contract. Rather, it is altering the performance required of the appellants.

f [76] There appears to be no authority in which the application of s 3(2)(b)(i) to a situation similar to that which exists in this case has been considered. The editors of *Chitty on Contracts* (28th edn, 1999) offer this view at para 14-071:

'Nevertheless it seems unlikely that a contract term entitling one party to terminate the contract in the event of a material breach by the other (e.g.
g failure to pay by the due date) would fall within paragraph (b), or, if it did so, would be adjudged not to satisfy the requirement of reasonableness. Nor, it is submitted, would that provision extend to a contract term which entitled one party, not to alter the performance expected of himself, but to alter the performance required of the other party (e.g. a term by which a seller of
h goods is entitled to increase the price payable by the buyer to the price ruling at the date of delivery, or a term by which a person advancing a loan is entitled to vary the interest payable by the borrower on the loan).'

[77] In my judgment, this passage accurately states the law. The contract term must be one which has an effect (indeed a substantial effect) on
j contractual performance reasonably expected of the party who relies on the term. The key word is 'performance'. A good example of what would come within the scope of the statute is given at para 14-070 of *Chitty*. The editors postulate a person dealing as a consumer with a holiday tour operator who agrees to provide a holiday at a certain hotel at a certain resort, but who claims to be entitled, by reference to a term of the contract to that effect, to be able to accommodate the consumer at a different hotel, or to change the resort, or to

cancel the holiday in whole or in part. In that example, the operator has an obligation
to provide a holiday. The provision of the holiday is the 'contractual performance'.
But that does not apply here.

MR AND MRS STAUNTON: THE STABILISED RATE FACILITY

[78] As I explained at [5], above, the stabilised rate facility enabled Mr and Mrs
Staunton to cap the amount of interest payable each month and defer payment of the
excess by granting a 'monthly credit' and converting the credit (up to a maximum of
£10,500) into part of the capital amount of the loan. The offer of loan incorporated
certain special conditions in respect of the stabilised rate facility. Condition 2 provided
that:

> 'The Company's obligation to credit any Monthly Credit shall cease if the
> amount of the next Monthly Credit when aggregated with Monthly Credits
> previously paid and amounts of Interest capitalised or accrued in accordance
> with Condition 5 would equal or be greater than the Maximum Deferred
> Interest shown on the Offer of Loan.'

[79] In other words, once the maximum deferred interest of £10,500 was reached,
Mr and Mrs Staunton ceased to be entitled to the benefit of the cap. If that occurred,
they would inevitably face a jump in interest rates.

[80] Mr Falkowski submits that they were not warned of the jump in interest rates
that would occur once the stabilised rate period came to an end. What was required
was an explanation in plain and intelligible language of the way in which the facility
would operate. The failure of the contract documents to do this rendered the credit
bargain extortionate, since it grossly contravened ordinary principles of fair dealing:
see s 138(1)(b) of the 1974 Act.

[81] In my view, there is nothing misleading or underhand about the contract
documentation. It may not be especially easy for a lay person to understand. But it
does clearly describe the way in which the stabilised rate facility works. It does not
even contravene ordinary principles of fair dealing, let alone contravene them grossly.
I would reject Mr Falkowski's argument.

CONCLUSION

[82] In my judgment, therefore, these appeals must be dismissed. This may seem
a harsh result, since it is clear that the appellants have suffered serious hardship as a
result of the increases in interest rates. But the 1974 Act provides borrowers with only
limited protection from the working of the free market. Parliament has empowered
the court to intervene only where a bargain is *grossly* unfair to the borrower, either
because the payments required to be made are grossly exorbitant, or because it
otherwise grossly contravenes ordinary principles of fair dealing. Nothing less will do.
For the reasons that I have explained, moneylending agreements which contain
provisions for variable rates of interest are also subject to an implied term of limited
scope, but that cannot avail the appellants in this case. If greater protection is to be
accorded to borrowers, that is a matter for Parliament.

ASTILL J. I agree.

THORPE LJ. I also agree.

Appeals dismissed.

Kate O'Hanlon   Barrister.

a # Brown and another v Bennett and others

CHANCERY DIVISION

NEUBERGER J

5, 8, 9 OCTOBER, 16 NOVEMBER 2001

Counsel – Payment of costs by counsel personally – Costs incurred improperly, unreasonably or negligently – Whether court having power to make wasted costs orders only against lawyers of party applying for such an order – Whether liability of barristers for wasted costs limited to conduct of case in court – Whether court to apply 'but for' test or loss of chance approach in wasted costs application – Supreme Court Act 1981, s 51(6), (7), (13).

The respondents, a firm of solicitors and three barristers, had advised and/or represented the claimants at various stages of an action against the applicants, which had been commenced, with the benefit of legal aid, in March 1996. The claims in that action involved allegations of dishonesty against the applicants. In September 2000, four days before the trial, the applicants' solicitors were informed that the claimants' legal aid certificates would not be extended to cover it. The claimants represented themselves at trial, but the judge found that the applicants had no case to answer and duly dismissed the action. Subsequently, the applicants sought orders against the respondents under s 51(6)[a] of the Supreme Court Act 1981 which empowered the court to order 'legal representatives' to meet wasted costs, such costs being defined in sub-s (7) as costs incurred by 'a party as a result' of any improper, unreasonable or negligent act or omission on the part of 'any' legal representative. Section 51(13) defined 'legal representative', in relation to 'a party to proceedings', as any person 'exercising a right of audience or a right to conduct litigation on his behalf'. The applicants sought orders in respect of the costs, or a substantial proportion of the costs, of the whole of the action, contending that the respondents should have appreciated that it stood no chance of success and, in particular, that there were no grounds for alleging dishonesty. Some of the applicants further submitted that, in any event, they should be entitled to recover from the claimants' solicitors and two of the barristers the costs incurred by them in securing the discharge, on the grounds of insufficient evidence, of an interlocutory injunction obtained by the claimants at an early stage of the proceedings. The claimants refused to waive privilege for the purposes of the application. On the first stage of the application, in which the court had to consider whether it was likely that wasted costs orders would be made, the barristers contended that s 51 of the 1981 Act empowered the court to make such orders only against a litigant's own legal representatives, not against the legal representatives of his opponent or of any other party to the proceedings, since the latter did not fall within the definition of 'legal representative' in s 51(13). They further contended that barristers could only be liable for wasted costs orders in respect of costs incurred as a result of their conduct of the case in court since the phrase 'exercising a right of audience' in s 51(13) was confined to such conduct and barristers did not 'conduct litigation' within the meaning of that provision. All the respondents contended that the making of a wasted costs order against them could not be justified on the facts

---

a   Section 51, so far as material, is set out at [20], below

since, inter alia, the claimants would have brought their action and taken it to trial even if they lacked legal representation, and accordingly the applicants could not establish that the costs claimed were incurred 'as a result' of the respondents' advice and actions. On that issue, the question arose whether, as the respondents contended, the court should deal with causation by applying a 'but for' test on the balance of probabilities or whether, as the applicants contended, causation should be dealt with on the basis of the loss of a chance by awarding a proportion of the total costs. A further issue arose as to the circumstances in which a pleading of dishonesty would breach a barrister's obligation under the Bar Code of Conduct not to plead an allegation of fraud unless the barrister had before him reasonably credible material which, as it stood, established a prima facie case of fraud.

Held – (1) On its true construction, s 51 of the 1981 Act extended to wasted costs applications by one party against the legal representatives of another party to the same proceedings. A conclusion to the contrary would be inconsistent with the policy behind s 51 which was aimed against the mischief of causing loss and expense to litigants by the unjustifiable conduct of litigation by their or the other side's lawyers. Moreover, when read together with s 51(13), the reference to 'any' legal representative in s 51(7) more naturally meant a representative of any party to the proceedings rather than being limited to the party making the claim for wasted costs. Nor was there any need to equate the 'party' in s 51(7) with the 'party to proceedings' in s 51(13). That conclusion was not vitiated by the words 'on his behalf' at the end of s 51(13), which served to emphasise that a wasted costs order could only be made against a legal representative who was acting on behalf of a party to the proceedings in respect of which the wasted costs order was sought (see [28], [29], [33], [35], [36], [187], below); *Ridehalgh v Horsefield* [1994] 3 All ER 848 considered.

(2) The liability of a barrister for a wasted costs order under s 51 of the 1981 Act was not limited to his conduct of the proceedings in court, but extended to his involvement in connection with acting or advising on the proceedings in any respect, including his involvement in drafting or settling any document in connection with the proceedings. In carrying on such activities, a barrister was exercising a right to conduct litigation within the meaning of s 51(13). Although the concept of conducting litigation would in many circumstances be understood to involve the traditional litigation activities of a solicitor, it was appropriate, bearing in mind that a 'right to conduct litigation' was not defined in the 1981 Act, to give that expression a meaning that was less technical and more vernacular. On that basis, it was impossible to see why it should not extend to all the activities involved in providing litigation services in a wide sense, whether taking formal steps in proceedings, appearing in court or being a party to preparatory and connected activities, such as drafting or settling of documents and advising on prospects or procedure. Alternatively, the phrase 'any person exercising a right of audience or a right to conduct litigation on his behalf' was to be treated as a single composite expression extending to all lawyers who were engaged in acting before, or advising, the client in connection with the relevant proceedings. A narrower interpretation of s 51(13) would considerably emasculate s 51 in so far as it related to the conduct of barristers. It would also discriminate in favour of barristers and against solicitors in an invidious and unfair way (see [45]–[48], [50], [187], below).

a (3) In wasted costs applications, the court should ask itself whether, on the balance of probabilities, the costs in question would have been incurred but for the conduct on the part of the lawyers which formed the subject matter of the complaint. That conclusion was the correct construction of s 51(7). In contrast, it would be inconsistent with the approach to be adopted to wasted costs applications if the court had to assess the level of costs to be awarded on the loss
b of a chance basis. It would increase both the number of wasted costs applications and the level of inquiry involved in such applications. In the instant case, the claimants would either not have brought the action at all or proceeded with it to anything like the extent they had done without the benefit of legal aid, and even if they had proceeded with it to trial the costs of the action to the applicants would have been substantially less (see [54], [59], [65], [187], below); *Allied Maples*
c *Group Ltd v Simmons & Simmons (a firm)* [1995] 4 All ER 907 distinguished.

(4) Although there was no doubt as to counsel's duty not to plead a claim of dishonesty in circumstances which infringed the Bar Code of Conduct, such a pleading would be improper only if counsel's view that he could plead dishonesty was unreasonable or reckless. In other words, such a pleading could be criticised
d as improper only if the lawyer's conclusion that he could plead a claim for dishonesty was one which no reasonable lawyer, properly considering matters, could have reached. In the instant case, the pleading of dishonesty could be justified against all but one of the applicants and, in any event, there was a real risk of unfairness to the respondents in light of the claimants' insistence on privilege. Accordingly, all the general applications for wasted costs would be
e dismissed, but the application in relation to the injunction would be allowed to proceed to the second stage since it was more likely than not that a wasted costs order would be made in respect of the costs of discharging the injunction (see [113], [133], [137], [142]–[144], [149], [152], [181], [187], below); *Medcalf v Mardell* [2001] Lloyd's Rep PN 146 and *Three Rivers DC v Bank of England (No 3)* [2001] 2 All
f ER 513 considered.

Notes

For personal liability of legal representatives for costs in civil proceedings, see 44(1) *Halsbury's Laws* (4th edn reissue) para 171.

For the Supreme Court Act 1981, s 51, see 11 *Halsbury's Statutes* (4th edn) (2000
g reissue) 1094.

Cases referred to in judgment

Allied Maples Group Ltd v Simmons & Simmons (a firm) [1995] 4 All ER 907, [1995] 1 WLR 1602, CA.
h *Barclays Bank plc v Eustice* [1995] 4 All ER 511, [1995] 1 WLR 1238, CA.
Cornwall Gardens PTE Ltd v R O Garrard & Co Ltd [2001] EWCA Civ 699.
Davy-Chiesman v Davy-Chiesman [1984] 1 All ER 321, [1984] Fam 48, [1984] 2 WLR 291, CA.
Drums and Packaging Ltd v Freeman [1999] All ER (D) 964.
j *Fryer v Royal Institution of Chartered Surveyors* [2000] Lloyd's Rep PN 534, CA.
Harley v McDonald, Glasgow Harley (a firm) v McDonald [2001] UKPC 18, [2001] 2 AC 678, [2001] 2 WLR 1749.
Locke v Camberwell Health Authority [1991] 2 Med LR 249, CA.
Medcalf v Mardell [2001] Lloyd's Rep PN 146, CA.
Orchard v South Eastern Electricity Board [1987] 1 All ER 95, [1987] QB 565, [1987] 2 WLR 102, CA.

R v Derby Magistrates' Court, ex p B [1995] 4 All ER 526, [1996] AC 487, [1995] 3 WLR 681, HL.

Ridehalgh v Horsefield [1994] 3 All ER 848, sub nom *Ridehalgh v Horsefield, Allen v Unigate Dairies Ltd, Roberts v Coverite (Asphalters) Ltd, Philex plc v Golban (t/a Capital Estates), Watson v Watson, Antonelli v Wade Gery Farr (a firm)* [1994] Ch 205, [1994] 3 WLR 462, CA.

Siporex Trade SA v Comdel Commodities Ltd [1986] 2 Lloyd's Rep 428.

Three Rivers DC v Bank of England (No 3) [2001] UKHL 16, [2001] 2 All ER 513; *rvsg in part* [1999] 4 All ER 800n, [2000] 2 WLR 15, CA.

Veasey v Millfeed Co Ltd [1997] PNLR 100, CA.

Wilsher v Essex Area Health Authority [1988] 1 All ER 871, [1988] AC 1074, [1988] 2 WLR 557, HL.

Worsley v Tambrands Ltd (8 November 2000, unreported), QBD.

Cases also cited or referred to in skeleton arguments

Abermeadow Ltd, Re [2000] 2 BCLC 824.

Baden v Société Générale pour Favoriser le Développement du Commerce et l'Industrie en France SA (1982) [1992] 4 All ER 161, [1993] 1 WLR 509, Ch D.

Bank of Credit and Commerce International (Overseas) Ltd (in liq) v Akindele [2000] 4 All ER 221, [2001] Ch 437, CA.

Barings plc, Re (No 5), Secretary of State for Trade and Industry v Baker (No 5) [1999] 1 BCLC 433, CA.

Barnes v Addy (1874) LR 9 Ch App 244, CA.

Barrister (wasted costs order), Re A (No 1 of 1991) [1992] 3 All ER 429, [1993] QB 293, CA.

Boardman v Phipps [1966] 3 All ER 721, [1967] 2 AC 46, HL.

Boyce v Wyatt Engineering [2001] EWCA Civ 692, [2001] CPLR 343.

Brinks Ltd (formerly Brink's-Mat Ltd) v Abu-Saleh [1996] CLC 133.

Canadian Aero Service Ltd v O'Malley (1973) 40 DLR (3d) 371, Can SC.

Caparo Industries plc v Dickman [1990] 1 All ER 568, [1990] 2 AC 605, HL.

Connolly-Martin v Davis [1999] Lloyd's Rep PN 790, CA.

Cook v G S Deeks [1916] 1 AC 554, [1916–17] All ER Rep 285, PC.

CPS v Tweddell [2001] EWHC Admin 188, [2001] ACD 83, DC.

Credit Lyonnais Bank Nederland NV (now known as Generale Bank Nederland NV) v Export Credits Guarantee Department [1999] 1 All ER 929, [2000] 1 AC 486, HL.

Daniels (formerly Deloitte Haskins & Sells) v Anderson (1995) 16 ACSR 607, NSW SC.

El Ajou v Dollar Land Holdings plc [1994] 2 All ER 685, CA.

Estill v Cowling Swift & Kitchin [2000] Lloyd's Rep PN 378.

General Mediterranean Holdings SA v Patel [1999] 3 All ER 673, [2000] 1 WLR 272.

Hall (Arthur J S) & Co (a firm) v Simons, Barratt v Ansell (t/a Woolf Seddon (a firm)), Harris v Scholfield Roberts & Hill (a firm) [2000] 3 All ER 673, [2000] 3 WLR 543, HL.

Industrial Development Consultants Ltd v Cooley [1972] 2 All ER 162, [1972] 1 WLR 443.

Lowline (PSV) v Direct Aviation Ltd (8 March 1999, unreported), QBD.

Manzanilla Ltd v Corton Property and Investments Ltd [1997] 3 FCR 389, CA.

Matrix Securities Ltd v Theodore Goddard (a firm) [1998] PNLR 290.

McDonald's Corp v Steel [1995] 3 All ER 615, CA.

McFarlane v Wilkinson, Hegarty v E E Caledonia Ltd [1997] PNLR 578, CA.

Meridian Global Funds Management Asia Ltd v Securites Commission [1995] 3 All ER 918, [1995] 2 AC 500, PC.

Myers v Elman [1939] 4 All ER 484, [1940] AC 282, HL.

Panatown Ltd v Alfred McAlpine Construction Ltd [2000] 4 All ER 97, [2001] 1 AC 518, HL.

a *R (Fleurose) v Securities and Futures Authority Ltd* [2001] EWHC Admin 292, [2001] 2 All ER (Comm) 481.

R v Horsham DC, ex p Wenman [1994] 4 All ER 681, [1995] 1 WLR 680.

R v Mills [1999] 3 SCR 668, Can SC.

Regal (Hastings) Ltd v Gulliver [1942] 1 All ER 378, [1967] 2 AC 134, HL.

Royal Brunei Airlines Sdn Bhd v Tan [1995] 3 All ER 97, [1995] 2 AC 378, PC.

b *South Australia Asset Management Corp v York Montague Ltd, United Bank of Kuwait plc v Prudential Property Services Ltd, Nykredit Mortgage Bank plc v Edward Erdman Group Ltd* [1996] 3 All ER 365, [1997] AC 191, HL.

Sykes v Midland Bank Executor & Trustee Co Ltd [1970] 2 All ER 471, [1971] QB 113, CA.

Tate v Hart [1999] PNLR 787, CA.

Taylor v Midland Bank Trust Co Ltd [2002] WLTR 95, CA.

c *Twinsectra Ltd v Yardley* [2000] Lloyd's Rep PN 239, CA.

Wall v Lefever [1998] 1 FCR 605, CA.

Westmid Packaging Services Ltd, Re, Secretary of State for Trade and Industry v Griffiths [1998] 2 All ER 124, CA.

d **Applications for wasted costs orders**

The applicants, Maurice Bennett, Michael Bennett, Vivian Scott, Peter Evans, David Sarson, Oasis Stores plc (collectively the Oasis defendants), Apax Partners & Co Ventures Ltd, Apax Ventures III, APA Ventures III International Partners LP and Cyril Freedman (collectively the APA defendants), applied pursuant to s 51(6) of the Supreme Court Act 1981 for wasted costs orders against the respondents,

e David Oliver QC, Nicholas Asprey, Timothy Evans (collectively the Barristers), and Abrahamsons and Associates, who had advised and/or represented the claimants, Graham Brown and Edwina Brown, in an unsuccessful action brought by them against the applicants and one other defendant, Stephen Kane. Such orders were sought in respect of the whole of the proceedings, but Mr Michael

f Bennett, Mr Evans, Mr Sarson, Apax Partners, Apax Ventures and APA Ventures sought, in any event, wasted costs orders against Mr Oliver, Mr Asprey and Abrahamsons in respect of the costs incurred by them in relation to an interlocutory injunction, granted to the claimants ex parte by Ferris J on 17 May 1996, but which had been discharged by Knox J on 24 June 1996. The facts are set out in the judgment.

g

Barbara Dohmann QC and Robert Anderson (instructed by Berwin Leighton Paisner) for the Oasis defendants.

Richard Slowe and Paul Stanley (instructed by S J Berwin) for the APA defendants.

John L Powell QC, Roger Stewart QC and Amanda Savage (instructed by Richards

h Butler) for the Barristers.

Guy Mansfield QC and Derrick Dale (instructed by Reynolds Porter Chamberlain) for Abrahamsons.

Cur adv vult

j 16 November 2001. The following judgment was delivered.

NEUBERGER J.

(A) INTRODUCTION

[1] This case concerns applications for wasted costs orders against the solicitors and counsel who advised and/or represented the claimants, Mr and

Mrs Graham Brown, in connection with proceedings brought against the applicants (the action). The case raises some points of principle in relation to the wasted costs jurisdiction, and the application of principles, laid down in earlier cases concerned with wasted costs applications, in the context of a relatively complex case.

[2] I propose to begin by setting out the background and history of the action. I will then turn to the present applications, and to the relevant statutory and other material. Thereafter, I will deal with certain points of principle in connection with the ambit of the wasted costs jurisdiction, raised by Mr John Powell QC, who appears with Mr Roger Stewart QC and Ms Amanda Savage for the barrister respondents to the present applications. I will then discuss the applicants' claim for a wasted costs order in respect of the whole of the proceedings. Finally, I will turn to the applications in relation to two specific aspects of the proceedings, namely a claim which was struck out and an interlocutory injunction.

(B) THE BACKGROUND

[3] Until 4 August 1988, Mr and Mrs Brown (the Browns) were the only shareholders in Pinecord Ltd (the Company) and, together with Mr Peter Evans and Mr Stephen Kane, they were the directors. On 4 August 1988, they entered into an agreement whereby two brothers, Maurice and Michael Bennett (the Bennetts) became directors of the company and obtained a small shareholding, together with an option to acquire more shares. In March 1989, pursuant to funding arrangements, the Bennetts obtained options to acquire further shares. In September 1989, three venture capital companies, namely Apax Partners & Co Ventures Ltd, Apax Ventures III and APA Ventures III International Partners LP (together APA) subscribed a substantial sum for shares in the Company, and appointed Mr Cyril Freedman to the board of the Company. There was a rights issue of shares and loan stock in March 1990, in which the Browns participated only to a limited extent.

[4] As a result of the allotment of shares to the Bennetts and to APA, the Bennetts exercising their options and the rights issue, Mr and Mrs Browns' share in the Company was diluted to below 50%. On 19 July 1990, they ceased to be directors of the Company, and allege that they were forced to resign by the refusal of the Bennetts to implement economies. There was also a dispute as to the circumstances in which the Browns resigned, and, indeed, as to whether they were wrongly excluded from the Company's premises.

[5] On 24 January 1991, the Company went into administrative receivership, at a time when its directors (the directors) were the Bennetts, Mr Freedman, Mr Evans, Mr Kane, and Mr Vivian Scott (who had become a director in November 1990). The company secretary at that time was Mr David Sarson, who had been its financial controller since August 1988.

[6] Thereafter, the administrative receivers (the receivers) of the Company advertised its business for sale, and a number of offers were received, including from the Browns and from the Bennetts. The Bennetts' offer was accepted in principle by the receivers. The Bennetts then acquired all the shares in another company known as Oasis Stores plc (Oasis) of which they became the directors, and they entered into negotiations with various outside investors with a view to funding Oasis for the purpose of purchasing the business of the Company. Eventually, during March 1991, the issued share capital of Oasis was increased, and about 49% of its shares was issued to the Bennetts and Mr Scott, and the remainder to a new company called Tuneclass Ltd. In the same month, Oasis

a purchased the business of the Company from its administrative receivers for £1·5m. Thereafter, the Company went into insolvent liquidation on 9 June 1993. Meanwhile, Oasis prospered, and its shares were floated on the London Stock Exchange on 28 June 1995.

[7] Mr and Mrs Brown took an assignment of the Company's causes of action (if any) against various persons, and, having obtained legal aid for that purpose,
b they issued proceedings on 27 March 1996 against the Bennetts, Mr Scott, Mr Evans, Mr Sarson, and Oasis (the Oasis defendants), APA and Mr Freedman (the APA defendants), and Mr Kane. The writ was issued by the solicitors acting for Mr and Mrs Brown, Abrahamsons and Associates (Abrahamsons). In very rough terms, the writ alleged fraud, breach of fiduciary duty, and negligence against the various defendants in connection with the running of the Company
c and the sale of its assets to Oasis, and sought damages, restitution and rescission of the sale of the business to Oasis.

[8] After the issue of the writ, but before it was served on any of the defendants, Mr and Mrs Brown applied on 17 May 1996 without notice to Ferris J for what was then known as an Anton Piller order, and is now known as a search
d order, against Mr Michael Bennett, Mr Evans, Mr Sarson and APA. Ferris J refused the order sought, but granted a more limited injunction (the Injunction) against those defendants preventing them from destroying documents. Four days later, the writ and statement of claim were served, and on 24 May and 14 June 1996, the Injunction was continued by Ferris J and Lindsay J respectively by consent, but on 24 June 1996 it was discharged by Knox J, on grounds of
e insufficient evidence to support its grant or continuation.

[9] The statement of claim was a detailed document, signed by Mr Nicholas Asprey of counsel. It was subsequently amended (pursuant to an order of Rattee J on 25 November 1997) and comprehensively re-amended by Mr Asprey (pursuant to an order of the Court of Appeal on 1 December 1998).

f [10] It is unnecessary for me to describe the nature of the Browns' claims in great detail. They contended that the defendant directors and Mr Sarson had effectively conspired together to drive the Company into insolvency, with a view to achieving precisely what was achieved, namely the appointment of receivers and the purchase of the Company's business from the receivers through a vehicle, namely Oasis, in which some of the defendants had a direct or indirect interest.
g The main allegations advanced by Mr and Mrs Brown were that the directors deliberately decided (1) to maintain head office expenses at an insupportably high level; (2) not to progress the opening up of new shops; (3) to incur expenditure which the Company would not afford, and (4) to keep the Company under pressure with a view to increasing their share of the equity and driving it into
h receivership. Oasis was a defendant on the basis of having knowingly received dishonestly acquired assets. So far as APA was concerned, Mr and Mrs Brown alleged that it was party to this dishonest activity of the directors. It was also alleged, in brief terms, that the defendants were negligent.

[11] The precise nature and extent of the claims advanced against the
j defendants were complex, as can be appreciated from reading the judgments of Rattee J and the Court of Appeal (see [1998] 2 BCLC 97 and [1999] 1 BCLC 649). The Court of Appeal, in agreement with Rattee J, decided that the claim against Oasis should be struck out, but determined that all the other claims, at least on the face of the pleadings, were fit to go to trial. Mr and Mrs Brown were represented by Mr David Oliver QC and Mr Asprey, instructed by Abrahamsons both before Rattee J and before the Court of Appeal.

[12] Quite apart from the application for the Injunction, the action had a long, eventful, and expensive history between the issue of the writ and trial. I have already referred to the hearings before Rattee J and the Court of Appeal (which concerned applications to strike out some of the claims and applications by Mr and Mrs Brown to amend the statement of claim) and the consequential amended and re-amended statement of claim. Defences were served on behalf of the various defendants, all denying allegations of wrongdoing and the right of the Browns to any of the relief sought in their writ. There were various applications made by some of the defendants at different times for further and better particulars, security for costs, directions, and disclosure, as well as for permission to amend and to strike out. There were over 20 separate inter partes hearings between the issue of the writ and the trial. At many of these hearings Mr Asprey appeared for the Browns; he acted from the inception of the proceedings until shortly after 7 May 1999 (when he appeared for them before Master Moncaster). He was replaced by Mr Timothy Evans of counsel, who first appeared for the Browns at a case management conference on 15 May 2000, and who represented them at a number of further hearings up to and including the pre-trial review on 31 July 2000. Mr Oliver acted for the Browns from the inception: he appeared with Mr Asprey on the application before Ferris J which resulted in the grant of the Injunction on 17 May 1996, and similarly at the hearings before Rattee J and the Court of Appeal, as well as at two case management conferences.

[13] On 15 May 2000, a timetable was fixed for the exchange of factual and expert evidence, and preparation for trial, including exchange of skeleton arguments. This timetable was altered on 10 July 2000 and a final pre-trial review took place on 31 July 2000. Meanwhile, on 18 July 2000, expert reports (dealing with accountancy issues and retail property issues) were exchanged, and the two accountancy experts met and agreed a joint memorandum on 4 September 2000. On 20 September 2000, Abrahamsons provided a relatively brief skeleton argument on behalf of the Browns, signed by Mr Oliver and Mr Evans. Rather fuller skeleton arguments were provided on behalf of the Oasis defendants and on the APA defendants on 22 September 2000. On 28 September 2000, four days before the fixed trial date, the defendants' solicitors were notified that the Browns' legal aid certificates were not to be extended to cover the trial.

[14] In accordance with the directions which had been given, the action came on for hearing on 2 October 2000. Pursuant to an application by the Browns, I postponed the trial to 4 October 2000, and subsequently to 6 October, to enable them to prepare their case. The trial began on 6 October 2000 and, after Mr and Mrs Brown opened their case and (with one exception) called the evidence they wished to call, all the defendants submitted that there was no case to answer. I accepted that contention and therefore dismissed the claim on 18 October 2000. I refused Mr and Mrs Brown permission to appeal, and on their renewed application to appeal to the Court of Appeal, Aldous LJ refused them such permission.

(C) THE PRESENT APPLICATIONS

[15] The Oasis defendants, through Ms Barbara Dohmann QC and Mr Robert Anderson, and the APA defendants, through Mr Richard Slowe and Mr Paul Stanley, seek wasted costs orders against Mr Oliver, Mr Asprey and Mr Evans (the Barristers) and against Abrahamsons. Mr Kane, who represented himself at trial, made a similar applications against the Barristers and Abrahamsons (the

a respondents except in part (H) of this judgment), but that application has been compromised, and I need say no more about it.

[16] The primary case of the Oasis defendants and the APA defendants (the applicants) is that the respondents should be liable for all, or alternatively a very substantial proportion, of the costs incurred by both sets of applicants, on the basis that they should have appreciated that the action against each of the
b applicants stood no chance of success and, in particular, that there were no grounds for alleging dishonesty on the part of any of the applicants. In so far as the applicants fail to establish a claim based on the starting of the action, they alternatively contend that the respondents should not have continued to act in connection with the proceedings in light of the evidence as it transpired, the warnings as to the apparent weakness of the Browns' case from the representatives
c of various applicants and from the court. It is also contended that the respondents should have ensured that expert accountancy evidence was obtained long before it was in fact sought on behalf of the Browns. The Oasis defendants further contend that the claims against Mr Scott, Mr Evans and Mr Sarson were even more unjustifiable than the claim against the Bennetts.

d [17] There are two other more specific and limited claims against the respondents brought by only some of the applicants. Ms Dohmann contends on behalf of Oasis, against whom the claim was struck out by Rattee J and the Court of Appeal, that it was or should have been clear to the respondents that there was no cause of action against Oasis, and that therefore Oasis should in any event recover its costs from them. Secondly, Ms Dohmann on behalf of Mr Michael
e Bennett, Mr Evans and Mr Sarson, and Mr Slowe on behalf of APA, contend that those applicants (the injunction applicants) should in any event recover all the costs that they incurred in relation to the Injunction from Mr Oliver, Mr Asprey and Abrahamsons (the injunction respondents), because relevant evidence was not before Ferris J when the Injunction was granted on 17 May 1996.

f [18] Mr Powell contends that there is no jurisdiction to make a wasted costs order against the Barristers in the present case, or, if there is, that it is only limited to costs incurred by the applicants consequent upon the Barristers exercising their right of audience. On behalf of the solicitors, Mr Guy Mansfield QC, who appears with Mr Derrick Dale, contends that Abrahamsons relied on, and were entitled to rely on, the advice of the Barristers, and that they therefore should not
g be liable in any event for any of the costs of the applicants. Quite apart from this, Mr Powell and Mr Mansfield each contend that, even if their respective clients could as a matter of principle be rendered liable for any of the costs claimed by any of the applicants, the facts relied on by the applicants do not justify the making of a wasted costs order against any of the respondents.

h

(D) THE WASTED COSTS JURISDICTION

[19] The court always had an inherent power to make a wasted costs order against a solicitor (whether or not he was acting for the party seeking the order) but, despite one or two suggestions to the contrary, the court had no such
j inherent power in relation to barristers. The reason for this distinction was that, unlike a barrister, a solicitor is an officer of the court, and is therefore amenable to the inherent jurisdiction of the court. Subject to the points of principle raised by Mr Powell, to which I will turn in the next section of this judgment, the inherent jurisdiction of the court has effectively been replaced and extended by statute, and in particular by sub-ss (6) and (7) of s 51 of the Supreme Court Act 1981.

[20] Section 4(1) of the Courts and Legal Services Act 1990 is in these terms:

a

'The following section shall be substituted for section 51 of the Supreme Court Act 1981 (costs in civil division of Court of Appeal and High Court)—
"**51.** *Costs in civil division of the Court of Appeal, High Court and county courts.*—(1) Subject to the provisions of this or any other enactment and to rules of court, the costs of and incidental to all proceedings in—(a) the civil division of the Court of Appeal; (b) the High Court; and (c) any county court, shall be in the discretion of the court.

b

(2) Without prejudice to any general power to make rules of court, such rules may make provision for regulating matters relating to the costs of those proceedings including, in particular, prescribing scales of costs to be paid to legal or other representatives.

c

(3) The court shall have full power to determine by whom and to what extent the costs are to be paid ...

(6) In any proceedings mentioned in subsection (1), the court may disallow, or (as the case may be) order the legal or other representatives concerned to meet, the whole of any wasted costs or such part of them as may be determined in accordance with rules of court.

d

(7) In subsection (6), 'wasted costs' means any costs incurred by a party—(a) as a result of any improper, unreasonable or negligent act or omission on the part of any legal or other representative or any employee of such a representative; or (b) which, in light of any such act or omission occurring after they were incurred, the court considers it is unreasonable to expect that party to pay ...

e

(13) In this section 'legal or other representative', in relation to a party to proceedings, means any person exercising a right of audience or a right to conduct litigation on his behalf."'

[21] CPR PD 48, para 53.6 provides:

f

'As a general rule the court will consider whether to make a wasted costs order in two stages—
(1) in the first stage, the court must be satisfied—(a) that it has before it evidence or other material which, if unanswered, would be likely to lead to a wasted costs order being made; and (b) the wasted costs proceedings are justified notwithstanding the likely costs involved.

g

(2) At the second stage (even if the court is satisfied under paragraph (1)) the court will consider, after giving the legal representative an offer to give reasons why the court should not make a wasted costs order, whether it is appropriate to make a wasted costs order ...'

h

Paragraph 53.7 entitles the court to proceed immediately to the second stage without an adjournment 'if it is satisfied that the legal representative has already had a reasonable opportunity to give reasons why the court should not make a wasted costs order'.

[22] It follows that, in order to succeed in an application for wasted costs against a legal representative, an applicant must show that he has incurred wasted costs 'as a result of any improper unreasonable or negligent act or omission' on the part of the legal representative, that it is unreasonable that he should pay those costs, and that the court should order the legal representative to meet those costs. Procedurally speaking, para 53.6 indicates that there will normally be two hearings before a wasted costs order is made. At the first hearing, the court must,

j

a on the basis of the evidence and arguments put before it, decide whether it is 'likely' that the court will make a wasted costs order in favour of an applicant against a legal representative, and additionally whether proceeding to the second stage is justified. If it is not satisfied as to both requirements, then the application should be dismissed; if it is so satisfied, then the application proceeds to the second stage, namely an examination as to whether a wasted costs order should

b be made in favour of an applicant against the legal representative, and, if so, in what amount.

[23] In a case such as this, where there are a number of applicants, and a number of respondent legal representatives, the respondents contend, and I do not understand the applicants to challenge, that the court must consider the

c application of each applicant against each legal representative. There is therefore no question of some sort of 'broad brush' approach, although, of course, there will inevitably often be a degree of interrelationship between the claims, and in particular between claims by different applicants against the solicitors and the barristers representing another party at the proceedings.

d [24] In the present case, all parties have proceeded on the basis that the applications are to be dealt with on the normal two-stage process, and on the assumption that, if the applicants or any of them succeed to any extent at this first stage, there will be an adjournment before proceeding with the second stage. Given the issues of law, fact and discretion raised by the present applications, that seems to me to be right. However, effectively by consent between the parties

e rather than by specific order of the court, the hearing involved more evidence and argument than is usual for the first stage of a wasted costs application. It is not so much that the applicants have put forward quite a lot of evidence and argument; it is more that the respondents have put forward some (albeit not voluminous) evidence, and have addressed the court in some detail on the legal principles

f applicable and the way in which the court should exercise its power. I have been prepared to go along with this, not least because the parties had prepared their respective cases on the assumption that I would do so, but also because it seems to me at least arguably appropriate that the respondents should be permitted to take this course in the present case. I should add that the respondents' representatives have not taken unfair advantage of their de facto right to put in

g evidence and address the court. Indeed, I would like to express my gratitude to the representatives of all parties for the economic and good humoured way in which this potentially somewhat fraught hearing was conducted.

[25] Before turning to consider the guidance given in earlier cases, I propose to deal with two points of principle relating to the construction and effect of s 51

h of the 1981 Act raised by Mr Powell, and with the question of causation.

(E) THE EFFECT OF s 51(6) AND (7) OF THE 1981 ACT

[26] On behalf of the Barristers, Mr Powell has advanced two arguments of principle as to why the present claim against them should in principle fail wholly

j or to a substantial extent. Both points are of general significance. The first goes to the root of the statutory power of the court to make a wasted costs order against solicitors and barristers; the second has far-reaching effects as to the extent of the wasted costs jurisdiction in relation to barristers. There is a further point relating to the correct approach to causation under s 51(6) and (7) which, although it also raises an issue of fact (or inference from fact), can be conveniently considered at this juncture.

Are s 51(6) and (7) limited to claims against a litigant's own lawyers?

[27] Mr Powell says that, on its true construction, s 51 empowers the court to make an order for wasted costs only against a litigant's own legal representatives, and not against the legal representatives of his opponent or of any other party to the proceedings. If that is right, then the present application would be misconceived, not merely against the Barristers, but also against Abrahamsons; the applicants would only be able to claim a wasted costs order against their own solicitors and/or counsel (and it should be emphasised that there has been no suggestion of any basis whatsoever for raising such a claim). The argument proceeds in this way. By virtue of s 51(6), the court can order 'the legal or other representative' to meet 'wasted costs', which, according to s 51(7), must be incurred as a result of the failures of 'any legal or other representative'. The reference in each subsection to 'legal or other representative' brings one to the definition in s 51(13), which limits the definition to the representative exercising the relevant right 'in relation to a party to proceedings ... *on his behalf*'. Accordingly, runs the arraignment, the 'legal or other representative' referred to in s 51(7)(a), and against whom a wasted costs order can be sought, must be a legal or other representative of the 'party to proceedings' in question ie the party who is seeking the wasted costs order.

[28] As an academic exercise of statutory construction, this contention has some force. However, I am of the view that it is wrong. It appears to me that s 51 is at least as capable of bearing a wider construction, to the effect that it is open to a litigant to seek a wasted costs order against the legal representatives of any party (including, but not limited to, himself) to the proceedings. In this connection, it is to be noted that s 51(7)(a) refers to 'any' representative, which, when read together with s 51(13), is at least capable of meaning, and in my view more naturally means, a representative of any party in the proceedings, and is not limited to the party making the claim for the wasted costs. It also seems to me significant in this context that s 51(13) refers to '*a* party to proceedings' and not '*the* party to proceedings'.

[29] Further, there is no need to equate the 'party' in the first line of s 51(7) with the 'party to proceedings' in s 51(13) imported into s 51(7)(a). Indeed, the use of the indefinite article and the addition of the words 'to proceedings' in the latter expression suggests that it would be unsafe to equate it to the 'party' referred to earlier in s 51(7). I do not consider that this conclusion is vitiated by the words 'on his behalf' at the end of s 51(13). In my view, they serve to emphasise that a wasted costs order could only be made against a legal representative who was acting on behalf of a party to the proceedings in respect of which the wasted costs order is sought.

[30] Ms Dohmann contends that the reference in s 51(6) to the court ordering a representative to 'meet' the wasted costs is difficult to reconcile with Mr Powell's construction. She argues that the wasted costs as defined in s 51(7), on Mr Powell's argument, would not have to be 'met' because they would never be paid. I disagree. It seems to me that where a litigant had to repay the costs incurred by another party as a result of the litigant's own lawyers' failures, the court would have power, even on Mr Powell's construction to order the litigant's own lawyer to 'meet' those costs. None the less I agree with Ms Dohmann that Mr Powell's construction should be rejected.

[31] It is fair to say that s 51(6) and (7) do not lie particularly happily with the definition in s 51(13). In my judgment, that is explained by the fact that s 51 is intended not merely to deal with the wasted costs jurisdiction, but also, in its

a opening subsections, with the power of the court to award costs generally—see especially s 51(2). However, that does not call into question, or, indeed, support, my view, save to the extent that it may help to justify a purposive, rather than purely literal, construction, if that were necessary. I should add that I do not consider that my conclusion is in any way weakened by contrasting the definition of 'legal or other representative' in s 51(13) with the slightly different *b* definition of the same expression in s 19A(3) of the Prosecution of Offences Act 1985 and in s 145A(3) of the Magistrates' Courts Act 1980 (which were respectively added by ss 111 and 112 of the 1990 Act, and provide for wasted costs orders in the Crown Court and the magistrates' court respectively). First, although created by the same Act, namely the 1990 Act, they are insertions into different Acts from that into which s 51 is inserted, namely the 1981 Act. *c* Secondly, it is scarcely surprising that the definitions in these two sections are different from that in s 51, because the two sections are limited to wasted costs orders, whereas, as I have mentioned, s 51 casts its net much wider, and is concerned with the power of the civil courts to award costs generally. Thirdly, I do not consider that it is legitimate to construe a section of the 1981 Act by *d* reference to sections of the 1985 Act or the 1980 Act, even though the sections were all inserted into the relevant Acts by the same Act, namely the 1990 Act.

[32] As with any other question of statutory construction, one is not concerned merely with the language the legislature has employed; one must cast ones eyes more widely. The purpose of s 51 has been considered in a number of cases, most notably *Ridehalgh v Horsefield* [1994] 3 All ER 848, [1994] Ch 205, *e* where the Court of Appeal laid down principles and guidelines in relation to wasted costs applications, and considered and applied them in the context of six specific cases. In *Ridehalgh v Horsefield*, and in a number of subsequent cases, many of which have been reported, the courts have consistently proceeded on the basis that an order for wasted costs under s 51(6) can be made in favour of a *f* litigant against the legal representatives of another litigant in the same proceedings. Indeed, virtually every case on s 51(6) to which I have been referred involved such a claim, and in none of them was it suggested that the claim should fail because s 51 is limited to a claim by a litigant against his own legal representatives. Of course, as Mr Powell rightly says, the fact that the point has not been taken before does not mean that it is wrong, any more than the fact, that *g* many previous cases would have been decided differently if the point had been taken, demonstrates that it is wrong. None the less, the fact that the point has not been taken in a large number of previous cases by and on behalf of many experienced advocates and solicitors can be said to provide some support for the proposition that it leads to a somewhat surprising result.

h [33] However, I think that it goes further than that. The history and effect of s 51(6) as considered in *Ridehalgh v Horsefield* [1994] 3 All ER 848 at 856–861, [1994] Ch 205 at 226–231 strongly suggests to my mind that Mr Powell's submission is inconsistent with the policy behind s 51. After explaining that the court has always had an inherent jurisdiction to make a wasted costs order in favour of a *j* litigant against his own solicitor or against a solicitor acting for another party in the proceedings (but not against counsel), the Court of Appeal turned to the effect of s 51(6) and said:

'There can in our view be no room for doubt about the mischief against which these new provisions were aimed: this was the causing of loss and expense to litigants by the unjustifiable conduct of litigation by their *or the other side's* lawyers.' (See [1994] 3 All ER 848 at 860, [1994] Ch 205 at 231; my emphasis.)

[34] Further, while dealing with a slightly different aspect of the wasted costs jurisdiction, the Court of Appeal observed that it was 'inconceivable that by changing the language [from the law previous to s 51] Parliament intended to make it harder, rather than easier, for courts to make orders' (see [1994] 3 All ER 848 at 862, [1994] Ch 205 at 232).

[35] It appears to me that Mr Powell's argument would lead to an unjustified and undesirable degree of emasculation of s 51. It is true that, if he is right, a legal adviser or representative of one party, A, could in some cases be rendered indirectly liable for the costs of another party, B, by an order for costs in favour of B against A, followed by an order that A recover those costs from his own lawyers. However, that would not be particularly satisfactory, not least because A would presumably need to seek separate legal representation to raise a claim against his own lawyers, which would be particularly embarrassing and cumbersome if the application was being considered before the action had been disposed of. Further, it would scarcely work if A was legally aided: the order for costs in favour of B may not be enforceable against A, so A's lawyers may escape liability. The emasculative effect of Mr Powell's argument is underlined by the Privy Council's view that the wasted costs jurisdiction should rarely be invoked by a client against his own lawyers (see *Harley v McDonald, Glasgow Harley (a firm) v McDonald* [2001] UKPC 18 at [51]–[53], [2001] 2 AC 678 at [51]–[53], [2001] 2 WLR 1749).

[36] Bearing in mind the purpose of s 51 as explained in the cases, the fact that it was enacted at a time when the court had inherent jurisdiction to order the solicitors to one party pay the costs of another party, and the fact that s 51 is capable of bearing a wider meaning, I reject this first argument raised by Mr Powell as to the meaning and effect of s 51.

The scope of s 51 in relation to barristers

[37] Mr Powell also submitted that a wasted costs order can only be made against a barrister by virtue of his conduct when actually 'exercising a right of audience', that is, when actually conducting a case in court. This argument is based on the point that s 51(7)(a) enables a wasted costs order to be made only as a result of inappropriate conduct on the part of any 'legal or other representative' and s 51(13) limits that expression to 'any person exercising a right of audience or right to conduct litigation'. The argument involves contending that a barrister, unlike a solicitor, does not 'conduct litigation' but that he does exercise 'a right of audience', and that that latter expression is limited to the conduct of the case in court.

[38] In support of this argument, Mr Powell relies on what he says is the meaning, as normally understood among lawyers, of the words 'exercising a right of audience' and 'exercising ... a right to conduct litigation'; he says that a barrister can only exercise a right of audience, and does not conduct litigation, which is the traditional business of a solicitor. In connection with this point, Mr Powell also heavily relies on a number of provisions of the 1990 Act, including various definitions in s 119(1) thereof, and in particular the definitions therein of 'right of audience' and 'right to conduct litigation'.

[39] In my judgment, this second argument on behalf of the Barristers should be rejected. In the first place, it appears to me that any reliance on the definitions

a   in s 119(1) of the 1990 Act, and, indeed, contrasting the terms of s 51(13) with sections of the 1990 Act, is misconceived in principle. Section 119(1) of the 1990 Act introduces the various definitions that follow with the words 'In this Act'. The definitions in s 119(1) therefore apply to the provisions of (ie the sections of, and schedules to) that Act. However, in my judgment, the definitions do not, in the absence of some further specific provision or some principle of construction

b   to the contrary, apply to the provisions of another act, and in particular to the provisions of the 1981 Act. The effect of s 4(1) of the 1990 Act is to insert a new section, namely s 51, into the 1981 Act. Accordingly, s 51 is part of the 1981 Act, and not part of the 1990 Act, and therefore, at least on the face of it, the definitions in s 119(1) simply have no application or relevance to the construction of s 51, which is in the 1981 Act.

c   [40] By the same token, an exercise involving a comparison of s 51 with the provisions of certain sections of the 1990 Act, in order to assist in identifying the extent and effect of s 51, appears to me to be illegitimate. In the absence of special circumstances, one cannot normally construe a provision of one Act, such as the 1981 Act, by reference to the provisions of another Act, in this case the 1990 Act.

d   I believe that this conclusions is supported by an observation in *Bennion on Statutory Interpretation* (3rd edn, 1997) section 78 (p 213):

> 'It follows that the usual rule is that the function of the amending Act is to serve as an instrument for altering the text of the earlier Act, subject only to the need for commencement and transitional provisions. Unless the
e   contrary intention appears, the other provisions of the amending Act should not affect the construction of words inserted by it into the earlier Act.'

[41] *Bennion* accepts that there is an exception to this rule, namely as set out in section 234 (p 541): 'Where a later Act is *in pari materia* with an earlier Act, provisions of the later Act may be used to aid the construction of the earlier Act.'
f   In section 210 (pp 461–462), *Bennion* identifies four categories of cases where two or more Acts may be in pari materia, namely:

> '1. Acts which have been given a collective title … 2. Acts which are required to be construed as one … 3. Acts having short titles that are identical … 4. Other Acts which deal with the same subject matter on the
g   same lines. Here it must be remembered that the Latin word *par* or *paris* means equal, and not merely similar.'

Later in the same section, *Bennion* adds, somewhat mordantly, that 'it is however necessary to remain realistic'.

h   [42] The guidance given by *Bennion*, therefore, appears to confirm my view that it is illegitimate to invoke provisions of the 1990 Act in order to assist in the construction of s 51. In particular, although the 1981 Act and the 1990 Act are concerned with the same general area of law, as their short titles suggest, it cannot sensibly be said that they 'deal with the same subject matter on the same lines'. In these circumstances I do not propose to consider the detailed submissions

j   made by Mr Powell on this issue of construction, in so far as they rely on s 119, and other provisions, of the 1990 Act.

[43] However, this does not, without more, lead to a rejection of his argument. As I have mentioned, Mr Powell contends that a barrister does not exercise 'a right to conduct litigation', and that he only exercises 'a right of audience' when he is actually in court, and that he can therefore only be liable for

a wasted costs order in respect of costs incurred as a result of his conduct of the case in court.

[44] As with Mr Powell's first argument, I consider that he has a fairly powerful point as a matter of pure language, but that the point founders once one looks at the matter rather more widely, and considers whether the words of s 51(13) are capable of bearing another meaning. Ms Dohmann's primary argument is that the reference in s 51(13) to a 'person exercising a right of audience' should be read as a person entitled to exercise a right of audience, whether he actually does so or not; accordingly, a barrister signing pleadings, settling affidavits or witness statements, advising whether to bring proceedings, and what steps to take in the proceedings is within s 51(13) because he is a person who may exercise a right of audience, and could do so on his lay client's behalf. In other words, given that a barrister's traditional function is as an advocate, any work he does in anticipation of and/or in connection with that function is to be treated as falling within the expression 'exercising a right of audience'. That construction has its attractions and it may be right, but it does not involve giving the words 'a person exercising a right of audience' their natural meaning.

[45] Another reading, which effectively achieves the same result, but may do rather less violence to the words of s 51(13), is to conclude that a barrister carrying on such activities is 'exercising ... a right to conduct litigation'. It is true that the concept of conducting litigation will in many circumstances be understood to involve the traditional litigation activities of a solicitor (such as 'issuing a writ or otherwise commencing proceedings' or 'entering appearances', or, to put it in modem parlance, acknowledging service: the quoted expressions are part of the definition of 'right to conduct litigation' in s 119 of the 1990 Act). However, bearing in mind that 'a right to conduct litigation' is not defined in the 1981 Act, it seems to me that it is quite permissible, indeed appropriate, to give that expression a meaning which is less technical and more vernacular. On that basis, I do not see why it should not extend to all the activities involved in providing litigation services in a wide sense, whether taking formal steps in proceedings, such as starting proceedings, serving documents, giving disclosure, preparing a skeleton argument, or appearing in court, or being party to preparatory and connected activities, such as drafting or settling of documents and advising on prospects or procedure. In this connection, I think that the words 'a right to conduct litigation' in s 51(13) should not be read on their own, but should be read as part of the expression 'a right to conduct litigation on his behalf'; in other words, the right is one granted by the client to the lawyers to conduct litigation.

[46] An alternative way of reaching the same conclusion is that it is inappropriate to over-analyse the expression 'any person exercising a right of audience or a right to conduct litigation on his behalf', which should be treated as a single composite expression extending to all those lawyers who are engaged in acting before, or advising, the client in connection with the relevant proceedings.

[47] When one considers the purpose and effect of s 51, I consider that such a wider meaning of s 51(13) is to be preferred, and that the argument that a barrister can only be liable for a wasted costs order as a result of his conduct of the proceedings in court is wrong. First, it would considerably emasculate the effect of s 51, at least in so far as it related to the conduct of barristers. For instance, a barrister would only be liable for wasted costs caused by his actually appearing in court: that would not even cover the brief fee payable to counsel

a representing the applicant defendant. That in itself appears to me to be inconsistent with common sense and, indeed with the purpose of s 51 as explained in *Ridehalgh v Horsefield*. Indeed it is consistent with much of the reasoning and the level of wasted costs assessed by, the Court of Appeal in *Medcalf v Mardell* [2001] Lloyd's Rep PN 146, a case I shall refer to in more detail below. Secondly, it would discriminate in favour of barristers and against solicitors in an

b invidious and unfair way: a barrister's liability for a wasted costs order would be very much more limited than that of a solicitor. Mr Powell sought to justify the limitation of liability for barristers which his construction would involve, by reference to the problems thrown up if the barrister's lay client claimed privilege. However, it seems to me that that point would apply equally to a claim against solicitors, and therefore I do not believe that it assists his contention that s 51(6)

c should be treated as limited so far as barristers are concerned, when it is not so limited in relation to solicitors.

[48] Thirdly, Mr Powell's construction could lead to a most unsatisfactory situation where the conduct giving rise to a claim for wasted costs was that of a solicitor who had been advised by a barrister. The solicitor, who would otherwise

d be liable for a wasted costs order, may well be able to escape liability on the basis that he reasonably took and followed the advice of counsel (see *Ridehalgh v Horsefield* [1994] 3 All ER 848 at 866, [1994] Ch 205 at 237). If Mr Powell is right, an applicant who otherwise would have an unanswerable claim for a wasted costs order would find himself falling between two stools: he could not recover the wasted costs from the barrister either, because the costs would not have been

e incurred as a result of the conduct of the barrister in court. Fourthly, as Mr Slowe points out, the result of Mr Powell's construction leads to something of an anomaly when one considers the position of the solicitor advocate. If a wasted costs order is sought against a solicitor advocate on the basis of pleadings he improperly signed, he could not be liable, because he would not, on Mr Powell's

f argument, be 'exercising a right of audience'. On the other hand, if the pleadings were settled by a solicitor, who was not a solicitor advocate, it would be signed by the firm, who would be 'exercising ... a right to conduct litigation', and they could be liable for a wasted costs order.

[49] Fifthly, there is this point about Mr Powell's argument. Often, the conduct complained of against a barrister will be based on his allegedly improper

g advice that a particular claim or application be brought. Applied strictly, Mr Powell's analysis of s 51 would mean that, in such a case, no wasted costs application could ensue: the improper conduct of a barrister would not actually be in court. That would be little short of ridiculous both as a matter of common sense and because it would mean that s 51(6) was not merely emasculated in the

h case of barristers: it would have hardly any effect. Alternatively, if a somewhat looser approach is permissible, the barrister could be liable for wasted costs in such a case. However, if that is right, it is hard to see how, as a matter of logic, principle or language, a barrister should not be liable for wasted costs on the basis of other preparatory steps for which he was professionally responsible in

j connection with proceedings.

[50] In these circumstances, I conclude that the liability of a barrister for a wasted costs order is not limited to his conduct of the proceedings in court, but extends to his involvement in connection with acting or advising on the proceedings in any connection, including his involvement in drafting or settling any document in connection with the proceedings. This conclusion is the same as that reached by Leveson J in *Worsley v Tambrands Ltd* (8 November 2000,

unreported). While some of my reasons for rejecting the case advanced on behalf of the Barristers are different from those of Leveson J, I generally agree with his reasons for favouring the wider construction advanced on behalf of the applicants.

Causation: the law

[51] It is contended on behalf of the respondents that, even if all their other arguments on law and fact fail, the present application should not succeed, because the applicants cannot establish that the costs they are claiming were incurred 'as a result' of the advice and actions of the respondents. This is on the basis that, even if the Browns had not received legal aid (presumably on the basis of advice given by the respondents) and even if they had therefore not had the benefit of legal representation, they would still have started and proceeded with the action, and indeed would have taken it to trial. On this basis, therefore, the respondents contend that the applicants cannot show that their costs were incurred 'as a result' of any failure, advice or action on the part of the respondents. As a matter of principle, it seems to me that, if the Browns would have started and proceeded with the action without legal representation in the same way as they did with the benefit of legal representation, and if this would have led to the applicants incurring the same level of costs as they did, this contention would be well founded. That would appear to follow from the language of s 51(7). Further, in *Fryer v Royal Institution of Chartered Surveyors* [2000] Lloyd's Rep PN 534 at 547–548 (paras 85, 88), the Court of Appeal effectively confirmed the correctness of the proposition. That case also involved consideration that the applicant for the wasted costs order had to show that there was 'a strong prima facie case' that the alleged negligence of the legal advisors led to the grant of legal aid and that this had caused the applicant to incur costs which would not have been incurred if legal aid had not been granted.

[52] The question whether the applications in the present case should fail on this ground raises two points. The first is a point of principle and potentially of general application to wasted costs applications; the second turns on an analysis of the facts of this case. The first issue is the approach the court should adopt when deciding whether, if the legal representatives had not been guilty of the alleged improper or unreasonable or negligent act or omission, the claimants would none the less have preceded with their claim and the applicants would therefore have incurred the costs they are claiming. The respondents contend that the court must determine on the balance of probabilities whether, absent the legal representatives' alleged improper, unreasonable or negligent acts or omissions, the applicants would have incurred the costs. If they would, the respondents contend that the application for wasted costs must fail, and, they say, the onus of proof in this connection is, in the normal way, on the applicants. The applicants, on the other hand, argue that the court must ask itself whether there is a real prospect that the applicants would not have incurred all the costs that they did incur, if the claimants' legal representatives had not acted and advised as they did. If so, then, they say, provided the court is satisfied that there is a real prospect (an expression which includes an assessment of significantly worse than evens) then the application for wasted costs should not fail on this ground, albeit that the uncertainty would have to be taken into account when assessing the level of costs to order against the legal representatives. This argument of the applicants involves effectively applying the principle which was discussed and applied in

a *Allied Maples Group Ltd v Simmons & Simmons (a firm)* [1995] 4 All ER 907, [1995] 1
WLR 1602.

[53] The question of which of the two approaches is appropriate in a wasted
costs application was specifically left open by the Court of Appeal in *Veasey v
Millfeed Co Ltd* [1997] PNLR 100 where the judgment of Rose LJ proceeded on the
assumption that the approach based on the balance of probabilities, rather than
b loss of a chance, was correct, expressly 'without deciding' the issue. There is a
powerful argument in logic for applying the reasoning in the *Allied Maples* case to
the case of a wasted costs application, and therefore awarding, in many cases, a
proportion of the total costs on the 'loss of a chance' basis. After all, as was
explained in the *Allied Maples* case, such an approach to damages is appropriate
where the existence or size of the loss suffered by a claimant as a result of the
c defendant's negligence or breach of contract depends upon what a third party
would have done. In a wasted costs application, the claimant is the applicant and
the defendant is the respondent legal advisor, and one is considering how a third
party, namely the former client of the legal advisor, would have acted if the legal
advisor had not advised or acted in the way that he did.

d [54] However, I consider that that is not the appropriate approach to take in
wasted costs applications, and that the court should ask itself whether, on the
balance of probabilities, the applicant would have incurred the costs which he
claims from the legal representatives if they had not acted or advised as they did.
First, it seems to me that this is the correct construction of s 51(7)(a): the court
has to assess what, if 'any costs [were] incurred by a party ... as a result of [the
e conduct complained of] on the part of [the] legal ... representative'. To my mind,
that indicates that, applying the normal standard of proof applicable to civil
proceedings, the court should ask itself whether all or some of the costs incurred
by the applicant resulted from the conduct of the respondent legal representatives.
Secondly, it appears to me that this conclusion is consistent with the approach of
f the court in negligence actions: the question to be decided is whether, on the
balance of probabilities, the claimant's loss was caused by the defendant's alleged
breach of duty (see e g *Wilsher v Essex Area Health Authority* [1988] 1 All ER 871,
[1988] AC 1074). Thirdly, I consider that it would be inconsistent with the
approach to be adopted to wasted costs applications, as embodied in the cases to
which I have referred, if the court had to assess the level of costs to be awarded
g on the loss of a chance basis. If the question was to be based on the loss of a
chance basis, it would increase the number of wasted costs applications, and it
would increase the level of inquiry which be involved in any wasted costs
application. Instead of being able to take a relatively broad brush approach to the
likely attitude of the client (or former client) of the legal representative, the court
h would in many cases have to indulge in a fairly close examination of the attitude
of the client at various stages, which would lead to a much greater danger of a
wasted costs application representing a 'costly form of satellite litigation' (see
Ridehalgh v Horsefield [1994] 3 All ER 848 at 867, [1994] Ch 205 at 239), and it could
be said the issue would frequently not be 'apt for summary disposal by the court'
j (to quote from *Harley v McDonald, Glasgow Harley (a firm) v McDonald* [2001] 2 AC
678 at [50]).

[55] Fourthly, the wasted costs jurisdiction is now founded in s 51 which is
concerned with the award of costs generally, and which, of course, is far more
frequently invoked (albeit rarely expressly) in relation to familiar party and party
costs. Of course, it is by no means unusual for a court to award a proportion of
costs; indeed, it has become more frequent since the introduction of the CPR.

However, it is virtually unknown for the court to award only a proportion of costs on a party and party basis on the basis of the loss of chance approach.

[56] Fifthly, the Court of Appeal when considering the individual cases before it in *Ridehalgh v Horsefield* does not appear to have thought that the loss of a chance approach was right. In *Roberts v Coverite (Asphalters) Ltd* [1994] 3 All ER 848 at 877, [1994] Ch 205 at 249, the allegation made by the defendants against the legal representatives to the plaintiff was that they had failed to give proper notification that their clients were legally aided. The Court of Appeal said:

'We accept [the] submission that the history of events ... makes it impossible to conclude *on the balance of probabilities* that with knowledge that the plaintiff was legally aided ... the defendants would have made either a successful payment into court or an acceptable offer earlier than they did.' (My emphasis.)

The same point may be made (perhaps with a little less force) about the passages at [1994] 3 All ER 848 at 882j–883a, 890j–891a, [1994] Ch 205 at 255f–g and 264b–d dealing with the facts of *Philex plc v Golban (t/a Capital Estates)* and *Watson v Watson*. The same point may also be made about the view of the Court of Appeal in *Fryer*'s case [2000] Lloyd's Rep PN 534 at 547 (para 85), to which I have already alluded.

Causation: the facts

[57] Accordingly, I conclude that, in the present case, one has to ask whether it is more likely than not that the Browns would have proceeded with the action, if they had not obtained legal aid for that purpose, on the assumption that it is fair to assume that the Legal Aid Board (the Board) must have been told by the respondents that the Browns stood at least a reasonable chance of success in establishing their case. Two points are taken on behalf of the applicants. First, the Browns would never have undertaken and maintained the application unless they had obtained legal aid; secondly, even if that is not made out, the applicants would not have incurred the same level of costs against the Browns in person as they incurred as a result of the respondents acting for the Browns, and in particular it is contended on behalf the Oasis defendants that leading counsel would not have been engaged.

[58] Strictly speaking, the question at this first stage of the wasted costs application is whether it is likely that the court will hold that the Browns would none the less have proceeded with the action, and, if so, whether it is likely that the applicants would have incurred the same level of costs; indeed, that is the way the point is expressed in *Fryer*'s case [2000] Lloyd's Rep PN 534 at 547 (para 85). Although it may be wrong for me definitively at this stage to shut out the parties from arguing the issue at the second stage, if there is a second stage, of these applications, it is right to say that I think it very unlikely that there will be any further evidence or argument on this issue over and above what has been raised at this stage.

[59] While there is undoubtedly material to support the contention that the Browns would have proceeded with the action, even if legal aid had not been made available to them, I have reached the conclusion that they would not in fact have brought the action, and, if they had done so, they would not have proceeded with it to anything like the extent they in fact did so, without the benefit of legal aid. It is true that their conduct before the issue of proceedings could be said to suggest that they were concerned to do almost everything they could to obtain

a recompense for what they believed was serious wrong done to them by the applicants. Thus, they raised and pressed complaints to the Solicitors' Complaints Bureau, the Institute of Chartered Accountants for England and Wales, the City of London Police, the Thames Valley Police, the London Stock Exchange, IMPRO, the Securities and Investment Board, the DTI, the British Venture Capital Association, the liquidator of the Company, the Official Receiver, and

b Mr Michael Heseltine MP, all of which complaints were eventually dismissed. However, despite this, they did not bring the action until they obtained legal aid. The very fact that the Browns confined themselves to this myriad of complaints, until they obtained legal aid for the action, tends to support the view that, without legal aid, there would have been no action. The only way they could have confidently expected to recover substantial compensation to which they felt

c they were entitled would have been by successfully bringing and proceeding with the action, but, until they obtained legal aid, the bringing of the action was the one thing they did not do.

[60] Further, in an affidavit sworn during the action, Mr Brown stated that he and his wife needed legal aid, 'since we could not possibly afford to fund the

d action without it'. It is true that it was in the Browns' interest to make that statement, but it was not an issue of great significance at the time of the affidavit, and there is no reason to doubt its veracity. The statement amounts to this: that, without legal aid, the Browns could not have afforded the expense of running the action. That conclusion is reinforced by the fact that, by the time the action was started, the Browns had gone to live and work in the United States of America. It

e is one thing for American residents to instruct solicitors, counsel and experts in this country to conduct an action; it is quite another thing for residents in the United States to conduct complex litigation against many defendants in this country, particularly when they are not legally qualified and not particularly well-off. Indeed, I think Ms Dohmann was right to characterise the notion of the

f Browns conducting the action themselves from America as being quite unrealistic.

[61] It is true that, after legal aid was not extended to cover the trial, the Browns conducted the case themselves. However, that does not persuade me that they would have been prepared, or even in a position, to initiate and run the action if they had not had legal aid to do so. By the time legal aid was withdrawn,

g the Browns were prepared for trial, psychologically and in terms of pleadings, witness statements, bundles of documents, detailed knowledge of the case, and even counsel's skeleton arguments. It would have been quite a different thing for the Browns to have started the action, by producing a clearly pleaded case against all the applicants, and thereafter to have dealt with the significant number of

h interlocutory applications, the settling of pleadings, responding to the large number of requests, and to have prepared for trial, without legal representation and advice, and, indeed, to have done all this from America.

[62] My view that the Browns would not have started proceedings without legal aid is in no way called into question by the impression that they made on

j me during the presentation of their case. It would be wrong to suggest that my view, that they would not have begun or proceeded with the action if they had not obtained legal aid, receives much support from the impression they made during the trial, but it is certainly not called into question. It is by no means inconceivable that Mr Brown would have been deterred from bringing the action without legal aid, knowing that, in those circumstances, he would not be protected in relation to costs if he lost. As a legally-aided claimant, he would, I

think, have been told that normally any order for costs against him would not
been enforceable without the court's permission.

[63] Even if the Browns had sought to begin and proceed with the action
without legal aid, it is quite possible that it would not have proceeded very far.
On 30 October 1996, the Oasis defendants applied for an order that the Browns
give security for costs, and, due to various other applications and delays, that
application was only heard on 24 August 1999, when Master Moncaster dismissed
it. He no doubt had to balance the fact that the Browns were legally aided with
no contribution, so that the Oasis defendants would be unlikely to recover their
costs if they won, against the fact that any significant order for security against the
Browns would, as they themselves said, effectively stifle their claim. In reaching
the conclusion that the latter factor should outweigh the former, the master,
would in my view, inevitably have been influenced by the fact that counsel had
effectively underwritten the arguability of the serious allegations of dishonesty
made against the Oasis defendants. That would have been evident from the fact
that the Browns' pleadings had been signed by Mr Asprey, and impliedly when he
and Mr Oliver appeared before Ferris and Rattee JJ and the Court of Appeal.
Additionally, counsel's view that the Browns' case was arguable would have been
tolerably self-evident from the fact that the Browns were legally aided. While I
am certainly not suggesting that the master would or should have taken the view
that the Browns' claim was bound to fail simply because they were in person, he
would inevitably have borne in mind that allegations of dishonesty can only too
easily be made by litigants in person, who have suffered great loss and feel a very
great grievance, and who are not under any sort of duty in relation to the case
they plead or advance in court, unlike barristers and solicitors, who fall under a
particular duty when alleging dishonesty.

[64] The master may well also have borne in mind that an order for costs
against a legally-aided party cannot normally be enforced without the permission
of the court. It is fair to say that the extent to which that is a factor which should
weigh with the court when considering an application for security against a
legally-aided claimant is unclear. However, it would certainly not have been a
factor which the Browns, if not legally aided, could have relied on. I think it quite
possible that the master would, in those circumstances, have ordered security for
costs against the Browns, even knowing that it might well stifle the action.
However, I would not be comfortable about resting my decision, as to the
likelihood of the Browns being able to proceed without legal aid, on this point; it
is neither particularly attractive nor particularly strong.

[65] Finally, even if the Browns would have started the action and proceeded
to trial without legal aid, I am quite satisfied that the cost of the whole action to
the applicants would have been substantially less. The applicants and their
respective legal advisors, while obviously taking the action seriously, would not
have been concerned about it to the same extent as with the serious claims
advanced in the action being backed by solicitors and counsel. Rather than asking
for particulars or seeking to strike out, I think it far more likely that, if they had
not obtained security for costs, the applicants would have tried to get the action
on for hearing as quickly and as cheaply as possible. It would have been much
easier to achieve this perfectly properly if the Browns had not got legal
representation. Assuming in the respondents' favour, that the Browns had got
their pleaded case together sufficiently well not to be struck out, the applicants
would have been less likely to press for particulars than they were with counsel
responsible for the pleadings. Further, the Oasis defendants and the APA

a defendants would not each, I think, have employed two lawyers to represent them. I would have thought it likely that in those circumstances, Ms Dohmann, for the Oasis defendants, and Mr Stanley, for the APA defendants would not have been briefed to appear. Accordingly, even if I am wrong on all the other aspects for causation, I am firmly of the view that there would have been a substantial reduction in the costs incurred to the applicants if legal aid had not been accorded
b to the Browns, even if they had none the less proceeded to trial.

(F) THE PROPER APPROACH TO A WASTED COSTS APPLICATION

General considerations

[66] In *Ridehalgh v Horsefield*, as I have mentioned, the Court of Appeal gave
c guidance as to the proper approach to be adopted in relation to applications for wasted costs under s 51(6) and considered six cases where the first instance courts had made wasted costs orders. The purpose of s 51 was described as being 'that litigants should not be financially prejudiced by the unjustifiable conduct of litigation by their or their opponents' lawyers' (see [1994] 3 All ER 848 at 855, [1994] Ch 205 at 226). However, this principle, as the Court of Appeal had
d explained in an immediately preceding passage, must be balanced against the competing factors that 'lawyers should not be deterred from pursuing their clients' interests by fear of incurring a personal liability to their clients' opponents', that 'wasted costs orders should not become a back-door means of recovering costs not otherwise recoverable' and that 'the remedy should not
e grow unchecked to become more damaging than the disease'. The Court of Appeal affirmed the applicability of the familiar proposition that:

'Although a solicitor is in general entitled to rely on the advice of counsel properly instructed, he is not entitled to follow such advice blindly but is in the ordinary way obliged to apply his own expert professional mind to the
f substance of the advice received.' (See [1994] 3 All ER 848 at 858, [1994] Ch 205 at 228.)

This reflects the approach of the court to the defence of a solicitor, accused of professional negligence, to the effect that he had taken counsel's advice on the point at issue.
g [67] The Court of Appeal ([1994] 3 All ER 848 at 858, [1994] Ch 205 at 229) quoted with approval the observations of Donaldson MR in *Orchard v South Eastern Electricity Board* [1987] 1 All ER 95 at 100, [1987] QB 565 at 572 to the effect that:

h '... no solicitor or counsel should lend his assistance to a litigant if he is satisfied that the initiation or further prosecution of a claim is mala fide or for an ulterior purpose or ... if the proceedings would be, or have become, an abuse of the process of the court or unjustifiably oppressive.'

Just before that observation, however, Donaldson MR said: '[I]t must never be
j forgotten that it is not for solicitors or counsel to impose a pre-trial screen through which a litigant must pass before he can put his complaint or defence before the court.'
[68] Donaldson MR went on to warn against inferring that a legally-aided litigant's legal advisors had given inappropriately optimistic advice simply because legal aid had been granted or continued. That point was also taken up by Dillon LJ in *Orchard's* case. He said:

'[T]here is no indication that the legal aid authorities have ever complained or sought costs against the plaintiff's solicitors ... As to the [alleged] shortcomings of counsel's opinions, we have not seen those opinions. It may well be the duty of counsel primarily, but also of the solicitor with due regard to the views expressed by experienced counsel, to weigh the evidence available to his client, if a plaintiff, to see whether the plaintiff's claim raises a triable issue. It is not the duty of the solicitor to endeavour to assess the result where there is a likelihood of a conflict of evidence between his client's witnesses and those of the other side ... In the light of the apparent integrity of the plaintiff, the apparent evidence of his supporting witnesses ... and the reports of ... a qualified expert witness, I would not be prepared to hold, without ever knowing what the solicitors and counsel did advise their client and the legal aid committee, that the solicitors and counsel must have so fallen short of the proper discharge of their duty that the solicitors ought to be found guilty of a serious dereliction of duty or serious misconduct in allowing the case to proceed with the benefit of legal aid.' (See [1987] 1 All ER 95 at 105, [1987] QB 565 at 579–580.)

[69] In *Ridehalgh v Horsefield* [1994] 3 All ER 848 at 861–862, [1994] Ch 205 at 232–233, the Court of Appeal considered the meaning of the words 'improper, unreasonable or negligent' in s 51(7). As the court said, the first two adjectives do not seem to give rise to problems, but the third, 'negligent', is potentially more controversial. It is clear from the reasoning of the court that the concept of 'negligent' in s 51(7) is not directed towards the negligence of the legal representative in the sense of breach of his duty to his client. The observations at [1994] 3 All ER 848 at 862, [1994] Ch 205 at 233 indicate that it must be negligence which amounts to 'breach of [the respondent lawyer's] duty to the court' and 'failure to act with the competence reasonably to be expected of ordinary members of the profession'. Indeed the Court of Appeal applied this test when rejecting the wasted costs application in one of the cases before it, namely *Roberts v Coverite (Asphalters) Ltd* [1994] 3 All ER 848 at 877, [1994] Ch 205 at 249.

[70] The Court of Appeal ([1994] 3 All ER 848 at 863–864, [1994] Ch 205 at 233–234) considered 'pursuing a hopeless case'. After referring to the 'cab-rank rule', the Court of Appeal said:

'Legal representatives will, of course ... advise clients of the perceived weakness of their case and of the risk of failure. But clients are free to reject advice and insist that cases be litigated. It is rarely if ever safe for a court to assume that a hopeless case is being litigated on the advice of the lawyers involved ... It is, however, one thing for a legal representative to present, on instructions, a case which he regards as bound to fail; it is quite another to lend his assistance to proceedings which are an abuse of the process of the court.' (See [1994] 3 All ER 848 at 863, [1994] Ch 205 at 234.)

As the Court of Appeal went on to observe: 'It is not entirely easy to distinguish by definition between the hopeless case and the case which amounts to an abuse of the process ...'

Privilege and wasted costs orders

[71] The Court of Appeal ([1994] 3 All ER 848 at 866, [1994] Ch 205 at 236–237) dealt with the difficult question of privilege in relation to wasted costs orders. As they pointed out, in a wasted costs application, the privilege is not that of the

a respondent lawyers to waive: the privilege is that of their client or former client, and he may be reluctant to waive privilege. Further, it is difficult, indeed impossible, for the respondent lawyers to know whether, and indeed how, to advise their client or former client in relation to privilege. In such a case, the client's privilege may be a valuable asset, which he may even be able to trade. However, the applicant will, almost by definition, not know what the privileged
b material consists of, and therefore he will not know what he is 'buying' from the client of the respondent lawyers. So as the respondent lawyers are concerned, I would have thought that there would be a strong argument for saying that it would be unprofessional, even unlawful, for them to seek to pay their client or former client to maintain his claim for privilege.

c [72] The nature of privilege was considered in *R v Derby Magistrates' Court, ex p B* [1995] 4 All ER 526, [1996] AC 487. Lord Taylor of Gosforth CJ (with whom the other members of the House of Lords agreed) said this, after considering a number of earlier authorities:

d 'The principle which runs through all these cases, and the many other cases which were cited, is that a man must be able to consult his lawyer in confidence, since otherwise he might hold back half the truth. The client must be sure that what he tells his lawyer in confidence will never be revealed without his consent. Legal professional privilege is thus much more than an ordinary rule of evidence, limited in its application to the facts of a particular case. It is a fundamental condition on which the administration
e of justice as a whole rests.' (See [1995] 4 All ER 526 at 540–541, [1996] AC 487 at 507.)

[73] Thus, the privilege is absolute: there can be no question, as I see it, of the court being able to breach the privilege on the basis that the breach is trivial, and
f the justification for the breach in terms of the interests of justice is substantial. The one exception is where privilege is a cloak for fraud—see *Barclays Bank plc v Eustice* [1995] 4 All ER 511, [1995] 1 WLR 1238, possibly something of a high-water mark example of this exception.

[74] In *Ridehalgh v Horsefield*, there is this important passage about cases where
g privilege is not waived by the client or former client in a wasted costs application:

h 'Judges who are invited to make or contemplate making a wasted costs order must make full allowance for the inability of respondent lawyers to tell the whole story. Where there is room for doubt, the respondent lawyers are entitled to the benefit of it. It is again only when, with all allowances made, a lawyer's conduct of proceedings is quite plainly unjustifiable that it can be appropriate to make a wasted costs order.' (See [1994] 3 All ER 848 at 866, [1994] Ch 205 at 237.)

j [75] In *Medcalf v Mardell* [2001] Lloyd's Rep PN 146 at 153–154, the majority of the Court of Appeal made an order for wasted costs against counsel who had maintained allegations of fraud and other impropriety in pleadings and in oral argument, on the basis that the allegations 'were not supported by the reasonably credible evidence establishing a prima facie case of fraud' as required by section 606 of the Bar Code of Conduct (the Code). The Court of Appeal considered whether a wasted costs order could be resisted on the grounds that the client of the respondent legal advisors in the case had not waived privilege.

The conclusion of the majority (Peter Gibson and Schiemann LJJ) on this issue was in these terms (at 158): *a*

> '58. ... Try though we might, we have not found it possible to conceive of any circumstances in which the barristers in putting their names to the particular allegations of impropriety in the draft amended notice of appeal and supporting them in their skeleton and at the hearing had relevant privileged or confidential material which justified their conduct as compliant *b* with section 606 but had to be withheld from the court ... 59. In the particular circumstances of this case therefore in our judgment, having regard to section 606, the propriety of the pleaded allegations must be assessed in the light of the material put before the court.'

c

That material, as analysed earlier in the judgment, could not, in their view, justify at least some of the allegations of dishonesty pursued on behalf of the appellants.

[76] While the majority of the Court of Appeal in *Medcalf v Mardell* thought it right, therefore, to make an order for wasted costs against the legal advisors, it seems that they accepted that it would not have been right to make such an order if there was a real possibility of the legal advisors being able to justify their *d* allegations on the basis of material which they were prevented from laying before the court because their former client insisted on maintaining his privilege. In some wasted costs cases, therefore, the court can be confident that no evidence other than that before the court could have been available to the respondent lawyers. However, in many cases, the fact that the client (or former client) of the *e* respondent lawyers claims privilege means that the court cannot be reasonably confident that other relevant information was not available to the respondent lawyers, and which could justify conduct which, in the absence of such evidence, could not be justified. In such a case, although it may result in a considerable and understandable sense of grievance on the part of the applicant, a wasted costs order must be refused. That is because the court cannot properly characterise the *f* conduct of respondent lawyers as 'improper, unreasonable or negligent', as there could be material the court is not entitled to see, which could exonerate the lawyers. In broad terms, this outcome can be justified on the basis that the wider public interest requires litigants to be represented by lawyers who are not looking over their shoulders and worrying about potential applications for wasted costs, *g* and that that interest also requires the strict rules of privilege to be observed. I appreciate that is scant comfort to many unsuccessful applicants for wasted costs orders, or even to the court, at least in cases where there may be a strong suspicion that, if privilege had been waived, a wasted costs order would have been made.

[77] The risk of unfairness to the respondent lawyers of making a wasted costs *h* order when privilege has not been waived is demonstrated by the closing observations of Mr George Laurence QC (sitting as a deputy judge of the High Court) in a judgment refusing to make a wasted costs order. In *Drums and Packaging Ltd v Freeman* [1999] All ER (D) 964 he said:

j

> 'In *Ridehalgh v Horsefield* [1994] 3 All ER 848 at 866, [1994] Ch 205 at 237 Bingham MR said that "Judges who are invited to make or contemplate making a wasted costs order must make full allowance for the inability of respondent lawyers to tell the whole story". As it happens, privilege having been waived, the whole story has been told. I cannot help wondering whether I would have arrived at the same conclusion had privilege not been

a waived. It would not have been particularly easy, in that event, to make the necessary full allowance for the firm's inability to tell the whole story. On the facts known to D3 at the time it launched this application, D3 might very well have concluded that the firm would not be able to avoid a wasted costs order, even on the "every allowance" basis recommended by Bingham MR. If that is right, it would appear to me to indicate not merely that the

b jurisdiction to order wasted costs should be cautiously exercised: rather more seriously, it shows how the very existence of the jurisdiction can operate to put pressure, perhaps undue, on clients to waive privilege in order to permit their lawyers to tell the full story. That seems to me in principle a regrettable state of affairs.'

c *Procedure*

[78] In *Ridehalgh v Horsefield* [1994] 3 All ER 848 at 867–868, [1994] Ch 205 at 238–239, the Court of Appeal considered the appropriate procedure in relation to an application for wasted costs. They said that they—

d 'cannot imagine circumstances in which the applicant should be permitted to interrogate the respondent lawyer, or vice versa. Hearings should be measured in hours, and not in days or weeks. Judges must not reject a weapon which Parliament has intended to be used for the protection of those injured by the unjustifiable conduct of the other side's lawyers, but they must be astute to control what threatens to become a new and costly form

e of satellite litigation.' (See [1994] 3 All ER 848 at 867, [1994] Ch 205 at 238–239.)

[79] This view that the wasted costs jurisdiction should not normally lead to long or complex hearings is endorsed in a number of decisions. Most recently in *Harley v McDonald, Glasgow Harley (a firm) v McDonald* [2001] 2 AC 678 at [50], the

f Privy Council said: 'As a general rule allegations of breach of duty relating to the conduct of the case by a barrister or solicitor with a view to the making of a costs order should be confined strictly to questions which are apt for summary disposal by the court.' The Privy Council went on to explain that the wasted costs jurisdiction was therefore particularly appropriate for abusive conduct in the face of the court, e g failure to appear, wholly unjustifiable lengthening of a hearing

g etc.

[80] The Court of Appeal in *Ridehalgh v Horsefield* [1994] 3 All ER 848 at 866, [1994] Ch 205 at 239 said, consistently with the current provisions of CPR PD 48, para 53.6, that a wasted costs order should normally involve a two-stage process.

h They stated that, in order to get to the second stage, the applicant would have to make out 'an apparently strong prima facie case'. That seems to me to be substantially the same as the formulation now contained in para 53.6, but, if it is not, then, as I see it, the test in the practice direction has effectively replaced that laid down in *Ridehalgh v Horsefield*.

j (G) THE MAIN CLAIM FOR WASTED COSTS

Introductory

[81] The main case advanced by the Oasis defendants and the APA defendants in that they should recover the whole of their respective costs, or a substantial proportion thereof, incurred from the beginning of the action, up to its dismissal. The major plank upon which these applications are based is that, subject to the

brief claim based on negligence, the Browns' claims involved alleging dishonesty on the part of each of the applicants, and that it was improper for the Barristers to have pleaded and/or proceeded with and/or maintained in court those allegations of dishonesty, and it was equally wrong for Abrahamsons to have been associated therewith. Paragraphs 606 and 610 of the Code in force at the relevant time (now reproduced as paras 704 and 708 of the current Code) contain well-known and important requirements as to which counsel have to be satisfied before he can properly plead or advance in court a case based on dishonesty.

[82] The applicants' case starts with the point that I dismissed the Browns' case on the basis that none of the defendants had a case to answer. They rely on the fact that the only allegation of wrongdoing against any of the defendants, which I found the Browns' evidence and argument sufficient to found a case to answer, was negligence on the part of the Bennetts, and I did not let that claim proceed because the Browns did not establish any loss as a result of that alleged negligence. They also rely on certain observations in my judgment. I said that it seemed to me that there was 'substantial case for saying that this is a case which should never have brought and an even stronger case for saying that dishonesty should never have been pleaded against some, or even all, of the defendants'. I went on to say that the grounds for the allegations of dishonesty did not appear to me to exist. My judgment contained further costs observations about the particular weakness of the Browns' case against Mr Scott, Mr Evans and Mr Sarson.

[83] The applicants go on to rely on a number of other matters to support the contention that it was wrong to plead and allege dishonesty, but also as freestanding allegations. First, the allegation that the applicants failed to open stores when they should have done was not merely alleged in the original statement of claim, but it was maintained, so far as the applicants were aware, until just before counsel provided the Browns' skeleton argument for trial. It was then abandoned. It is said that this demonstrates that there never was any evidence to support the allegation. Secondly, the fact that the expert accountancy witness instructed on behalf of the Browns, Ms Callaghan, had concluded that there was no evidence to support this allegation, is said to demonstrate that the Browns' legal advisors ought to have recommended that expert evidence be obtained very early on, rather than, as happened, very late in the proceedings. That point, say the applicants, is underlined by the fact that, in her report, Ms Callaghan expressed the view that the Company might have avoided receivership in January 1991 if its bankers had continued to support its business and the Bennetts and APA had injected further money (either £500,000, if the Company's creditors had agreed a moratorium, or £2m, without a moratorium). Such a contention was not pleaded, and, anyway, it plainly made the Browns' case very difficult to sustain, bearing in mind that it could not be argued that the Bennetts or APA were under any obligation to provide further funding. Although Ms Callaghan considered that head office costs could, indeed should, have been reduced significantly, she said that this alone would not have avoided the Company going into receivership.

[84] Thirdly, the applicants draw attention to the warnings which were given to the legal advisors of the Browns by the court and by the solicitors acting for the applicants, during the currency of the proceedings. The reference to court warnings is to comments made by Rattee J during the hearing before him and in his judgment. Additionally, there were letters to Abrahamsons from Berwin Leighton Paisners, for the Oasis defendants, and S J Berwin & Co, for the APA

a defendants, which questioned the justification for continuing the proceedings against all or some of the applicants, and the appropriateness of alleging dishonesty. These letters were met by replies from Abrahamsons implying or expressing confidence in the success of the Browns, and, on one occasion, suggesting that counsel as well as Abrahamsons shared this optimism.

[85] Fourthly, the applicants point to the fact that the Browns were legally
b aided until very shortly before the trial, and they make two points in this connection. First, it is said that the Board must have been advised that the Browns' case stood a reasonably good chance of success. Indeed, it is said that the advice must have been that the claim stood a better than ever chance of success. That argument is based on the proposition that, if the prospects of success are below 50%, legal aid is likely to be refused (see para 7-02 of the 'Notes for
c Guidance' at p 117 of the *Legal Aid Handbook 1998/1999*, which identifies how the Board is likely to approach funding of claims in light of s 15 of the Legal Aid Act 1988). In this connection, s 15(2) provides that an applicant for legal aid has to satisfy the Board that he has 'reasonable grounds for taking ... the proceedings, and, under s 15(3)(a) legal aid for representation may be refused if it is
d 'unreasonable [for a litigant to] be granted representation' in the circumstances of his particular case. Secondly, the applicants point out that Mr Oliver, Mr Evans and Abrahamsons must have advised the Board that the Browns' case did not merit legal aid for trial shortly before the hearing, and that it was as a result of this that the Browns had to represent themselves at the trial before me.

[86] Finally, the applicants rely on the fact that a claim was pleaded and
e proceeded with against Mr Scott, Mr Evans and Mr Sarson. In my judgment, I described the allegation that Mr Scott was not honest as 'astonishing', not least because he only became a director of the Company on 22 November 1990. I also expressed surprise that the allegation of dishonesty was based on his alleged failure to raise objections to the level of head office costs, when, as Ms Callaghan,
f the Browns' expert acknowledges, he was responsible for immediately effecting a reduction in such expenses. I said that there was 'no evidence of any dishonesty on his part' nor 'of his failure to control head office expenses'. I also commented that he was not mentioned anywhere in the 600 paragraphs in the witness statements of the Browns.

[87] Mr Evans had been a director for a long time, but I still described the
g allegation of dishonesty against him as 'astonishing', as it appeared to be supported only by the fact that he did not support reductions in head office expenses during 1990, which was scarcely surprising as there was no resolution before the board proposing such a course. As to Mr Sarson, the Browns' allegation against him also dated from November 1990. I said that the only basis
h for alleging dishonesty against him appeared to be that he had prepared projections (the projections) in late 1990 and early 1991 for the business of the Company if it was acquired by another entity (as it eventually was), and that he was initially employed by Oasis, of which he later became a director and shareholder. The applicants also point out that there was no reason to sue
j Mr Evans, Mr Sarson or Mr Scott, because if the Browns' claim against the other defendants had been made out, they would have been undoubtedly good for the money.

[88] The two points most strongly emphasised by Mr Powell on behalf of the Barristers and Mr Mansfield on behalf of Abrahamsons were as follows. First, the Browns have not agreed to waive privilege; accordingly, even if it appears that, on the basis of the evidence available at trial, pleading dishonesty against the

applicants could not be justified, it would be impossible, fairly properly or
consistently with authority, to conclude that issue against the respondents. That
is because information, evidence, promises of evidence or expectations may have
been available to the respondents, which would have justified their conduct, but
one is not available to the court now because of the Browns' insisting on their
privilege. Secondly, and quite apart from this, on the evidence available, and
viewed in a fair, but (bearing in mind the nature of the jurisdiction) a tolerably
summary way, it can be seen that there was evidence upon which a member of
the Bar could properly have pleaded and maintained a claim based on dishonesty.
Further, on behalf of Abrahamsons, Mr Mansfield contends that they were
entitled to rely on the Barristers with regard to the pleading and maintaining of
the case against the Bennetts.

Peripheral points

[89] It may be convenient to get certain matters out of the way. First, I believe
that it is unhelpful, even dangerous, to consider what must or may have passed
between a legally-aided litigant's legal advisors and the Board, at least in an
application such as this, where the Board has taken no part in this application.
One simply does not know what factors influenced the Board, and in particular
what points may have been made by or on behalf of the Browns, quite apart from
the respondents' advice as to the prospects of success. For instance, the Board
may have been told that, if the strongly held and strongly expressed beliefs and
suspicions of the Browns were made out, then their claim could succeed, and that
in that event the claim, would be worth a substantial sum of money. The Board
accordingly might well have formed the view, or been advised, that the action
was therefore at least arguably worth taking, say, to discovery/disclosure or
exchange of witness statements, possibly with a view to seeking a substantial
offer to settle. It may well be that the court is entitled to assume that the Board
was told that the Browns' legal advisors thought that they had a real prospect of
success, but it cannot be safe, and therefore it cannot be fair to the respondents,
to assume that the advice on prospects ever went further than that. (In this
connection, I bear in mind the observations of Dillon LJ in *Orchard v South Eastern
Electricity Board* [1987] 1 All ER 95 at 105, [1987] QB 565 at 579–580, which I have
cited above.) If that conclusion is correct, then the fact that the Browns were
legally aided takes matters no further. The most it establishes is that some of the
respondents advised that the Browns had a real prospect of success, and that must
include a real prospect of establishing dishonesty on the part of the applicants.
Consideration of whether that advice was justifiable involves precisely the same
factors as consideration of whether maintaining or pleading the case of
dishonesty against each of the applicants was justifiable.

[90] Secondly, the fact that there were warnings to the respondents about the
weakness of the Browns' case, does not take matters further: either that case was
properly pleadable and maintainable or it was not. Further, although it does raise
a point of some interest, namely the extent to which solicitors are bound to be
strictly honest in such letters, it does not seem to me that the correspondence in
which Abrahamsons expressed confidence on the part of themselves and counsel
as to the Browns' eventual success in the action, takes the present issues any
further. If there were no reasonable grounds for believing that the Browns could
succeed at the time that the relevant letters were written, then that is tantamount
to saying that it was inappropriate to maintain the claims either on the pleadings
or in court. On the other hand, if there were grounds for believing that the

a Browns could succeed, the worst that could be said about these letters is that they were over-optimistic, to the point of being dishonest. Whether a solicitor writing to the other side can be said to be guilty of unprofessional conduct if he substantially overstates his view and that of counsel as to the prospects of success, and indeed whether counsel who sees the letter and does nothing about it can be accused of unprofessional conduct, raise points which are not easy to resolve.

b Morality and ethics point one way, whereas practicality and common sense tend to point the other. However, given the contents of these letters from Abrahamsons cannot be said to be causative of the applicants' incurring of costs, and given that the contents of the letters are not even referred to in the various wasted costs applications, I do not think that that correspondence needs to be considered further.

c [91] Thirdly, I am unimpressed with the contention that the case against the respondents is made out, or even significantly supported, by the contents of Ms Callaghan's report or the late stage at which it was obtained. It cannot be doubted that, with wisdom of hindsight, it is a great shame that Ms Callaghan's report was not obtained much earlier. It would, I think, almost inevitably have

d persuaded the respondents that they should not maintain the allegation that the applicants caused the Company to delay opening new shops. Indeed, I suspect that it would have gone further than that: the fact that Ms Callaghan took the view that, without the Bennetts and APA providing further funding, which they were not obliged to do, the Company would have gone into receivership, even in the absence of the matters which she thought could be complained of, would

e have rendered the Browns' case virtually doomed. While it is strictly a matter of speculation, it appears to me to be a fair inference that it was consideration by the respondents of Ms Callaghan's report, and, also perhaps, of the whole case with a view to advising the board on providing legal aid for the trial, that ultimately led to the Board's decision not to provide such legal aid to the Browns.

f [92] However, I do not consider that it follows that any of the respondents can be criticised for the fact that Ms Callaghan's report was not obtained earlier. Although a number of pre-action protocols now require a recommendation that a claimant obtains an expert report before or shortly after beginning proceedings, there were, of course, no such protocols available, let alone applicable, in relation to the action. It was, and indeed still is, quite common, in cases which require

g expert evidence at trial, for the claimant not to instruct an expert until fairly late in the proceedings, although in many cases, of course, expert advice is obtained early on, even before the proceedings are started. In the present case, the allegations of dishonest or negligent conduct upon which the Browns relied did not involve allegations which, to my mind, any reasonably competent barrister

h or solicitor would inevitably have advised required expert evidence from the beginning. The Browns contended that the applicants were engaged on a course of dishonest conduct involving doing or not doing things with a particular aim, and whether the applicants did or did not do those things, and whether or not they had that particular aim, were ultimately questions of fact, which would in

j the main be expected to be determined by reference to the documentary and oral evidence of fact. Indeed, the fact that the Browns' own expert accountant thought there was no evidence to support a particular factual allegation would not have precluded their representatives from maintaining that allegation, or, indeed, the court from accepting the allegation.

[93] As I have already mentioned, I believe that it is more significant that Ms Callaghan could have advised much earlier that the prospects of success were

substantially reduced by the fact that the Company would probably have gone into receivership anyway. However, although it is regrettable that this advice was not obtained earlier, I do not believe that it takes matters any further here. First, there is simply no evidence to suggest that any competent lawyer advising the Browns would have appreciated that there was no real prospect of establishing any damage, if their allegations of dishonesty were made out against the applicants. It may have been sensible for the Browns' legal advisors to suggest that that question was investigated at the start; it may even be that failure to give such advice would have been negligent, in the sense of being a breach of duty to the Browns. However, because all the legal advice given to the Browns, and indeed to the Board, is privileged, it may be that instructing an expert accountant early was raised as a possibility, even an advisable possibility, by one or more of the respondents at an early stage. Even if it was not raised, and even if it was a breach of the respondents' duty to the Browns not to have raised it, that would not of itself justify a wasted costs order in the present case (see *Ridehalgh v Horsefield* [1994] 3 All ER 848 at 862, 877, [1994] Ch 205 at 233, 249). The contention that the accountant's report should have been obtained earlier is also weakened by the fact that the parties agreed that there would be a split trial, so that the hearing before me was concerned only with liability. Given that the Browns' legal advisors would have appreciated the desire of the Board to keep costs to minimum, they may well have been hopeful that it would be unnecessary to instruct an expert accountant unless and until liability had been determined in favour of the Browns.

[94] In light of this analysis, it seems to me that the fact that Ms Callaghan's report was obtained at a late stage does not assist the applicants. If the respondents were entitled properly to plead and allege deceit without the expert's report, then the fact they did not obtain such a report until very late cannot have any bearing on the point: they were entitled to do that which they did. Indeed, once the expert's report was obtained, it was probably at least partially responsible for the legal advice which I expect resulted in the Board refusing to grant the Browns legal aid for the trial. On the other hand, if the respondents could not properly have concluded that there was a pleadable and arguable case based on dishonesty without an expert's report, then the applicants' case is made out, and the fact that an expert's report was obtained late merely provides confirmation for the conclusion which would have been reached anyway.

[95] I should make a small further point in relation to Ms Callaghan's report. It is said on behalf of the applicants that there was an unreasonable delay between the report being obtained and the advice to the Board which resulted in legal aid being discontinued. I am not impressed with that argument. Although I strongly suspect that the Board's decision not to provide legal aid for trial was influenced, and quite possibly ultimately caused, by the contents of the expert's report, I cannot be sure of that: I do not know what other factors may have weighed with the Board. Further, having seen the Browns present their case and give evidence, and having read many of the documents they have produced, I think it very likely that Mr Brown would have done everything he could to persuade the Board that his case was maintainable and should be supported at trial, notwithstanding the contents of Ms Callaghan's report. It is a matter of speculation as to what communications took place between Mr Brown and the Board, and between his legal advisors and the Board, before the Board decided not to continue supporting his case. It is therefore quite unsafe to assume that any delay in this connection was attributable to the respondents. Quite apart from this, the case

a was a complicated one, and it might have taken a little time for counsel and solicitors to appreciate the full effect of Ms Callaghan's report on the Browns' case as a whole.

[96] Fourthly, it seems to me irrelevant that the Board may well have been advised at some point between the finalisation of the expert's report and around two weeks before trial, that legal aid should not be accorded to the Browns for
b their legal representation at trial. The applicants contend that the giving of this advice confirms that it had always been inevitable that the Browns' claim would fail, and, indeed, that the respondents should always have appreciated that fact, and that it therefore strongly assists the contention that a wasted costs order should be made. I do not accept that point. An opinion, that there was or may have been evidence to justify an action being brought and maintained against the
c various applicants, is not undermined by the fact that, when the action is ready for trial, counsel advised the Board that the prospects, viewed as a whole, were so poor that legal aid for representation at trial could not be justified. In a case where starting an action could be justified, but by the conclusion of the action, it seems that at some point the action should have been discontinued, it will
d frequently be difficult to identify a precise moment at which counsel should have advised that the action was no longer maintainable. In circumstances where privilege has not been waived, it may often be impossible. Even in a substantial action involving dishonesty, there must be a limit to the extent to which the legal advisors to the claimant have to monitor the arguability of the case. Clearly, the weaker the case, the more alert the lawyers should be to monitor its arguability,
e but that cannot mean that there is a duty, for instance, on counsel to reconsider the point every time any aspect of it is sent back to him. It must be a question of fact and degree. If all the papers were sent back to him to review the strength of the case, he may well be obliged to consider whether he could properly advance a dishonesty allegation. On the other hand, if a few of the papers were sent back
f to him to advise on an aspect of further and better information, it would be unlikely that would be under such a duty.

[97] In the present case, I have seen the evidence which would have been available to the respondents, save to the extent that it is subject to privilege in favour of the Browns. I must determine whether that evidence was sufficient to justify pleading and maintaining a case of dishonesty against the applicants. If
g not, then I must decide whether the respondents can realistically contend that there may be privileged material which could justify their pleading and maintaining the action. I do not see how it assists me, in reaching a conclusion on these issues, to know or take into account that (if it be the case) the respondents initially considered legal aid could be justified for starting and
h maintaining the action, but that they subsequently concluded that it could not be justified for the trial.

[98] There is another reason for reaching that conclusion. It is quite possible that, from the inception, the legal advice given to the Board by counsel was not optimistic, but that it was sufficiently hopeful, taking into account the financial rewards of success, for the Board, possibly assisted by the strong representations
j of the Browns, to maintain legal aid with the view to seeing what came up on disclosure, exchange of witness statements, obtaining of experts reports, possibly in the hope of a beneficial settlement being achieved. It may well be that the advice given by counsel to the Board which resulted in legal aid being withdrawn was, apart from considering the effect of Ms Callaghan's report, not very different in its assessment of prospects, albeit significantly more firmly expressed, than it

had been from the beginning. The reason it could be more firmly expressed was because there would have been much less uncertainty in terms of what the documents would reveal (after disclosure) what the witnesses would say (after exchange of statements) and what the experts would say (after exchange of reports and meeting). It can fairly be said that this is all speculation, but that argument reveals the whole problem: it must be speculation because the Browns have not waived privilege, and once one is in the realms of such speculation, then, provided one does not stray into the fanciful, one is fairly within the territory which precludes the court determining the question of wasted costs.

[99] For these reasons, I do not consider that the applicants gain any assistance from the fact that the Board appears to have been advised either that legal aid should not be provided for the trial or that the prospects were such that legal aid was not provided for the trial. I reach the same conclusion in relation to the suggestion on behalf of the respondents, that the fact that they appear to have given this advice counted in their favour. This argument is advanced on the basis that the refusal of legal aid to the Browns for trial is indicative of the fact that the respondents were prepared to advise that the case was hopeless and/or were not prepared to advance the case once they were satisfied that it was inappropriate or hopeless to do so. In the first place, there is the obvious point that, if they ought never have pleaded and advanced the case in the first place, they may only have appreciated it at the last minute. Quite apart from this, as I have mentioned, one simply does not know what passed between the respondents and the Board, or the respondents and the Browns, from time to time, nor does one know to what extent, if any, their advice to the Board changed from the time they were first instructed to advise to the time when they last advised.

[100] Finally, the fact that the applications of Mr Evans, Mr Scott and Mr Sarson are stronger than those of the other applicants, does not assist the applications of those other applicants. If Mr Evans, Mr Scott and/or Mr Sarson's respective applications succeed, that does not mean that the applications of the other applicants should succeed, if they do not deserve success on their own merits. It would be quite unjust on the respondents if it were otherwise.

[101] Accordingly, it appears to me that the question whether the applications on behalf of the various applicants should be permitted to proceed to the second stage must depend on two questions. The first question is whether I am satisfied that there was no evidence upon which the claim on behalf of the Browns against each applicant could properly have been maintained by the respondents. The second question is whether, even if there is no such evidence available, the fact that the Browns had not waived privilege would make it impossible and therefore unfair on the respondents, to let the applications proceed to the second stage.

Reliance on the judgment in the action

[102] There is one further point I should mention about the applicants' approach to these applications. There are obvious dangers in considering an application for wasted costs based on what happened at trial, and on what was contained in the judgment. First, it is inherently unsatisfactory, particularly when the conduct of the legal representatives which is subject to criticism has accrued over a long period, to consider that conduct over that period retrospectively from the end point of the trial. One is looking at matters with the wisdom of hindsight, and also in a different perspective from those whose conduct is under scrutiny. In this case, Abrahamsons were acting for the Browns well before the proceedings were brought, and there is an obvious risk of unfairness to them if

a their conduct is judged backwards from the date of trial, rather than forwards from their first instructions. The same point in principle applies to the Barristers, although their involvement, particularly that of Mr Evans, was of more recent origin. Further, if one looks at the matter from or around the date of the final judgment, one runs the danger of concentrating on the evidence and the perceptions available at that time. On earlier occasions, a claimant's legal

b advisors may have reasonably expected, or have been reasonably led to believe, that evidence which did not in fact materialise might materialise. Indeed, they may have been given apparently reliable information which could not be used at trial, either because that evidence turned out to be unreliable or unavailable, or because it was privileged: in either event, it is not available to the legal representatives to explain their conduct, unless, of course, their former client

c waives his privilege, which the Browns have not done. It is, however, fair to add that, in this particular case, reliance on the arguments and facts as they came out at trial is less risky than it would be in most cases. What the Browns had been saying in their complaints to the 12 organisations, and individuals, and what was in the Company's files which were available to the Browns, before the action

d started, were very similar to their case and documentary evidence at trial.

[103] There is another danger in relying too heavily on the judgment in the matter in respect of which the wasted costs order is sought, in this case my judgment of 18 October 2000. First, any findings made in that judgment are only binding as between the parties to the proceedings, and therefore are not, as a matter of principle, binding on the respondents. Secondly, and relatively unusually,

e none of the respondents were professionally responsible for presenting the arguments and evidence at the hearing which led to the judgment (although it is right to record that a representative of Abrahamsons gave informal assistance to the Browns during the trial). Accordingly, it is important to bear in mind that the findings and observations made in my judgment were based on the evidence and

f arguments advanced by the Browns acting in person, and not by a barrister or solicitor acting on their behalf, let alone by any of the respondents to the present wasted costs applications. Clearly, that is a point which should not be permitted to get out of proportion, and, although they rightly rely on this point, neither Mr Powell nor Mr Mansfield have over-emphasised it. The Browns' case was

g fully pleaded by counsel with the assistance of Abrahamsons, and, as I have mentioned, all three counsel featured relatively frequently at various hearings, and, indeed, Mr Oliver and Mr Evans prepared the skeleton argument for trial, albeit that it was pretty brief.

h *Pleading and maintaining a claim of dishonesty*

[104] Paragraph 606 of the Code in force at that time (now para 704) provides:

'A practising barrister must not devise facts which will assist in advancing his lay client's case and must not draft any originating process, pleading

j affidavit witness statement or notice of appeal containing ... (c) any allegation of fraud unless he has clear instructions to make such allegation and has before him reasonably credible material which as it stands establishes a prima facie case of fraud ... provided that nothing in this paragraph will prevent a barrister drafting a document containing specific factual statements or contentions included by the barrister subject to confirmation of their accuracy by the lay client or witness.'

Paragraph 610 of the Code in force at the time (currently para 708) provides that counsel 'must not suggest that a witness or other person is guilty of ... fraud or misconduct ... unless such allegations ... appear to him to be supported on reasonable grounds'.

[105] The test in the two paragraphs is expressed in slightly different terms. There is force in the contention that the two provisions, concerned with the same sort of matter and so close to each other in the same document, namely the Code, do imply slightly different tests, on the basis that one must assume that the change of wording was deliberate. Although there is obviously a real argument to the effect that the two tests are identical, I am inclined at the moment to think that the hurdle is set at a slightly higher level at the first stage, namely pleading the case, than at the second stage, at least as a matter of language. It seems a little surprising at first sight, but there is a case for saying that, once dishonesty is pleaded, the starting gun has been fired, and, because the prospect of success can inevitably ebb and flow thereafter, it is appropriate to set a slightly less stringent test before counsel is professionally required to abandon the allegation of dishonesty. There was no argument on this difference in the language in the two paragraphs of the Code, and it does not appear to me to affect the outcome of the instant applications.

[106] The importance the court attaches to the principles in those paragraphs in the Code cannot be doubted. It was emphasised by the decision and reasoning in *Medcalf v Mardell* [2001] Lloyd's Rep PN 146. The significance of counsel's duty to the court in this connection has been re-emphasised by the Court of Appeal in *Cornwall Gardens PTE Ltd v R O Garrard & Co Ltd* [2001] EWCA Civ 699 where Lord Phillips of Worth Matravers MR approved the guidance given by the Bar Council following *Medcalf v Mardell*, and said that he had 'reservations as to whether there exists material which justifies the making of this serious allegation' of malicious falsehood in that case.

[107] I turn to consider recent observations made by the House of Lords in connection with allegations of dishonesty, in *Three Rivers DC v Bank of England (No 3)* [2001] UKHL 16, [2001] 2 All ER 513. Lord Hope of Craighead said:

'A party is not entitled to a finding of fraud if the pleader does not allege fraud directly and the facts on which he relies are equivocal. So too with dishonesty. If there is no specific allegation of dishonesty, it is not open to the court to make a finding to that effect if the facts pleaded are consistent with conduct which is not dishonest such as negligence.' (See [2001] 2 All ER 513 at [55].)

[108] That proposition is important and, one hopes, that it is part of the common general knowledge of any practising litigation lawyer. At the end of that paragraph, however, Lord Hope made a more subtle point:

'Of course, the allegation of fraud, dishonesty or bad faith must be supported by particulars. The other party is entitled to notice of the particulars on which the allegations is based. If they are not capable of supporting the allegation, the allegation itself may be struck out. But it is not a proper ground for striking out the allegation that the particulars may be found, after trial, to amount not to fraud, dishonesty or bad faith but to negligence.'

[109] Lord Hutton ([2001] 2 All ER 513 at [111]) who said he was 'in general agreement' with Lord Hope's conclusions and reasons, gave 'two further

a   considerations' for rejecting the contention 'that the plaintiffs have no real prospect of establishing' that the defendant knew of matters which rendered its conduct dishonest or reckless (see [2001] 2 All ER 562 at [144]). He then set out those reasons (at [144], [145]):

b   'One is that I think that it is reasonably possible that further material may become available to the plaintiffs before trial ... Secondly, I consider that the material already available to the plaintiffs provides reasonable grounds for thinking that they may be able to advance their case by the cross-examination of the [defendant's] officials.'

[110] In relation to the first point, he agreed with the dissenting judgment of Auld LJ in the Court of Appeal ([1999] 4 All ER 800n, [2000] 2 WLR 15) that the court 'was not entitled ... to conclude ... that all the available material evidence on those questions had been gathered in'. On the second point, he said ([2001] 2 All ER 513 at [147]): '[T]he assessment whether it is reasonable to take the view that evidence may emerge in cross-examination depends on the particular facts of the case.'

d   [111] Lord Steyn ([2001] 2 All ER 513 at [1]) agreed with Lord Hope and Lord Hutton.

[112] These observations in the House of Lords, when read together with the duty of counsel set out in the Code, serve to illustrate the potential difficulties for a barrister when pleading or maintaining an allegation of dishonesty. On the one hand, he cannot plead a claim based on dishonesty unless he can properly give
e   particulars which could, on their face, support the allegation of dishonesty and unless he has 'reasonably credible' material which appears to him to 'establish ... a prima facie case' of dishonesty. On the other hand, it is scarcely consistent with the observations of Lord Hope if, when considering whether he can properly plead or advance a claim of dishonesty, a barrister cannot plead fraud if his
f   pleaded particulars of dishonesty, if established as facts, might turn out not to support a claim of dishonesty. Equally, in light of Lord Hutton's observations, a barrister, considering whether to plead fraud, appears to be entitled to take into account that further facts and evidence of dishonesty may turn up before trial, or even during trial, at least in some cases. At first sight, the two competing sets of considerations seem almost contradictory, but I do not think they are. A
g   barrister's duty is to ask himself, whether bearing in mind the evidence currently available, but taking into account the possibility (whose value may be nil or significant depending on the particular case) of evidence which might come to light during the course of the proceedings or during trial, there is a strong enough case to justify pleading and maintaining dishonesty in accordance with the Code.
h   [113] A barrister instructed by a client to plead and maintain a claim of dishonesty has to face another judgment call, which will sometimes be of some nicety, arising out of competing duties. The first duty is that laid down by the Code to which I have referred, namely not to plead or maintain a claim of dishonesty unless it is properly warranted. However, as Mr Stewart points out,
j   a barrister has a more general duty to plead and advance his client's case in accordance with his client's instructions. Of course, in the event of a conflict, this latter general duty must yield to the former more specific duty, but that does not alter the fact that a lawyer who is in doubt as to whether he can properly plead a claim of dishonesty is in a position of some nicety. If he cannot properly plead it, then he would be in breach of the duty embodied in the Code if he pleads it; on the other hand, if he can properly plead it, then he would be in breach of his

general duty to his client if he did not maintain it. To my mind, these factors
serve to emphasise that, while there is no doubt as to the duty of counsel not to _a_
plead a claim of dishonesty in circumstances which infringe the provisions of the
Code, the importance of which principle is underlined by the decision in _Medcalf
v Mardell_, it must none the less be accepted that, whether there is sufficient
evidence to satisfy the barrister that he can properly plead a claim of dishonesty,
will sometimes be a matter of judgment, on which reasonable lawyers could _b_
differ. Accordingly, it would only be if the view reached by counsel that he could
plead dishonesty was unreasonable or reckless that it could be improper. In other
words, as I see it, it would only be if the lawyer's conclusion that he could plead
a claim for dishonesty was one which no reasonable lawyer, properly considering
matters, could have reached, that it can be criticised as being improper.

[114] Another point of possible difficulty for a lawyer rises where the _c_
allegations of dishonesty are largely, or even exclusively, based on what his client
tells him. Where this information consists of factual evidence of dishonesty, the
lawyer could be in a position of some difficulty if that evidence is thoroughly
inconsistent with a mass of apparently convincing other evidence. In general, as
Donaldson MR emphasised in _Orchard v South Eastern Electricity Board_ [1987] 1 All _d_
ER 95 at 100, [1987] QB 565 at 572, a lawyer is normally entitled to proceed on
the basis of his client's factual instructions being correct. However, that does not
mean that, when giving his views as to the likely outcome of the case, a lawyer
should not express his professional assessment as to the likelihood of the client's
case succeeding on the facts. None the less, I think that it would require strong
facts before a barrister could be said to be acting contrary to the standards laid _e_
down by the Code if he maintained a case of dishonesty which could be justified
on the basis of the facts put forward by his client, simply because there was
credible strong contrary evidence available.

[115] The position may, however, be different where the client's instruction
and evidence do not consist so much of hard facts, but are more expressions of _f_
opinion or inference. Much of what the Browns must have told the respondents
would have been in that category. The Browns were intimately involved in the
running of the Company until they ceased to be directors, and they had
considerable knowledge of both the running of the Company and of the Bennetts
and some of the other applicants. In my opinion, the impressions and belief of
the Browns, and the inferences they felt able to draw from what occurred, should _g_
have been regarded by their lawyers with greater scepticism than the factual
evidence given by the Browns. However, I consider that it would be wrong to
conclude that the lawyers advising the Browns should—or even could—properly
have ignored such impressions, belief and inferences. It appears to me that it
would have been part of the respondents' duty to their clients, the Browns, to _h_
consider and give weight to their impressions, belief and inferences, albeit that,
when considering whether there was a prima facie case of dishonesty, they would
have been bound to take into account all the evidence, including, albeit to an
inevitably less critical extent than the court at trial, their assessment of their
clients. _j_

[116] There is no doubt in my mind that Mr Scott, Mr Evans and Mr Sarson
have a stronger case for a wasted costs order than the APA defendants, and that
the APA defendants have a stronger case for a wasted costs order than the
Bennetts. I propose to start by considering whether the Bennetts establish that
their application should go to a second stage. If they do, then it would follow that
the other applicants should also succeed. If they do not, it will be necessary to

a consider whether some or all of the applicants have a sufficiently stronger case to justify their application going to the second stage.

The Bennetts

[117] At trial, although of the view that there was no case of dishonesty for the Bennetts to answer, I found that there would have been a case for them to answer
b in negligence, were it not for the fact that the Browns had failed to establish any damage. This was because Ms Callaghan's evidence was that, even with the complaints she thought could be established against the Bennetts, the Company would still have gone into receivership, and, unlike the claim based on dishonesty, the claim in negligence could not have extended to the profits made by the applicants when the business of Oasis proved successful.
c [118] The fact that a prima facie case was made out by the Browns at trial to the effect that the Bennetts were negligent is of some assistance to the respondents in the present applications, because it means that, even viewed from the date of trial, there was evidence to support the contention that there had been some sort of wrongdoing (albeit with no implications of impropriety) on the part
d of the Bennetts. I turn to the question of whether the court, at the second stage of the Bennetts' applications, would be likely to conclude that there was sufficient evidence for the Barristers to have pleaded a claim against the Bennetts based on dishonesty.

[119] At the time the action was started, the principal source of information available to Abrahamsons and Mr Asprey would have been the documents in the
e possession of the Company and statements and the instructions given by the Browns. Those statements would have been evidence in themselves, and it can fairly be said that the Browns would have appeared to have been in a very good position to give that evidence, and, indeed, to have opinion and to draw inferences. Further, as is implicit in the reasoning of the House of Lords in the
f *Three Rivers* case, it was in the very nature of the type of allegations of dishonesty made by the Browns that they would contend that inferences should be drawn against the Bennetts from a series of events. It would not have been particularly surprising if there had been no 'paper trail' because the Bennetts could have been expected to have ensured that all incriminating documents were destroyed. Further, although each individual event may have been insufficient to justify
g inferring dishonesty, it may not by any means have been unreasonable to expect or hope that the court would infer dishonesty from the whole history.

[120] So far as general allegations of dishonesty are concerned, the respondents would have known that Mr Brown not merely distrusted the Bennetts and believed that they would destroy documents, but that he had been prepared to
h go on oath to support that contention, in his affidavit in support of his claim for the search order. In that affidavit he also stated that he and Mrs Brown had been 'denied any opportunity to retrieve our own copies of Company documents and records' when they were locked out 'on the instructions of Michael Bennett'. The respondents would also have been told by the Browns that the Bennetts had
j not told the truth about the circumstances in which the Browns were locked out, and indeed had flagrantly breached Mr Brown's service contract as a result. In this connection there was a contemporary letter to the Midland Bank plc (the Bank), that disputed the Bennetts' version of facts relating to the lockout of the Browns.

[121] The respondents would presumably have been told, as is also stated in Mr Brown's affidavit, that, at least according to Mr Brown, Mr Freedman had not

been quite frank in what he told the Browns about the existence of private
arrangements in March 1990 between APA and the Bennetts in relation to their *a*
respective shareholdings in the Company as a result of the March 1990 rights
issue. As the evidence unfolded, it would have become clear that there was
something in this. The Browns regarded this behaviour as deceitful, and I do not
accept that the respondents would have been unreasonable in thinking that that
was a properly maintainable view. There was also evidence that the Bennetts and *b*
APA had misled the Browns in 1990 about their future in the Company. In a
report prepared by the accountants KPMG on 3 December 1993, which would
have been seen by the respondents, there was reference to the fact that APA 'felt
that it would have looked bad to reinvest in the Company post receivership and
might have added weight to [Mr Brown's] allegations' that APA were plotting
with the Bennetts to force him out of the Company. Further, Mr Brown would *c*
have told the respondents that, as was the case, the Bennetts and APA were
instrumental in removing the Browns from the board of the Company in June
1990.

[122] The Browns would also have made much of the central complaints
raised in their pleaded case. Thus, they would have explained that the Bennetts *d*
had been instrumental in not controlling head office costs and in failing to open
new shops. The Company's management accounts showed that its shops were
operating profitably, and that it was head office expenditure that was running the
Company into loss. There was evidence to show that the Bennetts knew that
head office costs were unjustifiably high. Further, when Oasis acquired the
business, head office expenses were substantially reduced from the start. The *e*
Browns would also have said that the Company's overheads in late 1990 could
only have been justified if new shops were opened, as was projected, but that
Bennetts appeared to have had no sense of urgency in connection with opening
such shops. There would also have been evidence from the Browns which could
be said to suggest that the Bennetts had dismissed the previous finance director, *f*
Mr Gunning, for expressing concerns in this connection, and that they then
refused to address the problem themselves. The Company's board minutes did
not record the Browns pressing for these problems to be dealt with, but their case
was that the minutes were inaccurate, and this was supported by their own
apparently accurate and contemporaneous notes.

[123] There was also evidence from the Browns to suggest that the Bennetts *g*
had stated to a number of people that, if they did not get what they wanted, they
would put the Company into receivership. On the basis of what the Browns said,
there was evidence to suggest that the Bennetts obtained control of the Company
by concealing their activities and not telling the truth. There was some
documentary evidence that the Bank considered that they might have been *h*
misled by the Bennetts (and indeed by APA) about the level of funding which the
Bennetts were prepared to provide. Furthermore, during late 1990, the Bennetts
were parties to the preparation of the projections, ie the plans for a new entity
which would acquire the business of the company (which ultimately turned out
to be Oasis) well in advance of the Company going into receivership. It was not *j*
merely that they had such plans prepared, and that the plans eventually came to
fruition; it was also that the projections they had prepared appeared to provide
for reductions in head office expenses. There was also evidence that, before the
end of November 1990, the Bennetts had resolved that the Company would go
into receivership after Christmas 1990, if the Bank withdrew its support. There
was some independent evidential support for the view the Bennetts had impeded

a the Browns' rescue plan for the Company in 1991, by dissuading one or two creditors from converting their debt into equity, and that the Bennetts subsequently paid off those who had agreed. Finally, there is the fact that the Bennetts profited to a very substantial extent, by the Company going into receivership, and its business being purchased by Oasis in which the Bennetts had a substantial shareholding; the business then prospered, and Oasis was b subsequently floated on the stock market.

[124] In many cases, where a defendant was at least arguably negligent, and the defendant might reasonably have anticipated benefiting from that behaviour, or, even more, he actually benefited from that behaviour, one does not have to go very far to justify a contention that the behaviour may have been worse than negligent, namely in some way dishonest. It would, of course, be quite wrong to c generalise, because each case must turn on its own particular facts. None the less, where there is credible evidence to suggest that the defendants managed a company in a way which was at least arguably negligent, and that they ultimately benefited financially from this, it does not involve a large leap to envisage that the behaviour may have been worse than negligent. In the present case, bearing in d mind the various factors which I have attempted to summarise, all of which the Browns strongly believed could be made out at trial, and some of which received a degree of support from documents, I do not think a court could fairly hold that no reasonable lawyer retained by the Browns could have formed the view that he could properly plead and maintain an allegation of dishonesty against the Bennetts.

e [125] For instance, however much the Browns might have appeared to be obsessed, it is by no means unknown for board minutes to be doctored or slanted at the suit of the more powerful directors. Indeed, the Browns' own notes of the meetings did not tally with the formal minutes. There were real grounds for thinking that the Browns were right in suggesting that the Bennetts did not tell f the truth about the lockout of the Browns, and that they concealed an arrangement with APA about shares in the Company in March 1990. Further, the projections for the new company prepared for the Bennetts, did exist, and there is force in the suggestion that they only ceased to look sinister after Ms Callaghan, the Browns' expert accountant, expressed the view that it was not unusual for directors and shareholders of companies in difficulties, to prepare projections g with a view to buying the business if the company went into receivership. The management accounts also could be viewed as supporting the urgent need during 1990 for cutting head office expenditure and opening new shops. There was also the curious fact that a report prepared for APA as late January 1991 suggested that the Company's position was healthy.

h [126] I accept that the great majority of these points were ultimately answered, or explained by the Browns' unreliability and by reference to other documents and witness statements. However, that does not justify the conclusion that the Barristers should not have been prepared to plead or maintain a case of dishonesty against the Bennetts. Bearing in mind that the allegations, j inferences, and suspicions of the Browns were based on their substantial involvement with the Company and of the Bennetts, and the fact that a number of independent factors tended to give some apparent possible justification for their views, it seems to me that counsel cannot fairly, let alone safely, be criticised for alleging dishonesty against the Bennetts. This view is reinforced by the fact that there were undoubtedly grounds for alleging negligence on the part of the Bennetts, which negligence redounded to their advantage, and by the fact that

one could not have been confident that this was not the sort of case where further
evidence might turn up during the period leading up to the trial, and even during
cross-examination of the Bennetts, or indeed of the other applicants.

[127] The extent to which the Barristers were under an obligation to go
through the voluminous documentation to check the evidence on each allegation
against the Bennetts also raises a problematic issue. Clearly, a barrister cannot
simply plead a case of dishonesty, in a case where there are masses of potentially
relevant documents, without looking at the documents first. On the other hand,
it is scarcely realistic to expect a barrister in such a case to scrutinise each
document with the same degree of detail as would be involved immediately
before, or indeed during, the trial. While he must satisfy himself as to the
propriety of pleading dishonesty by looking at and considering all the evidence,
he cannot be required to conduct the sort of detailed investigation, analysis and
critique which would amount to an intra cranial trial. It is not possible to lay
down any general rule as to the degree of detailed investigation that is
appropriate in each case. It must turn on the facts of the case and, within limits,
on the judgment of the barrister, which must be carefully and reasonably
exercised. Mr Slowe's contention, that there is an answer to each of the points
which would have been made against the Bennetts, is therefore not an answer.
In any event, I am far from persuaded that by any means all the points could be
met to the extent of saying that no reasonable lawyer acting for the Browns could
have thought that there was anything in them at all.

[128] In other words, assuming, in favour of the applicants, that each of the
points could have been answered, that would still leave open the question of
whether a barrister, when pleading the case of dishonesty or subsequently
maintaining it, could fairly be criticised for not having appreciated that that was
in fact the case. In my judgment, that contention would be difficult to establish,
and it is unlikely that the court would accept it. Over and above this, one cannot
be confident that there could have been no answer or possible answer by the
Browns to the respondents in relation to some or all of those apparent
explanations. There is a large and significant difference between this type of case,
where there are a number of points which may all turn out to be bad, but which,
when taken together may justify a pleading of dishonesty, and a case such as
Medcalf v Mardell [2001] Lloyd's Rep PN 146, where there was, according to the
Court of Appeal, simply no evidence upon which a claim of dishonesty could
properly have been maintained. Further, the particular allegations of dishonesty
in *Medcalf v Mardell* were somewhat extraordinary in the circumstances.

[129] I also consider that, once one concludes that there was a properly
pleadable case against the Bennetts, it is unrealistic to think that they could
establish that there was a point at which counsel should have come to the
conclusion that that case would have to be abandoned. It is unlikely that it would
be possible to identify a point in time, on the basis of a specific event, as the
moment when dishonesty could no longer properly be advanced, with the
possible exception of the receipt of Ms Callaghan's report. However, the report
takes matters no further for the reasons I have given. Accordingly, I believe that
the case against the Bennetts was properly pleadable and maintainable on the
information available to me.

[130] Over and above this, I consider that, even if I am wrong in this
conclusion, the Bennetts' application should not be allowed to proceed in any
event, because it would be impossible to find against the respondents in light of
the Browns' not waiving privilege. In many claims involving reasonably complex

a and detailed allegations of dishonest conduct over more than four-and-a-half years, the conclusion, that a wasted costs application could not fairly proceed in light of the inability of the court to look at privileged documents, would be almost self-evident. In the present case, it is fair to the applicants to say that it is not so clear. Because they took an assignment of the Company's claims, the Browns, and therefore the respondents, had all the Company's documents
b available from the inception of action. Furthermore, there are the 12 detailed complaints the Browns made against many of the applicants, and in which they set out their case before the action. Additionally, this is not one of those cases where it is immediately obvious that specific items or categories of evidence would have been available to counsel which were not available at trial, or that specific evidence counsel might have believed would come to light did not in fact
c become available. Ms Dohmann and Mr Slowe can fairly say that the specific examples of what evidence might or might not have been available at various times, as advanced on behalf of the respondents, were not particularly compelling.

d [131] However, I do not think that is quite the point. It is difficult for counsel for a respondent in a wasted costs application, where privilege is claimed by the respondent's former client, to give sensible examples of what might have been available but has not been disclosed. Either they have seen privileged material, in which case they cannot fairly give examples knowing them to be true, because they thereby risk breaching the privilege with a nod and a wink, or they have to
e give examples which they know are not true, in which case they could be misleading the court. Normally, as here, counsel representing the respondents will very sensibly have not looked at the privileged material, in which case they will be in the dark as to what evidence, facts and expectations might have been available to the respondents at various times before and during the progress of the action.
f
[132] Accordingly, I must take a reasonably robust approach, and consider whether there is no real possibility of there having been further facts, inferences arguments or expectations before counsel which may justify the course they adopted, which course could not, solely on the basis of evidence actually available to the court, be justified. In *Medcalf v Mardell*, the majority of the Court of Appeal
g felt able to answer the question in the affirmative on the special facts of the case. In the present case, I do not feel capable of answering the question with any reasonable degree of confidence. It may well be right that the Browns did not tell the respondents any more than they had said in the complaints and in their very full witness statements. It may well be that there were no documents available
h to the respondents other than those that I have seen. It may well be that there was no indication of further helpful witnesses. However, I do not know what explanations about some of the documents were given by the Browns; I do not know what further evidence, through witnesses, documents or cross-examination was reasonably anticipated by the respondents as a result of what they were told
j by the Browns or otherwise. The evidence as a whole would have been looked at by the respondents rather differently from the way I looked at it at trial. I had rejected the reliability of any evidence given by the Browns, which was very probably not sensibly open to lawyers advising and acting for the Browns, particularly as I heard argument and cross-examination on behalf of the applicants. Further, some of the allegations or suspicions advanced by the Browns may have been demolished by Ms Callaghan's report.

[133] In all these circumstances, I am satisfied that the respondents have made
out each of their two main grounds for contending that these applications by the
Bennetts should not be allowed to proceed. First, on the basis of the evidence
actually available, it seems to me that a barrister instructed by the Browns could
properly have pleaded and maintained a claim based on the dishonesty of the
Bennetts in connection with their running of the Company. Secondly, even if
that were not the case, in light of the fact that the Browns maintain their right to
privilege, it would not be possible for a court to conclude otherwise.

[134] There is also a real argument to the effect that, even if the various points
raised by the respondents might well be shown to be wrong at the second state
hearing, the number and nature of the points is such that it would scarcely be
appropriate hearing for a wasted costs application. As was emphasised in
Ridehalgh v Horsefield [1994] 3 All ER 848, [1994] Ch 205 and *Harley v McDonald,
Glasgow Harley (a firm) v McDonald* [2001] 2 AC 678, [2001] 2 WLR 1749, a wasted
costs application is 'satellite litigation', and is not normally to be regarded as a
jurisdiction which involves anything other than 'summary' hearing, which
should last hours rather than days, let alone weeks. It is difficult to assess how
long the second stage would last if the Bennetts were permitted to proceed with
their application against three barristers and one firm of solicitors, particularly
bearing in mind that there are also other applicants. Counsel for the respondents,
perhaps not surprisingly, took a rather more pessimistic view than counsel for the
applicants, and it is not any easy matter to assess. Bearing in mind the points at
issue and the mass of paper involved, I would be surprised if the application of all
the applicants against all the respondents on this main aspect could be disposed
of in a week. In the context of a claim for wasted costs which I am told could
exceed £3m in all, there is something to be said for the view that this factor of
itself should not, in the absence of any other factors, be sufficient to refuse the
Bennetts permission to proceed to the second stage. However, if I was in real
doubt about whether the Bennetts' main application should proceed to the
second stage, the likely length of the hearing of the second stage would have been
a factor which would have tended to support the conclusion that the Bennetts'
application should not proceed to the second stage.

The APA defendants

[135] As I have mentioned, the APA defendants have a stronger case than the
Bennetts, partly because I found that there was not even a prima facie case against
them in negligence, and partly because (in the case of APA, but not of
Mr Freedman) they were not directors of the Company, and therefore owed no
fiduciary duty to the Company. However, so far as Mr Freedman is concerned,
there is force in the contention that, if a claim of the sort actually pleaded and
maintained against the Bennetts could properly have been so pleaded and
maintained, then the same conclusion must apply to Mr Freedman. After all, if
the contention was that the Company was being run in breach of fiduciary duty
and dishonestly, then, if that allegation can properly be made against the
Bennetts, the two directors concerned with running the Company on a
day-to-day basis, it is not a large leap to suggest that this allegation can properly
be extended to another director who had been on the board for more than 15
months, ie during the whole of the crucial period. On its own, I doubt that this
point would suffice, but it does not stand alone.

[136] A number of possible further points would, I think, almost certainly
have been made against Mr Freedman by the Browns to the respondents. In this

a connection, it seems to me that it is not merely allegations against Mr Freedman, but also allegations against APA, which have to be considered. If there were grounds for pleading dishonesty against APA and the Bennetts, then it seems to me virtually a foregone conclusion that, in the absence of some very telling point or points to the contrary, dishonesty could properly have been pleaded against Mr Freedman: APA appointed him as a director of the Company, and he was a
b co-director with the Bennetts when they were allegedly dishonest in their running of the Company. When considering what might have been said against the Bennetts, I have already considered a number of points which involve APA and Mr Freedman. Additionally, although it turned out to be wrong, Mr Brown clearly believed that APA intended to participate in the new business, eventually embodied in Oasis, and this belief was not fanciful. It is supported by the extract
c from the KPMG report of 3 December 1993 from which I have quoted. It is also supported by the fact that there was a telephone conversation between Mr Freedman and Michael Bennett, at the time APA decided not to invest further, when Mr Freedman floated the possibility of APA none the less advancing £200,000. In addition, there was a newspaper report in which a
d reporter employed by Business Age magazine wrote that he had been informed on 11 May 1995, in an interview with the Bennetts and Mr Sarson, that APA had in fact offered to invest in Oasis. Subsequently, Mr Freedman denied saying this, but that could have inflamed, rather than hampered, doubts as to his credibility. Further, there was evidence, according to an affidavit sworn by Mr Brown in June 1997, that one of the Bennetts and his wife were trustees for shares in
e Oasis for beneficiaries who had the same surname as Mr Freedman.

[137] In all the circumstances, it seems to me that the application of the APA defendants must fail on the basis that there was sufficient to justify pleading and maintaining a claim for dishonesty against them. Even if that is wrong, for the same reasons as those given in relation to the Bennetts, I also believe that the APA
f defendants' application should in any event fail on the grounds that there could be material which justified the conduct of the respondents, but which they cannot put before the court because the Browns have not waived privilege.

Mr Scott, Mr Evans and Mr Sarson

g [138] The case of these three applicants for wasted costs orders is substantially stronger than that of the Bennetts or of the APA defendants. Each of them was a member of the board of the Company at least during the last two or three months of its trading, and it is said that, if the case based on dishonesty against the Bennetts and Mr Freedman could properly have been pleaded, then such a case could also properly have been pleaded against these three applicants. The
h argument runs thus. If there was a maintainable case against the Bennetts and Mr Freedman, as directors of the Company, for having been dishonest in their management of the Company, then there must be a maintainable case in dishonesty against the other directors, on the basis that it must be arguable that all the directors, as members of the same board with fiduciary duties to the
j Company, were or may have been parties to the dishonesty in running the Company into receivership. Bearing in mind the observations in *Three Rivers DC v Bank of England (No 3)* [2001] 2 All ER 513, and in particular the observations of Lord Hutton ([2001] 2 All ER 513 at [142]–[145]) to which I have referred, where there is a pleadable case in dishonesty against three members of a board in connection with their running of the Company, it may often be relatively easy to justify pleading a similar case against the other members of the board. However,

as his observations ([2001] 2 All ER 513 at [147]) demonstrate, each case must turn inevitably on its own facts.

[139] Mr Scott only joined the Company in October 1990, and he was not appointed as a director until 22 November 1990. Despite its substantial length, Mr Brown's witness statement in the action did not refer to Mr Scott even once. There was not a single document which so much as hinted at Mr Scott's involvement in any of the matters alleged against him. Ms Callaghan was actually complimentary about Mr Scott's involvement, and he was on the board when a reduction in head office costs of around 15% was achieved, as Ms Callaghan indicated. He came to the Company with a high reputation, and there was uncontradicted evidence to suggest that he was prepared to invest £50,000 of his own money into the Company. Further, as he was never on the board with the Browns, he would never have considered the question of opening new shops or cutting head office expenses on their raising the topics.

[140] These are undoubtedly powerful points, particularly when taken together. I turn to consider the answers advanced by the respondents. It is said that the fact that Mr Scott was not mentioned in Mr Brown's witness statement is not of itself surprising, as he became a director after Mr Brown had ceased to be a director. That is an explanation of why he is not referred to, but it does not meet the point that there was a lack of evidence against Mr Scott. Further, as I have mentioned, Mr Scott was, albeit only for a short time before receivers were appointed, on the Company's board with the Bennetts and Mr Freedman, against whom there was a pleadable case. He had been appointed a director at the instigation of APA, against whom there was a pleadable case in dishonesty in connection with the running of the Company. Those points are not very telling. He was a director for such a short time. Further, he did benefit as a result of the receivership, in that he became a director of, and shareholder in, Oasis, when it acquired the Company's business from the receivers. That shows a benefit from the events complained of, but on its own it is plainly not enough to justify alleging dishonesty against him.

[141] Further, although he allegedly intended to invest £50,000 in the Company, Mr Scott in fact never did so: the Browns believed that the intention was not genuine. That was merely their belief. During the short period that he was a director, Mr Scott did not, according to the Browns, cause the Company to cut head office costs by enough, and there was no direct evidence available to the respondents to show that Mr Scott could personally take credit for the cuts which were achieved. That is merely a negative point: it does not help establish his dishonesty. Although there was no documentary evidence showing Mr Scott's involvement in the projections for a possible buy out, it is said that it was reasonable to infer that he must have been involved in those projections, partly because of his expertise and partly because he would have been unlikely to join the Company without knowing of them. Again, that is conjecture.

[142] Whether or not a barrister can properly plead dishonesty is to be tested by reference to the standard laid down in the Code. However, as I have already mentioned it seems to me that the standard must allow for the possibility of different lawyers having different views, and I believe that it is only if a reasonable barrister could not have come to the conclusion that dishonesty could be pleaded or maintained, that the court can conclude that there was a breach of the Code. Even bearing in mind that degree of latitude, I have reached the conclusion, albeit with some hesitation, that, at least on the material which to my knowledge would have been available to the respondents from the time the case was pleaded

a   against Mr Scott onwards, there was simply insufficient material to justify an
    allegation of dishonesty being pleaded and maintained against Mr Scott.

    [143] Mr Powell and Mr Mansfield contend that the respondents could have
    relied on inference from primary facts, and could have hoped that further and
    better evidence would appear on discovery or exchange of witness statements, or
    even on cross-examination. However, as is clear from what was said by Lord
b   Hutton in the *Three Rivers* case ([2001] 2 All ER 513 at [147]) that sort of
    consideration does not automatically justify any allegation of dishonesty:
    whether it is justified 'depends on the particular facts of the case'. I do not
    consider that it did apply in the case of Mr Scott. His involvement was for such a
    short period. The evidence against him was not based on the Browns' knowledge
    of him or his activities, or any documentary evidence, or any witness statement.
c   There really was no more than the Browns' obsessive suspicions. If there was a
    pleadable case against the Bennetts and the APA defendants, the correct course
    would have been to start the action against them, and so add Mr Scott if
    subsequent evidence justified it. Accordingly, in the case of Mr Scott, I have
    reached the conclusion that, at least based on the evidence which can be looked
d   at, there was no proper basis for pleading or maintaining an allegation of
    dishonesty against him.

    [144] However, that is not the end of the matter so far as Mr Scott is
    concerned. I have to consider whether, none the less, Mr Scott's application
    should not proceed, in the light of the possibility of there having been material
    before the respondents, in respect of which the Browns are entitled to claim, and
e   do claim, privilege, which could or would justify their having pleaded and
    maintained the allegation of dishonesty against Mr Scott. I doubt that there
    would have been any such material, but I do not consider that doubt is enough.
    It seems to me that fairness to the respondents and the reasoning in *Ridehalgh v
    Horsefield* [1994] 3 All ER 848 at 866, [1994] Ch 205 at 237 require the conclusion
f   that there is no realistic possibility of there having been privileged material
    available to the respondents which have justified the pleading and maintaining
    the allegation of dishonesty against Mr Scott, before his application can proceed
    to the second stage.

    [145] The sort of possible factors which have persuaded me that the Bennetts'
    application should not be allowed to proceed on this ground apply, albeit with
g   significantly less force, but with sufficient force, to Mr Scott's application. Purely
    by way of hypothetical example, the Browns seem to me to have been prepared
    to exaggerate, or even to make up, facts in particular as to what was said
    contemporaneously. It is far from inconceivable, for instance, that they could
    have stated to the respondents that the discussion they had with Mr Evans about
h   the running of the Company in late 1990 included information which helped
    establish a claim in dishonesty against Mr Scott. Although any such statement
    would almost certainly have been inaccurate, it would have been something
    which the respondents were entitled, possibly even bound, to take into account.

    [146] Indeed, there is the obvious point that, after he was instructed,
j   Mr Asprey may well have been concerned about pleading dishonesty against
    Mr Scott in light of the scanty evidence against him (if based, for instance, on the
    contents of the 12 complaints made by the Browns). He may have sought specific
    instructions on that issue. He may have been given what amounted to factual
    evidence by the Browns which they did not subsequently seek to maintain. Or
    he may have been told by the Browns of evidence which they were confident, or
    even which they believed, a third party (eg Mr Evans) would give about

Mr Scott's involvement. I do not believe that this is a fanciful possibility; in other words, I cannot say that there is no real possibility of this sort of thing having *a* occurred. I think that the fact that the Browns were paranoid about their treatment, and obsessed with the fact that they had been dishonestly deprived of the value of their shares in the Company, renders it more likely than would otherwise be the case, that they would have put alleged facts, inferences or suspicions to the respondents, or promised or suggested to the respondents that *b* some further evidence would become available, which could have justified the respondents pleading and maintaining a claim for dishonesty against Mr Scott. As I have mentioned, the court should accord to counsel a margin of appreciation in relation to a decision as to whether it is proper to plead and maintain an allegation of dishonesty, and, while I consider that, on the known material, the respondents would have strayed outside that margin, it would not have been a very great *c* amount. I do not therefore think it would have required a great deal more material, or indication or promise of more material, before what appears, on the available evidence, to be unjustified could have been justified. In these circumstances, I have come to the conclusion that I should not let the wasted costs application against Mr Scott proceed. *d*

[147] I turn to Mr Evans, who, unlike Mr Scott, had been a long-serving director of the Company, having been appointed in 1978. Mr Brown said that he and Mr Evans were close friends, and that Mr Evans apparently had generally agreed with Mr Brown about the Bennetts (whom Mr Brown described as being 'single minded in their lust for control of the Company') and about the failure to *e* open new shops and to reduce head office costs. Although Mr Evans did not support Mr Brown when, according to Mr Brown, he raised these failures at board meetings, Mr Brown said he understood that this reticence was caused by Mr Evans' fear of losing his job. The highest any allegation made against him went in terms of acts or defaults was that he did not take steps to ensure that shops were opened more quickly or that head office expenses were reduced. The *f* case against him on the basis of available evidence looks very weak indeed.

[148] On the other hand, Mr Evans had been a director for a long time, and indeed had been a director throughout the time that the Bennetts and Mr Freeman were directors. It is therefore inherently more likely that he would have known of, or even been party to, any dishonest acts or plans than would *g* Mr Scott. Further, unlike in the case of Mr Scott, the Browns would have been able to say that head office costs had got out of control during the period Mr Evans was a director, and they could have said the same about the delay in opening new shops. Additionally, the fact (according to Mr Brown) that Mr Evans was frightened of losing his directorship could have been a reason why he did not *h* take steps to challenge what the Bennetts and Mr Freeman were dishonestly doing. Further, after the receivership, Mr Evans was employed by Oasis and was granted share options in that company, but the grant of these options must have been of little if any weight because they were only granted in March 1993.

[149] I am in some doubt as to whether, on the material I know was available *j* to the respondents, there was sufficient to justify pleading or maintaining an allegation of dishonesty against Mr Evans. On balance, I think there was sufficient evidence to justify that course. However, if I am wrong on that, then I would still not permit Mr Evans' application to proceed, for the same reason that Mr Scott's application is not to proceed. If I consider that there is a real possibility of there having been further material available to the respondents, but not known to me

a because it is privileged, which would have justified their drafting and maintaining proceedings against Mr Scott, then that must apply a fortiori to Mr Evans.

[150] Finally, there is Mr Sarson. He was the company secretary, but he was never a director of the Company. Consequently, a point was taken to the effect that there could have been no claim against him in any event. I do not consider that there is anything in that point so far as his application for a wasted costs order

b is concerned. In my judgment, even if it were to transpire that he had no fiduciary duty to the Company, it seems to me that he might still arguably have been a proper defendant in the conspiracy claim. In any event, it is arguable that an employee, particularly a senior employee, such as a company secretary, owes, at least in some circumstances, a fiduciary duty, or a duty akin thereto, to the company. After all, Rattee J only struck out one aspect of the claim against

c Mr Sarson, and even that aspect was reinstated by the Court of Appeal.

[151] So far as the material available in relation to Mr Sarson is concerned, the period of his alleged involvement was a little longer than that of Mr Scott: it was from about March 1990, when he became company secretary. In that position, the respondents say that he must have, at least arguably, appreciated the

d problems created by the Bennetts' failure to cut head office expenses or to open new shops. Further, Mr Sarson was involved with the Bennetts' lockout, and, according to the Browns, lied about it. He was also responsible for the board minutes which, according to the Browns, were inaccurate. Additionally, he prepared the three projections for carrying on the businesses of the Company through a new entity (eventually Oasis) following any potential receivership.

e Subsequently, he was employed by Oasis. He also received options in Oasis, but, again, that was only in March 1993. Mr Sarson was mentioned in Mr Brown's evidence, but his involvement in the dishonesty was really based on surmise: apart from the facts to which I have referred, there were the facts that he had attended board meetings, at which he must have realised the existence and cause

f of the Company's parlous financial state.

[152] In my view, the basis for raising a claim of dishonesty against Mr Sarson was stronger than in relation to Mr Scott. Although the grounds put forward for justifying an allegation of dishonesty against Mr Sarson were in some ways weaker (e g his relatively short tenure at the Company) and in other respects stronger (e g the fact that he was involved in the lockout) than against Mr Evans,

g it seems to me that the overall strength against him was not dissimilar. I think that the available material against Mr Sarson rendered it equally justifiable to allege dishonesty against him as it did in relation to Mr Evans. However, even if there was not sufficient evidence, on the basis of what I know, to justify pleading and maintaining an allegation of dishonesty against Mr Sarson, I consider that his

h application for a wasted costs order should not proceed, in light of the fact that there is a real possibility of there having been material, which is subject to privilege in favour of the Browns (and which I cannot therefore see), which could justify alleging and maintaining a plea of dishonesty against him.

j *The position of Abrahamsons and Mr Timothy Evans*

[153] For the reasons so far given, I do not think it right to let any of the wasted costs applications in relation to the main aspect proceed to the second stage. However, it is right to record that there is another reason why I would not have let these applications proceed against Abrahamsons. Although both solicitors and counsel can be responsible for a pleading, there will be circumstances in which the court may conclude that one or other of them bears substantially

more, or indeed all, of that responsibility. In relation to the present applications, if I had thought that any of them should otherwise proceed to the second stage, I would none the less have ordered that they should not proceed as against Abrahamsons. Although the question of whether or not dishonesty can properly be pleaded is a matter on which a solicitor will have responsibilities, the court will normally take the view that the main responsibility for the contents of a particular pleading is that of the advocate who signs the pleading. Similarly, while each case will depend on its facts, the primary responsibility for maintaining a case in court is that of the person exercising the right of audience. Of course, in any particular case, the pleader or advocate may be able to establish that, on the facts of the case, the responsibility for a particular impropriety was that of his instructing solicitor, and was not in any way his fault.

[154] When it comes to pleading dishonesty or maintaining dishonesty in court, it is plainly up to the person pleading or making the allegation to satisfy himself that there is sufficient material to justify the pleading or allegation. In some cases, even where the primary liability is that of the pleader or advocate, the responsibility for an improper allegation of dishonesty may lie with the solicitor as well as—or even instead of—with the advocate. In the present case, Abrahamsons were a relatively small firm, and although not inexperienced in litigation, it does not seem that they had much experience in substantial and complex proceedings of the sort exemplified by the action. They were quite closely involved with their clients, the Browns, in the sense of having acted for them for a significant time before the action started. They went to two successive respected and experienced Chancery junior counsel who were in highly-regarded chambers, who (in the case of Mr Asprey) settled and resettled the proceedings alleging dishonesty and effectively supported them in a number of appearances and a number of subsequent pleadings thereafter, and who (in the case of Mr Timothy Evans) impliedly supported the allegations on at least two court appearances. They also instructed a reputable and highly-experienced Queen's Counsel in highly-regarded chambers, who also effectively approved the allegations, by supporting the pleaded case and advancing it in court. Further, the Browns' case was funded by the Board, who would not have paid Abrahamsons for reviewing the advice of junior and leading counsel, particularly on a point which was more in the sphere of counsel than that of a solicitor.

[155] It is also right to say that, even if I had thought that any of the main applications should go to the second stage against Mr Oliver and Mr Asprey, I would not have permitted them to proceed to that stage against Mr Timothy Evans. It is true that he took on the responsibility (with Mr Oliver) for the Browns' case in the sense of appearing for them on at least two hearings as well as settling the skeleton argument. However, by the time he was instructed, the pleadings had all been settled and the action was well advanced; his involvement, at least in court, was on purely procedural matters; he had been brought into a case which a respected leader had been involved from the start, and remained involved. Further, it seems likely that he was party to advising the Board in such a way as to the discontinuance of legal aid. Bearing in mind these factors, it would, in any event, have been wrong to let the main application proceed against Mr Timothy Evans.

(H) THE MORE SPECIFIC CLAIMS FOR WASTED COSTS

[156] As I have mentioned, some of the applicants also have relatively specific and limited claims for wasted costs orders. First, it is contended on behalf of Oasis

a   in this part of the judgment that it is entitled to recover its costs from Mr Oliver, Mr Asprey (counsel) and/or Abrahamsons (in this part the respondents), because the claim against it stood no chance of success, essentially for the reason that it was struck out by Rattee J and the Court of Appeal. Secondly, the injunction applicants contend that they should recover their costs from the respondents, ie counsel and/or Abrahamsons in connection with discharge of the Injunction. I
b   shall deal with those arguments in turn.

The claim by Oasis
   [157] The claim pleaded on behalf of the Browns against Oasis was based on the contention that Oasis was liable in some way to account for the benefit it had enjoyed as a result of having received the business of the Company which was
c   purchased from the receivers, knowing that the receivership had been dishonestly engineered for this purpose by, or with the assistance of, the other applicants. Even though Rattee J and the Court of Appeal accepted that the Browns' claims against the other defendants, based on their alleged dishonesty, were maintainable on the face of the pleadings, they none the less struck out the
d   claim against Oasis on the basis that it could not be maintained, even on the face of the pleadings.
   [158] I accept that, at least in some circumstances, a lawyer who puts his name to a pleading against a defendant, and who is responsible for pursuing the claim against the defendant, in circumstances in which he appreciated or ought to have appreciated that the claim was completely hopeless, could be liable for a wasted
e   costs order. Such a proposition could be said to derive support from para 704(b) of the relevant edition of the Code which provided, so far as relevant, that: 'a barrister ... must not draft any statement of case, witness statement, affidavit, notice of appeal or other document containing ... any contention which he does not consider to be properly arguable.'
f   **[159]** On this basis reliance is placed on the fact that Rattee J and the Court of Appeal could only have reached their conclusions that the claim raised against Oasis was to be struck out on the basis that it was effectively hopeless.
   [160] In my judgment, the mere fact that the court considers it appropriate to strike out a claim against a defendant does not mean, without more, that it was therefore inappropriate for counsel or solicitors to have raised the claim. In many
g   cases, the court may think it right to strike out a claim, even where the striking out application raises a difficult point of law. The court may well conceive that it is right to determine a point of law on a strike-out application, on the basis that, particularly if the point is determined in favour of the defendant, it will eliminate or considerably cut down the cost, time and effort in pursuing the particular claim
h   or the particular defendant any further. Indeed, if a claim against a defendant is bound to fail as a matter of law, it is rarely appropriate to permit further cost, time and effort being expended in connection with the claim.
   [161] Accordingly, at least in many cases, I consider that there is no more justification in seeking a wasted costs order against a lawyer who has raised a
j   claim which is ultimately struck out, than in seeking a wasted costs order against any lawyer who has raised any point of law which turns out to be wrong. Of course, each case must be judged on its own facts: there may be some cases where the pleading and pursuing of a hopeless point does amount to misconduct—ie it is an abuse. However, in my firm view, the mere fact that a claim fails, even on a striking out application, is not enough to justify a wasted costs order. Indeed, as I read it, the Court of Appeal in *Ridehalgh v Horsefield* [1994] 3 All ER 848 at 863,

[1994] Ch 205 at 234 accepted that even pursuing a 'hopeless case' will not always be 'an abuse of process'. That point is underscored by what the Court of Appeal said in relation to the facts of *Ridehalgh v Horsefield* itself: $\quad$ *a*

> 'After two days of argument by counsel, and having reserved judgment, this court was able to take a clear view of the legal point at issue. This view was directly contrary to the solicitors; and is plainly right. But it does not follow that the solicitors were negligent in forming the opinion they did. We *b* do not think they were.' (See [1994] 3 All ER 848 at 872, [1994] Ch 205 at 244.)

[162] In the present case, I am firmly of the view that, although it is fair to say that (conceivably with the assistance of the wisdom of hindsight) the Browns' claim against Oasis was pretty optimistic, it was a long way from being an abuse. *c* It would be inappropriate to rehearse the reasons accepted by Rattee J and the Court of Appeal for striking out the claim against Oasis: they are set out at [1998] 2 BCLC 97 at 100–106 and [1999] 1 BCLC 649 at 653–659. While both the courts obviously reached a clear conclusion (because otherwise they would not have struck out the claim) and expressed themselves at times in firm terms, it is clear *d* both from the content and, indeed, from the length, of those passages, that there was a case against Oasis which was undoubtedly properly arguable, in the sense that it could be seriously maintained in argument. That seems to me to be the end of the matter so far as any claim for a wasted costs order in favour of Oasis on this ground is concerned. If that were not enough, it is to be noted that, although Rattee J refused the Browns permission to appeal his decision to strike *e* out the claim against Oasis, Robert Walker LJ obviously thought the point sufficiently arguable to justify giving permission to appeal (see [1999] 1 BCLC 649 at 650).

[163] So far as Abrahamsons are concerned, I believe that there is an additional defence, namely that this was, in any event, an aspect upon which they would *f* have been entitled to shelter behind their reliance upon counsel. As I have mentioned, whether or not the Browns had a valid claim against Oasis on the bases of their pleaded case, appears to me to turn on issues of law which were considered by Rattee J and the Court of Appeal in their respective judgments. Even if I am wrong in my view that the pleaded claim against Oasis was sufficiently arguable to be advanced and presented by counsel, I would still think *g* it wrong to hold Abrahamsons liable for the fact that the claim was pleaded and argued, in circumstances where counsel had plainly taken the view that it was appropriate to do so, as a matter of law. Liability for receipt of assets which were allegedly obtained dishonestly, which is how, in very general terms, the claim against Oasis was framed, raises points of principle on which a firm of solicitors, *h* particularly a small firm such as Abrahamsons, would be entitled to consult counsel, and in respect of which they would be entitled to proceed on the basis that counsel's advice was right, unless it was absurd or self-contradictory, and there is no suggestion of that in the present case. All the more so where legal aid was involved, and solicitors would not expect to be paid by the Board for *j* reviewing counsel's advice on a point of law.

The claim by the injunction applicants

[164] The injunction applicants contend that, if the respondent lawyers acting for the Browns had carried out their duty to the court when seeking injunctive relief from Ferris J on 17 May 1996, he would not have granted any injunction,

a and consequently all the costs incurred on behalf of the injunction applicants in connection with the Injunction, and in particular in connection with the discharge of the Injunction, would not have been incurred. On this basis, the injunction applicants contend that it is likely that the court would make a wasted costs order against the respondents in respect of the costs of discharging the Injunction.

b [165] I turn first to consider the breach of duty alleged by the injunction applicants in this connection. The duty is that of a claimant, who is seeking relief against a defendant in his absence, to give full disclosure to the court from which the claimant is seeking the relief. The existence of such a duty cannot be doubted, any more than the fact that such a duty was incumbent on the Browns and their legal advisors at the time of the hearing before Ferris J, or, indeed, any more than

c the fact that that duty was well established by that time. Thus, in *Siporex Trade SA v Comdel Commodities Ltd* [1986] 2 Lloyd's Rep 428 at 437, Bingham J emphasised that a claimant on such an application must 'identify the crucial points for and against the application', 'identify any likely defences', and 'disclose all facts which reasonably could or would be taken into account by the judge in

d deciding whether to grant the application'.

[166] Having identified the duty alleged to have been breached, I turn to the alleged breach. The injunction applicants contend that Ferris J should have been informed of letters before action (the letters) sent to the Bennetts and Oasis on 14 October by Jaques & Lewis, and to Mr Michael Bennett on 21 June 1995 by

e Silvermans, and of the complaints (the complaints) of which some or all of the defendants knew, made by the Browns to the nine organisations and three individuals to which I have referred.

[167] It appears clear, subject to one point, that neither of the letters and none of the complaints were drawn to the attention of Ferris J, and it also seems clear

f that the significance of those documents in relation to the claim before him was not drawn to his attention. It is fair to say that there was a reference to one or two of the complaints in the schedule to the draft of the Browns' statement of claim which was before Ferris J. However, it seems to me to be quite unrealistic to suggest that he should have been expected to spot the significance of a passing reference to a couple of the complaints let alone appreciated its potential

g significance in relation to the injunction sought from him.

[168] In my judgment, the letters and the complaints should have been drawn to the attention of Ferris J, and I do not understand Mr Powell or Mr Mansfield to argue otherwise. The Browns' case was that injunctive relief should be granted against the injunction applicants because there was a real risk that they would

h destroy, hide, or deface documents relevant to the Browns' claim, once they knew that an action based on their alleged dishonesty on connection with the Company was actually being brought against them. Where such an allegation is being made against a defendant who is not present and has had no notice of the application, it seems to me clear that the court should be told if some of the

j defendants had been warned of the action (as they had been in the letters) and that most of the defendants knew that at least some of the matters to be raised in the proceedings had been formally raised against them publicly (as they had been in the complaints). In other words, it would be highly germane for the court to know that at least one of the injunction applicants had actually been told that the proceedings concerned were to be issued, and that most of them knew that the Browns had been formally and publicly pursuing their allegations against them.

[169] The next issue is whether Ferris J would have granted the Injunction if
he had been told of these facts. That is inevitably a matter of speculation and, to *a*
some extent, a matter of impression based upon a reading of his judgment. At
least as currently advised, it seems to me unlikely that Ferris J would have granted
the Injunction had he been told of the letters and the complaints, or even any of
them. He had no hesitation in refusing to grant a search order, and he indicated
a preparedness to grant the Injunction almost as something as a consolation for *b*
the Browns. Lindsay and Knox JJ each expressed the view that there was (to
quote Knox J) 'something of a void in relation to the necessary evidence for the
continuation of the injunction'. Indeed, Knox J concluded that the evidence
before the court 'was inadequate to warrant the grant of the injunctive relief', a
view with which he thought Lindsay J would have agreed, in light of his earlier
judgment. In effect, Knox J and, as I read his judgment, Lindsay J were expressing *c*
the view that they would not have granted any injunctive relief at all. To my
mind, that tends to support the conclusion that Ferris J was likely to have been
close to refusing any injunctive relief, which renders it all the more likely that he
would have refused the Injunction if he had been shown some of the letters
and/or complaints. *d*

[170] On that basis, it seems to me to follow that it is likely that the injunction
applicants will establish that there was a breach of the duty to give full disclosure
to Ferris J, which resulted in his granting the Injunction, which in turn resulted in
costs being incurred by the injunction applicants, which would not otherwise
have been incurred, namely costs in connection with the discharge of the
Injunction. That leaves two questions to be considered. First, it is likely that in *e*
those circumstances the court would make a wasted costs order against some or
all of the respondents? Secondly, if so, is there any reason why the application for
wasted costs against them should not proceed to the second and final stage? I
shall take those two questions in turn.

[171] The likelihood of the court making a wasted costs order against the *f*
respondents must depend on whether they knew of or saw the letters or the
complaints. At the moment at any rate, I think it is very unlikely indeed that
Abrahamsons did not have to know about the letter before the action of 21 June
1995, ie the second of the letters. That is because it had been sent by Silvermans,
a firm of solicitors to which Mr Abrahamson of Abrahamsons was a consultant at
the time. I also consider it likely that Abrahamsons would have known about, *g*
and indeed would have had a copy of, the earlier letter before action. It also
seems to me likely, indeed very likely, that Abrahamsons knew of at least some
of the complaints.

[172] My view that Abrahamsons are likely to have been in possession of, and
to have known of, at least some of the letters and the complaints, is supported by *h*
an exchange of correspondence between Berwin Leighton Paisner, the solicitors
for the Oasis defendants, and Abrahamsons, shortly after the Injunction was
granted. In a letter of 30 May 1996 Berwin Leighton Paisner drew attention to
the non-disclosure, and Abrahamsons' reply on 11 June 1996 was that the letters
'were written long ago ... and their effect must have long since been spent' that *j*
two of the complaints had been referred to in the statement of claim, and one of
them had been discussed in front of Ferris J to explain the derivation of an exhibit,
and consequently that it was 'absurd to suppose that the details of those
complaints should have been put before the court'. Abrahamsons' argument
about the letters having been written some time ago misses the point in my view:
once the letters were received by the recipient, he was on notice as to the

a imminence of proceedings and he had the incentive and opportunity to destroy incriminating documents. I also consider their argument about the complaints is wrong for the reasons already given.

[173] So far as counsel are concerned, at the moment it seems to me likely that at least some of the letters and/or complaints were known to them. It is obviously probable that the papers sent down to counsel would have included a
b letter before action, and that counsel was presumably aware of two of the complaints, for the very reason advanced by Abrahamsons in their letter of 11 June 1996. I think there is a very powerful case for saying that, if counsel were aware of these documents, or even of some of these documents, it was not enough merely to refer to them for the purpose of explaining an exhibit, or even to refer to them specifically. They should have drawn to the attention of Ferris J
c the fact that the defendants, against whom an injunction was being sought on the basis that they might destroy evidence if they knew that proceedings were being brought, had knowingly been the subject of complaints in connection with the same matter some time ago, and, at least in some cases, knew that proceedings had been formally threatened in a letter before action. Merely to include relevant
d documents in the evidence given to the court is not enough; nor is merely to make a passing reference to such documents. The court's attention should be drawn to the fact that the documents give rise to an argument against the grant of an injunction, at least when it should have been pretty clear to counsel that that was so.

e [174] A point taken on behalf of Abrahamsons, and (to my mind much more strongly) on behalf of counsel, is that it is a matter of speculation as to what they knew about the letters before action and/or the complaints at the time of the application to Ferris J, and that it would be unfair to let the application proceed against them in circumstances where one has to rely on speculation, even if it is based on some evidence and inherent likelihood. In the case of Abrahamsons, I
f reject that argument, simply in light of the evidence already available, which seems to show, that at least some of the documents in question were in their possession and known to them. In the case of both Abrahamsons and counsel, I reject that argument because it appears to me likely that the court would not accept the whole basis on which it rests. The argument is based on the contention that the respondents are not entitled to inform the court as to which, if any, of the
g letters and complaints they saw or knew of prior to the hearing before Ferris J, on the grounds that they would only have known of these documents through what they were told by or on behalf of their lay client, that that information is privileged, and, as the privilege is that of the Browns, who do not waive it, the information cannot be put before the court. At least as at present advised, I think
h that argument is wrong.

[175] The documents concerned, namely the letters and the complaints, are of themselves plainly nor privileged. Of course, what might have been said about them to or by the Browns by or to their legal advisors, in connection with the action or the projected action, would be privileged. However, it seems to me that
j the question of whether counsel and/or Abrahamsons had seen or knew of some or all of these letters or complaints, and if so which, at the time of the hearing before Ferris J, was not the subject of privilege. As I have mentioned, the evidence that Abrahamsons knew of the letters and at least some of the complaints appears to me, at the moment, to be very strong. In all the circumstances, I find it hard to see why the court should not be entitled to know whether counsel had seen or knew of these documents at the time of the hearing before Ferris J.

[176] Given that it seems likely that it will be established that Abrahamsons
saw at least one of the two letters and at least some of the complaints, all of which   a
were in any event open documents in themselves, I find it hard to see how the
question of whether counsel saw the documents at or before the hearing in front
of Ferris J is a matter which of itself attracts client's privilege. I accept that the
mere fact that the question concerns not what the clients told their solicitors, but
what documents their solicitors passed on to counsel, does not of itself prevent   b
the strict rules of privilege applying. However, the point is that the court is
simply concerned to know whether, at a hearing without notice where counsel
were under a duty to the court to reveal the existence, terms and effect of
documents which might harm their client's application, they knew of or had in
their possession such documents. It is not concerned with when or whether the
documents were sent or shown to counsel by his instructing solicitor, let alone   c
what was said to or by counsel about the documents.

[177] Mr Stewart suggested that, even if privilege was not involved,
confidence might be invoked by the Browns in relation to the question of what
counsel saw or knew. This was not a point which was developed. As I see it, at
its highest, if the Browns could claim confidence in respect of that matter, it   d
would not be an absolute right, unlike privilege. I have no hesitation in
concluding that the court, at the second stage, would be likely to hold that such
a bare claim to confidence must yield to the strong and legitimate interest of the
injunction applicants being informed of the relevant factors. Indeed, there is a
public interest in the proper administration of justice that any such confidence
should be overridden in this case.   e

[178] I accept that it is conceivable that, at the second stage, the court might
conclude that it cannot, for one reason or another, safely conclude that counsel
saw either of the letters or any of the complaints, but, at any rate at this stage, I
think that is unlikely. In the event, given that neither of the two counsel involved
nor Abrahamsons have denied that they knew of the letters and of at least some   f
of the complaints, at the time that they were before Ferris J, I conclude that this
aspect of the application for wasted costs should proceed to the second stage
against each of them, unless there is a good reason to the contrary. It would
obviously be preferable to rule at this stage on the issue of privilege and I would
have done so, if it had not appeared that my present view may have taken
Mr Powell and Mr Mansfield by surprise, and, to be fair to them, the point was   g
not raised in terms in the skeleton arguments of Ms Dohmann or Mr Slowe.

[179] On behalf of Abrahamsons it is contended that, if counsel saw the letters
and complaints and did not draw them to the court's attention, then Abrahamsons
cannot be held liable, because they were entitled to leave the matter to counsel.
At the moment, I am inclined to reject that argument. The authorities establish   h
that, in many cases, a solicitor who has acted on the advice of counsel cannot be
open to criticism, provided, of course, he properly instructed counsel. However,
in some cases the court may conclude that the advice given was so plainly wrong
or absurd or in some other way dubious that the solicitor cannot escape liability
on this ground (for a well-known example see *Davy-Chiesman v Davy-Chiesman*   j
[1984] 1 All ER 321, [1984] Fam 48, considered, approved and expanded in *Locke
v Camberwell Health Authority* [1991] 2 Med LR 249 at 254). Further, in some
circumstances, particularly those involving a duty to do something, it can fairly
be said that a solicitor owes a duty which is parallel to the same duty of the
barrister. In my judgment, there is at least a powerful case, particularly where the
solicitor is likely to know the facts more intimately than the barrister, and

a particularly where the duty is owed to the court, that the solicitor should not escape liability on the ground that he left matters to counsel, even though the issue involved proceedings in court.

[180] In the present case, the duty in question was the duty to the court to give full disclosure on an application without notice. This is a duty which was and is well known, and is a very important principle of practice and justice: accordingly,

b it is a principle of which any solicitor involved in litigation should know and observe. Further, Mr Abrahamson was in a particularly good position to know of the documents and their comments. He had been involved in assisting, advising and acting for the Browns in connection with their concerns about the activities of some or all of the defendants in relation to the Company for a relatively long period, whereas counsel will only have been comparatively

c recently engaged.

[181] My view that the application of the injunction applicants should be permitted to proceed as against Abrahamsons, appears to me to reinforce the conclusion that the application should also be permitted to proceed against counsel. It seems to me to be likely on the evidence at the moment (bearing in

d mind inherent likelihood, the absence of any denial or alleged inability to recollect on the part of counsel despite having sworn affidavits, and my present view on the privilege point) that, at the second stage, the court will conclude that counsel saw or knew of at least one of the letters and some of the complaints. I must emphasise that, having heard full argument and considered the evidence then before it, the court might at the second stage decide differently. However,

e given that I think at the moment that it is likely that the court will so conclude, it appears to me that it could well be unfair on Abrahamsons if I permitted the injunction applicants' application to proceed against them, without also permitting the application to proceed against counsel. If a wasted costs order was made against Abrahamsons alone, because the applications had not

f been permitted to proceed against counsel, then Abrahamsons would have been deprived of the opportunity of sharing the liability of any wasted costs, and, quite conceivably, being able to claim plausibly that any criticism of them would be regarded as softened by the fact that they were not alone.

[182] There is another point, which is highlighted by the privilege argument raised by counsel and Abrahamsons' argument based on the advice they may

g have received from counsel. Where two counsel are involved, as here, each might be able to avoid liability on the basis that, for instance, leading counsel could say that he may not have seen the documents, and junior counsel could say that he may have been told in firm terms by leading counsel that the documents need not be revealed to the court. This leads me to mention a more general

h question not covered by the cases. If it is clear that one party's legal representatives, viewed as a group, must, between them, have been guilty of improper, unreasonable or negligent conduct, but it is not possible because of privilege (or some other reason) to identify which of the representatives it was, can the other party get a wasted costs order against 'the legal ... representatives' as a group and

j leave it to them to sort out how the liability is to be apportioned between them? One can see that such an order could be impracticable (how to apportion) and unfair (in many cases, some of the representatives will have been guiltless and yet they will be caught by the order). But the applicant could be forgiven for thinking that this unfairness would be much less marked than the unfairness of refusing him a wasted costs order, to which he is plainly otherwise entitled against at least one of the legal representatives, simply because of the structure of the legal profession (divided between barristers and solicitors, and between junior and leading counsel) simply because s 51(7) of the Supreme Court Act 1981 refers to a wasted costs order being made against 'any' legal representative.

[183] Finally, I turn to consider whether there is any other reason why the injunction applicants' application should not proceed to a second stage. Two arguments, in support of the contention that the matter should not proceed to a second stage, have been advanced. The first is based on delay and the second on cost. So far as delay is concerned it is certainly true that it is some time since the injunction proceedings were determined: as I have mentioned, Knox J discharged the Injunction more than five years ago. However, I think that the only issue of fact, which needs to be determined, is what knowledge Abrahamsons and counsel each had of the letters and complaints at the time of the application to Ferris J. That is something which, if necessary, Abrahamsons should be able to investigate through perusal of their files, and which counsel should be able to discover, if necessary, by calling for their briefs and documents enclosed therewith, which, as I see it, they have a right to ask to call for. I accept that it may transpire that, for one reason or another, it is not possible fairly to assess what counsel knew, or, conceivably, what Abrahamsons knew, in this connection. However, although evidence has been filed by each counsel, and Mr Abrahamson has had the opportunity to file evidence, none of them has suggested that there is a difficulty in identifying which of the letters and complaints he saw or knew of at the date if the hearing before Ferris J. Given that my current view is that privilege does not present a problem, I do not presently consider that the delay is likely to present any difficulty. I accept that it may present a difficulty, but that is something which could be raised at the next stage.

[184] Quite apart from this, the possibility of a wasted costs application based on non-disclosure was raised at an early stage. On 30 May 1996, Berwin Leighton Paisners wrote to Abrahamsons drawing their attention to the non-disclosure, and seeking their agreement 'to the withdrawal of the injunction before significant costs are incurred in discharging [it]', and this request was repeated in a later letter of 17 June 1996. Even more significantly, on 18 July 1996, Berwin Leighton Paisners wrote to Abrahamsons expressly to put them 'on notice that our clients intend to apply for a wasted costs order against your firm and against the counsel who represented your clients' on the application to Ferris J. This letter went on to say that the application would not be made immediately as 'this would not be a productive use of the parties' and the court's time at this stage' but the application would be made 'after trial'. No objection was made to that proposal by Abrahamsons. While that does not appear to me to dispose of the argument that the injunction applicants' application is made too late, it is a powerful factor in their favour. First Abrahamsons (and, presumably, through them, counsel) had an opportunity to object to that course. Secondly, we were on notice, almost from the start, that a wasted costs application would be made. Further, in *Ridehalgh v Horsefield* [1994] 3 All ER 848 at 867, [1994] Ch 205 at 238, the Court of Appeal stated that 'speaking generally ... in the ordinary way applications for wasted costs are best left until after the end of the trial'.

[185] The second argument raised against the application of the injunction applicants proceeding is that the cost would be disproportionate, particularly bearing in mind the costs of the present hearing. I am unimpressed with that argument. For the reasons I have given, it appears to me at the moment that the injunction applicants have a fairly strong case for seeking a wasted costs order in relation to the Injunction, and that the issues to be raised at the second stage are

a unlikely to be particularly complex and should not take a long time to determine. The issue of privilege may have to be considered; it may also be that some or all of the respondents may say that they cannot state whether they saw any of the letters of the complaints, despite having looked at those documents which they are entitled to look at and call for. If that happened, then it may well be that, unsatisfactory though it may seem to the court and unfair though it may seem to

b the injunction applicants, their application would have to be dismissed. The only alternative would seem to be to permit cross-examination of either or both counsel or Abrahamsons. First, that would almost certainly be inappropriate (in light of what was said in *Ridehalgh v Horsefield* [1994] 3 All ER 848 at 867, [1994] Ch 205 at 238 and by the Privy Council in *Harley v McDonald, Glasgow Harley (a firm) v McDonald* [2001] 2 AC 678 at [50]). Secondly, the exercise would be likely to be

c fruitless. Thirdly, it is difficult to see how cross-examination could proceed without quickly descending into privileged territory. It may be that, even in such circumstances, the court will be persuaded, on the balance of probabilities, that Abrahamsons, and indeed possibly both or one or both counsel, saw or had sufficient knowledge of the letters or complaints to justify a wasted costs order, but

d there are obvious possible difficulties with such a course. All I should say at this stage is that, bearing in mind the factors to which I have referred, and assuming that my present view on the privilege issue is correct, it does seem more 'likely' than not that a wasted costs order would be made in favour of the injunction applicants. Of course, if the application ultimately fails, then the court may well think it right to award costs against the injunction applicants: that is the risk they take.

e [186] A slightly different point is that the costs, indeed the court time, taken up by the present hearing have been substantial, and, leaving aside the present aspect, the applications have failed. In those circumstances, runs the argument, it would be wrong to let some of the applications proceed in relation to a comparatively small aspect, namely in relation to the costs of the Injunction. I am unimpressed

f with that argument. The balance of the applications have failed, and I will, no doubt, have to decide the issue of costs in relation to them, but, whatever is decided on that aspect, I cannot see how it logically impinges on the appropriate course to take in relation to the costs of the Injunction. If the injunction applicants would otherwise be entitled to those costs, and indeed to the costs of the present application so far as they relate to that aspect, it seems to me that it would result in

g real injustice to them if their application was barred in light of the fate of the balance of their applications. This conclusion is reinforced by two factors. First, I cannot see any injustice being caused to any of the respondents if the application is to proceed: if the injunction applicants are entitled to their costs, then it would seem to be something of a windfall for the respondents if the application is stayed; if they

h are not entitled to their costs, then the respondents would have a strong case for recovering their costs if and when the application fails. Quite apart from this, although I have dismissed the main application for a wasted costs order, it seems to me that at least some of the injunction applicants (especially Mr Evans and Mr Sarson) may have an understandable sense of grievance as a result; refusing to

j permit their application for the wasted costs in relation to the Injunction to proceed to the second stage would justifiably enhance that sense of grievance.

(I) CONCLUSIONS

[187] For these reasons, I conclude: (1) s 51 of the 1981 Act extends to wasted costs applications by one party against the legal representatives of another party to the same proceedings; (2) a barrister can be liable for wasted costs under s 51,

notwithstanding the fact that the conduct complained of against him was not
when he was actually exercising his rights of audience; (3) on the issue of
causation, liability for wasted costs is to be determined by reference to the
question of whether, but for the conduct complained of, the costs in question
would, on the balance of probabilities, have been incurred; in this case, I do not
think that they would have been; (4) with the exception of Mr Scott's application,
all the general applications for wasted costs fail, on the basis that the pleading of
dishonesty could be justified; (5) in any event, all the general applications
(including that of Mr Scott) fail because there is a real risk of unfairness to the
respondents in light of the Browns' insistence on privilege; (6) even if any of the
general applications had proceeded to the second stage against Mr Oliver and
Mr Asprey, I would not have thought it right that they should proceed against
Abrahamsons (who were entitled to rely on counsel) or Mr Timothy Evans
(whose involvement was late and limited); (7) Oasis' application based on the fact
that the claim against it was struck out fails: the mere fact that a claim pleaded and
maintained by counsel was struck out is insufficient to justify a wasted costs
order; (8) on the arguments I have heard it is, in my view, more likely (than not)
that a wasted costs order would be made in favour of Mr Michael Bennett,
Mr Evans, Mr Sarson and APA in relation to their costs of discharging the
Injunction granted by Ferris J, against Mr Oliver, Mr Asprey and Abrahamsons;
(9) accordingly, all the applications are dismissed, save on the application referred
to in (8) which can proceed to the second stage.

Order accordingly.

Celia Fox   Barrister.

a # Braymist Ltd and others v Wise Finance Company Ltd
[2002] EWCA Civ 127

b COURT OF APPEAL, CIVIL DIVISION

JUDGE, LATHAM AND ARDEN LJJ

15, 16 JANUARY, 20 FEBRUARY 2002

Contract – Parties – Unformed company – Solicitors to unformed company signing
c agreement for sale of land as its agents – Whether agent for unformed company entitled
to sue on contract – Whether agreement signed by and on behalf of party to agreement
– Companies Act 1985, s 36C(1) – Law of Property (Miscellaneous Provisions) Act 1989,
s 2.

d The respondent, as agents and solicitors for B Ltd, signed an agreement for the
sale of a piece of land to the appellant purchaser. Unbeknown to the purchaser,
B Ltd was then in the process of incorporation and accordingly it was not in
existence when the agreement was signed. The purchaser failed to complete. In
subsequent proceedings against the purchaser for breach of contract, the judge
held that B Ltd's solicitors could enforce the contract against the purchaser. He
e relied on s 36C(1)[a] of the Companies Act 1985 which provided that a contract that
purported to be made by or on behalf of a company at a time when it had not
been formed had effect as one made with the person purporting to act for the
company or as its agent, and that he was personally liable on the contract
accordingly. The judge further concluded that the solicitors were deemed to be
f the vendors even though they had signed the agreement as agents, and that
accordingly the execution of the agreement satisfied the requirement, in s 2[b] of
the Law of Property (Miscellaneous Provisions) Act 1989, for a contract for the
sale of land to be signed by and on behalf of each party to the contract. He
awarded damages to the solicitors, and the purchaser appealed. On its appeal, the
purchaser contended, inter alia, that s 36C(1) of the 1985 Act imposed contractual
g liability on an unformed company's agent, but did not allow the agent to sue on
the contract.

Held – On its true construction, s 36C(1) of the 1985 Act not only entitled a party
who had entered into a contract with an unformed company to enforce that
h contract against the person purporting to act for or as agent of the unformed
company, but also entitled such a person or agent to enforce the contract against
the other party unless such enforcement was otherwise precluded by the
ordinary common law principles governing contractual arrangements. In the
instant case, B Ltd's solicitors were entitled under s 36C(1) to enforce the
j agreement against the purchaser as a party to it. In those circumstances, the
solicitors were to be treated as having signed the agreement on their own behalf
for the purposes of s 2 of the 1989 Act, and the appeal would be dismissed (see
[66], [67], [72], [75]–[77], [83], [85], below).

---

a   Section 36C(1) is set out at [2], below
b   Section 2, so far as material, is set out at [11], below

Notes

For the enforceability of contracts entered into by an agent for an unformed   *a*
company and for the requirement for a signed contract in respect of agreements
for the sale of land, see respectively 1(2) *Halsbury's Laws* (4th edn reissue) para 76
and 42 *Halsbury's Laws* (4th edn reissue) para 33.

For the Companies Act 1985, s 36C, see 8 *Halsbury's Statutes* (4th edn) (1999
reissue) 137.   *b*

For the Law of Property (Miscellaneous Provisions) Act 1989, s 2, see 37
Halsbury's Statutes (4th edn) (1998 reissue) 661.

Cases referred to in judgments

Cundy v Lindsay (1878) 3 App Cas 459, [1874–80] All ER Rep 1149, HL.
East End Dwellings Co Ltd v Finsbury BC [1951] 2 All ER 587, [1952] AC 109, HL.   *c*
Elliott v Pierson [1948] 1 All ER 939, [1948] Ch 452.
Harper & Co v Vigers Bros [1909] 2 KB 549, [1908–10] All ER Rep Ext 1293.
Litster v Forth Dry Dock and Engineering Co Ltd [1989] 1 All ER 1134, [1990] 1 AC
    546, [1989] 2 WLR 634, HL.
Newborne v Sensolid (GB) Ltd [1953] 1 All ER 708, [1954] 1 QB 45, [1953] 2 WLR 596,   *d*
    HL; *affg* [1952] WN 491.
Peyman v Lanjani [1984] 3 All ER 703, [1985] Ch 457, [1985] 2 WLR 154, CA.
Phonogram Ltd v Lane [1981] 3 All ER 182, [1982] QB 938, [1981] 3 WLR 736, CA.
Pinekerry Ltd v Needs (Kenneth) Contractors Ltd (1992) 64 P & CR 245, CA.
Rayner v Grote (1846) 15 M & W 359, (1846) 153 ER 888.   *e*
Schmaltz v Avery (1851) 16 QB 655.
Ubbink Isolatie BV v Dak-en Wandtechniek BV Case 136/87 [1988] ECR 4665.
Universal Steam Navigation Co Ltd v James McKelvie & Co [1923] AC 492, HL.

Cases also cited or referred to in skeleton arguments

Aquis Estates Ltd v Minton [1975] 3 All ER 1043, [1975] 1 WLR 1452, CA.   *f*
Cotronic (UK) v Dezonie [1991] BCLC 721, CA.
Country and Metropolitan Homes Surrey Ltd v Topclaim Ltd [1997] 1 All ER 254,
    [1996] Ch 307.
Cox & Neve's Contract, Re [1891] 2 Ch 109.
Dimsdale Developments (South East) Ltd v De Haan (1983) 47 P & CR 1.   *g*
Marleasing SA v La Comercial Internacional de Alimentación SA Case C-106/89 [1990]
    ECR I-4153
Marshall v Southampton and South West Hampshire Area Health Authority (No 2) Case
    C-271/91 [1993] 4 All ER 586, [1993] ECR-I 4367, ECJ.
Pips (Leisure Productions) Ltd v Walton (1980) 43 P & CR 415.   *h*
Rightside Properties Ltd v Gray [1974] 2 All ER 1169, [1975] Ch 72.
Saxby v Thomas (1890) 64 LT 65, CA.
von Colson v Land Nordrhein-Westfalen Case 14/83 106 [1984] ECR 1891.
Warde v Dixon (1858) 28 LJ Ch 315.

                                                                                  j
Appeal

The defendant, Wise Finance Co Ltd (Wise), appealed with permission of
Etherton J from his order of 2 March 2001 ([2001] All ER (D) 20) declaring forfeit to
the second claimant, William Sturges & Co (Sturges), Wise's deposit under a
contract for the purchase by it of land forming part of Harcombe Wood, Chudleigh,
Devon, and requiring it to pay Sturges the sum of £67,700·58 in damages and

a interest for breach of that contract. The facts are set out in the judgment of Arden LJ.

Mark Blackett-Ord (instructed by *Harris & Co*, Crawley) for Wise.
Barbara Rich (instructed by *William Sturges & Co*) for Sturges.

b *Cur adv vult*

20 February 2002. The following judgments were delivered.

ARDEN LJ.
[1] This is an appeal with the permission of the judge from the order of
c Etherton J dated 2 March 2001 ([2001] All ER (D) 20). By this order the court declared that the respondent, William Sturges & Co (Sturges), had effectively rescinded an agreement dated 28 January 1993 made between (1) Braymist Ltd (Braymist) and (2) The Wise Finance Co Ltd (Wise), the appellant in this appeal, for the purchase by Wise of a parcel of land adjoining the A380, part of Harcombe
d Wood, Chudleigh, Devon (the property). The order also declared that Wise's deposit of £5,000 was forfeit to Sturges. The order dismissed the counterclaim of Wise and ordered Wise within 28 days to pay to Sturges the sum of £67,700·58 representing damages for breach of contract and interest.
[2] The relevant facts can be briefly stated. At the time of the relevant contract, Braymist was in process of incorporation. Its solicitors, Sturges, signed the
e agreement as agents and solicitors for it. The property comprised a piece of land next to a corner site (the adjoining land) where a minor road joined the A380. On part of the adjoining land there stood a filling station. Wise hoped to obtain planning permission to facilitate the removal of the filling station to the property, thus freeing the adjoining land for development. However, the contract was not
f conditional on this planning permission. The principal point in issue flows from the fact that Braymist, the vendor, was not in existence at the time the agreement was signed. Wise was not aware of this at the time the agreement was made. Sturges now seek to enforce the contract against the purchaser by virtue of s 36C(1) of the Companies Act 1985. Accordingly, the first question is whether an agent is not only liable on the contract where his principal is a company in course of formation but
g entitled to sue on it. Section 36C(1) provides:

'A contract which purports to be made by or on behalf of a company at a time when the company has not been formed has effect, subject to any agreement to the contrary, as one made with the person purporting to act for the company or as agent for it, and he is personally liable on the contract
h accordingly.'

I will refer to the concluding clause of this subsection, ie the words 'and he is personally liable on the contract accordingly', as 'the tailpiece'.
[3] Wise made an application for planning permission for the property to be
j purchased on 11 May 1993. On 21 September 1993, that application was refused. The reason given for the refusal was that the property was situated in an area designated as being of great landscape value and that it would be detrimental to the character and appearance of the area and contrary to local policies and planning guidelines. Notice to complete was served on 2 February 1994 pursuant to condition 22 of the National Conditions of Sale (20th edn) which were incorporated into the contract. The notice to complete expired on 21 February 1994. Wise failed

to complete on that day. On 4 March 1994 Sturges notified Wise's solicitor that Braymist had rescinded the agreement and forfeited the deposit.

THE JUDGMENT OF ETHERTON J

[4] Not all of the issues with which the judge dealt arise on this appeal and accordingly I need not summarise them.

[5] The first issue was whether Sturges were entitled to enforce the agreement by virtue of s 36C. The judge pointed out that s 36C(1) was first enacted in s 9(2) of the European Communities Act 1972 and was intended to give effect to art 7 of the First EC Company Law Directive (EEC) 68/151 (OJ 1968 L65 p 8 (S edn 1968(I) p 41)). He referred to the French and English texts of art 7:

'If, before a company being formed has acquired legal personality, action has been carried out in its name and the company does not assume the obligations arising from such action, the persons who acted shall, without limit, be jointly and severally liable therefor, unless otherwise agreed.'

'Si des actes ont été accomplis au nom d'une société en formation, avant l'acquisition par celle-ci de la personnalité morale, et si la société ne reprend pas les engagements résultant de ces actes, les personnes qui les ont accompli en sont solidairement et indéfiniment responsables, sauf convention contraire.'

[6] The judge held that s 36C(1) enabled the agent for the unformed company to enforce the contract. His reasons were as follows. First he held that this was the literal effect of the following words in s 36C: '[the] contract ... has effect ... as one made with the person purporting to act for the company or as agent for it ...' He held that s 36C did not reflect the directive as it could have done if it had provided merely that a person who purported to enter into a contract for and on behalf of an unformed company was liable to the same extent as if he had contracted personally.

[7] Second, he referred to *Phonogram Ltd v Lane* [1981] 3 All ER 182, [1982] QB 938, the first case to come before the Court of Appeal on construction of s 9(2) of the 1972 Act. In it the Court of Appeal expressly rejected the argument that s 9(2) should be construed solely by reference to the directive. Lord Denning MR said ([1981] 3 All ER 182 at 186, [1982] QB 938 at 943): 'Section 9(2) is in accordance with the spirit and intent of the directive. We should go by our own statute, and not by the directive.' The judge observed that the correctness of that approach was emphasised by the fact that s 36C failed to implement that part of art 7 which provides for a company to assume obligations arising from the contract.

[8] The judge's third reason was that the directive did not preclude a provision of national law imposing liability and conferring rights on agents.

[9] The judge's fourth reason was that his interpretation of s 36C resulted in both parties being mutually able to enforce the contract and in his judgment this was neither unworkable nor unfair. The judge considered that the concluding words of s 36C(1) would include specific performance and that supported his conclusion on mutuality.

[10] The judge's fifth reason was that the concluding words abolished the previous distinction made at common law between agents who made pre-incorporation contracts and on the true interpretation incurred personal liability and those who made such contracts but incurred no personal liability: see the *Phonogram* case [1981] 3 All ER 182 at 188, [1982] QB 938 at 946 in which Oliver LJ held that s 9(2) of the 1972 Act, from which s 36C(1) is derived, made these subtle distinctions irrelevant.

a [11] The third issue before the judge (and the second on this appeal) was whether the execution of the agreement by Sturges 'as solicitors and agents' for Braymist satisfied s 2(1) and (3) of the Law of Property (Miscellaneous Provisions) 1989. Section 2(1) and (3) provides:

b '(1) A contract for the sale or other disposition of an interest in land can only be made in writing and only by incorporating all the terms which the parties have expressly agreed in one document or, where contracts are exchanged, in each ...

(3) The document incorporating the terms or, where contracts are exchanged, one of the documents incorporating them (but not necessarily the same one) must be signed by or on behalf of each party to the contract.'

c [12] The judge held that it did not matter that Sturges signed as agents for Braymist. The effect of s 36C(1) was that they were deemed to be vendors even though they had signed as agents. Otherwise, s 36C(1) would be useless in the case of all contracts for the sale or other disposition of land. The statutory purpose of s 2 of the 1989 Act would not be served by that construction. Accordingly, the
d provisions of s 2(1) and (3) of the 1989 Act were satisfied.

[13] The fifth issue before the judge (and the third arising on this appeal) is whether Sturges were able to complete and thus able to serve a valid notice to complete under condition 22. Condition 22(1) provides:

e 'At any time on or after the completion date, either party being ready and willing to fulfil his own outstanding obligations under the contract, may (without prejudice to any other right or remedy available to him) give to the other party or his solicitors notice in writing requiring completion of the contract in conformity with this condition.'

[14] At the time notice to complete was served, Sturges were not the owners of
f the property nor were they directors or shareholders of Braymist or of Plumtree Ltd (Plumtree), the registered owner of the property, or its parent company Pique Holdings plc (Pique). The judge held that condition 22 was satisfied. The agreement provided for title to be deduced by production of a transfer from Plumtree to Braymist. Before notice to complete was served, Sturges held a transfer executed by Plumtree and Braymist in favour of Wise, being the form
g required by Wise's solicitor. In addition, as solicitors for Plumtree and instructed to act in the sale of the property, Sturges were entitled by virtue of their right against Plumtree and its parent company's majority shareholder, Mr Pool, to compel the transfer of the property from Plumtree to Wise. As Braymist had not been incorporated Mr Pool was personally liable on the contract of retainer and it
h was an implied term of the contract of retainer that if Sturges put in place the legal mechanisms for the transfer of the property to the defendant in accordance with their principal's instructions Plumtree and Mr Pool would secure the transfer of the property to Wise. It was an implied term of the contract that Plumtree and Mr Pool would not leave Sturges exposed to personal liability by virtue of s 36C(1).

j [15] Plumtree was a wholly-owned subsidiary of Pique. Mr Pool was entitled to 75% of Pique's share capital. He was also chairman and managing director of Pique. He was also chairman and managing director of Plumtree and he held a power of attorney in property matters for Mr Gerald Johnson, one of the two other directors of Plumtree. The judge held that neither Mr Pool or Plumtree was in a position to prevent Sturges from handing over on completion the executed transfer then in Sturges' possession.

[16] The next issue before the judge (and the fourth issue on this appeal) was whether Sturges' title was defective because the land was encumbered by a restrictive covenant in favour of the Minister of Agriculture, Food and Fisheries (MAFF).

[17] Clause 18 of the agreement dated 28 January 1993 provided that Wise should enter into a covenant with the Forestry Enterprise that—

'it will forthwith cease using and forever after not use the existing soakaway drainage from the property and all the adjoining filling station which system runs on to the adjoining property of the Forestry Enterprise ...'

[18] Clause 4 of the deed of covenant and surrender dated 10 December 1993 between (1) Plumtree and (2) MAFF provided as follows:

'Plumtree hereby further covenants with the Minister that if at any time within the period of 80 years from the date hereof the Adjoining Property shall come into the possession of Plumtree or its successors in title to the property then Plumtree and its successors in title shall cease forthwith and not thereafter use the existing drainage system on the Adjoining Property and shall not discharge sewage from such system into the septic tank situated on the west side of the A380 or as the case may be any overflow from the system so as to discharge sewage or surface water into any culvert or drainage ditch to the west of the A380.'

[19] The adjoining property for the purposes of this clause is the site which I have described above as the adjoining land.

[20] The judge held that cl 18 of the agreement was consistent with a restrictive covenant such as was imposed by cl 4 of the MAFF deed. In any event the MAFF deed was sent to Wise's solicitors on 22 December 1993. They did not raise any requisition on title in respect of cl 4 of the MAFF deed. On 10 January 1994, Wise's solicitors sent Sturges the engrossed transfer, cl 3 of which expressly provided that Wise would observe and perform the covenant in cl 4 of the MAFF deed. In these circumstances, Wise was precluded from objecting to those covenants in the MAFF deed by condition 9 of the National Conditions of Sale which provide for a purchaser to be deemed to accept the vendor's title unless he raises requisitions on title. Condition 9 was not overridden by cl 4 of the agreement.

[21] In any event, Wise had acted unequivocally under the agreement, notwithstanding its knowledge of cl 4 of the deed, by conducting itself on the basis that the transfer would be subject to the MAFF covenants. When sending the engrossed transfer Wise's solicitors stated that they were awaiting instructions in respect of completion but they gave no indication that if and when completion took place it would not be on the terms of the engrossed transfer.

[22] The judge, therefore, held that the notice to complete was valid and effective. He also held that, in any event, a reasonable time had elapsed from the contractual completion date before the contract was terminated on the ground of Wise's failure to complete.

THE ISSUES ON THIS APPEAL

[23] The following issues arise on this appeal: (1) Is the agreement binding on Wise by virtue of s 36C? In other words, can Sturges enforce it as against Wise? (2) Is the agreement unenforceable for want of writing under s 2 of the 1989 Act? (3) Did Sturges have title to the property so as to be able to serve a valid notice to complete under condition 22 of the National Conditions of Sale? (4) Was the

a vendor's title defective because the land was encumbered by a restrictive covenant in favour of MAFF? (5) If the notice to complete did not comply with condition 22, was it valid under the general law? (6) If the notice to complete was bad under condition 22, might it still be good because of lapse of time after the contractual completion date?

b APPELLANT'S SUBMISSIONS

Issue 1

[24] Mr Mark Blackett-Ord, for the appellant, places particular emphasis on the tailpiece (as defined above). He submits that these words are otiose on the judge's approach and that their purpose was, and was only, to make the agent liable. They provide no support for the proposition that the agent can enforce the contract. Mr c Blackett-Ord does not submit that because the directive does not provide for the agent to be entitled to enforce the contract s 36C(1) cannot have this effect. He submits that that submission is precluded by *Phonogram Ltd v Lane*.

[25] However, Mr Blackett-Ord submits that bizarre results might flow if the agent could sue on a contract to which s 36C(1) applies. He points that no agent has d succeeded on this basis and that there is no reported case in which the point has been taken. If the judge is right, agents for non-existent companies will get an advantage. They can take advantage of their own carelessness in making contracts on behalf of unformed companies. He submits that it is extraordinary to award damages to Sturges. A further bizarre result is that the third party becomes liable to a party with whom he did not intend to contract. That person may be a man of e straw or an infant. The effect may be to impose a contract on a party who particularly wished to contract with the company which was in course of incorporation. Moreover, the contract might be a contract to work for that party. There is no reason why Parliament should want to confer the benefit on agents. Sturges, as reputable solicitors, were likely to disgorge the profit to their principal f but they are not, on Mr Blackett-Ord's submission, required to do so.

[26] As respects mutuality, Mr Blackett-Ord submits that this concept is relevant only to specific performance and is not relevant to the present question. The sole effect of s 36C is to prevent the agent from denying the existence of a contract.

[27] In this case the identity of the vendor was of no particular concern to Wise.

g [28] The purpose of the tailpiece, on Sturges' submission, is to clarify and not to qualify the effect of the earlier words in s 36C(1). This is contrary to the presumption that words in a statute are always operative. The judge's fifth reason does not explain the concluding words of s 36C(1). These words do not so much emphasise the abolition of the common law distinction as create another distinction. The h preamble to the directive indicates that the object of art 7 of the directive is to protect third parties. A third party is fully protected by having someone whom he can hold liable. He is not protected by a deemed contract. Moreover, if the judge is right, there are several people who under the directive can enforce the contract—Mr Pool, Plumtree and William Sturges—and there is no mechanism in j s 36C(1) for determining who should be entitled to the benefit of the contract.

Issue 2

[29] Under s 2 of the 1989 Act the contract has to be signed by the parties to it. Here Sturges only signed as agents and solicitors for Braymist. It was not signed by Sturges in their own right. The effect of s 36C(1) is that the contract may be enforced against Sturges, but not by them. This result is not unknown in the law

(compare s 40 of the Law of Property Act 1925). It is an odd result if a deemed agent can be entitled to sell property which he does not own.

Issue 3

[30] Mr Blackett-Ord submits that Sturges must be able to show title to the land. The conveyancers in this case ignored the provisions of cl 4 of the agreement requiring a transfer of the land by Plumtree to Braymist to be produced. However, there could not be any estoppel against Wise preventing it from taking this point because it never knew that the other contracting party was really Sturges, not Braymist. Moreover, Mr Blackett-Ord submits that Sturges could not have compelled Braymist to deliver the land. The situation is different from that in *Elliott v Pierson* [1948] 1 All ER 939, [1948] Ch 452, where the title was vested in a company which the vendor owned. Harman J held that as the vendor was in a position to compel the company to execute the necessary conveyance he had a right to enforce a contract and accordingly the purchaser had no right to repudiate. The vendor had to have the legal estate before he became entitled to an order for specific performance of the contract of sale (see *Pinekerry Ltd v Needs (Kenneth) Contractors Ltd* (1992) 64 P & CR 245). In this case Mr Blackett-Ord submits, Sturges could not have compelled Plumtree to proceed with the transfer to themselves and therefore, they had no document in their favour so that they could not complete the agreement. Even if Mr Pool could have been compelled to execute the transfer, on Mr Blackett-Ord's submission, Mr Pool could not have compelled Plumtree because that company was insolvent because a loan account due to the minority shareholder of Pique (Mr Johnson) exceeded the value of its assets. Sturges was not, therefore, in a position to compel Plumtree to hand over title to it and accordingly, Sturges could not be said to be ready and willing to complete the contract.

Issue 4

[31] Mr Blackett-Ord submits that cl 4 of the MAFF deed was a restrictive covenant as to what could be done on the adjoining property. It went further than the agreement. Clause 18 deals only with the owner of the property and provides what drainage he may use. The restrictive covenant on the other hand restricts drainage when the purchaser becomes owner of the adjoining land. This is an additional restriction which affects drainage from the adjoining land. This additional restrictive covenant is fatal because it is not mentioned in the agreement.

[32] Mr Blackett-Ord submits that neither party appreciated that there was a new restrictive covenant and accordingly there could be no waiver (see *Peyman v Lanjani* [1984] 3 All ER 703, [1985] Ch 457). Mr Blackett-Ord particularly relies on the identification by Slade LJ of the issue which had to be determined with respect to affirmation in that case:

'The question is whether his conduct on 22 February 1979 would have led Mr Lanjani and his legal advisers reasonably to infer that he did not intend to object to *the particular defect in title which had arisen through the first impersonation.*' (See [1984] 3 All ER 703 at 735, [1985] Ch 457 at 502.)

[33] Mr Blackett-Ord submits that Wise's solicitors did not intend to object to the restrictive covenant created by cl 4 of the MAFF deed. The draft transfer which Wise's solicitors produced was ineptly drafted so its production could not amount to a waiver. He further submits that as the defect in title was fundamental, it could now be raised even though the time for raising requisitions on title under condition 9 had expired.

Issue 5

[34] If the notice did not comply with condition 22 it would for the same reason fail to be a valid notice to complete at common law.

RESPONDENTS' SUBMISSIONS

[35] Miss Barbara Rich, for the respondents, made the following submissions.

Issue 1

[36] Miss Rich attaches particular importance to the fact that s 36C states that the contract takes effect as a contract to which the agent is a party. The court must give effect to this wording. As Lord Asquith of Bishopstone said in *East End Dwellings Co Ltd v Finsbury BC* [1951] 2 All ER 587 at 599, [1952] AC 109 at 132–133:

> 'If one is bidden to treat an imaginary state of affairs as being real, one must surely, unless prohibited from doing so, also imagine as real the consequences and incidents which, if the putative state of affairs had in fact existed, must inevitably have flowed from or accompanied it. One of these in this case is emancipation from the 1939 level of rents. [The Town and Country Planning Act 1947] says that one must imagine a certain state of affairs. It does not say that, having done so, one must cause or permit one's imagination to boggle when it comes to the inevitable corollaries of that state of affairs.'

[37] Miss Rich submits that where identity is relevant, the counterparty can rescind the contract, but that is not the case here. This is the answer to Mr Blackett-Ord's submission that the effect of s 36C is to impose a contract even if the contract was one of employment.

[38] The tailpiece makes it clear that the common law distinction is abolished.

[39] Miss Rich supports the judge's five reasons. In particular, his construction of s 36C(1) does not make the provision unworkable or unfair. The defendant has no good reason for avoiding the contract in this case.

[40] Miss Rich submits that the United Kingdom fulfilled its obligation to implement the directive by implementing it to the minimum extent. Article 7 of the directive must be construed purposively. That article goes further than simply protecting the interests of third parties. The objective is to impose equivalent safeguards which restrict invalidity to the greatest possible extent.

[41] Miss Rich submits that the judge was correct with respect to mutuality. The end words of s 36C(1) are not restricted to damages and so it would be odd if there were no requirement for mutuality.

[42] On Miss Rich's submission, the effect of s 36C is to substitute Sturges for Braymist as Sturges can enforce any right conferred on Braymist. The effect of this section is to make the agent personally liable and to make the agent the principal.

[43] Miss Rich makes the point that the Report of the Company Law Committee (Cmnd 1749) (1962) under the chairmanship of the Rt Hon Lord Jenkins, (the Jenkins Committee) recommended (paras 44, 54(b)) that a company should be able unilaterally to adopt contracts which purport to be made on its behalf or in its name prior to incorporation and thereby become a party to the same extent as if the contract had been entered into after incorporation and that unless or until the company does adopt such a contract the persons who have purported to act for the company should be entitled to sue and liable to be sued thereon.

Issue 2

[44] Miss Rich adopts the judge's reasoning. In particular, the appellant's construction of s 2 would render s 36(C) of no effect in contracts for the sale or other disposition of land.

Issues 3, 4, 5

[45] Miss Rich adopts the judge's reasoning. She also submits that no notice to complete could have been served other than under condition 22.

CONCLUSIONS

Issue 1

[46] In *Newborne v Sensolid (GB) Ltd* [1953] 1 All ER 708, [1954] 1 QB 45, a company purported to sell goods at a time when it had not been incorporated. The company's name was appended to the contract as 'Leopold Newborne (London) Ltd' and underneath was the name of Leopold Newborne. When it was discovered that the company had not been formed, Leopold Newborne commenced proceedings for damages for breach of contract against the buyers in his own name. The Court of Appeal held that the plaintiff had never purported to contract to sell nor sold the goods either as principal or agent. The contract purported to be made by the company and Leopold Newborne had merely added his name to verify that the company was a party. In the circumstances, the contract was a nullity. In so deciding, the Court of Appeal distinguished the principle, applied in *Schmaltz v Avery* (1851) 16 QB 655 and other cases, that where a person purported to contract as agent he could nevertheless disclose himself as being in truth the principal and enforce the contract. The only person who had any contract with the defendants was the company and Mr Newborne's signature merely confirmed that of the company. At first instance ([1952] WN 491), Parker J expressed the view that if the principle had applied the defendants could have escaped liability if they could have shown that they would not have contracted with the agent. The contract would have been voidable and the defendants could have claimed rescission (see [1954] 1 QB 45 at 48–49). In the circumstances, however, it was not necessary for either Parker J or the Court of Appeal to determine the circumstances in which an agent could claim to be the principal and thus enforce a contract.

[47] *Newborne's* case was one of the decisions considered by the Jenkins Committee in their report (referred to above). Their recommendation, however, had two parts. Firstly, that the agent for a company in the course of incorporation should be entitled to sue and liable to be sued on a pre-incorporation contract and also that the company should be able unilaterally to adopt such a contract. On such adoption, the liability of the agent would cease. However, before this recommendation could be implemented, the United Kingdom became a member of the European Community. Article 54(1)(g) of the Treaty of Rome (now, after amendment, art 44(2)(g) EC) provides for co-ordination of safeguards for the protection of members and others, such as creditors, involved with companies. Before the United Kingdom became a member of the European Community, the other members had adopted the directive and accordingly on the accession of the United Kingdom it was necessary for the United Kingdom to implement this directive. Section 9 of the 1972 Act was designed to implement the directive.

[48] A change of approach has occurred in the interpretation of domestic directive-based legislation. Although in the *Phonogram* case [1981] 3 All ER 182, [1982] QB 938, Lord Denning MR held that the court should simply construe the

a English domestic statute and not look at the French version of the directive, the approach of the court now is to construe domestic legislation, if possible, in conformity with the directive which it aims to implement. As Miss Rich explains in her skeleton argument, this is required by the jurisprudence of the Court of Justice of the European Communities. As Lord Oliver of Aylmerton said in *Litster v Forth Dry Dock and Engineering Co Ltd* [1989] 1 All ER 1134 at 1140, [1990] 1 AC 546 at 559:

b   'If the legislation [enacted in effect to give the United Kingdom's obligations under the EEC Treaty] can reasonably be construed so as to conform with those obligations, obligations which are to be ascertained not only from the wording of the relevant directive, but from the interpretation placed upon it by the Court of Justice of the European Communities, such a purposive

c   construction will be applied even though, perhaps, it may involve some departure from the strict and literal application of the words which the legislature has elected to use.'

[49] In those circumstances, the starting point, in my judgment, is the meaning of the directive and any decision of the Court of Justice on it.

d [50] The judge set out above the English and French language versions of art 7 of the directive. The French version is silent on the question whether the agent can enforce the contract. Recourse should also be had to the other language versions of the directive, but they are not before us. Likewise there is no information as to the legal position in the other member states. The directive is to be construed in the light of its preamble which, having referred to art 54(3)(g) of the Treaty of Rome

e continues (in material part) as follows:

       'Whereas the co-ordination of national provisions concerning disclosure, the validity of obligations entered into by, and the nullity of, such companies is of special importance, particularly for the purpose of protecting the interests of those parties;

f   Whereas in these matters Community provisions must be adopted in respect of such companies simultaneously, since the only safeguards they offer to third parties are their assets;

       Whereas the basic documents should be disclosed ...

       Whereas the protection of third parties must be ensured by provisions which

g   restrict to the greatest possible extent the grounds on which obligations entered into in the name of the company are not valid;

       Whereas it is necessary, in order to ensure certainty in the law as regards relations between the company and third parties, and also between members, to limit the cases in which nullity can arise ...'

h [51] I deduce the following points on the preamble. First, the directive stems from art 54(3)(g). Accordingly the particular emphasis of the directive is on the co-ordination of provisions for the protection of shareholders and creditors. Second, a major concern of the preamble is the protection of third parties. It may, therefore, be taken that one of the main objectives of the directive is to make

j uniform in the laws of the member states the protection given to third parties in relation to pre-incorporation contracts. Third, the preamble refers to the validity of obligations entered into by companies, particularly for the purpose of protecting third-party interests, but does not refer to the validity of obligations entered into by agents who are rendered principals on such contracts.

[52] I then turn to the body of the directive itself. Article 7 is the first article under the heading 'Section II: Validity of obligations entered into by a company'.

This section also contains art 8 which prevents a company from relying on any
limitation in the powers of an organ of the company as against third parties unless   *a*
the company proves that such third parties had knowledge of that limitation.
Article 9 restricts the doctrine of ultra vires and in particular provides that acts done
by organs of the company are binding on it, even though those acts are not all in
the objects of the company unless such acts exceed the powers which the law
confers or allows to be conferred on those organs. Also by art 9, an option is given   *b*
to member states to permit a company not to be bound by such acts if it proves that
the third party knew that the act was outside those objects or could not have been
unaware of it.

[53] There are distinct doctrinal differences between the company laws of
various member states with respect to formation and ultra vires and arts 7, 8 and 9
bear all the hallmarks of compromise. It is to be noted that in art 7 the agents are   *c*
not liable if the company actually assumes the obligations arising from the contract
or if it is agreed that the agents should not be liable. Likewise in art 8, a company
can rely on irregularities in the appointment of agents (despite compliance with
publicity requirements) if it proves that third parties had knowledge thereof.
Article 9 deals with the well-known doctrine of ultra vires. Views differ as to the   *d*
value of that doctrine. Article 9 does not abolish the doctrine absolutely but does
so only subject to the qualification such as those to which I have referred. That arts
7, 8 and 9 should have been the subject of compromise is not surprising since the
directive was the first attempt at harmonising the company laws of the member
states. Significantly, it was negotiated before the United Kingdom entry into the
Community.   *e*

[54] From the above analysis I deduce that the directive has nothing to say on
the question whether or not an agent who becomes personally liable on a contract
under art 7 should be able to enforce it. The concern of the directive and the
concern of art 54(3)(g) was to provide for the protection of third parties. That is
obtained by the imposition of personal liability on the agents responsible for the   *f*
pre-incorporation acts.

[55] I then turn to consider whether any jurisprudence of the Court of Justice
throws doubt on this approach. In Edwards *EC Company Law* (1999), p 32,
Ms Edwards says:

> 'The Court of Justice briefly considered Article 7 in [*Ubbink Isolatie BV v*   *g*
> *Dak-en Wandtechniek BV* Case 136/87 [1988] ECR 4665], a case concerning acts
> performed in the name of a company not yet incorporated. The Court held
> that the rules on the nullity of companies in Section III of the Directive did not
> apply where acts had been performed in the name of a company whose
> existence was not confirmed by the public register because the formalities for   *h*
> incorporation required by national law had not been completed, and stated
> that: "in so far as acts performed in the name of a limited liability company not
> yet incorporated are regarded by the applicable national law as having been
> performed in the name of a company being formed within the meaning of
> Article 7 ... it is for the national law in question to provide, in accordance with   *j*
> that provision, that the persons who perform them are to be jointly and
> severally liable." (Para 18 of the judgment.) A further point as to the scope of
> Article 7 was made by Advocate General Cruz Vilaça, in whose view: "When
> the existence of a partnership is equivalent, under an express disposition of
> national law or in accordance with the interpretation given of it by legal
> doctrine or the courts, to a company in formation ... Article 7 ... must apply.

a   Were it otherwise, its aim of safeguarding the interests of third parties could be
      frustrated by the legal expedient of regarding such an organization as a
      partnership." (Para 42 of the Opinion.)'

      [56] Counsel have not referred us to any more recent authority. So far as I can
      see the Court of Justice has not suggested that the directive requires that the agents
      should become a party to the contract to be entitled to enforce it.

b   [57] It is, therefore, apparent that s 36C(1) goes further than the directive
      requires. However, I agree with counsel that it is not appropriate to read s 36C
      down so that it complies with the directive and does no more. Parliament has
      deliberately provided that the contract should take effect as a contract with the
      agent and the court must give effect to that wording.

c   [58] The only consequence for which s 36C(1) legislates is that the agents should
      be personally liable accordingly. Personal liability is necessary to ensure compliance
      with the directive. Situations in which a director is held merely to have appended
      his name to confirm that of the company, as in *Newborne v Sensolid (GB) Ltd* [1953]
      1 All ER 708, [1954] 1 QB 45, would be contrary to the directive. The decision in
      Newborne's case would have been in the mind of Parliament when enacting the
d   predecessor of s 36C(1). Parliament would, therefore, have been aware of the
      possibility that an agent might sue to enforce a contract which he had purported to
      make as agent when his principal did not exist. The desire to reverse *Newborne's*
      case accounts in my judgment, for the provision in the first part of s 36C(1) that the
      contract should take effect 'as one made with the person purporting to act for the
e   company or as agent for it'. It does not, however, explain the tailpiece.

      [59] I reject an approach to interpretation of s 36C(1) which would render the
      tailpiece non-operative or clarificatory only. Such an approach is contrary to
      well-established principle. In my judgment the words in the tailpiece are operative
      words and as I explain below the reason behind them can also be found in
      Newborne's case. As I see it, the function of the tailpiece is to establish liability only
f   and to leave the question whether the agent can enforce the contract to the general
      law. For, as the judge observed, the contract imposed by statute is to take effect not
      with Mr Newborne or the agent as if he were the principal and had been principal
      all along but on the footing that 'the person purporting to act for the company or
      as agent for it' is the contracting party. The common law thus applies to determine
g   whether such a person can enforce the contract. There is case law which deals with
      the question whether an agent can enforce a contract made by him as agent on
      behalf of his principal if he discloses himself as the true principal. The case law
      includes *Schmaltz v Avery* (1851) 16 QB 655, and other case law, to which *Newborne's*
      case refers.

h   [60] The matter is discussed in *Bowstead and Reynolds on Agency* (17th edn, 2001)
      pp 516–517 (paras 9–091 to 9–093). The learned editor says:

          '9-091 **Identified principal** ... it was held in *Rayner v. Grote* ((1846) 15 M &
          W 359, (1846) 153 ER 888) that a person who had purported to sell goods as
          agent for such a principal but who was really himself the seller could sue for
j   non-acceptance where the third party had become aware of the true position
          and nevertheless continued with the contract. On this basis it might be argued
          that such a person can do so in any case, if he gives notice that he is the
          principal, and provided that the third party is not clearly prejudiced. But in
          such a case the contract is with the named principal, an identified person
          different from the agent, the agent being by the wording of the contract
          excluded from being a party, and it is extremely difficult to see how the agent

can then intervene and claim the benefit of such a contract. For although
mistake is not relevant in the formation of contract where it is not material, it
should not be difficult for the third party to show that he intended to contract
with the named principal only. He should not be left to establish prejudice,
which, in view of the fact that the benefit of contracts is usually assignable,
might not be easy. It is submitted therefore that the case itself should be
explained on the basis of novation ... In other circumstances it is highly
doubtful whether [the agent] [*Bowstead* says "the principal" but this appears to
be a misprint] could intervene: this is supported by a dictum of Alderson B. in
the case ((1856 15 M &W 359 at 365, (1846) 153 ER 888 at 891), which has since
been cited with approval ... "In many such cases, such as, for instance, the case
of contracts in which the skill or solvency of the person who is named as the
principal may reasonably be considered as a material ingredient in the contract,
it is clear that the agent cannot then shew himself to be the real principal, and
sue in his own name; and perhaps it may be fairly urged that this, in all
executory contracts, if wholly unperformed, or if partly performed without the
knowledge of who is the real principal, may be the general rule."

9–92 Unidentified principal. It was decided in *Schmaltz v. Avery* ((1851) 16
QB 655) that an agent who signed a charterparty containing a cesser clause
purportedly as agent for an unidentified principal could show that he was
himself the principal and sue on the contract, on the grounds that it was not of
moment to the third party who contracted on such terms to whom he was
liable, and that the agent could say that he was his own principal. Such a right
is in danger of being inconsistent with the terms of the contract, especially
where the contract can be said to be embodied in a document. It is therefore
submitted that, even on the most favourable view of the situation, the true
analysis is that the contract in such cases is with the unidentified principal, and
that the agent can only intervene if he fits such description (if any) as has been
given of the supposed principal. Further, if the third party can establish that,
with whomsoever he was willing to contract, he was not willing to contract
with the agent, he should equally be able to say that he had no agreement with
the agent ...

9–93 Supposed rule doubtful. *Schmaltz v. Avery* is a case arising in the
context of particular form of the cesser clause, a very specialised charterparty
provision on which there is much case law. The purpose of such a clause is that
the charterer can substitute for himself shippers or consignees of cargo whose
positions are regulated by bills of lading and against whom the shipowner can
recover outstanding charges by the exercise of his lien. A charterer who uses
such a clause may well have no principals ... The general reasoning of the case
has been criticised in Scotland as being obsolete in view of the restatement of
the rules as to interpretation of written contracts by the House of Lords in
Universal Steam Navigation Co. v. McKelvie ([1923] AC 492), and is difficult to
reconcile with the principles of law established since that time. The right to
sue of an agent purporting to act for a *disclosed* principal is even more difficult
to justify ... Even if the third party cannot plead that he made no contract with
the agent, he can presumably plead misrepresentation in appropriate cases;
and all authorities agree that the agent cannot intervene when such
intervention would prejudice the third party, *e.g.* where the third party could
show that he relied on liability of both agent and principal, or where the agent's
liability as principal is by the terms of the contract less onerous than his liability
as agent. But this is similar to the rule preventing the intervention of the

a undisclosed principal in some situations, and it might well be more difficult for the third party to establish such prejudice than merely to plead that the contract was made with the supposed principal and not with the agent. *Harper & Co. v. Vigers Bros.* ([1909] 2 KB 549, [1908–10] All ER Rep Ext 1293), indeed, shows clearly the difficulty of establishing prejudice.'

b [61] *Chitty on Contracts* (28th edn, 1999) Vol 2, p 56 (para 32–095) is to similar effect:

c 'Where "agent" is in fact principal: his rights. It may also be that a party who has contracted "as agent," but in fact on his own account, may in certain cases be allowed to sue as principal on the contract which he has thus made. In the case of charterparties there is authority for the proposition that he can do so if he has not named anyone else as his true principal, on the ground that in such a case the other party cannot, in entering into the contract, have been influenced by the personal qualifications of the supposed principal. Secondly, where such a contract has been in part performed and that performance has been accepted by the other contracting party with full knowledge that the *d* party who was described as agent in the contract was the real principal, it has been held that the latter may after that sue for the completion of the contract. But these propositions also are not beyond criticism; and it has been held that an agent cannot sue as principal if the identity of the contracting party is material.'

e [62] From the above texts, it is clear that the position in the general law is not that an agent can in all circumstances come in and claim to be principal on a contract which he made as agent. The circumstances in which he can do so have yet to be fully defined and winnowed out by the courts. In my judgment Parliament intended to preserve the process of common law adjudication in this *f* respect and to leave it to the courts to complete the exercise of defining the relevant circumstances. Accordingly, as I see it, the purpose of s 36C was limited to: (i) complying with the United Kingdom's treaty obligations to implement art 7 of the directive, (ii) removing the possibility that the agent would be held not liable on the ground that he merely confirmed the company's signature and (iii) putting such persons or agents in the same position as regards the enforcement of the contract *g* as they would be at common law and in particular (in the case of agents) this is the same position as agents who contracted as agents.

[63] However, for the reasons explained I do not consider that Parliament intended in s 36C to determine the rules which should apply where an agent makes a contract as agent on behalf of a principal then claims to enforce the contract. As *h* *Bowstead and Reynolds on Agency* points out, in determining such rules the law has to have regard among other considerations to the position of third parties who claim that they would not have entered into a contract if they had known the other party was not the principal whom they thought they were contracting for some other party. It may be that they rely on the skill of that other party or on his solvency or *j* on some other quality altogether. Counsel found it difficult to think of an example where this might happen, but the following example may be supposed as a start. Suppose that the third party agrees to provide legal services as and when required at cost to a company with charitable objects. The contract is made at a time when the company is in the process of formation and is signed by a person who proposes to become a director of the company. The third party in that situation may very well say that the particular quality of the contracting party which induced him to be

bound to such a contract was the fact that the other party was a charity. In my judgment, it should not be assumed that Parliament intended in that situation that the agent should be able to enforce the contract to the same extent as if he had been the company itself.

[64] As to what the rules should be in a situation which I have postulated, that matter will have to await another case. It is clear that in this particular instance it is of no moment to the appellant whether the party selling the property is Braymist or Sturges.

[65] The United Kingdom's implementation of art 7 makes no reference to the possibility of the company enforcing the contract when it has been formed. Since so far as it was concerned the contract was a nullity it could only do this by entering into a contract of novation with the agent. Even then the agent would remain personally liable. While the issue does not arise in this case, my provisional view is that this possibility exists because s 36C only applies to the making of the contract and does not require that the contract remains the same throughout its currency. In those circumstances there was no need for Parliament to deal with this additional option. I agree with the view expressed by Ms Edwards in the work cited that the omission of Parliament to deal with this aspect of art 7 'is not a serious flaw'.

[66] In those circumstances, I conclude that Sturges are entitled to enforce the agreement.

Issue 2

[67] Section 2 of the 1989 Act refers to signature 'by or on behalf' of a party. In my judgment, having concluded that Sturges is a party to the agreement by virtue of s 36C and that there is no common law bar to enforcement of the contract by Sturges, in my judgment Sturges is properly to be treated as having signed the agreement on its own behalf for the purposes of s 2. I reach this construction in order to make both sections work properly together. Otherwise, Sturges having shown that it is entitled to enforce the contract under s 36C would be unable to do so because of over-literal construction of s 2 of the 1989 Act. I agree with the judge that this cannot be the policy of s 2. My interpretation does no violence to the language: Sturges did sign the contract. Because it renders ss 36C and 2 more efficacious, in my view the judge's consideration is to be preferred.

Issue 3

[68] I can deal with this matter shortly. In my judgment, Sturges were able to complete the contract because they were able to hand over a transfer executed on behalf of Braymist and Plumtree. This accorded with the contract and the purchaser's requirements. Section 36C does not affect the contractual provision for the delivery of title. The fact that Plumtree was insolvent would not place a restriction on the powers of the directors and there is no evidence to show that performance of the agreement was not in the best interests of Plumtree. Sturges had instructions from Mr Pool and Plumtree to effect the transaction, and Mr Pool could procure the way in which Plumtree acted with respect to the agreement.

Issue 4

[69] I agree with the judge that cl 18 of the agreement reflected cl 4 of the MAFF deed. It imposes an obligation not to use the existing soakaway drainage from either the property being sold or the adjoining filling station. It is not suggested that the drainage on the adjoining land occupied any area other than the filling station site. Clause 18 does not contain the refinements of cl 4, namely that the restriction

a   does not operate unless the adjoining property is acquired but that is implicit. Moreover the 80-year period in cl 4 is inserted merely to make the clause effective and should have been expected. In those circumstances I agree with the judge that cl 18 of the agreement is consistent with cl 4 of the MAFF deed.

[70] In any event, I agree with the judge that, if there was any defect, the defendant's solicitor waived it. He may not have appreciated that cl 4 of the MAFF

b   deed imposed a restrictive covenant, but by producing the transfer in the form he did, in my judgment, he clearly intended to waive any objection that he might have had to the fact that that cl 4 went beyond cl 18 of the agreement. The inept drafting of the transfer does not diminish this point.

Issue 5

c
[71] This issue does not arise.

DISPOSITION

[72] Accordingly, I would dismiss this appeal.

d **LATHAM LJ.**

[73] I agree that the appeal should be dismissed. As to the first issue identified by Arden LJ, I do so for the reasons given by the judge. It is common ground that s 36C of the Companies Act 1985, and its predecessor, was enacted in order to give effect to art 7 of the first EC Company Law Directive (EEC) 68/151 (OJ 1968 L65 p 8 (S edn 1968(I) p 41)) already referred to by Arden LJ in her judgment, and in

e   particular to reverse the decision of this court in *Newborne v Sensolid (GB) Ltd* [1953] 1 All ER 708, [1954] 1 QB 45. It also put to rest any doubts that there might have been as to the liability of a person who purports to act as an agent in such a situation (as to these doubts see *Chitty on Contracts* (28th edn, 1999) Vol 2, pp 55–56 (para 32–094 and n75)).

f   [74] The important question which is raised in this appeal is whether or not the person purporting to act for the company or as agent for it can sue, not merely be sued, on the contract. It is submitted that the final words of the section are restrictive, making it clear that the section is only concerned with the imposition of liability and does not affect entitlement to sue which must be determined by the ordinary rules of common law. I have great difficulty in accepting this submission.

g   The express imposition of liability in the final words of the section is said to follow 'accordingly' from the main principle set out in the section which is that the contract 'has effect … as one made with the person purporting to act for the company or as agent for it'. These words do not seem to me to be apt to be words of restriction. A contract can only, in my judgment, have 'effect' if both parties are

h   entitled to give it effect.

[75] I accept that the directive itself, in particular art 7 is concerned to ensure that obligations assumed in the name of a company yet to be formed should be respected in order to protect the rights of third parties who have apparently contracted in good faith. But there is also, it seems to me, a proper justification for

j   extending that protection to the nascent company by validating pre-incorporation contracts, and also to others who might have relied on the existence of an apparent contract in their dealings with that company; if it were otherwise the fortuitous date of the company's incorporation might affect a series of significant and important transactions. It is to be noted that the Report of the Company Law Committee (Cmnd 1749) (1962), again referred to by Arden LJ, recommended that pre-incorporation contracts should be mutually enforceable. It seems to me that

the ordinary common law rules as to the enforceability of contracts are both
sufficient and satisfactory to deal with any difficulties, one of which has been   *a*
described by Arden LJ, which the consequence of this section, construed as I believe
it should be construed, could give rise to. For example if the identity of the
contracting party is of critical significance, or if there has been a vitiating
representation, there could be no question of the contract being enforceable, on
ordinary principles.   *b*

[76] I would therefore hold that the section itself provides the answer as to
whether or not, in a case such as this, the person purporting to act as an agent for
the company should be entitled to enforce the contract, subject to the proviso that
I have just mentioned. Although my conclusion may appear to result in the last
phrase of the section being surplussage, I find it difficult to construe the main, and
operative part of the section otherwise. The result accords with the views of Parker *c*
J, with which the Court of Appeal agreed, in *Newborne v Sensolid (GB) Ltd* [1953] 1
All ER 708, [1954] 1 QB 45 that where a person contracts as an agent in
circumstances in which he is to be fixed with liability, he is also entitled to sue on
the contract. I would accordingly hold that the solicitors are entitled to rely upon
s 36C in order to enforce the contract in the present case. In my judgment, this   *d*
produces a just result in that there is no good reason why the defendants should be
entitled to resile from their obligations under the contract as a result of a pure
technicality when in truth they wish to do so because it proved a bad bargain.

JUDGE LJ.

[77] The critical question for decision is whether s 36C(1) of the Companies Act   *e*
1985 not only provides a remedy for a person (A) who has purported to enter into
a contract with a company when it was unformed (the narrow view) but also
imposes obligations enforceable against A's wishes by the person purporting to act
for or as agent of the unformed company (B). I describe this as the broad view. The
answer to this question is not straightforward, and for some time I was persuaded   *f*
by Mr Blackett-Ord that the narrow view was right. I should therefore explain why
I have reached the same conclusion as Arden and Latham LJJ.

[78] There is no difficulty when A chooses to proceed with the contract. He
cannot cherry-pick the parts which are convenient or favourable to him. If the
contract takes effect, it takes full effect, according to its terms, and the contractual
obligations as well as contractual benefits and remedies created by the purported *g*
contract, continue in accordance with the agreed terms. But what if B wishes to
enforce the contract against A? Is he entitled to do so, against A's wishes, and when
A has done nothing to affirm the contract or to indicate that he wishes to proceed
with it?

[79] Section 36C(1) provides: *h*

'A contract which purports to be made by or on behalf of a company at a
time when the company has not been formed has effect ... as one made with
the person purporting to act for the company or as agent for it, and he is
personally liable on the contract accordingly.'
                                                                                     j
At common law, if 'the company was not in existence when the contract was
signed, there never was a contract' (per Lord Goddard CJ in *Newborne v Sensolid (GB)
Ltd* [1953] 1 All ER 708 at 710, [1954] 1 QB 45 at 51: see also, the judgment of
Morris LJ, and the judgment of Parker J ([1952] WN 491) upheld by the Court of
Appeal). Section 36C(1) in effect abrogates this principle. There is deemed to be a
contract. The purported contract, otherwise a nullity, 'has effect', not as one made

a   with the unformed company but as one made with the purported agent, who is 'personally liable' to A on the contract.

[80] My difficulty is created by the concluding words of the subsection, 'and he is personally liable on the contract accordingly'. If the contract 'has effect' as one made with the purported agent of the company, B would become personally liable on the contract without the concluding words of the subsection. The contract 'has *b*   effect'. The language of s 36C(1) reflects the broad thrust of Council Directive (EEC) 68/151 (OJ 1968 L65 p 8 (S edn 1968(I) p 41)), first implemented domestically in its predecessor, s 9(2) of the European Communities Act 1972. The recital twice refers to 'protecting' third parties. In Section II, which concerns the validity of obligations entered into by a company, art 7 provides:

c   'If, before a company being formed has acquired legal personality, action has been carried out in its name and the company does not assume the obligations arising from such action, the persons who acted shall, without limit, be jointly and severally liable therefor, unless otherwise agreed.'

If the broad view is correct, the statute has gone much further than the creation of *d*   new protection for A. Plainly, as a matter of statutory construction, s 36C(1) may have extended beyond simple compliance with the directive. Nevertheless the concluding words add something: if surplusage, they would not be there. Their presence provides a clear indication that the highlight of s 36C(1) is protection for A.

[81] The second relevant feature of s 36C(1) is that its language is not apt to undermine or alter any of the well-understood principles which govern contractual *e*   arrangements. For example, if prior to the formation of the purported contract, and to induce it, B has misrepresented the material facts, A is entitled to the remedies appropriate for fraudulent or innocent misrepresentation. They are not to be ignored merely because the contract 'has effect'. Similarly if the purported contract were tainted by illegality, or for any other reason were unenforceable s 36C(1) *f*   would not remove the taint, or overcome the obstacles to enforceability. In short, the normal incidents appropriate to any contract apply equally to deemed or statutory contracts created by s 36C(1).

[82] This consideration leads me briefly to reflect on the position at common law where A discovers that he has entered into a contract with B when he intended to and believed that he was contracting not with B, but with C. This is not, or will *g*   not always be of mere academic interest to A. Sometimes personal, sometimes commercial considerations, sometimes both, may be important. As there was no lengthy citation of authority on this issue, it is instructive to reflect that in *Newborne*'s case, Parker J commented:

h   '... a contract of that sort would be clearly voidable when the other party found that the person with whom he thought he was contracting was not the real principal and he could then claim to have the contract rescinded.'

In the Court of Appeal both Morris and Romer LJJ expressly agreed with this judgment. In the classic case of *Cundy v Lindsay* (1878) 3 App Cas 459, [1874–80] All *j*   ER Rep 1149 the House of Lords held that a mistake as to the identity of the other party to the purported contract rendered it void.

[83] In principle, the identity of the other party to a contract often matters, sometimes very much indeed. A might happily contract with C, but not with either B, or even D, even if identical terms were available. He may have a complete antipathy to being beholden to or under any legal obligation personally to B, or indeed anyone other than C. There are, of course, well understood exceptions to

the principle that an individual is free to decide whether and with whom to enter or not to enter, a contract (for example, the legislation in relation to discrimination on the grounds of sex or race). But I may illustrate the difficulties by considering a contract of employment, underlining that so far as unformed companies are concerned, there are no limits to the contracts to which s 36C(1) applies: it applies to them all. A may welcome the opportunity of employment, as, say, an office manager for a particular company, with which he is contracting. If the company is unformed, is he bound to accept similar employment on identical contractual terms, with B? Or become liable to B for breach of contract if he refuses or fails to do so? Surely not. The answer however is not that the contract is automatically deprived of the 'effect' which s 36C(1) has created, but rather, that just as s 36C(1) is not apt to exclude considerations such as illegality, or misrepresentation, or other incidents of a contract, it is equally inappropriate to exclude relief on the basis of the identity of the contracting party, if relief would be available on ordinary contractual principles.

[84] The insurmountable difficulty with the narrow view is that it requires s 36C(1) to be read as if it created a complete option for someone in A's position, but never for someone in B's position, either to adopt or reject the contract, a choice to be made unilaterally by him, for good, bad, or no reason. The statutory language could, of course, have been drafted so to provide. Instead s 36C(1) specifies that contract has 'effect', language remote from the concept of an 'option' or, as here, the wish of the party in A's position to be protected from the consequences of the deemed contract simply because the bargain is no longer as commercially attractive as it once was.

[85] Accordingly, dealing with the issue as a matter of construction, I prefer the broad rather than the narrow view of the meaning and effect of s 36C(1). I am in complete agreement with the reasoning and conclusions of Arden LJ on the remaining issues which arise in this appeal. In my view therefore, the appeal should be dismissed.

Appeal dismissed.

Melanie Martyn   Barrister.

Taylor and another v Lawrence and another

[2002] EWCA Civ 90

COURT OF APPEAL, CIVIL DIVISION
LORD WOOLF CJ, LORD PHILLIPS OF WORTH MATRAVERS MR, WARD, BROOKE AND
CHADWICK LJJ
17, 18 DECEMBER 2001, 4 FEBRUARY 2002

Court of Appeal – Jurisdiction – Application to reopen appeal – Whether Court of Appeal having power to reopen appeal after final judgment given and drawn up.

Natural justice – Judge – Bias – Apparent bias – Circumstances capable of giving rise to possibility of bias on part of judge – Guidance.

At the trial of a boundary dispute, the judge informed the parties that he had been a client of the claimants' solicitors but that it had been many years since he had instructed them. Nobody objected to his continuing to hear the trial. After judgment was given for the claimants, the defendants appealed on the ground, inter alia, that there was an appearance of bias because of the judge's relationship with the claimants' solicitors. Before the hearing of the appeal, it was disclosed to the defendants that the judge and his wife had used the services of the solicitors to amend their wills the night before he had delivered judgment. The appeal was dismissed in January 2001. Subsequently, the defendants learned that the judge had not paid for the services of the solicitors. The defendants applied to reopen the appeal on the basis that the judge had received a financial benefit from the solicitors which he had failed to disclose, and that the earlier appeal had been dismissed in ignorance of that fact. On the application, the Court of Appeal considered (i) whether it had power to reopen an appeal after it had given a final judgment and that judgment had been drawn up, and (ii) the circumstances that were capable of giving rise to the possibility of bias on the part of a judge.

Held – (1) The Court of Appeal had a residual jurisdiction to reopen an appeal which it had already determined in order to avoid real injustice in exceptional circumstances. The court had implicit powers to do that which was necessary to achieve the dual objectives of an appellate court, namely to correct wrong decisions so as to ensure justice between the litigants involved, and to ensure public confidence in the administration of justice, not only by remedying wrong decisions, but also by clarifying and developing the law and setting precedents. A court had to have such powers in order to enforce its rules of practice, suppress any abuses of its process and defeat any attempted thwarting of its processes. The residual jurisdiction to reopen appeals was linked to a discretion which enabled the Court of Appeal to confine its use to the cases in which it was appropriate for the jurisdiction to be exercised. There was a tension between a court having such a residual jurisdiction and the need to have finality in litigation, so that it was necessary to have a procedure which would ensure that proceedings would only be reopened when there was a real requirement for that to happen. The need to maintain confidence in the administration of justice made it imperative that there should be a remedy in a case where bias had been established, and that might justify the Court of Appeal in taking the exceptional course of reopening proceedings which it had already heard and determined. It should,

however, be clearly established that a significant injustice had probably occurred and
that there was no alternative effective remedy. The effect of reopening the appeal on *a*
others and the extent to which the complaining party was the author of his own
misfortune would also be relevant considerations. Where the alternative remedy
would be an appeal to the House of Lords, the Court of Appeal would only give
permission to reopen an appeal which it had already determined if it were satisfied
that the House of Lords would not give permission to appeal (see [26], [50]–[55], *b*
below); *Connelly v DPP* [1964] 2 All ER 401, *Bremer Vulcan Schiffbau und Maschinenfabrik
v South India Shipping Corp* [1981] 1 All ER 289 and *R v Bow Street Metropolitan
Stipendiary Magistrate, ex p Pinochet Ugarte (No 2)* [1999] 1 All ER 577 considered.

(2) For the purpose of applying the test for apparent bias, namely whether in the
all the circumstances a fair-minded and informed observer would be led to conclude *c*
that there was a real possibility that the tribunal was biased, the informed observer
could be expected to be aware of the legal traditions and culture of the English
jurisdiction, and accordingly he would be aware that in the ordinary way contacts
between the judiciary and the legal profession should not be regarded as giving rise to
a possibility of bias. On the contrary, they promoted an atmosphere that was totally *d*
inimical to the existence of bias, and what was true of social relationships was equally
true of normal professional relationships between a judge and the lawyers he might
instruct in a private capacity. Judges should be circumspect about declaring the
existence of a relationship where there was no real possibility of it being regarded by
a fair-minded and informed observer as raising a possibility of bias. If such a
relationship was disclosed, it necessarily raised an implication that it could affect the *e*
judgment and approach of the judge. If that was not the position, no purpose was
served by mentioning the relationship. On the other hand, if the situation was one
where a fair-minded and informed person might regard the judge as biased, it was
important that disclosure should be made. If the position was borderline, disclosure
should be made so that the judge could consider, having heard the parties' *f*
submissions, whether or not he should withdraw. If disclosure was made, it should
be full disclosure. The instant case demonstrated the danger of making partial
disclosure, but no case of apparent bias had been made out. It was unthinkable that
an informed observer would regard it as conceivable that a judge would be influenced
to favour a party with whom he had no relationship merely because that party *g*
happened to be represented by solicitors who were acting for the judge in a purely
personal matter in connection with a will. If permission had been sought in
accordance with the procedure set out below, the court would not have given the
permission for the new evidence to be considered. The application for permission to
make the application would, however, be granted to enable the court's judgment to *h*
be the subject of an application for permission to appeal to the House of Lords. The
application itself would be dismissed (see [60]–[65], [72]–[76], below); *Porter v Magill*
[2002] 1 All ER 465 applied.

Per curiam. A party seeking permission to reopen a decision of the Court of
Appeal, whether refusing permission to appeal or dismissing a substantive appeal, *j*
must apply in writing for permission to do so. That application will then be
considered on paper and only allowed to proceed if, after the paper application is
considered, the Court of Appeal so directs. Unless it does so, there will be no right to
an oral hearing of the application. The court should exercise strong control over any
such application, so as to protect those who are reasonably entitled to believe that the
litigation is already at an end (see [56], below).

Notes

For apparent bias and for the jurisdiction of the Court of Appeal, see respectively 1(1) *Halsbury's Laws* (4th edn reissue) para 99 and 37 *Halsbury's Laws* (4th edn reissue) para 1541.

Cases referred to in judgment

b *Aden Refinery Co Ltd v Ugland Management Co, The Ugland Obo One* [1986] 3 All ER 737, [1987] QB 650, [1986] 3 WLR 949, CA.

Ampthill Peerage Case [1976] 2 All ER 411, [1977] AC 547, [1976] 2 WLR 777, HL.

BT v BT (rehearing: procedure) [1990] FCR 654.

Banco de Portugal, Ex p, Re Hooper (1880) 14 Ch D 1, CA.

Barrell Enterprises, Re [1972] 3 All ER 631, [1973] 1 WLR 19, CA.

c *Birmingham and District Land Co v London and North Western Rly Co* (1886) 34 Ch D 261, CA.

Bremer Vulcan Schiffbau und Maschinenfabrik v South India Shipping Corp [1981] 1 All ER 289, [1981] AC 909, [1981] 2 WLR 141, HL.

C (a Hague Convention case), Re [1999] CA Transcript 1785.

d *Cassell & Co Ltd v Broome (No 2)* [1972] 2 All ER 849n, [1972] AC 1136, [1972] 2 WLR 1214, HL.

Connelly v DPP [1964] 2 All ER 401, [1964] AC 1254, [1964] 2 WLR 1145, HL.

Daisystar Ltd v Town and Country Building Society, Townroots Ltd v Raja [1992] 2 All ER 321, [1992] 1 WLR 390, CA.

Falcke v Scottish Imperial Insurance Co (1887) 57 LT 39, [1886–90] All ER Rep 768.

e *Flower v Lloyd* (1877) 6 Ch D 297, CA.

Henderson v Henderson (1843) 3 Hare 100, [1843–60] All ER Rep 378, 13 ER 301.

Hession v Jones [1914] 2 KB 421, DC.

J (a minor), Re [2000] CA Transcript 230.

James v Williams [2001] CP Rep 42, CA.

f *Ladd v Marshall* [1954] 3 All ER 745, [1954] 1 WLR 1489, CA.

Lane v Esdaile [1891] AC 210, HL.

Locabail (UK) Ltd v Bayfield Properties Ltd, Locabail (UK) Ltd v Waldorf Investment Corp, Timmins v Gormley, Williams v HM Inspector of Taxes, R v Bristol Betting and Gaming Licensing Committee, ex p O'Callaghan [2000] 1 All ER 65, [2000] QB 451, [2000] 2 WLR 870, CA.

g *Medicaments and Related Classes of Goods (No 2), Re* [2001] 1 WLR 700, CA.

Porter v Magill [2001] UKHL 67, [2002] 1 All ER 465, [2002] 2 WLR 37.

R v Bow Street Metropolitan Stipendiary Magistrate, ex p Pinochet Ugarte (No 2) [1999] 1 All ER 577, [2000] 1 AC 119, [1999] 2 WLR 272, HL.

St Nazaire Co, Re (1879) 12 Ch D 88, CA.

h *Wood v Gahlings* [1996] TLR 684, CA.

Cases also cited or referred to in skeleton arguments

Ashingdane v UK (1985) 7 EHRR 528, [1985] ECHR 8225/78, ECt HR.

B (children) (abduction: new evidence), Re [2001] EWCA Civ 625, [2001] 2 FCR 531.

Banks v Cox [2000] CA Transcript 1476.

j *Barder v Barder (Caluori intervening)* [1987] 2 All ER 440, sub nom *Barder v Caluori* [1988] AC 20, HL.

Baron Kalman De Demko, Re [1958] 3 All ER 360, sub nom *R v Governor of Brixton Prison, ex p De Demko* [1959] 1 QB 268, CA; *affd* sub nom *De Demko v Home Secretary* [1959] 1 All ER 341, [1959] AC 654, HL.

Brown v Dean [1910] AC 373, [1908–10] All ER Rep 661, HL.

Calcraft v Guest (1898) 1 QB 759, [1895–9] All ER Rep 346, CA.

Commercial Acceptances Ltd v Townsend Investments Inc [2000] CPLR 421, CA.
Davis v Johnson [1978] 1 All ER 1132, [1979] AC 264, HL.   *a*
de Lasala v de Lasala [1979] 2 All ER 1146, [1980] AC 546, PC.
Director General of Fair Trading v Proprietary Association of Great Britain [2001] EWCA
   Civ 1217, [2002] 1 All ER 856, sub nom Re Medicaments and Related Classes of Goods
   (No 4) [2002] 1 WLR 269.
Goddard v Nationwide Building Society [1986] 3 All ER 264, [1987] QB 670, CA.   *b*
Great Northern Rly Co v Mossop (1855) 17 CB 130, 139 ER 1018, DC.
Hertfordshire Investments Ltd v Bubb [2000] 1 WLR 2318, CA.
ITC Film Distributors v Video Exchange Ltd [1982] 2 All ER 241, [1982] Ch 431.
Johnson v Gore Wood & Co (a firm) [2001] 1 All ER 481, [2001] 2 WLR 72, HL.
Jordan v Norfolk CC [1994] 4 All ER 218, [1994] 1 WLR 1353.
Kuwait Airways Corp v Iraqi Airways Co (No 2) [2001] 1 WLR 429, HL.   *c*
Leeson v General Council of Medical Education and Registration (1889) 43 Ch D 366,
   [1886–90] All ER Rep 78, CA.
Livesey (formerly Jenkins) v Jenkins [1985] 1 All ER 106, [1985] AC 424, HL.
Mulholland v Mitchell (by his next friend Hazel Doreen Mitchell) [1971] 1 All ER 307, [1971]
   AC 666, HL.   *d*
Murphy v Stone Wallwork (Charlton) Ltd [1969] 2 All ER 949, [1969] 1 WLR 1023, HL.
O'Connor v Din [1997] 1 FLR 226, CA.
R v DPP, ex p Kebeline, R v DPP, ex p Rechachi [1999] 4 All ER 801, [2000] 2 AC 326, HL.
R v Gray [1900] 2 QB 36, [1900–3] All ER Rep 59, DC.
R v His Honour Sir Shirley Worthington-Evan, Clerkenwell County Court, ex p Madan [1959] *e*
   2 All ER 457, DC.
R v Inner West London Coroner, ex p Dallaglio [1994] 4 All ER 139, CA.
R v Kansal (No 2) [2001] UKHL 62, [2002] 1 All ER 257, [2001] 3 WLR 1562.
R v Sussex JJ, ex p McCarthy [1924] 1 KB 256, [1923] All ER Rep 233, DC.
Racal Communications Ltd, Re [1980] 2 All ER 634, [1981] AC 374, HL.
Riniker v University College London [2001] 1 WLR 13n, CA.   *f*
Robinson v Robinson [1982] 2 All ER 699n, [1982] 1 WLR 786n, CA.
Royal Brompton Hospital NHS Trust v Hammond (No 5) [2001] EWCA Civ 550, [2001]
   EWCA Civ 778, (2001) 76 Con LR 62.
Skrzypkowski v Silvan Investments Ltd [1963] 1 All ER 886, [1963] 1 WLR 525, CA.
Stewart v Engel [2000] 3 All ER 518, [2000] 1 WLR 2268, CA.   *g*
Stubbings v UK (1997) 23 EHRR 213, [1996] ECHR 22083/93, ECt HR.
Tracy v Jones [2001] EWCA Civ 925.
Vernon v Bosley (No 2) [1997] 1 All ER 614, [1999] QB 18, CA.
X v Sweden (1982) 31 DR 223, E Com HR.
Young v Bristol Aeroplane Co Ltd [1944] 2 All ER 293, [1944] KB 718, CA; affd [1946] 1 All *h*
   ER 98, [1946] AC 163, HL.
Zincroft Civil Engineering Ltd v Sphere Drake Insurance plc (1996) TLR 722, CA.

Application to reopen appeal
The defendant appellants, Joseph Dwight Lawrence and Ruth Amanda Lawrence,
applied for the reopening of their appeal from the decision of His Honour Peter   *j*
Goldstone, sitting as Deputy Circuit Judge at Watford County Court on 12
November 1999, giving judgment for the claimant respondents, Richard Mark Taylor
and Kim Priscilla Taylor, in a boundary dispute between the parties, such appeal
having been dismissed by the Court of Appeal (Peter Gibson, Chadwick and
Keene LJJ) on 25 January 2001 ([2001] EWCA Civ 119, [2001] All ER (D) 180 (Jan)).
The facts are set out in the judgment of the court.

a   *Bernard Eder QC* and *David Scorey* (instructed through the *Bar Pro Bono Unit*) for the
     appellants.
     Tim Cowen (instructed by *Mathew Arnold & Baldwin*, Watford) for the respondents.
     Timothy Corner and *Sarah-Jane Davies* (instructed by the *Treasury Solicitor*) as advocates
     to the court.

b   *Cur adv vult*

4 February 2002. The following judgment of the court was delivered.

LORD WOOLF CJ.

c   INTRODUCTION
         [1] This application raises two important issues. The first relates to the jurisdiction
     of this court. It is whether the Court of Appeal has power to reopen an appeal after it
     has given a final judgment and that judgment has been drawn up (the jurisdiction
     issue). The second issue is as to the circumstances that are capable of giving rise to the
d   possibility of bias on the part of a judge (the bias issue). The judge against whom the
     allegations of bias were made was His Honour Peter Goldstone, who was sitting as a
     deputy circuit judge at Watford County Court at the trial of this action in November
     1999.
         [2] We are grateful for the assistance given by counsel in this case. We are
e   particularly grateful to Mr Bernard Eder QC and Mr David Scorey, who have
     appeared for the appellants, Mr Joseph Dwight Lawrence and Mrs Ruth Amanda
     Lawrence, as they have done so without charging any fees, and to Mr Timothy
     Corner and Miss Sarah-Jane Davies, whom the Attorney General, at our request,
     instructed to appear as advocates to the court. We are also grateful to Clifford
     Chance, who prepared the eight bundles of documents and authorities for use at the
f   hearing in an exemplary manner and without making any charge.
         [3] For a summary of the appellants' version of the background facts to this appeal
     we cannot improve upon that provided by counsel for the appellants in their skeleton
     argument. The summary is in these terms:

g   '1. The parties litigated a boundary dispute. A trial took place in 1999. At that
         trial, the appellants were not represented but the respondents had both solicitors
         and counsel. The trial judge informed the parties that he had been a client of the
         respondents' solicitors (referred to as MAB), but that it had been "many years"
         since he had last instructed them, and no one objected to him continuing to hear
         the trial. In November 1999, judgment was given against the appellants. An
h   appeal was made to the Court of Appeal. One ground of appeal was that there
         was an appearance of bias because of the judge's relationship with the other
         parties' solicitors, MAB. Subsequent to the permission being granted in March
         2000, it was disclosed to the appellants that the judge and his wife had in fact used
         the services of MAB the very night before judgment was given against the
j   appellants to amend their wills. Before the appeal, the judge provided further
         information as to his involvement with MAB. 2. The appeal failed in January
         2001. The appellants have subsequently learnt that the judge did not pay for the
         services provided by MAB. He therefore received a financial benefit from MAB
         in whose favour he gave judgment. The fact was never disclosed by the judge,
         despite his having the opportunity to do so. The earlier appeal was dismissed in
         ignorance of this fact …'

[4] The manner in which the appellants learnt that the judge had not paid for the
services provided by MAB is disgraceful. An inquiry agent telephoned MAB, *a*
pretending to be the judge's accountant, and elicited the information. This raises the
question of whether this court ought to entertain an appeal based on material
obtained in this way. There is a similar, but more general question. Why had the
appellants not discovered, before the Court of Appeal embarked on the hearing of
their case, that the judge had not paid for the services provided by MAB? Had they *b*
sought information about this it is likely they would have been told that MAB had
made no charge.

[5] It is a firm rule of practice that the Court of Appeal will not allow fresh evidence
to be adduced in support of an appeal if that evidence was reasonably accessible at the
time of the original hearing (see *Ladd v Marshall* [1954] 3 All ER 745, [1954] 1 WLR
1489). Counsel for the respondents argued that this rule should preclude the *c*
appellants from seeking at this stage to base an allegation of bias on material that they
could and should have deployed at the hearing of the original appeal. We consider
that there is force in this submission. Arguably, this application should have
been dismissed at the outset for this reason. A court of five judges has, however, been
constituted in order to address the important issue of jurisdiction that arises on the *d*
facts of this case. In these circumstances we have decided to proceed on the basis that
the appellants could not reasonably have become aware of the fact that the judge had
not paid for MAB's services at the time of the original appeal and to overlook the
discreditable manner in which that information was subsequently obtained. This will
enable us to address the issue of jurisdiction that is raised by this application.
e

THE JURISDICTION ISSUE

[6] The rule in *Ladd v Marshall* is an example of a fundamental principle of our
common law—that the outcome of litigation should be final. Where an issue has
been determined by a decision of the court, that decision should definitively
determine the issue as between those who were party to the litigation. Furthermore, *f*
parties who are involved in litigation are expected to put before the court all the issues
relevant to that litigation. If they do not, they will not normally be permitted to have
a second bite at the cherry (see *Henderson v Henderson* (1843) 3 Hare 100, [1843–60] All
ER Rep 378). The reasons for the general approach is vigorously proclaimed by Lord
Wilberforce and Lord Simon of Glaisdale in the *Ampthill Peerage Case* [1976] 2 All ER
411, [1977] AC 547. Both statements deserve the most careful attention. However, *g*
for reasons of economy we will cite only Lord Wilberforce, who presided, but we
give reference to Lord Simon's speech [1976] 2 All ER 411 at 423–424, [1977] AC 547
at 575–576. Lord Wilberforce said:

'English law, and it is safe to say, all comparable legal systems, place high in the *h*
category of essential principles that which requires that limits be placed on the
right of citizens to open or to reopen disputes. The principle which we find in
the (Legitimacy Declaration Act 1858) is the same principle as that which
requires judgments in the courts to be binding, and that which prohibits
litigation after the expiry of limitation periods. Any determination of disputable
fact may, the law recognises, be imperfect: the law aims at providing the best and *j*
safest solution compatible with human fallibility and having reached that
solution it closes the book. The law knows, and we all know, that sometimes
fresh material may be found, which perhaps might lead to a different result, but,
in the interest of peace, certainty and security it prevents further enquiry. It is
said that in doing this, the law is preferring justice to truth. That may be so; these
values cannot always coincide. The law does its best to reduce the gap. But there

are cases where the certainty of justice prevails over the possibility of truth (I do not say that this is such a case), and these are cases where the law insists on finality. For a policy of closure to be compatible with justice, it must be attended with safeguards: so the law allows appeals; so the law, exceptionally, allows appeals out of time; so the law still more exceptionally allows judgments to be attacked on the ground of fraud; so limitation periods may, exceptionally be extended. But these are exceptions to a general rule of high public importance, and as all the cases show, they are reserved for rare and limited cases, where the facts justifying them can be strictly proved.' (See [1976] 2 All ER 411 at 417–418, [1976] AC 547 at 569.)

[7] The creation by the Supreme Court of Judicature Act 1873 of the Court of Appeal recognised that justice required some qualification to the principle that the outcome of litigation should be final. The Court of Chancery had already demonstrated that this was so. It had been prepared to entertain a bill to impeach a judicial decree that had been obtained by fraud and, in some circumstances, where facts had come to light which showed that the decree should not have been made—see the observations of Jessel MR in *Flower v Lloyd* (1877) 6 Ch D 297 at 299–301.

[8] The right of appeal to the House of Lords, now subject to the Administration of Justice (Appeals) Act 1934, is further recognition of the need to temper the principle that the outcome of litigation should be final. In *R v Bow Street Metropolitan Stipendiary Magistrate, ex p Pinochet Ugarte (No 2)* [1999] 1 All ER 577, [2000] 1 AC 119 the House held that it had jurisdiction to rehear an appeal where an appearance of bias was demonstrated on the part of one of the members of the committee that had determined the appeal. The present application raises the question of whether the Court of Appeal has jurisdiction to reopen an appeal if an appearance of bias can be demonstrated on the part of the court below.

[9] It is not uncommon for fresh evidence to come to light after a judgment has been perfected which puts that judgment in doubt. In such circumstances the unsuccessful litigant may be able to invoke that evidence in order to challenge the judgment by an appeal. Once the judgment is perfected, however, the court that has delivered the judgment, be it a court of first instance or the Court of Appeal, would not entertain an application to reopen the judgment in order to consider the effect of the fresh evidence. This is not because of any express statutory prohibition. In considering the extent of their jurisdiction the courts have ruled that a perfected judgment exhausts their jurisdiction because this accords with the fundamental principle that the outcome of litigation should be final. This can be demonstrated by reference to the judgment of Russell LJ in *Re Barrell Enterprises* [1972] 3 All ER 631, [1973] 1 WLR 19 (see the passages of the judgment in [1972] 3 All ER 631 at 636e–g, 637b–c, [1973] 1 WLR 19 at 23h–24a, 24e–f).

[10] The appellant in this case was a contemnor who had appealed to the Court of Appeal against a committal order made by Pennycuick V-C and had her appeal dismissed. By what appears to have been an oversight the order of the Court of Appeal was not perfected. The contemnor then persuaded Brightman J to entertain an application to set aside the committal order on the ground of fresh evidence. That application was dismissed. She then sought to reopen her appeal on the ground of the fresh evidence.

[11] In the course of his judgment Russell LJ considered whether Brightman J had had jurisdiction to reopen the case on the ground of fresh evidence. He observed:

'We are reluctant to find carried forward into this century procedures which
were devised for review or rehearing or new trial at a time when the Court of   *a*
Appeal did not exist. We can accept without difficulty the notion that if a
judgment has been obtained by fraud an action can be brought to set it aside. But
when it comes to setting aside a judgment on the ground that fresh evidence has
been obtained it appears to us highly desirable that the Court of Appeal alone
should have jurisdiction. Then the rules as to time for appeal, with the discretion   *b*
to allow an appeal out of time, will apply. So will the code for deciding when
fresh evidence should be admitted, now enshrined in the judgment of
Denning LJ in *Ladd v Marshall* ([1954] 3 All ER 745, [1954] 1 WLR 1489). There
are however in the Supreme Court Practice and in textbooks statements to the
effect that an action will lie to set aside a judgment on the ground of fresh
evidence and it is necessary to consider whether these are well-founded. The   *c*
Supreme Court Practice 1970 has this sentence (p 327): "If a judgment or order
has been obtained by fraud or where evidence which could not possibly have
been adduced at the original hearing is forthcoming, a fresh action will lie to
impeach the original judgment."' (See [1972] 3 All ER 631 at 637, [1973] 1 WLR
19 at 24–25.)   *d*

[12] Russell LJ went on to consider the authorities that related to this passage in
the White Book. He found authorities that indicated that before 1873 litigants, by a
bill of review, had succeeded in reopening a decision on the ground that it had been
obtained by fraud or shown to be wrong by fresh evidence. So far as fraud was
concerned this jurisdiction had survived the 1873 Act in the form of an action to set   *e*
aside a judgment obtained by fraud. As to the effect of the discovery of fresh evidence,
he held:

'In none of the cases brought to our notice has an action to set aside a judgment
on the ground of fresh evidence succeeded. Indeed there is nothing to show that   *f*
in the last 100 years any such action has even been brought, although in *Falcke's*
case (*Falcke v Scottish Imperial Insurance Co* (1887) 57 LT 39, [1886–90] All ER Rep
768) in 1887 there was an unsuccessful attempt to bring one. Insofar as any of the
dicta tend to show that an action will lie they are obiter. The reason which Sir
George Jessel MR gave in *Re St Nazaire Co* ((1879) 12 Ch D 88) for the review that   *g*
the jurisdiction to order a rehearing was vested by the Judicature Act in the Court
of Appeal and not in the High Court is of equal weight in relation to fresh
evidence as to the type of case with which he was dealing. Even if, technically,
the High Court was at first clothed with this jurisdiction we are of opinion that
this cause of action has long since lapsed because applications for rehearing on
the ground of fresh evidence have for generations been made only to the Court   *h*
of Appeal.' (See [1972] 3 All ER 631 at 639, [1973] 1 WLR 19 at 26–27.)

[13] In refusing the contemnor's attempt to reopen her appeal, Russell LJ stated:

'When oral judgments have been given, either in a court of first instance or on   *j*
appeal, the successful party ought *save in most exceptional circumstances* to be able
to assume that the judgment is a valid and effective one. The cases to which we
were referred in which judgments in civil courts have been varied after delivery
(apart from the correction of slips) were all cases in which some most unusual
element was present.' (See [1972] 3 All ER 631 at 636, [1973] 1 WLR 19 at 23–24;
my emphasis.)

a Later Russell LJ added:

> 'It is clearly not permissible for a party to ask for a further hearing merely because he has thought of a possible ground of appeal that he originally overlooked. The discovery of fresh evidence has never been suggested as a ground for reopening the argument before the Court of Appeal. If fresh evidence
> b comes to light, of such a character as to call for further consideration of the issues, the right way to deal with the situation is by applying for leave to appeal to the House of Lords ...' (See [1972] 3 All ER 631 at 637, [1973] 1 WLR 19 at 24.)

[14] Does it follow that there are no circumstances in which the Court of Appeal can reopen an appeal once judgment has been given and perfected? Mr Corner submitted that this was indeed the case. He started by pointing out that the Court of
c Appeal owes its creation to statute and it has no inherent jurisdiction. He also helpfully traced the statutory history of s 15 of the Supreme Court Act 1981, which goes back to the 1873 Act. Section 15 describes the general jurisdiction of the Court of Appeal today. The critical part of s 15 is in these terms:

d   '(1) The Court of Appeal shall be a superior court of record.

(2) Subject to the provisions of this Act, there shall be exercisable by the Court of Appeal—(a) all such jurisdiction (whether civil or criminal) as is conferred on it by this or any other Act; and (b) all such other jurisdiction (whether civil or criminal) as was exercisable by it immediately before the commencement of this
e   Act.'

[15] The earlier statutory provisions demonstrate that when the Court of Appeal was established, it was not given any jurisdiction in relation to appeals from the county court. The jurisdiction to hear appeals from the county courts was transferred to the High Court by s 16 of the 1873 Act and was expressly conferred upon divisional
f courts of the High Court by s 45 of the 1873 Act. The Court of Appeal only acquired jurisdiction to hear appeals from the county court in 1934, such jurisdiction again being expressly conferred by statute (s 2 of the 1934 Act).

[16] Accordingly, it is accepted that the Court of Appeal does not have any inherent jurisdiction in respect of appeals from the county court but only that which
g is given by statute. However, the use of the word 'inherent' in this context means no more than that the Court of Appeal's jurisdiction depends on statute and it has no originating jurisdiction. The position is very much the same in relation to other appeals to the Court of Appeal. Its jurisdiction is to be determined solely by reference to the relevant statutory provisions.

h [17] We here emphasise that there is a distinction between the question whether a court has jurisdiction and how it exercises the jurisdiction which it is undoubtedly given by statute. So, for example, a court does not need to be given express power to decide upon the procedure which it wishes to adopt. Such a power is implicit in it being required to determine appeals. It is also important when considering authorities which, it is suggested, are laying down principles as to the jurisdiction of a
j court, to ascertain whether they are doing more than setting out statements of the current practice of the court, which can be changed as the requirements of practice change. These powers to determine its own procedure and practice which a court possesses are also referred to as being within the inherent jurisdiction of the court, and when the term 'inherent jurisdiction' is used in this sense (as to which see 'The Inherent Jurisdiction of the Court' by Master Sir Jack Jacob, (1970) 23 CLP 23 at 32 et seq), the Court of Appeal, as with other courts, has an inherent or implicit jurisdiction.

[18] As the appellants' case was originally heard in the county court, Mr Corner also referred to s 77 (as amended) of the County Courts Act 1984 which sets out the right of appeal from the county court to the Court of Appeal and provides, so far as material, as follows:

'*Appeals: general provisions.*—(1) Subject to the provisions of this section and the following provisions of this Part of this Act and to any order made by the Lord Chancellor under section 56(1) of the Access to Justice Act 1999, if any party to any proceedings in a county court is dissatisfied with the determination of the judge or jury, he may appeal from it to the Court of Appeal in such manner and subject to such conditions as may be provided by Civil Procedure Rules.'

[19] Section 81 of the 1984 Act sets out the powers of the Court of Appeal on an appeal from the county court. It provides, so far as material:

'*Powers of Court of Appeal on appeal from county court.*—(1) On the hearing of an appeal, the Court of Appeal—may draw any inference of fact and either—(a) order a new trial on such terms as the court thinks just; or (b) order judgment to be entered for any party; or (c) make a final or other order on such terms as the court thinks proper to ensure the determination on the merits of the real question in controversy between the parties.'

[20] Finally, Mr Corner referred us to s 15(3) of the 1981 Act which confers incidental jurisdiction on the Court of Appeal and provides:

'(3) For all purposes of or incidental to—(a) the hearing and determination of any appeal to the civil division of the Court of Appeal; and (b) the amendment, execution and enforcement of any judgment or order made on such an appeal, the Court of Appeal shall have all the authority and jurisdiction of the court or tribunal from which the appeal was brought.'

[21] Mr Corner then referred us to statements of principle which he submitted authoritatively determine that this court has no jurisdiction to reopen an appeal once it has been finally decided, and that the only course available to persons in the appellants' position is to seek to appeal to the House of Lords out of time.

[22] The earliest and perhaps the most important case upon which Mr Corner relied for this submission is the case of *Flower v Lloyd* (1877) 6 Ch D 297. *Flower v Lloyd* was decided early in the life of this court but it did exert a considerable influence on what was said in judgments in later cases. The court was presided over by the then Master of the Rolls, Sir George Jessel. The issue before the court was whether the claimant in that action was entitled by motion to apply for leave for rehearing of an appeal because of the 'subsequent discovery of facts which shew or tend to shew that the order of the Court of Appeal was obtained by a fraud practised on the Court below'.

[23] Jessel MR stated (at 299):

'If there were no other remedy I should be disposed to think that the relief now asked ought to be granted, for I should be slow to believe that there were no means whatever of rectifying such a miscarriage if it took place; but I am satisfied that there is another remedy.'

[24] Jessel MR then went on to point out that where a fraud has been practised on a court it is possible to bring a fresh action to impeach the original decree and obtain justice by so doing if the fraud is established to have occurred. Jessel MR added that as there was this alternative remedy there was 'no necessity for straining' the meaning

a   of the legislation which established the Court of Appeal. He then concluded that if the Court of Appeal 'has once determined an appeal, it has no further jurisdiction'. He added that the original jurisdiction of the Court of Appeal is 'limited to that which is necessary for the determination of any appeal, and the amendment, execution, and enforcement of any order made on such an appeal'. James LJ took the same view. The third member of the court, Baggallay LJ concurred, though he acknowledged

b   that initially he had 'felt great hesitation in negativing the proposition that there was jurisdiction in this Court to rehear an appeal' where a judgment had been pronounced or obtained by fraud.

[25] In contrast, there are dicta which suggest that, in exceptional circumstances, the Court of Appeal might have jurisdiction to reopen an appeal; see, for instance, the observations of Cotton LJ in *Birmingham and District Land Co v London and North*

c   *Western Rly Co* (1886) 34 Ch D 261 at 277 and in *Ex p Banco de Portugal, Re Hooper* (1880) 14 Ch D 1 at 6. We are about to refer to some more recent observations to similar effect, but we believe that Mr Corner is correct to submit that there is no decision which is in direct conflict with *Flower v Lloyd* and *Hession v Jones* [1914] 2 KB 421.

[26] Before turning to Mr Eder's argument, it is desirable to note that, while, if a

d   fraud has taken place a remedy can be obtained, even if the Court of Appeal has no 'jurisdiction', it does not necessarily follow that there are not other situations where serious injustice may occur if there is no power to reopen an appeal. We stress this point because this court was established with two principal objectives. The first is a private objective of correcting wrong decisions so as to ensure justice between the litigants involved. The second is a public objective, to ensure public confidence in the

e   administration of justice not only by remedying wrong decisions but also by clarifying and developing the law and setting precedents. (See *Civil Procedure* (White Book 2001) para 52.0.3.)

[27] There can, of course be an appeal to the House of Lords from decisions of the Court of Appeal. However, the House of Lords is not in a position to hear more than

f   a minority of the appeals which litigants would wish to bring. The number of Lords of Appeal in Ordinary is limited to 12, and they are required to sit both in the Appellate Committee of the House of Lords and the Judicial Committee of the Privy Council. It would not be practical nor proportionate or appropriate for the House of Lords to be involved in resolving the type of issue which is raised by Mr and Mrs Lawrence in this case, relying as it does essentially on fresh evidence for reopening the appeal.

g   [28] In addition, there are cases where there is no right of appeal to the House of Lords if the party seeking to have a decision of first instance set aside has been refused permission to appeal to the Court of Appeal. If there is no more appropriate form of relief, then in relation to decisions in the county court (but not the High Court), it is possible that a remedy might be available if an application for judicial review were

h   made. Such an application, however, would be subject to the limitations inherent in an application for judicial review, namely that it is not a procedure which is suited to the resolution of issues of fact.

[29] Against this backcloth, Mr Eder submitted that in the special circumstances of this case, the Court of Appeal does have jurisdiction to review its previous judgment

j   and to order a rehearing of the appeal. He advanced three alternative grounds for asserting that such a jurisdiction exists. They are: (i) that there is a jurisdiction conferred by the County Court Rules (CCR) as transposed to the Court of Appeal; (ii) that a jurisdiction exists by analogy with the Court of Appeal's apparent jurisdiction in the case of fraud, as suggested in *Wood v Gahlings* [1996] TLR 684; and (iii) that by analogy with cases where the implementation of an order needs supervision, the Court of Appeal retains jurisdiction to revisit an appeal judgment in special cases.

[30] We will deal with those three situations in turn.

a

JURISDICTION BASED UPON THE COUNTY COURT RULES

[31] This argument stems from s 15(3) of the 1981 Act (see [20], above), which provides that the Court of Appeal has 'all the authority and jurisdiction of the court or tribunal from which the appeal was brought' for all purposes of or incidental to an appeal. Unlike the position generally in the High Court, where there is no provision *b* of the rules giving the court power to order a retrial or to set aside a verdict, the county court has long had the power to order a rehearing. (See *BT v BT (rehearing: procedure)* [1990] FCR 654 at 660ff, 669ff for Ward J's historical account of the differences between the jurisdiction and powers of the High Court and county court in this context which was justifiably described by Mr Eder as masterly.)   *c*

[32] The power to order a rehearing in the county court is now contained in CCR Ord 37, r 1 which has been retained by CPR Pt 50.

[33] The existence of this power is undoubted. However, we cannot accept Mr Eder's submission that this power provides a solution to the jurisdictional problem we are considering in the case of appeals to the Court of Appeal from the *d* county court. The submission begs the question as to whether the Court of Appeal has jurisdiction. If, but only if, it has jurisdiction to reopen the appeal will the Court of Appeal be able to exercise the powers of the county court to order a rehearing. In other words, the difficulty is that unless the Court of Appeal retains jurisdiction to reopen the appeal it cannot exercise the county court's jurisdiction to order a rehearing. The argument rightly establishes the width of the court's powers if it has *e* jurisdiction, but it does not help to create the jurisdiction.

Grounds of jurisdiction 2 and 3; by analogy with Wood v Gahlings and retained jurisdiction

[34] Mr Eder's second and third grounds for establishing jurisdiction are *f* conveniently taken together. The second ground is founded upon dicta contained in judgments in this court in *Wood v Gahlings*.

[35] *Wood v Gahlings* is a case in which two members of the present constitution, namely Lord Woolf (then Master of the Rolls) and Brooke LJ, were sitting, together with Aldous LJ. It is a case where the Court of Appeal had ordered a retrial and as a *g* result of the decision on the retrial it was alleged on a further appeal to the Court of Appeal that a fraud had been practised, not on the court of trial but on the Court of Appeal. The relevant ground of decision of this court on the second appeal was that the allegation of fraud had not been sufficiently clearly made out but Lord Woolf MR and Aldous LJ made obiter remarks suggesting that there was power in this court in the appropriate circumstances to intervene if actual fraud could be *h* established.

[36] In *James v Williams* [2001] CP Rep 42 Peter Gibson LJ reviewed the authorities including *Wood v Gahlings* and assumed, without deciding, that the court had jurisdiction to entertain an application to set aside a perfected order of another division of the court on the ground that the opposing party had been guilty of fraud *j* that materially contributed to the decision sought to be set aside.

[37] Fraud has always been treated as an exceptional case, and the dicta in these cases do not provide a foundation for answering the issue of jurisdiction which is before us. If, however, it is arguable that the Court of Appeal is able to reopen a decision where it has been obtained by fraud, this opens the door to the argument that there is jurisdiction to reopen an appeal in other exceptional cases.

a [38] Mr Eder's third ground is founded upon the fact that in special and exceptional circumstances, the Court of Appeal has exercised a power to reopen its judgments, in order to oversee and regulate the implementation and enforcement of its own orders.

[39] These cases have involved appeals in family cases involving children. Dicta in some of the judgments address the possibility that this court's power of review might b extend as far as setting aside the order in question. Thus in Re C (a Hague Convention case) [1999] CA Transcript 1785, the House of Lords had refused to grant a petition and so the case rested with the Court of Appeal. The court decided in that case to hear the merits of an application to set aside the decision without determining the issue of the jurisdiction of the court to revisit its own final decisions. In relation to this point the President said:

c
'There is no doubt that there is a serious question mark, to say the least, as to whether or not the Court of Appeal has any jurisdiction to revisit its own final decisions. These are, of course, civil proceedings like any other civil proceedings. But, unlike other civil litigation, in all family cases there is a continuing situation ... Specifically, in Hague Convention cases, the court does not make a decision, d yes or no, and then wash its hands of the result. This court inevitably has a continuing jurisdiction for the purpose of implementation; as it has in other forms of civil litigation, but particularly in family cases.'

[40] In Re J (a minor) [2000] CA Transcript 230 an application was made to the Court of Appeal for leave to set aside an order of the court, after an oral hearing, e refusing permission to appeal. The application was dismissed on the ground that as it did no more than challenge the merits of the decision, the court had no jurisdiction to reopen the case. In the course of her judgment, however, the President said (at para 8):

f
'It is possible, though I would not like to be too encouraging about it, that this court, as the final court on applications for leave, may, in the most exceptional circumstances, have the power to revisit its own decisions. Miss Golden did pray in aid a decision of this court of which I was a member in Re C. But the point of that case was that we said that you could revisit an order for the purpose of implementing it, and there was no suggestion in the judgments in that court that g it would be for the purpose of setting aside an earlier order and substituting another. But I can see the possibility of a residual power in the court with the final decision-making process, which may extend to the Court of Appeal as the final court (as it is, since the decision in Lane v Esdaile [1891] AC 210) on applications for permission to appeal, that if it can be demonstrated that there is some factor outside the decision in the case itself that stands out, then it may be h necessary to set that order aside. It would have, in my view, to be a factor that flawed the decision, and a factor which was outside the ambit of the decision itself. For instance, that the court had read the wrong papers in order to come to a decision or the fact that the court might not be competent to hear the case.'

j [41] In agreeing that the application should be dismissed, Robert Walker LJ said (at paras 16–20):

'In my judgment the circumstances of this case come nowhere near to the very limited circumstances in which the refusal of permission to appeal by the full court, pronounced in open court, can subsequently be challenged (whether by way of further appeal, application to set aside the decision or in any other way). Without in any way attempting a comprehensive statement of what those circumstances might be, it is possible to note three categories which are exceptional. The first (which I mention only for completeness) is the familiar power under the slip rule to correct an order before it has been perfected; although in the circumstances of refusal of permission to appeal that is unlikely to be in point. Another case mentioned by my Lady, the President, is the possibility (which was noted in the Hague Convention case of *Re C*, decided by this court on 1 November 1999) that the working out of an order made by the full court might be varied under an express or implied liberty to apply for the purposes of implementing the previous order. That leaves the third, and for present purposes most relevant, category, that is a very limited residual class of cases in which in quite extraordinary circumstances a decision might be revisited. That class was tentatively described by Lord Donaldson of Lymington MR in *Daisystar Ltd v Town and Country Building Society, Townroots Ltd v Raja* [1992] 2 All ER 321 at 324, [1992] 1 WLR 390 at 394 when, after referring to a passage in the judgment of Mustill LJ in *Aden Refinery Co Ltd v Ugland Management Co, The Ugland Obo One* [1986] 3 All ER 737 at 747, [1987] QB 650 at 666, Lord Donaldson MR said: "For my part, I would affirm that comment by Mustill LJ. [That was a comment in relation to judicial impropriety.] While I cannot and do not contemplate bias, whimsy or personal interest in the judges of this court, mischance is always a remote possibility: if, for example, a Lord Justice had pre-read two cases and, owing to mischance and perhaps the absence of counsel or gross incompetence by counsel, in the course of the argument it was never borne in on him that the case upon which counsel was addressing him was not in fact the case to which he was applying his mind. I can see that, in those circumstances, it could be argued that there had not been a decision and, if there was no decision, quite plainly s 54(6) does not apply."'

(The reference was to s 54(6) of the 1981 Act.)

[42] In concurring, May LJ observed that if, which he did not decide, the Court of Appeal had a jurisdiction similar to that exercised by the House of Lords in *R v Bow Street Metropolitan Stipendiary Magistrate, ex p Pinochet Ugarte (No 2)* [1999] 1 All ER 577, [2000] 1 AC 119 (see [8], above), it was a power only to be exercised in exceptional circumstances.

[43] The history of the Pinochet litigation is so well known that no statement of the facts is necessary. However, in the special circumstances of that case the House of Lords exercised a jurisdiction to rehear an appeal because of the alleged bias of one of the members of the constitution who first heard the appeal.

[44] Lord Browne-Wilkinson stated the general principle in these terms:

'... it must be that your Lordships, as the ultimate court of appeal, have power to correct any injustice caused by an earlier order of the House. There is no relevant statutory limitation on the jurisdiction of this House in this regard and therefore its inherent jurisdiction remains unfettered. In *Cassell & Co Ltd v Broome (No 2)* [1972] 2 All ER 849n, [1972] AC 1136 your Lordships varied an order for costs already made by the House in circumstances where the parties had not had a fair opportunity to address argument on the point. However, it should be made clear that the House will not reopen any appeal save in circumstances where, through no fault of a party, he or she has been subjected to an unfair procedure. Where an order has been made by the House in a particular case there can be no question of that decision being varied or rescinded by a later order made in the same case just because it is thought that the first order is wrong.' (See [1999] 1 All ER 577 at 585–586, [2000] 1 AC 119 at 132.)

a [45] Those words of Lord Browne-Wilkinson are clearly focusing on the special position of the House of Lords as a final appellate court. They cannot therefore automatically be applied to this court. None the less as we have pointed out, in some cases no appeal will lie to the House of Lords and in others an appeal to the House of Lords will not be appropriate. Thus for practical purposes in many cases this court is the final court of appeal. The difference between this court and the House of Lords
b is therefore one of degree, and it has changed over the years. While there will be situations where this court could and will say, if it has this jurisdiction, that the would-be appellant must seek to appeal to the House of Lords, there are other situations where to require this would be wholly inappropriate because there would be no realistic prospect of the House of Lords hearing an appeal.

[46] The fact that the House of Lords is generally the final court of appeal and the
c Court of Appeal is generally an intermediate court of appeal is not the only distinction between the two tribunals. The approach which the Court of Appeal adopts to giving permission to appeal to this court differs from the approach which the House of Lords adopts when deciding whether to accept an appeal. In giving permission to appeal to this court, this court is primarily concerned with correcting injustice in the particular
d case to which the application for permission relates. If there is a sufficient prospect of the appeal succeeding permission to appeal will normally be given as a matter of course. In the case of an appeal to the House of Lords it is not enough to show a sufficient prospect of the appeal succeeding. The would-be appellant has to show in addition that the case is of such importance that it justifies the attention of the House of Lords.

e [47] It is the House of Lords which is the best judge of whether a particular case meets this test. It is the House of Lords which is the best judge of whether its limited judicial resources are properly deployed in hearing a particular appeal. That is why this court rarely exercises its jurisdiction to give permission to appeal to the House of Lords.

f [48] However, there are some cases where it is obvious that the House of Lords should hear an appeal and then this court gives permission. To do otherwise causes the litigants expense which is unnecessary and squanders the judicial resources of the House of Lords. Equally, there are some cases where it is obvious that the case is one where it is inappropriate for there to be an appeal to the House of Lords. In such a case it is obvious that permission, irrespective of the merits of the appellant, will not
g be given even if there is a petition to the House of Lords. If a case falls within this category, it would not be in accord with the purposes for which this court was established for it not to accept the reality of the situation and to decline to recognise a jurisdiction which it would otherwise have, because there is a theoretical, though not a real, right of appeal to the House of Lords. In such a case this court is for practical
h purposes the final court of appeal and if this court is not prepared to ensure justice is done, justice will not be done.

[49] We will set out later how we propose to reconcile the position of this court as an intermediate appellate court with the position of the House of Lords as the final court of appeal. It is the reality of the situation which means that we cannot, as
j Jessel MR did in *Flower v Lloyd* (1877) 6 Ch D 297, take refuge in the fact that there is an alternative remedy. If there is no effective right of appeal to the House of Lords and this court is the only court which can provide a remedy then in our judgment there can arise the 'exceptional circumstances' to which Russell LJ referred in *Re Barrell Enterprises* [1972] 3 All ER 631, [1973] 1 WLR 19.

[50] If, as we believe it is necessary to do, we go back to first principles, we start with the fact which is uncontroversial, that the Court of Appeal was established with a broad jurisdiction to hear appeals. Equally it was not established to exercise an

originating as opposed to an appellate jurisdiction. It is therefore appropriate to state that in that sense it has no inherent jurisdiction. It is, however, wrong to say that it has no implicit or implied jurisdiction arising out of the fact that it is an appellate court. As an appellate court it has the implicit powers to do that which is necessary to achieve the dual objectives of an appellate court to which we have referred already (see [26], above).

[51] As to these powers, Lord Diplock, who perhaps speaks on a subject of this nature with the greatest authority of any judge, has dealt with the inherent power conferred on a court, whether appellate or not, to control its own procedure so as to prevent it being used to achieve injustice.

[52] We would give an illustration of Lord Diplock's approach. It is taken from his speech in *Bremer Vulcan Schiffbau und Maschinenfabrik v South India Shipping Corp* [1981] 1 All ER 289 at 295, [1981] AC 909 at 977:

'The High Court's power to dismiss a pending action for want of prosecution is but an instance of a general power to control its own procedure so as to prevent its being used to achieve injustice. Such a power is inherent in its constitutional function as a court of justice. Every civilised system of government requires that the state should make available to all its citizens a means for the just and peaceful settlement of disputes between them as to their respective legal rights. The means provided are courts of justice to which every citizen has a constitutional right of access in the role of plaintiff to obtain the remedy to which he claims to be entitled in consequence of an alleged breach of his legal or equitable rights by some other citizen, the defendant. Whether or not to avail himself of this right of access to the court lies exclusively within the plaintiff's choice; if he chooses to do so, the defendant has no option in the matter; his subjection to the jurisdiction of the court is compulsory. So, it would stultify the constitutional role of the High Court as a court of justice if it were not armed with power to prevent its process being misused in such a way as to diminish its capability of arriving at a just decision of the dispute. The power to dismiss a pending action for want of prosecution in cases where to allow the action to continue would involve a substantial risk that justice could not be done is thus properly described as an "inherent power" the exercise of which is within the "inherent jurisdiction" of the High Court. It would I think be conducive to legal clarity if the use of these two expressions were confined to the doing by the court of acts which it needs must have power to do in order to maintain its character as a court of justice.'

[53] In our judgment the final words of Lord Diplock, 'the doing by the courts of acts which it needs must have power to do in order to maintain its character as a court of justice' express the situation here under consideration exactly. If more authority is required, reference may be made in a very different context to the speech of Lord Morris of Borth-Y-Gest in *Connelly v DPP* [1964] 2 All ER 401 at 409, [1964] AC 1254 at 1301 where Lord Morris said:

'There can be no doubt that a court which is endowed with particular jurisdiction has powers which are necessary to enable it to act effectively within such jurisdiction. I would regard them as powers which are inherent in its jurisdiction. A court must enjoy such powers in order to enforce its rules of practice and to suppress any abuses of its process and to defeat any attempted thwarting of its process.'

a [54] Earlier judgments referring to limits on the jurisdiction of this court must be read subject to this qualification. It is very easy to confuse questions as to what is the jurisdiction of a court and how that jurisdiction should be exercised. The residual jurisdiction which we are satisfied is vested in a court of appeal to avoid real injustice in exceptional circumstances is linked to a discretion which enables the court to confine the use of that jurisdiction to the cases in which it is appropriate for it to be

b exercised. There is a tension between a court having a residual jurisdiction of the type to which we are here referring and the need to have finality in litigation. The ability to reopen proceedings after the ordinary appeal process has been concluded can also create injustice. There therefore needs to be a procedure which will ensure that proceedings will only be reopened when there is a real requirement for this to happen.

c [55] One situation where this can occur is a situation where it is alleged, as here, that a decision is invalid because the court which made it was biased. If bias is established, there has been a breach of natural justice. The need to maintain confidence in the administration of justice makes it imperative that there should be a remedy. The need for an effective remedy in such a case may justify this court in

d taking the exceptional course of reopening proceedings which it has already heard and determined. What will be of the greatest importance is that it should be clearly established that a significant injustice has probably occurred and that there is no alternative effective remedy. The effect of reopening the appeal on others and the extent to which the complaining party is the author of his own misfortune will also be important considerations. Where the alternative remedy would be an appeal to

e the House of Lords this court will only give permission to reopen an appeal which it has already determined if it is satisfied that an appeal from this court is one for which the House of Lords would not give leave.

[56] Today, except in a few special cases, there is no right of appeal without permission. The residual jurisdiction which we have been considering, is one which

f should only be exercised with the permission of this court. Accordingly a party seeking to reopen a decision of this court, whether refusing permission to appeal or dismissing a substantive appeal, must apply in writing for permission to do so. The application will then be considered on paper and only allowed to proceed if after the paper application is considered this court so directs. Unless the court so directs, there will be no right to an oral hearing of the application. The court should exercise strong

g control over any such application, so as to protect those who are entitled reasonably to believe that the litigation is already at an end.

[57] In due course the Civil Procedure Rules Committee may wish to consider whether rules or a practice direction setting out the procedure should be introduced.

h THE BIAS ISSUE

[58] The bias which is alleged here is in the court of first instance and not the appellate court. This does not mean that the jurisdiction to which we have referred cannot exist. It is, however, important to have in mind that what the Lawrences are seeking to do is to adduce further evidence of bias after this court has already considered an appeal where the issue of bias was raised and it was decided that no case

j of bias on the part of the deputy circuit judge was made out.

[59] Before turning to examine in more detail the facts of this case, it is convenient to make some comments of a general nature as to how allegations of possible bias should be dealt with by the judiciary.

[60] While before the Pinochet litigation an allegation of bias in the court was a rare event, such complaints are now becoming increasingly prevalent. In *Locabail (UK) Ltd v Bayfield Properties Ltd, Locabail (UK) Ltd v Waldorf Investment Corp, Timmins v*

Gormley, Williams v HM Inspector of Taxes, R v Bristol Betting and Gaming Licensing Committee, ex p O' Callaghan [2000] 1 All ER 65, [2000] QB 451 after hearing a number *a* of appeals at the same time this court sought to give guidance as to the principles which should be applied. Fortunately, subsequently, in a speech of Lord Hope of Craighead in *Porter v Magill* [2001] UKHL 67 at [99]–[104], [2002] 1 All ER 465 at [99]–[104], [2002] 2 WLR 37, the House of Lords has put to rest the conflicting views as to how the test in cases of apparent bias should be expressed. It can now be said *b* that the approach should be:

> 'The court must first ascertain all the circumstances which have a bearing on the suggestion that the judge was biased. It must then ask whether those circumstances would lead a fair-minded and informed observer to conclude that there was a real possibility, or a real danger, the two being the same, that the *c* tribunal was biased.' (See *Re Medicaments and Related Classes of Goods (No 2)* [2001] 1 WLR 700 at 727 (para 85).)

[61] The fact that the observer has to be 'fair-minded and informed' is important. The informed observer can be expected to be aware of the legal traditions and culture of this jurisdiction. Those legal traditions and that culture have played an important *d* role in ensuring the high standards of integrity on the part of both the judiciary and the profession which happily still exist in this jurisdiction. Our experience over centuries is that this integrity is enhanced, not damaged, by the close relations that exist between the judiciary and the legal profession. Unlike some jurisdictions the judiciary here does not isolate itself from contact with the profession. Many examples *e* of the traditionally close relationship can be given: the practice of judges and advocates lunching and dining together at the Inns of Court; the Master of the Rolls' involvement in the activities of the Law Society; the fact that it is commonplace, particularly in specialist areas of litigation and on the circuits, for the practitioners to practise together in a small number of chambers and in a small number of firms of solicitors, and for members of the judiciary to be recruited from those chambers and *f* firms.

[62] It is also accepted that barristers from the same chambers may appear before judges who were former members of their chambers or on opposite sides in the same case. This close relationship has not prejudiced but enhanced the administration of justice. The advantages in terms of improved professional standards which can flow *g* from these practices have been recognised and admired in other jurisdictions. Again by way of example, in the United States they have in recent years established the rapidly expanding American Inns of Court modelled on their English counterparts with the objective of improving professional standards.

[63] The informed observer will therefore be aware that in the ordinary way *h* contacts between the judiciary and the profession should not be regarded as giving rise to a possibility of bias. On the contrary, they promote an atmosphere which is totally inimical to the existence of bias. What is true of social relationships is equally true of normal professional relationships between a judge and the lawyers he may instruct in a private capacity.

[64] A further general comment which we would make, is that judges should be *j* circumspect about declaring the existence of a relationship where there is no real possibility of it being regarded by a fair-minded and informed observer as raising a possibility of bias. If such a relationship is disclosed, it unnecessarily raises an implication that it could affect the judgment and approach of the judge. If this is not the position no purpose is served by mentioning the relationship. On the other hand, if the situation is one where a fair-minded and informed person might regard the

a judge as biased, it is important that disclosure should be made. If the position is
borderline, disclosure should be made because then the judge can consider, having
heard the submissions of the parties, whether or not he should withdraw. In other
situations disclosure can unnecessarily undermine the litigant's confidence in the
judge.

[65] If disclosure is made, then full disclosure must be made. This case
b demonstrates the danger of making partial disclosure. If there has been partial
disclosure and the litigant learns that this is the position, this is naturally likely to excite
suspicions in the mind of the litigant concerned even though those concerns are
unjustified.

[66] The facts of the present application have to be considered against the facts
which were already known to this court when it gave its judgment on 25 January 2001
c ([2001] EWCA Civ 119, [2001] All ER (D) 180 (Jan)). On that occasion the court was
presided over by Peter Gibson LJ sitting with Chadwick and Keene LJJ. The relevant
facts of which the court was then aware are set out in Peter Gibson LJ's judgment. He
stated:

d   '[14] The second ground of appeal relates to the appearance of bias, which, if
     established, would mean that the appeal must be allowed. The deputy judge,
     Mr Lawrence points out, was a client of the claimants' solicitors. That fact was
     not disclosed until the fourth hearing conducted by the deputy judge on 9
     November 1999. The deputy judge did not disclose the fact that at that time he
     was to meet with persons from the claimants' solicitors on 11 November 1999 to
e   execute a codicil and have it witnessed, that is to say immediately after hearing
     the closing submissions and the very day before he was to give judgment, and
     that he was to visit the offices of the claimants' solicitors.

     [15] Mr Lawrence adds to those points a number of other points. They
     include that the claimants' solicitors acted for the deputy judge first in November
f   1995 to draft his will and his wife's will; that they drafted a codicil for the deputy
     judge on his instructions in April 1998; that when rejecting the defendants'
     application on 21 September 1999 relating to whether Judge Viljoen should
     conduct the trial, the deputy judge did not mention his relationship with the
     solicitors, as he had not done at the time when the deputy judge was hearing the
     evidence of Mr Moore, nor did the deputy judge mention that relationship when
g   he rejected the application for summary judgment on 28 October, although it is
     clear that he was by then aware who the claimants' solicitors were; that the
     deputy judge, in late October or early November 1999, arranged with the private
     client partner who had drafted the will and codicil that that partner should
     prepare a further amendment to the wills of the deputy judge and his wife and
h   arrange to call on the solicitors to execute the further codicil on 11 November;
     that although the deputy judge at the start of the hearing on 9 November told the
     parties that the claimants' solicitors had prepared his will and held it, he had not
     revealed anything further about his relationship with the solicitors; so that when
     the defendants were asked, as they were, together with the claimants' counsel,
     whether the relationship that was revealed between the deputy judge
j   and the claimants' solicitors was of concern to them and obtained their
     acknowledgement that it was not, a less than full account had been given to the
     defendants.

     [16] Mr Lawrence further points to the fact that on 10 November counsel for
     the claimants, Mr Cowen, was approached by either the judge, or the judge's
     clerk, or the usher—Mr Cowen cannot remember which—in the area outside
     the robing room and was told of the judge's intention to impose a timetable for

the trial as a whole and was asked to pass on that statement to Mr Lawrence, which Mr Cowen did immediately. That, Mr Lawrence says, was an approach made by the deputy judge to counsel for the claimants not in the presence of the defendants.

[17] Mr Lawrence further points out that when the visit to the claimants' solicitors took place on 11 November for the deputy judge and his wife to complete their codicils, their signatures were witnessed by a partner in the claimants' solicitors and a secretary who had worked in the litigation department for six years and whose initials had appeared on some correspondence in the case. Mr Lawrence made vigorous protests over this. At the conclusion of the judgment he sought the deputy judge's assistance as to whether he had the basis of a complaint against the deputy judge for not telling the defendants of the deputy judge's association with the claimants' solicitors. Not surprisingly, the deputy judge did not proffer such advice. But Mr Lawrence has complained to the Lord Chancellor, who has investigated the matter. No doubt on the basis of what the Lord Chancellor was told by the deputy judge, the Lord Chancellor, in a lengthy letter to Mr Lawrence dated 7 April 2000, deals with the various matters of complaint, but rejects all of them. However, in that letter—and Mr Lawrence has drawn specific attention to this—the Lord Chancellor says of the occasion when the deputy judge, with his wife, called at the offices of the claimants' solicitors: "He spoke to nobody who had any connection with the case he was hearing, and he has given me his absolute assurance that at no point has he discussed your case, or indeed any case whilst he has been hearing it, with the solicitors."

[18] The deputy judge has set out in a letter to the Civil Appeals Office his reaction to the complaints of Mr Lawrence. He says that before 11 November he had not met either the partner or the secretary who witnessed his and his wife's signatures on the codicil, that the full extent of the deputy judge's association with the solicitors was in relation to the preparation and execution of the will and the two codicils, that he knew no partner or other employee of the solicitors personally, that he did not regard them as his personal solicitors as other firms in the City had acted for him, and that the claimants' solicitors were not his executors, trustees and administrators. He says that the solicitors were instructed because they were a large firm in Watford, where he was sitting, and he wished to save going to the City. He further says that he does not consider that there was any conflict of interest and that at the time when he heard the evidence of Mr Moore, he had no idea who were the claimants' solicitors. The deputy judge was a circuit judge from 1978 to 1997. The Lord Chancellor authorised him to continue to sit, even though he had reached the age of 73 at the beginning of November 1999. Mr Lawrence at one time was suggesting that the deputy judge had a conflict of interest; but that, in my judgment, was unsustainable. It is not suggested that the deputy judge was interested in any way in the outcome of the litigation …

[20] It is not altogether clear precisely what was said by the deputy judge to the defendants and Mr Cowen on 9 November in the deputy judge's room at the start of the case. Mr Lawrence has told us that the deputy judge said, or gave the impression, that his relationship with the claimants' solicitors over his will had ended some time previously. There can be no doubt that the defendants were told that the solicitors continued to hold the deputy judge's will. There is also no doubt that the deputy judge did not indicate that he would be meeting at least two people from the claimants' solicitors for the execution of his will. We are

a
told by Mr and Mrs Lawrence that the deputy judge said that he could not remember the name of the partner concerned.'

[67] The response of the court to those facts was:

b
'[21] What then is the fair-minded and informed observer to make of this? Is it, as Mr Lawrence submits, that the deputy judge was seeking to conceal his true relationship and that he had something to hide and indeed was leaving a misleading impression? Mr Lawrence submits that this is so. He points to the fact that the deputy judge for a long time was not prepared to reveal the names of the two witnesses to his codicil when it was executed on 12 November. He says that the deputy judge ought to have inquired as to who those persons were,

c
and if he did not know that one of the persons witnessing his signature worked in the litigation department and had been involved in some capacity in correspondence with the Lawrences, he should have made it his business to find out and should not have misled the Lord Chancellor into making the statement which he did.

d
[22] It seems to me that the fair-minded and informed observer would recognise that every judge lives in the community and that in his private life, away from his judicial life, he may need to use the service providers, including solicitors. That observer would also appreciate that solicitors, by the very nature of their work, have many clients the affairs of each of whom must be kept separate from those of another client. The use by a judge of the services of a firm

e
of solicitors for his personal purposes, such as for drafting his will, would not, I think, give rise to any expectation, or even any suspicion, in the fair-minded and informed observer that the judge in his judicial capacity would, by reason of that connection over his will, be untrue to his judicial oath and favour another client of those solicitors. The observer would take note of the fact that at the time when the deputy judge heard the evidence of Mr Moore he was not aware who were

f
the solicitors of the claimants and that, having heard that evidence, the deputy judge was the obvious person to complete the hearing of the trial. Indeed, if he had stood down, there would at least have been a risk that Mr Moore's evidence would have to be taken again in front of another judge, thereby adding disproportionately to the costs of what is essentially a very minor dispute. The

g
observer would take note of the fact that the deputy judge volunteered the information that the claimants' solicitors had acted for him in preparing his will and that the deputy judge had obtained the express confirmation of the parties that there was no objection to him continuing to preside in the case. The observer would, in my view, have attached particular importance to the fact that

h
the will, as the deputy judge told the defendants, was being kept by the claimants' solicitors. That in itself would indicate that there was a continuing relationship with the solicitors and that it was possible that the will might need to be altered in some way (and codicils are frequently made after a will has been executed), when probably there would be contact between the deputy judge and those solicitors. As the deputy judge obtained confirmation from the defendants that

j
despite his connection with the solicitors over his will there was no objection to him continuing to sit, the observer would reasonably regard the completion of a codicil, which the solicitors had been asked by the deputy judge to prepare, as within the reasonable scope of what had been cleared with the parties.

[23] The witnessing of the signature of the testator on a testamentary document, as the informed observer would know, is a mere ministerial task, and the fact that a secretary in the litigation department of the solicitors happened to

be available to be such a witness is in itself neither sinister nor significant. The observer would note that the deputy judge has made clear that he did not discuss the claimants' case against the defendants when he went to complete his codicil.

[24] The passing of a message to the claimants' counsel by the deputy judge, or the court usher, or the deputy judge's clerk would not, in my view, be regarded by the observer as of any significance whatsoever. There is no evidence that the deputy judge was consulting Mr Cowen in passing that message to Mr Cowen and Mr Lawrence. I have already stated what Mr Cowen has said occurred. In my judgment, it is impossible to regard that incident as indicating any appearance of bias.

[25] It is unfortunate that in the letter to Mr Lawrence from the Lord Chancellor a factual error has been made in the sentence which I have cited. But the mere fact that a witness of the deputy judge's signature to his codicil was a secretary who had some connection with the case, in that her initials appear (with the initials of another) on letters to the defendants in relation to this case, would not appear to the fair-minded observer to be of any importance. Nor, in my judgment, can there possibly be some sort of duty on the deputy judge to have investigated precisely what functions were performed in the affairs of the claimants' solicitors by a mere witness to his signature.

[26] Looking at the matter objectively, I am wholly unable to see that the fair-minded and informed observer would conclude from the various matters to which Mr Lawrence has attached importance that this was a case in which there has been an appearance of bias. For these reasons, therefore, I do not accept his arguments on this ground.'

[68] We respectfully endorse that approach.

[69] We also endorse the approach of Chadwick LJ:

'[32] In the present case the material facts included the disclosure by the judge that the solicitors instructed by the claimants held his will. Whether or not he needed to disclose that fact in the circumstances of this case is not a matter which I find it necessary to decide. The fact is that he did disclose that fact and that that disclosure led no one to object. What he did not disclose was that those solicitors had current instructions to amend that will or, perhaps more accurately, to prepare a codicil; nor did he disclose that he had made an appointment to attend on those solicitors at their offices for the purposes of executing the codicil. Whether or not, having disclosed that the solicitors held his will, he would have been wise to disclose those additional matters also, is, again, something which I do not think it necessary to decide. The relevant question is not whether the judge was wise to act as he did; nor whether other judges might have acted differently. The relevant question is whether, having disclosed that the solicitors held the will, his failure to disclose also that the solicitors were currently instructed in relation to it gives rise to a fear in a fair-minded and informed observer of a real danger that the judge's judgment would be influenced by that current relationship.

[33] In my view, no fair-minded observer would reach the conclusion that a judge would so far forget or disregard the obligations imposed by his judicial oath as to allow himself, consciously or unconsciously, to be influenced by the fact that one of the parties before him was represented by solicitors with whom he was himself dealing on a wholly unrelated matter. It is a matter of everyday experience that judges are acquainted, in one capacity or another, with those who appear before them as solicitors or advocates. That is a matter of which an

a   informed observer would be well aware. The informed observer would be well
    aware, also, that judges, solicitors and advocates can be expected to recognise
    that it is a matter of paramount importance that the public should retain
    confidence in the administration of justice; and to recognise that they are
    required to conduct themselves accordingly. But judges, solicitors and advocates
    are entitled to expect from a fair-minded and informed observer a corresponding
b   recognition that they will endeavour to be true to their judicial oath and to the
    standards set by their respective professional codes. It is not to be assumed,
    without cogent evidence to the contrary, that a judge's acquaintanceship,
    whether social or professional, with those conducting litigation before him in a
    professional capacity will lead him to reach a decision in that litigation that he
    would not otherwise reach on the evidence and the arguments.

c   [34] The judge kept the appointment which he had made. He executed his
    will at the solicitors' offices on the evening of 11 November 1999, after the
    completion of argument in the case and before giving judgment on the following
    morning. The mere fact that he attended to execute his will in accordance with
    the appointment which he had made adds nothing, in my view, to the matters to
d   which I have already referred. It was an incident of the current professional
    relationship between the judge and his solicitors.

        [35] The more relevant question is whether his attendance at the solicitors'
    offices would lead a fair-minded and informed observer to infer that he might use
    the opportunity to discuss the litigation which he had been hearing that day with
    someone in those offices whose views would impact upon his mind; or, to revert
e   to the test which is to be applied, that the fair-minded and informed observer
    would infer that there was a real danger that that might occur.

        [36] The chance of a judge meeting out of court a solicitor or advocate who
    is currently appearing before him in court is a chance which has to be accepted
    unless judges are to lead lives of cloistered isolation. The danger lies not in the
f   chance meeting—or even in a meeting planned for some purpose unrelated to
    the litigation—but in the discussion of the litigation in the course of that meeting.
    The fair-minded and informed observer would, in my view, credit both judge
    and solicitor (or advocate) with a recognition that discussion of current litigation
    would be wholly improper; and, indeed, would be likely to be embarrassing to
    either or both of them. He would not infer, without cogent evidence to the
g   contrary, that the judge, solicitor or advocate would forget the behavioural
    norms by reference to which their daily lives are conducted.

        [37] It may well be that, had this matter been handled differently, the
    suspicion that the appellants now undoubtedly hold of the judge's partiality
    would never have arisen. But I repeat that the test is not whether the appellants
h   think that the judge may have been biased; but whether a fair-minded and
    informed observer would conclude that there was a real danger of bias. I have
    no doubt that a fair-minded and informed observer, taking account of all the
    material facts, would not reach that conclusion.'

j   [70] The new evidence upon which the Lawrences would now seek to rely is the
    fact that it is now known that the judge was not rendered a bill for the work which
    the solicitors carried out on his behalf. Their explanation for this is that the work was
    so modest it would not have been economic for them to render an account, though
    it is right to note as Mr Lawrence points out, that on a previous occasion they did
    render an account for a relatively nominal sum.

        [71] It is forcefully urged by Mr Eder, in submissions which were endorsed by
    Mr Lawrence personally when we allowed him to make short oral submissions to us,

that the conduct of the deputy judge was 'outrageous'. The fact that disclosure, having been made in part, was not followed by full disclosure was described by Lord Chancellor in the correspondence as 'unfortunate'. We have already indicated the undesirability of partial disclosure. This undesirability is underlined if the disclosure which is made appears to be made reluctantly as happened here. No doubt in Mr Lawrence's mind everything was given a more sinister twist because he would have preferred another judge to have tried the case. He had already made an application, not based on bias, for the case to be heard by another judge which was refused by the deputy judge.

[72] However, we have not only carefully considered the 'new evidence' but we have also reviewed the facts as a whole, applying the now established test for bias, and having done so we do not accept that any case of apparent bias on the part of the judge is made out.

[73] We regard it as unthinkable that an informed observer would regard it as conceivable that a judge would be influenced to favour a party in litigation with whom he has no relationship merely because that party happens to be represented by a firm of solicitors who are acting for the judge in a purely personal matter in connection with a will. There is no reason to doubt the explanation for a bill not being rendered. There is no evidence that the judge knew that this was to be the case, but even if he did, it would not alter our view.

[74] This is not a situation where we would have given permission for the new evidence to be considered if permission had been sought in accordance with the procedure set out in [56], above. The judge was not required to raise his personal relations with the solicitors and it was a mistake to do so. After he had made that mistake, his subsequent conduct fuelled the Lawrences' suspicions. Regrettably the Lawrences' response to what has happened has been a wholly disproportionate suspicion. They are not in a position to be objective, as they cannot accept a court could decide this unfortunate litigation against them unless there was bias.

[75] The fact that their feelings are no doubt genuine cannot be allowed to dictate our conclusion. To decide that the circumstances on which they rely could give rise to a suspicion of bias would put at risk the way in which the judiciary and the legal profession conduct their relationship; a relationship which has long served the interests of justice in this country.

[76] The application for permission is granted to enable this judgment to be the subject of application for leave to appeal to the House of Lords. Permission having been granted to make the application, the application is dismissed.

Application for permission allowed, but substantive application dismissed. Permission to appeal refused.

Kate O'Hanlon   Barrister.

a
Twinsectra Ltd v Yardley and others
[2002] UKHL 12

HOUSE OF LORDS

b
LORD SLYNN OF HADLEY, LORD STEYN, LORD HOFFMANN, LORD HUTTON AND LORD MILLETT

15–18 OCTOBER 2001, 21 MARCH 2002

Trust and trustee – Constructive trust – Fraud – Knowing assistance in furtherance of dishonest breach of trust – Accessory liability – Test to be applied for determining
c *dishonesty.*

The appellant, L, was a solicitor who acted for Y in a transaction which included the negotiation of a loan of £1m from the respondent lender. L did not deal directly with the lender, and another firm of solicitors, S, represented themselves as acting
d on behalf of Y. They received the money in return for an undertaking that the money would be retained until such time as it was applied in the acquisition of property on behalf of Y and that it was to be utilised solely for that purpose. Contrary to the terms of the undertaking, S did not retain the money until it was so applied, but instead paid it to L on being given an assurance by Y that it would be. In his turn, L similarly took no steps to ensure that it was utilised solely for the
e acquisition of property on Y's behalf. He simply paid it out upon Y's instructions. As a result, Y used almost £358,000 for other purposes. The loan was not repaid, and the lender brought proceedings against, inter alia, L, contending that the payment by S to L in breach of the undertaking was a breach of trust and that the latter was liable for dishonestly assisting in that breach of trust. The trial judge did
f not accept that the moneys were subject to any form of trust in S's hands, holding, inter alia, that the terms of the undertaking were too vague. He also held that, in receiving the money and paying it to Y without concerning himself about its application, L had not been acting dishonestly because he had believed that he was holding the money to Y's order without restriction. The Court of Appeal reversed the judge on both issues, and L appealed to the House of Lords.
g
Held – (1) Money held in a solicitor's client account was held in trust, and the only question would be as to the terms of the trust. In the instant case, the effect of the undertaking was to provide that the money in S's client account should remain the lender's money until such time as it was applied for the acquisition of property in
h accordance with that undertaking. It followed that S had held the money in trust for the lender, but subject to a power to apply it by way of loan to Y in accordance with the undertaking. It was true that the undertaking was unusual because there was nothing to prevent Y, having acquired a property in accordance with the undertaking, from mortgaging it to the hilt and spending the proceeds on something else. However, that did not mean that it was void for uncertainty.
j Accordingly, the Court of Appeal had been correct to reverse the judge on the first issue (see [2], [7], [12], [13], [15], [16], [25], [103], below).

(2) (Lord Millett dissenting) For the purposes of accessory liability for breach of trust, a defendant would not be held to be dishonest unless it was established that his conduct had been dishonest by the ordinary standards of reasonable and honest people and that he himself had realised that by those standards his conduct was dishonest. Thus, in equity, a person could not escape a finding of dishonesty

because he set his own standards of honesty and did not regard as dishonest what he knew would offend the normally-accepted standards of honest conduct. It would, however, be less than just for the law to permit a finding that a defendant had been dishonest in assisting a breach of trust where he had known of the facts which created the trust and its breach, but had not been aware that what he was doing would be regarded by honest men as being dishonest. It followed in the instant case that a finding of accessory liability could only be made against L if, applying the combined objective and subjective test, it was established on the evidence that he had been dishonest. Although the judge had not stated the test that he had applied to determine dishonesty, it was probable that he had applied the correct combined test, not a purely subjective test. Since it was only in exceptional circumstances that an appellate court should reverse a finding by a trial judge on a question of fact (particularly on the state of mind of a party) when the judge had had the advantage of seeing the party giving evidence in the witness box, it had not been right for the Court of Appeal to come to a different conclusion from the judge and to have held that L had been dishonest in that, when he had transferred the moneys to Y, he had known that his conduct was dishonest by the standard of responsible and honest solicitors. Accordingly, the appeal would be allowed (see [5]–[8], [20], [22]–[24], [27], [32]–[36], [38], [42], [43], [49]–[51], below); *Royal Brunei Airlines Sdn Bhd v Tan* [1995] 3 All ER 97 explained and followed.

Notes
For accessory liability for knowing assistance in breach of trust, see 48 *Halsbury's Laws* (4th edn) (2000 reissue) para 603.

Cases referred to in opinions
Abbey National plc v Solicitors' Indemnity Fund Ltd [1997] PNLR 306.
Agip (Africa) Ltd v Jackson [1992] 4 All ER 385, [1990] Ch 265, [1989] 3 WLR 1367; *affd* [1992] 4 All ER 451, [1991] Ch 547, [1991] 3 WLR 116, CA.
Aktieselskabet Dansk Skibsfinansiering v Brothers [2001] 2 BCLC 324, HK CFA.
Australian Elizabethan Theatre Trust, Re (1991) 102 ALR 681, Aust Fed Ct.
Automatic Woodturning Co Ltd v Stringer [1957] 1 All ER 90, [1957] AC 544, [1957] 2 WLR 203, HL.
Baden v Société Générale pour Favoriser le Développement du Commerce et de l'Industrie en France SA (1983) [1992] 4 All ER 161, [1993] 1 WLR 509.
Barclays Bank Ltd v Quistclose Investments Ltd [1968] 3 All ER 651, [1970] AC 567, [1968] 3 WLR 1097, HL.
Barclays Bank plc v Weeks Legg & Dean (a firm), Barclays Bank plc v Layton Lougher & Co (a firm), Mohamed v Fahiya (N E Hopkin John & Co (a firm), third party) [1998] 3 All ER 213, [1999] QB 309, [1997] 3 WLR 656, CA.
Barnes v Addy (1874) LR 9 Ch App 244, LC and LJJ.
Beaman v ARTS Ltd [1949] 1 All ER 465, [1949] 1 KB 550, CA; *rvsg* [1948] 2 All ER 89.
Boscawen v Bajwa, Abbey National plc v Boscawen [1995] 4 All ER 769, [1996] 1 WLR 328, CA.
Bristol and West Building Society v Mothew (t/a Stapley & Co) [1996] 4 All ER 698, [1998] Ch 1, [1997] 2 WLR 436, CA.
British Motor Trade Association v Salvadori [1949] 1 All ER 208, [1949] Ch 556.
Carreras Rothmans Ltd v Freeman Mathews Treasure Ltd (in liq) [1985] 1 All ER 155, [1985] Ch 207, [1984] 3 WLR 1016.
Cowan de Groot Properties Ltd v Eagle Trust plc [1992] 4 All ER 700.
Denley's Trust Deed, Re, Holman v H H Martyn & Co Ltd [1968] 3 All ER 65, [1969] 1 Ch 373, [1968] 3 WLR 457.

a *Edwards v Glyn* (1859) 2 E & E 29, 121 ER 12.

EVTR, Re, Gilbert v Barber [1987] BCLC 646, CA.

General Communications Ltd v Development Finance Corp of New Zealand Ltd [1990] 3 NZLR 406, NZ CA.

Gibert v Gonard (1884) 54 LJ Ch 439.

b *Goldcorp Exchange Ltd (in receivership), Re* [1994] 2 All ER 806, [1995] 1 AC 74, [1994] 3 WLR 199, PC.

Grant's Will Trusts, Re [1979] 3 All ER 359, [1980] 1 WLR 360.

Grupo Torras SA v Al-Sabah [1999] CLC 1469.

Manifest Shipping Co Ltd v Uni-Polaris Shipping Co Ltd [2001] UKHL 1, [2001] 1 All ER 743, [2001] 2 WLR 170.

c *McPhail v Doulton* [1970] 2 All ER 228, [1971] AC 424, [1970] 2 WLR 1110, HL.

Mortgage Express Ltd v S Newman & Co (a firm) [2000] Lloyd's Rep PN 745, CA; *rvsg* [2000] PNLR 298.

Northern Developments (Holdings) Ltd, Re (6 October 1978, unreported), Ch D.

R v Ghosh [1982] 2 All ER 689, [1982] QB 1053, [1982] 3 WLR 110, CA.

d *Rogers, Re, ex p Holland & Hannen* (1891) 8 Morr 243, CA.

Rose v Rose (1986) 7 NSWLR 679, NSW SC.

Royal Brunei Airlines Sdn Bhd v Tan [1995] 3 All ER 97, [1995] 2 AC 378, [1995] 3 WLR 64, PC.

Sefton (Earl) v Tophams Ltd [1965] 3 All ER 1, [1965] Ch 1140, [1965] 3 WLR 523, CA; *e* *rvsd* [1966] 1 All ER 1039, [1967] 1 AC 50, [1966] 2 WLR 814, HL.

Thomson (D C) & Co Ltd v Deakin [1952] 2 All ER 361, [1952] Ch 646, CA.

Toovey v Milne (1819) 2 B & Ald 683, 106 ER 514.

United Bank of Kuwait Ltd v Hammoud, City Trust Ltd v Levy [1988] 3 All ER 418, [1988] 1 WLR 1051, CA.

f *Walker v Stones* [2000] 4 All ER 412, [2001] QB 902, [2001] 2 WLR 623, CA.

Westdeutsche Landesbank Girozentrale v Islington London BC [1996] 2 All ER 961, [1996] AC 669, [1996] 2 WLR 802, HL.

Appeal

g The sixth defendant, Paul Leach, trading as Paul Leach & Co, appealed with permission of the Appeal Committee of the House of Lords given on 4 November 1999 from that part of the order of the Court of Appeal (Potter LJ, Sir Iain Glidewell and Sir David Hirst) on 28 April 1999 ([1999] Lloyd's Rep Bank 438) allowing an appeal by the claimant, Twinsectra Ltd, from the decision of Carnwath J on 9 October 1997 dismissing its claim against Mr Leach for accessory liability for breach *h* of trust. The first to fifth defendants, Francis John Yardley, Yardley Commercial Vehicles Ltd, Maltsword Ltd, YC Sales Ltd and Maltsword Properties Ltd, took no part in the proceedings before the House of Lords. The facts are set out in the opinion of Lord Hoffmann.

j *David Oliver QC, Justin Fenwick QC* and *Sue Carr* (instructed by *Fairmays*) for Mr Leach.

Romie Tager QC and *Tony Oakley* (instructed by *Wallace & Partners*) for Twinsectra.

Their Lordships took time for consideration.

21 March 2002. The following opinions were delivered.

LORD SLYNN OF HADLEY.

[1] My Lords, my noble and learned friend Lord Hoffmann has referred to the facts relevant to the issues which arise on this appeal and I gratefully adopt them.

[2] The first main issue is whether the moneys received by Sims and Roper were held in trust. The judge found that they were not; the Court of Appeal ([1999] Lloyd's Rep Bank 438) held that they were. For the reasons given by Lord Hoffmann I agree firmly with the Court of Appeal.

[3] The second issue I have found more difficult. The judge found that Mr Leach had shut his eyes to the problems or the implications of what happened, yet he acquitted him of dishonesty. The Court of Appeal in a careful analysis by Potter LJ concluded that deliberately shutting his eyes in this way was dishonesty within the valuable analysis by Lord Nicholls of Birkenhead in *Royal Brunei Airlines Sdn Bhd v Tan* [1995] 3 All ER 97, [1995] 2 AC 378.

[4] There are conflicting arguments. Prima facie, shutting one's eyes to problems or implications and not following them up may well indicate dishonesty; on the other hand, prima facie, it needs a strong case to justify the Court of Appeal reversing the finding as to dishonesty of the trial judge who has heard the witness and gone in detail into all the facts.

[5] The real difficulty it seems to me is whether in view of these two conflicting arguments the case should go for a retrial with all the disadvantages that entails or whether one of the arguments was sufficiently strong for your Lordships to accept it and to conclude the question. In the end I am not satisfied that the Court of Appeal were entitled to substitute their assessment for that of the trial judge. Despite my doubts as to the implications to be drawn on a finding of 'shutting one's eyes' it seems to me clear that the judge was very conscious of Lord Nicholls' analysis and I do not think he can possibly have left out of account the question whether Mr Leach knew or realised that what he was doing fell below the required standards when he deliberately shut his eyes eg to the implications of the undertaking given by Mr Sims. Mr Leach may have been naive or misguided but I accept that the judge after hearing lengthy evidence from Mr Leach was entitled to conclude that he had not been dishonest.

[6] Accordingly it would be wrong to send the matter for retrial and for these brief reasons and the reasons given by Lord Hutton I would allow the appeal.

LORD STEYN.

[7] My Lords, I agree that the law is as stated in the judgments of my noble and learned friends Lord Hoffmann and Lord Hutton. In particular I agree with their interpretation of the decision in *Royal Brunei Airlines Sdn Bhd v Tan* [1995] 3 All ER 97, [1995] 2 AC 378. In other words, I agree that a finding of accessory liability against Mr Leach was only permissible if, applying what Lord Hutton has called the combined test, it were established on the evidence that Mr Leach had been dishonest.

[8] After a trial Carnwath J was not satisfied that Mr Leach had been dishonest. I agree with Lord Hutton's reasons for concluding that the Court of Appeal ([1999] Lloyd's Rep Bank 438) was not entitled to reverse the judge on the central issue of dishonesty. I too would allow the appeal.

LORD HOFFMANN.

[9] My Lords, Paul Leach is a solicitor practising in Godalming under the name Paul Leach & Co. Towards the end of 1992 he acted for a Mr Yardley in a transaction which included the negotiation of a loan of £1m from Twinsectra Ltd (Twinsectra). Mr Leach did not deal directly with Twinsectra. Another firm of

a solicitors, Sims and Roper of Dorset (Sims), represented themselves as acting on behalf of Mr Yardley. They received the money in return for the following undertaking:

b '1. The loan monies will be retained by us until such time as they are applied in the acquisition of property on behalf of our client. 2. The loan monies will be utilised solely for the acquisition of property on behalf of our client and for no other purpose. 3. We will repay to you the said sum of £1,000,000·00 together with interest calculated at the rate of £657·53 … such repayment to be made by us [within four calendar months after] receipt … of the loan monies …'

[10] Contrary to the terms of the undertaking, Sims did not retain the money
c until it was applied in the acquisition of property by Mr Yardley. On being given an assurance by Mr Yardley that it would be so applied, they paid it to Mr Leach. He in turn did not take steps to ensure that it was utilised solely for the acquisition of property on behalf of Mr Yardley. He simply paid it out upon Mr Yardley's instructions. The result was that £357,720·11 was used by Mr Yardley for purposes other than the acquisition of property.

d [11] The loan was not repaid. Twinsectra sued all the parties involved including Mr Leach. The claim against him was for the £357,720·11 which had not been used to buy property. The basis of the claim was that the payment by Sims to Mr Leach in breach of the undertaking was a breach of trust and that he was liable for dishonestly assisting in that breach of trust in accordance with the principles stated
e by Lord Nicholls of Birkenhead in *Royal Brunei Airlines Sdn Bhd v Tan* [1995] 3 All ER 97, [1995] 2 AC 378.

[12] The trial judge (Carnwath J) did not accept that the moneys were 'subject to any form of trust in Sims and Roper's hands'. I do not imagine that the judge could have meant this to be taken literally. Money in a solicitor's client account is
f held on trust. The only question is the terms of that trust. I should think that what Carnwath J meant was that Sims held the money on trust for Mr Yardley absolutely. That is the way it was put by Mr Oliver QC, who appeared for Mr Leach. But, like the Court of Appeal, I must respectfully disagree. The terms of the trust upon which Sims held the money must be found in the undertaking which they gave to Twinsectra as a condition of payment. Clauses 1 and 2 of that
g undertaking made it clear that the money was not to be at the free disposal of Mr Yardley. Sims were not to part with the money to Mr Yardley or anyone else except for the purpose of enabling him to acquire property.

[13] In my opinion the effect of the undertaking was to provide that the money in the Sims client account should remain Twinsectra's money until such time as it
h was applied for the acquisition of property in accordance with the undertaking. For example, if Mr Yardley went bankrupt before the money had been so applied, it would not have formed part of his estate, as it would have done if Sims had held it in trust for him absolutely. The undertaking would have ensured that Twinsectra could get it back. It follows that Sims held the money in *trust* for Twinsectra, but subject to a *power* to apply it by way of loan to Mr Yardley in accordance with the
j undertaking. No doubt Sims also owed fiduciary obligations to Mr Yardley in respect of the exercise of the power, but we need not concern ourselves with those obligations because in fact the money was applied wholly for Mr Yardley's benefit.

[14] The judge gave two reasons for rejecting a trust. The first was that the terms of the undertaking were too vague. It did not specify any particular property for which the money was to be used. The second was that Mr Ackerman, the moving spirit behind Twinsectra, did not intend to create a trust. He set no store

by cll 1 and 2 of the undertaking and was content to rely on the guarantee in cl 3 as Twinsectra's security for repayment.

[15] I agree that the terms of the undertaking are very unusual. Solicitors acting for both lender and borrower (for example, a building society and a house buyer) commonly give an undertaking to the lender that they will not part with the money save in exchange for a duly executed charge over the property which the money is being used to purchase. The undertaking protects the lender against finding himself unsecured. But Twinsectra was not asking for any security over the property. Its security was cl 3 of the Sims undertaking. So the purpose of the undertaking was unclear. There was nothing to prevent Mr Yardley, having acquired a property in accordance with the undertaking, from mortgaging it to the hilt and spending the proceeds on something else. So it is hard to see why it should have mattered to Twinsectra whether the immediate use of the money was to acquire property. The judge thought it might have been intended to give some protective colour to a claim against the Solicitors' Indemnity Fund if Sims failed to repay the loan in accordance with the undertaking. A claim against the fund would depend upon showing that the undertaking was given in the context of an underlying transaction within the usual business of a solicitor (see *United Bank of Kuwait Ltd v Hammoud, City Trust Ltd v Levy* [1988] 3 All ER 418, [1988] 1 WLR 1051). Nothing is more usual than for solicitors to act on behalf of clients in the acquisition of property. On the other hand, an undertaking to repay a straightforward unsecured loan might be more problematic.

[16] However, the fact that the undertaking was unusual does not mean that it was void for uncertainty. The charge of uncertainty is levelled against the terms of the power to apply the funds. 'The acquisition of property' was said to be too vague. But a power is sufficiently certain to be valid if the court can say that a given application of the money does or does not fall within its terms (see *McPhail v Doulton* [1970] 2 All ER 228, [1971] AC 424). And there is no dispute that the £357,720·11 was not applied for the acquisition of property.

[17] As for Mr Ackerman's understanding of the matter, that seems to me irrelevant. Whether a trust was created and what were its terms must depend upon the construction of the undertaking. Clauses 1 and 2 cannot be ignored just because Mr Ackerman was not particularly interested in them.

[18] The other question is whether Mr Leach, in receiving the money and paying it to Mr Yardley without concerning himself about its application, could be said to have acted dishonestly. The judge found that in so doing he was 'misguided' but not dishonest. He had 'shut his eyes' to some of the problems but thought he held the money to the order of Mr Yardley without restriction. The Court of Appeal reversed this finding and held that he had been dishonest.

[19] My noble and learned friend Lord Millett considers that the Court of Appeal was justified in taking this view because liability as an accessory to a breach of trust does not depend upon dishonesty in the normal sense of that expression. It is sufficient that the defendant knew all the facts which made it wrongful for him to participate in the way in which he did. In this case, Mr Leach knew the terms of the undertaking. He therefore knew all the facts which made it wrongful for him to deal with the money to the order of Mr Yardley without satisfying himself that it was for the acquisition of property.

[20] I do not think that it is fairly open to your Lordships to take this view of the law without departing from the principles laid down by the Privy Council in the *Royal Brunei* case. For the reasons given by my noble and learned friend Lord Hutton, I consider that those principles require more than knowledge of the facts which make the conduct wrongful. They require a dishonest state of mind, that is to say,

a consciousness that one is transgressing ordinary standards of honest behaviour. I also agree with Lord Hutton that the judge correctly applied this test and that the Court of Appeal was not entitled, on the basis of the written transcript, to make a finding of dishonesty which the judge who saw and heard Mr Leach did not.

[21] The ground upon which the Court of Appeal reversed the judge's finding was that he had misdirected himself in law. His finding about Mr Leach shutting
b his eyes to problems meant that he did not appreciate that a person may be dishonest without actually knowing all the facts if he suspects that he is about to do something wrongful and deliberately shuts his eyes to avoid finding out. As Lord Nicholls said in the *Royal Brunei* case ([1995] 3 All ER 97 at 106, [1995] 2 AC 378 at 389), an honest person does not 'deliberately close his eyes and ears, or deliberately not ask questions, lest he learn something he would rather not know,
c and then proceed regardless'. So the Court of Appeal said that, when the judge said that Mr Leach was not dishonest, he meant that he was not 'consciously dishonest'. But the finding about shutting his eyes meant that in law he had nevertheless been dishonest.

[22] I do not believe that the judge fell into such an elementary error. He had
d himself quoted the passage I have cited from the opinion of Lord Nicholls in the *Royal Brunei* case a little earlier in his judgment. He could not possibly have overlooked the principle. That said, I do respectfully think it was unfortunate that the judge three times used the expression 'shut his eyes' to 'the details', or 'the problems', or 'the implications'. The expression produces in judges a reflex image of Admiral Nelson at Copenhagen and the common use of this image by lawyers to
e signify a deliberate abstinence from inquiry in order to avoid certain knowledge of what one suspects to be the case (see *Manifest Shipping Co Ltd v Uni-Polaris Shipping Co Ltd* [2001] UKHL 1 at [25], [2001] 1 All ER 743 at [25], [2001] 2 WLR 170 per Lord Hobhouse of Woodborough, and Lord Scott of Foscote, at [112]–[120]). But, as my noble and learned friend Lord Millett points out, there were in this case no
f relevant facts of which Mr Leach was unaware. What I think the judge meant was that he took a blinkered approach to his professional duties as a solicitor, or buried his head in the sand (to invoke two different animal images). But neither of those would be dishonest.

[23] Mr Leach believed that the money was at the disposal of Mr Yardley. He thought that whether Mr Yardley's use of the money would be contrary to the
g assurance he had given Mr Sims or put Mr Sims in breach of his undertaking was a matter between those two gentlemen. Such a state of mind may have been wrong. It may have been, as the judge said, misguided. But if he honestly believed, as the judge found, that the money was at Mr Yardley's disposal, he was not dishonest.

[24] I do not suggest that one cannot be dishonest without a full appreciation of
h the legal analysis of the transaction. A person may dishonestly assist in the commission of a breach of trust without any idea of what a trust means. The necessary dishonest state of mind may be found to exist simply on the fact that he knew perfectly well that he was helping to pay away money to which the recipient was not entitled. But that was not the case here. I would therefore allow the appeal
j and restore the decision of Carnwath J.

LORD HUTTON.

[25] My Lords, I have had the advantage of reading in draft the speeches of my noble and learned friends Lord Hoffmann and Lord Millett. For the reasons which they give I agree that the undertaking given by Mr Sims to Twinsectra Ltd (Twinsectra) created a trust, and I turn to consider whether the Court of Appeal was right to hold that Mr Leach is liable for assisting in Mr Sims' breach of trust.

Carnwath J held that the undertaking did not create a trust, but he also held that
Mr Leach had not been dishonest. The Court of Appeal ([1999] Lloyd's Rep Bank
438) reversed his findings and held that the undertaking gave rise to a trust and that
Mr Leach had acted dishonestly and was liable as an accessory to Mr Sims' breach
of trust.

[26] My Lords, in my opinion, the issue whether the Court of Appeal was right
to hold that Mr Leach had acted dishonestly depends on the meaning to be given to
that term in the judgment of Lord Nicholls of Birkenhead in *Royal Brunei Airlines
Sdn Bhd v Tan* [1995] 3 All ER 97, [1995] 2 AC 378. In approaching this question it
will be helpful to consider the place of dishonesty in the pattern of that judgment.
Lord Nicholls ([1995] 3 All ER 97 at 101–102, [1995] 2 AC 378 at 384–385) considered
the position of the honest trustee and the dishonest third party and stated that
dishonesty on the part of the third party was a sufficient basis for his liability
notwithstanding that the trustee, although mistaken and in breach of trust, was
honest. He then turned to consider the basis on which the third party, who does
not receive trust property but who assists the trustee to commit a breach, should be
held liable. He rejected the possibility that such a third party should never be liable
and he also rejected the possibility that the liability of a third party should be strict
so that he would be liable even if he did not know or had no reason to suspect that
he was dealing with a trustee. Therefore Lord Nicholls concluded ([1995] 3 All ER
at 104, [1995] 2 AC 378 at 387) that the liability of the accessory must be fault-based
and in identifying the touchstone of liability he stated: 'By common accord
dishonesty fulfils this role.' Then, he cited a number of authorities and the views of
commentators and observed that the tide of authority in England had flowed
strongly in favour of the test of dishonesty and that most, but not all, commentators
also preferred that test (see [1995] 3 All ER 97 at 104–105, [1995] 2 AC 378 at
388–389).

[27] Whilst in discussing the term 'dishonesty' the courts often draw a
distinction between subjective dishonesty and objective dishonesty, there are three
possible standards which can be applied to determine whether a person has acted
dishonestly. There is a purely subjective standard, whereby a person is only
regarded as dishonest if he transgresses his own standard of honesty, even if that
standard is contrary to that of reasonable and honest people. This has been termed
the 'Robin Hood test' and has been rejected by the courts. As Sir Christopher Slade
stated in *Walker v Stones* [2000] 4 All ER 412 at 444, [2001] QB 902 at 939:

> 'A person may in some cases act dishonestly, according to the ordinary use
> of language, even though he genuinely believes that his action is morally
> justified. The penniless thief, for example, who picks the pocket of the
> multi-millionaire is dishonest even though he genuinely considers the theft is
> morally justified as a fair redistribution of wealth and that he is not therefore
> being dishonest.'

Secondly, there is a purely objective standard whereby a person acts dishonestly if
his conduct is dishonest by the ordinary standards of reasonable and honest people,
even if he does not realise this. Thirdly, there is a standard which combines an
objective test and a subjective test, and which requires that before there can be a
finding of dishonesty it must be established that the defendant's conduct was
dishonest by the ordinary standards of reasonable and honest people and that he
himself realised that by those standards his conduct was dishonest. I will term this
'the combined test'.

a [28] There is a passage in the earlier part of the judgment in the *Royal Brunei* case which suggests that Lord Nicholls considered that dishonesty has a subjective element. Thus in discussing the honest trustee and the dishonest third party he stated:

b 'These examples suggest that what matters is the state of mind of the third party ... But [the trustee's] state of mind is essentially irrelevant to the question whether the *third party* should be made liable to the beneficiaries for the breach of trust.' (See [1995] 3 All ER 97 at 102, [1995] 2 AC 378 at 385.)

[29] However, after stating that the touchstone of liability is dishonesty ([1995] 3 All ER 97 at 104, [1995] 2 AC 378 at 387), Lord Nicholls went on to discuss the meaning of dishonesty:

c 'Before considering this issue further it will be helpful to define the terms being used by looking more closely at what dishonesty means in this context. Whatever may be the position in some criminal or other contexts (see, for instance, *R v Ghosh* [1982] 2 All ER 689, [1982] QB 1053), in the context of the accessory liability principle acting dishonestly, or with a lack of probity, which is synonymous, means simply not acting as an honest person would in the d circumstances. This is an objective standard.' (See [1995] 3 All ER 97 at 105, [1995] 2 AC 378 at 389.)

[30] My noble and learned friend Lord Millett has subjected this passage and subsequent passages in the judgment to detailed analysis and is of the opinion that e Lord Nicholls used the term 'dishonesty' in a purely objective sense so that in this area of the law a person can be held to be dishonest even though he does not realise that what he is doing is dishonest by the ordinary standards of honest people. This leads Lord Millett on to the conclusion that in determining the liability of an accessory dishonesty is not necessary and that liability depends on knowledge.

[31] In *R v Ghosh* [1982] 2 All ER 689, [1982] QB 1053 Lord Lane CJ held that in f the law of theft dishonesty required that the defendant himself must have realised that what he was doing was dishonest by the ordinary standards of reasonable and honest people. The three sentences in Lord Nicholls' judgment ([1995] 3 All ER 97 at 105, [1995] 2 AC 378 at 389) which appear to draw a distinction between the position in criminal law and the position in equity, do give support to Lord Millett's g view. But considering those sentences in the context of the remainder of the paragraph and taking account of other passages in the judgment, I think that in referring to an objective standard Lord Nicholls was contrasting it with the purely subjective standard whereby a man sets his own standard of honesty and does not regard as dishonest what upright and responsible people would regard as dishonest. Thus after stating that dishonesty is assessed on an objective standard he continued:

h 'At first sight this may seem surprising. Honesty has a connotation of subjectivity, as distinct from the objectivity of negligence. Honesty, indeed, does have a strong subjective element in that it is a description of a type of conduct assessed in the light of what a person actually knew at the time, as j distinct from what a reasonable person would have known or appreciated. Further, honesty and its counterpart dishonesty are mostly concerned with advertent conduct, not inadvertent conduct. Carelessness is not dishonesty. Thus for the most part dishonesty is to be equated with conscious impropriety. However, these subjective characteristics of honesty do not mean that individuals are free to set their own standards of honesty in particular circumstances. The standard of what constitutes honest conduct is not subjective. Honesty is not an optional scale, with higher or lower values according to the moral standards of each individual. If a person knowingly appropriates another's property, he will not escape a finding of dishonesty simply because he sees nothing wrong in such behaviour.' (See [1995] 3 All ER 97 at 105–106, [1995] 2 AC 378 at 389.)

Further, Lord Nicholls said:

'Ultimately, in most cases, an honest person should have little difficulty in knowing whether a proposed transaction, or his participation in it, would offend the normally accepted standards of honest conduct. Likewise, when called upon to decide whether a person was acting honestly, a court will look at all the circumstances known to the third party at the time. The court will also have regard to personal attributes of the third party such as his experience and intelligence, and the reason why he acted as he did.' (See [1995] 3 All ER 97 at 107, [1995] 2 AC 378 at 391.)

[32] The use of the word 'knowing' in the first sentence would be superfluous if the defendant did not have to be aware that what he was doing would offend the normally accepted standards of honest conduct, and the need to look at the experience and intelligence of the defendant would also appear superfluous if all that was required was a purely objective standard of dishonesty. Therefore I do not think that Lord Nicholls was stating that in this sphere of equity a man can be dishonest even if he does not know that what he is doing would be regarded as dishonest by honest people.

[33] Then, Lord Nicholls stated the general principle that dishonesty is a necessary ingredient of accessory liability and that knowledge is not an appropriate test:

'The accessory liability principle

Drawing the threads together, their Lordships' overall conclusion is that dishonesty is a necessary ingredient of accessory liability. It is also a sufficient ingredient. A liability in equity to make good resulting loss attaches to a person who dishonestly procures or assists in a breach of trust or fiduciary obligation. It is not necessary that, in addition, the trustee or fiduciary was acting dishonestly, although this will usually be so where the third party who is assisting him is acting dishonestly. "Knowingly" is better avoided as a defining ingredient of the principle, and in the context of this principle the *Baden* scale of knowledge is best forgotten (see *Baden v Société Générale pour Favoriser le Developpement du Commerce et de l'Industrie en France SA* [1992] 4 All ER 161, [1993] 1 WLR 509).' (See [1995] 3 All ER 97 at 109, [1995] 2 AC 378 at 392.)

I consider that this was a statement of general principle and was not confined to the doubtful case when the propriety of the transaction in question was uncertain.

[34] Lord Nicholls stated ([1995] 3 All ER 97 at 104, [1995] 2 AC 378 at 387) that there is a close analogy between 'knowingly' interfering with the due performance of a contract and interfering with the relationship between a trustee and a beneficiary. But this observation was made in considering and rejecting the possibility that a third party who did not receive trust property should never be liable for assisting in a breach of trust. I do not think that in referring to 'knowingly' procuring a breach of contract Lord Nicholls was suggesting that knowingly assisting in a breach of trust was sufficient to give rise to liability. Such a view would be contrary to the later passage, dealing directly with this point (see [1995] 3 All ER 97 at 109, [1995] 2 AC 378 at 392).

a [35] There is, in my opinion, a further consideration which supports the view
that for liability as an accessory to arise the defendant must himself appreciate that
what he was doing was dishonest by the standards of honest and reasonable men.
A finding by a judge that a defendant has been dishonest is a grave finding, and it is
particularly grave against a professional man, such as a solicitor. Notwithstanding
that the issue arises in equity law and not in a criminal context, I think that it would
b be less than just for the law to permit a finding that a defendant had been 'dishonest'
in assisting in a breach of trust where he knew of the facts which created the trust
and its breach but had not been aware that what he was doing would be regarded
by honest men as being dishonest.

[36] It would be open to your Lordships to depart from the principle stated by
Lord Nicholls that dishonesty is a necessary ingredient of accessory liability and to
c hold that knowledge is a sufficient ingredient. But the statement of that principle by
Lord Nicholls has been widely regarded as clarifying this area of the law and, as he
observed, the tide of authority in England has flowed strongly in favour of the test
of dishonesty. Therefore I consider that the courts should continue to apply that
test and that your Lordships should state that dishonesty requires knowledge by the
d defendant that what he was doing would be regarded as dishonest by honest
people, although he should not escape a finding of dishonesty because he sets his
own standards of honesty and does not regard as dishonest what he knows would
offend the normally accepted standards of honest conduct.

[37] In cases subsequent to the *Royal Brunei* case there has been some further
consideration of the test to be applied to determine dishonesty (the cases being
e helpfully discussed in an article by Mr Andrew Stafford QC on 'Solicitors' liability
for knowing receipt and dishonest assistance in breach of trust' (2001) 17
Professional Negligence 3. For the reasons which I have given I consider that in
Abbey National plc v Solicitors Indemnity Fund Ltd [1997] PNLR 306 Steel J applied the
correct test. In that case, she referred to the test set out in *R v Ghosh* and to
f Lord Nicholls' judgment in the *Royal Brunei* case and observed that it was to the
effect that honesty is to be judged objectively, and she continued (at 310):

'What in this case, did, Mr Fallon do, and was he acting as a reasonable and
honest solicitor would do? In that case it was laid down that individuals are not
free to set their own standards. Mr Fenwick on behalf of the defendant says
g that if I find that by those standards Mr Fallon was dishonest that would be
enough. I need to consider what he did and ask the question: Was he acting as
an honest person should? Was what he did dishonest by the standards of a
reasonable and honest man or a reasonable and honest solicitor? Having read
that case, however, it seems to me that the judgment does not set down a
wholly objective test for civil cases. Lord Nicholls particularly refers to a
h conscious impropriety. The test there, it seems, does embrace a subjective
approach, and I have to look at the circumstances to see whether they were
such that Mr Fallon must have known that what he did was by the standards
of ordinary decent people dishonest. I accept totally that individuals should
not be free to set their own standards, but there is in my view a subjective
j element both in civil and in criminal cases.'

[38] Therefore I turn to consider the judgment of Carnwath J and the Court of
Appeal on the basis that a finding of accessory liability can only be made against
Mr Leach if, applying the combined test, it were established on the evidence that he
was dishonest.

[39] At the trial Mr Leach was cross-examined very closely and at length about
his state of mind when he paid to Mr Yardley the moneys transferred to him by

Mr Sims. The tenor of his replies was that he paid the moneys to his client because
his client instructed him to do so. Thus in the course of that cross-examination *a*
counsel for Twinsectra put the following questions to him:

'Q: That is not what you said in your pleading which is what I am putting to
you. In your pleading you said that with the exception of the Glibbery
payment every other payment was made by you in the belief that the money
was going to be used for the acquisition of property by companies of *b*
Mr Yardley. A: I had no reason to disbelieve that it was not. As I said, I
believed my client. He borrowed the money. I followed his instructions.

Q: £200,000 was being transferred to Y C Sales, you did not believe for a
moment that that company was going to use it to acquire property, did you?
A: My Lord, I merely followed my client's instructions. *c*

Carnwath J: I think there is a difference. I mean I understand you are saying
that, but there is a difference between saying: "I simply paid it in accordance
with my client's instructions", and saying, as is said in the pleading: "I paid it
in the belief it was going to be used on the acquisition of property". Now, if
your evidence that the former was true and the latter was not then fair enough,
but I think Mr Tager is entitled to ask you whether it is right positively to state *d*
that you paid the moneys in the belief that they were being applied in the
acquisition of property. A: I merely believed in the sense that the monies my
client had borrowed were being used for the purpose for which he borrowed
them. I actually didn't consider the point.

Q: No, so it is probably that pleading goes rather farther than your own *e*
recollection? A: Yes, I think it is probably ....

Mr Tager: You were putting forward a case in your pleading that Mr Sims
had confirmed with you on 23 December that it was going to be used for
property. You asked your client if that was so and you got him to confirm the
details. The money comes in, you pay it out and you believe each time that
that is how the money was used. A: I had no reason to disbelieve my client. *f*

Carnwath J: I think I am clear what the witness is saying, Mr Tager.'

[40] Carnwath J stated:

'I do not find Mr Leach to have been dishonest, but he was certainly
misguided. He found himself in a difficult position. His retainer for Mr Yardley *g*
on the Apperley Bridge transaction was very important to his practice (at a
time when large conveyancing jobs were few), and offered the prospect of
similar work in the future. When asked to review the documentation on the
Nigerian venture, he was understandably reluctant to prejudice his
relationship with his client. I do not accept his evidence that he paid no regard *h*
to the details. He was specifically asked to review the terms. He must have
realised that it was a very unusual venture, and that the returns of the kind
offered were very unlikely to be associated with a wholly legitimate business
transaction ... His attitude to the Twinsectra loan was not dissimilar. When
asked to give the undertaking himself, he regarded it as a very unusual request, *j*
and one outside the normal course of a solicitor's practice. This did not lead
him to advise Mr Yardley against it, but rather to distance himself from any
responsibility for its terms. He told Mr Sims that they were a matter for him.
This unease ought to have put him on notice of the need for caution when
dealing with the money received under the undertakings. He was clearly
aware of their terms. Indeed, his pleaded defence asserts (para 25(4)) that he
believed their "substance ... to be that the advance would be applied in the

a
acquisition of property" and that he had received them on the footing that they would be so applied. Yet, in evidence, he frankly admitted that he had regarded the money as held simply to the order of Mr Yardley, without restriction. Again, I have to conclude that he simply shut his eyes to the problems. As far as he was concerned, it was a matter solely for Mr Sims to satisfy himself whether he could release the money to Mr Yardley's account.'

b
Later in the judgment after holding that the undertaking given by Mr Sims did not create a trust the judge stated:

'Were any of the defendants knowing recipients or accessories?

The above conclusion makes it unnecessary to resolve the more difficult question whether any of the defendants (that is, the Yardley companies, or Mr Leach) had the necessary state of mind to make them liable under these headings. For these purposes the companies must realistically be taken to have had the same knowledge and state of mind as Mr Yardley. I have already given my views as to the extent to which I regard him as having acted dishonestly. In Mr Leach's case, I have found that he was not dishonest, but that he did deliberately shut his eyes to the implications of the undertaking. Whether in either case this would be sufficient to establish accessory liability depends on the application of the *Royal Brunei* principles to those facts (see *Royal Brunei Airlines Sdn Bhd v Tan* [1995] 3 All ER 97, [1995] 2 AC 378). Although that case was concerned with "knowing assistance" rather than "knowing receipt", I would find it very difficult, in the light of the current state of the authorities to which I have referred, to define the difference in the mental states required; and I doubt if there is one.'

[41] It would have been open to the judge to hold that Mr Leach was dishonest, in that he knew that he was transferring to Mr Yardley or to one of his companies moneys which were subject to an undertaking that they would be applied solely for the acquisition of property and that the moneys would not be so applied. But the experienced judge who was observing Mr Leach being cross-examined at length found that Mr Leach, although misguided, was not dishonest in carrying out his client's instructions.

[42] The judge did not give reasons for this finding or state what test he applied to determine dishonesty, but I think it probable that he applied the combined test and I infer that he considered that Mr Leach did not realise that in acting on his client's instructions in relation to the moneys he was acting in a way which a responsible and honest solicitor would regard as dishonest. The judge may also have been influenced by the consideration that as he did not find that Mr Sims' undertaking created a trust Mr Leach would not have realised that he was dealing with trust property.

[43] It is only in exceptional circumstances that an appellate court should reverse a finding by a trial judge on a question of fact (and particularly on the state of mind of a party) when the judge has had the advantage of seeing the party giving evidence in the witness box. Therefore I do not think that it would have been right for the Court of Appeal in this case to have come to a different conclusion from the judge and to have held that Mr Leach was dishonest in that when he transferred the moneys to Mr Yardley he knew that his conduct was dishonest by the standards of responsible and honest solicitors.

[44] This was the view taken by the Court of Appeal in *Mortgage Express Ltd v S Newman & Co (a firm)* [2000] Lloyd's Rep PN 745 where the issue before the court was not dissimilar to the issue in the present case. In that case it was alleged that

the defendant, a solicitor, had dishonestly taken part in a mortgage fraud. In the High Court ([2000] PNLR 298) the judge found that the defendant had not consciously suspected a mortgage fraud. Nevertheless he found that she had deliberately refrained from making inquiries and giving advice which an ordinary honest and competent solicitor would have made and given in all the circumstances, and that she had no excuse for doing so other than the fact that she had taken a highly restricted and blinkered view of the duties that she owed to her clients. The judge considered that the explanation for this behaviour was to be found in what she had been told by an insurance and mortgage broker, Mr Baruch, at the outset of the whole transaction, which was that a particular client was not the kind of client who required to be advised of the matters of which a purchaser would normally be advised. The judge found that the solicitor had not been dishonest. He said (at 321–322):

> 'Her fault thus lay in her grossly defective appreciation of the nature of the duties she owed to Mortgage Express and a determination *at the outset* not to concern herself with any matters which were not strictly within the tunnel of her vision. If she honestly believed that it was proper for her to take such a restricted view of her duties, and did not in fact come to suspect that a mortgage fraud was being committed, then in my judgment, however gross the negligence she was not guilty of a dishonest or fraudulent omission within the meaning of rule 14(f) (of the Solicitors' Indemnity Rules 1993). I have concluded that, unreasonable as it was for her to hold it, the view that she held of the very restricted ambit of her duties to Mortgage Express was honestly held ... My conclusion is that her whole approach to this problem was from the outset both naive and well below the standards which should be expected of her profession, but was not dishonest.'

[45] The Court of Appeal held that the judge's finding that the defendant's conduct was explained by instructions given to her by Mr Baruch was not one which he could have come to on the pleadings and the evidence and that therefore his judgment must be set aside. The plaintiff had submitted that in the absence of a conclusion as to the Baruch instructions, it was clear that the judge would have held that the defendant had been dishonest. Therefore the plaintiff submitted that the Court of Appeal should so hold. The Court of Appeal acknowledged the logic of this submission but observed that it did not take into account the important fact that the judge had concluded that the defendant had not been dishonest after having seen her cross-examined over one-and-a-half days, and Aldous LJ (with whose judgment Tuckey and Mance LJJ agreed) stated:

> 'It would not be right for this court to conclude that Ms Newman was dishonest when the judge had concluded to the contrary, albeit upon a basis which I have held to be flawed. A conclusion as to whether Ms Newman acted honestly can only be reached after seeing Ms Newman give her evidence.' (See [2000] Lloyd's Rep PN 745 at 752 (para 38).)

[46] However, in the present case, the Court of Appeal considered that it was entitled to differ from the judge and to find that Mr Leach had been dishonest on the ground that the judge had deliberately refrained from considering a particular aspect of the case, namely 'Nelsonian' dishonesty. In his judgment, Carnwath J cited the following passage from the judgment of Lord Nicholls in *Royal Brunei Airlines Sdn Bhd v Tan* [1995] 3 All ER 97 at 106, [1995] 2 AC 378 at 389:

a
'... an honest person does not participate in a transaction if he knows it involves a misapplication of trust assets to the detriment of the beneficiaries. Nor does an honest person in such a case deliberately close his eyes and ears, or deliberately not ask questions, lest he learn something he would rather not know, and then proceed regardless.'

b
Later in his judgment after holding that the undertaking did not create a trust the judge continued with the passage which I have already set out under the heading: 'Were any of the defendants knowing recipients or accessories?'

[47] Delivering the judgment of the Court of Appeal and after referring to the passage in the judgment of Carnwath J, citing Lord Nicholls, Potter LJ stated ([1999] Lloyd's Rep Bank 438 at 462):

c
'102. ... Bearing in mind the inclusion within Lord Nicholl's definition of dishonesty of the position where a party deliberately closes his eyes and ears, it can only be assumed that at that point, when the judge referred to Mr Leach as "not dishonest", he was referring to the state of conscious, as opposed to "Nelsonian", dishonesty, and it is plain that he deliberately refrained from
d
resolving the latter question on the basis that it was unnecessary to do so.

103. Had the judge undertaken that task, Mr Tager submits that he could only have been driven to one conclusion, namely that Nelsonian dishonesty was established.'

e
[48] At the conclusion of a detailed and careful consideration of the submissions advanced by the respective counsel Potter LJ concluded the portion of the judgment relating to Mr Leach by stating (at 465–466):

'109. ... It seems to me that, save perhaps in the most exceptional circumstances, it is not the action of an honest solicitor knowingly to assist or encourage another solicitor in a deliberate breach of his undertaking. At the
f
very least it seems to me that Mr Leach's conduct amounted, in the words of Lord Nicholls to "acting in reckless disregard of others' rights or possible rights [which] can be a tell-tale sign of dishonesty".

110. I do not consider that the points taken by Mr Jackson are sufficient to negative that tell-tale sign in this case. I have already dealt with his submissions
g
(1) and (3). So far as his submission (2) is concerned, for reasons already given it does not seem to me that the fact that Mr Leach was acting for Mr Yardley can of itself excuse the formers' refusal to consider the rights or possible rights of Twinsectra which came to his notice. Nor do I consider that the question whether Mr Leach acted dishonestly in the Nelsonian sense depends on whether he appreciated that what was anticipated was a "mere" breach of
h
undertaking or that it constituted a breach of trust. In such a case the vice seems to me to rest in deliberately closing his eyes to the rights of Twinsectra, whether legal or equitable, as the beneficiary of the undertaking, and his deliberate failure to follow matters up or take advice for fear of embarrassment or disadvantage.'

j
[49] I agree with Lord Hoffmann that it is unfortunate that Carnwath J referred to Mr Leach deliberately shutting his eyes to the problems and to the implications of the undertaking, but like Lord Hoffmann I do not think it probable that having cited the passage from the judgment of Lord Nicholls ([1995] 3 All ER 97 at 106, [1995] 2 AC 378 at 389) the judge then overlooked the issue of Nelsonian dishonesty in finding that Mr Leach was not dishonest. I also consider, as Lord Millett has observed, that this was not a case where Mr Leach deliberately closed his eyes and

ears, or deliberately did not ask questions, lest he learned something he would rather not know—he already knew all the facts, but the judge concluded that nevertheless he had not been dishonest. I also think that Potter LJ applied too strict a test when he stated (at 465):

'It seems to me that, save perhaps in the most exceptional circumstances, it is not the action of an honest solicitor knowingly to assist or encourage another solicitor in a deliberate breach of his undertaking.'

This test does not address the vital point whether Mr Leach realised that his action was dishonest by the standards of responsible and honest solicitors. In the light of the judge's finding, based as it clearly was, on an assessment of Mr Leach's evidence in cross-examination in the witness box before him, I consider the Court of Appeal should not have substituted its own finding of dishonesty.

[50] As I have stated, Carnwath J did not give reasons for his finding that Mr Leach was not dishonest and did not state the test which he applied to determine dishonesty. Therefore the question arises whether a new trial should be ordered. An argument of some force can be advanced that there should be a retrial, and in the *Mortgage Express* case the Court of Appeal ordered a new trial, although with considerable reluctance. However the present case can be distinguished from the *Mortgage Express* case on the ground that in that case the judge appears to have based his decision on a factual matter (Mr Baruch's instructions) which was not before him in evidence. In the present case the evidence was fully deployed before the judge and he saw Mr Leach rigorously cross-examined at length as to his state of mind. Whilst the judge did not define the test of dishonesty which he applied, I think it probable, as I have stated, that he applied the right test, ie the combined test, and did not apply a purely subjective test. In these circumstances I consider that it would not be right to order a retrial. Whilst the decision whether a new trial should be ordered will largely depend on the facts of the particular case, I find support for this view in the judgment of the House in *Automatic Woodturning Co Ltd v Stringer* [1957] 1 All ER 90, [1957] AC 544. In that case the Court of Appeal had ordered a new trial on the issue of negligence, but the order was set aside and Lord Morton of Henryton stated:

'My Lords, I cannot think that this order would have been made if the Court of Appeal had fully appreciated that OLIVER, J., after hearing all the evidence, had expressed his view that the appellants had not been guilty of negligence at common law. There is no indication in the record that the learned judge had not fully considered the evidence when he expressed this view.' (See [1957] 1 All ER 90 at 96, [1957] AC 544 at 555.)

[51] For the reasons which I have given I would allow Mr Leach's appeal and set aside the judgment of the Court of Appeal.

LORD MILLETT.
[52] My Lords, there are two issues in this appeal. The first is concerned with the nature of the so-called '*Quistclose* trust' and the requirements for its creation (see *Barclays Bank Ltd v Quistclose Investments Ltd* [1968] 3 All ER 651, [1970] AC 567). The second arises only if the first is answered adversely to the appellant. It is whether his conduct rendered him liable for having assisted in a breach of trust. This raises two questions of some importance. One concerns the extent of the knowledge of the existence of a trust which is required before a person can be found civilly liable for having assisted in its breach. In particular, is it sufficient that he was aware of the arrangements which created the trust or must he also have appreciated

a   that they did so? The other, which has led to a division of opinion among your
Lordships, is whether, in addition to knowledge, dishonesty is required and, if so,
the meaning of dishonesty in this context. For reasons which will appear a third
question, concerned with the ingredients of the equitable claim tendentiously
described as being in respect of the 'knowing receipt' of trust property, is no longer
alive. The much needed rationalisation of this branch of the law must, therefore,
b   await another occasion.

(1) THE FACTS
   [53] The appellant Mr Leach is a solicitor. At the material time he was in sole
practice. In October 1992 he was instructed by a Mr Yardley to act in the purchase
of residential land at Apperley Bridge, Bradford. The terms of the sale required the
c   payment of £950,000 on exchange of contracts. Exchange took place on 23
December 1992 with the use of moneys obtained from Barclays Bank.
   [54] Mr Yardley was an entrepreneur with a number of irons in the fire. He was
involved in several ongoing property transactions besides the purchase of the site at
Apperley Bridge, but his interests were not confined to the purchase and development
of property. He carried on business through a series of one-man companies.
d   [55] Delays occurred in securing the necessary finance from Barclays Bank, and
by December 1992 Mr Yardley was actively seeking an alternative source of funds.
In due course he obtained an offer of a short-term loan of £1m from the respondent
Twinsectra Ltd (Twinsectra).
   [56] Twinsectra was only prepared to make the loan if repayment was secured
e   by a solicitor's personal undertaking, a most unusual requirement. Mr Leach
refused to give such an undertaking. Mr Yardley then approached another solicitor,
a Mr Sims, who was a member of a two-partner firm. Mr Sims had been involved
in some dealings on his own behalf with Mr Yardley as a result of which he owed
Mr Yardley $US1·5 m He agreed to give the requisite undertaking.
   [57] By this time Barclays Bank had agreed to provide the finance for Apperley
f   Bridge, and the loan from Twinsectra was no longer needed. Mr Yardley and
Mr Sims decided to proceed with it nevertheless. They agreed between themselves
that Mr Sims would take up the loan on his own account and use it to repay his
personal indebtedness to Mr Yardley. Mr Sims' undertaking to repay the loan,
originally intended to be by way of guarantee of Mr Yardley's liability to repay the
g   money he was borrowing from Twinsectra, would (as between himself and
Mr Yardley) be given by Mr Sims as principal debtor. Mr Yardley knew that if
Twinsectra were told of the change the loan would be at risk. The judge found that
his failure to tell Twinsectra was dishonest but that he was not liable in deceit for
falsely holding Mr Sims out as his solicitor. In the judge's view the representation
h   was essentially true, since Mr Sims had authority to act as Mr Yardley's agent to
conclude the loan agreement on his behalf. The Court of Appeal ([1999] Lloyd's
Rep Bank 438) reversed this finding because it did not meet the gravamen of
Twinsectra's complaint. This was not that it was misled about the extent of
Mr Sims' authority to bind Mr Yardley to the contract of loan. It was that it would
not have made the loan if it had known that Mr Sims was no longer acting for
j   Mr Yardley as his client in a property transaction, for in those circumstances he
could not properly give a solicitor's undertaking (see *United Bank of Kuwait Ltd v
Hammoud, City Trust Ltd v Levy* [1988] 3 All ER 418, [1988] 1 WLR 1051). The judge
found that on this aspect of the case Mr Leach, too, was not dishonest, but that he
was 'certainly misguided'.
   [58] The undertaking was drafted by Twinsectra's solicitors and was signed by
Mr Sims on 24 December 1992. It was in the following terms:

'Dear Sirs,

In consideration of your providing a loan in the sum of £1,000,000·00 (one million pounds) to a client of this firm for the purpose of temporary bridging finance in the acquisition of property to be acquired by such client, we hereby personally and irrevocably undertake that:—1. The loan monies will be retained by us until such time as they are applied in the acquisition of property on behalf of our client. 2. The loan monies will be utilised *solely* for the acquisition of property on behalf of our client *and for no other purpose.* 3. We will repay to you the said sum of £1,000,000·00 together with interest calculated at the rate of £657·53 per day from the date you instruct your bankers to transfer the loan monies to our client account, such repayment to be made on the earlier of:—(a) the last day of the fourth calendar month from the date upon which you instruct your bankers to transfer the loan monies to our client account or (b) the seventh day following our giving written notice to your solicitors of intention to make such repayment. 4. We will pay to your solicitors upon receipt by us of the loan monies their charges in connection with the loan in the sum of £1,000·00 plus VAT and disbursements. We confirm that this undertaking is given by us in the course of our business as solicitors and in the context of an underlying transaction on behalf of our clients which is part of our usual business as solicitors.' (My emphasis.)

[59] The judge found that the letter was fundamentally untrue. Mr Sims was not acting for any client in any relevant property transaction and there was no 'underlying transaction on behalf of their clients' still less one which was 'part of the usual business of solicitors'. While Mr Sims obviously knew this, however, it cannot be assumed that Mr Leach did so. The judge found that Mr Leach 'should have been aware' of it if he had thought about it at all (though even this seems somewhat speculative); but he did not find that he was.

[60] Mr Sims had previously on 23 December 1992 forwarded a draft of the proposed undertaking to Mr Leach which Mr Leach placed on his file. It did not differ from the final version in any respect material to these proceedings, which are based exclusively on cll 1 and 2 of the undertaking. Those clauses were unchanged in the final version, the only substantive amendments being to cl 3.

[61] In the letter which accompanied the draft undertaking Mr Sims sought Mr Leach's confirmation on a number of points. These included the following: 'The matter that concerns me is paragraph 1 which strictly means that my firm has to retain this sum until another property has been acquired. Is the £1,000,000·00 to be used for another purchase?' Mr Sims' concern arose from the fact that, by pre-arrangement with Mr Leach, he intended to pay the money as soon as it was received to Mr Leach as Mr Yardley's solicitor, and realised that this would put him in breach of cl 1 of the undertaking. He evidently thought that this would not matter so long as the money was applied in the acquisition of property. Mr Leach clearly understood the reason for Mr Sims' concern, even if (as may be the case) he knew nothing of the arrangement by which Mr Sims had agreed with Mr Yardley that the payment would be treated as discharging his own personal debt.

[62] Mr Leach spoke to Mr Sims by telephone and discussed the proposed undertaking. He told Mr Sims that he would obtain confirmation from Mr Yardley as to the purpose of the loan. As for Mr Sims' undertaking to retain the money, 'that was a matter for him' and he 'appreciated his difficulty'. He told Mr Sims that the moneys would be held by his firm in a separate account 'until they are required by Mr Yardley'. It was, however, for Mr Sims to decide as he was giving the undertaking and must be satisfied with its wording.

a [63] Mr Leach then spoke to Mr Yardley and was told that the money would be used in connection with property acquisitions at Stourport, Apperley Bridge and Droitwich. Mr Leach duly faxed Mr Sims and told him that he had spoken to Mr Yardley and could confirm that the money was to be used for the purchase of property. Mr Leach sent a copy of the fax to Mr Yardley and asked for his instructions to be confirmed by fax. He told Mr Yardley that he would notify him

b as soon as the moneys were received 'so that the funds may be utilised in connection with the purchase of the property you have notified to me'. Mr Yardley faxed his confirmation.

[64] All this took place on 23 December 1992 before the undertaking was finally signed by Mr Sims on the following day. On the same day, and in anticipation of the receipt of the money from Twinsectra, Mr Sims gave the necessary instructions

c to his bank to make telegraphic transfers of the bulk of the money to Mr Leach's firm. They were implemented on 29 December 1992.

[65] Mr Leach received £949,985 on 29 December 1992 and a further sum of £14,810 on 19 January 1993. The money was credited to a client account. Over a period between 29 December 1992 and 31 March 1993 the money was disbursed in

d accordance with the instructions of Mr Yardley or one of his co-directors. Three of the payments totalling £580,875 were applied in the acquisition of property at Stourbridge, Droitwich and Apperley Bridge. The judge held that these payments were within the spirit if not the letter of the undertaking and his finding was upheld by the Court of Appeal. It has not been challenged before us. Three sums totalling £22,000 were retained by Mr Leach in payment of his conveyancing fees. These

e were the subject of a claim in 'knowing receipt'. Other sums totalling £357,720·11 were applied on Mr Yardley's instructions otherwise than in connection with the acquisition of property and in breach of cl 2 of the undertaking. These were the subject of a claim for 'dishonest assistance.'

f (2) THE JUDGMENTS BELOW

[66] The judge found that the undertaking did not create a trust and accordingly dismissed the action. As a result he did not need to make a specific finding of Mr Leach's state of mind in relation to the disbursements. But in summarising his conclusions he stated that he had found that 'he was not dishonest, but that he did deliberately shut his eyes to the implications of the undertaking'.

g [67] The Court of Appeal ([1999] Lloyd's Rep Bank 438) allowed Twinsectra's appeal. They held that cll 1 and 2 of the undertaking created a *Quistclose* trust or a trust analogous thereto (which they described as 'an express purpose trust') and upheld a tracing claim for proprietary relief against Mr Yardley's companies, which were in administration. They reversed the judge's conclusion that Mr Leach had

h not been dishonest, holding that the judge's conclusions were consistent only with a finding of what they described as 'Nelsonian dishonesty', and gave judgment against him for £379,720·11 and interest.

(3) WAS THERE A *QUISTCLOSE* TRUST?

j [68] Money advanced by way of loan normally becomes the property of the borrower. He is free to apply the money as he chooses, and save to the extent to which he may have taken security for repayment the lender takes the risk of the borrower's insolvency. But it is well established that a loan to a borrower for a specific purpose where the borrower is not free to apply the money for any other purpose gives rise to fiduciary obligations on the part of the borrower which a court of equity will enforce. In the earlier cases the purpose was to enable the borrower to pay his creditors or some of them, but the principle is not limited to such cases.

[69] Such arrangements are commonly described as creating 'a *Quistclose* trust', after the well-known decision of the House in *Barclays Bank Ltd v Quistclose Investments Ltd* [1968] 3 All ER 651, [1970] AC 567 in which Lord Wilberforce confirmed the validity of such arrangements and explained their legal consequences. When the money is advanced, the lender acquires a right, enforceable in equity, to see that it is applied for the stated purpose, or more accurately to prevent its application for any other purpose. This prevents the borrower from obtaining any beneficial interest in the money, at least while the designated purpose is still capable of being carried out. Once the purpose has been carried out, the lender has his normal remedy in debt. If for any reason the purpose cannot be carried out, the question arises whether the money falls within the general fund of the borrower's assets, in which case it passes to his trustee in bankruptcy in the event of his insolvency and the lender is merely a loan creditor; or whether it is held on a resulting trust for the lender. This depends on the intention of the parties collected from the terms of the arrangement and the circumstances of the case.

[70] In the present case Twinsectra contends that cll 1 and 2 of the undertaking which Mr Sims signed on 24 December 1992 created a *Quistclose* trust. Mr Leach denies this and advances a number of objections to the existence of a trust. He says that Twinsectra lacked the necessary intention to create a trust, and relies on evidence that Twinsectra looked exclusively to Mr Sims' personal undertaking to repay the loan as its security for repayment. He says that commercial life would be impossible if trusts were lightly inferred from slight material, and that it is not enough to agree that a loan is to be made for a particular purpose. There must be something more, for example, a requirement that the money be paid into a segregated account, before it is appropriate to infer that a trust has been created. In the present case the money was paid into Mr Sims' client account, but that is sufficiently explained by the fact that it was not Mr Sims' money but his client's; it provides no basis for an inference that the money was held in trust for anyone other than Mr Yardley. Then it is said that a trust requires certainty of objects and this was lacking, for the stated purpose 'to be applied in the purchase of property' is too uncertain to be enforced. Finally it is said that no trust in favour of Twinsectra could arise prior to the failure of the stated purpose, and this did not occur until the money was misapplied by Mr Yardley's companies.

Intention

[71] The first two objections are soon disposed of. A settlor must, of course, possess the necessary intention to create a trust, but his subjective intentions are irrelevant. If he enters into arrangements which have the effect of creating a trust, it is not necessary that he should appreciate that they do so; it is sufficient that he intends to enter into them. Whether cll 1 and 2 of the undertaking created a *Quistclose* trust turns on the true construction of those clauses.

[72] The fact that Twinsectra relied for its security exclusively on Mr Sims' personal liability to repay goes to Twinsectra's subjective intention and is not relevant to the construction of the undertaking, but it is in any case not inconsistent with the trust alleged. Arrangements of this kind are not intended to provide security for repayment of the loan, but to prevent the money from being applied otherwise than in accordance with the lender's wishes. If the money is properly applied the loan is unsecured. This was true of all the decided cases, including the *Quistclose* case itself.

The effect of the undertaking

[73] A *Quistclose* trust does not necessarily arise merely because money is paid for a particular purpose. A lender will often inquire into the purpose for which a

a loan is sought in order to decide whether he would be justified in making it. He may be said to lend the money for the purpose in question, but this is not enough to create a trust; once lent the money is at the free disposal of the borrower. Similarly payments in advance for goods or services are paid for a particular purpose, but such payments do not ordinarily create a trust. The money is intended to be at the free disposal of the supplier and may be used as part of his cash flow.

b Commercial life would be impossible if this were not the case.

[74] The question in every case is whether the parties intended the money to be at the free disposal of the recipient (see *Re Goldcorp Exchange Ltd (in receivership)* [1994] 2 All ER 806 at 823, [1995] 1 AC 74 at 100 per Lord Mustill). His freedom to dispose of the money is necessarily excluded by an arrangement that the money shall be used *exclusively* for the stated purpose, for as Lord Wilberforce observed in

c the *Quistclose* case:

'A necessary consequence from this, by a process simply of interpretation, must be that if, for any reason, [the purpose could not be carried out], the money was to be returned to [the lender]: the word "only" or "exclusively" can have no other meaning or effect.' (See [1968] 3 All ER 651 at 654, [1970] AC 567 at 580.)

d
In the *Quistclose* case a public quoted company in financial difficulties had declared a final dividend. Failure to pay the dividend, which had been approved by the shareholders, would cause a loss of confidence and almost certainly drive the company into liquidation. Accordingly the company arranged to borrow a sum of money 'on condition that it is used to pay the forthcoming dividend'. The money

e was paid into a special account at the company's bank, with which the company had an overdraft. The bank confirmed that the money would only be used for the purpose of paying the dividend due on 24 July 1964. The House held that the circumstances were sufficient to create a trust of which the bank had notice, and that when the company went into liquidation without having paid the dividend the

f money was repayable to the lender.

[75] In the present case cll 1 and 2 of the undertaking are crystal clear. Mr Sims undertook that the money would be used *solely* for the acquisition of property *and for no other purpose;* and was to be retained by his firm until so applied. It would not be held by Mr Sims simply to Mr Yardley's order; and it would not be at Mr Yardley's free disposition. Any payment by Mr Sims of the money,

g whether to Mr Yardley or anyone else, otherwise than for the acquisition of property would constitute a breach of trust.

[76] Mr Leach insisted that such a payment would, no doubt, constitute a breach of contract, but there was no reason to invoke equitable principles merely because Mr Sims was a solicitor. But Mr Sims' status as a solicitor has nothing to do

h with it. Equity's intervention is more principled than this. It is unconscionable for a man to obtain money on terms as to its application and then disregard the terms on which he received it. Such conduct goes beyond a mere breach of contract. As North J explained in *Gibert v Gonard* (1884) 54 LJ Ch 439 at 440:

'It is very well known law that if one person makes a payment to another for

j a certain purpose, and that person takes the money knowing that it is for that purpose, he must apply it to the purpose for which it was given. He may decline to take it if he likes; but if he chooses to accept the money tendered for a particular purpose, it is his duty, and there is a legal obligation on him, to apply it for that purpose.'

The duty is not contractual but fiduciary. It may exist despite the absence of any contract at all between the parties, as in *Rose v Rose* (1986) 7 NSWLR 679; and it binds third parties as in the *Quistclose* case itself. The duty is fiduciary in character because a person who makes money available on terms that it is to be used for a particular purpose only and not for any other purpose thereby places his trust and confidence in the recipient to ensure that it is properly applied. This is a classic situation in which a fiduciary relationship arises, and since it arises in respect of a specific fund it gives rise to a trust.

The nature of the trust

[77] The latter two objections cannot be so easily disposed of. They call for an exploration of the true nature of the *Quistclose* trust, and in particular the location of the beneficial interest while the purpose is still capable of being carried out.

[78] This has been the subject of much academic debate. The starting point is provided by two passages in Lord Wilberforce's speech in the *Quistclose* case. He said:

'That arrangements of this character for the payment of a person's creditors by a third person, give rise to a relationship of a fiduciary character or trust, in favour, as a primary trust, of the creditors, and secondarily, if the primary trust fails, of the third person, has been recognised in a series of cases over some 150 years.' (See [1968] 3 All ER 651 at 654, [1970] AC 567 at 580.)

Later, he said:

'... when the money is advanced, the lender acquires an equitable right to see that it is applied for the primary designated purpose (see (*Re Rogers, ex p Holland & Hannen* (1891) 8 Morr 243) where both LINDLEY and KAY, L.J.J., recognised this) ...' (See [1968] 3 All ER 651 at 656, [1970] AC 567 at 580.)

[79] These passages suggest that there are two successive trusts, a primary trust for payment to identifiable beneficiaries, such as creditors or shareholders, and a secondary trust in favour of the lender arising on the failure of the primary trust. But there are formidable difficulties in this analysis, which has little academic support. What if the primary trust is not for identifiable persons, but as in the present case to carry out an abstract purpose? Where in such a case is the beneficial interest pending the application of the money for the stated purpose or the failure of the purpose? There are four possibilities: (i) in the lender; (ii) in the borrower; (iii) in the contemplated beneficiary; or (iv) in suspense.

[80] (i) *The lender.* In 'The *Quistclose* Trust: Who Can Enforce It?' (1985) 101 LQR 269, I argued that the beneficial interest remained throughout in the lender. This analysis has received considerable though not universal academic support: see for example Priestley J 'The Romalpa Clause and the *Quistclose* Trust' in Finn (ed) *Equity and Commercial Transactions* (1987) p 217 at 237; and Professor M Bridge 'The *Quistclose* Trust in a World of Secured Transactions' (1992) 12 OJLS 333 at 352; and others. It was adopted by the New Zealand Court of Appeal in *General Communications Ltd v Development Finance Corp of New Zealand Ltd* [1990] 3 NZLR 406 and referred to with apparent approval by Gummow J in *Re Australian Elizabethan Theatre Trust* (1991) 102 ALR 681. Gummow J saw nothing special in the *Quistclose* trust, regarding it as essentially a security device to protect the lender against other creditors of the borrower pending the application of the money for the stated purpose.

[81] On this analysis, the *Quistclose* trust is a simple commercial arrangement akin (as Professor Bridge observes) to a retention of title clause (though with a different object) which enables the borrower to have recourse to the lender's money for a particular purpose without entrenching on the lender's property rights

a more than necessary to enable the purpose to be achieved. The money remains the property of the lender unless and until it is applied in accordance with his directions, and in so far as it is not so applied it must be returned to him. I am disposed, perhaps predisposed, to think that this is the only analysis which is consistent both with orthodox trust law and with commercial reality. Before reaching a concluded view that it should be adopted, however, I must consider the alternatives.

b [82] (ii) *The borrower.* It is plain that the beneficial interest is not vested unconditionally in the borrower so as to leave the money at his free disposal. That would defeat the whole purpose of the arrangements, which is to prevent the money from passing to the borrower's trustee in bankruptcy in the event of his insolvency. It would also be inconsistent with all the decided cases where the contest was between the lender and the borrower's trustee in bankruptcy, as well

c as with the *Quistclose* case itself (see in particular *Toovey v Milne* (1819) 2 B & Ald 683, 106 ER 514, *Re Rogers, ex p Holland & Hannen* (1891) 8 Morr 243).

[83] The borrower's interest pending the application of the money for the stated purpose or its return to the lender is minimal. He must keep the money separate; he cannot apply it except for the stated purpose; unless the terms of the loan

d otherwise provide he must return it to the lender if demanded; he cannot refuse to return it if the stated purpose cannot be achieved; and if he becomes bankrupt it does not vest in his trustee in bankruptcy. If there is any content to beneficial ownership at all, the lender is the beneficial owner and the borrower is not.

[84] In the present case the Court of Appeal adopted a variant, locating the beneficial interest in the borrower but subject to restrictions. I shall have to return

e to this analysis later.

[85] (iii) *In the contemplated beneficiary.* In the *Quistclose* case itself, as in all the reported cases which preceded it, either the primary purpose had been carried out and the contest was between the borrower's trustee in bankruptcy or liquidator and the person or persons to whom the borrower had paid the money; or it was treated

f as having failed, and the contest was between the borrower's trustee in bankruptcy and the lender. It was not necessary to explore the position while the primary purpose was still capable of being carried out and Lord Wilberforce's observations must be read in that light.

[86] The question whether the primary trust is accurately described as a trust for the creditors first arose in *Re Northern Developments (Holdings) Ltd* (6 October 1978,

g unreported), where the contest was between the lender and the creditors. The borrower, which was not in liquidation and made no claim to the money, was the parent company of a group one of whose subsidiaries was in financial difficulty. There was a danger that if it were wound up or ceased trading it would bring down the whole group. A consortium of the group's banks agreed to put up a fund of

h more than £500,000 in an attempt to rescue the subsidiary. They paid the money into a special account in the name of the parent company for the express purpose of 'providing money for the subsidiary's unsecured creditors over the ensuing weeks' and for no other purpose. The banks' object was to enable the subsidiary to continue trading, though on a reduced scale; it failed when the subsidiary was put into receivership at a time when some £350,000 remained unexpended. Relying on

j Lord Wilberforce's observations in the passages cited above, Megarry V-C held that the primary trust was a purpose trust enforceable (inter alios) by the subsidiaries' creditors as the persons for whose benefit the trust was created.

[87] There are several difficulties with this analysis. In the first place, Lord Wilberforce's reference to *Re Rogers* makes it plain that the equitable right he had in mind was not a mandatory order to compel performance, but a negative injunction to restrain improper application of the money; for neither Lindley nor

Kay LJJ recognised more than this. In the second place, the object of the
arrangements was to enable the subsidiary to continue trading, and this would a
necessarily involve it in incurring further liabilities to trade creditors. Accordingly
the application of the fund was not confined to existing creditors at the date when
the fund was established. The company secretary was given to understand that the
purpose of the arrangements was to keep the subsidiary trading, and that the fund
was 'as good as share capital'. Thus the purpose of the arrangements was not, as in b
other cases, to enable the debtor to avoid bankruptcy by paying off existing
creditors, but to enable the debtor to continue trading by providing it with working
capital with which to incur fresh liabilities. There is a powerful argument for saying
that the result of the arrangements was to vest a beneficial interest in the subsidiary
from the start. If so, then this was not a *Quistclose* trust at all.

[88] In the third place, it seems unlikely that the banks' object was to benefit the c
creditors (who included the Inland Revenue) except indirectly. The banks had their
own commercial interests to protect by enabling the subsidiary to trade out of its
difficulties. If so, then the primary trust cannot be supported as a valid
non-charitable purpose trust (see *Re Grant's Will Trusts* [1979] 3 All ER 359, [1980] 1
WLR 360 and cf *Re Denley's Trust Deed* [1968] 3 All ER 65, [1969] 1 Ch 373). d

[89] The most serious objection to this approach is exemplified by the facts of
the present case. In several of the cases the primary trust was for an abstract purpose
with no one but the lender to enforce performance or restrain misapplication of the
money. In *Edwards v Glyn* (1859) 2 E & E 29, 121 ER 12 the money was advanced
to a bank to enable the bank to meet a run. In *Re EVTR, Gilbert v Barber* [1987] BCLC e
646 it was advanced 'for the sole purpose of buying new equipment'. In *General
Communications Ltd v Development Finance Corp of New Zealand Ltd* [1990] 3 NZLR
406 the money was paid to the borrower's solicitors for the express purpose of
purchasing new equipment. The present case is another example. It is simply not
possible to hold money on trust to acquire unspecified property from an
unspecified vendor at an unspecified time. There is no reason to make an arbitrary f
distinction between money paid for an abstract purpose and money paid for a
purpose which can be said to benefit an ascertained class of beneficiaries, and the
cases rightly draw no such distinction. Any analysis of the *Quistclose* trust must be
able to accommodate gifts and loans for an abstract purpose.

[90] (iv) *In suspense.* As Peter Gibson J pointed out in *Carreras Rothmans Ltd v* g
Freeman Mathews Treasure Ltd (in liq) [1985] 1 All ER 155 at 166, [1985] Ch 207 at 223
the effect of adopting Megarry V-C's analysis is to leave the beneficial interest in
suspense until the stated purpose is carried out or fails. The difficulty with this
(apart from its unorthodoxy) is that it fails to have regard to the role which the
resulting trust plays in equity's scheme of things, or to explain why the money is not h
simply held on a resulting trust for the lender.

[91] Lord Browne-Wilkinson gave an authoritative explanation of the resulting
trust in *Westdeutsche Landesbank Girozentrale v Islington London BC* [1996] 2 All ER
961, [1996] AC 669 and its basis has been further illuminated by Dr R Chambers in
his book *Resulting Trusts* published in 1997. Lord Browne-Wilkinson explained that j
a resulting trust arises in two sets of circumstances. He described the second as
follows: 'Where A transfers property to B *on express trusts*, but the trusts declared do
not exhaust the whole beneficial interest ...' (see [1996] 2 All ER 961 at 990, [1996]
AC 669 at 708). The *Quistclose* case was among the cases he cited as examples. He
rejected the argument that there was a resulting trust in the case before him
because, unlike the situation in the present case, there was no transfer of money on
express trusts. But he also rejected the argument on a wider and, in my respectful

a opinion, surer ground that the money was paid and received with the intention that it should become the absolute property of the recipient.

[92] The central thesis of Dr Chambers' book is that a resulting trust arises whenever there is a transfer of property in circumstances in which the transferor (or more accurately the person at whose expense the property was provided) did not intend to benefit the recipient. It responds to the absence of an intention on the part
b of the transferor to pass the entire beneficial interest, not to a positive intention to retain it. In so far as the transfer does not exhaust the entire beneficial interest, the resulting trust is a default trust which fills the gap and leaves no room for any part to be in suspense. An analysis of the *Quistclose* trust as a resulting trust for the transferor with a mandate to the transferee to apply the money for the stated purpose sits comfortably with Dr Chambers' thesis, and it might be thought surprising that he does not adopt it.
c
[93] (v) *The Court of Appeal's analysis.* The Court of Appeal were content to treat the beneficial interest as in suspense, or (following Dr Chambers' analysis) to hold that it was in the borrower, the lender having merely a contractual right enforceable by injunction to prevent misapplication. Potter LJ put it in these terms:

d
'The purpose imposed at the time of the advance creates an enforceable restriction on the borrower's use of the money. Although the lender's right to enforce the restriction is treated as arising on the basis of a "trust", the use of that word does not enlarge the lender's interest in the fund. The borrower is entitled to the beneficial use of the money, subject to the lender's right to
e   prevent its misuse; the lender's limited interest in the fund is sufficient to prevent its use for other than the special purpose for which it was advanced.'
(See [1999] Lloyd's Rep Bank 438 at 456 (para 75).)

This analysis, with respect, is difficult to reconcile with the court's actual decision in so far as it granted Twinsectra a proprietary remedy against Mr Yardley's
f companies as recipients of the misapplied funds. Unless the money belonged to Twinsectra immediately before its misapplication, there is no basis on which a proprietary remedy against third party recipients can be justified.

[94] Dr Chambers' 'novel view' (as it has been described) is that the arrangements do not create a trust at all; the borrower receives the entire beneficial ownership in the money subject only to a contractual right in the lender to prevent
g the money being used otherwise than for the stated purpose. If the purpose fails, a resulting trust in the lender springs into being. In fact, he argues for a kind of restrictive covenant enforceable by negative injunction yet creating property rights in the money. But restrictive covenants, which began life as negative easements, are part of our land law. Contractual obligations do not run with money or a chose
h in action like money in a bank account.

[95] Dr Chambers' analysis has attracted academic comment, both favourable and unfavourable. For my own part, I do not think that it can survive the criticism levelled against it by Lusina Ho and P St J Smart 'Re-interpreting the *Quistclose* Trust: A Critique of Chambers' Analysis' (2001) 21 OJLS 267. It provides no solution to
j cases of non-contractual payment; is inconsistent with Lord Wilberforce's description of the borrower's obligation as fiduciary and not merely contractual; fails to explain the evidential significance of a requirement that the money should be kept in a separate account; cannot easily be reconciled with the availability of proprietary remedies against third parties; and while the existence of a mere equity to prevent misapplication would be sufficient to prevent the money from being available for distribution to the creditors on the borrower's insolvency (because the trustee in bankruptcy has no greater rights than his bankrupt) it would not prevail

over secured creditors. If the bank in the *Quistclose* case had held a floating charge (as it probably did) and had appointed a receiver, the adoption of Dr Chambers' analysis should have led to a different outcome.

[96] Thus all the alternative solutions have their difficulties. But there are two problems which they fail to solve, but which are easily solved if the beneficial interest remains throughout in the lender. One arises from the fact, well established by the authorities, that the primary trust is enforceable by the lender. But on what basis can he enforce it? He cannot do so as the beneficiary under the secondary trust, for if the primary purpose is fulfilled there is no secondary trust: the precondition of his claim is destructive of his standing to make it. He cannot do so as settlor, for a settlor who retains no beneficial interest cannot enforce the trust which he has created.

[97] Dr Chambers insists that the lender has merely a right to prevent the misapplication of the money, and attributes this to his contractual right to specific performance of a condition of the contract of loan. As I have already pointed out, this provides no solution where the arrangement is non-contractual. But Lord Wilberforce clearly based the borrower's obligation on an equitable or fiduciary basis and not a contractual one. He was concerned to justify the co-existence of equity's exclusive jurisdiction with the common law action for debt. Basing equity's intervention on its auxiliary jurisdiction to restrain a breach of contract would not have enabled the lender to succeed against the bank, which was a third party to the contract. There is only one explanation of the lender's fiduciary right to enforce the primary trust which can be reconciled with basic principle: he can do so because he is the beneficiary.

[98] The other problem is concerned with the basis on which the primary trust is said to have failed in several of the cases, particularly *Toovey v Milne* (1819) 2 B & Ald 683, 106 ER 514 and the *Quistclose* case itself. Given that the money did not belong to the borrower in either case, the borrower's insolvency should not have prevented the money from being paid in the manner contemplated. A man cannot pay some only of his creditors once he has been adjudicated bankrupt, but a third party can. A company cannot pay a dividend once it has gone into liquidation, but there is nothing to stop a third party from paying the disappointed shareholders. The reason why the purpose failed in each case must be because the lender's object in making the money available was to save the borrower from bankruptcy in the one case and collapse in the other. But this in itself is not enough. A trust does not fail merely because the settlor's purpose in creating it has been frustrated: the trust must become illegal or impossible to perform. The settlor's motives must not be confused with the purpose of the trust; the frustration of the former does not by itself cause the failure of the latter. But if the borrower is treated as holding the money on a resulting trust for the lender but with power (or in some cases a duty) to carry out the lender's revocable mandate, and the lender's object in giving the mandate is frustrated, he is entitled to revoke the mandate and demand the return of money which never ceased to be his beneficially.

[99] There is a further point which is well brought out in the judgment of the Court of Appeal. On a purchase of land it is a commonplace for the purchaser's mortgagee to pay the mortgage money to the purchaser's solicitor against his undertaking to apply it in the payment of the purchase price in return for a properly executed conveyance from the vendor and mortgage to the mortgagee. There is no doubt that the solicitor would commit a breach of trust if he were to apply it for any other purpose, or to apply it for the stated purpose if the mortgagee countermanded his instructions (see *Bristol and West Building Society v Mothew (t/a Stapley & Co)* [1996] 4 All ER 698 at 715, [1998] Ch 1 at 22). It is universally

a acknowledged that the beneficiary of the trust, usually described as an express or implied trust, is the mortgagee. Until paid in accordance with the mortgagee's instructions or returned it is the property of the mortgagee in equity, and the mortgagee may trace the money and obtain proprietary relief against a third party (see *Boscawen v Bajwa, Abbey National plc v Boscawen* [1995] 4 All ER 769, [1996] 1 WLR 328). It is often assumed that the trust arises because the solicitor has become
b the mortgagee's solicitor for the purpose of completion. But that was not the case in *Barclays Bank plc v Weeks Legg & Dean (a firm), Barclays Bank plc v Layton Lougher & Co (a firm), Mohamed v Fahiya (N E Hopkin John & Co (a firm), third party)* [1998] 3 All ER 213, [1999] QB 309, where the solicitor's undertaking was the only communication passing between the mortgagee and the solicitor. I said:

c   'The function of the undertaking is to prescribe the terms upon which the solicitor receives the money remitted by the bank. Such money is trust money which belongs in equity to the bank but which the solicitor is authorised to disburse in accordance with the terms of the undertaking but not otherwise. Parting with the money otherwise than in accordance with the undertaking
d   constitutes at one and the same time a breach of a contractual undertaking and a breach of the trust on which the money is held.' (See [1998] 3 All ER 213 at 221, [1999] QB 309 at 324.)

The case is, of course, even closer to the present than the traditional cases in which
e a *Quistclose* trust has been held to have been created. I do not think that subtle distinctions should be made between 'true' *Quistclose* trusts and trusts which are merely analogous to them. It depends on how widely or narrowly you choose to define the *Quistclose* trust. There is clearly a wide range of situations in which the parties enter into a commercial arrangement which permits one party to have a limited use of the other's money for a stated purpose, is not free to apply it for any
f other purpose, and must return it if for any reason the purpose cannot be carried out. The arrangement between the purchaser's solicitor and the purchaser's mortgagee is an example of just such an arrangement. All such arrangements should if possible be susceptible to the same analysis.

[100] As Sherlock Holmes reminded Dr Watson, when you have eliminated the
g impossible, whatever remains, however improbable, must be the truth. I would reject all the alternative analyses, which I find unconvincing for the reasons I have endeavoured to explain, and hold the *Quistclose* trust to be an entirely orthodox example of the kind of default trust known as a resulting trust. The lender pays the money to the borrower by way of loan, but he does not part with the entire beneficial interest in the money, and in so far as he does not it is held on a resulting
h trust for the lender from the outset. Contrary to the opinion of the Court of Appeal, it is the borrower who has a very limited use of the money, being obliged to apply it for the stated purpose or return it. He has no beneficial interest in the money, which remains throughout in the lender subject only to the borrower's power or duty to apply the money in accordance with the lender's instructions. When the
j purpose fails, the money is returnable to the lender, not under some new trust in his favour which only comes into being on the failure of the purpose, but because the resulting trust in his favour is no longer subject to any power on the part of the borrower to make use of the money. Whether the borrower is obliged to apply the money for the stated purpose or merely at liberty to do so, and whether the lender can countermand the borrower's mandate while it is still capable of being carried out, must depend on the circumstances of the particular case.

Certainty

[101] After this over-long exposition, it is possible to dispose of the remaining *a* objections to the creation of a *Quistclose* trust very shortly. A trust must have certainty of objects. But the only trust is the resulting trust for the lender. The borrower is authorised (or directed) to apply the money for a stated purpose, but this is a mere power and does not constitute a purpose trust. Provided the power is stated with sufficient clarity for the court to be able to determine whether it is still *b* capable of being carried out or whether the money has been misapplied, it is sufficiently certain to be enforced. If it is uncertain, however, then the borrower has no authority to make any use of the money at all and must return it to the lender under the resulting trust. Uncertainty works in favour of the lender, not the borrower; it cannot help a person in the position of Mr Leach.

c

When the trust in favour of the lender arises

[102] Like all resulting trusts, the trust in favour of the lender arises when the lender parts with the money on terms which do not exhaust the beneficial interest. It is not a contingent reversionary or future interest. It does not suddenly come into being like an eighteenth century use only when the stated purpose fails. It is a *d* default trust which fills the gap when some part of the beneficial interest is undisposed of and prevents it from being 'in suspense'.

Conclusion

[103] In my opinion the Court of Appeal were correct to find that the terms of cll 1 and 2 of the undertaking created a *Quistclose* trust. The money was never at *e* Mr Yardley's free disposal. It was never held to his order by Mr Sims. The money belonged throughout to Twinsectra, subject only to Mr Yardley's right to apply it for the acquisition of property. Twinsectra parted with the money to Mr Sims, relying on him to ensure that the money was properly applied or returned to it. Mr Sims' act in paying the money over to Mr Leach was a breach of trust, but it did *f* not in itself render the money incapable of being applied for the stated purpose. In so far as Mr Leach applied the money in the acquisition of property, the purpose was achieved.

(4) KNOWING (OR DISHONEST) ASSISTANCE

[104] Before turning to the critical questions concerning the extent of the *g* knowledge required and whether a finding of dishonesty is a necessary condition of liability, I ought to say a word about the distinction between the 'knowing receipt' of trust money and 'knowing (or dishonest) assistance' in a breach of trust; and about the meaning of 'assistance' in this context.

[105] Liability for 'knowing receipt' is receipt-based. It does not depend on fault. *h* The cause of action is restitutionary and is available only where the defendant received or applied the money in breach of trust for his own use and benefit (see *Agip (Africa) Ltd v Jackson* [1992] 4 All ER 385 at 403–404, [1990] Ch 265 at 291–292, *Royal Brunei Airlines Sdn Bhd v Tan* [1995] 3 All ER 97 at 103, [1995] 2 AC 378 at 386). There is no basis for requiring actual knowledge of the breach of trust, let alone *j* dishonesty, as a condition of liability. Constructive notice is sufficient, and may not even be necessary. There is powerful academic support for the proposition that the liability of the recipient is the same as in other cases of restitution, that is to say strict but subject to a change of position defence.

[106] Mr Leach received sums totalling £22,000 in payment of his costs for his own use and benefit, and Twinsectra seek their repayment on the ground of knowing receipt. But he did not receive the rest of the money for his own benefit

a at all. He never regarded himself as beneficially entitled to the money. He held it to Mr Yardley's order and paid it out to Mr Yardley or his companies. Twinsectra cannot and does not base its claim in respect of these moneys in knowing receipt, not for want of knowledge, but for want of the necessary receipt. It sues in respect of knowing (or dishonest) assistance.

[107] The accessory's liability for having assisted in a breach of trust is quite
b different. It is fault-based, not receipt-based. The defendant is not charged with having received trust moneys for his own benefit, but with having acted as an accessory to a breach of trust. The action is not restitutionary; the claimant seeks compensation for wrongdoing. The cause of action is concerned with attributing liability for misdirected funds. Liability is not restricted to the person whose breach of trust or fiduciary duty caused their original diversion. His liability is strict. Nor
c is it limited to those who assist him in the original breach. It extends to everyone who consciously assists in the continuing diversion of the money. Most of the cases have been concerned, not with assisting in the original breach, but in covering it up afterwards by helping to launder the money. Mr Leach's wrongdoing is not confined to the assistance he gave Mr Sims to commit a breach of trust by receiving
d the money from him knowing that Mr Sims should not have paid it to him (though this is sufficient to render him liable for any resulting loss); it extends to the assistance he gave in the subsequent misdirection of the money by paying it out to Mr Yardley's order without seeing to its proper application.

The ingredients of accessory liability

e [108] The classic formulation of this head of liability is that of Lord Selborne LC in *Barnes v Addy* (1874) LR 9 Ch App 244 at 251. Third parties who were not themselves trustees were liable if they were found 'either making themselves trustees *de son tort*, or actually participating in any fraudulent conduct of the trustee to the injury of the *cestui que trust*'. In the next passage of his judgment (at 252) he
f amplified this by referring to those who 'assist with knowledge in a dishonest and fraudulent design on the part of the trustees'.

[109] There were thus two conditions of liability: the defendant must have assisted (i) with knowledge (ii) in a fraudulent breach of trust. The second condition was discarded in the *Royal Brunei* case. Henceforth, it was sufficient that the defendant was accessory to any breach of trust whether fraudulent or not. The
g question for present decision is concerned with the first condition. Since that case it has been clear that actual knowledge is necessary; the question is whether it is sufficient, or whether there is an additional requirement of dishonesty in the subjective sense in which that term is used in criminal cases.

[110] Prior to the decision in the *Royal Brunei* case the equitable claim was
h described as 'knowing assistance'. It gave a remedy against third parties who knowingly assisted in the misdirection of funds. The accessory was liable if he knew all the relevant facts, in particular the fact that the principal was not entitled to deal with the funds entrusted to him as he had done or was proposing to do. Unfortunately, the distinction between this form of fault-based liability and the
j liability to make restitution for trust money received in breach of trust was not always observed, and it was even suggested from time to time that the requirements of liability should be the same in the two cases. Authorities on one head of liability were applied in cases which concerned the other, and judges embarked on sophisticated analyses of the kind of knowledge required to found liability.

[111] Behind the confusion there lay a critical issue: whether negligence alone was sufficient to impose liability on the accessory. If so, then it was unnecessary to

show that he possessed actual knowledge of the relevant facts. Despite a divergence of judicial opinion, by 1995 the tide was flowing strongly in favour of rejecting negligence. It was widely thought that the accessory should be liable only if he actually knew the relevant facts. It should not be sufficient that he ought to have known them or had the means of knowledge if he did not in fact know them.

[112] There was a gloss on this. It is dishonest for a man deliberately to shut his eyes to facts which he would prefer not to know. If he does so, he is taken to have actual knowledge of the facts to which he shut his eyes. Such knowledge has been described as 'Nelsonian knowledge', meaning knowledge which is attributed to a person as a consequence of his 'wilful blindness' or (as American lawyers describe it) 'contrived ignorance'. But a person's failure through negligence to make inquiry is insufficient to enable knowledge to be attributed to him (see *Agip (Africa) Ltd v Jackson* [1992] 4 All ER 385 at 405, [1990] Ch 265 at 293).

[113] In his magisterial opinion in the *Royal Brunei* case, every word of which merits close attention, Lord Nicholls firmly rejected negligence as a sufficient condition of accessory liability. The accessory must be guilty of intentional wrongdoing. But Lord Nicholls did not, in express terms at least, substitute intentional wrongdoing as the condition of liability. He substituted dishonesty. Dishonesty, he said, was a necessary and sufficient ingredient of accessory liability. 'Knowingly' was better avoided as a defining ingredient of the principle, and the scale of knowledge accepted in *Baden v Société Générale pour Favoriser le Développement du Commerce et de l'Industrie en France SA* [1992] 4 All ER 161, [1993] 1 WLR 509 was best forgotten. His purpose, as he made clear, was to get away from the refinements which had been introduced into the concept of knowledge in the context of accessory liability.

The meaning of dishonesty in this context

[114] In taking dishonesty to be the condition of liability, however, Lord Nicholls used the word in an objective sense. He did not employ the concept of dishonesty as it is understood in criminal cases. He explained the sense in which he was using the word as follows:

> 'Whatever may be the position in some criminal or other contexts (see, for instance, *R v Ghosh* [1982] 2 All ER 689, [1982] QB 1053), in the context of the accessory liability principle acting dishonestly, or with a lack of probity, which is synonymous, means simply not acting as an honest person would in the circumstances. This is an objective standard. At first sight this may seem surprising. Honesty has a connotation of subjectivity, as distinct from the objectivity of negligence. Honesty, indeed, does have a strong subjective element in that it is a description of a type of conduct assessed in the light of what a person actually knew at the time, as distinct from what a reasonable person would have known or appreciated. Further, honesty and its counterpart dishonesty are mostly concerned with advertent conduct, not inadvertent conduct. Carelessness is not dishonesty. Thus for the most part dishonesty is to be equated with conscious impropriety. However, these subjective characteristics of honesty do not mean that individuals are free to set their own standards of honesty in particular circumstances. The standard of what constitutes honest conduct is not subjective. Honesty is not an optional scale, with higher or lower values according to the moral standards of each individual. If a person knowingly appropriates another's property, he will not escape a finding of dishonesty simply because he sees nothing wrong in such behaviour. In most situations there is little difficulty in identifying how an

a honest person would behave. Honest people do not intentionally deceive others to their detriment. Honest people do not knowingly take others' property. Unless there is a very good and compelling reason, an honest person does not participate in a transaction if he knows it involves a misapplication of trust assets to the detriment of the beneficiaries. Nor does an honest person in such a case deliberately close his eyes and ears, or deliberately not ask

b questions, lest he learn something he would rather not know, and then proceed regardless.' (See [1995] 3 All ER 97 at 105–106, [1995] 2 AC 378 at 389.)

Dishonesty as a state of mind or as a course of conduct?

c [115] In *R v Ghosh* [1982] 2 All ER 689, [1982] QB 1053 Lord Lane CJ drew a distinction between dishonesty as a state of mind and dishonesty as a course of conduct, and held that dishonesty in s 1 of the Theft Act 1968 referred to dishonesty as a state of mind. The question was not whether the accused had in fact acted dishonestly but whether he was aware that he was acting dishonestly. The jury must first of all decide whether the conduct of the accused was dishonest according to the ordinary standards of reasonable and honest people. That was an objective

d test. If he was not dishonest by those standards, that was an end of the matter and the prosecution failed. If it was dishonest by those standards, the jury had secondly to consider whether the accused was aware that what he was doing was dishonest by those standards. That was a subjective test. Given his actual (subjective) knowledge the accused must have fallen below ordinary (objective) standards of

e honesty and (subjectively) have been aware that he was doing so.

[116] The same test of dishonesty is applicable in civil cases where, for example, liability depends upon intent to defraud, for this connotes a dishonest state of mind. *Aktieselskabet Dansk Skibsfinansiering v Brothers* [2001] 2 BCLC 324 was a case of this kind (trading with intent to defraud creditors). But it is not generally an appropriate

f condition of civil liability, which does not ordinarily require a guilty mind. Civil liability is usually predicated on the defendant's conduct rather than his state of mind; it results from his negligent or unreasonable behaviour or, where this is not sufficient, from intentional wrongdoing.

[117] A dishonest state of mind might logically have been required when it was thought that the accessory was liable only if the principal was guilty of a fraudulent

g breach of trust, for then the claim could have been regarded as the equitable counterpart of the common law conspiracy to defraud. But this requirement was discarded in the *Royal Brunei* case.

[118] It is, therefore, not surprising that Lord Nicholls rejected a dishonest state of mind as an appropriate condition of liability. This is evident from the opening

h sentence of the passage cited above, from his repeated references both in that passage and later in his judgment to the defendant's conduct in 'acting dishonestly' and 'advertent conduct', and from his statement that 'for the most part' (ie not always) it involves 'conscious impropriety'. 'Honesty', he said, 'is a description of a type of conduct assessed in the light of what a person actually knew at the time'.

j Usually ('for the most part'), no doubt, the defendant will have been guilty of 'conscious impropriety'; but this is not a condition of liability. The defendant, Lord Nicholls said ([1995] 3 All ER 97 at 107, [1995] 2 AC 378 at 390) was 'required to act honestly'; and he indicated that Knox J had captured the flavour of dishonesty in *Cowan de Groot Properties Ltd v Eagle Trust plc* [1992] 4 All ER 700 at 761 when he referred to a person who is 'guilty of commercially unacceptable conduct in the particular context involved'. There is no trace in Lord Nicholls' opinion that the defendant should have been aware that he was acting contrary to objective

conduct"—or in other words, if the concealment can be said to be "dishonest" ... the claimant must show that the defendant was being dishonest in [concealing information]. We do not consider that the concealment could be described as "dishonest" unless the person concealing it is aware of what is being concealed and does not wish the claimant to discover it ... by covering up shallow foundations the builder ... cannot be said to have been guilty of "dishonest concealment" unless he was aware that his work was defective or negligent, and does not want the claimant to discover this.' (My emphasis.)

In the context it is clear that the Law Commission are indicating requirements which are not only necessary but sufficient. It would be self-defeating to require the plaintiff to establish subjective dishonesty: many people would see nothing wrong, and certainly nothing dishonest, in seeking to avoid legal liability by refraining from disclosing their breach of duty to a potential plaintiff.

[125] The modern tendency is to deprecate the use of words like 'fraud' and 'dishonesty' as synonyms for moral turpitude or conduct which is morally reprehensible. There is much to be said for semantic reform, that is to say for changing the language while retaining the incidents of equitable liability; but there is nothing to be said for retaining the language and giving it the meaning it has in criminal cases so as to alter the incidents of equitable liability.

Should subjective dishonesty be required?

[126] The question for your Lordships is not whether Lord Nicholls was using the word dishonesty in a subjective or objective sense in the *Royal Brunei* case. The question is whether a plaintiff should be required to establish that an accessory to a breach of trust had a dishonest state of mind (so that he was subjectively dishonest in the *R v Ghosh* sense); or whether it should be sufficient to establish that he acted with the requisite knowledge (so that his conduct was objectively dishonest). This question is at large for us, and we are free to resolve it either way.

[127] I would resolve it by adopting the objective approach. I would do so because: (1) consciousness of wrongdoing is an aspect of mens rea and an appropriate condition of criminal liability: it is not an appropriate condition of civil liability. This generally results from negligent or intentional conduct. For the purpose of civil liability, it should not be necessary that the defendant realised that his conduct was dishonest; it should be sufficient that it constituted intentional wrongdoing. (2) The objective test is in accordance with Lord Selborne LC's statement in *Barnes v Addy* (1874) LR 9 Ch App 244 and traditional doctrine. This taught that a person who knowingly participates in the misdirection of money is liable to compensate the injured party. While negligence is not a sufficient condition of liability, intentional wrongdoing is. Such conduct is culpable and falls below the objective standards of honesty adopted by ordinary people. (3) The claim for 'knowing assistance' is the equitable counterpart of the economic torts. These are intentional torts; negligence is not sufficient and dishonesty is not necessary. Liability depends on knowledge. A requirement of subjective dishonesty introduces an unnecessary and unjustified distinction between the elements of the equitable claim and those of the tort of wrongful interference with the performance of a contract.

[128] If Mr Sims' undertaking was contractual, as Mr Leach thought it was, then Mr Leach's conduct would have been actionable as a wrongful interference with the performance of the contract. Where a third party with knowledge of a contract has dealings with the contract breaker which the third party knows will amount to a breach of contract and damage results, he commits an actionable interference

a with the contract (see *D C Thomson & Co Ltd v Deakin* [1952] 2 All ER 361 at 378, [1952] Ch 646 at 694, *Earl of Sefton v Tophams Ltd* [1965] 3 All ER 1, [1965] Ch 1140, where the action failed only because the plaintiff was unable to prove damage).

[129] In *British Motor Trade Association v Salvadori* [1949] 1 All ER 208, [1949] Ch 556 the defendant bought and took delivery of a car in the knowledge that it was offered to him by the vendor in breach of its contract with its supplier. There is a
b close analogy with the present case. Mr Leach accepted payment from Mr Sims in the knowledge that the payment was made in breach of his undertaking to Twinsectra to retain the money in his own client account until required for the acquisition of property.

[130] In the *Earl of Sefton's* case the defendant bought land in the knowledge that
c the use to which it intended to put the land would put the vendor in breach of his contractual obligations to the plaintiff. Again the analogy with the present case is compelling. Mr Leach knew that by accepting the money and placing it at Mr Yardley's free disposal he would put Mr Sims in breach of his contractual undertaking that it would be used only for the purpose of acquiring property.

[131] In both cases the defendant was liable for any resulting loss. Such liability
d is based on the actual interference with contractual relations, not on any inducement to break them, so that it is no defence that the contract-breaker was a willing party to the breach and needed no inducement to do so. Dishonesty is not an ingredient of the tort.

[132] It would be most undesirable if we were to introduce a distinction between
e the equitable claim and the tort, thereby inducing the claimant to attempt to spell a contractual obligation out of a fiduciary relationship in order to avoid the need to establish that the defendant had a dishonest state of mind. It would, moreover, be strange if equity made liability depend on subjective dishonesty when in a comparable situation the common law did not. This would be a reversal of the general rule that equity demands higher standards of behaviour than the common law.
f [133] If we were to reject subjective dishonesty as a requirement of civil liability in this branch of the law, the remaining question is merely a semantic one. Should we return to the traditional description of the claim as 'knowing assistance', reminding ourselves that nothing less than actual knowledge is sufficient; or should we adopt Lord Nicholls' description of the claim as 'dishonest assistance',
g reminding ourselves that the test is an objective one?

[134] For my own part, I have no difficulty in equating the knowing mishandling of money with dishonest conduct. But the introduction of dishonesty is an unnecessary distraction, and conducive to error. Many judges would be reluctant to brand a professional man as dishonest where he was unaware that
h honest people would consider his conduct to be so. If the condition of liability is intentional wrongdoing and not conscious dishonesty as understood in the criminal courts, I think that we should return to the traditional description of this head of equitable liability as arising from 'knowing assistance'.

Knowledge
j [135] The question here is whether it is sufficient that the accessory should have actual knowledge of the facts which created the trust, or must he also have appreciated that they did so? It is obviously not necessary that he should know the details of the trust or the identity of the beneficiary. It is sufficient that he knows that the money is not at the free disposal of the principal. In some circumstances it may not even be necessary that his knowledge should extend this far. It may be sufficient that he knows that he is assisting in a dishonest scheme.

[136] That is not this case, for in the absence of knowledge that his client is not entitled to receive it there is nothing intrinsically dishonest in a solicitor paying money to him. But I am satisfied that knowledge of the arrangements which constitute the trust is sufficient; it is not necessary that the defendant should appreciate that they do so. Of course, if they do not create a trust, then he will not be liable for having assisted in a breach of trust. But he takes the risk that they do.

[137] The gravamen of the charge against the principal is not that he has broken his word, but that having been entrusted with the control of a fund with limited powers of disposal he has betrayed the confidence placed in him by disposing of the money in an unauthorised manner. The gravamen of the charge against the accessory is not that he is handling stolen property, but that he is assisting a person who has been entrusted with the control of a fund to dispose of the fund in an unauthorised manner. He should be liable if he knows of the arrangements by which that person obtained control of the money and that his authority to deal with the money was limited, and participates in a dealing with the money in a manner which he knows is unauthorised. I do not believe that the man in the street would have any doubt that such conduct was culpable.

The findings below

[138] Mr Leach's pleaded case was that he parted with the money in the belief, no doubt engendered by Mr Yardley's assurances, that it would be applied in the acquisition of property. But he made no attempt to support this in his evidence. It was probably impossible to do so, since he was acting for Mr Yardley in the acquisition of the three properties which had been identified to him on 23 December 1992, and must have known that some of the payments he was making were not required for their acquisition. In his evidence he made it clear that he regarded the money as held by him to Mr Yardley's order, and that there was no obligation on his part to see that the terms of the arrangements between Twinsectra and Mr Sims were observed. That was Mr Sims' responsibility, not his.

[139] The judge found that Mr Leach was not dishonest. But he also found as follows:

'He was clearly aware of [the terms of the undertaking]. Indeed, his pleaded defence asserts ... that he believed their "substance ... to be that the advance would be applied in the acquisition of property" and that he had received them on the footing that they would be so applied. Yet, in evidence, he frankly admitted that he had regarded the money as held simply to the order of Mr Yardley, without restriction. Again, I have to conclude that he simply shut his eyes to the problems. As far as he was concerned, it was a matter solely for Mr Sims to satisfy himself whether he could release the money to Mr Yardley's account.'

[140] The Court of Appeal thought that the judge's two conclusions (i) that Mr Leach was not dishonest and (ii) that he 'simply shut his eyes to the problems' (or, as he put it later in his judgment 'deliberately shut his eyes to the implications') were inconsistent. They attempted to reconcile the two findings by saying that the judge had overlooked the possibility of wilful blindness. Potter LJ put it in these terms:

'Mr Leach clearly appreciated (indeed he recorded) that an undertaking in the form proposed created difficulties for Mr Sims (as Mr Sims himself recognised) yet, as from that point ... [he] deliberately closed his eyes to those difficulties in the sense that he treated them as a problem simply for Mr Sims a and not for himself or his client.' (See [1999] Lloyd's Rep Bank 438 at 465 (para 108).)

Conclusion

[141] I do not think that this was a case of wilful blindness, or that the judge overlooked the possibility of imputed knowledge. There was no need to impute b knowledge to Mr Leach, for there was no relevant fact of which he was unaware. He did not shut his eyes to any fact in case he might learn the truth. He knew of the terms of the undertaking, that the money was not to be at Mr Yardley's free disposal. He knew (i) that Mr Sims was not entitled to pay the money over to him (Mr Leach), and was only prepared to do so against confirmation that it was proposed to apply the money for the acquisition of property; and (ii) that it could not be paid to Mr Yardley except for the c acquisition of property. There were no inquiries which Mr Leach needed to make to satisfy himself that the money could properly be put at Mr Yardley's free disposal. He knew it could not. The only thing that he did not know was that the terms of the undertaking created a trust, still less a trust in favour of Twinsectra. He believed that Mr Sims' obligations to Twinsectra sounded in contract only. That was not an d unreasonable belief; certainly not a dishonest one; though if true it would not have absolved him from liability.

[142] Yet from the very first moment that he received the money he treated it as held to Mr Yardley's order and at Mr Yardley's free disposition. He did not shut his eyes to the facts, but to 'the implications', that is to say the impropriety of putting the money at e Mr Yardley's disposal. His explanation was that this was Mr Sims' problem, not his.

[143] Mr Leach knew that Twinsectra had entrusted the money to Mr Sims with only limited authority to dispose of it; that Twinsectra trusted Mr Sims to ensure that the money was not used except for the acquisition of property; that Mr Sims had betrayed the confidence placed in him by paying the money to him (Mr Leach) without seeing to its further application; and that by putting it at Mr Yardley's free disposal he f took the risk that the money would be applied for an unauthorised purpose and place Mr Sims in breach of his undertaking. But all that was Mr Sims' responsibility.

[144] In my opinion this is enough to make Mr Leach civilly liable as an accessory (i) for the tort of wrongful interference with the performance of Mr Sims' contractual obligations if this had been pleaded and the undertaking was contractual as well as g fiduciary; and (ii) for assisting in a breach of trust. It is unnecessary to consider whether Mr Leach realised that honest people would regard his conduct as dishonest. His knowledge that he was assisting Mr Sims to default in his undertaking to Twinsectra is sufficient.

Knowing receipt

h [145] Each of the sums which Mr Leach received for his own benefit was paid in respect of an acquisition of property, and as such was a proper disbursement. He thus received trust property, but not in breach of trust. This was very properly conceded by counsel for Twinsectra before your Lordships.

j *Conclusion*

[146] I would reduce the sum for which judgment was entered by the Court of Appeal by £22,000, and subject thereto dismiss the appeal.

Appeal allowed.

Dilys Tausz   Barrister.

Irvine and another v Talksport Ltd   *a*
[2002] EWHC 367 (Ch)

CHANCERY DIVISION

LADDIE J
                                                                        b
22, 23 28, 29 JANUARY, 13 MARCH 2002

*Passing off – Endorsement – False endorsement – Whether action for passing off
applying to cases of false endorsement.*

In 1999 the defendant company, which operated a commercial radio station,   *c*
obtained the rights to broadcast live coverage of the Formula 1 (F1) Grand Prix
World Championship. To generate interest among potential advertisers, the
defendant embarked upon a special promotional campaign. It engaged the
services of a marketing and communications agency to produce a boxed pack to
be sent to just under 1000 people who it was thought were likely to be
responsible, directly or indirectly, for the placement of advertisements. The   *d*
initial mailing was deliberately timed to take place shortly before the British
Grand Prix. The contents of the box included a brochure. The photograph on
the front of the brochure was of the first claimant, a prominent British driver on
the F1 racing circuit, who was then at the height of his career and attracting great
press and media interest. The right to use the photograph had been purchased   *e*
from a sporting photograph agency. As made available by that agency, the
photograph had shown the driver holding a mobile telephone. The marketing
and communications agency, however, had taken the image and manipulated it
to cut out the mobile telephone and replace it with an image of a portable radio
to which the name of the defendant's radio station had been added. The driver,   *f*
together with a number of companies through whom, or to whom, he had
contracted to offer various services, including endorsement services, brought an
action for passing off against the defendant in respect of the distribution of the
brochure. At the trial of the driver's claim for damages, the issue arose whether
the cause of action for passing off applied to false endorsements. In reaching its
conclusion on that issue, the court was required to consider whether, as had been   *g*
held in a long-established first instance authority, a claimant had to show that he
was engaged in a common field of activity as the defendant.

Held – There was no good reason why the law of passing off, in its modern form
and in modern trade circumstances, should not apply to cases of false
endorsement. If someone acquired a valuable reputation or goodwill, the law of   *h*
passing off would protect it from unlicensed use by other parties. Such use would
frequently be damaging in the direct sense that it would involve selling inferior
goods or services under the guise that they were from the claimant. However,
the action was not restricted to protecting against that sort of damage. The law
would vindicate the claimant's exclusive right to the reputation or goodwill.   *j*
It would not allow others to so use goodwill as to reduce, blur or diminish its
exclusivity. It followed that it was not necessary to show that the claimant and
the defendant shared a common field of activity or that sales of products or
services would be diminished either substantially or directly, at least in the short
term. Moreover, it was common for famous people to exploit their names and

a images by way of endorsement. It was common knowledge that for many sportsmen income received from endorsing a variety of products and services represented a very substantial part of their income. Businessmen had reason to believe that the lustre of a famous personality, if attached to their goods or services, would enhance the attractiveness of those goods or services to their target market. In that respect, the endorsee was taking the benefit of the
b attractive force which was the reputation or goodwill of the famous person. Manufacturers and retailers recognised the realities of the market place when they paid for well-known personalities to endorse their goods, and the law of passing off should do likewise. To succeed, however, the burden on the claimant included a need to prove at least two interrelated facts, namely (i) that at the time of the acts complained of he had a significant reputation or goodwill, and (ii) that
c the actions of the defendant gave rise to a false message which would be understood by a not insignificant section of the market that his goods had been endorsed, recommended or approved of by the claimant. In the instant case, the driver was able to prove those facts, and his claim succeeded (see [38], [39], [43], [46], [56], [57], [73], [76], below).

d   *British Medical Association v Marsh* (1931) 48 RPC 565 followed.
     McCulloch v Lewis A May (Produce Distributors) Ltd [1947] 2 All ER 845 not followed.

Notes

e For the action for passing off in general, see 48 *Halsbury's Laws* (4th edn) (2000 reissue) para 297.

Cases referred to in judgment

Annabel's (Berkeley Square) Ltd v G Schock (trading as Annabel's Escort Agency) [1972] RPC 838, CA.
f *British American Glass Co Ltd v Winton Products (Blackpool) Ltd* [1962] RPC 230.
British Medical Association v Marsh (1931) 48 RPC 565.
Burberrys v JC Cording & Co Ltd (1900) 26 RPC 693.
Cadbury-Schweppes Pty Ltd v Pub Squash Co Pty Ltd [1981] 1 All ER 213, [1981] 1 WLR 193, PC.
g *Campomar Sociedad, Limitada v Nike International Ltd* (2000) 169 ALR 677, Aust HC.
Chocosuisse Union des Fabricants de Chocolat v Cadbury Ltd [1999] RPC 826, CA.
Clark v Freeman (1848) 11 Beav 112.
Douglas v Hello! Ltd [2001] 2 All ER 289, [2001] QB 967, [2001] 2 WLR 992, CA.
Eastman Photographic Materials Co Ltd v John Griffiths Cycle Corp Ltd (1898) 15 RPC
h 105.
Elvis Presley Trade Marks, Re [1999] RPC 567, CA.
Erven Warnink BV v J Townend & Sons (Hull) Ltd [1979] 2 All ER 927, [1979] AC 731, [1979] 3 WLR 68, HL.
Harrods Ltd v Harrodian School Ltd [1996] RPC 697, CA.
j *Henderson v Radio Corp Pty Ltd* [1969] RPC 218, NSW HC and NSW HC (Appellate Jurisdiction).
IRC v Muller & Co's Margarine Ltd [1901] AC 217, [1900–1903] All ER Rep 413, HL.
McCulloch v Lewis A May (Produce Distributors) Ltd [1947] 2 All ER 845, (1947) 65 RPC 58.
Moorgate Tobacco Co Ltd v Philip Morris Ltd (No 2) (1984) 56 ALR 193, Aust HC.

Parker-Knoll Ltd v Knoll International Ltd [1962] RPC 265, HL.
Reddaway (Frank) & Co Ltd v George Banham & Co Ltd [1896] AC 199, [1895–9] All
  ER Rep 133, HL.   a
Taittinger v Allbev Ltd [1994] 4 All ER 75, CA; *rvsg* [1992] FSR 647.
Van Marle v Netherlands (1986) 8 EHRR 483, ECt HR.
Vine Products Ltd v MacKenzie & Co Ltd [1969] RPC 1.
Walter v Ashton [1902] 2 Ch 282.   b
Williams v Hodge & Co (1887) 4 TLR 175.

Action

By claim form issued on 22 December 2000, the claimants, Edmund Irvine and
Tidswell Ltd, sought damages for passing off from the defendant, Talksport Ltd,
in respect of a promotional brochure issued by the defendant. The facts are set   c
out in the judgment.

Lindsay Lane (instructed by *Fladgate Fielder*) for the claimants.
Michael Hicks (instructed by *Olswang*) for the defendant.

                                                    Cur adv vult   d

13 March 2002. The following judgment was delivered.

LADDIE J.

                                                                      e
Introduction

[1] This is the judgment in an action for passing off. It raises an important
point of principle. The first claimant is Mr Edmund Irvine. The remaining
claimants are a number of companies through whom or to whom he has
contracted to offer various services, including endorsement services. Save where   f
the context otherwise requires, I will refer to the claimants as 'Mr Irvine' or 'the
claimant'. The defendant is Talksport Ltd.

[2] The evidence shows, as anyone interested in motor racing would know,
that Mr Irvine, referred to generally as 'Eddie Irvine', is a prominent driver on the
Formula 1 (F1) racing circuit. He is one of a small group of British drivers who
have achieved some success in recent years in that sport. 1999 has proved his   g
most successful year to date. During that racing season, Mr Irvine was driving F1
cars made by Ferrari. By a narrow margin he missed being the F1 champion of
the year, coming second.

[3] Talksport Ltd runs an eponymous radio station. It is now one of the largest
commercial radio stations in the United Kingdom. Until the end of 1999, the   h
station bore the name 'Talk Radio'. Under that name it concentrated on what is
called commercial news and talk-back programmes. In 1998 or early 1999, it was
decided to re-focus the area of interest away from news and general talk
programmes towards sport. At the times material to this dispute, the company's
sales director was Mr Thomas Bleakley. He became managing director of TWG
Impact, another company within the same group as the defendant. More   j
recently he has moved on to other employment. He has explained that the
decision to move the centre of interest towards sport was motivated by a desire
to capture a larger audience consisting of men earning over £20,000 per year. Part
of the implementation of that decision was the rebranding of the station by
abandoning its existing name and adopting the name 'Talksport'. As Mr Bleakley

a explains, the defendant entered into a number of contracts which allowed it to broadcast live coverage of certain high-profile sporting events. In 1999 it obtained the rights to cover, inter alia, the F1 Grand Prix World Championship.

[4] To support the change of direction and to generate interest among potential advertisers, the defendant embarked on a special promotional campaign. As part of that, it engaged the services of a marketing and *b* communications agency called SMP Ltd (SMP) to produce a number of boxed packs to be sent to just under 1,000 people who it was thought were likely to be responsible, directly or indirectly, for the placement of advertisements. Three such boxed sets were produced. The first, concentrated on cricket, since the defendant had secured broadcasting rights relating to the England Cricket Winter Tour of South Africa. The third was a more general promotion covering a *c* number of sports. It is the second with which this action is concerned.

[5] The second promotion consisted of a box bearing the image depicted at Annex 1 to this judgment. The car in the middle of the photograph is a F1 racing car. The two small photographs at opposite corners of the main image are of another famous F1 driver, Mr Michael Schumacher. On the bottom right of the *d* image there is an instruction that, if undelivered, the box should be returned to an identified PO Box. There is no other marking on the box, save for the address of the addressee. Inside the box is a pair of white shorts and a brochure or 'flyer'. The shorts bear on the back an imitation of the skid mark left on the road when a car accelerates too forcefully. On the front there are the words 'Talk radio 1053/1089 am'. The brochure has four sides (ie it is one piece of card folded *e* down the middle). The front is shown in Annex 2 to this judgment. Inside and on the back there is advertising copy extolling the virtues of Talk Radio including, in particular, as a vehicle for carrying sport-related advertisements. The reader is invited to contact a website: www.talksport.net. In the middle of pp 2 and 3 is a partial photograph of an F1 car. On the back page is a further photograph of *f* another F1 car and a photograph of the winner's podium at the Monte Carlo F1 Grand Prix showing, amongst others, Michael Schumacher, Mika Hakkinen and Eddie Irvine. All three are F1 drivers. This page is shown in Annex 3.

[6] There was no dispute between the parties that the anonymous box and the shorts are likely to be discarded and the brochure retained, assuming that all three *g* are not immediately thrown away by the recipient. It is the brochure which will stay on the recipient's desk or may be passed to others.

[7] The photograph on the front of the brochure is of Eddie Irvine. There is no question of copyright infringement because the right to use this photograph was purchased from a sporting photograph agency. However the photograph as made available by the agency does not show Mr Irvine holding a radio. He is *h* holding a mobile telephone. SMP took that image and manipulated it to cut out the mobile telephone and to replace it by an image of a portable radio to which the words 'Talk Radio' had been added.

[8] It is Mr Irvine's case that the distribution of the defendant's brochure bearing a manipulated picture of him is an actionable passing off. He seeks *j* damages but not an injunction because, at a very early stage, the defendant wrote a letter which included the following:

'The flyer was part of a campaign promoting Talk Radio's live coverage of the FIA Grand Prix World Championship. The initial mailing itself was time critical to coincide with the British Grand Prix at Silverstone on 11 July 1999

... Without any admission of liability, we confirm that no more of these
flyers will be despatched.'

[9] Before considering the principles of law and the facts in this case, it will be
useful to clear up one issue of terminology. Throughout the trial reference was
made to sponsorship, endorsement and merchandising. The evidence sometimes
referred to one, sometimes another and at times to all of these. As Ms Lane, who
appeared for the claimants, explained, this case is concerned with endorsement.
When someone endorses a product or service he tells the relevant public that he
approves of the product or service or is happy to be associated with it. In effect
he adds his name as an encouragement to members of the relevant public to buy
or use the service or product. Merchandising is rather different. It involves
exploiting images, themes or articles which have become famous. To take a
topical example, when the recent film, *Star Wars Episode 1* was about to be
exhibited, a large number of toys, posters, garments and the like were put on sale,
each of which bore an image of or reproduced a character or object in the film.
The purpose of this was to make available a large number of products which
could be bought by members of the public who found the film enjoyable and
wanted a reminder of it. The manufacture and distribution of this type of spin-off
product is referred to as merchandising. It is not a necessary feature of
merchandising that members of the public will think the products are in any sense
endorsed by the film makers or actors in the film. Merchandised products will
include some where there is a perception of endorsement and some where there
may not be, but in all cases the products are tied into and are a reminder of the
film itself. An example of merchandising is the sale of memorabilia relating to the
late Diana, Princess of Wales. A porcelain plate bearing her image could hardly
be thought of as being endorsed by her, but the enhanced sales which may be
achieved by virtue of the presence of the image is a form of merchandising.

The relevant law

[10] As I have said, Ms Lane has argued that this is an endorsement case (or
more strictly a false endorsement case) and falls squarely within modern
application of the law of passing off. Mr Michael Hicks, who appears for the
defendant, argues that even as an endorsement case, this fails to fall within the
scope of passing off. At the forefront of his submission and encapsulating the
various strands of his argument he relied on the following passage from the
judgment of Simon Brown LJ in *Re Elvis Presley Trade Marks* [1999] RPC 567 at
597–598:

'On analysis, as it seems to me, all the English cases upon which [the
appellant] seeks to rely (*Mirage Studios* not least) can be seen to have turned
essentially upon the need to protect copyright or to prevent passing off (or
libel). None creates the broad right for which in effect [counsel for the
appellant] contends here, a free standing general right to character
exploitation enjoyable exclusively by the celebrity. As Robert Walker L.J.
has explained, just such a right, a new "character right" to fill a perceived gap
between the law of copyright (there being no copyright in a name) and the
law of passing off was considered and rejected by the Whitford Committee
in 1977. Thirty years earlier, indeed, when it was contended for as a corollary
of passing off law, it had been rejected in *McCulloch v. Lewis A. May* ([1947] 2
All ER 845, (1947) 65 RPC 58). I would assume to reject it. In addressing the

a critical issue of distinctiveness there should be no *a priori* assumption that only a celebrity or his successors may ever market (or licence the marketing of) his own character. Monopolies should not be so readily created.'

[11] At its heart, Mr Hicks' argument was that what Mr Irvine is trying to enforce here is just the sort of broad and novel right which Simon Brown LJ rejected.

b [12] This dispute raises important questions as to the nature of the cause of action in passing off and whether, as Ms Lane asserted, that cause of action can prevent unauthorised endorsements assuming, of course, that what has happened here amounts to such an endorsement.

[13] The sort of cases which come within the scope of a passing off action has c not remained stationary over the years. This is for two reasons. First, passing off is closely connected to and dependent upon what is happening in the market place. It is a judge-made law which tries to ensure, in its own limited way, a degree of honesty and fairness in the way trade is conducted. As Lord Morris of Borth-Y-Gest said in *Parker-Knoll Ltd v Knoll International Ltd* [1962] RPC 265 at 278:

d 'My Lords, in the interests of fair trading and in the interests of all who may wish to buy or to sell goods the law recognises that certain limitations upon freedom of action are necessary and desirable. In some situations the law has had to resolve what might at first appear to be conflicts between competing right. In solving the problems which have arisen there has been no need to e resort to any abstruse principles but rather, I think, to the straightforward principle that trading must not only be honest but must not even unintentionally be unfair.'

[14] That statement does not define the characteristics of a passing off action, but it does emphasise that an underlying principle is the maintenance of what is f currently regarded as fair trading. The law of passing off responds to changes in the nature of trade.

[15] Second, the law itself has refined over the years. As Lord Scarman said in *Cadbury-Schweppes Pty Ltd v Pub Squash Co Pty Ltd* [1981] 1 All ER 213 at 218, [1981] 1 WLR 193 at 200:

g 'The width of the principle now authoritatively recognised by the High Court of Australia and the House of Lords is, therefore, such that the tort is no longer anchored, as in its early nineteenth century formulation, to the name or trade mark of a product or business. It is wide enough to encompass other descriptive material, such as slogans or visual images, which radio, h television or newspaper advertising campaigns can lead the market to associate with a plaintiff's product, provided always that such descriptive material has become part of the goodwill of the product. And the test is whether the product has derived from the advertising a distinctive character which the market recognises.'

j [16] This passage, although dealing with matters which are not directly in issue in this case, illustrates at least one way in which the law of passing off has evolved over the years. The old cases provide us with the origin of the law. They do not illustrate more recent developments.

[17] As Professor Cornish explains in *Intellectual Property* (4th edn, 1999) p 619 (para 16–01), the passing off action was first developed to meet what he calls the

'classic case' the features of which were described, for example, in Lord Halsbury LC's speech in *Reddaway (Frank) & Co Ltd v George Banham & Co Ltd* [1896] AC 199 at 204, [1895–9] All ER Rep 133 at 137: '... the principle of law may be very plainly stated ... that nobody has any right to represent his goods as the goods of somebody else.'

[18] The need for goods-for-goods substitution as an essential ingredient in the tort was a feature in many nineteenth century cases and still can be discerned in some early decisions in the last century. Because the claimant had to show this substitution, it was inherent that he also had to show that he was in business selling goods. Perhaps, to modern eyes, one of the most stark and surprising illustrations of this is to be seen in *Clark v Freeman* (1848) 11 Beav 112, an early case of false endorsement. The plaintiff, Sir James Clark, was an eminent physician and physician-in-ordinary to Queen Victoria. The defendant sold certain pills under the name 'Sir J. Clarke's Consumption Pills'. Before Lord Langdale MR, the claim failed, a major reason being that the plaintiff did not carry on the business of selling pills so, it was held, he suffered no pecuniary injury by reason of the defendant's activities. It is interesting to note that Lord Langdale MR said that he could not conceive that anyone in the world would suppose that Sir James' professional name would be the least damaged by the defendant's 'unscrupulous' use of it. Presumably that view made sense in an era when physicians were treated as the sort of gentlemen who would not soil their hands or their reputation by being involved 'in trade'.

[19] *Clark's* case was followed, though without conspicuous enthusiasm, in *Williams v Hodge & Co* (1887) 4 TLR 175, a case in which another eminent physician tried, but failed, to secure interlocutory relief against a manufacturer of surgical equipment who used his name to boost sales.

[20] *Clark's* case was distinguished in another false endorsement case; *British Medical Association v Marsh* (1931) 48 RPC 565. Then as now, the plaintiff was the association for medical professionals. In 1874 it was registered as a company not for gain. It carried on no trade. Before the 1914–1918 war it had published two books which contained the results of analyses which had been carried out on a large number of proprietary medicines. It disclosed which ones were ineffective and which were dangerous. The defendant, a pharmacist, had two retail shops. He sold medicines which were supposed to have been manufactured in accordance with the analyses in the plaintiff's books. He used the initials 'BMA' as a trade mark for his medicines and made liberal reference to the British Medical Association. Maugham J came to the conclusion that the initials would be recognised as referring to the plaintiff.

[21] The defendant relied on the fact that the plaintiff was a non-trading company and had never manufactured or sold drugs or medical remedies and had never been associated with any firm or person who manufactured or sold such goods. The defendant said that it and its predecessors-in-title had been trading for seven years without complaint, so that the claim should fail as a result of delay and it argued that the plaintiff could not have suffered any damage and therefore was not entitled to relief (see (1931) 48 RPC 565 at 567–568). In holding that there was passing off, Maugham J had to address the issue of damage. He held that no actual damage had been proved or had been suggested as having occurred. Notwithstanding this, he found damage by assuming loss of membership, based on an assumption that association with a pharmacist would damage the reputation of the association. Thus it was damage to the reputation of the

a association which perfected the cause of action, the loss of memberships was the consequence in money terms of that damage. To the best of my understanding, the correctness of the *British Medical Association* case has never been doubted. It is therefore not necessary to consider a number of other professional association cases which went the same way.

b [22] Counsel agreed that the most recent endorsement case in England is *McCulloch v Lewis A May (Produce Distributors) Ltd* [1947] 2 All ER 845, (1947) 65 RPC 58 in which the plaintiff was a famous presenter of children's radio programmes. He was known as 'Uncle Mac'. He had lost one leg and the use of one eye and had limited mobility. The defendant sold cereal food under the same name. It also used various advertising copy on the cartons in which its product was sold. They included 'Uncle Mac loves children—and children love Uncle *c* Mac!' and:

'You know the difficulties of travel these days, and will understand that Uncle Mac can't get about as freely as he would like to, but rest assured that all will come right in time and that he will always do his best to please his many friends.'

d

[23] Apparently a considerable number of authorities were put before Wynn-Parry J, but he concentrated on an analysis of the *British Medical Association* case which had been relied on by the plaintiff. His analysis included the conclusion (at 851) that in the *British Medical Association* case, Maugham J had—

e 'felt it necessary to find that the plaintiffs had a business, and that, having regard to all the circumstances, it could properly be said that the acts of the defendant were likely to cause damage to the plaintiffs in that business, thus pointing, as I understand his Lordship's judgment, quite clearly to the necessity of showing connection between the two businesses.'

f [24] Wynn-Parry J then went on to say that, on the basis of the case law, including the *British Medical Association* case, the plaintiff needed to show the existence of a 'common field of activity' in which it and the defendant were engaged. Finding against the plaintiff he said (at 851):

g 'On the postulate that the plaintiff is not engaged in any degree in producing or marketing puffed wheat, how can the defendant, in using the fancy name used by the plaintiff, be said to be passing off the goods or the business of the plaintiff? I am utterly unable to see any element of passing off in this case.'

h [25] With respect, it is difficult to agree with the suggestion that in the *British Medical Association* case, Maugham J put forward the need to prove a common field of activity. If anything, that authority points decisively away from such a need. Further, if the last-quoted passage had been applied to the facts in the *British Medical Association* case it is difficult to see how the plaintiff could have succeeded. There the plaintiff was 'not engaged in any degree in producing or *j* marketing' medicines, yet it succeeded in its claim. Furthermore it does not appear to me to be accurate to say, as Wynn-Parry J did, that Maugham J's judgment demonstrated 'quite clearly ... the necessity of showing connection between the two businesses'. It appears to me that Maugham J accepted that there was no connection between the two businesses. The plaintiff was a non-trading association looking after the interests of the medical profession while the defendant was a retail pharmacist. The only connection between the parties was that the defendant's activities damaged the plaintiff's goodwill.

[26] *McCulloch's* case was considered and not followed by the High Court of New South Wales sitting in its appellate jurisdiction (Evatt CJ, Myers and Manning JJ) in *Henderson v Radio Corp Pty Ltd* [1969] RPC 218. The plaintiffs were well-known professional ballroom dancers. The defendant manufactured and distributed a record of ballroom dancing music. On the cover of the record was a photograph of the plaintiffs. The plaintiffs alleged that the use of a picture of them on the record would lead buyers to believe that they recommended the record. They said that this amounted to passing off. At first instance, Sugerman J found for the plaintiffs and granted an injunction but declined to order an inquiry because he was of the view that damages were nominal. The defendant appealed. There was no cross-appeal in relation to damages. In the appellate division, the court held as a fact that the photograph on the record would be understood as a representation that the Hendersons recommended the record and this was used to induce customers to buy it. Furthermore, the court cited with approval the *British Medical Association* case (1931) 48 RPC 565. On the other hand it subjected *McCulloch's* case [1947] 2 All ER 845, (1947) 65 RPC 58 to strong criticism. Noting that Wynn-Parry J had dismissed the action because there was no common field of activity, the High Court said (at 234):

'We find it impossible to accept this view without some qualification. The remedy in passing off is necessarily only available where the parties are engaged in business, using that expression in its widest sense to include professions and callings. If they are, there does not seem to be any reason why it should also be necessary that there be an area, actual or potential, in which their activities conflict. If it were so, then, subject only to the law of defamation, any businessman might falsely represent that his goods were produced by another provided that other was not engaged, or not reasonably likely to be engaged, in producing similar goods. This does not seem to be a sound general principle. The present case provides an illustration of the unjust consequences of such a principle. For the purposes of this part of its argument, the appellant concedes that it is falsely representing that the respondents recommend, favour or support its dance music record, but it claims that because the respondents are not engaged or likely to be engaged in making or selling gramophone records, it is entitled to appropriate their names and reputations for its own commercial advantage and that the court has no power to prevent it doing so. It would be a grave defect in the law if this were so. In our view, once it is proved that A. is falsely representing his goods as the goods of B., or his business to be the same as or connected with the business of B., the wrong of passing off has been established and B. is entitled to relief.'

It also said (at 233):

'We have some difficulty in accepting the proposition stated in *McCulloch's* case. If deception and damages are proved, it is not easy to see the justification for introducing another factor as a condition of the court's power to intervene.'

[27] *Henderson's* case has been followed not only in Australia, but at least in Canada as well. It has recently been cited with approval by the full High Court

a of Australia (Gleeson G, Gaudron, McHugh, Gummow, Kirby, Hayne and
Callinan JJ) in *Campomar Sociedad, Limitada v Nike International Ltd* (2000) 169 ALR
677 as was a passage in *Moorgate Tobacco Co Ltd v Philip Morris Ltd (No 2)* (1984) 56
ALR 193 at 214 in which Deane J approved of—

b
'the adaptation of the traditional doctrine of passing off to meet new
circumstances involving the deceptive or confusing use of names, descriptive
terms or other indicia to persuade purchasers or customers to believe that
the goods or services have an association, quality or endorsement which
belongs or would belong to goods or services of, or associated with, another
or others ...'

c **[28]** *McCulloch v Lewis A May (Produce Distributors) Ltd* [1947] 2 All ER 845,
(1947) 65 RPC 58 has also been disapproved of in this country. In *Harrods Ltd v
Harrodian School Ltd* [1996] RPC 697 at 714, Millett LJ, which whom Beldam LJ
agreed, said:

d
'There is no requirement that the defendant should be carrying on a
business which competes with that of the plaintiff or which would compete
with any natural extension of the plaintiff's business. The expression
"common field of activity" was coined by Wynn-Parry J. in *McCulloch v. May*
([1947] 2 All ER 845, (1947) 65 RPC 58), when he dismissed the plaintiff's
claim for want of this factor. This was contrary to numerous previous
authorities (see, for example, *Eastman Photographic Material Co. Ltd. v. John
e   Griffiths Cycle Corporation Ltd.* (1898) 15 R.P.C 105 (cameras and bicycles);
Walter v. Ashton [1902] 2 Ch. 282 (The Times newspaper and bicycles) and is
now discredited.'

f **[29]** With respect, I agree. The approach adopted by the High Court in New
South Wales in *Henderson v Radio Corp Pty Ltd* [1969] RPC 218, supported more
recently by the full court of the High Court of Australia in the *Campomar* case, are
to be preferred and seem to me to be consistent with a long line of English
authority both before and since *McCulloch*'s case. For example in *Annabel's
(Berkeley Square) Ltd v G Schock (trading as Annabel's Escort Agency)* [1972] RPC 838,
the Court of Appeal granted interlocutory relief to restrain the defendant from
g running an escort agency under the name 'Annabel's', a name which was used for
the plaintiff's high-class nightclub. *McCulloch*'s case was referred to the court
during argument. There was no question of the plaintiff running an escort
agency. Indeed it was anxious that the defendant's activities might lead people to
think that it had branched out into this new type of activity. The court declined
h to approach the issue on this basis. Instead it said (at 844) that looking at
overlapping fields of activity was simply a question which is involved in the
ultimate decision whether there is likely to be confusion.

[30] However, if the narrow approach in *McCulloch*'s case is not right, so that
identifying overlapping businesses is not a necessary ingredient in a passing off
action, and nor is goods-for-goods or service-for-service substitution, what is the
j scope of the cause of action in its current form and does it cover false
endorsement?

[31] The law of passing off is not designed to protect a trader from fair
competition. It is not even to protect him against others selling the same goods
or copied goods. If the latter is possible at all it is only as a result of the application
of the law of copyright, designs, patents or confidential information (see

British American Glass Co Ltd v Winton Products (Blackpool) Ltd [1962] RPC 230).
Furthermore, passing off does not create or protect a monopoly in a name or
get-up. The latter point was made clearly over 100 years ago by Parker J in
Burberrys v JC Cording & Co Ltd (1900) 26 RPC 693 at 701:

> 'The principles of law applicable to a case of this sort are well known. On
> the one hand, apart from the law as to trade marks, no one can claim
> monopoly rights in the use of a word or name. On the other hand, no one is
> entitled to the use of any word or name, or indeed in any other way, to
> represent his goods as being the goods of another to that other's injury. If an
> injunction be granted restraining the use of a word or name, it is no doubt
> granted to protect property, but the property, to protect which it is granted,
> is not property in the word or name, but property in the trade or good-will
> which will be injured by its use.'

[32] What is protected is goodwill. The nature of goodwill was described by
the House of Lords in *IRC v Muller & Co's Margarine Ltd* [1901] AC 217,
[1900–1903] All ER Rep 413. The oft-quoted passage from the speech of Lord
Macnaghton reads:

> 'What is goodwill? It is a thing very easy to describe, very difficult to
> define. It is the benefit and advantage of the good name, reputation, and
> connection of a business. It is the attractive force which brings in custom.'
> (See [1901] AC 217 at 223–224, [1900–1903] All ER Rep 413 at 416.)

[33] However, there is another passage in that speech which is just as
important and throws light on rights held by the owner of goodwill:

> 'It is very difficult, as it seems to me, to say that goodwill is not property.
> Goodwill is bought and sold every day. It may be acquired, I think, in any of
> the different ways in which property is usually acquired. When a man has
> got it he may keep it as his own. He may vindicate his exclusive right to it if
> necessary by process of law. He may dispose of it if he will—of course under
> the conditions attaching to property of that nature.' (See [1901] AC 217 at
> 223, [1900–1903] All ER Rep 413 at 416.)

[34] Expressed in these terms, the purpose of a passing off action is to
vindicate the claimant's exclusive right to goodwill and to protect it against
damage. When a defendant sells his inferior goods in substitution for the
claimant's, there is no difficulty in a court finding that there is passing off. The
substitution damages the goodwill and therefore the value of it to the claimant.
The passing off action is brought to protect the claimant's property. But goodwill
will be protected even if there is no immediate damage in the above sense. For
example, it has long been recognised that a defendant can not avoid a finding of
passing off by showing that his goods or services are of as good or better quality
than the claimant's. In such a case, although the defendant may not damage the
goodwill as such, what he does is damage the value of the goodwill to the
claimant because, instead of benefiting from exclusive rights to his property, the
latter now finds that someone else is squatting on it. It is for the owner of
goodwill to maintain, raise or lower the quality of his reputation or to decide
who, if anyone, can use it alongside him. The ability to do that is compromised
if another can use the reputation or goodwill without his permission and as he

a likes. Thus Fortnum & Mason is no more entitled to use the name FW Woolworth than FW Woolworth is entitled to use the name Fortnum & Mason.

[**35**] The point is particularly clearly demonstrated by the so-called 'champagne' cases in which the claimants share a reputation in the name under which their type of wine is sold. In such cases a defendant would not escape liability for use of the name 'Champagne' on a beverage which is not authentic *b* French champagne by showing either that his product was as good as or better than the claimants' or that he had not diverted any measurable sales from them. One type of damage which can support the modern form of passing-off action was explained in just such a case; *Taittinger v Allbev Ltd* [1994] 4 All ER 75. In that action the claimants were a number of champagne houses. The defendant made a non-alcoholic drink which it sold under the name 'Elderflower Champagne'. At *c* first instance ([1992] FSR 647) the court held that the use of the word 'champagne' on the defendant's product would give rise to a misrepresentation to members of the public and that the claimants had a protectable goodwill but dismissed the action on the basis that the claimants had failed to establish a likelihood of substantial damage, not least because it was of the view that the claimants would *d* lose very few, if any, sales. The decision was reversed on appeal. Peter Gibson LJ, with whom Bingham MR and Mann LJ agreed, analysed the nature of the harm to goodwill which is relevant in a passing off action. Having noted that in *Vine Products Ltd v MacKensie & Co Ltd* [1969] RPC 1 Dankwerts J was concerned about 'blurring' or 'diluting' of the plaintiff's goodwill and references to 'encroaching the reputation and goodwill' or 'erosion of distinctiveness' in certain New *e* Zealand cases, he said ([1994] 4 All ER 75 at 88):

> 'By parity of reasoning it seems to me no less obvious that erosion of the distinctiveness of the name champagne in this country is a form of damage to the goodwill of the business of the champagne houses.'

f [**36**] Much the same point was made by Sir Thomas Bingham MR. Having commented on how the cause of action for passing off had expanded over the years, he noted (at 93):

> 'But it is now, as I understand, clear that a defendant need not, to be liable, misrepresent his goods to be those of the plaintiff if he misrepresents his
g goods or his business as being in some way connected or associated with the plaintiff's.'

[**37**] He then went on to consider (at 95) the question of damage:

> 'Like the judge, I do not think the defendants' product would reduce the
h first plaintiffs' sales in any significant and direct way. But that is not, as it seems to me, the end of the matter. The first plaintiffs' reputation and goodwill in the description "Champagne" derive not only from the quality of their wine and its glamorous associations, but also from the very singularity and exclusiveness of the description, the absence of qualifying epithets and imitative descriptions. Any product which is not "Champagne"
j but is allowed to describe itself as such must inevitably, in my view, erode the singularity and exclusiveness of the description "Champagne" and so cause the first plaintiffs damage of an insidious but serious kind. The amount of damage which the defendants' product would cause would of course depend on the size of the defendants' operation. That is not negligible now, and it could become much bigger. But I cannot see, despite the defendants'

argument to the contrary, any rational basis upon which, if the defendants' product were allowed to be marketed under its present description, any other fruit cordial diluted with carbonated water could not be similarly marketed so as to incorporate the description "champagne". The damage to the first plaintiffs would then be incalculable but severe.'

[38] In my view these cases illustrate that the law of passing off now is of greater width than as applied by Wynn-Parry J in *McCulloch v Lewis A May (Produce Distributors) Ltd* [1947] 2 All ER 845, (1947) 65 RPC 58. If someone acquires a valuable reputation or goodwill, the law of passing off will protect it from unlicensed use by other parties. Such use will frequently be damaging in the direct sense that it will involve selling inferior goods or services under the guise that they are from the claimant. But the action is not restricted to protecting against that sort of damage. The law will vindicate the claimant's exclusive right to the reputation or goodwill. It will not allow others to so use goodwill as to reduce, blur or diminish its exclusivity. It follows that it is not necessary to show that the claimant and the defendant share a common field of activity or that sales of products or services will be diminished either substantially or directly, at least in the short term. Of course there is still a need to demonstrate a misrepresentation because it is that misrepresentation which enables the defendant to make use or take advantage of the claimant's reputation.

[39] Not only has the law of passing off expanded over the years, but the commercial environment in which it operates is in a constant state of flux. Even without the evidence given at the trial in this action, the court can take judicial notice of the fact that it is common for famous people to exploit their names and images by way of endorsement. They do it not only in their own field of expertise but, depending on the extent of their fame or notoriety, wider afield also. It is common knowledge that for many sportsmen, for example, income received from endorsing a variety of products and services represents a very substantial part of their total income. The reason large sums are paid for endorsement is because, no matter how irrational it may seem to a lawyer, those in business have reason to believe that the lustre of a famous personality, if attached to their goods or services, will enhance the attractiveness of those goods or services to their target market. In this respect, the endorsee is taking the benefit of the attractive force which is the reputation or goodwill of the famous person.

[40] This was supported by the evidence at the trial. Mr Bleakley, who gave evidence on behalf of the defendant, summed the position up neatly in his witness statement: 'Endorsement arrangements by sports stars are often entered into with a view to influencing the target audience's choice.'

[41] He also gave evidence on this subject under cross-examination. Other relevant passages will be referred to below. For present purposes I need only refer to one:

'Q. Presumably, if you could get it, if you told your recipients that you had celebrity endorsement that would attract them?

A. If we had celebrity endorsement, from a radio broadcaster's point of view that would mean somebody broadcasting on the radio; that would be something we would specifically shout about, yes, no doubt.

Q. It wouldn't necessarily have to be somebody broadcasting on the radio, it could be, say, David Beckham saying "I love listening to Talk Radio"?

a   A. That could be, and think there are famous people that listen to various radio stations and have made that public. That tends to be PR that you are not in control of, as opposed to something you would actively pursue.

Q. But if you could get celebrity endorsement that would help you?

A. Yes, association would definitely would of assistance [sic] to any brand, definitely, but from a radio station's point of view and for the advertising, *b*   media market, what I'm trying to influence, the most important thing is are you talking about people that influence the content, and therefore the listeners to the station—you know, a brand association with anybody or anything is not necessarily how the industry is driven, I would say, but by the very nature of it if David Beckham said he listened to Talk Radio that *c*   wouldn't be a bad thing.'

[42] This was supported by the evidence given by Mr Ian Phillips who has long been associated with F1 racing and, in 1999, was director of business affairs of Jordan Grand Prix Ltd, one of the 11 teams involved in the F1 World Championship. He has extensive knowledge of motor racing not only as a result *d*   of his own connection with a number of F1 teams, but also as a motor-sports journalist. He told me that over the last 15 years the receipt of endorsement fees had become a particularly important part of the income of F1 drivers and others whose period at the top of their respective sports was likely to be short-lived.

[43] Manufacturers and retailers recognise the realities of the market place *e*   when they pay for well-known personalities to endorse their goods. The law of passing off should do likewise. There appears to be no good reason why the law of passing off in its modern form and in modern trade circumstances should not apply to cases of false endorsement. Indeed, it seems to me that this is not a novel proposition in this country. *British Medical Association v Marsh* (1931) 48 RPC 565 *f*   and similar trade association cases are all ones in which passing off was used to prevent false endorsement. The most recent case which stands against this is *McCulloch*'s case which, as explained above, is discredited.

[44] In my view nothing said above touches on the quite separate issues which may arise in character merchandising cases, a considerable number of which were cited to me during the trial. In those cases the defendant's activities do not *g*   imply any endorsement. For example, although it was a trade mark registration case, in *Re Elvis Presley Trade Marks* [1999] RPC 567 much of the argument turned on whether the appellant had merchandising rights in the name Elvis Presley or in his image. It wanted to prevent third parties from selling products such as bars of soap and drinking mugs bearing the name of the performer and photographs *h*   of him. There could be no question of the performer endorsing anything since he had been dead for many years. So the argument being advanced was one which amounted to an attempt to create a quasi-copyright in the name and images. The Court of Appeal's rejection of that is, with respect, consistent with a long line of authority. As Robert Walker LJ said in *Re Elvis Presley Trade Marks* *j*   (at 582):

'However this appeal is not an appropriate occasion on which to attempt to define precisely how far the law of passing off has developed in response to the growth of character merchandising, still less to express views as to how much further it should develop or in what direction.'

[45] The same point can be made here. Whether such a new right may be created either by development of the common law or as a result of the passing of the Human Rights Act 1998, is not relevant to this action.

[46] It follows from the views expressed above that there is nothing which prevents an action for passing off succeeding in a false endorsement case. However, to succeed, the burden on the claimant includes a need to prove at least two, interrelated, facts. First that at the time of the acts complained of he had a significant reputation or goodwill. Second that the actions of the defendant gave rise to a false message which would be understood by a not insignificant section of his market that his goods have been endorsed, recommended or are approved of by the claimant. I shall turn to those two issues.

In 1999 did Mr Irvine have a substantial reputation or goodwill?

[47] In my view there can be little doubt on this score. Mr Irvine gave unchallenged evidence of the size and public exposure of F1 racing. He said that it represents the pinnacle of motor racing. Each race is watched by over 350m television viewers worldwide. There is a large following in England. Races take place in different locations around the world. There is one F1 race each year in England. At present there are 11 teams who compete in the FIA Formula 1 World Championship. Each team can race two cars in each race. The championship usually consists of 16 or 17 races during a season which lasts from March to October. These races take place throughout the world including one in the United Kingdom. One of the most famous teams is Ferrari. As noted above, in 1999 Mr Irvine was driving for that team.

[48] A driver and his team is awarded points according to how high up the field he finishes in each race. The aggregate of points determines who wins the Drivers' World Championship and the Constructors' (ie the teams') World Championship.

[49] Publicity plays a large part in the funding of the sport and its participants. In the United Kingdom, television broadcasting rights are held by ITV while radio broadcasting rights are held by BBC Radio 5. There is enormous print media coverage, with hundreds of journalists and photographers attending each race. Mr Irvine gave the following evidence concerning the general practice of sponsorship and endorsement:

'Drivers also benefit from the significant media coverage. The celebrity status of Formula 1 drivers means that there is demand for drivers to be involved with endorsements, private sponsorship and merchandising. Typically a driver will have some space on his race suit or cap for his own sponsors. Sponsorship is where a company will pay a driver a fee usually in return for the driver displaying the sponsor's logo on his race suit or cap. A driver will also endorse products and services that do not conflict with the team's sponsors. Endorsement is where the driver's image is used to promote a product or service typically in an advertisement. I would always obtain the consent of the team I drove for in respect of any such endorsements or sponsorships.'

[50] He also gave evidence about merchandising activities although, as I have indicated, no one has suggested that this is a merchandising case. The considerations which apply to merchandising and, in particular, whether our law offers protection to it is not before me.

a [51] Mr Irvine's first season with Ferrari was in 1996. He finished tenth in the Drivers' Championship. In 1997 he finished eighth. In 1998 he finished fourth. By the last race in 1999, he was in the lead of the championship but he came third in that race and was the runner-up in the championship. When a driver comes in the first three places in a race, he stands on the winners' podium at the end of the race and usually indulges in a tradition of spraying champagne over his co-drivers b and anyone within striking distance. In 1999, Mr Irvine was on the winners' podium for half the races in the season.

[52] Mr Irvine also explained that while he was driving for Ferrari, and particularly in 1999, he received what he described as an immense amount of press coverage. For example he was on the front page of a number of car-related and non-car related magazines and his book was serialised in the News of the c World. Some flavour of the enthusiasm generated in 1999 can be gathered from the front covers used on the magazine *Autosport* during that year. The 11 March issue has a front cover with a large picture of a smiling Mr Irvine holding aloft the victor's plate from the Australian F1 race. The copy on the cover reads 'EDDIE'S FINEST HOUR—We join Brit hero Irvine as he revels in glory of first win'. The d cover of the July 15 issue also carries a picture of a smiling Mr Irvine with the following copy 'FERRARI—EDDIE'S OUR MAN!—Irvine gets backing for title charge'. The cover of the 29 July issue carries a photograph of a F1 racing car (presumably being driven by Mr Irvine) with the banner headlines 'WHO NEEDS SCHUEY?—Ferrari star Irvine takes pressure cooker victory in Austria'. The reference to 'Schuey' is, no doubt, a reference to Mr Michael Schumacher, e another famous F1 driver. Examination of the examples of press coverage, whether in racing or non-racing publications, produced for the trial shows that it frequently includes large pictures of Mr Irvine. Furthermore, Mr Irvine has been engaged to sponsor a variety of products including, amongst others, sunglasses, mens' toiletries, fashion clothing, footwear and car-racing helmets.

f [53] This was supported by the evidence given by Mr Phillips. In his witness statement he said:

'In the summer of 1999 Eddie Irvine was at the height of his career with Ferrari. He had won three races and had a realistic chance of winning the Drivers' World Championship. During that year his image appeared in g numerous television, newspaper and magazine articles partly as a result of his racing success and partly, as I understand it, as a result of efforts by his management to exploit his position. I would say that he was easily and still is the most high-profile British driver in Formula 1 that year, as Damon Hill was in decline. He was also probably the next most recognisable of all h drivers after Michael Schumacher.'

[54] Although Mr Phillips was cross-examined by Mr Hicks, Mr Phillips' competence to give this evidence was not challenged. It was accepted that he had great knowledge both of F1 racing and the whole world of endorsement, sponsorship and merchandising. The only parts of the above evidence which j were challenged were the suggestions that Mr Irvine was the most high-profile British F1 driver in 1999 and was the second most recognisable driver. On the first of these points, the cross-examination went as follows:

'Q. Right. Now, what I want to suggest to you is that in July of 1999, I make the position quite clear, if you were a follower of Formula 1 you might well know the name Eddie Irvine, of course you would know it, and you might well be able to recognise his face, but that so far as the man in the street was concerned, in England, other drivers were much higher up on the *a* spectrum because they had had much longer careers at the top whereas Mr Irvine was a man who, at that point, was just about to break into the big time?

A. No, he broke into the big time when Jordan Grand Prix sold him to Ferrari. He made a bit of a name for himself when he made his Grand Prix *b* debut with Jordan in 1993. Having starred in the race he got physically assaulted by Ayrton Senna, which led to a disciplinary hearing against Mr Senna with a suspended ban, that's something pretty tough on a three times world champion, never happened before. Mr Irvine, himself, actually got a ban during 1994 for an alleged involvement in a huge accident which occurred in a British Grand Prix. We appealed on his behalf against the ban *c* that he was given. The ban was extended, so he achieved fame and notoriety from his very first drive in Formula 1. The week before the British Grand Prix, which was the French Grand Prix, he was actually leading the race which was eventually won by the Jordan team, but he arrived in the pits and the team were busy watching his team mate out on the circuit and left him *d* sitting in the pit for 45 seconds with no wheels on the car. Four-and-a-half million people watching television the week before the British Grand Prix, probably at the time this flyer had gone out would have known who he was, he was the top British driver at the time, the top British racing driver is a well-known person, not just in the sports pages.'

e

[55] Mr Hicks then went on to challenge the assertion that Mr Irvine would be recognised from a picture:

'*Q.* I agree for a moment that people might have heard of his name if they had heard about Formula 1, what I'm saying is that they would not necessarily recognise his face, that's the point I am making. The faces they *f* would recognise would be faces of people who over the year had got a bigger track record, Damon Hill, David Coulthard or Nigel Mansell, those were the names in 1999 that people could put a face to. That in mid-1999 putting a face to Eddie Irvine was something only a racing aficionado [sic]?

A. I disagree, he had been in gossip columns, fashion magazines, he had a *g* regular newspaper column which featured his photograph. Remember he's only the second British driver ever to have driven for Ferrari in 50 years. If you are a Ferrari Grand Prix driver you are known around the world, believe me.'

And: *h*

'*Q.* You, therefore, don't accept my proposition. I'll put it to you one more time: so far as members of the public are concerned, not a racing enthusiast, just a normal member of the public not specifically interested in Formula 1, in mid-1999 people could put faces, perhaps, to the name of Damon Hill, ex-world champion, David Coulthard or Michael Schumacher, or perhaps *j* even Ayrton Senna, but after that putting names to faces would be a difficult thing for just an average member of the public to do?

A. I would disagree with you, perhaps I'm too intimately involved in the sport. Eddie Irvine was a race winner that year, on and off the leadership of the championship for the whole of the year, plus the newspaper columns, his

a
outspokenness, his willingness to comment and make intelligent informed comment unlike some of the other personalities that you have mentioned, made him a much sought after, well-known and recognised sportsman.'

[56] I think it is necessary to bear in mind Mr Phillips' close connection with the F1 industry for many years. His knowledge of the personalities in the sport
b will inevitably be greater than that of many members of the public so his views will not accord with those of all members of the public. The public is not a homogenous mass. Some will have no interest in either F1 racing or the personalities involved in it. Others will be passionate supporters. A significant portion of the public will occupy the space between these two extremes.
c However, it must be remembered that stories about Mr Irvine and pictures of him have appeared in large numbers of publications, including many high volume non-specialist newspapers. For example the sample documents produced to the court show that Mr Irvine and his photograph have been featured prominently in, amongst others, the News of the World, the Yorkshire Evening Press, the Daily Mail, The Times and the Daily Telegraph. In my view
d it is proved that Mr Irvine was, in 1999, an extremely 'hot property' in the field of motor racing and was well known by name and appearance to a significant part of the public in this country. In my view he would have been even more well known among, or would be well known to an even greater proportion of, those who are concerned to seek endorsement of their goods from sports personalities.

[57] This conclusion is consistent with the actions of the defendant. Although
e it has not given a full explanation of how Mr Irvine's face ended up on its brochure, I think the only reasonable inference is that those who designed this promotion knew of Mr Irvine's fame and wanted it to be attached to the launch of the new sports-related programme. Indeed, I think that the suggestion that the addressees of the brochure would not have recognised the picture as being of
f Mr Irvine is not only contrary to common sense, it is also contrary to the defendant's own evidence. It should be remembered that the distribution of this brochure was deliberately timed to take place shortly before the British F1 Grand Prix. It need hardly be stated that the prospects of the leading British F1 driver in that event would be the subject of much press coverage at the time. If, as was suggested, few or none would recognise the picture of Mr Irvine, one is left with
g no adequate explanation of why a picture of him was bought from a specialist sports photographic library and why it was manipulated so as to remove the mobile phone and replace it with a radio bearing the words 'TALK RADIO'. If the photograph was really anonymous, the defendant could have used a photograph of anyone dressed up as a racing driver. Furthermore Mr Bleakley
h said in his witness statement that the manipulated image was 'designed to amuse the target audience, who would have instantly realised from the photograph and its context that it had been manipulated'. I will return to the issue of whether the manipulation of the image was obvious below, but it is difficult to see how the target audience could have been 'amused' if they did not know whose picture was being used. Mr Bleakley gave other evidence which also is consistent with the
j claimant's case that Mr Irvine was very well known at the time:

'Q. Going back to your answer in response to what you would have done if you had actually had a real genuine celebrity endorsement, you seem to be saying that you need to shout that from the tree tops otherwise your recipients would not have understood it?

A. There are a couple of things there. This is trade promotion so it's going to a very, very small select group of people. *Believe me, Eddie Irvine being part of Talksport's content would be big news—not trade news, this would be national news.* I suppose that's the difference really. There are lots of sports personalities on the station, in our literature, in brochures, photographs in various form, and that photograph could have been anyone. Indeed, after looking at the photograph on the box, another sales promotion agency could probably have done the same thing with Schumacher. Looking at that photo—they just selected the best shot to get the angle, it wasn't specific to any angle, it was specific to the sport really and *the people in it.*' (My emphasis.)

Did the actions of the defendant create a false message which would be understood by a not insignificant section of its market to mean that its radio programme or station had been endorsed, recommended or are approved of by Mr Irvine?

[58] As pointed out already, this case is concerned with endorsement, not merchandising rights. For that reason, Miss Lane does not argue that her client can succeed simply by showing that his image was used for commercial purposes on the defendant's brochure. She accepts that she must go further and show that there was an implicit representation of endorsement or that members of the target audience would believe that to be the case.

[59] This is an issue which, in the end, has to be determined by the court. Evidence may be helpful, but it is not determinative. In particular I must bear in mind that the likely impact of the brochure will differ from person to person. The question is whether, on a balance of probabilities, a significant proportion of those to whom this brochure was sent would think that Mr Irvine had endorsed or recommended Talk Radio. The approach I have tried to adopt is that sanctioned by the Court of Appeal in *Chocosuisse Union des Fabricants de Chocolat v Cadbury Ltd* [1999] RPC 826 at 837–838.

[60] On this issue there was some evidence relating to the reaction of at least one recipient, Mr Phillips. He was supplied with the brochure although he almost certainly did not receive the box in which it had been posted. The latter point makes no difference to the issues I have to decide, since it was accepted that the packaging would be expected to be discarded and only the brochure would be retained and passed around inside a recipient's office and studied. It is the brochure which is intended to do the marketing of the defendant's new sports-related business. In his witness statement, Mr Phillips said that when he received the brochure he thought it was authorised by Mr Irvine and he sent it on to Mr Irvine's manager, Mr Enrico Zanarini. This was not covered by Mr Zanarini in his two brief witness statements, which concentrated on detailing Mr Irvine's various commercial relationships. Both Mr Phillips and Mr Zanarini were cross-examined in relation to Mr Phillips' reaction to the brochure.

[61] Mr Phillips expanded on his written evidence under cross-examination. He said that he believed that, on receiving the brochure, he telephoned Mr Zanarini to congratulate him on having negotiated a sponsorship deal with the defendant. He said that Mr Zanarini denied any knowledge of the Talk Radio brochure. As a result Mr Phillips sent it to him. This and other matters are covered in the following extract from the cross-examination:

a
'Q. Now, I want to understand what you said to him on the telephone then, could you explain what happened in the course of that conversation?

A. Well, I was sort of congratulating him on having done a deal, it was quite clearly a personal endorsement and I quite fancied getting a personalised Talk Radio myself it being a sports person, I thought obviously as part of the deal he would have a few free radios to give away, that's

b
normally what you do with these things, it was so obviously a tampered or set-up photograph that I presumed that it just had to be a deal which had been done by Irvine or by Zanarini for Irvine.

Q. You say you thought it was authorised, if that was the case I don't understand whether you are saying you actually thought it was authorised, or are you saying in reality you thought it was something which ought to

c
have been authorised and he should be getting a fee for?

A. There are an awful lot of rogues in this business that are taking hold of images and using them for commercial gain, it's part of what I—I do police this sort of thing. I congratulated Mr Zanarini on having done a deal and he told me he knew nothing about it which is why I sent it to him.

d
Q. I want to say, it strikes me, if you thought it was obviously doctored that you might well have been sending it to him on this basis, "Look, I wonder whether you would be interested in chasing this up Mr Zanarini because it looks if there are some rogues out there", is that more precisely what happened?

A. Absolutely not at all. I said to Enrico, "Well done, it looks like a good

e
deal" and he said, "I don't know what you are talking about".'

[62] Although he was pressed on this issue, his evidence remained unshaken.

[63] Although Mr Zanarini gave no written evidence on this topic, he was cross-examined on it. He supported what Mr Phillips said but accepted that his recollection of what had been said during a telephone conversation some while

f
ago was not clear. I do not think that his evidence on this adds or subtracts much.

[64] Mr Hicks suggested that Mr Phillips' evidence should not be trusted for two reasons. First, as he put it, Mr Phillips was an enthusiastic supporter of Mr Irvine's case and knew him well. He had a vested interest in the claimant succeeding in this action since he is employed in organising sponsorship,

g
endorsement and merchandising deals for other F1 drivers. Second, Mr Phillips was not representative of the kind of person who received the brochure. He was too close to the individuals and the sport.

[65] As far as the first of these points is concerned, it would, perhaps, have been better had Mr Hicks put it to Mr Phillips that he was partisan. Nevertheless

h
I think Mr Hicks' point has merit. It is clear that a favourable outcome of this action as far as Mr Irvine is concerned would benefit Mr Phillips. I also accept that Mr Phillips would have been closer to the individuals and the sport than most of the recipients of the brochure. I am by no means convinced that the latter point makes him more likely to be confused than others. I would have thought his exposure to this market and (as Mr Hicks suggested to him in

j
cross-examination) his knowledge that there are many 'rogues' about, might have made him less likely to be confused.

[66] With these considerations as a background, I have considered carefully Mr Phillips' evidence. As will be seen from the extract from his cross-examination set out above, Mr Phillips told me that he not only thought that Mr Zanarini had procured an endorsement deal with the defendant but that, as a result,

Mr Zanarini would be likely to have some free radios, and Mr Phillips was hoping to get one of these. If Mr Hicks is right and Mr Phillips realised at all times that this was not authorised by or on behalf of Mr Irvine, it must mean that Mr Phillips' evidence on this issue was thoroughly misleading. There was nothing about Mr Phillips' evidence which led me to believe that he was being untruthful or was putting self-interest in front of honesty. I accept that he did think that Mr Irvine had endorsed the brochure.

[67] In coming to that conclusion, I do not think that Mr Phillips was being either hypersensitive or unreasonable. The brochure was put out at just the time when media interest in the British F1 Grand Prix, and in the most prominent British competitor, Mr Irvine, would be at its highest. As noted above, the defendant described this promotion as being 'time critical' to coincide with the British Grand Prix at Silverstone in early July 1999. The brochure showed Mr Irvine listening to Talk Radio. It was in a brochure which was designed to encourage the recipients to think of placing advertisements on Talk Radio's programmes. For that purpose it was beneficial to convince the recipients that Talk Radio would be likely to attract a large audience. It seems to me that letting people know, or suggesting to them, that Talk Radio enjoyed the endorsement of Mr Irvine would significantly help Talk Radio to deliver that message.

[68] What is at issue here is the likely effect of the brochure on those to whom it was sent. If it is likely to have the effect of conveying to a significant number of the recipients that Mr Irvine was endorsing Talk Radio, then it does not matter whether or not that was the defendant's intention. Nevertheless, what the defendant intended to achieve by the promotion can give some indication of what it was likely to achieve. After all, the promotion was designed by experts who probably had a good idea of the impact the promotion would make.

[69] Mr Bleakley's witness statement discloses that the defendant instructed SMP, an experienced marketing and communications agency to create material promoting the opportunities of advertising on Talk Radio. Talk Radio had used SMP to produce materials for previous campaigns it had run. SMP was provided with information on the extent and depth of the coverage which would be offered in respect of the various sporting events and the advantages of advertising on Talk Radio during the sports coverage concerned. From this material SMP were asked to create appropriate copy and artwork for the brochures. It appears that it was SMP which then designed the promotional literature and the packaging for it. Mr Bleakley said that it was SMP which was responsible for obtaining all the images which were to be included in the packs. Mock-ups were reviewed and approved by Talk Radio. In accordance with this procedure, the images which are featured in the brochure were obtained by SMP from a specialist motorsport image library that licensed the use of the images for this purpose. In the process of creating the mock-up of the brochure, it was SMP, not Talk Radio, which decided to alter the image of Mr Irvine so as to make it appear that he was listening to Talk Radio and I assume it was also SMP which decided to use that doctored image on the front cover.

[70] Unfortunately the defendant produced no evidence from SMP so one is left in the dark as to what it understood its brief to be and as to why it chose to use a photograph of Mr Irvine apparently listening to Talk Radio on a brochure designed to coincide with the British F1 Grand Prix. Miss Lane did cross-examine Mr Bleakley on this issue. He said that the promotion was intended to grab the attention of the target audience to which it was sent so that it would 'receive your

a message'. Mr Bleakley was not clear what that message was supposed to be. In his witness statement he said that the manipulated image was designed to amuse the target audience but under cross-examination he accepted that there was nothing particularly amusing about the doctored image of Mr Irvine. He was asked why the undoctored photograph, showing Mr Irvine talking into a mobile telephone, was not sufficient for the defendant's purposes. His answer was:

b 'The promotions agency are always specifically for—going back to your point about irreverence, some kind of catchy, twangy angle. I think talking into a mobile phone as opposed to listening to the radio with Talk Radio on caught the mood of that particular promotion. So they are looking for angles in any shot that is going to deliver that cut through. That would be their
c view of that.'

[71] I am not sure that that response really discloses what the defendant's purpose was behind using this photograph. It may well be that the defendant did not think too closely about this, leaving it to SMP to decide how to impress the target audience. It should be remembered that the defendant had expertise in
d running a radio station. SMP was the expert in marketing and making promotions and was trusted as a result of the work it had previously done for the defendant. The possibility that SMP was primarily responsible for the campaign while the defendant took a back seat is supported by another answer given by Mr Bleakley:

e 'Yes. SMP sourced the photographs from what I believe was a grand prix or F1 photograph agency, and with hindsight I probably wouldn't have done it but I assumed from SMP's point of view that that was okay. I didn't spot that as something which would be, you know, would have a detrimental effect down the line, personally, so I signed it off. I didn't see a problem with
f it.'

[72] Mr Bleakley did go on to say that it was not his intention to mislead the target audience. I accept that. But the fact is that the company which designed this promotion with the intention of grabbing the attention of the audience decided not to use a photograph of an unknown holding a radio with the
g defendant's name on, but selected a photograph of the most famous British driver at the time and manipulated the image so as to represent to the viewer that he was listening avidly to the defendant's programme. In the absence of evidence from SMP, I think it is legitimate to conclude that part at least of the intention was to convey the message to the audience that Talk Radio was so good that it was endorsed and listened to by Mr Irvine. Mr Irvine's support of Talk Radio would
h make it more attractive to potential listeners with the result that more would listen to its programmes and that would make Talk Radio an attractive medium in which to place advertisements.

[73] Taking into account the above matters, I have come to the conclusion that a not insignificant number of recipients of the brochure would have made
j the same assumption as to endorsement as Mr Phillips did. I should add that Mr Hicks argued that the photograph was obviously doctored and this meant that it was less likely that anyone would believe that Mr Irvine had endorsed his client. Even if it were true that the photograph was obviously doctored, I do not see how that could make any significant difference to the impact the brochure would have on its recipients. Furthermore I am unable to accept that the

doctoring was obvious. On the contrary, when I first saw the brochure it did not occur to me that the photograph was doctored. The replacement of the mobile telephone has been done so skillfully that, even now, it does not look like a doctored picture to me.

[74] The other major point relied on by Mr Hicks was the fact that the brochure was only distributed once to just under 1,000 recipients. This meant that the confusion, if any, was limited to only a comparatively few people. He said that the claimant needs to prove substantial damage (see *Erven Warnink BV v J Townend & Sons (Hull) Ltd* [1979] 2 All ER 927, [1979] AC 731) and has failed to do so here. It is true that, once it had received the claimant's complaint, the defendant indicated that it would not repeat the use of the brochure, but it maintained that it had not breached Mr Irvine's rights and clearly reserved the right to do something similar in the future. Furthermore, it appears to me that the approach adopted by Sir Thomas Bingham in *Taittinger v Allbev Ltd* [1994] 4 All ER 75 and set out at [37], above, applies here as well. It is possible that the damage already done to Mr Irvine may be negligible in direct money terms but the potential long-term damage is considerable.

[75] There was one other set of points relied on by Mr Hicks. I hope I do not do them a disservice if I lump them all together under the general heading of 'other people's rights'. Mr Hicks said that Mr Irvine had no rights because he provided his endorsement services through a network of companies. I do not think that there was anything in this. The fact that the claimant, no doubt for tax reasons, makes his endorsement available through companies does not alter the fact that it is his fame and personality which is being exploited and that the misrepresentation made to the relevant public, who would know nothing about his corporate arrangements, is that it is he who has endorsed the defendant's radio station. In any event, to counter this point Miss Lane sought and obtained permission to join Mr Irvine's other companies as claimants. The other part of this defence is that in 1999 Mr Irvine was under contract to Ferrari and one of the terms of that contract was that he could not appear in the distinctive Ferrari red clothing in an endorsement save where that endorsement was through and on behalf of Ferrari. It follows that since the photograph on the brochure shows Mr Irvine wearing Ferrari overalls and a Ferrari cap, he would not have been permitted to use it to support a private endorsement undertaken on his own behalf. Because of this, Mr Hicks argued that Mr Irvine had no goodwill in images of himself in Ferrari uniform. Accordingly he has suffered no damage. This argument fails for two reasons. First, on the evidence it was tolerably clear that in 1999, had they been asked, Ferrari would have permitted him to endorse a product by appearing in a photograph wearing its uniform. Second, even if that were not so, this has no relevance to Mr Irvine's claim. For reasons given above, Mr Irvine has a property right in his goodwill which he can protect from unlicensed appropriation consisting of a false claim or suggestion of endorsement of a third party's goods or business. The fact, if it be one, that he might not be free to engage in a particular form of endorsement when wearing particular clothes or because of some other contractual restraint between him and another, does not alter the fact that the goodwill remains his and can be protected against intruders.

[76] For the above reasons, I have come to the conclusion that Mr Irvine succeeds in this action.

a [77] By way of postscript I should refer to one other matter. At an early stage in the trial, I asked whether there was a Human Rights Act 1998 point in this case. I referred counsel to the provisions of art 8 of the European Convention for the Protection of Human Rights and Fundamental Freedoms 1950 (as set out in Sch 1 to the 1998 Act) and those relating to the protection of property in art 1 of the First Protocol, particularly in the light of *Van Marle v Netherlands* (1986) 8 EHRR

b 483. As a result Miss Lane and Mr Hicks addressed me on this interesting subject. Had I come to the conclusion that passing off had not developed sufficiently to cover false endorsements it would have been necessary to go on to consider whether this new strand of law was effective, to use the words of Sedley LJ in *Douglas v Hello! Ltd* [2001] 2 All ER 289 at 317, [2001] QB 967 at 998, to '[give] the final impetus' to reach that result. As it is, for reasons set out above, I have come

c to the conclusion that the law of passing off secures to Mr Irvine the protection he seeks and no recourse needs to be had to the provisions of the Act.

Order accordingly.

Celia Fox   Barrister.

Annex 1

Annex 2

Clearer image of area in which the photograph has been manipulated:

Annex 3

Win and wear...

the winning team's colours
with Talk Radio...

Not only is Talk Radio giving your brand an unbeatable
advertising opportunity, we're giving you the chance to
become a **WINNER** and get into team colours.

Whether you call Tim Bleakley to arrange a meeting, or
set up a meeting when a member of the sales team
contacts you direct, we will enter you into our free prize
draw. You could win fantastic merchandise including a
sweatshirt, cap and T-shirt of the British Grand Prix
winning team, plus a Magnum of Champagne.

To find out more information about putting your
advertising in pole position, contact Tim Bleakley on
0171 546 1004 or email: tbleakley@talk-radio.co.uk.

Pelling v Families Need Fathers Ltd

[2001] EWCA Civ 1280

COURT OF APPEAL, CIVIL DIVISION

MUMMERY, JONATHAN PARKER LJJ AND WILSON J

12 JULY, 1 AUGUST 2001

Company – Register of members – Disclosure – Court having statutory power to compel company to send copy of register of members' names to person whose request for such a copy had been refused by company – Whether court having discretion to refuse application for such an order – Factors governing exercise of discretion – Companies Act 1985, s 356(6).

(1) On the true construction of s 356(6)[a] of the Companies Act 1985, which provides that in the case of a refusal or default to cause a copy of the register to be sent to the person requesting it 'the court may compel an immediate inspection of the register and index, or direct that copies required be sent to the persons requiring them', the registrar has a discretion to refuse the order. That provision empowers the court to make the order where a refusal in contravention of the law has been established, but whether the power will be exercised depends upon the proper discretionary considerations affecting it in the light of the facts found by the court. As a general rule, the court will make a mandatory order to give effect to the legal right to be supplied with a copy of the register on request, but it is not a matter of unqualified right. There may be something special in the circumstances of the case which leads the court to refuse to make the usual order. Although the scope of the residual discretion to refuse such an order may be narrow, it does exist. There will be cases in which it will be pointless for the court to make an order, where, for example, it is no longer necessary to make one, because the request has been complied with after the application is issued but before it is heard, or where the request is physically impossible to comply with because the register has been destroyed or lost. There are other circumstances in which the court is entitled to refuse to make an order or to make one in unqualified terms. It is common, for example, for a court to decline to exercise its discretion to make a mandatory or prohibitory order when the person against whom it is sought has offered the other side or the court an undertaking which meets the justice of the case. Nor is the court deprived of its discretion to refuse to make an order under s 365(6) by the criminal penalties to which the company is exposed under sub-s (5) if it refuses a request for a copy of the register. Those penalties underscore the importance both of the right and of the obligation of the company to give effect to it, but they do not expressly or impliedly deprive the court of the discretion clearly conferred by s 356(6). The making of an order under subsection will not contravene the provisions of the Data Protection Act 1984 (see [23], below).

(2) In exercising its discretion under s 356(6) of the 1985 Act, the court can cater both for the applicant's wish to gain access to the register for the purpose of legitimately communicating with members and for the company's proper and understandable concerns about the detrimental effect of an unqualified order for

---

a   Section 356, so far as material, is set out at [3], below

a disclosure of the names and addresses of the members. Such a reconciliation can be achieved by attaching relevant and reasonable terms and conditions to the exercise of the discretion. It is possible to provide a practical and fair solution either by making an order in favour of the applicant on terms as to the confidentiality and use of the information made available or by declining to make an order for inspection on the company giving a suitably-worded undertaking to

b facilitate communication with members by acting as a postbox for mail between the applicant and the members (see [23], below).

Notes

For copies of the register of members, see 7(1) *Halsbury's Laws* (4th edn reissue) 391.

c For the Companies Act 1985, s 356, see 8 *Halsbury's Statutes* (4th edn) (1999 reissue) 413.

Cases referred to in judgment

Armstrong v Sheppard & Short Ltd [1959] 2 All ER 651, [1959] 2 QB 384, CA.

d *Davies v Gas Light and Coke Co* [1909] 1 Ch 248; *affd* [1909] 1 Ch 708, CA.

Julius v Lord Bishop of Oxford (1880) 5 App Cas 214, [1874–80] All ER Rep 43, HL.

O'Brien v Sporting Shooters Association of Australia (Victoria) [1999] 3 VR 251, Vic SC.

Phonographic Performance Ltd v AEI Redifussion Music Ltd [1999] 2 All ER 299, [1999]

e 1 WLR 1507, CA.

Appeal

Dr Michael John Pelling appealed with permission of Mr Registrar Buckley from his decision on 5 April 2001 refusing Dr Pelling's application for an order under s 356(6) of the Companies Act 1985 directing the respondent, Families Need

f Fathers Ltd (the Company), to send him a copy of part of its register of members in accordance with a requirement made by him on the Company in a letter dated 13 March 2001. The facts are set out in the judgment of the court.

Dr Pelling appeared in person.

g The Company was represented, with the court's permission, by its vice-chairman, Colin Hale.

Cur adv vult

h 1 August 2001. The following judgment was delivered.

MUMMERY LJ.

[1] This is the judgment of the court to which all members of the court have contributed.

j [2] The appeal is by Dr Michael Pelling against the decision of Mr Registrar Buckley on 5 April 2001. The registrar dismissed Dr Pelling's application under s 356(6) of the Companies Act 1985 for an order against Families Need Fathers Ltd (the Company), a company limited by guarantee and registered as a charity. Dr Pelling sought an order directing that a copy of part of the register of members be sent to Dr Pelling in accordance with a requirement made by him on the Company in a letter of 13 March 2001.

[3] Under s 356(3):

'Any member of the company or other person may require a copy of the register, or of any part of it, on payment of such fee as may be prescribed; and the company shall cause any copy so required by a person to be sent to him within 10 days beginning with the day next following that on which the requirement is received by the company.'

By sub-s (5), if the requirement is refused or a copy so required is not sent within the proper period, the company and every officer of it who is in default is liable in respect of each offence to a fine. Subsection (6) provides:

'In the case of such refusal or default, the court may by order compel an immediate inspection of the register and index, or direct that the copies required be sent to the persons requiring them.'

[4] There is no transcript of the registrar's judgment, but, according to a note approved by him, he gave these reasons for his decision:

'I have a discretion under Section 356 (6) of the Companies Act 1985 whether or not to make an order requiring disclosure of the Register of Members. Having read the evidence and submissions of the Trustee for Families Need Fathers Ltd, I consider this is a case in which it is not appropriate to require disclosure of the Register. Accordingly I refuse the order sought by the claimant.'

[5] The registrar granted permission to appeal.

[6] On the appeal the court was supplied with written submissions by each side. It heard oral argument from Dr Pelling, who acts in person, and from Mr Colin Hale, the vice-chairman of the Company and an elected trustee on its national council, who was granted permission by the court to represent the Company at the hearing. The court did not have the benefit of legal argument from counsel on the construction of the 1985 Act. Fortunately the Court of Appeal has at its disposal research resources in the form of the judicial assistants scheme. This facility is particularly valuable in cases such as this where the parties have not supplied, or been able to supply, to the court all the legal materials necessary for the determination of the appeal. Research has revealed, first, that provisions based on those contained in s 356(6) of the 1985 Act have been enacted with local variations in various Commonwealth jurisdictions, such as Australia, New Zealand and Canada and, secondly, that a very similar question came before the Supreme Court of Victoria two years ago in the case of *O'Brien v Sporting Shooters Association of Australia (Victoria)* [1999] 3 VR 251. The wording of the equivalent statutory provision (s 1303 of the Australian Corporations Law) was in almost the same terms as s 356(6). The case concerned a company limited by guarantee, which was required by law to keep a register of members showing their names and addresses. Three members, who were candidates for election to the executive council of the association, sought a court order to enforce their statutory rights to obtain a copy of the register, so that they could canvass members of the association for their votes at the forthcoming annual meeting. One of the grounds relied on by the association for opposing the order was that it was concerned to protect the confidentiality of the identity of the members, who were for the most part people who possessed guns which they kept at home. The association also challenged the bona fides of the applicant members, contending that the order was not sought for their professed purpose. Byrne J a concluded that he had a discretion to make an order. He also held that, on the facts of that particular case, he was satisfied that the applicants sought the information for a legitimate purpose and that there was no ground either to doubt their bona fides or to exercise his discretion adversely to them. We shall return to his ruling on the discretion issue later in this judgment. The court and the parties are indebted to the judicial assistant (Mr Richard Clegg) for his

b research.

Background facts

[7] The Company, described as 'the Charity', is incorporated for the following objects:

c '(i) For the relief of parents and their children and other close family members suffering from the consequences of divorce or separation by providing advice, assistance and other support and, in so doing, helping parents stay in touch with their children after divorce or separation; (ii) To further the emotional development of children whose parents have divorced or separated by encouraging shared parenting arrangements which enable

d such children to have continuing and meaningful relationships with both their parents; (iii) To conduct study and research into problems concerned with children who are deprived of the presence of a parent in their families, and into the problems concerned with establishing good relations between parents living apart from their children, and to publish the useful results of

e all such study and research in order to encourage appropriate changes in professional and public opinion; (iv) To relieve poor parents by helping to obtain and promoting the provision of free legal advice, assistance and other free legal services which such parents would be unable to obtain by reason of their lack of means.'

f [8] Clause 7 of the memorandum of association provides:

'Every member of the Charity undertakes to contribute such amount as may be required (not exceeding £10) to the Charity's assets if it should be wound up while he or she is a member or within 1 year after he or she ceases to be a member, for payment of the Charity's debts and liabilities contracted

g before he or she ceases to be a member, and of the costs, charges and expenses of winding up, and for the adjustment of the rights of the contributories among themselves.'

[9] Article 2 of the articles of association provides:

h '(1) The subscribers to the memorandum and such other persons or organisations as are admitted to membership in accordance with the rules made under Article 61 shall be members of the Charity. No person shall be admitted a member of the Charity unless his application for membership is approved by the trustees.'

j [10] The articles provide for the holding of general meetings of which members are entitled to be given notice and at which they are entitled to attend and vote. Article 61 provides:

'(1) The trustees may from time to time make such rules or bye laws as they may deem necessary or expedient or convenient for the proper conduct and management of the Charity and for the purposes of prescribing classes of and conditions of membership, and in particular but without prejudice to the generality of the foregoing, they may by such rules or bye laws regulate: (i) The admission and classification of members of the Charity (including the admission of organisations to membership) and the rights and privileges of such members, and the conditions of membership and the terms on which members may resign or have their membership terminated and the entrance fees, subscriptions and other fees or payments to be made by members ...'

[11] It does not appear from the evidence or from what the court was told by Mr Hale that any rules or byelaws have been made under art 61. The evidence does, however, indicate that there are about 3,000 members of the Company, yielding a subscription income, according to the accounts for the year ending 31 December 1999, of £58,455. It also appears that there are 12 trustees and directors of the Company.

[12] Dr Pelling became a member of the Company in 1990. As a result of recent disagreements the Company purported to suspend him from membership as from 22 February 2001 and to terminate his membership with effect from 24 April 2001. Dr Pelling informed the court that he has instituted proceedings in the Chancery Division challenging the validity of the steps taken against him. On 16 July 2001 Hart J declared that the purported suspension and termination were unlawful and void. Dr Pelling, along with some other members of the Company, takes the view that the Company is not well-served by the present directors. At about the beginning of March 2001 the 'FNF Reform Group' came into being. Dr Pelling is the secretary of that group. Its aim is to replace the existing board of directors at the annual general meeting of the Company, which was originally to be held on Sunday 20 May 2001, but has now been postponed to Sunday 23 September 2001.

[13] The nature of the present dispute between Dr Pelling and the Company is evident from the correspondence immediately preceding the issue of Dr Pelling's application under s 356(6) on 26 March 2001. On 13 March Dr Pelling wrote to the company at its registered office making an application under s 356(3) of the 1985 Act for, and requiring a copy of, that part of the register of members consisting of the entries of persons who were both currently members as at 13 March 2001 and had been continuously members since 31 December 1999. He enclosed a cheque for £37·50 to cover the prescribed fee if the number of such entries did not exceed 2,100 and an additional cheque for £15, if the number was more than 2,100 but not more than 3,100. His letter set out the provisions of the subsection under which he made the application.

[14] Mr Hale replied on behalf of the Company on 23 March asserting that the members of the charity were not registered as members of the Company, that the 1985 Act was not relevant to his request and that, as a long-standing and experienced member, he, Dr Pelling, would readily understand that the membership list was confidential and that he was therefore unable to comply with the request. The two cheques were returned.

The rival submissions

[15] Before this court Dr Pelling's initial stance was that the registrar had no discretion to refuse an application for an order under s 356(6), whether made by a member or other person, in a case in which a company had refused or was in default of complying with a requirement made under s 356(3). He submitted that he had a clear and incontestable legal right to be supplied with what he required

a   in his letter of 13 March; that his reasons for making that requirement were
irrelevant to his right to make and enforce it; that the registrar had had no option
but to make the order sought in his application; and that the registrar had erred
in law in holding that he had a discretion in the matter.

[16] In support of these submissions Dr Pelling cited *Davies v Gas Light and
Coke Co* [1909] 1 Ch 248, a decision of Warrington J on the construction of the
b   Companies Clauses Consolidation Act 1845, which did not include a provision in
the terms of s 356(6) or any equivalent provision. (That procedure for enforcing
the right to inspection was not introduced until s 32 of the Companies Act 1862.)
Under the 1845 Act only a member of the company could require a copy of the
register and the enforcement of that right was by way of ordinary action and not
under a specially prescribed statutory procedure. It was in that context that
c   Warrington J granted mandamus against the company, holding that the
member's right to inspect the register was incidental to his private right of
property as a holder of shares in the company, that the court had (at 254) 'no title
to inquire into the motives of the person who seeks to enforce that private right',
and that the court had no option but to grant him relief enforcing the right. The
d   decision was affirmed on appeal (see [1909] 1 Ch 708).

[17] Dr Pelling also contended that the court's jurisdiction under s 356(6)
could not be discretionary because the preceding subsection made the refusal or
default of the company a criminal offence. This feature of the statutory scheme,
he submitted, underlined the mandatory quality of the court's jurisdiction.

[18] Although Dr Pelling stated in his written argument that he was not going
e   to argue that, if there was a discretion, it should have been exercised in his favour,
he submitted at the hearing that, if he was wrong in his absolutist construction,
the registrar's exercise of his discretion was reviewable in this court, because he
had erred in principle in failing to give effect to the unqualified legal right
conferred on him by s 356(3).

f   [19] On behalf of the Company Mr Hale challenged the contention that the
registrar had no discretion to refuse to make an order. He pointed to the use of
'may' in s 356(6), in contrast to the use of 'shall' in sub-s (3) and other parts of
s 356, indicating that Parliament was fully aware of the difference between a
mandatory requirement and a discretionary power.

[20] He argued that the registrar was entitled, in all the circumstances, to
g   refuse to exercise his discretion in Dr Pelling's favour. He focused on the factors
highlighted in his evidence to the registrar, as amplified in further documents
submitted on the appeal. Mr Hale explained that since 1993 he had been
responsible for the development and registration of the Company's database and
the functioning of the London office of the Company. He emphasised that the
h   members join the Company at a time of great personal stress, seeking the help of
the confidential service offered by the Company to its members. It was implicit
in the sensitive nature of the Company's work and the confidentiality of the
service provided to the members that it would be obnoxious to them for their
names and addresses to be available to other members or to the world at large on
j   demand. He said that membership details had never been released before and, if
ordered now, would cause serious difficulties in the work of the Company,
putting the continuing existence of that work at risk. Dr Pelling did not challenge
this evidence, save to inform the court of his reason for wanting the names and
addresses of the members, to which we will refer in [22](iii). He continued to
insist on the unqualified proprietary nature of his legal right and the irrelevance
of the discretionary factors relied on by Mr Hale. Echoing the words of Lord

Coke he warned the court against substituting the crooked cord of discretion for the golden metwand of the law.

[21] Mr Hale added that compliance with an order of the kind sought by Dr Pelling would involve a potential breach of provisions of the Data Protection Act 1984. He also contended that, if s 356(6) had the mandatory effect contended for by Dr Pelling, that would be incompatible with the provisions of art 8 of the European Convention for the Protection of Human Rights and Fundamental Freedoms 1950 (as set out in Sch 1 to the Human Rights Act 1998) and that, if the court accepted Dr Pelling's construction, it should make a declaration of incompatibility under s 4 of the 1998 Act. Mr Hale also raised for the first time on the appeal the possibility of an order granting to officers of the Company relief under s 727 of the 1985 Act in respect of any breach of duty by them. It was pointed out to him that this court only had jurisdiction to hear appeals and that it would be necessary for the officers of the Company to issue an application, supported by evidence, in the Companies Court.

Issues on the appeal

[22] In the light of the rival submissions, the following questions arise for decision on this appeal. (i) Did the registrar have a discretion under s 356(6)? This is a question of the true construction of the provision. (ii) If the registrar did have a discretion, is this court entitled to interfere with his refusal to exercise it? In limited circumstances the Court of Appeal is entitled to interfere with the exercise of a judicial discretion. It has to be shown that the lower court has erred in principle in the approach to the exercise of the discretion, or has left out of account a factor which should have been taken into account, or has taken into account a factor which ought not to have been taken into account, or that the decision is plainly wrong and could only have been the result of a failure to balance the relevant factors fairly in the scale (see *Phonographic Performance Ltd v AEI Redifussion Music Ltd* [1999] 2 All ER 299 at 314, [1999] 1 WLR 1507 at 1523). (iii) If this court holds that the registrar erred in refusing to exercise the discretion, should this court exercise it in Dr Pelling's favour and, if so, on what terms? During the course of the argument we raised the question whether the Company was willing to circulate to its members material which Dr Pelling wished to put before the members in relation to the forthcoming annual general meeting. In his submissions Dr Pelling stressed the importance of the right of free communication with members of the Company. Although he had argued that the reasons for his requirement were irrelevant, he explained in his evidence that he required the names and addresses of members so that he could communicate with them and canvass their votes in advance of the forthcoming annual general meeting. While Mr Hale indicated that there would be no problem in the Company giving such an undertaking, Dr Pelling responded that the undertaking would be unacceptable to him in view of his lack of trust in those at present responsible for the running of the Company.

Conclusions

[23] We have reached the following conclusions. (i) On the true construction of s 356(6) the registrar had a discretion to refuse the order. In its ordinary and natural meaning the word 'may' is apt to confer a discretion or power. It is true that there are certain situations where a discretionary power is conferred for the purpose of enforcing a right and is coupled with an obligation or duty to exercise a power, when required to do so, for the benefit of the person who has the right

a (see *Julius v Lord Bishop of Oxford* (1880) 5 App Cas 214 at 223, 241, [1874–80] All ER Rep 43 at 47–48, 57). This is not such a case. The use of 'may' in sub-s (6) is in striking contrast to the mandatory force of 'shall' in other parts of the same section, such as sub-s (3). In *O'Brien v Sporting Shooters Association of Australia (Victoria)* [1999] 3 VR 251 at 255 Byrne J rejected the submission that the court had no discretion under the similarly-worded provision in s 1303 of the Australian *b* Corporations Law. It was submitted to him that the word 'may' in that section was not permissive, but merely signified that the jurisdiction of the court to make an order did not arise unless there had been a refusal or contravention of the Corporations Law. He held (at 255) that the drafting of the Law was such that—

c   'the word "may" means exactly that. It means that the court is empowered to make the order where a refusal in contravention of the Law has been established, as in the present case. Whether the power will be exercised must depend upon the proper discretionary considerations affecting the power in the light of the facts as are found by the court.'

We agree. For those reasons we reject the absolutist construction proposed by *d* Dr Pelling. (ii) The statutory discretion must be exercised judicially in accordance with established legal principles and having regard only to relevant considerations. We agree with Dr Pelling that, as a general rule, the court will make a mandatory order to give effect to a legal right. But, as stated by Lord Evershed MR in *Armstrong v Sheppard & Short Ltd* [1959] 2 All ER 651 at 656, [1959] 2 QB 384 at 396 '[i]t is not a matter of unqualified right'. There may be something *e* special in the circumstances of the case which leads the court to refuse to make the usual order. The scope of the residual discretion to refuse such an order may be narrow, but Dr Pelling is, in our view, wrong in his assertion that it is non-existent. Indeed, we understood him to accept that there would be cases in which it would be pointless for the court to make an order where, for example, it *f* was no longer necessary to make one, because the request had been complied with after the application was issued but before it was heard, or where the request was physically impossible to comply with because the register had been destroyed or lost. There are other circumstances in which the court is entitled to refuse to make any order or to make one in unqualified terms. It is common, for example, for a court to decline to exercise its discretion to make a mandatory or *g* prohibitory order when the person against whom it is sought has offered to the other side or to the court an undertaking which meets the justice of the case. (iii) We also reject Dr Pelling's contention that the criminal penalties to which the company is exposed under s 356(5) deprive the court of discretion to refuse to make an order under sub-s (6). It can certainly be said that the criminal penalties *h* underscore the importance both of the right and of the obligation of the Company to give effect to it, but they do not expressly or impliedly deprive the court of the discretion clearly conferred by the use of the word 'may'. The line of exceptional cases in which the assistance of the civil courts is invoked in aid of the criminal law amply demonstrates that the civil courts retain a discretion as to *j* whether or not it is an appropriate case for their intervention by making an order to enforce obedience to the criminal law. (iv) Having regard to specific exemption provisions in s 34 of the 1984 Act, we are satisfied that the making of an order would not contravene the provisions of the Act protecting personal data. Further the construction of s 356(6) so as to confer a discretion on the court would not involve any incompatibility with art 8 of the convention. (v) In our judgment, it is possible to cater for both Dr Pelling's wish to gain access to the register for the professed purpose of legitimately communicating with the members and the proper and understandable concerns of Mr Hale about the detrimental effect of an unqualified order for disclosure of the names and addresses of the members, particularly on the charitable purposes for which the Company was established. A reconciliation can be achieved by attaching relevant and reasonable terms and conditions to the exercise of the discretion. As indicated in *O'Brien's* case [1999] 3 VR 251 at 256, it is possible to provide a practical and fair solution either by making an order in favour of the applicant on terms as to the confidentiality and use of the information made available; or, as we suggested, and as was offered in *O'Brien's* case (at 255), by declining to make an order for inspection, on the Company giving a suitably-worded undertaking to facilitate communication with members by acting as a postbox for mail between the applicant and the members. (vi) The parties should be entitled to address the court further on this point before the final form of order is settled by the court.

Form of order

[24] On the handing down of the judgment the court invited submissions from the parties on the form of order which should be made in the light of the judgment, in particular [20] and [23](ii) and (v), above. Dr Pelling argued that the court should make an order in the terms of s 356(6) without imposing additional terms or accepting undertakings in lieu of such an order. He said that the court could not reasonably refuse to do as he asked. He repeated that he did not trust the Company's council. He referred to his recent success against the Company in the Chancery Division. As to an undertaking by the Company in lieu of a mandatory order under s 356(6), he submitted that the court could not accept an undertaking, unless it had power to make a corresponding injunction, which it did not have in this case. He also questioned the authority of Mr Hale to give an undertaking on behalf of the Company. Although he declined to give any undertakings himself in respect of the use of the register of members, he was willing to enter into contractual undertakings with the Company as set out in his written submissions, so that his use of the copy of the register was confined to the purpose of communicating with the members of the Company.

[25] Mr Hale confirmed that he was willing to give undertakings on behalf of the Company along the lines referred to in [22](iii) and [23](v) of this judgment and claimed that he had authority to give them on behalf of the Company. He was willing, if necessary, to obtain evidence of the requisite authority. He opposed the alternative form of order proposed by Dr Pelling and repeated his concerns, as set out in [20], above, about the effect of making copies of the register of members available. When he made his oral submissions Dr Pelling accepted the validity of those concerns, but disputed their impact on his right to an unqualified order.

[26] In the light of the undertakings offered by Mr Hale on behalf of the Company and his personal undertakings we dismiss the appeal against the refusal of the registrar to make an order under s 356(6). It is inappropriate to make such an order when there is available a satisfactory means of meeting the Company's valid concerns about the effect of the order on their members and their charitable activities, and of providing Dr Pelling with the desired opportunity of communicating with the other members of the Company ahead of the forthcoming annual general meeting.

Appeal dismissed.

Dilys Tausz   Barrister.

Re B (adult: refusal of medical treatment)
[2002] EWHC 429 (Fam)

FAMILY DIVISION

DAME ELIZABETH BUTLER-SLOSS P

6–8, 22 MARCH 2002

Medical treatment – Adult patient – Consent to treatment – Right to refuse treatment – Tetraplegic patient being kept alive by ventilator – Patient wishing to have ventilator turned off – Whether patient competent to refuse treatment – Whether treatment of patient unlawful.

In 1999 the claimant, who was then 41 years old, suffered a haemorrhage of the spinal column in her neck. She was admitted to a hospital run by the defendant NHS trust. Although the claimant recovered sufficiently to return to work, her condition deteriorated at the beginning of 2001. She was readmitted to the hospital after suffering an intramedullary cervical spine cavernoma. As a result of the cavernoma, she became tetraplegic and suffered complete paralysis from the neck down. She was transferred to the hospital's intensive care unit and began to experience respiratory problems. She was treated with a ventilator, upon which she had been entirely dependent ever since. After neurological surgery to remove the cavernous haematoma, she was able to move her head and articulate words. She gave formal instructions to the hospital through her solicitors that she wished artificial ventilation to be removed, even though she realised that that would almost certainly result in her death. She was assessed by two consultant psychiatrists at the hospital. They initially concluded that she had capacity to make a decision in respect of the withdrawal of treatment, and preparations were put in hand to turn the ventilator off. However, those preparations were called off after the psychiatrists changed their minds as to the claimant's capacity. She was prescribed anti-depressants, and said that she was relieved that the ventilator had not been switched off. Long-term plans were made for her rehabilitation, and she was referred to several spinal units. She was reassessed by the hospital psychiatrists, but they failed to reach a firm conclusion as to her mental capacity. An independent reassessment was carried out on 8 August 2001 by another doctor. He did not consider the claimant to be suffering from depression and concluded that she was competent to make the decision to discontinue treatment. Thereafter, the hospital treated the claimant as having capacity to make decisions. From September 2001 the claimant made it clear that she did not wish to go to a spinal rehabilitation unit as it offered no hope of recovery. However, the treating clinicians, who had developed a close relationship with the claimant, were not prepared to turn off the ventilator, and instead reluctantly agreed to a one-way weaning programme by which, over a period of time, assistance from the ventilator would be reduced, with the aim of allowing the claimant's body to become used to breathing again. There was, however, less than a 1% chance of independent ventilation, and the claimant rejected the weaning programme, fearing that it would lead to her suffering a long and painful death. Instead, she applied to the court for, inter alia, a declaration that she had been treated unlawfully from 8 August 2001. The treating clinicians gave evidence that they regarded her as competent to make decisions about her medical treatment, but could not contemplate bringing her

life to an end by turning off the ventilator. An independent consultant
psychiatrist, like all the other medical witnesses, also concluded that the claimant
was competent, but was concerned that if immediate priority was given to her
autonomy by acting on her wishes, there was a risk of depriving her of potential
benefits in the future. Despite the medical evidence, the trust did not accept that
the claimant had capacity. It relied, inter alia, on her alleged ambivalence
towards the withdrawal of treatment and her failure to experience the positive
experience of rehabilitation.

Held – (1) The right of a competent patient to request the cessation of treatment
had to prevail over the natural desire of the medical and nursing profession to try
to keep her alive. If mental capacity were not in issue and the patient, having
been given the relevant information and offered the available options, chose to
refuse treatment, that decision had to be respected by the doctors. If there were
difficulties in deciding whether the patient had sufficient mental capacity,
particularly if the refusal might have grave consequences for the patient, it was
most important that those considering the issue should not confuse the question
of mental capacity with the nature of the patient's decision, however grave the
consequences. The patient's view might reflect a difference in values rather than
an absence of competence, and the assessment of capacity should be approached
with that firmly in mind. The doctors were not to allow their emotional reaction
to, or strong disagreement with, the patient's decision to cloud their judgment in
answering the primary question whether the patient had the mental capacity to
make the decision. If the hospital were faced with a dilemma that the doctors did
not know how to resolve, it had to be recognised and further steps taken as a
matter of priority. Those in charge were not to allow a situation of deadlock or
drift to occur. If there were no disagreement about competence but the doctors
were, for any reason, unable to carry out the patient's wishes, their duty was to
find other doctors who would do so. If all appropriate steps to seek independent
assistance from medical experts outside the hospital had failed, the hospital trust
should not hesitate to make an application to the High Court or seek the advice
of the Official Solicitor. Furthermore, unless the gravity of illness had affected a
patient's capacity, a seriously-disabled patient had the same rights as a fit person
to respect for personal autonomy. There was a serious danger of a benevolent
paternalism which did not embrace recognition of the personal autonomy of the
severely-disabled patient. As regards the ambivalence of a patient about the
withdrawal of treatment, that might be relevant to the assessment of capacity if,
and only if, the ambivalence genuinely struck at the root of the patient's mental
capacity. Unless the case was exceptional, the judicial approach to
mental capacity had to be largely dependent upon the assessments of the medical
profession whose task it was, on a regular basis, to assess the competence of the
patient to consent to, or refuse, the recommended medical or surgical treatment
(see [27], [35], [89], [94], [100], below); *Re T (adult: refusal of medical treatment)*
[1992] 4 All ER 649 and *Airedale NHS Trust v Bland* [1993] 1 All ER 821 considered.

(2) In the instant case, the claimant was competent to make all the relevant
decisions about her medical treatment, including the decision whether to
seek to withdraw from artificial ventilation. Her mental competence was
commensurate with the gravity of the decision that she might wish to make.
She had had the mental capacity to make such decisions since 8 August 2001 and
she would remain competent to make them for the foreseeable future. Her lack
of experience in a spinal rehabilitation unit and, thereafter, in the community had

a not eroded her mental capacity to any degree whatsoever. Nor had she been
   ambivalent in her determination to choose her medical treatment and in her wish
   to cease to have artificial ventilation. She had looked at the alternatives and gone
   down the path of rehabilitation when she had been deemed incapable of making
   her own decision. It followed that the claimant had been treated unlawfully by
   the trust since 8 August 2001. It was, however, important to draw a distinction
b between the duties of the dedicated team in the intensive care unit caring for the
   claimant and those of the trust. The team had cared for her to the highest
   standards of medical competence and with devotion, and they deserved the
   highest praise. The request from the claimant, which would have been
   understood in a palliative care situation, appeared to have been outside the
   experience of the intensive care unit in relation to a mentally-competent patient.
c It was seen by some as killing the claimant or assisting her to die, and as ethically
   unacceptable. The claimant was placed in an impossible position, and the trust
   had been under a duty to do something effective to resolve the dilemma and to
   do so with some degree of urgency. Its failure to deal with the issue would result
   in the court making a small award of damages in addition to granting appropriate
d declarations (see [92], [94]–[99], below).

Notes
For the requirement of a patient's consent to treatment, see 30 *Halsbury's Laws*
(4th edn reissue) para 39.

e **Cases referred to in judgment**
   Airedale NHS Trust v Bland [1993] 1 All ER 821, [1993] AC 789, [1993] 2 WLR 316,
     Fam D, CA and HL.
   Bartling v Superior Court of Los Angeles County (1984) 163 Cal App 3d 186, Cal Ct of
     Apps.
f *C (adult: refusal of medical treatment), Re* [1994] 1 All ER 819, [1994] 1 WLR 290.
   Cruzan v Director, Missouri Department of Health (1990) 497 US 261, US SC.
   F v West Berkshire Health Authority (Mental Health Act Commission intervening) [1989]
     2 All ER 545, sub nom *Re F (mental patient: sterilisation)* [1990] 2 AC 1, [1989] 2
     WLR 1025, HL.
g *Lane v Candura* (1978) 376 NE 2d 1232, Mass Apps Ct.
   Malette v Shulman (1990) 67 DLR (4th) 321.
   MB (an adult: medical treatment), Re [1997] 2 FCR 541, CA.
   McKay v Bergstedt (1990) 801 P 2d 617, Nev SC.
   Nancy B v Hôtel-Dieu de Québec (1992) 86 DLR (4th) 385, Que Superior Ct.
h *S v S, W v Official Solicitor* [1970] 3 All ER 107, [1972] AC 24, [1970] 3 WLR 366,
     HL.
   Sidaway v Bethlem Royal Hospital Governors [1985] 1 All ER 643, [1985] AC 871,
     [1985] 2 WLR 480, HL.
   St George's Healthcare NHS Trust v S, R v Collins, ex p S [1998] 3 All ER 673, [1999]
     Fam 26, [1998] 3 WLR 936, CA.
j *T (adult: refusal of medical treatment), Re* [1992] 4 All ER 649, [1993] Fam 95, [1992]
     3 WLR 782, CΛ.

Application
The claimant, Ms B, applied for a declaration that she had had been treated
unlawfully by way of artificial ventilation by the defendant NHS hospital trust

since 8 August 2001 and also sought damages against the trust. The facts are set out in the judgment.

Philip Havers QC and *Jeremy Hyam* (instructed by *Leigh Day & Co*) for Ms B.
Robert Francis QC and *Michael Horne* (instructed by *Capsticks*) for the trust.
Peter Jackson QC (instructed by the *Official Solicitor*) as advocate to the court.

Cur adv vult

22 March 2002. The following judgment was delivered.

DAME ELIZABETH BUTLER-SLOSS P.

[1] The claimant, whom I shall call Ms B, seeks declarations from the High Court in its exercise of the inherent jurisdiction. She claims that the invasive treatment which is currently being given by the defendant by way of artificial ventilation is an unlawful trespass.

[2] The defendant is the NHS hospital trust (the trust) responsible for the hospital which is currently caring for Ms B (the hospital). At the request of the court the Official Solicitor instructed Mr Peter Jackson QC to act as advocate to the court. The main issue is whether Ms B has the capacity to make her own decision about her treatment in hospital. Underlying this important issue is the tragic story of an able and talented woman of 43 who has suffered a devastating illness which has caused her to become tetraplegic and whose expressed wish is not to be kept artificially alive by the use of a ventilator.

THE HISTORY

[3] Ms B was born on 6 August 1958 in Jamaica, and has lived in the United Kingdom since the age of eight. She had an unhappy childhood but triumphed over many difficulties to achieve a degree in social science and social work, and a Master's degree in public policy and administration. She is a qualified practice teacher for social work, and has a management diploma from a London college. She worked as a social worker for a number of local authorities and became a team manager. She was appointed in that role to a hospital and was promoted to head of department and principal officer for training and staff development. She is unmarried. She has a close circle of friends and a godchild to whom she is devoted.

Medical history

[4] On 26 August 1999, Ms B suffered a haemorrhage of the spinal column in her neck. She was admitted to the hospital and a cavernoma was diagnosed, a condition caused by a malformation of blood vessels in the spinal cord. She was transferred to another hospital where she stayed for five weeks. She was informed by doctors that there was a possibility of a further bleed, or surgical intervention, which would result in severe disability. On the basis of this advice she executed a living will (dated 4 September 1999). The terms of the will stated that should the time come when Ms B was unable to give instructions, she wished for treatment to be withdrawn if she was suffering from a life-threatening condition, permanent mental impairment or permanent unconsciousness. She was, however, also told that the risk of re-haemorrhage was not particularly great, and so she felt very optimistic about the future. Her condition gradually improved and after leaving hospital and a period of recuperation, she returned to

a   work. Thereafter Ms B was in generally good health although she had some
continued weakness in her left arm.

[5] At the beginning of 2001, Ms B began to suffer from general weakening on
the left side of her body, and experienced greater numbness in her legs. She felt
unwell on 12 February 2001, and was admitted to the hospital in the early hours
of 13 February 2001. She had suffered an intramedullary cervical spine cavernoma,

b   as a result of which she became tetraplegic, suffering complete paralysis from the
neck down. On 16 February 2001 she was transferred to the Intensive Care Unit
(the ICU) of the hospital. She began to experience respiratory problems, and was
treated with a ventilator, upon which she has been entirely dependent ever since.

[6] Ms B told Dr R (a consultant anaesthetist in the ICU of the hospital) and
another consultant anaesthetist on about 24 February 2001 that she had a living

c   will on file, and did not want to be ventilated. The doctors informed her that the
terms of the living will were not specific enough to authorise withdrawal of
ventilation. On 23 March 2001 at another hospital she underwent neurological
surgery to remove the cavernous haematoma. After the operation, her condition
improved slightly. She regained the ability to move her head, and to articulate

d   words. She was however, as she said, bitterly disappointed that the operation had
not been more successful. It was at that time that she first asked for the ventilator
to be switched off.

[7] On 26 March 2001 she was assessed by Dr RG, a consultant psychiatrist
from another hospital. On 28 March 2001 Ms B was returned to the ICU at the
hospital where she remains. She made a request to a consultant anaesthetist to

e   have the ventilator switched off. On 5 April 2001, Ms B gave formal instructions
to the hospital, via her solicitors, that she wished the artificial ventilation to be
removed. The trust got in touch by telephone with its solicitors, Capsticks, who
replied by a letter to the head of external relations. I shall return to that letter later
in this judgment. A case conference followed and it was arranged that two

f   independent psychiatric assessments would be conducted before any further
steps were taken.

[8] On 10 April 2001 she was assessed by Dr L, a consultant psychiatrist at the
hospital, who concluded she had capacity. On 11 April 2001 she was assessed by
another consultant psychiatrist at the hospital, Dr E, who initially found that
Ms B did have capacity. Dr E on 12 April 2001 then amended her report to state

g   that Ms B did *not* have capacity, after which Dr L amended his original
assessment so as to agree with Dr E. After Dr E's initial opinion, preparations had
begun to be made for the ventilator to be turned off. Ms B held discussions with
one of the doctors and a lead nurse of the hospital, and it was agreed that three
days should be allowed for Ms B to say goodbye to her family and friends and to

h   finalise her affairs. However, these preparations were called off after Dr E
changed her report.

[9] Ms B was prescribed anti-depressants on 13 April 2001. She was seen by
both Dr E and Dr R on 30 April 2001. Both doctors stated that on this occasion
Ms B said that she was relieved the ventilator had not been switched off. On

j   29 May 2001, Ms B participated in assessment for rehabilitation, and agreed to try
it. Long-term plans were made for her rehabilitation, with a view to eventually
returning home with 24-hour care, or alternatively a residential nursing home.
Dr R gave evidence that on 29 May 2001 Ms B, having been visited by the
rehabilitation specialists, was 'very cheerful' and 'upbeat'. She was referred to
several spinal units. She received help, which is continuing, from a clinical
psychologist. She was reassessed on 29 June 2001 by Dr L, and on 4 July 2001 by

Dr E. Their assessments did not provide a firm conclusion as to her mental capacity. On 12 July 2001 a bronchoscopy was carried out as part of treatment for a left lung collapse. At her request, an independent reassessment was conducted by Dr RG on 8 August 2001. He indicated that he did not consider her to be suffering from depression and that he considered her competent to make the decision to discontinue her treatment. Thereafter the hospital treated Ms B as having capacity to make decisions.

8 August to the hearing

[10] Ms B made a further living will on 15 August 2001. On 12 and 25 September two further bronchoscopies were performed with Ms B's consent. She was suffering respiratory distress at the time. The medical director considered that there should be involvement from an ethics committee and that assistance should be sought from outside. The trust did not have an ethics committee and the health authority was unable to consider the problem. Between August 2001 and the issue of these proceedings by Ms B on 16 January 2002 the trust sought advice from various outside sources. The possibility of a one-way weaning programme was suggested by Dr S, a consultant in neuroanaesthesia and intensive care from another hospital who was consulted. One-way weaning is a programme whereby over a period of time the number of breaths supplied by the ventilator is gradually reduced and the patient's body is allowed to become used to breathing on its own again. Generally if the patient cannot manage on his/her own then the number of breaths is increased. In a one-way weaning programme it would be reduced without going back on the support. Sedation would be given but not so as to cause respiratory depression unless clinically indicated. The clinicians were not prepared to turn off the ventilator. The one-way weaning programme was agreed by the clinicians but with reluctance as an acceptable compromise. It was also agreed that this could be achieved either by sending Ms B to a weaning centre or carrying it out in the ICU.

[11] On 12 November Ms B was offered referral to a weaning centre which she rejected. In the alternative she was offered the programme in the ICU. This she also rejected for two reasons, being the length of the process (about three weeks), and the omission of pain-killers as part of the treatment. Ms B made it clear from September 2001 that she did not want to go to a spinal rehabilitation unit. She refused the possibility of a referral to one clinic when her name was near the top of the waiting list in October. She also refused the possibility of a bed in a hospice in December since the hospice would not accept her wish to have her ventilator withdrawn.

THE ISSUES

[12] Mr Havers QC, for Ms B, has not, for the purpose of this hearing, challenged the conclusions of the psychiatrists as to her lack of mental capacity between April and August 2001 and it is not necessary for me to consider her ability to make decisions before 8 August. Although her capacity was not challenged by the treating doctors after 8 August nor was she again examined by a psychiatrist before the commencement of these proceedings, Mr Francis QC, for the trust, does not accept that Ms B did have capacity from 8 August nor that she has it now. I shall therefore have to consider in some detail her ability to make decisions and in particular the fundamental decision whether to require the removal of the artificial ventilation keeping her alive. It is important to underline

a that I am not asked directly to decide whether Ms B lives or dies but whether she, herself, is legally competent to make that decision. It is also important to recognise that this case is not about the best interests of the patient but about her mental capacity.

[13] The issues are therefore: (a) does the claimant, Ms B, have the mental capacity to choose whether to accept or refuse medical treatment, in *b* circumstances in which her refusal will, almost inevitably, lead to her death? If the answer is Yes, (b) did she have the capacity to choose from August 2001? Ms B seeks declarations from the court in respect of both questions. (c) If the answer to (b) is Yes, then Ms B seeks a declaration from the court that the hospital has been treating her unlawfully from 8 August 2001. (d) If the answer to (b) is Yes, then Ms B also seeks nominal damages to recognise the tort of trespass to the *c* person. (e) It will be necessary to continue injunctions in relation to publicity.

The law on mental capacity

[14] The general law on mental capacity is, in my judgment, clear and easily to be understood by lawyers. Its application to individual cases in the context of *d* a general practitioner's surgery, a hospital ward and especially in an intensive care unit is infinitely more difficult to achieve.

[15] In a series of cases during the 1990s the House of Lords and the Court of Appeal restated the long-established principles which govern the law on mental capacity of adults and provided some guidelines in complex medical situations.

e (a) The principle of autonomy

[16] In 1972 Lord Reid in *S v S, W v Official Solicitor* [1970] 3 All ER 107 at 111, [1972] AC 24 at 43 said:

f 'English law goes to great lengths to protect a person of full age and capacity from interference with his personal liberty. We have too often seen freedom disappear in other countries not only by coups d'état but by gradual erosion; and often it is the first step that counts. So it would be unwise to make even minor concessions.'

[17] In *F v West Berkshire Health Authority (Mental Health Act Commission* *g* *intervening)* [1989] 2 All ER 545 at 563, sub nom *Re F (mental patient: sterilisation)* [1990] 2 AC 1 at 72 Lord Goff of Chieveley said: 'I start with the fundamental principle, now long established, that every person's body is inviolate.'

[18] Lord Donaldson MR said in *Re T (adult: refusal of medical treatment)* [1992] 4 All ER 649 at 662, [1993] Fam 95 at 113: '... the patient's right of choice exists *h* whether the reasons for making that choice are rational, irrational, unknown or even non-existent.'

[19] In *Re T*, I cited Robins JA in *Malette v Shulman* (1990) 67 DLR (4th) 321 at 336, and said:

j 'The right to determine what shall be done with one's own body is a fundamental right in our society. The concepts inherent in this right are the bedrock upon which the principles of self-determination and individual autonomy are based. Free individual choice in matters affecting this right should, in my opinion, be accorded very high priority.' (See [1992] 4 All ER 649 at 665, [1993] Fam 95 at 116–117.)

[20] In *Re MB (an adult: medical treatment)* [1997] 2 FCR 541 at 549, I said:

'A mentally competent patient has an absolute right to refuse to consent to medical treatment for any reason, rational or irrational, or for no reason at all, even where that decision may lead to his or her own death, see *Sidaway v Board of Governors of the Bethlem Royal Hospital* ([1985] AC 871 at 904–905, [1985] 1 All ER 643 at 665 per Lord Templeman); see also *Re T (An Adult: Medical Treatment)* ([1992] 4 All ER 649 at 653, [1993] Fam 95 at 102 per Lord Donaldson MR).'

[21] This approach is identical with the jurisprudence in other parts of the world. In *Cruzan v Director, Missouri Department of Health* (1990) 497 US 261, the United States Supreme Court stated:

'No right is held more sacred, or is more carefully guarded ... than the right of every individual to the possession and control of his own person, free from all restraint or interference of others, unless by clear and unquestionable authority of law.'

(b) The sanctity of life

[22] Society and the medical profession in particular are concerned with the equally fundamental principle of the sanctity of life. The interface between the two principles of autonomy and sanctity of life is of great concern to the treating clinicians in the present case. Lord Keith of Kinkel in *Airedale NHS Trust v Bland* [1993] 1 All ER 821 at 861, [1993] AC 789 at 859 said:

'...the principle of the sanctity of life, which it is the concern of the state, and the judiciary as one of the arms of the state, to maintain ... is not an absolute one. It does not compel a medical practitioner on pain of criminal sanctions to treat a patient, who will die if he does not, contrary to the express wishes of the patient.'

[23] Lord Goff of Chieveley said ([1993] 1 All ER 821 at 866, [1993] AC 789 at 864):

'First, it is established that the principle of self-determination requires that respect must be given to the wishes of the patient, so that, if an adult patient of sound mind refuses, however unreasonably, to consent to treatment or care by which his life would or might be prolonged, the doctors responsible for his care must give effect to his wishes, even though they do not consider it to be in his best interests to do so ... To this extent, the principle of the sanctity of human life must yield to the principle of self-determination ... and, for present purposes perhaps more important, the doctor's duty to act in the best interests of his patient must likewise be qualified. On this basis, it has been held that a patient of sound mind may, if properly informed, require that life support should be discontinued: see *Nancy B v Hôtel-Dieu de Québec* (1992) 86 DLR (4th) 385 ... I wish to add that, in cases of this kind, there is no question of the patient having committed suicide, nor therefore of the doctor having aided or abetted him in doing so. It is simply that the patient has, as he is entitled to do, declined to consent to treatment which might or would have the effect of prolonging his life, and the doctor has, in accordance with his duty, complied with his patient's wishes.'

[24] Lord Mustill said ([1993] 1 All ER 821 at 889, [1993] AC 789 at 891):

a

'Any invasion of the body of one person by another is potentially both a crime and a tort … How is it that, consistently with the proposition just stated, a doctor can with immunity perform on a consenting patient an act which would be a very serious crime if done by someone else? The answer must be that bodily invasions in the course of proper medical treatment stand completely outside the criminal law. The reason why the consent of the patient is so important is not that it furnishes a defence in itself, but because it is usually essential to the propriety of medical treatment. Thus, if the consent is absent, and is not dispensed with in special circumstances by operation of law, the acts of the doctor lose their immunity … If the patient is capable of making a decision on whether to permit treatment and decides not to permit it his choice must be obeyed, even if on any objective view it is contrary to his best interests. A doctor has no right to proceed in the face of objection, even if it is plain to all, including the patient, that adverse consequences and even death will or may ensue.'

[25] In *Bland*'s case the issue concerned a patient in the permanent vegetative state. In *Re T* the issue was the state of competence of a pregnant young woman who had been injured in a car crash and was refusing a blood transfusion. Lord Donaldson MR said ([1992] 4 All ER 649 at 661, [1993] Fam 95 at 112):

'This situation gives rise to a conflict between two interests, that of the patient and that of the society in which he lives. The patient's interest consists of his right to self-determination—his right to live his own life how he wishes, even if it will damage his health or lead to his premature death. Society's interest is in upholding the concept that all human life is sacred and that it should be preserved if at all possible. It is well established that in the ultimate the right of the individual is paramount.'

[26] I note with interest that a situation similar to that of Ms B was considered by the Quebec Superior Court in *Nancy B v Hôtel-Dieu de Québec* (1992) 86 DLR (4th) 385, in which a competent 25-year-old woman with an incurable neurological disorder sought an injunction to enforce her refusal of artificial ventilation, without which she was incapable of breathing independently. The court in that case decided that the plaintiff was entitled to the injunction sought, and ordered that the treating doctor be permitted to stop ventilation if and when the plaintiff so instructed.

[27] In the evidence of Dr I, to which I refer later in this judgment, he said that, in his view, the principles of autonomy and beneficence would appear to be in conflict in this case. In accordance with the principle set out so clearly by Lord Mustill and Lord Donaldson MR (above), the right of the competent patient to request cessation of treatment must prevail over the natural desire of the medical and nursing profession to try to keep her alive.

(c) The presumption of mental capacity

[28] There is a presumption of capacity: 'Every person is presumed to have the capacity to consent to or to refuse medical treatment unless and until that presumption is rebutted' (see *Re MB (an adult: medical treatment)* [1997] 2 FCR 541 at 553 per Butler-Sloss LJ).

(d) Assessing Capacity

[29] In looking at this most difficult exercise which has to be carried out a
regularly by the medical profession and only occasionally by the judiciary, it is
instructive to read a passage in the opinion of Steffen J in *McKay v Bergstedt* (1990)
801 P 2d 617 at 621:

'One of the verities of human experience is that all life will eventually end b
in death. As the seasons of life progress through spring, summer and fall, to
the winter of our years, the expression unknown to youth is often heard
evincing the wish to one night pass away in the midst of a peaceful sleep. It
would appear, however, that as the scientific community continues to
increase human longevity and promote "the greying of America," prospects
for slipping away during peaceful slumber are decreasing. And, for c
significant numbers of citizens like Kenneth, misfortune may rob life of
much of its quality long before the onset of winter.'

[30] In that case Kenneth was 31 years old and had been tetraplegic since the
age of ten. As a result of the imminent death of his father who had cared for him,
Kenneth wanted to be released from 'a life of paralysis held intact by the d
life-sustaining properties of a respirator'.

[31] Lord Donaldson MR in *Re T* [1992] 4 All ER 649 at 661, [1993] Fam 95 at
113 said:

'What matters is that the doctors should consider whether at [the relevant e
time] he [the patient] had a capacity which was commensurate with the
gravity of the decision which he purported to make. The more serious the
decision, the greater the capacity required.'

[32] And he summarised the position ([1992] 4 All ER 649 at 664, [1993] Fam
95 at 115–116):   f

'(1) [is largely set out in the passage above]
(2) An adult patient may be deprived of his capacity to decide either by
long-term mental incapacity or retarded development or by temporary
factors such as unconsciousness or confusion or the effects of fatigue, shock,
pain or drugs.   g
(3) If an adult patient did not have the capacity to decide at the time of the
purported refusal and still does not have that capacity, it is the duty of the
doctors to treat him in whatever way they consider, in the exercise of their
clinical judgment, to be in his best interests.
(4) Doctors faced with a refusal of consent have to give very careful and h
detailed consideration to what was the patient's capacity to decide at the
time when the decision was made. It may not be a case of capacity or no
capacity. It may be a case of reduced capacity. What matters is whether at
that time the patient's capacity was reduced below the level needed in the
case of a refusal of that importance, for refusals can vary in importance.
Some may involve a risk to life or of irreparable damage to health. Others j
may not.'

[33] In *Re MB* the Court of Appeal adopted the criteria set out by Thorpe J in
Re C (adult: refusal of medical treatment) [1994] 1 All ER 819 at 824, [1994] 1 WLR
290 at 295 and I said ([1997] 2 FCR 541 at 553–554):

a 'A person lacks capacity if some impairment or disturbance of mental functioning renders the person unable to make a decision whether to consent to or to refuse treatment. That inability to make a decision will occur when

(a) The person is unable to comprehend and retain the information which is material to the decision, especially as to the likely consequences of having
b or not having the treatment in question;

(b) The patient is unable to use the information and weigh it in the balance as part of the process of arriving at a decision.'

[34] In *Bartling v Superior Court of Los Angeles County* (1984) 163 Cal App 3d 186, the superior court had to consider the issue of ambivalence. It held that the
c patient's previous ambivalence about withdrawal of treatment was not relevant to the assessment of his capacity:

'The fact that [a patient] periodically wavered from this posture [ie, preferring death to his intolerable life on the ventilator] because of severe
d depression or for any other reason does not justify the conclusion of [the hospital] and his treating physicians that his capacity to make such a decision was impaired to the point of legal incapacity [*Lane v Candura* (1978) 376 NE 2d 1232 at 1234, fn 3 referred to].'

[35] In my view, ambivalence may be relevant if, and only if, the ambivalence
e genuinely strikes at the root of the mental capacity of the patient. As I have already said the principles are clear and, in certain cases, their application to the individual case may be extremely difficult. To resolve disputed issues of capacity, as a last resort, there may have to be an application to the High Court for guidance.
f [36] I turn now to the evidence called before me.

THE EVIDENCE OF MS B

[37] I heard the evidence of Ms B in a side ward of the ICU of the treating hospital. She heard the remainder of the evidence through a video-conferencing link between the Royal Courts of Justice and the hospital.
g [38] Her present situation is that she is paralysed from the neck down. She is conscious and capable of speech with the assistance of a speaking valve. She can move her head and use some of her neck muscles, but cannot move her torso, arms or legs at all. She is able to eat and drink. She is totally dependent on her carers, who feed, clothe and wash her and assist with her bodily functions. Her
h life is supported by artificial ventilation through a tracheostomy, a tube in her windpipe. Without the help of artificial ventilation, according to the medical evidence, she would have a less than 1% chance of independent ventilation, and death would almost certainly follow.

[39] She provided two written statements and gave oral evidence for about an
j hour and a half. She gave a clear account of her wishes and her feelings. She made it clear in her written and oral evidence that she had never changed her view that she wanted the ventilator withdrawn. It was only during the period that she was assessed as not having capacity to decide that she agreed to consider other possibilities. For the purposes of this case I shall concentrate upon the issues of ambivalence over turning off the ventilator and her rejection of rehabilitation and the one-way weaning programme.

Ambivalence

[40] In her written statement Ms B said:

'I never changed my mind about wishing for the ventilator to be switched off with the inevitable consequence of death. Having expected the process towards death to be commenced, I was informed by the hospital that this would not now happen because of a change in psychiatric opinion that I no longer had capacity ... I was relieved to some extent by the fact that I would not have to deal with the undeniably stressful and difficult questions of saying goodbye to my friends and family. Although it is true that I felt some level of relief, at no stage did I feel that I either regretted my previous decision or wished to change my mind.'

[41] In her oral evidence, she repeated that explanation, stating: 'I did have some sense of relief, but it was not the sort of relief like, "I am really glad I am alive", it was a sort of relief that I had a very difficult task ahead of me.'

[42] She was asked why she had previously agreed to undergo bronchoscopies and said: 'Because if I had refused treatment, dying would have been similar to the ventilation—to being weaned ... it may have been very painful and slow.'

[43] In her statement Ms B explained why she looked at the possibility of rehabilitation: 'At this stage I had not been assessed as having capacity so I agreed to giving rehabilitation a try.'

[44] Ultimately, upon having her mental capacity accepted on 8 August, Ms B said that she 'rejected this option of rehabilitation as it offered no possibility of recovery. I had not changed my views, it is just that now I was assessed as being able to make a choice.'

One-way weaning programme

[45] In her written statement Ms B said:

'I have refused the specialist clinic because weaning is essentially a long-term treatment for patients who want to live without ventilation. This is not what I want as it has no positive benefits for me given my level of disability. [The one-way weaning programme] does not include pain control and would last for several weeks ... I have refused this option because this would be a slow and painful death and my view of this is not disputed by the doctors. I would also feel robbed of a certain amount of dignity ... My wish is to be sedated. I would expect it to be a quick and painless death and less distressing for my loved ones. Negative weaning [one-way weaning] would mean watching me die over a series of weeks, the thought of this is painful for me to accept.'

[46] In her oral evidence she said:

'My concern was that I would have a very long and uncomfortable, possibly painful, passage because the programme, as proposed to me, was not to gradually withdraw the ventilator, but to reduce it to a level where my ventilation would be inadequate. That would provide a situation where I would then develop a chest infection and, possibly, other complications, and then I would die from those complications. So, without being too graphic, I would actually be waiting to become septic. I have seen that happen and I know it is slow and I know it is painful. One of my other concerns is that I have experienced having sedation here for short procedures like when I had my lungs cleaned out, but I have also had sedation over a longer period during the earlier part of my illness when I was very ill. The type of sedation I had meant that I had very vivid dreams, was very disoriented and did not know where I was or what the nurses' roles were and was very frightened. I felt that if I was lightly sedated as part of the weaning programme, and I lay here for a period of weeks, I would possibly go quietly psychotic, quite frankly, apart from the physical discomfort. That just terrified me, the prospect of dying like that, really.'

Ms B's wishes

[47] She was asked by Mr Francis QC, for the hospital, whether it was her wish to die, or not to remain alive in her present condition. She replied:

'The latter ... Given the range of choices, I would want to recover and have my life back, or significant enough recovery to have a better quality of life. I am not convinced from the evidence that that is going to happen, and I find the idea of living like this intolerable ... My view [about rehabilitation] is that it offers me no real opportunity to recover physically, that, in actual fact, it will be more teaching me to live with my disability and to make use of the technologies available and that sort of thing, working with the carers. But, actually, I will not recover in any way. That is not acceptable to me.'

[48] She was asked by Mr Francis whether the independence gained through rehabilitation would be of value to her, and said:

'I think it is an improvement, certainly. Whether it is sufficient for me or not is where we probably disagree. I don't think it is sufficient, but I can see that it offers opportunities for communication ... I think it does make a difference to quality of life, but I do not think it is sufficient for me to want to pursue it.'

[49] She was asked by Mr Francis what stopped her from trying rehabilitation before making up her mind and replied:

'There are two things. One, I know what it has to offer and I know that what I want it cannot offer. It offers me no chance of recovery. That is not disputed by anybody. Two, there has not been a place available anyway to try it. At a time when I was going through it here and would have tried it, there was no place. And I think there is a logistical problem that, once you go to rehab, if my views did not change, it would be extremely difficult to get to a position of having my ventilation withdrawn.'

[50] She expressed some views on the hospital and the present proceedings. She said:

'I felt that I was being treated as if I was being unreasonable by putting people in this awkward position. I fully accept the doctor's right to say, "I personally will not do it", and I respect that position, but I was angered at the arrogance and complete refusal to allow me access to someone that would. I felt my path was being blocked and I was being pressurised to accept this option, to quietly go away conveniently, even though at tremendous cost to me and my family ... I felt that my rights were being eroded and that is not something I tolerate really; it is not within my character to go along with that.'   *a*

[51] She was then asked whether it would make a difference to her views if she were able to access a place in the near future on a trial basis subject to subsequent review as to whether she wished to remain on ventilation or not. She said:

> 'Six months ago I think I would have tried it, but my mind is made up. I   *b*
> would not, out of choice, do that now. I think I have sufficient
> understanding of what is available to be able to make an informed decision.
> Six months ago I was judged not to have capacity. I would have tried
> anything. But I think I have more options now. I think people are disabled
> by their own feelings about this ... That is a human response that I   *c*
> understand, but that is what I mean about being in professional mode and
> getting on with the difficult things you have to do.'

[52] At the end of her written statement she set out her feelings as a Christian:

> 'In many ways the decision to have my treatment withdrawn has been a   *d*
> very difficult one for me as I have been a Christian and a regular church
> attendee all my life. The dominant view in the church is that that I should
> wait for God to heal me. Withdrawing ventilation would be seen as
> throwing in the towel. I have questioned myself about this and it has
> challenged my integrity. It has been a very difficult process to rationalise   *e*
> what I am doing in the context of my faith but I feel there is no alternative,
> as I do not have any realistic hope of recovery. I have come to believe that
> people die and become disabled and God does not always intervene. It has
> also been difficult for me to contemplate leaving the people I love behind.
> There has been a lot of talking and crying as no one wants me to die but
> almost all of them empathise with me and my situation and sincerely wish to   *f*
> respect my wishes, which I have made clear to all.'

[53] Her wishes were clear and well-expressed. She had clearly done a considerable amount of investigation and was extremely well-informed about her condition. She has retained a sense of humour and, despite her feelings of frustration and   *g* irritation which she expressed in her oral evidence, a considerable degree of insight into the problems caused to the hospital clinicians and nursing staff by her decision not to remain on artificial ventilation. She is, in my judgment, an exceptionally impressive witness. Subject to the crucial evidence of the consultant psychiatrists, she appears to me to demonstrate a very high standard   *h* of mental competence, intelligence and ability.

THE MEDICAL EVIDENCE

[54] I heard oral evidence from five doctors. I also read other statements filed by the trust and a further report from Dr S, to whom I referred above. It is not,   *j* in my view, necessary to set out anything further from the written evidence other than from Dr B to whom I shall refer below. All the consultants, other than one whom I have named, either have been or may be in a clinical treating relationship with Ms B and, for that reason, none of them is identified in this judgment. Two consultant anaesthetists, Dr R and Dr C, who have been treating Ms B in the hospital ICU, gave oral evidence.

Dr R

[55] She made a statement and gave oral evidence. She said that, on the request of Ms B to stop the ventilator, she was not prepared to take that step in the way suggested. She accepted that from August 2001 Ms B had capacity and the right to withdraw treatment. She treated Ms B on the basis that she had capacity to make decisions. She asked for advice. Her main concern was for Ms B to be aware of all the options available. The position in the ICU was different from a rehabilitation clinic. The ICU was not an ideal place for decision-making.

[56] She questioned whether there was ambivalence. The main dilemma was around the legal and ethical issues of turning off the ventilator. She had never had to discuss a decision such as this before or be in such a situation. Ms B was not a common day-to-day patient. She was very unusual. Dr R had treated her for a year and would find it very difficult to turn off the ventilator. After artificial ventilation for a period it would take a few days for the body to adjust to breathing normally. The attempt at one-way weaning was over a period of about three weeks and if not successful she would not be able to breathe unaided. But if the ventilator were switched off, the end would be in a few hours. Immediate withdrawal would cause her death. She would be prepared to undergo the one-way weaning process and to sedate the patient to keep her calm. If there was no possibility of her breathing unaided, Dr R said she would reduce the length of time of the weaning and increase the sedation. There was a dilemma over the one-way weaning process. In the past she had put patients back on the ventilator when it was necessary. She had agreed to the weaning process. She accepted Mr G's judgment as to the unlikelihood of Ms B being weaned off the ventilator and that staged weaning was irrelevant.

Dr C

[57] She made a statement and gave oral evidence. She was the lead clinician and met regularly to discuss Ms B's case with the medical director of the hospital. She made inquiries of a consultant from another hospital (Dr D). He told her that it was a matter of consent. She felt that the clinicians always treated Ms B as competent to make decisions. It was however difficult for a patient to make a decision without experiencing a spinal rehabilitation unit. Her dilemma was not to be against the wishes of Ms B but to offer her anything to make her want to live. The four anaesthetists working in intensive care, Dr R, herself and two others, discussed how they should approach this situation. It was very difficult and they were and continued to be put under tremendous pressure by the circumstances of this case. She had reluctantly gone along with the proposal of a one-way weaning process. If it was up to her, she would not suggest or commence withdrawal of treatment from Ms B. She had studied and spent her professional life trying to do her best to improve and preserve life. She did not feel able to agree with simply switching off Ms B's ventilation. She would not be able to do it. She felt she was being asked to kill Ms B. They had all been looking after Ms B for a long time on a very intimate level. She felt that a lot more needed to be done for these patients.

[58] It was clear from their evidence that both the treating clinicians were deeply distressed by the dilemma which had faced them over the year that Ms B had spent in the ICU. They knew her well and respected and liked her. They considered her to be competent to make decisions about her medical treatment. They could not, however, bring themselves to contemplate that they should be part of bringing Ms B's life to an end by the dramatic (my word) step of turning

off the ventilator. As I listened to the evidence of each of them I had the greatest
possible sympathy for their position.

Mr G

[59] Mr G is a consultant surgeon in spinal injuries with particular experience
of patients in a spinal rehabilitation unit unconnected with the trust. He saw
Ms B on 8 February 2002 and made a report and gave oral evidence. He was very
impressed by Ms B. She appeared able to understand everything he said and to
respond appropriately to all questions. She did not appear to be depressed. She
told him that she had asked for the ventilator to be withdrawn at an early stage
as soon as she had been made aware of her prognosis. He discussed with her the
various rehabilitation options. She appeared to have given considerable thought
to her situation. She had done a great deal of research through the Internet. She
said that she still wanted the ventilation to be withdrawn. She said: 'I have given
it a fair try but I still feel the way I do.'

[60] Mr G considered that she was able to receive and retain information
given by him. She was able to converse in a rational manner and to explain
herself clearly and in an apparently balanced manner. She was able to weigh the
information in order for her to reach a decision. He said in his report:

> 'My main reservation in relation to the above three questions can be seen
> in the records. At certain times she enjoys herself and is glad that she is alive.
> At other times she expresses a wish that the ventilator should
> be switched off. I am, therefore, concerned that her wish to have the
> ventilator switched off stems not so much from a wish to be dead, as from
> her wish to be free from all that surrounds her current condition. I consider
> this is a most important aspect as I have seen it before in different forms and
> have seen patients change their minds. This change of mind is not usually a
> sudden event but rather an evolution of understanding and insight as the
> person comes to appreciate in greater depth the value of life to them. This
> tends to arise most often as the person leaves hospital for life in the
> community.'

[61] He discussed some of those issues with Ms B who pointed out that she did
not have a supportive family and might find herself on her own with carers or in
a nursing home. He accepted that she was permanently ventilator-dependent and
in his opinion she would never be weaned from the ventilator. He considered
that she had not experienced the full range of environmental control systems.
She might be aware of what was possible but she had not experienced what could
be done. He felt that the sooner she could be admitted into a comprehensive
spinal cord injury centre the better in order to experience the modern approaches
and to meet other patients in a similar position to her. She would be able to go
out into the community. Although the ICU looked after her extremely well,
ICUs were very abnormal environments for persons who were otherwise well
such as Ms B.

[62] He was aware from his personal experience and from research he had
carried out in 1984 that there were several patients who had expressed the wish
to die whilst in the acute phase following their injury but then changed their mind
later and were grateful that their wishes expressed earlier were ignored. He drew
the attention of the court to his article in the *British Medical Journal* (December
1985, p 1620) entitled 'Ventilation or dignified death for patients with high
tetraplegia'. He accepted that none of the patients in his study had gone home

a   still dependent on a ventilator. In his view patients needed to experience those
aspects in order to know what life would be like. He disagreed with Ms B's view
to the contrary. From his experience he doubted that she could come to a fully
informed decision without having actually experienced what was possible. The
wish to be off the ventilator reflected the total indignity, lack of control and
frustration that emanated from their severe disability rather than a specific wish

b   for death. When such patients left hospital and went into the community and
experienced life, the majority found that life was valuable to them. Perhaps
surprisingly most ventilator-dependent patients took a very positive view on life.
He felt that time was a factor; time, appropriate environment and exposure to the
technology available. He thought that it would take up to two years to gain the
experience necessary to have an informed opinion. Patients in the position of

c   Ms B, in his view, could only appreciate fully through experience.

[63] Mr G clearly has great experience in the field of spinal injuries and in the
process of rehabilitation. He accepted that Ms B had mental competence and his
one reservation was his conclusion that she was unable to give informed consent,
not because of a lack of capacity in general but her specific lack of knowledge and

d   experience of exposure to a spinal rehabilitation unit and thereafter to readjustment
to life in the community. Without that opportunity, which might take up to two
years to complete, Ms B did not have the requisite information to give informed
consent. On that aspect of his evidence, I have the gravest doubts as to its legal
validity and indeed its practicality. Even in issues of the utmost significance and
gravity, people, including patients, have to make decisions without experience of

e   the consequences and his requirement is unrealistic.

Dr I

f   [64] He is a consultant psychiatrist at a hospital unconnected with the trust.
He has extensive experience of patients with serious spinal injuries including
tetraplegia. He visited Ms B in the ICU on 8 February 2002 and read extensively
the documentation in this case. He spent three hours with Ms B. He reviewed
aspects of his instructions with Ms B. He did not elicit any evidence of cognitive
impairment. There was no evidence of persistent depression of mood. She gave
a sense of strong vitality in equal measure to the frustration and pain that have

g   led to being locked in her current state of disability. He wrote in his report:

'It appears difficult in this case to challenge Ms B's presumed capacity to
consent to or refuse medical treatment. She appears to be rational in relation
to her decision. The consequences of a decision to withdraw artificial
ventilation are grave. In the light of the gravity, I understand that a greater

h   level of competence is required in making the decision. I have found no
evidence that psychiatric disorder interferes with her capacity to receive and
retain information given to her, believe the information that has been
provided or weigh the information in order to reach a decision. Of particular
relevance here may be her attitude, in relation to information that suggests

j   that she may have a different outcome if assisted further in a model spinal
injuries system. She can understand that this is possible and believes that it
is possible for some people. She believes that it may be possible for her but
in her heart does not believe it is possible for her. Her deeply felt conviction
cannot be considered irrational. Indeed, it may turn out to be true and
suggestions to the contrary may turn out to be false. On the other hand, she
has not actually been in care in such a system and although Ms B, clearly

highly informed, cannot be considered to be 100% fully informed in view of the fact that she has not had the experience of being in such treatment. Being told about treatment is different to having experience of it.'

[65] Dr I identified a number of significant clinical factors which he said could be relevant and which he felt he ought to bring to the attention of the court. The situation in which Ms B was in an ICU in a general hospital might amount to a temporary factor so as to erode her capacity. The possibility was a significant one although he found it extremely difficult to determine whether it was more likely than unlikely. He felt that some aspects of the relationship between Ms B and those caring for her were strained.

[66] Dr I formed the view in his assessment that she did not wish to close the last door but was prepared to contemplate further treatment/rehabilitation provided she was assured that she had the final say. In his oral evidence Dr I said that he had discussed the case on three occasions with Dr Sensky. It was Dr I's understanding that Ms B had not closed the last door and would go to a rehabilitation unit. He was surprised that she was significantly more positive and it was an important part of his opinion to the court. It was his experience that patients expressed a wish to die when they were breathless or in pain but once the acute state was treated the underlying psychiatric state improved and the patient changed his mind. The statement of Dr Sensky on the consistency of Ms B's wishes weakened his concern about possible ambivalence.

[67] Another factor referred to by Dr I was that commonly patients who experienced serious illness might regress psychologically. He then referred to Ms B's childhood experiences. This was a very difficult area and in his report he was uncertain. Psychological regression needed to be considered as a possibility rather than that it was present. It was a relevant consideration in deciding capacity. He set out a group of possible regressive factors which I do not propose to repeat since he said in cross-examination: 'I accept that the evidence I offered does not establish regression.'

[68] He felt a considerable degree of uncertainty about the possibility of a temporary factor eroding the capacity of Ms B in the present case. Being in the ICU might affect her ability to make decisions. The ICU was not geared to rehabilitation and the ethos was different from a rehabilitation unit, where patients rarely die. There was no mental incapacity. There were however broader social considerations. He did not state that Ms B did not have capacity but that there were relevant issues to be considered by the court. He felt acutely the dilemma of how rational was a man or woman, whether the legal concept of autonomy gave due weight to the emotional factors which drive reason, and the potential force of feelings for Ms B if she were treated in one hospital or in another, for instance in the ICU or a rehabilitation unit. He agreed that for a fresh start the patient must want it.

[69] Dr I had discussed with Dr Sensky that it was more likely that considered judgment led Ms B to express her choice. He accepted that intellectually there was no inconsistency between Ms B's vitality and her wish to die, although emotionally it grieved him, which was not too strong a word. He concluded that he still held the view that it was difficult to challenge Ms B's capacity. There were some factual issues in dispute between Dr I and Ms B but in view of the overall picture, it is not necessary for me to adjudicate upon them.

[70] In his view the principles of autonomy and beneficence would appear to be in conflict in this case: 'If immediate priority is given to the patient's autonomy

a through acting according to her wishes, there is a risk of depriving her of potential
benefits in the future.'

[71] Dr I gave very careful and thoughtful evidence in which he wrestled with
the problems raised by Ms B in her request for the ventilator to be turned off. He
recognised that she was competent although he looked throughout for reasons
to demonstrate that she was not competent. Finally he accepted both in the
b telephone discussions with Dr Sensky and, in particular, in his oral evidence that
none of his reservations in fact applied and that Ms B did not lack capacity to
make decisions as to her medical care including the decision to have the
ventilator turned off.

Dr Sensky

c [72] The Official Solicitor instructed Dr Sensky, a consultant psychiatrist, who
is reader in psychological medicine at Imperial College of Science, Technology
and Medicine. He has special experience of mental disorder and long experience
in the assessment and management of psychiatric and psychological aspects of
physical illness. He examined Ms B on 5 February for an hour and a half and again
d for an hour on 5 March. He has written three reports; read the other reports;
discussed the issue with Dr I and gave the court a note of two telephone
conversations with Dr I on 2 and 4 March 2002. He gave oral evidence to the
court. The note of the telephone conversation included:

'Drs I and Sensky agree on the following:
e   a) Ms B can assimilate and understand information which has been given
to her.
     b) She is capable of discussing information in detail with experts and lay
people.
     c) She is capable of evaluating the information she has acquired and
forming judgments on the basis of a process of weighing up the information
f she has acquired.
     d) During their respective interviews with Ms B, Drs I and Sensky elicited
no evidence of a depressive illness, nor of any other specific mental state
abnormalities which would point to the presence of a mental illness.
The key difference in the opinions of Drs I and Sensky concerns the weight
g to be assigned to possible temporary factors on Ms B's capacity to express
autonomous wishes.'

[73] Dr Sensky was very clear in his impressions of Ms B. In his evidence he
said that there was no difference in the mental state of Ms B on either of the two
occasions he interviewed her. She had a considerable degree of self-awareness
h and self-knowledge. She was an immensely impressive woman.

[74] Dr Sensky was equally clear in his view as to Ms B's mental competence.
He concluded she had the mental capacity to make decisions. In his overall
judgment, Ms B was at the extreme end of competence, despite the limitations of
her physical state and her environment in the ICU. She was likely to remain
j competent to make decisions for the foreseeable future. Dr Sensky's discussions
with the clinical psychologist who had seen Ms B regularly and frequently since
Spring 2001, and with the senior nurse on the ICU and others who have cared for
Ms B, confirmed his assessment that Ms B was not suffering from depression and
was competent to reach the decision she had made. He excluded mental illness.
He considered that she had a good understanding of her circumstances and had
given a great deal of thought to her decision. She had gone to considerable

lengths to find out the relevant information on her condition. She told him that she was a fighter by nature but said: 'I cannot accept myself as disabled and dependent—it's too big a leap to make. The totality of dependence is intolerable.'

[75] Dr Sensky then addressed the concerns put forward by the trust about perceived ambivalence in Ms B's views. He considered whether she had not yet closed the door on further treatment as was suggested by Dr I. If she had not closed the door that might be an indication of ambivalence. Ms B made it clear to him that the discussion on rehabilitation with Dr I only arose if her request to have the ventilator turned off was declined by the court. Dr Sensky did not find any evidence of ambivalence. Ms B's clinical psychologist confirmed to him that Ms B had been entirely consistent in her views about her treatment and her wish to have her treatment discontinued.

[76] He also considered the opinion expressed by Mr G as to whether the environment in the ICU clouded her judgment. He did not consider that her judgment had been clouded either by her environment or by her professional carers. In the context of the decisions she wanted to make, despite expressing frustration, anger and criticism of some aspects of her management, she showed a good understanding of the position of the clinicians and was sensitive to them and to the nursing staff. He did not consider that her current views were unduly influenced by unresolved psychological problems in childhood and adolescence nor that there was any evidence of regression.

[77] Dr Sensky then offered helpful insight into the difficulties with the way in which decisions about Ms B's treatment had been managed. He recognised the complexities involved in this case arising from the decision made by Ms B. He agreed that it was a highly unusual decision. He pointed out that it could be seen from the clinicians' witness statements how stressful and distressing the present situation is for all concerned. He agreed that in a decision of this magnitude the highest degree of scrutiny was required.

[78] He pointed out that one thing which struck him forcibly was that the clinicians started from the decision made by Ms B, and not from the assessment of her competence. They looked too much at the decision, which was contrary to their advice and which they would not endorse, and not enough at the surrounding circumstances. The clinicians were not able to accept her views and deal with them. It was a fundamental principle that one should start with the individual's capacity to make decisions and values. There may have been some confusion over her values compared with other people's, and it was important to focus on the individual and respect that individual's values. The weight which an individual chooses to give competing factors is an essential part of the decision-making process. A key issue in this case was the weighing up by Ms B of artificial ventilation and the stopping of ventilation and almost inevitable death. She valued the ventilator and her handicap as worse than being dead. Her decision was made against the advice offered and was not understood. Subjective values have to be taken into account. If at an earlier stage there had been an acknowledgement of a clash of values it might possibly have led to a different approach to management of the case.

[79] Dr Sensky then offered some helpful observations on the proper management of these inevitably difficult cases. He recommended that the first step should be to recognise where the problem lay and the difference in values. It was a very complex decision with a potentially devastating outcome for clinicians. The second step was to get someone from outside, not in the first instance a lawyer, to help define the differences and to draw boundaries round the decisions to be

a taken. It was important that the patient came into contact with the outsider and the outsider should negotiate his/her involvement in the first place with the patient. It should be seen as a joint referral. When the impasse was identified, one should ask whether this is a problem of difference of values, or alternatively one of insufficient knowledge and understanding by the patient. If it were a case of a lack of information, the clinicians would manage it differently. He accepted

b that the level of physical disability might have an effect on capacity, as might the level of anger or inconsistent statements which should be looked at with great care.

[80] The circumstances of Ms B illustrate the conundrum and how difficult ethically and personally it is for doctors serving people who only remain alive with the help of medical technology. In palliative care this option often arises and

c is not unfamiliar but in the setting of the ICU this is unusual. The principle is to have appropriate respect for values and recognise the patient's equal right to autonomy.

[81] Dr Sensky referred to an article titled 'Autonomy and the Subjective Character of Experience' (*Journal of Applied Philosophy*, vol 17, no 1, 2000), written

d by Dr Kim Atkins, a member of the Department of Philosophy at the University of Tasmania. I found this article helpful in the context of the present case and consider it would be useful to include some passages from it in this judgment.

[82] Dr Atkins discussed the value of autonomy:

e 'If we accept that the subjective character of experience is irreducible and that it is grounded in the particularity of our points of view, then we are bound to realise that our respect for each other's differences and autonomy embodies a respect for the particularity of each other's points of view. Respect for autonomy is at the same time recognition of the irreducible differences that separate us as subjects ... While we can imagine, we cannot

f know objectively "what it is like to be" another person, no matter how many facts we are in possession of ...'

[83] Dr Atkins said of illness:

g '... the more extreme the experience of illness, the more profound are the implications of this view for patient autonomy, because of the increasing difficulty for carers to raise the spectre of the subjective character of very unpleasant experiences ... Making way for the subjective character of experience is *not* achieved by offering up more facts for the person to "face", it is achieved by allowing a place for the expression of a person's perspective

h on the nature of their illness and the treatment they are being offered ... We might want to criticise the practice of denying oneself life-saving treatment on some other grounds, for example, because of its effects on those the dying person expects to care for her, but it simply misses the point to criticise the practice on the grounds of insufficient objectivity ... However disturbing it

j is to see someone, especially one's loved one, on something like [a ventilator], it is essential that one tries to imagine what it is like to be *that particular* person on [a ventilator] if one is to attempt to act from respect for *that person's* autonomy. The difficulty here lies not in becoming *more* objective, but in being appropriately subjective ... I need to imagine not just what it would be like to *me* to be on [a ventilator], but what it would be like for [Ms B] ... Insisting that a decision be made from a fully objective perspective can only produce a decision that is further from the patient's own point of view, not closer to it.'

[84] I found Dr Sensky to be a most impressive witness. Dr I did not in any material particular really disagree with any of his reports. I accept unreservedly Dr Sensky's assessment of the mental capacity of Ms B. I am also very grateful to him for wise advice for the future where an intractable, painful and distressing situation such as the present might arise. I have set out his evidence in some detail since, in my judgment, it may be of assistance for clinicians in the future.

[85] I read the report of Professor B, a professor of Intensive Care Medicine from a hospital unconnected with the trust. Professor B was not called to give oral evidence, but from his reading of the statements and clinical records he considered that there was no doubt that Ms B was now mentally competent. He understood why the clinicians were not prepared to turn off the ventilator and that it was clear that close relationships had been built up between the patient and the nurses and doctors. In his view the only option was to arrange for the patient to be transferred to a hospital which would be willing to grant the patient her wish. It would probably be an unprecedented event, at least in the United Kingdom, and would have to be handled with the greatest delicacy and tact. He had discussed the situation with the senior medical, nursing and management staff at his hospital and they agreed that he should offer Ms B a bed at that hospital on the basis that he and his team would carry out Ms B's wishes in respect of her future medical care.

SUBMISSIONS

[86] Mr Havers submitted that the evidence conclusively proved that Ms B had the requisite mental capacity to make her own decision about her future medical care, and in particular, to decide whether artificial ventilation should be withdrawn. Mr Havers also submitted that from 8 August 2001 Ms B had been managed by the hospital on that basis. The doctors had however been reluctant to accede to her wish to have the ventilation withdrawn. The clear advice of the solicitors to the trust as to mental capacity in their letter of 5 April 2001 had been ignored and the hospital continued to treat her with artificial ventilation and to explore other alternatives which were unacceptable to Ms B. The clinicians at the hospital were unwilling to accede to Ms B's request and the trust failed altogether to take the key step, which should have been taken at the outset, namely to find another doctor prepared to carry out the wishes of Ms B for over five months. Accordingly Mr Havers submitted that I should find that the claimant had been treated unlawfully since August 2001 and that I should make a nominal award of damages in order for that situation to be recognised.

[87] Mr Francis sought to convince me that Ms B did not have legal capacity in and from August nor did she have it now, despite the conclusions of the treating clinicians. He relied upon the evidence of Mr G and Dr I. He argued that if there was the possibility that the patient did not have capacity to decide whether to accept or refuse medical treatment, it was lawful for the doctors to continue treating the patient until the issue was resolved and the doctors were satisfied about mental competence. He submitted that there were temporary factors which in this case eroded Ms B's ability to make this crucial decision. He adverted to the effect upon Ms B of the gravity of her physical disability and her reaction to being totally dependent upon others, the effect of the environment of the ICU, her relationship with the treating doctors and other carers, her anger at her treatment, and possible regression prompted by childhood experiences. He

a relied upon her refusal to consider rehabilitation. He suggested that she had been ambivalent in her intention to have treatment withdrawn, for example the agreement to the bronchoscopies which she could have refused. He accepted that it was an extremely unusual case and it was necessary to examine very carefully the reasons given by Ms B and the assertion that she had capacity.

b [88] Mr Jackson, as advocate to the court, supported the submissions of Mr Havers as to mental capacity. He reminded me that the question of the best interests of the patient did not arise in this case. She was competent now and on the evidence would be competent for the foreseeable future. The finding of mental capacity would leave the patient not with a past decision but with a future choice which she could consider freely when she was relieved of the burdens of litigation. He recommended a number of steps which the trust might have taken

c and which might be helpful to consider for the future. They are very helpful and I consider them below. On behalf of the Official Solicitor, he made the very helpful suggestion that where a trust finds itself in a serious dilemma it should not hesitate to approach the court. But in the first instance, if such a step were to be contemplated, he referred to the Official Solicitor's Practice Note annexed to

d *Practice Direction (declaratory proceedings: incapacitated adults)* [2002] 1 All ER 794, [2002] 1 WLR 325 and said that the Official Solicitor was available to give advice if asked.

CONCLUSION ON MENTAL CAPACITY

e [89] As I have already said Ms B was a most impressive witness. I therefore considered with especial care the evidence of the two psychiatrists and the submissions of Mr Francis for the trust. I start with the presumption that Ms B has mental capacity. That presumption was displaced between April and August 2001 in the light of the assessments by Dr E and Dr L, which have not been challenged in this court. Dr RG in August assessed her as mentally competent and

f the hospital thereafter treated her as such. Nevertheless, Mr Francis has argued that it is legal capacity which I must consider not the assessment of the mental capacity provided by the doctors. That may be so, but, unless it is an exceptional case, the judicial approach to mental capacity must be largely dependent upon the assessments of the medical profession whose task it is on a regular basis to assess the competence of the patient to consent or refuse the medical/surgical

g treatment recommended to the patient. If, as in the present case, two experienced and distinguished consultant psychiatrists give evidence that Ms B has the mental capacity to make decisions, even grave decisions about her future medical treatment, that is cogent evidence upon which I can and should rely. That evidence supports and reinforces the assessment of Ms B's competence

h in August 2001. No psychiatrist has suggested since August that Ms B is not competent.

[90] Mr Francis has pointed to a number of temporary factors which might affect Ms B's competence or erode her capacity: possible evidence of psychological regression; the effect of her grave physical disability; the absence of

j her experience of rehabilitation which was thought likely to be a positive experience; and the effect of her environment in the ICU. Mr Francis also points to concern about Ms B's history of ambivalence about ventilation and her consent to bronchoscopies.

[91] It is important to note from the outset, as Dr Sensky properly emphasised in his evidence to the court, the importance of avoiding generalisations about the possibilities for patients in Ms B's position for capacity to be diminished by one or

a number of temporary factors. Rather, the court's task in the instant case is to determine whether *in fact* Ms B's capacity is affected by any of the factors identified by the trust.

[92] I reject any suggestion that Ms B's capacity has been impaired by the advent of psychological regression. There is no evidence to support it. I do not consider that Ms B has been ambivalent in her determination to choose her medical treatment and in her wish to cease to have artificial ventilation. She did look at the alternatives and went down the path of rehabilitation when she was deemed incapable of making her own decision. As soon as she was deemed capable she made it clear that she did not want to go to a spinal rehabilitation unit and turned down the opportunity of a place in October last year. Her relief at not having to say goodbye to her family and friends in April is entirely explicable on two grounds. First, it must not be forgotten that she was deemed not competent at that time so it would be unjust of me to place great weight on her emotions. Second, if, contrary to the psychiatric assessment, she was competent, her explanation of relief in not undergoing painful and distressing final goodbyes to those she loves, does not seem to me to be incompatible with her long term objective of cessation of artificial ventilation. Equally there is no incompatability in consenting to the bronchoscopies, refusal of which she felt would involve pain and discomfort, which understandably she did not wish to undergo.

[93] Mr G's evidence to the effect that one must experience the advantages of rehabilitation is probably excellent advice for the vast majority of paraplegic and tetraplegic patients. His view that not to have experienced rehabilitation means that the patient lacks informed consent cannot be the basis for the legal concept of mental capacity. If Mr G were correct, the absence of experience in the spinal rehabilitation clinic would deny Ms B or any other similar patient the right to choose whether or not to go to one. It is not possible to experience before choosing in many medical situations. That is not the state of the law nor, I assume, would the medical profession accept it for many fundamental and practical reasons.

[94] One must allow for those as severely disabled as Ms B, for some of whom life in that condition may be worse than death. It is a question of values and, as Dr Sensky and Dr Atkins have pointed out, we have to try inadequately to put ourselves into the position of the gravely disabled person and respect the subjective character of experience. Unless the gravity of the illness has affected the patient's capacity, a seriously disabled patient has the same rights as the fit person to respect for personal autonomy. There is a serious danger, exemplified in this case, of a benevolent paternalism which does not embrace recognition of the personal autonomy of the severely disabled patient. I do not consider that either the lack of experience in a spinal rehabilitation unit and thereafter in the community or the unusual situation of being in an ICU for a year has had the effect of eroding Ms B's mental capacity to any degree whatsoever.

[95] I am therefore entirely satisfied that Ms B is competent to make all relevant decisions about her medical treatment including the decision whether to seek to withraw from artificial ventilation. Her mental competence is commensurate with the gravity of the decision she may wish to make. I find that she has had the mental capacity to make such decisions since 8 August 2001 and that she will remain competent to make such decisions for the foreseeable future. I should however like to underline the wise submission made to me by Mr Jackson that my decision leaves Ms B with a future choice which she can consider freely now that she will be relieved of the burdens of litigation. She is not bound by her past

a decision and when she goes to the hospital prepared to accept her, she has the right to reflect on what she may wish to do with her life. I would like to add how impressed I am with her as a person, with the great courage, strength of will and determination she has shown in the last year, with her sense of humour, and her understanding of the dilemma she has posed to the hospital. She is clearly a splendid person and it is tragic that someone of her ability has been struck down

b so cruelly. I hope she will forgive me for saying, diffidently, that if she did reconsider her decision, she would have a lot to offer the community at large.

REMEDIES

[96] In the light of my decision that the claimant has mental capacity and has had such capacity since August 2001 I shall be prepared to grant the appropriate

c declarations after discussions with counsel. I also find that the claimant has been treated unlawfully by the trust since August.

[97] Throughout the sad developments of this case, all those looking after Ms B have cared for her to the highest standards of medical competence and with devotion. They deserve the highest praise. Ironically this excellent care has to

d some extent contributed to the difficulties for the hospital. Ms B has been treated throughout in the ICU in which the medical and nursing team are dedicated to saving and preserving life, sometimes in adverse medical situations. As Dr C said, they are trained to save life. The request from Ms B, which would have been understood in a palliative care situation, appears to have been outside the experience of the ICU in relation to a mentally-competent patient. It was seen by

e some as killing the patient or assisting the patient to die and ethically unacceptable. The solicitors to the trust, Capsticks, wrote an excellent letter in April which set out with admirable clarity the legal position. As a result of the assessment of Ms B by Dr L and Dr E, the trust did not have to reconsider the situation until August. At that time it would appear that the letter was not

f re-read. The solicitors were not asked to advise further and the trust over a period of seven to eight months went down a number of ineffective paths.

[98] One route was the proposed one-way weaning process. Ms B was, in my view, placed in an impossible position by the treating clinicians who could not contemplate turning off the ventilator. If they had stopped to consider the likelihood of her being able to breathe unaided, they presumably would have

g endorsed the possibility of success at not greater than 1%. In which case, the one-way weaning process was inevitably going to fail and she would die over three weeks and not in a few hours. I have to say, with some sadness, that the one-way weaning process appears to have been designed to help the treating clinicians and the other carers and not in any way designed to help Ms B. If the

h one-way weaning process were to be carried out as suggested by the doctors, there would be a risk that she would die in discomfort and possibly in pain, even though that is not what they intended. It was obviously, to anyone looking at it from outside the hospital, an unrealistic and unhelpful programme. It was none the less supported by the hospital and by the trust. No one stood back, as the

j solicitors undoubtedly would have done, had they been asked, and considered in an objective way the best way to go forward. The clinicians had clearly become emotionally involved. That situation was entirely understandable. They had with the nursing staff kept Ms B alive and looked after her in every respect including her most intimate requirements. Obviously a relationship built up and it was, in my view, unjust to the team in the ICU that the burden of decision and responsibility for Ms B largely remained in their hands. Although the issue of capacity may be a grey area, it is one capable of resolution by one means or another. The trust had a duty to do something effective to resolve the dilemma and to do so with some degree of urgency for the sake of all concerned. This they consistently failed to do up to the hearing of the case in court. It fell to Ms B to initiate proceedings to get the issue resolved.

[99] It is important to draw a careful distinction between the duties of the dedicated team in the ICU of the hospital caring for Ms B and the trust responsible for the working of the hospital. In my view, the latter should have taken steps to deal with the issue. The failure to do so has led me to the conclusion that I should mark my finding that the claimant has been treated unlawfully by the NHS hospital trust by a small award of damages. I shall not decide the amount until Mr Francis has had an opportunity to make representations if he wishes to do so.

GUIDANCE

[100] Guidance has already been given by the Court of Appeal in *St George's Healthcare NHS Trust v S, R v Collins, ex p S* [1998] 3 All ER 673 at 703, [1999] Fam 26 at 63. The circumstances of the present case are however very different from the facts of that case. It might therefore be helpful if I restate some basic principles and offer additional guidelines in case a situation similar to the present should arise again.

(i) There is a presumption that a patient has the mental capacity to make decisions whether to consent to or refuse medical or surgical treatment offered to him/her.

(ii) If mental capacity is not in issue and the patient, having been given the relevant information and offered the available options, chooses to refuse the treatment, that decision has to be respected by the doctors. Considerations that the best interests of the patient would indicate that the decision should be to consent to treatment are irrelevant.

(iii) If there is concern or doubt about the mental capacity of the patient, that doubt should be resolved as soon as possible, by doctors within the hospital or NHS trust or by other normal medical procedures.

(iv) In the meantime, while the question of capacity is being resolved, the patient must, of course, be cared for in accordance with the judgment of the doctors as to the patient's best interests.

(v) If there are difficulties in deciding whether the patient has sufficient mental capacity, particularly if the refusal may have grave consequences for the patient, it is most important that those considering the issue should not confuse the question of mental capacity with the nature of the decision made by the patient, however grave the consequences. The view of the patient may reflect a difference in values rather than an absence of competence and the assessment of capacity should be approached with this firmly in mind. The doctors must not allow their emotional reaction to or strong disagreement with the decision of the patient to cloud their judgment in answering the primary question whether the patient has the mental capacity to make the decision.

(vi) In the rare case where disagreement still exists about competence, it is of the utmost importance that the patient is fully informed of the steps being taken and made a part of the process. If the option of enlisting independent outside expertise is being considered, the doctor should discuss this with the patient so that any referral to a doctor outside the hospital would be, if possible, on a joint basis with the aim of helping both sides to resolve the disagreement. It may be

^a crucial to the prospects of a good outcome that the patient is involved before the referral is made and feels equally engaged in the process.

(vii) If the hospital is faced with a dilemma which the doctors do not know how to resolve, it must be recognised and further steps taken as a matter of priority. Those in charge must not allow a situation of deadlock or drift to occur.

(viii) If there is no disagreement about competence but the doctors are for any
^b reason unable to carry out the wishes of the patient, their duty is to find other doctors who will do so.

(ix) If all appropriate steps to seek independent assistance from medical experts outside the hospital have failed, the NHS hospital trust should not hesitate to make an application to the High Court or seek the advice of the Official Solicitor.

^c (x) The treating clinicians and the hospital should always have in mind that a seriously physically-disabled patient who is mentally competent has the same right to personal autonomy and to make decisions as any other person with mental capacity.

[101] All those reading this judgment must be careful to recognise the
^d importance of complying with the publicity injunction set out in the annex to this judgment.

Order accordingly.

^e   Manjit Gheera   Barrister.

^f   *Annex*

IN THE HIGH COURT OF JUSTICE
FAMILY DIVISION
PRINCIPAL REGISTRY

^g Before the Rt Hon DAME ELIZABETH BUTLER-SLOSS   The President

In the matter of the Inherent Jurisdiction of the High Court

And in the matter of Ms B
^h
Between   Ms B   Claimant

and   An NHS HOSPITAL TRUST   Defendant

^j On the 22nd day of March 2002

UPON HEARING leading counsel and junior counsel for the claimant, leading and junior counsel for the defendant and leading counsel for the Official Solicitor

AND UPON READING the papers filed herein

IT IS ORDERED THAT:—   *a*

1. No written or photographic material shall be published or broadcast in any form whatsoever (save solely on a strictly confidential basis to any persons from whom the claimant wishes to receive advice) to any persons whether in writing or electronically from which any of the following could be identified as   *b* being connected with these proceedings:—

(a) The claimant;
(b) Any members of the claimant's family or friends;
(c) The defendant NHS trust;
(d) A hospital in which the claimant is being cared for or in which it is or has   *c* been proposed that she be cared for in the future;
(e) Any person caring for or treating the claimant or whom it is proposed shall care for or treat her in future;
(f) Any person who gives evidence in these proceedings whether written or oral except Dr T Sensky.   *d*

2. This order, unless varied by the court, shall continue to have effect notwithstanding the death of claimant.

3. There be liberty to any person affected by this order to apply to vary or discharge it.

a

R v Shayler
[2002] UKHL 11

HOUSE OF LORDS

LORD BINGHAM OF CORNHILL, LORD HOPE OF CRAIGHEAD, LORD HUTTON, LORD
HOBHOUSE OF WOODBOROUGH AND LORD SCOTT OF FOSCOTE

4–6 FEBRUARY, 21 MARCH 2002

*Criminal law – Official secrets – Communication of information – Statutory restriction
on disclosure of information by members or former members of security service –
Whether defence of public and national interest available in prosecution for disclosure
in breach of restriction – Whether restriction on disclosure infringing right to freedom
of expression – Official Secrets Act 1989, ss 1, 4, 7(3) – Human Rights Act 1998, Sch 1,
Pt I, art 10.*

The defendant, a former member of the security service, was charged with
unlawful disclosure of documents and information contrary to ss 1[a] and 4[b] of the
Official Secrets Act 1989. Those disclosures had been made to the press and not
in accordance with the provisions on disclosure in s 7(3)[c] of the 1989 Act. On his
arrest, the defendant asserted that his disclosures had been in the public and
national interest. The judge ordered a preparatory hearing under the Criminal
Procedure and Investigations Act 1996. At the hearing, he ruled under s 31(3)(b)[d]
of that Act that no public interest defence was open to the defendant under ss 1
and 4 of the 1989 Act, and further held that those provisions were compatible
with the right to freedom of expression under art 10[e] of the European
Convention for the Protection of Human Rights and Fundamental Freedoms
1950 (as set out in Sch 1 to the Human Rights Act 1998). He went on to consider
the common law defences of necessity and duress of circumstances, and was
prepared to accept that a conventional defence of duress was in theory open to a
former member of the service, but not a defence of necessity or duress of
circumstances. The defendant appealed to the Court of Appeal against the
judge's rulings, and also questioned whether it had been appropriate for him to
make rulings under the 1996 Act. The Court of Appeal held that the judge had
been entitled to make rulings under that Act, and upheld them. The court
differed from the judge on whether a defence of necessity or duress of
circumstances was open to a member of the service, but was of the opinion that
there was no material before the court to suggest that such a defence was open
to the defendant on the facts. The defendant appealed to the House of Lords.

Held – (1) The judge's decision to order a preparatory hearing in the case was
entirely sound. Substantial benefits were likely to accrue from such a hearing. It
was, however, important to stress that the judge's power under s 31(3)(b) of the

---

a   Section 1, so far as material, is set out at [13], below
b   Section 4, so far as material, is set out at [13], below
c   Section 7(3) is set out at [13], below
d   Section 31, so far as material, provides: '(1) At the preparatory hearing the judge may exercise any
    of the powers specified in this section …
    (3) He may make a ruling as to … (b) any … question of law relating to the case.'
e   Article 10, so far as material, is set out at [22], [23], below

1996 Act was limited to ruling on questions of law 'relating to the case'. That
limitation should be strictly observed. The defendant's case before the judge did   *a*
not raise any questions of necessity or duress of circumstances, and it was a little
unfortunate that the judge had ventured into that vexed and uncertain territory
not 'relating to the case', and that the Court of Appeal had followed him into it
(see [17], [39], [87], [119], [120], below).

(2) Giving ss 1(1)(a) and 4(1) and (3)(a) of the 1989 Act their natural and   *b*
ordinary meaning and reading them in the context of the Act as a whole, it was
plain that a defendant prosecuted under those provisions was not entitled to be
acquitted if he showed that it was, or he believed that it was, in the public or
national interest to make the disclosure in question or if the jury concluded that
it might have been, or that the defendant might have believed it to be, in the
national or public interest to make the disclosure in question. Those provisions   *c*
imposed no obligation on the prosecution to prove that the disclosure was not in
the public interest and gave the defendant no opportunity to show that the
disclosure was in the public interest or that he thought it was (see [20], [87], [119],
[120], below).

(3) Sections 1(1) and 4(1) and (3) of the 1989 Act were compatible with art 10   *d*
of the convention. Although there could be no doubt that the sections under
which the defendant was being prosecuted restricted his prima facie right to
freedom of expression, the need to preserve the secrecy of information relating
to intelligence and military operations in order to counter terrorism, criminal
activity, hostile activity and subversion had been recognised by the European   *e*
Commission and the European Court of Human Rights in relation to complaints
made under art 10 and other articles. The acid test was whether, in all the
circumstances, the interference with the individual's convention right prescribed
by national law was greater than was required to meet the legitimate object
which the state sought to achieve. The 1989 Act, as it applied to the defendant,
had to be considered in that context. The ban on disclosure of information or   *f*
documents relating to security or intelligence imposed by the Act on a former
member of the service was not absolute. Rather, it was a ban on disclosure
without lawful authority. In effect, it was a ban subject to two conditions. First,
the former member might, under s 7(3)(a) of the Act, make disclosure as
appropriate to the staff counsellor, the Attorney General, the Director of Public   *g*
Prosecutions, the Commissioner of Metropolitan Police, and the Prime Minister
and other ministers, if he had anxieties relating to the work of the service which it
had not been possible to allay through the ordinary processes of management/staff
relations, or concerns about the lawfulness of what the service had done or was
doing, or concerns about misbehaviour, irregularity, maladministration, waste of   *h*
resources or incompetence in the service. Secondly, if, following disclosure to
one of those persons, effective action were not taken or there remained facts
which should in the public interest be revealed to a wider audience, the former
member might, under s 7(3)(b), seek official authorisation to make disclosure to
such an audience. Consideration of such a request should be undertaken bearing
in mind the importance attached to the right of free expression and the need for   *j*
any restriction to be necessary, responsive to a pressing social need and
proportionate. If the request were refused without adequate justification or, at
any rate, the former member firmly believed there was no such justification, he
was entitled to seek judicial review of the decision to refuse. Moreover, by s 9(1)
of the 1989 Act, the consent of the Attorney General was required before any

a prosecution was instituted under the Act. Those procedures, properly applied, provided sufficient and effective safeguards to ensure that unlawfulness and irregularity could be reported to those with the power and duty to take effective action, that the power to withhold authorisation to publish was not abused and that proper disclosures were not stifled. It was necessary, however, that a member or former member of a relevant service should avail himself of the

b procedures available to him under the 1989 Act. A former member of a relevant service, prosecuted for making an unauthorised disclosure, could not defend himself by contending that if he had made disclosure under s 7(3)(a) no notice or action would have been taken or that if had sought authorisation under s 7(3)(b) it would have been refused. Accordingly, the appeal would be dismissed (see [24], [26], [27], [29]–[31], [35], [36], [38], [63], [72], [85], [86], [105], [111], [117]–[120],

c below).

Notes
For the convention right to freedom of expression and for disclosure of security or intelligence information, see respectively 8(2) *Halsbury's Laws* (4th edn reissue)

d para 158 and 11(1) *Halsbury's Laws* (4th edn reissue) paras 246, 251.

For the Official Secrets Act 1989, ss 1, 4, 7, see 12 *Halsbury's Statutes* (4th edn) (1997 reissue) 1211, 1215, 1218.

For the Criminal Procedure and Investigations Act 1996, s 31, see 12 *Halsbury's Statutes* (4th edn) (1997 reissue) 1814.

For the Human Rights Act 1998, Sch 1, Pt I, art 10, see 7 *Halsbury's Statutes* (4th

e edn) (1999 reissue) 524.

Cases referred to in opinions
A v The Scottish Ministers 2001 SLT 1331, PC.
A-G v Blake (Jonathan Cape Ltd, third party) [2000] 4 All ER 385, [2001] 1 AC 268,

f   [2000] 3 WLR 625, HL.
A-G v Guardian Newspapers Ltd (No 2) [1988] 3 All ER 545, [1990] 1 AC 109, [1988] 3 WLR 776, HL.
A-G v Guardian Newspapers Ltd [1987] 3 All ER 316, [1987] 1 WLR 1248, HL.
Associated Provincial Picture Houses Ltd v Wednesbury Corp [1947] 2 All ER 680, [1948] 1 KB 223, CA.

g *Barthold v Germany* (1985) 7 EHRR 383, ECt HR.
Brind v UK (1994) 18 EHRR CD 76, E Com HR.
Bryan v UK (1995) 21 EHRR 342, ECt HR.
Chahal v UK (1997) 1 BHRC 405, ECt HR.
Chassagnou v France (2000) 7 BHRC 151, ECt HR.

h *Connolly v Commission of the European Communities* Case C-274/99 (6 March 2001, unreported), ECJ.
de Freitas v Permanent Secretary of Ministry of Agriculture, Fisheries, Lands and Housing [1999] 1 AC 6, [1998] 3 WLR 675, PC.
Engel v The Netherlands (No 1) (1976) 1 EHRR 647, ECt HR.

j *Esbester v UK* (1994) 18 EHRR CD 72, E Com HR.
Fitt v UK (2000) 30 EHRR 480, ECt HR.
Hadjianastassiou v Greece (1993) 16 EHRR 219.
Handyside v UK (1979) 1 EHRR 737, ECt HR.
Jasper v UK (2000) 30 EHRR 441, ECt HR.
Kingsley v UK (2001) 33 EHRR 288, ECt HR.

Klass v Federal Republic of Germany (1978) 2 EHRR 214, ECt HR.

Leander v Sweden (1987) 9 EHRR 433, ECt HR.

Lingens v Austria (1986) 8 EHRR 407, ECt HR.

McCartan Turkington Breen (a firm) v Times Newspapers Ltd [2000] 4 All ER 913, [2001] 2 AC 277, [2000] 3 WLR 1670, HL.

Murray v UK (1995) 19 EHRR 193, ECt HR.

New York Times v United States (1971) 403 US 713.

Nyambirai v National Social Security Authority [1996] 1 LRC 64, Zim SC.

Porter v Magill [2001] UKHL 67, [2002] 1 All ER 465, [2002] 2 WLR 37.

R (on the application of Daly) v Secretary of State for the Home Dept [2001] UKHL 26, [2001] 3 All ER 433, [2001] 2 AC 532, [2001] 2 WLR 1622.

R (on the application of DPP) v Acton Youth Court [2001] All ER (D) 267.

R (on the application of Pretty) v DPP [2001] UKHL 61, [2002] 1 All ER 1, [2001] 3 WLR 1598.

R v A (No 2) [2001] UKHL 25, [2001] 3 All ER 1, [2002] 1 AC 45, [2001] 2 WLR 1546, HL.

R v Carass [2001] EWCA Crim 2845, [2001] All ER (D) 300.

R v Lambert [2001] UKHL 37, [2001] 3 All ER 577, [2001] 3 WLR 206, HL.

R v Ministry of Defence, ex p Smith [1996] 1 All ER 257, [1996] QB 517, [1996] 2 WLR 305, CA.

R v Secretary of State for the Home Dept, ex p Simms [1999] 3 All ER 400, [2000] 2 AC 115, [1999] 3 WLR 328, HL.

Rowe v UK (2000) 30 EHRR 1, ECt HR.

Secretary of State for the Home Dept v Rehman [2000] 3 All ER 778, [2000] 3 WLR 1240, CA; *affd* [2001] UKHL 47, [2002] 1 All ER 122, [2001] 3 WLR 877.

Smith v UK (1999) 29 EHRR 493, ECt HR.

Sunday Times v UK (1979) 2 EHRR 245, ECt HR.

Tinnelly & Sons Ltd v UK (1999) 27 EHRR 249, ECt HR.

Vereniging Weekblad Bluf! v Netherlands (1995) 20 EHRR 189, ECt HR.

Vogt v Germany (1996) 21 EHRR 205, ECt HR.

Winterwerp v Netherlands (1979) 2 EHRR 387, ECt HR.

Appeal

The appellant, David Michael Shayler, appealed with leave of the Appeal Committee of the House of Lords given on 1 November 2001 from the order of the Court of Appeal (Lord Woolf CJ, Wright and Leveson JJ) on 28 September 2001 ([2001] EWCA Crim 1977, [2001] 1 WLR 2206) dismissing his appeal from the decision of Moses J on 16 May 2001 whereby, on a preparatory hearing under s 29 of the Criminal Procedure and Investigations Act 1996, he ruled (i) that the appellant had no public interest defence available to him in his prosecution for alleged offences under ss 1 and 4 of the Official Secrets Act 1989, and (ii) that those provisions were compatible with art 10 of the European Convention for the Protection of Human Rights and Fundamental Freedoms 1950 (as set out in Sch 1 to the Human Rights Act 1998). The Secretary of State for the Home Department intervened in the appeal to the House of Lords, and submissions were also received on behalf of The Times, The Sunday Times, The Observer, The Guardian, The Mirror, The Sunday People, The Mail on Sunday, The Independent, The Independent on Sunday, Channel 4, Channel 5 and the Newspaper Society (the press). The Court of Appeal certified that points of law of general public importance were involved in its decision, namely: '1. Whether a the offence of disclosing information relating to security or intelligence without lawful authority contrary to s 1 of the Official Secrets Act 1989 is committed if, or is subject to a defence that (a) the disclosure was necessary in the public interest to avert damage to life or limb, or serious damage to property; or (b) to expose serious and pervasive illegality in the obtaining of warrants and surveillance of suspected persons; either at common law or as a result of the coming into force

b of the Human Rights Act 1998. (2) Whether the offence of disclosing information obtained under warrants issued under the Interception of Communications Act 1985, contrary to s 4(1) of the Official Secrets Act 1989, is not committed if, or is subject to a defence that (a) the disclosure was necessary in the public interest to avert damage to life or limb, or serious damage to property; or (b) to expose serious and pervasive illegality in the obtaining of

c warrants and surveillance of suspected persons; either at common law or as a result of the coming into force of the Human Rights Act 1998. 3. Whether an "extended" defence based on the doctrine of necessity is available to a defendant charged under ss 1(1) and 4(1) of the Official Secrets Act 1989 and, if so, what is the scope of the "extended defence" of necessity.' The facts are set out in the

d opinion of Lord Bingham of Cornhill.

Geoffrey Robertson QC and *Keir Starmer* (instructed by *Liberty* and *Birnberg Peirce & Partners*) for the appellant.
Michael Tugendhat QC and *Sapna Jethani* (instructed by *Alastair Brett*, Times Newspapers Ltd) for the press.

e *Nigel Sweeney QC, Jason Coppel* and *Jonathan Laidlaw* (instructed by the *Crown Prosecution Service*) for the Crown.
Jonathan Crow (instructed by the *Treasury Solicitor*) for the Secretary of State.

f Their Lordships took time for consideration.

21 March 2002. The following opinions were delivered.

LORD BINGHAM OF CORNHILL.

[1] My Lords, Mr David Shayler, the appellant, is a former member of the

g Security Service. He has been indicted on three counts charging him with unlawful disclosure of documents and information contrary to ss 1 and 4 of the Official Secrets Act 1989 (OSA 1989). Moses J, exercising a power conferred by s 29(1) of the Criminal Procedure and Investigations Act 1996, ordered that a preparatory hearing be held before him. At that hearing the judge ruled under

h s 31(3)(b) of that Act that no public interest defence was open to the appellant under those sections, which he held to be compatible with art 10 of the European Convention for the Protection of Human Rights and Fundamental Freedoms 1950 (as set out in Sch 1 to the Human Rights Act 1998). The appellant appealed to the Court of Appeal (Criminal Division) ([2001] EWCA Crim 1977, [2001] 1 WLR 2206) against those rulings, and also questioned

j whether it had been appropriate for the judge to make rulings under the 1996 Act. The Court of Appeal held that the judge had been entitled to make rulings under the 1996 Act, and upheld his rulings both on the absence of a public interest defence and on the compatibility with art 10 of the convention of ss 1 and 4 of the OSA 1989. The appellant now challenges these rulings of the judge and the Court of Appeal before the House. At the hearing of this appeal the

House had the benefit of submissions on behalf of media interests and the
Home Secretary.

The facts

[2] The appellant faces trial on indictment and his right to a fair trial must of
course be protected. No evidence has yet been called and no facts proved. In
summarising the facts giving rise to the appeal it is appropriate to rely very
heavily on the statement of facts agreed between the parties.

[3] The appellant was a member of the security service (the service) from
November 1991 to October 1996. At the outset of his service he signed an OSA
1989 declaration acknowledging the confidential nature of documents and
other information relating to security or intelligence, defence or international
relations that might come into his possession as a result of his position; he also
signed an acknowledgment that he was under a contractual obligation not to
disclose, without authority, any information that came into his possession by
virtue of his employment. On leaving the service he signed a further OSA
declaration acknowledging that the provisions of the OSA 1989 continued to
apply to him notwithstanding the termination of his appointment, and that the
same requirements of confidentiality continued to apply to any information,
documents or other articles relating to security or intelligence, defence or
international relations which might have come into his possession as a result of
his previous employment. He made a written declaration that he had
surrendered any and all information in material form (whether classified or not)
made or acquired by him owing to his official position, save such as he had the
written authority of the service to retain.

[4] Before August 1997, the appellant disclosed a number of documents to
journalists from the Mail on Sunday. Some 29 different documents were later
returned by the newspaper to the Treasury Solicitor in March 1998. Most of
them appeared to relate to security and intelligence matters and were classified
at levels ranging from 'Classified' up to and including 'Top Secret'. The
prosecution allege that certain of the documents included material obtained by
or relating to the interception of communications in obedience to warrants
issued under s 2 of the Interception of Communications Act 1985.

[5] On 24 August 1997, the Mail on Sunday published an article written by
the appellant himself (according to the by-line) and a number of other articles
by journalists purporting to be based on information disclosed by the appellant.
The prosecution allege that the appellant was paid a substantial sum of money
by the newspaper for these activities. The prosecution also allege that the
information contained in and referred to in the articles relates to matters of
security and intelligence to which the appellant could only have had access by
reason of his employment with the service.

[6] Just before the articles were published, the appellant left the country and
a subsequent attempt to extradite him from France failed. He returned on 21
August 2000 and was arrested on his arrival at Dover. He was cautioned and
made no reply. He was not interviewed at any stage, but was taken to London
and charged at Charing Cross Police Station that same afternoon. In reply to
the charge he said:

> 'I have been living in Paris for three years and I have decided voluntarily
> to return to Britain to face charges under the Official Secrets Act. I have
> done this to clear my name and to allow a jury of twelve of my fellow

citizens to judge me. I have also returned to challenge the cover-ups and complacency that have followed my disclosures. I admit that as an officer of the Security Service, I was a Crown Servant from November 1991 to October 1996. However, I do not admit making any disclosures which were contrary to the criminal law. Any disclosures made by me were in the public and national interests. In my defence I will rely on my right of freedom of expression as guaranteed by the common law, the Human Rights Act and Article 10 of the European Convention on Human Rights.'

[7] The first count in the indictment against the appellant alleges that, on or before 24 August 1997, being a person who had been a member of the security and intelligence services, he disclosed documents relating to security or intelligence without lawful authority contrary to s 1(1) of the OSA 1989. The second count alleges that, on or before 24 August 1997, being a person who had been a Crown servant, he without lawful authority disclosed information obtained by reason of warrants issued under the 1985 Act, contrary to s 4(1) of the OSA 1989. The third count alleges that on 24 August 1997, being a person who had been a member of the security and intelligence services, he without lawful authority disclosed information relating to security or intelligence, contrary to s 1(1) of the OSA 1989. The appellant has pleaded not guilty to these charges.

[8] At the preparatory hearing before the judge the first issue was whether, in law, the appellant would be entitled to be acquitted of the charges against him if (as he asserted on his arrest) his disclosures had (or, one should add, might have) been made in the public and national interest. In his judgment Moses J referred to the assertion made by the appellant on his arrest and quoted the written submission made on the appellant's behalf:

'Any disclosures made by him were intended to draw attention to the illegal, unlawful and inefficient workings of the security and intelligence services, which, on occasion risked, and continued to risk, life and limb.'

The judge recorded (at [4]) the appellant as seeking—

'to contend that his disclosures were necessary to expose serious illegality by the security and intelligence services, and, in particular such disclosure was necessary to avert threat to life or limb or serious damage to property.'

The judge's conclusion expressed at the end of his judgment, was unequivocal:

'Sections 1(1) and 4 of the OSA 1989 do not permit a defendant to raise a defence that his disclosure was necessary in the public interest to avert damage to life or limb or serious damage to property.'

The judge developed at some length his reasons for holding that the sections as so construed were not incompatible with art 10 and in his judgment (at [82]), under the heading 'Extending the Common Law', said:

'Were I to have concluded that the absence of any public interest offence is incompatible with the convention, Mr Fitzgerald QC's argument that the common law principle of necessity should be developed in the light of art 10 seems to me to afford a more fruitful basis for the courts to permit such a defence.'

He then went on to consider the common law defences of necessity and duress of circumstances.   He was prepared to accept that a conventional defence of _a_ duress was in theory open to a former member of the service, but could not accept that a defence of necessity or duress of circumstances was open.   The Court of Appeal took a different legal view on this latter issue, to which much of its judgment was directed, but it was of the opinion that there was no material before the court to suggest that a defence of necessity or duress of _b_ circumstances was open to the appellant on the facts.

The OSA 1989

[9] Section 2 of the Official Secrets Act 1911, enacted in great haste, was the subject of sustained criticism over many years.   Its excessive scope had proved an obstacle to its effective enforcement.   For this reason, and in fulfilment of a _c_ pledge to get rid of unnecessary secrecy, a departmental committee under the distinguished chairmanship of Lord Franks was established in 1971 to consider and recommend an effective and enforceable alternative.   The committee reported in 1972 (*Departmental Committee on Section 2 of the Official Secrets Act 1911* (Cmnd 5104)).   The committee recognised (p 9 (para 1))—   _d_

'the concern of democratic governments to see that information is widely diffused, for this enables citizens to play a part in controlling their common affairs.   There is an inevitable tension between the democratic requirement of openness, and the continuing need to keep some matters secret.'   _e_

The committee went on to observe (pp 47–48):

'122.   It is generally accepted that secrecy is an important element in the effectiveness of defence measures and equipment, and that a breach of secrecy could seriously damage the nation ...   _f_
123.   Defence is traditionally thought of in terms of troops, weapons and equipment, and plans.   Intelligence is also an important aspect of defence, and comprises both our own intelligence operations and measures taken against the intelligence operations of others.   All defence matters must be treated in terms not just of this country, but of the United Kingdom and her allies taken together.   The Government are under an obligation to _g_ protect the defence information of our allies in the same way as our own.   For the purposes of our broad categories, we regard defence as including home defence and internal security.'

After observing (p 49 (para 127)) that in the field of international relations _h_ secrecy is mutual, since one country cannot breach secrecy unilaterally without damaging its relations with others, the committee said (p 50 (para 130)):

'Exchanges between governments not amounting to negotiations are often on a confidential basis.   One nation may entrust to a second nation or to its friends or allies information which it is on no account prepared to _j_ allow to go further.   A breach of this trust could have a seriously adverse effect on relations between the countries concerned, which might extend well beyond the particular matter which leaked.'

[10] A White Paper based on the Franks recommendations was published in July 1978 and a Bill was introduced in Parliament in the following year.   The

a   Bill was, however, criticised for its reliance on conclusive ministerial certificates and the excessive width of the prohibition it imposed. In the face of strong criticism it was withdrawn. Unsuccessful attempts to reform the law were made by private members, and in 1987 the government of the day again sought to devise an acceptable reform. A further White Paper (*Reform of Section 2 of the Official Secrets Act 1911* (Cm 408)) was published in June 1988.

b   [11] This White Paper was the immediate precursor of the OSA 1989 and its recommendations bear directly on the interpretation of the Act. The following paragraphs are particularly relevant (pp 7–12):

> 'Defence, security and intelligence—25. The most obvious areas in which the public interest needs to be protected are those where the *c* protection of the nation from attack from outside or from within is involved. Clearly new legislation must protect information relating to defence (including civil preparedness) and information relating to security and intelligence ...
>
> Interception—30. There is a particular sensitivity about the interception *d* of telephone calls, mail and other forms of communication. It is an exceptional but vital instrument which is used, for the protection of society, when other means are not available. Successive Governments have recognised that properly controlled interception for limited purposes, such as national security or the prevention and detection of crime, is not only justified but essential in the public interest. The effectiveness of *e* interception would be much reduced if details of the practice were readily available. But it is not only the means by which interception is practised which need to be protected. The information gathered by its use, even where it is not covered by one of the other categories already mentioned, ought not to be publicly available. Interception inevitably involves *f* interference, without their knowledge, with the privacy of those whose communications are intercepted. Such interference is acceptable in the public interest only if those responsible for interception maintain the privacy of the information obtained ...
>
> Security and intelligence matters—38. [The government] proposes *g* instead that legislation should make a distinction between disclosures by members and former members of the security and intelligence services and disclosures by other persons; and that, in the latter case, the prosecution should have to show that the disclosure was likely to damage the operation of the security or intelligence services.
>
> *h* 39. Because of the exceptional sensitivity of this area of information, however, there is a particular difficulty in bringing prosecutions in some cases which would be exacerbated by the need to show that the proposed test of harm had been met. In order to prove the truth of the information at present, and in order to satisfy the test of harm if the Government's proposal is adopted, evidence may need to be adduced which involves a *j* disclosure which is as harmful as or more harmful than the disclosure which is the subject of the prosecution. Because of this danger it is not always possible to bring a prosecution at all. The Government considers that it is not in the public interest that those who wish to disclose information which damages the operation of the security or intelligence services (for example by revealing details of their operations or identifying

personnel) should be able to do so with impunity, simply by reason of the
sensitivity of the subject matter ... *a*

41. While the Government believes that this proposed test of harm is in
general adequate to safeguard the interests both of the defendant and of
the security and intelligence services, it considers that different arguments
apply to the unauthorised disclosure of information by members or former
members of those services. It takes the view that all such disclosures are *b*
harmful to the public interest and ought to be criminal. They are harmful
because they carry a credibility which the disclosure of the same
information by any other person does not, and because they reduce public
confidence in the services' ability and willingness to carry out their
essentially secret duties effectively and loyally. They ought to be criminal
because those who become members of the services know that *c*
membership carries with it a special and inescapable duty of secrecy about
their work. Unauthorised disclosures betray that duty and the trust placed
in the members concerned, both by the State and by people who give
information to the services.

42. The Government accordingly proposes that it should not be *d*
necessary for the prosecution to adduce evidence of the likely damage to
the operation of the security or intelligence services when information
relating to security or intelligence has been disclosed by a member or
former member of one of those services.

43. The difficulties described in paragraph 39, arising from the fact that *e*
a trial may lead to the disclosure of information more sensitive than has
already been disclosed, need particularly to be overcome where the
defendant is a member or former member of the security or intelligence
services. It is clearly not in the public interest that a person who is
entrusted with the protection of the security of the country, and who
betrays that trust, should be able to escape prosecution because of the very *f*
sensitivity of the information with which he has been entrusted.
Furthermore, as a general policy, Governments do not comment on
assertions about security or intelligence: true statements will generally go
unconfirmed, and false statements will normally go undenied. As a result,
and because of the particular credibility attaching to statements about
security or intelligence by members of the services concerned, the *g*
circulation of misinformation by a member of the services may, in a
different way, be as harmful as his disclosure of genuine information.

44. The Government proposes to meet these problems by making it an
offence for a member or former member of the security or intelligence
services to make any disclosure which is either of information relating to *h*
security or intelligence or which purports to be of such information or
which is intended to be taken as such ...

Interception—53. Finally, paragraph 30 sets out the reasons why the
disclosure of information relating to the process of interception or
obtained by that means is harmful. It seems to the Government that no *j*
information relating to this process can be disclosed without the possibility
of damaging this essential weapon against terrorism and crime and vital
safeguard of national security. Similarly no information obtained by
means of interception can be disclosed without assisting terrorism or
crime, damaging national security or seriously breaching the privacy of

a private citizens. The Government does not therefore consider that a specific test of harm can be formulated or, indeed, is necessary or appropriate for this category of information.'

Under the heading 'A Public Interest Defence', the White Paper continued (p 13):

b '58. Suggestions have been made that the law should provide a general defence that disclosure was in the public interest. The object would be to enable the courts to consider the benefit of the unauthorised disclosure of particular information, and the motives of the person disclosing it, as well as the harm which it was likely to cause. It is suggested, in particular, that such a defence is necessary in order to enable suggestions of misconduct or malpractice to be properly investigated or brought to public attention.

c 59. The Government recognises that some people who make unauthorised disclosures do so for what they themselves see as altruistic reasons and without desire for personal gain. But that is equally true of some people who commit other criminal offences. The general principle which the law follows is that the criminality of what people do ought not

d to depend on their ultimate motives—though these may be a factor to be taken into account in sentencing—but on the nature and degree of the harm which their acts may cause.

60. In the Government's view, there are good grounds for not departing from the general model in this context; and two features of the present proposals particularly reinforce this conclusion. First, a central objective

e of reform is to achieve maximum clarity in the law and in its application. A general public interest defence would make it impossible to achieve such clarity. Secondly, the proposals in this White Paper are designed to concentrate the protection of the criminal law on information which demonstrably requires its protection in the public interest. It cannot be

f acceptable that a person can lawfully disclose information which he knows may, for example, lead to loss of life simply because he conceives that he has a general reason of a public character for doing so.

61. So far as the criminal law relating to the protection of official information is concerned, therefore, the Government is of the mind that there should be no general public interest defence and that any argument

g as to the effect of disclosure on the public interest should take place within the context of the proposed damage tests where applicable.'

What became the OSA 1989 was debated in both Houses during its passage through Parliament. An amendment designed to introduce a public interest

h defence was rejected. The OSA 1989 as passed gives general effect to the proposals in the White Paper.

[12] As enacted the OSA 1989 makes important distinctions leading to differences of treatment: (1) The Act distinguishes between different classes of discloser. Thus, in s 1, members and former members of the intelligence and security services and persons notified that they are subject to the subsection are

j covered by sub-s (1), whereas past and present Crown servants and government contractors are covered by sub-s (3). (2) The Act distinguishes between different kinds of information. Section 1 deals with security and intelligence information. Successive sections deal with information relating to defence, international relations and crime. (3) The Act provides specific defences on which reliance may be placed in different circumstances: thus, in

addition to the defence expressly provided in s 1(5) quoted below, further
defences are provided in ss 2(3), 3(4), 4(4) and (5), 5(3) and (4), 6(3), 7(4) and
8(2). (4) The requirement to prove damage differs according to the nature of
the disclosure and the information disclosed. Thus the provisions in s 1(3) and
(4) are to be contrasted with the lack of any express requirement of damage in
s 1(1), and are in line with similar provisions in ss 2(1) and (2), 3(1), (2) and (3),
4(2), 5(3) and 6(2).

[13] Section 1 under which counts 1 and 3 of the indictment against the
appellant have been laid, provides (so far as relevant) as follows:

'(1) A person who is or has been—(a) a member of the security and
intelligence services; or (b) a person notified that he is subject to the
provisions of this subsection, is guilty of an offence if without lawful
authority he discloses any information, document or other article relating
to security or intelligence which is or has been in his possession by virtue
of his position as a member of any of those services or in the course of his
work while the notification is or was in force.

(2) The reference in subsection (1), above to disclosing information
relating to security or intelligence includes a reference to making any
statement which purports to be a disclosure of such information or is
intended to be taken by those to whom it is addressed as being such a
disclosure.

(3) A person who is or has been a Crown servant or government
contractor is guilty of an offence if without lawful authority he makes a
damaging disclosure of any information, document or other article relating
to security or intelligence which is or has been in his possession by virtue
of his position as such but otherwise than as mentioned in subsection (1),
above.

(4) For the purposes of subsection (3) above a disclosure is damaging
if—(a) it causes damage to the work of, or of any part of, the security and
intelligence services; or (b) it is of information or a document or other
article which is such that its unauthorised disclosure would be likely to
cause such damage or which falls within a class or description of
information, documents or articles the unauthorised disclosure of which
would be likely to have that effect.

(5) It is a defence for a person charged with an offence under this section
to prove that at the time of the alleged offence he did not know, and had
no reasonable cause to believe, that the information, document or article
in question related to security or intelligence or, in the case of an offence
under subsection (3), that the disclosure would be damaging within the
meaning of that subsection ...

(9) In this section "security or intelligence" means the work of, or in
support of, the security and intelligence services or any part of them, and
references to information relating to security or intelligence include
references to information held or transmitted by those services or by
persons in support of, or of any part of, them.'

Section 4, under which count two of the indictment is laid, provides (so far as
material, and as amended) as follows:

'(1) A person who is or has been a Crown servant or government
contractor is guilty of an offence if without lawful authority he discloses

a any information, document or other article to which this section applies and which is or has been in his possession by virtue of his position as such ...

(3) This section also applies to—(a) any information obtained by reason of the interception of any communication in obedience to a warrant issued under section 2 of the Interception of Communications Act 1985 ... any

b information relating to the obtaining of information by reason of any such interception and any document or other article which is or has been used or held for use in, or has been obtained by reason of, any such interception; and (b) any information obtained by reason of action authorised by a warrant issued under section 3 of the Security Service Act 1989 or under section 5 of the Intelligence Services Act 1994 or by an authorisation given

c under section 7 of that Act, any information relating to the obtaining of information by reason of any such action and any document or other article which is or has been used or held for use in, or has been obtained by reason of, any such action ...

(5) It is a defence for a person charged with an offence under this section in respect of any other disclosure to prove that at the time of the alleged

d offence he did not know, and had no reasonable cause to believe, that the information, document or article in question was information or a document or article to which this section applies.'

Section 7 governs the authorisation of disclosures. It deals first with disclosures
e by Crown servants and persons subject to notification under s 1(1), then with government contractors, and then in sub-s (3) provides:

'For the purposes of this Act a disclosure made by any other person is made with lawful authority if, and only if, it is made—(a) to a Crown servant for the purposes of his functions as such; or (b) in accordance with

f an official authorisation.'

'Official authorisation' is defined to mean an authorisation duly given by a Crown servant or by or on behalf of a prescribed body or a body of a prescribed class. These expressions are defined in s 12. A 'Crown servant' includes any minister, civil servant, member of the armed forces or constable, and any

g holder of an office or body or member of a body prescribed by the secretary of state. In s 13 'disclose' and 'disclosure' are defined to include parting with possession of a document.

The Security Service Act 1989

h [14] The Security Service Act 1989 was enacted, very shortly before the OSA 1989, to put the service on a statutory basis. Its functions are defined in s 1 (as amended):

'(2) The function of the Service shall be the protection of national security and, in particular, its protection against threats from espionage,

j terrorism and sabotage, from the activities of agents of foreign powers and from actions intended to overthrow or undermine parliamentary democracy by political, industrial or violent means.

(3) It shall also be the function of the Service to safeguard the economic well-being of the United Kingdom against threats posed by the actions or intentions of persons outside the British Islands.

(4) It shall also be the function of the Service to act in support of the
activities of police forces, the National Criminal Intelligence Service, the
National Crime Squad and other law enforcement agencies in the
prevention and detection of serious crime.'

Under s 2 (as amended), the Director General is to be responsible for the
efficiency of the service and it is to be his duty to ensure—

'(a) that there are arrangements for securing that no information is
obtained by the Service except so far as necessary for the proper discharge
of its functions or disclosed by it except so far as necessary for that purpose
or for the purpose of the prevention or detection of serious crime or for the
purpose of any criminal proceedings; and (b) that the Service does not take
any action to further the interests of any political party; and (c) that there
are arrangements, agreed with the Director General of the National
Criminal Intelligence Service, for co-ordinating the activities of the Service
in pursuance of section 1(4) of this Act with the activities of police forces,
the National Criminal Intelligence Service, the National Crime Squad and
other law enforcement agencies.'

The preparatory hearing

[15] Section 29(1) of the 1996 Act confers powers on a judge of the Crown
Court to order a preparatory hearing where it appears to him that an
indictment reveals a case of such complexity, or a case whose trial is likely to
be of such length, that substantial benefits are likely to accrue from a hearing
before the jury are sworn for any of the purposes listed in sub-s (2). These
purposes are those of—

'(a) identifying issues which are likely to be material to the verdict of the
jury; (b) assisting their comprehension of any such issues; (c) expediting the
proceedings before the jury; (d) assisting the judge's management of the
trial.'

The order may be made on the application of the prosecutor or the defendant
or of the judge's own motion, and at the hearing the judge may under s 31(3)
make a ruling as to '(a) any question as to the admissibility of evidence' or '(b)
any other question of law relating to the case'. An appeal lies to the Court of
Appeal, with leave, against any ruling given (see s 35(1)).

[16] As s 29 makes clear, resort to this procedure is only permissible where
the case appears complex or likely to lead to a lengthy trial. But in such cases
the procedure can be highly beneficial. The process of disclosure can be
conducted, and the marshalling of evidence prepared, with direct reference to
the live issues in the case. Jurors and witnesses, summoned to court for the
trial, can be spared hours or days of frustrating inaction while issues of law are
argued out in their absence. The risk of sudden adjournments to deal with
unforeseen contingencies can be reduced. And, perhaps most important of all,
the risk that the trial will be conducted on what an appellate court later rules to
be a mistaken legal basis, leading to the necessarily undesirable consequence of
a retrial, can be minimised if not eliminated. If there is an issue on the proper
interpretation of a section or the correct direction to be given to a jury, it may
be better to resolve the question sooner rather than later (see *R v Carass* [2001]
EWCA Crim 2845 at [22], [2001] All ER (D) 300 at [22]).

a   [17] The judge's decision to order a preparatory hearing in this case, not
challenged at the time, was entirely sound. Substantial benefits were indeed
likely to accrue. It was faintly suggested in argument before the House that the
case did not meet the statutory criteria of complexity and likely length. But the
legal argument occupied four days before the judge, three days in the Court of
Appeal and three days before the House. There are eight substantial bundles
b   of authorities before the House. The test of complexity is comfortably satisfied,
and the likely length of the trial in large measure depended on how the main
legal issue was resolved. It is, however, important to stress that the judge's
power under s 31(3)(b) is limited to ruling on questions of law 'relating to the
case'. This limitation must be strictly observed. Here, the issues of law before
the judge were whether the sections under which the appellant was charged,
c   on a proper construction, afford him a public interest defence; whether, if not,
those sections are compatible with art 10 of the convention; and whether, if
they are not, they can or should be read conformably with the convention or a
declaration of incompatibility made. The appellant's case before the judge did
not raise any question of necessity or duress of circumstances, and it is a little
d   unfortunate that the judge ventured into this vexed and uncertain territory not
'relating to the case'. It is a little unfortunate, for the same reason, that the
Court of Appeal followed him into it. I should not for my part be taken to
accept all that the Court of Appeal said on these difficult topics, but in my
opinion it is unnecessary to explore them in this case. The appellant's case, put
very broadly, is understood to be that he was appalled at the unlawfulness,
e   irregularity, incompetence, misbehaviour and waste of resources in the service,
which he thought was failing to perform its public duty; he believed that unless
these failings were exposed and remedied dire consequences would follow; and
he therefore believed it in the public and national interest to make the
disclosure he did. This omnibus contention may or may not afford him a
f   defence under the OSA 1989, depending on whether a public interest defence is
available; but it is not within measurable distance of affording him a defence of
necessity or duress of circumstances.

Construction of ss 1(2) and 4(1) of the OSA 1989

g   [18] Section 1(1)(a) of the OSA 1989 imposes criminal liability on a member
or former member of the security and intelligence services if, without lawful
authority (as defined in s 7), he discloses any information or document relating
to security or intelligence which is or has been in his possession by virtue of his
position as a member of any of those services. The only defence expressly
provided is, under sub-s (5), that at the time of the disclosure he did not know
h   and had no reasonable cause to believe that the information or documents in
question related to security or intelligence. As already demonstrated, a
member or former member of the security and intelligence services is treated
differently under the Act from other persons, and information and documents
relating to security and intelligence are treated differently from information
j   and documents relating to other matters. Importantly, the section does not
require the prosecution to prove that any disclosure made by a member or
former member of the security and intelligence services was damaging to the
interests of that service or the public service generally.

   [19] Section 4(1), read in conjunction with s 4(3)(a), imposes criminal
liability on a serving or former Crown servant if, without lawful authority (as

defined in s 7), he discloses any information obtained by reason of the interception of any communication in obedience to a warrant issued under s 2 of the 1985 Act which has been in his possession by virtue of his position as a serving or former Crown servant. The only defence expressly provided is, under sub-s (5), that at the time of the disclosure he did not know and had no reasonable cause to believe that any information or document disclosed was information or a document to which the section applied. In a prosecution under the subsections referred to the prosecution do not have to prove damage or the likelihood of damage (as required under s 4(2)) and a limited defence based on lack of knowledge that damage would be caused (as provided under s 4(4)) does not apply.

[20] It is in my opinion plain, giving ss 1(1)(a), 4(1) and (3)(a) their natural and ordinary meaning and reading them in the context of the OSA 1989 as a whole, that a defendant prosecuted under these sections is not entitled to be acquitted if he shows that it was or that he believed that it was in the public or national interest to make the disclosure in question or if the jury conclude that it may have been or that the defendant may have believed it to be in the public or national interest to make the disclosure in question. The sections impose no obligation on the prosecution to prove that the disclosure was not in the public interest and give the defendant no opportunity to show that the disclosure was in the public interest or that he thought it was. The sections leave no room for doubt, and if they did the 1988 White Paper quoted above, which is a legitimate aid to construction, makes the intention of Parliament clear beyond argument.

The right to free expression

[21] The fundamental right of free expression has been recognised at common law for very many years: see, among many other statements to similar effect *A-G v Guardian Newspapers Ltd* [1987] 3 All ER 316 at 331, 376 [1987] 1 WLR 1248 at 1269, 1320; *A-G v Guardian Newspapers Ltd (No 2)* [1988] 3 All ER 545 at 596, 627, 628, 632, 660, [1990] 1 AC 109 at 178, 218, 220, 226, 283; *R v Secretary of State for the Home Dept, ex p Simms* [1999] 3 All ER 400 at 408, [2000] 2 AC 115 at 126; *McCartan Turkington Breen (a firm) v Times Newspapers Ltd* [2000] 4 All ER 913 at 922, [2001] 2 AC 277 at 290–291. The reasons why the right to free expression is regarded as fundamental are familiar, but merit brief restatement in the present context. Modern democratic government means government of the people by the people for the people. But there can be no government by the people if they are ignorant of the issues to be resolved, the arguments for and against different solutions and the facts underlying those arguments. The business of government is not an activity about which only those professionally engaged are entitled to receive information and express opinions. It is, or should be, a participatory process. But there can be no assurance that government is carried out for the people unless the facts are made known, the issues publicly ventilated. Sometimes, inevitably, those involved in the conduct of government, as in any other walk of life, are guilty of error, incompetence, misbehaviour, dereliction of duty, even dishonesty and malpractice. Those concerned may very strongly wish that the facts relating to such matters are not made public. Publicity may reflect discredit on them or their predecessors. It may embarrass the authorities. It may impede the process of administration. Experience however shows, in this country and elsewhere, that publicity is a powerful disinfectant.

a Where abuses are exposed, they can be remedied. Even where abuses have already been remedied, the public may be entitled to know that they occurred. The role of the press in exposing abuses and miscarriages of justice has been a potent and honourable one. But the press cannot expose that of which it is denied knowledge.

b [22] Despite the high value placed by the common law on freedom of expression, it was not until incorporation of the convention into our domestic law by the Human Rights Act 1998 that this fundamental right was underpinned by statute. Article 10(1) of the convention, so far as relevant, provides:

c   'Everyone has the right to freedom of expression. This right shall include freedom to hold opinions and to receive and impart information and ideas without interference by public authority and regardless of frontiers.'

Section 12 of the 1998 Act reflects the central importance which attaches to the right to freedom of expression. The European Court of Human Rights for its part has not wavered in asserting the fundamental nature of this right. In its *d* judgment in *Vogt v Germany* (1996) 21 EHRR 205 at 234 (para 52), the court said:

      'The court reiterates the basic principles laid down in its judgments concerning Article 10: (i) Freedom of expression constitutes one of the essential foundations of a democratic society and one of the basic conditions for its progress and each individual's self-fulfilment. Subject to *e*   Article 10(2), it is applicable not only to "information" or "ideas" that are favourably received or regarded as inoffensive or as a matter of indifference, but also to those that offend, shock or disturb; such are the demands of that pluralism, tolerance and broadmindedness without which there is no "democratic society".'

f It is unnecessary to multiply citations to the same effect. Thus for purposes of the present proceedings the starting point must be that the appellant is entitled if he wishes to disclose information and documents in his possession unless the law imposes a valid restraint upon his doing so.

g *Article 10(2)*
[23] Despite the high importance attached to it, the right to free expression was never regarded in domestic law as absolute. Publication could render a party liable to civil or criminal penalties or restraints on a number of grounds which included, for instance, libel, breach of confidence, incitement to racial *h* hatred, blasphemy, publication of pornography and, as noted above, disclosure of official secrets. The convention similarly recognises that the right is not absolute: art 10(2) qualifies the broad language of art 10(1) by providing, so far as relevant to this case:

j   'The exercise of these freedoms, since it carries with it duties and responsibilities, may be subject to such formalities, conditions, restrictions or penalties as are prescribed by law and are necessary in a democratic society, in the interests of national security, territorial integrity or public safety, for the prevention of disorder or crime ... for the protection of the ... rights of others, for preventing the disclosure of information received in confidence ...'

It is plain from the language of art 10(2), and the European Court has repeatedly
held, that any national restriction on freedom of expression can be consistent
with art 10(2) only if it is prescribed by law, is directed to one or more of the
objectives specified in the article and is shown by the state concerned to be
necessary in a democratic society. 'Necessary' has been strongly interpreted: it is
not synonymous with 'indispensable', neither has it the flexibility of such
expressions as 'admissible', 'ordinary', 'useful', 'reasonable' or 'desirable' (see
Handyside v UK (1979) 1 EHRR 737 at 754 (para 48)). One must consider whether
the interference complained of corresponded to a pressing social need, whether
it was proportionate to the legitimate aim pursued and whether the reasons given
by the national authority to justify it are relevant and sufficient under art 10(2)
(see *Sunday Times v UK* (1979) 2 EHRR 245 at 277–278 (para 62)).

[24] In the present case there can be no doubt but that the sections under
which the appellant has been prosecuted, construed as I have construed them,
restricted his prima facie right to free expression. There can equally be no
doubt but that the restriction was directed to objectives specified in art 10(2) as
quoted above. It was suggested in argument that the restriction was
not prescribed by law because the procedure for obtaining authorisation
was not precisely specified in the OSA 1989, but I cannot accept this. The
restriction on disclosure is prescribed with complete clarity. A member or
former member of any of the security or intelligence services wishing to obtain
authority to disclose could be in no doubt but that he should seek authorisation
from his superior or former superior in the relevant service or the head of that
service, either of whom might no doubt refer the request to higher authority.
It was common ground below, in my view, rightly, that the relevant restriction
was prescribed by law. It is on the question of necessity, pressing social need
and proportionality that the real issue between the parties arises.

[25] There is much domestic authority pointing to the need for a security or
intelligence service to be secure. The commodity in which such a service deals
is secret and confidential information. If the service is not secure those working
against the interests of the state, whether terrorists, other criminals or foreign
agents, will be alerted, and able to take evasive action; its own agents may be
unmasked; members of the service will feel unable to rely on each other; those
upon whom the service relies as sources of information will feel unable to rely
on their identity remaining secret; and foreign countries will decline to entrust
their own secrets to an insecure recipient (see, for example, *A-G v Guardian
Newspapers Ltd (No 2)* [1988] 3 All ER 545 at 550, 623, 642, 647, [1990] 1 AC 109
at 118, 213–214, 259, 265; *A-G v Blake (Jonathan Cape Ltd, third party)* [2000] 4 All
ER 385 at 399–400, [2001] 1 AC 268 at 287). In the *Guardian Newspapers'* case
[1988] 3 All ER 545 at 650, [1990] 1 AC 109 at 269, Lord Griffiths expressed the
accepted rule very pithily:

'The security and intelligence services are necessary for our national
security. They are, and must remain, secret services if they are to operate
efficiently. The only practical way to achieve this objective is a brightline
rule that forbids any member or ex-member of the service to publish any
material relating to his service experience unless he has had the material
cleared by his employers. There is, in my view, no room for an exception
to this rule dealing with trivia that should not be regarded as confidential.

a What may appear to the writer to be trivial may in fact be the one missing piece in the jigsaw sought by some hostile intelligence agency.'

As already shown, this judicial approach is reflected in the rule laid down, after prolonged consideration and debate, by the legislature.

[26] The need to preserve the secrecy of information relating to intelligence and military operations in order to counter terrorism, criminal activity, hostile

b activity and subversion has been recognised by the European Commission and the Court in relation to complaints made under art 10 and other articles under the convention (see *Engel v The Netherlands (No 1)* (1976) 1 EHRR 647 at 684–686 (paras 100–103); *Klass v Federal Republic of Germany* (1978) 2 EHRR 214 at 232 (para 48); *Leander v Sweden* (1987) 9 EHRR 433 at 452–453 (para 59);

c *Hadjianastassiou v Greece* (1993) 16 EHRR 219 at 239–240 (paras 45–47); *Esbester v UK* (1994) 18 EHRR CD 72 at CD 74; *Brind v United Kingdom* (1994) 18 EHRR CD 76 at CD 83–84; *Murray v United Kingdom* (1995) 19 EHRR 193 at 226 (para 58); *Vereniging Weekblad Bluf! v The Netherlands* (1995) 20 EHRR 189 at 201–202, 203 (paras 35, 40)). The thrust of these decisions and judgments has not been to discount or disparage the need for strict and enforceable rules but to insist

d on adequate safeguards to ensure that the restriction does not exceed what is necessary to achieve the end in question. The acid test is whether, in all the circumstances, the interference with the individual's convention right prescribed by national law is greater than is required to meet the legitimate object which the state seeks to achieve. The OSA 1989, as it applies to the

e appellant, must be considered in that context.

[27] The OSA 1989 imposes a ban on disclosure of information or documents relating to security or intelligence by a former member of the service. But it is not an absolute ban. It is a ban on disclosure without lawful authority. It is in effect a ban subject to two conditions. First of all, the former member may, under s 7(3)(a), make disclosure to a Crown servant for the

f purposes of his functions as such: (1) The former member may make disclosure to the staff counsellor, whose appointment was announced in the House of Commons in November 1987 (see 121 HC Official Report (6th series) col 508), before enactment of the OSA 1989 and in obvious response to the grievances ventilated by Mr Peter Wright in *Spycatcher*. The staff counsellor, a high

g ranking former civil servant, is available to be consulted—

'by any member of the security and intelligence services who has anxieties relating to the work of his or her service which it has not been possible to allay through the ordinary processes of management-staff relations.'

h In February 1989 the role of the staff counsellor was further explained (see the judgment of the Court of Appeal ([2001] 1 WLR 2206 at [39])). (2) If the former member has concerns about the lawfulness of what the service has done or is doing, he may disclose his concerns to (among others) the Attorney General, the Director of Public Prosecutions or the Commissioner of Metropolitan

j Police. These officers are subject to a clear duty, in the public interest, to uphold the law, investigate alleged infractions and prosecute where offences appear to have been committed, irrespective of any party affiliation or service loyalty. (3) If a former member has concerns about misbehaviour, irregularity, maladministration, waste of resources or incompetence in the service he may disclose these to the Home Secretary, the Foreign Secretary, the Secretary of

State for Northern Ireland or Scotland, the Prime Minister, the Secretary to the Cabinet or the Joint Intelligence Committee. He may also make disclosure to the secretariat, provided (as the House was told) by the Home Office, of the Parliamentary Intelligence and Security Committee. He may further make disclosure, by virtue of art 3 of and Sch 2 to the Official Secrets Act 1989 (Prescription) Order 1990, SI 1990/200 to the staff of the Controller and Auditor General, the National Audit Office and the Parliamentary Commissioner for Administration.

[28] Since one count of the indictment against the appellant is laid under s 4(1) and (3) of the OSA 1989, considerable attention was directed by the judge and the Court of Appeal to the role of the commissioners appointed under s 8(1) of the Interception of Communications Act 1985, s 4(1) of the Security Service Act 1989 and s 8(1) of the Intelligence Services Act 1994. The appellant submits, correctly, that none of these commissioners is a minister or a civil servant, that their functions defined by the three statutes do not include general oversight of the three security services, and that the secretariat serving the commissioners is, or was, of modest size. But under each of the three Acts, the commissioner was given power to require documents and information to be supplied to him by any Crown servant or member of the relevant services for the purposes of his functions (see s 8(3) of the 1985 Act, s 4(4) of the Security Service Act 1989, s 8(4) of the 1994 Act), and if it were intimated to the commissioner, in terms so general as to involve no disclosure, that serious abuse of the power to intercept communications or enter premises to obtain information was taking or had taken place, it seems unlikely that the commissioner would not exercise his power to obtain information or at least refer the warning to the Home Secretary or (as the case might be) the Foreign Secretary.

[29] One would hope that, if disclosure were made to one or other of the persons listed above, effective action would be taken to ensure that abuses were remedied and offenders punished. But the possibility must exist that such action would not be taken when it should be taken or that, despite the taking of effective action to remedy past abuses and punish past delinquencies, there would remain facts which should in the public interest be revealed to a wider audience. This is where, under the OSA 1989, the second condition comes into play: the former member may seek official authorisation to make disclosure to a wider audience.

[30] As already indicated, it is open to a former member of the service to seek authorisation from his former superior or the head of the service, who may no doubt seek authority from the Secretary to the Cabinet or a minister. Whoever is called upon to consider the grant of authorisation must consider with care the particular information or document which the former member seeks to disclose and weigh the merits of that request bearing in mind (and if necessary taking advice on) the object or objects which the statutory ban on disclosure seeks to achieve and the harm (if any) which would be done by the disclosure in question. If the information or document in question were liable to disclose the identity of agents or compromise the security of informers, one would not expect authorisation to be given. If, on the other hand, the document or information revealed matters which, however scandalous or embarrassing, would not damage any security or intelligence interest or impede the effective discharge by the service of its very important public

a functions, another decision might be appropriate. Consideration of a request for authorisation should never be a routine or mechanical process: it should be undertaken bearing in mind the importance attached to the right of free expression and the need for any restriction to be necessary, responsive to a pressing social need and proportionate.

[31] One would, again, hope that requests for authorisation to disclose b would be granted where no adequate justification existed for denying it and that authorisation would be refused only where such justification existed. But the possibility would of course exist that authority might be refused where no adequate justification existed for refusal, or at any rate where the former member firmly believed that no adequate justification existed. In this situation the former member is entitled to seek judicial review of the decision to refuse, c a course which the OSA 1989 does not seek to inhibit. In considering an application for judicial review of a decision to refuse authorisation to disclose, the court must apply (albeit from a judicial standpoint, and on the evidence before it) the same tests as are described in the last paragraph. It also will bear in mind the importance attached to the convention right of free expression. It d also will bear in mind the need for any restriction to be necessary to achieve one or more of the ends specified in art 10(2), to be responsive to a pressing social need and to be no more restrictive than is necessary to achieve that end.

[32] For the appellant it was argued that judicial review offered a person in his position no effective protection, since courts were reluctant to intervene in matters concerning national security and the threshold of showing a decision e to be irrational was so high as to give the applicant little chance of crossing it. Reliance was placed on the cases of *Chahal v UK* (1997) 1 BHRC 405 and *Tinnelly & Sons Ltd v UK* (1999) 27 EHRR 249, in each of which the European Court was critical of the effectiveness of the judicial review carried out.

[33] There are in my opinion two answers to this submission. First the f court's willingness to intervene will very much depend on the nature of the material which it is sought to disclose. If the issue concerns the disclosure of documents bearing a high security classification and there is apparently credible unchallenged evidence that disclosure is liable to lead to the identification of agents or the compromise of informers, the court may very well be unwilling to intervene. If, at the other end of the spectrum, it appears that while g disclosure of the material may cause embarrassment or arouse criticism, it will not damage any security or intelligence interest, the court's reaction is likely to be very different. Usually, a proposed disclosure will fall between these two extremes and the court must exercise its judgment, informed by art 10 considerations. The second answer is that in any application for judicial review h alleging an alleged violation of a convention right the court will now conduct a much more rigorous and intrusive review than was once thought to be permissible. The change was described by Lord Steyn in *R (on the application of Daly) v Secretary of State for the Home Dept* [2001] UKHL 26, [2001] 3 All ER 433, [2001] 2 AC 532 where after referring to the standards of review reflected in j *Associated Provincial Picture Houses Ltd v Wednesbury Corp* [1947] 2 All ER 680, [1948] 1 KB 223 and *R v Ministry of Defence, ex p Smith* [1996] 1 All ER 257, [1996] QB 517, he said:

'[26] ... There is a material difference between the *Wednesbury* and *Ex p Smith* grounds of review and the approach of proportionality applicable in respect of review where convention rights are at stake.

[27] The contours of the principle of proportionality are familiar. In *de Freitas v Permanent Secretary of Ministry of Agriculture, Fisheries, Lands and Housing* [1999] 1 AC 69, [1998] 3 WLR 675 the Privy Council adopted a three-stage test. Lord Clyde observed that in determining whether a limitation (by an act, rule or decision) is arbitrary or excessive the court should ask itself: "whether: (i) the legislative objective is sufficiently important to justify limiting a fundamental right; (ii) the measures designed to meet the legislative objective are rationally connected to it; and (iii) the means used to impair the right or freedom are no more than is necessary to accomplish the objective." (See [1999] 1 AC 69 at 80, [1998] 3 WLR 675 at 684.) Clearly, these criteria are more precise and more sophisticated than the traditional grounds of review. What is the difference for the disposal of concrete cases? Academic public lawyers have in remarkably similar terms elucidated the difference between the traditional grounds of review and the proportionality approach (see Professor Jeffrey Jowell QC "Beyond the Rule of Law: Towards Constitutional Judicial Review" [2000] PL 671; Craig *Administrative Law* (4th edn, 1999) pp 561–563; Professor David Feldman "Proportionality and the Human Rights Act 1998" in *The Principle of Proportionality in the Laws of Europe* (1999) pp 117, 127 et seq). The starting point is that there is an overlap between the traditional grounds of review and the approach of proportionality. Most cases would be decided in the same way whichever approach is adopted. But the intensity of review is somewhat greater under the proportionality approach. Making due allowance for important structural differences between various convention rights, which I do not propose to discuss, a few generalisations are perhaps permissible. I would mention three concrete differences without suggesting that my statement is exhaustive. First, the doctrine of proportionality may require the reviewing court to assess the balance which the decision maker has struck, not merely whether it is within the range of rational or reasonable decisions. Secondly, the proportionality test may go further than the traditional grounds of review in as much as it may require attention to be directed to the relative weight accorded to interests and considerations. Thirdly, even the heightened scrutiny test developed in *R v Ministry of Defence, ex p Smith* [1996] 1 All ER 257 at 263, [1996] QB 517 at 554 is not necessarily appropriate to the protection of human rights. It will be recalled that in *Ex p Smith* the Court of Appeal reluctantly felt compelled to reject a limitation on homosexuals in the army. The challenge based on art 8 of the [c]onvention ... (the right to respect for private and family life) foundered on the threshold required even by the anxious scrutiny test. The European Court of Human Rights came to the opposite conclusion: *Smith and Grady v UK* (1999) 29 EHRR 493. The court concluded (at 543 (para 138)): "the threshold at which the High Court and the Court of Appeal could find the Ministry of Defence policy irrational was placed so high that it effectively excluded any consideration by the domestic courts of the question of whether the interference with the applicants' rights answered a pressing social need or was proportionate to the national security and public order aims pursued, principles which lie at the heart of the Court's analysis of complaints under Article 8 of the Convention." In other words, the intensity of the review, in similar cases, is guaranteed by

a the twin requirements that the limitation of the right was necessary in a democratic society, in the sense of meeting a pressing social need, and the question whether the interference was really proportionate to the legitimate aim being pursued.

[28] The differences in approach between the traditional grounds of review and the proportionality approach may therefore sometimes yield

b different results. It is therefore important that cases involving convention rights must be analysed in the correct way.'

This approach contrasts sharply with that adopted in the authorities on which the appellant based his submission. In *Chahal v UK* (1997) 1 BHRC 405, on applications for both habeas corpus and judicial review, there was no effective

c judicial inquiry into the legality of the applicant's detention, and this was of even greater importance where the applicant faced the risk of torture or inhuman or degrading treatment (see (1997) 1 BHRC 405 at 433, 437 (paras 132, 150–151)). In *Tinnelly & Sons Ltd v UK* (1999) 27 EHRR 249 the issue of conclusive certificates had effectively prevented any judicial determination of the merits of the applicants' complaints (see (1999) 27 EHRR 249 at 290–291

d (para 77)).

[34] The appellant contended that even if, theoretically, judicial review offered a means of challenging an allegedly wrongful refusal of authorisation to disclose, it was in practice an unavailable means since private lawyers were not among those to whom disclosure could lawfully be made under s 7(3)(a), and a

e former member of the service could not be expected to initiate proceedings for judicial review without the benefit of legal advice and assistance. I would for my part accept that the fair hearing guaranteed by art 6(1) of the convention to everyone in the determination of their civil rights and obligations must ordinarily carry with it the right to seek legal advice and assistance from a lawyer outside the government service. But this is a matter to be resolved by

f seeking official authorisation under s 7(3)(b). The service would at that stage, depending on the nature of the material sought to be disclosed, be fully entitled to limit its authorisation to material in a redacted or anonymised or schematic form, to be specified by the service; but I cannot envisage circumstances in which it would be proper for the service to refuse its authorisation for any

g disclosure at all to a qualified lawyer from whom the former member wished to seek advice. If, at the hearing of an application for judicial review, it were necessary for the court to examine material said to be too sensitive to be disclosed to the former member's legal advisors, special arrangements could be made for the appointment of counsel to represent the applicant's interests as

h envisaged by the Court of Appeal in *Secretary of State for the Home Dept v Rehman* [2000] 3 All ER 778 at 788, [2000] 3 WLR 1240 at 1250–1251.

[35] There is one further safeguard which deserves mention. By s 9(1) of the OSA 1989 the consent of the Attorney General is required before any prosecution is instituted for an offence under (among other sections) ss 1(1),

j 4(1) and (3). The appellant submitted that this is not an effective safeguard since there are no criteria to govern the giving of consent. Successive Directors of Public Prosecutions, acting under the general superintendence of the Attorney General, have, however, published codes for the guidance of Crown prosecutors, and the practice of the Attorney General is to follow this guidance, although he may of course take a broader view of the public interest. The tests laid down comprise a merits or evidential test, requiring a realistic prospect of securing a conviction, and a public interest test. The Attorney General will not give his consent to prosecution unless he judges prosecution to be in the public interest. He is unlikely to consent if the disclosure alleged is trivial or the information disclosed stale and notorious or the facts are such as would not be thought by reasonable jurors or judges to merit the imposition of criminal sanctions. The consent of the Attorney General is required as a safeguard against ill-judged or ill-founded or improperly motivated or unnecessary prosecutions.

[36] The special position of those employed in the security and intelligence services, and the special nature of the work they carry out, impose duties and responsibilities on them within the meaning of art 10 (2) (see *Engel v The Netherlands (No 1)* (1976) 1 EHRR 647 at 684–685 (para 100); *Hadjianastassiou v Greece* (1993) 16 EHRR 219 at 240 (para 46)). These justify what Lord Griffiths called a bright line rule against disclosure of information of documents relating to security or intelligence obtained in the course of their duties by members or former members of those services. (While Lord Griffiths was willing to accept the theoretical possibility of a public interest defence, he made no allowance for judicial review (see *A-G v Guardian Newspapers Ltd (No 2)* [1988] 3 All ER 545 at 650, [1990] 1 AC 109 at 269).) If, within this limited category of case, a defendant is prosecuted for making an unauthorised disclosure it is necessary to relieve the prosecutor of the need to prove damage (beyond the damage inherent in disclosure by a former member of these services) and to deny the defendant a defence based on the public interest; otherwise the detailed facts concerning the disclosure and the arguments for and against making it would be canvassed before the court and the cure would be even worse than the disease. But it is plain that a sweeping, blanket ban, permitting of no exceptions, would be inconsistent with the general right guaranteed by art 10(1) and would not survive the rigorous and particular scrutiny required to give effect to art 10(2). The crux of this case is whether the safeguards built into the OSA 1989 are sufficient to ensure that unlawfulness and irregularity can be reported to those with the power and duty to take effective action, that the power to withhold authorisation to publish is not abused and that proper disclosures are not stifled. In my opinion the procedures discussed above, properly applied, provide sufficient and effective safeguards. It is, however, necessary that a member or former member of a relevant service should avail himself of the procedures available to him under the OSA 1989. A former member of a relevant service, prosecuted for making an unauthorised disclosure, cannot defend himself by contending that if he had made disclosure under s 7(3)(a) no notice or action would have been taken or that if he had sought authorisation under s 7(3)(b) it would have been refused. If a person who has given a binding undertaking of confidentiality seeks to be relieved, even in part, from that undertaking he must seek authorisation and, if so advised, challenge any refusal of authorisation. If that refusal is upheld by the courts, it must, however, reluctantly, be accepted. I am satisfied that ss 1(1), 4(1) and (3) of the OSA 1989 are compatible with art 10 of the convention; no question of reading those sections conformably with the convention or making a declaration of incompatibility therefore arises. On these crucial issues I am in agreement with both the judge and the Court of Appeal. They are issues on which the House can form its own opinion. But they are also issues on which Parliament has expressed a clear democratic judgment.

a [37] The House received and heard interesting submissions on behalf of the
Newspaper Society, nine newspapers and two television channels. But this
appeal calls for decision of no issue directly affecting the media and I think it
would be undesirable to attempt to give guidance in the context of this appeal.

[38] I would dismiss the appeal. I do not think it necessary to address the
specific questions certified by the Court of Appeal. When the matter returns to
b the judge he will direct the jury on the law, sum up the evidence as it then
stands, identify the issues which the jury have to decide and invite the jury to
return their verdict in the ordinary way.

LORD HOPE OF CRAIGHEAD.

c [39] My Lords, I have had the advantage of reading in draft the speech of my
noble and learned friend, Lord Bingham of Cornhill. I gratefully adopt his
narrative of the facts and of the legislative background. I respectfully agree
with all that he has said about the decision of the trial judge to make a
preparatory ruling and the defences of duress and necessity of circumstances. I
shall concentrate on the points which lie at the heart of this case.

d [40] It has been obvious ever since the publication of the government's
proposals for reform in its White Paper (*Reform of Section 2 of the Official Secrets
Act 1911* (Cm 408)) that it was not going to be easy to reconcile its rejection of
any proposal for a general defence that a disclosure of information was in the
public interest with art 10 (2) of the European Convention for the Protection of
e Human Rights and Fundamental Freedoms 1950 (as set out in Sch 1 to the
Human Rights Act 1998), which allows restrictions to be imposed upon the
right to freedom of expression if, but only if, the restriction is prescribed by law
and is necessary in a democratic society in the interests of national security.

[41] The fact that the White Paper did not mention the art 10 convention
f right leaves one with the uneasy feeling that, although the right of individual
petition under art 25 had been available to persons in this country since 1966,
the problems which it raises were overlooked. Many attempts were made in
both Houses of Parliament to introduce a public interest defence in one form
or another when the Bill was being discussed there, but they were all
unsuccessful. The Official Secrets Act 1989 (OSA 1989), when it finally
g emerged from the Parliamentary process, contained no such defence. The
effect of s 1(1) of the Act, construed according to the ordinary principles of
statutory interpretation, is that any unauthorised disclosure of information,
documents or articles relating to security or intelligence by anyone who is or
has been a member of the security and intelligence services is an offence,
h irrespective of whether or not its disclosure is or is likely to be harmful to the
interests of national security.

[42] The coming into force of the 1998 Act has revived interest in the
apparent lack of harmony between s 1(1) of the OSA 1989 and art 10(2) of the
convention. There appears to be general agreement among those writers who
have commented on the issue that it is likely to be difficult to reconcile them.
j For example, Clayton and Tomlinson *The Law of Human Rights* (2000) p 1105
state:

'**15.261** The Official Secrets Act 1989 is also difficult to reconcile with
Article 10. In particular, where restrictions on freedom of expression are
permissible without the need to prove damage, it is arguable that such

restrictions are unnecessary. Under section 1 the defendant could be liable
for disclosing information which is already in the public domain.   *a*

15.262 The 1989 Act does not include a "public interest defence". This
contrasts with proceedings for breach of confidence in which such a
defence is available. As Feldman points out (Feldman *Civil Liberties and
Human Rights in England and Wales* (1993)), this means that: "under all
provisions of the 1989 Act criminal liability may be imposed in   *b*
circumstances when no injunction could have been obtained to restrain
publication." (Feldman ... 669.) The result of these considerations is that:
"It seems likely ... that ... the restraints on freedom of expression resulting
from the [Official Secrets Act 1989 go] ... further than is necessary in a
democratic society." (R Stone, *Textbook on Civil Liberties* (2nd edn,
Blackstone 1997) 184.)'   *c*

[43] The White Paper noted that it had been difficult to find agreement on
the precise nature of the reform (see p 5 (para 13)). It acknowledged that there
was a case for a public interest defence, but it rejected it (see para 61). It did so
for two main reasons. The first was that a central objective of the reform was
to achieve maximum clarity in the law and its application. The view was taken   *d*
that a general public interest would make it impossible to achieve such clarity.
The second was that its proposals were designed to concentrate the
protection of the criminal law on information which demonstrably required
its protection in the public interest. It was recognised that what justifies the
application of the criminal law is the degree of harm to the public interest   *e*
which may result (see p 6 (para 14)). But the proposed test of harm was not
regarded as appropriate in the case of unauthorised disclosure of information
by members or former members of the security and intelligence services (see p
10 (para 41)). The view was taken that all such disclosures are harmful to the
public interest and ought to be criminal. This was because they reduce public
confidence in the services' ability to carry out their duties effectively and   *f*
loyally, and because they betray the members' duty of secrecy about their work
and the trust placed in them by people who give information to these services.
Under its proposals it would be for the courts to decide whether the disclosure
of particular information was criminal, and it was to be left to the jury to
safeguard the public interest (see p 16 (para 79)).   *g*

[44] These are powerful arguments. But they do not meet the points on
which the measure has been criticised, and there is no discussion in the White
Paper of the system under which the disclosure of information which it was in
the public interest to know about by former members of the security and
intelligence services might be officially authorised. Professor Stone points out   *h*
that those who support a public interest defence do not argue that it should
permit disclosures that are harmful, and he finds it hard to accept that there
could be no circumstances in which a public interest in disclosure would
outweigh the possible damage that might be caused by it (see *Civil Liberties and
Human Rights* (3rd edn, 2000) (para 5.6.6.3)). He concludes that the lack of any
public interest defence must make the OSA 1989 vulnerable.   *j*

[45] Against this background I would approach the question which lies at
the heart of this case from a position of considerable doubt as to whether the
problems which it raises have really been faced up to by the legislature. I would
place the onus firmly on those who seek to rely on art 10(2) to show that ss 1(1)
and 4(1) are compatible with the convention right.

[46] Two points in particular must be made at the outset. The first is that the construction that must be put on Mr Shayler's explanation for making the unauthorised disclosures with which he has been charged must be the most favourable to him, as he has not yet had an opportunity of giving evidence. The context is that of a preparatory hearing under s 29 of the Criminal Procedure and Investigations Act 1996, one of the purposes of which is to identify the issues that are likely to be material at the trial. At this stage he is entitled under art 6(2) of the convention, as well as under the common law, to the presumption of innocence. The second point is indicated by the jurisprudence of the Strasbourg Court. The provisions of ss 1(1) and 4(1) of the OSA 1989 under which Mr Shayler has been charged must be subjected to very close scrutiny in order to determine whether or not they are compatible.

The explanation

[47] When he was charged at Charing Cross Police Station after his arrest on 21 August 2000 Mr Shayler replied that he did not admit to making any disclosures which were contrary to the criminal law, that any disclosures made by him were made in the public and national interests and that in his defence he would rely on his right of freedom of expression as guaranteed by the common law, the 1998 Act and art 10 of the convention. He had not previously been interviewed, and he has made no other statement to the police.

[48] It is agreed in the statement of facts and issues that the bulk of the documents which he disclosed to the Mail on Sunday newspaper appeared to relate to security and defence matters and that they were classified at levels ranging from 'Classified' to 'Top Secret'. It is also agreed that certain of these documents included material obtained by or relating to the interception of communications in obedience to warrants issued by the Secretary of State under s 2 of the Interception of Communications Act 1985. But Mr Shayler does not admit that the disclosure of any of these documents was or would be likely to be damaging. It must be assumed in his favour at this stage, for the purposes of the public interest argument, that none of them was of that character. It is alleged that he was paid a substantial sum of money for his activities. But this fact also is not admitted, and I would regard it too as something that has yet to be proved.

[49] The public interest which Mr Shayler seeks to assert is the right of the public to be provided with information which will enable it to assess whether the powers given to the security and intelligence services are being abused and whether the services are being run properly. He seeks to draw attention to past incidents of misconduct. His point is that, unless the services are reformed, they will continue to be operated in a manner which creates a danger to the public in respect of life, limb and property. At the heart of the matter is the right of the public to make informed decisions about behaviour on the part of those who are responsible for these services. It is the right of the public to call the government to account wherever there is dishonesty, malpractice or inefficiency.

[50] The disclosures were made by Mr Shayler to the press. I narrate that simply as a fact, not as a ground for criticism. As Black J said in *New York Times v United States* (1971) 403 US 713 at 717, only a free and unrestrained press can effectively expose deception in government. Its role is to act as the eyes and ears of the people. Facts should not be withheld from it simply on the ground

that they are inconvenient or embarrassing. It is not suggested that Mr Shayler attempted to obtain official authorisation before making the disclosures. His position is that there were no effective steps that he could have taken through official channels to address his concerns, or that would have resulted in his being authorised to make the disclosures to the press. As the Court of Appeal said, there must be some doubt as to whether authorisation would have been given by the authorities if he had asked for it (see [2001] EWCA Crim 1977 at [23], [2001] 1 WLR 2206 at [23]). I think that it is equally doubtful whether all the ends which he was seeking to achieve could have been achieved by addressing his concerns to those to whom he could address them without being officially authorised.

[51] I would approach this case therefore on the basis that Mr Shayler may have good grounds for arguing that it was in the public interest that the matters which were of concern to him should be disclosed, and that the fact that he decided to disclose his concerns to the press is not in itself a ground for criticism.

The 1998 Act

[52] The context for the discussion about the compatibility of ss 1(1) and 4(1) of the OSA 1989 with art 10 of the convention can be stated quite simply. So far as it is possible to do so, these provisions must be read and given effect in a way that is compatible with convention rights (see s 3(1) of the 1998 Act). The word 'must' indicates, as Lord Steyn said in *R v A (No 2)* [2001] UKHL 25 at [44], [2001] 3 All ER 1 at [44], [2002] 1 AC 45, that the court must strive to read the statute in a way that is compatible. But the same word is also qualified by the phrase 'so far as it is possible to do so'. The obligation, powerful as it is, is not to be performed without regard to its limitations (see *R v Lambert* [2001] UKHL 37 at [79], [2001] 3 All ER 577 at [79], [2001] 3 WLR 206). The techniques of judicial interpretation on the one hand and of legislation on the other are different, and this fact must be respected. If compatibility cannot be achieved without overruling decisions which have already been taken on the very point at issue by the legislator, or if to do so would make the statute unintelligible or unworkable, it will be necessary to leave it to Parliament to amend the statute. The only option left to the court will be to make a declaration of incompatibility under s 4(2) of the Act.

[53] Mr Robertson QC for Mr Shayler did not suggest that a public interest defence as such could be read in to ss 1(1) and 4(1) of the 1989 Act. He did suggest that the word 'lawful' should be inserted into ss 1(9) and 4(3)(a) in a way which might achieve this result. But Moses J said that it was not possible to interpret the 1989 Act in this way (see his judgment at [78]–[81]). Mr Crow for the Secretary of State joined with the respondent in submitting that, if the Act is incompatible with Mr Shayler's convention rights, it cannot be interpreted compatibly with those rights by virtue of s 3 of the 1998 Act. I agree that, if the legislation is incompatible with Mr Shayler's convention rights, the position whether it should be amended so as to remove the incompatibility must be left to Parliament. This means that the issue of incompatibility can be addressed directly in this case, without the distraction of trying to resolve the issue by means of the technique of judicial interpretation.

The Strasbourg jurisprudence

a [54] Article 10(1) of the convention states that the right to freedom of expression includes the right to impart information and ideas without interference by public authorities. Article 10(2) states, by way of qualification, that the exercise of this right—

b 'since it carries with it duties and responsibilities, may be subject to such formalities, conditions, restrictions or penalties as are prescribed by law and are necessary ... in the interests of national security ...'

[55] The wording of art 10(2) as applied to this case indicates that any such restriction, if it is to be compatible with the convention right, must satisfy two basic requirements. First, the restriction must be 'prescribed by law'. So it c must satisfy the principle of legality. The second is that it must be such as is 'necessary' in the interests of national security. This raises the question of proportionality. The jurisprudence of the European Court of Human Rights explains how these principles are to be understood and applied in the context of the facts of this case. As any restriction with the right to freedom of d expression must be subjected to very close scrutiny, it is important to identify the requirements of that jurisprudence before undertaking that exercise.

[56] The principle of legality requires the court to address itself to three distinct questions. The first is whether there is a legal basis in domestic law for the restriction. The second is whether the law or rule in question is e sufficiently accessible to the individual who is affected by the restriction, and sufficiently precise to enable him to understand its scope and foresee the consequences of his actions so that he can regulate his conduct without breaking the law. The third is whether, assuming that these two requirements are satisfied, it is nevertheless open to the criticism on the convention ground that it was applied in a way that is arbitrary because, for example, it has been f resorted to in bad faith or in a way that is not proportionate. I derive these principles, which have been mentioned many times in subsequent cases, from *Sunday Times v UK* (1979) 2 EHRR 245 at 271 (para 49) and also from *Winterwerp v The Netherlands* (1979) 2 EHRR 387 at 402–403 (para 39) and *Engel v The Netherlands (No 1)* (1976) 1 EHRR 647 at 669–670 (paras 58–59) which were g concerned with the principle of legality in the context of art 5(1) (see also *A v The Scottish Ministers* 2001 SLT 1331 at 1336–1337).

[57] The phrase 'necessary ... in the interests of national security' has to be read in the light of art 18, which provides that the restrictions permitted under the convention must not be applied for any purpose other than those for which h they have been prescribed. The word 'necessary' in art 10(2) introduces the principle of proportionality, although the word as such does not appear anywhere in the convention: see *Handyside v UK* (1979) 1 EHRR 737 at 753–755 (paras 48–49). In its judgment the court said (para 49):

j 'The Court's supervisory functions oblige it to pay the utmost attention to the principles characterising a "democratic society". Freedom of expression constitutes one of the essential foundations of such a society, one of the basic conditions for its progress and for the development of every man ... This means, amongst other things, that every "formality", "condition", "restriction" or "penalty" imposed in this sphere must be proportionate to the legitimate aim pursued.'

[58] Applied to the circumstances of this case, this means that a restriction on the disclosure of information cannot be said to be 'necessary' in the interests of national security unless (a) 'relevant and sufficient reasons' are given by the national authority to justify the restriction, (b) the restriction on disclosure corresponds to a 'pressing social need' and (c) it is 'proportionate to the legitimate aim pursued' (see *Sunday Times v UK* (1979) 2 EHRR 245 at 277–278 (para 62)).

[59] The principle involves a question of balance between competing interests. But it is important to appreciate that there is a process of analysis that must be carried through. The starting point is that an authority which seeks to justify a restriction on a fundamental right on the ground of a pressing social need has a burden to discharge. There is a burden on the state to show that the legislative means adopted were no greater than necessary (see *R v Lambert* [2001] 3 All ER 577 at [37], [2001] 3 WLR 206 per Lord Steyn). As Sir Sydney Kentridge QC observed in his Tanner Lecture at Oxford, 'Human Rights: A Sense of Proportion', 26 February 2001:

> '"Necessary" does not mean indispensable, but it does connote the existence of a pressing social need ... It is only on the showing of such need that the question of proportionality or "balancing" should arise.'

[60] The European Court has not identified a consistent or uniform set of principles when considering the doctrine of proportionality (see Richard Clayton 'Regaining a Sense of Proportion: The Human Rights Act and the Proportionality Principle' [2001] EHRLR 504 at 510). But there is a general international understanding as to the matters which should be considered where a question is raised as to whether an interference with a fundamental right is proportionate.

[61] These matters were identified in the Privy Council case of *de Freitas v Permanent Secretary of Ministry of Agriculture, Fisheries, Lands and Housing* [1999] 1 AC 6, [1998] 3 WLR 675 by Lord Clyde. He adopted the three-stage test which is to be found in the analysis of Gubbay CJ in *Nyambirai v National Social Security Authority* [1996] 1 LRC 64, where he drew on jurisprudence from South Africa and Canada (see also *R (on the application of Daly) v Secretary of State for the Home Dept* [2001] UKHL 26 at [26], [27], [2001] 3 All ER 433 at [26], [27], [2001] 2 AC 532 per Lord Steyn; *R (on the application of Pretty) v DPP* [2001] UKHL 61 at [93], [2002] 1 All ER 1 at [93], [2001] 3 WLR 1598). The first is whether the objective which is sought to be achieved—the pressing social need—is sufficiently important to justify limiting the fundamental right. The second is whether the means chosen to limit that right are rational, fair and not arbitrary. The third is whether the means used impair the right as minimally as is reasonably possible. As these propositions indicate, it is not enough to assert that the decision that was taken was a reasonable one. A close and penetrating examination of the factual justification for the restriction is needed if the fundamental rights enshrined in the convention are to remain practical and effective for everyone who wishes to exercise them.

Further analysis: legality

[62] It is plain that the first requirement of the principle of legality is satisfied in this case, because the restrictions on the fundamental right are set out in ss 1 and 4 of the 1989 Act. We are dealing here with a statutory scheme for the

a protection of information relating to the security and intelligence services. In order to see whether the second and third requirements relating to accessibility, precision and lack of arbitrariness are satisfied it is necessary to look more closely at that scheme.

[63] Although there is no general public interest defence, the restriction on disclosure is certainly not a blanket restriction. The offences which are created *b* by ss 1(1) and 4(1) of the 1989 Act both relate only to the disclosure of information, documents or other articles to which those sections apply 'without lawful authority'. The meaning of the phrase 'lawful authority' is explained by s 7, which defines the circumstances in which the disclosure of any information to which the Act applies may be made with lawful authority. The relevant provision in the case of someone in Mr Shayler's position, who is no *c* longer a Crown servant as he is no longer a member of the security or intelligence services, is s 7(3). It provides:

> 'For the purposes of this Act a disclosure made by any other person is made with lawful authority if, and only if, it is made—(a) to a Crown servant for the purposes of his functions as such; or (b) in accordance with *d* an official authorisation.'

[64] The expression 'Crown servant' is defined in s 12(1). It includes a minster of the Crown, any person employed in the civil service of the Crown, any constable and any person who is a member or employee of a prescribed body or a body of a prescribed class or is the holder of a prescribed office. The *e* word 'prescribed' means prescribed by an order made for the purposes of that subsection (see s 12(3)). Opportunities also exist for disclosure through their civil service staff to the Security Service Commissioner appointed under s 4 of the Security Service Act 1989, the Commissioner for the Secret Intelligence Service under s 8 of the Intelligence Services Act 1994, the Commissioner *f* appointed under s 7 of the Interception of Communications Act 1985 and the Intelligence and Security Committee. I do not think that a person who has read the relevant provisions of these statutes and the orders made under them can be said to have been left in any doubt as to the wide range of persons to whom an authorised disclosure may be made for the purposes of their respective *g* functions without having first obtained an official authorisation. Section 2(2)(b) of the Security Service Act 1989 imposes a duty on the Director General of the security service to secure that disclosures are made for the discharge of the service's functions. In *Esbester v UK* (1994) 18 EHRR CD 72 at 74 the Commission rejected an argument that the fact that the guidelines relating to the Director General's supervision of information obtained by the security *h* service were unpublished meant that they were not sufficiently accessible to the individual.

[65] In this connection it should be noted that Mr Shayler signed a declaration on leaving the service in which he acknowledged that his attention had been drawn to the OSA 1989 and the consequences that might follow any *j* breach, and that he understood he was liable to be prosecuted if he disclosed either orally or in writing any information or material which had come into his possession as a result of his employment as a Crown servant on terms requiring it to be held in confidence unless he had previously obtained the official sanction in writing of the service by which he was appointed. He also acknowledged that to obtain such sanction—

'two copies of the manuscript of any article, book, play, film, speech or broadcast, intended for publication, which contains such information or material shall be submitted to the Director General.'

In fact, the class of person from whom official authorisation may be obtained in terms of s 7(5) of the OSA 1989 is very wide.

[66] Whether making use of the opportunities of disclosure to Crown servants would have been a practical and effective means of addressing the points which Mr Shayler wished to raise is another matter. The alternative, which requires the seeking of an official authorisation duly given by a Crown servant, is not further explained in the Act. It too requires more careful examination. I shall have to return to these points once I have set the scene for their examination more precisely.

Further analysis: proportionality

[67] The objective which is sought to be achieved by the Act is to safeguard national security by preventing the disclosure to unauthorised persons of information relating to the work of the security and intelligence services. Long before the horrific events of 11 September 2001 in New York and Washington it was recognised by the European Court of Human Rights that democratic societies are threatened by highly sophisticated forms of espionage and by terrorism. The court held that they have to be able to take measures which will enable them to counter such threats effectively (see *Klass v Germany* (1978) 2 EHRR 214 at 232 (para 48)). But it stressed in the same case (at 232–233 (para 50)) that it must be satisfied that there exist adequate and effective guarantees that such measures will not be abused. An assessment of their adequacy and effectiveness depends on all the circumstances of the case, such as the scope and duration of the possible measures, the grounds required for ordering such measures, the authorities competent to permit, carry out and supervise such measures, and the kind of remedy provided by the national law.

[68] So it is not enough for the authorities to show in general terms that a restriction on disclosure is needed in the interests of national security. There is, of course, an obvious risk that unauthorised disclosures will impair the efficiency of the work done by the security and intelligence services. Lives may be put at risk, sources of information compromised, operations undermined and vital contacts with friendly foreign intelligence agencies terminated. These points need not be elaborated. It is clear that the state is entitled to impose restrictions on the disclosure of information by members or former members of those services who have had access to information relating to national security, having regard to their specific duties and responsibilities and the obligation of discretion by which they are bound (see *Leander v Sweden* (1987) 9 EHRR 433 at 452–453 (para 59); *Hadjianastassiou v Greece* (1993) 16 EHRR 219 at 239–240 (paras 45–47)). The margin of appreciation which is available to the contracting states in assessing the pressing social need and choosing the means of achieving the legitimate aim is a wide one (see *Leander's* case (1987) 9 EHRR 433 at 452–453 (para 59); *Esbester v UK* (1994) 18 EHRR CD 72 at 74). The special nature of terrorist crime, the threat which it presents to a democratic society and the exigencies of dealing with it must also be brought into account (see *Murray v UK* (1995) 19 EHRR 193 at 222 (para 47)).

[69] The problem is that, if they are to be compatible with the convention right, the nature of the restrictions must be sensitive to the facts of each case if

a they are to satisfy the second and third requirements of proportionality. The restrictions must be rational, fair and not arbitrary, and they must impair the fundamental right no more than is necessary.

[70] As I see it, the scheme of the Act is vulnerable to criticism on the ground that it lacks the necessary degree of sensitivity. There must, as I have said, be some doubt as to whether a whistle-blower who believes that he has good *b* grounds for asserting that abuses are being perpetrated by the security or intelligence services will be able to persuade those to whom he can make disclosures to take his allegations seriously, to persevere with them and to effect the changes which, if there is substance in them, are necessary. The integrity and energy of Crown servants, as defined in s 12(1) of the OSA 1989, *c* of the commissioners and members of the Intelligence and Security Committee is not in question. But one must be realistic, as the Court of Appeal recognised. Institutions tend to protect their own and to resist criticism from wherever it may come. Where this occurs it may require the injection of a breath of fresh air from outside before institutional defects are recognised and rectified. On the other hand, the sensitivity and effectiveness of this system has not been *d* tested, as Mr Shayler chose not to make use of any of these opportunities.

[71] The official authorisation system provides the final opportunity. It too has not been tested by Mr Shayler. But it must be effective, if the restrictions are not to be regarded as arbitrary and as having impaired the fundamental right to an extent that is more than necessary. Here too there must be some *e* doubt as to its adequacy. I do not regard the fact that the Act does not define the process of official authorisation beyond referring in s 7(5) to the persons by or on behalf of whom it is to be given as a serious defect. The Court of Justice of the European Communities has held that art 17 of the Staff Regulations, which requires an official of the Commission of the European Communities to obtain prior permission for the publication of material dealing with the work of *f* the Commission, is compatible with the right of freedom of expression in art 10 (see *Connolly v Commission of the European Communities* Case C-274/99 (6 March 2001, unreported)). Members and former members of the security and intelligence services are unlikely to be in doubt as to whom they should turn for this purpose, and common sense suggests that no further formalities require *g* to be laid down (see [64], [65], above). The defect lies in the fact that the Act does not identify the criteria that officials should bear in mind when taking decisions as to whether or not a disclosure should be authorised.

[72] But the scheme of the Act does not stand alone. Any decision to decline an official authorisation will be subject to judicial review. The European Court *h* of Human Rights has recognised, in the context of a complaint of lack of impartiality in breach of the art 6(1) convention right, the value which is to be attached to a process of review by a judicial body that has full jurisdiction and provides the guarantees of that article (see *Bryan v UK* (1995) 21 EHRR 342 at 360–361 (paras 44, 46); *Kingsley v UK* (2001) 33 EHRR 288; *Porter v Magill* [2001] UKHL 67 at [93], [2002] 1 All ER 465 at [93], [2002] 2 WLR 37). I would apply *j* that reasoning to the present case. An effective system of judicial review can provide the guarantees that appear to be lacking in the statute. Two questions then arise. First, there is a procedural point. The list of Crown servants in s 12(1), to whom disclosures may be made under s 7(3)(a) without an official authorisation, does not include those to whom the applicant may wish to turn for legal assistance. The second is a point of substance. Is the process of judicial

review capable of providing the intensity of review that is needed to satisfy the
requirements of the convention right?

[73] The procedural point can, I think, be met by the authorisation system
itself with judicial review with regard to it as the ultimate safeguard. Each case
will have to be taken on its own facts, but the basic principle is that everyone is
entitled to a lawyer of his own choosing in the determination of his civil rights
and obligations or of any criminal charge against him. This is a matter of
express provision in art 6(3)(c) in the case of a person who has been charged
with a criminal offence. At the stage when authorisation is being sought the
matter to be determined still lies within the scope of the person's civil rights and
obligations. But he is nevertheless entitled to a fair hearing under art 6(1). I
think that it follows that he has an implied right to legal assistance of his own
choosing, especially if his dispute is with the state. Access to legal advice is one
of the fundamental rights enjoyed by every citizen under the common law.

[74] It was suggested to your Lordships that, if the matter was particularly
sensitive, authorisation could be given on condition that the person who is to
provide legal assistance agrees to be notified under s 1(6) of the Act that he is
subject to the provisions of s 1(1). That solution carries with it the risk of
criminal sanctions in the event of any breach of the statutory restriction, and it
would be open to objection on convention grounds if freedom of choice was at
risk of being inhibited. But the same objection is unlikely to be present if all that
is sought is the giving of undertakings sufficient to ensure that any information
is properly safeguarded.

[75] As for the point of substance, it has now been recognised that, although
there is an overlap between them, a greater intensity of review is available
under the proportionality approach to issues relating to alleged breaches of
convention rights than is the case where the review is conducted on the
traditional *Wednesbury* grounds (see *Associated Provincial Picture Houses Ltd v
Wednesbury Corp* [1947] 2 All ER 680, [1948] 1 KB 223): see *R (on the application
of Daly) v Secretary of State for the Home Dept* [2001] 3 All ER 433 at [23] per Lord
Bingham of Cornhill and Lord Steyn (at [27]). As Lord Steyn explained in that
case (at [27]), the doctrine of proportionality may require the reviewing court
to assess the balance which the decision maker has struck, not merely whether
it is within the range of rational or reasonable decisions. It may also require
attention to be directed to the relative weight which is to be accorded to
different interests and considerations. It is, above all, important that cases
involving convention rights are analysed in the right way.

[76] As Lord Steyn acknowledged in his judgment in *Daly's* case (at [27]),
much useful guidance on the difference between the traditional grounds of
judicial review and the proportionality approach can be found in the work of
academic public lawyers on this subject. Professor David Feldman points out
in his essay, 'Proportionality and the Human Rights Act 1998', in *The Principle
of Proportionality in the Laws of Europe* edited by Evelyn Ellis (1999), pp 123–124
that it is necessary first clearly to understand the place which the doctrine of
proportionality occupies in the structure of analysis under the Human Rights
Act 1998 (see also Feldman *Civil Liberties and Human Rights in England and Wales*
(2nd edn, 2002), pp 55–57). As Professor Feldman explains, the principle is
relevant only at a very late stage in the analysis of a case, when the court has
decided that that a convention right has been interfered with and that the
justification offered by the state has a basis in domestic law and was or may

a have been for a legitimate purpose. At the end of the process of reasoning, where there is doubt about the justifiability of an established infringement of a convention right, the principle allows the court to balance the reasons for and against regarding the infringement as justifiable. In his essay he made these points which have a particular bearing on the present case (p 134):

b   'In some cases, then, no balancing of rights against security will be permitted. Even where non-absolute rights are in issue, the careful balancing required by a doctrine of proportionality should become a major check on the acceptability of claims to the shield of national security, both in relation to the existence of threats to national security and their significance in relation to the interference with rights in the particular case.
c   There will be some cases in which the national security considerations are so sensitive and important that the courts will still decline to intervene, but the doctrine of proportionality should be able to operate (giving appropriate but not unquestioning weight to national security) whenever the court is not satisfied that it ought to treat the particular type of national
d   security consideration as being of such overriding sensitivity and importance as to make the decision in respect of it essentially non-justiciable.'

[77] Professor Jeffrey Jowell QC has also emphasised the importance of the carefully constructed set of criteria which the process of analysis involves. In
e 'Beyond the Rule of Law: Towards Constitutional Judicial Review' [2000] PL 671 at 679 he explains that a test for proportionality is more sophisticated than that undertaken in English administrative law. As he puts it, the administrative law test is not rooted in any particular criteria but is, by and large, a test as to whether relevant considerations have been properly weighed or balanced. As
f for proportionality, it is a test of constitutionality. It is both too simple and wrong to equate it with a merits test, but it involves more than a heightened scrutiny of the decision in question:

     'It starts by asking whether the breach is justifiable in terms of the aims it seeks. Some Convention rights can only be violated for a specific purpose
g   (such as national security) and therefore other aims would not be legitimate, whatever their rationale. It then proceeds to consider whether in reality those aims are capable of being achieved. Spurious or impractical aims will not suffice. It then goes on to consider whether less restrictive means could have been employed. The breach must be the minimum
h   necessary. Finally it asks whether the breach is necessary (not merely desirable or reasonable) in the interest of democracy. Only a "pressing social need" can justify the breach of a fundamental right.'

[78] In *Smith v UK* (1999) 29 EHRR 493 at 543 (para 138) the European Court
j said that the threshold of review had been placed so high in that case by the High Court and the Court of Appeal that it effectively excluded any consideration by the domestic courts of the question whether the interference with the applicants' rights answered a pressing social need or was proportionate to the national security and public order claims pursued by the Ministry of Defence policy which placed a limitation on homosexuals in the army. It is now clear that, if the approach which was explained and approved in *Daly*'s case

is adopted, the more precise method of analysis which is provided by the test of proportionality will be a much more effective safeguard.

[79] So I would hold that, where a refusal of official authorisation under s 7(3)(b) to disclose information is in issue, the court should address the following questions: (1) what, with respect to that information, was the justification for the interference with the convention right? (2) If the justification was that this was in the interests of national security, was there a pressing social need for that information not to be disclosed? And (3) if there was such a need, was the interference with the convention right which was involved in withholding authorisation for the disclosure of that information no more than was necessary. This structured approach to judicial control of the question whether official authorisation should or should not be given will enable the court to give proper weight to the public interest considerations in favour of disclosure, while taking into account at the same time the informed view of the primary decision maker. By adopting this approach the court will be giving effect to its duty under s 6(1) of the Human Rights Act 1998 to act in a way that is compatible with the convention rights (see [58], above).

Where the balance lies

[80] The question is whether the scheme of the OSA 1989, safeguarded by a system of judicial review which applies the test of proportionality, falls within the wide margin of discretion which is to be accorded to the legislature in matters relating to national security especially where the convention rights of others such as the right to life may be put in jeopardy (see *Leander v Sweden* (1987) 9 EHRR 433 at 452–453 (para 59); *Chassagnou v France* (2000) 7 BHRC 151 at 184–185 (paras 112–113)). I do not think that it can be answered without taking into account the alternatives.

[81] It has not been suggested that the disclosure of information relating to the work of the security and intelligence services should be unrestricted. The European Court has held that a democratic state is entitled to impose a duty of discretion on civil servants, on account of their status provided that a fair balance is struck between their fundamental right to freedom of expression and the legitimate interests of the state (see *Vogt v Germany* (1996) 21 EHRR 205 at 235 (para 53)). On the one hand there is the system of control laid down by s 7(3) of the Act, which permits disclosure to Crown servants as defined in s 12(1) for the purposes of their functions as such but not otherwise unless the disclosure is officially authorised. As part of this system undertakings to abide by it are given by members of the security and intelligence services on taking up their employment, so that they are left in no doubt about the restrictions. On the other there is a system of individual decision as to what it is in the public interest to disclose. This is subject to control of wider publication by the court on the grounds discussed in *A-G v Guardian Newspapers Ltd (No 2)* [1988] 3 All ER 545, [1990] 1 AC 109. It would be subject also to the imposition of the criminal sanction, if there was a general defence to an unauthorised disclosure on public interest grounds and the prosecution could prove that there was no public interest to be served by the disclosure.

[82] It was suggested in the course of the argument that a contrast should be drawn between judicial review of a decision to withhold authorisation and the factors to be taken into account where an injunction is sought to prevent the publication of disclosed material. Reference was made to Lord Griffiths' speech

a in *A-G v Guardian Newspapers Ltd (No 2)* [1988] 3 All ER 545 at 652, [1990] 1 AC 109 at 273 where he said that, while the court cannot brush aside claims that publication will imperil national security, it must examine and weigh against the countervailing public interest of freedom of speech and the right of people in a democracy to be informed by a free press. The suggestion was that judicial review on traditional *Wednesbury* grounds would fall short of the degree of

b scrutiny which the court can bring to bear in injunction cases. But once the full scope and intensity of judicial review of individual decisions to withhold official authorisation on proportionality grounds is recognised, there is parity on this point between the two systems. The essential difference between the two systems is between the taking of decisions on public interest grounds before disclosure on the one hand and taking those decisions after disclosure on the

c other.

[83] It is plain that these two alternatives are not exactly two sides of the same coin. One system of control depends ultimately on judicial review of decisions taken beforehand by administrators. Control under the other system would depend ultimately on decisions taken after the event by judges and juries

d in the criminal process. There is a choice to be made, and it seems to me that the choice of a system which favours official authorisation before disclosure subject to judicial review on grounds of proportionality is within the margin of discretion which ought to be accorded to the legislature.

[84] In favour of that choice there are a number of important factors.

e However well-intentioned he or she may be, a member or former member of the security or intelligence services may not be equipped with sufficient information to understand the potential impact of any disclosure. It may cause far more damage than the person making the disclosure was ever in a position to anticipate. The criminal process risks compounding the potential for

f damage to the operations of these services, if the prosecution have to prove beyond reasonable doubt the damaging nature of the disclosures.

[85] As Mr Crow for the Secretary of State pointed out, there is for this reason a serious risk that disclosures of security and intelligence material would go unprosecuted if the strict controls of ss 1(1) and 4(1) of the OSA 1989 were not in place. This is not a new point, as it was mentioned in the White Paper

g (see para 39). And it has to be borne in mind that a successful prosecution will do nothing to remedy the damage that a disclosure of security or intelligence information may have caused. Damage already done may well be irreparable, and the gathering together and disclosure of evidence to prove the nature and extent of the damage may compound its effects to the further detriment of

h national security. I think therefore that there is in the end a strong case for insisting upon a system which provides for the matter to be addressed by requiring that official authorisation be obtained by former members of the security and intelligence services, if necessary after judicial review of any refusal on grounds of proportionality, before any disclosures are made by them

j other than to Crown servants of information, documents or other articles to which ss 1(1) and 4(1) of the Act apply.

Conclusion

[86] For these reasons, and for those given by my noble and learned friend, Lord Bingham, with which I agree, I would hold that the provisions of the OSA

1989 under which Mr Shayler has been charged are not incompatible with his art 10 convention right. I would dismiss the appeal.

LORD HUTTON.

[87] My Lords, I have had the advantage of reading in draft the speech of my noble and learned friend, Lord Bingham of Cornhill. For the reasons which he gives I agree that the judge, Moses J, was fully entitled to hold a preparatory hearing pursuant to s 29 of the Criminal Procedure and Investigations Act 1996 and that the judge acted within his powers in the course of that hearing. I further agree that on ordinary principles of construction ss 1 and 4 of the Official Secrets Act 1989 (OSA 1989) do not permit a defendant to raise a defence that the information which he disclosed without lawful authority was disclosed by him in the public interest when those sections are considered without regard to art 10 of the European Convention for the Protection of Human Rights and Fundamental Freedoms 1950 (as set out in Sch 1 to the Human Rights Act 1998).

[88] Therefore I turn to consider the principal issue which arose before your Lordships, which is whether this construction infringes the provisions of art 10. Article 10(1) provides:

'Everyone has the right to freedom of expression. This right shall include freedom to hold opinions and to receive and impart information and ideas without interference by public authority and regardless of frontiers. This Article shall not prevent States from requiring the licensing of broadcasting, television or cinema enterprises.'

[89] The appellant submitted that the prohibitions imposed by ss 1 and 4 and his prosecution under those sections infringe his right to impart information about the security service of which he was formerly a member without interference by public authority. He further submitted that the infringement is the more serious because the information which he disclosed was given by him to the press, and the freedom of the press to receive information of public interest and to publish it is one of the great bulwarks of democracy.

[90] I commence the consideration of these submissions and the submissions of the Crown by observing, as did Bingham LJ in *A-G v Guardian Newspapers Ltd (No 2)* [1988] 3 All ER 545 at 623, [1990] 1 AC 109 at 213 (the *Spycatcher* case), that they represent a clash between two competing aspects of the public interest. On the one hand there is the assertion by the appellant of the public interest in freedom of speech and the exercise of that freedom by those who give information to the press so that the press may publish it and comment on it for the public benefit. On the other hand there is the reliance by the Crown on the public interest in the maintenance of the secrecy of the work of the Security Service so that it can operate effectively to protect national security. Both interests are valid and important and it is for the courts to resolve the clash of interests and to decide how the balance is to be struck.

[91] In carrying out this function in the present case the courts must look for guidance to the terms of art 10 and also to the decisions of the European Court of Human Rights in applying that article to the cases which have come before it.

[92] Article 10 itself recognises in express terms that there will be clashes between the right to impart information without interference by public

a authority and the interests of national security and that in some circumstances the interests of national security must prevail and art 10(2) provides:

> 'The exercise of these freedoms, since it carries with it duties and responsibilities, may be subject to such formalities, conditions, restrictions or penalties as are prescribed by law and are necessary in a democratic society, in the interests of national security, territorial integrity or public
b safety, for the prevention of disorder or crime, for the protection of health or morals, for the protection of the reputation or rights of others, for preventing the disclosure of information received in confidence, or for maintaining the authority and impartiality of the judiciary.'

c The wording of art 10(2) directs attention to a number of matters and requirements and I propose to consider them in turn.

Duties and responsibilities

[93] Article 10(2) recognises that the exercise of the freedoms set out in art 10(1) carries with it duties and responsibilities which may give rise to
d restrictions. It is clear that in its decisions determining whether restrictions on the freedom of expression are justified under art 10(2) the European Court recognises that the particular position which a person holds and the work which he carries out may impose special duties and responsibilities upon him. In *Engel v The Netherlands (No 1)* (1976) 1 EHRR 647 the European Court found there had been no violation of art 10. In that case two soldiers had been
e committed to a disciplinary unit for having taken part in the publication and distribution of a writing tending to undermine discipline. The court stated in its decision (at 685 (para 100)):

> 'The court doubtless has jurisdiction to supervise, under the Convention,
f the manner in which the domestic law of the Netherlands has been applied in the present case, but it must not in this respect disregard either the particular characteristics of military life (para. 54 *in fine* above), the specific "duties" and "responsibilities" incumbent on members of the armed forces, or the margin of appreciation that Article 10(2), like Article 8(2), leaves to the Contracting States.'

g And the court stated (at 685):

> '102. [Two of the applicants] allege a dual breach of Articles 10 and 14 taken together. They stress that a civilian in the Netherlands in a comparable situation does not risk the slightest penalty. In addition, they
h claim to have been punished more severely than a number of Netherlands servicemen, not belonging to the V.V.D.M. [(Conscript Servicemen's Association)], who had also been prosecuted for writing or distribution material likely to undermine military discipline.
>
> 103. On the first question, the court emphasises that the distinction at
j issue is explicable by the differences between the conditions of military and of civil life and, more specifically, by the "duties" and "responsibilities" peculiar to members of the armed forces in the field of freedom of expression.'

[94] In *Hadjianastassiou v Greece* (1993) 16 EHRR 219 the applicant, a serving officer, was in charge of a project for the design and production of a guided

missile and he submitted a report to the air force on the missile on which he had been working. The following year he communicated to a private company another technical study on guided missiles which he had prepared himself. He was convicted and sentenced for having disclosed military information relating to the design and produce of guided missiles to a private company. The domestic court concluded that although the disclosed study differed from the one used by the air force, none the less some transfer of technical knowledge had inevitably occurred. The European Court found that there had been no violation of art 10. In its decision the court stated (at 240):

'46. It is also necessary to take into account the special conditions attaching to military life and the specific "duties" and "responsibilities" incumbent on the members of the armed forces. The applicant, as the officer at the KETA [(Air Force Technical Research Centre)] in charge of an experimental missile programme, as bound by an obligation of discretion in relation to anything concerning the performance of his duties.

47. In the light of these considerations, the Greek military courts cannot be said to have overstepped the limits of the margin of appreciation which is to be left to the domestic authorities in matters of national security. Nor does the evidence disclose the lack of a reasonable relationship of proportionality between the means employed and the legitimate aim pursued.'

[95] In the present case also there were special conditions attached to life in the security service and there were special duties and responsibilities incumbent on the appellant whereby, unlike the great majority of other citizens, he was prohibited by statute from disclosing information about his work or about the actions of others engaged in the same work. Moreover these duties and responsibilities were specifically acknowledged and accepted by the appellant. The agreed statement of facts in the present case states:

'The appellant was a member of the Security Service ("the Service") from November 1991 to October 1996. At the outset of his service he signed an Official Secrets Act 1989 ("OSA") declaration acknowledging the confidential nature of documents and other information relating to security or intelligence, defence or international relations that might come into his possession as a result of his position; he also signed an acknowledgment that he was under a contractual obligation not to disclose, without authority, any information that came into his possession by virtue of his employment. On leaving the Service he signed a further OSA declaration acknowledging that the provisions of the Act continued to apply to him notwithstanding the termination of his appointment, and that the same requirements of confidentiality continued to apply to any information, documents or other articles relating to security or intelligence, defence or international relations which might have come into his possession as a result of his previous employment.'

Therefore in considering whether the restrictions contained in ss 1 and 4 of the OSA 1989 were permissible under art 10(2) it is relevant to take into account that the appellant was subject to particular duties and responsibilities arising from his membership of the security service.

Such restrictions or penalties as are prescribed by law

a [96] In my opinion the restrictions and penalties to which the appellant was subject are prescribed by law. The terms of ss 1 and 4 of the Act are clear. Each section prohibits the disclosure of information 'without lawful authority' and s 7(3) of the Act provides:

b 'For the purposes of this Act a disclosure made by any other person which includes a former member of the Security Service is made with lawful authority if, and only if, it is made—(a) to a Crown servant for the purposes of his functions as such; or (b) in accordance with an official authorisation.'

c Section 12(1) defines who is a 'Crown servant':

'(1) In this Act "Crown servant" means—(a) a Minister of the Crown; (b) a person appointed under section 8 of the Northern Ireland Constitution Act 1973 (the Northern Ireland Executive etc); (c) any person employed in the civil service of the Crown, including Her Majesty's Diplomatic Service,
d Her Majesty's Overseas Civil Service, the civil service of Northern Ireland and the Northern Ireland Court Service; (d) any member of the naval, military or air forces of the Crown, including any person employed by an association established for the purposes of Part XI of the Reserve Forces Act 1996; (e) any constable and any other person employed or appointed in or for the purposes of any police force (including a police force within the
e meaning of the Police Act (Northern Ireland) 1970); (f) any person who is a member or employee of a prescribed body or a body of a prescribed class and either is prescribed for the purposes of this paragraph or belongs to a prescribed class of members or employees of any such body; (g) any person who is the holder of a prescribed office or who is an employee of such a
f holder and either is prescribed for the purposes of this paragraph or belongs to a prescribed class of such employees.'

Section 13(1) defines the meaning of 'prescribed': '"prescribed" means prescribed by an order made by the Secretary of State.' And s 7(5) defines the meaning of 'official authorisation':

g 'In this section "official authorisation" and "official restriction" mean, subject to subsection (6) below, an authorisation or restriction duly given or imposed by a Crown servant or government contractor or by or on behalf of a prescribed body or a body of a prescribed class.'

h It is also relevant to note that the declaration which the appellant signed on leaving the security service stated that in order to obtain the official sanction of the service to publish any material two copies of the manuscript of the work containing such information should be submitted to the Director General.

Necessary in a democratic society in the interests of national security

j [97] The judgments of the European Court have established that these words contain two requirements. First, the restrictions on the imparting of information must pursue a legitimate aim and, secondly, the requirements must be necessary in a democratic society. In addition the reasons given by the national authority to justify the restrictions must be relevant and sufficient under art 10(2) (see *Sunday Times v UK* (1979) 2 EHRR 245 at 277–278 (para 62),

Barthold v Germany (1985) 7 EHRR 383 at 402 (para 55) and *Lingens v Austria* (1986) 8 EHRR 407 at 418 (para 39)).

A legitimate aim

[98] The function of the security service is to protect national security against threats from espionage, terrorism and sabotage and from actions intended to overthrow or undermine Parliamentary democracy (see s 1 of the Security Service Act 1989). In order to carry out this function effectively I consider it to be clear that the security service must operate under and be protected by a cloak of secrecy. This view is in conformity with the judgment of the European Court in *Vereniging Weekblad Bluf! v Netherlands* (1995) 20 EHRR 189 which related to the restriction on a publication of a report prepared by the BVD, the internal security service of the Netherlands. The court stated in its decision (at 201–202):

'35. The Court recognises that the proper functioning of a democratic society based on the rule of law may call for institutions like the BVD which, in order to be effective, must operate in secret and be afforded the necessary protection. In this way a state may protect itself against the activities of individuals and groups attempting to undermine the basic values of a democratic society.

36. In view of the particular circumstances of the case and the actual terms of the decisions of the relevant courts, the interferences were unquestionably designed to protect national security, a legitimate aim under Article 10(2).'

Therefore I consider that the restrictions imposed by ss 1 and 4 of the OSA 1989 were imposed for a legitimate aim.

Necessary in a democratic society

[99] As regards the second requirement, the judgments of the European Court have also established that a restriction which is necessary in a democratic society must be one which is required by a pressing social need and is proportionate to the legitimate aim pursued. On these issues the appellant advanced two principal arguments. One argument was that whilst there are many matters relating to the work of the security service which require to be kept secret in the interests of national security, there are other matters where there is no pressing need for secrecy and where the prohibition of disclosure and the sanction of criminal punishment are a disproportionate response. An example of such a matter would be where a political figure in the United Kingdom had been under surveillance for a period a considerable number of years ago. It was submitted that the disclosure of such information could not constitute any impairment of national security or hinder in any way the efficient working of the security service.

[100] I am unable to accept this submission. It has been recognised in decisions in this jurisdiction that the disclosure of any part of the work or activities of the security service by a member or past member would have a detrimental effect upon the service and its members because it would impair the confidence of the members in each other and would also impair the confidence of those, whether informers or the intelligence services of other states, who would entrust secret information to the security service of the

United Kingdom on the understanding and expectation that such information
would never be revealed to the outside world. As Lord Nicholls of Birkenhead
stated in *A-G v Blake (Jonathan Cape Ltd, third party)* [2000] 4 All ER 385 at
399–400, [2001] 1 AC 268 at 287:

> 'It is of paramount importance that members of the service should have
> complete confidence in all their dealings with each other, and that those
> recruited as informers should have the like confidence. Undermining the
> willingness of prospective informers to co-operate with the services, or
> undermining the morale and trust between members of the services when
> engaged on secret and dangerous operations, would jeopardise the
> effectiveness of the service. An absolute rule against disclosure, visible to
> all, makes good sense.'

[101] Moreover the appellant's submission is advanced on the basis that it
would be for the individual member or past member of the security service
who wished to make public a particular piece of information to decide himself
whether its disclosure would or would not be damaging to the work of the
service. But such a decision could not safely be left to that individual because
he may not have a full appreciation of how that piece of information fits into a
wider picture and of what effect the disclosure might have on other aspects of
the work of the service of which he is unaware or of which he lacks a full
appreciation. Moreover there is the risk that on some occasions the individual
making the decision may be motivated in varying degrees by desire for money
or by spite or by some similar emotion.

[102] The second submission advanced by the appellant was that the
restrictions contained in ss 1 and 4 of the OSA 1989 were too wide and were
therefore disproportionate because they prevented a member or past member
of the security service from revealing to the public through the press or other
sections of the media information that the security service had engaged in
illegal activities or that its work was conducted in an incompetent and
disorganised way. The appellant submitted that the disclosure of such matters
was required in the public interest, because unless such matters were disclosed
the public would be unable to demand that steps should be taken to stop such
conduct and to ensure that the work of the service was lawfully and
competently carried out.

[103] In answer to this submission the Crown made the reply that under
s 7(3)(a) there are a considerable number of senior and responsible Crown
servants to whom the appellant could have gone with his concerns and with a
request that the conduct of which he complained should be investigated and
that, if established, appropriate steps should be taken to punish it or to stop it.
If he were concerned about unlawful activity he could have given information
to the Attorney General, the Director of Public Prosecutions or the Commissioner
of the Metropolitan Police. If he were concerned about incompetence or
maladministration he could have brought his concerns to any one of the wide
range of Crown servants, including government ministers and senior civil
servants who are listed in s 12(1) of the OSA 1989.

[104] The appellant's response to this reply by the Crown was that if
members of the security service have deliberately carried out illegal actions (it
may be with the approval of their superior officers) which they consider to be
necessary to further the work of the service it is probable that complaints to law

enforcement officers or to senior civil servants or to a government minister
would not be acted upon or would be met by the eventual response that the   *a*
activities complained of had been investigated and that no wrongdoing had
been discovered. He also submitted that senior civil servants or ministers
might be reluctant to investigate complaints of incompetence or
maladministration.

[105] In my opinion these arguments should be rejected. In *Klass v Federal*   *b*
Republic of Germany (1978) 2 EHRR 214, where the applicants claimed that
surveillance of letters and telephone conversations constituted a violation of
art 8 of the convention, the state claimed that the surveillance was necessary in
a democratic state in the interests of national security and for the prevention of
disorder and crime, and that the administrative procedures in place were
designed to ensure that surveillance was not ordered improperly. The   *c*
applicants advanced the argument, similar to the argument advanced by the
present appellant, that the safeguards were inadequate because they did not
provide protection against dishonesty or negligence on the part of the
supervising officials. The European Court rejected this submission stating (at
236–237 (para 59)):   *d*

'Both in general and in relation to the question of subsequent
notification, the applicants have constantly invoked the danger of abuse as
a ground for their contention that the legislation they challenge does not
fulfil the requirements of Article 8(2) of the Convention. While the
possibility of improper action by a dishonest, negligent or over-zealous   *e*
official can never be completely ruled out whatever the system, the
considerations that matter for the purposes of the Court's present review
are the likelihood of such action and the safeguards provided to protect
against it. The Court has examined above (at paras. 51 to 58) the contested
legislation in the light, *inter alia*, of these considerations. The Court notes
in particular that the [German legislation] contains various provisions   *f*
designed to reduce the effect of surveillance measures to an unavoidable
minimum and to ensure that the surveillance is carried out in strict
accordance with the law. In the absence of any evidence or indication that
the actual practice followed is otherwise, the Court must assume that, in
the democratic society of the Federal Republic of Germany, the relevant   *g*
authorities are properly applying the legislation in issue.'

[106] In the present case there is no suggestion in the agreed statement of
facts that the appellant sought to place his concerns before the Director General
of the security service or before the Home Secretary or any other Crown
servant. Therefore there is no evidence that the persons to whom the appellant   *h*
could have made complaints would not have considered and, if necessary,
investigated them in an honest and proper way and taken steps to remedy any
wrongs revealed. Accordingly there is no basis for concluding that the
safeguard provided by the ability to make such complaints are inadequate to
protect the public interest. In my opinion the reasoning of Moses J in his   *j*
judgment (at [54]), was correct and fully in accordance with the judgment of the
European Court in *Klass'* case:

'I accept that, in general, a restriction on disclosure cannot be justified as
being proportionate without regard to the public interest in the particular
disclosure. However, that proposition must be considered in the context

a of the statutory scheme in the instant case. There is no blanket ban on disclosure by a former member of the security services. Where a former member of a security service seeks to expose illegality or avert a risk of injury to persons or property, he is entitled to approach any Crown servant identified in s 12(1) of the OSA 1989 for the purposes of that Crown servant's functions (see s 7(3)). It is not therefore correct to say that a

b restriction is imposed irrespective of the public interest in disclosure. If there is a public interest in disclosure, it is, at the very least, not unreasonable to expect at least one of the very large number identified to recognise the public interest, if it is well-founded, and to act upon it.'

c [107] Moreover, if complaints to Crown servants were to prove fruitless and the appellant considered that the public interest required that he should disclose the information in his possession about alleged wrongdoing or incompetence to the press or other sections of the media the Crown argued that he would have another course open to him. This would be to apply, pursuant to s 7(3)(b), for official authorisation to disclose the information to the

d public. If his complaints to official quarters had been fruitless and if official authorisation were not granted, the appellant could apply to the High Court for a judicial review of the refusal to give official authorisation.

[108] The appellant submitted that such an application would be fruitless. He argued that in order to present his case in an effective way to the High Court it would be necessary for him to make disclosure to his own lawyers and to the

e judge of the information which he wished to bring to the attention of the public, but the refusal of official authorisation (which was the subject matter of his complaint) would prevent such disclosure.

[109] In considering this argument it is necessary to take account of the judgment of the European Court in *Tinnelly & Sons Ltd v UK* (1999) 27 EHRR

f 249. The principal point decided in that case was that a certificate issued pursuant to statute by the Secretary of State that an act was done for the purpose of safeguarding national security cannot exclude access to a court to determine a dispute as to a citizen's rights: the right guaranteed by art 6(1) 'cannot be displaced by the *ipse dixit* of the executive' (see (1998) 27 EHRR 249

g at 290 (para 77)). But the court also recognised that the right of access to a court may be subject to limitations in the interests of national security provided that the very essence of the right is not impaired and that there is a reasonable relationship of proportionality between the means employed and the aims sought to be achieved (see (1998) 27 EHRR 249 at 271 (para 72)). The court also

h noted that in other contexts it had been found possible to modify judicial procedures in such a way as to safeguard national security concerns about the nature and sources of intelligence information and yet accord the individual a substantial degree of procedural justice (see (1998) 27 EHRR 249 at 273–274 (para 78)).

j [110] In *Jasper v UK* (2000) 30 EHRR 441 the European Court again recognised that national security may require certain information not to be disclosed and stated that the fact that the issue of whether there should be disclosure was monitored by a judge was an important safeguard which could lead to the conclusion that there had not been a violation of art 6(1). The court stated (at 472, 472–473):

'52. However, as the applicant recognised, the entitlement to disclosure
of relevant evidence is not an absolute right. In any criminal proceedings ᵃ
there may be competing interests, such as national security or the need to
protect witnesses at risk of reprisals or keep secret police methods of
investigation of crime, which must be weighed against the rights of the
accused. In some cases it may be necessary to withhold certain evidence
from the defence so as to preserve the fundamental rights of another ᵇ
individual or to safeguard an important public interest. However, only
such measures restricting the rights of the defence which are strictly
necessary are permissible under Article 6(1). Moreover, in order to ensure
that the accused receives a fair trial, any difficulties caused to the defence
by a limitation on its rights must be sufficiently counterbalanced by the
procedures followed by the judicial authorities ...	ᶜ

56. The fact that the need for disclosure was at all times under
assessment by the trial judge provided a further, important, safeguard in
that it was his duty to monitor throughout the trial the fairness or
otherwise of the evidence being withheld.'

ᵈ

[111] In the light of these principles stated by the European Court, I consider
that if the appellant were refused official authorisation to disclose information
to the public and applied for judicial review of that decision, a judge of the High
Court would be able to conduct an inquiry into the refusal in such a way that
the hearing would ensure justice to the appellant and uphold his rights under
art 6(1) whilst also guarding against the disclosure of information which would ᵉ
be harmful to national security. The intensity of the review, involving as it
would do convention rights, would be greater than a review conducted under
the *Wednesbury* principle (see per Lord Steyn in *R (on the application of Daly) v
Secretary of State for the Home Dept* [2001] 3 All ER 433 at 445–446, [2001] 2 AC
532 at 547).	ᶠ

[112] In a recent judgment of the Divisional Court in *R (on the application of
Director of Public Prosecutions) v Acton Youth Court* [2001] All ER (D) 267, after
referring to *Jasper's* case, *Rowe v UK* (2000) 30 EHRR 1, and *Fitt v UK* (2000) 30
EHRR 480, Lord Woolf CJ said (at [34]):

'... the European Court of Human Rights is prepared to accept the ᵍ
obvious need in limited circumstances for the courts to protect in the
public interest immunity from production of documents ...'

[113] It would not be appropriate or practicable in this speech to specify the
steps which a judge, before whom an application for judicial review was ʰ
brought, should take to achieve the objective of giving substantial protection
to the convention rights of a past member of the security service in a way which
would not result in the disclosure of information which would be harmful to
national security. But just as it is possible to devise a procedure to be followed
in the Crown Court for upholding a claim to public interest immunity whilst
not impairing the essential rights of the accused under art 6(1), so I consider ʲ
that the High Court could devise a procedure to achieve a similar objective in
applications for judicial review of a refusal of official authorisation. A possible
course might be for the judge to appoint a special counsel to represent the
interests of the person seeking disclosure. This procedure was referred to by
Lord Woolf MR, in his judgment in the Court of Appeal in *Secretary of State for*

the Home Dept v Rehman [2000] 3 All ER 778 at 788, [2000] 3 WLR 1240 at 1250,
where an issue of national security arose:

> 'As it was possible that part of the hearing would have to be in closed
> session, Mr Nicholas Blake appeared at the request of the court. The
> [Special Immigration Appeals Commission Act 1997] makes no provision
> for a special advocate on an appeal. However, it seemed to us that, if it was
> necessary for the court in order to dispose justly of the appeal to hear
> submissions in the absence of Mr Rehman and his counsel, under the
> inherent jurisdiction of the court, counsel instructed by the Treasury
> Solicitor, with the agreement of the Attorney-General, would be able to
> perform a similar role to a special advocate without the advantage of
> statutory backing for this being done. A court will only hear submissions
> on a substantive appeal in the absence of a party in the most extreme
> circumstances. However, considerations of national security can create
> situations where this is necessary. If this happens, the court should use its
> inherent power to reduce the risk of prejudice to the absent party so far as
> possible ...'

[114] Another possible course might be for the past member of the security
service, as a preparatory step before instituting an application for judicial
review, to seek official authorisation to disclose the information only to a
specified solicitor and counsel, and in the course of his submissions on behalf of
the Crown Mr Sweeney QC stated that he was instructed to say that if such an
application for authorisation were made it would be looked at sympathetically.
If authorisation for such restricted disclosure were refused the past member
could seek judicial review of that refusal.

[115] There would, of course, be no substance in the argument by the
Crown that the appellant would have a remedy in judicial review to challenge
an improper refusal of authorisation to make disclosure to the public, if the
right to apply for judicial review was merely a formal right where the
application would be bound to fail because the applicant could place no
information before the court to support it. But, notwithstanding the difficulties
which could arise in relation to placing the necessary information before the
High Court, I consider that those difficulties would not be insurmountable and
that the High Court would be able to assist the appellant to overcome those
difficulties and to ensure that justice was done to him.

[116] It is to be observed that the appellant took no steps to apply for official
authorisation to publish the information which he wished to disclose to the
public and for the reasons which I have given I consider that he cannot argue
that, if there had been a refusal of authorisation, an application for judicial
review would have been fruitless and would not have provided an effective
remedy.

[117] Therefore I consider that ss 1 and 4 of the OSA 1989 are not
incompatible with art 10. I am in agreement with Lord Bingham that the
defence of necessity or duress of circumstances did not arise for consideration
in this case and, like him, I would not wish to be taken to agree with all that the
Court of Appeal said on this issue. I am also in agreement with him that no
issue directly affecting the media arises in this case and therefore it would be
undesirable to express an opinion on the interesting submissions advanced on
their behalf to the House.

[118] I would dismiss this appeal.

LORD HOBHOUSE OF WOODBOROUGH.
[119] My Lords, for the reason given by my noble and learned friend Lord Bingham of Cornhill, I too would dismiss this appeal.

LORD SCOTT OF FOSCOTE.
[120] My Lords, I have had the advantage of reading in draft the opinions of my noble and learned friends Lord Bingham of Cornhill, Lord Hope of Craighead and Lord Hutton. Save that on the matters referred to in Lord Hutton's opinion at [99], [100] I would wish to reserve my opinion as to how the balance between the requirements of national security on the one hand and freedom of expression and freedom of the press on the other hand should be struck, I am in full agreement with them and for the reasons they give I, too, would dismiss this appeal.

Appeal dismissed.

Kate O'Hanlon   Barrister.

Knauf UK GmbH v British Gypsum Ltd and another

[2001] EWCA Civ 1570

a

COURT OF APPEAL, CIVIL DIVISION
b HENRY, ROBERT WALKER AND RIX LJJ
31 JULY, 24 OCTOBER 2001

Practice – Service out of the jurisdiction – Service by alternative means – Service on German defendant via English solicitors – Whether 'good reason' for authorisation of
c *alternative service shown – CPR 6.8(1).*

The appellant company, P, and the respondent company, K, were both domiciled in Germany, although K's operations were based exclusively in England. Between March 1997 and July 1998 P supplied K with products used in the making of plasterboard. Plasterboard sold by K was used in the construction of
d homes in the north of England. In the course of construction a skim plaster finish was applied to the exposed surface of the plasterboard, most of which was supplied by an English company, BG Ltd. In December 1997 complaints began to be received that delamination of the plaster skim coat was occurring. K and BG Ltd entered into an agreement whereby claims involving their products would be settled on a 50/50 basis without prejudice to liability as between
e themselves. BG Ltd's position was that the delamination was caused by defects in the plasterboard made by K, whether caused in turn by P's products or otherwise, while K's view was that the problem was caused by or at least contributed to by P's products. K wished to avoid being sued by BG Ltd in England and then having to carry its claim against P to Germany and thus, in July
f 2000, issued a claim form against BG Ltd and P and applied under CPR 6.8(1)[a] for service of the claim form on P by an alternative method, namely by service within the jurisdiction on P's English solicitors. CPR 6.8(1) provided that service by an alternative method might be permitted where it appeared to the court that there was a good reason to do so. K submitted that although there was no difficulty in
g serving BG Ltd in England, or in bringing P within the English jurisdiction because it could rely on art 6(1) of the Convention on Jurisdiction and the Enforcement of Judgments in Civil and Commercial Matters 1968 (the Brussels Convention) (as set out in Sch 1 to the Civil Jurisdiction and Judgments Act 1982), there would be difficulty in obtaining priority under the Brussels Convention for
h its suit against P in England over any suit brought by P against it in Germany, because, in the absence of an order for alternative service on the English solicitors, K would have to serve the English proceedings on P in Germany by a method permitted under the Hague Convention on the Service Abroad of Judicial and Extrajudicial Documents in Civil or Commercial Matters 1965 or under the 1928 bilateral treaty between the United Kingdom and Germany (the
j Convention regarding Legal Proceedings in Civil and Commercial Matters), which could take up to three months, and that that consideration constituted 'good reason.' The judge granted the application for alternative service. P subsequently applied, inter alia, to have the order for alternative service set aside. The judge

---

a   Rule 6.8(1) is set out at [9], below

held that there had been good reason for making the order for alternative service, and P appealed.

Held – There could not be a good reason for ordering service in England by an alternative method on a foreign defendant when such an order subverted, and was designed to subvert, in the absence of any difficulty about effecting service, the principles on which service and jurisdiction were regulated by agreement between the United Kingdom and her convention partners. That was not a matter of mere discretion, but of principle. The application made to the judge under CPR 6.8(1) was put specifically on the basis that it was the best and perhaps the only means of bringing all parties into a single forum. The unusual form of service had been requested, not for the sake of effecting service, but for the sake of establishing jurisdiction over a foreign party, namely P, which was prima facie entitled to be sued in the courts of its domicile. The conventions controlling service between the United Kingdom and Germany were therefore being bypassed not in the interest of effecting service by some alternative method when the agreed method was not possible, but so as to establish jurisdiction in England. Although the means used for effecting jurisdiction in England purported to find justification in the Brussels Convention's rule of strict chronological precedence and in its interest in seeing all related actions tried together, in truth such means subverted the rules of that convention, since such precedence was achieved only by taking an a priori view of where it was convenient for the litigation to be conducted. Moreover, that view had been taken in the absence of P, which, because it was served before it had opportunity to address the court on the manner of service, had had the question of chronological precedence decided in its absence. The court's rationale for taking such action was a view as to where the litigation could best be canalised, whereas the convention dictated other rules for deciding such questions. Accordingly, the appeal would be allowed and the order for service by an alternative method set aside (see [58]–[60], below).

Per curiam. Where the court is being asked to make an exceptional order, in the exercise of its discretion, for the making of which a 'good reason' must be found, and that order is designed to affect and does affect the jurisdiction or potential jurisdiction of the English court in respect of foreign parties, it is absolutely necessary to bring to the court's attention the possible existence of an exclusive jurisdiction clause in favour of a foreign jurisdiction (see [70], below).

Decision of David Steel J [2001] 2 All ER (Comm) 332 reversed.

Cases referred to in judgment

Behbehani v Salem [1989] 2 All ER 143, [1989] 1 WLR 723, CA.

Brink's-MAT Ltd v Elcombe [1988] 3 All ER 188, [1988] 1 WLR 1350, CA.

Canada Trust Co v Stolzenberg (No 2) [2000] 4 All ER 481, [2000] 3 WLR 1376, HL.

Continental Bank NA v Aeokos Cia Naviera SA [1994] 2 All ER 540, [1994] 1 WLR 588, CA.

Custom Made Commercial Ltd v Stawa Metallbau GmbH Case C-288/92 [1994] ECR I-2913.

Dresser UK Ltd v Falcongate Freight Management Ltd, The Duke of Yare [1992] 2 All ER 450, [1992] QB 502, [1992] 2 WLR 319, CA.

Kleinwort Benson Ltd v Glasgow City Council [1997] 4 All ER 641, [1999] 1 AC 153, [1997] 3 WLR 923, HL.

a *Neste Chemicals SA v DK Line SA, The Sargasso* [1994] 3 All ER 180, CA.
Zelger v Salinitri Case 129/83 [1984] ECR 2397.

Cases also cited or referred to in skeleton arguments
Berghoefer GmbH & Co KG v ASA SA Case 221/84 [1985] ECR 2699.
Coreck Maritime GmbH v Handelsveen BV Case C-387/98 [2000] ECR I-9337.
b *Galeries Segoura SPRL v Firma Rahim Bonakdarian* Case 25/76 [1976] ECR 1851.
IP Metal Ltd v Ruote OZ SpA [1993] 2 Lloyd's Rep 60.
Interfoto Picture Library Ltd v Stiletto Visual Programmes Ltd [1988] 1 All ER 348,
[1989] QB 433, CA.
Lafarge Plasterboard Ltd v Fritz Peters & Co KG [2000] 2 Lloyd's Rep 689.
c *Partenreederei ms Tilly Russ v Haven & Vervoebedrijf Nova NV* Case 71/83 [1985] QB
931, [1985] 3 WLR 179, ECJ.
Powell Duffryn plc v Petereit Case C-214/89 [1992] ECR I-1745.

Notes
d For service by an alternative method, see 37 *Halsbury's Laws* (4th edn reissue) para
324.

Appeal
By notice dated 5 April 2001 Wellkisten Papierfabriken Fritz Peters KG (Peters)
appealed with permission of David Steel J from his decision of 27 March 2001
e refusing to set aside the order of Aikens J on 14 July 2000 granting an application
without notice made by the respondent, Knauf UK GmbH, for an order under
CPR 6.8 permitting service by an alternative method to be made on Peters. The
first defendant to the action, British Gypsum Ltd, took no part in the appeal. The
facts are set out in the judgment of the court.

f
Howard Palmer QC and *Timothy Otty* (instructed by *Fishburn Morgan Cole*) for
Peters.
Alexander Layton QC and *Sara Masters* (instructed by *Gregory, Rowcliffe & Milners*)
for Knauf UK.

g   *Cur adv vult*

24 October 2001. The following judgment was delivered.

HENRY LJ.
h [1] This is a judgment of the court prepared by Rix LJ.
[2] This appeal concerns two German companies, one of which wishes to
conduct its litigation in England, while the other wishes to do so in Germany.
Each invokes in its favour the Convention on Jurisdiction and the Enforcement
of Judgments in Civil and Commercial Matters 1968 (as set out in Sch 1 to the
Civil Jurisdiction and Judgments Act 1982) (the Brussels Convention). In
j particular, three issues arise. (1) Can the desire to advance the date on which the
English court is seised of proceedings over a foreign domiciliary of another
convention state be a 'good reason' for the purpose of ordering alternative service
on that person under CPR 6.8? (2) Does an exclusive jurisdiction clause bind the
parties so that art 17 of the convention in any event mandates jurisdiction in
Germany rather than England? (3) Ought the failure of the claimant in England

to disclose the existence of the exclusive jurisdiction clause to the court at the time when it sought and obtained, without notice to the intended defendant, the order for alternative service on that defendant to lead in any event to the setting aside of that order?

[3] The two German companies are respectively claimant and second defendant in these proceedings. The claimant is Knauf UK GmbH (Knauf UK), and the second defendant is Wellkisten und Papierfabriken Fritz Peters & Co KG (Peters). Knauf UK is a manufacturer of plasterboard. It is incorporated in Germany but its operations are based exclusively in England. It is common ground that it is domiciled in Germany. Peters is a German limited partnership, also domiciled in Germany. It manufactures lining paper which is used in the plasterboard manufacturing process. Between March 1997 and July 1998 Peters supplied Knauf UK with light grade ivory and green lining paper which Knauf UK used in the making of plasterboard. Knauf UK sold its plasterboard into the market, and it was used in the construction of homes in the north of England. In the course of construction a skim plaster finish was applied to the exposed surface of the plasterboard. This finish was supplied (in very large part) by the first defendant, British Gypsum Ltd (Gypsum). There was at this stage no contractual relationship between Knauf UK and Gypsum.

[4] In December 1997 complaints started to be received that delamination of the plaster skim coat was occurring. It was not clear what the cause of this delamination was, but it exposed Knauf UK to large claims. In order to satisfy their market, Knauf UK and Gypsum entered into an agreement under the auspices of the Gypsum Products Development Association (GPDA) whereby claims involving their products were settled on a 50/50 basis by the two of them, without prejudice to their liability as between themselves. This agreement is the only contractual relationship between Knauf UK and Gypsum.

[5] As between Knauf UK and Gypsum, it is Gypsum's view that the delamination was caused by defects in the plasterboard made by Knauf UK, whether as a consequence of the lining paper supplied by Peters or otherwise. As between Knauf UK and Peters, it is Knauf UK's view that the problem was caused or at least contributed to by defects in Peters' lining paper. In June 1998 Knauf UK informed Peters of that view. On 11 November 1998 its London solicitors wrote to Peters—

'to notify you formally of this claim and to inform you that our clients have no alternative but to bring a claim in Court for recovery of their losses as a result of your failure to supply goods in accordance with the specification and which were in any event not suitable for the purpose.'

On 15 March 1999 Knauf UK's technical manager wrote directly in reply to Peters' German insurers and said that Knauf UK was prepared to seek its recovery through the German courts. On 8 April 1999 those insurers wrote to Knauf UK's German solicitors to say that 'to avoid a premature court case' they would confirm that the limitation period for a claim would not end until 31 December 2000 (unless the claim were already barred). On 29 June 1999 Knauf UK's German solicitors quantified its claim in the sum of £1,140,363 so far paid to buyers in compensation, in the further sum of almost £3·7m paid to Peters for the paper supplied, and in an unspecified amount for loss of profits arising out of reduced turnover. The solicitors cited provisions of the German Code in support *a* of Knauf UK's claim. The letter, which was addressed to Peters' insurers, ended with a further threat of legal proceedings.

[6] The matter then appears to have gone comparatively quiet. At any rate, over a year later on 5 July 2000 Peters' English solicitors, Messrs Morgan Cole, wrote to Knauf UK following a telephone conversation earlier that day to confirm that they had been instructed 'to consider both liability and quantum in *b* relation to supplies to you by Peters'. The letter continued:

'You outlined the problems and the nature of the claims and I assured you that I would look into the documents which I had as soon as possible, coming back to you following your return from the Far East.'

c [7] What was happening meanwhile between Knauf UK and Gypsum is not known, but there is evidence that shortly before the commencement of these proceedings Gypsum wrote a letter before action to Knauf UK threatening proceedings in the very near future. The letter itself is not before the court. It seems that negotiations between Knauf UK and Gypsum to avoid court proceedings had broken down. That letter caused a flurry of activity on the part *d* of Knauf UK, who did not want to be sued in England by Gypsum and then have to carry its claim against Peters to Germany. Knauf UK therefore sought to find a way to canalise its litigation with both Gypsum and Peters in one jurisdiction, viz England.

[8] Thus by 11 July 2000 a claim form had been issued against Gypsum and *e* Peters. On 13 July Mr Christopher Harper, a partner of Gregory, Rowcliffe & Milners, made a witness statement in support of Knauf UK's application under CPR 6.8 for service of the claim form on Peters by an alternative method, namely by service within the jurisdiction on Peters' solicitors, Morgan Cole.

[9] CPR 6.8(1) provides:

f 'Where it appears to the court that there is a *good reason* to authorise service by a method not permitted by these Rules, the court may make an order permitting service by an alternative method.' (My emphasis.)

[10] That application came before Aikens J without notice on 14 July 2000. Mr Harper's witness statement put forward the following account of the 'good *g* reason' which Knauf UK was presenting to the court in support of its application. Knauf UK feared imminent suit by Gypsum. It therefore wished to ensure that it could bring both Gypsum and Peters into one set of proceedings. There was no difficulty in serving Gypsum in England. Nor was there any difficulty in bringing Peters within the English jurisdiction, because Knauf UK could rely on art 6(1) of *h* the Brussels Convention (which enables a person domiciled in a contracting state to be sued in the courts for the place where any one of a number of defendants is domiciled). Therefore Gypsum's domicile in England would give jurisdiction over Peters in England. The difficulty was in obtaining priority for Knauf UK's suit against Peters in England over any suit brought by Peters against Knauf UK in Germany. Since Knauf UK was a German company, Peters could serve *j* German proceedings against Knauf UK in Germany as easily as Knauf UK could serve English proceedings on Gypsum in England. However, in the absence of an order for alternative service on Morgan Cole in England, Knauf UK would have to serve the English proceedings on Peters in Germany by a method allowed under either the Hague Convention on the Service Abroad of Judicial and Extrajudicial Documents in Civil or Commercial Matters (15 November 1965; TS

50 (1969); Cmnd 3986) or the 1928 bilateral treaty between the United Kingdom and Germany (the Convention regarding Legal Proceedings in Civil and Commercial Matters) (the Bilateral Convention). Service under the Hague Convention would take up to three months. In the meantime, any service of the claim form on Gypsum would probably result in news of the claim leaking to Peters in Germany. If Peters were tipped off about Knauf UK's English claim before it had been served with the claim form in Germany, then it would seek to obtain priority in Germany by commencing German proceedings and serving them on Knauf UK in Germany. Article 21 of the Brussels Convention assured priority for the first set of proceedings involving the same cause of action and between the same parties to come before the court, which then became the court 'first seised'. That would occur upon service of the defendant. The only way therefore to ensure that Peters was served for the purpose of the English proceedings before Knauf UK was served by Peters for the purpose of proceedings in Germany was to serve Peters before it could find out anything about the action, and before Gypsum could sue Knauf UK in England. That could be achieved by serving Peters' English solicitors, Morgan Cole. Albeit those solicitors had not been authorised to accept service, they had been instructed to investigate the claim and would certainly give notice of the proceedings to Peters. Therefore the court should make an order for service on Morgan Cole by an alternative method. Knauf UK also offered to effect service on Peters in Germany under the Hague Convention and to send a copy of the claim form to Peters at its address in Germany. Mr Harper's witness statement concluded as follows:

'26. In summary, therefore, the only effect of the present order sought will be to advance the date upon which Peters are served with the Claim Form and, as a result, the date upon which this Court is 'seised' with these proceedings for the purpose of Article 21 of the Brussels Convention. This is an appropriate and legitimate course for Knauf UK to take so as to prevent Peters from seeking to take advantage of the three month delay in service of process in Germany and thereby depriving Knauf UK from their right (pursuant to Article 6(1) of the Brussels Convention) to bring their claim against Peters before this Court. Moreover, by permitting Knauf UK to take this course, this Court will ensure that all of the disputes between all of the parties concerned (Knauf UK, British Gypsum and Peters) are determined by the same court, in the same set of proceedings, and will avoid the risk of separate concurrent proceedings with the consequent danger of inconsistent judgments on the same issues.'

[11] Aikens J acceded to the application. He made the following order:

'(1) The second defendant will be deemed to have been personally served with the claim form in this action by serving the said claim form on Messrs Morgan Cole of Suffolk House, George Street, Croydon, Surrey CR0 1PE.
PROVIDED THAT:
(a) The second defendant is also served with the claim form in accordance with the Hague Service Convention.
(b) A copy of the claim form is also sent by post to the second defendant at Industriestrasse 5, 47447 Moers, Germany.
(2) The documents will be deemed to have been personally served on the second defendant one day after they are served upon Messrs Morgan Cole at the address specified at (1) above.'

[12] In the event Peters was deemed to have been served within a matter of days. Gypsum was served by post on 19 July. On the same day the claim papers were lodged with the foreign process section of the High Court for service under the Hague Convention, and a copy of the claim form was posted to Peters in Germany.

[13] At about the same time as these events were occurring, a Mr Ingenillem of Knauf UK's German parent (Gebruder Knauf Westdeutsche Gipswerke, or 'Knauf Germany') made a courtesy telephone call to Mr Volkmar Peters, one of Peters' principals, in which he informed him of what was happening, and why. Mr Peters recorded this information in an internal note of 20 July. Mr Peters wrote:

'This is an unfortunate escalation of the whole situation which has to be taken very seriously. The legal dispute which will then be determined in accordance with Anglo-Saxon law ["angelsächsischen Recht"] would also be against us because the plaster produced by [Gypsum] did not adhere to our products.'

[14] In the event, Peters did what Knauf UK anticipated it would do on hearing of the English proceedings, namely it commenced its own proceedings in Germany. It sued both Knauf Germany and Knauf UK. Its complaint is dated 18 August 2000. It seeks negative declarations of non-liability. It alleges that its supply contracts were with the parent, Knauf Germany, not with the subsidiary Knauf UK. These proceedings were served on Knauf Germany on 5 September, and on Knauf UK on 18 September 2000.

[15] It was only after service of Peters' German proceedings on Knauf UK that the latter's English proceedings were served on Peters under the Hague Convention, on 5 October 2000. But for errors committed by the foreign process section of the High Court, service under the Hague Convention would have been effected somewhat earlier. If Knauf UK had simply gone ahead and served Peters under the Hague Convention without warning them in advance that it was doing so, and if such service had been effected without error, it is perfectly feasible that Knauf UK's service would have been well in advance of service of any proceedings brought by Peters.

[16] As it is, Gypsum in England has brought Pt 20 proceedings against Peters, and Peters has sought to bring proceedings for negative declaratory relief against Gypsum in Germany.

Peters' application to attack service and jurisdiction

[17] On 15 September 2000 Peters brought an application designed to set aside the alternative service which Aikens J had ordered and to challenge English jurisdiction. It relied on four separate points. It said, first, that there was no good reason to order service by an alternative method; secondly, that Knauf UK had failed to give full and frank disclosure to the court when requesting the special order as to service; thirdly, that the court should stay the proceedings against it or decline jurisdiction pursuant to arts 21 and/or 22 of the convention; and fourthly, that any contracts between Knauf UK and Peters were governed by an exclusive jurisdiction clause in favour of the courts of Germany within the meaning of art 17.

[18] It was common ground that if service were to be set aside either on the ground that there was no good reason for it, or because of non-disclosure, then

the English action should be stayed under art 21. Three grounds of
non-disclosure were argued, but the only one which has been raised again in this *a*
court is Knauf UK's failure to disclose to Aikens J the presence of an exclusive
jurisdiction clause in Peters' standard terms and conditions. The logic of the
application was that, even if service on Peters survived, jurisdiction should be
declined in favour of the German courts under art 17.

b

The Brussels Convention
[19] The relevant terms of the Brussels Convention are as follows:

'ARTICLE 2
Subject to the provisions of this Convention, persons domiciled in a
Contracting State shall, whatever their nationality, be sued in the courts of *c*
that State ...

ARTICLE 6
A person domiciled in a Contracting State may also be sued:
(1) where he is one of a number of defendants, in the courts for the place *d*
where any one of them is domiciled;
(2) as a third party in an action on a warranty or guarantee or in any other
third party proceedings, in the court seised of the original proceedings,
unless these were instituted solely with the object of removing him from the
jurisdiction of the court which would be competent in his case ...

e
ARTICLE 17
If the parties, one or more of whom is domiciled in a Contracting State,
have agreed that a court or the courts of a Contracting State are to have
jurisdiction to settle any disputes which have arisen or which may arise in
connection with a particular legal relationship, that court or those courts
shall have exclusive jurisdiction. Such an agreement conferring jurisdiction *f*
shall be either—(a) in writing or evidenced in writing or, (b) in a form which
accords with practices which the parties have established between
themselves ...

ARTICLE 21
Where proceedings involving the same cause of action and between the *g*
same parties are brought in the courts of different Contracting States, any
court other than the court first seised shall of its own motion stay its
proceedings until such time as the jurisdiction of the court first seised is
established. Where the jurisdiction of the court first seised is established, any
court other than the court first seised shall decline jurisdiction in favour of *h*
that court.

ARTICLE 22
Where related actions are brought in the courts of different Contracting
States, any court other than the court first seised may, while the actions are
pending at first instance, stay its proceedings. A court other than the court *j*
first seised may also, on the application of one of the parties, decline
jurisdiction if the law of that court permits the consolidation of related
actions and the court first seised has jurisdiction over both actions. For the
purposes of this Article, actions are deemed to be related where they are so
closely connected that it is expedient to hear and determine them together

a   to avoid the risk of irreconcilable judgments resulting from separate proceedings.'

The exclusive jurisdiction clause and German law

[20] Peters' primary case is that it has no contractual relations with Knauf UK, only with its parent, Knauf Germany. If, however, there is any contractual
b   relationship directly with Knauf UK, its alternative case is that it is governed by standard conditions which include an exclusive jurisdiction clause in the following terms:

c   'For all our business and rights and duties flowing from this contract as well as delivery and payment the place of performance is Gelsenkirchen. The court of Krefeld shall have exclusive jurisdiction in all these cases on the condition that nevertheless we are entitled to invoke any other court which may have legal jurisdiction: this rule as to jurisdiction applies also to claims on cheques. In our relationship with our client German law is to be applied.'

d   [21] In the court below David Steel J ([2001] 2 All ER (Comm) 332) found the following facts in connection with Peters' alternative case. During an earlier period between 1989 and 1993 when Peters supplied lining paper to Knauf UK, it was standard procedure for all order confirmations sent by Peters to Knauf UK to be on a printed form whose box headings were in both German and English, and in the body of which was to be found (in typescript) this notation (as translated
e   from the German): 'We thank you for your order which we will carry out in accordance with our trading conditions to be found overleaf.' Those conditions were to be found in small print, in German, and began with a clause in these terms:

f   '1. For all business transactions between ourselves and our clients the following terms shall apply. The content of the contract should be determined exclusively by our written confirmation of order and our terms and conditions [of] contract ... Contracts between us and our clients shall only come into existence through our confirmation of orders. Clients' terms and conditions shall not apply even if we have not repudiated them.'

g   [22] From 1993 to 1996 Knauf UK sourced their lining paper elsewhere and there was no trade whatsoever between Peters and Knauf UK. Trade between the two companies only restarted following a letter from Peters dated 21 May 1996 which drew attention to what was claimed to be a reduction in paper weight and invited Knauf UK to try out samples. In due course this approach led to a
h   resumption of business. Peters now had a confirmation of order in a new format. The body of the confirmation filled up in typescript was now almost entirely in English. It no longer contained the typed-in reference to the conditions on the reverse. Instead it merely stated, in English: 'Thank you for your order, which we are pleased to accept.' The reverse continued to contain terms and conditions
j   printed in German, including the cl 1 and the jurisdiction clause cited above.

[23] The judge also made findings about German law. It was common ground between the parties that, at any rate for present purposes, any contracts between Peters and Knauf UK were governed by German law. The judge, who was provided with expert reports on German law, found that the critical issue under that law narrowed to one of fact, namely whether German was one of the

languages of the relevant contracts. On that issue he concluded that English was
the only language of the contract. He said: *a*

'... Following a break of several years, Peters opened negotiations with a
view to seeking orders for a new brand of paper. The negotiations were
conducted entirely in English. Furthermore, in stark contrast to the position
prior to 1993, the order confirmations were expressed in English without any   *b*
cross-reference to the German conditions of contract. It is true that there
were a few German words used on the form but in the overall context they
were de minimis.

[45] I conclude, therefore, that as a matter of German law the clauses were
not incorporated.'
                                                                               c
There has been no appeal from that conclusion.

The judgment of David Steel J

[24] Peters' application came before David Steel J. On the four issues before
him, his conclusions were as follows.   *d*

[25] First, he found that there was good reason for making the order for
alternative service. He reasoned that matter as follows. The discretion under
CPR 6.8 was unfettered save for the need for 'good reason'; there was no need for
the applicant to establish that it was *impracticable* to serve the proceedings in the
prescribed manner. In the circumstances, the best prospect for ensuring that all
issues arising from the failure of the plasterboard in use were decided in one *e*
jurisdiction was Knauf UK's action in England. With that in mind, it was not
illegitimate to seek to forestall any attempt by Peters to take advantage of the
disparity in periods needed to accomplish service and thus introduce the
complication of a second forum first seised of only part of the dispute. He
continued (at [32]):   *f*

'To the contrary, in my judgment there were good reasons for authorising
the alternative method. (i) Knauf UK was not in a position to ensure that
proceedings against both British Gypsum and Peters were successfully
instituted in Germany. The overwhelming probability was that British
Gypsum would commence proceedings first in England. (ii) Once   *g*
proceedings were instituted against British Gypsum Knauf UK could pray in
aid art 6 of the convention to override art 2. (iii) Whilst it is true that the risk
of proceedings in Germany could not be (and indeed has not been)
eliminated, the proceedings instituted by Peters would necessarily be in the
form of an application for a negative declaration itself susceptible to an   *h*
application for a stay under art 22.'

[26] Finally, he rejected the submission that the period needed to effect service
under the Hague Convention constituted a substantive safeguard to Peters' right
to be sued in Germany. He regarded the disparities between the jurisdictions as
regards the time needed to effect service as 'purely technical in nature'.   *j*

[27] As for non-disclosure, he regarded (at [35]) Knauf UK's failure to disclose
the exclusive jurisdiction clause as 'potentially material', but ultimately
concluded (at [52]) that it was immaterial in the light of his separate decision that
there was no good arguable case that the clause had been properly agreed for the
purposes of art 17.

a [28] As for the argument in relation to art 17, he held that German law was irrelevant since the test of agreement of a jurisdiction clause under art 17 was autonomous law which displaced national law; that the standard of proof was that of a good arguable case, not that of the balance of probabilities; that there was no good arguable case that the clause had been agreed in writing or evidenced in writing for the purposes of art 17(a); and that there was also no good

b arguable case that good faith prevented Knauf UK from denying the applicability of the clause for the purposes of art 17(b). Peters' case on art 17 therefore failed (see [41]–[52]).

[29] In the circumstances, there was no question of staying Knauf UK's claim against Peters or of declining jurisdiction for it.

c [30] The judge gave permission to appeal, although his reasons indicated that he regarded the first issue (good reason) as essentially one of discretion.

Good reason

[31] The first and most important issue re-argued in this court is whether there was good reason within CPR 6.8. If there was not, it was common ground

d that the action against Peters in England should be stayed. That would make the other issues moot. It would still be relevant, even if unnecessary, to determine the issue of non-disclosure. But in our judgment it would not be right to determine the third issue relating to art 17: for if the court first seised (as between Peters and Knauf UK) is the German court, it would be for that court to

e determine the art 17 point, if necessary. It is not as though art 17 is being relied on to maintain the jurisdiction of the English court, but the reverse. It would, it seems, only be necessary to determine the art 17 point if there was an application to the German court to stay its proceedings under art 22 on the basis that ultimately the court first seised of any of the related actions was the English court, by reason of its earliest service on Gypsum.

f [32] On behalf of Peters, Mr Howard Palmer QC submitted that the judge erred. It was only if there was 'good reason' that the court had a discretion to exercise under the rule. However wide the ambit of 'good reason' or of that discretion, it needed to be remembered that the historical background of a rule for alternative service lay in RSC Ord 65, r 4 ('Substituted service') and its test of

g impracticability. The modern rule remained to deal with cases where there was some unexpected impediment or difficulty in effecting service by the primary method contemplated by the Rules. There was no such impediment or difficulty in the present case. On the contrary, the primary method of service of a German company in Germany was regulated by the Hague Convention and the Bilateral

h Convention. The requirements of these conventions should not be lightly evaded by an order for service within the jurisdiction. Moreover, although there might be jurisdiction over Peters under art 6(1) of the Brussels Convention, the primary rule of that convention was art 2, namely that persons should be sued in the country of their domicile. Where there were proceedings in more than one country, the convention had devised its own principles, set out in arts 21 and 22,

j for resolving the issue of lis alibi pendens. It was a mere stratagem to use the domestic rule relating to alternative service to seek to undermine the operation of those principles, which reflected the Brussels Convention's desire for clear and certain tests to operate in this field. Such tests were distinct from the common law's approach by way of discretionary rules and the doctrine of forum non conveniens.

[33] On behalf of Knauf UK, on the other hand, Mr Alexander Layton QC
submitted that the reasons put forward in Mr Harper's witness statement were
indeed good reasons, and that the judge was right to recognise them as such.
CPR 6.8 was a new departure, there was no restriction on what could be
considered a good reason for the purposes of that rule, and the test of
impracticability had been left behind. It was mere technicality that produced the
situation where it was quicker to serve a home defendant than a defendant
abroad. In the interests of achieving a single jurisdiction where all parties could
litigate together the court was entitled to ensure a level playing field as to the
technique of service. In that way the peculiar imbalance in the procedures for
service here and abroad was avoided. That was not a stratagem designed to
undermine the policy of the Brussels Convention, but a means for achieving that
policy, spoken to in art 22, of bringing related actions into a single forum. In any
event, service was one thing and jurisdiction another. The rule that an English
court was seised not on issue of the claim form but only on service was a domestic
rule, not an autonomous rule of the convention. It was because of that rule that
in a deserving case, such as this, English law could find an alternative method of
service to ensure that the convention's policy of canalising related actions into a
single jurisdiction could be achieved. Article 2 was not the primary rule of
jurisdiction under the convention, for that rule was 'subject to the provisions of
this Convention' and thus subject to art 6(1), which, where as here it applied, was
mandatory.

[34] The resolution of these competing submissions requires consideration of
the policies and purposes of the rules relating to service and to the founding of
jurisdiction.

Service in English law

[35] Service in English law is now governed by CPR Pt 6. Section I of that Part
is headed 'General Rules about Service', and those rules apply in all circumstances
save where another enactment, rule or practice direction or a court order
provides otherwise (r 6.1). Section II is headed 'Special Provisions about Service
of the Claim Form', and section III is headed 'Special Provisions about Service out
of the Jurisdiction'.

[36] The most basic rule is that service may be effected by any of the methods
identified in CPR 6.2, which includes both personal service and first class post.
Rule 6.2(2) makes it clear that any such method applies equally to companies.
The permission of postal service is a departure from the traditional rule, which
had required personal service. Turning to service out of the jurisdiction, we can
confine our comments to the case, such as that in the present claim against Peters
governed by the 1982 Act, where permission is not required (r 6.19). Rule 6.24,
headed 'Method of service—general provisions', states that where a claim form
is to be served out of the jurisdiction 'it may be served by any
method—(a) permitted by the law of the country in which it is to be served' or
provided for by r 6.25. Rule 6.25 (headed 'Service through foreign governments,
judicial authorities and British Consular authorities') provides for service under
the Hague Convention, and also provides that where a claim form is to be served
on a defendant in any country which is a party to a 'Civil Procedure Convention'
providing for service in that country, it 'may be served' through the judicial
authorities of that country or through the British consular authority in that
country. 'Civil Procedure Convention' is defined in r 6.18(e) as meaning the

a   Brussels and Lugano Conventions and any other conventions entered into by the
    United Kingdom regarding service outside the jurisdiction. The Brussels
    Convention itself has no provisions regarding service (but art IV of its Annexed
    Protocol does: see below). Rule 6.25 appears to be permissive, not mandatory,
    although of course, where any convention is utilised to effect service, its
    provisions will need to be complied with.

b   [37] Although it was common ground between the parties that, as a matter of
    English law, it was not permitted to serve Peters outside the jurisdiction by post
    in the absence of an order for alternative service, we are not sure why that is said
    to be so. There is a general rule that permits service by first class post as an
    alternative to personal service, and we are not sure why that is said not to apply
    to service on Peters in this case.

c   [38] It was also common ground before David Steel J below that amendments
    to the CPR regime had, perhaps inadvertently, eliminated the provision
    permitting an order for alternative (or substituted) service out of the jurisdiction.
    The judge commented ([2001] 2 All ER (Comm) 332 at [28]): 'I am not convinced
    that it is material to the present dispute but I would not wish to be thought as
d   concurring with that view.' We would echo that sentiment.

    [39] The question then is whether the Hague Convention or the Bilateral
    Convention, or German law, prevents such postal service being effected in
    Germany.

The Hague Convention
e   [40] Article 10 of the Hague Convention provides as follows:

> 'Provided the State of destination does not object, the present Convention
> shall not interfere with—(a) the freedom to send judicial documents, by
> postal channels, directly to persons abroad ...'

f   [41] Article 25 provides:

> '... the present Convention shall not derogate from Conventions
> containing provisions on the matters governed by this Convention to which
> the Contracting States are, or shall become, Parties.'

g   [42] Nevertheless the skeleton argument of Peters put before David Steel J
    asserted (citing Layton and O'Malley *European Civil Practice* (1989) p 109 n 23) that
    Germany has objected to postal service for the purposes of art 10. That appears
    to be common ground.

h   *The Bilateral Convention*
    [43] Article 6 provides as follows:

> 'Documents may also be transmitted by post in case where this method of
> transmission is permitted by the law of the country from which the
j   document emanates.'

    [44] As stated above, we do not see why English law, relevant as the 'law of
    the country from which the document emanates', does not permit service by post
    abroad. If it does, then we do not see why art 6 of the Bilateral Convention does
    not permit service by post on a defendant in Germany. However, it is common
    ground that Peters cannot be served by post in Germany.

The Protocol to the Brussels Convention

[45] Article IV provides:

> 'Judicial and extrajudicial documents drawn up in one Contracting State which have to be served on persons in another Contracting State shall be transmitted in accordance with the procedures laid down in the conventions and agreements concluded between the Contracting States.
>
> Unless the State in which service is to take place objects by declaration to the Secretary-General of the Council of the European Communities, such documents may also be sent by the appropriate public officers of the State in which the document has been drawn up directly to the appropriate public officers of the State in which the addressee is to be found. In this case the officer of the State of origin shall send a copy of the document to the officer of the State applied to who is competent to forward it to the addressee. The document shall be forwarded in the manner specified by the law of the State applied to. The forwarding shall be recorded by a certificate sent directly to the officer of the State of origin.'

That appears to take matters no further. In any event there were no submissions with relation to the Protocol. But we note that Germany has apparently declared its objection under the second paragraph of art IV (see Layton and O'Malley p 109, n 22).

The rule as to service

[46] The long and short of all this is that, whether it is due to a rule of English law or to a rule of German law (that as we say is opaque), it is common ground that it is not permissible under either the Hague Convention or the Bilateral Convention to effect postal service upon Peters from England to Germany. It follows that Knauf UK accepts that without an order for service *within* England by an alternative method, viz upon Messrs Morgan Cole, Peters could not have been served save by methods which would have involved delay. Indeed, Knauf UK asserts and relies upon such delay as a critical part of its 'good reason'.

[47] It was argued by Peters before the judge that the Hague Convention and the Bilateral Convention were a 'mandatory and exhaustive code of the proper means of service on German domiciled defendants', which therefore excluded alternative service in England. The judge did not accept that submission, pointing out that those conventions were simply not concerned with service *within* the English jurisdiction. Peters did not repeat that submission on its appeal. Nevertheless, it follows in our judgment that to use CPR 6.8 as a means for turning the flank of those conventions, when it is common ground that they do not permit service by a direct and speedy method such as post, is to subvert the conventions which govern the service rule as between claimants in England and defendants in Germany. It may be necessary to make exceptional orders for service by an alternative method where there is 'good reason': but a consideration of what is common ground as to the primary method for service of English process in Germany suggests that a mere desire for speed is unlikely to amount to good reason, for else, since claimants nearly always desire speed, the alternative method would become the primary way.

The Brussels Convention and the rule of jurisdiction

[48] Where jurisdiction, as distinct from service, is concerned, there is, generally speaking, no need to distinguish between an English rule and a German rule since, in a case such as this, jurisdiction is governed by the Brussels

a Convention. (We say 'generally speaking', because there are areas in which domestic rules are allowed to play a subsidiary role within the context of the Convention's autonomous doctrines.)

[49] The basic and primary rule is that a defendant should be sued in the courts of his domicile (art 2). It is not merely that a claimant is entitled to sue his defendant where he is domiciled: the defendant is entitled to be sued there. It is b true, as Mr Layton submits, that art 2 is expressed to be subject to the other provisions of the convention, but that does not stop art 2 expressing the convention's basic philosophy. Thus art 2 falls within s 1 of the convention, headed 'General provisions', whereas s 2 is headed 'Special jurisdiction'. In other words such special rules are exceptions to the general rule. This distinction is recognised in the jurisprudence: see *Kleinwort Benson Ltd v Glasgow City Council* c [1997] 4 All ER 641 at 646–647, [1999] 1 AC 153 at 163–164 per Lord Goff of Chieveley.

[50] Since it is possible for the identical causes or related actions to be commenced in more than one jurisdiction, the convention contains its own rules to deal with such situations. Those rules are contained in s 8, headed 'Lis d pendens— related actions' and include arts 21 and 22. Those articles have been described by both Bingham LJ and Lord Steyn as 'tie-break rules' (*Dresser UK Ltd v Falcongate Freight Management Ltd, The Duke of Yare* [1992] 2 All ER 450 at 460, [1992] QB 502 at 514 and *Canada Trust Co v Stolzenberg (No 2)* [2000] 4 All ER 481 at 483–484, [2000] 3 WLR 1376 at 1379).

[51] Article 21, which concerns proceedings involving the same cause of e actions and the same parties (as here Knauf UK's English claim against Peters and Peters' action in Germany for a negative declaration of non-liability) is a precise rule which depends on strict chronological precedence. As Steyn LJ put it in *Neste Chemicals SA v DK Line SA, The Sargasso* [1994] 3 All ER 180 at 184:

f   'The analysis of the problem must start with the language of art 21. The 1968 convention does not contain the traditional English discretionary principle of lis alibi pendens. As between the courts of two contracting states having jurisdiction under the scheme of the convention, a rule dependent on strict chronological priority was adopted. Commentators have variously described the rule as rigid, mechanical and crude. So it is. On the other hand, g the framers of the convention wanted to avoid the uncertainties and disputes inherent in a discretionary principle of lis alibi pendens. Their preference was for what Bingham LJ in *Dresser UK Ltd v Falcongate Freight Management Ltd, The Duke of Yare* [1992] 2 All ER 450 at 460, [1992] QB 502 at 514 described as a simple "tie-break rule". In other words the framers of the convention h put their faith in the simplicity, certainty and predictability of a rule of chronological priority. That principle in their view best served the objective of avoiding as far as possible inconsistent judgments, and the non-recognition of a judgment on the ground that it is irreconcilable with the judgment of the court of another contracting state. It promoted the free j circulation of readily enforceable judgments.'

[52] Mr Layton submits that in *Zelger v Salinitri* Case 129/83 [1984] ECR 2397 the Court of Justice of the European Communities did not adopt an autonomous rule as to when national courts became seised for the purpose of arts 21/22, and that the adoption of a 'date of service' rule for seisin in England was a matter of English law. The suggestion was that what English law had adopted for the

purpose of the Brussels Convention it could feel free to affect by other procedural rules, such as CPR 6.8's doctrine of service by an alternative method. However, we do not accept that submission, which does scant justice to the policy of the convention, the significance of the decision in *Zelger's* case, or to the considerations which led English law to adopt the date of service rule. As to *Zelger's* case, we would refer to Lord Hoffmann's speech in the *Canada Trust* case ([2000] 4 All ER 481 at 494–497, [2000] 3 WLR 1376 at 1390–1393) and in particular to the passage [2000] 4 All ER 481 at 495–496, [2000] 3 WLR 1376 at 1391–1392. Lord Hoffmann there points out that the domestic rule had to reflect the policy of the convention in finding a rule that 'had to be fixed and ascertainable, not discretionary as under the common law forum non conveniens doctrine'; and also that it should not be a rule which limited the rights of the defence. As to the considerations which led English law to adopt the date of service rule, they are spelled out by Bingham LJ in *Dresser's* case [1992] 2 All ER 450 at 467–468, [1992] QB 502 at 523 and by Steyn LJ in *The Sargasso* [1994] 3 All ER 180 at 188, for instance where the latter said:

'On the other hand in *Zelger v Salinitri* ... the European Court did emphasise the importance of certainty in national procedural laws. And it seems to me that a "date of service" rule will be readily comprehensible not only in England but also in other contracting states ...

And it is in the interests of the proper working of the convention that the provisions of national systems should be simple and readily comprehensible. In the continental contracting states there is no problem: a simple solution of the date of service of the writ applies ... For my part I prefer the simple solution of saying that an English court only becomes definitively seised on service of the writ.'

[53] Peter Gibson LJ (at 189) cited with approval a comment by Adrian Briggs in [1992] LMCLQ 150 at 153:

'Far better a clear and workable rule than an opaque, if doctrinally purer, rule. Especially when the rule is being constructed for the benefit of foreign, as much as for English, courts.'

[54] In these circumstances we do not think that it is open, save perhaps in very special circumstances which we do not presently have in mind, for English law to arrogate to itself a discretionary approach, under the rubric of 'good reason', to advance the normal date at which the English court would be seised for the purpose of arts 21 and 22. Although the principle of date of service would have been nominally preserved through the device of the alternative method of service, it would have been abandoned in essence: and not for the sake of *service* (as under the old RSC Ord 65, r 4, because normal service had been found impracticable) but for the sake of arriving at a state of being first seised in order to oust the jurisdiction of a competing forum, in other words for the sake of *jurisdiction*.

[55] Where it is only the same parties and the same cause of action which are concerned (as in art 21), the matter is simpler than in the case of related actions involving different parties or different causes of action. Nevertheless, the principle of the convention approach remains the same. Article 22 recognises in its own language the desirability of hearing related actions together in one jurisdiction 'to avoid the risk of irreconcilable judgments resulting from separate

a proceedings'. Again, however, it does not adopt the common law approach of forum non conveniens (although an element of discretion is apparent in the 'may' which appears in both the first and second paragraphs of the article): instead it proceeds on the basis that the jurisdiction of the court first seised will be preserved, whereas the court 'other than the court first seised' may stay its proceedings or decline jurisdiction.

b [56] How the regime of arts 21 and 22 works in any situation may be hard to foresee, and it may well be said in complaint that its and the convention's rigid rules have the ability of bifurcating litigation which should all be heard in a single forum. Nevertheless, those are the rules which bind the contracting states. In the present case, Mr Layton submits that even if, as between Knauf UK and Peters, the German court turns out to be the court first seised (because the order of *c* Aikens J for alternative service has to be set aside), nevertheless ultimately the court first seised of any of the related actions is the English court, because service on Gypsum takes priority over every other claim. He therefore contemplates an application to the German court to stay the proceedings before it in favour of the English court. That remains to be seen.

d [57] It is possible therefore that a form of canalisation of this transnational litigation will be achieved, perhaps however only after a series of further disputed applications. It is also possible that, at any rate in the eyes of English lawyers familiar with the doctrine of forum non conveniens, the position achieved by Aikens J is the simplest way of achieving litigation in a single forum: although Knauf Germany is not at present a party in England. Be that as it may, it seems *e* to us that the 'good reason' which appealed to Aikens J and again to David Steel J sits uneasily with the principles of the Brussels Convention (and of the service conventions).

[58] In the light of these considerations we would seek to sum up the issue of whether or not there was good reason in this case under CPR 6.8 as follows. The *f* application to Aikens J was put specifically on the basis that it was the best, perhaps the only means of bringing all parties into a single forum. An unusual form of service was requested, not for the sake of effecting service (for instance because of some difficulty about that), but for the sake of establishing jurisdiction over a foreign party (Peters) which was prima facie entitled to be sued in the *g* courts of its domicile. The conventions controlling service between the United Kingdom and Germany were therefore being bypassed not in the interest of effecting service by some alternative method where the agreed method was not possible, but for the sake of establishing jurisdiction in England. Although the means used for effecting jurisdiction in England purported to find justification in *h* the Brussels Convention's rule of strict chronological precedence and in its interest in seeing all related actions tried together, in truth such means subverted the principles of that convention: for precedence was achieved only by taking an a priori view of where it was convenient for the litigation to be conducted. Moreover that view was taken in the absence of the defendant, who, because it was served before it even had a chance to address the court on the manner of its *j* service, had the question of chronological precedence decided in its absence (otherwise than in the normal way mandated by the service conventions in force between the states concerned). The court's rationale for taking such action was a view as to where the litigation could best be canalised; whereas the convention dictates other rules for deciding such questions. The devices sought were not therefore a means of finding a level playing field, but were designed to subvert

the agreed principles by which the United Kingdom and Germany regulated   a
service of process and jurisdiction.

[59] In our judgment there cannot be a good reason for ordering service in
England by an alternative method on a foreign defendant when such an order
subverts, and is designed to subvert, in the absence of any difficulty about
effecting service, the principles on which service and jurisdiction are regulated by
agreement between the United Kingdom and its convention partners. This is not   b
a matter of mere discretion, but of principle.

[60] We would therefore allow the appeal against the judgment and order of
David Steel J and set aside the order for service by an alternative method made
by Aikens J.

Article 17   c

[61] In the circumstances we do not think that it is appropriate to form a
decided view on the questions which arise under art 17 of the Brussels
Convention. In any event, it would not be possible to do so without reconvening
a further hearing, since the court was unable in the time available to hear Mr
Layton on Knauf UK's respondent's notice. That raised two interesting   d
submissions which were decided against Knauf UK by the judge: that the
standard of proof is not that of a good arguable case, but that of the balance of
probabilities, and that the question of the agreement or not of an exclusive
jurisdiction clause does not depend *only* on the autonomous test of art 17 but also
on the national law of the parties' contract. Mr Layton wished to argue that,   e
despite what was said in the *Canada Trust* case, the good arguable case test is
inappropriate where a litigant seeks to use art 17 to derogate from a jurisdiction
otherwise established under the convention; and that, despite the opinion of
Advocate General Lenz in *Custom Made Commercial Ltd v Stawa Metallbau GmbH*
Case C-288/92 [1994] ECR I-2913 at 2948, a jurisdiction agreement cannot be
proved unless it is valid by its proper law as well as by the autonomous test of   f
art 17. Those arguments must therefore await another day.

Non-disclosure

[62] Finally, there is the issue of non-disclosure, which is a free-standing
ground on which Peters seeks to have the order of Aikens J set aside.   g
[63] Mr Palmer submits that, having found the possible existence of an
exclusive jurisdiction clause which, if valid, would have bound Knauf UK to
proceed against Peters in Germany in any event, to be 'potentially material', the
judge erred in concluding that it was not material just because, on the merits of
the issue as to its effectiveness, he had decided that it did not bind the parties. On   h
that basis the question of non-disclosure would always be decided on the merits
of any issue and never on the failure to disclose. Since the clause, if it did bind the
parties, would have had an overriding effect, its disclosure must have entered into
the balance of the decision which Aikens J had been called upon to make.
[64] Mr Layton, however, submitted that the clause was not material at all.
There was not even a good arguable case that it had been agreed. In any event it   j
could not enter into any exercise of discretion which Aikens J had to perform,
since, if effective, it was mandatory and overriding. In that respect nothing done
by Aikens J could affect Peters' right to avail itself of the clause, if effective. It was
always open to Peters to raise the matter of the clause and seek to establish it.
The present case was unlike other examples of judicial intervention which were

a invoked without notice: such as a freezing order which could affect a litigant's property or liberties, or an application for permission to serve out of the jurisdiction where ex hypothesi the defendant was only within the court's reach if the order was made.

[65] The leading cases remain *Brink's-MAT Ltd v Elcombe* [1988] 3 All ER 188, [1988] 1 WLR 1350 and *Behbehani v Salem* [1989] 2 All ER 143, [1989] 1 WLR 723.

b Those authorities in this court bring their reminder of the essential principles: that there is a 'golden rule' that an applicant for relief without notice must disclose to the court all matters relevant to the exercise of the court's discretion; that failure to observe this rule entitles the court to discharge the order obtained even if the circumstances would otherwise justify the grant of such relief; that a due sense of proportion must be maintained between the desiderata of marking

c the court's displeasure at the non-disclosure and doing justice between the litigants; that for these purposes the degree of any culpability on the part of the applicant or of any prejudice on the part of the respondent are relevant to the reviewing court's discretion; and that a balance must be maintained between undermining 'the heavy duty of candour and care' which falls on applicants and

d promoting a 'tabula in naufragio' to save respondents who lack substantial merits.

[66] In these circumstances, of particular relevance is the explanation given to the court of the non-disclosure complained of. What explanation did Knauf UK give in the present case? In essence none, other than that the presence of the exclusive jurisdiction clause among the rest of Peters' terms and conditions was

e irrelevant as a matter both of German and of convention law. Thus it was not suggested that the presence of the clause was unknown, or overlooked. On the contrary, Mr Harper, in his second witness statement, once the non-disclosure had been challenged, took his stand on the submission that 'the relevance of these matters depends on the exercise being undertaken by Aikens J being *jurisdictional*

f in nature, rather than being concerned with the fair and balanced application of the rules relating to service'.

[67] We therefore infer that the existence of the clause was known about and that there was a deliberate decision not to disclose it, on the basis that it was irrelevant.

g [68] Peters has not appealed David Steel J's conclusions that Peters' terms and conditions were not incorporated into the parties' contracts (if any) as a matter of German law. David Steel J has also held that the same was true as a matter of the autonomous rules of art 17. The latter point is still in issue, but will not be decided in this court. Therefore we are prepared to assume that David Steel J was right. Nevertheless, it is not true that such considerations were irrelevant on the

h ground that Aikens J was concerned only with matters of service and not with matters of jurisdiction. On that point David Steel J was against Knauf UK ('potentially material'), and in our judgment correctly so. The whole point of the application to Aikens J to order service by an alternative method was in order to steal a march on anticipated German proceedings so as to achieve a firm

j jurisdictional foundation for Knauf UK's proceedings in England and to render them immune from jurisdictional attack under the 'tie-break rules' of the convention. A submission to the contrary is in our judgment misconceived.

[69] What is more, although it is true that the art 17 point remains as an overriding point (at any rate in England, on the basis that art 17 overrides art 21, see *Continental Bank NA v Aeokos Cia Naviera SA* [1994] 2 All ER 540, [1994] 1 WLR

588, a controversial point in the jurisprudence of the convention), in Germany our understanding is that the view would be that art 21 overrides art 17. Thus, if the English court were to become the court first seised, then the validity of the art 17 point would be debated in England rather than in Germany. That demonstrates what is true even irrespective of any argument about art 17, and that is that the order for which Aikens J was requested is self-fulfilling: if it is made, it achieves that chronological priority which assures jurisdiction in England rather than in Germany; whereas the question whether such an order should be made at all is the very matter in issue.

[70] It seems to us that when a court is being asked to make an exceptional order, in the exercise of its discretion, for the making of which a 'good reason' must be found, and that order is designed to affect and does affect the jurisdiction or potential jurisdiction of the English court in respect of foreign parties, it is absolutely necessary to bring to the court's attention the possible existence of an exclusive jurisdiction clause in favour of a foreign jurisdiction. Nothing else would vindicate that 'heavy duty of candour and care' which is required. Moreover, it is impossible to say that knowledge of the clause's existence would not have affected Aikens J's decision. If it did not, it would be because the court was willing to act with its eyes open to the potential dispute between the parties as to the effect of the clause. But knowledge of the clause, albeit accompanied by all or some of the arguments for disputing its applicability, may well have led a court to decide that Knauf UK must take its chances in the ordinary course of things, rather than to make an exceptional order in its favour.

[71] In truth, the clause was not a wooden plank grasped in desperation by a drowning litigant nor was Peters shipwrecked (cf 'si tabulam de naufragio stultus arripuerit' (Cicero, Off 3, 23)). The ultimate merits of the litigation are wholly unknown. There is a dispute about where the litigation should take place. There is an exclusive jurisdiction clause which points towards Germany. There is a valid dispute as to its applicability. In such circumstances the English court should not be asked to act as it were blindfolded. In our judgment this is one of those cases where, unless the 'golden rule' is to fall into disrespect, a failure to disclose should be met by the sanction of the court. We would therefore have set aside the order of Aikens J even if we had concluded that there was good reason for his order.

Appeal allowed.

Kate O'Hanlon   Barrister.

A v B (a company) and another
[2002] EWCA Civ 337

COURT OF APPEAL, CIVIL DIVISION

LORD WOOLF CJ, LAWS AND DYSON LJJ

b 11, 12 FEBRUARY, 11 MARCH 2002

Confidential information – Injunction against disclosure of information – Interim injunction – Application for interim injunction restraining publication by press of confidential information which would allegedly infringe claimant's privacy – Guidelines – Human Rights Act 1998, s 12, Sch 1, Pt I, arts 8, 10.

The claimant, a Premier League footballer with a responsible position at his club, was a married man with children. He had transient adulterous relationships with the second defendant, C, and another woman, D, who both sold their stories to the first defendant, a national newspaper. In order to prevent his wife learning of his adultery, the claimant sought an interim injunction restraining the newspaper from publishing the stories. The judge granted the injunction, but the newspaper subsequently applied to have it discharged on the merits. The judge held, inter alia, that the protection of confidentiality which applied to sexual relations in marriage should, in the context of modern sexual relations, also be applied outside marriage; that there was a substantial distinction between communication of information to family and friends and to the press; that the claimant had a right to respect for his private life and there was no countervailing public interest in the publication of the proposed articles; and that the claimant was likely to succeed at trial in establishing his claim. On that basis, he reimposed the injunction, though on terms that did not prevent C from disclosing her story to her friends or the claimant's wife. On the newspaper's appeal, in which numerous judicial authorities and decisions of the Press Complaints Commission were put before the Court of Appeal, the latter gave guidelines on the approach to be adopted in the majority of cases in which interim injunctions were sought to protect claimants from the publication by the media of confidential information which would allegedly infringe their privacy. In doing so, it considered how the courts were to balance two potentially conflicting provisions of the European Convention for the Protection of Human Rights and Fundamental Freedoms 1950 (as set out in Sch 1 to the Human Rights Act 1998)—the right to respect for private life in art 8[a] and the right to freedom of expression in art 10[b]. In particular, it considered the impact of s 12[c] of the 1998 Act which applied where the court was considering whether to grant any relief which, if granted, might affect the exercise of the convention right to freedom of expression. Under s 12(3), no such relief was to be granted so as to restrain publication before trial unless the court was satisfied that the applicant was likely

---

j a   Article 8, so far as material, provides: '1. Everyone has the right to respect for his private ... life ...'
   b   Article 10, so far as material, provides: '1. Everyone has the right to freedom of expression. This right shall include freedom ... to receive and impart information ...
       2. The exercise of these freedoms, since it carries with it duties and responsibilities, may be subject to such ... restrictions ... as are prescribed by law and are necessary in a democratic society ... for the protection of the ... rights of others, for preventing the disclosure of information received in confidence ...'
   c   Section 12, so far as material, is set out at [11](ii), below

to establish that publication should not be allowed. Section 12(4) required the
court to have particular regard to the importance of the convention right to
freedom of expression and, where the case appeared to involve journalistic
material, to the extent to which, inter alia, it was or would be in the public
interest for the material to be published, and any relevant privacy code.

Held – (1) When the court was seeking to balance the conflicting rights on
applications for interim injunctions to restrain publication by the media of
confidential information which would allegedly infringe a claimant's privacy, a
balancing of the facts was frequently required, not a technical approach to the
law. The weight which should be attached to each relevant consideration would
vary depending on the precise circumstances, and in many situations the balance
might not point clearly in either direction. If that were the position, interim relief
should be refused. Consideration of the application should generally begin with
recognition that whether an interim injunction was granted at all was a matter
for the discretion of the judge on well-established principles which included the
need to establish that, after a trial, it was likely that an injunction would be
granted, while recognising that the grant or refusal of an interim injunction could
well determine the outcome of the entire proceedings. The fact that the injunction
was being sought to protect the privacy of the claimant, and that without it he
might be deprived of the only remedy which would be of any value, was a
relevant consideration, but had to be weighed against the defendant's right to
freedom of expression, the importance of which had been enhanced by s 12 of the
1998 Act. Any interference with the press had to be justified, irrespective of
whether a particular publication was desirable in the public interest. The fact that
under s 12(4) the court was required to have particular regard to whether it
would be in the public interest for the material to be published did not mean that
the court was justified in interfering with the freedom of the press because there
was no identifiable special public interest in any particular material being
published. Such an approach would turn s 12(4) upside down. Regardless of the
quality of the material which it was intended to publish, the court should not,
prima facie, interfere with its publication. It was most unlikely that any purpose
would be served by a judge seeking to decide whether there existed a new cause
of action in tort which protected privacy. In the great majority of situations, if
not all, where the protection of privacy was justified in relation to events after the
implementation of the 1998 Act, an action for breach of confidence would
provide the necessary protection. Furthermore, in the majority of cases the
question whether there was an interest capable of being the subject of a claim for
privacy should not be allowed to be the subject of detailed argument. The same
was true in cases in which the public interest in publication was relied on to
oppose the grant of an injunction. The need for the existence of a confidential
relationship should not give rise to problems as to the law. The difficulty would
be as to the relevant facts. A duty of confidence would arise whenever the party
subject to the duty either knew or ought to have known that the other person
could reasonably expect his privacy to be protected. If there was an intrusion in
a situation where a person could reasonably expect his privacy to be respected,
that intrusion would be capable of giving rise to a liability in an action for breach
of confidence unless the intrusion could be justified. The situation would be
more difficult where the alleged intrusion into privacy was as a result of the
reporting of the information to a third party by a party to the relationship which
created the privacy. That was a material factor where two people had shared a

a sexual relationship outside marriage. If one party wished to exercise his or her rights under art 10 of the convention, that had to impact on the other's right to maintain confidentiality. Where the parties were not married, the fact that the confidence was a shared confidence which only one of the parties wished to preserve did not extinguish the other party's right to have the confidence respected, but it did undermine that right. While recognising the special status of

b a lawful marriage under the law, the courts, for present purposes, had to recognise and give appropriate weight to the extensive range of relationships which now existed. Obviously, the more stable the relationship, the greater would be the significance which was attached to it. A public figure was entitled to have his privacy respected in appropriate circumstances, but should recognise that because of his public position he had to expect and accept that his or her

c actions would be more closely scrutinised by the media. Conduct which, in the case of a private individual, would not be the appropriate subject of comment, could be the proper subject of comment in the case of a public figure. Such a person might be a legitimate subject of public attention whether or not he had courted publicity. In balancing the respective interests of the parties, the court

d should not act as censors or arbiters of taste. Courts might well find of assistance the statement of practice in relation to privacy in the Press Complaints Commission Code of Practice, but they should discourage advocates from seeking to rely on individual decisions of the commission. If judges directed themselves in accordance with those guidelines, in many cases they would not need to be burdened by copious reference to other authorities (see [11], [12],

e below); *Venables v News Group Newspapers Ltd* [2001] 1 All ER 908 and *Douglas v Hello! Ltd* [2001] 2 All ER 289 considered.

(2) In the instant case, there had been important flaws in the judge's approach. He had made no reference to the fact that any interference by way of an injunction had to be justified. His approach had been to assume that, as the

f claimant had a right to privacy with regard to his relationships with C and D, the proposed publication should be restrained unless the newspaper could show that there was a public interest in what was proposed to be published. His view that the confidentiality which applied to facts concerning sexual relations within marriage also applied in the modern context to relationships outside marriage was objectionable, because it made no allowance for the very different nature

g between the relationship that the claimant had had, on his own account, with the two women and that which would exist within marriage. Quite apart from the recognition which the law gave to the status of marriage, there was a significant difference between the confidentiality which attached to what was intended to be a permanent relationship and that which attached to the category of relationships

h with which the claimant was involved. Furthermore, the fact that the women had chosen to disclose their relationships with the claimant affected his right to protection of the information. A conclusion to the contrary would not acknowledge their right to freedom of expression. The judge apparently did not regard disclosure by C and D to their friends as being objectionable, but only publication

j to the media. That approach ignored the importance to be attached to a free press. Moreover, the judge had been wrong to reject any question of there being a public interest in the proposed publications. It was not self-evident that the way in which a well-known Premiership footballer, who had a position of responsibility within his club, chose to spend his time off the football field lacked a modicum of public interest. Footballers were role models for young people, and undesirable behaviour on their part could set an unfortunate example.

Whilst the claimant had not courted publicity, someone in his position was inevitably a figure in whom a section of the public and the media would be *a* interested. Furthermore, relationships of the sort that the claimant had had with the two women were not the categories of relationship which the court should be astute to protect when the other parties to the relationships did not want them to remain confidential. It was most unlikely that a permanent injunction after a trial would ever be granted. In those circumstances, the grant of an injunction would *b* be an unjustified interference with the freedom of the press. Accordingly, the appeal would be allowed (see [43]–[47], [50], below); *Theakston v MGN Ltd* [2002] All ER (D) 182 (Feb) considered.

Decision of Jack J [2002] 1 All ER 449 reversed.

Notes   *c*

For the convention rights to respect for private life and to freedom of expression, see 8(2) *Halsbury's Laws* (4th edn reissue) paras 149–150, 158.

For the Human Rights Act 1998, s 12, Sch 1, Pt I, arts 8, 10, see 7 *Halsbury's Statutes* (4th edn) (1999 reissue) 510, 524.

Cases referred to in judgment   *d*

A-G v Guardian Newspapers Ltd (No 2) [1988] 3 All ER 545, [1990] 1 AC 109, [1988] 3 WLR 776, HL.

American Cyanamid Co v Ethicon Ltd [1975] 1 All ER 504, [1975] AC 396, [1975] 2 WLR 316, HL.

Argyll (Duchess of) v Duke of Argyll [1965] 1 All ER 611, [1967] Ch 302, [1965] 2 WLR   *e* 790.

Australian Broadcasting Corp v Lenah Game Meats Pty Ltd (2001) 185 ALR 1, Aust HC.

Douglas v Hello! Ltd [2001] 2 All ER 289, [2001] QB 967, [2001] 2 WLR 992, CA.

Imutran Ltd v Uncaged Campaigns Ltd [2001] 2 All ER 385.

Kaye v Robertson [1991] FSR 62, CA.   *f*

R v Central Independent Television plc [1994] 3 All ER 641, [1994] Fam 192, [1994] 3 WLR 20, CA.

Stephens v Avery [1988] 2 All ER 477, [1988] Ch 449, [1988] 2 WLR 1280.

Theakston v MGN Ltd [2002] EWHC 137 (QB), [2002] All ER (D) 182 (Feb).

Venables v News Group Newspapers Ltd [2001] 1 All ER 908, [2001] Fam 430, [2001] 2 WLR 1038.   *g*

Appeals

The first defendant, B, a national newspaper, appealed (i) with permission of Rix LJ granted on 13 September 2001 from the decision of Jack J on 5 July 2001 reversing his decision of 20 June 2001 discharging an injunction granted by him on 27 April *h* 2001 restraining B from publishing two articles relating to the sexual relationships of the claimant, A, with the second defendant, C, and another woman, D, (the procedural appeal), and (ii) with permission of Jack J from his decision on 10 September 2001 ([2002] 1 All ER 449, [2001] 1 WLR 2341) reimposing the interim injunction on B and C in modified terms (the substantive appeal). The facts are set *j* out in the judgment of the court.

Richard Spearman QC (instructed by *Marcus Partington*) for B.

Alastair Wilson QC, Stephen Bate and *Jeremy Reed* (instructed by *George Davies*, Manchester) for A.

C did not appear and was not represented.

a

Cur adv vult

11 March 2002. The following judgment of the court was delivered.

LORD WOOLF CJ.

b   *The background*

[1] The case involves two linked appeals. They relate to four interim judgments which Jack J gave in the same proceedings. The substantive appeal is against the fourth judgment of 10 September 2001 ([2002] 1 All ER 449, [2001] 1 WLR 2341) which granted A an interim injunction against B and C. That injunction had been previously granted on 27 April 2001 in different terms by Jack J for reasons which he set out in his first judgment of 30 April 2001. The second appeal is an appeal against the third judgment of Jack J. The third judgment was given on 5 July 2001. That decision reversed his second judgment of 20 June 2001 which had discharged the injunction which Jack J had originally granted on 27 April 2001.

c

d   [2] A is a footballer with a Premier League football club. B is a national newspaper. C is one of two women with whom A, who is a married man, had affairs. The injunction was granted to restrain B from publishing the stories which C and the other woman, D, had sold to B recounting their affairs with A. In using initials to describe the parties we are following the course adopted in the court below to protect the identity of A. D has taken no part in the proceedings.

e

[3] Since the coming into force of the Human Rights Act 1998 there has been an increase in the number of actions in which injunctions are being sought to protect the claimants from the publication of articles in newspapers on the grounds that the articles contain confidential information concerning the claimants, the publication of which, it is alleged, would infringe their privacy. Such actions can

f   be against any part of the media.

[4] The applications for interim injunctions have now to be considered in the context of arts 8 and 10 of the European Convention for the Protection of Human Rights and Fundamental Freedoms 1950 (as set out in Sch 1 to the 1998 Act). These articles have provided new parameters within which the court will decide,

g   in an action for breach of confidence, whether a person is entitled to have his privacy protected by the court or whether the restriction of freedom of expression which such protection involves cannot be justified. The court's approach to the issues which the applications raise has been modified because under s 6 of the 1998 Act, the court, as a public authority, is required not to act 'in a way which is incompatible with a Convention right'. The court is able to achieve this by

h   absorbing the rights which arts 8 and 10 protect into the long-established action for breach of confidence. This involves giving a new strength and breadth to the action so that it accommodates the requirements of those articles.

[5] The court is assisted in achieving this because the equitable origins of the action for breach of confidence mean that historically the remedy for breach of

j   confidence will only be granted when it is equitable for this to happen. As the headnote makes clear, in *Duchess of Argyll v Duke of Argyll* [1967] Ch 302 Ungoed-Thomas J decided that—

> 'a contract or obligation of confidence need not be expressed, but could be implied, and a breach of contract or trust or faith could arise independently of any right of property or contract (other than any contract which the

imparting of the confidence might itself create); and that the court, in the exercise of its equitable jurisdiction, would restrain a breach of confidence independently of any right at law ...' (See also [1965] 1 All ER 611.)

In *Stephens v Avery* [1988] 2 All ER 477, [1988] Ch 449, Browne-Wilkinson V-C made it clear that this approach could be extended to other relationships apart from that between husband and wife, though it would not necessarily apply in the same way.

[6] The manner in which the two articles operate is entirely different. Article 8 operates so as to extend the areas in which an action for breach of confidence can provide protection for privacy. It requires a generous approach to the situations in which privacy is to be protected. Article 10 operates in the opposite direction. This is because it protects freedom of expression and to achieve this it is necessary to restrict the area in which remedies are available for breaches of confidence. There is a tension between the two articles which requires the court to hold the balance between the conflicting interests they are designed to protect. This is not an easy task but it can be achieved by the courts if, when holding the balance, they attach proper weight to the important rights both articles are designed to protect. Each article is qualified expressly in a way which allows the interests under the other article to be taken into account.

[7] Actions for breach of confidence are usually brought at short notice and are followed by an immediate application for an interim injunction (as happened here) which has to be heard urgently without adequate time either for preparation or for the hearing of the application. If an interim injunction is to be granted it is essential that it is granted promptly because otherwise the newspaper will be published and then, from the claimant's point of view, the damage will have been done. Notwithstanding these constraints of time, the applications for injunctions in this class of action are frequently marked by the citation of very large numbers of authorities which the unfortunate judge has to do his best to digest prior to announcing his decision as to where the balance falls in the particular case.

[8] In the present appeals the parties have placed before us three lever arch files of authorities. In addition, during the course of the hearing we were handed a number of other domestic and Strasbourg decisions. Finally we have another file which contains what was described as 'Press Complaints Commission Material', which includes 17 decisions of the Press Complaints Commission, as well as the Code of Practice of the commission and a further judgment. It is understandable that, in what is a developing area of the law, citation of authority is necessary, but we would hope that the law has now, at least at the level below the House of Lords, become sufficiently clear to make the citation of authority on this scale unnecessary. This comment is not to be understood as a criticism of the counsel appearing before us on these appeals. They were seeking guidance as to the proper approach to the granting of injunctions in this sort of action. We do, however, hope that as a result of our decision the citation of authorities on this scale will be regarded as unnecessary and not accepted by judges of first instance who have to hear these applications. This action on the part of judges is necessary and part of their responsibilities because of the overriding objective to deal with cases justly in accordance with CPR 1.1(2). The need for control of the excessive citation of authority should be borne in mind in deciding questions of costs since it leads to disproportionate expense which can in turn make litigation beyond the means of the ordinary person.

[9] The authorities largely fall into two categories. The first category consists
of the decisions of the Strasbourg court on arts 8 and 10. These decisions are
valuable sources of the principles which the articles embrace. The decisions do
however tend to repeat the same principles in successive cases in order to apply
them to different situations. The citation of a single case may therefore be all
that is required. The application of the principles to the facts of a particular
situation is largely unhelpful because that is primarily the task of the domestic
court. The other category of cases are decisions given in this jurisdiction. If they
are authorities which relate to the action for breach of confidence prior to the
coming into force of the 1998 Act then they are largely of historic interest only.

[10] The citation of authorities on the present scale adds hugely to the costs of
litigation which is already inevitably high. It also creates huge problems for the
judges hearing the applications, particularly in view of the urgency with which
they have to be dealt. In order to assist the parties we now set out guidelines
which are intended to assist the judiciary and the parties to deal with the majority
of these applications in a more proportionate manner.

The guidelines
[11] We suggest that if judges direct themselves in accordance with the
following paragraphs in many cases they will not need to be burdened by copious
reference to other authorities:

(i) The consideration of this type of application should generally begin with
recognition that what is being considered is an interim application for an
injunction. This means that whether any injunction is granted at all is a matter
of discretion for the judge, to be exercised in accordance with what are now
well-established principles which include the need to establish, as we will explain
later, that after a trial it is likely that an injunction would be granted after a
substantive hearing, while recognising that the grant or refusal of an interim
injunction could well determine the outcome of the entire proceedings.

(ii) The fact that the injunction is being sought to protect the privacy of the
claimant, and if the injunction is not granted, the claimant may be deprived of the
only remedy which is of any value is a relevant consideration. However, this
consideration has to be weighed against the defendant's rights of freedom of
expression. Even before the 1998 Act this would have been an important
consideration. Its importance has been enhanced by s 12 of the 1998 Act. The
relevant provisions of s 12 are:

'(1) This section applies if a court is considering whether to grant any relief
which, if granted, might affect the exercise of the Convention right to
freedom of expression ...

(3) No such relief is to be granted so as to restrain publication before trial
unless the court is satisfied that the applicant is likely to establish that
publication should not be allowed.

(4) The court must have particular regard to the importance of the
Convention right to freedom of expression and, where the proceedings
relate to material which the respondent claims, or which appears to the
court, to be journalistic, literary or artistic material (or to conduct connected
with such material), to—(a) the extent to which—(i) the material has, or is
about to, become available to the public; or (ii) it is, or would be, in the
public interest for the material to be published; (b) any relevant privacy
code.'

(iii) As to the word 'likely' in s 12(3) useful guidance is provided by Sir Andrew Morritt V-C in *Imutran Ltd v Uncaged Campaigns Ltd* [2001] 2 All ER 385. He said of s 12 (at [17]):

> 'Counsel for the defendants submitted that the requirement of likelihood imposed a higher standard than that formulated in [*American Cyanamid Co v Ethicon Ltd* [1975] 1 All ER 504, [1975] AC 396]. I did not understand this to be disputed by counsel for Imutran. He submitted that whatever the standard was his case satisfied it. Theoretically and as a matter of language likelihood is slightly higher in the scale of probability than a real prospect of success. But the difference between the two is so small that I cannot believe that there will be many (if any) cases which would have succeeded under the *American Cyanamid* test but will now fail because of the terms of s 12(3) of the 1998 Act. Accordingly I propose to apply the test of likelihood without any further consideration of how much more probable that now has to be.'

There is no conflict between s 12(3) and the convention. (See *Douglas v Hello! Ltd* [2001] 2 All ER 289 at 326–327, [2001] QB 967 at 1008 (para 150) per Keene LJ.)

(iv) The fact that if the injunction is granted it will interfere with the freedom of expression of others and in particular the freedom of the press is a matter of particular importance. This well-established common law principle is underlined by s 12(4). Any interference with the press has to be justified because it inevitably has some effect on the ability of the press to perform its role in society. This is the position irrespective of whether a particular publication is desirable in the public interest. The existence of a free press is in itself desirable and so any interference with it has to be justified. Here we would endorse the approach of Hoffmann LJ in *R v Central Independent Television plc* [1994] 3 All ER 641 at 652, 653, [1994] Fam 192 at 203, 204, where he said:

> '... publication may cause needless pain, distress and damage to individuals or harm to other aspects of the public interest. But a freedom which is restricted to what judges think to be responsible or in the public interest is no freedom. Freedom means the right to publish things which government and judges, however well motivated, think should not be published. It means the right to say things which "right-thinking people" regard as dangerous or irresponsible. This freedom is subject only to clearly defined exceptions laid down by common law or statute ... The principle that the press is free from both government and judicial control is more important than the particular case.'

(v) The fact that under s 12(4) the court is required to have particular regard to whether it would be in the public interest for the material to be published does not mean that the court is justified in interfering with the freedom of the press where there is no identifiable special public interest in any particular material being published. Such an approach would turn s 12(4) upside down. Regardless of the quality of the material which it is intended to publish prima facie the court should not interfere with its publication. Any interference with publication must be justified.

(vi) It is most unlikely that any purpose will be served by a judge seeking to decide whether there exists a new cause of action in tort which protects privacy. In the great majority of situations, if not all situations, where the protection of privacy is justified, relating to events after the 1998 Act came into force, an action for breach of confidence now will, where this is appropriate, provide the *a*   necessary protection. This means that at first instance it can be readily accepted that it is not necessary to tackle the vexed question of whether there is a separate cause of action based upon a new tort involving the infringement of privacy.

(vii) Furthermore in the majority of cases the question of whether there is an interest capable of being the subject of a claim for privacy should not be allowed to be the subject of detailed argument. There must be some interest of a private

b   nature which the claimant wishes to protect, but usually the answer to the question whether there exists a private interest worthy of protection will be obvious. In those cases in which the answer is not obvious, an answer will often be unnecessary. This is because the weaker the claim for privacy the more likely that the claim for privacy will be outweighed by the claim based on freedom of expression. The advantage of not having to distinguish between acts which are

c   public and those which are private in a difficult case is made clear by what Gleeson CJ had to say on the subject in *Australian Broadcasting Corp v Lenah Game Meats Pty Ltd* (2001) 185 ALR 1. He explained the difficulty of distinguishing between public and private information when he said (at 13):

d   '[42] There is no bright line which can be drawn between what is private and what is not. Use of the term "public" is often a convenient method of contrast, but there is a large area in between what is necessarily public and what is necessarily private. An activity is not private simply because it is not done in public. It does not suffice to make an act private that, because it occurs on private property, it has such measure of protection from the public

e   gaze as the characteristics of the property, the nature of the activity, the locality, and the disposition of the property owner combine to afford. Certain kinds of information about a person, such as information relating to health, personal relationships, or finances, may be easy to identify as private; as may certain kinds of activity, which a reasonable person, applying contemporary standards of morals and behaviour, would understand to be

f   meant to be unobserved. The requirement that disclosure or observation of information or conduct would be highly offensive to a reasonable person of ordinary sensibilities is in many circumstances a useful practical test of what is private.'

g   (viii) The same is true in cases in which the public interest in publication is relied on to oppose the grant of an injunction. We have already made clear that even where there is no public interest in a particular publication interference with freedom of expression has to be justified. However, the existence of a public interest in publication strengthens the case for not granting an injunction. Again in the majority of situations whether the public interest is involved or not will be

h   obvious. In the grey area cases the public interest, if it exists, is unlikely to be decisive. Judges should therefore be reluctant in the difficult borderline cases to become involved in detailed argument as to whether the public interest is involved. In a borderline case the application will usually be capable of being resolved without deciding whether there is a public interest in publication. In any

j   event, the citation of authority is unlikely to be helpful. The circumstances in any particular case under consideration can vary so much that a judgment in one case is unlikely to be decisive in another case, though it may be illustrative of an approach.

(ix) The need for the existence of a confidential relationship should not give rise to problems as to the law. The difficulty will be as to the relevant facts. A duty of confidence will arise whenever the party subject to the duty is in a

situation where he either knows or ought to know that the other person can
reasonably expect his privacy to be protected.　(See Lord Goff of Chieveley in　*a*
A-G v Guardian Newspapers Ltd (No 2) [1988] 3 All ER 545 at 658, [1990] 1 AC 109
at 281.) The range of situations in which protection can be provided is therefore
extensive.　Obviously, the necessary relationship can be expressly created.　More
often its existence will have to be inferred from the facts.　Whether a duty of
confidence does exist which courts can protect, if it is right to do so, will depend　*b*
on all the circumstances of the relationship between the parties at the time of the
threatened or actual breach of the alleged duty of confidence.

　(x)　If there is an intrusion in a situation where a person can reasonably expect
his privacy to be respected then that intrusion will be capable of giving rise to
liability in an action for breach of confidence unless the intrusion can be justified.
(See the approach of Dame Elizabeth Butler-Sloss P in *Venables v News Group*　*c*
Newspapers Ltd [2001] 1 All ER 908 at 933, [2001] Fam 430 at 462 (para 81).)　The
bugging of someone's home or the use of other surveillance techniques are
obvious examples of such an intrusion.　But the fact that the information is
obtained as a result of unlawful activities does not mean that its publication
should necessarily be restrained by injunction on the grounds of breach of　*d*
confidence (see the *Australian Broadcasting* case (2001) 185 ALR 1).　Dependent on
the nature of the unlawful activity there may be other remedies.　On the other
hand, the fact that unlawful means have been used to obtain the information
could well be a compelling factor when it comes to exercising discretion.

　(xi)　More difficult is the situation where the alleged intrusion into privacy is as
a result of the reporting of the information to a third party by a party to the　*e*
relationship which creates the privacy.　This is a material factor in situations
where two people have shared a sexual relationship outside marriage.　If one
wishes to exercise his or her art 10 rights that must impact on the other's right to
maintain confidentiality.　For example the information may relate, as in this case,
to a situation where there is a sexual relationship between two parties and one of　*f*
the parties informs the media about the relationship without the consent of the
other party.　Here the conflict between one party's right to privacy and the other
party's right of freedom of expression is especially acute.　In situations where the
parties are not married (when they are, special considerations may arise) the fact
that the confidence was a shared confidence which only one of the parties wishes
to preserve does not extinguish the other party's right to have the confidence　*g*
respected, but it does undermine that right.　While recognising the special status
of a lawful marriage under our law, the courts, for present purposes, have to
recognise and give appropriate weight to the extensive range of relationships
which now exist.　Obviously, the more stable the relationship the greater will be
the significance which is attached to it.

　(xii)　Where an individual is a public figure he is entitled to have his privacy　*h*
respected in the appropriate circumstances.　A public figure is entitled to a private
life. The individual, however, should recognise that because of his public position
he must expect and accept that his actions will be more closely scrutinised by the
media.　Even trivial facts relating to a public figure can be of great interest to　*j*
readers and other observers of the media.　Conduct which in the case of a private
individual would not be the appropriate subject of comment can be the proper
subject of comment in the case of a public figure.　The public figure may hold a
position where higher standards of conduct can be rightly expected by the public.
The public figure may be a role model whose conduct could well be emulated by
others.　He may set the fashion.　The higher the profile of the individual

concerned the more likely that this will be the position. Whether you have courted publicity or not you may be a legitimate subject of public attention. If you have courted public attention then you have less ground to object to the intrusion which follows. In many of these situations it would be overstating the position to say that there is a public interest in the information being published. It would be more accurate to say that the public have an understandable and so

b a legitimate interest in being told the information. If this is the situation then it can be appropriately taken into account by a court when deciding on which side of the line a case falls. The courts must not ignore the fact that if newspapers do not publish information which the public are interested in, there will be fewer newspapers published, which will not be in the public interest. The same is true in relation to other parts of the media. On the difficult issue of finding the right

c balance, useful guidance of a general nature is provided by the Council of Europe Resolution 1165 of 1998. We set out paras 6–12 which are in these terms:

'6. The Assembly is aware that personal privacy is often invaded, even in countries with specific legislation to protect it, as people's private lives have become a highly lucrative commodity for certain sectors of the media. The

d victims are essentially public figures, since details of their private lives serve as a stimulus to sales. At the same time, public figures must recognise that the special position they occupy in society—in many cases by choice—automatically entails increased pressure on their privacy.

7. Public figures are persons holding public office and/or using public resources and, more broadly speaking, all those who play a role in public life,

e whether in politics, the economy, the arts, the social sphere, sport or in any other domain.

8. It is often in the name of a one-sided interpretation of the right to freedom of expression, which is guaranteed in Article 10 of the European Convention on Human Rights, that the media invade people's privacy,

f claiming that their readers are entitled to know about public figures.

9. Certain facts relating to the private lives of public figures, particularly politicians, may indeed be of interest to citizens, and it may therefore be legitimate for readers, who are also voters, to be informed of those facts.

10. It is therefore necessary to find a way of balancing the exercise of two

g fundamental rights, both of which are guaranteed by the European Convention on Human Rights: the right to respect for one's private life and the right to freedom of expression.

11. The Assembly reaffirms the importance of every person's right to privacy, and of the right to freedom of expression, as fundamental to a

h democratic society. These rights are neither absolute nor in any hierarchical order, since they are of equal value.

12. However, the Assembly points out that the right to privacy afforded by Article 8 of the European Convention on Human Rights should not only protect an individual against interference by public authorities, but also against interference by private persons or institutions, including the mass

j media.'

(xiii) In drawing up a balance sheet between the respective interests of the parties courts should not act as censors or arbiters of taste. This is the task of others. If there is not a sufficient case for restraining publication the fact that a more lurid approach will be adopted by the publication than the court would regard as acceptable is not relevant. If the contents of the publication are untrue the law of defamation provides prohibition. Whether the publication will be attractive or unattractive should not affect the result of an application if the information is otherwise not the proper subject of restraint.

(xiv) Section 12(4) of the 1998 Act requires the court to take into account 'any relevant privacy code' but it is only one of a number of factors to be taken into account. The Press Complaints Commission Code of Practice provides:

'It is essential to the workings of an agreed code that it be honoured not only to the letter but in the full spirit. The Code should not be interpreted so narrowly as to compromise its commitment to respect the rights of the individual, nor so broadly that it prevents publication in the public interest ...

3 **Privacy**
(i) Everyone is entitled to respect for his or her private and family life, home, health and correspondence. A publication will be expected to justify intrusions into any individual's private life without consent. (ii) The use of long lens photography to take pictures of people in private places without their consent is unacceptable. Note—Private places are public or private property where there is a reasonable expectation of privacy.

4 **Harassment**
... They must not photograph individuals in private places (as defined by the note to clause 3) without their consent; must not persist in telephoning, questioning, pursuing or photographing individuals after having been asked to desist; must not remain on their property after having been asked to leave and must not follow them ...

The public interest
... 1. The public interest includes: (i) Detecting or exposing crime or a serious misdemeanour. (ii) Protecting public health and safety. (iii) Preventing the public from being misled by some statement or action of an individual or organisation.'

Courts may well find this statement of practice of assistance. While recognising that s 12(4) was primarily concerned with preserving the freedom of the press regard should be had to the guidance given by Brooke LJ in *Douglas v Hello! Ltd* [2001] 2 All ER 289 at 313–314, [2001] QB 967 at 994 (para 94), where he says:

'It appears to me that the existence of these statutory provisions, coupled with the current wording of the relevant privacy code, mean that in any case where the court is concerned with issues of freedom of expression in a journalistic, literary or artistic context, it is bound to pay particular regard to any breach of the rules set out in cl 3 of the code, especially where none of the public interest claims set out in the preamble to the code is asserted. A newspaper which flouts cl 3 of the code is likely in those circumstances to have its claim to an entitlement to freedom of expression trumped by art 10(2) considerations of privacy. Unlike the court in *Kaye v Robertson* [1991] FSR 62, Parliament recognised that it had to acknowledge the importance of the art 8(1) respect for private life, and it was able to do so untrammelled by any concerns that the law of confidence might not stretch to protect every aspect of private life.'

(xv) However, the court should discourage advocates seeking to rely on individual decisions of the Press Complaints Commission which at best are no *a* more than illustrative of how the Press Complaints Commission performs its different responsibilities.

[12] In the above paragraphs we have attempted to assist courts as to how they should go about the task of holding the balance between the conflicting rights when hearing these applications. We are suggesting that frequently what is required is not a technical approach to the law but a balancing of the facts. The

b weight which should be attached to each relevant consideration will vary depending on the precise circumstances. In many situations the balance may not point clearly in either direction. If this is the position, interim relief should be refused. We turn to deal with the present case.

c *The facts*

[13] We have already indicated the general nature of the relationships between A and C, and A and D. A is married and he and his wife have two children. There is no dispute that A had adulterous relationships with both C and D. There is a dispute as to the detail of the relationships. By bringing these proceedings and obtaining the injunction A hopes to prevent his wife learning of his adultery since,

d if she were to learn of this, it could prejudice his marriage and his long-standing relationship with his wife and also indirectly harm his children.

[14] There was never any question so far as A is concerned of his leaving his wife for C or D. It does however appear that at different times there was a fairly intimate relationship between, first, D and A and then C and A. A held a

e responsible position in his team and was in the habit of going out drinking from time to time in the evening with fellow members of the team with the object of improving team spirit. It was as a result of this that he became involved first with one girl and then with the other.

[15] D worked as a lap-dancer in a bar and A went to the bar in November 1999 and she danced for him. He again visited the bar on 15 December 1999 and

f again they met. There were meetings from time to time thereafter, including one where they spent the night together in a hotel and another on 21 November 2000 when he stayed the night at her flat. In addition there were a few other meetings which took place over a period of approximately a year, from December 1999 to December 2000. A and D were also in frequent contact on the telephone or

g sending telephone text messages.

[16] A and C first met in late January 2001 at a bar and later the same night at a club. He visited her house on one occasion and on another two occasions they spent the night together at a hotel. In March 2001, there was a further occasion when they spent the night together at her house but C says that she became angry

h with A because of his lying and on 31 March she posted through the door of A's parents' house a transcript of a text message he had sent saying that he was married which she had kept. She indicated that it should be shown to his wife and referred to photographs of him at the second hotel at which they had stayed. This brought that relationship to an end.

j [17] There were numerous telephone messages between A and C. An analysis of telephone bills showed that between 31 January and 21 April 2001, A called C 438 times. Because a long text message can be transmitted as several short messages, the total number of calls may give an exaggerated picture of the number of communications.

[18] In late April 2001 there was a telephone conversation between A and D in which reference was made to the fact that C was involved with a newspaper. D

accepts that during that telephone conversation she suggested to A that he give
her £5,000 for her story.   *a*

[19] The next development was the hearing of the application for the injunction
which was granted on 27 April 2001. The application was designed to restrain B
from printing a story intended to run on 29 April 2001.

[20] There are available to this court, as there were available to the judge,
drafts of the two articles which B proposed to publish. One concerned his   *b*
relationship with C and the other concerned his relationship with D. In the
judge's words, much of each is concerned with 'the salacious description of the
sexual activity between the claimant and C or D. They are both intended for the
prurient.'

[21] The judge having given his reasons for his decision on 30 April 2001 (the
first judgment), on 17 May 2001 B made an application that the injunction which   *c*
had been granted should be discharged on two grounds. The first was that new
legal and factual material made it inappropriate for the injunction to be maintained.
The second ground was that A had failed to make a full and frank disclosure in his
first witness statement relied on in support of the original application for an
interim injunction and therefore regardless of the merits of the original order the   *d*
injunction should be discharged.

[22] B served three witness statements in support of its application,
including a second witness statement by Marcus Partington, a lawyer acting on
behalf of B, a second witness statement by C and a witness statement by D, all
dated 18 May 2001. These witness statements set out in full C's and D's versions
of their relationships with A. Marcus Partington's second witness statement   *e*
exhibited an attendance note from a telephone conversation he had with a
member of staff at the Hoole House Hotel on 10 May 2001 during which it was
confirmed to him that A had stayed there with D on 10 February 2001. C's second
witness statement sets out, inter alia, the detail of the night she spent with A on
10 February 2001 and the afternoon meetings she had with him on 14 and 15   *f*
February 2001. D's witness statement sets out the detail of the relationship she
says that she had with A

[23] In response A filed a second witness statement dated 23 May 2001. In this
witness statement A admits meeting up with C on 10 February 2001. It also
includes an apology for not having mentioned this in his first witness statement
but states that he 'did not realise that it could be regarded as material'. This   *g*
should be contrasted with his first witness statement in which A says that he did
not see C from 9 to 17 February.

[24] Jack J heard the application over three days on 24, 25 May and 4 June 2001
and judgment was handed down on 20 June 2001 (the second judgment) in which
he discharged the injunction on the basis of A's material non-disclosure. Jack J   *h*
found that A had deliberately not disclosed his meetings with C between 9 and 17
February 2001 in order to minimise the relationship. In the light of this decision
Jack J considered that it was unnecessary for him to consider the substantive
ground put forward by B for having the injunction discharged.

[25] Following the handing down of judgment on the morning of 20 June   *j*
2001, two further witness statements, both dated 20 June 2001, were filed on
behalf of A: a third witness statement by A and a witness statement by Gareth
Dando, the solicitor who had prepared A's second (but not his first) witness
statement. These witness statements sought to explain the discrepancy between
A's first and second witness statements in relation to the meeting with C of 10
February 2001.

a   [26] A applied to Jack J to consider the new evidence and to reconsider his judgment on two grounds. First that the judge had misunderstood A's evidence in his first and second witness statement. Secondly that in the light of the further evidence, Jack J's findings of fact were wrong and the decision to discharge the injunction ought to be reversed.

b   [27] Jack J invited the parties to provide written submissions and oral submissions were also made in a telephone hearing by counsel for both sides on 27 June 2001. In the light of these submissions Jack J delivered his judgment dated 5 July 2001 (the third judgment) in which he held that he had jurisdiction to reopen his second judgment, that the exceptional circumstances of the case meant that he ought so to do, that the new evidence was simply explanatory and ought to be admitted and that in the light of that new evidence the injunction restraining B

c   should be reimposed. It is this decision which forms the basis of one of B's appeals (the procedural appeal).

[28] Having made this decision, B's application to set aside the injunction on the merits, which had not needed to be decided on 20 June 2001, fell to be considered. Jack J reserved judgment on this application.

d   [29] On 10 September 2001 Jack J delivered his judgment on B's application to set aside the injunction on the merits (the fourth judgment) (see [2002] 1 All ER 449, [2001] 1 WLR 2341). In this judgment Jack J reimposed the injunction against B in narrower terms than previously. In doing so he held: the law affords the protection of confidentiality to facts concerning sexual relations in marriage (see *Duchess of Argyll v Duke of Argyll* [1965] 1 All ER 611, [1967] Ch 302) and in the

e   context of modern sexual relations, it should be no different outside marriage (see [2002] 1 All ER 449 at [56]); it was a breach of confidence for C and D to provide information about their sexual relationships with A to B with a view to publication and it would be a further breach of confidence for B to publish the information (see [59]); there is a substantial distinction between communication

f   of information to family and friends and communication of information to the press (see [60]); aspects of A's relationships with C and D were conducted in public, but the fact that they were having sexual intercourse and the detail of that intercourse were not known by anyone other than the participants. The information is therefore not in the public domain and is capable of protection (see [63]); s 12(4) of the 1998 Act requires the court to have particular regard to

g   the importance under the convention of art 10 (see [64]); art 10(2) places restrictions on freedom of expression which includes breach of confidences. Any such restriction must be necessary in a democratic society, inter alia, for the protection of the rights of others, or for preventing the disclosure of information received in confidence. In this case A has a right to respect for his private life. C

h   and D as participants have not received information in the literal sense, but giving the words a purposive construction in the light of art 8(1), they are to be treated as having received the information as the events occurred (see [65]); there is a pressing social need for protection of a person's private life (see [66]); there is no countervailing public interest in the publication of the proposed articles by B.

j   The public interest is to be interpreted in the sense of being in the interests of the public, approximating to public benefit. A is only a public figure to the extent that he is a professional footballer. He has not courted publicity or laid his life open to public scrutiny (see [67]); in accordance with the judgment of Brooke LJ on the application of s 12(4) of the 1998 Act and art 10 in *Douglas v Hello! Ltd* [2001] 2 All ER 289, [2001] QB 967 A is likely to succeed at trial in establishing that his right to privacy should prevail over the newspaper's right to freedom of expression

(see [68]); the discretion of the court to award an injunction should be exercised;
in respect of a free-standing right of privacy, in the light of the finding on breach
of confidence and Dame Elizabeth Butler-Sloss P's judgment in *Venables v News
Group Newspapers Ltd* [2001] 1 All ER 908, [2001] Fam 430, the views expressed in
the first judgment should be revisited and no view is now expressed.

[30] It is this judgment which forms the subject matter of the second appeal
(the substantive appeal).

The procedural appeal

[31] B makes the procedural appeal with the permission of Rix LJ against the
third judgment of Jack J in which he reconsidered and reversed his second
judgment.

[32] It is accepted by B that there is a jurisdiction in the court which enables
the judge to reconsider and if necessary reverse a judgment order during the
period between the delivery of the judgment and the moment when the order is
sealed or otherwise perfected. However, it is argued that this jurisdiction is an
exceptional jurisdiction and could not appropriately be exercised in this situation.
It is argued that it was wrong to allow A to introduce further evidence subsequent
to the second judgment being handed down. It is submitted that A was
represented by leading and junior counsel, he had ample opportunity to consider
the evidence he placed before the court and the issue of A's non-disclosure had
been raised at the end of the hearing on 27 April 2001 and also taken up in
correspondence by B's solicitor from 1 May 2001 onwards. It could not be
suggested that A's further evidence was not available at the time of the hearing
and while A's third statement explained his failure to deal with the events of 14
and 15 February 2001 in his first witness statement no explanation was given for
his failure to deal with these events in his second witness statement. The
evidence was certainly not capable of properly being described as fresh evidence.

[33] A contends in broad terms either the judge's third judgment was correct
or, if it was not, his second judgment of 20 June 2001 to discharge the injunction
was wrong and this court should give permission for the fresh evidence to be
readmitted.

[34] We did not hear oral argument on the procedural appeal. Time allocated
to the appeal was exhausted in considering the substantive appeal. It would have
probably extended the hearing of the appeal by at least a day and possibly two
days if we had heard the matter argued fully. However, we are urged to give a
decision on the procedural appeal for two reasons. First it is contended that there
are issues of principle involved and secondly it could be relevant on the question
of costs.

[35] Considering the circumstances in which he had to give his decisions,
Jack J dealt with all the arguments which the parties advanced before him at the
different hearings with commendable conscientiousness. We are particularly
appreciative of his willingness to hear argument over the telephone so as to
accommodate the parties. We are none the less extremely concerned about what
is likely to be the scale of the costs involved in this litigation so far. Whatever the
scale of A's means, neither he nor B were entitled to conduct the proceedings in
a disproportionate manner and the judge should have been astute to prevent this
happening. Despite the judge's efforts the issues have been dealt with in a manner
which bears no relation to the significance of what was at issue.

[36] In relation to each application, in the forefront of the judge's mind should
have been the fact that he had originally given a decision on an interim application.

a It is true, as we have indicated already, his interim decision could have been the end of the proceedings. However, he was aware that there were issues of fact which could only be resolved satisfactorily at a hearing of oral evidence and although A indicates he would have preferred to be cross-examined this was never a viable option.

b [37] In the circumstances, the judge's approach should have been one where unless there are circumstances which justify this, such as a defendant has had no proper opportunity to be heard, the parties either accept a decision or appeal. We do not underestimate the importance in appropriate circumstances of a court taking a firm view about non-disclosure in an interim application. However, the matters of non-disclosure which were being relied upon by B for setting aside the first judgment of 30 April 2001 were not of any particular relevance. The number c of occasions that A met C and D and the number of occasions upon which he may have committed adultery were of marginal, if any, relevance to the substantive decision. We would have expected many judges to have taken the view, having considered the nature of the application, that it was one which could have been disposed of summarily without the disproportionate expenditure of costs. If it d was to be resolved, it would be more appropriately resolved at a speedy trial.

[38] Having been persuaded to deal with the application and having granted it, the subsequent events in our judgment were the consequences of the inappropriate initial decision. We understand why the judge was persuaded to have second thoughts, and his reasons for coming to the decisions which he did, but the resulting decisions are hardly an example of the efficient handling of legal e proceedings.

[39] Behind the parties' reasons for asking us to give a decision on the individual steps which were taken is apparently the belief that there are points of principle involved. These are as to when a decision can be reconsidered and when additional evidence is or is not admissible. In a case where an interim f injunction has been granted, we reject the suggestion that there are technicalities which require one outcome or another. Each application has to be decided on its merits as to which the only guidance which is required is that contained in CPR Pt 1. On this aspect of the appeal the parties had prepared a core bundle of 11 authorities, but we do not consider that they throw any decisive light on the very different issues that are before us.

g [40] Jack J had jurisdiction to come to the decisions he did which resulted in his having to give his four judgments, but we consider he was wrong to set aside his original decision to grant the injunction of 27 April 2001, even if there were circumstances which meant it was reasonable to have a further hearing before Jack J, as to which we make no finding, and that all his subsequent decisions were h tainted by this decision. However, in view of our conclusions as to the substantive appeal, we are not prepared to go into academic questions as to whether the procedural appeal should be allowed or refused.

The substantive appeal

j [41] The injunction which was granted in consequence of the fourth judgment was different from that originally granted. The main provisions were contained in paras 2 and 3 of the order and were in these terms:

'2. Until after judgment in this action or further order in the meantime, the first defendant must not publish or disclose information concerning the facts: (a) that the claimant was having sexual relations with C and with D;

(b) relating to the sexual intercourse and other private sexual conduct which occurred with C and with D.

3. Until after judgment in this action or further order in the meantime, the second defendant must not publish or disclose any of the said information to any person with a view to its publication in the media.'

[42] The order makes it clear that the injunction on B is wider in its application than that on C which prevents her from making disclosure with a view to publication in the media. C could for example inform A's wife of their adultery. B contends that the terms of the injunction indicate its inappropriate nature. We recognise that the terms are unusual but do not attach any particular significance to this, though it does illustrate the difficulty involved in restraining publication.

[43] Mr Spearman QC subjected Jack J's fourth judgment to detailed criticism. We would not accept all the criticisms but we do detect important flaws in his approach. These are as follows: (i) Jack J makes no reference to the fact that any interference of the court by way of an injunction has to be justified. His approach is to assume that, as A has a right to privacy with regard to his relationship with C and D, it is in order to restrain the proposed publications unless B can show that there is a public interest in what it is proposed to publish. (ii) Jack J appears to regard A as being entitled to the same protection in respect of his transient relationships with C and D as would be available to facts concerning 'sexual relations within marriage' (see [2002] 1 All ER 449 at [56]). Thus Jack J states, undoubtedly correctly, that confidentiality applies to facts concerning sexual relations within marriage but then adds that 'in the context of modern sexual relations, it should be no different with relationships outside marriage'. This approach is objectionable because it makes no allowance for the very different nature of the relationship that A had, on his own account, with C and D from that which would exist within marriage. Quite apart from the recognition which the law gives to the status of marriage, there is a significant difference in our judgment between the confidentiality which attaches to what is intended to be a permanent relationship and that which attaches to the category of relationships which A was involved with here. We would refer here to a judgment of Ouseley J in *Theakston v MGN Ltd* [2002] EWHC 137, [2002] All ER (D) 182 (Feb):

'[59] I consider it impossible however to invest with the protection of confidentiality all acts of physical intimacy regardless of circumstances. I consider it artificial to draw a line at full sexual intercourse in the context of confidentiality, such that anything short of that is not confidential. Whilst the degree of intimacy is a very relevant factor, it cannot be taken in isolation from the relationship within which the physical intimacy occurs and from the other circumstances particularly the location. I do consider Jack J is right to point out that the protection of confidentiality in relation to any particular set of circumstances is also affected by the nature of the person to whom disclosure is proposed to be made, whether to partner, friend or lawyer or to the press for wider publication. The impact of disclosure on others, for example the children of a relationship, may also be relevant to the very existence of confidentiality.

[60] Sexual relations within marriage at home would be at one end of the range or matrix of circumstances to be protected from most forms of disclosure; a one night stand with a recent acquaintance in a hotel bedroom might very well be protected from press publicity. A transitory engagement in a brothel is yet further away.'

a (iii) Furthermore, although again we would not go so far as to say there can be no confidentiality where one party to a relationship does not want confidentiality, the fact that C and D chose to disclose their relationships to B does affect A's right to protection of the information. For the position to be otherwise would not acknowledge C and D's own right to freedom of expression. (iv) Jack J ([2002] 1 All ER 449 at [59]) did not apparently regard a disclosure by C and D to their

b friends as being objectionable but only publication to the media. This approach ignores the importance to be attached to a free press. (v) Jack J also appears in his first judgment to have been influenced by the need to not only protect A but his family as well. At the end of his judgment, he states: '... but if it is published the damage to the claimant and his family is done and will be difficult to quantify in terms of money'. The judge should not, in our view, assume that it was in the

c interests of A's wife to be kept in ignorance of A's relationships. This is an issue on which the court is not in a position to reach a judgment. (vi) Again Jack J rejected any question of there being a public interest in B's proposed publications. Ignoring, as one must, the literary quality of what it was proposed to publish, it is not self-evident that how a well-known Premiership football player, who has a

d position of responsibility within his club, chooses to spend his time off the football field does not have a modicum of public interest. Footballers are role models for young people and undesirable behaviour on their part can set an unfortunate example. While Jack J was right to say on the evidence which was before him that A had not courted publicity, the fact is that someone holding his position was inevitably a figure in whom a section of the public and the media

e would be interested.

[44] Although the criticisms which we make of the approach of Jack J are not individually of great significance, collectively we do believe they resulted in his coming to a wrong decision. The degree of confidentiality to which A was entitled, notwithstanding that C and D did not wish their relationships with A to

f be confidential, was very modest.

[45] Relationships of the sort which A had with C and D are not the categories of relationships which the court should be astute to protect when the other parties to the relationships do not want them to remain confidential. Any injunction granted after a trial would have to be permanent. It is most unlikely such an injunction would ever be granted.

g [46] On an issue which depends to such a substantial extent on the discretion of the judge, his decision is entitled to a considerable degree of deference from an appellate court. However here, it can be shown there are significant flaws in Jack J's approach and we are satisfied that his decision is wrong.

[47] Ouseley J in Theakston's case [2002] All ER (D) 182 (Feb) made reference

h to this case, saying (at [61]) that if the relationship between A and C and D was entitled to confidentiality 'that degree of protection represents to my mind the outer limit of what is confidential'. We do not go so far as to say the relationships of the class being considered here can never be entitled to any confidentiality. We prefer to adopt Ouseley J's view that the situation is one at the outer limits of

j relationships which require the protection of the law. The fact that it attracts the protection of the law does not mean, however, that an injunction should be granted to provide that protection. In our view to grant an injunction would be an unjustified interference with the freedom of the press.

[48] Once it is accepted that the freedom of the press should prevail, then the form of reporting in the press is not a matter for the courts but for the Press Complaints Commission and the customers of the newspaper concerned.

[49] In relation to certain communications between A and C and D, A could be in a position to contend that their publication would constitute a breach of copyright. Restraining B in respect of the limited area to which the law of copyright would apply would serve no purpose if that was the only relief granted to A, and so the claim based on copyright is accepted as being of no practical significance.

[50] We set aside the injunction and allow this appeal.

Substantive appeal allowed. Permission to appeal refused.

Kate O'Hanlon   Barrister

Morris v KLM Royal Dutch Airlines
King v Bristow Helicopters Ltd

[2002] UKHL 7

HOUSE OF LORDS

LORD NICHOLLS OF BIRKENHEAD, LORD MACKAY OF CLASHFERN, LORD STEYN, LORD
HOPE OF CRAIGHEAD AND LORD HOBHOUSE OF WOODBOROUGH

19–21 NOVEMBER 2001, 28 FEBRUARY 2002

*Carriage by air – Carriage of passengers – Liability of carrier – International convention
imposing liability on carrier for 'bodily injury' to passenger – Whether 'bodily injury'
including purely mental injury – Carriage by Air Act 1961, Sch 1, Pt I, art 17.*

In two conjoined appeals to the House of Lords, the question arose as to whether,
and if so to what extent, an air carrier was liable under art 17[a] of the Warsaw
Convention 1929, as amended at The Hague in 1955 and set out in Sch 1 to the
Carriage by Air Act 1961, for an injury sustained by a passenger in an accident
where that injury was a mental injury rather than a physical injury. Article 17
imposed liability on the carrier for damage sustained in the event of the death or
wounding of a passenger or any other 'bodily injury'—'lésion corporelle' in the
original French text of the convention—suffered by a passenger, if the accident
which had caused that damage had taken place on board the aircraft or in the
course of any of the operations of embarking or disembarking. In the first appeal,
the claimant, M, had been flying as an unaccompanied minor on a long-distance
flight. After falling asleep, she had woken to discover her thigh being caressed by
the man sitting next to her. Although she suffered no physical illness or injury,
she was very distressed and was subsequently diagnosed as suffering from clinical
depression amounting to a single episode of a major depressive illness. In the
second appeal, the pursuer, K, had been a passenger on a helicopter which had
taken off in poor weather from the helideck of a floating platform in a North Sea
oilfield. Shortly after take-off, two of the helicopter's engines flamed out, there
was a loud bang and the helicopter descended rapidly, landing heavily on the
helideck. K did not sustain any physical injury, but was extremely frightened and
developed several psychiatric conditions as a result of the accident, including a
moderate post-traumatic stress disorder. The stress led to the onset of peptic
ulcer disease. Both M and K claimed damages from the respective carriers under
art 17. No attempt was made in either case to show that the mental illness or
injury had been caused to any extent by physical injury. In M's case, the Court of
Appeal, reversing the judge at first instance, held that her depressive illness did
not constitute a 'bodily injury' within the meaning of art 17 and that accordingly
she was not entitled to damages under that provision. M appealed. In K's case,
the First Division of the Court of Session reversed the decision of the
Lord Ordinary that K's claim under art 17 was confined to his peptic ulcer disease,
and held instead that he was also entitled to claim damages for his psychiatric
conditions. The carrier appealed.

---

a   Article 17 is set out at [13], below

Held – Where a mental injury or illness lacked a physical cause or origin, it could not constitute a 'bodily injury' within the meaning of art 17 of the convention, but that term did cover physical manifestations of a mental injury and (per Lord Nicholls, Lord Mackay and Lord Hobhouse) psychiatric disorders arising from injury to the brain or nervous system. The use of the adjective 'bodily' suggested that art 17 had not been intended to cover everything that might possibly be described as an injury to the passenger sustained on board the aircraft or in the course of embarking or disembarking. The word 'corporelle' in the French text directed attention to physical changes in the body rather than to something that affected the mind, and it had been chosen to qualify, and thus restrict, the meaning of the word 'lésion'. The phrase was therefore to be read in a way that would confine its application to the skin, bones or other tissues of the body and exclude mental injury. That interpretation was not contradicted by anything in the travaux préparatoires, and there was a consistent body of judicial opinion in the United States that the phrase 'any other bodily injury' did not permit compensation for an emotional reaction which had not been shown to be a manifestation of physical injury. Emotional distress was excluded, but so also was a psychiatric illness which affected the mind only and was not capable of being described as a physical injury. However, if the brain could be shown to have been injured and the other conditions for compensation under art 17 were satisfied, such compensation could not be refused on the ground that in 1929 an injury of that kind would not have been capable of being demonstrated and medical opinion would then have concluded that the passenger had suffered only mental injury. Whether or not there was such an injury to the brain would always depend on the evidence. In the instant cases, there had been no attempt to demonstrate that the passengers' depressive illnesses had a physical cause or origin, and it had not been shown that their mental injuries fell within the scope of the expression 'bodily injury'. Accordingly, M's appeal would be dismissed, while the appeal of the carrier in K's case would be allowed and the decision of the Lord Ordinary restored (see [1], [3], [6]–[8], [20], [21], [32], [83], [85], [88], [97], [118], [125], [128]–[130], [152], [156], [175], [179], [181], [183], [184], below).

Decision of the Court of Appeal [2001] 3 All ER 126 affirmed.

Notes

For liability of carriers for injury to passengers, see 2 *Halsbury's Laws* (4th edn reissue) para 1559.

For the Carriage by Air Act 1961, Sch 1, Pt I, art 17, see 4 *Halsbury's Statutes* (4th edn) (1998 reissue) 33.

Cases referred to in opinions

Air Crash at Little Rock, Arkansas on 1 June 1999, Re (2000) 118 F Supp 2d 916, Arkansas DC.

Air France v Saks (1985) 470 US 392, US SC.

Alvarez v American Airlines Inc (1999) 27 Avi 17,214; *affd* (2000) 27 Avi 17,475, NY DC.

Buchanan (James) & Co Ltd v Babco Forwarding and Shipping (UK) Ltd [1977] 3 All ER 1048, [1978] AC 141, [1977] 3 WLR 907, HL.

Burnett v Trans World Airlines Inc (1973) 12 Avi 18,405, US DC.

Carey v United Airlines (2001) 28 Avi 15,408, US Ct of Apps (9th Circuit).

Chaudhari v British Airways plc (1997) Times, 7 May, [1997] CA Transcript 590.

Cockburn v Chief Adjudication Officer [1997] 3 All ER 844, [1997] 1 WLR 799, HL.

a *Commonwealth of Australia v Baume* (1905) 2 CLR 405, Aust HC.
Daddon v Air France (1984) 1 S & B Av R VII/141, Israel SC.
Eastern Airlines Inc v Floyd (1991) 499 US 530, US SC.
El Al Israel Airlines Ltd v Tsui Yuan Tseng (1999) 525 US 155, US SC.
Fellowes (or Herd) v Clyde Helicopters Ltd [1997] 1 All ER 775, [1997] AC 534, [1997] 2 WLR 380, HL.
b *Fothergill v Monarch Airlines Ltd* [1980] 2 All ER 696, [1981] AC 251, [1980] 3 WLR 209, HL.
Georgeopoulos v American Airlines Inc (26 September 1996, unreported), NSW CA.
Georgeopoulos v American Airlines Inc (No 2) [1998] NSWSC 463.
Grein v Imperial Airways Ltd [1936] 2 All ER 1258, [1937] 1 KB 50, CA.
c *Hay (or Bourhill) v Young* [1942] 2 All ER 396, sub nom *Bourhill v Young* [1943] AC 92, HL.
Holmes v Bangladesh Biman Corp [1989] 1 All ER 852, [1989] AC 1112, [1989] 2 WLR 481, HL.
Jack v Trans World Airlines Inc (1994) 854 F Supp 654, California DC.
d *Kotsambasis v Singapore Airlines Ltd* (1997) 42 NSWLR 110, NSW SC.
McLoughlin v O'Brian [1982] 2 All ER 298, [1983] 1 AC 410, [1982] 2 WLR 982, HL.
Page v Smith [1995] 2 All ER 736, [1996] AC 155, [1995] 2 WLR 644, HL.
R v Chan-Fook [1994] 2 All ER 552, [1994] 1 WLR 689, CA.
R v Ireland, R v Burstow [1997] 4 All ER 225, [1998] AC 147, [1997] 3 WLR 534, HL.
e *R v Secretary of State for the Home Dept, ex p Adan* [2001] 2 AC 477, [2001] 1 All ER 593, [2001] 2 WLR 143, HL.
Randwick Municipal Council v Rutledge (1959) 102 CLR 54, Aust HC.
Rosman v Trans World Airlines Inc (1974) 34 NY 2d 385, NY Ct of Apps.
Sidhu v British Airways plc, Abnett (known as Sykes) v British Airways plc [1997] 1 All ER 193, [1997] AC 430, [1997] 2 WLR 26, HL.
f *Stag Line Ltd v Foscolo, Mango & Co Ltd* [1932] AC 328, [1931] All ER Rep 666, HL.
Swiss Bank Corp v Brink's-MAT Ltd [1986] 2 All ER 188, [1986] QB 853, [1986] 3 WLR 12.
Terrafranca v Virgin Atlantic Airways Ltd (1998) 151 F 3d 108, US Ct of Apps (3rd Circuit).
g *Turturro v Continental Airlines* (2001) 27 Avi 18,414, NY DC.
Weaver v Delta Airlines (1999) 56 F Supp 2d 1190, Montana DC.
White v Chief Constable of the South Yorkshire Police [1999] 1 All ER 1, sub nom *Frost v Chief Constable of South Yorkshire Police* [1999] 2 AC 455, [1998] 3 WLR 1509, HL.

h **Appeals**

Morris v KLM Royal Dutch Airlines

The claimant, Kelly Morris, appealed with permission of the Court of Appeal (Lord Phillips of Worth Matravers MR, Peter Gibson and Latham LJJ) from its
j decision on 17 May 2001 ([2001] EWCA Civ 790, [2001] 3 All ER 126, [2002] QB 100) allowing an appeal by the defendant, KLM Royal Dutch Airlines (KLM), from the decision of Judge Carter QC at Bury County Court on 1 December 2000 giving summary judgment on liability for Miss Kelly in her action for damages against KLM under art 17 of the Warsaw Convention 1929, as amended at The Hague in 1955 and set out in Sch 1 to the Carriage by Air Act 1961. The facts are set out in the opinion of Lord Steyn.

King v Bristow Helicopters Ltd

The defender, Bristow Helicopters Ltd (Bristow), appealed from the decision of   *a*
the First Division of the Inner House of the Court of Session (Lord President
(Lord Rodger of Earlsferry) and Lord Cameron of Lochbroom, Lord Reed
dissenting) on 12 July 2000 (2001 SLT 126) allowing a reclaiming motion by the
pursuer, Philip King, from the decision of the Lord Ordinary (Lord Philip) on 13
November 1998 (1999 SLT 919) excluding from probation in Mr King's action   *b*
against Bristow for damages under art 17 of the Warsaw Convention 1929, as
amended at The Hague in 1955 and set out in Sch 1 to the Carriage by Air Act
1961, all averments about the psychiatric conditions sustained by Mr King as a
result of the accident which formed the subject matter of the action. The facts
are set out in the opinion of Lord Steyn.

                                                                                  c
Nicholas Braslavsky QC and *Andrew Singer* (instructed by *Kippax Beaumont Lewis*,
    Bolton) for Miss Morris.
Charles Haddon-Cave QC and *Robert Lawson* (instructed by *Beaumont & Son*) for
    KLM.
Colin Campbell QC and *Marian Gilmore* (both of the Scottish Bar) (instructed by   *d*
    Beaumont & Son as agents for *Shepherd & Wedderburn WS*, Edinburgh) for
    Bristow.
Michael S Jones QC (of the Scottish and English Bars) and *Shona Haldane* (of the
    Scottish Bar) (instructed by *Balfour & Manson*, Edinburgh, as agents for
    Burnside Kemp Fraser, Aberdeen) for Mr King.
                                                                                  e
Their Lordships took time for consideration.

28 February 2002. The following opinions were delivered.

LORD NICHOLLS OF BIRKENHEAD.   *f*
    [1] My Lords, the facts and issues in these two appeals are set out fully in the
speeches of my noble and learned friends Lord Steyn, Lord Hope of Craighead,
and Lord Hobhouse of Woodborough. Your Lordships are agreed on the outcome
of these appeals: the appeal in *King's* case should be allowed, and the decision of
the Lord Ordinary (Lord Philip) (1999 SLT 919) restored, and the appeal in
Morris's case should be dismissed. I also agree.   *g*
    [2] There is a measure of disagreement between your Lordships on whether
inherent in art 17 of the Warsaw Convention (as set out in Sch 1 to the Carriage
by Air Act 1961) is an antithesis between bodily injury and mental injury, the
latter being outside the scope of art 17. I can state my own view shortly.
    [3] The expression 'bodily injury', or 'lésion corporelle', in art 17 means, simply,   *h*
injury to the passenger's body. The contrast is with absence of injury to a passenger's
body. This simple meaning propounds a coherent and workable test. None of
the submissions urged upon your Lordships has persuaded me that this phrase
should be given a different, more limited meaning. In particular, I see no occasion
for limiting art 17 to bodily injuries which are 'palpable and conspicuous', whatever   *j*
those two ambiguous expressions are taken to mean in this context. The brain is
part of the body. Injury to a passenger's brain is an injury to a passenger's body
just as much as an injury to any other part of his body. Whether injury to a part
of a person's body has occurred is, today as much as in 1929, essentially a question
of medical evidence. It may be that, in the less advanced state of medical and
scientific knowledge 70 years ago, psychiatric disorders would not have been

a related to physical impairment of the brain or nervous system. But even if that is so, this cannot be a good reason for now excluding this type of bodily injury, if proved by satisfactory evidence, from the scope of art 17.

[4] This does not mean that shock, anxiety, fear, distress, grief or other emotional disturbances will as such now fall within art 17. It is all a question of medical evidence. In *Weaver v Delta Airlines* (1999) 56 F Supp 2d 1190 the
b uncontradicted medical evidence was that extreme stress could cause actual physical brain damage. The judge observed (at 1192) that 'fright alone is not compensable, but brain injury from fright is'.

[5] It really goes without saying that international uniformity of interpretation of art 17 is highly desirable. Like Lord Mackay of Clashfern, I have been much concerned that the interpretation of art 17 espoused by this House should, if
c possible, be consistent with the mainstream views expressed in leading overseas authorities. Most notable in this respect, given the important position of the United States in carriage by air, is the decision of the United States Supreme Court in *Eastern Airlines Inc v Floyd* (1991) 499 US 530. I consider the view I have expressed above is consistent with *Floyd*'s case and the other leading cases. I agree with
d Lord Hobhouse's analysis of the authorities.

LORD MACKAY OF CLASHFERN.

[6] My Lords, I have had the advantage of reading in draft the speech to be delivered by my noble and learned friend Lord Hope of Craighead. I agree with his conclusion on the disposal of these appeals and with the reasons he gives for
e it, subject to the following comment.

[7] Because I consider it important that the Warsaw Convention (as set out in Sch 1 to the Carriage by Air Act 1961) should have a common construction in all the jurisdictions of the countries that have adopted the convention, I attach crucial importance to the decisions of the United States Supreme Court in *Eastern*
f *Airlines Inc v Floyd* (1991) 499 US 530 and *El Al Israel Airlines Ltd v Tsui Yuan Tseng* (1999) 525 US 155, particularly as the United States is such a large participant in carriage by air. But for these decisions, I would have given more weight than does my learned friend to the argument that the word 'bodily' and its French counterpart 'corporelle' were directed to the distinction between injury to a passenger through loss of baggage or delay on the one hand and injury to his
g person on the other, rather than to the distinction between bodily injury and mental injury.

[8] I wish also to say that in my opinion if an injury to the brain of a passenger is found to have occurred, and the other conditions requisite to qualify for compensation under art 17 are present, compensation under the article cannot be
h refused on the ground that in 1929 this fact would not have been known, with the result that at that time medical opinion would have been that the passenger had suffered only mental injury. Like my noble and learned friend Lord Nicholls of Birkenhead I do not see merit in adding words to the description of injury which are not present in the convention text and I would apply the simple test, does the
j evidence demonstrate injury to the body, including in that expression the brain, the central nervous system and all the other components of the body?

LORD STEYN.

[9] My Lords, in the context of two appeals, one English and one Scottish, the question before the House concerns the phrase 'bodily injury' in art 17 of the Warsaw Convention as amended at The Hague in 1955 which was incorporated

into the law of the United Kingdom as Sch 1 to the Carriage by Air Act 1961. The
principal question of law in both appeals is whether a person who suffers no   *a*
physical injury but who does suffer mental injury or illness (such as clinical
depression) as a result of an accident on board an aircraft has a claim against the
carrier under art 17 of the convention. It is a point of construction of the relevant
words in their context. It is common ground that no question of implying words
into art 17 arises. The Court of Appeal (Lord Phillips of Worth Matravers MR,   *b*
Peter Gibson and Latham LJJ) answered the question in the negative: *Morris v
KLM Royal Dutch Airlines* [2001] EWCA Civ 790, [2001] 3 All ER 126, [2002] QB
100. By a majority the First Division (the Lord President (Lord Rodger of
Earlsferry) and Lord Cameron of Lochbroom; Lord Reed dissenting) answered it
in the affirmative: *King v Bristow Helicopters Ltd* 2001 SLT 126. Depending on the
view of the House, the further question may arise in *King's* case whether an   *c*
adverse physical manifestation, such as a peptic ulcer caused by mental illness,
may be within art 17.

(I) *The assumed facts*

[10] In *Morris's* case the alleged facts were as follows. On 6 September 1998 the   *d*
appellant was a passenger carried for reward on a KLM flight from Kuala Lumpur
to Amsterdam. At the time, she was not yet 16 years of age and was travelling on
her own. She was seated next to two men. After a meal, she fell asleep and woke
to discover the hand of the man next to her caressing her left thigh from the hip to
the knee. She got up, and told an air hostess what had happened and was moved
to another seat. She was very distressed. On her return to England a doctor found   *e*
that she was suffering from clinical depression amounting to a single episode of a
major depressive illness. She does not allege that she suffered any physical illness.
Her claim for mental injury under art 17 was upheld by a judge. The Court of
Appeal held that what befell the appellant was an accident within art 17. But the
Court of Appeal held that a mental injury falls outside art 17. Only the latter ruling   *f*
is before the House.

[11] In *King's* case the alleged facts were as follows. On 22 December 1993,
King was a passenger on board a helicopter, owned and operated by Bristow
Helicopters Ltd. The helicopter took off from a floating platform in the North
Sea in poor weather. The helicopter ascended and hovered for a short period, at
which point its two engines failed. It descended and landed on the helideck.   *g*
Smoke engulfed the helicopter; there was panic on board; and passengers feared
that the helicopter was about to crash into the sea. The door was opened and the
passengers disembarked. The passenger developed post-traumatic stress disorder.
As a result of the stress he suffered an onset of peptic ulcer disease. The Lord
Ordinary (Lord Philip) (1999 SLT 919) allowed the claim to go to proof only in   *h*
respect of the allegations concerning the peptic ulcer. The First Division allowed
the appeal and ordered that the entire claim should go to proof.

(II) *The scheme of the convention*

[12] It is important to understand the major objective of the Warsaw Convention.   *j*
Before it came into operation passengers were free to claim under a diversity of
applicable national laws in respect of damage caused by death, wounding and
bodily injury; loss of or damage to property; and delay. On the other hand,
carriers were free to limit their liability to passengers by exception and limitation
clauses. The liability insurance premiums charged by insurers to carriers no
doubt reflected the exception and limitation clauses imposed. Taking into

a account exception and limitation clauses, prudent passengers would have had to take out appropriate direct insurance cover. This system was unsatisfactory from the point of view of the public, who wanted to travel by air, and for the fledgling and still fragile aviation industry. The purpose of the Warsaw Convention, following the precedent of the earlier Hague Rules governing carriage by sea, was to bring some order to a fragmented system by a partial harmonisation of the b applicable laws.

[13] For present purposes the compromise agreed on at Warsaw involved the imposition of a form of strict liability on carriers in respect of accidents causing death, wounding or bodily injury to passengers in return for the limitations of liability expressed in the Warsaw Convention. Chapter III of the Warsaw Convention reflects the bargain struck at Warsaw. The relevant articles of Ch III c (as amended) read as follows:

Article 17
The carrier is liable for damage sustained in the event of the death or wounding of a passenger or any other bodily injury suffered by a passenger, if the accident which caused the damage so sustained took place on board the d aircraft or in the course of any of the operations of embarking or disembarking.

Article 18
The carrier is liable for damage sustained in the event of the destruction or loss of, or of damage to, any registered baggage or any cargo, if the occurrence which caused the damage so sustained took place during the carriage by air ...

Article 19
The carrier is liable for damage occasioned by delay in the carriage by air f of passengers, baggage or cargo.

Article 20
The carrier is not liable if he proves that he and his servants or agents have taken all necessary measures to avoid the damage or that it was impossible for him or them to take such measures.

Article 21
If the carrier proves that the damage was caused by or contributed to by the negligence of the injured person the court may, in accordance with the provisions of its own law, exonerate the carrier wholly or partly from his h liability.

Article 22
(1) In the carriage of persons the liability of the carrier for each passenger is limited to the sum of 100,000 special drawing rights ...
(2)—(a) In the carriage of registered baggage and of cargo, the liability of j the carrier is limited to a sum of 17 special drawing rights per kilogramme ...

Article 23
(1) Any provision tending to relieve the carrier of liability or to fix a lower limit than that which is laid down in this Convention shall be null and void, but the nullity of any such provision does not involve the nullity of the whole contract, which shall remain subject to the provisions of this Convention.

(2) Paragraph (1) of this Article shall not apply to provisions governing loss or damage resulting from the inherent defect, quality or vice of the cargo carried.

Article 24

(1) In the cases covered by Articles 18 and 19 any action for damages, however founded, can only be brought subject to the conditions and limits set out in this Convention.

(2) In the cases covered by Article 17 the provisions of the preceding paragraph also apply, without prejudice to the questions as to who are the persons who have the right to bring suit and what are their respective rights.

Article 25

The limits of liability specified in Article 22 shall not apply if it is proved that the damage resulted from an act or omission of the carrier, his servants or agents, done with intent to cause damage or recklessly and with knowledge that damage would probably result; provided that, in the case of such act or omission of a servant or agent, it is also proved that he was acting within the scope of his employment.'

Since, in the event of inconsistency between the English and French texts of the convention, s 1 of the 1961 Act provides that the French text shall prevail, I cite the French wording of art 17:

'Le transporteur est responsable du dommage survenu en cas de mort, de blessure ou de toute autre lésion corporelle subie par un voyageur lorsque l'accident qui a causé le dommage s'est produit à bord de l'aéronef ou au cours de toutes opérations d'embarquement et de débarquement.'

[14] The effect of the convention was described by Lord Hope of Craighead in *Sidhu v British Airways plc, Abnett (known as Sykes) v British Airways plc* [1997] 1 All ER 193, [1997] AC 430. Speaking on behalf of a unanimous House Lord Hope observed:

'On the one hand, the carrier surrenders his freedom to exclude or to limit his liability. On the other hand, the passenger or other party to the contract is restricted in the claims which he can bring in an action for damages by the conditions and limits set out in the convention. The idea that an action for damages may be brought by a passenger against the carrier outside the convention in the cases covered by art 17, which is the issue in the present case, seems to be entirely contrary to the system which these two articles were designed to create ... In my opinion, the answer to it is to be found not by an exact analysis of the particular words used but by a consideration of the whole purpose of the article. In its context, the purpose seems to me to be to prescribe the circumstances, that is to say the only circumstances, in which a carrier will be liable in damages to the passenger for claims arising out of his international carriage by air.' (See [1997] 1 All ER 193 at 206–207, [1997] AC 430 at 447.)

In *El Al Israel Airlines Ltd v Tsui Yuan Tseng* (1999) 525 US 155 the United States Supreme Court followed *Sidhu's* case on this point. I respectfully adopt this analysis.

[15] The Warsaw Convention is an exclusive code of limited liability of carriers to passengers. On the other hand, it enables passengers to recover damages even though, in the absence of the convention and the Act, they might have no cause of action which would entitle them to succeed: *Swiss Bank Corp v*

a *Brink's-MAT Ltd* [1986] 2 All ER 188 at 189, [1986] QB 853 at 856, per Bingham J (now Lord Bingham of Cornhill). It is therefore not necessarily right to approach the meaning of the phrase 'bodily injury' in art 17 of the convention through the spectacles of full corrective justice.

[16] It follows from the scheme of the convention, and indeed from its very nature as an international trade law convention, that the basic concepts it
b employs to achieve its purpose are autonomous concepts. It is irrelevant what 'bodily injury' means in other contexts in national legal systems. The correct inquiry is to determine the autonomous or independent meaning of 'bodily injury' in the convention: *R v Secretary of State for the Home Dept, ex p Adan* [2001] 2 AC 477, [2001] 1 All ER 593. And the premise is that something that does not qualify as a 'bodily injury' in the convention sense does not meet the relevant
c threshold for recovery under it.

(III) *Indications of the meaning of art 17*

[17] If the matter was untrammelled by precedent, my approach to the interpretation of 'bodily injury' in art 17 would have been influenced by six
d factors. (1) The contextual scene is that in 1929 in legal systems generally there was compensation available for physical injuries. By contrast in 1929 the position was different in regard to mental injury and illness. The best view is that except in a few states mental injuries and illnesses were not compensatable or were a matter of controversy. In these circumstances one would have expected, if it was intended to cover mental injuries and illnesses by art 17, that it would have been
e debated in working sessions at Warsaw and expressly provided for. (2) The importance of the factor mentioned in (1) is underlined if one takes into account that many untoward occurrences affecting aircraft may cause mental injury or illness alone but not physical injuries. An IATA position paper presented at the Montreal Conference 1999 (2000 Aviation Quarterly) list by way of example such
f circumstances as follows:

> 'warning of possible in-flight turbulence; a missing approach due to weather, or obstruction on the runway; near miss with other aircraft en route, on approach, or on departure; lightning strike on aircraft or thunderstorm activity in vicinity of aircraft; "accidental" emergency landing announcement;
g decompression of aircraft; hijacking of aircraft; bomb threat; emergency landing; gear malfunction resulting in passengers being warned to prepare for gear collapse on landing; engine malfunction; aborted take-off due to engine failure, tyre failure, conflicting traffic; encountering in-flight turbulence; diversion to alternative airport due to weather, traffic congestion, fuel shortage; delayed gate departure due to announced mechanical problem
h with aircraft or engine; return to gate due to announced mechanical problem with aircraft or engine; unruly passenger behaviour in-flight and crew handling of situation.'

Such occurrences and consequent mental injuries or illnesses would already have
j been a reality in 1929. I accept that the medical explanation for mental injuries, and their physical connection, is today somewhat better informed. No competent psychiatrist would, however, assert that this knowledge is complete. The psychiatric nostrums of today may become the scientific heresies of tomorrow. The textually relevant circumstance is that in 1929 it would already have been appreciated that the imposition of strict liability for mental injury and illness would have opened the door to an avalanche of intangible claims, greatly

in excess of the number of claims for physical injuries. For the fledgling aviation industry this would have involved a large exposure to (i) judgments and awards, (ii) the cost of expert evidence to sort out what were cognisable claims, and (iii) the cost of litigation, the latter being irrecoverable in the United States. This might have meant larger liability insurance premiums and a resultant increase in passenger fares. In these circumstances Professor Malcolm Clarke, a specialist in this area of the law, commented that the expansive interpretation of the First Division in *King*'s case as including purely psychological injury 'caused shock waves': 'Air rage–businessmen behaving badly: civil liability for uncivil passengers' [2001] LMCLQ 369. (3) In this context it is reasonable to expect that if it had been intended to cover mental injury or illness, it would have been provided for expressly. In the absence of such an express reference it is reasonable to interpret 'bodily injury' and 'lésion corporelle' as words of restriction, ie as referring to non-fatal injury which is physical rather than mental: contrast the wide term 'personal injury' in the Guatemala Protocol which never came into force: see Protocol to Amend the Convention for the Unification of Certain Rules Relating to International Carriage by Air, signed at Warsaw on 12 October 1929, as amended by the Protocol done at The Hague on 28 September 1955, signed at Guatemala City on 8 March 1971. His interpretation involves reading the phrase 'bodily injury' or 'lésion corporelle' ejusdem generis with death (mort) and wounding (blessure). It has the merit, unlike the contrary interpretation, of interpreting 'lésion corporelle' and '*bodily* injury' in a meaningful sense. As a matter of first impression as well as common sense there is inherent in these phrases the antithesis between '*bodily* injury' and mental injury. These phrases are prima facie inapposite to convey a meaning wide enough to include mental illness: see Dr Georgette Miller in her work *Liability in International Air Transport* (1977) pp 127–128 which was cited by Lord Phillips of Worth Matravers MR in *Morris*'s case [2001] 3 All ER 126 at [45]–[46]. (4) It is common ground that the travaux préparatoires reveal no discussion or mention of liability for mental injury or illness. Given the spectre of enormous exposure to liability for carriers if claims for mental injury or illness were held to be within art 17, the omission of a reference to such claims during working sessions is revealing. Undoubtedly, at Warsaw and before carriers, aircraft insurers and countries whose national systems did not recognise liability for mental injury or illness would have been likely to argue against including such claims. This is not a case of mere silence: if the idea of including claims for mental injury was under consideration it would have demanded discussion. This indicates clearly and convincingly that the idea of covering mental injury or illness was never contemplated: see *Fothergill v Monarch Airlines Ltd* [1980] 2 All ER 696 at 703, [1981] AC 251 at 278 per Lord Wilberforce. (5) While the domestic law position in France is irrelevant, Professor Malcolm Clarke in a book with the title *Carriage of Goods by Air* to be published in 2002 has shown that the amendments to the French text of the parallel Convention concerning International Carriage by Rail are instructive. In 1952, the text of art 26, the liability provision corresponding to art 17, read 'de la mort, les blessures et toute autre atteinte a l'integrite corporelle'. However, in 1961 the text was amended to read 'de la mort, les blessures et toute autre atteinte a l'integrite corporelle ou mentale'. The expression in both the current text of 1980 and the revision of 1999 is 'dommage resultant de la mort, des blessures ou toute autre atteinte a l'integrite physique ou psychique du voyageur'. It follows that successive French drafters of the convention over the last 50 years did not consider that, in the text of an international convention, 'corporelle' was wide a enough to cover purely psychic injury. Moreover, this factor cogently reinforces the proposition that for the framers of the Warsaw Convention the natural and obvious antithesis would have been between bodily injury and mental injury. And it shows how unrealistic it is to describe mental injury as an unscientific term. In using the phrase 'bodily injury' the framers were not selecting a scientific term. Rather they adopted a term which in ordinary signification, experience and acceptance had a restrictive meaning. (6) Lastly, there is also the fact that until

b some 50 years after the Warsaw Convention no claims for mental injury or illness against carriers were ever brought to judgment anywhere in the world: see *Daddon v Air France* (1984) 1 S & B Av R VII/141. Given that claims for mental injury and illness are inherently likely to occur more frequently and be more controversial than claims for physical injuries, the suggestion that such claims

c may for decades have been paid or settled is fanciful. The truth is that until the 1970s the view that such claims were not covered was the orthodox view throughout the commercial world. The Court of Appeal rightly attached importance to the fact that decades elapsed after 1929 before such claims were ever advanced against carriers. (7) In combination these factors indicate that a

d line was drawn in art 17 which excludes liability where a person suffers no physical injury but only mental injury or illness, such as clinical depression.

(IV) *Comparative jurisprudence*

[18] Leaving aside for the moment the decisions under appeal, there are decisions of courts of high standing to be considered. Lord Hope has reviewed

e the case law comprehensively and accurately. I can therefore deal with the major cases quite shortly. In *Daddon's* case the Israeli Supreme Court held that claims for mental anguish suffered by passengers which was caused by the Entebbe hijacking was covered by the phrase 'bodily injury' in art 17 of the Warsaw Convention. Unfortunately, the Israeli Supreme Court impermissibly relied on

f changes in the aviation industry since 1929 and the current domestic law view of mental and psychological injury. In the two appeals under consideration the Court of Appeal and the Court of Session rejected this reasoning. Counsel for the passengers in the two appeals before the House placed no reliance on *Daddon's* case. Profound as my respect is for the Supreme Court of Israel, I am driven to the same position in regard to this decision.

g [19] The most important decision is that of the United States Supreme Court in *Eastern Airlines Inc v Floyd* (1991) 499 US 530. On a flight between the Bahamas and Miami a plane experienced engine failure. The crew announced that 'the plane would be ditched'. Fortunately, the engine was restarted and the plane landed safely. Passengers sued for emotional injury. The judgment of the

h Supreme Court addressed in detail the question whether art 17 of the Warsaw Convention permits recovery for mental injury unaccompanied by physical injury. For reasons substantially similar to those I have already given the Supreme Court answered this question in the negative. Marshall J, writing for a unanimous court, expressed the ratio of the decision (at 552–553):

j 'We conclude that an air carrier cannot be held liable under Article 17 when an accident has not caused a passenger to suffer death, physical injury, or physical manifestation of injury. Although Article 17 renders air carriers liable for "damage sustained in the event of" ("domage survenu en cas de") such injuries ... we express no view as to whether passengers can recover for mental injuries that are accompanied by physical injuries. That issue is not presented here because respondents do not allege physical injury or physical manifestation of injury.'

a

Since then in *Tseng's* case the United States Supreme Court by an 8:1 decision followed *Floyd's* case and reiterated that without bodily injury there could be no recovery under art 17 for solely psychic or psychosomatic injury. That plainly excludes mental injury or illnesses. In a subsequent decision of a lower court in *Weaver v Delta Airlines Inc* (1999) 56 F Supp 2d 1190 there appears to be a development to outflank *Floyd's* case and *Tseng's* case by alleging that psychiatric injury or illness involves physical changes to the body. It is not strictly relevant on the issues before the House but I will briefly comment on it. But there is another decision of high authority on the principal point. In *Kotsambasis v Singapore Airlines Ltd* (1997) 42 NSWLR 110 the New South Wales Court of Appeal followed *Floyd's* case and held that bodily injury in art 17 does not include purely psychological injury.

b

c

[20] For my part the trilogy of decisions of high authority which I have mentioned in the last paragraph, and the reasoning in those decisions, reinforce the view that somebody who suffered no physical injuries but suffered mental injury or illness has no claim under art 17. On the other hand, I would hold that in two respects mental injury and illness may be relevant. First, there is no reason in principle to exclude from consideration pain and suffering caused by physical injury. It may therefore cover mental injury caused by a physical injury. In such cases the threshold requirement of bodily injury under the convention is satisfied. It is therefore not an exception to the rule as I have stated it. Secondly, I would hold that if a relevant accident causes mental injury or illness which in turn causes adverse physical symptoms, such as strokes, miscarriages or peptic ulcers, the threshold requirement of bodily injury under the convention is also satisfied. In *Rosman v Trans World Airlines Inc* (1974) 34 NY 2d 385 at 399 the Court of Appeals of New York ruled by a majority of six to one that—

d

e

f

'as we read article 17, the compensable injuries must be "bodily" but there may be an intermediate causal link which is "mental" between the cause—the "accident"—and the effect—the "bodily injury". And once that predicate of liability—the "bodily injury"—is established, then the damages sustained as a result of the "bodily injury" are compensable including mental suffering.'

g

For my part this reasoning in *Rosman's* case is faithful to the intent of the Warsaw Convention and I would adopt it. This too is not an exception. But mental injury or illness, such as clinical depression, is excluded.

h

(V) *Applying the distinction*

[21] The outcome of applying the interpretation which I have preferred is that the claim in *Morris's* case falls outside art 17 because it involves mental injury or illness only and that the claim in *King's* case is within art 17 in as much as it involves a peptic ulcer together with pain and suffering associated with it.

j

(VI) *The new point: Weaver's case*

[22] Towards the end of the hearing in the House a new and important point emerged. It was based on *Weaver's* case. The potential effect of it was that psychiatric injury or illness involved physical changes to the body and is therefore 'bodily injury'. Given the decisions announced in the speeches today this point

a does not arise on the appeals under consideration. While the House, of course, has a broad discretion to deal with a point which does not strictly arise, it usually only does so when the point has been considered by courts below and addressed in written and oral argument before the House.

b [23] It is necessary to explain the forensic background. In *Morris*'s case, *Weaver*'s case was not cited to the first instance judge or considered by him. According to the law report it was not cited in argument in the Court of Appeal. It is not referred to in the judgment of the Court of Appeal. It is not referred to in the printed cases for the appellant or the respondent. In *King*'s case there is no reference to *Weaver*'s case in the first instance judgment. In the First Division judgment there are two passing references by Lord Rodger of Earlsferry (2001 SLT 126 at 129 (para 3 of the opinion)) and Lord Reed (at 169 (para 64 of his

c dissenting opinion)) but it was not an issue addressed by the First Division. *Weaver*'s case is not referred to in the printed cases of the appellant or respondent. The submissions to the House on *Weaver*'s case were meagre. In the result the discussion of *Weaver*'s case in the substantial speeches today contain many matters on which the House has not had the benefit of adversarial argument.

d That judges are not mere cyphers and may make their independent investigation into matters of law, I do not doubt. Indeed to some extent I have done so in this case. But it is reassuring if an important new issue, on which the House rules, has been properly investigated and debated by counsel. It has not happened in this case. It will be necessary to revisit *Weaver*'s case when it is directly in issue and with the benefit of a proper exploration of the issues. My discussion of *Weaver*'s

e case must be read subject to this caveat.

(VII) *The merits of the Weaver point*

[24] In *Weaver*'s case, the United States District Court for the District of Montana, Billings Division, was faced with a claim by a passenger to recover compensation for

f post-traumatic stress disorder resulting from an emergency landing. The issue was whether the plaintiff suffered bodily injury. The judge observed ((1999) 56 F Supp 2d 1190 at 1192):

'Weaver's action here is distinguishable from previous cases, because her claim is presented as a physical injury and she relies on recent scientific

g research explaining that post-traumatic stress disorder evidences actual trauma to brain cell structures. Weaver's post-traumatic stress disorder evidences an injury to her brain, and the only reasonable conclusion is that it is, in fact, a bodily injury. More particularly, the injury to her brain should be considered a "bodily injury" as defined under the Warsaw Convention.

h Granted, Weaver's injury manifests itself in ways that are similar to the "injuries" previously found not compensatable in similar cases under the Warsaw Convention. However, the central factor here is not legal, but medical. The legal question in this case is simply whether the Warsaw Convention allows recovery for this particular kind of bodily injury, ie a

j brain injury (even with slight physical effects). The answer must be yes. The court is cognizant that the Warsaw Convention chose to preclude recovery for purely psychic injuries, and the court respects the Supreme Court's determination in *Floyd* that such was a legislative choice. Moreover, the present holding has the potential of allowing for more valid actions under the Warsaw Convention, with the increase attributable only to the increased sophistication of medical science. However, no floodgates of litigation will be opened by allowing for claims such as Weaver's, which are based on a definite diagnosis of a disorder that arises from a physical injury that is medically verifiable. Fright alone is not compensatable, but brain injury from fright is. Unlike the plaintiffs in *Floyd* and its progeny, Weaver's injury is a "bodily injury" as defined by the Warsaw Convention.' *a*

The Ninth Circuit is the appellate court which supervises the *Weaver* court. Last year the Ninth Circuit followed *Floyd*'s case and *Tseng*'s case in a post-traumatic stress syndrome case where there was no evidence of physical injury but left open the issue whether such a physical injury would satisfy the requirements of art 17: *Carey v United Airlines* (2001) 28 Avi 15,408 at 15,415 (footnote 47). On the other hand, *Weaver*'s case was followed in *Re Air Crash at Little Rock, Arkansas* (2000) 118 F Supp 2d 916. There are also lower court decisions the other way: *Jack v Trans World Airlines Inc* (1994) 854 F Supp 654; *Terrafranca v Virgin Atlantic Airways Ltd* (1998) 151 F 3d 108; *Alvarez v American Airlines Inc* (1999) 27 Avi 17,214; (2000) 27 Avi 17,475. As a matter of precedent *Weaver*'s case hardly rests on secure foundations. *b* *c*

[25] In aid of the argument based on *Weaver*'s case points have been made which I would not dispute. First, there is the undoubted fact that medical science generally and psychiatry in particular have advanced since 1929. While it is a matter for expert opinion—and there was none before the House—I accept that in cases of recognisable psychiatric illnesses, such as clinical depression (as in the case of *Morris*) and post-traumatic stress disorder (as in *Weaver*'s case) there is a physical connection between the illness of the mind and the body in as much as the central nervous system, which includes the nervous tissue of the brain, is involved: see *Black's Medical Dictionary* (39th edn, 1999), sv 'central nervous system', 'brain', 'depression' and 'post-traumatic stress disorder'; and Gelder, Mayou and Cowen *Shorter Oxford Textbook of Psychiatry* (4th edn, 2001) passim. Secondly, I accept that courts of law cannot ignore advances in scientific knowledge. In *R v Ireland, R v Burstow* [1997] 4 All ER 225 at 231, [1998] AC 147 at 156, and in *White v Chief Constable of the South Yorkshire Police* [1999] 1 All ER 1 at 31, [1999] 2 AC 455 at 492, I observed that courts of law must act on the best medical insight of the day. This is also an uncontroversial point and does not provide the answer to the point of interpretation before the House. Thirdly, statutes are generally always speaking, and ought therefore to be interpreted in light of the contemporary social and scientific world. This is not a rule of law but a principle of construction, which may be displaced by a contrary intent revealed by a particular statutory context: *R v Ireland* [1997] 4 All ER 225 at 233, [1998] AC 147 at 158. Given that the rationale of the principle is that statutes are generally intended to endure for a long time, one can readily accept that multilateral international trade conventions, which are by statute incorporated in our law, should be approached in a similar way. Indeed one may say that a fortiori they ought to be so interpreted. Again, this principle does not provide an answer to the question before the House. *d* *e* *f* *g* *h*

[26] None of these points, nor a combination of them, undermines the conclusion that at the time of the Warsaw Convention a line was drawn between bodily injury (that is, involving non-fatal physical injury) and mental injury or illness. If this view is correct the argument based on *Weaver*'s case cannot succeed. To accept it would be to ignore the contextual meaning of the Warsaw Convention. It is no answer to say that the distinction between the body and the mind is arbitrary. To some extent it is. Nevertheless, scientifically and in *j*

a common sense there is a real distinction between physical injuries and mental injury or illness. In *Weaver's* case the threshold requirement of a bodily injury within the meaning of the convention was absent. For reasons already explained *Weaver's* case (involving only alleged psychiatric injury) is quite different from the two qualifications which I mentioned in [20], above, (involving physical manifestations). If cases of mental injuries and illnesses are to be brought within

b the convention system, it must be done by amendment of the convention system and not by judicial creativity. In my view *Weaver's* case was wrong in holding that there is no legal issue but only a medical question. *Weaver's* case was not faithful to the law as settled in *Floyd's* case and *Tseng's* case by the United States Supreme Court. And the acceptability of the *Weaver* line of authority is not saved by restricting it to recognisable psychiatric illnesses. That is a legal concept taken

c from post-1929 English case law: see *McLoughlin v O'Brian* [1982] 2 All ER 298 at 301, [1983] 1 AC 410 at 418; *R v Chan-Fook* [1994] 2 All ER 552, [1994] 1 WLR 689; *R v Ireland*. It was not available at Warsaw to serve as an autonomous concept in art 17. It does not satisfy the criterion of approaching the interpretation of a multilateral trade convention 'unconstrained by technical rules of English law, or

d by English legal precedent, but on broad principles of general acceptation': *James Buchanan & Co Ltd v Babco Forwarding and Shipping (UK) Ltd* [1977] 3 All ER 1048 at 1052, [1978] AC 141 at 152.

[27] Moreover, the court in *Weaver's* case failed to take into account that to this day the extension of the Warsaw system to include mental injury and illnesses is too controversial to command sufficient international support. In part

e this must be due to policy factors, namely the expected escalation of claims, far beyond the incidence of physical claims, if mental injuries and illnesses are held to be included in art 17. The potential range of such cases is one factor. The cost of meeting such claims is likely to be huge. Another aspect is the cost of psychiatric evidence by rival experts to determine whether claims are cognisable.

f Finally, there is the cost of legal proceedings. It may be that large countries, and major airlines, could cope with such additional exposure. For smaller countries, and smaller airlines, it could be a serious matter. In 1929 the aviation industry was fragile as it apparently is today. In 1929 the world was not ready to include mental injuries and illnesses within the scope of art 17. It is not ready to do so in

g 2002.

[28] It is true, of course, that a judge's instinct must be for full corrective justice. But the language and contextual scene of art 17 rule out the *Weaver* approach to its interpretation. Courts of law must avoid the reproach that they are becoming the redrafters of the convention.

h [29] I would hold that *Weaver's* case should not be followed.

(VIII) *The judgments below*

[30] I am much indebted to the judgments of the Court of Appeal and the First Division for a careful and analytical exploration of the issues in the cases under

j consideration. It will be clear, however, that I prefer the opinion of the Court of Appeal to the views of the majority of the First Division.

(IX) *Conclusion*

[31] In *Morris's* case [2001] 3 All ER 126 at [103] Lord Phillips of Worth Matravers MR observed:

'If and when the 1999 Montreal Convention comes into force there may be
scope for argument, on the basis of the travaux préparatoires evidencing the   *a*
consideration that was given to mental injury, that those who drafted the
convention intended the meaning of the phrase "bodily injury" to turn on
the jurisprudence of the individual state applying that convention. We do
not consider that this course is open to those who have to interpret that
phrase in the Warsaw Convention. In that convention the phrase means   *b*
"physical injury"'.

A statement to Parliament by the Government further elucidated the position.
The relevant House of Commons Written Answers (Hansard (HC debates) 3 July
2000, cols 87 and 88) were as follows:

'Montreal Convention   *c*
Mr Dismore: To ask the Secretary of State for the Environment, Transport
and the Regions what representations he has made in relation to the
Montreal Convention to ensure UK passengers will be able to claim
compensation for psychiatric injury caused by air accidents; and if he will
make a statement.   *d*
Mr Hill: Damages for mental injury caused by air accidents are already
recoverable in the UK when associated with physical injury. In preparation
for the Diplomatic Conference held in Montreal in May 1999, at which the
Convention was signed, the UK supported a proposal by Sweden for a
separate head of claim for mental injury. Prior to the Conference, however,   *e*
that proposal was withdrawn from the draft text of the Convention. Our
position was that a separate claim for mental injury could be advocated only
if there was sufficient support to gain global agreement. There was not
sufficient support so, in the interest of securing the best deal for the UK, it
was decided to support the text of the Convention without a separate
reference to mental injury. The Conference "travaux préparatoires",   *f*
nevertheless, indicate that damages for mental injury can be recovered in
certain states and that jurisprudence in this area is developing.'

This is how matters stand at present. Limited progress towards the admission of
claims for mental injury and illness must await the coming into operation of the
Montreal Convention.   *g*

(X) *Disposal*
[32] For the reasons I have given I would dismiss the appeal in *Morris's* case.
For the same reasons I would allow the appeal in *King's* case and restore the
decision of the Lord Ordinary. I am in agreement with the speech of my noble   *h*
and learned friend Lord Hope of Craighead.

LORD HOPE OF CRAIGHEAD.
[33] My Lords, the question in these appeals relates to the meaning of the
phrase 'bodily injury' in art 17 of the Warsaw Convention of 1929 as amended at   *j*
The Hague in 1955, which was incorporated into the law of the United Kingdom
as Sch 1 to the Carriage by Air Act 1961. To what extent, if at all, is the carrier
liable under this article where the injury which the passenger sustained in the
accident was a mental injury and not a physical injury?
[34] Although both cases raise the same question, they arose out of different
facts and circumstances and they have arrived here by different routes. I shall

give a brief summary of the cases in their historical order before examining the point of law which they have raised.

MR KING'S CASE

[35] On 22 December 1993 Philip King was a passenger on a helicopter which Bristow Helicopters Ltd were operating in poor weather in the North Sea. It took off from the helideck of a floating production platform in the Beryl oilfield, rose to a height of about 35 feet and hovered for a short period. Suddenly its two engines flamed out, there was a loud bang and the helicopter descended rapidly and landed heavily on the helideck. It was engulfed in smoke which prevented the passengers from seeing out. They did not know whether it had landed safely or was on the edge of the helideck and liable to fall off into the sea. There was panic on board and the passengers were shouting. Mr King did not sustain any physical injury while he was on board or when he disembarked from the helicopter. But he was extremely frightened, and he developed several psychiatric conditions including a moderate post-traumatic stress disorder as a result of the accident. The stress led to the onset of peptic ulcer disease, which caused him severe pain and an exacerbation of pre-existing dyspeptic symptoms.

[36] Mr King raised an action of damages in the Court of Session against Bristow Helicopters Ltd (Bristow). His flight was non-international carriage by air within the meaning of the Carriage by Air Acts (Application of Provisions) Order 1967, SI 1967/480. Schedule 1 to the 1967 order applies to such carriage the Warsaw Convention as amended by the Hague Protocol. He claimed damages under art 17 of the convention both for the psychiatric conditions and for the peptic ulcer disease.

[37] On 13 November 1998 the Lord Ordinary (Lord Philip) (1999 SLT 919), having heard a debate on the procedure roll, excluded from probation all the averments about the psychiatric conditions which Mr King sustained as a result of the accident. He also dismissed actions which had been raised by two other passengers which had been heard at the same time: *Hammond v Bristow Helicopters Ltd* 1999 SLT 919. But he allowed the averments about Mr King's peptic ulcer disease to go to proof before answer. A reclaiming motion was marked by Mr King in which he sought a proof before answer of all his averments. A cross-reclaiming motion was marked by Bristow in which they asked the court to dismiss the action. On 12 July 2000 the First Division (the Lord President (Lord Rodger of Earlsferry) and Lord Cameron of Lochbroom, Lord Reed dissenting) allowed Mr King's reclaiming motion, refused the cross-reclaiming motion and allowed the parties a proof before answer of their averments: 2001 SLT 126. It is against that interlocutor that Bristow have appealed to this House.

[38] During the hearing before the First Division Mr King's counsel said that his averments should be interpreted as disclosing that Mr King was suffering from three psychiatric conditions: post-traumatic stress disorder, chronic depression and fear of flying, and that his peptic ulcer disease was caused, or materially contributed to, by his psychiatric conditions: 2001 SLT 126 at 129. He also stressed that he was not offering to prove that Mr King's psychiatric conditions were caused by any physiological changes in his body. That position was maintained in the hearing before your Lordships. The appeal in this case was argued on the basis that Mr King suffered two distinct kinds of injury as a result of the accident when he was on board the helicopter. The first was a mental injury which led to the three psychiatric conditions described in the averments.

The second was a physical disorder consisting of the peptic ulcer disease which
the psychiatric conditions had caused.   *a*

MISS MORRIS'S CASE

[39] On 6 September 1998 Miss Morris was on an international flight which
was being operated by KLM Royal Dutch Airlines from Kuala Lumpur to
Amsterdam. She was just under 16 years old and was travelling as an   *b*
unaccompanied minor. She was seated next to two men who were speaking
French to each other. After a meal she fell asleep and woke to discover the hand
of the man next to her touching her left thigh from the hip to the knee. He was
caressing her between her hip and knee and his fingers dug into her thigh. She
got up, walked away and told an air hostess what had occurred. She became very
distressed and on her return went to see a doctor. He found that she was   *c*
suffering from a clinical depression amounting to a single episode of a major
depressive illness. She has now made a full recovery.

[40] Miss Morris brought a claim for damages against KLM in Bury County
Court. The flight on which she was travelling was international carriage by air
for reward within the meaning of art 1 of the Warsaw Convention as amended   *d*
by the Hague Protocol. She claimed damages under art 17 of the convention as
incorporated into English law by Sch 1 to the 1961 Act. In the particulars of
injuries annexed to her claim form she stated that she relied for particulars of her
injury on reports from Dr NJ Cooling, a consultant psychiatrist. In his report Dr
Cooling said that in his opinion Miss Morris was emotionally shocked by what
happened to her, that since returning home she had shown the characteristic   *e*
features of a clinical depression and that the diagnosis according to DSM-IV
criteria was one of a single episode of a major depressive illness (296.2) for which
her general practitioner, recognising the very dramatic change in her mental
state, had started her on anti-depressant treatment.

[41] By consent the issue of liability was treated in the county court as a   *f*
preliminary issue. This issue was heard on the basis of agreed facts before Judge
Carter QC. On 1 December 2000 he gave judgment for Miss Morris for damages
to be assessed, but gave KLM permission to appeal. In the appeal the meaning of
'accident' and 'bodily injury' in art 17 were both in issue. On 17 May 2001 the
Court of Appeal (Lord Phillips of Worth Matravers MR, Peter Gibson and
Latham LJJ) allowed the appeal: [2001] EWCA Civ 790, [2001] 3 All ER 126, [2002]   *g*
QB 100. Miss Morris now appeals against that order to this House.

[42] Before Judge Carter both parties had claimed that the issue between them
fell to be determined in a manner that entitled each party to summary judgment.
The hearing in the Court of Appeal also proceeded on the agreed premise that
there is a distinction between physical injury and mental injury: that is to say, that   *h*
physical injury involves damage or adverse change to the structure of the body,
whereas mental illness adversely affects the well-being of the mind without
organic change to the body: [2001] 3 All ER 126 at [35]. Lord Phillips of Worth
Matravers MR said (at [40]) that the appeal had to be approached on the premise
that mental illness and physical injury are distinguishable and that the claimant   *j*
had accepted that she suffered no physical injury.

[43] It can be seen from this summary that no attempt has been made in
either case to show that the mental illness or injury was caused to any extent
by physical injury. The only physical injury which is said to have been
sustained in either case is what may conveniently be described as the physical
manifestation of a mental injury in Mr King's case. This is the peptic ulcer

a disease which he claims to have developed as a result of the psychiatric conditions described in his averments.

TERMINOLOGY

[44] As this brief summary has demonstrated, various expressions may be used to describe an injury which affects the mind but is not accompanied by any
b physical injury. In Mr King's case, the Lord President observed that among the expressions used in the extensive case law and literature on this subject are 'shock', 'mental distress', 'mental injury', 'psychic injury', 'psychological injury' and 'psychiatric injury'. For the sake of consistency he chose to adopt the term 'psychological injury': 2001 SLT 126 at 129. In Miss Morris's case, Lord Phillips of Worth Matravers MR used the expressions 'mental injury' and 'mental illness':
c [2001] 3 All ER 126 at [35], [40].

[45] For the purposes of this judgment, except when I am dealing which Mr King's peptic ulcer disease, I propose to adopt the phrase 'mental injury'. I think that it is preferable to adhere to the noun 'injury', which is the word used in art 17. Moreover, I would wish to recognise at the outset that the word 'injury'
d does not extend to the reactions which a passenger may experience during or as a result of an accident such as fright, fear or anxiety. Emotional upsets of that kind seem to me to be clearly outside the scope of the article. Article 17 is concerned only with something that can properly be described as an injury.

[46] As for the choice of adjective, I would prefer to use the word 'mental' to 'psychological', although I adopted the latter expression in *Sidhu v British Airways*
e *plc, Abnett (known as Sykes) v British Airways plc* [1997] 1 All ER 193 at 201, [1997] AC 430 at 441. In that case it was suggested that the phrase 'bodily injury' in art 17 ought to be construed as including psychological damage, especially if it were shown to have a physiological basis by medical evidence. But the point did not require decision in that case. I recognise at once that the phrase 'mental
f injury' is open to criticism for the reasons which have been so carefully explained by my noble and learned friend, Lord Hobhouse of Woodborough. But, for the purpose of these appeals, all I am looking for is a convenient expression to embrace those conditions affecting the mind which are sufficiently serious to fall within the concept of injury. The words 'physical' and 'mental' seem to me to provide a sufficient contrast to mark the broad dividing line which has been
g identified between the two sides of the argument. The question where that line is to be drawn is a difficult one, but is not the question to which the passengers' counsel addressed their principal argument. Their argument was that it was sufficient for them to show that the passengers sustained a mental injury.

h ARE THE TWO TYPES OF INJURY DISTINGUISHABLE?

[47] Underlying the problem of terminology there is a more fundamental question. It has for a long time been recognised that it is not possible to maintain a rigid distinction between the body and the mind in the law relating to liability in damages for negligence. In *Hay (or Bourhill) v Young* [1942] 2 All ER 396 at 402,
j [1943] AC 92 at 103 Lord Macmillan recognised that the crude view that the law should take cognisance only of physical injury resulting from actual impact had been discarded and that it was recognised that an action will lie for injury by shock sustained without direct contact. As he put it, the distinction between mental shock and bodily injury was never a scientific one.

[48] This theme was developed in *Page v Smith* [1995] 2 All ER 736 at 752, [1996] AC 155 at 181 by Lord Browne-Wilkinson, where he observed that

medical science has demonstrated that the body can suffer injuries which are not demonstrably attributable to physical injury:

'Injuries of this type may take two forms. First, physical illness or injury not brought about by a chain of demonstrable physical events but by mental or emotional stresses ie by a psychiatric route. Examples are a heart attack or a miscarriage produced by shock. In this case, the end-product is a physical condition although it has been brought about by a process which is not demonstrably a physical one but lies in the mental or nervous system. The second form is psychiatric illness itself which is brought about by mental or emotional stresses, ie by a psychiatric route. Because medical science has so far been less successful in demonstrating the nature of psychiatric illness and the processes whereby it is brought about by the psychiatric route, the courts have been more reluctant to accept the risk of such illness as being foreseeable. But since the decision of this House in *McLoughlin v O'Brian* [1982] 2 All ER 298, [1983] 1 AC 410 it has been established that, in certain circumstances, a defendant can be liable for illness or injury, whether psychiatric or physical, produced in a plaintiff by purely psychiatric processes, without any direct physical impact on, or injury to, the limbs or organs of the plaintiff.'

[49] This passage helps to set the scene for these appeals. The branch of medical science which is concerned with psychiatric disorders and disturbances is still in the process of development. It is not yet fully understood. We are able to identify physical conditions which have been brought about by a psychiatric route. Mr King's peptic ulcer disorder is a physical condition of this type. We can also identify various psychiatric illnesses which, according to our present state of knowledge, appear not to have been the product of any kind of physical injury. But the distinction between what I have described as a mental injury and a physical injury is unclear, and the extent to which it can be maintained is debatable. It may now be possible to show objectively, by means of expert medical evidence, that a psychiatric illness is due to a disturbance within the patient's own central nervous system which drugs can control or alleviate. As I shall show later, this has been the basis for some recent decisions in the Federal courts in the United States that a psychiatric illness of that kind is a physical injury. It is of some importance therefore to appreciate the basis on which counsel for the passengers in these cases presented their argument.

[50] The argument in the courts below has assumed that the mental injury which Mr King and Miss Morris sustained is one which cannot be attributed to any kind of physical injury. This point was expressly conceded in Mr King's case. Lord Phillips of Worth Matravers MR acknowledged in Miss Morris's case that the stage may one day be reached when a physical cause can be demonstrated for these kinds of psychiatric illnesses: [2001] 3 All ER 126 at [40]. But he said her appeal had to be approached on the assumption that that stage had not yet been reached. I understand the point to have been a matter of express concession in her case also. Mr Braslavsky was content to present her appeal to this House on the same basis. He did not attempt to link her mental injury to any physical condition affecting the tissues of her body. He maintained that it was sufficient for her to show that Dr Cooling's diagnosis was that she was suffering from a depressive illness which had a recognised international classification. He said that his case was that she was suffering from a recognised mental disorder, not that her disorder could be linked to any injury to her body.

DOMESTIC JURISPRUDENCE

a   [51] It may be helpful, before embarking upon an examination of the words 'any other bodily injury' in art 17 of the convention, to examine the present state of our own jurisprudence as to how similar words in domestic legislation are to be interpreted. This is not to say that the approach which we take when we are construing our own legislation is the approach which we should take when we are construing the convention. The construction of an international convention

b   proceeds upon different principles. But this exercise may help to put the problem in its current context.

[52] The word 'bodily' is not unknown in the legislation of the United Kingdom. The phrase 'bodily functions' in modern social security legislation has received a broad interpretation: see *Cockburn v Chief Adjudication Officer* [1997]

c   3 All ER 844, [1997] 1 WLR 799. Lord Slynn of Hadley said that this phrase could extend to the operation of the senses and their communication to the brain (see [1997] 3 All ER 844 at 858–859, [1997] 1 WLR 799 at 813). But the concept of function is not the same as that of injury. More in point is the use of the phrase 'bodily harm' in English criminal law to describe various categories of offences

d   against the person: see ss 18, 20 and 47 of the Offences against the Person Act 1861. The phrase 'grievous bodily harm' is used in ss 18 and 20 of that Act. The phrase 'actual bodily harm' is used in s 47.

[53] The meaning of the phrase 'actual bodily harm' in that context was considered in *R v Chan-Fook* [1994] 2 All ER 552, [1994] 1 WLR 689. The issue was whether an assault which caused no physical injury but caused an hysterical and

e   nervous condition in the victim was an assault occasioning actual bodily harm. It was held by the Court of Appeal that, while the phrase did not include emotions such as fear or panic, it was capable of including psychiatric injury. Hobhouse LJ, delivering the judgment of the court, said:

f   'These are three words of the English language which require no elaboration and in the ordinary course should not receive any. The word "harm" is a synonym for injury. The word "actual" indicates that the injury (although there is no need for it to be permanent) should not be so trivial as to be wholly insignificant.' (See [1994] 2 All ER 552 at 557, [1994] 1 WLR 689 at 694.)

g   [54] Later, he said that in certain cases an explanation might be required of what is involved in the word 'bodily'. Rejecting the argument that inclusion of the word in the phrase 'actual bodily harm' limits harm to harm to the skin, flesh and bones of the victim, he said:

h   'The body of the victim includes all parts of his body, including his organs, his nervous system and his brain. Bodily injury therefore may include injury to any of those parts of his body responsible for his mental and other faculties.' (See [1994] 2 All ER 552 at 558–559, [1994] 1 WLR 689 at 696.)

j   He recognised that there was a line to be drawn between mere emotions on the one hand and some psychiatric illness on the other, and that this was a matter for expert evidence. He concluded his discussion of this issue with these words:

'Accordingly the phrase "actual bodily harm" is capable of including psychiatric injury. But it does not include mere emotions such as fear or distress or panic nor does it include, as such, states of mind that are not themselves evidence of some identifiable clinical condition.' (See [1994] 2 All ER 552 at 559, [1994] 1 WLR 689 at 696.)

[55] In *R v Ireland, R v Burstow* [1997] 4 All ER 225 at 233, [1998] AC 147 the question was whether psychiatric illness was capable of amounting to bodily harm in terms of ss 18, 20 and 47 of the 1861 Act. Two appeals were before the House. In neither case had the victims suffered from structural injuries to the brain such as might require the intervention of a neurologist, nor was it suggested that they had developed psychotic or psychoneurotic conditions. The case was that they had developed anxiety and depressive disorders, which could be distinguished from simple states of fear or problems in coping with everyday life. It was held, in the light of contemporary knowledge covering recognisable psychiatric injuries, that injuries of that kind fell within the phrase 'bodily harm' as used in the 1861 Act. Having examined the progress in scientific understanding since that date and the recognition in recent English case law that in the relevant context the distinction between physical and mental injury is by no means clear-cut, Lord Steyn said:

'The proposition that the Victorian legislator when enacting ss 18, 20 and 47 of the 1861 Act, would not have had in mind psychiatric illness is no doubt correct. Psychiatry was in its infancy in 1861. But the subjective intention of the draftsman is immaterial. The only relevant inquiry is as to the sense of the words in the context in which they are used. Moreover the 1861 Act is a statute of the "always speaking" type: the statute must be interpreted in the light of the best current scientific appreciation of the link between the body and psychiatric injury.' (See [1997] 4 All ER 225 at 233, [1998] AC 147 at 158–159.)

He concluded ([1997] 4 All ER 225 at 234, [1998] AC 147 at 159) that the word 'bodily harm' must be interpreted in the context of the 1861 Act so as to include recognisable psychiatric illness.

[56] In the light of these decisions and the reasoning which was used to support them, I think that there is little doubt that, if same words as those in art 17 were used in a United Kingdom statute to describe the kinds of personal injury caused by an accident that would entitle the victim to recover damages, they would now be held to extend to those kinds of mental injury that could be shown to amount to a recognisable psychiatric illness or injury by expert evidence. The depressive illness which Dr Cooling has diagnosed in Miss Morris's case according to DSM IV criteria (296.2) would seem to fall readily into that category. This brings me to the question whether the words used in the convention can be construed in the same way.

THE CONVENTION

[57] The history of the convention and its incorporation into our law which I shall now outline has been fully described elsewhere and is not controversial. But it is necessary to place it on record in this judgment by way of background.

[58] The Warsaw Convention was concluded in French on 12 October 1929. Arrangements were made for it to be received into the law of the United Kingdom by the Carriage by Air Act 1932, and the French text was ratified by the United Kingdom on 14 February 1933. The 1932 Act gave the force of law to a translation of the French text into English. Only the English text was set out in the First Schedule to that Act. Section 4 of the 1932 Act gave power by order in council to apply the provisions of the First Schedule to non-international carriage by air, subject to such exceptions, adaptations and modifications, if any, as might

a be specified. The provisions of the First Schedule were applied, in a modified form, to non-international carriage by air by the Carriage by Air (Non-international Carriage) (United Kingdom) Order 1952, SI 1952/158.

[59] The Warsaw Convention was amended by a Protocol which was concluded at The Hague in 1955. The Carriage by Air Act 1961 gave effect to the Convention concerning international carriage by air, now known as 'The *b* Warsaw Convention as Amended at The Hague, 1955', so that it too might have the force of law in the United Kingdom in relation to any carriage by air to which the convention applied. Force of law to the convention in regard to international carriage by air is given by s 1(1) of the 1961 Act, read together with Sch 1. Part I of the Schedule to that Act sets out a translation of the convention into English. Part II sets out the text in French. Section 1(2) of the Act provides that, if there is *c* an inconsistency between the text in English in Pt I of the Schedule and the text in French in Pt II, the text in French shall prevail.

[60] Once again steps were taken to enable the provisions of the convention, in their amended form, to be applied to carriage by air, not being carriage to which the convention applies: see s 10(1). This was done by the Carriage by Air *d* Acts (Application of Provisions) Order 1967, SI 1967/480, for the purposes of which the expression 'the amended convention' is defined by art 2(1) of the order as meaning the English text of the Warsaw Convention as amended by the Hague Protocol. The order applies to all carriage by air, not being carriage to which the amended convention applies: art 3. Article 4(a) provides that Sch 1 to that order is to have effect in respect to carriage which is not 'international carriage' as *e* defined in Sch 2 to the order. Schedule 2 sets out the provisions relating to international carriage in the unamended Warsaw Convention, to which continuing force had to be given as some states party to the Warsaw Convention had not adopted the Hague Convention.

[61] The carriage of Miss Morris on the KLM flight from Kuala Lumpur to *f* Amsterdam was plainly international carriage by air to which the rules in Sch 1 to the 1961 Act (the Hague Rules) apply. In her case the position is straightforward. The statute provides that the French text is to prevail over the English text if there is any inconsistency: s 1(2).

[62] The carriage of Mr King in the helicopter when it took off from the Beryl platform in the North Sea was not international carriage as defined in Sch 2 to the *g* 1967 order. The rules which applied to that carriage were those set out in Sch 1 to that order (the United Kingdom rules). But the parties in Mr King's case are agreed that, although the Hague Rules do not apply in his case, it is proper in his case too to look at the French text of the convention when construing the articles in Sch 1.

h [63] For the reasons which I gave in *Fellowes (or Herd) v Clyde Helicopters Ltd* [1997] 1 All ER 775 at 790–791, [1997] AC 534 at 552 I would endorse this approach. The long title of the 1961 Act states that it is—

'An Act to give effect to the Convention concerning international carriage by air known as "the Warsaw Convention as amended at The Hague, 1955", *j* to enable the rules contained in that Convention to be applied, with or without modification, in other cases and, in particular, to non-international carriage by air; and for connected purposes.'

One of the primary objectives of the United Kingdom rules, as in the case of the convention itself, was to eliminate conflict of laws problems which are just as likely to arise from non-convention as from convention carriage. As Lord Reed said in Mr King's case, the practical advantages of construing identical provisions in all three sets of rules, including those in Sch 2 to the 1961 order (the Warsaw rules), in the same sense are manifest: 2001 SLT 126 at 159.

[64] Chapter III of the convention contains the provisions which are relevant to these appeals. It is headed 'Liability of the Carrier'. The articles in this chapter are numbered from 17 to 30. Article 17 is concerned with the carrier's liability for death or injury suffered by a passenger. Article 18 is concerned with the carrier's liability for destruction or loss of or damage to registered baggage or cargo. Article 19 is concerned with damage caused by delay in the carriage by air of passengers, baggage or cargo. Article 20 provides that the carrier is not liable if he proves that he and his servants or agents have taken all necessary measures to avoid the damage or that it was impossible for him or them to take such measures. These provisions must be read together with art 24, which provides that, in the cases covered by these articles, any action for damages, however founded, can only be brought subject to the conditions and limits set out in the convention.

[65] The general character and purpose of the Hague Rules, which were authorised to be applied by order in council to non-international carriage by air by s 10(1) of the 1961 Act, were described in *Holmes v Bangladesh Biman Corp* [1989] 1 All ER 852 at 858, [1989] AC 1112 at 1129 by Lord Bridge of Harwich; see also *Sidhu's* case [1997] 1 All ER 193 at 212, [1997] AC 430 at 453–454. They impose liability on the carrier without proof of fault in respect of the death of or injury to passengers, damage to or loss of baggage or cargo and delay to passengers, baggage or cargo. They impose limits on the amount recoverable in respect of the death, injury, damage, loss or delay. They nullify contractual provisions tending to relieve the carrier of liability or to lower the limits of liability. Actions for damages to enforce the rights given by the rules can only be brought subject to the rules, and they exclude other remedies. What was sought to be achieved was a uniform international code which could be applied by the courts of all the high contracting parties. In those areas with which it deals the rules which it lays down were intended to be uniform and exclusive of resort to domestic law.

[66] From the point of view of the passenger or the owner of baggage or cargo, the imposition of liability without proof of fault on the carrier and the nullification of provisions relieving him of liability or restricting the amount of his liability are very significant advantages. From the point of view of the carrier too, however, there are significant advantages in the system laid down by the convention. A principal consequence of that system is the exposure of the carrier to liabilities without the freedom to contract out of them. But it defines those situations in which compensation is to be available, and it sets out the limits of liability and the conditions under which claims to establish liability, if disputed, are to be made. A balance has been struck between these competing interests, in the interests of certainty and uniformity.

THE ISSUE

[67] As Lord Phillips of Worth Matravers MR said in Miss Morris's case [2001] 3 All ER 126 at [67], it is not difficult to see that the convention was intended to create a uniform set of circumstances in which a carrier by air would be obliged to pay compensation for damage sustained by a passenger. But this raises the question, what damage? To answer this question it is necessary to turn to the wording of the articles.

a [68] I must first set out the relevant articles in Ch III of the convention, using the English text as set out in Pt I of the Schedule to the 1961 Act:

'Article 17

The carrier is liable for damage sustained in the event of the death or wounding of a passenger or any other bodily injury suffered by a passenger,
b if the accident which caused the damage so sustained took place on board the aircraft or in the course of any of the operations of embarking or disembarking.

Article 18

(1) The carrier is liable for damage sustained in the event of the
c destruction or loss of, or of damage to, any registered baggage or any cargo, if the occurrence which caused the damage so sustained took place during the carriage by air ...

Article 19

The carrier is liable for damage occasioned by delay in the carriage by air
d of passengers, baggage or cargo.

Article 20

The carrier is not liable if he proves that he and his servants or agents have taken all necessary measures to avoid the damage or that it was impossible for him or them to take such measures.

e Article 21

If the carrier proves that the damage was caused by or contributed to by the negligence of the injured person the court may, in accordance with the provisions of its own law, exonerate the carrier wholly or partly from his liability ...

f Article 24

(1) In the cases covered by articles 18 and 19 any action for damages, however founded, can only be brought subject to the conditions and limits set out in this Convention.

(2) In the cases covered by article 17, the provisions of the preceding
g paragraph also apply, without prejudice to the questions as to who are the persons who have the right to bring suit and what are their respective rights.'

[69] The art 17 in the French text as set out in Pt II of the Schedule is in these terms:

h 'Le transporteur est responsable du dommage survenu en cas de mort, de blessure ou de toute autre lésion corporelle subie par un voyageur lorsque l'accident qui a causé le dommage s'est produit à bord de l'aéronef ou au cours de toutes opérations d'embarquement et de débarquement.'

j [70] The wording of art 17 indicates that three things must be established in order to demonstrate that the carrier is liable. The first is that the passenger must have sustained death or wounding or other bodily injury. The second is that there must have been an accident which took place on board the aircraft or in the course of any of the operations of embarking or disembarking. The third is that the passenger's death, wounding or bodily injury must have been caused by the accident.

[71] In *Air France v Saks* (1985) 470 US 392 at 398–399 the United States Supreme Court said that the text of the convention implies that, however the word 'accident' is defined, it is the cause of the injury that must satisfy that definition rather that the occurrence of the injury alone. The court concluded (at 405) that liability under art 17 arises only if a passenger's injury is caused by an unexpected or unusual event that is external to the passenger. This interpretation of the article was approved by the Court of Appeal in *Chaudhari v British Airways plc* (1997) Times, 7 May, [1997] CA Transcript 590. It was also approved and applied by Lord Phillips of Worth Matravers MR in Miss Morris's case [2001] 3 All ER 126 at [24]. I agree that it gives the word 'accident' a natural and sensible meaning in the context of art 17, and I too would adopt this approach.

[72] In Mr King's case it was accepted that the incident which he describes in his averments was an accident. In Miss Morris's case the defendant argued that the indecent assault which she suffered could not reasonably be described as an accident. The Court of Appeal held that it was not necessary to show that the event had any relationship with the operation of the aircraft or carriage by air, that the incident in which Miss Morris was involved exemplified a special risk inherent in air travel and that she had sustained an accident within the meaning of the article: [2001] 3 All ER 126 at [31]. So long as it occurred during the time when the passenger was in the charge of the carrier, the passenger was entitled to be compensated for its consequences if the carrier was not able to discharge the burden imposed by art 20 of showing that he and his servants or agents had taken all necessary measures to avoid the damage or that it was impossible for him or them to take such measures. There has been no appeal against this finding by the Court of Appeal.

[73] The remaining question, which is common to both cases, is whether the mental injury which the passengers sustained falls within the scope of the expression 'bodily injury'. That is the central issue in these appeals.

[74] I propose to approach this question by examining first the principles of interpretation that are relevant to this issue. I shall then discuss the natural meaning of the words used in both the English and the French texts. I shall then look at the travaux préparatoires in order to see what light, if any, they may cast on this issue. Finally I shall examine the jurisprudence of other jurisdictions in order to see whether a settled practice has developed as to the meaning of this phrase and, if not, what guidance can be obtained from the approach which has been taken to the problem in the United States. Before undertaking this exercise I should like to pay tribute to the researches of counsel, to the quality of the judgments both in the Court of Session and in the Court of Appeal and to the diligence and attention to detail with which they have set out and examined the relevant material.

PRINCIPLES OF INTERPRETATION

[75] Almost everything that needs to be said on this subject was referred to in *Sidhu*'s case, and it is necessary here to provide only a brief summary.

[76] We are concerned in this case with the meaning of words used in an international convention. The convention must be considered as a whole, and it should receive a purposive construction: *Grein v Imperial Airways Ltd* [1936] 2 All ER 1258 at 1277–1279, [1937] 1 KB 50 at 74–76 per Greene LJ; *Fothergill v Monarch Airlines Ltd* [1980] 2 All ER 696 at 704, [1981] AC 251 at 279 per Lord Diplock. The ordinary and natural meaning of the words used in the English text in Pt I of the Schedule provides the starting point. But these words must also be compared

a with their equivalents in the French text in Pt II of the Schedule, as s 1(2) of the 1961 Act tells us that if there is any inconsistency the text in French shall prevail.

[77] As the language was not chosen by English draftsmen and was not designed to be construed exclusively by English judges, it should not be interpreted according to the idiom of English law. What one is looking for is a meaning which can be taken to be consistent with the common intention of the *b* states which were represented at the international conference. The exercise is not to be controlled by technical rules of English law or domestic precedent. It would not be right to search for the legal meaning of the words used, as the convention was not based on the legal system of any of the contracting states. It was intended to be applicable in a uniform way across legal boundaries.

[78] In situations of this kind the language used should be construed on broad *c* principles leading to a result that is generally acceptable: see *Stag Line Ltd v Foscolo Mango & Co Ltd* [1932] AC 328 at 350, [1931] All ER Rep 666 at 677 per Lord Macmillan; *James Buchanan & Co Ltd v Babco Forwarding and Shipping (UK) Ltd* [1977] 3 All ER 1048 at 1052, [1978] AC 141 at 152 per Lord Wilberforce. But this does not mean that a broad construction has to be given to the words used in *d* the convention. As Lord Phillips of Worth Matravers MR said in Miss Morris's case ([2001] 3 All ER 126 at [90]), it is not axiomatic that the broad principle of 'general acceptation' described in these cases militates in favour of a broad rather than a narrow interpretation of the phrase 'any other bodily injury'.

[79] It is legitimate to have regard to the travaux préparatoires in order to resolve ambiguities or obscurities: *Fothergill's* case [1980] 2 All ER 696 at 703, *e* [1981] AC 251 at 278 per Lord Wilberforce. But caution is needed in the use of this material, as the delegates may not have shared a common view. An expression by one of them as to his own view is likely be of little value if it was met simply by silence on the part of the other delegates. It will only be helpful if, after proper analysis, the travaux clearly and indisputably point to a definite *f* intention on the part of the delegates as to how the point at issue should be resolved.

[80] It is also legitimate to have regard to subsequent practice in the application of the convention, if this shows that the contracting parties were in agreement as to its interpretation when it was entered into. General guidance to this effect is given, albeit only prospectively, in the Vienna Convention on the *g* Law of Treaties (Vienna, 23 May 1969, TS 58 (1980); Cmnd 7964), arts 31(1) and 32.

[81] In an ideal world the convention should be accorded the same meaning by all who are party to it. So case law provides a further potential source of evidence. Careful consideration needs to be given to the reasoning of courts of other jurisdictions which have been called upon to deal with the point at issue, *h* particularly those which are of high standing. Considerable weight should be given to an interpretation which has received general acceptance in other jurisdictions. On the other hand a discriminating approach is required if the decisions conflict, or if there is no clear agreement between them.

[82] The question was raised whether the convention must be approached on *j* the basis that it is a document of the 'always speaking' type described by Lord Steyn in *R v Ireland, R v Burstow* [1997] 4 All ER 225 at 233, [1998] AC 147 at 158–159, whose meaning should be interpreted in the light of the current scientific evidence. I would answer that question in this way. The meaning that is to be given to the words used in the convention must be the meaning which was to be attributed to them when the convention was entered into in 1929. But it must always have been intended that the application of that meaning to the

facts would depend on the evidence. The proper approach is to make use of the best current medical and scientific knowledge that is available. An important question therefore is whether, if the position has now been reached where a physical basis for a mental injury can be demonstrated objectively by the evidence, the framers of the convention intended to include a condition of that kind within the scope of art 17 when they used the expression 'bodily injury'.

NATURAL MEANING

[83] It is necessary to start by considering the natural meaning of the words 'any other bodily injury'. At first sight the words 'bodily injury' appear to envisage injury of a physical nature, similar in kind to that which is encompassed by the words 'death or wounding'. Both phrases may be thought to contemplate some kind of physical injury, some physiological damage to the structure of the body. While the phrase as a whole seems to have been intended to extend the scope of the article beyond 'wounding', the adjective 'bodily' appears to have been included to restrict or limit the extent of the word 'injury'. The use of this adjective suggests that not everything that might possibly be described as an injury to the passenger which he sustains on board the aircraft or in the course of embarking or disembarking was intended to be covered by art 17. The possibilities for experiencing emotions such as fear, fright or anxiety due to unexpected events during air travel must have been many in 1929 when the airline industry was in its infancy and the ability of unpressurised aircraft to avoid thunderstorms and other adverse weather conditions was limited. It is reasonable to think that they were familiar to the draftsmen of the convention and to the signatories. But their use of language suggests not only that they did not intend art 17 to apply to emotional reactions of that kind but that they had in mind injuries which were manifestly physical.

[84] On the other hand the Lord President said in Mr King's case (2001 SLT 126 at 136) that he saw no reason why the phrase 'any other bodily injury' should be interpreted narrowly; rather that it should be interpreted as covering any injury whatever which can properly be regarded as affecting the body. So construed, it seemed to him that the phrase was capable of including psychological injury. Lord Reed recognised (at 168) that a wider construction, which would include any impairment to health, was possible. I agree that the words are sufficiently imprecise to permit that interpretation. On that approach it would be sufficient to show that the passenger was suffering from a specific mental illness which had diagnostic features that could be objectively demonstrated. But I think that, in its context, the phrase points to some injury to the body and not to a mental injury.

[85] The equivalent phrase in the French text is 'de toute autre lésion corporelle'. It follows the word 'de mort, de blessure'. 'Blessure' is defined by the Le Petit Robert (1970 edn) as 'lésion faite aux tissus vivants par une cause extérieure (pression, instrument tranchant ou contondant, arme à feu; chaleur)'. 'Lésion' has two meanings, one legal, the other medical. In the medical sense it is defined as 'changement grave dans les caractères anatomiques et histologiques d'un organe sous l'influence d'une maladie, d'un accident'. This points to an injury which affects the tissues of the body. 'Corporelle' is defined in the relevant sense as 'relatif au corps'. This tends to confirm that the word 'lésion' should be interpreted in this context as meaning a physical injury: see Dr Georgette Miller Liability in International Air Transport (1977) pp 127–128. The phrase 'lésion corporelle' in the French text seems to convey the same meaning as that which I

a would be inclined to draw from the English text. It appears to relate to those changes in the tissues of the body which are not covered by the word 'blessure'. The word 'corporelle' directs attention to physical changes in the body rather than something that affects the mind.

[86] It was suggested that the phrase 'bodily injury' was intended to extend to all harm that the passenger might sustain in his person, and to distinguish that b kind of injury from an injury to his property or his business. The Lord President saw this explanation as more plausible: 2001 SLT 126 at 144. This argument is based on the proposition that art 17 must be read in the context of Ch III of the convention as a whole. Article 18 deals with damage to registered baggage. Article 19 deals with delay. The juxtaposition of these articles suggests that the intention was to include in art 17 everything that could be regarded as personal c injury, while patrimonial loss consisting of damage to property and economic loss was left to be covered by the following articles.

[87] On the other hand I should have thought that, if this was indeed the intention, the word 'lésion' on its own would have done and that the adjective 'corporelle' would have been unnecessary. It would have been plain from its d association with the word 'blessure', and the reference to presence on board the aircraft and to the actions of embarking and disembarking, that the phrase 'toute autre lésion' in art 17 was being used in the sense of an injury to the person of the passenger. The fact that the word 'corporelle' was included appears to me to indicate that the word 'lésion' was intended to describe a physical injury to the passenger as distinct from a mental injury.

e [88] The Lord President recognised (at 135) that the argument that the word 'corporelle' was included to exclude mental as opposed to physical injury had an immediate appeal to the reader of the article. But he said that it would be superfluous to add the word 'corporelle' to the word 'lésion' if the latter word were to be given a meaning which contains within itself a reference to injury to f the body. In his view therefore the word 'lésion' in the relevant phrase must be taken to have been used in the wider legal sense, indicated in the dictionary by the words 'dommage, préjudice, tort'. The fact remains, however, that the adjective 'corporelle' was chosen to qualify, and thus to restrict, the meaning of the word 'lésion'. Its ordinary meaning tends to exclude any other form of injury to the body other than a physical injury. And I would hold that the word 'lésion' g is used in its medical sense in art 17.

[89] I would be inclined therefore to read the phrase in a way that would confine its application to an injury to the skin, bones or other tissues of the body and exclude mental injury. But its meaning is not so clear that that one need look no further. I turn therefore to see what guidance is available in the other h material.

THE TRAVAUX PRÉPARATOIRES

[90] It must be said at once that, despite diligent research, no indication has been found that there was any discussion of the meaning to be attached to the j phrase 'any other bodily injury' by any of the delegates in the course of their negotiations at the Warsaw conference. But there are some points about these negotiations that are of interest.

[91] As Lord Reed noted (at 166) the text of the convention went through previous drafts before the matter reached the stage of the final negotiations. They originated in the French Government's Draft Protocol which was circulated prior to the Paris Conference of 1925. It dealt with liability in

extremely general terms, which focused solely on loss, damage and delay without
discussing the nature of the accidents which would give rise to liability. Article 3 a
of that draft said simply: 'Le transporteur est responsable des pertes, avaries et
retards qui résultent de ses fautes personelles et du vice propre de l'appareil.'

[92] Following various modifications a more detailed provision was produced
by the Comité International Technique d'Experts Juridiques Aériens (CITEJA),
which introduced the three categories which were later to appear in the b
convention in three separate articles:

> 'Le transporteur est responsable du dommage pendant le transport: a) en
> cas de mort, de blessures ou de toute autre lésion corporelle subie par un
> voyaguer; b) en cas de destruction, perte ou avarie de marchandises ou de
> bagages; c) en cas de retard subi par un voyageur, des marchandises ou c
> des bagages.'

As Lord Reed said (at 167), it is perhaps easier in this context to appreciate that
'lésion corporelle' might be intended to demarcate category (a) from the other
two categories.   But discussions which then followed during the Warsaw d
conference, which are fully described in Lord Reed's speech, focused on other
matters. There was no discussion of what was meant by the expression 'lésion
corporelle'. Nor was there a discussion of any issue which could be related in any
way to the issue whether it was intended to include mental injury as well as
physical injury.

[93] The Lord President said in Mr King's case that the court would have to e
conclude that the travaux préparatoires were of no assistance, as it was accepted
by both sides that the question of psychological injury was not discussed in them.
This was the primary conclusion that he too had reached and that he would apply
(see 2001 SLT 126 at 137). Lord Cameron of Lochbroom said (at 147) that it was
accepted that during the course of the preparatory work which led to the f
determination of the final text there was no debate minuted which indicated, one
way or the other, which meaning the delegates intended to give to the words
'toute autre lésion corporelle' as they appeared in the final text. Lord Reed said
(at 167) that in his opinion the travaux préparatoires did not support any theory
that the signatories to the Warsaw Convention had a specific intention either to
include or to exclude liability for psychiatric disorders. But he added that they g
did, on the other hand, confirm that arts 17, 18 and 19 should be read as a whole,
concerned respectively with passengers, goods and delay.

[94] In Miss Morris's case Lord Phillips of Worth Matravers MR said the court
in her case also agreed that the travaux préparatoires did not afford the type of
clear indication that enabled them to be used to resolve the ambiguity: [2001] 3 h
All ER 126 at [50]. But he went on to say that the fact that no mention was made
of mental injury was not without significance when one came to consider the
overall purpose and scheme of the convention.

[95] What inference is it proper to draw from the silence? It is clear that the
importance of these articles was not overlooked. The president of the drafting j
committee, Mr Giannini, is recorded as having said when he drew attention to
art 17, and in particular to the fact that it had been decided to divide what had
originally appeared in a single article into three articles setting out the causes for
liability for person, goods and baggage and delay: 'As our colleagues certainly
recall, these are perhaps the most important articles of the Convention.'
Nevertheless the draft art 17 was approved without discussion (*II Conference*

a *International de Droit Privé Aérien*, Minutes, translated by Horner & Legraz (1975) pp 204–205).

[96] It seems reasonable to conclude from their silence that the delegates did not feel it necessary to discuss what was meant by the words 'lésion corporelle'. None of them appears to have anticipated that there would be any difficulty in applying the wording of art 17 to the facts in practice. Nor was it suggested that *b* the formula which they were adopting would cause serious concern to the airlines or to their insurers. This suggests that the meaning which they gave to the words was the simplest and least troublesome meaning that they would ordinarily bear.

[97] As to the conclusion to be drawn from this material, I can at least say that I have not found anything so far which contradicts the impression which I have *c* already formed on reading the convention that the word 'bodily' restricts the scope of the word 'injury' to injuries which are manifestly physical and that it excludes emotional reactions and mental injury.

SUBSEQUENT PRACTICE

d [98] The search is for the meaning which was to be attributed to the words 'bodily injury' in 1929 when the convention was entered into. So I think that we should be cautious in the use of subsequent practice. It would not be right to use subsequent practice to show that the meaning of these words has been changed. The proper way to change the meaning used in an international convention is by amending the convention. But it would be helpful if there was some evidence of *e* a settled practice on the part of all the contracting states to show what they have always understood the words to mean. The point does not appear to have been raised in any reported case until a series of hijackings in the 1970s led to the making of claims in the United States for damages for emotional distress and mental injury. I shall come back later to the case law. At this stage, however, I *f* wish to refer to some other material to which our attention has been drawn.

[99] The Lord President in Mr King's case drew support for a broader interpretation of the phrase from the fact that from the very beginning in the German-speaking countries the phrase was interpreted in a way that would have permitted recovery for mental injury: 2001 SLT 126 at 136. An official German-language translation was prepared as the result of co-operation among *g* officials of Germany, Austria and Switzerland and published in 1933. It interprets the phrase 'blessure ou toute autre lésion corporelle' as 'körperlich verletzt oder sonst gesundheitlich geschädigt'. According to this translation, which uses the adjective 'körperlich' to qualify the equivalent to the word 'blessure' in the French text rather than the word 'lésion', the article applies where the passenger *h* is bodily wounded or otherwise damaged in his health.

[100] For the reasons which the Lord President described (at 136) it is thought that one of those who had a hand in the translation was Dr Otto Riese. He was a member of the German delegation in all the negotiations from the Paris conference in 1925 onwards. He continued to take an interest in and write about *j* aviation matters after the Warsaw conference. He had already indicated in an article which he wrote shortly after it ended that the phrase should be given a wide scope. In subsequent articles he adhered to the view that it applied to damage to health, although he acknowledged in his *Luftrecht* (1949) p 442 that this was a somewhat free translation of 'lésion corporelle'. In a French text which appeared in 1951, *Riese and Lacour, Précis de droit Aérien* p 264, para 323, he said that the difference between the words 'blessure' and 'lésion corporelle' was that the

convention applied not only to wounding properly so called but also to all injury
or the health of the passenger, 'telles que les conséquences d'un choc psychique   *a*
ou d'un mal de l'air'. The Lord President said (2001 SLT 126 at 137) that he did
not think that either the official German translation or Dr Riese's views, which
tended to confirm that the expression 'lésion corporelle' was not used with the
intention of excluding mental or physical injury, could be dismissed lightly.

[101] Commenting on this chapter of evidence, Lord Reed pointed out (at   *b*
165) that the official German translation was of no greater weight than the
English translation and of less weight than the French text, and he noted
Dr Riese's own description of the German version as a somewhat free translation
of it. Lord Phillips of Worth Matravers MR made similar comments in
Miss Morris's case: [2001] 3 All ER 126 at [85]. I also agree with him that caution
must be applied to the views expressed subsequently by one delegate, for the   *c*
reason which the Lord President himself gave (2001 SLT 126 at 137) that
delegates at a conference may not actually all share a common view on the point
at issue.

[102] I can see that there is force in the point which the Lord President made
(at 136–137) that it would be surprising if Dr Riese had felt able consistently to   *d*
advance his interpretation while conscious either that his fellow delegates at
Warsaw had chosen the phrase with the settled intention of excluding mental
injury or that his interpretation was wholly inconsistent with the meaning of
these words. But the fact remains that, so far as the records show, the question
whether the phrase extended to mental injury was simply not discussed at the
Warsaw conference.   *e*

[103] CITEJA was dissolved in 1947, and its work was taken over by the
International Civil Aviation Organisation (ICAO). The legal committee of the
ICAO met at Madrid in 1951 as part of the programme of work of revision of the
Warsaw Convention which led to the Hague Conference in 1955. The French
representative, M Garnault, proposed as an amendment to art 17 the substitution   *f*
of the words 'affection corporelle' for 'lésion corporelle'. His reason, as recorded
in the minutes, was that the word 'lésion' presupposed a rupture in the tissue and
that he thought that there could be cases where, without there being a 'lésion' in
the tissues or a break in their continuity, there could be a mental illness.

[104] As Lord Reed observed (2001 SLT 126 at 166) the French representative's   *g*
explanation adopted the medical, rather than the legal, meaning of the word
'lésion' and it indicates that he did not think that the words 'lésion corporelle'
covered mental illness. The Lord President agreed (at 140) that M Garnault's
views do indeed support the narrower interpretation of those words and that, as
he would be a native speaker of the language, they must carry a certain weight.   *h*
His view was that, taken as a whole, the legal debate at Madrid showed that by
1951 there was no settled view that the words in art 17 were to be interpreted as
excluding psychological injury. I would agree with this assessment. But it does
not persuade me that it was thought in 1929 by the signatories to the Warsaw
Convention that the phrase 'any other bodily injury' would include cases where
the only injury sustained was a mental injury.   *j*

[105] The Montreal Convention on Air Carrier Liability was signed on 28 May
1999, but it is not yet in force. One of the issues which was discussed was whether
mental injury could be included in any new, revised system of liability. A
document produced under the aegis of the chairman included the following
statement with regard to art 17:

a   'With reference to article 17, paragraph 1 of the Convention, the
     expression "bodily injury" is included on the basis of the fact that in some
     states damages for mental injuries are recoverable under certain
     circumstances, that jurisprudence in this area is developing and that it is not
     intended to interfere with this development, having regard to jurisprudence
     in areas other than international carriage by air.'

b   [106] The Lord President said (2001 SLT 126 at 141) that the delegates' official
     view showed that they were quite prepared to countenance the situation, which
     had developed since the Warsaw Convention, where courts of different states
     deal with damages for psychological harm in different ways. He said that this
     seemed to him to be consistent with the intention of the delegates at the Warsaw
c   conference who did not seek to impose a uniform system of assessing damages,
     being content that the cap on the recoverable damages provided sufficient
     uniformity for carriers and their insurers. On the other hand, as Lord Reed
     pointed out (at 166), the position in 1999 was that national courts, including in
     particular those in the United States where the point was of particular importance
     in view of the size of its air market, had interpreted the words 'any other bodily
d   injury' as excluding mental injury. This brings me to the relevant case law.

DECISIONS OF FOREIGN COURTS

(a) *United States*
e   [107] The first reported case in the United States which was drawn our
     attention arose out of an incident when an aircraft en route from Tel Aviv to New
     York was hijacked, diverted to the Middle East and forced to land in the desert in
     Jordan: *Rosman v Trans World Airlines Inc* (1974) 34 NY 2d 385. The passengers
     were not struck or personally assaulted by any of the hijackers, but they claimed
     to have suffered severe psychic trauma during the ordeal. The question was
f   whether they were entitled to compensation for their psychic trauma under the
     convention. The case came before the Court of Appeals of New York, which held
     that the defendant was liable for the plaintiff's palpable, objective bodily injuries,
     including those caused by the psychic trauma of the hijacking, and for the
     damages flowing from these bodily injuries, but not for the trauma as such or for
     the non-bodily or behavioural manifestations of the trauma.
g   [108] Delivering the judgment of the majority, Rabin J recognised (at 397) that
     the relationship between the mind and the body was a difficult issue. But he said
     that it was not one that the court had to decide:

h   'Rather, in seeking to apply the treaty's terms to the facts before us, we ask
     whether the treaty's use of the word "bodily", in its ordinary meaning, can
     fairly be said to include "mental". We deal with the term as used in an
     international agreement written almost 50 years ago, a term which even
     today would have little significance in the treaty as an adjective modifying
     "injury" except to import a distinction from "mental". In our view, therefore,
j   the ordinary, natural meaning of "bodily injury" as used in article 17 connotes
     palpable, conspicuous physical injury, and excludes mental injury with no
     observable "bodily", as distinguished from "behavioural", manifestations.' (My
     emphasis.)

He dealt (at 399) with the need for a causal connection between the injury and
the accident, and with the question whether the expression 'bodily injury' could
extend to an injury such as a skin rash which was caused or aggravated by fright

experienced during the incident. Disagreeing on this point with Stevens J, who
dissented, he said:

> 'In our view, this connection can be established whether the bodily injury
> was caused by physical impact, by the physical circumstances of the
> confinement or by psychic trauma. If the accident—the hijacking—caused
> severe fright, which in turn manifested itself in some objective "bodily
> injury", then we would conclude that the Convention's requirement of the
> causal connection is satisfied.'

[109] I have quoted these passages from the majority judgment in *Rosman's*
case, and added emphasis to the words 'palpable', 'conspicuous' and 'observable',
because they provide important guidance about the scope, on what it described
(at 399) as a liberal interpretation, which can be given to the phrase 'any other
bodily injury'. As Rabin J put it in a later passage on the same, the predicate of
liability is to establish the 'bodily injury'. Once this is established, then the
damages sustained as a result of the bodily injury can be compensated, including
mental suffering. It treats as 'bodily injury' physical injuries consequent upon
shock or distress such as heart attacks, rashes and strokes and damage to the
brain. But it excludes manifestations of fear, anxiety or other mental problems
which cannot be described as physical injuries, such as sleeplessness, headaches
and loss of weight: see Lord Reed's analysis in Mr King's case (2001 SLT 126 at
169). It also excludes conditions affecting the mind which are not due to a
palpable, conspicuous or observable physical injury

[110] The first case to come before the Supreme Court of the United States on
this issue was *Eastern Airlines Inc v Floyd* (1991) 499 US 530. Passengers on an
aircraft which narrowly avoided crashing during a flight between Miami and the
Bahamas claimed damages solely for mental distress arising out of the accident.
A conflict had arisen between the decision of the Court of Appeals in that case
that the phrase 'lésion corporelle' encompasses purely emotional distress and the
decision in *Rosman's* case. The Supreme Court held that art 17 does not allow
recovery for what it described as mental or psychic injuries unaccompanied by
physical injury or physical manifestation of injury.

[111] The court used the French text to guide its analysis. It examined the
meaning which was given to the words in the French dictionaries, observed that
the phrase was not used in any French legislation in force in 1929, that there were
no French court decisions in or before 1929 which explained its meaning or had
allowed recovery for injury caused by fright or shock absent an incident in which
someone sustained physical injury and that there were no materials in French
treatises which indicated that 'lésion corporelle' embraced psychic injury. The
court observed (at 540) that the cause of action that evidently was possible in
principle under French law in 1929 would not have been recognised in many
other countries represented at the Warsaw Convention. The court said (at
544–545) that the unavailability of compensation for purely psychic injury in
many common and civil law countries at the time of the Warsaw Convention
persuaded it that the signatories had no specific intent to include such a remedy
in the convention. It said (at 551–552):

> 'Even if we were to agree that allowing recovery for purely psychic injury
> is desirable as a policy goal, we cannot give effect to such policy without
> convincing evidence that the signatories' intent with respect to Article 17
> would allow such recovery. As discussed, neither the language, negotiating

a   history, nor postenactment interpretations of Article 17 clearly evidences
    such intent ... Moreover, we believe our construction of Article 17 better
    accords with the Warsaw Convention's stated purpose of achieving
    uniformity of rules governing claims arising from international air
    transportation ... We have no doubt that subjecting international air carriers
    to *strict* liability for purely mental distress would be controversial for most
b   signatory countries. Our construction avoids this potential source of divergence.'

[112] The court summarised (at 552–553) the view that it had reached in terms
which specifically left open the question whether compensation might be
available where mental injury was accompanied by physical injury:

c   'We conclude that an air carrier cannot be held liable under Article 17
        when an accident has not caused a passenger to suffer death, physical injury,
        or physical manifestation of injury. Although Article 17 renders air carriers
        liable for "damage sustained in the event of" ("*dommage survenu en cas de*")
        such injuries ... we express no view as to whether passengers can recover for
        mental injuries that are accompanied by physical injuries. That issue is not
d   presented here because respondents do not allege physical injury or physical
        manifestation of injury.'

[113] The decision in *Floyd*'s case was followed in *El Al Israel Airlines v Tseng*
(1999) 525 US 155 in which the Supreme Court confirmed (at 166, note 9) the
conclusion reached in *Floyd*'s case that the convention provides for compensation
e   only when the passenger suffers 'death, physical injury, or physical manifestation
of injury'. The passenger claimed that she had sustained psychic or psychosomatic
injuries as a result of an intrusive body search but accepted that there had been
no 'bodily injury' as that term is used in the convention. Her claim was that, as
the convention allowed no recovery, it did not preclude her from maintaining a
f   separate action for damages. It was rejected by the Supreme Court. The same
result would be reached in this jurisdiction: see *Fellowes (or Herd) v Clyde
Helicopters Ltd* [1997] 1 All ER 775, [1997] AC 534.

[114] Judicial thinking in the United States has been developed further in a
series of cases in the Federal courts. In *Jack v Trans World Airlines Inc* (1994)
854 F Supp 654 there had been a crash and a fire following an aborted take-off.
g   The court distinguished three different kinds of injury (at 664):

        '"Impact injuries" refer to the bodily injuries (such as bruises, lacerations
        and broken bones) that passengers suffer during an airplane accident (here,
        the aborted take off and evacuation of the plane). "Physical manifestations"
        refer to those bodily injuries or illnesses (such as skin rashes and heart attacks)
h   that result from the distress one experiences during or after an accident.
        "Emotional distress" refers to the psychic trauma that one experiences either
        during or after the accident.'

It was not disputed that 'impact injuries' and 'physical manifestations' were
j   within the scope of the expression 'bodily injury'. But the court noted (at 665)
that there were four possible approaches to emotional distress: (1) no recovery
allowed for emotional distress; (2) recovery allowed for all distress, as long as
bodily injury occurs; (3) emotional distress allowed as damages for bodily injury,
but distress may include distress about the accident; and (4) only emotional
distress flowing from the bodily injury is recoverable. The court adopted the
fourth approach (at 668). It held that the emotional distress recoverable was

limited to the distress about the physical impact or manifestation, ie the bodily injury, but that recovery was not allowed for the distress about the accident itself.

[115] In *Alvarez v American Airlines Inc* (2000) 27 Avi 17,475 the court held that a passenger's claim for psychological and emotional injuries was properly dismissed because the physical manifestations of his post-traumatic stress disorder, including increased heart rate and elevated blood pressure, were directly related to his emotional trauma and not to a physical injury suffered during the evacuation from the aircraft. The court said (at 17,478) that, if these physical manifestations could support a recovery, a passenger frightened by air turbulence could recover on the basis of his increased heart rate which would convert the rule established in *Floyd*'s case into a mere pleading formality. This decision supports the view that emotions and other mental disturbances which cannot be related to a palpable, conspicuous or observable physical injury are outside the scope of art 17. But it is not wholly consistent with what was said in *Rosman*'s case about the physical manifestations of a mental injury.

[116] In *Weaver v Delta Airlines Inc* (1999) 56 F Supp 2d 1190 a passenger brought an action to recover damages for chronic post-traumatic stress disorder which she attributed to terror which she felt during an emergency landing of the aircraft in which she was a passenger. But in this case there was an affidavit from the passenger's doctor which stated that the impact of the event included bio-chemical reactions which had physical impacts upon her brain and neurological system. In response, the airline did not present sufficient evidence to raise a factual issue on this point. The scientific research relied on by the passenger was criticised, but it was not explained and its expert had not examined the passenger. In the light of this evidence the court held that she had met her burden of showing that the emergency landing physically impacted on her brain and that there was no genuine issue on the facts. The court said (at 1192):

'Weaver's action here is distinguishable from previous cases, because her claim is presented as a physical injury and she relies on recent scientific research explaining that post-traumatic stress disorder evidences actual trauma to brain cell structures. Weaver's post-traumatic stress disorder evidences an injury to her brain, and the only reasonable conclusion is that it is, in fact, a bodily injury ... The legal question in this case is simply whether the Warsaw Convention allows recovery for this particular kind of bodily injury, ie, a brain injury (even with slight physical effects). The answer must be yes.'

[117] In *Re Air Crash at Little Rock, Arkansas, on 1 June 1999* (2000) 27 Avi 18,428 the passenger suffered from smoke inhalation, knee, leg and ankle injuries in a crash and her subsequent escape from the aircraft. But her primary claim was for emotional and psychological injuries consisting of serious chronic post-traumatic stress disorder and major depression. The judge observed (at 18,431) that Federal courts had come to different conclusions as to the nexus required between physical and psychic injuries. He referred to *Jack's, Alvarez's* and *Weaver's* cases and to *Terrafranca v Virgin Atlantic Airways Ltd* (1998) 151 F 3d 108, in which it was held that there could be no recovery unless the passenger demonstrated direct, concrete bodily injury as opposed to manifestations of fear or anxiety. He held ((2000) 27 Avi 18,428 at 18,433) that, once the threshold of liability had been crossed by proving a physical injury, then all damages available under the passenger's domicile are recoverable. As to whether post-traumatic stress disorder was a physical manifestation of injury, the judge noted that different

a results had been reached in several recent cases on this point. He held in favour of the passenger, regarding this as a matter of evidence. The passenger's doctor said in his evidence that research had shown brain dysfunction in people with post-traumatic stress disorder and that, while it could not be said that everybody would demonstrate the same abnormality, the consistent theme was that post-traumatic stress disorder was both a biological and a psychological syndrome.

b As the judge put it (at 18,436):

'The *Terrafranca* and *Jack* decisions reflect our nascent understanding of the nature of mental illness. It is not clear that those courts were presented with the scientific literature to underpin a finding that PTSD is a biological as well as an emotional and psychological illness ... Furthermore, the evidence

c presented at the trial, both in the form of expert testimony and exhibits, established that PTSD is a biological/physical as well as a psychological injury.'

[118] The conclusion which I would draw from these cases is that there is a consistent body of judicial opinion in the United States that the phrase 'any other

d bodily injury' does not permit compensation for an emotional reaction which has not been shown to be a manifestation of physical injury. Emotional distress is excluded, but so also is a psychiatric illness which affects the mind only and is not capable of being described as a physical injury. The decisions in *Weaver's* case and the *Little Rock* case appear to have broken new ground. They have applied the

e phrase to a mental injury which was shown by expert medical evidence to have been accompanied by physical changes to the patient's brain cell structures. In those cases, in the light of the evidence, the passengers' post-traumatic stress disorder was held to be a physical as well as a psychological injury. This extends the meaning of the phrase 'bodily injury' beyond that which was recognised in *Rosman's* case, because changes of that kind are plainly not palpable, conspicuous

f or observable.

(b) *Australia and Israel*

[119] I have grouped these two countries together because they have produced the only judicial decisions outside the United States which were drawn

g to our attention.

[120] In *Daddon v Air France* (1984) 1 S & B Av R VII/141 the Supreme Court of Israel was concerned with claims by passengers in respect of the mental anguish which they had suffered while being held captive at Entebbe Airport by hijackers. It held that 'bodily injury' in art 17 included mental anguish which was

h not accompanied by any physical injury. It reached this conclusion after recognising (at 152) that the parties to the convention apparently had no intention whatsoever in that regard, either because most states at that time had not recognised mental anguish as a cause of action or because the possibility of mental anguish which was not accompanied by physical injury had not been

j contemplated. What the court sought to do was to develop the meaning of the word by judicial policy in the light of subsequent developments. This approach has received no support in the other jurisdictions. It has been criticised on the ground that it is impermissible to construe the convention in the light of changes since 1929. The question is whether purely mental injury was within the intention of the draftsmen and the signatories: *Floyd's* case (1991) 499 US 530 at 544.

[121] In *Kotsambasis v Singapore Airlines Ltd* (1997) 42 NSWLR 110, a decision of the Court of Appeal of New South Wales, the passenger claimed that she had suffered psychological injuries when shortly after take-off a fire broke out in one of the engines of the aircraft, which returned safely to the airport after fuel had been jettisoned. Meagher JA, with whose judgment Powell and Stein JJA agreed, said (at 114) that the words 'bodily injury' both in English and in French were ambiguous and that the ambiguity could only be resolved by looking at the intention of the contracting parties and adopting a purposive approach to the convention:

'It is immediately apparent that the adjective "bodily" is a word of qualification or limitation. It is a general principle of statutory interpretation, equally applicable to the interpretation of international agreements, that courts are not at liberty to consider any word as superfluous or insignificant—*Commonwealth v Baume* ((1905) 2 CLR 405 at 414)—and, more specifically, that effect is to be given to words of limitation: *Randwick Municipal Council v Rutledge* (1959) 102 CLR 54, 94. It is clear that the draftsmen of the Convention did not intend to impose absolute liability in respect of all forms of injury.'

Following *Floyd's* case he held (at 115) that the term 'bodily injury' was not intended to, and on a proper interpretation of the convention does not, include purely psychological injury. He noted that the question whether recovery might be available where psychological injury was accompanied by physical injury was left open in *Floyd's* case and said that, in view of the findings of the trial judge, it was not necessary for him to decide that point. This decision supports the view that art 17 does not provide compensation for mental injury.

DISCUSSION

[122] I find myself in agreement with the conclusions which Lord Reed reached in Mr King's case and those of the Court of Appeal in Miss Morris's case. The Lord President said in Mr King's case that, on the approach suitable to an international convention, the phrase 'any other bodily injury' was apt to cover all injuries of any kind which affected a person in his body, and that these would include purely psychological injuries which an individual suffers, in a certain sense at least, in his body: 2001 SLT 126 at 144. I regret that I cannot agree with this view. It seems to me to give too little weight to the limiting effect of the word 'bodily' and to the difficulties that would have been apparent in 1929 if it had been the intention to extend liability to that kind of injury. It is inconsistent with the decision in *Floyd's* case, which has been followed in New South Wales and which I too would wish to follow. It is also inconsistent with the decision in *Rosman's* case, which I regard as the other leading authority in this field.

[123] The evidence indicates that there was no uniform approach among the contracting states in 1929 to recovery in damages for mental injury. As the court noted in *Floyd's* case (1996) 499 US 530 at 540, a cause of action for mental injury would not have been recognised in many of them. In this situation clear words would have been needed to ensure that a uniform approach to this problem was adopted in all jurisdictions. The absence of clear words allowing recovery for a purely mental injury is telling. The introduction of the word 'corporelle' was not the way to make this point clear. The absence of discussion suggests that the contracting parties were content to use this word as a word of limitation to qualify the otherwise unrestricted scope of the word 'lésion', and that they

a intended to restrict it to physical injury of a kind that was manifest and observable.

[124] Insurance practice has not been the subject of evidence. But it is commonplace for insurers to seek to exclude or restrict liability. One of the central points in the convention was the surrendering of the opportunity to do this in the case of carriage to which the convention applies. Part of the process of compromise *b* lay in the choice of language for the articles in Pt III, including art 17. This adds further weight to the point that the words 'bodily' and 'corporelle' were used as words of modification or restriction. It would have been a reasonable compromise to provide strict liability for physical injury of a kind that was manifest and observable, but not to extend this to an emotional reaction or any kind of mental injury. Practice since then suggests that this was what the compromise was *c* understood to be, as there was a marked absence of claims of this character until the 1970s despite the many alarming or distressing events that may be encountered during air travel.

[125] The search is for the meaning which the words were understood to have when the convention was entered into. It would be wrong to regard art 17 as limited *d* by the state of medical and scientific knowledge that was current in the 1920s. There is no reason to think that the contracting parties intended that no account should be taken of developments in medical science in determining the question whether a passenger has sustained a bodily injury. I agree with my noble and learned friend Lord Mackay of Clashfern that, if the brain could be shown to have been injured and *e* the other conditions for compensation under art 17 are satisfied, it would not be right to refuse compensation under the article on the ground only that in 1929 an injury of that kind would not have been capable of being demonstrated. Whether or not there is such an injury will always depend on the evidence. But the fact remains that a bodily injury is conceptually distinct from any injury which affects the mind: Mullany and Handford *Tort Liability for Psychiatric Damage* (1993) p 18.

f [126] The words 'palpable' and 'conspicuous' were used by the court in *Rosman's* case to describe the kind of injury that they envisaged as falling within the expression 'bodily injury'. But the use of such strong language risks substituting a new test for that used in the convention. The question whether there is any better way of explaining what the convention meant is best left over for another occasion, as my *g* noble and learned friend Lord Steyn has indicated. For the time being I would venture to suggest that one would expect an injury falling within the expression 'bodily injury' to be capable of being demonstrated by an examination of the body of the passenger, making the best use of the most sophisticated means that are now available. *Weaver's* case and the *Little Rock* case, as I understand them, did not *h* proceed on that kind of evidence. There was no evidence in either case that the passengers had suffered an injury to the brain that was capable of being demonstrated by means of an examination of the body of the passenger. The argument was that the post-traumatic stress disorder itself constituted a manifestation of a physical injury. In my opinion evidence of the kind that was available in those *j* cases is not enough to satisfy the test of showing that a psychiatric illness is or includes a 'bodily injury' for the purposes of art 17.

[127] I believe that this approach is consistent with the mainstream views in *Floyd's* case and other leading cases in the United States whose interpretation of art 17, like my noble and learned friend, Lord Nicholls of Birkenhead, I too would wish that this House should follow if possible. I regret that I am unable to agree with the opinion of Lord Hobhouse of Woodborough as to the effect of these authorities.

[128] In any event there has been no attempt in either case to demonstrate that the passengers' depressive illnesses had a physical cause or origin. It would not be right to speculate as to whether, in view of the fact that a clinical diagnosis has been achieved in each case and that treatment has been prescribed for them, their illnesses could be shown to have had a physical origin which could be causally linked to the accident. That would have been a matter for proof. But there has been no offer to lead any such evidence. It is sufficient for the decision in these cases to say that it has not been shown that the mental injury which the passengers sustained falls within the scope of the expression 'bodily injury'.

[129] I would, however, follow the indications in *Rosman*'s case and *Jack*'s case that compensation may be awarded to a passenger under art 17 for the physical manifestations of a mental injury. A peptic ulcer disorder involves the tissues of the body, and it is not difficult to see that it is a kind of bodily injury. The requirement of a causal link to the accident will be satisfied if it can be shown, as Mr King seeks to do, that the disorder was caused by a mental illness which was itself caused by the accident. Thus, while there is no general right to recover damages under art 17 for mental injury sustained by a passenger, damages for the physical manifestations of a mental injury will be recoverable. I would hold that the Lord Ordinary was right to allow Mr King a proof of his averments about the peptic ulcer disease.

CONCLUSIONS

[130] I would allow the appeal in Mr King's case and restore the interlocutor of the Lord Ordinary. I have considered whether an opportunity should be given in Miss Morris's case to re-open the question whether her depressive illness was linked to changes in her brain cell structures and could be said on this ground to have amounted to a physical injury. But I have come to the conclusion, in view of the way her case was expressly argued both in the Court of Appeal and in this House and because I do not think that even with the benefit of such evidence it could be shown that she has suffered a 'bodily injury', that this would not be appropriate. I would dismiss her appeal.

LORD HOBHOUSE OF WOODBOROUGH.

[131] My Lords, these two appeals, the one from the Court of Session (the Lord President (Lord Rodger of Earlsferry) and Lord Cameron of Lochbroom, Lord Reed dissenting) (2001 SLT 126) and the other from the English Court of Appeal (Lord Phillips of Worth Matravers MR, Peter Gibson and Latham LJJ) ([2001] EWCA Civ 790, [2001] 3 All ER 126, [2002] QB 100), raise a question of the correct meaning to be given to art 17 of the Warsaw Convention 1929, and the 1955 Hague Amendment, as incorporated into the law of the United Kingdom by the Carriage by Air Act 1961. In one case the flight was internal to the United Kingdom and in the other was international. As more fully explained by my noble and learned friend Lord Hope of Craighead, nothing turns on this difference and no argument has been advanced based on making such a distinction. Point is lent to the relevant question by the fact that the two courts reached irreconcilable and opposing decisions as to the meaning of art 17. The question is one upon which the highest courts of other countries have also expressed opinions using language which has been relied upon by one or more of the parties to these appeals to support their submissions and which will need to be carefully examined. The question is one of importance to the air transport

a industry worldwide since it affects the division of risk between passengers and carriers and the settlement of claims.

[132] The authoritative text of art 17 of the Warsaw Convention is that in the French language: art 36 of the convention. The United Kingdom Act schedules both an English text and the French text. Section 1(2) of the 1961 Act provides 'if there is any inconsistency between the text in English ... and the text in French

b ... the text in French shall prevail'. The English text, which is the same as that used in other English-speaking countries and that used for the purposes of later air carriage conventions, reads:

c 'The carrier is liable for damage sustained in the event of the death or wounding of a passenger or any other bodily injury suffered by a passenger, if the accident which caused the damage so sustained took place on board the aircraft or in the course of any of the operations of embarking or disembarking.'

The relevant phrase in French reads 'dommage survenu en cas de mort, de blessure ou de toute autre lésion corporelle subie par un voyageur' which has the

d same connotations as the English. Thus the word 'lésion' has a similar breadth of meaning as the English word 'injury'. Your Lordships were referred to various dictionaries, both French and English, but these did not disclose any inconsistency between the French and English texts and therefore did not raise any question under s 1(2).

e [133] Before coming to the rival arguments it is necessary to give an example of a factual situation in order to illustrate the significance of the question raised before us. It is convenient to take the pleaded facts of Morris's case for this purpose. The passenger was a 15-year-old girl travelling on an overnight international flight as an unaccompanied minor. She was placed in a seat next to a male passenger of a different nationality. During the night she woke up to find

f herself being indecently assaulted by her neighbour. Unsurprisingly she was deeply disturbed by this. The stewardess moved her to another part of the aeroplane where the girl completed the flight without further incident. The man had not physically injured the girl in any visible way. She had not been scratched or bruised. The seriousness of the assault lay in its indecency. It was a traumatic

g experience for the girl which had a lasting effect upon her. As a direct result of the incident she became clinically depressed. She was referred to a consultant psychiatrist, Dr Cooling, and he diagnosed her to be suffering from the illness 'major depressive disorder, single episode', 296.2[x] in the 'DSM-IV'. 'DSM-IV' is the fourth edition of the *Diagnostic and Statistical Manual of Mental Disorders*

h published by the American Psychiatric Association. This manual contains the authoritative classification of psychiatric illnesses defining the signs and symptoms upon which the diagnosis of the various illnesses and disorders should be based. The manual explains the terminology used and its purpose. The phrase 'mental disorder' is used for reasons of convenience although it 'unfortunately implies a distinction between "mental" and "physical" disorders that is a

j reductionist anachronism of mind/body dualism' (see p xxx). The word 'disorder' is used to describe what is clinically significant and mark the boundary between normality and pathology:

'In DSM-IV, each of the mental disorders is conceptualized as a clinically significant behavioral or psychological syndrome or pattern that occurs in an individual and that is associated with present distress (e.g., a painful symptom) or disability (i.e., impairment in one or more important areas of functioning) or with a significantly increased risk of suffering death, pain, disability, or an important loss of freedom. In addition, this syndrome or pattern must not be merely an expectable and culturally sanctioned response to a particular event, for example, the death of a loved one, Whatever its original cause, it must currently be considered a manifestation of a behavioral, psychological, or biological dysfunction in the individual. Neither deviant behavior (e.g., political, religious or sexual) nor conflicts that are primarily between the indivi-dual and society are mental disorders unless the deviance or conflict is a symptom of a dysfunction in the individual, as described above.' (See p xxxi.)

[134] So, there had been an incident during the course of the flight which qualified as an accident for the purposes of art 17 (see the judgment of the Court of Appeal [2001] 3 All ER 126 at [13]–[31], following *Air France v Saks* (1985) 470 US 392). The incident is alleged to have caused the girl to suffer a recognised psychiatric illness displaying observable dysfunctional symptoms as a result of which she suffered damage. Is the psychiatric illness alleged a 'bodily injury'? The passenger submits that it is: the carrier submits that cannot be.

[135] The arguments advanced by each side as to what was required for the passenger to have suffered a 'bodily injury' ranged over a spectrum of alternative submissions. These submissions covered not only the 'injury' itself but also how it may have been caused. It was correctly accepted by the parties that the three elements in the first sentence of art 17 must be causally linked. The use of the phrase 'in the event of' (en cas de) does not mean that any wound suffered by the passenger at any time between the commencement of embarkation and the completion of disembarkation will suffice to permit any claim for damages. Thus, there must have been an accident which has caused the death, the wounding or the 'bodily injury' suffered by the passenger which caused the damage complained of. Some of the submissions sought to distinguish between different ways in which the relevant death, wounding or 'bodily injury', as the case might be, had been caused. Such submissions have been consistently rejected by the courts though they have undoubtedly affected the reasoning. The simplest form of the argument has been the 'impact' argument: there must have been an actual impact between some physical object and the passenger. Another form of the argument is that the causal link must have been through the medium of some physical object coming into contact with the passenger as, for example, the inhalation of smoke. These arguments, which were advanced again on these appeals by the carriers, were directed to excluding any injury other than one so caused and many psychiatric illnesses would not have been so caused. Ironically, in *Morris*'s case, there was such physical contact—the indecent touching. However, a traumatic experience can be something the passenger merely witnesses such as passively witnessing a life-threatening emergency or a hijacking. The difficulty with the carriers' causation arguments is that they would seek to make an unwarranted distinction between death and injury. The death of a susceptible individual can be caused by being involved in a sufficiently traumatic incident, such as a very severe fright, and the same applies to non-fatal injuries (though not to woundings). The causal link is a link made through the passenger's senses. Once the 'causation' arguments are rejected, it is necessary to examine carefully the carriers' arguments upon bodily injury, since they tend to equate 'bodily' with 'physical' and then apply criteria which would have the effect

of including or excluding injuries of the same character on the basis that they were fatal or non-fatal.

[136] Each side preferred the extreme form of its argument and in so doing had received support from one or other of the courts below. Thus, they variously argued as to the meaning of 'bodily injury' (using the term 'flight' as including embarkation and disembarkation and including the carriers' causation arguments): (1) only a palpable physical injury inflicted during the flight by some physical impact upon the passenger would suffice, eg a crash injuring the passenger, a bag falling on the head of the passenger; 'the impact test'; (2) the physical infliction of some such physical injury during the flight and palpably in existence at the conclusion of the flight whether or not any actual impact was involved, eg anoxia and immediate brain damage caused by the failure of the pressurisation system or carbon monoxide poisoning; 'in-flight injury without impact'; (3) any palpable injury physically caused during the flight, ie, an injury caused by some direct physical cause, not being an injury caused through the senses like a fatal or non-fatal heart attack or stroke caused by observing a hijacking or experiencing a sudden loss of altitude; 'the physical causation test'; (4) a physical injury which does not have any mental aspect or mental manifestations: not a 'mental injury' (the Court of Appeal view); (5) the physical infliction of physical injury during the flight even though not already manifested at the conclusion of the flight, for example, (a) a heart attack suffered after having disembarked, (b) a disease or illness contracted upon the plane say through the contamination of the plane's air supply or on-flight food; 'the delayed effect injury'; (6) an injury, even if it was caused through the senses, which has physical consequences or physical manifestations, even if they are not already manifest at the conclusion of the flight; (7) any injury which could properly be described as a personal injury; (8) any emotional upset or reaction—distress, fright, mental anguish, anxiety, grief, etc.

[137] The majority of the First Division preferred argument (7), largely basing themselves on an examination of the various texts and how the article had been viewed, especially by a German jurist who had attended the Warsaw conference and some of the later conferences. They considered the history of the convention and concluded that art 17 should be given a wide and generous meaning: there is little difference between this and argument (8) as the Israeli case, *Daddon v Air France* (1984) 1 S & B Av R VII/141, demonstrates. The dissenting opinion of Lord Reed comes closest to argument (6). The Court of Appeal adopted argument (4), having broadly the same result as argument (2), viewing the phrase 'bodily injury' as pointing a contrast with what they described as 'mental injury'. This argument was developed by the carriers before your Lordships as an argument that, in 1929, those attending the conference at Warsaw would have contemplated only a crude mind-body dualism and the words used implicitly demonstrate an actual intention to exclude anything which would in popular diction be referred to as of the mind. By contrast argument (6) can be developed by reference to basic medical knowledge of the brain and the way it works as an integral part of the whole body so as to show why psychiatric illnesses may come within the term 'bodily injury' and therefore, provided the other conditions are satisfied, should be understood as falling within art 17.

[138] The diversity of the judicial statements within the United Kingdom and to some extent elsewhere, all expressed in relation to the same two simple English words 'bodily injury' as used in art 17, disclose a legal confusion and even, it may be thought, a failure of method. The range of the arguments advanced

lead to a similar conclusion. My Lords, I believe that it is possible to identify the explanations for this. I will attempt to classify them under three headings: first, the adoption of a subjective approach to the construction of the words and the misuse of national law concepts and rules; second, the assumptions made by the lawyers as to medical science and the change of environment between 1929 and the present day and its relevance; third, the misuse of language and the errors which result.

[139] But I will start by stating briefly what I consider to be the correct reading of these words and how it is supported, not contradicted, by the United States authorities.

Brief overview

[140] The composite expression 'bodily injury' involves a combination of two elements. The word 'injury' in the context of personal injury involves a condition which departs from the normal, which is not a mere transitory discomfort or inconvenience and which, whilst not permanent or incurable, has, in conjunction with its degree of seriousness, a sufficient duration. It includes a loss of function. A person who is concussed or who is in clinical shock or who is made deaf or blind is properly described as injured. (As to deafness, see, for example, *Daddon*'s case.) A condition which requires treatment to enable the person to return to the normal is typical of an injury though not essential; many injuries heal over time without intervention. Contracting an illness may amount to an injury depending upon the degree to which the illness departs from the normal. One would not normally describe a person who caught a cold as having suffered an injury but, on the other hand, one would certainly describe someone who contracted a serious disease or condition, say, 'AIDS' or hepatitis, as the result of the deliberate or negligent act of another as having suffered an injury.

[141] The word 'bodily' is simpler. It means pertaining to the body. There must be an injury to the body. It is, as it must be, accepted that the brain, the central nervous system and the glands which secrete the hormones which enable the brain and the rest of the central nervous system to operate are all integral parts of the body just as much as are the toes, heart, stomach and liver. They are all susceptible to injury. The mechanisms by which they can be injured vary. An ingested poison might injure the stomach or liver. A lack of oxygen will injure the brain by causing the death of brain cells. An injury to the heart may be caused by a blow or by a traumatic experience or by over-exertion. In every case there is a cause, external to the organ in question, which produces a change in the structure or ability to function of the organ. If the change, either alone or in conjunction with changes in other organs, is properly described as an injury, it is a 'bodily' injury. Since the body is a complex organism depending for its functioning and survival upon the interaction of a large number of parts, the injury may be subtle and a matter of inference not direct observation. The medical science of diagnosis exists to enable the appropriate inferences to be drawn from the observed evidence. Medicinal treatments (as with drugs) are prescribed on the basis that there is a physical condition which can be reversed or alleviated by physical means.

[142] 'Bodily injury' does not import visibility nor palpability nor externality. Its use in art 17 in addition to the use of the words 'death' and 'wounding' (blessure) and the inclusion of the word 'any' confirm this. Take an incident which ruptures a spleen or causes some other internal injury. The doctor infers that the injury has been caused from other signs and symptoms and ultimately

a confirms it by an invasive (surgery) or non-invasive (ultrascan or X-ray) procedure. An incident may damage someone's optic nerve in a location or manner which cannot be observed; the person may as a result have no sight in that eye; this will be a 'bodily injury' even though there is no thing palpable, conspicuous or visible. The use of the word 'palpable' in the discussion of the meaning of art 17 typifies the dangers of the use of loose terminology which does

b not aid clarity but, rather, creates ambiguity. 'Palpable' is a term which has a precise meaning—capable of being felt by touch—which is its medical meaning. But it also has a metaphorical usage—readily perceived by the senses or the mind. It will be readily understood that the precise meaning is too restrictive and cannot be justified as a gloss upon the simple phrase 'bodily injury'. The metaphorical usage likewise cannot be justified and is impractical and unprincipled. Is the

c judge or arbitrator to say: 'Having heard the evidence I am satisfied that the passenger suffered an injury but I cannot say that I readily perceived it?' The obvious attraction of using words such as 'palpable' is that they give an illusion of clarity when in truth they enable the user to avoid clarity and simply serve to detract from the clarity of the primary terminology.

d   [143] Thus, 'bodily injury' simply and unambiguously means a change in some part or parts of the body of the passenger which is sufficiently serious to be described as an injury. It does not include mere emotional upset such as fear, distress, grief or mental anguish (cf argument (8)). A psychiatric illness may often be evidence of a 'bodily injury' or the description of a condition which includes 'bodily injury'. But the passenger must be prepared to prove this, not just prove

e a psychiatric illness without evidence of its significance for the existence of a 'bodily injury'.

     [144] Turning to the United States authorities, the leading and subsequently influential case which first brought the relevant points to the fore was *Rosman v Trans World Airlines Inc* (1974) 34 NY 2d 385, decided in the Court of Appeals in

f New York in 1974 with the leading judgment given by Judge Rabin. The plaintiff passengers sought to recover damages from the carrier for 'psychic' (sic) trauma suffered on board a hijacked aircraft. None of the passengers had been shot or struck or personally assaulted but they said that they had feared, as was natural in the circumstances, that their lives were in grave danger. They complained of being subjected to emotional stress (and physical deprivation in being kept

g without adequate food and water in excessively hot and arid conditions). The court rejected the claim for emotional stress but held that it would allow damages for any—

h   'palpable, objective bodily injuries, including those caused by the psychic trauma of the hijacking, and for the damages flowing from those bodily injuries, but not for the trauma as such or for the nonbodily or behavioral manifestations of that trauma.' (See (1974) 34 NY 2d 385 at 400.)

They explained their reasoning in a passage (at 399–400) which it is worth quoting in full:

j   'A faithful reading of the terms of the Convention leads, we believe, to the following conclusions. A claim for damages under article 17 arises "in the event of ... bodily injury". The claim must therefore be predicated upon some *objective identifiable injury* to the body. In addition, there must be some causal connection between the bodily injury and the "accident". In our view, this connection can be established whether the bodily injury was caused by physical impact, by the physical circumstances of the confinement *or by psychic trauma*. If the accident—the hijacking—caused severe fright, which *a* in turn manifested itself in some *objective "bodily injury"*, then we would conclude that the Convention's requirement of the causal connection is satisfied. For example, if plaintiff Herman's *skin rash* was caused or aggravated by the fright she experienced on board the aircraft, then she should be compensated for the rash and the damages flowing from the rash. *b* It follows that, *if proved at trial*, she should be compensated for her mental anguish, *suffered as a result* of the rash, since this anguish would have flowed from the "bodily injury" ... only the damages flowing from the "bodily injury", whatever the causal link, are compensable. We are drawn to these conclusions by the clear import of the terms of article 17. Those terms, in their ordinary meaning, will not support plaintiffs' claim that *psychic trauma* *c* *alone*, or even the psychic trauma which caused the bodily injury, is compensable under the Warsaw Convention.' (My emphasis.)

[145] I have italicised certain phrases in this quotation in order to illustrate certain of the points being made. Emotional distress is not compensable as such; *d* it is *bodily injury* which is compensable. Therefore the passenger must prove that he has suffered a bodily injury. That is what art 17 says. That is what Judge Rabin is saying when he says there must be some 'objective identifiable injury'; the passenger must prove the bodily injury. (He later refers to the need for proof at the trial.) Thus, if an injury to the brain can be proved, we can substitute for the phrase 'skin rash' the words 'brain damage'. He is holding that proved brain *e* damage and its sequelae would be compensable. Given causation, it comes down to a question of proof. Judge Rabin rejects the 'causation' and 'impact' tests. 'Psychic' trauma experienced through the senses can be the route by which the 'bodily injury' can be caused by the 'accident'. The course upon which Judge Rabin is setting the United States courts is one which is fully consistent with the *f* reading of art 17 which I have adopted in [143], above. I will return to the American authorities (including *Rosman's* case) later in this opinion.

The convention: construction

[146] The historical context in which the Warsaw Convention of 1929 is set was not only the emergent business of commercial international carriage by air *g* of passengers and goods but also the framework of existing international conventions and agreements covering carriage by sea which was at the time and was, for the following decades, to continue to be the dominant means of international transport. The Warsaw Convention substantially incorporated the same scheme and the same main features as those earlier conventions. Thus *h* there is a recognition of the basic contractual relationship pursuant to which the transport is being performed and the requirement of the compulsory application of the internationally agreed terms to the contracts of carriage and the compulsory inclusion of statements to that effect into the contractual documentation. The substantive provisions provide a division of risk between *j* the carrier on the one hand and the goods or baggage owner or passenger on the other. In relation to carriage by sea, the salient features of this division of risk are provisions which impose evidential burdens on the carrier, give him limited exceptions which he can rely on and which give him either an absolute or qualified right to limit his liability. In the Warsaw Convention effectively the same scheme is followed for the carriage of passengers, their baggage and

a commercial cargo. In each case an agreed code divides the risk between the carrier and his customer. It provides uniformity and certainty; conflicts of laws problems are avoided as far as possible; the incidents of where any accident or litigation may occur are sought to be removed as far as possible; the negotiation and acceptance of the 'five freedoms' of international air transport were facilitated.

b [147] It follows from this that considerations of national or local law should not be allowed to intrude upon, let alone govern, any question of construction that may arise on the provisions for division of risk. As Lord Hope of Craighead said in *Sidhu v British Airways plc, Abnett (known as Sykes) v British Airways plc* [1997] 1 All ER 193 at 212, [1997] AC 430 at 453: '... the code is intended to be uniform and to be exclusive also of any resort to the rules of domestic law.' It is not right to attempt *c* to construe the words of the convention by reference to the rules of any domestic law, English, American, German or even French. We know that those rules were and are not all identical. The purpose of uniformity means that it is the duty of the national court to put to one side its views about its own law and other countries' laws. Quite apart from defeating uniformity, such a course can only lead to the *d* complication of simple issues, the inadequately informed investigation of other legal systems and, most importantly, to uncertainty. In few areas can this be more deleterious than in relation to the historical treatment by various legal systems, including our own, of the topic of so-called 'nervous shock'. Nor can it be acceptable, as was urged upon your Lordships by the carriers, to seek to find the 'lowest common denominator' of the delegates' national laws in 1929 and adopt *e* that. Whilst it is important to have regard to the international consensus upon the understanding of the provisions of international conventions and hence to what the courts in other jurisdictions have had to say about the provision in question, the relevant point for decision always remains: what do the actual words used mean? (*Stag Line Ltd v Foscolo, Mango & Co Ltd* [1932] AC 328, [1931] All ER Rep 666, the *f* Hague Rules; *James Buchanan & Co Ltd v Babco Forwarding and Shipping (UK) Ltd* [1977] 3 All ER 1048, [1978] AC 141, CMR, *Fothergill v Monarch Airlines Ltd* [1980] 2 All ER 696, [1981] AC 251, the amended Warsaw Convention; *Sidhu's* case, Warsaw.)

[148] Further things follow. First, the words used should receive an objective interpretation. It is equally mistaken to try and find out what the individual *g* delegates thought they were agreeing to as it is to investigate the various domestic laws of the signatory countries. The investigation is equally liable to be based on incomplete or imperfect evidence. It may well be that different delegates may have had different beliefs. The views of one delegate, however distinguished, articulate and well-published, may not represent the views of *h* others. The examination must be an objective one. The disciplined liberty to make use of travaux préparatoires regulates this. It is common ground that in the present case, to quote Lord Reed (2001 SLT 126 at 167 (para 56)):

> 'The travaux préparatoires do not support any theory that the signatories to the Warsaw Convention had a specific intention either to include or to *j* exclude liability for psychiatric disorders.'

Therefore, it is the unadorned language of the article to which attention must be directed. It is again a descent into unprincipled subjectivism to use, as do the Court of Appeal ([2001] 3 All ER 126 at [50], [96]) and others have done before them, the absence of travaux préparatoires as a tool of construction. Thus the Court of Appeal say: 'We consider that it is highly significant that no mention was made of liability for mental injury [sic] in the course of the negotiations that resulted in the Warsaw Convention.' This is reasoning which speculates about the subjective intentions of the delegates and is not directed to the objective autonomous meaning of the words used. Likewise it is erroneous, in the absence of cogent travaux, to infer that a particular interpretation of a provision is intended from the fact that on a later occasion the convention was amended without making any change to the provision in question. All it shows is that on the later occasion the parties were content to leave the wording of the provision unaltered. The motives or beliefs of the individual delegates for so doing are irrelevant. Similarly, it is unprincipled to say, as the Court of Appeal say also in [96], that it is 'equally significant' that no claim was made for 'mental injury' until the 1970s. One can only ask how can it be relevant to the question of the construction of the convention. In fact there are simple explanations arising from the development of mass passenger air transport, the outbreak of terrorist hijacking and probably developments in United States domestic law.

[149] Secondly it is also mistaken to interpret a convention such as the Warsaw Convention, or the various amended versions of it, as if they were intended to be historical documents frozen in time. They are intended to provide an enduring uniform code which will govern contractual and, where relevant, delictual relationships not just for a finite time but for the future as the transactions to which they apply are entered into. The contracts into which the code is to be incorporated are to be made and will be performed at dates in the future, maybe long into the future. Notionally to relate them back to a supposed state of affairs existing in 1929 is not only wrong but wholly impractical. It leads to the complication and confusion to which I have already referred. It is also destructive of uniformity since when a convention has later been amended, logic would require that one starts the clock again and asks what was in the minds of the delegates at the later conference. It is not necessary in order to understand this point to have regard to the principles applicable to 'always speaking' constitutional documents. The principle is more simple. Words have a meaning which does not change but the application of those words to the decision of any question depends on the facts and circumstances of the case in which that question arises. It is the facts and circumstances of the cases that change, not the meaning of the contractual words.

[150] Thirdly, the code involves a division of risk. It strikes a balance. It is wrong to construe it as a code designed to advantage one interest or the other, the carrier or the customer. Like any code of this character, it contains familiar types of provision assisting one interest balanced against others assisting the other interest. For the passenger, a simple criterion of causation by an 'accident' is adopted but counterbalanced by strong provisions enabling the carrier to limit his liability. These are not like exemption clauses to be construed against one or other party. The phrase 'bodily injury' simply enters the picture as part of the balanced code regardless of which interest it is thought to assist.

[151] I have elaborated the question of the approach to the construction of art 17 because, in my view, all the courts below were drawn into an essentially mistaken consideration of material which was nationally-based, historical, and subjective. It has resulted in an over-complication of the relevant question. It has necessitated a display of the most impressive scholarship and research but has led to the wrong questions being asked and the wrong answers given.

Medical science

a   [152] It is a feature of the brain and the central nervous system that the manner in which it works has inevitably limited the knowledge and understanding of how the organ functions and its pathology. It is an interrelated and interdependent system. Only limited knowledge could be gained from the examination of the anatomy of a corpse. In the living subject, the scope for
b   intrusive investigation was very limited. In the popular perception, this has led to the perpetuation of theories of psychic disembodiment long after they have any scientific justification. There now exist techniques for investigating the functioning of the living brain and the central nervous system together with the roles played by neurotransmitters, hormones and electrical impulses. Physical changes can be scanned and observed using sophisticated instruments and the
c   alterations in the normal chemistry of the brain can now be detected by sophisticated sampling techniques. What was previously invisible can now be made visible. These developments have two relevant results. It can now be shown by valid scientific techniques that certain psychiatric symptoms correspond to physical changes in the brain. Psychiatry (the science of mental
d   illness) has been able to develop a more reliable classification and aetiology enabling better diagnoses to be made and more reliable opinions to be given as to the probable causation of observed disorders. What these developments have changed is not the phenomena nor the meaning of the language used in the article but the ability to adduce evidence relevant to the factual issues raised by the article.

e   [153] The judgments of Lord Philip and Lord Reed in the Court of Session both show an awareness of these developments. The judgment of Lord Phillips of Worth Matravers MR in the Court of Appeal ([2001] 3 All ER 126 at [35]–[40]), in a section headed 'The distinction between physical injury and mental injury', from which it is necessary to quote certain passages in full since they are
f   fundamental to the thinking of the Court of Appeal, says:

> '[35] This appeal has proceeded on the premise that there is a distinction between physical injury and mental injury; that physical injury involves damage or adverse change to the structure of the body, whereas mental illness adversely affects the wellbeing of the mind without organic change to
g   the body.
> [36] This was undoubtedly the general belief in the 1920s, when the terms of the Warsaw Convention were negotiated.'

Then, having quoted from two speeches in the House of Lords in two tort cases and two English textbooks on English tort law, the judgment continues:

h   '[40] These passages lead to the reflection that it is possible that every mental illness may, in time, be shown to be accompanied by and consequent upon some change to the physical structure of the body, so that mental illness can properly be described as a type of physical injury. That stage has not yet been reached, however, and this appeal must be approached on the
j   premise that mental illness and physical injury are distinguishable and that the claimant, as she accepts, suffered no physical injury.'

[154] Lord Phillips of Worth Matravers MR says, referring to the time when 'mental illness can properly be described as a type of physical injury', that 'that stage has not yet been reached'. This is in truth a statement about medical science. It is contentious and needs to be made good by qualified expert evidence.

Evidence to the contrary was successfully adduced in the American case of
Weaver v Delta Airlines Inc (1999) 56 Fed Supp 2d 1190. Before Lord Philip, in the
Outer House, where there were three actions before the court, the unsuccessful
argument was that the cases should proceed to proof so that the pursuers could
call just such evidence: see 1999 SLT 919 at 922, 925. The argument apparently
failed (at 926) for want of particularity in the pleading. The argument was not
pursued on the solitary appeal by King to the First Division of the Inner House,
where any reliance upon *Weaver's* case was disclaimed: see 2001 SLT 126 at 129 per
Lord Rodger. So far as United Kingdom judges are concerned there has long been
an appreciation that given mental functions correspond to and depend upon a given
physical state of the body. In the Outer House, Lord Philip gave citations going
back to the nineteenth century: 1999 SLT 919 at 925–926 and there are others which
he could have cited: for example, *McLoughlin v O'Brian* [1982] 2 All ER 298 at 301,
[1983] 1 AC 410 at 418 and *R v Ireland, R v Burstow* [1997] 4 All ER 225, [1998] AC
147. These citations and a simple perusal of such basic but authoritative textbooks
such as *The Shorter Oxford Textbook of Psychiatry* (4th edn, 2001), written by Professor
Gelder and two other professors of psychiatry at Oxford University, show that
there is respectable medical support for the view that, for example, a major
depressive disorder is the expression of physical changes in the brain and its
hormonal chemistry. Such physical changes are capable of amounting to an injury
and, if they do, they are on any ordinary usage of language bodily injuries. The
passenger needs to prove by qualified expert evidence that these changes have
occurred, that they were caused by the accident and that they have led to the
psychiatric condition which constitutes the damage complained of. If he discharges
this burden of proof he has satisfied the requirements of the article and the
explanation given of it in *Rosman's* case and *Weaver's* case. For the court to shut out
the passenger from his opportunity to prove his case is both wrong in law and
involves assuming the role of prejudging an expert issue which it is not for the court
to assume.

[155] I recognise that under the procedural rules which governed the proceedings
before him in the Outer House, Lord Philip may have been justified in refusing to
allow the cases before him to go to proof and it seems that the subsequent history
of the actions bears out that the parties apparently shared this view. As regards the
proceedings in *Morris's* case, the situation was less clear-cut and I will have to revert
to this point later in this opinion.

[156] But two mistakes in the reasoning of the courts below need to be
emphasised. The scientific developments have not changed the meaning of the
article. The meaning of the phrase 'bodily injury' has not changed. The criterion
or test remains the same. All that has changed is the ability of certain plaintiffs to
bring their cases within it. The historical argument of saying one must look to
some meaning existing in 1929 is, quite apart from the other objections to the
argument, simply misconceived. Air transport has been transformed since 1929,
mainly because of the invention of the jet engine and its use in civilian aircraft.
Land-based planes are no longer confined to a range of 500 miles or less nor civilian
aircraft to daytime flight and an operating height of three or four thousand feet. A
delegate to the Warsaw conference asked what he thought about jet engines,
helicopters or pressurised aircraft flying at 30,000 feet or more carrying hundreds of
passengers or the risk of hijacking would probably have merely looked bemused, as
he no doubt would have if asked about monamine neurotransmitters,
noradrenaline or changes in the size of the hippocampus. But this ignorance or lack

a   of imagination does not affect the meaning of the words which for better or worse they decided in 1929 to use in the text of the convention.

The use of language

[157] The third point leads on from the second. Lawyers are not expert scientists nor are they always familiar with the accurate use of medical language. b   This is no criticism of them unless they have had the assistance of expert evidence. For example, they cannot be expected to know the character of the DSM classification unless they have at one time or another been informed of it or have had the professional opportunity to inform themselves. But, on the other hand, it should be possible to detect the shortcomings of arguments which, citing c   from the works of Descartes (as did counsel for the carriers in these appeals), invoke primitive and patently unscientific dualist theories. Similarly it is not sound to use such expressions as 'mental injury', an expression which forms the cornerstone of the reasoning of the Court of Appeal. The adjective 'mental' means relating to the mind. The mind is a metaphysical concept associated with the self-consciousness of human beings. The word can be used in a descriptive d   but not a substantive sense. One can have a mental illness or disorder just as one can have a respiratory illness or disorder. But one cannot usefully refer to having a mental injury. Little more helpful is the expression 'psychic injury' (though it may have the meaning 'psychological injury' in the United States, where it seems to have its main currency). However, none of these expressions, nor the e   confusion of psychiatry with psychology, assist to answer the question what is a bodily injury. At the best they identify that class of complaints which represent normal responses to external experiences, fright, grief, anguish, feeling sad or unhappy, feeling depressed but not clinically, and so on. These emotional upsets are real and unpleasant but they are not bodily injuries. Indeed they will not cross the threshold into what are properly described as injuries at all. It is this class of f   unpleasant experiences which, without more, do not suffice to ground a recovery under art 17 and which, as I read them, the American authorities are seeking to exclude.

[158] The reasoning of the Court of Appeal discloses a striking combination of the various features to which I have referred, most fundamentally, the errors g   which arise from the use of a phrase which does not occur in the convention, 'mental injury', and which is devoid of actual meaning. This phrase is then used to create a false antithesis with a phrase which is used, 'bodily injury', bolstered by a supposed investigation of what delegates to the 1929 conference would have actually had in mind when they agreed to the convention and the proposition h   that the absence of travaux préparatoires to support a particular reading should be treated as if there were such travaux préparatoires. The conclusion then arrived at is that although a passenger may be able to adduce evidence to prove that she has suffered an injury which comes within the ordinary meaning of 'bodily injury', she must be precluded from doing so. The quotations which I j   have made from the judgment of Lord Phillips of Worth Matravers MR also illustrate a use of language which inevitably tends to confuse the reasoning. 'Mental injury' is used interchangeably with 'mental illness' and then 'mental illness' is contrasted with 'physical injury' and 'physical' is apparently being used as a substitute for 'bodily'. The picture is not made any clearer by the fact that in intervening passages the phrases 'damage to the mind' and 'mental disorders' are used.

[159] I therefore disagree with the reasoning and conclusion of the Court of Appeal. Whilst I agree with much of the language and reasoning of Lord Philip *a* and Lord Reed, I do not agree with them that the correct reading of the American cases is that they would exclude more than emotional upset.

The overseas authorities

[160] As stated in the judgments of the courts below, the relevant question *b* under art 17 has been discussed by jurists in civilian jurisdictions but without disclosing a consistent view independent of domestic law considerations. For present purposes I believe that the most useful assistance can be found in the reported decisions of courts. However, here as well there are difficulties since the decision may have been given on the basis of assumed facts, imprecisely defined, or without a clear statement in the report of the actual facts found. *c*

[161] The first cases to which your Lordships were referred were ones which arose from the hijacking in 1970 of a TWA flight from Frankfurt to New York. It gave rise to *Rosman's* case, already referred to, and to a case in the United States District Court, *Burnett v Trans World Airlines Inc* (1973) 12 Avi 18,405. It has been suggested that the fact that there do not seem to have been earlier cases under *d* this part of art 17 shows the artificiality of a construction which had never previously been thought to be arguable. The reports do not bear this out. The new factor appears to have been the occurrence of very unpleasant experiences without any actual impact but causing temporary distress and mental anguish. Until the first spate of terrorist hijackings occurred there was little scope for any such incident or claim. The metamorphosis of the carriage of passengers by air *e* into a mass market serving consumers from a wide range of backgrounds also led to novel situations giving rise to the possibility to argue that damage had been caused by an 'accident'.

[162] *Burnett's* case arrived at similar conclusions to those of the New York Court of Appeals in *Rosman's* case. Thus the claim for 'mental anguish' *not* caused *f* by any bodily injury was held to be irrecoverable (at 18,409): 'Therefore, plaintiffs may recover in this action for any such emotional anxiety that they can demonstrate resulted from a bodily injury suffered as a consequence of the hijacking'. The 'contact' argument was rejected—'that any bodily injury sustained must be the result of physical contact between the body and another object'—described as 'a sterile interpretation': 'Brief reflection allows one to pose *g* many instances in which a bodily injury may result without any physical contact whatsoever'. The decision therefore is fully consistent with *Rosman's* case though the discussion of the convention is different, drawing on various French materials.

[163] In *Rosman's* case, an argument based upon French domestic law was *h* specifically rejected:

'It does not follow from the fact that the treaty is written in French that in interpreting it we are forever chained to French law, either as it existed when the treaty was written or in its present state of development.' (See (1974) 34 NY 2d 385 at 394.) *j*

In the same vein they rejected the subjective approach to construction (at 395): 'Nor do we see any useful purpose to be served by [an investigation of French law] to search out the intent of the drafters of Warsaw.' The conclusions in *Rosman's* case can be summarised: (a) mere 'psychic' trauma, mental anguish and emotional distress are not 'bodily injury' and do not on their own give a basis of a recovery under art 17. But, (b) such trauma etc may provide the causal link between the accident and the 'bodily injury'. (c) If a 'bodily injury' is proved, all the consequences of that 'bodily injury' should be taken into account in assessing the passenger's damage, including any consequential mental suffering. This, if I may respectfully say so, is a coherent scheme which reflects the language of the article and is one with which I agree.

b [164] The penultimate paragraph of the judgment of Judge Rabin draws a distinction between the 'non-bodily or behavioral manifestations' of the psychic trauma of the accident and the 'palpable, objective bodily injuries' which may have been caused by that trauma. The former does not, without more, amount to a 'bodily injury' whereas the latter clearly does. I do not read the word 'palpable' (the use of which I have already commented upon in [142], above) as adding anything
c more than emphasis and a requirement for proof to the phrase 'objective bodily injuries'. However, the carriers relied before your Lordships in this connection upon some of the language which Judge Rabin had used earlier on (at 397):

d 'Rather, in seeking to apply the treaty's terms to the facts before us, we ask whether the treaty's use of the word "bodily", in its ordinary meaning, can fairly be said to include "mental". We deal with the term as used in an international agreement written almost 50 years ago, a term which even today would have little significance in the treaty as an adjective modifying "injury" except to import a distinction from "mental". In our view, therefore, the ordinary, natural meaning of "bodily injury" as used in
e article 17 connotes palpable, conspicuous, physical injury and excludes mental injury with no observable bodily, as distinguished from "behavioral", manifestations.'

This passage is expressly governed by the context of the facts of *Rosman's* case and the limited question which it raised. It is not evident what is the justification for
f the inclusion of the words 'palpable' and 'conspicuous' or what is gained by substituting 'physical' for 'bodily'. The passage is open to the same criticisms as those which I have made of the reasoning of the Court of Appeal in *Morris's* case. I do not accept that this passage of the judgment is meant to contradict what Judge Rabin says more cogently (at 399, 400) which I have quoted in [144], above.

[165] Next in time came a decision of the Israel Supreme Court, *Daddon v Air*
g *France* (1984) 1 S&B Av R VII/141. It arose out of the Entebbe hijacking of 1976. The passengers were eventually rescued. The passengers, after nearly six years' delay, sued the airline for 'damages in respect of the mental anguish caused to them and for the pain and suffering sustained by them due to what was involved' in the hijacking. The court held (in anticipation of *Sidhu's* case and *El Al Israel*
h *Airlines Ltd v Tsui Yuan Tseng* (1999) 525 US 155) that the Warsaw Convention (with the Guatemala Protocol) was exhaustive of the passengers' rights. The court concluded that, in view of the objects of the convention and its background, art 17 should be interpreted 'in the widest possible way so that it would be possible in pursuance thereof to award compensation also for pure mental
j anguish' ((1984) 1 S & B Av R VII/141 at 153). This interpretation stands alone internationally and is not one I would agree with. It deprives the words 'bodily injury' of their ordinary meaning and equates them with a legal category, personal injury.

[166] The leading decision of the Supreme Court of the United States, *Eastern Airlines Inc v Floyd* (1991) 499 US 530, arose from an incident during a flight to the Bahamas from Miami. Shortly after take-off, all three of the plane's engines

failed. It lost height and a crash landing into the sea seemed inevitable. However, at the last moment one of the engines restarted and the plane was able to land safely at Miami. No one was hurt but the passengers claimed 'damages solely for mental distress arising out of the incident'. The court held (at 533–534) that 'Article 17 does not allow recovery for purely mental injuries'. The decision of the case therefore poses no problems for any save those who would support the extreme *Daddon* view, as had the Eleventh Circuit Court of Appeals. The subject matter of the case naturally governed the language used in the judgment delivered by Marshall J (at 536–537)—'when a passenger has suffered only a mental or psychic injury'—'recovery for purely psychic injuries'. In a footnote (at 540) he seems to have equated these expressions with 'emotional distress' and 'grief'. No doubt because of the judgment below and the arguments presented to them, the judgment spends some time considering the French text and the jurist's commentaries before coming to the conclusion (at 542) that the French legal sources were ambiguous and did not help to resolve the relevant question. After a historical review, taking in subsequent conferences and conventions and *Daddon's* case, the court declined to agree with the Israel Supreme Court and rejected its wide interpretation of art 17. Reverting to the expression 'mental distress', they consider how recovery in respect of it has been treated in America and elsewhere and adds (at 552):

> 'We have no doubt that subjecting international carriers to *strict* liability for purely mental distress would be controversial for most signatory countries.'

[167] Marshall J concluded (at 552–553):

> '... an air carrier cannot be held liable under Article 17 when an accident has not caused a passenger to suffer death, physical injury or physical manifestation of injury ... we express no view as to whether passengers can recover for mental injuries that are accompanied by physical injuries. That issue is not presented here because [the passengers] do not allege physical injury or physical manifestation of injury.'

He also declined to decide the question whether the convention was exhaustive of the parties' rights and liabilities. Thus the Supreme Court strictly confined their decision to the facts of the case before them and the question whether to follow *Daddon's* case and reverse to that extent *Rosman's* case. They rejected *Daddon's* case and preferred *Rosman's* case although they chose to leave open some of the points *Rosman's* case had decided.

[168] *Jack v Trans World Airlines Inc* (1994) 854 F Supp 654, District Judge Caulfield. This case arose from an incident at John F Kennedy airport, New York, when a plane was taking off for a flight to San Francisco. The take-off had to be aborted and the plane caught fire. During the evacuation of the plane some passengers suffered minor injuries and many passengers claimed to have suffered 'emotional distress' as a result of the incident, which was undoubtedly traumatic. The carrier sought to strike out the claims for 'emotional distress', in respect of those who had not been injured at all, on the ground that the claims were barred by *Floyd's* case and, in respect of those who had been injured during the evacuation, on the ground that emotional distress damages are not allowed. The carrier also complained that the evidence relied upon by the passengers in connection with their emotional distress claims was self-contradictory and sham, a submission which the judge accepted (at 661). The judge did not accept the

a evidence of the psychiatrist relied upon by the passengers, describing it as speculative (at 663–664). The judge, however, went on to discuss the right to recover for emotional distress following on an injury. His conclusion was to adopt a similar analysis to that in *Rosman's* case: see [163], above. Damages for emotional distress are not recoverable as such but may be recovered if consequent upon a bodily injury. The judge, notwithstanding his views about

b the passengers' evidence, declined to strike out the claims by passengers who were alleging 'physical manifestations' of their emotional distress or had suffered impact injuries (at 668). This case therefore provides an example of the application of the decisions in *Floyd's* case and *Rosman's* case but no more. The judge (at 664) sought to define his terms; his definitions do not assist as they raise as many questions as they purport to answer.

c [169] *Georgeopoulos v American Airlines Inc (No 2)* [1998] NSWSC 463, Supreme Court of Appeal, New South Wales. This case first came before the Court of Appeal on agreed findings which included 'that the [passenger] claims damages for nervous shock or mental suffering and no other basis': *Georgeopoulos v American Airlines Inc* (26 September 1996, unreported). The carriage was agreed

d to be governed by the Warsaw Convention. The appeal therefore raised the bare question whether the Australian courts should follow *Daddon's* case or *Floyd's* case. The court preferred *Floyd's* case. They held the question of liability could not be decided without further findings of fact; absent such findings it was impossible to decide whether the passenger suffered 'bodily injury' within the meaning of the article. To quote the headnote:

e
 '"Nervous shock" as a condition or a cause of a condition for which a defendant may be liable in negligence describes a non-impact injury which may or may not give rise to a body tissue alteration. Assuming shock occurs, the question is whether that shock caused injury and the nature of that

f injury. These evidentiary findings are essential to any conclusion whether the injury complained of was a "bodily injury" for the purposes of article 17.'

This decision is therefore in line with the view I have expressed. The case was remitted.

[170] Before *Georgeopoulos's* case returned to the Court of Appeal for the

g second time, the case of *Kotsambasis v Singapore Airlines Ltd* (1997) 42 NSWLR 110 had come before it. The plaintiff in this case had been a passenger on a flight from Athens to Sydney. Shortly after take-off one of the engines caught fire and, after dumping fuel, the plane returned safely to Athens. The trial judge accepted that the plaintiff had been severely frightened and anxious during the incident. Her onward flight was diverted via Paris and she strained her back carrying her heavy

h luggage. Meagher JA said (at 115):

 'I am of the opinion that the term "bodily injury" was not intended to, and on a proper interpretation of the Convention does not, include purely psychological injury. I note that the decision in *Eastern Airlines Inc v Floyd*

j specifically left open the possibility that recovery might be available where psychological injury was accompanied by physical injury.'

On the judge's findings she had not suffered any injury which had anything to do with the fright and anxiety of which she complained nor was it in the course of any embarkation or disembarkation. Powell JA agreed. Stein JA, also agreeing, followed the first *Georgeopoulos* case and expressly preferred *Floyd's* case to

Daddon's case. He said that *Floyd's* case 'held that there could be no recovery for "psychic" injury unaccompanied by physical injury' and continued (at 121):

> 'However where mental anguish follows and is caused by physical injury, recovery for both injuries is covered. I would agree with this latter statement. Moreover, if the psychological injury is proven to be a species of bodily injury, then it would constitute "bodily injury" within the article.'

He later summarised his view as being that bodily injury in art 17 was not intended to include '*purely* psychological injury' (at 122; Stein JA's emphasis).

[171] On the return of *Georgeopoulos's* case for the second time to the Court of Appeal ([1998] NSWSC 463), the court included Sheller JA, who had given the leading judgment on the first appeal, and Meagher JA, who had presided on *Kotsambasis's* case. The additional facts found by the magistrate were not helpful to the passengers. He found that all they had suffered was a 'mild post-traumatic stress disorder' which had not resulted from 'any physical or bodily injury' to either passenger nor 'any structural alteration to body tissues or alteration in the function of an organ or neurochemical change or any other form of damage to tissues or organs'. Sheller JA, again delivering the agreed leading judgment, expressly adopted and approved what Stein JA had said ((1997) 42 NSWLR 110 at 121) and accordingly dismissed the passengers' appeals.

[172] The importance of these Australian cases is that they follow the lead given by the United States cases; they reject the proposition that there can be a recovery for emotional distress as such; they accept that an accident can cause a 'psychological' (sic, clearly meaning 'psychiatric') injury which may be proved to be a 'bodily injury'; they do not criticise the criteria 'structural alteration in bodily tissues', 'alteration in the function of an organ or neurochemical change' and 'any other form of damage to tissues or organs'; they see no inconsistency between this and what was said in *Floyd's* case.

[173] It is not necessary to refer to *Tseng's* case, United States Supreme Court, the case of the over-intrusive security search, as it was deliberately argued as a case which fell outside of art 17. There probably had been no accident. It was doubtful whether the material events occurred within the period covered by art 17. The plaintiff's evidence was that she was 'emotionally traumatised and disturbed', 'really sick and very upset' and that is all (at 587). The decision in *Floyd's* case was not questioned. The plaintiff's argument was that she should be allowed to bring a tort claim. The question for the decision of the Supreme Court was that left open in *Saks's* case and *Floyd's* case.

> 'Her case presents a question of the Convention's exclusivity: When the Convention allows no recovery for the episode-in-suit, does it correspondingly preclude the passenger from maintaining an action for damages under another source of law, in this case, New York tort law?' (See (1999) 525 US 155 at 160 per Ginsberg J.)

The Supreme Court, following, among other authorities, *Sidhu's* case, held that the convention was exhaustive. It adds nothing presently material to *Rosman's* case and *Floyd's* case.

[174] Of the later United States cases, only a few need be referred to since most are merely examples of the application of *Floyd's* case to facts which were not materially different from those on which *Floyd's* case was based. Where those facts have included some injury, the injury had no causative or other relevance to the emotional distress (e g *Alvarez v American Airlines* (1999) 27 Avi 17,214 and

a   (2000) 27 Avi 17,475).   In two cases *Terrafranca v Virgin Atlantic Airways Ltd* (1998) 151 F Supp 3d 108, Third Circuit Court of Appeals, and *Carey v United Airlines* (2001) 28 Avi 15,408, Ninth Circuit Court of Appeals, the passenger sought to satisfy the criteria in *Floyd*'s case by saying that the accident had caused emotional distress and the emotional distress had caused physical symptoms like, in *Terrafranca*'s case, loss of weight and, in *Carey*'s case, sleeplessness, nausea, perspiration etc.   These consequences it was argued amounted to 'physical

b   manifestations' for the purpose of art 17 so as to bring what would otherwise be mere emotional stress within the terms of that article.   It will be appreciated at once that I myself would not accept that argument.   What the passenger has to prove is a 'bodily injury', not something less but with physical manifestations. The argument was based upon the language used in *Floyd*'s case: but the phrase

c   used there is 'physical injury or physical manifestation of injury' ((1991) 499 US 530 at 552–553).   If it is simply emotional stress which is causing the person to lose weight, no injury, bodily or otherwise, is proved.   For the argument to succeed the plaintiff must prove either that the manifestation proves that there is or has been an underlying 'bodily injury' or that the manifestation itself is a 'bodily

d   injury'.   As *Rosman*'s case shows, provided that causation by the accident can also be proved, in the former instance the plaintiff can recover damages for the underlying bodily injury and its consequences and in the latter for the bodily injury but not what preceded it.   What I have said corresponds to the reasoning of the Court of Appeals in *Terrafranca*'s case: see (1998) 151 F 3d 108 at 110–111 where *Rosman*'s case is cited.   In *Carey*'s case (2001) 28 Avi 15,408 at 15,414 Circuit

e   Judge Nelson followed *Terrafranca*'s case, saying:

'The Third Circuit concluded … that there was no support for the argument that the plaintiff's physical manifestations of her emotional injury satisfied the "bodily injury" requirement.   Because the plaintiff could not "demonstrate direct, concrete, bodily injury as opposed to mere

f   manifestation of fear or anxiety", the court held that she did not satisfy the conditions for liability under Article 17 and thus could not recover for her emotional distress.   For reasons similar to those articulated by the Third Circuit in *Terrafranca*, we hold that physical manifestations of emotional and mental distress do not satisfy the "bodily injury" requirement in Article 17.'

g   *Carey*'s case came after *Weaver*'s case and the Court of Appeals referred to it in footnote 47 to its opinion without expressing either approval or disapproval.   The value of *Terrafranca*'s case and *Carey*'s case is that they implicitly approve *Rosman*'s case and confirm the primacy of the simple 'bodily injury' criterion, not any gloss or paraphrase of it.

h   [175]   There have been two cases where the passenger claimants took upon themselves and discharged the burden of proof contemplated by *Rosman*'s case and the Australian cases.   The first is *Weaver v Delta Airlines Inc* (1999) 56 F Supp 2d 1190, Chief Judge Shanstrom.   The plaintiff was a passenger on a flight from London to Billings.   Mechanical problems necessitated an emergency landing at

j   Dayton, Ohio.   She claimed that during the landing she had been terrified and had subsequently had to be medically treated for emotional and physical problems attributable to her flight experiences with a diagnosis of post-traumatic stress disorder.   The carrier sought to strike out her claim, relying on *Floyd*'s case.   The judge refused the application.   The plaintiff filed affidavits providing uncontradicted expert evidence that 'extreme stress causes actual physical brain damage, i e, physical destruction or atrophy of portions of the hippocampus of the brain'. 'The impact upon [the plaintiff] of the events which occurred on that flight was extreme and included biochemical reactions which had physical *a* impacts upon her brain and neurological system'. She had thus presented evidence of 'physical injury' and was entitled to say that 'her diagnosed post-traumatic stress disorder arose from the physical changes in her brain brought on during the extreme stress of the emergency landing' (see 1191). The judge therefore distinguished her case from 'Floyd and its progeny': she was *b* relying upon 'an injury to her brain, and the only reasonable conclusion is that it is, in fact, a bodily injury' (see 1192). It is hard to see any basis for disagreeing with the conclusion that, if the passenger can prove that his or her brain was damaged as a result of the accident, the passenger has suffered a 'bodily injury'.

[176] On 1 June 1999 a plane crashed on the runway at Little Rock, Arkansas. One of the passengers, Mrs Lloyd, was wounded in the crash, suffering multiple *c* though not, in themselves, life-threatening injuries. She was trapped for a while in the burning plane and claimed that she also had suffered debilitating emotional and psychological injuries which led to chronic post-traumatic stress disorder and major depression. The judge found that a sufficient causal connection had been established between her physical injuries and her 'mental injuries' (sic) (*Re Air* *d* *Crash at Little Rock, Arkansas on 1 June 1999* (2000) 27 Avi 18,428 at 18,433). This sufficed for her to succeed in full on her claim. However, he went on to consider briefly what would have been the case if that causal connection had not been established: could she prove that her post-traumatic stress disorder was a physical manifestation of injury? He followed *Weaver's* case, considered the expert evidence and found sufficient cause to find that her chronic post-traumatic stress *e* disorder caused biological, physical changes in brain function (see 18,435). Evidence is necessary to underpin the finding that post-traumatic stress disorder is 'a biological as well as an emotional and psychological illness' (see 18,436).

[177] District Judge Knapp reached similar conclusions in *Turturro v* *Continental Airlines* (2001) 27 Avi 18,414. In a careful review of the earlier *f* decisions, he concluded (at 18,419) that the Supreme Court's line drawing in *Floyd's* case had worked well. He also referred (at 18,420) to *Weaver's* case and the *Little Rock* case as cases where plaintiffs had successfully tendered evidence that extreme stress such as that experienced in near-death situations or being taken hostage may actually change brain cell structure and cause a specific area of the brain to atrophy. He recognised that it will not be in every case of *g* post-traumatic stress disorder that such biological abnormalities will have been caused and it will be necessary to prove by objective evidence that in the given case brain damage has ensued. He therefore endorsed the course which the United States cases were following. He decided the case before him in favour of the carrier because the plaintiff had neither pleaded nor shown she could prove a *h* case of 'bodily injury'.

[178] To summarise, there is clear support in the overseas authorities for the view I have expressed. I believe that these authorities show an international acceptability for giving a natural meaning to the words 'bodily injury' without imposing any artificial or restrictive gloss upon them. This is the direction in *j* which the jurisdiction which has to deal with the greatest volume of air passenger litigation, the United States, has moved. It is supported by the decisions of the courts of New South Wales. If your Lordships adopt the same view as I have of the effect of art 17, you will be promoting international uniformity rather than creating a risk that the law of the United Kingdom will be at odds with that elsewhere. The decision in *Weaver's* case was, given the evidence there before

a   the court, wholly unexceptionable. It is in line with the United States law and the natural meaning of the words 'bodily injury'. I accept that the judgment of the Court of Appeal in *Morris*'s case is inconsistent with it. I prefer the reasoning in *Weaver*'s case.

The arguments

b   [179] What I have already said has covered most of the points raised in the argument of the appeals before us. The extreme arguments in favour of the passengers cannot be accepted (nos (7) and (8)). There is insufficient reason for reading the words of the first sentence of art 17 as embracing everything which might be described as 'personal injury' as opposed to damage to property or mere financial loss. The actual language of art 17 must be given effect to. *Floyd*'s case
c   is to be preferred to *Daddon*'s case. I disagree with the majority of the First Division on this point.

[180] Similarly, the various forms of the causation argument relied on by the carriers are likewise not acceptable (nos (1), (2) and (3)). Argument no (6) which was also relied upon by the carriers conforms most closely to what I consider to
d   be the correct understanding of the use of the words 'bodily injury' but because it represents a paraphrase of them can give rise to error and the adoption of argument no (4).

[181] An argument advanced by the carriers in support of their submissions was that if the Court of Appeal view was not accepted, there would be a flood of claims of non-specific injury which it would be expensive for carriers and their
e   insurers to investigate and would be difficult for them to rebut. This argument would have some force if the *Daddon* approach was to be adopted and mere emotional stress and upset were to be recoverable. But the argument has no force if the passenger has to prove by the appropriate expert evidence some actual bodily injury in the sense which I have identified and is illustrated by *Weaver*'s
f   case. The passenger will have to be able to make a specific claim of injury consequent upon the accident and support it by convincing expert evidence. Any forensic difficulties for the carriers should be no greater than with, say, an alleged painful spinal injury.

[182] But there is a further version of the carriers' argument to which I should refer: it accepts that the criterion 'bodily injury' provides a threshold which the
g   passenger must cross (by the adducing the necessary evidence) but then argues that, even though the passenger has crossed the threshold, he is to be precluded from recovering for any 'mental injury'. This argument seeks to use as an excluding criterion an unscientific expression ('mental injury') which lacks definition and fails to provide the requisite certainty. An injury to the brain (or, indeed, some other
h   part of the body) may cause a mental disorder, say some form of dementia or amnesia. Suppose that the injury to the brain is accompanied by a fractured skull or merely was the result of some concussion or a minor stress-induced stroke. In a proportion of such cases the sole external evidence of the injury may be the mental disorder. The reasoning that seeks to exclude such a consequence from the scope
j   of art 17 encounters problems and it is these which the argument fails adequately to address. What is the distinction between the fractured skull case and the concussion or minor stroke case unless it is to be some causal distinction (the causation argument) which is rightly rejected as unsound? On the other hand, if all mental disorder cases are to be excluded, contrary to the United States cases, what is the distinction between a brain injury which causes paralysis of a limb and one which causes amnesia? The reality is that the use of the term 'mental injury'

serves no useful defining purpose and is inconsistent with the United States cases. It has to be analysed down into some form of the causation argument or it has to become a restriction on the damages that can be recovered even though the threshold has been crossed. Given an injury to the brain which was caused by the accident and which in its turn causes a mental disorder, the only way in which compensation for the mental disorder can be excluded is by introducing an arbitrary limit upon the consequences of the physical injury—the brain injury—which can be taken into account. If of course there has been no injury to the brain, there will have been on these hypotheses no 'bodily injury' and therefore no right to claim. The 'bodily injury' criterion as I have defined it provides a criterion whereas 'mental injury' does not.

King's case

[183] On this appeal to the Inner House, the majority adopted the *Daddon* view with which I have said I disagree. The pursuer specifically disclaimed any reliance upon the *Weaver* decision and, by necessary implication, declined to make any allegation of having suffered a bodily injury involving his brain. Therefore I agree that the appeal to the Inner House should have failed and the order of the Lord Ordinary allowed to stand.

Morris's case

[184] The Court of Appeal applied the wrong test and their reading of art 17 cannot stand. However, where that leaves the plaintiff's case is another matter. She had adequately pleaded a prima facie case of 'bodily injury' in relation to the psychiatric element in her case. But she had also pleaded and accepted that the assault did not cause her any physical injury. On the view adopted by the Court of Appeal, she was bound to fail. According to the law reports, the court was not referred to *Weaver's* case even though that case had been referred to in *King's* case to which they had been referred. In any event, it is clear that no argument can have been advanced based upon a physical brain injury. In these circumstances, would it be right to leave Miss Morris without any possibility of recovery? The appeal to this House was brought in order to try to obtain the adoption of the *Daddon* interpretation of the article and that was the manner in which her appeal was argued. Her printed case submitted that she should not be left without a remedy for her depressive disorder 'merely because she is unable to identify any ... physiological damage to her head'. Therefore I do not consider that it would be appropriate to remit her case to the county court when she has implicitly stated that she will not be able to prove any 'bodily injury'. I accordingly agree that her appeal should be dismissed.

Miss Morris's appeal dismissed. Bristow's appeal allowed.

Kate O'Hanlon   Barrister.

R (on the application of Quintavalle) v Secretary of State for Health

[2002] EWCA Civ 29

COURT OF APPEAL, CIVIL DIVISION
LORD PHILLIPS OF WORTH MATRAVERS MR, THORPE AND BUXTON LJJ
16, 18 JANUARY 2002

Medical treatment – Human reproduction – Embryo – Cell nuclear replacement – Cell nuclear replacement not involving fertilisation – Statute defining embryo as 'live human embryo where fertilisation is complete' – Whether embryo created by cell nuclear replacement falling within statutory definition – Human Fertilisation and Embryology Act 1990, s 1(1).

The Human Fertilisation and Embryology Act 1990 regulated the creation and use of human embryos outside the body. When it was enacted, the only known way of producing an embryo was by fertilisation. That was reflected in s 1(1)[a] of the 1990 Act which defined 'embryo' as 'a live human embryo where fertilisation is complete'. Since the introduction of the Act, however, scientists had developed a method of creating an embryo that did not involve fertilisation, but instead involved introducing a nucleus, taken from an adult human, into an unfertilised egg. That method, which had the potential for producing a clone, was known as cell nuclear replacement (CNR). The government believed that creating an embryo by CNR was a process covered by the 1990 Act, and that, while it would be abhorrent to use it to produce a clone, it was desirable that the process be licensed for the purpose of certain types of research which were not permitted by provisions scheduled to the Act. Regulations under the Act, expanding the areas of research involving the use of embryos that could be licensed, were therefore placed before Parliament in January 2001 and approved. Subsequently, the claimant organisation, which was opposed both to human cloning and to the use of human embryos for research, brought proceedings for judicial review, contending that the Act applied only to embryos created by fertilisation and that accordingly embryos created by CNR fell outside its scope. That contention was accepted by the judge whose decision meant that no licence was required for the creation or use of embryos created by CNR. In response, Parliament passed the Human Reproductive Cloning Act 2001 which made it unlawful to place in a woman a human embryo that had been created other than by fertilisation. The government had not sought to impose any other restriction on the creation of embryos by CNR or on their use. Instead, the Secretary of State appealed against the judge's decision with the object of demonstrating that the creation of embryos by CNR was subject to the regulatory regime imposed by the 1990 Act. The issue arose whether, as the Secretary of State contended, it was permissible and appropriate to imply the words 'if it is produced by fertilisation' into the definition of 'embryo' in s 1(1) so that it embraced an embryo produced by CNR.

Held – An organism created by CNR fell within the definition of 'embryo' in s 1(1) of the 1990 Act which was to be construed as if it read 'a live human embryo

---

a   Section 1, so far as material, is set out at [14], below

where [*if it is produced by fertilisation*] fertilisation is complete'. That construction
was permissible provided that it was plainly necessary to give effect to the
Parliamentary intention. In considering that question, the court had to
ask whether embryos created by CNR fell within the genus covered by the
legislation and whether the legislation's clear purpose would be defeated if the
extension were not made. An embryo created by CNR was of the same genus as
an embryo created by fertilisation. They were essentially identical as far as
structure was concerned and each was capable of developing into a full grown
example of the relevant species. Moreover, it was necessary to bring embryos
created by CNR within the regulatory regime created by the 1990 Act in order to
give effect to the intention of Parliament, the legislative policy being that it was
essential to bring the creation and use of embryos under strict regulatory control
for ethical reasons. The prospect of a regulatory regime which excluded embryos
created by CNR was both startling and alarming, and those considerations
provided the most cogent reason to reach an interpretation of the Act which
embraced embryos produced by CNR, subject to any countervailing
considerations, or incoherence. No such considerations existed and there was
very little that weighed against the construction for which the Secretary of State
contended. Accordingly, the appeal would be allowed (see [27], [34], [37], [38],
[42], [43], [49], [52]–[54], [56], [57], [60]–[62], below).

Dictum of Lord Wilberforce in *Royal College of Nursing of the UK v Dept of Health
and Social Security* [1981] 1 All ER 545 at 564–565 applied.

Decision of Crane J [2001] 4 All ER 1013 reversed.

Notes
For the meaning of 'embryo', see 30 *Halsbury's Laws* (4th edn reissue) para 59 n1.

For the Human Fertilisation and Embryology Act 1990, s 1, see 28 *Halsbury's
Statutes* (4th edn) (2001 reissue) 290.

Cases referred to in judgments
A-G v Edison Telephone Co of London (Ltd) (1880) 6 QBD 244.
Fitzpatrick v Sterling Housing Association Ltd [1999] 4 All ER 705, [2001] 1 AC 27,
[1999] 3 WLR 113, HL.
Royal College of Nursing of the UK v Dept of Health and Social Security [1981] 1 All ER
545, [1981] AC 800, [1981] 2 WLR 279, QBD, CA and HL.

Cases also cited or referred to in skeleton arguments
Birmingham City Council v Oakley [2001] 1 All ER 385, [2001] 1 AC 617, HL.
Litster v Forth Dry Dock and Engineering Co Ltd [1989] 1 All ER 1134, [1990] 1 AC
546, HL.
R v A [2001] UKHL 25, [2001] 3 All ER 1, [2001] 2 WLR 1546.

Appeal
The defendant, the Secretary of State for Health, appealed with permission of
Crane J from his decision on 15 November 2001 ([2001] EWHC Admin 918,
[2001] 4 All ER 1013) allowing an application for judical review by the claimant,
the ProLife Alliance (acting through its director, Bruno Quintavalle), by way of a
declaration that human embryos created by the cell nuclear replacement technique
were not embryos within the meaning of s 1(1) of the Human Fertilisation and
Embryology Act 1990, and were therefore not subject to regulation under that
Act. The facts are set out in the judgment of Lord Phillips of Worth Matravers MR.

a Kenneth Parker QC and James Eadie (instructed by the Solicitor to the Department of Health) for the Secretary of State.

David Anderson QC and Martin Chamberlain (instructed by Brown Cooper) for the ProLife Alliance.

Cur adv vult

b 18 January 2002. The following judgments were delivered.

LORD PHILLIPS OF WORTH MATRAVERS MR.

Introduction

c [1] The first stage of reproduction of a human being involves the creation of an embryo. An embryo is a live organism containing a full set of 46 chromosomes that has the potential to develop into a foetus and subsequently into a person. In 1990 the only way in which an embryo had ever been created was by the fertilisation of the female egg by the male sperm. Such fertilisation takes place d naturally as a result of sexual union between man and woman. Scientists have, however, developed other methods of fertilising a female egg with a male sperm so as to produce an embryo and can, in particular, achieve this outside the body (in vitro).

[2] In 1984 a committee of inquiry, chaired by Dame Mary Warnock, published a *Report of the Committee of Inquiry into Human Fertilisation and Embryology* (Cmnd e 9314) (the Warnock report) which dealt, in particular, with the ethical problems raised by scientific intervention in these processes. The report made a large number of recommendations which included, in particular, that the creation of embryos outside the body, and the use of these, should be regulated by a statutory licensing authority. The government published a White Paper that f proposed the implementation of the Warnock recommendations and, in accordance with this, introduced the Human Fertilisation and Embryology Act 1990.

[3] The 1990 Act contains a definition of an embryo, and a number of provisions, which reflect the fact that it was drafted at a time when the only known way of producing an embryo was by fertilisation.

[4] The Warnock report had identified the fact that it might prove possible to g substitute the nucleus of a fertilised egg with the nucleus taken from an adult human, thereby producing an embryo that would develop into a carbon copy clone of that human. Because this would involve making use of an embryo that had been created by fertilisation, such a process would unquestionably be covered by the licensing requirement imposed by the 1990 Act. There has been h included within the 1990 Act a clause which specifically prohibits the licensing of the creation of an embryo in this way.

[5] Since the introduction of the 1990 Act, scientists have developed a method of creating an embryo that does not involve fertilisation. It bears a close resemblance to the nucleus substitution that the Warnock report had identified j as a possibility and has the same potential for producing a clone. The difference is that it involves introducing a nucleus taken from an adult human into an egg that has not been fertilised. This method of creating an embryo is known as cell nuclear replacement or CNR. I have described the organism produced by CNR as an embryo because it is now common ground that the nature of that organism so resembles that of an embryo produced by fertilisation that it is appropriate to describe it by the same term. Certainly, it is generally so described by scientists.

[6] The government, and the scientists advising the government, believed that
creating an embryo by CNR was a process which was covered by the 1990 Act.
They also believed that, while it would be abhorrent to use this process to
produce a clone, it was desirable that the process be licensed for the purpose of
certain types of research which were not permitted by provisions scheduled to the
1990 Act. These provisions were, however, susceptible to alteration by regulations.
Accordingly regulations under the 1990 Act were placed before Parliament in
January 2001 which expanded the areas of research involving the use of embryos
that could be licensed. These regulations were approved by affirmative resolution
of each House.

[7] These developments were viewed with dismay by the ProLife Alliance,
which is opposed both to human cloning and to using human embryos for the
purpose of research. They brought proceedings for judicial review, contending
that the 1990 Act only applied to embryos created by fertilisation, so that embryos
created by CNR were not subject to the provisions of that Act. This contention
succeeded before Crane J, sitting in the Administrative Court. His decision, handed
down on 15 November 2001 ([2001] EWHC Admin 918, [2001] 4 All ER 1013),
meant that the licensing authority had no jurisdiction to license the creation of
embryos by CNR. But more fundamentally, his decision meant that no licence
was required for the creation or use of embryos created by CNR.

[8] On the face of it, the motivation of the ProLife Alliance was not easy to
follow. They had caused the baby to be expelled with the bath water. They had
established that CNR embryos could be created and used for any purpose
without regulation or restriction. As I understand the position, however, the
ProLife Alliance had assumed that, if their application for judicial review
succeeded, the government would be forced to introduce legislation to deal with
the practice of creating embryos by CNR. There would be a full Parliamentary
debate on the topic which might well result in the prohibition of the process.

[9] In the event, the government's reaction to Crane J's judgment was to
introduce a single clause bill making it unlawful to place in a woman a human
embryo which had been created otherwise than by fertilisation. This became the
Human Reproductive Cloning Act 2001. Apart from this, the government has not
sought to impose any restriction on the creation of embryos by CNR or the use
that can be made of these. The Secretary of State has, however, appealed against
Crane J's judgment with the object of demonstrating that creation of embryos by
CNR is, after all, subject to the regulatory regime imposed by the 1990 Act. The
ProLife Alliance has sought to uphold Crane J's judgment. Whether the 1990 Act
applies to embryos created by CNR is the principal issue raised by this appeal.

[10] There is a subsidiary issue raised by ProLife Alliance as an alternative
case. I have referred to the fact that a clause of the 1990 Act prohibits the licensing
of nucleus substitution within a fertilised embryo. The ProLife Alliance contends
that, if the 1990 Act applies to embryos created by CNR in an unfertilised egg, the
clause in question falls to be construed so as to extend this prohibition to the
licensing of the creation of embryos by CNR. Crane J indicated that he would not
have accepted this submission and it is challenged by the Secretary of State.

The relevant science

[11] It is not possible to understand the relevant statutory provisions without
a more detailed description of the science to which they relate than the simplified
account that I have given. Crane J included in his judgment an admirable
synthesis of the expert evidence presented to him which I shall gratefully adopt:

'[13] In the ovary the egg is a diploid germ (or reproductive) cell. It is described as "diploid" because its nucleus contains a full set of 46 chromosomes. By the process of meiotic division the nucleus divides into two parts. Only one of these, a pronucleus containing only 23 chromosomes (described as "haploid"), plays any further part in the process. Fertilisation begins when the male germ cell, the sperm, whose pronucleus contains 23 chromosomes, meets the haploid female germ cell and is a continuous process taking up to 24 hours. As part of the process the male and female pronuclei fuse to form one nucleus with a full complement of 46 chromosomes, a process known as syngamy. The one-cell structure that exists following syngamy is the zygote. After several hours the cell divides to create a two-cell zygote. At this stage it is generally referred to as an embryo. At about 15 days after fertilisation a heaping-up of cells occurs which is described as the "primitive streak".

[14] Fertilisation may of course take place in the normal way or in vitro.

[15] CNR is a process by which the nucleus, which is diploid, from one cell is transplanted into an unfertilised egg, from which ... the nucleus has been removed. The nucleus is derived from either an embryonic or a foetal or an adult cell. The cell is then treated to encourage it to grow and divide, forming first a two-cell structure and then developing in a similar way to an ordinary embryo.

[16] CNR is a form of cloning. Clones are organisms that are genetically identical to each other. When CNR is used, if the embryo develops into a live individual, that individual is genetically identical to the nucleus transplanted into the egg. There are other methods of cloning, for example, embryo splitting, which may occur naturally or be encouraged. Identical twins are the result of embryo splitting.

[17] The famous Dolly the sheep was produced by CNR. Live young have since been produced by CNR in some other mammals. It has not yet been attempted in humans.

[18] ... CNR of the kind under consideration does not involve fertilisation.'

[12] The possible implications for human health of CNR are dramatic. I quote from a report of the Human Genetics Advisory Commission and the Human Fertilisation and Embryology Authority (the authority) in December 1998 (*Cloning Issues in Reproduction, Science and Medicine*):

'5.3 The most likely objective of a research project involving the use of CNR would be to create a cultured cell line for the purposes of cell or tissue therapy. People who have tissues or organs damaged by injury or disease (e.g. skin, heart muscle, nervous tissue) could provide their own somatic nuclei and, by using these to replace nuclei in their own or donated eggs, individual stem cells (not embryos) could be produced in culture. These cells could then be induced (by exposure to appropriate growth factors) to form whichever type of cell or tissue was required for therapeutic purposes with no risk of tissue rejection and no need for treatment of the patient with immunosuppressive drugs.'

The 1990 Act

[13] The purposes of the 1990 Act set out in the long title include the following:

'... to make provision in connection with human embryos and any
subsequent development of such embryos; to prohibit certain practices in
connection with embryos and gametes; to establish a Human Fertilisation
and Embryology Authority.'

[14] The relevant provisions of the 1990 Act are the following:

'1. *Meaning of "embryo", "gamete" and associated expressions.*—(1) In this
Act, except where otherwise stated—(a) embryo means a live human
embryo where fertilisation is complete, and (b) references to an embryo
include an egg in the process of fertilisation and, for this purpose, fertilisation
is not complete until the appearance of a two cell zygote.

(2) This Act, so far as it governs bringing about the creation of an embryo,
applies only to bringing about the creation of an embryo outside the human
body ...

3. *Prohibitions in connection with embryos.*—(1) No person shall—(a) bring
about the creation of an embryo, or (b) keep or use an embryo, except in
pursuance of a licence.

(2) No person shall place in a woman—(a) a live embryo other than a
human embryo, or (b) any live gametes other than human gametes.

(3) A licence cannot authorise—(a) keeping or using an embryo after the
appearance of the primitive streak, (b) placing an embryo in any animal,
(c) keeping or using an embryo in any circumstances in which regulations
prohibit its keeping or use, or (d) replacing a nucleus of a cell of an embryo
with a nucleus taken from a cell of any person, embryo or subsequent
development of an embryo.

(4) For the purposes of subsection (3)(a) above, the primitive streak is to
be taken to have appeared in an embryo not later than the end of the period
of 14 days beginning with the day when the gametes are mixed, not counting
any time during which the embryo is stored ...

5. *The Human Fertilisation and Embryology Authority.*—(1) There shall be a
body corporate called the Human Fertilisation and Embryology Authority.'

[15] The functions of the authority include the grant of licences in accordance
with the provisions of Sch 2 to the 1990 Act.

[16] Section 41 of the 1990 Act lays down the maximum penalties for
contravention of that Act. The most serious offences carry a potential sentence
of ten years imprisonment.

[17] Schedule 2 to the 1990 Act lays down the various activities for which a
licence may be granted and some for which a licence cannot be given.

[18] Schedule 3 to the 1990 Act makes the following provisions in relation to
the consents that must be obtained to in vitro fertilisation and the subsequent use
of the embryo so produced:

'6.—(1) A person's gametes must not be used to bring about the creation
of any embryo *in vitro* unless there is an effective consent by that person to
any embryo the creation of which may be brought about with the use of
those gametes being used for one or more of the purposes mentioned in
paragraph 2(1) above.

(2) An embryo the creation of which was brought about *in vitro* must not
be received by any person unless there is an effective consent by each person
whose gametes were used to bring about the creation of the embryo to the

a   use for one or more of the purposes mentioned in paragraph 2(1) above of
the embryo.

(3) An embryo the creation of which was brought about *in vitro* must not
be used for any purpose unless there is an effective consent by each person
whose gametes were used to bring about the creation of the embryo to the
use for that purpose of the embryo and the embryo is used in accordance
b   with those consents.'

The need to strain the language

[19] The definition of an embryo in s 1(1) of the 1990 Act is manifestly designed
to identify the stage at which the process of fertilisation produces, or should be
c   deemed to produce, a live human embryo. References to fertilisation can have
no application to an embryo produced by CNR. Arguably, the term 'two cell
zygote' is not appropriate to describe the embryo produced at the stage at which
the single cell organism produced by CNR divides into two cells.

[20] On behalf of the Secretary of State, Mr Parker QC has submitted that it is
d   permissible and appropriate to imply words into the definition of an embryo in
s 1(1) in order to embrace an embryo produced by CNR. This he would achieve
by implying a phrase into the subsection, so that it defines embryo as 'a live
human embryo where [*if it is produced by fertilisation*] fertilisation is complete'.
Mr Parker accepts that this construction involves 'straining' the natural meaning
of the words of the subsection, but submits that a purposive approach to
e   construction requires such an approach.

Crane J's decision

[21] I am about to turn to the arguments advanced by Mr Parker in support of
his construction. They are arguments which did not persuade the judge ([2001] 4
All ER 1013) to adopt that construction. The judge's conclusions were as follows:
f

'[59] The defendant argues for a purposive interpretation of s 1. The
argument is a powerful one. The Warnock committee was appointed to
examine the social, ethical and legal implications of recent, and potential
developments in the field of human assisted reproduction. Its report was, in
the light of knowledge at the time, comprehensive. Had the discoveries of
g   1997 been known, they would have been considered. Similarly the White
Paper and the Act itself was clearly intended to provide comprehensive
control, either by prohibition or licensing, of human reproduction. The
parties differ about whether CNR would have fallen under the licensing
provisions or under the prohibition in s 3(3)(d), but it is inconceivable that
h   Parliament would have ignored CNR.

[60] The claimant nevertheless argues that the words of s 1(1) cannot be
stretched to cover organisms produced by CNR, involving no fertilisation.
Its argument is in my view supported by the way in which the provisions of
s 3(3)(d) and Sch 3 are worded. I place less weight on the fact that ss 1(1)(b)
j   and 3(4) would not apply and that the authority would be left to make
decisions in areas not explicitly covered by the Act.

[61] I decline any invitation to attempt to rewrite any of the sections of
the 1990 Act to make them apply by analogy to organisms produced by CNR.

[62] I accept the defendant's argument that the reason for inserting in
s 1(1)(a) the words "where fertilisation is complete" and the following words
in s 1(1)(b) was to define the moment at which the Act's protection applied

to the organism. Nevertheless the words are there. The question is whether to insert the additional words is permissible: "a live human embryo where [if it is produced by fertilisation] fertilisation is complete".   With some reluctance, since it would leave organisms produced by CNR outside the statutory and licensing framework, I have come to the conclusion that to insert these words would involve an impermissible rewriting and extension of the definition.'

[22] In challenging Crane J's conclusions, Mr Parker advanced his submissions under four heads: (1) unforeseen scientific developments can carry with them the necessity to strain statutory language; (2) the purpose of the legislation is of prime importance; (3) no countervailing considerations conflict with a purposive construction; (4) incoherence of other parts of the 1990 Act is no bar to a purposive construction of s 1(1).

The need to cater for unforeseen developments

[23] By way of example of the interpretation of a statute in the light of a subsequent scientific development, Mr Parker placed before us the case of *A-G v Edison Telephone Co of London (Ltd)* (1880) 6 QBD 244. The Telegraph Act 1869 gave the Postmaster General a monopoly of transmitting telegrams. Telegrams were defined as messages transmitted by telegraph. A telegraph was defined to include 'any apparatus for transmitting messages or other communications by means of electric signals'. When the 1869 Act was introduced the only such means of communication functioned by interrupting and re-establishing electric current, thereby causing a series of clicks which conveyed information by morse code. Then Bell and Edison invented the telephone which conveyed the human voice by wire by means of an entirely novel process. It was argued that because this process was unknown when the 1869 Act was passed, the Act could not apply to it. The court rejected this submission, observing (at 254):

'Of course no one supposes that the legislature intended to refer specifically to telephones many years before they were invented, but it is highly probable that they would, and it seems to us clear that they actually did, use language embracing future discoveries as to the use of electricity for the purpose of conveying intelligence. The great object of the Act of 1863 [the Telegraph Act 1863] was to give special powers to telegraph companies to enable them to open streets, lay down wires, take land, suspend wires over highways, connect wires, erect posts on the roofs of houses, and do many other things of the same sort. The Act, in short, was intended to confer powers and to impose duties upon companies established for the purpose of communicating information by the action of electricity upon wires, and absurd consequences would follow if the nature and extent of those powers and duties were made dependent upon the means employed for the purpose of giving the information.'

[24] This is an early example of a purposive approach to statutory interpretation. But the decision did not involve straining the natural meaning of the language of the statute.

[25] It is not simply in the field of science that developments subsequent to the introduction of a statute can raise problems as to its interpretation. In *Fitzpatrick v Sterling Housing Association Ltd* [1999] 4 All ER 705, [2001] 1 AC 27 the issue was whether a homosexual partner of a tenant enjoyed rights conferred under the

a   Rent Act 1977 on 'a member of ... the tenant's family'. The majority of the Judicial
    Committee held that he did. Since 1977 changing social attitudes had brought a
    same sex partner within the intention that Parliament had had when using the
    word 'family'.

    [26] In the course of their speeches, three members of the Committee referred,
    with approval, to the following statement of principle made by Lord Wilberforce
b   in a dissenting speech in *Royal College of Nursing of the UK v Dept of Health and Social
    Security* [1981] 1 All ER 545 at 564–565, [1981] AC 800 at 822:

        'In interpreting an Act of Parliament it is proper, and indeed necessary, to
        have regard to the state of affairs existing, and known by Parliament to be
        existing, at the time. It is a fair presumption that Parliament's policy or
c   intention is directed to that state of affairs. Leaving aside cases of omission
        by inadvertence, this being not such a case, when a new state of affairs, or a
        fresh set of facts bearing on policy, comes into existence, the courts have to
        consider whether they fall within the parliamentary intention. They may be
        held to do so if they fall within the same genus of facts as those to which the
        expressed policy has been formulated. They may also be held to do so if
d   there can be detected a clear purpose in the legislation which can only be
        fulfilled if the extension is made. How liberally these principles may be
        applied must depend on the nature of the enactment, and the strictness or
        otherwise of the words in which it has been expressed. The courts should be
        less willing to extend expressed meanings if it is clear that the Act in question
e   was designed to be restrictive or circumscribed in its operation rather than
        liberal or permissive. They will be much less willing to do so where the
        subject matter is different in kind or dimension from that for which the
        legislation was passed. In any event there is one course which the courts
        cannot take, under the law of this country: they cannot fill gaps; they cannot
f   by asking the question "What would Parliament have done in this current
        case, not being one in contemplation, if the facts had been before it?",
        attempt themselves to supply the answer, if the answer is not to be found in
        the terms of the Act itself.'

    [27] The guidance to be found in Lord Wilberforce's speech is highly relevant
    in the present context. One important consideration is plainly, as he said, the
g   strictness of the words of the relevant enactment. Does the implicit addition for
    which Mr Parker contends strain the language of s 1(1) to breaking point so that,
    however cogent the other relevant factors, the construction for which he
    contends is simply not viable? In my judgment it does not. In the context of the
    Human Rights Act 1998 the boundaries of purposive interpretation have been
h   extended where needs must. I consider that the construction for which Mr Parker
    contends is viable provided that this is plainly necessary to give effect to
    Parliamentary intention. When considering that question the court has to ask,
    not what would Parliament have enacted if it had foreseen the creation of
    embryos by CNR, but, do such embryos plainly fall within the genus covered by
j   the legislation and will the clear purpose of the legislation be defeated if the
    extension is not made?

    The genus
    [28] The legislation is very largely about the treatment of embryos. The embryos
    expressly contemplated by the legislation are embryos created by fertilisation.
    To what extent do embryos created by CNR fall into the same genus? This

depends in part on the policy of the legislation, which I have yet to consider. If the manner of the creation of the embryo is a significant factor in giving rise to the need for regulation, then the genus is significantly different. If it is not, then the relevant comparison is between the embryo created by fertilisation and the embryo created by CNR.

[29] The judge held that the express reference to fertilisation in s 1 of the 1990 Act was in order to define the moment at which the Act's protection applied to the organism. I agree. The fact that the organism was created by fertilisation was not a factor of particular relevance to the desirability of regulation.

[30] How then does the embryo created by CNR compare with the embryo created by fertilisation? Mr Parker submits that they are essentially identical— 'morphologically indistinguishable' and 'functionally indistinguishable'. These phrases, he submits, are supported by the expert evidence. By way of example he quotes from Professor Templeton:

> '... the one cell structure [created by CNR] can appropriately be described as a zygote. It is a single cell with full complement of chromosomes with potential to develop by division (ultimately to create a living being such as in the sheep, Dolly). Similarly, the two cell structure (each cell with a full complement of chromosomes) which exists once division or cleavage occurs can correctly be described as a two cell zygote or embryo, and I believe that most professionals in the field would regard that description as correct and appropriate.'

[31] Mr Anderson QC, on behalf of ProLife Alliance, has sought to persuade us that an embryo created by CNR is very different from an embryo created by fertilisation. There are some differences in the periphery of an egg that has been fertilised and the periphery of an egg that has had its nucleus replaced, but these are not functionally significant.

[32] It has to date proved more difficult to get an embryo created by CNR to develop into a live mammal than to achieve this from an embryo created by in vitro fertilisation. Mr Parker submits that this factor reflects the fact that scientists, through experience, have acquired greater expertise in the latter process and that this factor will change. This explanation is supported by the experts and seems reasonable.

[33] Some CNR embryos have grown to large sizes in mammals, but this does not demonstrate any morphological or functional difference.

[34] Mr Anderson has not persuaded me that any or all of these matters indicate that the embryo created by CNR is of a different genus from the embryo created by fertilisation. The two are essentially identical as far as structure is concerned, and each is capable of developing into a full grown example of the relevant species. So far as the human embryo is concerned, it is this capacity to develop into a human being that is the significant factor and it is one that is shared by both types of embryo.

[35] There is one difference between an embryo produced by CNR and one produced by fertilisation. The former, if it is permitted to develop, will grow into a clone of the donor of the implanted nucleus. This factor is one that Mr Anderson has emphasised when making submissions on legislative policy, the topic to which I now turn.

The policy of the legislation

a [36] The 1990 Act brings the creation and use of embryos within a regulatory regime which very severely restricts the right to indulge in those activities. The reasons for legislating to impose those restrictions are not in doubt. They are essentially ethical. I quote from the 1987 White Paper *Human Fertilisation and Embryology: A Framework for Legislation* (Cm 259) which set out the policy
b underlying the legislation. Dealing with the remit of the statutory licensing authority, this stated:

'13. The Government accepts the basic principle underlying the Warnock Report recommendations—namely the need "to regulate and monitor practice in relation to those sensitive areas which raise fundamental ethical
c questions". This is taken to go beyond just those medical or professional ethical questions relating to the safety or efficacy of certain clinical practices, to wider ethical issues such as are raised by the artificial creation of life outside the body or use of donated gametes.'

[37] The White Paper recognised that some practices, such as the creation of
d hybrids, were unacceptable and had to be forbidden. Whether the creation and use of embryos for research should be permitted at all was controversial and a matter that would be left to Parliament. If research was to be permitted, it would need to be strictly regulated. In the event Parliament opted for regulated research. Broadly speaking it can be said that the legislative policy was that it was essential to bring the creation and use of embryos under strict regulatory control
e for ethical reasons.

[38] To the question of whether it is necessary to bring embryos created by CNR within the regulatory regime created by the 1990 Act in order to give effect to the intention of Parliament, there can only be one answer. It is essential. There is no factor that takes embryos created by CNR outside the need, recognised by
f Parliament, to control the creation and use of human organisms. The consequence of Crane J's judgment is that anyone is free to create embryos by CNR and to experiment with these without limitation of time or any other restriction. There is no bar to placing a human embryo created in this way inside an animal. There is no bar to placing an animal embryo created in this way inside a woman. Until the government intervened with the 2001 Act, it was legal to use the process of CNR to
g produce and use an embryo to create a human clone. It is clear that these results are wholly at odds with the intention of Parliament when introducing the 1990 Act.

[39] Mr Anderson has challenged this conclusion. His reasoning is as follows. Under the heading 'Prohibited Research' the White Paper dealt with a number of concerns. In particular, it stated:

h
'38. Similar concerns arise from fears that it will one day be possible to produce artificially two or more genetically identical individuals by nucleus substitution (sometimes known as cloning). The Warnock Report (paragraph 12.11 and 12.14) described techniques by which such results might theoretically be achieved, although there is no knowledge of such work
j being carried out artificially with human embryos. The Bill will make such practices a criminal offence.'

[40] Effect was given to this statement by s 3(3)(d) of the 1990 Act. This prohibited the substitution of the nucleus of an embryo because this was the only cloning process that was envisaged as a possibility. It demonstrated, however, a policy of placing an absolute prohibition on the creation of an embryo that could

result in a clone. To apply the 1990 Act to embryos produced by CNR would
not result in the prohibition of creating or carrying out research on such   *a*
embryos. It followed that it would not accord with the legislative policy to bring
embryos produced by CNR within the ambit of the 1990 Act.

[41] I believe that this reasoning is at fault. The issue is whether it would
accord with the policy of Parliament at the time that the 1990 Act was passed to
bring embryos created by CNR within the regulatory framework rather than to   *b*
leave them unregulated. I will accept, for purposes of argument, that it was the
intention of Parliament to prohibit the creation of an embryo that might develop
into a clone, but the reason for this was, as the White Paper indicates, to prevent
the production artificially of two or more genetically identical individuals. This
policy would be put in jeopardy if the creation and use of embryos by CNR were
unregulated. It would be furthered by making the production of embryos by   *c*
CNR subject to the regulatory regime under the 1990 Act, for it is inconceivable
that the licensing authority would permit such an embryo to be used for the
purpose of reproduction.

[42] For the reasons that I have given, I consider that a regulatory regime that
excludes from its ambit embryos created by CNR is contrary to the intention of   *d*
Parliament in introducing the 1990 Act. The prospect of such a regime is both
startling and alarming. These considerations provide the most cogent reason to
reach an interpretation of the 1990 Act which embraces embryos produced by
CNR, subject to consideration of any countervailing considerations, or incoherence.

Countervailing considerations   *e*

[43] Mr Parker submitted that there were no countervailing considerations to
the construction for which he contended. Mr Anderson was not able to point to
any, other than the suggestion that if embryos produced by CNR were not
covered by the 1990 Act, this was likely to lead to a detailed debate in Parliament
and elsewhere, which might lead to the banning of the creation of such embryos   *f*
altogether. It does not seem to me that this is a matter which can validly be
invoked as a countervailing consideration to the construction for which Mr Parker
contends. On the contrary, it merely underlines how serious are the consequences
of the construction reached by the judge.

Incoherence   *g*

[44] There are some provisions of the 1990 Act which cannot be applied to an
embryo produced by CNR. This is not surprising, as such an embryo was not
within the contemplation of those who drafted that Act. If, however, the
provisions of the Act cannot sensibly be made to work in relation to an embryo
created by CNR, this must be a powerful reason for concluding that that Act does   *h*
not apply at all to such embryos.

[45] The first point that arises in this context is that there is a degree of
uncertainty as to whether an embryo created by CNR comes into existence at the
single cell stage, or only when that cell divides, so as to resemble a two-cell
zygote. Section 1(1)(b) resolves this problem in relation to an embryo created by   *j*
fertilisation. It seems to me that, so far as an embryo produced by CNR is
concerned, this problem is purely theoretical. I cannot conceive of any circumstance
in which it would have any practical significance to the working of the 1990 Act.

[46] It is then rightly said that s 3(4) cannot operate in respect of an embryo
created by CNR, for such an embryo is not created by the mixing of gametes.
Once again it does not seem to me that this is a point of significance. A stage will

a be reached in relation to an embryo created by CNR when the primitive streak appears, and s 3(3)(a) is thus effective. Further, it will always be open to the authority to stipulate a shorter period beyond which an embryo created by CNR cannot be kept or used.

[47] The point made by Mr Anderson in relation to s 3(3)(d) can also be invoked as an example of incoherence. I have already dealt with that point.

b [48] Finally, the point is made that no provision requires the person from whom the nucleus that is used for CNR is taken to consent to the process for which it is used. This contrasts with the provisions for consent in relation to those providing gametes for the creation of an embryo by fertilisation, which are set out in Sch 3. This is an anomaly, but it is one that can be cured by a requirement imposed by the authority. In any event, it provides little support for an argument

c that embryos produced by CNR should be excluded from the entirety of the regulatory regime under the 1990 Act.

[49] My conclusion is that there are most compelling reasons for giving s 1 of the 1990 Act the strained construction for which Mr Parker contends, and very little that weighs against this. I would reverse the decision reached by the judge

d and hold that an organism created by cell nuclear replacement falls within the definition of 'embryo' in s 1(1) of that Act.

The second issue

[50] My conclusion makes it necessary to consider the alternative case advanced by Mr Anderson. This case is pleaded in their grounds of cross-appeal

e as follows:

'(1) Section 3(3)(d) provides that a licence cannot authorise "replacing a nucleus of a cell of an embryo with a nucleus taken from a cell of any person, embryo or subsequent development of an embryo". (2) On its face, this

f provision does not prohibit cloning of the type described in the Donaldson report (*Stem Cell Research: Medical Progress with Responsibility* (2000)) because that type of cloning does not involve "replacing the nucleus of a cell of an embryo"; rather, it involves replacing the nucleus of an oocyte with adult genetic material. (3) Section 1(1) provides that "references to an embryo include an egg in the process of *fertilisation*", not an egg or oocyte in the

g process of CNR. But, if the Secretary of State is correct that fertilisation is unimportant, it must follow that it is possible to substitute for "fertilisation" any other similar process (such as CNR) by which the "embryo" comes into being. (4) The consequence is that, just as an egg in the process of fertilisation is an "embryo", so is an egg in the process of CNR. (5) Therefore, a licence

h cannot authorise the replacing of the nucleus of an egg or oocyte with adult genetic material.'

[51] It seems to me that several of the links in this chain of logic are unconnected. Looking at the third proposition, I do not see how one can compare an egg which the sperm has already started to fertilise with an egg which

j is about to receive, but has not yet received, a nucleus under the process of CNR. Nor do I see how the fourth proposition is said to follow from the third. Assuming that the 1990 Act applies to the process of creating an embryo by CNR, I can see no basis for arguing that an unfertilised egg, prior to the insertion of the nucleus under the CNR process, is required to be treated under that Act as if it is an embryo. I agree with the judge that ProLife Alliance's alternative case is unsound.

[52] For these reasons I would allow the appeal and dismiss the cross-appeal.   *a*

THORPE LJ.

[53] I agree.

BUXTON LJ.

[54] I also agree. Lord Phillips of Worth Matravers MR has set out the guidance   *b*
that was given by Lord Wilberforce in *Royal College of Nursing of the UK v Dept of
Health and Social Security* [1981] 1 All ER 545, [1981] AC 800, guidance that was
relied upon in this appeal by ProLife Alliance. It seems to me, with respect, that
this guidance is of direct help and relevance to the task before us. Lord
Wilberforce was specifically addressing a case such as ours where an Act of   *c*
Parliament is passed having regard to the state of affairs existing at the time, and
then a new state of affairs or a fresh set of facts bearing upon the policy informing
that Act comes into existence. It is for the court to consider whether the new facts
fall within the Parliamentary intention.

[55] If we apply to our case, and to the present Act (the Human Fertilisation   *d*
and Embryology Act 1990), the tests and guidance set out by Lord Wilberforce,
it seems to me that the solution is clear. First, we are to ask ourselves whether
there can be detected a clear purpose in the legislation which can only be fulfilled
if what Lord Wilberforce describes as the 'extension' (that is to say the application
of the words of the Act and use of the facts) is made.

[56] It is self-evident in this case, both from the background to this Act, which   *e*
has been set out by Lord Phillips MR, and more particularly from its long title,
that the purpose of the legislation was to protect and to make provision in respect
of embryos, they being seen as a form of life particularly deserving of protection
and control; and to bring dealings with such forms of life within the control of the
newly set up Human Fertilisation and Embryology Authority. That purpose   *f*
should extend, and there is no reason why it should not extend, to embryos
created by CNR as well as to embryos created by what I would call orthodox
fertilisation.

[57] Secondly, we are to ask ourselves whether CNR falls within the same
genus of facts as to those in the context of which the statutory policy has been
formulated. For the reason given by Lord Phillips MR, it is in my view also clear   *g*
that CNR do indeed fall within the same genus of facts as those to which the
legislation was originally directed.

[58] Bearing in mind this guidance, and the circumstances I have indicated, I
am bound to say that I think the Secretary of State may have, to a limited extent,
undervalued the force of his case when he accepted that the approach that he   *h*
advocated involved a strained construction of the terms, in particular of s 1, of the
1990 Act. The 1990 Act was passed at a time when the only class of embryos that
was known to exist were embryos produced by fertilisation; so that Act
concentrated on them. The draftsman used a form of words in s 1(1) that might
be read as putting the particular rules formulated in respect of fertilised embryos   *j*
into the definition of the overall reach of the section. But to regard those parts of
s 1(1) as definition is not only inconsistent with the principles set out by Lord
Wilberforce, but also, in my judgment, inconsistent with the long title of the 1990
Act. That view is supported by the conclusion of the judge, agreed by Lord
Phillips MR in [29], above that the express references to fertilisation in s 1 of the
Act are there included for the purpose, and I would say only for the purpose, of

a defining the moment at which the Act's protection extends to an embryo created by fertilisation.

[59] I see force in Mr Anderson QC's argument that if Parliament had known about CNR in 1990, it would probably simply have banned the process altogether, so none of the present statutory rules would apply because there would be no subject matter for them to bite upon. But to regard that as a guide
b to the construction of the statute as actually passed is to infringe against the latter part of the guidance given to us by Lord Wilberforce. We are not to ask, what would Parliament have done or said in this current case if the new facts had been before it? Rather, we are to interpret the words which Parliament did in fact use in the context of the new facts that have now come to light.

[60] I also agree that some parts of this Act cannot be applied in their narrow
c terms to CNR. An example is the prohibition to be found in s 3(3)(d); and other examples that Lord Phillips MR has mentioned. That objection, it seems to me, is not met by the argument advanced by the Secretary of State, however forceful that argument was as a matter of policy or of practicality, that a case such as that of s 3(3)(d) would in fact be met by use of the powers of the Human Fertilisation
d and Embryology Authority. It is clear from the structure of the Act that Parliament intended certain questions to be taken entirely outside the judgment of that authority. But the fact that there are certain parts of this Act which cannot easily be applied to the case of CNR does not mean that the Act is incoherent to the extent that the whole of the rest of the scheme that it lays down has to be withheld from embryos produced by CNR: with the startling and alarming
e overall consequences that Lord Phillips MR has pointed out.

[61] For those reasons, in addition to those given by Lord Phillips MR with which I agree, I am constrained to find that in his extremely helpful and clear judgment, which has been of particular assistance to this court in understanding the medical and scientific background, the judge in fact erred.

[62] I therefore agree that this appeal should be allowed.

Appeal allowed. Permission to appeal refused.

Kate O'Hanlon   Barrister.

Practice Direction

a

FAMILY DIVISION

Probate – Practice – Non-contentious probate – Grant of representation – Probate records – Required information – Revision.

b

The information appearing on grants of representation and in probate records as required by *Practice Direction* [1999] 1 All ER 384, [1998] 1 WLR 1699 dated 3 November 1998 shall be revised, as from 15 April 2002, as follows: (i) in relation to addresses (referred to in sub-para (b) of the practice direction), the postcode, if known, shall be stated; (ii) in relation to excepted estates (referred to in sub-para (f) of the practice direction), the net value of the estate shall be stated, rounded up to the next whole thousand, and expressed as 'not exceeding £ ...'

c

DAME ELIZABETH BUTLER-SLOSS
President

22 March 2002

a # Cave v Robinson Jarvis & Rolf (a firm)
[2002] UKHL 18

HOUSE OF LORDS

b LORD SLYNN OF HADLEY, LORD MACKAY OF CLASHFERN, LORD HOBHOUSE OF WOODBOROUGH, LORD MILLETT AND LORD SCOTT OF FOSCOTE

28 FEBRUARY, 25 APRIL 2002

c *Limitation of action – Concealment of right of action – Breach of duty – Defendant solicitors raising limitation defence in action for negligence – Claimant relying on statutory provision postponing limitation period where defendant had concealed from claimant any fact relevant to his right of action – Statute providing that deliberate commission of breach of duty amounting to concealment if claimant unlikely to discover it for some time – Whether defendant committing deliberate breach of duty for limitation purposes if unaware of breach – Limitation Act 1980, s 32(2).*

d The claimant instructed the defendant firm of solicitors to act for him in connection with a transaction under which a company was to grant him mooring rights over its land for 100 years. The solicitors drafted, or approved the drafting of, the document by which the rights were to be granted, and the transaction was e completed in March 1989. The company later went into receivership, and in February 1994 the receivers informed the claimant that his mooring rights were no longer exercisable. In January 1998 the claimant commenced proceedings for negligence against the solicitors, claiming that the document drafted or approved by them had granted him merely contractual rights instead of rights that would f be enforceable both against the company and its successors in title, and that the solicitors had failed to protect the rights by entry in the Land Registry. The solicitors pleaded, inter alia, that the action was time-barred. In his reply, the claimant relied on s 32[a] of the Limitation Act 1980. Section 32(1)(b) provided that, where any fact relevant to the plaintiff's right of action had been deliberately concealed from him by the defendant, the period of limitation did not begin to g run until the plaintiff had discovered the concealment or could with reasonable diligence have discovered it. Section 32(2) provided that, for the purposes of sub-s (1), 'deliberate commission of a breach of duty' in circumstances in which it was unlikely to be discovered for some time amounted to deliberate concealment of the facts involved in that breach of duty. The claimant pleaded, inter alia, that, h for the purposes of s 32(2), the negligent drafting of the agreement by the solicitors, though not done in the knowledge that it constituted a breach of duty, had been an intentional act done in circumstances in which the breach was unlikely to be discovered for some time. On the determination of a preliminary issue, the judge accepted the claimant's contention that s 32(2) applied and that j accordingly the six-year limitation period had not begun to run until February 1994 at the earliest. That decision was affirmed by the Court of Appeal. On the solicitors' appeal to the House of Lords, the issue was whether s 32(2) applied even where the defendant had not been aware that he had been committing a breach of duty. In contending that that was indeed the effect of s 32(2), the

_____

a   Section 32, so far as material, is set out at [8], [9], below

claimant argued that a conclusion to the contrary would mean that sub-s (2) added nothing to sub-s (1)(b).

Held – On its true construction, s 32(2) of the 1980 Act did not apply where the defendant had been unaware that he had been committing a breach of duty. Section 32 deprived a defendant of a limitation defence in two situations: first, where he took active steps to conceal his own breach of duty after he had become aware of it; and secondly, where he was guilty of deliberate wrongdoing, and, he concealed or failed to disclose it in circumstances where it was unlikely to be discovered for some time. It did not, however, deprive a defendant of a limitation defence where he was charged with negligence if, being unaware of his error or his failure to take proper care, there had been nothing for him to disclose. Section 32(2) itself distinguished between the breach of duty and the facts involved in the breach of duty. Moreover, where a defendant was charged with negligence, his breach of duty consisted of his failure to take reasonable care. Such a breach was unlikely to be deliberate and the defendant was unlikely to be aware of it. If, afterwards, he discovered the error and deliberately concealed it from the claimant, his conduct might come within s 32(1)(b); but while he remained ignorant of the error and of his own inadvertent breach of duty, there was nothing for him to disclose. Such conduct could not be brought within s 32(2). The correct construction did not not render that provision otiose. Section 32(2) provided an alternative, and in some cases what might well be an easier, means of establishing the facts necessary to bring the case within s 32(1)(b). There was, however, no reason at all why Parliament, in prescribing the circumstances in which the person injured by the act or omission could escape from a limitation defence, should not have distinguished between the case where the defendant knew he was committing a breach of duty and the case where he did not. The clear words of s 32(2)—'deliberate commission of a breach of duty'—showed that Parliament had made that distinction. Accordingly, the appeal would be allowed (see [1]–[3], [24]–[26], [30], [58], [60]–[62], [67], [68], below).

Brocklesby v Armitage & Guest (a firm) [2001] 1 All ER 172 disapproved.

Liverpool Roman Catholic Archdiocese Trustees Inc v Goldberg [2001] 1 All ER 182 overruled.

Notes

For the postponement of the limitation period by deliberate concealment, see 8(2) *Halsbury's Laws* (4th edn reissue) paras 1125–1127.

For the Limitation Act 1980, s 32, see 24 *Halsbury's Statutes* (4th edn) (1998 reissue) 733.

Cases referred to in opinions

A'Court v Cross (1825) 3 Bing 329, 130 ER 540.

Archer v Moss, Applegate v Moss [1971] 1 All ER 747, [1971] 1 QB 406, [1971] 2 WLR 541, CA.

Beaman v ARTS Ltd [1949] 1 All ER 465, [1949] 1 KB 550, CA.

Brocklesby v Armitage & Guest (a firm) [2001] 1 All ER 172, [2002] 1 WLR 598n, CA.

Bulli Coal Mining Co v Osborne [1899] AC 351, [1895–99] All ER Rep 506, PC.

Donovan v Gwentoys Ltd [1990] 1 All ER 1018, [1990] 1 WLR 472, HL.

Farrell v Alexander [1976] 2 All ER 721, [1977] AC 59, [1976] 3 WLR 145, HL.

King v Victor Parsons & Co (a firm) [1973] 1 All ER 206, [1973] 1 WLR 29, CA.

a   *Kitchen v Royal Air Forces Association* [1958] 2 All ER 241, [1958] 1 WLR 563, CA.
Liverpool Roman Catholic Archdiocese Trustees Inc v Goldberg [2001] 1 All ER 182.
Sheldon v R H M Outhwaite (Underwriting Agencies) Ltd [1995] 2 All ER 558, [1996]
      AC 102, [1995] 2 WLR 570, HL.

Appeal

b The defendant firm of solicitors, Robinson Jarvis & Rolf, appealed with
permission of the Appeal Committee of the House of Lords given on 24 May 2001
from the order of the Court of Appeal (Potter, Sedley and Jonathan Parker LJJ) on
20 February 2001 ([2001] EWCA Civ 245, [2002] 1 WLR 581) dismissing the
solicitors' appeal from the order of Newman J sitting in Winchester on 17
February 2000 whereby, on the determination of a preliminary issue, he declared
c that, by virtue of s 32(2) of the Limitation Act 1980, the period of limitation
commenced from February 1994 in respect of the action for negligence brought
against the solicitors by the claimant, Martin William Cave. The facts are set out
in the opinion of Lord Scott of Foscote.

d   *Nicholas Davidson QC* and *David Drake* (instructed by *Beachcroft Wansbroughs*,
      Bristol) for the solicitors.
      Brian Doctor QC and *Patrick Lawrence* (instructed by *Roach Pittis*, Newport, Isle of
      Wight) for Mr Cave.

Their Lordships took time for consideration.
e

25 April 2002. The following opinions were delivered.

LORD SLYNN OF HADLEY.

   [1] My Lords, I have had the advantage of reading in draft the opinion of my
f noble and learned friend Lord Scott of Foscote. I agree with him for the reasons
he gives that the appeal should be allowed.

LORD MACKAY OF CLASHFERN.

   [2] My Lords, I have had the advantage of reading in draft the speeches
prepared by my noble and learned friends Lord Millett and Lord Scott of Foscote.
g I agree that this appeal should be allowed for the reasons which they have given.

LORD HOBHOUSE OF WOODBOROUGH.

   [3] My Lords, I agree that this appeal should be allowed for the reasons to be
given by my noble and learned friends Lord Millett and Lord Scott of Foscote
h whose opinion I have read in draft.

LORD MILLETT.

   [4] My Lords, I have had the advantage of reading in draft the speech of my
noble and learned friend Lord Scott of Foscote. I gratefully adopt his narrative of
j the facts and the procedural history of these proceedings.
   [5] The limitation of actions is entirely statutory. The first statute was the
Limitation Act 1623. For almost four centuries, therefore, it has been the policy
of the legislature that legal proceedings should be brought, if at all, within a
prescribed period from the accrual of the cause of action. The statutes of
limitation have been described as 'statutes of peace'. They are regarded as
beneficial enactments and are construed liberally.

[6] The underlying policy to which they give effect is that a defendant should
be spared the injustice of having to face a stale claim, that is to say one with which   *a*
he never expected to have to deal (see *Donovan v Gwentoys Ltd* [1990] 1 All ER
1018 at 1024, [1990] 1 WLR 472 at 479 per Lord Griffiths). As Best CJ observed
nearly 200 years ago, long dormant claims have often more of cruelty than of
justice in them (see *A'Court v Cross* (1825) 3 Bing 329 at 332–333, 130 ER 540 at
541). With the passage of time cases become more difficult to try and the   *b*
evidence which might have enabled the defendant to rebut the claim may no
longer be available. It is in the public interest that a person with a good cause of
action should pursue it within a reasonable period.

[7] But this assumes that the plaintiff knows or ought to know that he has a
cause of action. In common justice a plaintiff ought not to find that his action is
statute-barred before he has had a reasonable opportunity to bring it. To this end   *c*
the Limitation Acts contain provisions which extend, suspend or postpone the
commencement of the limitation period in prescribed circumstances. The
particular provision with which your Lordships are concerned is contained in
s 32(2) of the Limitation Act 1980.

[8] Section 32(1)(b) postpones the commencement of the limitation period   *d*
where 'any fact relevant to the plaintiff's right of action has been deliberately
concealed from him by the defendant'. In such a case the period of limitation
does not begin to run until the plaintiff discovers the concealment or could with
reasonable diligence discover it. The rationale for this provision is plain: if the
defendant is not sued earlier, he has only himself to blame.

[9] Section 32(2) provides: *e*

'For the purposes of subsection (1) above, deliberate commission of a
breach of duty in circumstances in which it is unlikely to be discovered for
some time amounts to deliberate concealment of the facts involved in that
breach of duty.'   *f*

The rationale for this is less clear, but becomes apparent from the case law on
earlier statutes.

[10] In *Brocklesby v Armitage & Guest (a firm)* [2001] 1 All ER 172, [2002] 1 WLR
598n the plaintiff claimed that the defendants, who were a firm of solicitors, had
negligently failed to procure his release from his mortgage obligations. The   *g*
defendants were not accused of any impropriety or deliberate wrongdoing or of
having deliberately concealed anything from the plaintiff. They denied that the
plaintiff was their client or that they owed him any duty of care, and denied that
they had been negligent in any event. They also pleaded that the action was
statute-barred. In his reply the plaintiff sought to rely on s 32(2), but he did not   *h*
and could not allege that the defendants were aware of the fact that they had been
negligent.

[11] Despite the absence of any allegation of deliberate wrongdoing, a
two-man Court of Appeal held that the plaintiff had sufficiently pleaded a
'deliberate commission of a breach of duty' within the meaning of s 32(2). In the   *j*
course of an ex tempore judgment Morritt LJ held that ignorance of the law is no
defence, and that it is sufficient to bring the case within the subsection that the
defendant should have known that he was acting (or presumably failing to act); it
was not necessary that he should also have known that his act (or failure to act)
gave rise to a breach of duty. It was sufficient that 'the commission of the act was
deliberate in the sense of being intentional and that that act or omission, as the

case may be, did involve a breach of duty whether or not the actor appreciated that legal consequence' (see [2001] 1 All ER 172 at 181, [2002] 1 WLR 598n at 605).

[12] On this footing a person who sets out conscientiously to perform his duty but does so in a way which is subsequently found to have been negligent, thus constituting a breach of his duty of care, is liable to be sued without limit of time even where he denies that his conduct was negligent.

b   [13] *Brocklesby's* case was followed in *Liverpool Roman Catholic Archdiocese Trustees Inc v Goldberg* [2001] 1 All ER 182, where the plaintiff alleged that the defendant had given it negligent tax advice. The defendant denied that his advice had been wrong, let alone negligently wrong. Following the decision in *Brocklesby's* case, Laddie J held that it was sufficient to bring the case within s 32(2) that the defendant had intentionally given the advice in question and that (if c   negligent) it amounted to a breach of duty; it was not necessary that he should have appreciated that his advice was wrong or that he had been negligent. Even if all the facts are known to a plaintiff, the judge held, the intentional commission of a breach of duty in circumstances where the breach is unlikely to be discovered for some time results in a legal fiction, namely that the facts are unknown.

d   [14] In the present case counsel for Mr Cave has found himself unable to support this reasoning. He points out that the legal fiction, if any, is not that the facts are unknown to the plaintiff, but that they have been deliberately concealed from him by the defendant. In such circumstances, however, the start of the limitation period is postponed only until the plaintiff discovers the concealment or could with reasonable diligence have discovered it. If the relevant facts are e   already known to him, counsel concedes, treating them as deliberately concealed from him is of no effect. The start of the limitation period is not postponed even momentarily, for the facts which are deemed to be concealed from the plaintiff are at once discovered.

[15] For my own part, I do not accept that all the facts were known to the f   plaintiff in *Goldberg's* case, for it did not know that the advice was wrong. But neither did the defendant. Nor will that fact be known to either party until the case is tried on the merits. The effect of *Brocklesby's* case is to deprive a professional man, charged with having given negligent advice and who denies that his advice was wrong let alone negligent, of any effective limitation defence. However stale the claim, he must defend the action on the merits, for he will not g   have the benefit of a limitation defence unless he can show that his advice was not negligent. This subverts the whole purpose of the Limitation Acts. The harshness of the rule is evident. In the absence of any intentional wrongdoing on his part, it is neither just nor consistent with the policy of the Limitation Acts to expose a professional man to a claim for negligence long after he has retired from h   practice and has ceased to be covered by indemnity insurance.

[16] The decision in *Brocklesby's* case has been the subject of much criticism, not least by the Law Commission. In the present case a full Court of Appeal ([2001] EWCA Civ 245, [2002] 1 WLR 581) expressed strong reservations about the decision but considered themselves bound by it. They noted (at [14]) that it j   was an unreserved judgment in a case in which numerous authorities, both judicial and textbook, were not cited.

[17] The question is whether the words 'deliberate commission of a breach of duty' in s 32(2) of the 1980 Act mean 'deliberate commission of [an act or omission, being an act or omission which gives rise to] a breach of duty' or simply mean 'deliberate breach of duty'. If the latter, then they refer only to a breach of duty which has been committed intentionally. The distinction is between

intentional wrongdoing on the one hand and negligence or inadvertent
wrongdoing on the other.

[18] In a vigorous defence of the decision in *Brocklesby's* case counsel for
Mr Cave conducted a sustained analysis of the relationship between s 32(1)(b)
and s 32(2). He submitted that, on the defendants' construction, s 32(2) is otiose.
If it is limited to deliberate wrongdoing of which the defendant was aware but the
plaintiff was not, then this must be the result of deliberate concealment which is
already covered by s 32(1)(b). 'Concealment' means 'keeping secret', and (he
said) the pre-1980 case law showed that it covered non-disclosure as well as active
concealment.

[19] A defendant was formerly unable to take advantage of the Limitation
Acts if he had been guilty of 'concealed fraud'. This equitable doctrine was given
statutory effect by s 26(b) of the Limitation Act 1939, which postponed the start
of the limitation period where the plaintiff's right of action had been 'concealed
by the fraud of [the defendant or his agent]'. This was an inapt and inelegant
expression which caused much difficulty. It put the emphasis on the fraud rather
than the concealment. Section 32(1)(b) and s 32(2) of the 1980 Act were designed
to clarify and, if necessary, change the law by removing all reference to fraud and
substituting the more appropriate concept of 'deliberate concealment'. In such
circumstances reference to the antecedent statute and case law is of limited value,
since there can be no assumption that the later statute merely reproduced the
pre-existing law. But in my opinion it can be referred to if it helps either to
identify the mischief which the later statute set out to remedy or to explain why
Parliament chose to adopt the particular language or drafting technique which it
did when enacting the later statute.

[20] Lord Denning MR explained the meaning of the expression 'concealed by
the fraud of [the defendant or his agent]' in *King v Victor Parsons & Co (a firm)*
[1973] 1 All ER 206 at 209–210, [1973] 1 WLR 29 at 33–34 as follows:

'The word "fraud" here is not used in the common law sense. It is used in
the equitable sense to denote conduct by the defendant or his agent such that
it would be "against conscience" for him to avail himself of the lapse of time.
The cases show that, if a man *knowingly* commits a wrong (such as digging
underground another man's coal); or a breach of contract (such as putting in
bad foundations to a house), in such circumstances that it is unlikely to be
found out for many a long day, he cannot rely on the Statute of Limitations
as a bar to the claim: see *Bulli Coal Mining Co v Osborne* [1899] AC 351,
[1895–99] All ER Rep 506 and *Archer v Moss, Applegate v Moss* [1971] 1 All ER
747, [1971] 1 QB 406. In order to show that he "concealed" the right of action
"by fraud", it is not necessary to show that he took active steps to conceal his
wrongdoing or his breach of contract. It is sufficient that he *knowingly*
committed it and did not tell the owner anything about it. He did the wrong
or committed the breach secretly. By saying nothing he keeps it secret. He
conceals the right of action. He conceals it by "fraud" as those words have
been interpreted in the cases. To this word "knowingly" there must be
added "recklessly": see *Beaman v ARTS Ltd* [1949] 1 All ER 465 at 469, 470,
[1949] 1 KB 550 at 565, 566. Like the man who turns a blind eye. He is aware
that what he is doing may well be a wrong, or a breach of contract, but he
takes the risk of it being so. He refrains from further enquiry lest it should
prove to be correct; and says nothing about it. The court will not allow him
to get away with conduct of that kind. It may be that he has no dishonest

a motive; but that does not matter. He has kept the plaintiff out of the knowledge of his right of action; and that is enough: see *Kitchen v Royal Air Forces Association* [1958] 2 All ER 241, [1958] 1 WLR 563. *If the defendant was, however, quite unaware that he was committing a wrong or a breach of contract, it would be different. So if, by an honest blunder, he unwittingly commits a wrong (by digging another man's coal), or a breach of contract (by putting in an insufficient*
b *foundation) then he could avail himself of the Statute of Limitations.'* (My emphasis.)

[21] Concealment and non-disclosure are different concepts, but they have this much in common; they both require knowledge of the fact which is to be kept secret. A man cannot sensibly be said either to conceal or to fail to disclose
c something of which he is ignorant. In *King's* case the Court of Appeal unanimously held that s 26(b) of the 1939 Act did not extend to the case where the defendant ought to have known but did not in fact know the relevant facts which constituted the cause of action against him.

[22] In *Beaman v ARTS Ltd* [1949] 1 All ER 465, [1949] 1 KB 550 active
d concealment was not alleged. But the defendants were guilty of conversion, an intentional tort, and had failed to inform the plaintiff of what they had done. Quoting from the judgment of Lord James of Hereford in *Bulli Coal Mining Co v Osborne* [1899] AC 351 at 363–364, [1895–99] All ER Rep 506 at 510 the Court of Appeal held ([1949] 1 All ER 465 at 468, [1949] 1 KB 550 at 559–560) that active
e concealment was not necessary if the defendant was accused of intentional wrongdoing in circumstances where he could 'safely calculate on not being found out for many a long day'.

[23] As I have explained, in enacting the 1980 Act Parliament substituted 'deliberate concealment' for 'concealed fraud'. This is a different and more appropriate concept. It cannot be assumed that the law remained the same. But
f reference to the old law explains why Parliament enacted s 32(2) and did not rely on s 32(1)(b) alone to cover the whole ground. With all reference to fraud or conscious impropriety omitted, there was an obvious risk that 'deliberate concealment' might be construed in its natural sense as meaning 'active concealment' and not as embracing mere non-disclosure. Section 32(2) was therefore enacted to cover cases
g where active concealment should not be required. But such cases were limited in two respects: first, the defendant must have been guilty of a deliberate commission of a breach of duty; and secondly, the circumstances must make it unlikely that the breach of duty will be discovered for some time.

[24] Given that s 32(2) is (or at least may be) required to cover cases of
h non-disclosure rather than active concealment, the reason for limiting it to the deliberate commission of a breach of duty becomes clear. It is only where the defendant is aware of his own deliberate wrongdoing that it is appropriate to penalise him for failing to disclose it.

[25] In my opinion, s 32 of the 1980 Act deprives a defendant of a limitation
j defence in two situations: (i) where he takes active steps to conceal his own breach of duty after he has become aware of it; and (ii) where he is guilty of deliberate wrongdoing and conceals or fails to disclose it in circumstances where it is unlikely to be discovered for some time. But it does not deprive a defendant of a limitation defence where he is charged with negligence if, being unaware of his error or that he has failed to take proper care, there has been nothing for him to disclose.

[26] That this is the meaning of s 32(2) is supported by the text. In the first place, the subsection itself distinguishes between the breach of duty and the facts involved in the breach of duty. In the second place, where a defendant is charged with negligence, his breach of duty consists of his failure to take reasonable care. The tax adviser who inadvertently fails to take account of a provision in the latest Finance Act may well incur liability for negligence. But his breach of duty does not consist of giving the advice (which is deliberate and of which he is aware) or even of giving erroneous advice (which is not deliberate and of which he is unaware). It consists of his failure to take reasonable care, which is unlikely to be deliberate and of which he is unlikely to be aware. If he afterwards discovers the error and deliberately conceals it from the plaintiff, his conduct may come within s 32(1)(b); but while he remains ignorant of the error and of his own inadvertent breach of duty, there is nothing for him to disclose. In my opinion such conduct cannot be brought within s 32(2).

[27] A further consideration is even more telling. There is no rational justification for depriving a defendant of a limitation defence where neither his original wrongdoing nor his failure to disclose it to the plaintiff was deliberate. If *Brocklesby v Armitage & Guest (a firm)* [2001] 1 All ER 172, [2002] 1 WLR 598n is correct, then a surgeon who negligently leaves a swab in a patient's stomach but does not realise that he has done so can plead a limitation defence; but a solicitor who gives his client negligent advice cannot plead such a defence because he knows what advice he has given, even though he does not realise that it was wrong. There is no sensible basis for such a distinction.

[28] Another example will illustrate the anomalies to which the reasoning in *Brocklesby*'s case gives rise. Take the case of the anaesthetist who negligently administers the wrong drug, with consequent harm to his patient. The anaesthetist's selection of the wrong drug may be variously explained. He may have administered the drug deliberately, knowing perfectly well what drug he was administering and intending to administer it, but having negligently overlooked the fact that in the particular circumstances of the case it was dangerous to use it. Or he may simply have picked up the wrong bottle, and negligently but inadvertently administered one drug when he intended to administer another. There can be no rational justification for distinguishing between the two cases by allowing the anaesthetist in the second case a limitation defence which is denied to the anaesthetist in the first.

[29] The Court of Appeal justified the construction which it placed upon s 32(2) in *Brocklesby*'s case by reference to the maxim that ignorance of the law is no defence. But the defendant solicitors in that case were not relying on their ignorance of the law. The negligent solicitor or tax adviser is well aware that he is subject to a duty of care and generally does not deny it. In *Brocklesby*'s case itself the defendants denied that the plaintiff was their client; but they did not deny that, if he was, they owed him a duty of care. In cases of professional negligence the defendant is normally aware of his legal duty to take care but unaware of the fact that he has broken it. Of course, if he is giving legal advice he may have failed in his duty of care because he inadvertently overlooked the existence of a particular legal rule, but the fact that he has done so or otherwise misstated the law is as much a fact as any other, of which he may be or become aware or remain ignorant. The maxim that ignorance of the law is no defence does not operate to convert a lawyer's inadvertent want of care into an intentional tort.

[30] In agreement with my noble and learned friend Lord Scott of Foscote, I too would allow the appeal.

LORD SCOTT OF FOSCOTE.

[31] My Lords, this appeal comes to your Lordships' House on a preliminary point in a solicitors' negligence action. The point is whether the claim is barred by the Limitation Act 1980. The cause of action sued on accrued in March 1989. The action was not commenced until 16 January 1998. So unless the claimant is able to rely on one or other of the provisions of the 1980 Act extending time or postponing the running of time, his action is time-barred.

[32] In his pleading the claimant put forward three grounds on which, he contended, his time for commencing the action was extended. For reasons that I will explain later, two of these do not raise issues that are live before your Lordships. It is the third ground that raises the issue your Lordships must decide. The issue is whether the claimant can take advantage of s 32(2) of the 1980 Act. The Court of Appeal, expressing some disquiet but regarding themselves as bound by the exposition of the meaning and effect of s 32(2) given by Morritt LJ (as he then was) in *Brocklesby v Armitage & Guest (a firm)* [2001] 1 All ER 172, [2002] 1 WLR 598n, found in favour of the claimant. This appeal is, therefore, in effect an appeal against the construction of s 32(2) adopted in *Brocklesby's* case.

The facts

[33] The essential facts of the present case that are relevant to the s 32(2) issue can be shortly stated.

[34] The claimant, Mr Cave, the respondent in this House, instructed a firm of solicitors, Robinson Jarvis & Rolf, the appellants, to act for him in connection with a transaction under which a company, Hyde Securities Ltd, was to grant him mooring rights for a period of 100 years over land of the company at Fishbourne, Isle of Wight. A Mr Clarke of Robinson Jarvis & Rolf acted for Mr Cave in the transaction. Mr Clarke drafted, or approved the drafting of, the document by which the mooring rights were to be granted and the transaction was completed in March 1989.

[35] In January 1994 receivers of the company were appointed by the company's bank and in early February 1994 the receivers informed Mr Cave that his moorings rights were no longer exercisable. For a while Mr Cave did nothing about the information he had received but in November 1995 he wrote to Mr Clarke. Your Lordships have not seen the letter but, presumably, Mr Cave complained that the mooring rights he thought he had been granted were being challenged and asked for Mr Clarke's assistance in resisting the challenge or for an explanation as to what had gone wrong. Mr Cave received no answer to his letter. He wrote again on a number of occasions in 1996 but still did not receive any answer. He eventually consulted other solicitors and his writ claiming damages in negligence from the appellants was issued on 16 January 1998.

The pleadings

[36] Mr Cave's main pleaded complaints of negligence are, first, that the document drafted or approved by Mr Clarke granted him merely contractual rights instead of rights that would be enforceable both against the company and against its successors in title, and, secondly, that Mr Clarke failed to protect the rights by registration in the Land Registry. He also pleaded in his statement of claim, in reliance on s 14A of the 1980 Act, that he had not had the knowledge required for bringing his action until March 1996 when he received a letter from the Tunbridge Wells District Land Registry informing him that there was no entry on the register relating to his mooring rights. He contended that he had

therefore had three years from March 1996 within which to bring his action (see s 14A(4)(b)).

[37] The solicitors, in their defence, denied negligence but pleaded also that the action was time-barred. As to the s 14A point, they contended that, even if s 14A(4)(b) did apply, the three-year limitation period would have run from February 1994, when Mr Cave had been told that his mooring rights were no longer exercisable, and would, therefore, have expired before the action had been commenced.

[38] Mr Cave served a reply that, in its re-amended form, took two s 32 points. It was alleged, first, that the solicitors' failure to answer Mr Cave's letters in 1995 and 1996 constituted 'deliberate concealment' for the purposes of s 32(1)(b). The second point was the s 32(2) point. The reply alleged:

'3.A Further, the negligent drafting by the Defendant of an agreement which did not confer on the Claimant the rights which it ought to have conferred was (i) an intentional act (although, for the avoidance of doubt, it is not alleged that it was done in the knowledge that it was a breach of duty); and (ii) done in circumstances in which the breach of duty was unlikely to be discovered for some time. In the premises, pursuant to Section 32(1) and (2) of the Limitation Act 1980, time did not begin to run until the Claimant discovered or could with the exercise of reasonable diligence have discovered the breach. Even on the Defendant's case, that date was not before February 1994. Accordingly the proceedings were issued within the primary limitation period.'

Paragraph 3.A raises the *Brocklesby* point.

The Brocklesby point

[39] Section 32 of the 1980 Act provides, so far as relevant:

'(1) ... where in the case of any action for which a period of limitation is prescribed by this Act, either—(a) the action is based upon the fraud of the defendant; or (b) any fact relevant to the plaintiff's right of action has been deliberately concealed from him by the defendant; or (c) the action is for relief from the consequences of a mistake; the period of limitation shall not begin to run until the plaintiff has discovered the fraud, concealment or mistake (as the case may be) or could with reasonable diligence have discovered it ...
(2) For the purposes of subsection (1) above, deliberate commission of a breach of duty in circumstances in which it is unlikely to be discovered for some time amounts to deliberate concealment of the facts involved in that breach of duty ...
(5) Sections 14A and 14B of this Act shall not apply to any action to which subsection (1)(b) above applies (and accordingly the period of limitation referred to in that subsection, in any case to which either of those sections would otherwise apply, is the period applicable under section 2 of this Act).'

[40] The statutory predecessor of s 32 was (via s 7 of the Limitation Amendment Act 1980) s 26 of the Limitation Act 1939. The wording of s 26 of the 1939 Act was not the same as the wording of s 32 of the 1980 Act and, in particular, s 26 had no provision comparable to s 32(2). Nonetheless it was generally believed that the broad effect of s 26 had been continued under s 32. *Clerk and Lindsell on Torts*

a (17th edn, 1995) p 1593, para 31–19, (18th edn, 2000) p 1723, para 33–25 said that s 32(2)—

> 'preserves and confirms the case law on section 26 of the Limitation Act 1939, according to which the start of the limitation period is postponed whenever the defendant has committed the wrong, knowingly or recklessly, in circumstances such as to prevent the plaintiff coming to know of his cause *b* of action.'

(Cited by Janet O'Sullivan in her article 'Intentional acts, breaches of duty and the Limitation Act—a warning for negligent professionals' [2000] Professional Negligence 241 at 242, n 4.)

c [41] The case law on s 26 of the 1939 Act had established that a merely negligent act was insufficient to enable the benefit of the section to be claimed (see, for example, *Kitchen v Royal Air Forces Association* [1958] 2 All ER 241, [1958] 1 WLR 563). In *King v Victor Parsons & Co (a firm)* [1973] 1 All ER 206 at 209–210, [1973] 1 WLR 29 at 34, Lord Denning MR emphasised that if the benefit of s 26 was to be available there must be something more than mere negligence. He *d* said: 'So if, by an honest blunder, he unwittingly commits a wrong (by digging another man's coal), or a breach of contract (by putting in an insufficient foundation) then he could avail himself of the Statute of Limitations.'

[42] It is clear, therefore, that, under the pre-1980 law, a pleading on the lines of para 3.A of the re-amended reply would have been unsustainable. The pleader *e* would have had to have alleged something more than an intentional but negligent act or omission in order to claim the benefit of s 26.

[43] The approach to construction of s 32 of the 1980 Act was considered by this House in *Sheldon v R H M Outhwaite (Underwriting Agencies) Ltd* [1995] 2 All ER 558, [1996] AC 102. The case was concerned not with s 32(2) but with *f* s 32(1). Deliberate concealment of relevant facts (see s 32(1)(b)) had been relied on by the plaintiffs in their pleaded reply to the defendants' Limitation Act defence and was based on acts or omissions by the defendants which had taken place after the date on which the plaintiffs' cause of action had accrued. The question was whether the deliberate concealment merely suspended the running of time for Limitation Act purposes until the date when the plaintiffs could *g* reasonably have discovered the relevant facts or whether a complete new limitation period, three years or six years as the case might be, would start afresh from that date. This is not a point which arises in the present case, nor did it arise in *Brocklesby*'s case, but it is the guidance given by the House to the approach to construction of s 32 that is in point.

h [44] Lord Browne-Wilkinson, noting that the 1980 Act was a consolidating Act, said ([1995] 2 All ER 558 at 567, [1996] AC 102 at 144) that 'unless there is an ambiguity, it is not permissible to construe consolidating Acts in the light of their statutory history' and that 'much of the difficulty in this case is raised by the investigation of the statutory history and the decisions of the courts on earlier *j* statutes'. He held:

> 'Section 32 of the Act of 1980 is not ambiguous. On the plain meaning of the words any deliberate concealment of relevant facts falls within s 32(1)(b) with the consequence that, in applying the statutory time limits, time does not start to run until the concealment is discovered.' (See [1995] 2 All ER 558 at 568, [1996] AC 102 at 145.)

Lord Keith of Kinkel expressed himself in much the same terms. He said: *a*

'Recourse to the antecedents of a consolidation statute should only be had
when there is a real difficulty or ambiguity incapable of being resolved by
classical methods of construction: see *Farrell v Alexander* [1976] 2 All ER 721
at 726, [1977] AC 59 at 73 per Lord Wilberforce ... there is no such difficulty
or ambiguity here.' (See [1995] 2 All ER 558 at 563, 564, [1996] AC 102 at
140.)   *b*

[45] Lord Lloyd of Berwick, however, with whose opinion Lord Mustill
agreed ([1995] 2 All ER 558 at 568, [1996] AC 102 at 146), thought that 'Parliament
has left a gap' and that in order to try to fill the gap recourse to the history of the
legislation was necessary and, therefore, legitimate (see [1995] 2 All ER 558 at 569,
574, [1996] AC 102 at 146, 151–152). Lord Nicholls of Birkenhead, too ([1995] 2   *c*
All ER 558 at 575, [1996] AC 102 at 153), discerned an ambiguity in s 32(1) but he
joined Lord Keith and Lord Browne-Wilkinson in the result.

[46] The importance of *Sheldon's* case for present purposes is that it insists that
if the language of s 32 is clear, effect must be given to that language without
regard to the section's legislative history. This was the point taken up in   *d*
Brocklesby v Armitage & Guest (a firm) [2001] 1 All ER 172, [2002] 1 WLR 598n.

[47] For the purpose of establishing an important point of principle on the
construction and effect of s 32, *Brocklesby's* case is, in my opinion, a very unsatisfactory
vehicle. It was an interlocutory appeal on a pleading point, and heard by a
two-man Court of Appeal. The case was completed within the day and one ex
tempore judgment, by Morritt LJ, was delivered. The issue in the case was   *e*
whether sufficient particulars of a pleaded allegation of deliberate concealment
had been given. The case was, like the present, a solicitors' negligence case. The
transaction in respect of which it was alleged that the solicitors had been
negligent was a conveyancing transaction. In January 1989 a company in which
Mr Brocklesby held a minority interest had sold some commercial premises to   *f*
him. He had obtained a building society advance secured on the premises and
repayable by instalments over 25 years. The defendant solicitors had acted for all
three parties, ie the seller, the buyer and the building society. A few months later
it was agreed between Mr Brocklesby and the company that the company would
repurchase the premises from Mr Brocklesby on terms that it would procure the
release of Mr Brocklesby from his obligations to the building society. The   *g*
solicitors who had acted on the previous transaction were instructed to act on this
transaction for Mr Brocklesby and the company. Mr Brocklesby signed a
contract, executed a transfer of the property to the company, went out of
possession of the premises and stopped paying the mortgage instalments to the
building society. The company took over the payment of the mortgage   *h*
instalments. But the solicitors took no steps to procure the release of
Mr Brocklesby from his mortgage obligations. In November 1990 the company
stopped paying the mortgage instalments and went into compulsory liquidation.
The building society sold the premises and sued Mr Brocklesby for the balance
due to them. Mr Brocklesby sued the solicitors for negligence. His action was   *j*
commenced in June 1997, more than six years after his cause of action had
accrued. The solicitors pleaded in their defence that the action was time-barred
and applied to strike it out. Mr Brocklesby served a reply in which it was pleaded
that the solicitors' breaches of duty had been deliberately committed in
circumstances in which they had been unlikely to be discovered and had not in
fact been discovered until mid-1992. Such particulars as were given relating to

a these allegations indicated that Mr Brocklesby's case was that the solicitors had known that the resale to the company would not be completed but had failed to inform him of this.

[48] Morritt LJ summarised Mr Brocklesby's case thus:

b 'Mr Brocklesby relies on para (b) of s 32(1) [of the 1980 Act] as expanded by sub-s (2). He contends that there were three breaches of duty, that is the failure to take steps to procure Mr Brocklesby's release from the obligations to the building society; the failure to do anything with the executed contract/transfer; and the failure to inform Mr Brocklesby of either of the first or second breaches of duty. He suggests that each of them was deliberate in the sense of being intentional and each was committed in *c* circumstances where, by their nature, they were unlikely to be discovered for some time.' (See [2001] 1 All ER 172 at 177, [2002] 1 WLR 598n at 602.)

[49] After referring to *Sheldon's* case and *King's* case and to para 2.9 of the Law Reform Committee's *Final Report on Limitation of Actions* (Cmnd 6923 (1977)) that had preceded the 1980 Act, Morritt LJ expressed his conclusions in the following *d* passage:

'When one turns to the terms of s 32 of the 1980 Act itself, under sub-s (1) there is a clear contrast between the action based on fraud and para (b), the concealment of any fact relevant to the plaintiff's right of action being deliberate. The requirement is that the fact relevant to the cause of action *e* has been deliberately concealed from him by the defendant. But sub-s (2) amplifies what is meant by deliberate concealment and requires that for the purposes of sub-s (1) deliberate commission of a breach of duty, etc, amounts to deliberate concealment of the facts involved in the breach of duty. Generally speaking, and I do not say that there may not be exceptions, the civil law and, so far as I know, the criminal law, does not require that a *f* person should know the legal consequences of the act which he commits. Generally speaking, if he knows of the act and he intends the act, but is unaware of the legal consequences, his unawareness is immaterial for it is trite law that ignorance of the law is no defence. It appears to me that had Parliament intended in the case of a deliberate concealment under s 32(1)(b) *g* of the 1980 Act, as amplified by sub-s (2), that there should be both deliberate commission of an act in the sense of knowingly and intentionally committing the act and also knowledge that such commission gave rise to a particular legal consequence, then it required clearer words to spell that out than are to be found in sub-ss (2) or (1). Accordingly, the conclusion I reach is that it is *h* not necessary for the purpose of extending the limitation period pursuant to s 32(1)(b) of the 1980 Act to demonstrate that the fact relevant to the claimant's right of action has been deliberately concealed in any sense greater than that the commission of the act was deliberate in the sense of being intentional and that that act or omission, as the case may be, did involve a breach of duty whether or not the actor appreciated that legal *j* consequence.' (See [2001] 1 All ER 172 at 180–181, [2002] 1 WLR 598n at 605.)

[50] The result of this interpretation of s 32(2) is that whenever there is an intentional act which constitutes, whether or not to the knowledge of the actor, a breach of duty in circumstances in which it, ie the breach of duty, is unlikely to be discovered for some time, sub-s (2) comes into play. This interpretation

reversed what previously had been believed to be the position, namely that mere negligence would never by itself be enough to bring about a s 32(1) postponement of time.

[51] Basing himself on the view of s 32(2) that I have described, Morritt LJ concluded that the pleaded particulars of Mr Brocklesby's case were sufficient to sustain his cause of action against the Limitation Act defence and to resist the strike-out application.

[52] It is worth noting, however, that Morritt LJ then went on to give an alternative, uncontroversial and, if I may respectfully say so, plainly sound reason for coming to the same conclusion. He said:

'... in addition ... I am concerned that the judge imposed too high a standard of particularity for the reply to be served at the stage which the action had reached. Discovery of documents has not yet taken place. Most of the relevant facts were inevitably in the knowledge of the solicitors rather than Mr Brocklesby. There was no imminent trial such that an insufficiently particularised pleading might be embarrassing ... It may be that in the light of what is disclosed on discovery he will be able to supplement the particulars already given but without such supplementation I do not consider that his case as pleaded is so thin that the court is justified in, in effect, striking it out.' (See [2001] 1 All ER 172 at 181, [2002] 1 WLR 598n at 606.)

The other member of the court, Wilson J, simply agreed.

[53] The Brocklesby decision was followed by Laddie J in Liverpool Roman Catholic Archdiocese Trustees Inc v Goldberg [2001] 1 All ER 182. The defendant, Mr David Goldberg QC, a well-known specialist in tax law, had given certain tax advice to the archdiocese. The archdiocese contended that the advice was wrong, had been negligently given and had caused the archdiocese financial loss. A negligence action was commenced. The problem was that the allegedly negligent advice had been given in 1989 and 1992 but the action was not commenced until 1997. Mr Goldberg pleaded that an action in respect of his 1989 advice was time-barred. The archdiocese, in answer, sought to rely on the Brocklesby interpretation of s 32(2). They proposed to amend their pleading so as to allege, inter alia:

'(a) The acts and omissions pleaded in paragraph 14 of the Statement of Claim [ie in relation to the 1989 advice] constituted the deliberate commission of a breach of duty within the meaning of Section 32(2) of the Act in that they were intentional. For the avoidance of doubt it is not alleged that the Defendant knew that he was thereby committing a breach of duty.' (See [2001] 1 All ER 182 at 187 (para 13).)

[54] The second sentence of the cited paragraph uses the same language as the passage in parenthesis in para 3.A(i) of the re-amended reply in the present case. This pleading might now, I suppose, be called the Brocklesby disclaimer. Laddie J applied, as he had to, the interpretation of s 32(2) adopted in Brocklesby's case. He said ([2001] 1 All ER 182 at 190–191 (para 22)):

'... "deliberate commission of a breach of duty" should be read consistently with Brocklesby's case. Any intentional act which amounts to a breach of duty amounts to a deliberate commission of a breach of duty and triggers s 32(2) of the 1980 Act. The fact that in the proposed amendment to the reply, the a   Archdiocese concedes that Mr Goldberg did not know he was committing a breach of duty does not, therefore, exclude operation of the section. Mr Goldberg's advice was given intentionally. On the assumption, which I have to make for the purpose of this application, namely that it amounted to a breach of duty, that breach was committed deliberately within the meaning of the section.'

b

The present case: Newman J

[55] In the present case Newman J at first instance, applying *Brocklesby*'s case and concluding on the facts that the solicitors' assumed breach of duty would have been unlikely to have been discovered for some time, held that s 32(2) c   applied and that the six-year limitation period did not begin to run until, at earliest, February 1994. So the action was commenced well within the six-year period.

[56] The judge held, also, that the three-year period prescribed by s 14A of the 1980 Act would have started to run from February 1994. It followed that Mr Cave was unable to rely on s 14A as a ground for resisting the solicitors' d   Limitation Act defence. Mr Cave did not appeal against this finding.

The Court of Appeal

[57] The bulk of the argument in the Court of Appeal (Potter, Sedley and Jonathan Parker LJJ) ([2001] EWCA Civ 245, [2002] 1 WLR 581) appears to have e   centred on the question whether the court was bound by the decision of the two-man Court of Appeal in *Brocklesby*'s case. They held that they were. That being so, the decision to dismiss the solicitors' appeal was inevitable. Jonathan Parker LJ, however, confessed to being uneasy about the decision in *Brocklesby*'s case. He noted that in *Sheldon v R H M Outhwaite (Underwriting Agencies) Ltd* [1995] 2 All ER 558, [1996] AC 102 both Lord Browne-Wilkinson and Lord f   Nicholls of Birkenhead had regarded unconscionability and impropriety as the 'underlying rationale' of s 32 (see eg [1995] 2 All ER 558 at 568, [1996] AC 102 at 145). 'Yet', observed Jonathan Parker LJ ([2002] 1 WLR 581 at [47]), 'if the *Brocklesby* case is right, a wholly innocent act or omission may suffice to deprive a defendant of a limitation defence.' That this may be so is demonstrated by g   *Goldberg*'s case and, indeed, also the present case.

Was the Brocklesby construction of s 32(2) correct?

[58] In my opinion it was not. I would start by adopting the approach prescribed by Lord Browne-Wilkinson in *Sheldon*'s case. Unless there is some ambiguity in the statutory language, recourse to legislative history is unnecessary and h   impermissible. The relevant words in s 32(2) are: 'deliberate commission of a breach of duty ... amounts to deliberate concealment of the facts involved in that breach of duty'. These are clear words of English. 'Deliberate commission of a breach of duty' is to be contrasted with a commission of a breach of duty which is not deliberate, ie a breach of duty which is inadvertent, accidental, j   unintended—there is a number of adjectives that can be chosen for the purpose of the contrast, and it does not matter which is chosen. Each would exclude a breach of duty that the actor was not aware he was committing.

[59] Mr Doctor QC, counsel for Mr Cave, the respondent, submitted that in order for a fact to be 'deliberately concealed' for s 32(1)(b) purposes, the concealment must be an intended concealment. I would respectfully agree with that. He followed with the submission that in every case in which there was a

deliberate commission of a breach of duty in circumstances in which the victim
was unlikely to discover for some time that there had been a breach, there must
have been a deliberate concealment for sub-s (1)(b) purposes. In which case, he
concluded, sub-s (2) would add nothing to sub-s (1)(b). But Parliament must have
intended sub-s (2) to add something of significance to sub-s (1)(b) and the
Brocklesby interpretation does add something to sub-s (1)(b).

[60] I hope I have done justice to the argument but, in my opinion, it cannot
be accepted. I find it easy to accept that Mr Doctor's submissions as to the
meaning of s 32(1)(b) are correct. I agree that deliberate concealment for
s 32(1)(b) purposes may be brought about by an act or an omission and that, in
either case, the result of the act or omission, ie the concealment, must be an
intended result. But I do not agree that that renders sub-s (2) otiose. A claimant
who proposes to invoke s 32(1)(b) in order to defeat a Limitation Act defence
must prove the facts necessary to bring the case within the paragraph. He can do
so if he can show that some fact relevant to his right of action has been concealed
from him either by a positive act of concealment or by a withholding of relevant
information, but, in either case, with the intention of concealing the fact or facts
in question. In many cases the requisite proof of intention might be quite difficult
to provide. The standard of proof would be the usual balance of probabilities
standard and inferences could of course be drawn from suitable primary facts but,
nonetheless, proof of intention, particularly where an omission rather than a
positive act is relied on, is often very difficult. Subsection (2), however, provides
an alternative route. The claimant need not concentrate on the allegedly
concealed facts but can instead concentrate on the commission of the breach of
duty. If the claimant can show that the defendant knew he was committing a
breach of duty, or intended to commit the breach of duty—I can discern no
difference between the two formulations; each would constitute, in my opinion,
a deliberate commission of the breach—then, if the circumstances are such that
the claimant is unlikely to discover for some time that the breach of duty has been
committed, the facts involved in the breach are taken to have been deliberately
concealed for sub-s (1)(b) purposes. I do not agree with Mr Doctor that the
subsection, thus construed, adds nothing. It provides an alternative, and in some
cases what may well be an easier, means of establishing the facts necessary to
bring the case within s 32(1)(b).

[61] Morritt LJ in *Brocklesby*'s case said, in a passage I have cited at [49], above,
that in general a person is assumed to know the legal consequences of his actions
and that, therefore, if an act has been done intentionally, the actor's unawareness
of its legal consequences would be immaterial and no defence. The premise is, in
my opinion, much too wide to constitute a satisfactory approach to construction
of a statutory provision such as s 32(2). A person may or may not know that an
act of his or an omission to do or say something or other constitutes a breach of
tortious or contractual duty. His knowledge or lack of it may well be immaterial
to the question whether a cause of action for which he is liable has accrued to the
person injured by the act or omission. But that is no reason at all why Parliament,
in prescribing the circumstances in which the person injured by the act or
omission can escape from a Limitation Act defence, should not distinguish
between the case where the actor knows he is committing a breach of duty and
the case where he does not. The clear words of s 32(2)—'deliberate commission
of a breach of duty'—show that Parliament has made that distinction.

[62] It follows that, in my opinion, the construction of s 32(2) adopted in
Brocklesby's case was wrong. I wish to make clear that I do not think the case was

a   wrongly decided. As I have already said, Morritt LJ's alternative ground for reaching the same decision seems to me to have been sound.

[63] I do, however, think that *Goldberg's* case was wrongly decided. The *Brocklesby* disclaimer required, in my opinion, the conclusion that s 32(2) could not apply and that the archdiocese's claim in respect of the 1989 advice was time-barred.

b   [64] There is one further point I want to make on the construction of s 32(1)(b) and s 32(2). Mr Davidson QC, counsel for the solicitors, submitted that some degree of unconscionability in the conduct of a defendant was necessary before the defendant could be deprived under s 32(1)(b), with or without the help of s 32(2), of a Limitation Act defence. This was, I think, based mainly on Lord Browne-Wilkinson's comment in *Sheldon v R H M Outhwaite (Underwriting*
c   *Agencies) Ltd* [1995] 2 All ER 558 at 568, [1996] AC 102 at 145 that 'unconscionable behaviour by deliberately concealing the facts relevant to the plaintiffs' cause of action' was 'the underlying rationale' of s 32.

[65] I respectfully agree that it is difficult to think of a case of deliberate concealment for s 32(1)(b) purposes that would not involve unconscionable
d   behaviour and that most cases of deliberate commission of breach of duty for s 32(2) purposes would be in the same state. But the statutory language does not require that the behaviour of the defendant be unconscionable and its addition as a criterion to be satisfied before a case can be brought within s 32 is, in my opinion, unnecessary and unjustified. The plain words of the statutory requirements, 'deliberately concealed' and 'deliberate commission of a breach of duty', need no
e   embellishment.

The authority of the Brocklesby decision

[66] Your Lordships have not heard any argument on the question whether the Court of Appeal in the present case was correct to hold itself bound by the
f   *Brocklesby* decision and I do not wish to express any view on that issue.

The result

[67] In the present case the *Brocklesby* disclaimer in para 3.A of the re-amended reply means that that paragraph of the reply cannot succeed. Mr Cave still has, however, his para 3 point and, under a conditional compromise agreed between
g   the parties after the Court of Appeal judgments but before the hearing in this House, Mr Cave is entitled to recover an agreed sum from the appellant solicitors, albeit less than the agreed sum he would have been entitled to recover had your Lordships upheld the *Brocklesby* construction.

[68] I would allow the appeal accordingly.

Appeal allowed.

Kate O'Hanlon   Barrister.

Pine v The Law Society   *a*

[2002] EWCA Civ 175

COURT OF APPEAL, CIVIL DIVISION

SIR ANDREW MORRITT V-C, ROBERT WALKER AND RIX LJJ

6, 7, 20 FEBRUARY 2002   *b*

Solicitor – Dishonesty – Intervention by Law Society in solicitor's practice – Nomination or appointment of solicitor to act as agent of Law Society in intervention – Nominated solicitor submitting bills to Law Society in respect of costs of acting in intervention – Law Society seeking under statutory provision reimbursement from solicitor in whose practice it had intervened – Solicitor seeking taxation of bills – Whether bills submitted to Law Society solicitor's bills – Whether solicitor's right to seek taxation of bills excluded by provision rendering him liable for Law Society's costs of intervention – Solicitors Act 1974, ss 70, 71, Sch 1, Pt II, para 13.   *c*

The Law Society resolved, pursuant to powers conferred on it by s 35 of, and   *d*
Sch 1 to, the Solicitors Act 1974, to intervene in the claimant's practice as a solicitor on the grounds of suspected dishonesty. In that connection, the Society resolved to nominate or appoint a solicitor to hold the moneys or take possession of the documents to which certain parts of the 1974 Act applied. The Society duly appointed H to be that solicitor and otherwise to act as their agent in the   *e*
intervention. In due course, H's firm submitted five bills to the Society for their professional charges for acting on its behalf. After paying the bills, the Society sought reimbursement from the claimant under para 13[a] of Pt II of Sch 1 to the 1974 Act, which provided that any costs incurred by it for the purposes of that Schedule, including the costs of any person exercising powers under Pt II of Sch 1 on its behalf, were to be paid by the solicitor in whose practice the Society had   *f*
intervened, and were recoverable from him as a debt owing to the Society. The claimant brought proceedings against the Society, seeking an order under s 71[b] of the 1974 Act for a detailed assessment of the bills. Section 71 provided that where a person other than the party chargeable with the bill for the purposes of s 70[c] (ie a solicitor's bill) had paid it or was liable to pay it he could apply for taxation of   *g*
the bill as if he were the party chargeable with it. The Society applied for an order that the claim be struck out or summarily dismissed. The judge refused the application. On its appeal, the Society contended that (i) H's bills were not solicitor's bills within the meaning of s 70 since it had not retained him to act as its solicitor either to give advice or to conduct proceedings, and (ii) in any event,   *h*
the provisions of s 71 were overriden or excluded by para 13.

Held – (1) In deciding whether a bill was 'a solicitor's bill' within the meaning of s 70(1) of the 1974 Act, the court was required to consider whether the business was connected with the profession of a solicitor; whether the solicitor had been employed because he was a solicitor; and whether the solicitor would not have   *j*
been appointed if he had not been a solicitor or the relation of solicitor and client had not subsisted between him and his employer. For the purposes of that test,

---

a   Paragraph 13 is set out at [3], below
b   Section 71, so far as material, is set out at [5], below
c   Section 70, so far as material is set out at [5], below

a it could hardly be doubted that acting as agent for the Law Society under Sch 1 of the 1974 Act was business connected with the profession of a solicitor, and it was incorrect to regard the profession of solicitor as confined to advice on specific legal problems or the prosecution or defence of particular claims. Although the Society was under no obligation to appoint a solicitor as its agent in an intervention, and there might well be cases in which an accountant or office
b manager would be more appropriate, that consideration highlighted the importance of its decision to appoint a solicitor in the instant case. The form of the Society's resolution showed that the decision had been to appoint a solicitor, and it was clear that H would not have been appointed if he had not been a solicitor. Accordingly, each of the bills submitted by H was 'a solicitor's bill' (see [19]–[21], [23], [37], [38], below); *Allen v Aldridge, Re Ward* (1844) 5 Beav 401
c applied.

(2) Paragraph 13 of Pt II of Sch 1 to the 1974 Act did not override or exclude the right conferred by s 71 of the Act. Section 71 was of general application. It recognised that the person chargeable with the bill might not be ultimately liable to pay the costs thereby claimed. Its evident purpose was to confer on one with
d a secondary liability for those costs a right comparable to that possessed by the person primarily liable. Given that the Law Society was entitled to have the bills taxed under s 70 of the Act, it was unlikely that Parliament had intended that there should be degrees of secondary liability, some of which were excluded from the ambit of s 71. Accordingly, the appeal would be dismissed (see [27], [34], [36]–[38], below); *Law Society v McKanan-Jones* (14 July 1992, unreported)
e disapproved.

Notes

For persons entitled to taxation of a solicitor's bill and for reimbursement of the costs of a Law Society intervention, see 44(1) *Halsbury's Laws* (4th edn reissue)
f paras 207, 483.

For the Solicitors Act 1974, ss 70, 71, Sch 1, Pt II, para 13, see 41 *Halsbury's Statutes* (4th edn) (2000 reissue) 95, 98, 121.

Cases referred to in judgments

Allen v Aldridge, Re Ward (1844) 5 Beav 401, (1843) 49 ER 633.
g *Inderwick, Re* (1883) 25 Ch D 279, CA.
Law Society v McKanan-Jones (14 July 1992, unreported), Ch D.
Llewellyn v Law Society (10 December 1993, unreported), Ch D.
Osborne, Re (1858) 25 Beav 353, (1858) 27 LJ Ch 532, (1858) 53 ER 671.

h ### Cases also cited or referred to in skeleton arguments

Boddington v British Transport Police [1998] 2 All ER 203, [1999] 2 AC 143, HL.
Bradford v Law Society (31 July 1995, unreported).
Chassagnou v France (1999) 7 BHRC 151, ECt HR.
Cove v Law Society (1988) Times, 26 July, CA.
j *Giles v Law Society* (1996) 8 Admin LR 105, CA.
Harrison v Tew [1990] 1 All ER 321, [1990] 2 AC 523, HL.
Law Society v KPMG Peat Marwick (sued as KPMG Peat Marwick McLintock) [2000] 1 All ER 515; *affd* [2000] 4 All ER 540, [2000] 1 WLR 1921, CA.
Osman v UK (1998) 5 BHRC 293, ECt HR.
Shilson Goode & Co, Re [1904] 1 Ch 837.

Wilson v First County Trust Ltd [2001] EWCA Civ 633, [2001] 3 All ER 229, [2002] QB 74.

Appeal

The Law Society appealed with permission of Judge Maddocks granted on 2 March 2001 from his decision on 23 February 2001 dismissing its application for an order striking out under CPR 3.4 or summarily dismissing under CPR 24.5(1) proceedings brought by the claimant, Simon John Pine, for an order under s 71 of the Solicitors Act 1974 for a detailed assessment of bills submitted to the Society by Davis Blank Furniss, a firm of solicitors, in respect of the costs incurred by one of its partners in acting as the Society's agent in an intervention in Mr Pine's practice as a solicitor. The facts are set out in the judgment of Sir Andrew Morritt V-C.

Timothy Dutton QC (instructed by *Wright Son & Pepper*) for the Law Society.
Jeremy Morgan (instructed by *Irwin Mitchell*) for Mr Pine.

Cur adv vult

20 February 2002. The following judgments were delivered.

SIR ANDREW MORRITT V-C.

Introduction

[1] The claimant (Mr Pine) was admitted a solicitor in 1985. In September 1994 he set up in practice as a sole practitioner in the name of Pine & Co. On 24 March 1999 the defendant, the Law Society, resolved to intervene in the practice of Mr Pine pursuant to the powers conferred on them by s 35 of and Sch 1 to the Solicitors Act 1974. They did so on the ground specified in Sch 1, Pt I, para 1(1)(a), namely suspected dishonesty. In that connection they resolved to nominate or appoint a solicitor to hold the moneys or take possession of the documents to which Sch 1, Pt II, paras 6 and 9 thereof applied.

[2] On the same day the Law Society nominated or appointed Mr Heginbotham, a partner in the firm of Davis Blank Furniss, to be that solicitor and otherwise to act as the agent of the Law Society in the intervention. In due course Davis Blank Furniss submitted five bills to the Law Society for their 'professional charges for acting on your behalf' for the five months from 25 March to 25 August 1999. The bills specify the time spent by Mr Heginbotham and other partners or employees of Davis Blank Furniss and their respective charging rates. On the reverse is to be found the information required by art 6 of the Solicitors (Non-Contentious Business) Remuneration Order 1994, SI 1994/2616. The sums claimed in the bills, totalling £16,319·08, were paid, we do not know when, by the Law Society who, later in the same year, sought reimbursement from Mr Pine under Sch 1, Pt II, para 13 of the 1974 Act.

[3] Paragraph 13 provides:

> 'Subject to any order for the payment of costs that may be made on an application to the court under this Schedule, any costs incurred by the Society for the purposes of this Schedule, including, without prejudice to the generality of this paragraph, the costs of any person exercising powers under this Part of this Schedule on behalf of the Society, shall be paid by the

a Solicitor or his personal representatives and shall be recoverable from him or them as a debt owing to the Society.'

[4] On 8 February 2000 Mr Pine was struck off. On 28 February 2000 the Law Society served a statutory demand on Mr Pine seeking payment of £16,319·08. Mr Pine's attempt to have the statutory demand set aside was unsuccessful before District Judge Britlin, on appeal before Judge Maddocks and, finally, on 14 *b* November 2000, on an application for permission to appeal before Chadwick LJ.

[5] In the meantime, on 26 September 2000, Mr Pine instituted proceedings against the Law Society seeking an order under s 71 of the 1974 Act for a detailed assessment of the bills submitted to the Law Society by Davis Blank Furniss. Section 71(1) provides:

c   'Where a person other than the party chargeable with the bill for the purposes of section 70 has paid, or is or was liable to pay, a bill either to the solicitor or to the party chargeable with the bill, that person, or his executors, administrators or assignees may apply to the High Court for an order for the taxation of the bill as if he were the party chargeable with it, and the court *d*   may make the same order (if any) as it might have made if the application had been made by the party chargeable with the bill.'

Section 70(1) provides:

'Where before the expiration of one month from the delivery of a solicitor's bill an application is made by the party chargeable with the bill, the *e*   High Court shall, without requiring any sum to be paid into court, order that the bill be taxed and that no action be commenced on the bill until the taxation is completed.'

By sub-s (2) if the application is made after the expiration of the month it is provided that the High Court may, in its discretion, order a taxation. In that *f* event no action may be commenced on the bill and any action already commenced is stayed until the taxation is completed but subject to the limits and on the conditions prescribed by sub-ss (3) and (4).

[6] On 6 October 2000 the Law Society applied for an order that the claim be struck out under CPR 3.4 or summarily dismissed under CPR 24.5(1). That *g* application came before Judge Maddocks, sitting as a deputy High Court judge of the Chancery Division. He dismissed it but gave the Law Society permission to appeal. This is the hearing of that appeal.

The issues

h [7] The issue, whether the provisions of para 13 of Pt II of Sch 1, exclude or override the provisions of s 71 of the 1974 Act came before Mummery J in *Law Society v McKanan-Jones* (14 July 1992, unreported). His conclusion was:

'The 1974 Act contains provisions for taxation on application by a party chargeable, or solicitor, under s 70 and taxation on application of third *j* parties under s 71. Both provisions deal with the taxation of a solicitor's bill. The wording of para 13 of Sch 1 makes no reference to a bill of a solicitor; it simply refers to the costs of any person exercising powers under the section. The Law Society is a person who has incurred those costs and the paragraph provides in clear terms that those costs shall be paid by the solicitor, and recoverable from him as a debt owed to the Society. The machinery as to taxation in s 70, and more particularly s 71 appears to me to have no application to a provision that costs shall constitute a debt recoverable by the Society.'

That decision was followed by Judge Maddocks, sitting as a deputy judge of the Chancery Division in *Llewellyn v Law Society* (10 December 1993, unreported).

[8] In his judgment in this case Judge Maddocks took a different view. He analysed the problem into two questions:

'... one, whether the bill of the person exercising the powers of the Law Society, the agent, is a solicitor's bill, and if so, two, whether the terms of para 13 exclude or leave no room for the application of s 71.'

[9] With regard to the first question Judge Maddocks concluded:

'... the agent [Mr Heginbotham], although not giving legal advice to the Law Society, was nevertheless exercising his professional skills as a solicitor in carrying out the work and charging accordingly.'

[10] With regard to the second, Judge Maddocks considered that 'para 13 does no more than create the liability to pay which, in turn, if the bill is a solicitor's bill, leads to the right to apply for taxation under s 71'. He noted that in *McKanan-Jones'* case Mummery J did not have the benefit of opposing submissions as the solicitor did not appear and was not represented. He, Judge Maddocks, was persuaded that Mummery J was wrong and that it was his duty not to follow that decision.

[11] The Law Society contends that the judge was wrong to conclude that any of the bills in question came within the description of 'a solicitor's bill' within the meaning of those words in s 70(1) of the 1974 Act, or, if they did, that the rights conferred by s 71 were exercisable in respect of a liability arising under para 13 of Sch 1. By his respondent's notice Mr Pine contends that the result for which the Law Society contends would constitute a breach of art 6(1) of the European Convention for the Protection of Human Rights and Fundamental Freedoms 1950 (as set out in Sch 1 to the Human Rights Act 1998) or art 1 of the First Protocol thereto and, in either case, also of art 14 of the convention. Consequently, as he submits, the court is obliged to read and give effect to para 13 of Sch 1 to the 1974 Act 'so far as it is possible to do so' in a sense contrary to that for which the Law Society contends (see s 3 of the 1998 Act). Thus there are three issues for our determination: (1) whether the bills submitted by Davis Blank Furniss to the Law Society are solicitor's bills for the purposes of s 70(1) of the 1974 Act; and if so (2) whether the rights conferred by s 71 are excluded by the terms of para 13 of Sch 1; and if so (3) whether s 3 of the 1998 Act applies and if so with what consequence. Before dealing with those issues I should refer briefly to the nature of an intervention and the powers conferred on the Law Society to intervene.

[12] The Law Society is entitled to intervene in a solicitor's practice in a wide variety of circumstances ranging from suspected dishonesty to incapacity by illness or accident. The purpose of such intervention is the protection of the public and the limitation, by prompt preventive action, of claims on the compensation fund regulated in accordance with s 36 of the 1974 Act. We were told that in any given year there are likely to be about 100 interventions at an average cost of £30,000, of which a partial recovery from the solicitor concerned is made in about 30% of the interventions. The costs of intervention on the grounds of suspected dishonesty, in so far as not recovered from the solicitor, are

a   payable out of the compensation fund (see para 7(e) of Sch 2 to the 1974 Act). Costs of an intervention on other grounds, so far as not recovered, are an expense falling on the Law Society's general funds.

[13] In the event of an intervention Pt II of Sch 1 to the 1974 Act confers extensive powers on the Law Society or a person nominated by the Society in relation to moneys held by or due to the solicitor (paras 5 and 6), documents in
b   the possession of the solicitor (para 9), the redirection of mail addressed to the solicitor (para 10), the appointment of a new trustee in place of the solicitor (para 11) and all other matters reasonably necessary for exercising those powers (para 16). The Schedule authorises applications to the court by the solicitor (paras 6(4) and 9(8)) and the Law Society (paras 5(1), 9(10), 10(1) and 11) for the specific relief which those paragraphs authorise, namely the withdrawal of an
c   unjustified intervention, an order to deliver documents, the approval of a payment, authority to dispose of or destroy documents and the appointment of a new trustee.

Are the bills solicitor's bills?

d   [14] By s 87(1) of the 1974 Act, subject to the context, '"costs" includes fees, charges, disbursements, expenses and remuneration'. Section 69 contains restrictions on the ability of a solicitor to recover costs due to him. First, the bill of such costs must satisfy the conditions imposed by s 69(2) as to verification and delivery of the bill. Second, s 69(1) precludes any action to recover costs due to a solicitor
e   before the expiration of one month from delivery of such a bill save in cases where there is reason to believe that the client is about to abscond. That is the context in which to consider the meaning of the words 'a solicitor's bill' in s 70(1).

[15] The relevant provisions are not new; they may be traced back to s 37 of the Solicitors Act 1843. There are a number of decided cases on what constitutes a solicitor's bill for the purposes of the earlier enactments. The first is *Allen v*
f   *Aldridge, Re Ward* (1844) 5 Beav 401, (1843) 49 ER 633. That case concerned the recovery of costs by a solicitor for acting as steward of a manor. The claim to tax such costs failed. Lord Langdale MR said:

g   'The statute does not authorise the taxation of every pecuniary demand or bill which may be made or delivered by a person who is a solicitor, for every species of employment in which he may happen to be engaged. The business contained in a taxable bill may be business of which no part was transacted in any Court of law or equity; but I am of opinion that it must be business connected with the profession of an attorney or solicitor—business in which the attorney or solicitor was employed, because he was an attorney or
h   solicitor, or in which he would not have been employed, if he had not been an attorney or solicitor, or if the relation of attorney or solicitor and client had not subsisted between him and his employer. It may perhaps, on some occasions, be questionable, whether the business contained in a solicitor's bill be or be not such as to make the bill taxable under the act; but in the
j   present case I do not see any reason to doubt. The relation of solicitor and client did not subsist between Mr. *Ward* and the petitioners, or any of them, or between Mr. *Ward* and any other person in relation to this matter. He was not employed by the petitioners because he was a solicitor, but because he was steward of the manor, and he might have been steward of the manor without being a solicitor. His bill is not as to any part of it a solicitor's bill; it is the bill of charges claimed to be payable to the steward of a manor, and

nothing else; and I am of opinion that the statute gives me no jurisdiction over it.' (See (1843) 5 Beav 401 at 405–406, (1843) 49 ER 633 at 635.)   a

[16] The later cases to which we were referred exemplify the application of that principle. In *Re Osborne* (1858) 25 Beav 353, (1858) 53 ER 671 solicitors sought to recover costs due to them for having acted as election agents. One bill specified the work done as canvassing, looking up voters and conveying them to the polling booth. The other bill related to work in their office and in committee rooms. Romilly MR considered the character in which the solicitors had been employed. He concluded that they were employed as solicitors because their—   b

'duties required [their] attendance ... at the committee rooms, to see, amongst other things, that nothing should be done contrary to law, or which would infringe any of the provisions in the numerous statutes relative to elections; to secure that everything should be done in a legal and proper manner, and to detect the defects of the opposite party. It was therefore necessary for [the solicitors] to exercise their legal knowledge in the best manner they could for the gentlemen by whom they were employed.' (See (1858) 25 Beav 353 at 359–360, (1858) 53 ER 671 at 674.)   c

      d

From this report and from another which counsel found ((1858) 27 LJ Ch 532) it seems likely that the orders related only to the second bill. By contrast in *Re Inderwick* (1883) 25 Ch D 279 a commission of 100 guineas for negotiating a loan of £2,000 was not so clearly subject to taxation as to warrant an ex parte order for taxation.   e

[17] For the Law Society it is submitted that Mr Heginbotham was employed by the Law Society to act as its agent in the exercise of the powers conferred by Pt II of Sch 1 to the 1974 Act, but was not retained to act as its solicitor either to give advice or to conduct proceedings. The Law Society accepts that it normally appoints a solicitor as its intervention agent because of his knowledge and skill as such. It contends that there is no obligation to appoint a solicitor and that, in many cases, an accountant or office manager would do.   f

[18] Counsel for Mr Pine accepts that the costs must be incurred in the capacity of a solicitor but submits that the test formulated by Lord Langdale MR in *Allen*'s case (1844) 5 Beav 401, (1843) 49 ER 633 has been satisfied. For my part I prefer the submissions of counsel for Mr Pine.   g

[19] The test as formulated by Lord Langdale MR, which both parties accept to be correct, requires the court to consider (a) whether the business was connected with the profession of a solicitor, (b) whether the solicitor was employed because he was a solicitor and (c) whether the solicitor would not have been appointed if he had not been a solicitor or the relation of solicitor and client had not subsisted between him and his employer. In my view the answers to all three questions is in the affirmative.   h

[20] The business which Mr Heginbotham and his firm undertook was the winding up of the solicitor's practice of Mr Pine by the orderly collection and distribution of his files and the proper collection, application and distribution of Mr Pine's and his clients' moneys. It is true that Mr Heginbotham was not retained for the purpose of advising the Law Society in relation to a specific legal problem or conducting any particular claim or defence on their behalf. But his knowledge and skills as a solicitor were used for the benefit of the Law Society in the intervention in Mr Pine's practice. The nature of the business connected with the profession of solicitor will change with time. It is not, in my view, correct to   j

a regard the profession of a solicitor as confined to advice on specific legal problems or the prosecution or defence of particular claims. It can hardly be doubted that acting as agent for the Law Society under Sch 1 to the 1974 Act is business connected with the profession of solicitor for the purpose of the test formulated by Lord Langdale MR.

[21] It is not suggested that the Law Society is obliged to appoint a solicitor.
b There may well be cases in which an accountant or office manager would be more appropriate. But that consideration highlights the importance of the decision of the Law Society to appoint a solicitor in this case. The form of resolution shows that the decision was to appoint a solicitor. The choice of Mr Heginbotham to be that solicitor came later. Thus it is clear that Mr Heginbotham was appointed because he was a solicitor and that he would not have been appointed if he had not been.
c [22] The bills submitted by Davis Blank Furniss were in the form appropriate to a bill for professional services as a solicitor. They were so described and bore the information required by art 6 of the 1994 order. I do not suggest that this is enough but it is consistent with all the other indications.

[23] For all these reasons I conclude that each of the five bills submitted by
d Davis Blank Furniss to the Law Society in connection with the intervention in Mr Pine's practice is 'a solicitor's bill' for the purposes of ss 69 to 71 of the 1974 Act.

Does para 13 of Sch 1 exclude s 71?

[24] Given my conclusion on the first issue the five bills fall within s 70.
e Accordingly it would have been open to the Law Society to apply for an order that they be taxed in accordance with the conditions prescribed by that section. It is contended on their behalf that if they choose not to and provided that they act in good faith and not irrationally then they are entitled, without more, to recover the costs of the intervention from the solicitor in whose practice they
f intervened. In other words the terms of para 13 of Sch 1 exclude from the ambit of s 71 solicitors bills for services rendered in an intervention.

[25] I have quoted the relevant provisions in [3] and [5], above. Counsel for the Law Society emphasises that para 13 both creates a statutory debt and provides for the mechanism by which it is recoverable by the creditor. He stresses four aspects of that paragraph. First, the costs to which para 13 applies
g are those incurred by the Society for the purposes of the Schedule not those specified in the bills. Second, the liability arises under para 13 because the costs have been so incurred by the Society, not because of any retainer between the Society and Mr Heginbotham. Third, para 13 imposes a statutory duty to pay in contrast to the contractual duty to which s 71 would apply. Fourth, the liability
h is recoverable as a debt without further qualification. It is suggested that it would be inconsistent with the opening words of para 13, providing expressly for a potential exception, to imply another one in respect of rights arising under s 71. Counsel contended that the judge was wrong when, in the passage I have quoted in [10], above, he failed to recognise that para 13 also provided for a mechanism
j by which the liability might be enforced.

[26] Counsel for Mr Pine challenged these propositions. He contended that all that paragraph did was to create a liability by the mechanism of a debt. The potential exceptions for which the opening words of para 13 provide are necessary because the circumstances to which they apply will arise under the terms of the Schedule. He submitted that no such potential exception is necessary in relation to s 71 which is applicable to all solicitors' bills. In other words, as the

latter right does not arise under the Schedule so no provision in the Schedule is needed. He submitted that the public law rights were inadequate protection because the Law Society had neither the information nor the incentive to challenge the amount of the bills.

[27] I prefer the submissions of counsel for Mr Pine. Section 71 is of general application. It recognises that the person chargeable with the bill may not be ultimately liable to pay the costs thereby claimed. Its evident purpose is to confer on one with a secondary liability for those costs a right comparable to that possessed by the person primarily liable. Given that, for the reasons I have already explained, the Law Society is entitled to have the bills taxed under s 70 Parliament is unlikely to have intended that there should be degrees of secondary liability, some of which are excluded from the ambit of s 71.

[28] It is true that Sch 1 to the 1974 Act provides a code for an intervention. Provision is therein made for the costs of applications to the court sanctioned by that code. To preserve the primacy of the court's orders some such provision as that contained in the opening words of para 13 is needed. But no such provision is needed in respect of a general right created outside that code. In the case of such a right clear words or an obvious implication are needed to exclude, not create, it.

[29] I do not consider that any of the other factors relied on by counsel for the Law Society, either alone or together, are sufficient to exclude that right. First, if the purpose of the provision is to create a secondary liability it is natural to do so by reference to the primary liability. This is what the reference to 'costs incurred by the Society' achieves by identifying the subject matter of the provision. There is no reason to think that the primary liability was so identified for the purpose of excluding a defence otherwise available to the person secondarily liable.

[30] Second the requirement in para 13 that the costs so incurred 'shall be paid by the Solicitor' creates the secondary liability. But if the paragraph had stopped there it would have left open the question of whether the obligation was owed to the Society alone or to the Society or, in the alternative, the person to whom the Society had incurred the liability. In those circumstances there is good reason to conclude with the stipulation that the costs incurred are recoverable by the Society. I see no reason why this requirement should be regarded as excluding the right conferred by s 71.

[31] Finally there is the reference to the costs being recoverable 'as a debt owing to the Society'. This specifies the legal process for recovery and may be contrasted with other statutory formulae of 'recoverable as damages' or 'recoverable as a penalty'. But the fact that money is recoverable as a debt is not inconsistent with a reduction in the amount of the claim. Thus a claim for remuneration for services rendered or goods supplied at the defendant's request is a claim in debt notwithstanding that the defendant is entitled to defend it on the ground that the sum claimed is excessive (see *Chitty on Contracts* (28th edn, 1999) vol 1, pp 1464–1465 (para 30–005)). It is for this reason that I respectfully disagree with the view of Mummery J in *Law Society v McKanan-Jones* (14 July 1992, unreported) which I have quoted in [7], above.

[32] I should also refer to the practical considerations urged on us by counsel for the Law Society. As he pointed out the powers of intervention are conferred on and exercised by the Law Society in the public interest. The Law Society is amenable to the normal public law remedies if, having intervened into a solicitor's practice, it seeks to recover costs from the solicitor in bad faith, irrationally or otherwise than in exercise of those powers. Counsel pointed out that

a the Law Society is also concerned to keep costs down. He submitted that the Law Society should not, in addition, be vexed by applications for taxation under s 71 made by solicitors who seek to postpone liability or impede the Law Society in the prompt exercise of its powers and cannot pay the costs when they lose.

[33] I do not think that these considerations, which are of real and justified concern to the Law Society, should be allowed to affect the question of *b* construction. Unless the taxation is one to which the solicitor is entitled as of right, because the circumstances fall within s 70(1) as applied by s 71, the court will have a discretion whether and if so on what terms to order the taxation of the bill, s 70(2). In exercising that discretion the court will, no doubt, consider whether the applicant has made out a prima facie case for a reduction in the amount of the bill. Even if he has an order for taxation may be made on terms that all or a substantial *c* part of the sum claimed is paid to the Law Society or into court. Similarly in cases falling within s 70(3), but not s 70(2), the court is entitled to impose a condition requiring the solicitor into whose practice the Law Society has intervened to give security for the costs of the taxation. In my view these safeguards are sufficient to protect the Law Society and the courts from unmeritorious applications under s 71.

d [34] For all these reasons I conclude that the provisions of para 13 do not override or exclude the right conferred by s 71. In those circumstances I would dismiss this appeal. I should add that it was agreed between counsel for the parties that the questions whether the application of Mr Pine for an order for taxation of costs is precluded by s 70(4) and whether the discretion conferred by s 70(2) and (3), in each case as imported into s 71, should be exercised in favour of Mr Pine should *e* not be determined at this stage. Accordingly those issues will arise on the further hearing of Mr Pine's application.

Does s 3 of the 1998 Act apply and if so with what result?

[35] In the light of my conclusions the short answer to this question is that s 3 of *f* the 1998 Act does not apply because Mr Pine is, in my view, entitled to the rights for which he contends. It follows that there could have been no breach of arts 6(1) or 14 of the convention or of art 1 of the First Protocol. I see no useful purpose to be served by addressing these questions on the converse assumption.

Conclusion

g [36] For all these reasons I would dismiss this appeal.

ROBERT WALKER LJ.
[37] I agree.

h **RIX LJ.**
[38] I also agree.

Appeal dismissed.

Kate O'Hanlon   Barrister.

Runa Begum v Tower Hamlets London Borough Council

[2002] EWCA Civ 239

COURT OF APPEAL, CIVIL DIVISION

LORD WOOLF CJ, LAWS AND DYSON LJJ

13 FEBRUARY, 6 MARCH 2002

Housing – Homeless person – Duty of housing authority to provide accommodation – Appeals procedure – Whether decision of local authority reviewing officer constituting a determination of claimant's 'civil rights' – Whether local authority reviewing officer constituting 'independent and impartial tribunal' – Whether county court on appeal from reviewing officer's decision possessing 'full jurisdiction' so as to guarantee compliance with right to fair hearing – Housing Act 1996, ss 202, 204 – Human Rights Act 1998, Sch 1, Pt I, art 6(1).

Human rights – Right to a fair hearing – Impartial and independent tribunal – Proper approach to determining whether court having 'full jurisdiction' for purposes of ensuring compliance with right to fair hearing – Human Rights Act 1998, Sch 1, Pt I, art 6(1).

The claimant was a homeless person in respect of whom the defendant local housing authority accepted that it owed the full housing duty provided for in s 193(2) of the Housing Act 1996. She was given temporary accommodation, and was subsequently offered permanent accommodation. The claimant viewed the accommodation but turned it down, claiming that it was in a drug-addicted and racist area, that she had been attacked by two youths shortly after viewing the property, that she was worried for her two young children and that her estranged husband frequently visited the property. An officer of the authority conducted, under s 202[a] of the 1996 Act, an internal review of the decision to offer that accommodation to the claimant. The reviewing officer rejected or expressed doubts about the claimant's factual allegations, and concluded that the accommodation was suitable for the claimant and her household. The claimant appealed against that decision to the county court under s 204(1)[b] of the Act. The judge held that, on what was effectively a judicial review, he could not determine whether the reviewing officer's findings had been affected by her connection with the authority; that the authority should have at least considered whether to refer the matter to a wholly independent tribunal; and that their failure to do so meant that the appeal had to succeed because the procedure adopted contravened the claimant's right to a fair hearing in the determination of her 'civil rights' before an 'independent and impartial tribunal' under art 6(1)[c] of the European Convention for the Protection of Human Rights and Fundamental Freedoms 1950 (as set out in Sch 1 to the Human Rights Act 1998). On the authority's appeal, the Court of Appeal was required to determine (i) whether the reviewing officer's decision under s 202 of the 1996 Act was a determination of

---

a Section 202, so far as material, is set out at [5], below
b Section 204, so far as material, is set out at [5], below
c Article 6(1) is set out at [1], below

a the claimant's 'civil rights' within the meaning of art 6(1) of the convention; (ii) if so, whether the reviewing officer constituted an 'independent and impartial tribunal' for the purposes of art 6(1); and (iii) if not, whether the county court, on an appeal under s 204 of the 1996 Act, possessed 'full jurisdiction' so as to guarantee compliance with art 6(1), given that s 204 only enabled the county court to examine questions of law.

b **Held** – (1) A determination under s 202 of the 1996 Act engaged a homeless person's 'civil rights' for the purposes of art 6(1) of the convention. Such a determination led to the grant or withholding of a tenancy. Moreover, the subject matter of the statutory scheme, dealing with the urgent provision of living accommodation for persons who would often be gravely disadvantaged, so c touched their well-being that as a matter of the domestic law of human rights the art 6(1) discipline should be applied to it. It followed in the instant case that the reviewing officer's decision under s 202 constituted a determination of the claimant's 'civil rights' within the meaning of art 6(1) (see [25], [26], [47], [48], below); dicta of Stanley Burnton J in *R (on the application of Husain) v Asylum* d *Support Adjudicator* [2001] All ER (D) 107 (Oct) at [26], [27] approved.

(2) The reviewing officer did not constitute an 'independent and impartial tribunal' for the purposes of art 6(1) of the convention. If the officer's role under s 202 were looked at in isolation, there were not sufficient objective guarantees, visible to the outside world, to clothe it with the qualities of independence and impartiality required by art 6(1). Moreover, the reviewing officer sat in private, e and a public hearing was one of the conditions of art 6(1) (see [30], [47], [48], below).

(3) Section 204 of the 1996 Act conferred 'full jurisdiction' on the county court, and satisfied the requirements of the developing domestic law of human rights. Where, in a setting or regime created by Act of Parliament, a first instance f decision-maker, whose determination touched a citizen's civil rights, did not meet the standards imposed by art 6(1), there would generally be access to a court by way of review or appeal against the first decision, either provided by the statute itself or by way of judicial review. If the Act gave a right of appeal to a court on the merits, factual as well as legal, art 6 was plainly complied with, since on any view such a court possessed 'full jurisdiction'. Where, however, the right g of appeal was on a question of law only, equivalent to judicial review, the extent to which the first instance process might be relied on to produce fair and reasonable decisions was plainly an important element. It was not, however, to be viewed in isolation. The matter could only be judged by an examination of the statutory scheme as a whole. Where the scheme's subject matter generally h or systematically involved the resolution of primary fact, the court would incline to look for procedures akin to the conventional mechanisms for finding facts: rights of cross-examination, access to documents, a strictly independent decision-maker. To the extent that procedures of that kind were not given by the first instance process, the court would look to see how far they were given by the j appeal or review; and the judicial review jurisdiction (or its equivalent in the shape of a statutory appeal on law) might not suffice. Where, however, the subject matter of the scheme generally or systematically required the application of judgment or the exercise of discretion, especially if it involved the weighing of policy issues and regard being had to the interests of others who were not before the decision-maker, the court would, for the purposes of art 6, incline to be satisfied with a form of inquisition at first instance in which the decision-maker

was more of an expert than a judge, and the second instance appeal was in the
nature of a judicial review. Between those paradigms, there would lie instances   a
sharing in different degrees characteristics of each, and in judging a particular
scheme the court would, without compromising its duty to vindicate convention
rights, pay a degree of respect on democratic grounds to Parliament as the
scheme's author. In the instant case, there were sharp issues of primary fact
falling for determination, but that was not a necessary feature of a s 202 review,   b
and certainly not a systematic one. The compliance of the statutory scheme with
art 6(1) could not vary case by case, according to the degree of factual dispute
arising. Judged as a whole, the statutory scheme lay towards that end of the
spectrum where judgment and discretion, rather than fact-finding, played the
predominant part. Moreover, the judge had ample power under s 204 to decide   c
whether the review officer's decision was one that was properly available to her
on the evidence. Accordingly, the appeal would be allowed (see [39], [40],
[43]–[48], below); R (on the application of Alconbury Developments Ltd) v Secretary of
State for the Environment, Transport and the Regions [2001] 2 All ER 929 and R (on the
application of McLellan) v Bracknell Forest BC, Reigate and Banstead BC v Benfield   d
[2002] 1 All ER 899 applied; dicta of Brooke, Hale LJJ and David Steel J in Adan v
Newham London BC [2002] 1 All ER 931 at [43], [47], [80], [94] disapproved.

Notes

For the right to a fair hearing before an independent and impartial tribunal, see
8(2) Halsbury's Laws (4th edn reissue) paras 134, 140, and for reviews of a housing   e
authority's decision and appeals to the county court on a point of law from
a reviewing officer's decision, see 22 Halsbury's Laws (4th edn reissue)
paras 263–264.

For the Housing Act 1996, ss 202, 204, see 21 Halsbury's Statutes (4th edn) (1997
reissue) 910, 911.   f

For the Human Rights Act 1998, Sch 1, Pt 1, art 6, see 7 Halsbury's Statutes (4th
edn) (1999 reissue) 523.

Cases referred to in judgments

Adan v Newham London BC [2001] EWCA Civ 1916, [2002] 1 All ER 931.   g

Albert v Belgium (1983) 5 EHRR 533, [1983] ECHR 7299/75, ECt HR.

Associated Provincial Picture Houses Ltd v Wednesbury Corp [1947] 2 All ER 680,
[1948] 1 KB 223, CA.

Awua v Brent London BC [1995] 3 All ER 493, [1996] AC 55, [1995] 3 WLR 215, HL.   h

Begum v Tower Hamlets London BC [2000] 1 WLR 306, CA.

Bryan v UK (1996) 21 EHRR 342, [1995] ECHR 19178/91, ECt HR.

Cocks v Thanet DC [1982] 3 All ER 1135, [1983] 2 AC 286, [1982] 3 WLR 1121, HL.

Findlay v UK (1997) 24 EHRR 221, [1997] ECHR 22107/93, ECt HR.

Hague v Deputy Governor of Parkhurst Prison, Weldon v Home Office [1991] 3 All ER   j
733, [1992] 1 AC 58, [1991] 3 WLR 388, HL.

König v Germany (1980) 2 EHRR 170, [1978] ECHR 6232/73, ECt HR.

O'Rourke v Camden London BC [1997] 3 All ER 23, [1998] AC 188, [1997] 3 WLR 86,
HL; rvsg (1996) 28 HLR 600, CA.

Pudas v Sweden (1988) 10 EHRR 380, [1987] ECHR 10426/83, ECt HR.

a   *Puhlhofer v Hillingdon London BC* [1986] 1 All ER 467, [1986] AC 484, [1986] 2 WLR
     259, HL.

     *R (on the application of Alconbury Developments Ltd) v Secretary of State for the
     Environment, Transport and the Regions* [2001] UKHL 23, [2001] 2 All ER 929,
     [2001] 2 WLR 1389.

     R (on the application of the Personal Representatives of Beeson) v Dorset CC [2001]
b   EWHC Admin 986, [2002] HRLR 368.

     R (on the application of Bewry) v Norwich City Council [2001] EWHC Admin 657,
     [2002] HRLR 21.

     R (on the application of Husain) v Asylum Support Adjudicator [2001] EWHC Admin
     852, [2001] All ER (D) 107 (Oct).

c   *R (on the application of Kathro) v Rhondda Cynon Taff County BC* [2001] EWHC
     Admin 527, [2001] 4 PLR 83.

     *R (on the application of McLellan) v Bracknell Forest BC, Reigate and Banstead BC v
     Benfield* [2001] EWCA Civ 1510, [2002] 1 All ER 899.

d   *R v A* [2001] UKHL 25, [2001] 3 All ER 1, [2002] 1 AC 45, [2001] 2 WLR 1546.

     R v Camden London BC, ex p Pereira (1999) 31 HLR 317, CA.

     R v Kensington and Chelsea London BC, ex p Kihara (1996) 29 HLR 147, CA.

     Salesi v Italy (1998) 26 EHRR 187, [1993] ECHR 13023/87, ECt HR.

     Zumtobel v Austria (1993) 17 EHRR 116, [1993] ECHR 12235/86, ECt HR.

e   **Cases also cited or referred to in skeleton arguments**

     Garlick v Oldham Metropolitan BC [1993] 2 All ER 65; sub nom *R v Oldham
     Metropolitan BC, ex p Garlick, R v Bexley London BC, ex p Bentun, R v Tower
     Hamlets London BC, ex p Begum* [1993] AC 509, HL.

f   *Kaplan v UK* (1980) 4 EHRR 64, E Com HR.

     Medicaments and Related Classes of Goods (No 2), Re [2001] 1 WLR 700, CA.

     Sheffield City Council v Smart, Central Housing Co Ltd v Wilson [2002] EWCA Civ 4,
     [2002] All ER (D) 226 (Jan).

     *X (minors) v Bedfordshire CC, M (a minor) v Newham London BC, E (a minor) v
g   Dorset CC* [1995] 3 All ER 353, [1995] 2 AC 633, HL.

     Appeal

     Tower Hamlets London Borough Council appealed with permission of
     Schiemann LJ granted on 10 January 2002 from the decision of Judge Roberts at
h   Bow County Court on 21 December 2001 allowing an appeal, under s 204(1) of
     the Housing Act 1996, by the respondent, Runa Begum, from the determination,
     communicated by letter dated 27 July 2001, of an officer of the appellant, on a
     review under s 202 of the 1996 Act, that accommodation offered by the appellant
     to the respondent was suitable for her and her family. The facts are set out in the
j   judgment of Laws LJ.

     Ashley Underwood QC and *Kelvin Rutledge* (instructed by *Helen Sidwell*) for the
     appellant.

     Paul Morgan QC and *Steven Woolf* (instructed by *Maxim*) for the respondent.

                                                                    Cur adv vult

6 March 2002. The following judgments were delivered.

a

LAWS LJ (giving the first judgment at the invitation of Lord Woolf CJ).

Introductory

[1] As is well known, art 6(1) of the European Convention for the Protection of Human Rights and Fundamental Freedoms 1950 (as set out in Sch 1 to the *b* Human Rights Act 1998) (ECHR) provides in part:

'In the determination of his civil rights and obligations or of any criminal charge against him, everyone is entitled to a fair and public hearing within a reasonable time by an independent and impartial tribunal established by law.' *c*

This appeal has required the court to look again at the scope of the expression 'civil rights' in the context of the homeless persons legislation. In particular, we have had to examine the impact of the statutory setting in which a civil right is said to arise upon the nature and quality of independent adjudication required to satisfy art 6(1). *d*

[2] The appeal is brought against the decision of Judge Roberts given in the Bow County Court on 21 December 2001, when he allowed the respondent's appeal under s 204(1) of the Housing Act 1996 (HA) against the determination of Mrs Hayes, an officer of the appellant local authority, to the effect that certain premises in Tower Hamlets were suitable for the appellant and her family, and that it would have been reasonable for her to accept that accommodation. *e* Permission to appeal was granted by Schiemann LJ on 10 January 2002.

[3] At the invitation of the respondent and without objection from the appellant local authority the judge determined the appeal before him upon a preliminary issue, namely whether the procedure for internal review of a local authority's decision relating to its homelessness functions, provided for by HA *f* s 202, is compliant with ECHR art 6(1). The judge held that on facts such as those of the present case it was not, considering he was bound to arrive at that conclusion in light of what had been said in this court only seven days before in *Adan v Newham London BC* [2001] EWCA Civ 1916, [2002] 1 All ER 931.

The legislation *g*

[4] I have already set out ECHR art 6(1). I need not cite any of the provisions of the Human Rights Act 1998 (HRA). It is obvious that the local authority respondent is a 'public authority' within HRA s 6(3). Accordingly by HRA s 6(1) it may not 'act in a way which is incompatible with a Convention right'. Thus its procedures must comply with the convention standards so far as they touch *h* convention rights; and it is the court's duty, also by s 6(1), to see that they do so.

[5] The homeless persons legislation is now contained in HA Pt VII. I should set out these following provisions:

'**175.**—(1) A person is homeless if he has no accommodation available for *j* his occupation, in the United Kingdom or elsewhere ...

(2) A person is also homeless if he has accommodation but—(a) he cannot secure entry to it ...

(3) A person shall not be treated as having accommodation unless it is accommodation which it would be reasonable for him to continue to occupy ...

177. ... (2) In determining whether it would be, or would have been, reasonable for a person to continue to occupy accommodation, regard may be had to the general circumstances prevailing in relation to housing in the district of the local housing authority to whom he has applied for accommodation or for assistance in obtaining accommodation ...

179.—(1) Every local housing authority shall secure that advice and information about homelessness, and the prevention of homelessness, is available free of charge to any person in their district ...

182.—(1) In the exercise of their functions relating to homelessness and the prevention of homelessness, a local housing authority or social services authority shall have regard to such guidance as may from time to time be given by the Secretary of State ...

184.—(1) If the local housing authority have reason to believe that an applicant may be homeless or threatened with homelessness, they shall make such inquiries as are necessary to satisfy themselves—(a) whether he is eligible for assistance, and (b) if so, whether any duty, and if so what duty, is owed to him under the following provisions of this Part.

(2) They may also make inquiries whether he has a local connection with the district of another local housing authority in England, Wales or Scotland.

(3) On completing their inquiries the authority shall notify the applicant of their decision and, so far as any issue is decided against his interests, inform him of the reasons for their decision ...

188.—(1) If the local housing authority have reason to believe that an applicant may be homeless, eligible for assistance and have a priority need, they shall secure that accommodation is available for his occupation pending a decision as to the duty (if any) owed to him under the following provisions of this Part ...

189.—(1) The following have a priority need for accommodation—(a) a pregnant woman or a person with whom she resides or might reasonably be expected to reside; (b) a person with whom dependent children reside or might reasonably be expected to reside; (c) a person who is vulnerable as a result of old age, mental illness or handicap or physical disability or other special reason, or with whom such a person resides or might reasonably be expected to reside; (d) a person who is homeless or threatened with homelessness as a result of an emergency such as flood, fire or other disaster ...

191.—(1) A person becomes homeless intentionally if he deliberately does or fails to do anything in consequence of which he ceases to occupy accommodation which is available for his occupation and which it would have been reasonable for him to continue to occupy ...

193.—(1) This section applies where the local housing authority are satisfied that an applicant is homeless, eligible for assistance and has a priority need, and are not satisfied that he became homeless intentionally. This section has effect subject to section 197 (duty where other suitable accommodation available).

(2) Unless the authority refer the application to another local housing authority (see section 198), they shall secure that accommodation is available for occupation by the applicant ...

(5) The local housing authority shall cease to be subject to the duty under this section if the applicant, having been informed by the authority of the possible consequence of refusal, refuses an offer of accommodation which

the authority are satisfied is suitable for him and the authority notify him that they regard themselves as having discharged their duty under this section ...

197.—(1) This section applies if the local housing authority would be under a duty under this Part—(a) to secure that accommodation is available for occupation by an applicant, or (b) to secure that accommodation does not cease to be available for his occupation, but are satisfied that other suitable accommodation is available for occupation by him in their district.

(2) In that case, their duty is to provide the applicant with such advice and assistance as the authority consider is reasonably required to enable him to secure such accommodation ...

198.—(1) If the local housing authority would be subject to the duty under section 193 (accommodation for those with priority need who are not homeless intentionally) but consider that the conditions are met for referral of the case to another local housing authority, they may notify that other authority of their opinion. The authority need not consider under section 197 whether other suitable accommodation is available before proceeding under this section.

(2) The conditions for referral of the case to another authority are met if—(a) neither the applicant nor any person who might reasonably be expected to reside with him has a local connection with the district of the authority to whom his application was made, (b) the applicant or person who might reasonably be expected to reside with him has a local connection with the district of that other authority, and (c) neither the applicant nor any person who might reasonably be expected to reside with him will run the risk of domestic violence in that other district ...

202.—(1) An applicant has the right to request a review of ... (b) any decision of a local housing authority as to what duty (if any) is owed to him under sections 190 to 193 and 195 to 197 (duties to persons found to be homeless or threatened with homelessness) ... (f) any decision of a local housing authority as to the suitability of accommodation offered to him in discharge of their duty under any of the provisions mentioned in paragraph (b) ...

(4) On a request being duly made to them, the authority or authorities concerned shall review their decision.

203.—(1) The Secretary of State may make provision by regulations as to the procedure to be followed in connection with a review under section 202. Nothing in the following provisions affects the generality of this power.

(2) Provision may be made by regulations—(a) requiring the decision on review to be made by a person of appropriate seniority who was not involved in the original decision, and (b) as to the circumstances in which the applicant is entitled to an oral hearing, and whether and by whom he may be represented at such a hearing.

(3) The authority, or as the case may be either of the authorities, concerned shall notify the applicant of the decision on the review.

(4) If the decision is—(a) to confirm the original decision on any issue against the interests of the applicant, or (b) to confirm a previous decision—(i) to notify another authority under section 198 (referral of cases), or (ii) that the conditions are met for the referral of his case, they shall also notify him of the reasons for the decision.

a

(5) In any case they shall inform the applicant of his right to appeal to a county court on a point of law, and of the period within which such an appeal must be made (see section 204) ...

(8) Notice required to be given to a person under this section shall be given in writing ...

b

204.—(1) If an applicant who has requested a review under section 202—(a) is dissatisfied with the decision on the review, or (b) is not notified of the decision on the review within the time prescribed under section 203, he may appeal to the county court on any point of law arising from the decision or, as the case may be, the original decision ...

(3) On appeal the court may make such order confirming, quashing or varying the decision as it thinks fit ...

c

206.—(1) A local housing authority may discharge their housing functions under this Part only in the following ways—(a) by securing that suitable accommodation provided by them is available, (b) by securing that he obtains suitable accommodation from some other person, or (c) by giving him such advice and assistance as will secure that suitable accommodation is

d

available from some other person.

(2) A local housing authority may require a person in relation to whom they are discharging such functions—(a) to pay such reasonable charges as they may determine in respect of accommodation which they secure for his occupation (either by making it available themselves or otherwise), or (b) to pay such reasonable amount as they may determine in respect of sums

e

payable by them for accommodation made available by another person.'

[6] The Secretary of State has made regulations under s 203. Those current at the times material to this case are the Allocation of Housing and Homelessness (Review Procedures) Regulations 1999, SI 1999/71. (The judge below was

f

mistakenly referred to earlier regulations made in 1996, but nothing turns on that.) I should set out these following provisions:

'2. Where the decision of the authority on a review of an original decision made by an officer of the authority is also to be made by an officer, that officer shall be someone who was not involved in the original decision and

g

who is senior to the officer who made the original decision ...

6. ... (2) ... the authority to whom a request for a review under section 202 has been made shall—(a) notify the applicant that he, or someone acting on his behalf, may make representations in writing to the authority in connection with the review; and (b) if they have not already done so, notify the applicant of the procedure to be followed in connection with the review

h

...

8.—(1) The reviewer shall, subject to compliance with the provisions of regulation 9, consider—(a) any representations made under regulation 6 ... (b) any representations made under paragraph (2) below.

j

(2) If the reviewer considers that there is a deficiency or irregularity in the original decision, or in the manner in which it was made, but is minded nonetheless to make a decision which is against the interests of the applicant on one or more issues, the reviewer shall notify the applicant—(a) that the reviewer is so minded and the reasons why; and (b) that the applicant, or someone acting on his behalf, may make representations to the reviewer orally or in writing or both orally and in writing.'

Regulation 9 makes provision for the notification of the review decision within stipulated time limits.

[7] I should also refer to art 3 of the Local Authorities (Contracting Out of Allocation of Housing and Homelessness Functions) Order 1996, SI 1996/3205, which provides:

'Any function of an authority which is conferred by or under Part VII of the Act (homelessness) ... may be exercised by, or by employees of, such person (if any) as may be authorised in that behalf by the authority whose function it is.'

The facts

[8] The respondent is a homeless person. On 11 April 2000 the appellant notified her that it had accepted that it owed her the full housing duty as provided for in HA s 193(2). She was given temporary accommodation, of which she took a non-secure tenancy on 15 May 2000. On 6 July 2001 she was offered permanent accommodation in the shape of a two-bedroom third floor flat at 19 Balfron Towers, St Leonard's Road, London E14. The letter stated:

'If you have been accepted as homeless under section 184 of the Housing Act 1996 and you unreasonably refuse this offer, responsibility will be discharged by the homelessness service and you will be required to leave any accommodation provided by the council under Part VII of the Housing Act.'

[9] The respondent viewed the accommodation, but turned it down. She wrote to explain why. She said 'this place is [a] drug addicted area'. She said she was worried for her two young children. She claimed the area was racist, and that she had been attacked by two youths shortly after viewing the property. Lastly she said that her estranged husband frequently visited the building.

[10] So it was that Mrs Hayes came to conduct an internal review, under HA s 202, of the appellant's offer of the flat at 19 Balfron Towers. She gave her decision by letter of 27 July 2001. This was the subject of the appeal to the county court. Mrs Hayes said that she was satisfied that the offered accommodation was suitable for the respondent and her household. I will set out the bulk of the reasons given, as follows:

'2. Following receipt of your representations, information was requested from the estate office regarding your allegation that a drug problem exists at the above block, and also your allegation that the area suffers from racial problems. The estate officer advises that it has been reported that there are no drug problems at the block, and that this block is served by a concierge facility and is secure in that the entry phone system is extended to cover each individual landing, so that movement through the block is restricted, allowing only unauthorised access to particular areas. The estate officer also confirmed that there have not been any major racial incidents at the block in question, your allegations therefore appear unfounded and unsubstantiated.
3. Your letter of 12 July 2001 gives details of an alleged attack by two youths on yourself, which you later reported to the police. However, I note that there are discrepancies in the details provided by yourself in respect of this incident, in that your letter advises that your purse was taken, but during an interview with one of our officers, you advised that your purse was not taken, indeed you used money from your purse in order to return to your interim accommodation. Information was sought from the police in respect

a of the attack reported by yourself in order that further investigations could be made, however we were informed that attempts have been made to contact yourself, but thus far you have remained rather illusive [sic] to the enquiries being made by the police, and I am advised that there were also discrepancies in the original report you made to them. 4. You advised that your husband frequently visits friends at Balfron Towers, however, you are *b* unable to provide specific names and addresses of those friends in order to corroborate your suggestions. Notwithstanding this you have advised that you saw your husband on the day of the viewing and state that you do not wish to see him again. You have given no reason for this other than that you are no longer on friendly terms with him. I note from your application file my rehousing officer phoned your home on 13 July 2001 to discuss your *c* refusal of the offered tenancy, and a gentleman answered who stated that he was your husband and that you had taken your children to the hospital. When asked about this later in the day when you returned her call, firstly you advised that there was nobody in your house, when asked again about who the gentleman was you failed to respond. On balance I consider it strange *d* that a supposedly identified gentleman would answer your telephone whilst you are out, and you are unable to confirm who this person was. I consider that the property offered is both suitable for you and your children in that the physical attributes are in accordance with the council's allocation criteria, and I further consider that it is reasonable to expect yourself and your household to occupy the property offered as I consider that the area in which *e* Balfron Towers is located is no different to any other area within the London Borough of Tower Hamlets. You seem to suggest that you are on bad terms with your husband, and perhaps this would render the property unsuitable for you given an apparent frequency of which he is supposed to visit friends there, however you also report that on the day you met him there was no *f* incident or unpleasantness. Further, you are unable to substantiate this claim by providing details of his friends, and I do not accept that frequent visits to the block by your husband renders the property offered unsuitable.'

[11] The respondent's appeal against this decision came as I have said before Judge Roberts sitting at the Bow County Court. The judge said:

g 'The preliminary point which the appellant [respondent in this court] wished to argue and which the court has considered put very simply is this. It is said in this case that there were here disputed issues of fact which were material to the decision of the council and that accordingly the local authority could not, if the procedure was to be compatible with art 6(1) of *h* the European Convention for the Protection of Human Rights and Fundamental Freedoms 1950, have conducted a final review by its own officer, but was bound to at least have given consideration to using its powers to direct a review by an independent body [sc under art 3 of the 1996 order].'

j Having been referred to *Adan v Newham London BC* [2002] 1 All ER 931, and also to the decision of Richards J in *R (on the application of the Personal Representatives of Beeson) v Dorset CC* [2001] EWHC Admin 986, [2002] HRLR 368, he concluded:

'... the fact of the matter is that I cannot, on what is effectively a judicial review, determine whether or not those findings [sc of Mrs Hayes] have been affected by her connection with one of the parties, namely the local authority in this case. It therefore follows, in my judgment, that the failure on the part of the local authority either to refer this matter to a wholly independent tribunal for review ... or at least to give consideration to doing so, is fatal to their opposition to this appeal. As a matter of law they should have considered at least referring it to an independent tribunal and their failure to do so means that the appellant, in my judgment, must succeed on this appeal because the procedure adopted by the local authority is in contravention of art 6 of the European Convention on Human Rights.'

The issues

[12] Counsel are agreed that these three following issues arise. (1) Was Mrs Hayes' decision of 27 July 2001 taken under HA s 202 a determination of the respondent's 'civil rights' within the meaning of ECHR art 6(1)? (2) If so, did Mrs Hayes constitute an 'independent and impartial tribunal' for the purposes of art 6(1)? (3) If not, did the county court, on appeal to it under HA s 204, possess 'full jurisdiction' (I shall explain the quotation) so as to guarantee compliance with art 6(1)?

[13] Before I address these issues individually, there are some general observations I should make. By way of introduction, I should indicate at this stage one aspect of the case which is important though uncontentious. It is that the substance of the county court's jurisdiction under HA s 204, in the limited field to which it relates, is in effect the same as that of the High Court in judicial review save as regards the forms of relief that may be granted. This court so held in *Begum v Tower Hamlets London BC* [2000] 1 WLR 306.

[14] The first consideration to which I draw attention is this. By the law of England the quality of independent adjudication to which the individual is entitled at the hands of our courts, in any case where a public authority arrives at a decision of which (possessing a sufficient interest) he seeks to complain in court proceedings, is by no means dependent upon the authority's decision being categorised in terms of the individual's 'civil rights and obligations'. If he has a good judicial review case, for the purposes of the standards of judicial determination which will apply it is a matter of indifference whether or not it might fall to be so categorised.

[15] Secondly, it is of course true that the judicial review procedure is not generally apt for the adjudication of factual disputes. That is in contrast to the procedure for private law claims, which is precisely suited to that very task. The reason is that judicial review is primarily directed (there are exceptions) to the legality of decisions as regards which it is the duty or province of a body other than the court to find the necessary facts; whereas in private law claims it is generally the court's duty—more often than not, its most important duty—to ascertain the facts. The distinctions between these procedures are founded, simply, on what is in practice required for the just and efficient judicial disposal of different forms of legal dispute. There is no necessary match between on the one hand the contrast of private and public law forms of process in our domestic system, and on the other the contrast for ECHR art 6 purposes of forms of process which involve 'civil rights and obligations' with others which do not.

[16] Having all these considerations in mind, I shall with great respect be more interested in what procedures are needed to arrive at fair resolutions of the real issues arising, having regard to the nature of the scheme that Parliament has put in place in HA Pt VII, than in the categorisation of any stage of the process as touching the affected person's 'civil rights'.

a   **[17]** I acknowledge, however, that the exercise of categorisation cannot be ignored. The terms of art 6 require it to be undertaken, and I shall proceed to deal with it. But I should say that I think it important to have in mind that the court's task under the HRA, in this context as in many others, is not simply to add on the Strasbourg learning to the corpus of English law, as if it were a compulsory adjunct taken from an alien source, but to develop a municipal law of human b   rights by the incremental method of the common law, case by case, taking account of the Strasbourg jurisprudence as HRA s 2 enjoins us to do.

The first question: HA s 202 and 'civil rights'

[18] In *Adan*'s case, to which I have already referred, it was conceded that 'the procedure under Pt VII of the 1996 Act involved the determination of Mrs Adan's c   civil rights within the meaning of art 6(1) of the convention' (see [2002] 1 All ER 931 at [9], per Brooke LJ). However no such concession is made before us by Mr Underwood QC for the appellant. Mr Morgan QC for the respondent, plainly rightly, does not suggest that we are bound by the court's acceptance of the concession in *Adan*'s case. The issue is open to be determined afresh, and we have d   had the advantage of substantive argument on the point.

[19] It is convenient to start with what Lord Hoffmann said in *R (on the application of Alconbury Developments Ltd) v Secretary of State for the Environment, Transport and the Regions* [2001] UKHL 23 at [79], [2001] 2 All ER 929 at [79], [2001] 2 WLR 1389:

e   '... as we shall see, the European Court of Human Rights has not restricted art 6(1) to the determination of rights in private law. The probable original meaning, which Judge Wiarda said, in (*König v Germany* (1978) 2 EHRR 170 at 205) was the "classical meaning" of the term "civil rights" in a civilian system of law, is nevertheless important. It explains the process of f   reasoning, unfamiliar to an English lawyer, by which the Strasbourg court has arrived at the conclusion that art 6(1) can have application to administrative decisions. The court has not simply said, as I have suggested one might say in English law, that one can have a "civil right" to a lawful decision by an administrator. Instead, the court has accepted that "civil rights" means only rights in private law and has applied art 6(1) to g   administrative decisions on the ground that they can determine or affect rights in private law.'

[20] So the question is whether the review decision taken by Mrs Hayes under s 202 has determined or affected the respondent's rights in private law. But this is what I may call a loose question: that is, there is no sharp criterion by which to h   judge whether the s 202 decision *has* determined or affected such rights of the respondent. I should notice also that the category of civil rights in art 6 is not to be understood merely as referring to such rights and obligations as arise in the private law of the member states of the Council of Europe (or administrative decisions which determine or affect such rights). By the Strasbourg jurisprudence, j   'civil rights and obligations' is an autonomous concept, at any rate to the extent indicated by the European Court of Human Rights in *Pudas v Sweden* (1988) 10 EHRR 380 at 388–389 (para 35):

        'According to the well established case law of the Court, the concept of "civil rights and obligations" is not to be interpreted solely by reference to the respondent State's domestic law and Article 6(1) applies irrespective of

the status of parties, as of the character of the legislation which governs how
the dispute is to be determined and the character of the authority which is
invested with jurisdiction in the matter; it is enough that the outcome of the
proceedings should be decisive for private rights and obligations.'

With great respect I find this a little difficult to fathom (I am sure the fault is
mine). I take it to refer, partly at least, to the different courts, and court processes,
established respectively for the resolution of private and public law disputes in
civilian systems, and to indicate that differences of that kind cannot conclude the
question whether 'civil rights and obligations' are at stake. At all events I see no
reason here not to apply the touchstone described by Lord Hoffmann in the
Alconbury Developments case [2001] 2 All ER 929 at [79].

[21] On this issue Mr Underwood accepts, plainly rightly, that once a
homeless person becomes a tenant he or she thereby enjoys and owes civil rights
and obligations: the rights and obligations which are incidents of the tenancy as a
matter of private law. However he submits that an acceptance by the council of
the full housing duty under HA s 193(2) does not of itself 'determine or affect' (the
Alconbury Developments case) such rights nor is it 'decisive' of it (*Pudas v Sweden*),
because it remains open to the council, after the s 193(2) stage, to determine the
mode in which they will perform the duty they have accepted. There are three
such modes (see HA s 206(1) which I have set out at [5], above). Mr Underwood
says that the homeless person's civil rights (that is, those flowing from the
tenancy) are inchoate until a specific property has been identified for his
occupation. If these arguments are right, a review decision under s 202 cannot
amount to a determination of a civil right if the s 193(2) decision does not.

[22] More broadly Mr Underwood submits that it is clear from authority of
their Lordships' House that decisions under these provisions of the HA do not
determine civil rights and obligations. He referred to *O'Rourke v Camden
London BC* [1997] 3 All ER 23, [1998] AC 188. In that case the plaintiff brought an
action for damages against the council following his eviction from temporary
accommodation provided for him pursuant to s 63(1) of the Housing Act 1985
(the predecessor of HA s 188(1)). The defendant council applied to strike out the
claim. The Court of Appeal ((1996) 28 HLR 600) held that s 63(1) created a private
law duty sounding in damages. Their Lordships' House disagreed. Lord
Hoffmann emphasised particular features of the legislation. First, it was a scheme
of social welfare intended to confer benefits in the general public interest (see
[1997] 3 All ER 23 at 26, [1998] AC 188 at 193). Secondly, the duty to provide
accommodation depended upon 'a good deal of judgment on the part of the local
housing authority' (see [1997] 3 All ER 23 at 26, [1998] AC 188 at 194). Then this
passage:

'Lord Bridge went on [sc in *Cocks v Thanet DC* [1982] 3 All ER 1135, [1983]
2 AC 286] ... to say that a duty in private law would arise once the housing
authority had made a decision in the applicant's favour. He said ([1982] 3 All
ER 1135 at 1138, [1983] 2 AC 286 at 292–293): "On the other hand, the
housing authority are charged with executive functions. Once a decision has
been reached by the housing authority which gives rise to the temporary, the
limited or the full housing duty, rights and obligations are immediately
created in the field of private law. Each of the duties referred to, once
established, is capable of being enforced by injunction and the breach of it
will give rise to a liability in damages. But it is inherent in the scheme of the
1977 Act that an appropriate public law decision of the housing authority is

a   a condition precedent to the establishment of the private law duty." My
Lords, I must say with all respect that I cannot accept this reasoning. There
is no examination of the legislative intent, the various considerations which
I have discussed earlier as indicating whether or not a statute was intended
to create a duty in private law sounding in damages. The fact that the
housing authority is "charged with executive functions" is treated as
b   sufficient to establish a private law duty. No doubt because the question did
not have to be decided, Lord Bridge did not undertake a careful examination
of the statutory intent such as he afterwards made in *Hague v Deputy Governor
of Parkhurst Prison, Weldon v Home Office* [1991] 3 All ER 733 at 739–742, [1992]
1 AC 58 at 157–161. I feel sure that if he had, he would have expressed a
different opinion. The concept of a duty in private law which arises only
c   when it has been acknowledged to exist is anomalous. It means that a
housing authority which accepts that it has a duty to house the applicant but
does so inadequately will be liable in damages, but an authority which
perversely refuses to accept that it has any such duty will not. This seems to
me wrong. Of course a private law relationship may arise from the
d   implementation of the housing authority's duty. The applicant may become
the authority's tenant or licensee and so brought into a contractual relationship.
But there seems to me no need to interpose a statutory duty actionable in
tort merely to bridge the gap between the acknowledgement of the duty and
its implementation.' (See [1997] 3 All ER 23 at 28–29, [1998] AC 188 at 196.)

e   [23] It is instructive also to look at the decision of Stanley Burnton J in *R (on
the application of Husain) v Asylum Support Adjudicator* [2001] EWHC Admin 852,
[2001] All ER (D) 107 (Oct), a case whose subject matter was far distant from the
housing legislation. It was concerned (as the judge put it at the beginning of his
judgment) with 'the constitutionality of the office of asylum support adjudicators'.
f   But the judge made some general observations:

'[26] … art 6 does not apply to the exercise by public authorities of their
discretion, as distinguished from their compliance with their obligations
owed to citizens. Obligations give rise to rights; discretionary payments and
discretionary support do not …

g   [27] … A line has to be drawn between those decisions which, in a
democratic society, must be given to an independent tribunal and those
which need not. Article 6 draws this line by restricting the requirement to
the determination of criminal charges and civil rights and obligations. A
right by definition is something to which the citizen is entitled, to which he
has an enforceable claim. A discretionary benefit, one that a government
h   may give or refuse as it wishes, cannot be the subject of a right.'

[24] This reasoning of Stanley Burnton J seems to me to be correct. And it
touches, though it cannot determine, the present issue. The regime established
by HA Pt VII is by no means confined to the conferment of discretions upon the
j   local authority. Giving full weight, with respect, to Lord Hoffmann's emphasis
on what may be called the judgmental characteristics of the scheme (*O'Rourke's
case* [1997] 3 All ER 23 at 26–27, [1998] AC 188 at 194), it is to my mind clear that
in administering it the authority has to resolve a series of matters which sit at
different points on a spectrum between what is wholly objective and what is
wholly subjective. The issues arising under HA s 193(1)—non-intentional
homelessness, eligibility for assistance, priority need—are good examples. They

may include the question, obviously objective, whether a woman applicant is
pregnant (see HA s 189(1)(a)). But whether an applicant is intentionally homeless
within the statute's meaning involves matters far less hard-edged. And whether
the council is satisfied that other suitable accommodation is available for an
applicant comes closer to an exercise of discretion (see HA ss 193(1), 197(1)). So the
system has some elements akin to a discretionary regime, others distant from it.

[25] In these circumstances the court has to make a judgment as to the
engagement of 'civil rights and obligations' which cannot be arrived at by the
application of any brightline rule; as I have already said, Lord Hoffmann's
formulation in the *Alconbury Developments* case raises a loose question—whether
the decision in issue 'can determine or affect rights in private law'—not
susceptible of answer by reference to any sharp criterion. I prefer the view that
the homeless person's civil rights and obligations are engaged by a determination
under HA s 202. Such a determination leads to the grant or withholding of a
tenancy. And I think that the subject matter of the scheme, dealing with the
urgent provision of living accommodation for persons who will often be gravely
disadvantaged (or the refusal to provide it) so touches their well-being that as a
matter of our domestic law of human rights we should lean towards the
application of the ECHR art 6(1) discipline. This conclusion is in no sense
inconsistent with their Lordships' decision in *O'Rourke's* case, since it is not a
necessary incident of a 'civil right' attracting the protections of art 6(1) that the
law allows its owner to maintain an action for damages to make the right good.
In addition it is, I think, supported by the holding of this court in *R (on the
application of McLellan) v Bracknell Forest BC, Reigate and Banstead BC v Benfield*
[2001] EWCA Civ 1510 at [79]–[83], [2002] 1 All ER 899 at [79]–[83] (per Waller LJ)
that the function of the review panel under HA s 129(2), in the context not of
homelessness but of the introductory tenancy regime created by HA Pt V,
engages art 6 civil rights and obligations. Further support is to be found in the
approach of the European Court of Human Rights to the application of art 6(1)
to a statutory regime for welfare assistance in *Salesi v Italy* (1998) 26 EHRR 187 at
199 (para 19). Finally it is to be noted that in *Husain's* case ([2001] All ER (D) 107
(Oct)), to which I have referred, Stanley Burnton J concluded (at [54], [55]) that
there was a 'civil right' to asylum support. The jurisprudence in England and
Strasbourg alike demonstrate that 'civil right', for the purpose of art 6, may and
often does travel wider than the common law conception of cause of action.

[26] For these reasons I would conclude that Mrs Hayes' decision of 27 July
2001 taken under HA s 202 constitutes a determination of the respondent's 'civil
rights' within the meaning of art 6(1).

The second question: s 202 and 'independent and impartial tribunal'

[27] In *Adan v Newham London BC* [2002] 1 All ER 931 it was common ground
that an officer conducting a review under HA s 202 could not constitute an
'independent and impartial tribunal' within the meaning of art 6(1) (see, again,
[2002] 1 All ER 931 at [9], per Brooke LJ). In this case Mr Underwood makes no
such concession.

[28] The Strasbourg jurisprudence is clear and consistent. Purely by way of
example, the court stated in *Findlay v UK* (1997) 24 EHRR 221 at 244–245 (para 73):

'... in order to establish whether a tribunal can be considered
"independent", regard must be had *inter alia* to the manner of appointment
of its members and their term of office, the existence of guarantees against

a outside pressures and the question whether the body presents an appearance of independence. As to the question of "impartiality", there are two aspects to this requirement. First, the tribunal must be subjectively free of personal prejudice or bias. Secondly, it must also be impartial from an objective viewpoint, that is, it must offer sufficient guarantees to exclude any legitimate doubt in this respect. The concepts of independence and impartiality are

b closely linked ...'

[29] There is no suggestion of actual bias on the part of Mrs Hayes. The question is as to the appearance of the thing, in light of the manner of her appointment and the presence or absence of 'objective guarantees' of independence and impartiality. Mr Underwood emphasises in particular the rule as to seniority

c and no previous involvement in the case (see reg 2 of the 1999 regulations). He submits also that the appellant council had no or no substantial financial interest in the outcome of the HA s 202 review, and there is no reason to suppose that a council officer in Mrs Hayes' position would entertain any inclination to support the original decision-maker.

d [30] In my judgment there are not here sufficient objective guarantees, visible as it were to the outside world, so as to clothe the reviewing officer's role under s 202 with the necessary qualities of independence and impartiality, if it is looked at in isolation. This is not the slightest criticism of Mrs Hayes. I have already said that this is a question of appearances; but this is a context in which appearances are very significant. It is also to be noted that (as I understand it) the review

e officer sits in private, and a public hearing is one of the conditions of art 6(1). I should add that this conclusion by no means sidelines the s 202 review process so as to deprive it of any real significance for the problems which this appeal exposes. As I will show, the machinery of HA s 203 and of regs 6 and 8 of the regulations, which I have set out (see [5] and [6] respectively, above), is of considerable importance for the correct resolution of the third question, to which

f I now turn.

The third question: the county court and 'full jurisdiction'

[31] There is of course no contest as to the independence and impartiality of the county court. The issue on this part of the case, which I regard as the nub of

g the appeal, is whether or not HA s 204 suffices to satisfy ECHR art 6(1), given that the section only enables the county court to examine questions of law; the court does not revisit the review officer's decision under s 202 with full power to decide the factual merits for itself. The approach in Strasbourg to cases where a first instance decision-maker does not of itself satisfy art 6(1), but it is claimed that the

h defect is as it were cured by a right of appeal to or review by an independent court, is to ascertain whether in the circumstances the court possesses what has been called 'full jurisdiction'. The genesis of this expression is I think to be found in *Albert v Belgium* (1983) 5 EHRR 533. That was a case in which doctors suspended from practice by a disciplinary tribunal complained of violations of art 6(1). It is convenient to refer to the relevant passage as it is quoted by Lord Hoffmann in *R*

j *(on the application of Alconbury Developments Ltd) v Secretary of State for the Environment, Transport and the Regions* [2001] 2 All ER 929 at [86]–[88], where it is followed by reasoning to which with respect I would attach considerable importance in the context of the present case:

'[86] In ... *Albert v Belgium* (1983) 5 EHRR 533 at 542 (para 29) ... the court said, that although disciplinary jurisdiction could be conferred upon professional bodies which did not meet the requirements of art 6(1) (e g because they were not "established by law" or did not sit in public)—"Nonetheless, in such circumstances the Convention calls at least for one of the two following systems: either the jurisdictional organs themselves comply with the requirements of Article 6(1), or they do not so comply but are subject to subsequent control by a judicial body that has full jurisdiction and does provide the guarantees of Article 6(1)."

[87] The reference to "full jurisdiction" has been frequently cited in subsequent cases and sometimes relied upon in argument as if it were authority for saying that a policy decision affecting civil rights by an administrator who does not comply with art 6(1) has to be reviewable on its merits by an independent and impartial tribunal. It was certainly so relied upon by counsel for the respondents in these appeals. But subsequent European authority shows that "full jurisdiction" does not mean full decision-making power. It means full jurisdiction to deal with the case as the nature of the decision requires.

[88] This emerges most clearly from the decisions on the English planning cases ... But the leading European authority for the proposition that it is not necessary to have a review of the merits of a policy decision is *Zumtobel v Austria* (1993) 17 EHRR 116. The Zumtobel partnership objected to the compulsory purchase of their farming land to build the L52 by-pass road in the Austrian Vorarlberg. The appropriate government committee heard their objections but confirmed the order. They appealed to an administrative court which said that the government had taken proper matters into account and that it was not entitled to substitute its decision for that of the administrative authority. They complained to the commission and the European Court of Human Rights that, as the administrative court could not "independently assess the merits and the facts of the case", it did not have "full jurisdiction" within the meaning of the *Albert* formula. The European Court of Human Rights said (at 133 (para 32)) that its jurisdiction was sufficient in the circumstances of the case, "[r]egard being had to the respect which must be accorded to decisions taken by the administrative authorities on grounds of expediency and to the nature of the complaints made by the Zumtobel partnership."'

[32] Later in his speech in the *Alconbury Developments* case Lord Hoffmann referred to the case of *Bryan v UK* (1996) 21 EHRR 342, and in particular to the opinion of Mr Nicolas Bratza (as he then was) in the European Commission of Human Rights:

'[107] ... [Mr Bratza] said (at 354): "It appears to me that the requirement that a court or tribunal should have 'full jurisdiction' cannot be mechanically applied with the result that, in all circumstances and whatever the subject matter of the dispute, the court or tribunal must have full power to substitute its own findings of fact, and its own inferences from those facts, for that of the administrative authority concerned. Whether the power of judicial review is sufficiently wide to satisfy the requirements of Article 6 must in my view depend on a number of considerations, including the subject matter of the dispute, the nature of the decision of the administrative authorities which is in question, the procedure, if any, which exists for review of the decision by a person or body acting independently of the authority concerned and the scope of that power of review." ...

[110] Mr Bratza's particular insight, if I may respectfully say so, was to see that a tribunal may be more or less independent, depending upon the question it is being called upon to decide. On matters of policy, the inspector was no more independent than the Secretary of State himself. But this was a matter on which independence was unnecessary—indeed, on democratic principles, undesirable—and in which the power of judicial review, paying full respect to the views of the inspector or Secretary of State on questions of policy or expediency, was sufficient to satisfy art 6(1). On the other hand, in deciding the questions of primary fact or fact and degree which arose in enforcement notice appeals, the inspector was no mere bureaucrat. He was an expert tribunal acting in a quasi-judicial manner and therefore sufficiently independent to make it unnecessary that the High Court should have a broad jurisdiction to review his decisions on questions of fact.'

Lord Hoffmann (at [116]) proceeded to point out that Mr Bratza's opinion had influenced the decision of the court in *Bryan v UK* (at 360 (para 45)), which said:

'… in assessing the sufficiency of the review available to Mr Bryan on appeal to the High Court, it is necessary to have regard to matters such as the subject matter of the decision appealed against, the manner in which that decision was arrived at, and the content of the dispute, including the desired and actual grounds of appeal.'

[33] Against this background, we have to consider whether, in light of the nature and details of the scheme established in HA Pt VII, the county court's function under HA s 204 fulfils the ECHR art 6(1) standards: in the language of Strasbourg, whether in the context of Pt VII it possesses 'full jurisdiction'. In *Adan's* case this court concluded by a majority that it did not. That conclusion was obiter, though of course entitled to great respect. I should briefly explain how it was that the court came to pronounce on the matter. The appellant, who was a Dutch lady, applied to the local authority for accommodation as a homeless person. She was turned down on the ground that she was not habitually resident in this country (that being a requirement under regulations). She sought a review under HA s 202, but the original decision was upheld. She appealed to the county court under s 204. Her appeal was allowed. The judge directed that a further s 202 review should be conducted by a different reviewing officer who should be compliant with art 6(1). That direction was challenged on appeal by the council. This court concluded that there was no power to make such a direction. That was the end of the live appeal. But the court was invited, on pressing and responsible grounds, to deliver an opinion upon the question whether the procedures given by HA Pt VII fulfilled art 6. It was conceded (as I have said) that the respondent's civil rights were engaged. It was conceded also that the review officer did not constitute an 'independent and impartial tribunal' (see [2002] 1 All ER 931 at [9]). There remained the question, the very question arising in this case, whether the county court's function under s 204 validated the Pt VII process for the purpose of art 6(1).

[34] I should cite these passages from the judgment of Brooke LJ:

'[43] It follows that if a case arises on a s 202 review where there is a dispute about the primary facts of a kind which has to be resolved because it is material to the decision-making process, then the danger will arise that the proceedings, taken as a whole, will not be convention compliant. The reviewing officer will lack the independent status of the planning inspector

in the *Alconbury Developments* case and the county court does not have full
jurisdiction to decide questions of disputed fact (except in a *Wednesbury,* or
super-*Wednesbury,* sense) (see *Associated Provincial Picture Houses Ltd v
Wednesbury Corp* [1947] 2 All ER 680, [1948] 1 KB 223). If such a case arises
before the law is changed in order to correct the deficiencies identified in this
judgment, then it appears to me that the local authority will have to exercise
its contracting-out powers so as to ensure that any such dispute is
determined by a tribunal with the appropriate attributes of independence
and impartiality ...

[47] ... we were shown three recent judgments in the Administrative
Court in which conclusions were reached which are similar to that to which
I have found myself driven in the present case. I refer to the judgments of
Richards J in *R (on the application of Kathro) v Rhondda Cynon Taff County BC*
[2001] EWHC Admin 527 ([2001] 4 PLR 83) at [28], [29], Moses J in *R (on the
application of Bewry) v Norwich City Council* [2001] EWHC Admin 657 ([2002]
HRLR 21) at [58]–[62], and Stanley Burnton J in *R (on the application of
Husain) v Asylum Support Adjudicator* [2001] EWHC Admin 852 at [78], [79],
[2001] All ER (D) 107 (Oct) at [78], [79]. It is sufficient for present purposes
to recite a passage in the last of these judgments. In *Husain's* case Stanley
Burnton J said:

"[78] ... where the decisions of a tribunal are likely to depend to a
substantial extent on disputed questions of primary fact, and the tribunal
is clearly not independent, judicial review should not suffice to produce
compliance with art 6. The scope for review of findings of primary facts is
too narrow to be considered a 'full jurisdiction' in such a context. Fact-
dependent decisions must be made by fully independent tribunals: the
scope for judicial review of primary findings of fact, and particularly of
findings as to the credibility of witnesses, is generally too narrow to cure a
want of independence at the lower level.

[79] I think that the courts should lean against accepting judicial review
as a substitute for the independence of tribunals. If the availability of
judicial review is too easily regarded as curing a want of independence on
the part of administrative tribunals, the incentive for the executive and the
legislature to ensure the independence of tribunals is considerably
weakened."

I agree.'

[35] Hale LJ took a different view. She said:

'[61] An appeal which is limited to points of law as that has traditionally
been understood cannot fill all the gaps. Until this case, the understanding
was that the county court acted on the same principles as the High Court had
previously acted when judicial review was the only remedy in homelessness
cases (see *Begum v Tower Hamlets London BC* [2000] 1 WLR 306). This means
that it has a jurisdiction over errors both in procedure and in law which is, as
Sedley LJ observed (at 327) "at least as wide as that of a court of judicial
review". Its powers are in some respects wider, as s 204(3) permits it to
"make such order confirming, quashing or varying the decisions as it thinks
fit" ...

[79] ... if the local authority for whatever reason do not provide a
reviewing system which is adequate to comply with art 6 in the particular

a case, the county court would have to say so. As we are agreed that the court cannot send the case back with a direction to comply, the court is required to fill the gap itself. This is no more radical an interpretation of s 204 of the 1996 Act as a whole than is the suggestion that the local authority be required as a matter of law to adopt a different decision-making process. Of course, if they were so required, but did not do so, this would clearly be a question of
b law for the court to resolve.

[80] ... I am prepared to accept that the local authority may choose to contract out some or all of its reviews to a body whose constitution and procedures enable the decision to comply with art 6 (even though this would change the character of reviews and deprive applicants of much that is valuable in them). But if they do not do so, and the particular issues in the
c case require an independent decision, then the court should fill the gap.'

The third member of the court was David Steel J, who agreed with Brooke LJ:

'[94] Whatever may be the true analysis of the decision [sc in *R v A* [2001] UKHL 25, [2001] 3 All ER 1, [2002] 1 AC 45], I still agree with the conclusion
d of Brooke LJ that it does not permit an interpretation, so as to allow the county court to fill any "gap", that renders the words "appeal on a point of law" as including "appeal on a point of fact". Straining the language cannot achieve that end. Nor is a dispute of fact rendered a dispute of law by reason of what would otherwise be a shortfall in convention compliance as regards the provision for resolution of that dispute. Nor, in the further alternative,
e is there any need to imply words to that effect. The court is simply not boxed into a corner where the only option is the implication of the words "fact or" or a declaration of incompatibility. The local authority simply has to contract out the review process, either generally or in appropriate cases.'

f [36] We were referred to the three cases which Brooke LJ mentions in *Adan*'s case [2002] 1 All ER 931 at [47], and I have already cited extracts from Stanley Burnton J's decision in *R (on the application of Husain) v Asylum Support Adjudicator* [2001] All ER (D) 107 (Oct) in considering the first issue in the appeal. I mean no disrespect if I do not travel further into the detail of those judgments save for the decision of Moses J in *R (on the application of Bewry) v Norwich City Council* [2001]
g EWHC Admin 657, [2002] HRLR 21. That case was concerned with the functions of a review board, manned by local councillors, to which a person refused housing benefit by the local authority might apply for a fresh determination. Moses J said:

'57 But [counsel for the claimant] asserts that at the heart of this case lay
h an issue of credibility. The Secretary of State submits that the reasoning of the Review Board makes it plain that their decision was based upon the questions to which the documents gave rise which the claimant singularly failed to answer or to clarify. The question of credibility, he submits, did not depend upon oral evidence but upon inferences to be drawn from the
j documents to which the Review Board referred. Had the reasons for rejecting the claimant's assertions not stacked up, this court would have been in a good position to identify that failure. The reasoning demonstrates, it is submitted, an independence of approach.

58 There is however, in my judgment, one insuperable difficulty. Unlike an inspector, whose position was described by Lord Hoffman[n] as independent, the same cannot be said of a councillor who is directly

connected to one of the parties to the dispute, namely the Council. In my *a*
judgment, the position of councillors chosen to sit on a Review Board cannot
be likened to that of the Planning Inspectorate ...

62 ... The lack of independence [sc of the councillors on the Board] may
infect the independence of judgment in relation to the finding of primary fact
in a manner which cannot be adequately scrutinised or rectified by this court
... *b*

64 ... This court cannot cure the often imperceptible effects of the
influence of the connection between the fact-finding body and a party to the
dispute since it has no jurisdiction to reach its own conclusion on the primary
facts; still less any power to weigh the evidence.'

I should say that these conclusions were arrived at by the judge through what he *c*
saw as the application of common law principle, the relevant events having
happened before the ECHR rights were patriated by the HRA on 2 October 2000.
Moses J's judgment, and much of the other learning in this area, was cited at
some length by Richards J in R (*on the application of the Personal Representatives of
Beeson*) *v Dorset CC* [2002] HRLR 368 (to which as I have said the judge in the
present case referred). *Beeson's* case concerned certain statutory arrangements *d*
for the provision of residential accommodation under the National Assistance Act
1948. The judge found that like considerations to those which moved Moses J
applied in the circumstances before him.

[37] These decisions (right or wrong: Moses J's judgment was doubted,
though very much in passing and as was acknowledged without hearing full *e*
argument, by Waller LJ in R (*on the application of McLellan*) *v Bracknell Forest BC,
Reigate and Banstead BC v Benfield* [2002] 1 All ER 899 at [75], and we were told that
Beeson's case is currently subject to appeal) seem to me to reflect an important
truth about the relationship between the 'first instance' decision and the decision
of the court on appeal or review, in this class of case where it is said that the later
court process guarantees ECHR art 6 compliance where that is not satisfied by *f*
the earlier determination. We have seen that in such cases the later court must
possess 'full jurisdiction' (see *Albert v Belgium* (1983) 5 EHRR 533), and that this
means 'full jurisdiction to deal with the case as the nature of the decision requires'
(the *Alconbury Developments* case [2001] 2 All ER 929 at [87]). But what 'the nature
of the decision requires' is by no means limited to a consideration of the question *g*
whether, in light of the subject matter of the case, a court compliant with art 6
standards must possess the power to investigate and decide the facts for itself.
Assuming only that in any particular milieu disputes of fact may arise, it is
necessary also to confront the question whether the 'first instance' decision-
maker—internal review, review board, whatever it may be—is established and *h*
constituted in such a way that it may be expected to arrive at fair and reasonable
decisions. That may be a live and real question even though, for want of
sufficient independence, or publicity, or any other factor, such a first instance
decision-maker does not itself satisfy art 6. Its failure to meet the art 6 standards
by no means closes off the relevance of its processes for the *overall* judgment that
has to be made which takes account also of the second stage review or appeal in *j*
an independent court.

[38] This aspect of cases like the present is I think reflected in Waller LJ's
reasoning in *McLellan's* case [2002] 1 All ER 899:

'[99] It is in my view legitimate to take into account in this context that the
review panel is a body chosen by Parliament. If, of course, it was simply

a   impossible for such a tribunal to reach a fair decision, that would lead
inevitably to the conclusion that the scheme could not work without
infringement of art 6. Would it be impossible for there to be a fair decision
from any person who would be appointed to review matters under the
introductory tenancy scheme? Would a court inevitably come to the
conclusion that any officer, however senior, could not constitute a fair
b   tribunal for hearing the matter? Is the position such that judicial review
could not provide the check as to whether a decision had been reached
fairly and lawfully?

[100] One has to remember that the council are in reality making
decisions which are not simply decisions as to whether it has a right to
terminate. The council is not anxious to terminate unless other
c   considerations prevail. The council is having to have regard to competing
interests of other tenants and the competing interest of others who need
the housing that they can supply. In my view there is no reason to think
that such a decision cannot be taken fairly at a senior level of the council
reviewing the decisions already reached by less senior people.
d   Furthermore it seems to me that judicial review will be able to check the
fairness and legality of decisions taken.'

[39] Now I may gather the threads together. We are dealing with a state of
affairs in which a first instance decision-maker, whose determination touches
the citizen's civil rights, does not meet the standards imposed by art 6(1). Such
e   a state of affairs arises within a setting or regime created by Act of Parliament.
There will generally be access to a court by way of review or appeal against the
first decision. It may be provided (as it is by HA s 204) by the Act itself. If the
Act is silent, then at common law recourse may be had to the judicial review
court. If the Act gives a right of appeal to a court on the merits, factual as well
f   as legal, art 6 is plainly complied with: such a court on any view possesses 'full
jurisdiction'. But the commoner situation is where the right of appeal is on law
only. Subject to the remedies provided for (and to any points of procedure),
that will be equivalent to judicial review. The critical question, then, is this: in
these two-tier cases, what are the conditions which determine whether the
court process at the second tier, taken with the first instance process,
g   guarantees compliance with art 6(1)?

[40] As I have shown, the extent to which the first instance process may be
relied on to produce fair and reasonable decisions is plainly an important
element. But it is not to be viewed in isolation. The matter can only be judged
by an examination of the statutory scheme as a whole; that is the necessary
h   setting for any intelligent view as to what is fair and reasonable. Where the
scheme's subject matter generally or systematically involves the resolution of
primary fact, the court will incline to look for procedures akin to our
conventional mechanisms for finding facts: rights of cross-examination, access
to documents, a strictly independent decision-maker. To the extent that
j   procedures of that kind are not given by the first instance process, the court will
look to see how far they are given by the appeal or review; and the judicial
review jurisdiction (or its equivalent in the shape of a statutory appeal on law)
may not suffice. Where however the subject matter of the scheme generally or
systematically requires the application of judgment or the exercise of
discretion, especially if it involves the weighing of policy issues and regard
being had to the interests of others who are not before the decision-maker, then

for the purposes of art 6 the court will incline to be satisfied with a form of inquisition at first instance in which the decision-maker is more of an expert than a judge (I use the terms loosely), and the second instance appeal is in the nature of a judicial review. It is inevitable that across the legislative board there will lie instances between these paradigms, sharing in different degrees the characteristics of each. In judging a particular scheme the court, without compromise of its duty to vindicate the ECHR rights, will pay a degree of respect on democratic grounds to Parliament as the scheme's author.

[41] I intend the whole of this approach to be consonant with Lord Hoffmann's reasoning in *R (on the application of Alconbury Developments Ltd) v Secretary of State for the Environment, Transport and the Regions* [2001] 2 All ER 929, [2001] 2 WLR 1389, and with Waller LJ's reasoning in *McLellan*'s case, and I believe it to be so. And what was said by Lord Hoffmann in the *Alconbury Developments* case [2001] 2 All ER 929 at [79] (see [19], above) is, I think, reflected by the circumstance that civil rights are more likely to be directly engaged in a scheme where the finding of fact is a general or systematic feature; but where judgment, discretion, and issues of policy predominate, the scheme is more likely to be one in which decisions made under it 'determine or affect' civil rights.

[42] There remains of course the task of applying these principles to the present case. In *R v Camden London BC, ex p Pereira* (1999) 31 HLR 317 Hobhouse LJ as he then was cited what Lord Brightman had said about the homeless persons legislation, and made further observations in addition (at 320, 321):

'In *ex parte Puhlhofer* (*Puhlhofer v Hillingdon London BC* [1986] 1 All ER 467 at 473, [1986] AC 484 at 517), Lord Brightman said: "It is an Act to assist persons who are homeless, not an Act to provide them with homes ... It is intended to provide for the homeless a lifeline of last resort; not to enable them to make inroads into the local authority's waiting list of applicants for housing. Some inroads there probably are bound to be, but in the end the local authority will have to balance the priority needs of the homeless on the one hand and the legitimate aspirations of those on their housing waiting list on the other hand." (See also *ex parte Awua* (*Awua v Brent London BC* [1995] 3 All ER 493 at 501, [1996] AC 55 at 71–72) and *ex parte Kihara* (*R v Kensington and Chelsea London BC, ex p Kihara* (1996) 29 HLR 147 at 155).) It, thus, has to be borne in mind that any priority system involves striking a balance between the needs of one group of homeless persons and another. To grant priority to one person involves the deferment of another ... In the context of old age, the guidance [sc given by the Secretary of State under what is now HA s 182(1)] directs the authority to consider the extent to which the age of the applicant makes it hard for him to fend for himself ... In relation to mental illness or handicap or physical disability, the guidance states that the authority should consider the "relationship between the illness or handicap and the individual's housing difficulties" ... In relation to "victims of violence or abuse or sexual and/or racial harassment", the guidance demonstrates the breadth of the factors to be taken into account—"authorities should secure wherever possible that accommodation is available for men and women without children who have suffered violence at home or are at risk of further violence if they return home".'

a For my own part I have already stated (at [24], above) that the issues which may fall for decision on a homeless person's application lie across a spectrum between questions of fact and questions of judgment or discretion. It is important also to have in mind the procedures given by HA s 203 and regs 2, 6 and 8 of the 1999 regulations. I have already set out this material. It seems to me to provide very significant safeguards, in the applicant's interest, for the integrity
b of the HA s 202 process.

[43] I should indicate moreover that although there were sharp issues of primary fact falling for determination in the present case, that is not a necessary feature in a s 202 review, and certainly not a systematic one. As often as not there will be no real question of fact, and the decision will turn on the weight to be
c given to this or that factor against an undisputed background: whether the offered accommodation is too far from the children's school; whether there are too many stairs given the claimant's ill health; whether there are enough bedrooms given the size of the family; and so on. Now, clearly the statutory scheme is either compliant with ECHR art 6 or it is not. Its compliance or
d otherwise cannot vary case by case, according to the degree of factual dispute arising. That would involve a wholly unsustainable departure from the principle of legal certainty. In my opinion, judged as a whole, this statutory scheme lies towards that end of the spectrum where judgment and discretion, rather than fact-finding, play the predominant part.

[44] I think it important also to recognise the potential scope of the judicial
e review jurisdiction, replicated in this scheme in HA s 204. The judge has ample power to decide whether the review officer's decision was one which was properly available to her on the evidence which she had. In this particular case it will be open to the judge to scrutinise the s 202 decision letter of 27 July 2001, which I have set out at [10], above, to see whether it really dealt with the points
f which concerned the respondent. Given that (as I would find) the s 202 process does not of itself fulfil art 6, the judge is perfectly entitled, within the jurisdiction given him by s 204, to subject the earlier decision to a close and rigorous analysis.

[45] For all these reasons I conclude that s 204 in its context confers 'full jurisdiction' on the county court within the meaning of *Albert v Belgium*, and
g satisfies the requirements of our developing domestic law of human rights. I am conscious that in so holding I am propounding a view which is contrary to the conclusions of the majority in this court in *Adan v Newham London BC* [2002] 1 All ER 931; contrary also to the view of Hale LJ ([2002] 1 All ER 931 at [80]) that the county court should 'fill the gap' by assuming a fact-finding role as necessary. On
h the approach I favour, there is no gap to fill. I take this position with real diffidence. I would venture only to emphasise the concessions made in that case, that s 202 engages the claimant's civil rights, and that the s 202 review does not satisfy art 6. I do so without the least criticism, since as will be plain both concessions are in my view entirely correct. But had they not been made the
j court might have found it necessary to undertake a more specific examination of the statutory scheme, and in doing so might have arrived at a different conclusion as to the bite of art 6. One of the most important insights which in my view the authorities furnish is that the three issues which I have identified and addressed in this judgment are not hermetically sealed, each from the others. They engage overlapping considerations; the edge between administration and adjudication is cousin to the edge between judgment and fact-finding.

[46] I would allow the appeal. If my Lords agree, we should no doubt hear *a*
argument as to what orders should be made in consequence.

DYSON LJ.
[47] I agree.

LORD WOOLF CJ.   *b*
[48] I also agree.

Appeal allowed. Permission to appeal refused.

Kate O'Hanlon   Barrister.

a # Ako v Rothschild Asset Management Ltd and another
[2002] EWCA Civ 236

b COURT OF APPEAL, CIVIL DIVISION
MUMMERY, JONATHAN PARKER AND DYSON LJJ
25 JANUARY, 1 MARCH 2002

c

Employment tribunal – Decision – Res judicata – Complainant withdrawing complaint against employer but intending to bring fresh complaint arising out of same circumstances against employer and transferee of employer's undertaking – Tribunal formally dismissing complaint on withdrawal and complainant bringing fresh complaint – Tribunal holding fresh complaint barred by cause of action estoppel – Whether cause of action estoppel applying to employment tribunal cases where withdrawal of complaint tantamount to discontinuance of proceedings – Employment

d *Tribunals (Constitution and Rules of Procedure) Regulations 1993, Sch 1, r 13(2)(a).*

The complainant brought a complaint to an employment tribunal of unfair dismissal and race discrimination against her former employer. Shortly afterwards, she wrote to the tribunal to withdraw her application. The chairman of the

e tribunal subsequently made an order under r 13(2)(a)[a] of Sch 1 to the Employment Tribunals (Constitution and Rules of Procedure) Regulations 1993 that the application was 'dismissed on withdrawal by the applicant'. The chairman had heard no evidence or argument, and was not even sitting in the open tribunal room when he made the order. Within a week, the complainant presented a fresh application to the tribunal, repeating the same allegations against the

f employer, but also making allegations against a bank which she believed to be the transferee of the undertaking of the part of the employer's business in which she had worked. She claimed unfair dismissal by reason of the transfer and of race discrimination. The employer applied for the application to be struck out, contending that the complainant was barred by the principles of estoppel and res judicata from bringing the second application. The tribunal found that the

g complainant had never intended to abandon her claim against the employer, that at all material times she had intended to replace the withdrawn application with one naming both the employer and the bank, and that she would not have withdrawn the application against the employer if she had known that the withdrawal would preclude her from pursuing her claims. The tribunal

h nevertheless held that the complainant's claim against the employer had already been disposed of judicially, and that cause of action estoppel prevented the claim from being pursued. The complainant's appeal was allowed by the Employment Appeal Tribunal, and the employer appealed to the Court of Appeal.

j **Held** – There was no requirement that cause of action estoppel, as applied in the ordinary courts, should apply to employment tribunal cases where it was clear, on an examination of the surrounding circumstances, that the withdrawal of the application was in substance a discontinuance of the proceedings. In the ordinary

---

a   Rule 13, so far as material, provides: '... (2) A tribunal may—(a) if the applicant at any time gives notice of the withdrawal of his originating application, dismiss the proceedings ...'

courts there was a significant distinction in the rules of procedure governing
withdrawal of proceedings between (i) an order dismissing proceedings, which
was capable of creating cause of action estoppel, and (ii) discontinuance of
proceedings under CPR 38.7[b], which did not operate as a release or extinction of
a cause of action and as a bar to further proceedings. Under that provision, the
permission of the court was required to make another claim against the same
defendant when the claim arose out of facts which were the same or substantially
the same as those relating to a claim that had been discontinued after the
defendant had filed a defence. The court would very likely give permission in a
case such as the instant case. The procedural rules of the employment tribunal
did not, however, make the same distinction or contain similar provisions. That
omission might be a trap for the unwary if the doctrine of cause of action estoppel
were strictly applied. The only procedure for withdrawing an application in the
employment tribunal was by an order dismissing the proceedings, but there
could be cases in which a discontinuance of the tribunal proceedings, if that
procedure were available, would be more appropriate than dismissal. It did not
make any sense that the position should be more strict in its application in
employment tribunals, which were less formal than the ordinary courts.
Accordingly, the appeal would be dismissed (see [29], [30], [32], [33], [42], below);
Barber v Staffordshire CC [1996] 2 All ER 748 and *Lennon v Birmingham City Council*
[2001] IRLR 826 explained and distinguished.

Per curiam. Unless and until the regulations relating to employment tribunals
are amended to deal with the point, it is advisable for employment tribunals, on
being notified of the withdrawal of an originating application, to ask the applicant
for a statement of the circumstances of the decision to withdraw before deciding
whether to make an order dismissing the proceedings (see [30], below).

Notes
For res judicata in the context of employment tribunal proceedings, see Supp to
16 *Halsbury's Laws* (4th edn reissue) para 977.

For the Employment Tribunals (Constitution and Rules of Procedure)
Regulations 1993, Sch 1, r 13, see 7 *Halsbury's Statutory Instruments* (2001 Issue) 303.
With effect from 16 July 2001, r 13(2)(a) has been replaced by r 15(2)(a) of Sch 1 to
the Employment Tribunals (Constitution and Rules of Procedure) Regulations
2001, SI 2001/1171.

Cases referred to in judgments
Arnold v National Westminster Bank plc [1991] 3 All ER 41, [1991] 2 AC 93, [1991] 2
WLR 1177, HL.
Barber v Staffordshire CC [1996] 2 All ER 748, [1996] ICR 379, CA.
Henderson v Henderson (1843) 3 Hare 100, [1843–60] All ER Rep 378, (1843) 67 ER
313, VC Ct.
*Investors Compensation Scheme Ltd v West Bromwich Building Society, Investors
Compensation Scheme Ltd v Hopkin & Sons (a firm), Alford v West Bromwich
Building Society, Armitage v West Bromwich Building Society* [1998] 1 All ER 98,
[1998] 1 WLR 896, HL.

b   CPR 38.7, so far as material, provides: 'A claimant who discontinues a claim needs the permission of
the court to make another claim against the same defendant if—(a) he discontinued the claim after
the defendant filed a defence; and (b) the other claim arises out of facts which are the same or
substantially the same as those relating to the discontinued claim.'

a   *Khan v Goleccha International Ltd* [1980] 2 All ER 259, [1980] 1 WLR 1482, CA.
    Kronprinz (Cargo Owners) v Kronprinz (Owners), The Ardandhu (1887) 12 App Cas
       256, HL.
    Lennon v Birmingham City Council [2001] EWCA Civ 435, [2001] IRLR 826.
    Sajid v Sussex Muslim Society [2001] EWCA Civ 1684, [2002] IRLR 113.
    SCF Finance Co Ltd v Masri (No 3) [1987] 1 All ER 194, [1987] QB 1028, [1987] 2
b   WLR 81, CA.
    Sidney v Watts Countrymade Foods (unreported (EAT 453/78)), EAT.

    Cases also cited or referred to in skeleton arguments
    Abdulaziz v UK (1985) 7 EHRR 471, ECt HR.
    Ashingdane v UK (1985) 7 EHRR 528, ECt HR.
c   *Bradford and Bingley Building Society v Seddon (Hancock, t/a Hancocks (a firm), third
       parties)* [1999] 4 All ER 217, [1999] 1 WLR 1482, CA.
    Brumarescu v Romania App No 28342/95 (28 October 1999, unreported), ECt HR.
    Campbell v UK (1992) 15 EHRR 137, ECt HR.
    Deweer v Belgium (1980) 2 EHRR 439, ECt HR.
d   *Golder v UK* (1975) 1 EHRR 524,ECt HR.
    Håkansson v Sweden (1990) 13 EHRR 1, ECt HR.
    Mulvaney v London Transport Executive [1981] ICR 351, EAT.
    Neumeister v Austria (No 2) (1974) 1 EHRR 136, ECt HR.
    Pfeifer v Austria (1992) 14 EHRR 692, ECt HR.
    R v Lambert [2001] UKHL 37, [2001] 3 All ER 577, [2001] 3 WLR 206.
e   *Valve (Engineering) Services Ltd v Osborne* (unreported, 24 November 2000 (EAT
       0236/00)), EAT.
    Young v Bristol Aeroplane Co Ltd [1944] 2 All ER 293, [1944] KB 718, CA; *affd* [1946]
       1 All ER 98, [1946] AC 163, HL.

f   **Appeal**
    Rothschild Asset Management Ltd (Rothschild) appealed with permission of the
    Employment Appeal Tribunal (Lindsay J (President), Miss Holroyd and
    Mr Springer) from its decision on 8 February 2001 allowing an appeal by the
    complainant, Kate Ako, from the decision of an employment tribunal sitting at
    Stratford, communicated to the parties on 20 October 1999, that her claim for
g   unfair dismissal and race discrimination against Rothschild had already been
    disposed of judicially and that cause of action estoppel prevented the claim from
    being pursued. Boston Safe Deposit Trust Co, the second respondent to Ms
    Ako's complaint, took no part in the proceedings. The facts are set out in the
    judgment of Mummery LJ.

h
    Deshpal Panesar (instructed by *Eversheds*) for Rothschild.
    Karon Monaghan (instructed by the *Commission for Racial Equality*) for Ms Ako.

                                                                    Cur adv vult

j   1 March 2002. The following judgments were delivered.

    MUMMERY LJ.

    Introduction
    [1] The principle of cause of action estoppel has presented problems for
    employment tribunals in cases in which the initial originating application is

withdrawn before a full hearing on the merits and the complainant subsequently *a*
attempts to pursue fresh proceedings based on substantially the same facts against
the same party. It is desirable for the law to strike a sensible balance between (a)
the application of the principle of finality in legal proceedings and (b) the public
interest in full and fair public hearings of grievances in the relatively informal
setting of tribunal procedures. The facts of this case shine a spotlight on the
glaring injustices which could arise from the mechanical application of cause of *b*
action estoppel to all cases in which proceedings are withdrawn from the
tribunal.

The background

[2] Ms Kate Ako, who is black and of African origin, was employed by
Rothschild Asset Management Ltd (Rothschild) as a secretary in the Settlement *c*
Department and in the Institutional Sales Department from July 1993. She was
dismissed on 11 May 1999 in circumstances which led her to present to the
employment tribunal on 17 June 1999 a complaint of unfair dismissal and a
complaint of race discrimination throughout her employment (the first
application). *d*

[3] On 28 June 1999 she wrote to the employment tribunal at Stratford 'to
withdraw her application against Rothschild'.

[4] On 2 July 1999 the chairman of the tribunal signed a decision, which was
sent to the parties and entered on the register on 6 July 1999. The document
bearing the case number is headed 'Decision' and simply states: 'The application
is dismissed on withdrawal by the applicant.' *e*

[5] The chairman heard no evidence or argument. He was not even sitting in
the open tribunal room when he made the order. The order was made by the
chairman in exercise of his discretion under r 13(2)(a) of Sch 1 to the Employment
Tribunals (Constitution and Rules of Procedure) Regulations 1993, SI 1993/2687
which were then in force. They have since been replaced by the Employment *f*
Tribunals (Constitution and Rules of Procedure) Regulations 2001, SI 2001/1171,
which contain a similar provision.

[6] Within less than a week Ms Ako presented a fresh application dated 8 July
1999 to the employment tribunal (the second application) repeating the same
allegations against Rothschild. She also made allegations against Mellon Bank, in
the belief that it was the transferee of the undertaking of the Institutional Sales *g*
Department. She claimed unfair dismissal by reason of the transfer and of race
discrimination. Mellon Bank was later struck out and Boston Safe Deposit &
Trust Co, a subsidiary of Mellon and said to be the actual transferee, was
substituted as second respondent. It has not taken any part in this aspect of the
proceedings. *h*

[7] Rothschild's response in its grounds of resistance on 5 August 1999 was
that Ms Ako was 'barred by the principles of estoppel and res judicata from
bringing the second application'.

[8] Rothschild applied for the application to be struck out, relying on the
decision of this court in *Barber v Staffordshire CC* [1996] 2 All ER 748, [1996] ICR 379. *j*

The employment tribunal

[9] The employment tribunal hearing the matter as a preliminary issue
unanimously decided in extended reasons sent to the parties on 20 October 1999
that Ms Ako's claim against Rothschild had already been disposed of judicially
and that cause of action estoppel prevented the claim from being pursued.

a [10] The tribunal made important findings of fact about the circumstances in which the order was made. At the time of the first application Ms Ako sought assistance from the Commission for Racial Equality (the CRE). She sent them a copy of her originating application. At an interview with an employee of the CRE she was advised to name Mellon Bank as a respondent in addition to Rothschild and to send a letter to the employment tribunal withdrawing the originating

b application. Shortly after the interview Ms Ako telephoned the tribunal and inquired whether Rothschild had put in a notice of appearance. On being told that it had not she said that she would withdraw her application and would confirm that in writing. The tribunal found:

c 'The applicant never intended not to proceed against Rothschild Asset Management Ltd. It was at all material times her intention to replace the originating application which she had withdrawn with one which named both Rothschild Asset Management and the present second respondent.'

[11] Before writing to withdraw the application she checked with colleagues

d that it was all right to do so. She also checked the legal position in a book on employment law in the library of the college where she was studying law. The book, which was published in 1980, was out of date. It indicated that a second application could be made after the withdrawal of an application, provided that it was presented in time, citing the unreported case of *Sidney v Watts Countrymade*

e *Foods* (unreported (EAT 453/78)).

[12] The tribunal concluded that, although Ms Ako intended to withdraw the application against Rothschild, she—

'did not intend, understand or know that she would not be permitted to pursue those claims further and she would not have asked for the application

f to be withdrawn had she known that.'

[13] While expressing considerable regret for the position in which Ms Ako found herself, the employment tribunal held that, on the binding authority of *Barber*'s case, the decision of the chairman was a judicial act; and that the claim against Rothschild having been dismissed by that decision, each of her claims

g against Rothschild was res judicata. It was not open to the tribunal to find that the 'confused advice' or the out of date textbook on which she relied were special or exceptional circumstances which would enable the tribunal to exercise a discretion.

h [14] Ms Ako was refused a review of the decision of the tribunal on 18 November 1999. On 8 May 2000 she made an out of time application for the review of the decision of the chairman dated 2 July 1999. That was refused on 30 May 2000.

j *The appeals*

[15] Ms Ako appealed to the Employment Appeal Tribunal (EAT). On 8 February 2001 the EAT allowed her appeal, holding that *Barber*'s case was distinguishable. The case was remitted to the employment tribunal for a hearing on the merits. Rothschild now appeals on the ground that there was no error of law in the decision of the employment tribunal and that the EAT should have dismissed the appeal.

The appellant's submissions

[16] Mr Panesar, on behalf of Rothschild, contended that *Barber's* case, which
is binding on this court as well as on the tribunals below, is authority for the
proposition that an order of an employment tribunal dismissing an originating
application on withdrawal is a judicial act of a competent court giving rise to
cause of action estoppel, regardless of the reason for the withdrawal of the
application and regardless of the prejudice suffered by Ms Ako and the absence of
any evidence of prejudice to Rothschild. In support of the strict and absolute
nature of the principle he cited the recent decision of this court in *Lennon v
Birmingham City Council* [2001] EWCA Civ 435, [2001] IRLR 826, in which Buxton
LJ said:

'[30] Secondly, it was argued that *Barber* is distinguishable from the
present case because in that case the court knew the reasons for the
withdrawal of the original claim. In this case, we do not know the reasons.
That is, in my judgment, an incorrect argument. The doctrine turns not on
the reason why the court's decision to dismiss the claim was consented to by
the party making the claim, nor on the reason why a court made the order,
but on the simple fact that the order was in fact made. It is for that reason
that, in the case of issue estoppel, the court will not re-enter the merits or
justice of allowing the proceedings to continue, whereas in the wider
jurisdiction under *Henderson v Henderson* ((1843) 3 Hare 100, [1843–60] All ER
Rep 378), which turns on abuse of process and not simply on a comparison
of one order or another, the court may do that.'

[17] Mantell and Pill LJJ agreed with the judgment of Buxton LJ.

[18] In these circumstances, Mr Panesar submitted, it is not permissible to
look behind the terms of the order. The matters raised in the second application
were rightly held by the employment tribunal to be res judicata.

The authorities

[19] A review of the recent authorities is required in order to ascertain the
limits of the application of the doctrine to cases in the employment tribunals.

[20] The principal authority is *Barber v Staffordshire CC* [1996] 2 All ER 748,
[1996] ICR 379, in which the complainant argued that no cause of action estoppel
could arise from an order made by a chairman dismissing an application in the
employment tribunal on withdrawal, because it was an administrative procedure
and did not involve any reasoned judicial decision or determination on the facts
or the law of the case. It was in the context of that submission that the Court of
Appeal concluded that the order of the tribunal was a judicial decision, not a mere
administrative act, holding that there was nothing—

'in the principles of cause of action or issue estoppel which stipulated that
they could only apply in cases where a tribunal has given a reasoned decision
on the issues of fact and law in the previous litigation.' (See [1996] 2 All ER
748 at 756, [1996] ICR 379 at 397 per Neill LJ.)

[21] The Court of Appeal also rejected a subsidiary argument that there were
exceptional circumstances which prevented the application of the ordinary rules
of res judicata and cause of action estoppel. Neill LJ ([1996] 2 All ER 748 at 756,
[1996] ICR 379 at 397) cited the following passage from the opinion of Lord Keith
of Kinkel in *Arnold v National Westminster Bank plc* [1991] 3 All ER 41 at 46, [1991]
2 AC 93 at 104 as demonstrating that that argument was bound to fail:

a   'Cause of action estoppel arises where the cause of action in the latter
    proceedings is identical to that in the earlier proceedings, the latter having
    been between the same parties or their privies and having involved the same
    subject matter. In such a case the bar is absolute in relation to all points
    decided unless fraud or collusion is alleged, such as to justify setting aside the
    earlier judgment. The discovery of new factual matter which could not have
b   been found out by reasonable diligence for use in the earlier proceedings
    does not, according to the law of England, permit the latter to be reopened.'

[22] Although the formulation of general legal principles of cause of action
estoppel in *Barber's* case did not expressly refer to the relevance of the reason for
the withdrawal of the complaint, it should be noted that in his account of the
c   particular circumstances of that case Neill LJ said:

    'The reason why Mrs Barber withdrew her claim was because without
    aggregation she could not satisfy the statutory conditions relating to the
    minimum hours of work per week required to support her claim.' (See
    [1996] 2 All ER 748 at 751, [1996] ICR 379 at 392.)
d
[23] That was a case in which the application was withdrawn because the
applicant had decided to abandon a claim which she considered she could not
successfully pursue.

[24] That is to be contrasted with the circumstances of withdrawal in *Sajid v
Sussex Muslim Society* [2001] EWCA Civ 1684, [2002] IRLR 113. The Court of
e   Appeal distinguished *Barber's* case and held that cause of action estoppel did not
apply where on an application to the employment tribunal based on breach of
contract the complainant made it clear that he would pursue that claim in the
High Court rather than in the tribunal. The complainant had expressly reserved
his right to bring proceedings for breach of contract other than in the tribunal; he
f   withdrew his application because the tribunal did not have the jurisdiction to
award the full amount of damages claimed by him. The dismissal of the
proceedings on withdrawal was relied on by the defendant in the High Court as
creating a cause of action estoppel. The Court of Appeal held that the order of
the employment tribunal did not prevent him from pursuing the breach of
contract claim in the High Court proceedings.

g   [25] The judgments in *Sajid's* case were given on 2 October 2001. The
judgments of the Court of Appeal in *Lennon v Birmingham City Council* [2001] IRLR
826, given on 27 March 2001, were not cited and the court hearing *Sajid's* case was
unaware of them. Mr Panesar contended that the reasoning in the judgments in
Sajid's case was per incuriam and that in any event the decision was distinguishable,
h   as there was an express reservation in the originating application and on the
withdrawal, signifying that proceedings for breach of contract would be brought
in the High Court. In those circumstances it was known to all that the
withdrawal was not unequivocal. The appropriate order would have been a stay
rather than a dismissal of proceedings.

j
Conclusion

[26] I start with *Lennon's* case in which cause of action estoppel was discussed
in the context of refuting the argument that *Barber's* case was distinguishable,
because in *Barber's* case the court knew the reasons for the withdrawal of the
application, whereas in *Lennon's* case the reasons were not known. As Buxton LJ
said ([2001] IRLR 826 at [30]) the doctrine 'turns ... on the simple fact that the

order was in fact made' and not on the reasons why the court's decision to dismiss
was consented to by the party making the claim or the reason why the court
made the order.   *a*

[27] Although that part of the judgment of Buxton LJ, with which Mantell and
Pill LJJ agreed, might appear to present a serious legal difficulty for Ms Ako, I find
that, on a careful reading, it is not insuperable. *Lennon's* case is, of course, binding
on this court. I do not doubt for a moment that it was correctly decided. I do not, *b*
however, agree with Mr Panesar that it has the determinative effect on this case
for which he contends. Although *Lennon's* case highlights the importance of the
fact that an order for dismissal has been made, the decision does not preclude the
application of the general principle that a court may have regard to the factual
circumstances surrounding a consensual legal act (the matrix of fact) in order to
understand its meaning and effect (see *Investors Compensation Scheme Ltd v West* *c*
Bromwich Building Society, Investors Compensation Scheme Ltd v Hopkin & Sons (a
firm), Alford v West Bromwich Building Society, Armitage v West Bromwich Building
Society [1998] 1 All ER 98 at 114–115, [1998] 1 WLR 896 at 912–913). An order
dismissing an action by consent operates in the same way as dismissal by
adjudication: the cause of action expires with the dismissal and the fact of the *d*
order being made precludes fresh proceedings based upon the same or substantially
the same grounds. However, in the event of a subsequent disagreement as to the
extent of the disputes settled by a consent order, evidence of the objective
background to the consent and to the making of the order would be admissible,
even though direct evidence of the parties as to their subjective intentions would
not be (see Foskett *The Law and Practice of Compromise* (4th edn, 1996) p 92 (para *e*
6-05)). In my judgment, neither *Barber's* case nor *Lennon's* case is authority for the
proposition that it is never permissible to have regard to the circumstances
surrounding a consent order in order to determine the extent of the consent
given to the making of the order and the extent of the estoppel arising from it.

[28] In most cases in the ordinary courts of law no problem arises. The *f*
making of a consent order dismissing an action will bar further proceedings
between the same parties for the same cause of action. The order is binding until
it is set aside on appeal or in other proceedings brought for the purpose of
having it set aside. The reasons for the consent of the parties will be irrelevant and
it will not normally be necessary to look beyond the order itself in order to
determine the application of cause of action estoppel. *g*

[29] There is, however, a procedural problem peculiar to the employment
tribunals, which has not been mentioned in the authorities. Its importance only
became apparent to me in the course of the excellent submissions of Ms Monaghan
in support of this appeal. In the ordinary courts there is a significant distinction in
the rules of procedure governing withdrawal of proceedings between (a) an order *h*
dismissing proceedings, which is capable of creating cause of action estoppel, and
(b) discontinuance of proceedings under CPR 38.7 (and previously, with the leave
of the court, under RSC Ord 21, rr 3 and 4), which does not operate as a release
or extinction of a cause of action and as a bar to further proceedings (see *Kronprinz*
(Cargo Owners) v Kronprinz (Owners), The Ardandhu (1887) 12 App Cas 256 at 259 *j*
and *The Law and Practice of Compromise* p 247–249 (paras 15-24, 15-25)). The
permission of the court is now required to make another claim against the same
defendant when the claim arises out of facts, which are the same or substantially
the same as those relating to a claim which has been discontinued after the
defendant has filed a defence. The court would be very likely to give permission
in a case such as the present. The procedural rules in the employment tribunal

a do not, however, make the same distinction or contain similar provisions. This omission may be a trap for the unwary, if the doctrine of cause of action estoppel is strictly applied. The only procedure for withdrawing an application is by an order dismissing the proceedings. There may, however, be cases in which a discontinuance of the tribunal proceedings, if that procedure were available, would be more appropriate than dismissal: *Sajid v Sussex Muslim Society* [2002]

b IRLR 113 is one such case, where the evident purpose of withdrawal was to put an end to the particular proceedings without releasing or discharging the cause of action on which those proceedings were based.

[30] In my judgment, the reasoning in *Barber's* and *Lennon's* cases does not require that cause of action estoppel, as applied in the ordinary courts, should apply to employment tribunal cases where it is clear, on an examination of the

c surrounding circumstances, that the withdrawal of the application is in substance a discontinuance of the proceedings. Discontinuance does not release or discharge the cause of action. It preserves the right to establish an untried claim on the merits in other proceedings. If, as I have explained, this is so in ordinary courts, it does not make any sense that the position should be more strict in its

d application in the less formal setting of the employment tribunals. Unless and until the regulations of the employment tribunals are amended to deal with this point, it would be advisable for employment tribunals, on being notified of the withdrawal of an originating application, to ask the applicant for a statement of the circumstances of the decision to withdraw before deciding whether to make an order dismissing the proceedings.

e [31] I do not find it necessary to express a concluded view on the imaginative submissions of Miss Monaghan based on the Human Rights Act 1998 and art 6 of the European Convention for the Protection of Human Rights and Fundamental Freedoms 1950 (as set out in Sch 1 to the 1998 Act).

[32] I would dismiss the appeal.

f **DYSON LJ.**

[33] I agree that this appeal should be dismissed for the reasons given by Mummery LJ. I only add a few words of my own because it might seem at first blush that the decisions in *Barber v Staffordshire CC* [1996] 2 All ER 748, [1996] ICR 379 and *Lennon v Birmingham City Council* [2001] EWCA Civ 435, [2001] IRLR 826,

g and in particular the passage of the judgment of Buxton LJ in *Lennon's* case (at [30]), which has already been quoted by Mummery LJ, present an insurmountable obstacle for Ms Ako. Buxton LJ said:

h 'The doctrine turns not on the reason why the court's decision to dismiss the claim was consented to by the party making the claim, nor on the reason why a court made the order, but on the simple fact that the order was made.'

The argument advanced on behalf of Rothschild is quite simply that the reason why Ms Ako withdrew her application is irrelevant. Accordingly, the fact that she withdrew her application because she had been advised that it was necessary

j to take this step so as to enable her to make a properly constituted application, joining both companies as respondents, is irrelevant. Accordingly, the decision of the tribunal dismissing the application is an absolute bar to the subsequent proceedings.

[34] The passage in the judgment of Buxton LJ is capable of being misunderstood. A person may withdraw a claim or (in litigation) consent to judgment for many different reasons. He may do so because he has accepted advice that his claim will

fail; or because he cannot afford to continue; or because he wants to defer
proceedings until some other avenue of resolving the matter has been explored; *a*
or because he has decided that he is not yet in a position to proceed; or that he
ought to proceed before a different tribunal (as in *Sajid v Sussex Muslim Society*
[2001] EWCA Civ 1684, [2002] IRLR 113) or add another party (as in the present
case). In some cases, the reasons will indicate that the party has decided to
abandon the claim. In others not so. In relation to the question whether a *b*
dismissal following withdrawal (or a consent judgment) gives rise to a cause of
action or issue estoppel, I consider that the reasons for the withdrawal or consent
are not relevant, unless they shed light on the crucial issue of whether the person
withdrawing the application or consenting to judgment intended thereby to
abandon his claim or cause of action.

[35] I do not believe that Buxton LJ was saying that the dismissal of an *c*
application following withdrawal gives rise to a cause of action or issue estoppel
even if it is clear that the applicant did not intend to abandon his claim or cause
of action. No authority was cited to us for such a proposition which is both so
starkly far-reaching and capable of giving rise to serious injustice.

[36] Two decisions of this court were cited to us which, I believe, do shed *d*
some light on the problem. In *Khan v Goleccha International Ltd* [1980] 2 All ER
259, [1980] 1 WLR 1482, the plaintiff conceded on appeal that the transaction was
not one of moneylending within the meaning of the Moneylenders Act 1927 and
the appeal was dismissed by consent. He then brought another action against the
same defendant and alleged that the transaction was a loan to which the 1927 Act
applied. It was held on appeal that he was estopped by his concessions in the *e*
previous proceedings from asserting that the transaction was a loan. Brightman LJ
said:

> 'The judgment was given by consent and the consent was given because
> the defendant claimed, and the plaintiff accepted, that there was *no* lending
> of money. In my view, that admission by the plaintiff, given to the court and *f*
> founding the judgment by consent, was just as efficacious for the purpose of
> issue estoppel as a judicial decision by the court after argument founding a
> similar judgment.' (See [1980] 2 All ER 259 at 266, [1980] 1 WLR 1482 at
> 1490.)

[37] And he said: *g*

> 'In this case Mr Khan had his opportunity, in support of his appeal on the
> previous occasion, of establishing that money was lent. He chose not to
> establish that position. His counsel got up in court and deliberately
> abandoned it. So it seems to me that he loses his right of establishing that *h*
> same position before another tribunal'. (See [1980] 2 All ER 259 at 267, [1980]
> 1 WLR 1482 at 1491.)

[38] Similarly, Bridge LJ said:

> 'In the event what happened was that Mr Khan, through his counsel, quite
> specifically and categorically chose to withdraw that issue from the consideration *j*
> of the court on the basis that, in relation to that issue, he was bound to accept
> defeat and acknowledge that the case against him was unanswerable.' (See
> [1980] 2 All ER 259 at 268, [1980] 1 WLR 1482 at 1493.)

[39] It is clear from these passages that the court was emphasising the fact that
the plaintiff had expressly abandoned the claim that the transaction was a loan.

a

[40] The second authority is *SCF Finance Co Ltd v Masri (No 3)* [1987] 1 All ER 194, [1987] QB 1028. In that case, a wife decided not to proceed with her application to discharge a Mareva injunction that had been granted in relation to money standing in bank accounts on the basis that the money belonged to her husband. In not proceeding with her application and consenting to its dismissal, her counsel told the court that he did not concede that the money

b

belonged to her husband. The plaintiff then applied for leave to serve a garnishee order on the wife. In the garnishee proceedings, she sought to argue that the money did not belong to her husband. This court decided that, since the wife had chosen not to take advantage of the opportunity to have the issue of the ownership of the money determined in the earlier proceedings, she was barred from raising that issue in the later proceedings even though she had previously

c

purported not to concede the issue. It was argued on behalf of the wife that *Khan's* case could be distinguished because in that case it had been expressly stated that the wife did not concede that the money belonged to her husband. The court said ([1987] 1 All ER 194 at 208–209, [1987] QB 1028 at 1048) that it was not possible to decide that such a reservation is to be given in all such cases some

d

defined effect. The court was applying principles which were intended to treat an issue as laid to rest 'where it would be unfair and unjust between the parties to treat it otherwise; and, in particular, the court is concerned to prevent abuse of the court's procedure by any party'. The court then considered the facts in that case, and decided ([1987] 1 All ER 194 at 209, [1987] QB 1028 at 1049) that to allow the statement by counsel for the wife that she did not concede the issue, which

e

she declined to have tried, would be to permit the process of the court to be abused by her for her own advantage.

[41] In my view, what emerges from these authorities is that there is no inflexible rule to the effect that a withdrawal or judgment by consent invariably gives rise to a cause of action or issue estoppel. If it is clear that the party

f

withdrawing is not intending to abandon the claim or issue that is being withdrawn, then he or she will not be barred from raising the point in subsequent proceedings unless it would be an abuse of process to permit that to occur. On the facts of the present case, it is clear that Ms Ako did not intend to abandon her claim. Nor would it be unjust or unfair as between the parties to permit her to start again: no abuse of process is involved here.

g

JONATHAN PARKER LJ.

[42] I agree that this appeal should be dismissed, for the reasons which Mummery LJ has given. I also agree with the judgment of Dyson LJ (which I have had the advantage of reading in draft).

h

[43] Had Ms Ako expressed an intention to abandon her claim, I would have had no difficulty in concluding that the doctrine of issue estoppel operated to bar her from subsequently seeking to revive it. However, as the tribunal found, she—

j

'never intended not to proceed against [Rothschild]. It was at all material times her intention to replace the originating application which she had withdrawn with one which named both [Rothschild] and [Boston Safe Deposit & Trust Co].'

[44] Nor, in my judgment, does the mere fact that she sought the withdrawal of the application say anything as to her intentions in this respect. In the context of the procedural rules applicable in the employment tribunal, to

which Mummery LJ has referred, a withdrawal of proceedings is equivocal as
between an intention to abandon, on the one hand, and an intention to continue
with the claim in another form, on the other. Accordingly, the doctrine of issue
estoppel is not brought into play, in my judgment.

[45] Buxton LJ's observation in his judgment in *Lennon v Birmingham City
Council* [2001] EWCA Civ 435 at [30], [2001] IRLR 826 at [30] that—

> 'The doctrine [of issue estoppel] turns not on the reason why the court's
> decision to dismiss the claim was consented to by the party making the
> claim, nor on the reason why a court made the order, but on the simple fact
> that the order was in fact made'—

was made in the context of a clear expression of an intention to abandon the
claim. As Buxton LJ makes clear, where a party has expressed such an intention,
the court is not concerned with the reasons which may have led him to do so. In
the instant case that stage is not reached, because Ms Ako neither held nor
expressed any such an intention.

Appeal dismissed. Permission to appeal refused.

Kate O'Hanlon　Barrister.

a
Henderson v Jaouen and another
[2002] EWCA Civ 75

COURT OF APPEAL, CIVIL DIVISION

b PETER GIBSON, MANTELL LJJ AND WALL J

18 DECEMBER 2001, 1 FEBRUARY 2002

Conflict of laws – Jurisdiction – Civil and commercial matters – Special jurisdiction in matters relating to tort, delict or quasi-delict – 'Harmful event' – French court awarding claimant damages against defendants domiciled in France for personal injuries arising
c *from accident in France – Claimant having right under French law to bring new cause of action for further damages 'en cas d'aggravation' – Claimant's condition deteriorating while domiciled in England – Claimant bringing claim for further damages in England on basis that 'harmful event' had occurred in England – Whether 'aggravation' in French law constituting 'harmful event' for purposes of jurisdiction convention – Civil*
d *Jurisdiction and Judgments Act 1982, Sch 1, art 5(3).*

In 1978 the claimant was seriously injured in a road traffic accident in France. In 1981 he issued civil proceedings in France against the other driver, a French national resident in France, and his insurers, a French company. In 1983 the claimant was awarded damages which, under French law, were assessed on the
e basis of his disability at the date of the award. However, the French court expressly gave the claimant the right to return to seek a further award in the event of a subsequent deterioration in his condition. In French law that constituted a fresh cause of action designated 'en cas d'aggravation'. In 1995 the claimant commenced fresh proceedings in the French court claiming
f 'aggravation', but those proceedings were not pursued. Instead, in May 2000 he commenced proceedings against the defendants in England where any award of damages in his favour was likely to be greater than an award in France. The claimant, who had been domiciled in England since 1983, claimed that the English court had jurisdiction under art 5(3)[a] of the Brussels Convention on Jurisdiction and the Enforcement of Judgments in Civil and Commercial Matters
g 1968 (as set out in Sch 1 to the Civil Jurisdiction and Judgments Act 1982). Article 5(3) provided that a person domiciled in a contracting state could, in another contracting state, be sued in matters relating to tort, delict or quasi-delict, in the courts for the place where the 'harmful event' had occurred. It therefore constituted an exception to the general rule under the convention that persons
h domiciled in a contracting state should, whatever their nationality, be sued in the courts of that state. The claimant argued that because 'aggravation' was a new cause of action, and the deterioration in his condition on which that cause of action was based had occurred in England, the 'harmful event' for the purposes of art 5(3) had occurred in England. The defendants applied to have the English
j action struck out for want of jurisdiction. The master dismissed the application, holding (i) that he was bound to apply French substantive law, under which there was a fresh cause of action, and (ii) that, on the basis of an authority of the European Court of Justice, the claimant had the option of commencing proceedings either in France, because that was the place which had given rise to

---

a   Article 5(3) is set out at [4], below

and was the origin of the damage, or in England, because that was the place where the damage had occurred. The defendants appealed.

Held – Although the 'aggravation' was a fresh cause of action in French law, it did not constitute a 'harmful event' within the meaning of art 5(3) of the convention. That term was an autonomous convention concept, not to be determined by reference to national law. The 'harmful event' in the instant case was the original 'tort, delict or quasi-delict' which had occurred in France in 1978. The 'aggravation' was not a fresh wrong done to the claimant: it was a worsening of his condition deriving directly from the original wrong. The fact that in French law it constituted a fresh cause of action was, at best, procedural. There was nothing in that process which required the court to equate the 'aggravation' with a new and different 'harmful event' for the purposes of art 5(3). A conclusion to the contrary could result in forum shopping at will by a claimant simply moving to live in a different jurisdiction. Moreover, the authority on which the master had relied was apt for situations in which the wrongful act committed in one state had an extra-territorial effect directly giving rise to a liability for the same act in another state. It did not, however, apply where the harmful event was a traffic accident which self-evidently was an event occurring only in one jurisdiction at a particular time. Accordingly, the appeal would be allowed, and the proceedings dismissed (see [15], [19], [20], [28], [30], [44], [45], below).

Handelskwekerij GJ Bier BV v Mines de Potasse D'Alsace SA Case 21/76 [1978] QB 708 distinguished.

Notes

For the special jurisdiction in relation to torts, see 8(1) *Halsbury's Laws* (4th edn reissue) para 642.

For the Civil Jurisdiction and Judgments Act 1982, Sch 1, art 5, see 11 *Halsbury's Statutes* (4th edn) (2000 reissue) 1185.

Cases referred to in judgment

Handelskwekerij GJ Bier BV v Mines de Potasse D'Alsace SA Case 21/76 [1978] QB 708, [1977] 3 WLR 479, [1976] ECR 1735, ECJ.

Domicrest Ltd v Swiss Bank Corp [1998] 3 All ER 577, [1999] QB 548, [1999] 2 WLR 364.

Dumez France v Hessische Landesbank Case 220/88 [1990] ECR I-49.

Marinari v Lloyds Bank plc (Zubadi Trading Co, intervening) Case C-364/93 [1996] All ER (EC) 84, [1996] QB 217, [1996] 2 WLR 159, [1995] ECR I-2719, ECJ.

Réunion Européenne SA v Spliethoff's Bevrachtingskantoor BV Case C-51/97 [2000] QB 690, [2000] 3 WLR 1213, [1998] ECR I-6511, ECJ.

Shevil v Presse Alliance SA Case C-68/93 [1995] All ER (EC) 289, [1995] 2 AC 18, [1995] 2 WLR 499, [1995] ECR I-415, ECJ.

Cases also cited or referred to in skeleton arguments

Australia New Zealand Banking Group Ltd v Société Générale [2000] 1 All ER (Comm) 682, CA.

Chaplin v Boys [1969] 2 All ER 1085, [1971] AC 356, HL.

Connelly v RTZ Corp plc, Connelly v RTZ Corp plc [1997] 4 All ER 335, [1998] AC 854, HL.

Cowan v Trésor Public Case 186/87 [1989] ECR 195.

a   *Custom Made Commercial Ltd v Stawa Metallbau GmbH* Case C-288/92 [1994] ECR I-2913.

de Wolf v Harry Cox BV Case 42/76 [1976] ECR 1759.

Decker v Caisse de Maladie des Employé Privés Case C-120/95, *Kohll v Union des Caisses de Maladie* Case C-158/96 [1998] All ER (EC) 673, [1998] ECR I-1931, ECJ.

b   *Dresser UK Ltd v Falcongate Freight Management Ltd, The Duke of Yare* [1992] 2 All ER 450, [1992] QB 502, CA.

F v Belgium Case 7/75 [1975] ECR 679.

Fox v Taher [1997] IL Pr 441, CA.

Gubisch Maschinenfabrik AG v Palumbo Case 144/86 [1987] ECR 4861.

c   *Ivenel v Schwab* Case 133/81 [1982] ECR 1891.

Kalfelis v Bankhaus Schröder, Münchmeyer, Hengst & Co Case 189/87 [1988] ECR 5565.

Luisi v Ministero del Tesoro Case 286/82, 26/83 [1984] ECR 377, ECJ.

Maciej Rataj, The, Tatry (cargo owners) v Maciej Rataj (Owners) Case C-406/92 [1995] All ER (EC) 229, [1994] ECR I-5439, ECJ.

d   *Mecklermedia Corp v DC Congress GmbH* [1998] 1 All ER 148, [1998] Ch 40.

Ministère Public v Mutsch Case 137/84 [1985] ECR 2681.

Overseas Union Insurance Ltd v New Hampshire Insurance Co C-351/89 [1992] 2 All ER 138, [1991] ECR I-3317, ECJ.

Somafer SA v Saar-Ferngas AG Case 33/78 [1978] ECR 2183.

e   *Zelger v Salinitri (No 2)* Case 129/83 [1984] ECR 2397.

Appeal

The defendants, Michel Eugene Jaouen and Mutuelle Assurance des Instituteurs de France, appealed with permission of Senior Master Turner from his decision

f   on 9 March 2001 refusing their application to strike out for want of jurisdiction an action for damages brought against them by the claimant, John William Henderson. The facts are set out in the judgment of the court.

Adrian Brunner QC and *Patrick Green* (instructed by *Pierre Thomas & Partners*) for the defendants.

g   *Michael Brooke QC* and *Hugh Mercer* (instructed by *Teacher Stern Selby*) for Mr Henderson.

Cur adv vult

h   1 February 2002. The following judgment of the court was delivered.

WALL J.

The issue

j   [1] This appeal arises from the refusal by the Senior Master of the Queen's Bench Division (Senior Master Turner), in a judgment given on 9 March 2001, to strike out, for want of jurisdiction, an action for damages for personal injuries brought by John William Henderson (the claimant below and the respondent to the appeal in this court) against Michel Eugene Jaouen (M Jaouen) and Mutuelle Assurance des Instituteurs de France (MAIF) (respectively the first and second defendants in the court below and the appellants in this court).

[2] The case, which arises out of a traffic accident involving Mr Henderson and M Jaouen in France in 1978, raises a short point under art 5(3) of the Convention on Jurisdiction and the Enforcement of Judgments in Civil and Commercial Matters signed at Brussels on 27 September 1968 (the convention) as incorporated into English law by the Civil Jurisdiction and Judgments Act 1982.

The relevant articles of the convention

[3] For the purposes of this case, only two articles of the convention are directly relevant. Article 2 states the general rule:

'Subject to the provisions of this Convention, persons domiciled in a Contracting State shall, whatever their nationality, be sued in the courts of that State.'

[4] Article 5 provides for exceptions to the general rule. The relevant article is 5(3):

'A person domiciled in a Contracting State may, in another Contracting State, be sued ...
(3) in matters relating to tort, delict or quasi-delict, in the courts for the place where the harmful event occurred ...'

The question we have to resolve is: what is meant in this case by the phrase 'the place where the harmful event occurred'?

The facts

[5] The facts are straightforward. On 8 July 1978, Mr Henderson had the misfortune to be involved in a road traffic accident in the region of Cherbourg in France. He was seriously injured. M Jaouen was the other driver. On 20 February 1979 the French criminal court, *le Tribunal Correctionel de Cherbourg*, found that M Jaouen, who is a French national resident in France, was wholly responsible for the accident. In addition to imposing criminal penalties (including a two month suspended sentence of imprisonment) the court ordered M Jaouen to make payments in respect of special damages to Mr Henderson, who had been joined in the proceedings as *partie civile*.

[6] On 27 April 1981, Mr Henderson issued proceedings in a civil court, the *Tribunal de Grande Instance de Cherbourg* (the tribunal) against both M Jaouen and MAIF, which is a French insurance company and which insured M Jaouen. Dr Jacques Fresquet was appointed by the tribunal as the court expert and he examined Mr Henderson. On 14 March 1983 Mr Henderson was awarded damages by the tribunal. For present purposes, it is unnecessary for us consider the detail of either Mr Henderson's injuries, or the sum of damages awarded to him in 1983. Two points, however, need to be noted. The first is that under French law, damages for personal injuries are based on the court's assessment of the victim's disability at the date of the award. Thus it is common ground between the experts in French law in this case that the award made to Mr Henderson by the tribunal on 14 March 1983 was based on the degree of disability which Mr Henderson had suffered as at that date, and was a final award in relation to that degree of disability.

a   [7] However, the second point to be noted is that the judgment of the tribunal expressly gave Mr Henderson the right to return to the tribunal to seek a further award in the event of a subsequent deterioration in his condition. In French law this is a fresh cause of action designated *en cas d'aggravation*.

[8] On 12 December 1995, Mr Henderson, acting through French lawyers, issued fresh proceedings in the tribunal, claiming *aggravation* and seeking, inter

b   alia, an interim payment. On 26 February 1996, the tribunal directed a further medical examination by Dr Fresquet of Mr Henderson (for which he was ordered to pay the fee of F 4,200) and made a provisional award of damages of F 4,000. This appears, somewhat surprisingly to English eyes, to have been less than the fee for the medical examination.

c   [9] The medical report obtained pursuant to the direction of the tribunal is dated 22 May 1996. Mr Henderson does not, however, appear to have pursued his proceedings before the tribunal. Rather, following unsuccessful negotiations between English solicitors instructed on his behalf and English solicitors instructed by MAIF, the present claim was issued in the Queen's Bench Division of the High Court on 30 May 2000.

d   [10] In the particulars of claim, the case is pleaded as follows:

'11. As a matter of French law (a) it is open to a claimant to return to [the tribunal] following a judgment for damages to seek a further award if there has been a subsequent deterioration in his condition (*aggravation*); (b) when

e   a claimant makes a claim for (*aggravation*), this is by way of a new action based on the new fact, viz the deterioration in the claimant's medical condition since the previous award; (c) in accordance with art L124-3 of the French Insurance Code, the claimant is entitled to sue the second defendant [the first defendant's insurers] directly.

f   12. At all material times and, in particular, since 14 March 1983 the claimant has been resident and domiciled in England. Since 1983, the claimant's condition has deteriorated to a significant extent. The symptoms of such deterioration are directly related to the accident in question and would not have arisen but for that accident.'

g   Jurisdiction is then claimed under art 5(3) of the convention on the basis that the 'harmful event' occurred in England.

[11] None of the propositions pleaded in paras 11 and 12 of the particulars of claim is, as we understand it, controversial. Furthermore, as this is an argument about jurisdiction, the case, of course, proceeds on the basis that the claimant has

h   indeed suffered a deterioration in his medical condition, and thus has a valid action in French law *en cas d'aggravation*. The only question is whether or not he is entitled to bring that action in England.

[12] Three points were argued before the Senior Master one of which is not now pursued. Firstly, the claimant argued that he was entitled to bring

j   proceedings in England against MAIF pursuant to art 5(5) of the convention[b]. The Senior Master rejected that argument; there is no cross-appeal against his decision and we need say no more about it.

---

b   'A person domiciled in a Contracting State may, in another Contracting State, be sued ... (5) as regards a dispute arising out of the operations of a branch, agency or other establishment, in the courts for the place in which the branch, agency or other establishment is situated ...'

[13] Secondly, M Jaouen and MAIF argued that the proceedings before the
tribunal were lis pendens for the purposes of arts 21 and 22 of the convention. *a*
The Senior Master rejected that argument and his decision on the point is the
subject of amended additional grounds of appeal. It was, however, common
ground at the hearing before us that arts 21 and 22 only became relevant if the
appellants failed on the third point, namely the argument under art 5(3). It is,
accordingly, to that which we now turn.   *b*

The argument under art 5(3)
[14] We have already set out the terms of art 5(3) and identified the critical
phrase: 'the place where the harmful event occurred ...'
[15] It is common ground that the term 'harmful event' is an autonomous
convention concept, not to be determined by reference to national law. As we *c*
think is already apparent, Mr Henderson's case, in summary, is as follows.
Self-evidently, the accident occurred in France, and the original action, which
concluded in 1983, was properly brought in France. However, *aggravation* is a
fresh cause of action under French law. Mr Henderson has been domiciled and
has lived in England throughout the period from 1983 to date. Therefore, the *d*
deterioration in his condition which founds the basis for his cause of action *en cas
d'aggravation* occurred exclusively in England. Accordingly, the 'harmful event'
identified by art 5(3) has occurred exclusively in England, and the English courts
have jurisdiction to entertain his claim.
[16] This is the reasoning which persuaded the Senior Master that the English
courts had jurisdiction. He said: *e*

'The defendant's argument is that the harmful event took place solely in
France in that the accident and the initial injuries occurred at the same time
and that the deterioration is no more than a consequence of those initial
injuries. In a sense that is true, but it ignores that the French law prescribes
two separate causes of action to these two sets of injuries. The first certainly *f*
occurred in France and was properly dealt with there by the award of the
French court. At that stage there were no additional injuries for which the
claimant could claim damages. It was only in later years that the
deterioration occurred and this is the further harmful event on which the
claimant relies.'
                                                                           g
[17] The Senior Master then considered a decision of the Court of Justice of
the European Communities, *Handelskwekerij GJ Bier BV v Mines de Potasse D'Alsace
SA* Case 21/76 [1978] QB 708, [1976] ECR 1735 and continued:

'Because I am bound to apply French substantive law and because of the *h*
agreement of the French lawyers that there are two causes of action and that
the claimant must commence fresh proceedings in order to recover damages
for the deterioration of his health since the original award in Cherbourg, I
find that this case is on all fours [with] the *Bier* case, and the claimant has the
option to commence proceedings in either France or in England, because the
former was the place which gave rise to and was the origin of the damage *j*
and the latter was the place where the damage occurred.'

[18] The Senior Master did not consider that any of the later cases in the
European Court of Justice took the matter further. He regarded his conclusion
as according with the official report on the convention (see the Jenard Report on
the Convention on jurisdiction and the enforcement of judgments in civil and

a commercial matters 1968 (OJ 1979 C59 p 1)) which, he said, 'supported the option of the choice of two possible jurisdictions in cross-frontier torts and noted in particular that most such claims would result out of traffic accidents'.

[19] We are unable to accept the Senior Master's conclusions for a number of reasons. First and foremost, we are satisfied that for the purposes of art 5(3) of the convention the 'harmful event' in this case was the original 'tort, delict or

b quasi-delict', which occurred in France on 8 July 1978. The *aggravation*, in our judgment, is not a fresh wrong done to the claimant: it is a worsening of his condition deriving directly from the original wrong. The fact that in French law it constitutes a fresh cause of action is, in our judgment, at best procedural. We see nothing in this process which requires the court to equate the *aggravation* with a new and different 'harmful event' for the purposes of art 5(3).

c [20] Secondly, we do not agree with the Senior Master that the instant case is 'on all fours' with the *Bier* case, nor do we think that the subsequent European jurisprudence is neutral on the point: in our view it supports a restrictive interpretation of the *Bier* case which is unhelpful to Mr Henderson.

[21] Thirdly, we think there is considerable force in the point made by the

d appellants that the Senior Master's statement that he was 'bound to apply French substantive law' led him to overlook the fact that 'the place where the harmful event occurred' is an autonomous convention concept, which is not to be identified by reference to national law.

[22] Fourthly, the Senior Master was, in our judgment, mistaken in thinking that the Jenard Report, and in particular its reference to road traffic accidents,

e supported his conclusion.

The authorities

[23] Mr Brooke QC, in a well-structured argument, sought to persuade us that the Senior Master's construction of art 5(3) was supported by the *Bier* case and by

f several other decisions of the European Court of Justice; and that it accorded with the overarching objectives of the convention, namely the sound administration of justice and the efficacious conduct of proceedings in member states. We turn, accordingly, to examine the authorities to see if there is anything in them which either requires or enables us to construe art 5(3) in the manner for which

g Mr Brooke argues.

[24] The principal authority on which Mr Brooke relied was the *Bier* case [1978] QB 708, [1976] ECR 1735. In that case, a French industrial company unlawfully polluted the Rhine by discharging chlorides into it. When the river water was extracted downstream in Holland and used to irrigate a Dutch market

h garden, it caused serious damage to the garden's seed and plant beds. The Dutch market gardener sought to sue the French company in Holland. The Dutch court of first instance held, under art 5(3) of the convention that it had no jurisdiction, as the event which had caused the damage had been the act of polluting the river, which had occurred in France. On appeal, the Dutch *Gerechtshof* stayed the proceedings until the European Court of Justice had given a preliminary ruling

j on the meaning of the phrase 'the place where the harmful event occurred' in art 5(3).

[25] The European Court's decision is neatly encapsulated in the headnote to the case ([1976] ECR 1735):

'Where the place of the happening of the event which may give rise to liability in tort, delict or quasi-delict and the place where that event results in damage are not identical, the expression "place where the harmful event occurred", in Article 5(3) of the Convention ... must be understood as being intended to cover both the place where the damage occurred and the place of the event giving rise to it. The result is that the defendant may be sued, at the option of the plaintiff, either in the courts for the place where the damage occurred or in the courts for the place of the event which gives rise to and is at the origin of that damage.'

[26] Paragraph 11 of the judgment states that the freedom of choice given to claimants by art 5 and as exceptions to art 2 was introduced—

'having regard to the existence, in certain clearly defined situations, of a particularly close connecting factor between a dispute and the court which may be called upon to hear it, with a view to the efficacious conduct of the proceedings.' (See [1978] QB 708 at 729, [1976] ECR 1735 at 1746.)

[27] Paragraph 13 of the judgment gives a helpful insight into the type of situation, in the context of the convention, in which the phrase 'where the harmful event occurred' is unclear and in which, accordingly jurisdiction in either one of two places may be established. One such situation is—

'when the place of the event which is at the origin of the damage is situated in a state other than the one in which the place where the damage occurred is situated, as is the case, inter alia, with atmospheric or water pollution beyond the frontiers of a state.' (See [1978] QB 708 at 730, [1976] ECR 1735 at 1736.)

[28] In our judgment, what may be described as the Bier exception to art 2 is plainly apt for situations in which the wrongful act committed in one state has an extra-territorial effect directly giving rise to a liability for the same act in another state. The Bier case is, of course, the classic example. The tortious act of polluting the river, which occurred in France, did not cause any damage until the water reached Holland. In such circumstances, 'the place where the harmful event occurred' fits as easily with Holland as it does with France.

[29] Another clear example is provided by Shevil v Presse Alliance SA Case C-68/93 [1995] All ER (EC) 289, [1995] ECR I-415, in which the European Court decided that the victim of a libel published in various contracting states was not restricted to an action against the publisher in the state in which the publisher was established, but could sue in each of the states in which the libellous publication had been distributed, albeit solely in relation to the damage suffered to his reputation in each of the states in question.

[30] However, in our judgment, the Bier exception does not apply where the harmful event is a traffic accident which self-evidently is an event occurring only in one jurisdiction at a particular time. In our view, the harmful event in this case was M Jaouen's negligence in causing the accident and injury to Mr Henderson. That act had no extra-territorial effect. It gave Mr Henderson no cause of action in England. He could not choose where to sue in 1981: his only cause of action was in France.

[31] We do not think that the deterioration in Mr Henderson's condition can properly be described as a fresh 'harmful event'. It is a most unfortunate consequence which flows directly from the original tort, delict or quasi-delict and is recognised as such by the French court, which provides a fresh cause of action to cater for it.

a [32] We find nothing in the jurisprudence of the European Court which supports the broad interpretation of art 5(3) for which Mr Brooke argues. To the contrary, the limited scope given by the European Court of Justice to the *Bier* exception to art 2 is demonstrated in a number of the authorities, principal amongst which is *Dumez France v Hessische Landesbank* Case 220/88 [1990] ECR I-49.

b [33] In the *Dumez* case, French companies brought an action in France against a German bank. They sought compensation for damage which they said they had suffered in France consequent upon the insolvency of one of their subsidiaries in Germany. This followed the German bank cancelling loans made to the prime contractor of the development project in Germany in which the subsidiary companies were involved. The claimants argued that in the *Bier* case the court

c had not drawn any distinction in its interpretation of art 5(3) between direct and indirect victims of damage, and that as a consequence, where an indirect victim claims to have suffered personal damage, the court of competent jurisdiction should be the place where the victim suffered that damage.

[34] The European Court rejected that approach. Having reminded itself that

d art 5(3) was an exception to the general rule contained in art 2, the court continued (at 79–80):

> '17 ... those cases of special jurisdiction, the choice of which is a matter for the plaintiff, are based on the existence of a particularly close connecting factor between the dispute and courts other than those of the State of the
>
> e defendant's domicile, which justifies the attribution of jurisdiction to those courts for reasons relating to the sound administration of justice and the efficacious conduct of proceedings.
>
> 18 In order to meet that objective, which is of fundamental importance in a convention which has essentially to promote the recognition and enforcement of judgments in States other than those in which they were
>
> f delivered, it is necessary to avoid the multiplication of courts of competent jurisdiction which would heighten the risk of irreconcilable decisions, this being the reason for which recognition or an order for enforcement is withheld by virtue of Article 27(3) of the Convention.
>
> 19 Furthermore, that objective militates against any interpretation of the
>
> g Convention which, otherwise than in the cases expressly provided for, might lead to recognition of the jurisdiction of the courts of the plaintiff's domicile and would enable a plaintiff to determine the competent court by his choice of domicile.
>
> 20 It follows from the foregoing considerations that although, by virtue of
>
> h [the *Bier* case] the expression "place where the harmful event occurred" contained in Article 5(3) of the Convention may refer to the place where the damage occurred, the latter concept can be understood only as indicating the place where the event giving rise to the damage, and entailing tortious, delictual or quasi-delictual liability, directly produced its harmful effects upon the person who is the immediate victim of that event.
>
> j 21 Moreover, whilst the place where the initial damage manifested itself is usually closely related to the other components of the liability, in most cases the domicile of the indirect victim is not so related.'

[35] In *Marinari v Lloyds Bank plc (Zubadi Trading Co, intervening)* Case C-364/93 [1996] All ER (EC) 84, [1995] ECR I-2719, Mr Marinari lodged promissory notes with a face value in excess of $750m with a branch of Lloyds

Bank in Manchester. The bank refused to return them to Mr Marinari and informed the police. This led to Mr Marinari's arrest and the sequestration of the promissory notes. Mr Marinari brought an action against the bank in Italy seeking compensation for the damage caused to him in Italy by the bank.

[36] Basing itself on its decisions in the *Bier* case [1978] QB 708, [1976] ECR 1735, the *Dumez* case [1990] ECR I-49 and *Shevil's* case [1995] All ER (EC) 289, [1995] ECR 415, the European Court of Justice made clear that the rule which gave a claimant a choice of jurisdictions in which to sue was based on the existence of a particularly close connecting factor between the dispute and courts other than those of the state of the defendant's domicile which justifies the attribution of jurisdiction to those courts for reasons relating to the sound administration of justice and the efficacious conduct of proceedings. The court continued ([1996] All ER (EC) 84 at 95, [1995] ECR I-2719 at 2739–2740):

'13. The choice thus available to the plaintiff cannot however be extended beyond the particular circumstances which justify it: such an extension would negate the general principle laid down in the first para of art 2 of the convention that the courts of the contracting state where the defendant is domiciled are to have jurisdiction would lead to recognition, in cases other than those expressly indicated, of the jurisdiction of the courts for the plaintiff's domicile, which the convention militates against by excluding, in the second para of art 3, the application of national provisions which make such jurisdiction available for proceedings against defendants domiciled in the territory of a contracting state.

14. Whilst it is thus recognised that the term "place where the harmful event occurred" within the meaning of art 5(3) of the convention may cover both the place where the damage occurred and the place of the event giving rise to it, that term cannot, however, be construed so extensively as to encompass any place where the adverse consequences of an event that has already caused actual damage elsewhere can be felt.

15. Consequently, that term cannot be construed as including the place where, as in the present case, the victim claims to have suffered financial damage consequential upon initial damage arising and suffered by him in another contracting state.'

[37] Although *Marinari's* case is dealing with economic loss, it seems to us that the reasoning in paras 14 and 15 of the judgment is apt to cover the instant case, where Mr Henderson has suffered a deterioration in his condition whilst living in England following upon initial damage caused in France.

[38] Although we were referred to other cases, including *Réunion Européenne SA v Spliethoff's Bevrachtingskantoor BV* Case C-51/97 [2000] QB 690, [1998] ECR I-6511 and *Domicrest Ltd v Swiss Bank Corp* [1998] 3 All ER 577, [1999] QB 548, we do not feel these cases either advance Mr Brooke's argument or shed any further light on the question. There is, accordingly, in our judgment, nothing in the European jurisprudence which supports Mr Brooke's attempt to render art 5(3) applicable to the facts of this case, and the passages which we have cited from *Marinari's* case in particular are against it. We see nothing in the authorities, therefore, which causes us to change the view which we expressed earlier in this judgment.

[39] As to Mr Brooke's reliance on the official report on the convention (the Jenard Report on the Convention on jurisdiction and the enforcement of judgments in civil and commercial matters 1968 (OJ 1979 C59 p 1)), we do not think that this assists him. The relevant passage, headed *'Forum delicti commissi'*, deals with both arts 5(3) and (4)^c, and is largely taken up in setting out the countries and bi-lateral treaties in which the jurisdiction was recognised before the convention came into force. The fact that the jurisdiction was so widely recognised, M Jenard states (p 26), was 'a ground for including it in the convention, especially in view of the high number of road accidents'.

[40] The only paragraph dealing specifically with art 5(3) reads (p 26):

'Article 5(3) uses the expression "the place where the harmful event occurred". The Committee did not think it should specify whether that place is the place where the event which resulted in damage or injury occurred, or whether it is the place where the damage or injury was sustained. The Committee preferred to keep to a formula which has already been adopted by a number of legal systems (Germany, France).'

[41] This is plainly a formulation into which the *Bier* case fits neatly, but, in our judgment it is no more than that. It simply provides a template for the court to use when examining the facts of a given case to see if they fit within art 5(3). It cannot, we think, add anything to, or detract from the jurisprudence of the European Court of Justice to which we have referred.

[42] Accordingly, if and to the extent that the Senior Master prayed the Jenard Report in aid in reaching his conclusion, he was wrong to do so.

[43] Mr Brooke frankly acknowledged, in argument, that one of the reasons Mr Henderson had been advised to bring proceedings in England was that the award he was likely to receive in this jurisdiction would be greater than the award he would receive in France. At the same time he acknowledged that were there to be still further *aggravation* and were the French law to change to produce more generous awards, Mr Henderson might well be advised to return to the tribunal.

[44] Whilst we cannot but have sympathy for Mr Henderson, whose life has been blighted by his injuries sustained in the accident, we think there is some force in the submission made by the appellants that the definition of 'harmful event' for which Mr Brooke argues could result in forum shopping at will simply by a claimant moving to live in a different jurisdiction. Were a choice of jurisdictions genuinely open to Mr Henderson, he would plainly be well advised to choose that which was likely to give him the greater award. The fact that he would get more in England than in France cannot otherwise, however, be a good reason for conferring jurisdiction on England.

[45] For all these reasons, the Senior Master was in our judgment wrong to find that the English courts had jurisdiction to entertain Mr Henderson's claim. His order must, accordingly, be set aside and the proceedings dismissed.

[46] It also follows that we do not need to address the additional grounds of appeal in relation to lis pendens and arts 21 and 22 of the convention.

---

c   'A person domiciled in a Contracting State may, in another Contracting State, be sued ... (4) as regards a civil claim for damages or restitution which is based on an act giving rise to criminal proceedings, in the court seised of those proceedings, to the extent that that court has jurisdiction under its own law to entertain civil proceedings ...'

[47] For completeness we should add that we were invited by Mr Brooke, if
we felt it necessary, to adjourn the proceedings for a reference to be made to
the European Court of Justice on the applicability of art 5(3) of the convention
to the facts of this case. Mr Brooke helpfully produced draft questions to be put
to the court. In the event, we think that the European jurisprudence on the
issue is clear, and that the view which we have formed is consistent with it. We
do not, accordingly, think it necessary to make such a reference.

Appeal allowed. Permission to appeal refused.

Kate O'Hanlon   Barrister.

Re Ciro Citterio Menswear plc (in administration)
Ciro Citterio Menswear plc and others v Thakrar and others
[2002] EWHC 662 (Ch)

CHANCERY DIVISION

ANTHONY MANN QC (SITTING AS A DEPUTY JUDGE OF THE HIGH COURT)

14, 15, 18, 27 FEBRUARY 2002

Company – Director – Loan to director – Whether unlawful loan by company to director automatically making director constructive trustee – Companies Act 1985, ss 330, 341.

The first and third respondents, N and K, were shareholders and directors of a company. In 1999 a property was purchased by (or at least in the name of) N for £562,000. Of that sum, £250,000 was borrowed from a building society, but the balance came from funds paid over by the company and reflected in debit entries on the ledger for N's director's account with the company. Subsequently, K obtained a charging order over the property in support of a judgment in his favour against the other shareholders in proceedings under s 459 of the Companies Act 1985. Shortly afterwards, the company went into administration, and the administrators brought proceedings in which they claimed an interest in the property based on the application of the company's money. Those proceedings were resisted by K who asserted N's title to the property and relied on his own charging order. At the hearing, the administrators contended, inter alia, that if the transaction between N and the company had been a loan, it was unlawful under s 330[a] of the 1985 Act as a loan to a director; that it therefore constituted a misapplication of company moneys; that, as a result, N had held the moneys as constructive trustee; and that accordingly those moneys could be traced into the property so that N held it as constructive trustee. In particular, the administrators contended that either the loan itself had been a misfeasance which gave rise to a tracing remedy or, if that were not true when the loan had been made, that it had occurred when the loan had been avoided under s 341[b] of the 1985 Act; that the avoidance had occurred when the proceedings had been served on N; and that accordingly a constructive trust had arisen at that point. Section 341(1) provided that, if a company entered into a transaction or arrangement in contravention of s 330, the transaction was voidable at the instance of the company. Where such an arrangement or transaction had been made for a director of the company, s 341(2)(a) provided that the director was liable to account to the company for any gain which he had made directly or indirectly by the arrangement or transaction.

Held – A loan to a director in contravention of s 330 of the 1985 Act did not automatically make the director a constructive trustee. A loan to a director was not of itself the sort of transaction that was inevitably a misapplication of

---

a   Section 330, so far as material, is set out at [28], below
b   Section 341, so far as material, is set out at [30], below

company moneys. There was nothing inherently wrong with such a transaction
in the abstract. It might or might not be a misapplication on any particular set of *a*
facts, but it was not, as such, a breach by a director of his trusteeship of company
assets. It was not until 1985 that statute had specified civil consequences, namely
that the loan was voidable. If a loan were voidable, it stood until avoided and
accordingly the property in the money paid under the loan passed to the borrower.
That concept was inimical to the existence of a constructive trusteeship, or to any *b*
form of tracing claim, at least in the absence of special circumstances. In the case of
s 330, that conclusion was reinforced by the terms of s 341. That set out the civil
consequences, and, in the absence of special facts making the loan a breach of
fiduciary duty, they left no room for constructive trusteeship. Section 341(2)(a)
seemed to presuppose the absence of constructive trusteeship because it expressly
provided for what would otherwise be one of the consequences of constructive *c*
trusteeship, namely an obligation to account for gains made. Nor was there any
authority which bound the court to conclude that there was a constructive
trusteeship in every s 330 case where a director received the loan. There might be
accompanying facts that justified adding that, but the instant case was not such a
case. That reasoning and conclusion applied whether or not the loan contract had *d*
been avoided, and it was therefore unnecessary to consider whether, and if so
when, it had been avoided. Accordingly, the company and the administrators were
not entitled to claim the equity in the property on the footing that N was a
constructive trustee or by virtue of any other form of tracing (see [32]–[34],
[39]–[41], below).

    Guinness plc v Saunders [1990] 1 All ER 652 applied. *e*

    Wallersteiner v Moir, Moir v Wallersteiner [1974] 3 All ER 217 and *Budge v A F
Budge (Contractors) Ltd (in receivership and liq)* [1997] BPIR 366 distinguished.

Notes

For prohibition of loans to directors and for civil remedies for breach of that *f*
prohibition, see 7(1) *Halsbury's Laws* (4th edn reissue) paras 598, 604.

    For the Companies Act 1985, ss 330, 341, see 8 *Halsbury's Statutes* (4th edn)
(1999 reissue) 393, 401.

Cases referred to in judgment

Budge v A F Budge (Contractors) Ltd (in receivership and liq) [1997] BPIR 366, CA. *g*
Guinness plc v Saunders [1990] 1 All ER 652, [1990] 2 AC 663, [1990] 2 WLR 324,
    HL; *affg on other grounds* [1988] 2 All ER 940, [1988] 1 WLR 863, CA.
Hosack v Robins (No 2) [1918] 2 Ch 339, [1918–19] All ER Rep 565, CA.
Wallersteiner v Moir, Moir v Wallersteiner [1974] 3 All ER 217, [1974] 1 WLR 991,
    CA. *h*

Cases also cited or referred to in skeleton arguments

Bacon (M C) Ltd, Re [1990] BCLC 324.
Foskett v McKeown [2000] 3 All ER 97, [2001] 1 AC 102, HL.
Gill v Continental Union Gas Co Ltd (1872) LR 7 Exch 332.
Jones (F C) & Sons (a firm) (trustee of the property of) v Jones [1996] 4 All ER 721, *j*
    [1997] Ch 159, CA.
Paramount Airways Ltd, Re [1992] 3 All ER 1, [1993] Ch 223, CA.
Pierson (Brian D) (Contractors) Ltd, Re, Penn v Pierson [2001] 1 BCLC 275.
Tait Consibee (Oxford) Ltd v Tait [1997] 2 BCLC 349, CA.
Yagerphone Ltd, Re [1935] Ch 392, [1935] All ER Rep 803.

Application

The applicants, Gurpal Singh Johal and Simon Vincent Freakley, the joint administrators of Ciro Citterio Menswear plc (in administration), sought relief in respect of company funds which had been applied in the purchase by, or in the name of, the first respondent, Nilesh Rasik Thakrar, of a property known as 39 Farquhar Road, Edgbaston, Birmingham, such property being the subject of a charging order in favour of the third respondent, Kirit Lalji Thakrar. Neither the first respondent nor the remaining respondents, Surbhi Thakrar, Richard John Hill (as trustee in bankruptcy of Nilesh Rasik Thakrar and Rasik Lalji Thakrar), Rasik Lalji Thakrar and Vinod Lalji Thakrar, played any active part in the proceedings. The facts are set out in the judgment.

Stephen Moverley Smith (instructed by *DLA*) for the administrators.

John Randall QC and *Lance Ashworth* (instructed by *Wragge & Co*, Birmingham) for Kirit Thakrar.

Cur adv vult

27 February 2002. The following judgment was delivered.

ANTHONY MANN QC.

[1] This is an application brought by the administrators of Ciro Citterio Menswear plc (the company) claiming relief in respect of company funds which were applied in and towards the purchase of a property known as 39 Farquhar Road, Edgbaston, Birmingham (Farquhar Road). The property was purchased by (or at least in the name of) the first respondent Nilesh Thakrar (Nilesh) in a transaction completed on 15 October 1999. The purchase price was about £562,000—the precise figure does not matter. Of that sum, £250,000 was borrowed from Cheltenham and Gloucester Building Society (the building society) and secured by a mortgage. The balance, together with the costs and stamp duty involved, came from funds paid over by the company and reflected in debit entries on the ledger for Nilesh's director's account with the company. The administrators on behalf of the company claim an interest in the property based on that application of the money. In summary they say that the application of the money was a misapplication of company money; alternatively it was an improper loan to a director (Nilesh was a director at the time, as will appear below); in the further alternative it was a transaction at an undervalue entitling the company to follow the money into the company; in the yet further alternative they say that the process involved a wrongful preference of another director which again gives rise to relief involving the following of the money into the property.

Background

[2] The background to the application is as follows. The company was at the time a menswear company with over 150 retail branches. The shareholders at the material time were members of the Thakrar family—using their first names they were Rasik, Vinod, Kirit (all brothers) and Nilesh (the son of Rasik). They were all directors, and there were a couple of non-Thakrar directors as well. In 1999 relations became strained as between Kirit on the one hand and his brothers on the other. He claimed to have been excluded from the company in February 1999 and this led him to bring proceedings under s 459 of the Companies Act 1985 against his brothers and Nilesh. These proceedings were compromised by an order

dated 20 January 2000 on terms that the respondents to the proceedings, *a* including the company, would purchase Kirit's shareholding at a price to be determined under a mechanism involving valuations by accountants. Unfortunately that mechanism broke down and the parties returned to court for the valuation to be carried out. Having ordered an interim payment of £500,000 on 5 September 2000, on 17 October 2000 Judge Boggis QC sitting in the High Court in Birmingham valued the shareholding at £6·14m, and on 13 November *b* 2000 he ordered that £3·5m of that sum be paid to Kirit by 29 December 2000.

[3] What happened then involved the obtaining of charging orders by Kirit which in turn will bring me to some of the issues in this application. However, in order to show how one arrives there it is necessary to step back in time and deal with the history of the acquisition of Farquhar Road. At the beginning of 1999 Nilesh was living in Canada. It is said that his father required him to take more *c* of an active role in the company and so he decided to buy a house here. Farquhar Road was chosen. On 24 September 1999 the sum of £56,250 was transferred from company funds to the solicitors acting for Nilesh in the purchase (Martyn Amey & Co) to be applied as the deposit for the purchase. On 15 October 1999 the company transferred a further sum of £256,250 to Martyn Amey & Co for the *d* purpose of its being applied towards the balance of the purchase price. The remainder of the purchase price was, as I have said above, raised by way of mortgage from the building society. Lastly, on 12 November 1999 the company drew a cheque payable to Martyn Amey & Co in the amount of £20,636·52 for the stamp duty and professional fees due in relation to the house purchase. In this manner was the property purchased; it was at all times held in the name of Nilesh *e* and the entirety of the funds used to acquire it, other than those borrowed from the building society, came from the company.

[4] The order in which Judge Boggis QC fixed the value of the shares incorporated undertakings given by the individual defendants (ie Rasik, Vinod and Nilesh) to make disclosure of their assets. In those affidavits they made *f* reference to loans made to Nilesh which, as a matter of evidence, are highly germane to the issues which I have to decide. I shall return to those affidavits in due course but I shall, for the time being, continue the basic chronology. As appears from the story so far, by the time that Kirit obtained his order quantifying the amount to be paid for his shares, Nilesh owned Farquhar Road. The company also owned a number of properties, and Kirit set about obtaining charging orders *g* over all those properties (ie the company properties) in order to obtain payment for his shares. On 13 December 2000 Judge Boggis QC made charging orders nisi over 33 properties owned by the company. Those orders were made absolute on 22 December 2000. The orders secured the sums hitherto ordered to be paid by Judge Boggis QC. On 7 February 2001 Judge Boggis QC ordered that completion *h* of the acquisition of Kirit's shares should take place on 16 March 2001, at which date payment of the balance of the purchase price, not hitherto ordered by the judge, should take place. On 14 February 2001 the judge made charging orders nisi over the 33 company properties, and this time over properties owned by the individual respondents, to secure the sums due and payable on completion. One *j* of those properties was Farquhar Road. Those orders were made absolute on 26 February 2001. No sums have been paid under the judge's orders other than the interim payment of £500,000. It is as chargee under a charging order that Kirit is interested in these proceedings, and it is in that capacity that he has been joined.

[5] Surbhi Thakrar, the second respondent, is the wife of Nilesh. On 19 April 2001 Kirit started proceedings pursuant to his charging order seeking an order for

a sale of Farquhar Road. Surbhi claimed an interest in that property and was joined as a party to those proceedings by an order made by Judge Boggis QC on 14 May 2001. There was a trial of those proceedings on 26 and 27 June 2001, at the end of which Judge Boggis QC found that Surbhi was entitled to 22% of the equity in Farquhar Road, and he made an order for sale. Meanwhile, on 12 March 2001 the company had gone into administration. Having come to the conclusion that the

b circumstances of the purchase of Farquhar Road might entitle the company to claim an interest in Farquhar Road, the administrators sought to intervene in the order for sale proceedings, but on 10 September 2001 Judge Boggis QC refused to allow them to intervene on the basis that they could and should have intervened before if they were going to do so. It has not been suggested that that in any way prevented them from commencing their own proceedings, and that is what they

c have done in this application.

[6] Thus we arrived at the present application. The applicants are the two joint administrators (namely Mr Gurpal Johal and Mr Simon Freakley) and the company. The respondents are, in this order, Nilesh, Surbhi, Kirit, Richard John Hill, Rasik and Vinod. Mr Hill is the trustee in bankruptcy of Nilesh and Rasik;

d Rasik was bankrupted on his own petition on 11 May 2001 and Nilesh on his petition on 22 May 2001. The only one of the respondents to have played any active part in these proceedings is Kirit who defends the claim of the administrators by asserting the title of Nilesh to Farquhar Road and relying on his own charging order. Surbhi sent a letter to the court, received on 14 February 2002 (that is to say very shortly before the hearing commenced), ostensibly

e written from Canada to where she says she has moved permanently, explaining that she does not have funds to represent herself and setting out her version of the background to the purchase of Farquhar Road. I should say that I do not rely on this letter as being evidence before me for the purposes of this case. The principal effect of the letter, so far as I am concerned, is to confirm that she has

f been properly served with these proceedings and is properly joined.

[7] For the sake of completeness I should add that, as if the proceedings described above were not enough, there have been at least three further sets of proceedings brought by Kirit under s 423 of the Insolvency Act 1986 against various members of the Thakrar family and their wives. In relation to those I need say no more than that they are irrelevant to these proceedings other than to

g confirm (if confirmation were necessary) that there has been a very comprehensive falling-out between Kirit on the one hand and the other members of the family on the other. That goes to explain, in part, the paucity of the oral evidence which I received in this case.

h *The claims made in these proceedings*

[8] In these proceedings the administrators put their case in a number of ways. (1) They say that the application of company moneys in the purchase of Farquhar Road was a straight misapplication of company funds by the directors which leads to a constructive trust of the money and of the property bought with it so that Nilesh holds Farquhar Road on trust for the company (subject, of

j course, to the building society mortgage). They say that that interest is not caught or defeated by the charging order obtained by Kirit; nor does Surbhi's interest beat it. (2) In the alternative, if, as alleged by Kirit on one analysis of the facts, the true analysis of the transaction between Nilesh and the company was that there was a loan by the company to Nilesh, that loan was unlawful pursuant to s 330 of the 1985 Act and that unlawfulness again gives rise to a constructive

trusteeship of the property which beats both Kirit and Surbhi. (3) In the
alternative the administrators say that any gift or loan of the moneys to Kirit (if
either is the true analysis of what took place) was a transaction at an undervalue
which, they say, entitles the court to make an order following the money into the
property under s 241(1)(b) of the 1986 Act. (4) In the yet further alternative, they
say that if the analysis is as Kirit says it is, namely that the transaction involves a
repayment of Rasik's own director's account followed by a loan of the relevant
moneys by Rasik to Nilesh, then the repayment of Rasik was a voidable
preference under s 239 of the 1986 Act which again entitles the court to make an
order following the money into the property under s 241(1)(b) of that Act. (5) In
the application further relief is claimed against Rasik and Vinod (though now
abandoned against the latter) claiming the money which the administrators say
was misapplied by one or both of them in the purchase of Farquhar Road. I
should record that the leave of the court was given for the bringing of these
proceedings against the bankrupt respondents.

The application of the moneys—evidence
    [9] Obviously the correct analysis of the transaction, and the answers to the
issues raised by these claims, depends on an analysis of what happened at the time
as a matter of law, which in turn depends on a fuller consideration of the facts. I
therefore turn to that.
    [10] There is no dispute that the three sums of money that I have referred to
moved from the company, out of company funds, to the solicitors acting for
Nilesh. The movement itself is clearly documented. However, the documentation
relating to how the matter was dealt with as between Nilesh and the company,
and as between Nilesh and the other directors, is extremely thin. There is, in
effect, just one document. It is a print of part of the company's computerised
nominal ledger produced, according to its 'run date', on 29 December 1999. It is
headed 'Account 243301 Directors Account NRT'. It shows the three
contributions made towards the purchase of Farquhar Road as three debit items
but not entered on their proper dates—they were entered after the actual dates,
and not in the correct order. The entries are made under seven columns, namely
period, date, reference, type, debit, credit and comment. In respect of the three
items the entries in those columns are, taking the items in the order in which they
are entered on the ledger, as follows:

Period	Date	Reference	Type	Debit	Credit	Comment
9/99	06/11/99	PAYMETS	CASH BOOK	256250		PYMT OCT 99
10/99	4/12/99	CASH BK	CASH BOOK	20636.52		PAYMTS NOV 99
11/99	31/12/99	PAYEMTS	CASH BOOK	56250		ADD DEC'99 PAY

(The transcriptions are literal; the mistypings are in the ledger.)

[11] No live witness was produced by either side to explain how those entries came to be made or who directed them. There are a number of other debit and credit entries on that ledger before, after and between those entries; the provenance of many of those other entries is obscure. However, for present purposes it is significant to note that at the date of each of the entries there was no credit balance on this ledger so the payments cannot be viewed as repayments by the company of sums owing to Nilesh.

[12] It is around this central document that much of the case of the administrators hinges. They say that the document shows that when Nilesh took, or was provided with, the money he was at best receiving an unlawful loan or at worst involving himself in a misappropriation of the money of the company. Kirit, however, does not accept this. He has not adduced any evidence of the participants in the form of witness statements produced for the purposes of these proceedings which explain what happened, and in the light of the history of litigation between him on the one side and the rest of his family on the other that is not at all surprising. However, he has relied on various statements made by Nilesh, Rasik, Surbhi and Vinod in other litigious contexts which, he says, explain the matter in a way which demonstrates that the transaction was entirely proper. What he relies on is an arrangement between principally Nilesh and Rasik which enabled Nilesh to have the benefit of substantial credit balances which existed on Rasik's account with the company. In summary, it is said that the directors on this occasion were doing what they had done in the past, which is effectively to give a director without a credit balance on his account with the company the benefit of the credit balances on other directors' accounts if those others agreed. What happened in other contexts, and ultimately in this, was that the director without a credit balance (here Nilesh) was allowed to draw against the credit balances of others and the matter was put right by appropriate entries in the latter's accounts at the end of the financial year when the audited accounts were being drawn. In this case it was Rasik who had the credit balance. The strict analysis of the transaction was, it is said by Mr John Randall QC who appeared for Kirit, that the company repaid Rasik the debt it owed him, in the amount of the money used by Nilesh in the purchase of Farquhar Road, and that amount was lent by Rasik to Nilesh.

[13] It is necessary to examine the evidence relied on by Mr Randall to see what that evidence establishes, and then to consider the effect in law of my findings of fact.

[14] First, it is clear on the evidence that Rasik did, at that time, have sufficient sums owing to him on his account with the company to match the sums drawn by Nilesh for the purchase of Farquhar Road. It is not necessary for me to go through the calculations carried out by Mr Randall to prove that; at the end of the day I do not think that Mr Moverley Smith, who appeared for the administrators and for the company, disputed it. More problematic, however, is establishing what the arrangement between the parties was and what its legal effect was. The evidence relied on by Mr Randall was as follows. (1) The three director respondents filed witness statements and affidavits disclosing their means in the post-judgment proceedings in the s 459 petition. In his witness statement of 16 October 2000 Rasik said: 'Nilesh Thakrar has a property worth £562,000 subject to borrowings of £250,000 (including £200,000 borrowed from myself).' Mr Randall relies on that as supporting the case of a loan by Rasik while accepting that the statement of its amount is inaccurate. (2) In a further disclosure affidavit sworn on 27 October 2000, Rasik said: '... whilst I have a director's loan account

showing some of £438,653·81 at the end of September 2000, I have allowed Nilesh
to draw these funds from the company against my director's loan account
without payment of interest.' An exhibit to that affidavit describes his loan
account as being 'subject to loan in full to Nilesh'. (3) In a disclosure affidavit
sworn on 27 October 2000, Nilesh said:

'... as at end September 2000 I had drawn from the company a total of
£485,459·18 against the directors loan accounts for Rasik and Vinod. I have
used these funds to acquire the family home in Birmingham and to pay for
living expenses. No interest is payable by me to the company or by the
company to Rasik and Vinod in respect of their loan accounts.'

(4) In a similar affidavit, sworn on the same date, Vinod disclosed a schedule of
his assets in which he described his 'Directors Loan Account' in the company as
being '£59,538·89. Against this amount I allowed [Nilesh] to borrow £46,805·37
from the company as at end September 2000, with no interest payable.' (5) In an
affidavit sworn by her in order to support her claim to a share in the equity of
Farquhar Road, and to resist the application by Kirit for an order for sale, Surbhi
said: 'As on all previous occasions the deposit for the property was paid out of the
company against the money deposited by Rasik Thakrar into the company.'
(6) In his witness statement filed in these proceedings, Kirit said it will not have
been unusual for Rasik and Vinod to have made a loan to Nilesh from a
repayment to them of money they had lent to the company. He said that if,
during the period of his involvement with the company, he needed funds he
asked for authorisation from Rasik to withdraw funds from his director's loan
account. If the withdrawal resulted in his account becoming overdrawn, Rasik,
or Nilesh, or Vinod would lend to him from their loan accounts to ensure that his
account remained in credit. This, he says, occurred on a number of occasions and
involved a number of directors. He was not challenged on that in cross-
examination. (7) Kirit produced several documents which tended to indicate, or
were consistent with, a process by which what would otherwise be debit balances
on directors' loan accounts at the end of a year were cancelled out by debits to
other accounts of other directors which were at that time in credit. These
documents were accountants' summaries, accountants' working figures or, in
one case, figures prepared by the finance director of the company (who was not
a member of the Thakrar family) which, when compared with other available
figures, showed a general netting-off process of this nature. Kirit frankly admits
that he had no knowledge of how these transactions were actually written up into
the books of the company, but says that he was told by two sets of auditors that
the inter-account loans, as he describes them, were written up at the end of the
financial year in the manner just referred to. (8) During the course of the hearing,
Kirit served a Civil Evidence Act notice relying on a transcript of the oral evidence
given by Nilesh in the hearing before Judge Boggis QC in the order for sale
proceedings. Mr Moverley Smith did not oppose the introduction of that
evidence; nor did he seek to cross-examine Nilesh as he might have done under
CPR 33.4 (though since there is a possibility that Nilesh has moved to Canada it
may be that that failure was of no practical significance). During the course of
that evidence Nilesh gave positive evidence of a conversation between himself
and Rasik in which Rasik expressly permitted Nilesh to 'borrow against' Rasik's
credit balance in the company. (9) Mr Randall also relied on findings made by
Judge Boggis QC when he made the order for sale over Farquhar Road. In his
judgment Judge Boggis QC said: '[the balance of the purchase moneys] appears

a to have been drawn out of directors' loan accounts, certainly in the name of Rasik and possibly in the name of one of the other Thakrars as well.' I should say at this stage that I am not assisted by that finding. As I understand it, the precise basis on which money was drawn from the company was not the issue before him, and the sort of points that have to be debated as between the company on the one hand and its directors on the other in relation to the propriety of the transaction, b and its true analysis, simply did not arise in his proceedings. Furthermore, a finding such as that would not in any event bind the company or the administrators.

[15] Mr Moverley Smith invited me to reject the evidence as to what the members of the Thakrar family said was happening at the time. He points out that it is hearsay and says that no good reason has been advanced for not calling c the relevant deponents. In addition, he relies on inconsistencies of expression as to what the basis of the application of the moneys was, and a statement of affairs prepared by Nilesh which does not refer to an outstanding loan to Rasik. At its highest his case involves my looking at little more than the ledger entries showing the payment of the moneys from the company, debited to Nilesh's account, and d saying that since there was no justification for the payment of the money in the purchase of Farquhar Road then the application was inevitably a misapplication of company moneys.

The facts—my findings

[16] The evidence in this case is in an unsatisfactory state. While it is perfectly e understandable that Kirit himself would not know what happened at the time (because it happened during the period of his exclusion from the affairs of the company), there are three other directors who would have some knowledge (although one of them, namely Nilesh, may now be in Canada). They have spoken only through their evidence given in other proceedings where the focus f was different. Each side had its reasons for not calling them. Presumably Kirit was concerned at the prospect of calling as witnesses those against whom he has been conducting bitter litigation, even though the mechanism of witness summonses was available to him and even though he had in good solid form the evidence-in-chief that he would expect (and want) them to give. For their part the administrators were presumably wary of calling directors who might simply g be concerned to exculpate themselves, and in any event the evidence given by them before would not be a promising start for the administrators. In those circumstances I face obvious difficulties in coming to conclusions as to what the agreed basis was, if any, for the application of the moneys in the purchase of Farquhar Road.

h [17] Mr Moverley Smith has urged on me that I should not accept the principal evidence relied on by Mr Randall because it is hearsay and because Mr Randall did not call the witnesses. For his part, Mr Randall has said that I should not make a finding which effectively brands the directors as dishonest (if I were to find that the descriptions of arrangements in their various witness j statements were factually untrue) without their having been cross-examined. I have to say that my sympathies lie more with Mr Randall than with Mr Moverley Smith. Mr Moverley Smith took no point on the hearsay presentation of the witness statements of the other members of the Thakrar family—the statements were exhibited to a witness statement of Kirit in these proceedings. It would have been open to Mr Moverley Smith to have sought to call those witnesses for cross-examination under CPR 33.4, at least so far as those still within the jurisdiction are concerned (Rasik and Vinod—query Nilesh). Furthermore, Vinod attended on the first day of this hearing, representing himself. I was told that an agreement had been reached with him and that he would withdraw unless he was required to give evidence. I think there was some sort of implicit invitation for me to consider whether I thought he should give evidence; for obvious reasons I declined the invitation. Neither Mr Randall nor Mr Moverley Smith said they wished him to remain to give evidence, and in the circumstances he withdrew. Questions were then raised by Mr Randall as to the terms of the compromise between Vinod and the administrators, and it transpired that the terms were that the claim against him would not be proceeded with, that neither party would seek costs against the other, and (most significantly for these purposes) he would attend to give evidence if required. Accordingly, it seems to me that he was not only a witness who was theoretically available to the administrators, he was a witness who was *actually* available to them. Yet they made no attempt to call him. In those circumstances I am not prepared to disregard his evidence or the evidence of his brother Rasik and nephew Nilesh.

[18] In those circumstances, and in the light of their evidence (and the evidence of Kirit) I find that there was some sort of casual understanding between Nilesh and Rasik, which took place against the background of prior dealings between the directors which had, in previous years, involved one director to whom the company did not owe money drawing money from the company with a balancing transaction being carried out in other directors' accounts (those in credit) at the end of the company's financial year. From one or two other documents we have, it is reasonably clear that that had happened in the past. Against that background I think it is likely, and I am prepared to find, that there was a similar arrangement, albeit very casual, between Nilesh and Rasik when Nilesh bought Farquhar Road. In other words, Nilesh was permitted to draw the moneys from the company because Rasik, and perhaps Vinod, had credit balances which could be adjusted in due course to put Nilesh's account back in credit.

[19] As to the implementation of that arrangement, I also find that no balancing entries were in fact passed in the other directors' accounts before the company's year end (5 February 2000), after the year end or indeed at any time before the administration intervened. No documentation has been produced to suggest that they were entered, and there is some positive evidence that they were not. The ledger balance for Rasik's account as at 29 December 1999 shows a credit balance of £361,653·81. I have a print-out for the company's year 2001–2002 which shows an opening balance for that year of the same amount. There are no entries in his account which would be necessary to achieve the loans and transfers contemplated by the informal arrangements between the directors. It is true that there are documents, relied on by Mr Randall, which assume some sort of netting-off. For example, the finance director produced a manuscript document showing what he thought the balances on the accounts of Rasik, Vinod and Nilesh were in September 2000, presumably for the purposes of enabling them to give details to Judge Boggis QC, and that document probably assumes some sort of netting-off. The figures given by the directors, or some of them, to Judge Boggis QC assume the same thing. On 18 January 2001 the auditors of the company, Harben Barker, produced draft accounts for the period ended 5 February 2000, and Mr Randall pointed out, correctly, that in accordance with previous years the figure for directors' accounts was an overall netted figure, encompassing all accounts. Mr Randall relies on this as further support for his

a case that there was an implemented arrangement for making appropriate debits to Rasik's account (and if necessary Vinod's account, though on the figures it would not have been necessary to have resort to his) to balance the drawings by Nilesh. However, the impact of this submission in relation to the draft accounts is very much diminished by the manuscript on the first page which reads: 'VERY DRAFT, FIRST COMPUTER RUN, NOTES TO BE SORTED OUT.' All in all I do not consider

b that the evidence relied on by Mr Randall justifies a finding that the company actually did what it was planned it would do after the year end.

The legal effect of those findings

[20] I now turn to deal with some of the legal consequences of these findings. Mr Moverley Smith says that all that has happened, in the light of my findings, is

c that Nilesh drew the money, but any steps needed to 'legitimise' (my word) those drawings did not take place because there were no entries in the relevant ledgers and whatever netting-off process ought to have taken place did not take place. This means that there was an appropriation of company moneys without any legal justification; alternatively he says that the company in effect gave the money

d to Nilesh; alternatively there was a loan by the company to Nilesh. Mr Randall urges on me that there was in substance and in law an agreement by Rasik to make the relevant loans straight away (on drawdown by Nilesh from the company) so that all that happened was that there was a failure to record that. On this analysis any entry at the year end would be merely a formal record of that which had already taken place, so that there could be no question of any

e misappropriation of company money or an unlawful loan to Nilesh. I should find for that analysis, he says, because that is a fair overall reading of what the parties were saying they agreed; it would be wrong to make a finding which involved a potential criminal offence (an unlawful loan to a director) if there was another explanation; that I should apply the maxim omnia praesumuntur rite esse acta (if

f I am allowed to, given that it is Latin); and that is what Judge Boggis QC found.

[21] Despite Mr Randall's cogent submissions, I do not think his analysis is right. It is quite true that the parties could have carried out the transaction by the company repaying Rasik and Rasik lending on to Nilesh. Had they done so the company's ledgers would have shown no entry at all in Nilesh's account, and it would have shown debits in Rasik's. But the books do not show those entries.

g Of course, that is not determinative, because errors can be made, but there was no evidence that the entries that were made were mistakes. The failure to write them up in Rasik's account at the time was actually deliberate. There was no arrangement to make an immediate loan. There was an arrangement to pass entries at the end of the year to make sure that there was no outstanding debit

h balance on Nilesh's account. Since other entries could be anticipated (the ledger shows that there were others, and the whole arrangement between the directors, as I have found it to be, lends itself to fluidity in the accounts with various debits and credits during the course of the year) the debit entries to be passed on Rasik's account at the end of the year might or might not correspond to the debit entries

j passed on Nilesh's in connection with the purchase of Farquhar Road, or the debit balance on his account that resulted from those entries. Whether there was an exact correspondence or not would or might depend on what other entries occurred in the meanwhile to affect the balance.

[22] I therefore think that the arrangement between the parties was different from an immediate loan by Rasik to Nilesh. It was an arrangement to pass entries so as to give rise to loans at the end of the year so as to make sure that there were

no debit balances on Nilesh's account. That may or may not amount to a
binding contract to make a future loan; but it certainly does not amount to an
immediate contract of loan. Mr Randall described the difference between this
analysis and the analysis of immediate loan as being a fine or technical one. I do
not think it is. Directors have an important responsibility in relation to the funds
under their control. That responsibility is hedged around with legal obligations
and criminal offences. If one director has no credit on his account with a company
he (and the other directors) cannot simply treat the credit balance of another
director as something against which he can draw and rely on the matter being put
right at the end of the year. If the directors agree that the one in credit will
provide his credit for the benefit of the other so as to create a loan, then that is
permissible and easily achieved, but it does require some sort of agreement that
that is what should happen, and it requires real transactions to take place and to
be documented. The company has a right to expect that such matters are
properly documented and that the transaction is properly carried out. The
directors are not entitled to deal with matters informally and sort it out later. If
they do that they are at risk, as this case demonstrates, of being found to have
failed to have carried out the transaction in a permissible manner, thereby leaving
themselves exposed to the possibility of their having carried it out in an
impermissible manner. In this context the omnia praesumuntur maxim does not
apply. There is no reason to presume regularity in favour of someone who fails
to take the opportunity to carry out a transaction in a regular fashion.

[23] I therefore find that on the facts of this case the moneys applied in the
purchase were company moneys which passed to Nilesh and not Rasik's moneys
lent to Nilesh. It is therefore necessary to go on to consider what the nature of
that drawing was. Was it a straight misapplication of company money, that is to
say a director helping himself to company money in an impermissible way, was
it a gift (which amounts to the same thing) or was it in the nature of a loan by the
company to Nilesh? On this question may turn the relief to which the company
is entitled. Mr Moverley Smith's case is as follows. (a) The transaction was
simply a misapplication which gives the company a right to trace into the
property at common law or alternatively in equity via a constructive trusteeship
that would arise by virtue of the misapplication. (b) If it was not a simple
misapplication, then it was a loan. Being a loan to a director it was an unlawful
loan under s 330 of the 1985 Act, and if that is right then it is again a misapplication.
As a result of that the moneys were held by Nilesh as constructive trustee and via
that route the moneys can again be traced into Farquhar Road so that Nilesh
holds it (subject to the building society mortgage) as constructive trustee. (c) In
each case, the interest taken by Kirit under his charging order was not an
acquisition of an interest for value, so that the company's interest beats Kirit's
interest.

[24] In response to this Mr Randall makes the following points. (a) If (as I
have found) the transaction is not treated as a loan by Rasik then it was a loan by
the company to Nilesh. Even though that loan was made unlawful by s 330 of the
1985 Act, that still did not give rise to any constructive trusteeship, so that Nilesh
(and Surbhi) owned the beneficial interest in the house and Kirit's charge still had
an interest to bite on. The company has no competing interest. (b) As a
concomitant of that he denies that there was a straight misapplication, but if there
were then he would say that there was no right to trace at common law. He
would, I think, accept that a straight misapplication would give rise to constructive
trusteeship. However, he questions whether the court should enforce it when in

a the present circumstances a combination of a secured bank debt, the realisations to date and Kirit's right of marshalling would mean that enforcement makes absolutely no difference to the company in money terms because if the company takes this property then Kirit gets the same value elsewhere by virtue of marshalling.

b [25] It is therefore necessary to consider what the effect of the arrangement as to the drawing of the moneys was.

[26] I have already found that the moneys were taken as a result of an express adoption by Nilesh and Rasik of the arrangement that had operated in previous years of allowing one director to draw moneys from the company in anticipation of an adjustment from the accounts of other directors at or after the year end. It is pertinent to examine the situation immediately after the money was drawn.

c Nilesh had no intention of keeping company money for his own purposes with no mechanism for repayment. It was not an out and out misappropriation in the nature of theft. The money would not have been taken if there had not been other money available to, in effect, replace it. It, or any outstanding balance after any intervening transactions had been taken into account, would be replaced by

d the adjustments involving other directors' accounts. The nature of such an arrangement is, I think, an informal loan, with repayment coming at or shortly after the year end. The directors did not in terms agree that the moneys should be treated as loans, but that is not the point. The question is, what is the nature of the transaction that did occur, looked at objectively. Subject to questions of authority and consensuality, I think that they should be characterised as loans.

e [27] Mr Moverley Smith says that they should not be treated as loans because the necessary element of consensuality was missing. There was no loan agreement, no board resolution and no agreement by the board, or a director with authority, to make such a loan. It is true that there was no documentation, and that there was no formal board minute. However, in relation to this company, I do not

f think that that is necessarily determinative. The evidence, thin though it was, tended to show that what happened on this occasion was part of a historical pattern, and there was no suggestion that previous instances of the same sort of thing had been dealt with formally by the board. At the end of the year the balances were sorted out with the assistance of the auditors. That suggests, and I find, that Thakrar directors were informally authorised to give effect to these sort

g of arrangements, so that Rasik and Nilesh (in this case) had sufficient authority to give rise to this particular loan. The sort of casual disposal of company finances that went on in this case is not to be encouraged, but that does not mean that the relevant consensual element was lacking. I find it to have been present; and I therefore find that what technically happened in this case was a loan, or a

h transaction in the nature of a loan, to Nilesh by the company.

[28] That being the case, it is necessary to consider the legal consequences. The loan is rendered unlawful by s 330 of the 1985 Act. That section provides:

j '(2) A company shall not—(a) make a loan to a director of the company or of its holding company; (b) enter into any guarantee or provide any security in connection with a loan made by any person to such a director.

(3) A relevant company shall not—(a) make a quasi-loan to a director of the company or of its holding company; (b) make a loan or a quasi-loan to a person connected with such a director; (c) enter into a guarantee or provide any security in connection with a loan or quasi-loan made by any other person for such a director or a person so connected.'

[29] The expression 'quasi-loan' is defined in s 331:

'(3) A quasi-loan is a transaction under which one party ("the creditor") agrees to pay, or pays otherwise than in pursuance of an agreement, a sum for another ("the borrower") or agrees to reimburse, or reimburses otherwise than in pursuance of an agreement, expenditure incurred by another party for another ("the borrower")—(a) on terms that the borrower (or a person on his behalf) will reimburse the creditor; or (b) in circumstances giving rise to a liability on the borrower to reimburse the creditor.'

(The transaction in this case may be said to fall more naturally within that description than the concept of loan, but that does not matter for these purposes.)

[30] There are various exceptions to the bar, none of which applies in this case. Section 341 deals with remedies:

'(1) If a company enters into a transaction or arrangement in contravention of section 330, the transaction or arrangement is voidable at the instance of the company unless—(a) restitution of any money or any other asset which is the subject matter of the arrangement or transaction is no longer possible, or the company has been indemnified in pursuance of subsection (2)(b) below for the loss or damage suffered by it, or (b) any rights acquired bona fide for value and without actual notice of the contravention by a person other than the person for whom the transaction or arrangement was made would be affected by its avoidance.

(2) Where an arrangement or transaction is made by a company for a director of the company or its holding company or a person connected with such a director in contravention of section 330, that director and the person so connected and any other director of the company who authorised the transaction or arrangement (whether or not it has been avoided in pursuance of subsection (1)) is liable—(a) to account to the company for any gain which he has made directly or indirectly by the arrangement or transaction; and (b) (jointly and severally with any other person liable under this subsection) to indemnify the company for any loss or damage resulting from the arrangement or transaction.'

[31] Mr Moverley Smith puts his case on loan in two ways. First, he says, it is a misfeasance which gives rise to a tracing remedy. Second, if that was not true when the loan was made, then it occurs when the loan is avoided under s 341, so that a constructive trust arises at that point. He says that avoidance occurred in this case on the service of the present proceedings on Nilesh. Mr Randall, on the other hand, disputes that any breach of s 330 gives rise to constructive trusteeship. He says the loan is a voidable transaction, not a void one, and it stands until avoidance, at which point money is payable but no constructive trust arises. In this case there has not even been any avoidance on the facts.

[32] The principal question in this part of this case is whether an unlawful loan gives rise to constructive trusteeship at any stage. I take as a starting point that a loan to a director is not of itself the sort of transaction that is inevitably a misapplication of company moneys. There is nothing inherently wrong with such a transaction in the abstract. It may or may not be a misapplication on any particular set of facts, but it is not, as such, a breach by a director of his trusteeship of company assets. Statute did not intervene until the Companies Act 1929, when the predecessor of s 330 made its first appearance. The bar was repeated in s 190

a of the Companies Act 1948, but without the civil consequences of the bar being spelled out. It was not until 1985 that statute specified civil consequences.

[33] The civil consequences are specified as being that the loan is voidable. That is of obvious significance to this part of the case. If a loan is voidable, it stands until avoided. That means that property in the money paid under the loan passes to the borrower. In my view that concept is inimical to the existence of a

b constructive trusteeship, or any form of tracing claim, at least in the absence of special circumstances. That view is supported by the speech of Lord Goff of Chieveley in *Guinness plc v Saunders* [1990] 1 All ER 652, [1990] 2 AC 663. Lord Goff was considering a breach by a Guinness director of the disclosure rules in s 317 of the 1985 Act. The consequences of that breach were that the contract in question, under which the director took considerable financial benefits, was

c voidable, not void. The Court of Appeal ([1988] 2 All ER 940, [1988] 1 WLR 863) had held that the director therefore became a constructive trustee of the moneys he had received under that contract and had to pay them back. Lord Goff, with whom Lord Griffiths agreed, held that this part of the analysis could not be sustained. A voidable contract stood until avoided. He considered an argument

d by counsel for Guinness to the effect that the director—

'having received the money as constructive trustee, must pay it back. This appears to have formed, in part at least, the basis of the decision of the Court of Appeal. But the insuperable difficulty in the way of this proposition is again that the money was on this approach paid not under a void, but under

e a voidable, contract. Under such a contract, the property in the money would have vested in Mr Ward (who, I repeat, was ex hypothesi acting in good faith); and Guinness cannot short circuit an unrescinded contract simply by alleging a constructive trust.' (See [1990] 1 All ER 652 at 665, [1990] 2 AC 663 at 698.)

f [34] In my view that reasoning applies in this case. Until any avoidance by the company the loan stood, and there was no constructive trust. In the case of s 330 of the 1985 Act that conclusion is reinforced by the terms of s 341. That sets out the civil consequences, and it seems to me that in the absence of special facts making the loan a breach of fiduciary duty they leave no room for constructive trusteeship. Section 341(2)(a) seems to presuppose the absence of constructive

g trusteeship, because it expressly provides for what would otherwise be one of the consequences of constructive trusteeship, namely an obligation to account for gains made.

[35] That is the position looking at the 1985 Act and the *Guinness* case. However, Mr Moverley Smith relies on two cases which he says are binding on me and

h which require the conclusion that a breach of s 330, in the case of a loan to a director, makes the receiving director a constructive trustee. The first is *Wallersteiner v Moir, Moir v Wallersteiner* [1974] 3 All ER 217, [1974] 1 WLR 991. Lord Denning MR referred to a breach of s 190 of the 1948 Act (the predecessor of s 330 of the 1985 Act) and said ([1974] 3 All ER 217 at 239–240, [1974] 1 WLR

j 991 at 1015): 'The loans would be unlawful under s 190. He [the director] would be guilty of a misfeasance and liable to indemnify the company against any loss arising therefrom.'

[36] Lord Denning MR clearly says nothing there about constructive trusteeship, but Mr Moverley Smith says that the fact that there is a misfeasance means that such liability must arise. I do not agree. There may be many misfeasances which give rise to constructive trusteeship, but I do not think that *all* misfeasance has

that consequence. Lord Denning MR specified the remedy he saw as applicable
to that case, namely an indemnity against losses arising. That is a different   a
remedy from constructive trust.

[37] The second case is at first sight closer to the point. Mr Randall, in answer
to a question that I had posed about the consequences of a breach of s 330, had
very properly drawn my attention to a case reported only on Lexis even though
that case might be taken as being against him. That case is *Budge v A F Budge*   b
(Contractors) Ltd (in receivership and liq), which I have since been told is reported at
[1997] BPIR 366. In that case a company served a statutory demand on a former
director in respect of moneys owing on what the report describes as his 'loan
account'. The demand was not set aside by the district judge, or the judge
(Jonathan Parker J) on appeal, and the matter arrived in the Court of Appeal as
an application for leave to appeal. Apparently the director had habitually drawn   c
moneys from the company in anticipation of dividends declared in his favour by
the holding company. At some point there arose, and remained, a balance owing
by the director of over £1m, and it was in respect of that that the statutory
demand was served. The facts do not appear in any great detail, but it appears
that at least part of the indebtedness arose because the company paid interest and   d
other payments that were otherwise the liability of the director. Various points
were debated, and the point that Mr Randall drew to my attention, and that is
relied on by Mr Moverley Smith, is the last of them. The director argued that
certain payments were made by the company in breach of the relevant bank
mandate because more than one signature was required and the payment
authorisations only had one (presumably that of the director in question). He   e
seems to have made the brave submission that instead of suing him, the company
ought to sue the bank for breach of the mandate so he should not be held liable.
That submission was rejected for two reasons. The first was a ratification point,
which does not arise in the present case. Then Peter Gibson LJ set out the
reasoning of Jonathan Parker J below, who had said: f

"'In the second place, even if breaches of mandate occurred which were
not ratified, given that the payments in question were admittedly for the
benefit of Mr Budge, as a director of Contractors [ie the company] he was
and remains a constructive trustee of such moneys and under an obligation
to repay them to Contractors. Mr Budge, as a director of Contractors,   g
cannot be heard to say that instead of requiring him to repay moneys
wrongly applied for his benefit, Contractors should sue Barclays for the
money, leaving it to Barclays to join him as third party."' (See [1997] BPIR
366 at 376.)

And then Peter Gibson LJ himself said as follows: h

'[Counsel for the director] was unable to advance any argument to suggest
that the judge was wrong on that point. Indeed, it seems to me that he was
plainly right and on this point as well there is, in truth, no defence to the
claim made by Contractors.'
                                                                                      j
[38] That, Mr Moverley Smith says, shows that a director who wrongfully
takes a loan in contravention of s 330 of the 1985 Act, holds the money as
constructive trustee.

[39] That part of that decision obviously gives one pause for thought, but I do
not think it compels me to change the view at which I arrived as a result of
considering the statute and the *Guinness* case. It is impossible to see what the full

a facts were from the judgment. It may well be that the consensual element which I have found to be present in this case was lacking in that one, so although the case was described as a claim on a director's loan account it was in truth a claim based on improper drawings which could not be properly described as a loan. One gets the impression that that was a case of a principal director just helping himself without much reference to anyone else, an impression which is *b* strengthened by the 'breach of mandate' point (on the assumption that he, by himself, effected those particular drawings). The official receiver apparently treated the case as involving s 330 of the 1985 Act (part of his report in disqualification proceedings is set out in the Lexis report) but it does not follow that that was necessarily the correct analysis. The difference between constructive trusteeship and requiring the return of moneys does not seem to have been *c* focussed on in the report, since on any footing the director owed or was liable for the money. For whatever reason the judge below had concluded that the moneys were 'wrongly applied for his benefit'; that smacks to me much more of a case which goes beyond straight breaches of s 330 and gets into the territory of straightforward misappropriation. It may even be that Jonathan Parker J had in *d* mind that the director could not blow hot and cold—if there was a breach of mandate then he (the director) was not entitled to the money either because the drawing was not properly authorised as a matter of the company's internal authorities. That would give rise to constructive trusteeship if it were the case. All in all, therefore, I do not consider that this authority binds me to say that in every s 330 case where a director receives the loan (or quasi-loan) there is *e* constructive trusteeship. There may be accompanying facts which justify adding that, but the present is not, in my view, such a case.

[40] My reasoning and conclusion applies whether or not the loan contract has been avoided. It is therefore not necessary to consider the rival submissions as to whether, and if so when, it was.

f [41] I therefore conclude that the company and the administrators are not entitled to claim the equity in Farquhar Road on the footing that Nilesh was a constructive trustee or by virtue of any other form of tracing.

Transaction at an undervalue

g [42] That does not end Mr Moverley Smith's case. He has another weapon in his armoury. In the event that the transaction is found to have been a loan he says it was a transaction at an undervalue under s 238 of the Insolvency Act 1986, and the relief to be granted should be an order under s 241(1)(b) of that Act requiring Farquhar Road to be vested in the company as representing in Nilesh's hands the *h* application of moneys transferred pursuant to the transaction.

[43] The first question is whether the transaction was indeed at an undervalue. Part of the case on undervalue does not arise. Mr Moverley Smith argued that the transaction amounted to a gift to Nilesh but in the light of my findings above there was no gift, so that limb of s 238 does not arise. The second limb, however, probably does. Under s 238(4)—

j

> 'a company enters into a transaction with a person at an undervalue if ...
> (b) the company enters into a transaction with that person for a consideration
> the value of which, in money or money's worth, is significantly less than the
> value, in money or money's worth, of the consideration provided by the
> company.'

Mr Moverley Smith's case is that the company lent £100,000, and in exchange got *a* a covenant which is worth less than £100,000, and no provision to pay interest, so that on both counts there was an undervalue. I dismiss the first of those as the basis of undervalue. There was no evidence as to the value of Nilesh's covenant, and it is far from obvious that it was not worth £100,000. The second, however, is more material. On my findings there was no agreement for interest. There was no evidence that anyone ever paid interest under the casual drawing *b* arrangements the directors had, and I find that no interest was contractually payable. To that extent I think that the transaction falls within the definition and was a transaction at an undervalue—the company lent £100,000 on which it could have obtained interest to someone who was not going to pay interest on it. The considerations do not match, and undervalue is proved.

[44] However, the transaction is only one in respect of which relief can be *c* granted if it was carried out at a relevant time within the meaning of the statute. Section 240 of the 1986 Act contains two elements in this respect—a time element and an insolvency element. The time requirement is fulfilled—the transaction was within two years of the administration. In relation to solvency, s 240(2) provides that if the transaction is with a connected person (which it was—Nilesh *d* was a director and that makes him connected for these purposes under s 249 of the 1986 Act) then it is to be presumed that the company was unable to pay its debts at the time or became unable to do so as a result of the transaction. The next question therefore becomes whether Kirit (who claims through Nilesh) has rebutted that presumption.

[45] The evidence in relation to solvency in this case might be described as *e* rather thin. Had I found that the transaction had taken effect as a repayment by the company to Rasik and a loan by Rasik to Nilesh then the administrators would have sought to say that the repayment of Rasik was a voidable preference under s 239 of the 1986 Act. That would have required them to prove that the company was insolvent at the time. There was no real evidence of that. There *f* was no attempt by them to draw a balance sheet to show balance sheet insolvency, and there was none of the familiar evidence of unpaid bills, pressing creditors and recent writs that one so often sees in preference cases as demonstrating creditor pressure. I am prepared to infer from the absence of that sort of evidence in that context (ie in the context of a claim in which the administrators would have been expected to have produced that sort of evidence *g* if it had existed) that the evidence did not exist—in other words, to assume and find that creditors were being paid on time. No one has ever suggested they were not. I am confident that in any event, even in the absence of the voidable preference claim the administrators would have disclosed the evidence had it existed. On balance sheet solvency, the audited accounts as at 6 February 1999 *h* showed a balance sheet surplus of over £13m, and a trading profit after tax but before dividends of £1·72m. That is evidence of balance sheet solvency at that date. The accounts were signed off on 27 August 1999, and no post-balance sheet event of solvency-affecting proportions is disclosed in the accounts up to that date. No later accounts were audited but no draft accounts have been produced *j* suggesting insolvency. During the course of 1999 and 2000 the Thakrars were litigating the s 459 petition over the question of the price to be paid to Kirit for his shares. In December 1999 the respondents to those proceedings offered him over £2m for his shares, which he turned down. Judge Boggis QC ordered that he should receive over £6m, after having heard evidence which was obviously detailed, and which involved him hearing evidence on various accounts. I have

a not seen that evidence, though I have seen a draft profit and loss account produced by the auditors on 1 September 2000 showing a profit for the 12 months to 5 February 2000 of £1·09m. Nothing in Judge Boggis QC's judgment suggests insolvency in either of the statutory senses, or even the existence of evidence pointing that way; it all points the other way. While it is true that by the time of the administration petition the company was said to be insolvent, it is impossible

b to work out from the 2.2 report by what mechanism and when that occurred. The 2.2 report annexes a balance sheet which still shows a £9m surplus. Mr Moverley Smith, who admittedly did not have the burden in this respect, was not really able to point to any evidence of insolvency. He did point out that the company was insolvent when it went into administration; but that does not help much in relation to October 1999. He also pointed out that the draft accounts of

c 18 January 2001 showed the company making serious losses; but again that does not help in relation to October 1999. And he relied on the fact that in the intervening period the directors had themselves made further loans to the company; but that does not demonstrate insolvency any more than taking any other loan does. In the light of all the evidence I consider that Kirit (who

d shoulders Nilesh's burden for these purposes, since he claims through Nilesh) has satisfied me that the company was able to pay its debts as they arose within the meaning of the statute. In those circumstances the loan cannot be challenged as a payment at an undervalue.

[46] That means that I do not have to consider whether it would be

e appropriate to order the relief sought by Mr Moverley Smith, namely an order for the vesting in the company of Farquhar Road under s 241(1)(b) of the 1986 Act. However, I should say that I am far from convinced that such an order would have been appropriate bearing in mind that the purpose of the order is 'for restoring the position to what it would have been if the company had not entered into that transaction' (see s 238(3)). Depending on its value, to make such an

f order might well have resulted in doing more than that, even if as part of the transaction one cancelled the loan (a point which was not canvassed in argument).

[47] In the circumstances I find against the administrators on the claim based on a transaction at an undervalue.

g
Other matters

[48] The application in this case adds claims for repayment from Rasik and Vinod of the equivalent of the moneys advanced to Nilesh in so far as they 'co-operated in the disbursement of the company's money'. The claim against

h Vinod has been settled and I am not asked to make any order against him. That leaves a potential claim against Rasik. The application is framed so as to suggest that the claim against Rasik is based on a wrongful misappropriation by Nilesh in which he (Rasik) participated. I have found that not to be the analysis so on that footing that particular claim against Rasik fails. However, I have found that there

j was an unlawful loan, and under s 341(2)(b) of the 1985 Act Rasik, whom I find to have participated in and authorised it, would be liable to indemnify the company. During the course of the proceedings I allowed an amendment so that the s 330 point could be taken against Nilesh/Kirit (up to that point it was referred to in the evidence but not pleaded) but the amendment does not make reference to Rasik. It may be that in the light of Rasik's bankruptcy the company would not be particularly interested in a judgment on the point; or it may be that his trustee in

bankruptcy would not dispute it in the light of my findings. I invite the claimants
and the trustee to consider what should happen about this.

[49] This application, whose central facts (that is to say the application of
moneys in the autumn of 1999) are relatively simple, has raised a great number
of claims, defences and other points. The course and contents of this judgment
means that I have not dealt with them all because I have not had to. My failure
to do so should not be taken as any sort of indication that I have not considered
them to the extent that was appropriate. It is right, however, that I should refer
to one of them. If my findings had been otherwise in relation to the beneficial
ownership of Farquhar Road then the question might have arisen as to whether
or not Kirit, under his charging order, took for value so as to beat the interest of
the company. Mr Randall accepted that the case of *Hosack v Robins (No 2)* [1918]
2 Ch 339, [1918–19] All ER Rep 565 seemed to determine the point against him,
but had an argument that it was decided per incuriam. He indicated to me that
he did not intend to advance that point at this level but would effectively want it
kept live in case this case went further. I think it is right that I should record that
in case it should matter in the future.

Order accordingly.

Celia Fox   Barrister.

a
Woodhouse v Consignia plc
Steliou v Compton
[2002] EWCA Civ 275

b COURT OF APPEAL, CIVIL DIVISION
BROOKE, LAWS AND DYSON LJJ
4 FEBRUARY, 7 MARCH 2002

Practice – Stay of proceedings – Automatic stay of proceedings under CPR transitional
c *provisions – Lifting of stay – Considerations to be taken into account – CPR 3.9 –*
CPR PD 51, para 19.

Estoppel – Issue estoppel – Pre-trial application – Relevance of rule on finality of
litigation to successive pre-trial applications for same relief.

d
In two appeals to the Court of Appeal which were heard separately but on the
same day, issues of general importance arose in relation to the transitional
arrangements in CPR Pt 51 and the relevance of the Human Rights Act 1998 in
cases where the court was minded to make an order that had the effect of barring
a claimant from pursuing his case without a trial on the merits. Both appeals
e were second-tier appeals against the automatic stay, imposed under para 19[a] of
CPR PD 51, in existing proceedings which had not come before a judge between
26 April 1999 and 25 April 2000. In the first appeal, the district judge had
dismissed the claimant's application for the stay to be lifted solely on the grounds
of inordinate delay, even though CPR 3.9[b] provided that, on an application for
f relief from any sanction imposed for a failure to comply with any rule, practice
direction or court order, the court 'will' consider all the circumstances, including
nine specified items. The district judge's decision was upheld on appeal by the
judge who concluded that he was unable to interfere with her conclusion that the
delay was inordinate.

In the second appeal, the claimant had obtained judgment for damages to be
g assessed following a trial on liability in his action for personal injury. The
proceedings were subsequently automatically stayed under para 19 of CPR PD 51.
In response, the claimant applied for an order for an interim payment and
directions. A proposed directions order, annexed to the application notice, began
with a draft direction to remove any stay in respect of the proceedings. On the
h application, the claimant's counsel contended primarily that the action had not
been stayed. The district judge rejected that argument, and further held that if
the application could properly be treated as an application to lift the stay, he
would refuse it on the grounds that it had not been supported by any evidence.
After that decision was upheld by the judge on appeal, the claimant made a fresh
application to the district judge, asking in terms for an order removing the stay.
j The district judge dismissed the application as an abuse of process, and his

---

a   Paragraph 19, so far as material, provides: '(1) If any existing proceedings have not come before a
    judge, at a hearing or on paper, between 26 April 1999 and 25 April 2000, those proceedings shall be
    stayed.
    (2) Any party to those proceedings may apply for the stay to be lifted ...'
b   Rule 3.9 is set out at [31], below

decision was again affirmed by the judge who held that all the matters relied on by the claimant could and should have been raised on the first application, and that accordingly the second application fell foul of the principle that barred a party from relitigating at a later stage a matter that could have been litigated at an earlier stage. No consideration was given to the effect of CPR 3.9. On the appeals of both claimants, the Court of Appeal considered whether the courts below had properly exercised their discretion in light of the provisions of r 3.9. On the second appeal, the court was also required to consider the relevance, to pre-trial applications for the same relief, of the rule that, in the absence of special circumstances, parties should bring their whole case before the court so that all aspects of it might be decided once and for all (the finality of litigation rule).

Held – (1) The automatic stay imposed by para 19 of CPR PD 51 fell to be treated as a sanction imposed for a failure to comply with any rule, practice direction or court order within the meaning of CPR 3.9, and it followed that judges had to take into account the provisions of that rule when determining whether to lift an automatic stay. One of the great demerits of the former procedural regimes was that simple rules became barnacled with case law. Under the new regime, the draftsman had sought to dispense with the need for litigants to be familiar with judge-made case law by drawing into one place the most common of the considerations a court had to take into account when deciding whether a litigant should be granted relief from a sanction imposed on him. The circumstances in which a court might be asked to make a decision of that kind were infinitely varied. That was why r 3.9 instructed the court to consider all the circumstances of the particular case, including the nine items listed. On the other hand, r 3.9 would lose much of its praiseworthy purpose of encouraging structured decision-making if courts did not consciously go through the exercise of considering all the items on the list when determining how, on balance, they should exercise their discretion. Notwithstanding that the directory word 'will' was used in r 3.9 rather than the mandatory word 'must', judges (and particularly less experienced judges) should submit themselves to the discipline of considering each of the matters listed in r 3.9 which appeared to them to be relevant to the case that they had to decide. If they failed to do so, there might be a serious danger that an appeal court might overturn their decision for omitting to take a material consideration into account. It followed that in future judges should not simply latch onto one or two considerations (such as the length of any delay) to the exclusion of all others, when deciding whether it was just to remove an automatic stay. They should remember that if a stay remained in place, they were depriving the claimant of access to the court, a concept which now had particular resonance under art 6 of the European Convention for the Protection of Human Rights and Fundamental Freedoms 1950 (as set out in Sch 1 to the Human Rights Act 1998). Judges should carry out the necessary balancing exercise methodically and explain how they had reached their ultimate decision. In the first appeal, the district judge had been wrong to concentrate only on the length of the delay, and it fell to the Court of Appeal to exercise the discretion afresh. All the specific matters to be considered under CPR 3.9 were either fairly neutral or tended to favour the further progress of the claimant's action to trial. Accordingly, the appeal would be allowed (see [29], [31]–[33], [41], [42], [48], [50], [51], below); *Audergon v La Baguette Ltd* [2002] All ER (D) 166 (Jan) explained and applied.

a (2) Although the policy that underpinned the finality of litigation rule had
relevance as regards successive pre-trial applications for the same relief, it should
be applied less strictly than in relation to a final decision of the court, at least
where the earlier pre-trial application had been dismissed. In the second appeal,
both the district judge and the judge had been wrong to regard as decisive the fact
that the claimant's fresh application was a second bite at the cherry. They had
b failed to consider the cogency of the case for lifting the stay, having regard in
particular to the provisions of CPR 3.9. It therefore fell to the court to exercise
the discretion afresh, and that discretion would be exercised in favour of lifting
the stay. Accordingly, the second appeal would also be allowed (see [56], [58],
[62], below); *Henderson v Henderson* [1843–60] All ER Rep 378 and *Securum
Finance Ltd v Ashton* [2001] Ch 291 considered.

c

Notes
For the rule precluding the raising of issues that could have been raised previously,
see 16 *Halsbury's Laws* (4th edn reissue) para 980, and for automatic stays of
proceedings under the transitional provisions of the CPR, see 37 *Halsbury's Laws*
d (4th edn reissue) para 929.

Cases referred to in judgment
*Arbuthnot Latham Bank Ltd v Trafalgar Holdings Ltd, Chishty Coveney & Co (a firm) v
    Raja* [1998] 2 All ER 181, [1998] 1 WLR 1426, CA.
Ashingdane v UK (1985) 7 EHRR 528, [1985] ECHR 8225/78, ECt HR.
e *Audergon v La Baguette Ltd* [2002] EWCA Civ 10, [2002] All ER (D) 166 (Jan).
Axtell-Powell v Labor [2000] CLY 223.
Bansal v Cheema [2000] CA Transcript 358.
Barrow v Bankside Members Agency Ltd [1996] 1 All ER 981, [1996] 1 WLR 257, CA.
Biguzzi v Rank Leisure plc [1999] 4 All ER 934, [1999] 1 WLR 1926, CA.
f *Birkett v James* [1977] 2 All ER 801, [1978] AC 297, [1977] 3 WLR 38, HL.
G v G [1985] 2 All ER 225, [1985] 1 WLR 647, HL.
Henderson v Henderson (1843) 3 Hare 100, [1843–60] All ER Rep 378, 13 ER 301.
Janov v Morris [1981] 3 All ER 780, [1981] 1 WLR 1389, CA.
Keith v CPM Field Marketing Ltd [2000] CA Transcript 1311, (2000) Times, 29 August.
g *Securum Finance Ltd v Ashton* [2001] Ch 291, [2000] 3 WLR 1400, CA.
Stanford v Stanford [2001] EWCA Civ 1289, [2001] All ER (D) 261 (Jul).
Tanfern Ltd v Cameron-Macdonald [2000] 2 All ER 801, [2000] 1 WLR 1311, CA.
Tinnelly & Sons Ltd v UK, McElduff & Sons Ltd v UK (1999) 27 EHRR 249, [1998]
    EHCR 20390/92, ECt HR.

h

Appeals

Woodhouse v Consignia plc
The claimant, Tracey Woodhouse (suing as widow and administratrix of the
j estate of Mark Woodhouse, deceased), appealed with permission of Arden LJ
granted on 30 July 2001 from the order of Judge Coningsby QC made in the
Croydon County Court on 29 February 2001 dismissing her appeal from the
order of District Judge Fink on 4 September 2000 dismissing her application to
lift the automatic stay on her proceedings against the defendant, Consignia plc,
imposed under para 19 of CPR PD 51. The facts are set out in the judgment of
the court.

Steliou v Compton

The claimant, Martin Steliou, appealed from the order of Judge Thompson QC
made in the Basingstoke County Court on 27 April 2001 dismissing his appeal
from the order of District Judge Fuller on 19 January 2001 dismissing as an abuse
of process his application to lift the automatic stay on his proceedings against the
defendant, Nicola Jane Compton, imposed under para 19 of CPR PD 51. The
facts are set out in the judgment of the court.

Nicholas Dean (instructed by *Bhatia Best*, Mansfield) for Mrs Woodhouse.
Jonathan Spicer (instructed by *Eversheds*, Nottingham) for Consignia.
Colin Challenger (instructed by *Collins, Stone & Thompson*) for Mr Steliou.
Paul Russell (instructed by *Jacobs*) for Ms Compton.

Cur adv vult

7 March 2002. The following judgment of the court, to which all its members
contributed, was delivered.

INDEX

BROOKE LJ.

(1) INTRODUCTION

[1] We heard these two appeals separately on the same day, but because they
raise issues of general importance in relation to the transitional arrangements in
CPR Pt 51 and the relevance of the Human Rights Act 1998 in cases where a court
is minded to make an order which has the effect of barring a claimant from
pursuing his case without a trial on the merits, we are now giving a single
judgment of the court on the two appeals. We have structured our judgment so
that it will begin with a statement of the facts in each appeal, continue with a
consideration of the principles a court must apply when determining issues of this
kind, and end with the application of those principles to the two cases before us.
The *Steliou* case also raised an additional issue which we consider in the final part
of this judgment.

(2) WOODHOUSE v CONSIGNIA PLC

[2] This is an appeal by the claimant Tracey Woodhouse, who sues as widow
and administratrix of her dead husband Mark Woodhouse's estate, against an
order of Judge Coningsby QC at the Croydon County Court on 29 February 2001
when he dismissed her appeal against an order of District Judge Fink on 4 September

a 2000 whereby she had refused to lift the automatic stay imposed on the proceedings pursuant to para 19 of the practice direction to Pt 51 (CPR PD 51).

[3] This action was started on 30 April 1998. Mr Woodhouse committed suicide 17 days later. It appears that he had been suffering from paranoid psychosis prior to his death. He was claiming damages against the defendants, who were his employers, arising out of a reference they had written for him when b he was applying for a job with the local council. He had been offered the job subject to satisfactory references, and he complained because he said that the unsatisfactory reference, which lost him the job, contained false information about his disciplinary record and otherwise failed to give a fair and accurate view of his employment history.

c [4] This episode occurred in November 1997. Mr Woodhouse obtained legal aid in February 1998 and commenced this action less than six months after his alleged cause of action arose. Following his death on 17 May 1998, the defence was filed on 18 May, and Mr Woodhouse's solicitors told the defendants' solicitors of their client's death on 21 May 1998. Thereafter nothing happened in the action as between the parties for more than two years. On 28 June 2000 d Mrs Woodhouse's solicitors made an application for an order removing the automatic stay imposed by virtue of the transitional provisions contained in Pt 51 and its practice direction, and also for an order amending the particulars of claim so that she was substituted for her husband as the claimant.

[5] The only evidence she placed before the court in support of her application e for the stay to be removed was in these terms: 'The untimely death of Mr Woodhouse caused her immense grief and distress. She now, however, feels able to continue this action on behalf of Mr Woodhouse's estate.'

[6] The judge observed that although the formal evidence (apart from a reference to Mr Woodhouse's paranoid psychosis prior to death) was otherwise silent, it was possible to ascertain from the papers before the court that letters of f administration had been granted to Mrs Woodhouse as long ago as 25 August 1998 and her husband's legal aid certificate was amended in her favour a month later. It also appeared that counsel had made the necessary amendments to the particulars of claim in December 1999, six months before the application to the court was made.

g [7] When the matter came before the district judge, she observed that this was a difficult area of law because it was still comparatively new. She considered that CPR PD 51 did have the effect of imposing a stay in this case, and she went on to say that this was an inordinate delay. She accepted that the claimant was upset, but this was far too long a delay. She therefore refused to remove the stay.

h [8] The claimant appealed, and at the hearing of the appeal she sought permission to adduce new evidence in support of her case that the stay should be removed. She also asked that the judge should treat the appeal as a complete rehearing rather than merely a review of the district judge's judgment. The judge refused both these applications, and on this second appeal there is no challenge j to either of those rulings. Although he dismissed the appeal, Judge Coningsby indicated that there was an area of law raised by the case on which he believed that further guidance from this court would be valuable. He expressed it in this way:

'Whether on an application to lift a stay imposed by CPR PD 51, para 19 the criterion is the same as for an application to strike out for want of prosecution (ie inordinate delay) as stated in the footnote on p 1334 of *Jordans' Civil Court Service* for November 2000, or some other criterion.'   *a*

[9] In saying this he made it clear that he did not wish to encourage an appeal to this court, because of the relatively small value of the claim and principles of proportionality. On 30 July 2001, however, Arden LJ granted permission to appeal. She said: *b*

'There is an important point of practice raised by this case for the purposes of CPR 52.13, and a real prospect of success, in respect of the argument that in the light of CPR 1.1 and the decision of this court in *Biguzzi v Rank Leisure plc* [1999] 4 All ER 934, [1999] 1 WLR 1926 the test applied by the judge was too narrow.'   *c*

[10] When the matter came before the judge in January 2001, he had only two sources of guidance as to the manner in which a court should exercise its discretion whether to lift an automatic stay pursuant to para 19(2) of CPR PD 51, the practice direction itself being silent on this subject.

[11] The first was the footnote in *Jordans' Civil Court Service* (November 2000   *d* edn, p 1334) (see [8], above). This was in these terms:

'A party may apply under CPR Pt 23, supported by evidence, to lift the stay ... and the provisions in the checklist set out in CPR r 3.9, dealing with relief from sanctions, would apply to any such application. Notwithstanding the   *e* clear guidance in *Biguzzi v Rank Leisure plc* ([1999] 4 All ER 934, [1999] 1 WLR 1926) that compliance with time limits is more important under the CPR than under the old regime, a judge must still consider all the circumstances of the case before deciding whether to reinstate an action ... similar considerations will no doubt apply to an application to lift a stay. *It is unlikely that the courts will decline to lift a stay introduced by PD51, para 19 unless the delay*   *f* *involved in the individual case brings it within the criteria which would otherwise justify an order striking out the case for want of prosecution.'* (My emphasis.)

[12] The other was a note of a judgment of Judge Adams, the former Registrar of Civil Appeals, in *Axtell-Powell v Labor* [2000] CLY 223, to the following effect: *g*

'The purpose of CPR Pt 51 was not to kill off those cases which fall within its ambit but to require any party wishing to continue with the case to ask the court for permission to do so. The two factors of significance in deciding whether or not to lift the stay were: (i) whether the request to lift the stay was made timeously; (ii) whether it was still possible for a fair trial to be   *h* conducted.'

[13] Judge Coningsby said that he had no reason to dissent from what Judge Adams had said, but it did not seem to him to be a complete statement of the law. In particular, he said, it did not pick up the point made in the footnote in *Jordans'*   *j* *Civil Court Service* which we have emphasised in the extract from that footnote cited in [11], above.

[14] Because he was concerned only to review the way in which the district judge had exercised her discretion, he found that he was unable to interfere with her conclusion that the delay had been inordinate. He therefore dismissed the appeal. The claimant now appeals to this court.

(3) STELIOU v COMPTON

a

[**15**] This is an appeal by the claimant Martin Steliou against an order of Judge Thompson QC in the Basingstoke County Court on 27 April 2001 whereby he dismissed Mr Steliou's appeal against an order made by District Judge Fuller in the same court on 19 January 2001 striking out as an abuse of court process an application he had made on 8 November 2000 for the removal of an automatic

b stay imposed on the proceedings through the operation of CPR PD 51, para 19. There had been an earlier application (and subsequent appeal) by the claimant to the same two judges in connection with this matter on 4 August and 27 October 2000 which were made in the unusual circumstances we describe in [21]–[24], below.

c [**16**] Mr Steliou was seriously injured in a road accident on 3 February 1994. He suffered injury to both legs and hips. He underwent a number of operations in 1994, 1996 and 1998. The most recent medical report, by Mr Hook, a consultant orthopaedic surgeon, is dated 28 March 2000. On the basis of this report it is clear that, despite the passage of time and the operations, Mr Steliou continues to suffer from some pain and disability as a result of the injuries that he

d sustained in the accident.

[**17**] He started proceedings on 3 November 1995 in the Basingstoke County Court. On 26 February 1996 the court ordered that there be 'a split trial dealing first with the issue of liability'. As is explained in the statement of Mr Collins (the solicitor who represents Mr Steliou), the reason for ordering a split trial was that

e it was already clear in 1996 that it would be a very long time before the prognosis for the injuries would be sufficiently clear for damages to be assessed. Following a trial, Mr Recorder Boyle decided that the defendant, Ms Compton, had been negligent, but held that the damages should be reduced by 40% to reflect the contributory negligence of Mr Steliou. On 21 August 1996 he ordered that there be judgment in favour of Mr Steliou, with damages to be assessed. It is clear that

f Mr Steliou was entitled to a substantial award of damages. Indeed, it was submitted on his behalf that the figure will exceed £100,000, even allowing for the 40% discount for contributory negligence. Some small payments into court have been made by the defendant during the course of these proceedings.

[**18**] Following the decision on liability, Mr Collins did not seek directions

g from the court in relation to the trial of the assessment of damages. He decided not to make any application to the court until the prognosis became clearer. But as is apparent from the bundle of correspondence that has been placed before the court, he took active steps to clarify the medical position, and the defendant's solicitors were kept informed. Since no criticism has been made of Mr Collins, it

h is unnecessary to consider the details of this correspondence. In his statement, he says that it was common ground between the defendant's solicitors and himself that progress with the action could not be made until it was determined whether the operation for the reconstruction of Mr Steliou's left knee had been a success, and that this would not be known until at least six months after the operation had been carried out. The operation was carried out in October 1998. In March 1999

j Mr Steliou was still complaining of pain, and further surgical intervention remained a possibility. The parties agreed, therefore, to instruct an expert jointly. That is how Mr Hook came to be instructed on 11 June 1999.

[**19**] Mr Hook produced his first report on 3 August 1999. He required X-rays before he could give a firm prognosis. Mr Collins received his final report of 28 March on 3 April 2000. On 13 April 2000 he instructed Keith Carter (an employment

consultant) to advise on Mr Steliou's employment prospects. He received
Mr Carter's report on 9 June.

[20] Crucially for the purposes of this appeal, the proceedings had not come
before a judge, at a hearing or on paper, between 26 April 1999 and 25 April 2000.
The proceedings were, therefore, automatically stayed. It is not clear on the
evidence when Mr Collins first appreciated that the proceedings had been
automatically stayed. The procedural twists and turns that the case then
followed were unusual, to say the least.

[21] On 13 July 2000 Mr Collins gave notice of intention to apply for 'an order
for a further interim payment and directions', because—

> 'the liability trial in this action was heard on 21 August 1996 since when the
> claimant has undergone further surgery three operations. As a result the
> claimant is still not able to provide the court with a long-term prognosis.
> The claimant has not been able to return to full-time working since the
> accident and is suffering severe financial loss.'

In Part C of the application notice, Mr Collins identified the evidence on which
he wished to rely in support of the application. That evidence was Mr Hook's
latest report, coupled with the information that Mr Steliou had now been advised
that further surgery would be needed to his left knee. A proposed directions
order, annexed to the application notice, began with a draft direction to the effect
that 'any stay in respect of these proceedings be removed'.

[22] The application came before District Judge Fuller on 4 August 2000.
Mr Livesey of counsel appeared on behalf of Mr Steliou. His primary submission
was that the proceedings had not been stayed, since para 19 of CPR PD 51 was
ultra vires. During the course of argument, the district judge made it clear that
he was unimpressed with this submission. Mr Livesey submitted in the alternative
that, if the proceedings had been stayed, the stay should be lifted. The district
judge pointed out that an application to lift a stay under para 19(2) must be
supported by evidence (see CPR 3.9(2)), and that no evidence had been adduced
in support of the application in this case. Mr Livesey was asked twice whether he
wished to apply for an adjournment, but he refused on each occasion. He sought
to persuade the district judge to treat the bundle of correspondence that he produced
as being sufficient. We have not been shown the bundle of correspondence, but
we infer from the exchanges between the district judge and counsel that it
included most, if not all, of the documents that are in the bundle that has been
produced by Mr Collins.

[23] In a short judgment the district judge rejected Mr Livesey's ultra vires
argument, and further held that, even if the application that was before him could
properly be treated as an application to lift the stay, he would refuse it on the
grounds that it was not supported by any evidence.

[24] The claimant appealed to Judge Thompson on 27 October 2000. Mr Livesey
repeated his ultra vires argument, but apparently with less vigour than before the
district judge. His main point was that the stay should be lifted. The judge read
the correspondence, but observed that there had been nothing to stop the
claimant's solicitors from bringing the matter before the court before 25 April
2000. He decided that the district judge was right to hold that there was no
evidence before him on which he could have acted. The appeal was dismissed.

[25] On 8 November 2000 Mr Collins made a fresh application. This time he
asked in terms for an order that the stay imposed by operation of CPR PD 51,
para 19(1) should be removed. He also asked for a further interim payment of

a £20,000 and directions in relation to the trial of the issue of damages. He supported the application with the statement to which we have earlier referred, to which were annexed substantial exhibits, including the correspondence.

[26] The application was heard by District Judge Fuller on 17 January 2001. This time, Mr Steliou was represented by Mr Woodhouse of counsel. Mr Woodhouse submitted that there had never been an application to lift the stay of the

b proceedings. In refusing to lift the stay, the district judge said:

'I lean very strongly to the procedural management of this case. The matter was there in August. The question of the removal of the stay was discussed. It is inconceivable that learned counsel did not ask for the stay to be removed. The second part of the order is the reason why it was not.

c There was no evidence. Given the extreme pressure on the court service to supply adequate judicial resources, given the directive about allocation of time, I do not think it is within the spirit of the CPR that once the solicitor for the claimant has got it wrong, as he did, and gone to appeal, he can then totally abandon all the arguments and go back on those principles and say:

d "Oh, yes, I know about it all the way and it has cost me money and time, but I now see what I should have done, and I am now going to do it." It is too late for that. I have the greatest sympathy for the claimant. This is not an insignificant case. I am bearing that one in mind. Nobody has ventured to tell me what the likely amount of the claim is. There is no argument that he is not entitled to run it. Substantial sums have already been paid on account.

e But at the end of the day it is very difficult to say that it is not the case that it has already been dealt with on this point of the removal of the stay and res judicata. They cannot come and put it again on issue estoppel. More importantly, if the new rules are to work they have got to be complied with. The spirit is there. It is quite clear we have had two years almost to get to

f grips with these things. On that doctrine I could not support learned counsel for the claimant. The main emphasis is on the case management powers. It does not mean to say that the plaintiff will [not] get his money, but he will get it from the solicitors' insurance company, and the insurance company will pay. I would strike this matter out on the basis of an abuse of the court

g process pursuant to my management.'

[27] Once again, Mr Steliou appealed. Once again, the appeal was heard by Judge Thompson. This time, Mr Steliou was represented by Mr Challenger, who has also appeared before us. On 27 April 2001 Judge Thompson dismissed the appeal. He said: 'If something could and should have been brought forward before

h the court on the previous occasion, then it is not open to a party to relitigate that at a later stage, when it could have been litigated at the earlier stage.'

[28] He went on to say that the district judge had treated the application as an application to lift the stay, and that there could only be a further application to lift the stay 'if something new had arisen subsequently'. In the present case, all the

j matters relied on by Mr Steliou had arisen before the first application had been made to the district judge. Since all of them could and should have been raised before the district judge at the first application, the second application had to fail, and the appeal was 'doomed to failure for that reason'. The judge concluded that the decision of the district judge was right, and that the passage from the judgment of the district judge which we cited 'very succinctly encapsulates the position here'.

(4) THE PRINCIPLES TO BE APPLIED IN CASES OF THIS TYPE

a

(i) *The removal of an automatic stay*

[29] Another division of this court has now resolved the important point of practice identified by Arden LJ when she granted permission to appeal in the first of these appeals. In *Audergon v La Baguette Ltd* [2002] EWCA Civ 10 at [97]–[102], [2002] All ER (D) 166 (Jan) at [97]–[102] Jonathan Parker LJ, with whom Pill and Tuckey LJJ agreed, held that the automatic stay imposed by para 19 of CPR PD 51 fell to be treated as a sanction 'imposed for a failure to comply with any rule, practice direction or court order' within the meaning of r 3.9.

b

[30] He followed in this respect an earlier indication to the same effect made by Latham LJ, with whom Longmore and Potter LJJ had agreed, in *Stanford v Stanford* [2001] EWCA Civ 1289, [2001] All ER (D) 261 (Jul).

c

(ii) *CPR 3.9*

[31] It follows that it is now r 3.9, and not a footnote in a textbook, that judges must take into account when determining whether to lift an automatic stay imposed by virtue of the transitional provisions of Pt 51 and its practice direction. This rule reads:

d

'(1) On an application for relief from any sanction imposed for a failure to comply with any rule, practice direction or court order the court will consider all the circumstances including—
(a) the interests of the administration of justice;

e

(b) whether the application for relief has been made promptly;
(c) whether the failure to comply was intentional;
(d) whether there is a good explanation for the failure;
(e) the extent to which the party in default has complied with other rules, practice directions, court orders and any relevant pre-action protocol;
(f) whether the failure to comply was caused by the party or his legal representative;

f

(g) whether the trial date or the likely trial date can still be met if relief is granted;
(h) the effect which the failure to comply had on each party; and
(i) the effect which the granting of relief would have on each party.

g

(2) An application for relief must be supported by evidence.'

[32] This rule is a good example of the way in which the draftsman of the CPR has sometimes endeavoured to set out in a codified form the various matters which the court may have to take into account when deciding how to exercise its discretion in a context with which it will be all too familiar. One of the great demerits of the former procedural regimes was that simple rules got barnacled with case law. Under the new regime the draftsman has sought to dispense with the need for litigants to be familiar with judge-made case law by drawing into one place the most common of the considerations a court must take into account when deciding whether a litigant should be granted relief from a sanction imposed on him.

h

j

[33] The circumstances in which a court may be asked to make a decision of this kind are infinitely varied. This is why the rule instructs the court to consider all the circumstances of the particular case, including the nine listed items. On the other hand, the rule would lose much of its praiseworthy purpose of encouraging structured decision-making if courts did not consciously go through

a the exercise of considering all the items on the list when determining how, on balance, it should exercise its discretion. Provided it does so, and in this way ensures that the risk of omitting any material consideration is minimised, it is most unlikely that an appeal court will interfere with its decision. If it fails to do so, an appeal court may not be able to detect that it has taken all material matters into account, and it may be obliged to exercise its discretion afresh for this reason.

b [34] The two cases at present before the court were simpler than many, because in neither of them was there any evidence that the claimant had intentionally failed to comply with the sanction imposed by the practice direction; a trial date and/or a likely trial date had not been fixed in either case; and the party in default, namely the claimant, had not previously failed to comply with any other rule, practice direction, court order or relevant pre-action

c protocol. If any of these features are present, they may tend to incline a court in an appropriate case to bar a claimant from pursuing a case, or from pursuing a chosen course of action within a case, after incurring a sanction of a type described at the beginning of r 3.9(1).

[35] At the end of his judgment in *Audergon*'s case [2002] All ER (D) 166 (Jan),
d Jonathan Parker LJ, with whom Pill and Tuckey LJJ agreed, made two comments of general application about the application of r 3.9. We have no difficulty in adopting and endorsing his aversion to 'a judicially-created checklist, which does not appear in the rule itself' for the reasons he gave in his judgment (at [107]):

e 'Inherent in such an approach, as it seems to me, is the danger that a body of satellite authority may be built up, rather as it was under the old rules in relation to the dismissal of an action for want of prosecution, leading in effect to the rewriting of the relevant rule through the medium of judicial decision. That would seem to me to be just the kind of undesirable consequence which the CPR were designed to avoid.'

f We wholeheartedly agree.

[36] It appears to us, however, that paras [103]–[106] of the judgment in *Audergon*'s case, which are clearly correct in the context in which they appeared, may give rise to misunderstandings if they are taken out of context, particularly as there is earlier Court of Appeal authority, to which the court does not appear
g to have been referred, which tended the other way. In *Audergon*'s case, the court was concerned with a submission that the Chief Chancery Master (and Rimer J on an appeal from the Chief Chancery Master) were so much in error in failing to refer specifically to r 3.9 (and in not referring specifically to the list of matters contained in para (1) of that rule) when deciding whether or not to remove an automatic stay, that this court should exercise its discretion in the matter afresh.
h In this context, Jonathan Parker LJ said:

'[103] However, it does not follow that the master was in error in not referring specifically to the rule in his judgment and/or in not framing his judgment specifically by reference to the list of matters contained in para (1)
j of the rule. In my judgment the rule does not *require* the court to adopt such an artificial and mechanistic approach.

[104] I reach that conclusion for two main reasons. In the first place, I reject [counsel for the defendants'] submission that the word "will" in CPR 3.9 imposes a *mandatory* duty on the court to deal specifically and separately in its judgment with each of the matters listed in para (1). As in the case of CPR 52.11, the word "will" in r 3.9(1) is not an imperative: the

paragraph merely identifies a number of specific matters which the court "will" consider in every case. No doubt one of the reasons why the rule refers specifically to such matters is to assist litigants to focus their evidence and their arguments on relevant aspects of the particular case.

[105] In the second place, one must not lose sight of the fact that the overriding objective of the court in considering applications under the rule is to determine in each case where the justice of the case lies (see CPR 1.1). The discharge of that task involves, by definition, a consideration of all the relevant circumstances (as the opening words of r 3.9(1) make clear); and that will in turn include a consideration of the various matters listed in the paragraph. But provided always that the court gives sufficient reasons to enable those affected by its decision to understand the basis for that decision, it is not in my judgment a legitimate criticism of the court's judgment that it does not refer specifically to the rule, or that its judgment is not framed specifically by reference to the list of matters contained in para (1) of the rule.

[106] Accordingly in the instant case it is not, in my judgment, a legitimate criticism of the master (or, for that matter, of the judge) that in their judgments they did not address themselves specifically to r 3.9.' (Emphasis added.)

[37] This judgment related to judicial decisions made by two very experienced judges. It was also made at a time when there was a good deal of judicial uncertainty about the criteria to be applied when a court considered whether to remove an automatic stay imposed by virtue of CPR PD 51. It would, however, in our judgment, be in the highest degree unfortunate if the judgment was to be interpreted as giving any sort of green light to the abandonment of a practice recommended by this court on two previous occasions, even though the practice is not mandatory in the sense that a decision is defective if it has not been expressly followed.

[38] In *Bansal v Cheema* [2000] CA Transcript 358, in an unreported judgment whose effect is noted in the current (2001) editions of both the White Book *Civil Procedure* and the Green Book *Civil Court Practice* in the notes to r 3.9, this court was concerned with a case in which a judge's refusal to extend the time for serving a witness statement had the practical effect of preventing the claimant from giving evidence in support of his case at the forthcoming trial. The claimant's counsel argued that the judge's order was very nearly the harshest order that he could have made, that in the absence of any previous serious or persistent default by his client he should not have acted so peremptorily, and that he should have confined himself to an 'unless' order, which would have had the effect that the action would be struck out if the witness statement was not delivered and served by a date that fell just over nine weeks before the date fixed for trial.

[39] This court did not know the thought processes which had led the judge to make such a peremptory order. In a judgment with which Roch LJ and Ferris J agreed, Brooke LJ said:

'The principal ground which is urged upon us by [counsel] today is that the judge failed to take into account all the matters which he was under an obligation to take into account under CPR 3.9(1). In my judgment [counsel] had made a good point. Although Judge Wakefield gave an ex tempore judgment, it is essential for courts, exercising their discretion on an occasion like this, to consider each matter listed under r 3.9(1) systematically in the same way as it is now well known that courts go systematically through the matters listed when an application is made for the exercise of the court's discretion under s 33 of the Limitation Act 1980. In the present case there is no sign in the judge's brief ex tempore judgment that he took into account the matters which he was bound to take into account under the rules which are set out in r 3.9(1)(g), (h) and (i) ... So far as the effect which the granting of relief would have on each party (r 3.9(1)(g)), if relief was not granted the defendant would have the unsolicited windfall that this substantial action against him would be dismissed. On the other hand, this would have been an unsolicited windfall, particularly as the judge did not know when he made the order why it was that the claimant had suddenly had to go to India. The effect of the refusal of relief would clearly have a catastrophic effect on the claimant whose action would have been struck out. He would also face the Mangat action without being able to compensate himself from any money that he might have succeeded in recovering from the defendant. There is no sign at all that the judge took that into consideration. I am always very reluctant for this court to interfere with a decision made by a judge in the exercise of his case management powers under CPR Pt 3. The responsibility for managing these actions is given fairly and squarely to the judge. The role of the Court of Appeal should only be seen as a longstop, to be called in aid when things appear to have gone seriously wrong. If the judge had systematically gone through the list of matters he had to take into account under r 3.9(1), and come to the conclusion that the order he was making was a just order, it would be very difficult for this court to interfere with it, because he would manifestly have taken into account all the matters he was obliged to take into account. A circuit judge in a busy court like the Central County Court would have much greater experience of the problems and difficulties of controlling litigation in that court than this court necessarily has. I am of the clear view, however, that on this occasion the judge did not do what the rules required of him, and that a substantial injustice was done as a result. Accordingly this court should interfere.'

[40] In *Keith v CPM Field Marketing Ltd* [2000] CA Transcript 1311, (2000) Times, 29 August this court criticised a judge who had debarred the defendants from defending a claim when they had failed to produce some articles required of them by an earlier court order which set a deadline for compliance. In a judgment with which Swinton Thomas LJ and Gage J agreed, Brooke LJ referred to *Bansal v Cheema*, and commented that there was no sign in the judge's brief ex tempore judgment that he had taken into account any of the matters which he was bound to take into account under the rules which are set out in r 3.9(1)(g), (h) and (i). In addition, some of the other matters mentioned in that rule appeared to have been overlooked. He continued:

'[The judge] had been confronted with an application to extend time for compliance with an unless order in a context in which, if time was not extended, relief would be sought from the sanction imposed by the order. In my judgment, it is obligatory for the court in such a situation, in pursuance of its obligation to deal with the case justly (see CPR 1.1 and 1.2), to take into account the matters set out in r 3.9. This rule sets out a very convenient list of many of the matters which a judge should take into account when considering whether to make an order as draconian as the order that Judge Overend made on 29 February. Of course, *Bansal v Cheema* was decided two days afterwards and this, strictly, was not a r 3.9 case. But in my judgment, when he was exercising his discretion pursuant to the overriding objective, it should have been plain to the judge that he should take into account the matters set out in r 3.9 in all the circumstances of the case.'

[41] The comments in these two cases were made in ex tempore judgments when the court did not have the benefit of the argument addressed to the court in *Audergon*'s case about the legal effect of any failure by a judge to make it clear that he had taken express notice of the matters mentioned in r 3.9. To that extent, such expressions as 'bound', 'required' and 'obligatory' are in a very strict sense inappropriate when used in the explanation of a rule which deploys the directory word 'will' rather than the mandatory word 'must'. Subject to that caveat we would reiterate the message given by the court in the two earlier cases. Judges (and, particularly, less experienced judges) should submit themselves to the discipline of considering each of the matters listed in r 3.9 which appear to them to be relevant to the case they have to decide. If they fail to do so, there may be a serious danger that an appeal court may overturn their decision for omitting to take a material consideration into account.

[42] It follows that in future judges should not simply latch onto one or two considerations (such as the length of any delay) to the exclusion of all others, when deciding whether it is just to remove a stay imposed on an action by the operation of CPR PD 51, para 19. They must remember that if a stay remains in place, they are depriving the claimant of access to the court, a concept which now has particular resonance under art 6 of the European Convention for the Protection of Human Rights and Fundamental Freedoms 1950 (as set out in Sch 1 to the Human Rights Act 1998). They must carry out the necessary balancing exercise methodically and explain how they reached their ultimate decision.

[43] Provided that judges make their decisions in these cases within the general framework provided by rr 3.9 and 1.1, they are unlikely to fall foul of the convention in this regard. In *Ashingdane v UK* (1985) 7 EHRR 528 at 546 (para 57), the European Court of Human Rights said:

'Certainly, the right of access to the courts is not absolute but may be subject to limitations; these are permitted by implication since the right of access, "by its very nature calls for regulation by the State, regulation which may vary in time and place according to the needs and resources of the community and of individuals".'

[44] More recently the court emphasised the need for proportionality when it said in *Tinnelly & Sons Ltd v UK, McElduff & Sons Ltd v UK* (1999) 27 EHRR 249 at 271 (para 74):

'... a limitation will not be compatible with Article 6(1) if it does not pursue a legitimate aim and if there is not a reasonable relationship of proportionality between the means employed and the aim sought to be achieved.'

[45] There is one further matter of general practice which we need to mention in relation to applications of this kind. Under the new CPR appeals regime, the original decision of the district judge or master takes on a much greater significance than it ever did prior to 26 April 1999, because the role of the appeal court is now that of a court of record and not of a court which conducts a complete rehearing of the application and exercises its discretion afresh (see

a   *Tanfern Ltd v Cameron-Macdonald* [2000] 2 All ER 801 at 808, [2000] 1 WLR 1311 at 1317 (para 31)).

[46] It may be that in an effort to save expense, particularly in relation to small claims, a party's solicitors may prepare and serve quite a short witness statement in support of their application for the removal of the stay, and this may suffice in most cases, particularly if their application is unopposed. If, however, it is
b   opposed, they would do well to reconsider the adequacy of their evidence before embarking on the hearing before the district judge or master.

[47] The *Woodhouse* case provides a very good illustration of what may happen if they do not. The evidence before the district judge was very sparse, and the circuit judge refused to admit a much fuller witness statement on the appeal.
c   The moral of this story is that greater attention needs to be paid to the quality of the evidence adduced at the first hearing, because there may not be a second chance on appeal.

(5) THE APPLICATION OF THE PRINCIPLES IN THE WOODHOUSE CASE

[48] It will now be evident that the district judge was wrong to concentrate
d   only on the length of the delay in this case. None of the features we mentioned in [34], above, were present, so that there is no need to comment any further on r 3.9(1)(c), (e) or (g). So far as the other matters listed in the rule are concerned, we can deal with them quite briefly in turn. (a) The interests of the administration of justice are not directly affected either way. (b) The application for relief was made only two months after the guillotine fell. (d) There was an explanation for
e   the failure, although it could not be described as a 'good' one in the absence of greater particularisation. (f) The court did not really know if Mrs Woodhouse or her solicitor was responsible for the failure to comply. (h) The failure to comply improved the defendants' case to the detriment of Mrs Woodhouse's case, because they would be given the benefit of the doubt in the event of any failure
f   of recollection. (i) The granting of relief would mean that the defendants would have to go on defending a claim which was brought soon after the cause of action arose, and when the primary limitation period still had a long time to run. The refusal of relief would bar this widow from access to the court in a case in which none of the features mentioned in [34], above, were present.

[49] The court is also charged under r 3.9(1) to consider all the circumstances.
g   Judge Coningsby touched on these towards the end of his judgment, when he referred to the following additional considerations: (i) this was a small claim, less than £6,000 plus interest, being lost wages for 27 weeks until the date of death; (ii) since Mr Woodhouse was suffering from paranoid psychosis prior to his death, his damages might be reduced still further because of this fact; (iii) the
h   claim appeared to be a problematic one, because it seemed to be admitted that Mr Woodhouse was in fact away from work on 58 days in the previous 11 months (a reference to his poor attendance record being one of the matters complained of) and there was a dispute of fact, which the claimant might have difficulty in proving, as to whether the defendants told the council that Mr Woodhouse was
j   subject to a final written warning; (iv) in a case where there were going to be difficulties of proof, and difficulties with regard to damage, and the claim was relatively small, the costs which would be incurred on either side would be vastly in excess of the amount likely to be recovered. On the other hand, the judge accepted that even a small claim, if it has merits, should be allowed to go forward, provided that the rules have been complied with and there has not been inordinate delay.

[50] These are matters which should be weighed in the balance when deciding
whether to allow a claim to proceed. We have to exercise our discretion afresh,
and it seems to be wrong to bar this widow, who has the assistance of the Legal
Services Commission, from access to the court because of the problematic merits
of the claim, when all the specific matters to be considered under r 3.9 are either
fairly neutral or tend to favour the further progress of her action to trial.

[51] We would therefore allow this appeal and set aside the orders in the
courts below.

(6) THE APPLICATION OF THE PRINCIPLES IN THE STELIOU CASE

[52] Mr Challenger submitted quite simply that the district judge and the
judge had misdirected themselves. They had wrongly considered that the fact
that the application could and should have been made on the first occasion was
determinative of the outcome of the application on the second occasion. What
they should have done was to exercise their discretion taking into consideration
the factors enumerated in r 3.9(1), and had they done so, they should have lifted
the stay on the facts of this case.

[53] Mr Russell submitted that it was immaterial whether there was or was
not an application to lift the stay on the first occasion. If no such application was
made at that time, one could and should have been made. If such an application
was made, it was made incompetently since it was not supported by evidence.
There was no reason why an application could not have been made, supported
by evidence, on the first occasion. Either way, the second application was an
abuse of the process of the court. In the exercise of its case management powers,
the court has a discretion whether to allow or refuse a 'second bite at the cherry'
in such cases. The judge was right to regard the decision of the district judge as
a proper exercise of discretion. That exercise of discretion can only be upset on
appeal on familiar grounds (see *G v G* [1985] 2 All ER 225, [1985] 1 WLR 647).
There are no grounds for interference in the present case.

[54] Mr Russell has drawn our attention to *Securum Finance Ltd v Ashton* [2001]
Ch 291, [2000] 3 WLR 1400, and in particular to the judgment of Chadwick LJ:

'For my part, I think that the time has come for this court to hold that the
"change of culture" which has taken place in the last three years—and, in
particular, the advent of the Civil Procedure Rules—has led to a position in
which it is no longer open to a litigant whose action has been struck out on
the grounds of inordinate and inexcusable delay to rely on the principle that
a second action commenced within the limitation period will not be struck
out save in exceptional cases. The position, now, is that the court must
address the application to strike out the second action with the overriding
objective of the Civil Procedure Rules in mind—and must consider whether
the claimant's wish to have "a second bite at the cherry" outweighs the need
to allot its own limited resources to other cases. The courts should now
follow the guidance given by this court in the *Arbuthnot Latham* case
(*Arbuthnot Latham Bank Ltd v Trafalgar Holdings Ltd, Chishty Coveney & Co (a
firm) v Raja* [1998] 2 All ER 181 at 192, [1998] 1 WLR 1426 at 1436–1437): "The
question whether a fresh action can be commenced will then be a matter for
the discretion of the court when considering any application to strike out
that action, and any excuse given for the misconduct of the previous action:
see *Janov v Morris* ([1981] 3 All ER 780, [1981] 1 WLR 1389). The position is
the same as it is under the first limb of *Birkett v James* ([1977] 2 All ER 801,
[1978] AC 297). In exercising its discretion as to whether to strike out the

second action, that court should start with the assumption that if a party has had one action struck out for abuse of process some special reason has to be identified to justify a second action being allowed to proceed."' (See [2001] Ch 291 at 309, [2000] 3 WLR 1400 at 1414–1415 (para 34).)

Mr Russell submits that the district judge carried out the balancing exercise referred to by Chadwick LJ, and that the judge was right not to interfere with that exercise, and this court should be similarly self-denying.

[55] The application of 8 November 2000 was undoubtedly a 'second bite at the cherry'. It was supported by evidence that was available at the time of the first application. There was no good reason for the failure to place that evidence before the court on the first occasion. We accept that the fact that the evidence relied on in support of the application that was made on 8 November could and should have been put before the court in support of the earlier application is material to the exercise of the discretion conferred by r 3.9(1). There is a public interest in discouraging a party who makes an unsuccessful interlocutory application from making a subsequent application for the same relief, based on material which was not, but could have been, deployed in support of the first application. In some contexts, this is partly because, as Chadwick LJ said in the *Securum Finance* case, there is a need for the court to allot its limited resources to other cases. But at least as important is the general need, in the interests of justice, to protect the respondents to successive applications in such circumstances from oppression. The rationale for the rule in *Henderson v Henderson* (1843) 3 Hare 100, [1843–60] All ER Rep 378 that, in the absence of special circumstances, parties should bring their whole case before the court so that all aspects of it may be decided (subject to appeal) once and for all, is a rule of public policy based on the desirability, in the general interest as well as that of the parties themselves, that litigation should not drag on for ever, and that a defendant should not be oppressed by successive suits when one would do (see *Barrow v Bankside Members Agency Ltd* [1996] 1 All ER 981 at 983, [1996] 1 WLR 257 at 260 per Bingham MR).

[56] In our view, although the policy that underpins the rule in *Henderson v Henderson* has relevance as regards successive pre-trial applications for the same relief, it should be applied less strictly than in relation to a final decision of the court, at any rate where the earlier pre-trial application has been dismissed.

[57] To take an example: suppose that an application for summary judgment in a substantial multi-track case under CPR Pt 24 is dismissed, and the unsuccessful party then makes a second application based on material that was available at the time of the first application, but which through incompetence was not deployed at that time. The new material makes the case for summary judgment unanswerable on the merits. In so extreme a case, it could not be right to dismiss the second application solely because it was a second bite at the cherry. In those circumstances, the overriding objective of dealing with cases justly, having regard to the various factors mentioned in CPR 1.1(2), would surely demand that the second application should succeed, and that the proceedings be disposed of summarily. In such a case, the failure to deploy the new material at the time of the first application can properly and proportionately be reflected by suitable orders for costs, and (if appropriate) interest. The judge would, of course, be perfectly entitled to dismiss the second application without ceremony unless it could be speedily and categorically demonstrated that the new material was indeed conclusive of the case.

[58] In the present case, it is clear that both the district judge and the judge considered that the fact that the application of 8 November 2000 was a second bite at the cherry was decisive. In our view, they were wrong to do so. They failed to take into account the evidence of Mr Collins, and to consider how cogent the case was for lifting the stay, having regard in particular to the provisions of r 3.9(1). In short, they failed to exercise their discretion at all. In these circumstances, it is necessary for us to exercise our discretion afresh.

[59] As in the case of *Woodhouse*, none of the features mentioned in [34], above were present, so that there is no need to comment further on r 3.9(1)(c), (e) or (g). As regards the other matters listed in the rule, we comment as follows. (a) The interests of the administration of justice are affected since, in the absence of special circumstances, it is contrary to the good administration of justice to permit parties to have a second bite at the cherry on the basis of evidence that was available on the first occasion. (b) The first application was made about ten weeks and the second a little more than six months after the guillotine fell. (d) There was an understandable explanation for the failure to comply, even if it was not a good one. In his statement, Mr Collins said that the reason why he did not take account of the provisions of CPR PD 51, para 19(1) was because he believed that there would not be an automatic stay since this was a personal injury case 'where there is no issue on liability but the proceedings have been adjourned by court order to determine the prognosis' (CPR PD 51, para 19(3)(b)). (f) The failure to comply was not caused by Mr Steliou, but by his legal representatives. (h) The failure to comply had no effect on either party, since liability had been resolved, and the issues of damages would turn very largely on the evidence of jointly instructed experts. (i) The granting of relief would mean that the defendant would continue to be faced with the liability to pay such damages as (if not previously agreed) were assessed by the court. The refusal of relief would deprive the claimant of his (no longer disputed) right to substantial damages. Since the primary limitation period has now expired, he would almost certainly start proceedings against his legal representatives claiming damages for professional negligence.

[60] In our view, if the first application had been supported by the evidence of Mr Collins, the district judge could not reasonably have refused to lift the stay. The case in favour of allowing the application would have been overwhelming. On any view, Mr Steliou has an unanswerable claim to substantial damages. Moreover, although Mr Collins was wrong to believe that CPR PD 51, para 19(3)(b) applied, the spirit of that provision was engaged by the facts of the case. The reason why the court ordered a split trial in the first place was that it would be some time before the court would be able to determine the prognosis. Once liability had been decided, there was no issue on liability. The court could have adjourned the proceedings on 21 August 1996 to determine the prognosis, but it did not do so. If it had done so, no stay would have been automatically imposed on 26 April 2000. In these circumstances, and in the light of the factors which we have mentioned when going through the list in r 3.9(1), the case in favour of allowing the first application if it had been supported by the evidence relied on in support of the second application would have been irresistible. Mr Russell does not contend otherwise.

[61] The question that arises, therefore, is whether the fact that there was a second bite at the cherry leads to a different result. We have no doubt that this additional factor is an important matter that must be taken into account in considering how the discretion given by r 3.9 should be exercised. Although there

a was no good explanation for the failure to adduce the evidence of Mr Collins on the first occasion, the mistake he made in misreading CPR PD 51, para 19(3)(b) in the context of this case was not one which should be visited with a disproportionate penalty. After all, the facts of the case would have justified a court order being made in terms which would have meant that CPR PD 51, para 19 did not apply: it was fortuitous that the court order was not expressed in words which achieved

b that effect.

[62] Moreover, the result of a stay would unquestionably be (a) to deprive Mr Steliou of substantial damages in a case which would be very likely to settle out of court (in view of the fact that the principal evidence was that of jointly instructed experts), and (b) to encourage him to start proceedings against his legal advisers. In our view, such an outcome would not further the overriding

c objective of enabling the court to deal with cases justly, nor would it reduce the call on the court's resources. Nor would it be a proportionate response to the failure to make a proper application to lift the stay on the first occasion. We have no doubt that on the facts of this case, the discretion given to the court should be exercised so as to lift the stay.

d [63] This court is always very reluctant to interfere with the way in which district judges and circuit judges exercise their case management powers. They have a difficult task to perform, and the judges in the Basingstoke County Court were right to be reluctant to devote an excessive amount of the court's resources on a single case. On this occasion, however, it appears that the penalty they imposed on a seriously injured claimant whose solicitor had made a pardonable

e mistake in his interpretation of a transitional rule was disproportionate to the error that was made. The error could be remedied by orders for costs, and these have already been paid. It deserved no greater penalty on the unusual facts of this case.

[64] We would therefore allow this appeal and set aside the orders in the

f courts below.

Appeals allowed.

Kate O'Hanlon   Barrister.

R (on the application of ProLife Alliance) v British Broadcasting Corporation

[2002] EWCA Civ 297

COURT OF APPEAL, CIVIL DIVISION

SIMON BROWN, LAWS AND JONATHAN PARKER LJJ

30, 31 JANUARY, 14 MARCH 2002

Elections – Parliamentary – Party election broadcasts – Claimant political party opposing abortion – Party having statutory right to party election broadcast and submitting video showing graphic but honest footage of aborted foetuses – Broadcasters declining to transmit election broadcast on grounds of taste, decency and offensiveness – Whether broadcasters entitled to ban proposed party election broadcast on such grounds – Broadcasting Act 1990, s 6(1) – Human Rights Act 1998, Sch 1, Pt I, art 10(2).

Human rights – Freedom of expression – Restriction on freedom of expression – Proper approach to determining whether restriction on free speech justified in context of political debate – Human Rights Act 1998, Sch 1, Pt I, art 10(2).

The claimant was a registered political party which was opposed to abortion. In the 2001 general election the party fielded sufficient candidates in Wales to entitle it, under certain statutory provisions, to a party election broadcast (PEB) in that part of the country. It submitted a video to the broadcasters that illustrated graphically, but honestly and unsensationally, what was involved in abortion processes and included clear images of aborted foetuses in a mangled and mutilated state. The broadcasters unanimously refused transmission of the video on the grounds of taste and decency, concluding that it would be offensive to a very large number of viewers, and that transmission of the broadcast would plainly breach both the independent broadcasters' obligations under s 6(1)[a] of the Broadcasting Act 1990 not to include anything in their programmes which offended against good taste and decency, and the effectively identical obligations of the BBC under its agreement with the Secretary of State for National Heritage (the BBC agreement). The party's application for permission to apply for judicial review was refused by the judge, but permission to appeal against that decision was granted by a single Lord Justice. At the hearing, the Court of Appeal granted permission to seek judicial review, regarded the hearing before the judge as the disposal of the judicial review at first instance and treated the hearing before it as the substantive appeal. The issue for the court's determination was whether those considerations of taste and offensiveness, which had moved the broadcasters, constituted a legal justification for the act of censorship involved in banning the party's proposed PEB, or, as the party put it, whether the ban was 'necessary in a democratic society' under art 10(2)[b] of the European Convention for the Protection of Human Rights and Fundamental Freedoms 1950 (as set out in Sch 1 to the Human Rights Act 1998). In reaching its conclusion, the court considered the correct approach to determining whether there was legal justification for

---

a   Section 6, so far as material, is set out at [14], below
b   Article 10 is set out at [23], below

a censorship in the context of political debate. The BBC submitted that deference
   had to be given to the broadcasters' judgment.

   Held – When considering whether there was legal justification for censorship in
   the context of political debate, the court should not treat the text of the
   convention as a template for domestic law, since that ran the risk of an over-rigid
b approach. The court's duty in confronting the claims of free speech, and the
   claims that might be ranged against it, was very far distant from any exercise of
   textual interpretation. It was dealing with bedrock principles. It was concerned
   with the protection of free expression in the context of political debate. In the
   rancour and asperity of a general election, that duty, owed to the people, was at
c its highest. That position was wholly consistent with the domestic learning on
   freedom of expression, which established that the courts owed a special
   responsibility to the public as the constitutional guardian of the freedom of
   political debate. That responsibility was most acute at the time and in the context
   of a public election, especially a general election. It had its origin in a deeper trust,
   namely that the courts were ultimately the trustees of the country's framework
d of democracy. That view was consonant with the common law's general
   recognition of a category of fundamental or constitutional rights. Freedom of
   expression was plainly such a constitutional right, and its enjoyment by an
   accredited political party in an election context had to call for especially heightened
   protection. In such a context, the broadcasters' views were entitled to be respected,
e but their force and weight were modest at best. The court's constitutional
   responsibility to protect political speech was overarching. It amounted to a duty
   which lay on the court's shoulders to decide for itself whether the censorship was
   justified. Furthermore, the common law required that the freedom of political
   speech to be enjoyed by an accredited party at a public election, most especially
   a general election, was not to be interfered with save on the most pressing
f grounds. Such grounds would very rarely be shown by an appeal to
   considerations of taste and decency alone, and the BBC agreement, the 1990 Act
   and the Broadcasting Act 1996 had to be read conformably with that principle. In
   the instant case, there were no such grounds. The party's intended PEB was
   certainly graphic and disturbing, but if political free speech was to be taken
g seriously those characteristics could not begin to justify the censorship that had
   been carried out. The broadcasters had failed altogether to give sufficient weight
   to the pressing imperative of free political expression, and accordingly the appeal
   would be allowed (see [34]–[37], [43]–[46], [57], [59], [63], below); *R v Central
   Independent Television plc* [1994] 3 All ER 641 and *R v Secretary of State for the Home
   Department, ex p Simms* [1999] 3 All ER 400 considered.
h   Per curiam. There may be instances, even in the context of a general election,
   in which political speech may justifiably be censored on the grounds of taste or
   offensiveness, but it would take a very extreme case, most likely involving factors
   such as gratuitous sensationalism and dishonesty (see [44], [46], [63], below).

j **Notes**

   For the right to freedom of expression at common law and under the convention,
   and for party election broadcasts, see 8(2) *Halsbury's Laws* (4th edn reissue)
   paras 107, 158–159, 223.

   For the Broadcasting Act 1990, s 6, see 45 *Halsbury's Statutes* (4th edn) (1999
   reissue) 324.

For the Human Rights Act 1998, Sch 1, Pt I, art 10, see 7 *Halsbury's Statutes* (4th
edn) (1999 reissue) 524.

Cases referred to in judgments

A-G v Guardian Newspapers Ltd [1987] 3 All ER 316, [1987] 1 WLR 1248, Ch D, CA
and HL.

Associated Provincial Picture Houses Ltd v Wednesbury Corp [1947] 2 All ER 680,
[1948] 1 KB 223, CA.

Bowman v UK (1998) 4 BHRC 25, ECt HR.

Chapman v UK (2001) 10 BHRC 48, ECt HR.

Chassagnou v France (1999) 7 BHRC 151, ECt HR.

Council of Civil Service Unions v Minister for the Civil Service [1984] 3 All ER 935,
[1985] AC 374, [1984] 3 WLR 1174, HL.

Derbyshire CC v Times Newspapers Ltd [1993] 1 All ER 1011, [1993] AC 534, [1993] 2
WLR 449, HL.

International Transport Roth GmbH v Secretary of State for the Home Dept [2002]
EWCA Civ 158, [2002] All ER (D) 325 (Feb).

Kommunistischen Partei Deustchlands/Marxisten (1978) 2 BvR 523/75, Germ Fed
Const Ct.

McCartan Turkington Breen (a firm) v Times Newspapers Ltd [2000] 4 All ER 913,
[2001] 2 AC 277, [2000] 3 WLR 1670, HL.

Minister of Home Affairs v Fisher [1979] 3 All ER 21, [1980] AC 319, [1979] 2 WLR
889, PC.

Muller v Switzerland (1988) 13 EHRR 212, ECt HR.

Observer v UK (1991) 14 EHRR 153, [1991] ECHR 13585/88, ECt HR.

Pierson v Secretary of State for the Home Dept [1997] 3 All ER 577, [1998] AC 539,
[1997] 3 WLR 492, HL.

R v Central Independent Television plc [1994] 3 All ER 641, [1994] Fam 192, [1994] 3
WLR 20, CA.

R v DPP, ex p Kebeline, R v DPP, ex p Rechachi [1999] 4 All ER 801, [2000] 2 AC 326,
[1999] 3 WLR 972, DC and HL.

R v Lord Chancellor, ex p Witham [1997] 2 All ER 779, [1998] QB 575, [1998] 2 WLR
849, DC.

R v Secretary of State for the Home Dept, ex p Daly [2001] UKHL 26, [2001] 3 All ER
433, [2001] 2 WLR 1622.

R v Secretary of State for the Home Dept, ex p Leech [1993] 4 All ER 539, [1994] QB 198,
[1993] 3 WLR 1125, CA.

R v Secretary of State for the Home Dept, ex p Simms [1999] 3 All ER 400, [2000] 2 AC
115, [1999] 3 WLR 328, HL.

Reynolds v Times Newspapers Ltd [1999] 4 All ER 609, [2001] 2 AC 127, [1999] 3
WLR 1010, HL.

Sunday Times v UK (1979) 2 EHRR 245, [1979] ECHR 6538/74, ECt HR.

Vgt Verein gegen Tierfabriken v Switzerland (2001) 10 BHRC 473, ECt HR.

Wingrove v UK (1996) 1 BHRC 509, ECt HR.

Cases also cited or referred to in skeleton arguments

A-G v BBC [1980] 3 All ER 161, [1981] AC 303, HL.

Alberta Statutes Reference, Re [1938] SCR 100, Can SC.

Becker v Federal Communications Commission (1996) 95 F 3d 75, US Ct of Apps.

Bonnard v Perryman [1891] 2 Ch 269, [1891–4] All ER Rep 965, CA.

Brown v Stott (Procurator Fiscal, Dunfermline) [2001] 2 All ER 97, [2001] 2 WLR 817, PC.

a   *Brutus v Cozens* [1972] 2 All ER 1297, [1973] AC 854, HL.
     Buckley v Valeo (1976) 424 US 1, US SC.
     Castells v Spain (1992) 14 EHRR 445, [1992] ECHR 11798/85, ECt HR.
     Curtis v Minister of Safety and Security (1996) 1 BHRC 541, SA Const Ct.
     Gundem v Turkey App No 23144/93 (16 March 2000, unreported), ECt HR.
     Handyside v UK (1976) 1 EHRR 737, [1976] ECHR 5493/72, ECt HR.
b   *Holley v Smyth* [1998] 1 All ER 853, [1998] QB 726, CA.
     Living Word Distributors Ltd v Human Rights Action Group Inc [2001] 2 LRC 233,
          NZ CA.
     Moonen v Film and Literature Board of Review [2000] 4 LRC 158, NZ CA.
     Ontario Film & Video and Ontario Board of Censors, Re (1983) 147 DLR (3d) 58,
          Can HC; *affd* (1984) 5 DLR (4th) 766, Ont CA.
c   *ProLife Alliance v UK* App No 41869/98 (24 October 2000, unreported), ECt HR.
     R (on the application of Craven) v Secretary of State for the Home Dept [2001] EWHC
          Admin 850, [2001] All ER (D) 74 (Oct).
     R (on the application of Mahmood) v Secretary of State for the Home Dept [2001] 1 WLR
          840, CA.
d   *R v A* [2001] UKHL 25, [2001] 3 All ER 1, [2002] 1 AC 45.
     R v BBC, ex p Quintavalle (1998) 10 Admin LR 425.
     R v BBC, ex p Referendum Party (1997) 9 Admin LR 553, DC.
     R v Keegstra [1990] 3 SCR 697, Can SC.
     R v Ministry of Defence, ex p Smith [1996] 1 All ER 257, [1996] QB 517, CA.
e   *R v Radio Authority, ex p Bull* [1997] 2 All ER 561, [1998] QB 294, CA.
     R v Secretary of State for Health, ex p Wagstaff 0[2001] 1 WLR 292.
     Redmond-Bate v DPP (1999) 7 BHRC 375, DC.
     Schering Chemicals Ltd v Falkman Ltd [1981] 2 All ER 321, [1982] QB 1, CA.
     Sporrong v Sweden (1982) 5 EHRR 35, [1982] ECHR 7151/75, ECt HR.
     Surek v Turkey (1999) 7 BHRC 339, ECt HR.
f   *Terminiello v Chicago* (1949) 337 US 1, US SC.
     Texas v Johnson (1989) 491 US 397, US SC.
     Thomson Newspapers Co v Canada [1998] 1 SCR 877, Can SC.
     United Communist Party of Turkey v Turkey (1997) 4 BHRC 1, ECt HR.
     Verrall v Great Yarmouth BC [1980] 1 All ER 839, [1981] QB 202, CA.
g   *Wheeler v Leicester City Council* [1985] 2 All ER 1106, [1985] AC 1054, HL.

Appeal

The appellant claimant, the ProLife Alliance, appealed with permission of
Mummery LJ granted on 9 August 2001 from the decision of Scott Baker J on
h   24 May 2001 refusing it permission to apply for judicial review of the decision of
the defendant respondent, the British Broadcating Corporation, communicated
by letters dated 17 and 21 May 2001, refusing to broadcast the appellant's
proposed party election broadcast on grounds that it offended against good taste
and decency and/or was offensive to public feeling. The facts are set out in the
opinion of Laws LJ.
j

David Anderson QC, Martin Chamberlain and Maya Lester (instructed by Brown
     Cooper) for the appellant.
David Pannick QC and Mark Shaw (instructed by Head of BBC Litigation Dept) for
     the respondent.

Cur adv vult

14 March 2002. The following judgments were delivered.

a

LAWS LJ (giving the first judgment at the invitation of Simon Brown LJ).

INTRODUCTORY

[1] This case is about the censorship of political speech. It concerns the question, what constraints may lawfully be imposed upon the choice of a *b* registered political party as to the content of a party election broadcast (PEB) to be transmitted on television on its behalf at the time of a general election. It is difficult to think of a context in which the claims of free expression are more pressing.

[2] The appeal is brought against the order of Scott Baker J, delivered after oral *c* argument by counsel for both parties on 23 and 24 May 2001, by which he refused the appellant permission to apply for judicial review of the decision by the BBC and other terrestrial broadcasters to decline to transmit in Wales a PEB which had been made on video by the appellants. After the learned judge had given judgment, revised videos were submitted to the broadcasters and rejected by them on two further occasions. A fourth version of the PEB, with a voiceover *d* but an entirely blank screen, was transmitted on Saturday 2 June 2001. I shall deal with the facts in greater detail shortly. On 9 August 2001 Mummery LJ granted permission to appeal against Scott Baker J's decision. He stated:

'The application for permission to apply for judicial review, which was *e* refused by Scott Baker J, raises important issues which should be argued before the full court. The importance of those issues is a compelling reason for hearing the appeal. I express no view on the prospects of the appeal succeeding.'

[3] On the first morning of the hearing this court indicated to counsel that it *f* would grant permission to seek judicial review, regard the hearing before Scott Baker J as the disposal of the judicial review at first instance, and treat the hearing in this court as the substantive appeal. Mr Pannick QC for the respondent BBC has made it clear that for the purposes of the appeal there is no suggestion that the BBC is not amenable to the judicial review jurisdiction.

g

THE FACTS

[4] The appellant is a political party registered under the provisions of Pt II of the Political Parties, Elections and Referendums Act 2000. As it is put in the skeleton argument prepared on its behalf by Mr Anderson QC, it campaigns for absolute respect for innocent human life from fertilisation until natural death and *h* therefore opposes abortion, euthanasia, destructive embryo research and human cloning. In so summarising the appellant's platform, in particular by use of the phrase 'innocent human life', I mean to beg no question such as whether a foetus should be regarded as a person, far less a person with rights. To do so would be to take a position (or at least a preliminary position) as to the merits of the *j* appellant's policy. I hope that readers of this judgment will understand that in the context of these proceedings the court has no authoritative voice whatever on such matters. By contrast its authority, as I shall explain, rests in its constitutional duty to protect and enhance the democratic process, irrespective of the wisdom or the rightness of any or all the diverse political opinions which in the course of that process are paraded before the people.

a [5] The appellant is committed to working within the democratic structures of society and repudiates all forms of violence, unduly provocative action and harassment of individuals. Its 2001 election manifesto is before the court. As the learned judge recorded, its motives and good faith are not in question. Certainly they have not been put in question by Mr Pannick.

[6] The appellant has offered the following short summary of the contemporary
b facts and figures relating to abortion in the United Kingdom, which I do not understand to be disputed. Each year approximately 200,000 abortions are carried out in the United Kingdom, some 70% of them funded by the taxpayer. The great majority are performed on the third of the five permitted grounds under the Abortion Act 1967 as amended: that is that the continuance of the pregnancy would involve risk, greater than if the pregnancy were terminated, of
c injury to the physical or mental health of the pregnant woman. There is some evidence that many doctors maintain that the continuance of a pregnancy is always more dangerous to the physical welfare of a woman than having an abortion, a state of affairs which is said to allow a situation of de facto abortion on demand to prevail. The commonest form of abortion is suction
d abortion (vacuum aspiration), used on foetuses from 7–15 weeks' gestation. Suction abortion always causes the foetus to be mutilated to a greater or lesser extent. Larger foetuses must be dismembered prior to extraction. A technique known as D and E (dilation and extraction) is used to effect this, either in conjunction with vacuum aspiration, or (after 13 weeks) on its own. In the second and third trimester, drugs (prostaglandins) can be used to induce
e premature labour. However before labour is induced there is a requirement, under Royal College of Obstetricians and Gynaecologists guidelines, to kill the foetus in the womb. This is usually done by the injection of potassium chloride into the foetal heart, or of saline solution into the amniotic fluid. The latter causes a slow death. It is said that the purpose is to avoid the possibility of a live
f birth which, if followed by death, could result in criminal charges.

[7] The appellant has in the past put up candidates at local elections, Scottish Parliamentary elections and the general election of 1997. For the 1997 general election it fielded enough Parliamentary candidates to qualify for a PEB in England, Scotland and Wales under the rules established by the BBC, the Independent Television Commission (ITC) and the Electoral Commission. It
g submitted a video for the purpose. The broadcasters declined to broadcast it. The appellant sought permission for judicial review of this decision. That was refused by Dyson J, as he then was. A further application to the Court of Appeal was also refused. The appellant applied to the European Court of Human Rights, alleging a violation of art 10 of the European Convention for the Protection of
h Human Rights and Fundamental Freedoms 1950 (as now set out in Sch 1 to the Human Rights Act 1998) (ECHR). The application was declared inadmissible without the United Kingdom government being called on to put in observations.

[8] For the general election of 7 June 2001 the appellant put up enough candidates in Wales to entitle it to a single PEB of up to 4 minutes 40 seconds, to
j be screened in the principality (but not in England, Scotland or Northern Ireland) by the BBC, ITV and S4C. Accordingly on 2 May 2001 a video was delivered to the BBC. I shall summarise its content shortly. First I will describe the decision-making process leading to the broadcasters' refusal to put the PEB (and the later two modified versions) on air.

[9] On 8 May 2001 representatives of all the terrestrial broadcasters, that is the BBC, ITV, Channel 4 and Channel 5, met and viewed the first video. Mr Anderson

has a point about the constitution of this meeting, so I should identify the
representatives who were present.   They were the BBC's chief political advisor   *a*
Ms Anne Sloman, Channel 4's head of news and current affairs and business, and
executives in the legal and compliance departments of the other broadcasters.
On 10 May the BBC wrote to the appellant explaining, on behalf of all the
terrestrial broadcasters, why the preliminary view was that a significant
proportion of the proposed PEB would not comply with the relevant provisions   *b*
of the BBC's producers' guidelines and the Programme Code of the Independent
Television Commission (ITC) in respect of matters of taste and decency.   The
letter ended by inviting written submissions from the appellant. On 13 May the
appellant sent submissions to the BBC.   On 15 May 2001 the appellant's solicitors
wrote asking for a 'formal decision' on the proposed PEB, given the submissions
made, by noon on 17 May 2001.   On 16 May the representatives of the terrestrial   *c*
broadcasters (now joined by a BBC solicitor) held a further meeting and viewed
the video again in the light of the submissions.

[10]   On 17 May the BBC wrote to the appellant on behalf of all the terrestrial
broadcasters maintaining their preliminary view. This important letter constitutes
the primary object of the appellant's challenge. It included these passages: *d*

'4. In reaching our conclusions, we have certainly taken into account the
importance of the images to the political campaign of the ProLife Alliance.
We have also proceeded on the basis that we should seek the minimum
changes necessary to ensure compliance with the obligations of the BBC as
set out in paragraph 5(1)(d) of the Agreement, and the producers' Guidelines,   *e*
and the obligations of the other broadcasters under the ITC Code.

5. We have had regard to the guidelines on taste and decency, prevailing
standards of taste and decency, broadcasters' criteria on the portrayal of
violence, and public interest considerations, as well as the other points made
in your client's letter of 13 May and the accompanying written submissions.   *f*
But none of these factors leads us to conclude other than that it would be
wrong to broadcast these images which would be offensive to very large
numbers of viewers. None of the broadcasters regards this as a case at the
margin. We all regard it as a clear case in which it would plainly be a breach
of our obligations to transmit this broadcast.'

g

The letter went on to indicate the broadcasters' view that the images were 'so
offensive' that their objections could not be met by putting out the broadcast
after 10 pm with a warning, as had been suggested in the submissions.

[11]   On 18 May the appellant wrote to the BBC asking more questions about
the acceptability of the proposed PEB.   On 21 May there was a reply giving a   *h*
further explanation of the broadcasters' position, and repeating their willingness
to give urgent consideration to any revised broadcast. This was the second
challenged decision. On 21 May the appellant wrote informing the BBC that it
would be commencing judicial review proceedings the next day, and on 22 May
it did so. So the matter came before Scott Baker J on 23 and 24 May, and as I have   *j*
said he dismissed the application.

[12]   On 31 May a second version of the proposed PEB was submitted to, but
rejected by, all the terrestrial broadcasters for Wales. On 1 June a third version
was submitted and suffered the same fate.   On 2 June a fourth version was
submitted. It was approved and transmitted. This was the version with no visual
images whatever.

a **[13]** I have watched the first, second and third videos. It is only necessary to describe the first in any detail. It shows the products of a suction abortion: tiny limbs, bloodied and dismembered, a separated head, their human shape and form plainly recognisable. There are some pictures showing the results of the procedures undertaken to procure an abortion at later stages. There is no sound on the video. There is some introductory text. Then the words of arts 2, 3 and 14

b of the ECHR are cut into the visual images at various points. There is also some text briefly describing different abortion techniques. The pictures are real footage of real cases. They are not a reconstruction, nor in any way fictitious. Nor are they in any way sensationalised. They are, I think, certainly disturbing to any person of ordinary sensibilities. The second and third videos are edited versions of some of the same pictures which however in these later versions appear fuzzy,

c with no sharp focus.

THE LEGISLATION, THE BBC AGREEMENT, CODES OF GUIDANCE

[14] The broadcasters' decisions, of which the appellant complains, were made having regard (in the case of the BBC) to the obligation imposed by para 5(1)(d) of the then current agreement between the BBC and the Secretary of

d State, and (in the case of the independent broadcasters) to the obligation imposed by s 6(1)(a) of the Broadcasting Act 1990 (BA 1990). These obligations are in substance identical one with the other. Section 6(1)(a)–(c) of the BA 1990 provides:

'**6.**—(1) The Commission [viz the ITC, established by s 1 of the BA 1990] shall do all that they can to secure that every licensed service complies with

e the following requirements, namely—(a) that nothing is included in its programmes which offends against good taste or decency or is likely to encourage or incite to crime or to lead to disorder or to be offensive to public feeling; (b) that any news given (in whatever form) in its programmes is presented with due accuracy and impartiality; (c) that due impartiality is

f preserved on the part of the person providing the service as respects matters of political or industrial controversy or relating to current public policy ...'

Paragraph 5(1)(d) of the BBC agreement mirrors s 6(1)(a), and I need not give its text. These are the core provisions for the issues which fall to be determined on this appeal. But I should also set out certain other legislative measures. First,

g these parts of s 36 of the BA 1990:

'(1) Subject to subsection (2), any regional Channel 3 licence or licence to provide Channel 4 or 5 shall include—(a) conditions requiring the licence holder to include party political broadcasts in the licensed service; and (b) conditions requiring the licence holder to observe such rules with respect

h to party political broadcasts as the Commission may determine ...

(3) Without prejudice to the generality of paragraph (b) of subsection (1) but subject to section 37 of the Political Parties, Elections and Referendums Act 2000 (prohibition of broadcasts by unregistered parties), the Commission may determine for the purposes of that subsection—(a) the political parties

j on whose behalf party political broadcasts may be made; and (b) in relation to any political party on whose behalf such broadcasts may be made, the length and frequency of such broadcasts.'

Next, these following provisions of the Broadcasting Act 1996 (BA 1996):

'**109.**—(1) It shall be the duty of the BSC [Broadcasting Standards Commission] to monitor programmes to which section 108 applies with a view to enabling the BSC to make reports on the portrayal of violence and sexual conduct in, and the standards of taste and decency attained by, such programmes generally ...

110.—(1) Subject to the provisions of this Part, it shall be the duty of the BSC to consider and adjudicate on complaints which are made to them in accordance with sections 111 and 114 and relate—(a) to unjust or unfair treatment in programmes to which section 107 applies, or (b) to unwarranted infringement of privacy in, or in connection with the obtaining of material included in, such programmes.

(2) Subject to those provisions, it shall also be the duty of the BSC to consider, and make findings on, complaints which are made to them in accordance with sections 113 and 114 and relate ... (b) to alleged failures on the part of such programmes to attain standards of taste and decency.'

[15] Given its duty arising under para 5(1)(d) of the agreement with the Secretary of State, the BBC has produced a code, entitled 'The BBC producers' guidelines', ch 6 of which deals with issues of taste and decency. Likewise, given s 6(1)(a) of the BA 1990, the ITC has produced 'The ITC Programme Code'. Section 1 is headed 'Family Viewing Policy, Offence to Good Taste and Decency, Portrayal of Violence and Respect for Human Dignity'. There is also a document produced jointly by the BBC and the independent broadcasters entitled 'Guidelines for the Production of Party Election Broadcasts'. It indicates that PEBs must comply with the ITC Programme Code and the BBC producers' guidelines, 'having regard to the political context of the broadcast'; and then:

'Subject to the matters set out above, accuracy is the responsibility of the parties making the broadcasts ... Impartiality is achieved over the series of PEBs as a whole. There is, of course, no obligation on the parties to achieve impartiality within each broadcast.'

Although there is no issue in this case as to the 'accuracy' of the appellant's video, it is to be noted that s 6(1)(b) of the BA 1990 does not apply to PEBs, and impartiality (s 6(1)(c)) is achieved by the broadcasters' evenhandedness in providing airtime for PEBs, consistently with s 36 of the BA 1990, according to criteria framed by reference to the number of candidates fielded by the parties. As for the BSC, some of its adjudications on complaints are before the court and were referred to in the course of argument. In addition, the BSC is enjoined by ss 107 and 108 of the BA 1996 (which I have not set out) to draw up codes of guidance dealing with unjust or unfair treatment in programmes, unwarranted infringement of privacy, the portrayal of violence and of sexual conduct, and standards of taste and decency.

[16] I have looked at the relevant parts of the BBC producers' guidelines and the ITC programme code. As one would expect there is a good deal of reference to the broadcast of violent or sexual material, and to the 9 pm 'watershed'. While the content of the appellant's video obviously engages the s 6(1)(a)/para 5(1)(d) duty, there is I think nothing in these texts which bears on it specifically. One is thrown back on the words of the duty itself, 'offends against good taste or decency or is likely ... to be offensive to public feeling'. Nor I think is there anything to which I need refer in the BSC code, which was put before us as an exhibit to the third witness statement of Mr Quintavalle for the appellant. Mr Quintavalle (along with another witness, Mr Dorenbos) also produced some material dealing with the extent to which images of the kind shown in the

a appellant's video have been broadcast in other jurisdictions, principally in Europe. This was done at the invitation of the court, and I am sure my Lords, as well as I, are grateful for its having been done. In the event, however, after looking carefully at this evidence, I do not with respect find it necessary to describe it in this judgment.

b 1997

[17] The other matter which needs to be addressed before I deal with the issues in the case is the course of events in 1997, when as I have indicated the broadcasters declined to broadcast the video then put forward by the appellant to be put out as their PEB for the general election of that year, and the appellant's challenges here and in Strasbourg came to nothing. This is of some importance, c given Mr Pannick's reliance on the rejection of the appellant's case by the European Court of Human Rights without calling on the United Kingdom government to put in any answer, and the observation of Scott Baker J below that the Strasbourg decision was 'the death knell of the claimant's application' (transcript, para 54).

d [18] I should make it clear that I have not seen the 1997 video. By comparison with it the 2001 video was considerably modified, according to Mr Quintavalle. He describes the latter as a 'radically revised version' of the former. He says this in para 25 of his witness statement of 22 May 2001:

e 'All the most challenging images from the 1997 PEB were removed, including a scene of an actual abortion procedure. All images of third trimester abortions were also removed, as were other distressing sequences, including graphic images of severed heads.'

On 24 March 1997 Dyson J (as he then was), refusing judicial review leave, stated (transcript, p 8):

f 'I have no hesitation whatsoever in deciding that it is not arguable that the decision of the BBC that the offending parts of this transmission did not meet the requirements of decency and taste, is perverse.'

The learned judge proceeded to consider a separate argument, to the effect that g the curtailment of freedom of expression could only be allowed if 'a distinct and positive justification' were shown; and the court 'should give anxious scrutiny before upholding such an interference' (p 9). It seems this argument had been advanced both on the basis of a common law requirement and the provisions of the ECHR. The latter had, of course, not by then been incorporated into our h domestic law. Dyson J said (p 10): 'I am not persuaded that I ought to adopt an approach other than the conventional *Wednesbury* approach to these matters.' And so he dismissed the leave application. The application was renewed in the Court of Appeal, which also refused it on 20 October 1997. Lord Woolf MR, as he then was, stated (transcript, p 4) that there was no need for clarification of the law and in any event there were reservations as to whether this case was a j suitable vehicle for the giving of guidance.

[19] The appellant applied to the European Court of Human Rights. On 2 June 2000 a legal secretary at the court wrote to the appellant's lawyer, saying:

'In accordance with the general instructions received from the Court, I write to draw your attention to certain shortcomings in your application … The information given here is not intended to take the place of a decision, which only the Court can take, and is provided in order to explain, in the light of the case-law and practice, the conditions for admissibility and your application's prospects of success. The principal complaint in the case is that any interference with Article 10 was not proportionate to a legitimate aim.

However, the Court is likely to bear in mind, in assessing whether an appropriate balance was struck, that the essence of the Alliance's message was not affected: it was permitted to make its party political broadcast (even though Article 10 does not guarantee specific rights of access to television time), and, subject to the limitation complained of, was able to make what use of the time it wished. The Court may consider thus that the interference in the case was not arbitrary or unreasonable.'

There followed on 24 October 2000 a formal unanimous decision of the court, declaring the application inadmissible. It stated:

'The court has examined the application and has noted that the applicants have been informed of the possible obstacles to its admissibility. In the light of all the material in its possession, and in so far as the matters complained of are within its competence, the court finds that they do not disclose any appearance of a violation of the rights and freedoms set out in the convention or its protocols. It follows that the application must be rejected, in accordance with art 35(4) of the convention.'

THE JUDGMENT BELOW
[20] It is clear that Scott Baker J regarded his task as lying within conventional public law territory. He considered that his duty was to decide whether the broadcasters' decision was irrational. Given the view I take of the case, it is important to see how the judge put it:

'26. The broadcasters in this case had a difficult balancing exercise to perform between, on the one hand, allowing freedom of speech and expression and the pursuit of lawful political objectives and, on the other, meeting its own commitment not to offend good taste or decency, or broadcast something offensive to public feeling.

27. The balancing exercise, as Dyson J pointed out, necessarily involves a subjective judgment. Views will differ as to where the dividing line should be drawn. It is, however, in my judgment a decision that broadcasters are particularly experienced in making ... It seems to me ... that in this area the broadcasters are in a peculiarly good position to make judgments of this kind. It is also plain that it is the type of judgment to which the law accords a wide margin of discretion or appreciation ...

62. In 1997 Dyson J adopted a conventional *Wednesbury* approach [see *Associated Provincial Picture Houses Ltd v Wednesbury Corp* [1947] 2 All ER 680, [1948] 1 KB 223], having in mind, however, that freedom of expression was an important human right. Since then the Human Rights Act 1998 has become law ... It is clear that anxious scrutiny is required where human rights issues are involved and, furthermore, that interference with human rights can only be justified to the extent permitted by the convention itself.

63. However even today, in cases such [as] the present, the court's role remains supervisory. Great care must be taken to ensure that the Administrative Court does not assume the mantle of decision-taker. It is plain in the present case that the BBC has given careful consideration to the balancing exercise that is required. Even with the most anxious scrutiny it is

a impossible in my judgment to conclude that the BBC's decision was near the margin, let alone irrational.'

I should notice also that the learned judge expressed the view (at paras 53–54) that the Strasbourg court's conclusion 'that the claimant had no arguable case in respect of the 1997 party election broadcast' was 'the death knell' of the appellant's application before him in 2001.

b [21] That is a sufficient account of the facts of the case and its background, including the material statutory provisions, for the purposes of confronting the issues which we have to decide.

THE REAL ISSUE FORESHADOWED

c [22] It is convenient at this stage to state in outline what in my judgment is the real question in this case. In my view the court has to decide whether those considerations of taste and offensiveness, which moved the broadcasters, constituted a legal justification for the act of censorship involved in banning the appellant's proposed PEB (primarily as it was contained in the first video which was submitted). It will at once be clear that this formulation does not treat the
d reasonableness or rationality of the broadcasters' decision as conclusive of the issue falling for decision. That would have been the approach upon the conventional jurisprudence dealing with judicial review of a public body's exercise of discretionary power: *Associated Provincial Picture Houses Ltd v Wednesbury Corp* [1947] 2 All ER 680, [1948] 1 KB 223 and *Council of Civil Service Unions v Minister for the Civil Service* [1984] 3 All ER 935, [1985] AC 374. It was the
e approach taken by Dyson J in 1997 and Scott Baker J in 2001. However, with great respect, it was in my view a profoundly mistaken approach. At least it falls to be so regarded today. When I come to deal with the whole substance of this principal issue, I will explain why that is so. First, however, I must clear out of the way other points which were raised in argument but which in my judgment
f carry the case nowhere. I shall do it as shortly as I may.

PRELIMINARY POINTS

[23] The framework of the submissions advanced by Mr Anderson QC for the appellant was largely fashioned by reference to the terms of the second paragraph of the ECHR, art 10. I should set out the whole article:
g
'1. Everyone has the right to freedom of expression. This right shall include freedom to hold opinions and to receive and impart information and ideas without interference by public authority and regardless of frontiers. This Article shall not prevent States from requiring the licensing of
h broadcasting, television or cinema enterprises.
2. The exercise of these freedoms, since it carries with it duties and responsibilities, may be subject to such formalities, conditions, restrictions or penalties as are prescribed by law and are necessary in a democratic society, in the interests of national security, territorial integrity or public safety, for the prevention of disorder or crime, for the protection of health or morals,
j for the protection of the reputation or rights of others, for preventing the disclosure of information received in confidence, or for maintaining the authority and impartiality of the judiciary.'

[24] Mr Anderson's first argument was that the prohibition of his client's PEB was not 'prescribed by law' within art 10(2). He submitted that (a) there was no basis for the prohibition in domestic law, alternatively (b) the tests of taste,

decency and potential offence are so vague as not to satisfy the standard of legal certainty upon which the European Court of Human Rights insists as a measure of legality. This is a bad point. As for (a), the obligations of the BBC and the independent broadcasters, respectively arising under the agreement and the BA 1990, 'to secure that ... nothing is included in its programmes which offends against good taste or decency or is likely... to be offensive to public feeling' to my mind obviously empower the imposition of prior restraints as a matter of municipal law in a proper case, and with respect to Mr Anderson I do not find it necessary to say anything more about the submission. The question, of course, is whether this is a proper case. As for (b), it is clear from *Muller v Switzerland* (1988) 13 EHRR 212 at 226 (para 29) that the Strasbourg court accepts that laws whose subject matter touches areas of subjective judgment where public opinion may shift, cannot be expected to be rigid or over-precise. We are not of course bound to follow the Strasbourg cases; by s 2 of the Human Rights Act 1998 (HRA) we are obliged to take them into account. Here, I am quite satisfied that the terms of the BBC agreement and the BA 1990 do not offend any required standard of legal certainty.

[25] Mr Anderson's next argument was that the prohibition of his clients' PEB served no legitimate aim within art 10(2). The only candidate in this case, in the list there given of legitimate aims, was the 'rights of others'. Mr Anderson submitted that the prohibition could not possibly be justified in the name of the protection of 'the rights of others'. He cited *Chassagnou v France* (1999) 7 BHRC 151 for the proposition that where restrictions are imposed on the enjoyment of convention rights for the protection of other rights not guaranteed by the ECHR, 'only indisputable imperatives can justify interference with enjoyment of a convention right' (at 185 (para 113)). But the context of that observation by the court was its consideration of what measures in the particular case were justified as being 'necessary in a democratic society'. I do not consider, with respect, that the court was seeking to establish what would be a new and special rule. And there is a fair body of learning in Strasbourg to the effect that a broad approach is to be taken to the meaning of 'rights of others'. It is clearly by no means limited to the convention rights. Mr Pannick QC cited *Vgt Verein gegen Tierfabriken v Switzerland* (2001) 10 BHRC 473 at 486–487 (paras 59–62) and *Chapman v UK* (2001) 10 BHRC 48 at 68 (paras 80–82). With respect I need not set out those texts.

[26] This argument advanced by the appellant, like the first relating to the rubric 'prescribed by law', is an attempt to persuade the court that it has no need or business to inquire into the merits of the PEB's prohibition *at all*, because it falls at first base as lying wholly outside any application of art 10(2). That is in my judgment a mistaken approach. It is now well accepted that a common thread runs through the convention: the search for the means to strike a balance between private right and public interest. I cannot believe that the Strasbourg court, in any *lis* conducted there, would nonsuit the respondent on the footing that issues of taste, decency and offence were in principle *never* capable (however stark the facts) of providing a justification for a prior restraint under art 10(2) by reference to 'the rights of others'. All would depend on the facts and the context, and I believe with respect that the European Court of Human Rights would look at the case as a whole. Its jurisprudence has always exhibited a strong pragmatic philosophy. Even if that were wrong, given the nature of our obligation under s 2 of the HRA to which I have referred in [24], above, I would hold in any event (for the purposes of our developing municipal law of human rights) that the

a factors of taste, decency and offence cannot be treated as categorically irrelevant to the judgment of a prohibition upon free expression. I shall deal later with the different, and much more pertinent, question what force those factors possess in the present case.

[27] The third argument for the appellant was that it is the court's own task to decide whether the restriction of free expression complained of was justified as *b* falling within the scope of art 10(2) of the ECHR. Mr Pannick accepts that that is so in principle; his submission is that the court in arriving at its conclusion will pay great respect and deference (a) to the view of the primary legislature in imposing (by s 6(1)(a) of the BA 1990: para 5(1)(d) of the BBC agreement, though not given by statute, cannot sensibly be in any different case) requirements of taste and decency which are in no sense disapplied in cases like the present, and *c* (b) to the combined expertise of the broadcasters who made the impugned decision. I find it more convenient to address the issues arising under this head in dealing with what I have called the real question in the case.

[28] Mr Anderson's skeleton argument for the appellant contained a further submission, to the effect that the broadcasters' decision was insufficiently *d* reasoned, principally on the ground that they made no attempt to identify what particular images in the video were judged unacceptable. There is nothing in this. The broadcasters plainly looked at the video as a whole. They could not have done otherwise. Its impact, over the short period it runs, is inevitably cumulative. I have said that the images it contains are disturbing to anyone of ordinary sensibilities. The appellant, perhaps more than anyone, knows that that *e* is so. The outcome of this case does not depend on the quality of the broadcasters' reasons as a self-standing issue (though I shall refer again to the letter of 17 May 2001, which I have cited at [10], above, in looking at the *premise* on which the decision was made). Its outcome depends on the answer to the question, as I have described it in [22], above, whether those considerations of *f* taste and offensiveness, which moved the broadcasters, constituted a legal justification for the act of censorship involved in banning the appellant's proposed PEB. To this I now turn.

THE REAL ISSUE CONFRONTED: JUSTIFIED CENSORSHIP?

g (1) *Strasbourg*
[29] This issue was framed by the appellant in such a way as to ask the question, whether the prohibition was 'necessary in a democratic society' (sc for the protection of the rights of others), which is, of course, the language of art 10(2) of the ECHR. I need cite no authority for the proposition, which is very *h* generally accepted, that the term 'necessary in a democratic society' imports a test of proportionality into the court's judgment whether the interference complained of may be justified in light of any of the particular considerations set out in art 10(2). It is also well recognised that where a public authority seeks to justify an interference with the right of free expression, its restriction of the right will not be regarded as proportionate unless it fulfils a 'pressing social need': see *j* for example *Sunday Times v UK* (1979) 2 EHRR 245, and *Observer v UK* (1991) 14 EHRR 153 (the 'Spycatcher' case) in which the Court of Human Rights stated (at 191 (para 59)):

'Freedom of expression constitutes one of the essential foundations of a democratic society; subject to paragraph (2) of Article 10, it is applicable not only to "information" or "ideas" that are favourably received or regarded as inoffensive or as a matter of indifference, but also to those that offend, shock or disturb. Freedom of expression, as enshrined in Article 10, is subject to a number of exceptions which, however, must be narrowly interpreted and the necessity for any restrictions must be convincingly established.'

[30] There are many other judgments of the court in which the particular value of the right of free speech is emphasised. Often they deal with the special importance to be accorded to press freedom. But the imperative of free expression in the context of democratic elections is also heavily underlined. In *Bowman v UK* (1998) 4 BHRC 25 at 34 (para 42) the court said:

'Free elections and freedom of expression, particularly freedom of political debate, together form the bedrock of any democratic system ... The two rights are interrelated and operate to reinforce each other: for example, as the court has observed in the past, freedom of expression is one of the "conditions" necessary to "ensure the free expression of the opinion of the people in the choice of the legislature". For this reason, it is particularly important in the period preceding an election that opinions and information of all kinds are permitted to circulate freely.'

[31] There is also much learning on another dimension in the jurisprudence to which I need to refer if only to get it out of the way. This is the doctrine of the 'margin of appreciation' which the Strasbourg court will accord to national authorities so far as they seek to rely on the exempting or (more accurately) qualifying provisions contained in para 2 of each of arts 8–11. As is well known, this doctrine is a function of the Court of Human Rights' status as an international tribunal. In *R v DPP, ex p Kebeline, R v DPP, ex p Rechachi* [1999] 4 All ER 801 at 844, [2000] 2 AC 326 at 380 Lord Hope of Craighead stated:

'This doctrine is an integral part of the supervisory jurisdiction which is exercised over state conduct by the international court. By conceding a margin of appreciation to each national system, the court has recognised that the convention, as a living system, does not need to be applied uniformly by all states but may vary in its application according to local needs and conditions. This technique is not available to the national courts when they are considering convention issues arising within their own countries.'

We are not, therefore, bidden to accord a 'margin of appreciation' properly so called to the broadcasters, and we should fall into confusion and error if we did so. That is not to say that some margin of *discretion* or *deference* is not to be paid by this court to the statutory decision maker. As I have foreshadowed, it is Mr Pannick's submission that the authority of the BA 1990, being main legislation passed by Parliament, and the authority of the broadcasters who decided not to allow the PEB, being experts in judging matters of taste for broadcasting purposes, are entitled to a great degree of deference on democratic and practical grounds. Immediately after the passage I have just cited from *Ex p Kebeline*, Lord Hope continued:

'But in the hands of the national courts also the convention should be seen as an expression of fundamental principles rather than as a set of mere rules. The questions which the courts will have to decide in the application of these principles will involve questions of balance between competing interests and issues of proportionality. In this area difficult choices may have to be made by the executive or the legislature between the rights of the individual and *a* the needs of society. In some circumstances it will be appropriate for the courts to recognise that there is an area of judgment within which the judiciary will defer, on democratic grounds, to the considered opinion of the elected body or person whose act or decision is said to be incompatible with the convention.'

b [32] There is much other domestic learning on this question of deference. (A good deal of it is collected in a dissenting judgment given by myself in the recent case of *International Transport Roth GmbH v Secretary of State for the Home Dept* [2002] EWCA Civ 158, [2002] All ER (D) 325 (Feb).) There is, I think, some relationship between the margin of appreciation doctrine and the judgment of a domestic court upon the margin of discretion to be accorded to the domestic *c* decision-maker. In *Wingrove v UK* (1996) 1 BHRC 509, which was concerned with a blasphemous video called *Visions of Ecstasy*, the court held (at 526 (para 58)):

d 'Whereas there is little scope under art 10(2) of the convention for restrictions on political speech or on debate of questions of public interest … a wider margin of appreciation is generally available to the contracting states when regulating freedom of expression in relation to matters liable to offend intimate personal convictions within the sphere of morals or, especially, religion.'

While this reasoning is compressed, it tends in my judgment to show that in the Strasbourg court's view the state in principle should possess little discretion to *e* interfere with free political speech: especially at the time of an election (see *Bowman v UK* cited above). That view is not a function of the margin of appreciation. On the contrary it expresses a standard which the signatory states must fulfil for compliance with art 10. The reference to a 'wider margin of appreciation' in the context of speech liable to offend personal moral or religious *f* convictions indicates that in such matters the signatory states, consistently with their obligations under the ECHR, are at greater liberty to choose between more or less liberal or conservative regimes. The insight which this provides is that the scope or width of the margin of appreciation which in any given case the European Court of Human Rights will accord to the national authorities depends at least in part upon the court's judgment of the extent to which, giving full *g* weight to municipal culture and practice, there may in principle be a range of different views and approaches relating to the matter in hand.

(2) Domestic law

[33] These reflections furnish a convenient gateway to the proper approach to *h* be taken by the court to this appeal. The English court is not a Strasbourg surrogate. The very difference between the international margin of appreciation and the municipal margin of discretion illustrates the confusion that would arise if the court so regarded itself. Our duty is to develop, by the common law's incremental method, a coherent and principled domestic law of human rights. In *j* doing it, we are directed by the HRA (s 6) to insist on compliance by public authorities with the standards of the convention, and to comply with them ourselves. We are given new powers and duties (ss 3 and 4 of the HRA) to see that that is done. In all this we are to take account of the Strasbourg cases (s 2, to which I have already referred).

[34] The need to make good an autonomous human rights jurisprudence is promoted by a further consideration. Treating the ECHR text as a template for

our own law runs the risk of an over-rigid approach. Travelling through the words of provisions like art 10(2), with stops along the way to pronounce that this or that condition is met or not met, smacks to my mind of what Lord Wilberforce once condemned as the 'austerity of tabulated legalism' (see *Minister of Home Affairs v Fisher* [1979] 3 All ER 21 at 25, [1980] AC 319 at 328). I accept of course that such a wintry process would be tempered by what I have called (at [26], above) the strong pragmatic philosophy of the Strasbourg court. Even so, while great respect is to be paid to the way in which the ECHR is framed, and therefore to the structure of provisions such as art 10, I think the court's duty in confronting the claims of free speech, and the claims that may be ranged against it, in a context like that of the present case is very far distant from any exercise of textual interpretation. We are dealing here with bedrock principles. We are concerned with the protection of free expression in the context of political debate. In the rancour and asperity of a general election this duty, owed to the people, is surely at its highest.

[35] This position is in my judgment wholly consistent with the domestic learning on freedom of expression. It has often been said that the core rights enshrined in the ECHR by and large reflect principles which the common law itself espouses. This is especially demonstrated in the field of free speech by decisions in this jurisdiction over a period of years before incorporation of the convention rights by the HRA. We may have been slow—organs of the press would certainly so accuse us—to recognise the sometimes debilitating effect of prior restraint injunctions. But our courts have accorded a vigorous endorsement of the importance of free expression, not least in the political field. This is very well established and I need only give some leading instances from the authorities. I make no apology for starting with the dissenting opinion of Lord Bridge of Harwich in *A-G v Guardian Newspapers Ltd* [1987] 3 All ER 316, [1987] 1 WLR 1248, the *Spycatcher* case. In *Observer v UK*, which I have already cited, the Court of Human Rights vindicated his view that the extant injunctions against the newspapers, prohibiting the publication of material from the text of the book *Spycatcher*, should not have been continued. Lord Bridge stated:

> 'Freedom of speech is always the first casualty under a totalitarian regime. Such a regime cannot afford to allow the free circulation of information and ideas among its citizens. Censorship is the indispensable tool to regulate what the public may and what they may not know. The present attempt to insulate the public in this country from information which is freely available elsewhere is a significant step down that very dangerous road.' (See [1987] 3 All ER 316 at 346–347, [1987] 1 WLR 1248 at 1286.)

In *R v Central Independent Television plc* [1994] 3 All ER 641 at 651–652, [1994] Fam 192 at 202–203 Hoffmann LJ, as he then was, said:

> 'The motives which impel judges to assume a power to balance freedom of speech against other interests are almost always understandable and humane on the facts of the particular case before them ... [P]ublication may cause needless pain, distress and damage to individuals or harm to other aspects of the public interest. But a freedom which is restricted to what judges think to be responsible or in the public interest is no freedom. Freedom means the right to publish things which government and judges, however well motivated, think should not be published. It means the right

a to say things which "right-thinking people" regard as dangerous or irresponsible.'

In *R v Secretary of State for the Home Dept, ex p Simms* [1999] 3 All ER 400, [2000] 2 AC 115 these observations of Lord Steyn are especially pertinent for the importance of political speech:

b '... freedom of speech is the lifeblood of democracy. The free flow of information and ideas informs political debate. It is a safety valve: people are more ready to accept decisions that go against them if they can in principle seek to influence them. It acts as a brake on the abuse of power by public officials. It facilitates the exposure of errors in the governance and

c administration of justice of the country ...' (See [1999] 3 All ER 400 at 408, [2000] 2 AC 115 at 126.)

[36] Supported by such authority as this I would assert that as a matter of domestic law the courts owe a special responsibility to the public as the constitutional guardian of the freedom of political debate. This responsibility is

d most acute at the time and in the context of a public election, especially a general election. It has its origin in a deeper truth, which is that the courts are ultimately the trustees of our democracy's framework. I consider that this view is consonant with the common law's general recognition, apparent in recent years, of a category of fundamental or constitutional rights: see for example *Derbyshire CC v Times Newspapers Ltd* [1993] 1 All ER 1011, [1993] AC 534, *R v Secretary of State for*

e *the Home Dept, ex p Leech* [1993] 4 All ER 539, [1994] QB 198, *R v Lord Chancellor, ex p Witham* [1997] 2 All ER 779, [1998] QB 575, *Pierson v Secretary of State for the Home Dept* [1997] 3 All ER 577, [1998] AC 539, *Reynolds v Times Newspapers Ltd* [1999] 4 All ER 609, [2001] 2 AC 127, and with respect perhaps especially *Ex p Simms* [1999] 3 All ER 400 at 412, [2000] 2 AC 115 at 131 per Lord Hoffmann.

f Freedom of expression is plainly such a constitutional right, and its enjoyment by an accredited political party in an election contest must call, if anything, for especially heightened protection. We are in any case long past the point when interference with fundamental rights by public authorities can be justified by a bare demonstration of rationality or reasonableness: see *R v Secretary of State for the Home Dept, ex p Daly* [2001] UKHL 26, [2001] 3 All ER 433, [2001] 2 WLR 1622.

g [37] These considerations, with respect, give the lie to Mr Pannick's plea for deference to the decision-makers. If a producer were so insensitive as to authorise the inclusion of what is to be seen in the appellant's PEB video in an episode of a TV soap, the broadcasters would of course forbid its being shown and the courts would of course uphold them. That is at the extreme. There might be other

h more marginal situations, in which the courts would incline to defer to the broadcasters' judgment. Where the context is broadcast entertainment, I would accept without cavil that in the event of a legal challenge to a prohibition the courts should pay a very high degree of respect to the broadcasters' judgment, given the background of the BA 1990, the BA 1996, the BBC agreement, the codes

j of guidance and the BSC adjudications. Where the context is day-to-day news reporting, the broadcasters' margin of discretion may be somewhat more constrained but will remain very considerable. But the milieu we are concerned with in this case, the cockpit of a general election, is inside the veins and arteries of the democratic process. The broadcasters' views are entitled to be respected, but their force and weight are modest at best. I emphasise this is in no sense a slur on their expertise: having looked through the evidence I am very conscious, if I may say so, of the experience and professionalism clearly possessed by Ms Sloman, and her colleagues were no doubt likewise qualified. But in this context the court's constitutional responsibility to protect political speech is over-arching. It amounts to a duty which lies on the court's shoulders to decide for itself whether this censorship was justified. This is why, in my respectful view, the decisions of Dyson J and Scott Baker J went off on a mistaken footing.

[38] The reader of this judgment will see that I have used the word 'censorship' from the first sentence. I have well in mind that the broadcasters do not at all accept that their decision should be so categorised. Maybe the feathers of their liberal credentials are ruffled at the word's overtones; maybe there is an implicit plea for the comfort of a euphemism. However in my judgment this court must, and I hope the broadcasters will, recognise unblinking that censorship is exactly what this case is about. I should say that I do not mean it as a term of abuse; there are of course contexts in which Parliament and the common law have accepted that some forms of censorship are well justified. But we should know the beast we are dealing with. In the context of political speech, it needs to be kept in its cage.

(3) Application of the law to the facts

[39] Mr Anderson's case is very simple. The PEB video encapsulated his clients' case against abortion vividly but honestly. The suggestion that the message could as well be put over in words is unreal—it is inherent in any reasonable advocacy of the appellant's position that the public should be confronted with what an abortion actually entails. That is only effectively done by putting out the video, which is truthful and unsensational. Even if considerations of taste, decency and offensiveness might in some theoretical case justify the prohibition of a PEB, they cannot possibly do so on the facts here.

[40] A primary emphasis of Mr Pannick's submissions for the respondent was his plea for deference to Parliament and to the decision-makers, and I have already rejected that. On the substantive merits of the case Mr Pannick first drew attention to what he described as the limited nature of the restriction of free expression actually entailed by the broadcasters' decision. He was at pains to emphasise that the appellant was in no sense disabled from putting over its message in words, including words which might graphically describe the procedures involved in abortions. He submitted that we should infer that this factor was instrumental, or at least influential, in the Strasbourg court's admissibility ruling against the appellant. He did so by reference to the documents which I have cited at [19], above.

[41] There is nothing in this. As regards the Strasbourg decision I am by no means confident that the ruling of the court, as it was very shortly expressed on 24 October 2000, was necessarily intended to endorse the reasoning in the Secretariat's letter of 2 June 2000. Of course it may have been; but in any event it would be quite wrong to elevate this summary determination of a claim's admissibility to the status of persuasive jurisprudence. I do not think it possesses any particular force whatever. In my view Scott Baker J was in error in describing it as the 'death knell' of the appellant's application (see [20], above).

[42] Further, however, I am in profound disagreement with the very suggestion that the appellant's freedom to put its case in words somehow mitigates—no, *excuses*—this censorship of its case in pictures. I acknowledge of course that it is possible to construct instances in which a political party may seek to put over its message by images which are gratuitous and sensational. Even in

a such a case, I would not wish to be taken to accept that a prohibition of the proposed broadcast would necessarily be lawful; but at least a more colourable justification of censorship might be advanced than can be advanced here. All the more so if the image proposed for broadcast were deceitful or misleading as to the true facts.

b [43] I have already made it plain that there is nothing gratuitous or sensational or untrue in the appellant's intended PEB. It is certainly graphic; and, as I have said, disturbing. But if we are to take political free speech seriously, those characteristics cannot begin to justify the censorship that was done in this case. Here the image is the message, or at least an important part of it. Certainly I would accept that the pictures do not answer the deep philosophical questions which the abortion debate generates. But they show what actually happens. I c can see no answer to the claim that the appellant is entitled to show—not just tell—what happens.

[44] There may be instances, even in the context of a general election, in which political speech may justifiably be censored on grounds of taste or offensiveness. But in my judgment it would take a very extreme case, most likely d involving factors, to which I have already referred, such as gratuitous sensationalism and dishonesty. It is unhelpful to try to conjure instances. On the facts of this case the broadcasters have in my judgment failed altogether to give sufficient weight to the pressing imperative of free political expression. The letter of 17 May 2001 (see [10], above) demonstrates as much. There is no recognition of the critical truth, the legal principle, that considerations of taste and decency e cannot prevail over free speech by a political party at election time save wholly exceptionally. The premise of the letter is that the appellant's message is something merely to be taken into account in judging whether the taste and decency standards are breached. That is a profoundly mistaken approach. The common law requires that the freedom of political speech to be enjoyed by an f accredited party at a public election, most especially a general election, must not be interfered with save on the most pressing grounds, and such grounds will very rarely be shown by appeal to considerations of taste and decency alone. The BBC agreement and the BA 1990 and the BA 1996 have to be read conformably with this principle.

[45] I am entirely clear that no such grounds are shown in the present case. I g would accordingly allow the appeal. Since we are obviously long past the 2001 general election, I would assume that some form of declaration will be appropriate if my Lords agree with the substance of this judgment.

JONATHAN PARKER LJ.

h [46] I agree that this appeal should be allowed, for the reasons which Laws LJ has given. I also agree with the judgment of Simon Brown LJ, which I have had the advantage of reading in draft.

SIMON BROWN LJ.

j [47] The appellant is a registered political party committed to absolute respect for human life from fertilisation till death. Amongst its principal policies is the prohibition of abortion.

[48] In the 2001 general election the appellant fielded sufficient candidates to be entitled, pursuant to arrangements made under s 36 of the Broadcasting Act 1990 and s 3 of the Political Parties, Elections and Referendums Act 2000, to a four-minute party election broadcast (PEB) to be seen in Wales. The video it

submitted for transmission makes disturbing viewing. It graphically illustrates what is involved in first and second trimester abortion processes and includes clear images of aborted foetuses in a mangled and mutilated state. Under challenge in these proceedings is the broadcasters' unanimous decision to refuse transmission of the video on grounds of taste and decency and because it would offend public feeling. The respondent's decision letter of 17 May 2001 reads:

'We have had regard to the guidelines on taste and decency, prevailing standards of taste and decency, broadcasters' criteria on the portrayal of violence, and public interest considerations, as well as [all the points made on the appellant's behalf]. But none of these factors leads us to conclude other than that it would be wrong to broadcast these images which would be offensive to very large numbers of viewers. None of the broadcasters regard this as a case at the margin. We all regard it as a clear case in which it would plainly be a breach of our obligations to transmit this broadcast.'

[49] The broadcasters' 'obligations' there referred to were, for independent television, those prescribed by s 6(1) of the 1990 Act, and, for the BBC, effectively identical obligations under their agreement with the Secretary of State for National Heritage. Section 6(1) provides:

'The Commission shall do all that they can to secure that every licensed service complies with the following requirements, namely—(a) that nothing is included in its programmes which offends against good taste or decency or is likely to encourage of incite to crime or to lead to disorder or to be offensive to public feeling ...'

[50] The issue in this appeal is whether the appellant's proposed broadcast was properly refused on that ground, an issue falling for determination in the light of art 10 of the European Convention for the Protection of Human Rights and Fundamental Freedoms 1950 (as set out in Sch 1 to the Human Rights Act 1998). The ultimate question for decision is whether the ban was 'necessary in a democratic society' under art 10(2).

[51] Before addressing that central question, however, it is convenient to touch briefly on some of the appellant's wider submissions.

[52] That broadcasting, and therefore the right to freedom of expression under art 10(1), on occasion properly *can* be restricted on grounds of taste and decency and to avoid offending public feeling, I have not the least doubt. By the same token that the European Court of Human Rights in *Chapman v UK* (2001) 10 BHRC 48 at 68 (para 82) (a gypsy case under art 8) found that the planning controls there in question 'pursue the legitimate aim of protecting the "rights of others" through preservation of the environment', so too here, in my judgment, there is a legitimate interest in preserving what may be called the moral environment. People's sensibilities are affected no less by images broadcast into their homes than by those which confront them outside. Both affect the quality of life. The analogy must not, of course, be taken too far, but it seems to me sufficient to dispose of any suggestion that restriction on free speech can never be justified on these grounds. That said, the rights of others which are being protected by this measure are not themselves convention rights and are less potent as a justification for interference with convention rights than if they were. As the European Court of Human Rights in *Chassagnou v France* (1999) 7 BHRC 151 at 185 (para 113) said: 'In such a case only indisputable imperatives can justify interference with enjoyment of a convention right.' Although I respectfully

a question the usefulness of the phrase 'indisputable imperatives', preferring instead the well-established concept of 'pressing social need', it is plain that in this sort of case pressing need will not readily be found satisfied.

[53] Similarly I have no doubt, despite the appellant's sustained arguments to the contrary, that the legislation here in question is sufficiently clear and specific to permit of the prior restraint of broadcasts, rather than merely the retrospective
b operation of a complaints system. Again, however, that said, there is force in the appellant's argument that the objections which in any event ordinarily militate against prior restraint are substantially heightened in the context of a PEB. As the German Federal Constitutional Court pointed out in *Kommunistischen Partei Deustchlands/Marxisten* (1978) 2 BvR 523/75:

c '… it must not be forgotten that it is impossible to compensate for the serious legal disadvantages that arise where an election broadcast is rejected after a summary consideration and this is subsequently proved wrong … owing to the proximity of the broadcasting slots in time to the election date, the latter will usually have passed.'

d [54] That indeed is what happened here. Only, therefore, in the most clear and obvious cases should PEBs be refused transmission. All the broadcasters here, of course, thought that this case *was* clear and obvious.

[55] The third argument to be cleared out of the way before focusing on the central issue is the appellant's contention that concepts of taste, decency and offensiveness are intrinsically too vague and uncertain to satisfy the requirement
e under art 10(2) that any restrictive measure must be 'prescribed by law'. The answer to this is to be found in the European Court of Human Rights' judgment in *Muller v Switzerland* (1988) 13 EHRR 212 at 226 (para 29):

'A norm cannot be regarded as a "law" unless it is formulated with
f sufficient precision to enable the citizen–if need be, with appropriate advice–to foresee, to a degree that is reasonable in the circumstances, the consequences which a given action may entail. The Court has, however, already emphasised the impossibility of attaining absolute precision in the framing of laws, particularly in fields in which the situation changes according to the prevailing views of society. The need to avoid excessive
g rigidity and keep pace with changing circumstances means that many laws are inevitably couched in terms which, to a greater or lesser extent, are vague. Criminal law provisions on obscenity fall within this category.'

[56] There is no less 'need to avoid excessive rigidity and keep pace with changing circumstances' in the present context than with regard to the law of
h obscenity. In any event the uncertainty is to some extent lessened by codes of guidance drawn up by the Independent Television Commission (ITC) and the Broadcasting Standards Commission (BSC) suggesting how, with regard to various types of programme, questions of taste, decency and offensiveness should be approached. Ultimately, however, the crucial point to bear in mind is that
j these concepts are not absolute. They cannot be detached from their surrounding circumstances. The context in which they fall to be applied is all-important. Images or other material which if broadcast in one context would quite clearly be distasteful and offensive would be quite differently regarded in another. Take the appellant's video. The transmission of images of mutilated foetuses on a quiz programme or game show would be unthinkable; it would lack any possible justification and quite properly be condemned by all as utterly

tasteless and offensive. But in the context of a PEB, the essential and legitimate
purpose of which is to communicate a political message, different considerations   *a*
clearly apply. As the European Court of Human Rights held in *Bowman v UK*
(1998) 4 BHRC 25 at 34 (para 42) (another case concerning the distribution of
campaign literature about abortion at election time):

> 'Free elections and freedom of expression, particularly freedom of political
> debate, together form the bedrock of any democratic system ... The two   *b*
> rights are interrelated and operate to reinforce each other: for example, as
> the court has observed in the past, freedom of expression is one of the
> "conditions" necessary to "ensure the free expression of the opinion of the
> people in the choice of the legislature". For this reason, it is particularly
> important in the period preceding an election that opinions and information   *c*
> of all kinds are permitted to circulate freely.'

[57] Against that broad background, let me now turn to the critical issue
arising here. Was there a pressing social need to ban this broadcast? I have
reached the clear conclusion that there was not. Disturbing, perhaps shocking,
though the images on this video undoubtedly are, they represent the reality, the   *d*
actuality, of what is involved in the abortion process. To campaign for the
prohibition of abortion is a legitimate political programme. The pictures are in a
real sense the message. Words alone cannot convey (particularly to the less
verbally adept) the essentially human character of the foetus and the nature of its
destruction by abortion. This video provides a truthful, factual and, it is right to
say, unsensational account of the process. As the appellant's evidence explains: *e*

> 'All the most challenging images from the 1997 PEB were removed,
> including a scene of an actual abortion procedure. All images of third
> trimester abortions were also removed, as were other distressing sequences,
> including graphic images of severed heads.'
                                                                                    f
[58] The appellants were, moreover, always prepared for the broadcast to be
shown late in the evening and with all appropriate warnings.

[59] The importance of freedom of expression in the context of political
speech is hard to exaggerate. I have already cited *Bowman v UK* but in truth it is
unnecessary to travel to Strasbourg to find statements of compelling force at the
highest level emphasising the vital importance of free political communication.   *g*
The principle is resoundingly articulated by the House of Lords in *R v Secretary of
State for the Home Dept, ex p Simms* [1999] 3 All ER 400, [2000] 2 AC 115, *Reynolds v
Times Newspapers Ltd* [1999] 4 All ER 609, [2001] 2 AC 127, and *McCartan
Turkington Breen (a firm) v Times Newspapers Ltd* [2000] 4 All ER 913, [2001] 2 AC
277. When it comes to election time and PEBs, of course, the need for freedom   *h*
of expression is at its very highest.

[60] Although I think it possible to contemplate circumstances in which the
broadcasting authorities might properly decline to transmit a PEB on grounds of
taste, decency and offensiveness—that indeed may well have been true of the 1997
video which Mr Anderson QC acknowledges was significantly different—I am   *j*
quite certain that this was not such a case.

[61] It is an irony of these proceedings that the respondent broadcasters,
natural campaigners for media freedom and ordinarily concerned to resist
complaints about programmes which they themselves have thought suitable for
transmission, are here in the very different position of defending a decision *not* to
broadcast. It seems to me instructive in this connection to note some of the BSC's

_a_ and the ITC's adjudications. Although, as I recognise, none of the transmissions in question are directly comparable to this video, it is nevertheless worth noting certain of the considerations taken into account in determining the individual complaints. Let me instance just three. First, a complaint about a _Newsnight_ broadcast showing footage of animals being killed for their fur which the BBC successfully resisted on the basis of 'a strong public interest in making viewers _b_ aware of the full horror of the situation'. Second, a programme showing badgers being killed which Channel 5 successfully defended on the footing that it secured the conviction of those involved and brought about a change in the law, the BSC accepting that 'the report had served a valuable public purpose that would have been lost by simply describing the practice'. Thirdly, an ITV programme containing harrowing scenes of the victims of a Nairobi bomb explosion which _c_ the BSC found acceptable in these terms:

> '[The] images shown were, indeed, shocking, with a level of explicitness not usually depicted by broadcasters when acts of terrorism have occurred in the United Kingdom ... In the committee's view, the use of such powerful scenes was neither gratuitous nor sensationalist, but represented the true _d_ horror of terrorism. It therefore served an important public interest and educative function.'

[62] It may well be the case—I readily acknowledge that it probably _is_ the case—that none of those three programmes, or indeed any of the other programmes drawn to our attention to illustrate the kind of potentially offensive _e_ material already shown on television, contained quite such prolonged and deeply disturbing images as the appellant's video. But is there not the same 'strong public interest in making viewers aware' of the true nature (I refrain from using the expression 'the full horror' lest it be thought to imply a moral view) of the practice depicted, 'a valuable purpose that would have been lost by simply _f_ describing the practice'? And can it not equally be said here, as of the Nairobi bomb programme, that the use of these images 'was neither gratuitous nor sensationalist' and 'served an important public interest and educative function'? And do not the appellants too by their broadcast legitimately attempt to '[bring] about a change in the law'?

[63] Whatever public interest is recognised to justify the sort of shocking _g_ material shown in existing programmes is to my mind more pronounced still when it comes to PEBs. Provided only and always that such broadcasts are truthful and unsensational (not, be it noted, conditions which the broadcasters ordinarily impose on PEBs), only in the rarest of circumstances could they properly be rejected. Almost always the balance will fall to be struck in favour of _h_ the free communication of political aims and ideas. That certainly is the position here. I too would allow this appeal.

Appeal allowed. Permission to appeal refused.

Dilys Tausz   Barrister.

A Health Authority v X

[2001] EWCA Civ 2014

COURT OF APPEAL, CIVIL DIVISION

THORPE, LAWS LJJ AND HARRISON J

26 NOVEMBER, 21 DECEMBER 2001

Medical practitioner – Doctor and patient – Disclosure of confidential information – Health authority seeking disclosure of medical records and case papers relating to Children Act proceedings in Family Division – Disclosure sought in connection with disciplinary proceedings – Judge ordering disclosure of documents subject to conditions – Whether judge in error – National Health Service (General Medical Services) Regulations 1992, Sch 2, para 36(6).

After the hearing of a long and complex public law case in the Family Division under the Children Act 1989, the local authority involved reported to its area health authority facts that had emerged in the case and which it considered relevant to the discharge of the health authority's duties. It also applied to the trial judge for permission to release to the health authority a selection of papers in the case. The judge ruled that the health authority should make the application. With a view to possible disciplinary proceedings, the health authority duly sought an order for production of specified case papers and the general practitioner records of two named individuals who had been involved in the case. The health authority's application was heard not by the trial judge, but by another judge. He concluded that the health authority was entitled to disclosure of the selected case papers, including the judgment, and to an order requiring the respondent doctor to produce to the health authority the medical records relating to the named patients, whose consent to production had been refused or not obtained. The judge further concluded that in each instance disclosure should be subject to express conditions, designed to ensure that, as far as possible, the health authority should maintain the confidentiality of the documents and not disclose them to any other person without prior permission of the court. He held that the doctor's duty of confidentiality was ultimately to comply with whatever order the court might make. Prior to that point, his duty, like that of any other professional or person who owed a duty of confidentiality to his patient or client, was to assert that confidentiality in answer to any claim by a third party for disclosure and to put before the court every argument that could properly be put against disclosure. That was all the more so when, as in the instant case, he knew that the patient or client was refusing disclosure. The health authority appealed against the imposition of the conditions, and in particular against a condition which precluded it, save with the prior leave of the court, from disclosing any of the documents or communicating any information contained in them to any person other than (a) a medical disciplinary committee or the National Health Service Tribunal or the General Medical Council and (b) in accordance with regs 4 and 5 of the National Health Service (Service Committees and Tribunal) Regulations 1992. It submitted that far from the doctor having any duty to require the court's determination, his plain duty, save in the unlikely event that he had reason to doubt compliance with any one of the preconditions set out in the judge's judgment, was to comply with the health authority's request for the patient a records in accordance with para 36(6)[a] of Sch 2 to the National Health Service (General Medical Services) Regulations 1992 (the General Medical Services Regulations). It further submitted that the NHS depended upon free internal exchange of confidential information, and that the service would grind to a halt if the judge's definition of a doctor's duty were to be extensively applied.

b Alternatively, the health authority submitted that the judge was both wrong in principle and unjustified in imposing upon it the conditions set out in his judgment since there were already more than sufficient safeguards for the patient; that there was no evidence to suggest that the health authority was unaware of its obligations or that it was in breach of its own arrangements; and that the consequences of imposing the conditions would be prejudicial to the health authority and disproportionate to the underlying objective of para 36(6).

c The issue arose as to whether the conflict between the private/public interests in the confidentiality of medical records and some other public interest should be decided by the health authority or by a judge of the Family Division.

Held – A judge of the Family Division, not the area health authority, should
d resolve the conflict between the private/public interests in the confidentiality of medical records and some other public interest. There was obviously a high public interest, analogous to the public interest in the due administration of criminal justice, in the proper administration of professional disciplinary hearings, particularly in the field of medicine, and in the instant case the judge had
e properly ordered the release of the case materials. Although the patient records had been separately categorised because of the application of para 36(6) of Sch 2 to the General Medical Services Regulations, they were inextricably connected with the case materials, and in those circumstances the objection to their production fell to be decided in accordance with the same principle, namely whether the public interest in effective disciplinary procedures for the investigation
f and eradication of medical malpractice outweighed the confidentiality of the records. The application for production was not much enhanced by the para 36(6) duty. A balance still had to be struck between competing interests, and that balance came down in favour of production, as it invariably did save in exceptional circumstances. Moreover, the court did have a power to attach
g conditions to an order directing the release of case papers in proceedings under the 1989 Act to a third party. Without that power, the court would be left with a crude choice between directing or refusing release. Striking a balance between competing public interests, often across the interface of distinct justice systems, required much more sophisticated powers. It followed the judge had been
h correct in law to claim that power and equally correct to proceed to a discretionary exercise of the power having regard to the relevant facts and circumstances in so far as they were revealed to him. Furthermore, he had not overstated the doctor's duty to his patient, and the spectres of cost and administrative overload, developed by the health authority, were no more than
j speculation which good sense and management could contain. Accordingly, the health authority had not demonstrated any error of law or principle in the judge's decision which would justify the court's intervention, nor had it demonstrated that the discretionary bounds set by the judge were plainly wrong. The appeal would therefore be dismissed (see [19], [20], [22], [25]–[28], below); dictum of

---

a   Paragraph 36(6) is set out at [4], below

Cazalet J in *Re A (a minor) (disclosure of medical records to the General Medical Council)*
[1999] 1 FCR 30 at 35 approved.

Per curiam. Where a trial has been conducted by a judge of the Family
Division, a subsequent application by a third party for the release of case papers
must be made to that judge rather than to another judge of the Family Division,
absent exceptional circumstances (see [23], [27], [28], below).

Notes
For doctors' obligation of confidence to their patients and the circumstances
where the patient's consent is not a prerequisite to disclosure, see 8(1) *Halsbury's
Laws* (4th edn reissue) paras 437, 441.

For the National Health Service (General Medical Services) Regulations 1992,
see 14 *Halsbury's Statutory Instruments* (2001 Issue) 53.

Cases referred to in judgments
A (a minor) (disclosure of medical records to the General Medical Council), Re [1999] 1
FCR 30.

C (a minor) (care proceedings: disclosure), Re [1997] Fam 76, [1997] 2 WLR 322, CA.

D (minors) (wardship: disclosure), Re [1992] 1 FCR 297, CA.

L (a minor) (police investigation: privilege), Re [1996] 2 All ER 78, [1997] AC 16, [1996]
2 WLR 395, HL.

MS v Sweden (1997) 3 BHRC 248, ECt HR.

Parry Jones v Law Society [1968] 1 All ER 177, [1969] 1 Ch 1, [1968] 2 WLR 397, CA.

Z v Finland (1997) 25 EHRR 371, [1997] ECHR 22009/93, ECt HR.

Appeal
The appellant area health authority appealed from the decision of Munby J on 10
May 2001 ([2001] 2 FCR 634) to impose conditions on the health authority when
granting its application for an order (i) permitting disclosure to it of selected case
papers in proceedings under the Children Act 1989 in which Hughes J had given
judgment on 16 March 2000, and (ii) requiring the respondent doctor to produce
to the health authority, within seven days, records relating to two patients who
had been directly or indirectly involved in the proceedings under the 1989 Act.
The Association of Community Health Councils appeared on the appeal as an
interested party. The facts are set out in the judgment of Thorpe LJ.

Philip Havers QC and *Angus McCullough* (instructed by *Le Brasseur J Tickle*) for the
health authority.
David Pannick QC and *Angus Moon* (instructed by *Christina Milne*) for the
respondent.
Tim Ward (instructed by *Marion Chester*) as an interested party.

Cur adv vult

21 December 2001. The following judgments were delivered.

THORPE LJ.
[1] There was a long and complex public law Children Act case tried by
Hughes J in the Family Division which culminated in his judgment of 16 March
2000. When the case was over the local authority reported to its area health
authority facts that had emerged in the case which it considered relevant to the
discharge of the authority's duties. The local authority also applied to Hughes J

a for permission to release to the health authority a selection of the papers in the case. The judge ruled that the application should be made by the health authority. Accordingly by an application of 30 January 2001 the health authority sought an order for the production of both specified case papers and the GP records of two named individuals who had been involved in the case. For reasons which are not clear to me the application was not listed in front of the trial judge
b but in front of Munby J. He heard counsel for the health authority and counsel for the respondent doctors. On 10 May he handed down his judgment and made his orders upon the application.

[2] His learned and lucid judgment is now reported at [2001] 2 FCR 634. His first conclusion was that the health authority were entitled to the disclosure of the selected case papers, including the judgment of Hughes J. His second conclusion
c was that the authority was entitled to an order requiring the respondent to produce to the authority within seven days the medical records relating to the two named patients, whose consent to that production had been refused or had not been obtained. However his conclusion was that in each instance disclosure should be subject to express conditions set out in the second schedule of his order
d and designed to ensure that as far as possible the health authority should maintain the confidentiality of the documents and not disclose them to any other person without prior permission of the court. It is against the imposition of those conditions that the health authority appeals. In reality their challenge is directed to the third condition:

e 'Save with the prior leave of this court the Authority shall not disclose any of the documents or communicate any information contained in them to any person other than (a) to a medical discipline committee or the National Health Service Tribunal or the General Medical Council and (b) in accordance with regulations 4 and 5 of The National Health Service (Service Committees and Tribunal) Regulations 1992, SI 1992/664 as amended.'

f [3] The appeal is brought with leave of the judge. With the leave of this court the General Medical Council has lodged evidence in support of the respondent's case. The respondents have received further support from the Association of Community Health Councils for England and Wales. The association also filed evidence and appeared at the hearing by counsel, Mr Ward, who adopted the
g submissions of Mr Pannick QC for the respondents.

[4] The case for the appellant authority was skilfully argued by Mr Havers QC. The statutory framework for the application for the disclosure of the medical records in relation to the two patients who had not consented to production is fully and carefully set out in the judgment of Munby J. Accordingly
h Mr Havers was able to restrict himself to a reference to para 36(6) of Sch 2 to the National Health Service (General Medical Services) Regulations 1992, SI 1992/635 as amended. Paragraph 36(6) provides:

'A doctor shall send the records relating to a patient to the Health Authority—(a) as soon as possible, at the request of the Health Authority; or
j (b) before the end of the period of 14 days beginning with the date on which he was informed by the Health Authority of the death, or (in any other case) before the end of the period of one month beginning with the date on which he learned of the death.'

[5] Mr Havers' first submission was that that statutory language was sufficiently clear and unqualified to override the ordinary duty of confidentiality

owed by a GP to the patient. He submitted that that construction was supported
by authority, namely the case of *Parry Jones v Law Society* [1968] 1 All ER 177,
[1969] 1 Ch 1 and the European case of *MS v Sweden* (1997) 3 BHRC 248,
particularly at 256–257 (paras 41–44). Mr Havers accepted the conclusion of
Munby J that its right to demand production under para 36(6) was subject to three
preconditions set out in judgment, namely:

> '(i) if the documents are bona fide and reasonably required for the purpose
> of the proper exercise by the authority of one of its functions under Pt II of
> the 1977 Act; (ii) if, where the documents are to be used otherwise than in
> the particular patient's best interests—eg, for disciplinary or regulatory
> purposes—there is a compelling public interest in their disclosure which
> satisfies the usual Convention criteria of "necessity" and "proportionality";
> and (iii) if there are effective and adequate safeguards against abuse,
> including effective and adequate safeguards of the particular patient's
> confidentiality and anonymity.' (See [2001] 2 FCR 634 at [71].)

[6] Mr Havers submitted these preconditions are comparable to the built-in
safeguards accepted by the Strasbourg Court in *MS v Sweden* in rejecting that
applicant's claim to a breach of her convention rights.

[7] Mr Havers attacked Munby J's statement of the doctor's duty of
confidentiality which appears thus:

> 'Now of course in the final analysis … Dr X's ultimate obligation is to
> comply with whatever order the court may make. But prior to that point
> being reached his duty, like that of any other professional or other person
> who owes a duty of confidentiality to his patient or client, is to assert that
> confidentiality in answer to any claim by a third party for disclosure and to
> put before the court every argument that can properly be put against
> disclosure. All the more so when, as in the present case, he knows, because
> he has asked, that his patient or client is refusing to consent to disclosure.'
> (See [2001] 2 FCR 634 at [9].)

[8] Mr Havers' submission is that far from the doctor having any duty to
require the court's determination, his plain duty is to comply with a para 36(6)
request save in the unlikely event that he has reason to doubt compliance with
any one of the three preconditions set by Munby J (at [71]).

[9] Mr Havers submits that were we to uphold the doctor's duty as defined by
Munby J there would be a number of undesirable consequences. First applications
to the court are expensive and impractical. Second they involve inevitable delay
which could not be bridged in any case of urgency, still less in a case of
emergency. Third the creation of an unnecessary superstructure on the
production mechanism created by para 36(6) would not only impede the health
authority but any successive holder who would in turn be obliged to assert
confidence and to make yet another application to the court.

[10] In summary Mr Havers submitted that the National Health Service
depended upon free internal exchange of confidential information. He warned
that the service would grind to a halt were Munby J's judgment extensively
construed and applied.

[11] Mr Havers' alternative submission was that the judge was both wrong in
principle and unjustified in imposing upon the health authority the conditions set
out in Sch II to the judgment. In support of that submission he advanced three
reasons. The first was that there are already more than sufficient safeguards for

a the patient. He listed and elaborated in turn: (a) the duty of confidence as defined by our domestic law; (b) art 8 convention rights as recognised in the case of *MS v Sweden* as well as the case of *Z v Finland* (1997) 25 EHRR 371; (c) additional protection given by the Data Protection Act 1998; (d) the strong emphasis on confidentiality given in the Department of Health guidance: *The Protection and Use of Patient Information–Guidance from the Department of Health* HSG (96)
b 18/LASS L (95) 5 as updated; and (e) the creation of the structure of Caldicott guardians created in response to recommendation 3 of the Caldicott Report of December 1997.

[12] Secondly Mr Havers advanced the negative proposition that there was no evidence to suggest that the health authority was unaware of its obligations or that it was in breach of its own arrangements.
c
[13] Thirdly he submitted that the consequences of imposing the conditions would be prejudicial to the health authority and disproportionate to the underlying objective of para 36(6). In support of this third submission he submitted a bundle of papers to demonstrate a subsequent consequence of the imposition of the Sch II conditions. In the continuing management of the
d aftermath of the proceedings before Hughes J there had been a statutory review and his clients had been obliged to launch an application for permission to bring into the Pt 8 review documents produced pursuant to Munby J's order. The additional bundle which he submitted contained an application served on Dr X for permission and a directions order made by Bracewell J. However when
e pressed Mr Havers conceded that this third ground was his last and he did not seek to make too much of it.

[14] In responding to Mr Havers' submissions Mr Pannick essentially submitted that Munby J had been correct in principle because the need for patient protection required a decision of a High Court judge to decide the balance
f between the private/public interest in confidentiality and any competing public interest. Such a decision had to be objective and could not be left to the health authority acting in good faith. Alternatively Mr Pannick submitted that the imposition of conditions by Munby J was a proper exercise of a judicial discretion without any error of principle and accordingly not a discretion with which this court should interfere.

g [15] As to Mr Havers' first ground Mr Pannick emphasised the importance of the doctor's duty of confidentiality. As explained in *Z v Finland* it is not just the private interest of the patient which is at stake but the wider interest of the public in the proper treatment of transmissible diseases which depends in part upon the individual's sense of security in seeking help and in revealing private matters.
h Mr Havers' construction would impose an impossible burden on the GP in assessing whether or not the preconditions are satisfied without the requisite expertise or information. It would in practice amount to an absolute duty to disclose which would in turn deprive the court of any opportunity to strike a balance. He submitted that the *Parry Jones* case has been overtaken by European jurisprudence and that the case of *Z v Finland* emphasises the importance attached
j to the role of the court in weighing whether the state is in breach of convention rights.

[16] As to Mr Havers' spectres of costs and delay, whether in support of his first or second principal submissions, Mr Pannick foresaw that the majority of the applications would proceed by consent at little cost and urgent cases would be accommodated.

[17] As to Mr Havers' second principal submission, the attack on the imposition of conditions, Mr Pannick submitted that the central issue remains who should exercise the balance when a conflict of interests arises. If that exercise must be performed by the judge then none of Mr Havers' three objections arose. But in any event the safeguards advanced were insufficient. The domestic law of confidence was not yet clear. Of the two European cases greater account should be taken of the approach of the court in the case of Z v Finland. The Data Protection Act 1998 contained many exceptions, as the Department of Health guidance demonstrated. Finally Mr Pannick submitted that the arrival of Caldicott guardians was no substitute for judicial control. The concern was not that health authorities might act in bad faith or negligently but that a proper exercise of such a balance must be an independent exercise.

[18] I have summarised the argument in this court in some detail partly to demonstrate that it canvasses wide ranging issues that I do not consider to be directly raised in the present case. The strict confidentiality attaching to litigation material in children's cases has long been upheld both according to common law and statute. Of course that strict confidentiality is not absolute. There are many instances in which it must yield to a conflicting public interest. Most commonly the reported cases consider the release of case papers in Children Act proceedings for use in a criminal prosecution that requires investigation of the same facts and circumstances examined in the prior Children Act proceedings. There are a number of reported cases at first instance. In this court two significant cases are those cited by Munby J, namely Re D (minors) (wardship: disclosure) [1992] 1 FCR 297 and Re C (a minor) (care proceedings: disclosure) [1997] Fam 76, [1997] 2 WLR 322. There is also the case of Re L (a minor) (police investigation: privilege) [1996] 2 All ER 78, [1997] AC 16 reported in the House of Lords. At that level the decision set the balance between the claim of the area police authority to a sight of an expert report to assist in their criminal investigation and the mother's claim to litigation privilege in respect of the report. However in this court the judgment of the Master of the Rolls gives clear guidance as to how the balance should be set where either the prosecution or the defence seek the release of papers in Children Act proceedings for the proper conduct of a pending criminal case. Here we are not concerned with the administration of criminal justice but with possible disciplinary proceedings. Within the appellant's evidence in the court below was the explanation that—

'The Authority may wish to investigate through a Discipline Committee or NHS Tribunal ... (i) the possibility that there has been serious over-dispensing of medicines; (ii) the completeness of the records ... (iii) whether there may have been an inappropriate delegation of responsibility in relation to the medical care of patients ... (iv) the adequacy of the consent sought before performing medical procedures ...'

[19] There is obviously a high public interest, analogous to the public interest in the due administration of criminal justice, in the proper administration of professional disciplinary hearings, particularly in the field of medicine. In the application of the authorities which he had cited, Munby J properly ordered the release of the case material, namely the list A documents.

[20] Although the list B documents are separately categorised because of the application of para 36(6), the list B documents were inextricably connected in two respects: first because the patients in question had been directly or indirectly

involved in the Children Act proceedings and second because, as Munby J recorded ([2001] 2 FCR 634 at [6]):

'There is or may be a certain amount of overlap between the list A and the list B documents inasmuch as some of the general practitioner records were apparently before the judge who heard the care proceedings.'

In those circumstances in my opinion the objection to production fell to be decided in accordance with the principle that determined the application for the release of the list A documents, namely whether the public interest in effective disciplinary procedures for the investigation and eradication of medical malpractice outweighed the confidentiality of the records. I do not regard the application for production much enhanced by the para 36(6) duty. A balance still had to be struck between competing interests. The balance came down in favour of production as it invariably does, save in exceptional cases.

[21] In relation to the attachment of conditions to the orders for release and production Munby J cited and followed the prior decision of Cazalet J in *Re A (a minor) (disclosure of medical records to the General Medical Council)* [1999] 1 FCR 30. In that case Cazalet J heard an application by the General Medical Council for the disclosure of case papers pursuant to its statutory duty to investigate allegations of serious professional misconduct. To that extent there is common factual ground. However the majority of the judgment of Cazalet J deals with practice issues which are of no relevance to what we decide. But in the course of his judgment Cazalet J stated (at 35):

'It must be emphasised that the protection of the child's anonymity in the course of any hearing before the GMC Professional Conduct Committee will always be a matter of primary importance and necessary conditions, protective measures and assurances as to this will almost always be required from the GMC ...'

[22] In my opinion Cazalet J was right to claim the power to attach conditions to an order directing the release of case papers in Children Act proceedings to a third party. Without that power the court would be left with a crude choice between directing or refusing release. Striking a balance between competing public interests, often across the interface of distinct justice systems, requires much more sophisticated powers. In my opinion Munby J was correct in law to claim that power and equally correct to proceed to a discretionary exercise of that power having regard to the relevant facts and circumstances in so far as they were revealed to him.

[23] I add that qualification since Munby J was not the judge who had tried the Children Act proceedings. Accordingly he had no option but to deal with the application in abstract and without reference to the concrete context. Obviously the knowledge that Hughes J had gained from conducting the trial would have been of great advantage in determining the health authority's application. Therefore despite the administrative difficulties that may result I am of the strong opinion that where the trial has been conducted by a judge of the Division, then a subsequent application by a third party for the release of case papers must be to that judge rather than to another judge of the Division, absent exceptional circumstances.

[24] Accordingly in my judgment this appeal can and should be decided within those parameters. I would not want this judgment to be construed or used as

laying down any general propositions beyond the context of Children Act
proceedings and their aftermath.

[25] However I would add that I am not persuaded that Munby J overstated
the doctor's duty to his patient ([2001] 2 FCR 634 at [9]). I accept the analysis that
the only real issue in the present appeal is whether the conflict between the
private/public interest in the confidentiality of medical records and some other
public interest should be decided by the health authority or a judge of the
Division. I accept Mr Pannick's submission that the importance of the resolution
of such a conflict requires the independence of a judge. I conclude that the
spectres developed by Mr Havers, cost and delay and administrative overload,
are no more than speculations which good sense and management can contain.
I do not accept that the safeguards defined by Mr Havers, not all of which were
relied on below, are adequate to protect the private/public interest in
confidentiality after the judge's initial order for production to the health
authority.

[26] Accordingly, despite Mr Havers' cogent submissions I conclude that he
has not demonstrated any error of law or principle that would justify our
intervention nor has he demonstrated that the discretionary bounds set by
Munby J were plainly wrong. In the circumstances of this application listed
before a judge other than the trial judge the ambit of the judicial discretion is
necessarily wide. The judge elected for a cautious approach. In my opinion he
was not only entitled but wise so to do. (After all the health authority are not
precluded from further application should circumstances change or unexpected
difficulties arise.) We must, of course, ourselves be cautious in interfering with
such an exercise of discretion. I would dismiss this appeal.

LAWS LJ.
[27] I agree.

HARRISON J.
[28] I also agree.

Appeal dismissed. Permission to appeal refused.

Kate O'Hanlon   Barrister.

Attorney General v Ebert

[2001] EWHC Admin 695

QUEEN'S BENCH DIVISION (DIVISIONAL COURT)

BROOKE LJ AND HARRISON J

11 JULY, 21 SEPTEMBER 2001

High Court – Jurisdiction – Injunction – Injunction to protect integrity of administration of justice – Attorney General seeking injunction barring vexatious litigant from entering Royal Courts of Justice without permission – Whether injunction appropriate.

The respondent, E, was a bankrupt who had been declared a vexatious litigant and was subject, inter alia, to an order under s 42 of the Supreme Court Act 1981. On up to ten different occasions, E had been removed from the court by security guards. He had visited bankruptcy chambers and said that if the registrar did not break off what he was doing and hear an application made without notice, the police would be called. On many occasions, he had made requests of court staff to the effect that one or other of the many applications he was making should be dealt with by the judge immediately. He had also written many letters to the judge who had heard nearly all of his applications, making serious allegations against the judge in many of those letters. The Attorney General sought injunctive relief against E, contending that, since the making of the s 42 order, his conduct had been such that further constraints had to be imposed on him in order to prevent him interfering with the proper administration of justice. In particular, the Attorney General sought an order which, inter alia, (i) barred E from entering the Royal Courts of Justice without express permission, except for the purposes of attending a hearing for which he had been granted permission, and (ii) barred him from communicating in any form with anyone at the court except for the purpose of making the formal applications mentioned in the draft order. On the application, the Divisional Court considered the principles applicable when the court was being asked to exercise unusual powers in order to protect the integrity of the administration of justice.

Held – The court's supervisory role extended beyond the mere regulation of litigation and of litigants who had submitted themselves to the compulsory jurisdiction of the court, and included the regulation of the manner in which the court process could in general be utilised. The advent of the CPR only served to bolster the principle that, in the exercise of its inherent jurisdiction, the court had the power to restrain litigants from wasting the time of court staff and disturbing the orderly conduct of court processes in a completely obsessive pursuit of their own litigation, taking it forward by one unmeritorious application after another and insisting that they should be afforded priority over other litigants. It was, however, incumbent on the court in the exercise of its power to control its own procedure, or prevent future contempts of court, to ensure that nothing it might do amounted to an improper hindrance or interference with a litigant's right of access to the court or was otherwise disproportionate. In the instant case, the Attorney General was entitled to the relief sought. A distinction had to be made between E's practice of making innumerable applications (which could be kept under control by other techniques) and matters that amounted to disturbances of

the process of the court. The existing orders had not prevented E from wasting
the time of court staff and disrupting the conduct of court business. There was a
substantial risk that the process of the court would continue to be seriously
abused, and that the proper administration of justice in the future would be
seriously impeded by E unless the court intervened now with appropriate
injunctive relief. In the light of his past conduct, there was no reason why E
should be permitted to enter any part of the Royal Courts of Justice except to the
extent allowed for in the injunction that would be granted. That injunction
would be limited to three years in the first instance. An order limited in time in
that way would be a proportionate response to the nuisance of which the
Attorney General made complaint (see [35], [36], [41], [43], below).

Notes

For the High Court's jurisdiction in relation to injunctions generally, see 24
Halsbury's Laws (4th edn reissue) para 810.

Cases referred to in judgment

A-G v Ebert (7 July 2000, unreported), DC.

A-G v Times Newspapers Ltd [1973] 3 All ER 54, [1974] AC 273, [1973] 3 WLR 298,
  HL.

Binder v Binder [2000] CA Transcript 402.

Bremer Vulkan Schiffbau Und Maschinenfabrik v South India Shipping Corp Ltd [1981]
  1 All ER 289, [1981] AC 909, [1981] 2 WLR 141, HL.

de Court, Re [1997] TLR 604.

Ebert v Venvil, Ebert v Birch [2000] Ch 484, [1999] 3 WLR 670, CA.

Grepe v Loam (1887) 37 Ch D 168, CA.

Leachman, Ex p (16 January 1998, unreported), QBD.

Stubbings v UK (1997) 23 EHRR 213, [1997] ECHR 22083/93, 22095/93, ECt HR.

Application

The Attorney General applied for an order (i) barring the respondent, Gedaljahu
Ebert, from entering the Royal Courts of Justice without express permission,
except for the purposes of attending a hearing for which he had been granted
permission; (ii) barring him from any form of communication with anyone at the
court except for the purpose of making the formal applications mentioned in the
draft order; (iii) requiring him to make in writing in a particular form any
application he might make and providing that any such application be
determined in writing unless the court directed an oral hearing, and
(iv) providing for the dismissal without being heard of any application of any kind
which was not made in that form. The facts are set out in the judgment of the
court.

Neil Garnham QC (instructed by the *Treasury Solicitor*) for the Attorney General.
Mr Ebert in person.
Hugo Keith (instructed by the *Treasury Solicitor*) as friend to the court.

Cur adv vult

a 21 September 2001. The following judgment of the court was delivered.

BROOKE LJ.

[1] This is in many respects a sad case. Mr Ebert has been before the courts, or has made applications to the courts, many, many times during the last eight years. He has been made bankrupt. A *Grepe v Loam* order (see *Grepe v Loam* (1887) 37

b Ch D 168) was made against him as early as September 1997. This order has been renewed from time to time in even more restrictive terms. He was declared a vexatious litigant by this court in July 2000. Now, by an application made only ten months later, the Attorney General seeks further injunctive relief against him.

[2] The story which led to all this litigation has been told many times in earlier

c judgments. In particular, it was told in the judgment of Laws LJ in this court in July last year (see *A-G v Ebert* (7 July 2000, unreported)). Mr Ebert went into a property development venture with a man called Morris Wolff through the vehicle of a company called Europride Ltd in the late 1980s. When the property market went sour, the company's undertaking was sold by administrative receivers, and it went into insolvent liquidation in July 1993. Both Mr Ebert and Mr Morris Wolff had

d given joint and several guarantees to the Midland Bank in support of advances made by that bank to their company. The bank in due course demanded payment under its guarantees, and in 1995 it commenced separate actions against the two former directors to recover the debt owed to it.

[3] What we will call action 156 was brought against Mr Ebert. Summary

e judgment was entered against him by a deputy master in June 1995, and an appeal against that judgment was dismissed in July 1995. On each occasion a small adjustment was made to the amount of the bank's claim. The judgment in the sum awarded by the deputy master (for £55,894·70) was entered in the cause book, and it was never formally altered to show the slight reduction ordered by the deputy

f judge. This judgment was not drawn up or otherwise perfected. Last year the bank's solicitors agreed that the cause book should be amended to show the correct amount of £54,374·78.

[4] In action 9906 the bank obtained summary judgment against Morris Wolff for £55,894·70. Morris Wolff's brother Ralph came to his rescue, and made arrangements whereby his brother was able to pay this sum to the bank on terms

g that the bank assigned the benefit of its judgment in the other action to Ralph Wolff. Ralph Wolff then made a statutory demand on Mr Ebert for payment of the assigned judgment debt. After Mr Ebert had made an unsuccessful challenge to the validity of the statutory demand, Ralph Wolff presented a bankruptcy petition which was contested on much the same grounds. On 22 July 1997 Lloyd J made a

h bankruptcy order.

[5] The subsequent history is set out in paras 21–42 of Laws LJ's judgment. Mr Ebert maintained that this judgment contained inaccuracies on points of detail, but the judgment contains a good broad description of the events that took place. We do not need to refer to the first of the seven sets of proceedings on which the

j Attorney General relied (which was effectively dismissed in March 1996). The last five (whose effect is summarised in paras 35–42 of Laws LJ's judgment) pale into comparative insignificance compared with the course of events he describes in relation to the second set of proceedings, although they must have represented a costly and time-consuming nuisance to the other parties who were involved with them. They all arose out of what Laws LJ described (at para 38) as 'the Europride saga'.

[6] The second set of proceedings related to Ralph Wolff's statutory demand and bankruptcy petition. Laws LJ understandably said (at para 17) that it was in this litigation that the 'astonishing' nature of Mr Ebert's conduct was most patently apparent. The key events in the history which followed the bankruptcy order in July 1997 can be summarised in these terms: (i) On 18 September 1997 Laddie J dismissed a motion by Mr Ebert to commit Ralph Wolff's solicitor to prison for contempt of court. He said that the allegations on which the motion was based constituted an example of Mr Ebert's willingness to make wild and unsupportable allegations of the most damning nature against not just his former business partner but anybody associated with him. He made a *Grepe v Loam* order. (ii) On 10 December 1997 Neuberger J dismissed an application by Mr Ebert for annulment of the bankruptcy order. He said that concerns he had once had that matters had not been fairly investigated before the bankruptcy order was upheld were now at rest. (iii) On 19 January 1998 Rimer J dismissed an application by Mr Ebert to commit Ralph Wolff and his solicitor to prison. He said it constituted a gross abuse of the process of the court. (iv) On 25 March 1998 the Court of Appeal dismissed an application by Mr Ebert for permission to appeal Neuberger J's order at (ii), above. During the course of his judgment Potter LJ dismissed as a technicality Mr Ebert's complaints that the judgment entered in the cause book by the deputy master had never been reduced downwards and had never been perfected. He also rejected as a curable irregularity the point that although the Midland Bank's judgment against Morris Wolff was for a slightly higher amount than the bank's reduced judgment against Mr Ebert, the bankruptcy order was made on the larger of these two sums. (v) On 30 April and 7 July 1998 Neuberger J dismissed further applications by Mr Ebert, in which he was contending that Ralph Wolff should only be entitled to prove for half the amount Mr Ebert owed to Midland Bank, and seeking to set aside the assignment and the transaction between Ralph Wolff and the Midland Bank. The judge made a third *Grepe v Loam* order (a second having been made by Carnwath J on 5 February 1998). In future, any applications by Mr Ebert for leave were to be made to Rimer J or Neuberger J and dealt with on paper. (vi) On 10 September 1998 the Court of Appeal dismissed an application by Mr Ebert for permission to appeal Neuberger J's order of 7 July 1998 on the basis that he could not raise again the same matters which he had raised unsuccessfully so often before. It adjourned for later consideration an issue relating to the scope of the *Grepe v Loam* order made on 7 July. (vii) On 1 October 1998 Neuberger J refused an application by Mr Ebert for permission to raise an issue as to whether Ralph Wolff had paid the consideration for the assignment, and three weeks later he struck out as abusive an application by Mr Ebert against the liquidator of Europride Ltd and the Midland Bank. He also made a fourth *Grepe v Loam* order. (viii) On 14 January and 29 March 1999 Neuberger J dismissed two further attempts by Mr Ebert to set aside the bankruptcy order. On the second occasion he said that this appeared to be yet another attempt by Mr Ebert to raise points which had been gone over time and again. The Court of Appeal on 20 April 1999 refused permission to appeal the first of these orders. (ix) On 30 March 1999 the Court of Appeal (*Ebert v Venvil, Ebert v Birch* [2000] Ch 484, [1999] 3 WLR 670) dismissed Mr Ebert's challenge to the width of the *Grepe v Loam* orders. Lord Woolf MR said that the court was prepared to accept that Mr Ebert might initially have been hard done by, because his co-guarantor had avoided all liability, but that it was clear that he had already brought vexatious proceedings and that he would continue to bring vexatious proceedings unless he was restrained from doing so. (x) On 25 May 1999 Neuberger J dismissed three applications by Mr Ebert which represented an effort

a to set aside earlier orders made against him. He said that they were all hopeless. (xi) On 14 July 1999 Neuberger J refused an application by Mr Ebert for permission to challenge the statutory demand, the petition and the bankruptcy order. Mr Ebert was now suggesting that the judge was guilty of 'fraud and blackmail', and made other aspersions against him. The judge declined to recuse himself for reasons set out on pp 3 and 4 of his short written statement of that date. He said he

b did not think Mr Ebert was making the allegations against him out of malice. (xii) In his judgment Laws LJ described (at para 30) two further orders by the Court of Appeal and two further orders made by Neuberger J between July and October 1999, all dismissing various applications made by Mr Ebert in respect of different aspects of 'the Europride saga'. In December 1999, in a further judgment, Neuberger J referred to the fact that Mr Ebert had made a total of 50 (possibly over

c 80) applications of various sorts, all of which had failed. (xiii) On 6 March 2000, Laddie and Neuberger JJ, sitting as a Divisional Court of the Chancery Division, dismissed a further application by Mr Ebert in the bankruptcy proceedings. On this occasion Mr Ebert was seeking to re-litigate a point concerned with an alleged forgery which had been decided against him by Rimer J two years earlier. The

d court now directed that Mr Ebert should not be allowed to make applications under the *Grepe v Loam* orders more frequently than once every two months unless he could demonstrate in writing that a more urgent application was called for. (xiv) On three occasions between 14 March and 12 April 2000 Neuberger J dismissed further applications by Mr Ebert under the *Grepe v Loam* orders.

e [7] In paras 48–53 of his judgment, with which Silber J agreed, Laws LJ explained why he considered that an order under s 42 of the Supreme Court Act 1981 was required. He said that Mr Ebert's obsessions had cut him away from reality, and that he was entirely unable to appreciate the hopelessness of any further process he might commence in relation to the judgment, the assignment or the bankruptcy order. His vexatious proceedings had been very damaging to the public interest,

f because scarce and valuable judicial resources had been extravagantly wasted on barren and misconceived litigation, to the detriment of other litigants with real cases to try. He identified four advantages to be obtained from a s 42 order: (i) his judgment would provide a compendious overview of the whole of the relevant litigation history, to which any judge dealing with an application under s 42(1A)(a) would be able to refer; (ii) there is no appeal against a first instance decision under

g s 42(3); (iii) the court will avoid being vexed with arguments as to whether a particular fresh process is or is not caught by an extant *Grepe v Loam* order; (iv) if the judge was in any doubt as to whether Mr Ebert should be granted permission to pursue an application, he could seek assistance from the Attorney General, and it would not be necessary for Mr Ebert's adversaries to mount argument to dispel the

h doubt, as had happened on 6 March 2000.

[8] In his short supporting judgment, Silber J said (at para 64) that this case was uniquely strong in the light of Mr Ebert's burning determination to continue with these claims against the Wolff brothers and those connected with his bankruptcy in the face of many defeats in the courts. This was a very extreme instance of extreme

j litigation.

[9] We have summarised this earlier history in some detail because, as Mr Keith has rightly reminded us, on this application for injunctive relief the court should be concerned not so much by what has happened in the past, but by what is likely to happen in the future if Mr Ebert's litigious activities are not further restrained.

[10] The present application is supported by an affidavit and a witness statement made by Mr John Selch, the Group Manager of the Royal Courts of Justice, and a

witness statement by Mr Donald Bennett, who is Neuberger J's clerk. The form
this evidence took caused us some difficulty, because while it was all admissible, *a*
Mr Selch could not give any direct evidence about the matters to which he deposed
and Mr Bennett merely exhibited a great many documents. Mr Ebert disputed a
number of Mr Selch's assertions, and an order requiring Mr Selch to attend for
cross-examination would not have taken matters any further, because he would
only have been able to say that he was recording what he had been told by others. *b*
In view of the scale of the restraints now sought by the Attorney General, we
decided to proceed on the basis of the facts which were not or could not properly
be in dispute. Mr Garnham QC, who appeared for the Attorney General, did not
try to deflect us from this course once he had appreciated the difficulty.

[11] Mr Selch told us that in the course of about three-and-a-half-years Mr Ebert
had made at least 151 applications to the court for permission to issue fresh *c*
proceedings or applications in existing proceedings. All but five of these 151
applications were adjudicated on by Neuberger J and all were dismissed because they
were without merit and generally repetitive of previous applications. He had made
applications to the Court of Appeal for permission to appeal, all of which were
refused, on at least 20 occasions. We did not understand Mr Ebert to dispute these *d*
figures. Twenty to thirty further applications of one kind or another have been made.
Sometimes his wife made applications in connection with the same general subject
matter.

[12] The main thrust of Mr Selch's affidavit is set out in seven paragraphs headed
'Disruption to the Administration of Justice'. In so far as the facts are not in dispute,
the history they describe runs along the following lines. *e*

[13] Mr Ebert has been in the habit of requesting that his applications to
Neuberger J should be dealt with immediately or within 24 hours of his making
them. Mr Ebert told us that this was his right, pursuant to the bankruptcy rules or
the European Convention for the Protection of Human Rights and Fundamental
Freedoms 1950 (as set out in Sch 1 to the Human Rights Act 1998). When his *f*
applications were not dealt with within this timescale, he and his wife regularly
followed them up with letters and telephone calls to court staff. Mr Ebert said that
he could see nothing wrong in this, and that they had not been abusive to staff.

[14] Next, Mr Ebert has on at least four occasions sat in court in cases before
Neuberger J which did not involve him. He has often been accompanied by his *g*
wife. He denied that on his attendances at court he had frequently risen to interrupt
the proceedings and to demand that Neuberger J dealt with his application first. On
the other hand he did not dispute that security staff or the court tipstaff had been
called on a number of occasions to remove him from the court at the request of the
judge, his clerk or his usher. He said that this had happened on five, six or ten
different occasions. *h*

[15] We were shown correspondence from Mr Ebert to Neuberger J in which
he accused the judge of being corrupt and having accepted bribes. His complaints
about the judge's conduct (which contained references to conspiracy, high treason,
perjury and crimes against humanity) became more and more shrill as time went
on. In February 2001 Mr Ebert exhibited a notice outside the Royal Courts of *j*
Justice which contained allegations that Neuberger J and two other members of the
judiciary concerned with his bankruptcy case had a profit share in a multi-million
pound fraud.

[16] On 22 March 2001 Mr Ebert and his wife, accompanied by the president and
chairman of the Litigants in Person Society, came to the counter in room 110 of the
Thomas More Building and requested that an urgent application by Mrs Ebert

a should be heard immediately by Mr Registrar James, who was working in his private room. When the registrar declined to deal with the matter immediately, Mr and Mrs Ebert said that if their application to have a roof over their head was not heard immediately they would call the police in respect of the registrar's non-obedience of the law.

[17] The registrar eventually agreed to hear Mrs Ebert's application with two *b* security guards present. One of them had already escorted Mr and Mrs Ebert out of court 54 earlier in the morning. The application was dismissed because Mrs Ebert, who was also subject to a *Grepe v Loam* order, had not obtained permission from a High Court judge to make her application.

[18] We omit reference to the facts set out in paras 11 and 12 of Mr Selch's affidavit because they are in dispute. The final incident relied on occurred when a *c* member of the court's security staff was summoned outside the Royal Courts of Justice, where he found Mr Ebert holding a barrister who had appeared against him on the basis that he had obtained a possession order by fraud and that Mr Ebert was entitled to make a citizen's arrest for theft. The police were called, and the parties to the incident went to the local police station, where the barrister declined to make *d* a formal complaint. Mr Ebert did not dispute that this incident had occurred, but he maintained that he had effected the arrest outside the court gates and not, as alleged, in the West Green car park. He told us that so long as he was outside the court precincts he was entitled to effect a citizen's arrest on anyone, whether an opposing lawyer or even Neuberger J, who had deprived him of his property dishonestly in connection with these proceedings.

e [19] We have read with care all the documents exhibited by Mr Bennett which relate to the period after the s 42 order. Neuberger J appears to have dealt with the torrent of applications and correspondence which continued to flow from Mr Ebert with exemplary courtesy and patience. On at least one occasion he gave permission to Mr Ebert to seek permission to appeal, because of the accusations of corruption *f* which Mr Ebert was making against him. Jonathan Parker LJ ruled that the proposed appeal would stand no chance of success. On many occasions Neuberger J dismissed Mr Ebert's applications on the basis that they raised no new points.

[20] In his acknowledgment of service Mr Ebert said that he intended to contest the claim and to dispute the jurisdiction of the court. He sought a direction that the *g* application be transferred to the Central Criminal Court. He referred to abuse of the process, torture, fraud and perjury as details of directions he was seeking from the court. He also objected to the Attorney General issuing under this procedure. In addition to the other matters he mentioned he said that the procedure was defective and did not comply with CPR 3.4. We are satisfied that the claim is *h* properly brought, that this court has jurisdiction to hear it, and that it is inappropriate to transfer it to the Central Criminal Court as Mr Ebert suggests.

[21] Mr Ebert appeared in person at the hearing of the Attorney General's application. He produced a file containing 139 documents which related in one way or other to incidents in the Europride saga. He repeated points (such as those *j* which Potter LJ had dismissed as curable irregularities or technicalities) which had already been litigated unsuccessfully before. He was particularly anxious that we should consider the effect of some bank statements which had recently come to light, which related to the 1993–1995 history.

[22] In view of the previous history of this matter, we consider that it would be very unwise for this court to attempt an analysis of the documents Mr Ebert showed us unless it is necessary to do so for the proper disposal of the Attorney

General's application. There have been judgments in favour of the Midland Bank in relation to the amount demanded of Mr Ebert and Morris Wolff under their guarantees in December 1992, with adjustments made for the incidence of interest and the receipt of sums totalling £41,356 from receivers in 1993–1994, and it is futile for Mr Ebert to reopen issues relating to the Midland Bank indebtedness on an application of this kind. If he has any genuinely new point, we understand that Patten J has now been assigned by the Vice-Chancellor to handle any applications by Mr Ebert, and he will be able to consider it. It was, incidentally, evident to us that many of the very technical matters to which Mr Ebert drew our attention had already been decided against him on one or more occasions in the past.

[23] On this application we are concerned with issues relating to Mr Ebert's behaviour. The case for the Attorney General on this application is that since the s 42 order was made against him, Mr Ebert's conduct has been such that further constraints must now be imposed on him to stop his interfering with the proper administration of justice. The Attorney General accepts that Mr Ebert has a constitutional right of access to a court, and he does not seek to deny him that right. It is the manner in which Mr Ebert conducts himself in the pursuit of his various contentions of which complaint is made.

[24] The Attorney General seeks fourfold relief, which we will summarise in the following terms. First, that Mr Ebert should be barred from entering the Royal Courts of Justice without express permission, except for the purposes of attending a hearing for which he has been granted permission. Secondly, that he should be barred from any form of communication with anyone at the court except for the purpose of making the formal applications mentioned in the draft order. Thirdly, that any application he makes must be made in writing in a particular form and determined in writing (unless the court directs an oral hearing). And finally, that any application of any kind which is not made in that form should stand dismissed without being heard.

[25] It is evident that at the heart of the Attorney General's concerns is the worry that if Mr Ebert is not restrained in this way, he will continue to visit the Royal Courts of Justice and disrupt proceedings or waste the time of court staff, either by personal attendance in court offices or over the telephone, by making requests that his multitudinous applications should be given precedence over other court business. The evidence on which the court may act is less powerful than the evidence originally presented by Mr Selch, for the reasons given in [10], above, so that it is necessary to look with some care at the undisputed evidence.

[26] It is not in dispute that on up to ten different occasions Mr Ebert has had to be removed from court by security guards. He asserted that he was not disturbing the court, but security guards are not requested to remove a litigant from court without some good reason. It is also not in dispute that he visited bankruptcy chambers and said that if the registrar did not break off what he was doing and hear an application made without notice, the police would be called.

[27] It is also not in dispute that Mr Ebert on many occasions made requests of court staff to the effect that one or other of the many applications he was making should be dealt with by the judge immediately. It is possible to obtain a flavour of the peremptory demands Mr Ebert was in the habit of making by referring to the documents numbered 462, 495, 496, 530, 539, 554, 560, 577, 580, 599, 603, 611 and 612 in the main court bundle.

[28] It is also not in dispute that Mr Ebert made many serious accusations against Neuberger J in many of the letters he wrote to him. Judges have to have broad shoulders, and the relevance of this evidence goes to the contention that

a Mr Ebert is now so completely obsessed by this litigation that he does not cavil about making allegations of corruption, high treason and crimes against humanity against the judge who has been handling the case with remarkable patience and sensitivity. He also published the notice outside the Royal Courts of Justice to which mention is made in [15], above. This illustrates how Mr Ebert's sense of perspective is now seriously out of kilter.

b [29] While we are willing to accept that Mr Ebert performed the citizen's arrest we have described in [18], above, outside the precincts of the court, in the absence of direct evidence to contrary effect, the obsessive zeal with which he maintained that he was entitled to effect such an arrest on anyone connected with this litigation who had in his opinion defrauded him, even if it be the judge himself, provides evidence on which we can act to the effect that he has now lost all sense of proper
c perspective in the conduct of this litigation.

[30] Mr Garnham showed us three judgments in which courts have had to exercise unusual powers in order to protect the integrity of the administration of justice. In *Re de Court* [1997] TLR 604 Scott V-C was concerned with a litigant who had spat at the Chancery clerk of the lists. A medical certificate showed that
d he should be regarded as a person under disability: he had made over 100 attempts at instituting ridiculous or incomprehensible legal proceedings. Scott V-C held that he was in contempt of court. The Times report continues:

'His Lordship had a duty to provide protection to court officials not just in the High Court but also in any court where Mr de Court might seek to
e institute proceedings. He had an inherent power and duty to take those steps as a judge and Vice-Chancellor of the Chancery Division ... In the exercise of that power he would make an order in two parts: First to restrain Mr de Court from pursuing any action in court except by a next friend who could act for him; second, to restrain him from entering any civil court premises
f save as necessary to answer court subpoenas.'

[31] In *Ex p Leachman* (16 January 1998, unreported) this court was concerned with a litigant who had become wholly obsessed with the habeas corpus process and had lost all touch with reality. His behaviour in some ways mirrored that of Mr Ebert. Simon Brown LJ said that the court was told that he frequently
g telephoned Crown Office staff and demanded that they arranged immediate hearings for his applications. An order was made that no further application concerning his detention arising out of a 1993 conviction should be made, or (if made) be accepted or processed by the Crown Office, and that the litigant should not thereafter communicate with the Crown Office, save only in writing marked for the attention of a particular member of their staff.

h [32] In *Binder v Binder* [2000] CA Transcript 402, a litigant had instituted innumerable proceedings in the Family Division in relation to his children. The Court of Appeal, in a judgment given by Thorpe LJ, with whom Laws LJ agreed, upheld an order made by the President of the Family Division in terms similar to the relief now being sought by the Attorney General against Mr Ebert. The court
j of its own motion made an order protecting the staff of the Court of Appeal in terms similar to the President's order, which protected the staff of the Family Division.

[33] Mr Garnham told us that although it might well be that Mr Ebert's conduct justified committal for contempt, the Attorney General took the view that it would be preferable to regulate his future conduct rather than to seek to punish his past actions. Mr Ebert disputed that the Attorney General was entitled to adopt this approach, and invited the court to direct him to take committal

proceedings, but we see no reason why we should adopt this course. It is for the Attorney General to identify the relief he seeks and not for this court to dictate to him what he should do.

[34] Mr Keith, acting as the friend of the court, accepted the proposition that the court had the general power to control its own procedure so as to prevent its being used to achieve injustice and in order to maintain its character as a court of law (see *Bremer Vulkan Schiffbau Und Maschinenfabrik v South India Shipping Corp Ltd* [1981] 1 All ER 289 at 295, [1981] AC 909 at 977). He reminded us that in *Ebert v Venvil, Ebert v Birch* [2000] Ch 484, [1999] 3 WLR 670 the Court of Appeal extended the jurisdiction of the court to the prohibition, without the leave of the court, of new proceedings which are likely to constitute an abuse of process.

[35] We accept Mr Keith's submission that the court's supervisory role now extends beyond the mere regulation of litigation and of litigants who have submitted themselves to the compulsory jurisdiction of the court. It includes the regulation of the manner in which the court process may in general be utilised. It is of course well-established that the High Court may, in appropriate circumstances, grant an injunction to restrain an anticipated interference with the administration of justice, amounting to a contempt (see *A-G v Times Newspapers Ltd* [1973] 3 All ER 54 at 59, 69–70, [1974] AC 273 at 293–294, 306). The advent of the CPR only serves to bolster the principle that in the exercise of its inherent jurisdiction the court has the power to restrain litigants from wasting the time of court staff and disturbing the orderly conduct of court processes in a completely obsessive pursuit of their own litigation, taking it forward by one unmeritorious application after another and insisting that they should be afforded priority over other litigants.

[36] It goes without saying that every citizen has a right of access to a court both at common law and pursuant to art 6 of the convention. It is, however, implicit in the English case law (see *Grepe v Loam* (1887) 37 Ch D 168 and *Ebert v Venvil*) that this right of access is not absolute. This is also the effect of convention jurisprudence, which requires only that any limitations imposed on it must not impair the very essence of the right (see *Stubbings v UK* (1997) 23 EHRR 213 at 233 (para 48)). It is therefore incumbent on the court in the exercise of its power to control its own procedure, or to prevent future contempts of court, to ensure that nothing it may do amounts to an improper hindrance or interference with a litigant's right of access or is otherwise disproportionate.

[37] Mr Ebert presented his case in response to the Attorney General's application with moderation. He said that it was quite unreasonable to prevent him from using the library or the coffee shop or the toilets at the Royal Courts of Justice. He thought he enjoyed a good relationship with judges, apart from a few of them. He was, however, concerned and frustrated by the way in which Neuberger J treated him. He maintained that Neuberger J was incompetent and biased. He went on to make a number of points about the detailed contents of Mr Selch's affidavit, which we have already taken into account in this judgment. He maintained that the rules entitled him to a ruling forthwith whenever he made an application, and that he had been entitled to behave in the way he did when he urged court staff to list his cases. He said he had not threatened or abused court staff.

[38] Mr Ebert argued that if he made unreasonable applications, jurisdiction already existed to control him. Even if he had misbehaved in Neuberger J's court, this was no reason to ban him from the entire court complex. He intended to go

a on making applications until he achieved a breakthrough and was allowed his day in court.

[39] In our judgment a distinction must be made between Mr Ebert's practice of making innumerable applications (which can be kept under control by other techniques), and the matters set out in this judgment which amount to disturbances of the process of the court. Mr Garnham accepted that some of the

b matters on which he relied could have been regarded as contempts of court and been the subject of committal proceedings, if that course had seemed desirable. He said he was asking us to make an order restraining future conduct by Mr Ebert which was likely to constitute a contempt of court or an unwarrantable disruption of the administration of justice. For this purpose, he had to show a substantial likelihood that such misconduct would occur.

c [40] We have taken into account everything Mr Ebert has said to us and showed us, and we have already praised the moderate terms in which he addressed us. It is clear that he has developed an irrational obsession about the manner in which Neuberger J has dealt with the many applications he has made. We have already described how a different High Court judge has been appointed

d to deal with any further applications which Mr Ebert may make, and it is to be hoped that he will desist in future from the intemperate abuse he heaped upon his predecessor.

[41] Notwithstanding this change, we consider that the Attorney General is entitled to the relief he seeks. It is completely clear that neither the *Grepe v Loam* orders nor the s 42 order have prevented Mr Ebert from wasting the time of court

e staff and disrupting the conduct of court business, even if they have succeeded in taking the burden off the many other parties to the Europride saga whom he has plagued with unmeritorious litigation during the last five years. A careful study of the papers produced by Neuberger J's clerk and of the judgments of different courts (including the judgment of Laws LJ last year) has persuaded us that there

f is a substantial risk that the process of the court will continue to be seriously abused, and that the proper administration of justice in the future will be seriously impeded by Mr Ebert in future unless we intervene now with appropriate injunctive relief. We see no reason, in the light of his conduct in the past, why Mr Ebert should be permitted to enter any part of the Royal Courts of Justice except to the extent allowed for in the injunction we will grant.

g [42] We also consider that Mr Ebert's past conduct is so exceptional that it is more appropriate that he be restrained by injunction than by the process of committal for contempt for individual acts, a process we would regard as completely pointless in the context of this case.

[43] When we have handed down this judgment we will hear the parties in

h relation to the precise form the relief should take. We consider that any injunction should be for a period of three years in the first instance, with liberty to the Attorney General to apply thereafter if, as events turn out, an extension of the duration of the injunction proves to be necessary. An order which is, in the first instance, limited in time in this way will be a proportionate response to the nuisance of which the Attorney General makes complaint.

Order accordingly.

Martyn Gurr   Barrister.

Note
a

Rowe v Sanders

[2002] EWCA Civ 242

COURT OF APPEAL, CIVIL DIVISION
b
SCHIEMANN, MAY AND JONATHAN PARKER LJJ
7 FEBRUARY 2002

*Insolvency – Bankrupt's estate – Vesting in trustee – Annuity income under
occupational pension scheme – Whether annuity income vesting in trustee in*
c
*bankruptcy as part of bankrupt's estate – Whether statutory provisions compatible
with right to peaceful enjoyment of possessions – Insolvency Act 1986, ss 306, 310, 436
– Human Rights Act 1998, Sch 1, Pt II, art 1.*

The Court of Appeal dismissed an appeal by Ian Alistair Rowe, a discharged
bankrupt, from the order of Kevin Garnett QC, sitting as a deputy judge of the   d
Chancery Division on 20 February 2001, dismissing Mr Rowe's application for a
declaration that his trustee in bankruptcy, Michael Sanders, was not entitled to
annuity income under a policy issued pursuant to an occupational pension
scheme of which Mr Rowe had at all material times been a member. In doing so,
the Court of Appeal held that its earlier decisions in *Krasner v Dennison, Lawrence
v Lesser* [2000] 3 All ER 234, [2001] Ch 76 and *Jones v Patel* [2001] EWCA Civ 779,   e
[2001] BPIR 919 had not been per incuriam in holding that annuity income was
not 'income' within the meaning of s 310 of the Insolvency Act 1986, but rather
fell within the definition of 'property' in s 436 of the Act and therefore vested in
the trustee in bankruptcy, under s 306, as part of the bankrupt's estate. The court
also approved dicta of Chadwick LJ in *Krasner's* case [2000] 3 All ER 234 at   f
255–256, [2001] Ch 76 at 107–109 that the relevant statutory provisions were not
incompatible with the right to the peaceful enjoyment of possessions under art 1
of the First Protocol to the European Convention for the Protection of Human
Rights and Fundamental Freedoms 1950 (as set out in Sch 1 to the Human Rights
Act 1998).

James Brooks   Barrister.

Royal Brompton Hospital NHS Trust v Hammond and others (Taylor Woodrow Construction (Holdings) Ltd, Pt 20 defendant)

[2002] UKHL 14

HOUSE OF LORDS

LORD BINGHAM OF CORNHILL, LORD MACKAY OF CLASHFERN, LORD STEYN, LORD HOPE OF CRAIGHEAD AND LORD RODGER OF EARLSFERRY

6, 7 MARCH, 25 APRIL 2002

Contribution – Third party proceedings – Claim 'in respect of the same damage' – Whether 'same damage' meaning 'substantially or materially similar damage' – Civil Liability (Contribution) Act 1978, s 1(1).

Under a contract for the construction of new hospital premises, the contractor had to pay or allow the employer liquidated and ascertained damages at a specified weekly rate if the contractor failed to complete the works by the completion date. Practical completion was certified over 43 weeks later than the contractual completion date, but the architects under the contract granted the contractor extensions of time up to the date on which practical completion was certified. Those extensions had the effect of relieving the contractor of its obligation to pay or allow liquidated and ascertained damages for any of the delay. The contractor claimed for loss and expense, and the employer paid some £5·2m, which the architects had certified as due. The contractor commenced arbitration proceedings, claiming a further sum, while the employer counterclaimed. Those proceedings were settled on terms that the employer paid the contractor some £6·2m and agreed to indemnify it against any claim for contribution made against it by, amongst others, the architects. The employer brought proceedings against the architects, alleging that they had been negligent (i) in issuing to the contractor an instruction that had formed the basis of its claims for loss and expense, and (ii) in granting the extensions of time that had deprived the employer of its entitlement to liquidated damages from the contractor. The architects issued Pt 20 proceedings against the contractor to recover a contribution on the grounds that the contractor was liable 'in respect of the same damage' within the meaning of s 1(1)[a] of the Civil Liability (Contribution) Act 1978. On an application by the contractor to strike out the Pt 20 claim, the judge held that the contractor was not liable in respect of the same damage as the architects and therefore struck out the third party notice. His decision was affirmed by the Court of Appeal. On the architects' appeal to the House of Lords, their Lordships considered whether s 1(1) was to be given a broad interpretation, so that the words 'the same damage' were to be taken to mean 'substantially or materially similar damage'.

Held – On the true construction of s 1(1) of the 1978 Act, the words 'the same damage' did not mean 'substantially or materially similar damage'. The legislative

---

a   Section 1(1) is set out at [1], below

technique of limiting the contribution principle under the 1978 Act to the same damage was a considered policy decision. The context did not therefore justify an expansive interpretation of the words 'the *same* damage'. No glosses, extensive or restrictive, were warranted. The natural and ordinary meaning of 'the same damage' was controlling. It had been a constant theme of the law of contribution from the beginning that B's claim to share with others his liability to A rested upon the fact that they, whether equally with B or not, were subject to a common liability to A. There was nothing in s 1(1) which in any way weakened that requirement. Indeed the use of the words 'in respect of the same damage' emphasised the need for one loss to be apportioned among those liable. Thus, when any claim for contribution fell to be decided, the questions which arose for consideration were (i) what damage had A suffered, (ii) was B liable in respect of that damage and (iii) was C also liable to A in respect of that damage or some of it? At the striking-out stage, the questions had to be recast to reflect the rule that it was arguability and not liability that fell for decision, but their essential thrust was the same. In phrasing those questions, it did not matter greatly whether one spoke of 'damage' or 'loss' or 'harm', provided that it was borne in mind that 'damage' did not mean 'damages' and that B's right to contribution by C depended on the damage, loss or harm for which B was liable to A corresponding (even if in part only) with the damage, loss or harm for which C was liable to A. It followed that in order to determine whether claims were for the same damage it was necessary to conduct a legal analysis of those claims. In the instant case, the employer's claim against the contractor was for late delivery of the building, while the essence of the case against the architects was that their breach of duty had changed detrimentally the employer's contractual position against the contractor. Accordingly, neither head of claim satisfied the statutory criterion, and the appeal would therefore be dismissed (see [5]–[9], [22], [23], [27], [30]–[32], [35], [36], [46]–[49], below).

Hurstwood Developments Ltd v Motor & General & Andersley & Co Insurance Services (H B Boring & Co Ltd (Pt 20 defendants)) [2002] Lloyd's Rep IR 185 overruled.

Dictum of Auld LJ in *Friends' Provident Life Office v Hillier Parker May & Rowden (a firm) (Estates and General plc, third party)* [1995] 4 All ER 260 at 272 disapproved.

Dictum of Scott V-C in *Howkins & Harrison (a firm) v Tyler* [2001] Lloyd's Rep PN 1 at 4 considered.

Notes

For contribution in respect of the same damage, see 12(1) *Halsbury's Laws* (4th edn reissue) para 839.

For the Civil Liability (Contribution) Act 1978, s 1, see 13 *Halsbury's Statutes* (4th edn) (2000 reissue) 604.

Cases referred to in opinions

Adamson v Jarvis (1827) 4 Bing 66, [1824–34] All ER Rep 120, 130 ER 693, CP.
Arneil v Paterson [1931] AC 560, [1931] All ER Rep 90, HL.
Birse Construction Ltd v Haiste Ltd (Watson and ors, third parties) [1996] 2 All ER 1, [1996] 1 WLR 675, CA.
Bovis Construction Ltd v Commercial Union Assurance Co plc [2001] 1 Lloyd's Rep 416.
Bovis Lend Lease Ltd (formerly Bovis Construction Ltd) v Saillard Fuller & Partners (2001) 77 Con LR 134.

Dering v Earl of Winchelsea (1787) 1 Cox Eq Cas 318, [1775–1802] All ER Rep 140,
    29 ER 1184, Ex Ct.
*Eastgate Group Ltd v Lindsey Morden Group Inc (Smith & Williamson (a firm), Pt 20
    defendant)* [2001] EWCA Civ 1446, [2001] 2 All ER (Comm) 1050, [2002] 1 WLR
    642.
*Friends' Provident Life Office v Hillier Parker May & Rowden (a firm) (Estates and
    General plc and ors, third parties)* [1995] 4 All ER 260, [1997] QB 85, [1996] 2 WLR
    123, CA.
Grunwald v Hughes 1965 SLT 209, Ct of Sess.
Howkins & Harrison (a firm) v Tyler [2001] Lloyd's Rep PN 1, CA.
*Hurstwood Developments Ltd v Motor & General & Andersley & Co Insurance Services
    (H B Boring & Co Ltd (Pt 20 defendants))* [2001] EWCA Civ 1785, [2002] Lloyd's
    Rep IR 185.
Koursk, The [1924] P 140, [1924] All ER Rep 168, CA.
McConnell v Lynch-Robinson, Coulter & Son, third party [1957] NI 70, CA.
Merryweather v Nixan (1799) 8 Term Rep 186, 101 ER 1337.
National Coal Board v Thomson 1959 SC 353.
Palmer v Wick & Pulteneytown Steam Shipping Co Ltd [1894] AC 318, HL.
Turnbull v Frame 1966 SLT 24, Ct of Sess.
Wallace v Litwiniuk (2001) 92 Alta LR (3d) 249, Alta CA.
Weld-Blundell v Stephens [1920] AC 956, [1920] All ER Rep 32, HL.

Appeal

The eighth, fourteenth and fifteenth defendants, Watkins Gray International
(UK), Ivor Gordon Berresford and Keith Pegden Smith (collectively the
architect), appealed with permission of the Appeal Committee of the House of
Lords given on 8 March 2001 from the order of the Court of Appeal (Stuart-Smith,
Ward and Buxton LJJ) on 10 April 2000 ((2000) 69 Con LR 145 at 156) dismissing
their appeal from the order of Judge Hicks QC in the Technology and
Construction Court on 9 July 1999 ((2000) 69 Con LR 145) striking out their
proceedings under CPR Pt 20 against the respondent, Taylor Woodrow
Construction (Holdings) Ltd (the contractor). Neither the claimant, Royal
Brompton Hospital NHS Trust, nor the other defendants to its claim took any
part in the proceedings. The facts are set out in the opinion of Lord Steyn.

Marcus Taverner QC and *Richard Edwards* (instructed by *Fishburn Morgan Cole*) for
    the architect.
Antony Edwards-Stuart QC and *Mark Cannon* (instructed by *Masons*) for the
    contractor.

Their Lordships took time for consideration.

25 April 2002. The following opinions were delivered.

LORD BINGHAM OF CORNHILL.

[1] My Lords, s 1(1) of the Civil Liability (Contribution) Act 1978 provides:

'Subject to the following provisions of this section, any person liable in
respect of any damage suffered by another person may recover contribution
from any other person liable *in respect of the same damage* (whether jointly
with him or otherwise).' (My emphasis.)

This appeal turns on the interpretation of the six words I have emphasised and their application to the facts of this case. I am indebted to my noble and learned friend Lord Steyn for his account of the factual, contractual and legislative background to the case, which I adopt and need not repeat.

[2] The law has for many centuries recognised the existence of situations in which, if B is called upon to discharge a legal obligation owed to A, fairness demands that B should be entitled to claim a contribution from other parties subject with him to that obligation. Thus a rule first developed to cover parties to a common maritime adventure was over time extended to cover co-sureties, co-trustees, co-contractors, partners, co-insurers, co-mortgagors, co-directors and co-owners (see Goff and Jones *The Law of Restitution* (5th edn, 1998) pp 394, 399, 409, 413, 415, 421, 424, 425 and 427). The common link between all these situations was the obvious justice of requiring that a common liability should be shared between those liable.

[3] The advent of the motor car however highlighted a situation in which B, if called upon to discharge a liability to A, could not seek any contribution from others also subject to the same liability to A. The old rule in *Merryweather v Nixan* (1799) 8 Term Rep 186, 101 ER 1337 forbade claims for contribution or indemnity between joint tortfeasors and a more recent decision in *The Koursk* [1924] P 140, [1924] All ER Rep 168 showed that even where independent acts of negligence by different parties resulted in one injury and gave rise to a cause of action against each party there could be no contribution between them. The Law Revision Committee in its *Third Interim Report* (Cmd 4637) (1934) addressed this problem. In para 7 of its report the committee said (pp 5–6):

'We think that the common law rule should be altered as speedily as possible. The simplest way of altering the law would seem to be to follow the lines of Section 37(3) of the Companies Act [1929], and to give a right of contribution in the case of wrongs as in cases of contract. If this were done, joint tort-feasors in the strict sense would be given a right of contribution inter se. We think, however, that such a right might with advantage also be conferred where the tort is not joint (i.e., the same act committed by several persons) but where the same damage is caused to the Plaintiff by the separate wrongful acts of several persons. This is the position which frequently arises where the plaintiff sustains a single damage from the combined negligence of two motor car drivers, and recovers judgment against both … We think therefore that when two persons each contribute to the same damage suffered by a third the one who pays more than his share should be entitled to recover contribution from the other.'

The committee included (at p 8) the following among its recommendations:

'(II) Any person who is adjudged to be liable to make any payment … in respect of an actionable wrong may recover contribution … from any other person who has been made liable in respect of the same wrong, or who, if sued separately, would have been so liable, unless …

(III) Where two or more persons have committed independent wrongful acts which have been the cause of the same damage they shall have the same right to contribution among themselves but subject to the same exception as in the case of persons liable in respect of the same wrong.'

a Effect was given to these recommendations in s 6(1)(c) of the Law Reform (Married Women and Tortfeasors) Act 1935 which provided:

'Where damage is suffered by any person as a result of a tort ... (c) any tortfeasor liable in respect of that damage may recover contribution from any other tortfeasor who is, or would if sued have been, liable in respect of the same damage, whether as a joint tortfeasor or otherwise ...'

b [4] The Law Revision Committee's *Third Interim Report* and s 6(1)(c) of the 1935 Act were directed only to the liability, as between each other, of those who had committed tortious acts, whether jointly or concurrently. This limited field of application came in time to be recognised as a weakness, for s 6(1)(c) did not apply to wrongdoers other than tortfeasors and did not apply if only one of the *c* wrongdoers was a tortfeasor. This was one of the weaknesses addressed by the Law Commission in its *Law of Contract: Report on Contribution* (Law Com No 79) published in March 1977. A number of recommendations were made with the main aim of widening the jurisdiction given to the courts by the 1935 Act (see p 23 (para 81)) and specific recommendations were made:

d '(a) ... that statutory rights of contribution should not be confined, as at present, to cases where damage is suffered as a result of a tort, but should cover cases where it is suffered as a result of tort, breach of contract, breach of trust or other breach of duty ... (d) ... that the statutory right to recover contribution should be available to any person liable in respect of the *e* damage, not just persons liable in tort ...'

In the draft bill appended to its report the Law Commission proposed a subsection (in cl 3(1)) which differed from s 1(1) of the 1978 Act quoted at the outset of this opinion only in its reference to the time when the damage occurred, a reference which has been omitted in the subsection as enacted. The words *f* which I have emphasised at the outset were included in the Law Commission draft. Section 1(1) of the 1978 Act is supplemented by s 6(1):

'A person is liable in respect of any damage for the purposes of this Act if the person who suffered it ... is entitled to recover compensation from him in respect of that damage (whatever the legal basis of his liability, whether *g* tort, breach of contract, breach of trust or otherwise).'

This differs more obviously, at least in wording, from the interpretation clause proposed by the Law Commission (p 38, App C):

'For the purposes of this Act—(a) a person is liable in respect of any *h* damage if he is subject to a duty enforceable by action to compensate for that damage, whether or not he has in fact been held to be so liable in any action actually brought against him; and (b) it is immaterial whether he is liable in respect of a tort, breach of contract, breach of trust or on any other ground whatsoever which gives rise to a cause of action against him in respect of the damage in question.'

j [5] It is plain beyond argument that one important object of the 1978 Act was to widen the classes of person between whom claims for contribution would lie and to enlarge the hitherto restricted category of causes of action capable of giving rise to such a claim. It is, however, as I understand, a constant theme of the law of contribution from the beginning that B's claim to share with others his liability to A rests upon the fact that they (whether equally with B or not) are

subject to a common liability to A. I find nothing in s 6(1)(c) of the 1935 Act or in
s 1(1) of the 1978 Act, or in the reports which preceded those Acts, which in any
way weakens that requirement. Indeed both sections, by using the words 'in
respect of the same damage', emphasise the need for one loss to be apportioned
among those liable.

[6] When any claim for contribution falls to be decided the following
questions in my opinion arise: (1) What damage has A suffered? (2) Is B liable
to A in respect of that damage? (3) Is C also liable to A in respect of that damage
or some of it? At the striking-out stage the questions must be recast to reflect the
rule that it is arguability and not liability which then falls for decision, but their
essential thrust is the same. I do not think it matters greatly whether, in phrasing
these questions, one speaks (as the 1978 Act does) of 'damage' or of 'loss' or
'harm', provided it is borne in mind that 'damage' does not mean 'damages' (as
pointed out by Roch LJ in *Birse Construction Ltd v Haiste Ltd (Watson and ors, third
parties)* [1996] 2 All ER 1 at 8, [1996] 1 WLR 675 at 682) and that B's right to
contribution by C depends on the damage, loss or harm for which B is liable to A
corresponding (even if in part only) with the damage, loss or harm for which C is
liable to A. This seems to me to accord with the underlying equity of the
situation: it is obviously fair that C contributes to B a fair share of what both B
and C owe in law to A, but obviously unfair that C should contribute to B any
share of what B may owe in law to A but C does not.

[7] Approached in this way, the claim made by the architect against the
contractor must in my opinion fail in principle. It so happens that the employer
and the contractor have resolved their mutual claims and counterclaims in
arbitration whereas the employer seeks redress against the architect in the High
Court. But for purposes of contribution the parties' rights must be the same as if
the employer had sued both the contractor and the architect in the High Court
and they had exchanged contribution notices. The question would then be
whether the employer was advancing a claim for damage, loss or harm for which
both the contractor and the architect were liable, in which case (if the claim were
established) the court would have to apportion the common liability between the
two parties responsible, or whether the employer was advancing separate claims
for damage, loss or harm for which the contractor and the architect were
independently liable, in which case (if the claims were established) the court
would have to assess the sum for which each party was liable but could not
apportion a single liability between the two. It would seem to me clear that any
liability the employer might prove against the contractor and the architect would
be independent and not common. The employer's claim against the contractor
would be based on the contractor's delay in performing the contract and the
disruption caused by the delay, and the employer's damage would be the
increased cost it incurred, the sums it overpaid and the liquidated damages to
which it was entitled. Its claim against the architect, based on negligent advice
and certification, would not lead to the same damage because it could not be
suggested that the architect's negligence had led to any delay in performing the
contract.

[8] For the reasons given by Lord Steyn, and also for these reasons, I conclude
that Judge Hicks QC and the Court of Appeal made correct decisions and I would
dismiss this appeal.

LORD MACKAY OF CLASHFERN.

a
[9] My Lords, I have had the advantage of reading in draft the speeches prepared by my noble and learned friends Lord Bingham of Cornhill and Lord Steyn. I agree that this appeal should be dismissed for the reasons they have given.

b **LORD STEYN.**

[10] My Lords, in a tripartite relationship under a building contract between an employer, a contractor and an architect a question of the correct interpretation of s 1(1) of the Civil Liability (Contribution) Act 1978 arises. Subject to its other provisions s 1 provides: '... any person liable in respect of any *c* damage suffered by another person may recover contribution from any other person liable in respect of the same damage (whether jointly with him or otherwise).' The issue centres on the meaning of the words 'in respect of the same damage' read in the context of the language and purpose of the 1978 Act. Having ascertained the meaning of the operative words of s 1 the application of *d* the statute requires a close examination of the nature of claims by the employer against the contractor and the architect respectively in order to decide whether they are 'in respect of the same damage'.

(I) The history of the contract

e
[11] By a contract incorporating the articles of agreement and other conditions of the JCT Standard Form of Building Contract (1980 edn), Local Authorities with Quantities, with Amendment No 1 of 1984, the Royal Brompton Hospital National Health Service Trust (the employer) employed Taylor Woodrow Construction (Holdings) Ltd (the contractor) as the main contractor in the development and construction of phase 1 of new hospital premises in *f* Sydney Street, Chelsea. Watkins Gray International (UK), and two named architects, acted as architects under the contract. Collectively, I will call them 'the architect'. This is a well-known standard form of contract, which is readily available to interested parties, and it is therefore unnecessary to set out its provisions verbatim (see *Keating on Building Contracts* (7th edn, 2001) p 591 et seq).

g
[12] The contract between the employer and the contractor was not dated but it came into effect on about 2 March 1987 when the contractor took possession of the site. The contract fixed the date for the completion of the works as 23 July 1989. Under cl 24 of the contract the contractor had to pay or allow the employer liquidated and ascertained damages at the rate of £47,000 per week if the *h* contractor failed to complete the works by the completion date. In the event practical completion was certified 43 weeks and 2 days later than the contractual completion date. The contractor made numerous applications on a variety of grounds for extensions of time under cl 25 of the contract and for the payment of loss and expense for prolongation and disruption under cl 26 of the contract, for *j* variations and other matters. The architect granted extensions of time totalling 43 weeks, 2 days, ie up to the date on which practical completion was certified, ie on 22 May 1990. The effect of this was to relieve the contractor of its obligation to pay or allow liquidated and ascertained damages for any of the delay. The contractor claimed for loss and expense amounting to some £22m. The architect certified as due and the employer paid some £5·2m of which about £2·3m related to prolongation and the balance to disruption.

(II) *The proceedings*

[13] The contractor commenced arbitration proceedings, claiming a further £17·1m. The employer disputed the claim and counterclaimed for a sum of some £6·6m. The employer was able to make these claims notwithstanding the extensions of time granted by the architect because by art 5.3 of the contract the arbitrator had power to open up, review and revise any certificate to determine all matters in dispute in the same manner as if no such certificate had been given. On 19 December 1995 the parties settled the arbitration on terms that the employer paid to the contractor some £6·2m and agreed to indemnify the contractor against any claim for contribution made against the contractor by, amongst others, the architect.

[14] On 21 January 1993 the employer issued a writ against the architect and others. Between 1993 and 1997 the action was by consent stayed. On 5 August 1997 the statement of claim was served. The employer alleged that the architect had been negligent. The relevant heads of claim are summarised in the agreed statement of facts and issues. Subject to minor alterations the relevant paragraphs read:

'(b) **Hydrotite (section F of the re-amended statement of claim).** The contractor had responsibility for drying out the floor slabs. By April 1989 it had become apparent that the slabs would not dry out for a very long time. On 18 May 1989 the architect issued an instruction to lay a proprietary damp-proof membrane called Hydrotite so that the contractor could proceed to lay the floor coverings before the concrete was dry. The contractor made claims for loss and expense incurred by reason of the instruction to lay Hydrotite, for which the contractor was paid £669,070 (for prolongation) and £189,062 (for disruption) before the arbitration and claimed further sums in the arbitration. The architect granted extensions of time totalling 12 weeks (including two for Christmas) by reason of delay caused by the application of Hydrotite. The employer counterclaimed in the arbitration to recover the sums paid for prolongation and damages in respect of the sums paid for disruption. The employer claims that the architect was negligent in failing to give adequate advice as to the options available to the employer (and in particular in failing to advise of the option of holding the contractor to its now undoubted contractual responsibility for the drying out of the works) or as to the possible consequences of issuing an architect's instruction to lay Hydrotite in terms of claims for extension of time and loss and expense.

(c) **Extensions of time (section G of the re-amended statement of claim).** The contractor claimed loss and expense by reason of the events giving rise to the extensions of time, for which the contractor was paid £2,319,169 before the arbitration and claimed further sums in the arbitration. The employer counterclaimed to set aside the extensions of time and to recover the sums paid before the arbitration. The employer also claimed liquidated damages for which, but for the extensions of time, the contractor would have been liable. The total claim for liquidated damages was £2,021,000 at the contractual rate of £47,000 per week.'

The architect issued CPR Pt 20 proceedings to recover a contribution from the contractor under the 1978 Act. In respect of section F (Hydrotite) the architect alleged in the third party notice:

a   '[The employer] alleges that [the architect], inter alia, was negligent in that [the architect] should have known that [the contractor] was not therefore entitled to an architect's instruction to lay a moisture resistant membrane ... and [the employer] seeks to recover damages from [the architect]. If [the employer] is right in its allegations made against [the architect], which is denied, and in its allegations against [the contractor], then it was entitled ...
b   to recover £858,132 paid to [the contractor] in respect of and consequential upon the instruction; the recovery of liquidated damages in the sum of £564,000 and/or any other sums allegedly paid to [the contractor] in consequence of the instruction, extensions of time and/or prolongation. In the premises [the contractor] is and/or was liable to [the employer] in respect of the same damage, the subject matter of this part of the action
c   against [the architect] and thus liable to contribute to the extent of an indemnity for such loss as [the architect] may be held liable to [the employer] pursuant to the provisions of the Civil Liability (Contribution) Act 1978.'

In respect of section G (extensions of time) the architect alleged in the third party
d   notice:

    'If, which is denied, [the architect] was negligent as alleged by [the employer] in granting extensions of time to [the contractor] to which [the contractor] was not entitled and liable to [the employer] for the liquidated damages and/or loss and expense paid to [the contractor] as alleged in the amended statement of claim, then [the contractor] is and/or was also liable
e   to [the employer] in respect of the same damage the subject matter of this part of the action against [the architect] and thus liable to contribute to the extent of an indemnity for such loss as [the architect] may be held liable to [the employer] pursuant to the provisions of the Civil Liability (Contribution) Act 1978.'

f   The contractor applied to strike out the Pt 20 claim. Given the indemnity given by the employer to the contractor in the settlement of the arbitration, the contractor was represented by the same solicitors and counsel as the employer.

(III) The decisions of Judge Hicks QC and the Court of Appeal
g   [15] Sitting in the Technology and Construction Court, Judge Hicks QC ((2000) 69 Con LR 145) held that in respect of sections F and G, as described above, the contractor was not liable in respect of the same damage as the architect. He therefore struck out the third party notice of the architect against the contractor. The architect appealed to the Court of Appeal ((2000) 69 Con LR
h   145). By agreement the argument concentrated on the architect's claim for a contribution in respect of the section G (extensions of time). It was assumed that if the architect failed in the arguments on section G he must necessarily also to fail in his arguments on section F (Hydrotite). Dismissing the appeal Stuart-Smith LJ held that the contractor's breach consisted in the failure to deliver
j   the building on time whereas the damage caused by the architect occurred at the time of the certification of extensions and was the impairment of the ability of the employer to obtain financial recompense in full from the contractor; and, accordingly, it was not a claim in respect of 'the same damage'. Buxton LJ agreed. With some hesitation Ward LJ also agreed.
    [16] Since the Court of Appeal decision a trial has taken place of the employer's claims against the architect in respect of section G (extensions of

time). The architect was held to have been negligent in granting five weeks for laying Hydrotite on 24 November 1989. The issues on quantum still await decision. The trial in respect of section F (Hydrotite) has not yet taken place.

(IV) *The issues*

[17] On appeal to the House counsel for the architect broadened his case by making submissions both on section F (Hydrotite) and section G (extensions of time). Both aspects arise for decision in the context of a striking-out application: the focus is therefore on the arguability of claims. The agreed statement of facts and issues formulates the issues as follows:

> 'In the [case] ... of Hydrotite (section F): on the assumptions (i) that the relevant facts and matters alleged in the third party statement of claim were established at trial against [the contractor] and (ii) that the relevant facts and matters alleged in the re-amended statement of claim were established at trial against [the architect], would [the contractor] be liable to [the employer] "in respect of the same damage" as that in respect of which [the architect] would be liable for the purposes of s 1(1) of the Civil Liability (Contribution) Act 1978? ... In the case of the second extension of time in relation to Hydrotite (ie the extension in respect of which [the architect] has been found to have been in breach of duty: section G): on the assumption that the relevant facts and matters alleged in the third party statement of claim were established at trial against [the contractor], would [the contractor] be liable to [the employer] "in respect of the same damage" as that in respect of which [the architect] has been found to be liable for the purposes of s 1(1) of the Civil Liability (Contribution) Act 1978?'

It will be convenient first to consider the position under section G (extensions of time) which was the subject matter to which the judgments in the Court of Appeal were directed.

(V) *The operation of the contract.*

[18] It is necessary at the outset to describe in uncontroversial fashion how this standard form JCT contract operates. Drawing on a helpful summary in the contractor's printed case, the position is as follows. The contractor is obliged to proceed regularly and diligently with the works and to complete them by the completion date (cl 23.1). If he fails to do so, he is liable to pay or allow to the employer a sum by way of liquidated and ascertained damages calculated at the agreed rate (cl 24). Those damages are either deducted from sums otherwise payable to the contractor or the employer may recover them 'as a debt' (cl 24.2.1).

[19] If the works are delayed, or are likely to be delayed, beyond the completion date by a relevant event as defined by cl 25.4, the contractor is entitled to an extension of time; if, on the contractor's application, the architect is satisfied that there has been a relevant event and that the completion of the works is likely to be delayed thereby beyond the completion date, he must give an extension of time by fixing such a later date as the completion date which he considers fair and reasonable (cl 25.3). Thus the effect of giving an extension of time is twofold. First, the employer no longer has the right to take possession of the works on the original date for completion, but only on the later date fixed by the architect. Secondly, the contractor becomes relieved from any liability to pay liquidated damages in respect of the delay between the two dates. In addition, where the regular progress of the works is materially affected by one or more of

a the matters listed in cl 26.2 and the contractor has thereby incurred loss and/or expense for which he would not be reimbursed under any other provision of the contract, the contractor is entitled to have such loss and expense ascertained (by the architect or quantity surveyor) and paid to him.

[20] Each of the matters listed in cl 26.2. is also a relevant event under cl 25. Thus if an extension of time is given for one or more of those events, this will *b* entitle the contractor to recover any loss and expense under cl 26. In practice, when the architect gives an extension of time because of a relevant event that entitles the contractor to loss and expense, he will also ascertain (or instruct the quantity surveyor to ascertain) the amount of that loss and expense. The loss and expense so ascertained then becomes added to the contract sum (cll 26.5 and 30.6.2.13). At the conclusion of the contract (before the expiry of the defects *c* liability period) the architect must issue a final certificate stating (1) the sum of the amounts already due by way of interim certificates and (2) the contract sum as adjusted in accordance with the contractual provisions. The balance representing the difference between these two sums becomes (subject to any further deductions authorised by the contract) a debt payable by the employer to the *d* contractor, or vice versa, as the case may be (cl 30.8). The liability of either the employer or the contractor is to pay the balance.

[21] The arbitration clause in the main contract gives the arbitrator power to 'open up, review and revise any certificate, opinion, decision ... and to determine all matters in dispute ... as if no such certificate, opinion, decision ... had been given' (art 5.3). If either the employer or the contractor is dissatisfied with the *e* extension of time given by the architect then, not later than 15 days after the issue of the final certificate, he may commence an arbitration against the other and seek an award setting aside the extension of time. If the employer is successful in any arbitration, the final certificate (if already issued) will be subject to the terms of the award or any settlement so that any balance stated in it to be due by one *f* party to the other will be adjusted accordingly. If, for example, the balance was nil, and the arbitrator sets aside the extension of time, then the balance will be adjusted so that a sum representing the amount of liquidated damages referable to the extension of time, and the associated loss and expense overpaid, will become due to the employer as a debt (cll 30.8 and 30.9). In any event, the liability of the contractor will be the contractual liability to pay whatever balance *g* is due, after all relevant matters have been taken into account.

(VI) *A description of the claims*

[22] The characterisation of the employer's claim against the contractor is straightforward. It is for the late delivery of the building. This is not a claim *h* which the employer has made against the architect. Moreover, notionally it is not damage for which the architect could be liable merely by reason of a negligent grant of an extension of time. It is conceivable that an architect could negligently cause or contribute to the delay in completion of works, eg by condoning inadequate progress of the work or by failing to chivvy the contractor. *j* In such a case the contractor and the architect could be liable for the same damage. There are, however, no such allegations in the present case.

[23] The essence of the case against the architect is the allegation that his breach of duty changed the employer's contractual position detrimentally as against the contractor. The employer's case is that the architect wrongly evaluated the contractor's claim for an extension of time. It is alleged that by negligently giving an extension of time in respect of an unmeritorious claim by

the contractor, the architect presented the contractor with a defence to a
previously straightforward claim by the employer for breach of contract in   *a*
respect of delay. The employer lost the right under the contract to claim or
deduct liquidated damages for the delayed delivery of the building. The
contractor committed no wrong by retaining the money until the extension of
time had been set aside in an arbitration. The detrimental effect on the
employer's contractual position took place when the extension of time was   *b*
negligently given. In such a case the employer must go to arbitration in order to
restore his position. He has the burden of proof in the arbitration and has to face
the uncertain prospect of succeeding in what may perhaps be a complex
arbitration. The employer's bargaining position against the contractor is weakened.
A reasonable settlement with the contractor may reflect this changed position: a
case with a 100% prospect of success may become, for example, a case with only   *c*
a 70% prospect of success.

(VII) *Civil Liability (Contribution) Act 1978*

[24] The long title of the 1978 Act states that its purpose is—

d

'to make new provision for contribution between persons who are jointly
or severally, or both jointly and severally, liable for the same damage and in
certain other similar cases where two or more persons have paid or may be
required to pay compensation for the same damage; and to amend the law
relating to proceedings against persons jointly liable for the same debt or
jointly or severally, or both jointly and severally, liable for the same damage.'   *e*

[25] Section 1 creates the entitlement to contribution:

'(1) Subject to the following provisions of this section, any person liable in
respect of any damage suffered by another person may recover contribution
from any other person liable in respect of the same damage (whether jointly   *f*
with him or otherwise).'

For present purposes it is unnecessary to set out the remaining provisions of s 1.
It is, however, necessary to read s 1(1) with the interpretation provision in s 6(1).
It provides:

g

'A person is liable in respect of any damage for the purposes of this Act if
the person who suffered it (or anyone representing his estate or dependants)
is entitled to recover compensation from him in respect of that damage
(whatever the legal basis of his liability, whether tort, breach of contract,
breach of trust or otherwise).'   *h*

The court's power of assessing contributions is contained in s 2. So far as it is
material it provides:

'(1) ... in any proceedings for contribution under section 1 above the
amount of the contribution recoverable from any person shall be such as   *j*
may be found by the court to be just and equitable having regard to the
extent of that person's responsibility for the damage in question.
(2) ... the court shall have power in any such proceedings to exempt any
person from liability to make contribution, or to direct that the contribution
to be recovered from any person shall amount to a complete indemnity.'

(VIII) *The meaning of 'the same damage'*

[26] Counsel for the architect reminded the House that the 1978 Act is a reforming measure. He argued that it ought to be given a broad and purposive interpretation so as to achieve the legislative intent. He said that the wide power of the court under s 2(1) and (2) to impose a 'just and equitable' solution reinforces the appropriateness of such an approach. He cited dicta in two Court of Appeal decisions in favour of this approach. In *Friends' Provident Life Office v Hillier Parker May & Rowden (a firm) (Estates and General plc and ors, third parties)* [1995] 4 All ER 260 at 272, [1997] QB 85 at 102–103 Auld LJ, with the agreement of the other members of the court, observed in respect of ss 1(1) and 6(1):

> 'The contribution is as to "compensation" recoverable against a person in respect of "any damage suffered by another" (s 1(1)) "whatever the legal basis of his liability, whether tort, breach of contract, breach of trust or otherwise"(s 6(1)). It is difficult to imagine a broader formulation of an entitlement to contribution. It clearly spans a variety of causes of action, forms of damage in the sense of loss of some sort, and remedies, the last of which are gathered together under the umbrella of "compensation". The 1978 Act was clearly intended to be given a wide interpretation …'

This passage was cited with approval in *Hurstwood Developments Ltd v Motor & General & Andersley & Co Insurance Services (H B Boring & Co Ltd (Pt 20 defendants))* [2001] EWCA Civ 1785, [2002] Lloyd's Rep IR 185 by Keene LJ, who, having set out the passage from the judgment of Auld LJ, went on to say, at [19]:

> 'It is necessary, therefore, not to be over-influenced by the possibility of formulating the measure of damages or even the damage, for which one party is liable to the Claimant, in different words from that which may be employed to define or describe that for which another party is liable. Since the cause of action against each of them may differ, a different formulation of the damage for which they are liable may be possible.'

This observation was made with the agreement of the other members of the court. It will be necessary to return to these two decisions. At this stage I concentrate on the proposition that the 1978 Act ought to be given a broad interpretation. In large measure this statement is correct. This view can in particular be accepted to the extent that the 1978 Act extended the reach of the contribution principle to a wider range of cases 'whatever the legal basis of his liability, whether tort, breach of contract, breach of trust or otherwise' (s 6(1)) and in the light of the comprehensive powers of the court under s 2(1) and (2).

[27] But this purposive and enlarged view of the reach of the statute does not assist on the central issue of construction before the House. The critical words are 'liable in respect of the same damage'. Section 1(1) refers to 'damage' and not to 'damages' (see *Birse Construction Ltd v Haiste Ltd (Watson, third party)* [1996] 2 All ER 1 at 8, [1996] 1 WLR 675 at 682 per Roch LJ). It was common ground that the closest synonym of 'damage' is 'harm'. The focus is, however, on the composite expression 'the same damage'. As my noble and learned friend Lord Bingham of Cornhill has convincingly shown by an historical examination the notion of a common liability, and of sharing that common liability, lies at the root of the principle of contribution: see also *Current Law Statutes Annotated* (1978) ch 47 'Background to the Act'. The legislative technique of limiting the contribution principle under the 1978 Act to the same damage was a considered policy decision. The context does not therefore justify an expansive

interpretation of the words 'the same damage' so as to mean substantially or materially similar damage. Such solutions could have been adopted but considerations of unfairness to parties who did not in truth cause or contribute to the same damage would have militated against them. Moreover, the adoption of such solutions would have led to uncertainty in the application of the law. That is the context of s 1(1) and the phrase 'the same damage'. It must be interpreted and applied on a correct evaluation and comparison of claims alleged to qualify for contribution under s 1(1). No glosses, extensive or restrictive, are warranted. The natural and ordinary meaning of 'the *same* damage' is controlling.

[28] In *Howkins & Harrison (a firm) v Tyler* [2001] Lloyd's Rep PN 1 at 4 (para 17), Scott V-C (now Lord Scott of Foscote) suggested a test to be applied to determine the statutory criterion of 'the same damage'. With the agreement of Aldous and Sedley LJJ he observed:

'Suppose that A and B are the two parties who are said each to be liable to C in respect of "the same damage" that has been suffered by C. So C must have a right of action of some sort against A and a right of action of some sort against B. There are two questions that should then be asked. If A pays C a sum of money in satisfaction, or on account, of A's liability to C, will that sum operate to reduce or extinguish, depending upon the amount, B's liability to C? Secondly, if B pays C a sum of money in satisfaction or on account of B's liability to C, would that operate to reduce or extinguish A's liability to C? It seems to me that unless both of those questions can be given an affirmative answer, the case is not one to which the 1978 Act can be applied. If the payment by A or B to C does not *pro tanto* relieve the other of his obligations to C, there cannot, it seems to me, possibly be a case for contending that the non-paying party, whose liability to C remains un-reduced, will also have an obligation under section 1(1) to contribute to the payment made by the paying party.'

If this test is regarded as a necessary threshold question for the purpose of identifying whether a claim for contribution is capable of being a claim to which the 1978 Act could apply, questions of contribution might become unnecessarily complex: see on this point *Eastgate Group Ltd v Lindsey Morden Group Inc (Smith & Williamson (a firm), Pt 20 defendant)* [2001] EWCA Civ 1446 at [19], [2001] 2 All ER (Comm) 1050 at [19], [2002] 1 WLR 642, per Longmore LJ. It is best regarded as a practical test to be used in considering the very statutory question whether two claims under consideration are for 'the same damage'. Its usefulness may, however, vary depending on the circumstances of individual cases. Ultimately, the safest course is to apply the statutory test.

[29] Before the judge and in the Court of Appeal counsel for the contractor deployed in support of his argument that the two claims were different a hypothetical case not covered by direct English precedent (see the judge's observations (2000) 69 Con LR 145 at 153 (para 29); and Stuart-Smith LJ's observations (2000) 69 Con LR 145 at 161 (para 20)). Since then a report of a Canadian decision on the point has become available. It is the decision of the Alberta Court of Appeal in *Wallace v Litwiniuk* (2001) 92 Alta LR (3d) 249. In that case the plaintiff sustained injuries in a motor vehicle collision. She wanted to sue the driver of the other vehicle. Her lawyers allowed the claim to become time barred. She sued her lawyers. They issued a third party notice against the driver of the other car. Section 3(1) of the Canadian Tort-Feasors Act 1980 provides:

a 'When damage is suffered by any person as a result of a tort, whether a
crime or not ... (c) any tort-feasor liable in respect of that damage may
recover contribution from any other tort-feasor who is or would, if sued,
have been liable in respect *of the same damage,* whether as a joint tort-feasor
or otherwise, but no person is entitled to recover contribution under this
section from any person entitled to be indemnified by him in respect of the
b liability regarding which the contribution is sought.' (My emphasis.)

The court held (at 257):

'32 The compensation which she [the claimant] presently seeks from the
respondents [the lawyers] is not damages for her physical injuries, but
c damages for what she would have obtained had the original claim been
brought. In both cases, she sought *damages,* but that is not to say she sought
the *same damage.* The damage is different ...

33 The pleadings in [the claimant's] statement of claim against [the
lawyers] only superficially look as though she is claiming the same damages
she would have claimed against [the negligent driver]. This seeming
d similarity results from the usual method for calculating damages in a
professional negligence claim where a lawyer failed to bring litigation which
might otherwise have been pursued. Damages for the professional negligence
are calculated by reference to the damages which would have been obtained
in the original claim: Dugdale and Stanton, *Professional Negligence* (London:
e Butterworths, 1989) at pp. 363–364.

34 The distinct nature of the original claim and the professional
negligence claim is recognised by the need to estimate the value of the
original claim, and then discount for the costs of pursuing the original
litigation, and allow for any chance that the original claim might not have
f succeeded.'

Counsel for the architect rightly conceded that this is a correct analysis which in
a similar situation an English court would be bound to follow. He asserted that
the present case is different, apparently on the basis that there is greater proximity
between the two claims. This is, however, not a material distinction. The
g analogy of *Wallace v Litwiniuk* militates strongly against the claims in the present
case being for 'the same damage'. A further analogy was put forward by counsel
for the contractor. He postulated a sale of the shares in a company. An
accountant had negligently valued the shares at £7·5m. The vendor warranted
that the shares were worth the price of £10m. In truth the shares were worth only
h £5m. The vendor was liable for damages in the sum of £5m. Counsel for the
contractor said that the accountant could only be liable to the extent of the
common liability, ie £2·5m. Counsel for the architect accepted that this analysis
is correct. Again, the architect is in difficulties because the example demonstrates
the unavailability of a right of contribution to the extent that there is no common
liability. It points in the present case to the conclusion that the architect is not
j liable for 'the same damage' as the contractor.

[30] Counsel for the architect urged the House to eschew an overly analytical
approach to the nature of the claims. He said that in the application of the statute
a flexible and broad view should be adopted. But loyalty to the statutory criterion
of 'the same damage' demands legal analysis of claims. Moreover, counsel for the
architect rightly did not contest the legal characterisation of the claims set out in

[13] and [14], above in respect of section G (extensions of time). In my view the
conclusion is inescapable that the claims are not for the same damage.   *a*

(IX) *Conclusions on section G (extensions of time)*

[31] In agreement with the Court of Appeal I would hold that the criterion
that the two claims must be for 'the same damage' is not satisfied in respect of
section G (extensions of time).   *b*

(X) *Section F (Hydrotite)*

[32] As between the employer and the architect it has been held that the
contractor was contractually responsible for drying out the floor slabs. However,
the architect issued an instruction to lay Hydrotite. The effect of the instruction
was to transfer the cost of the solution to the problem from the contractor to the   *c*
employer. The pleaded case of the employer against the architect is that the
employer authorised the issue of the instruction on the negligent advice of the
architect. The damage or harm for which the architect is liable is the change in
the employer's contractual position vis-à-vis the contractor. This claim is
fundamentally different from the employer's claim against the contractor in   *d*
respect of the delay in completion of the building. On a correct analysis of the
claims the architect's argument does not satisfy the criterion that the claims must
be for 'the same damage'.

(XI) *Earlier decisions*

[33] It is necessary to refer to dicta in four earlier decisions. In *Friends'*   *e*
*Provident Life Office v Hillier Parker May & Rowden (a firm) (Estates and General plc
and ors, third parties)* [1995] 4 All ER 260, [1997] QB 85 to which I have already
referred Auld LJ observed:

> 'In my judgment, despite the distinction between a claim for restitution
> and one for damages, each may be a claim for compensation for damage   *f*
> under ss 1(1) and 6(1) of the 1978 Act. The difference between asking for a
> particular sum of money back or for an equivalent sum of money for the
> damage suffered because of the withholding of it is immaterial in this
> statutory context, which is concerned with "compensation" for "damage".'
> (See [1995] 4 All ER 260 at 272, [1997] QB 85 at 102.)   *g*

Goff and Jones *The Law of Restitution* (5th edn, 1998) p 396, commented on this
dictum:

> 'To conclude that a restitutionary claim is one for "damage suffered"
> cannot be justified in principle; nor is it, in our view, consistent with the   *h*
> natural meaning of the statutory language. A claim for restitution cannot be
> said to be a claim to recover *compensation* within the meaning of section 1(1).'

I am in respectful agreement with this criticism of the *Friends' Provident* case. To
this extent it cannot be accepted as a correct statement of the law. Secondly, it is
necessary to refer again to *Hurstwood Developments Ltd v Motor & General &*   *j*
Andersley & Co Insurance Services (H B Boring & Co Ltd (Pt 20 defendants)) [2001]
EWCA Civ 1785, [2002] Lloyd's Rep IR 185. Relying on the observations in the
Friends' Provident case the Court of Appeal held that the claim by an employer
against a contractor for negligent site investigation services and a claim by the
employer against insurance brokers for failure to insure against the contingency
are claims for 'the same damage', entitling the insurance brokers to claim a

a contribution against the contractor. The fact is, however, that the insurance brokers had no responsibility for the remedial work. In my view the extensive interpretation of s 1(1) adopted by the Court of Appeal led to a conclusion not warranted by the language of the statute. If my conclusions in respect of the claims under consideration in the present case are correct it follows that the *Hurstwood* case was wrongly decided.

b [34] In two first instance decisions a difference of opinion on s 1(1) arose. In *Bovis Construction Ltd v Commercial Union Assurance Co plc* [2001] 1 Lloyd's Rep 416 the question arose whether a claim against a builder for defective work was 'the same damage' under s 1(1) as an insurance company's liability under a policy of insurance. David Steel J held (at 420 (para 28)):

c   'Bovis was liable for the flood damage to Friendly House: CU was liable under a policy of insurance. It is a misconception to describe those as liabilities "in respect of the same damage". The damage inflicted by the builder was a defective building susceptible to flooding damage and consequential loss of rent. CU has not inflicted that damage: the only damage it could inflict would have been a refusal to pay on the policy (which

d   in any event excluded consequential loss), thereby imposing financial loss. This is not the same damage: see [the Court of Appeal decision in the *Royal Brompton* case (2000) 69 Con LR 145].'

In a careful and detailed judgment in *Bovis Lend Lease Ltd (formerly Bovis*
e *Construction Ltd) v Saillard Fuller & Partners* (2001) 77 Con LR 134 at 181–182 (paras 128–130) Judge Anthony Thornton QC took a contrary view. It will be obvious that on this point I prefer the view of David Steel J. It is unnecessary, however, to examine the discussion by Judge Thornton of other matters.

f (XII) *Disposal*
[35] For these reasons, as well as the reasons given by Lord Bingham, I would hold that the architect's claims were rightly struck out and I would dismiss the appeal.

LORD HOPE OF CRAIGHEAD.
g [36] My Lords, I have had the advantage of reading in draft the speeches of my noble and learned friends Lord Bingham of Cornhill and Lord Steyn. I agree with them and for the reasons which they have given I too would dismiss the appeal. I should like however to add a few observations of my own on the meaning and effect of ss 1(1) and 6(1) of the Civil Liability (Contribution) Act 1978.

h [37] The purpose of the Act, as its long title indicates, was to make new provision for contribution between persons who are jointly or severally, or both jointly and severally, liable for the same damage, and in certain other similar cases where two or more persons have paid or may be required to pay compensation for the same damage. The word 'contribution' is used where the cost of making

j good damage which has to be compensated is distributed equitably among a number of persons who are responsible in one way or another for causing the damage. The starting point for the exercise is the assumption that two or more persons have contributed, albeit in different ways, to the same wrong. The Act is concerned only with liability for damage, so the rules which apply to contribution between two or more persons who are liable for the same debts are not affected by it.

[**38**] As my noble and learned friend Lord Bingham has explained, the common law did not favour the remedy of relief between joint tortfeasors (see *Merryweather v Nixan* (1799) 8 Term Rep 186, 101 ER 1337). The principle upon which the decision in that case was based appears to have been that a wrongdoer could not seek redress from another where he is presumed to have known that what he was doing was wrong (see *Adamson v Jarvis* (1827) 4 Bing 66, [1824–34] All ER Rep 120, *Weld-Blundell v Stephens* [1920] AC 956 at 976, [1920] All ER Rep 32 at 42 per Lord Dunedin). It is plain from the comments on it in *Palmer v Wick & Pulteneytown Steam Shipping Co Ltd* [1894] AC 318 by Lord Herschell LC (at 324), Lord Watson and Lord Halsbury (both at 333), that the rule was not one which they regarded with much favour. That was a case where damages had been claimed by the widow of a man who was killed by the fall of part of the tackle when the cargo of a vessel was being discharged at Grangemouth. Both the shipowner and the stevedore had been found liable to the widow in damages and expenses. It was held that the shipowner was entitled to recover half of the damages and expenses from the stevedore, as the rule that there was no contribution between wrongdoers did not apply in Scotland. But, as Lord Herschell LC said (at 324) it was too late for the decision in *Merryweather v Nixan* to be questioned in England. It was not until the rule was removed by s 6 of the Law Reform (Married Women and Tortfeasors) Act 1935 that it became possible in this jurisdiction for the liability in damages to be distributed between joint or concurrent tortfeasors. Section 6(2) of the 1935 Act went one step further, as it enabled the liability to be apportioned equitably between them and not just equally. This reform was extended to Scotland by s 3 of the Law Reform (Miscellaneous Provisions) (Scotland) Act 1940.

[**39**] The 1978 Act extended these reforms still further so as to provide for relief by way of contribution between wrongdoers whatever the basis of their liability. The major innovation introduced by the 1978 Act is to be found in s 6(1), which provides:

'A person is liable in respect of any damage for the purposes of this Act if the person who suffered it (or anyone representing his estate or dependants) is entitled to recover compensation from him in respect of that damage (whatever the legal basis of his liability, whether tort, breach of contract, breach of trust or otherwise).'

[**40**] This further reform was designed to close the gap in the law which had been identified by the Law Commission in *Law of Contract: Report on Contribution* (1977) (Law Com no 79). It affected all wrongdoers other than tortfeasors (see p 2 (paras 5–7)). The Law Commission could see no policy reason for leaving this gap unfilled (see p 10 (para 33)). The problem which it had in mind was illustrated in the report by two simple examples. The first example was taken from *McConnell v Lynch-Robinson, Coulter & Son, third party* [1957] NI 70. It assumes that an architect was employed to draw plans for and supervise the building of a new house, and that a builder was employed under a separate contract to undertake the work. The builder in breach of his contract failed to install the damp proof course properly, and the architect in breach of his contract failed to notice this error. The building owner sued the architect, who failed in his attempt to have the builder joined as a third party as the claim lay not in tort but in contract. Although the architect and the builder had both caused the same damage, there was no right to contribution as they were not liable in contract to the same demand (see *Dering v Earl of Winchelsea* (1787) 1 Cox Eq Cas 318, [1775–1802] All

ER Rep 140). The second example assumes that the house falls down due to the
architect's breach of contract, and that this was due also to the fault of the local
authority whose inspector negligently approved the work for the house. In this
case the architect would have been disabled from obtaining a contribution from
the local authority under s 6 of the 1935 Act, as his liability was for breach of
contract while the liability of the local authority was as a tortfeasor. It was in
order to close this gap that the Law Commission recommended in para 58
(pp 17–18) of its report that 'wrongdoers other than tortfeasors' should be
brought within the ambit of contribution.

[41] This is the background against which s 1(1) of the 1978 Act should be
understood. This subsection provides:

'Subject to the following provisions of this section, any person liable in
respect of any damage suffered by another person may recover contribution
from any other person liable in respect of the same damage (whether jointly
with him or otherwise).'

The words 'any other person' must be read together with s 6(1). So the right to
contribution applies whatever the legal basis of that other person's liability. The
words 'whether jointly with him or otherwise' extend the wording of s 6(1)(c) of
the 1935 Act to all such persons. That subsection provided that any tortfeasor
was entitled to recover a contribution from any other tortfeasor liable in respect
of the same damage 'whether as a joint tortfeasor or otherwise'. Section 2 of the
1978 Act provides that in any proceedings for contribution under s 1 the amount
of the contribution recoverable from any person shall be such as may be found
by the court to be just and equitable 'having regard to the extent of that person's
responsibility for the damage in question'.

[42] Paragraph 1 of Sch 1 to the 1978 Act is the only provision in that Act
which extends to Scotland. It provides:

'For section 5(b) of the Law Reform (Contributory Negligence) Act 1945
(application to Scotland) there shall be substituted—(b) section 3 of the Law
Reform (Miscellaneous Provisions) (Scotland) Act 1940 (contribution among
joint wrongdoers) shall apply in any case where two or more persons are
liable, or would if they had all been sued be liable, by virtue of section 1(1) of
this Act in respect of the damage suffered by any person.'

[43] The effect of para 1 of Sch 1 is not easy to grasp at first sight, as s 1(1) of
the 1945 Act deals with the apportionment of liability between the claimant and
the wrongdoer in a case of contributory negligence. But I think that the reference
in para 1 of Sch 1 to the 1978 Act to s 1(1) of the 1945 Act must be read together
with s 1(3) of that Act, which provides:

'Section six of the Law Reform (Married Women and Tortfeasors) Act,
1935 (which relates to proceedings against, and contribution between, joint
and several tortfeasors), shall apply in any case where two or more persons
are liable or would, if they had all been sued, be liable by virtue of subsection
(1) of this section in respect of the damage suffered by any person.'

Section 1(3) of the 1945 Act was repealed by s 9(2) of and Sch 2 to the 1978 Act.
But s 10(3) of the 1978 Act provides that that Act, with the exception of para 1 of
Sch 1 thereto, does not apply to Scotland. I understand this to mean that the
repeal of s 1(3) of the 1945 Act does not extend to Scotland.

[44] The effect of these provisions would appear to be that s 3 of the 1940 Act, which enables the liability between wrongdoers in Scotland to be apportioned equitably between them, now applies in any case where two or more persons are jointly or severally or both jointly and severally liable for the same damage, whatever the basis in law of the wrongdoers' liability. It had already been held that the doctrine of joint and several liability applies in cases of breach of contract as well as in delict (see *Grunwald v Hughes* 1965 SLT 209). As the Lord Justice-Clerk (Grant) put it (at 211) the test is the same whether the action is based on delict or on contract. It is whether the two persons have contributed, albeit in different ways, to cause a single wrong.

[45] In *Friends' Provident Life Office v Hillier Parker May & Rowden (a firm) (Estates and General plc and ors, third parties)* [1995] 4 All ER 260 at 272, [1997] QB 85 at 102–103 Auld LJ referred to the words 'any damage suffered by another' and 'whatever the legal basis of his liability, whether tort, breach of contract, breach of trust or otherwise'. He said that it was difficult to imagine a broader formulation of an entitlement to contribution and that the 1978 Act was clearly intended to be given a wide interpretation. Keene LJ followed those observations in *Hurstwood Developments Ltd v Motor & General & Andersley & Co Insurance Services (H B Boring & Co Ltd (Pt 20 defendants))* [2001] EWCA Civ 1785 at [19], [2002] Lloyd's Rep IR 185, when he said that it is necessary not to be over-influenced by the possibility of formulating the damage for which one party is liable in different language from that which is employed to define or describe that for which another party is liable. It is clear that the purpose of the 1978 Act was to extend the law to enable a contribution to be recovered in situations where it was not previously available. In that respect the wording in s 6(1) is undoubtedly very wide. But I think that it is a misconception to regard the Act as a whole as being open to the widest possible interpretation.

[46] I do not detect either in the Law Commission's report or in the wording of the Act itself an intention to depart from the assumption which has always been made in contribution cases that this relief is available only where two or more persons have contributed, albeit in different ways, to the same harm or damage—that is, where a single harm has resulted from what they have done. Where this occurs it may be said (loosely, as their liability is not common in the strict sense, as in the case of co-trustees or co-owners) that they share a common liability to pay compensation for having inflicted the same harm. Prior to *Palmer v Wick & Pulteneytown Steam Shipping Co Ltd* [1894] AC 318 it was not settled whether the statement that there shall be no contribution between wrongdoers was part of the law of Scotland (see *National Coal Board v Thomson* 1959 SC 353 at 368 per Lord Patrick. But Lord Watson said in *Palmer's* case (at 327) that it had been recognised in Scots law that a right of relief inter se was competent to all persons concerned in and responsible for the civil consequences of the same delict. This was said to be because payment and reparation by one wrongdoer liberates the rest and he ought in equity to have relief against the others proportionately, since by his money the others are freed from their obligation (see Bankton *Institute of the Laws of Scotland* (1751–1753) I.10, 4). The words 'liable in respect of the same damage', which first appeared in s 6(1)(c) of the 1935 Act and were repeated in s 1(1) of the 1978 Act, confirm that the concept of a common liability remains the basis of the entitlement to contribution in English law.

[47] The effect of those words is that the entitlement to contribution applies only where the person from whom the contribution is sought is liable for the

a same harm or damage, whatever the legal basis of his liability. But the mere fact that two or more wrongs lead to a common result does not of itself mean that the wrongdoers are liable in respect of the same damage. The facts must be examined more closely in order to determine whether or not the damage is the same. As Lord Fraser pointed out in *Turnbull v Frame* 1966 SLT 24 at 25, each utterance of a slander may be said to lead to a common result in the sense that

b they each cause damage to a man's reputation. It may be difficult to identify the particular damage caused by each utterance. But that does not mean that they are not separate wrongs, each of which causes its own damage. That is equally true of separate physical assaults by different persons at different but closely consecutive times. Unless they were acting in combination, each would be liable only for the damage caused by his own attack. Those examples may be

c contrasted with *Arneil v Paterson* [1931] AC 560, [1931] All ER Rep 90, where two dogs which were the property of different owners, acting together, attacked a flock of black-faced ewes and killed some of them. It was held that each of the owners was liable jointly and severally for the whole of the damage done to the flock, as the whole of the damage was the result of the action of the two dogs

d acting together.

[48] In the present case, for the reasons explained by my noble and learned friend Lord Steyn, the contractor and the architect did not cause the same damage. The basis for a finding that this was so is entirely absent. The harm done by the contractor's breach of contract was the product of delay in the completion of the contract. The harm done by the architect's breach of contract was due to

e the certificates which the architect granted to the prejudice of the rights of the employer under the contract. I agree that the harm, or the damage, which was done in each case was different. The conclusion must be that the prerequisite for entitlement to contribution under s 1(1) of the 1978 Act is not satisfied.

f **LORD RODGER OF EARLSFERRY.**

[49] My Lords, I have had the advantage of reading in draft the speeches of my noble and learned friends Lord Bingham of Cornhill and Lord Steyn. I agree with them and, for the reasons that they give, I too would dismiss the appeal.

Appeal dismissed.

Dilys Tausz   Barrister.

Spring House (Freehold) Ltd v Mount Cook Land Ltd

[2001] EWCA Civ 1833

COURT OF APPEAL, CIVIL DIVISION

WARD AND RIX LJJ

5 OCTOBER, 12 DECEMBER 2001

Landlord and tenant – Lease – Construction – Clause in lease providing that no 'goods' were to be 'placed outside the said premises' if forbidden by landlord – Demised premises originally having open basement but that area later being completely covered by skylights at pavement level – Whether clause preventing lessee from parking cars on skylights outside building but within demised premises.

In 1924 the defendant lessor's predecessor in title granted a 999-year lease of a property on the corner of two streets in central London. The concluding part of cl II(9) of the lease provided that 'no goods shall at any time be or remain placed outside the said premises which or of any nature which the Lessor shall have forbidden to be or to remain so placed'. The preceding words of the clause placed a restriction on any placard, advertisement or announcement relating to goods actually dealt in by, and in the ordinary course of, the business or occupation of the occupants of the premises. The property was originally used as a school, but later became an office block and shop. Basement areas that had originally been open had since been completely covered by skylights at the same level as the pavement, railings had been removed and there was no obvious boundary between the property and the pavement. As a consequence of those alterations, it had become possible to park a motor car on the covered areas, and for many years the occupiers had parked one or more motor cars on the skylights. The claimant lessee and its licensees had done so ever since it had acquired the lease in 1980. In April 1999 the lessor's solicitors wrote to the lessee giving formal notice, in reliance on cl II(9), that it was forbidden with immediate effect to place any motor vehicles, motor cycles or other goods outside of the premises demised to it pursuant to the lease. The lessor also gave notice that if the parking continued action might be taken, including forfeiture of the lease. After service of a notice under s 146 of the Law of Property Act 1925, the parties agreed that the lessee would bring proceedings in the county court for a declaration that it and its licensees were entitled to park vehicles on the demised premises. At the hearing, the judge was required to determine whether motor vehicles were 'goods' within the meaning of the subclause; whether it was apt to say that a motor car was 'placed' outside the said premises; and whether the motor cars were placed 'outside the said premises'. The judge held, in agreement with the lessor, that it was not inappropriate to say that a motor car was 'placed' outside the said premises and that the words 'outside the said premises' meant outside the building even though within the demise, thereby incorporating the area where the vehicles were parked. He also concluded, however, that motor vehicles were not 'goods' within the meaning of cl II(9) since the meaning of that word was restricted by the context of the subclause as a whole. Accordingly, he granted the declaration sought by the lessee. The lessor appealed against the judge's ruling a on the meaning of 'goods', while the lessee cross-appealed against his interpretation of 'placed' and 'outside the said premises'.

Held – (1) On the true construction of cl II(9) of the lease, 'goods' included motor cars. Such a construction gave affect to the ordinary and natural meaning of that word, which covered a wide range of property or possessions. That width

b was not restricted by the context of cl II(9) as a whole to merchandise or wares or goods offered for sale, or even more narrowly to the goods actually dealt in by the occupant. On the contrary, the word had to be given its wide meaning. Accordingly, the plain and ordinary meaning prevailed. The judge had, however, been correct in his interpretation of 'placed' as covering both vehicles and other things. It followed that the words 'goods ... placed' were capable of extending to

c motor cars parked outside the premises (see [10], [11], [17], [22], below).

(2) The expression 'outside the said premises' in cl II(9) meant outside the boundaries of the demise, not outside the building. 'Premises' was a chameleon-like word that took its meaning from its context. It could bear one meaning at one time and another at another time in the same lease and even in the same

d clause. The task of the court was, therefore, to give the word the meaning that it most naturally bore in its context and as reasonably understood by the commercial men who had entered into the agreement. In the instant case, uncertainty pervaded the meaning of cl II(9), leaving real doubt as to what had been intended. It followed that the expression 'outside the said premises' was ambiguous, and the clause would have to be construed against the grantor.

e Accordingly, the declaration made by the judge would stand, and the lessor's appeal would therefore be dismissed (see [28], [52], [53], below); *Whitley v Stumbles* [1930] AC 544 and *Bracey v Read* [1962] 3 All ER 472 considered.

Notes

f For premises in lease, see 27(1) *Halsbury's Laws* (4th edn reissue) para 103.

Cases referred to in judgment

Bank of Nova Scotia v Hellenic Mutual War Risks (Bermuda) Ltd, The Good Luck [1989] 3 All ER 628, [1990] 1 QB 818, [1990] 2 WLR 547, CA; *rvsd* [1991] 3 All ER 1,

g [1992] 1 AC 233, [1991] 2 WLR 1279, HL.

Bracey v Read [1962] 3 All ER 472, [1963] Ch 88, [1962] 3 WLR 1194.

Lonsdale (Earl) v A-G [1982] 3 All ER 579, [1982] 1 WLR 887.

Stadium Finance Ltd v Robbins [1962] 2 All ER 633, [1962] 2 QB 664, [1962] 3 WLR 453, CA.

h *Whitley v Stumbles* [1930] AC 544, HL.

Cases also cited or referred to in skeleton arguments

Antaios Cia Naviera SA v Salen Rederierna AB, The Antaios [1984] 3 All ER 229, [1985] 1 AC 191, HL.

j *Behnke v Bede Shipping Co Ltd* [1927] 1 KB 649, [1927] All ER Rep 689.

Investers Compensation Scheme Ltd v West Bromwich Building Society, Investors Compensation Scheme Ltd v Hopkin & Sons (a firm), Alford v West Bromwich Building Society, Armitage v West Bromwich Building Society [1998] 1 All ER 98, [1998] 1 WLR 896, HL.

Macey v Qazi (1987) Times, 13 January, CA.

Mannai Investment Co Ltd v Eagle Star Life Assurance Co Ltd [1997] 3 All ER 352,
    [1997] AC 749, HL.
Scott v Martin [1987] 2 All ER 813, [1987] 1 WLR 841, CA.

Appeal and cross-appeal
The appellant, Mount Cook Land Ltd, the lessor of premises on the corner of
Wells Street and Margaret Street, London, W1, appealed with permission of
Judge Rich QC from his order of 17 November 2000 granting the respondent
lessee, Spring House (Freehold) Ltd, a declaration that it and its licensees were
entitled to park vehicles on the demised premises. The lessee cross-appealed
from two rulings made by the judge on the interpretation of cl II(9) of the lease.
The facts are set out in the judgment of the court.

David Hodge QC (instructed by *Hamlins*) for the appellant lessor.
Andrew Walker (insructed by *Finers Stephens Innocent*) for the respondent lessee.

Cur adv vult

12 December 2001. The following judgment of the court, to which both of its
members contributed, was delivered.

WARD and RIX LJJ.
[1] The appeal raises questions of the interpretation of a 999-year lease granted
in 1924 of a property on the corner of Wells Street and Margaret Street in London
W1. The property is, or perhaps at the time was, part of the Howard de Walden
estates in the West End and Lord Howard de Walden in whom the legal estate
was vested on trust for the lessor was as such trustee a party to the indenture.
The lessee at the time was the London Diocesan Fund and their successor in title,
whom we shall continue to call 'the lessee', is the respondent Spring House
(Freehold) Ltd who acquired the lease in 1980. Mount Cook Land Ltd, the
appellant, is the lessor's successor in title and we shall call it 'the lessor' where
convenient.
[2] The hereditaments demised by the lease dated 23 September 1924 were
described in these terms:

> 'All that piece or parcel of ground with the messuage or dwelling house
> and all other erections thereupon built situate and being on the West side of
> and numbered 70 and 71 in Wells Street and on the South side of Margaret
> Street in the Parish of St Marylebone in the County of London and which
> said premises are known as St Andrews National Schools and with the
> dimensions and abuttals thereof are more particularly delineated and
> described in the Plan in the margin hereof together with all yards areas vaults
> ways lights easements watercourses and appurtenances to the said premises
> belonging (except the free passage of water and soil from other premises of
> the Trustee or the Lessor or his or their tenants through the channels and
> drains appertaining to the said premises hereby demised and commonly used
> for that purpose) TO HOLD the said demised premises unto the said Lessees ...'

[3] The plan shows marked in red what was or what had been the school
buildings which are, however, there described as 'business premises'. There are
party walls to the south and to the west and in the south-western corner there is
an 'area' so described coloured grey and pink which presumably was the old

a enclosed schoolyard. On the eastern or the Wells Street boundary there is a strip marked 'area' between the edge of the building and what were probably the railings on the pavement. This is shown to be 36 ft 5 ins long, though upon closer examination of the plan this is actually the length of that side of the building. The strip is 4 ft 1 in wide. Between the western or Margaret Street edge of the building, which is there 43 ft 11 ins long, and the probable railings marking the
b boundary there is another 'area' 5 ft 11 ins wide. These two 'areas' converge at the corner into a quadrilateral shape created by the building itself being indented. The measurements of the building at this point of indent are again precisely given as 9 ft 2 ins x 13 ft 2 ins but no measurements are given for the other two sides of this quadrilateral shape which narrows as it reaches the corner. It would seem that together these two strips and the quadrilateral shape marked a basement area
c below the level of the pavement. Access would have been gained to this basement by steps leading down from Margaret Street near the corner. Steps are also shown on the plan from the street (or more accurately probably the pavement) giving two points of access to the building itself from Wells Street, one over the Wells Street basement area and the other at the corner at the indented
d configuration.

[4] Things have changed since 1924. The old school as such has gone and the building is now an office block and shop. Whether this is a conversion of the old school buildings or whether it is a new building erected at some time between 1924 and about 1955 is not established by the evidence. The photographs suggest that it might be a new building but nothing turns upon that. The important
e change is that the old basement areas have now been completely covered by pavement lights at the same level as the pavement itself. Although railings are still seen to be in place at the adjoining property in Margaret Street, they have been removed from this property and there is no obvious boundary between the property and the pavement. Entrance to the basement areas is now obtained
f through the building itself at basement level and access is no longer available directly from the street. Whereas it would originally have been possible to look over the railings into the basement areas, it is now impossible to see into them through the skylights. The photographs suggest that the main entrance to the building is now from Margaret Street, not at the corner as originally shown. For the purposes of this appeal, the important consequence of these alterations to the
g layout is that it has become possible to park a motor car on these covered areas and the evidence is that for many years the occupiers have parked one or more motor cars on these skylights by driving off the roadway, over the pavement and with care stationing one car on the Wells Street corner, and two over the Margaret Street pavement lights. The lessee and its licensees have continued to
h park motor cars in that way ever since it acquired the lease in 1980.

[5] Relying on cl II(9) of the lease, the lessor's solicitors wrote to the lessee on 6 April 1999 giving formal notice that the lessee was with immediate effect forbidden to place 'any motor vehicles, motor cycles or other goods outside of the premises demised to (it) pursuant to the above mentioned lease'. The lessor
j also gave notice that if the parking continued then action including forfeiture of the lease might be taken. We do not know why this stance was adopted by the lessor, and it does not matter for the purpose of this appeal why it sought to impose the ban. The issue is only whether it is entitled to do so. One does not have to be unduly cynical to observe that parking on one's doorstep is a great advantage and that the cost of parking in the West End of London is very expensive; so the right to park probably has quite a significant value. After service

of a notice under s 146 of the Law of Property Act 1925, the parties sensibly agreed that the lessee would bring proceedings in the Central London County Court for a declaration that it and its licensees are entitled to park vehicles on the demised premises. On 17 November 2000 Judge Rich QC granted that declaration but gave permission to appeal. So the matter comes to us.

[6] The appeal gives rise to three questions of construction of the concluding part of cl II(9). Reading the subclause in full, it provides with emphasis given to the material part:

'That (without such previous written consent as aforesaid) no placard advertisement or announcement of any description shall at any time be exhibited on the outside of the said premises (save and except that there may be exhibited in the windows of the ground floor of the said demised premises any placard advertisement or announcement relating to goods actually dealt in by and in the ordinary course of the business or occupation of the occupant or occupants of the said premises and except that there may be placed on the outside of the said ground floor by means of a suitable fascia board permanently fixed either above the windows and door or on the window sill an inscription showing the name or names or business or occupation or businesses or occupations of the said occupant or occupants) *And that no goods shall at any time be or remain placed outside the said premises which or of any nature which the Lessor shall have forbidden to be or to remain so placed.*'

(The use of a capital 'A' is a faithful transcription of the copperplate manuscript in which the lease is drawn even though it otherwise appears to be part of one sentence.)

[7] Three questions arise in the construction of those italicised words. (i) Are motor vehicles 'goods' within the meaning of that clause? The judge held that they were not. This ruling is the subject of the appeal. (ii) Is it apt to say that a motor car is 'placed' outside the said premises? The judge held that the word is not inappropriate. There is a cross-appeal by the lessee against that part of the decision. (iii) Are the motor cars placed 'outside the said premises'? The judge held that the words meant outside the building even though within the demise. The lessee also challenges this ruling in its respondent's notice.

The meaning of 'no goods shall at any time be or remain placed'

[8] We find it convenient to deal with questions (i) and (ii) together but to start with the meaning of 'placed'.

As for the meaning of 'placed'

[9] Mr Andrew Walker, counsel for the lessee, submits that the word 'placed' is important when reading the covenant as a whole because it throws light on the meaning of 'goods'. He submits that the activity of parking motor cars is not 'placing' goods outside the said premises. He contends that if the parties had intended to include parking cars, they would have selected a different noun (eg 'things' or 'items' or 'goods and chattels') and would also have used a different verb (eg 'put' or 'left').

[10] The judge dealt with this as follows:

'"Placed" is a general word which may be apt to describe vehicles which would be parked. I accept, of course, that if one were using a phrase specifically directed to the parking of vehicles, one would be unlikely to use the word "placed" and "park" would be the apt word. But if one needs a generic word to cover both vehicles and other things, "placing" is as apt a description of leaving them in a position on the ground as any and is the most general word available.'

Conclusions as to the meaning of 'placed'

[11] (1) We agree with the judge. As the *Oxford English Dictionary* observes, 'place' is 'often a mere synonym of *put*' (our emphasis). In ordinary discourse when asking, 'Where shall I park?', the answer may well be, 'Put your car over there'. When Mr Walker submits that placing has a connotation of arranging goods for a purpose, Mr David Hodge QC for the appellant, observes that the task of parking these three cars in the quite tight space available involves exactly that skilful arrangement. (2) In our judgment 'place' is such a colourless, general word that it throws no light on the shades of meaning to be given to 'goods'.

As for the meaning of 'goods'

[12] The judge held:

'There is no doubt at all in my mind that the word "goods" can be used to include a motor vehicle and there can be little doubt that, in certain circumstances, it must necessarily be apt to include a motor vehicle. An example would be where the premises were used for the sale of motor vehicles which is indeed one of the uses which is contemplated as a possibility and therefore specifically prohibited in cl II(8) of this lease. But, the word "goods", in my judgment, is as citations from dictionaries indicate, capable of meaning not only any possessions or personal property, but also more specifically property which is used as merchandise or wares offered for sale. The subclause which I have to construe is in the context of a clause which so far as its first words are concerned, deals with the display of advertisement for business and for goods. The part to which I have already referred deals, amongst other things, with a placard advertisement or announcement relating to goods actually dealt in by the occupant of the premises. It appears to me that in the context of this clause, the use of the word "goods" is intended to be more limited than a word such as "thing" which would have been apt to exclude any item of property by which the lessor might have thought it appropriate to prohibit. I can see the objective in terms of a restriction in the use of the premises, which might embrace the display or accommodation of goods in this more limited sense, falling sensibly within cl II(9). If the clause had been intended to restrict in every way anything that might have a visual impact upon the passer by or might be restrictive of the use of the premises, more generally than is already provided by the long list of prohibitions in cl II(8), I think that it would have been necessary to use more specific words than those that have been chosen by the draftsman of this clause. In case of ambiguity it is accepted that the words must be construed restrictively against the grantor rather than extensively. Goods normally is commonly used with a restricted meaning, albeit that it is capable of a wider and less restricted meaning. In this context, I construe it as having a restricted meaning and vehicles parked on the property as not being goods in the sense used in cl II(9) ...'

[13] Mr Hodge submits that the judge erred in placing undue emphasis on the earlier words of the clause. He failed to give significance to the capital letter in 'And' which hints at a more free-standing provision. If a link was intended it was an easy matter of draftsmanship to make that clear. He submits that the purpose of the clause was to give the landlord a flexibility over the long term of the lease to promote the appearance of the landlord's estate. There was no sufficient ambiguity to justify a resort to a construction against the grantor.

[14] Mr Walker concedes that goods can include cars but, construed in the context of the surrounding text, the implicit limitation is to goods, ie merchandise or wares offered for sale so as to prohibit, as was common in older leases, the activity of putting goods for sale outside the premises. He submits that for a purposive construction to be applied, the purpose must be the purpose of both parties and not just one of them (see *Bank of Nova Scotia v Hellenic Mutual War Risks (Bermuda) Ltd, The Good Luck* [1989] 3 All ER 628, [1990] 1 QB 818).

Conclusions as to the meaning of 'goods'

[15] It is common ground, as the dictionary definition makes clear, that 'goods' can be widely understood to mean 'property or possessions', or more narrowly 'saleable commodities, merchandise, wares' or, as Mr Walker puts it, 'tangible moveable property viewed as an item or items of commerce'. There is clear authority that a motor car was goods for the purposes of the Factors Act 1889 (see *Stadium Finance Ltd v Robbins* [1962] 2 All ER 633, [1962] 2 QB 664). There Ormerod LJ ([1962] 2 All ER 633 at 636, [1962] 2 QB 664 at 670) said: 'The word "goods" in the section does not appear to have anything other than the ordinary meaning ... I cannot see why ... [a motor car] does not come within the definition "goods".' Danckwerts LJ ([1962] 2 All ER 633 at 639, [1962] 2 QB 664 at 676) agreed with that judgment and said: 'In my view, the word "goods" must include all chattels of which physical possession is possible, notwithstanding that they are not easily moveable ...' The case was, of course, one concerned with the meaning of the word in the statute but the reference to the ordinary meaning of the word is at least persuasive even if it is not conclusive.

[16] The issue for us is whether a motor car is excluded from the wide range of property or possessions ordinarily encompassed within the meaning of 'goods'. That task of interpretation has to be carried out against the background knowledge which would reasonably be available to the contracting parties in the situation in which they were at the time of the execution of this lease (see *Earl of Lonsdale v A-G* [1982] 3 All ER 579, [1982] 1 WLR 887). Because the basement areas were open in 1924, parking motor cars was not likely to have been in the immediate contemplation of the parties. Motor cars were, however, familiar on the streets of London in 1924 and the user clause at cl II(8) contains a prohibition against the premises being used for the business of 'Dealer in Motors or Hirer Out or keeper of Motors'. This was a 999-year lease so it must have been within the contemplation of the parties that the premises might be altered perhaps in a way to make a motor business feasible and allow the display of motor cars in the way in which they are presently parked. We do not consider that the physical state of the property at the time of the lease takes the vexed question of interpretation much further.

[17] In our view the crucial question is whether or not the words taken in the whole context of the clause are limited by the preceding words which place a restriction on any placard, advertisement or announcement 'relating to goods actually dealt in by and in the ordinary course of the business or occupation of the

a occupant or occupants of the said premises'. We conclude the words are not so restricted.

[18] First, if it had been intended to qualify 'goods' in the part of the clause under our microscope, then it would have been perfectly simple to say 'no *such* goods' as that would make it plain that the veto was limited to the goods actually dealt in by the occupant. On the contrary the expression is 'no goods', which
b prima facie is unlimited.

[19] Secondly, although we cannot treat the use of the capital letter 'A' as importing a free self-standing provision, none the less the absence of any additional words which clarify 'goods' in the latter part of the clause and the absence of any apparent link between the two parts suggest to us that the limitation for which the lessee contends cannot properly be imputed.
c
[20] Thirdly, the immediate context of the word 'goods' in its two appearances in the clause is different. In its first appearance the context is dealing with a grant of permission to exhibit advertisements in the ground floor windows, and that permission is naturally limited to advertisements about goods actually dealt in by the tenant: otherwise the building might become a hoarding
d for mere advertising. Whereas in its second appearance, the word is found in the context of a restriction on goods themselves which may be physically placed outside the premises: in that context, there is no reason to limit the restriction to goods actually dealt in by the tenant, or to merchandise at all. On the contrary, if anything might be placed outside the premises, it might be thought to be things which were part of the tenant's business stock in trade, rather than things which
e were not.

[21] Fourthly, if one asks what the purpose of the restrictions in cl II(9) might be, the answer would seem to be that the clause as a whole is concerned with the appearance of the exterior of the building. Thus the clause limits what advertisements or notices may be exhibited on the outside of the premises or in the windows and
f what may be placed outside the premises. On that basis it would make no sense to limit the landlord's power to prohibit what the tenant may place outside the premises. Some examples will illustrate the point. It would be odd if the landlord could prevent a tenant from selling his wares outside the premises, but could not prevent him from leaving his office furniture there while he decorated inside. Moreover, if permission were given to a tenant to operate a café in the premises
g (the lease contains a general prohibition on that and other trades in cl II(8)), it would be odd if the tenant could not place food outside the premises, but could place tables, chairs and umbrellas there. Similarly, it would be odd that under cl II(8) the landlord is entitled to prevent a tenant from dealing in or garaging motor cars, but under cl II(9) cannot prevent a tenant parking cars outside the
h premises. Examples of this kind could be multiplied. Such considerations may well be thought to apply a fortiori to the open basement area which in 1924 when the lease was executed existed beneath today's pavement lights. Thus the construction favoured by the judge and supported by Mr Walker leads to uncommercial, unbusinesslike and surprising results.

j [22] We are, therefore, left in the position that the word by its natural and ordinary meaning covers a wide range of property or possessions and we are not satisfied that that width is restricted by the context of the clause as a whole to merchandise or wares or goods offered for sale, as Mr Walker contends, or even more narrowly to the goods actually dealt in by the occupant, which seems to be the judge's interpretation. On the contrary, we are satisfied that the word must be given its wide meaning. Accordingly, the plain and ordinary meaning prevails

and 'goods' includes motor cars. There is no ambiguity and thus no need to resort
to the contra proferentem rule. On this aspect of the case, the appellant's arguments
prevail and the words are therefore capable of extending to motor cars being
parked outside the premises.

The meaning of 'outside the said premises'

[23] The judge accepted that the ordinary meaning of the word 'premises' is
the subject matter of the demise as Mr Walker had submitted. Yet he held that
the habendum drew a 'coherent distinction between "premises" meaning building
and "demised premises" meaning the whole subject matter of the demise'. He
recognised that the words were not used consistently throughout the lease and it
was, therefore, necessary to construe the phrase as it appeared in cl II(9) in its
context. He concluded as follows:

'It is first to be noted that (the earlier) part of the subclause uses
indiscriminately "premises" and "demised premises" in the same way as they
are used in other clauses which it is not necessary for me to recite also. That
part of the clause, however, is directed to the prohibition of advertisement
or the like, visible from outside the premises, whichever premises means in
this context. It uses the phrase "*on* the outside of the said premises" whereas
the phrase in the part of the clause which I have to construe uses the phrase
"outside the said premises". In my judgment, in each case, the reference is
to the area which is outside the building, albeit that the placards and
advertisements for display "*on* the outside of the said premises" would
include, in my judgment, exhibits on the outside railings as they then were,
or on the forecourt as it now is. I construe "outside the said premises" in the
subclause which I have to construe as certainly incorporating the area where
the vehicles are in fact parked as being outside the building.'

[24] There is, as I understand counsels' submissions, no substantial dispute
about the principles to be applied. First, both agree that, to adopt the judgment
of Slade J in the *Earl of Lonsdale*'s case, when construing the relevant words of the
1924 indenture it will be necessary to attempt to do so in the way in which
commercial men would have interpreted them in 1924 when used in relation to
a commercial transaction of this kind.

[25] Secondly, the standard conveyancing meaning of the word 'premises' has
long been established as meaning the subject matter of the habendum of the
lease. We were referred to *Whitley v Stumbles* [1930] AC 544 where Viscount
Hailsham observed (at 546): 'It is, of course, conceded that in strict conveyancing
language the word "premises" is used as meaning the subject-matter of the
habendum in a lease ...' In *Bracey v Read* [1962] 3 All ER 472, [1963] Ch 88 at 92,
Cross J said:

'The word "premises" is not defined in the Act (Landlord and Tenant Act
1954). Its strict legal meaning is the subject-matter of the habendum in a
lease, and it would cover any sort of property of which a lease is granted ...'

[26] Both those cases recognise, however, that 'premises' may have another
meaning. *Whitley v Stumbles* [1930] AC 544 was concerned not with a lease but
with the Landlord and Tenant Act 1927. The question was whether an
incorporeal right of fishing, demised as part of a lease, was part of the 'premises'
for the purpose of the 1927 Act. Viscount Hailsham gave the only reasoned
speech, with which the rest of their Lordships agreed. It was held that

a 'premises' in the vital part of the statute had its strict legal meaning of the subject matter of the habendum of a lease, which would include incorporeal rights. Nevertheless, in reviewing the 1927 Act, Viscount Hailsham accepted (at 546) that in certain sections 'premises' was used in 'a colloquial sense ... as meaning merely the physical buildings and land which are included in the lease'. He said (at 546–547):

b

'My Lords, I think it is fair to say that in some of the earlier sections of the Act it is plain that the Legislature is considering primarily physical premises such as buildings. We find, for instance, in s. 4, sub-s. 1(a), a reference to the possibility of "the premises" being demolished; and we find in s. 5, sub-s. 3(b)(ii.), that the landlord can prove that he intends to pull down or remodel

c
    "the premises," and it was argued on behalf of the appellant that this phrase and other similar instances showed that the Legislature, when it used the word "premises," meant only buildings. That contention proves too much. It is conceded—indeed it must be conceded—that the word "premises" does not mean only buildings; it means also at least the land on which the

d
    buildings are erected and the land immediately surrounding the buildings, and yet the expression "pull down or remodel the premises" would be wholly inept for such a purpose. It was conceded in argument also that it must include some incorporeal hereditaments such as, for instance, easements. When one gets that concession, which I think was quite properly

e
    and necessarily made, then it is manifest that although the word "premises" is being used in a narrow sense to this extent that the Legislature is at times contemplating rather the buildings in which the trade is carried on than the whole of the subject-matter of the lease, yet it does not intend to exclude other things which are properly described as premises in the strict legal sense

f
    when it is appropriate that they should be included.'

[27] In *Bracey v Read*, where the issue was whether the letting of gallops for exercising racehorses was a business tenancy within the Landlord and Tenant Act 1954, Cross J, after referring to the legal meaning which we have cited, went on to qualify that statement by adding:

g

'... but no doubt the word is used sometimes in a popular sense which is considerably more restricted, in the sense of buildings, or buildings with land immediately adjoining them, and I do not think that in the popular sense anybody would call some gallops on a downland, with no buildings on or

h
    near them, "premises". Undoubtedly sometimes in legislation "premises" has been construed in a popular rather than in a legal sense.' (See [1962] 3 All ER 472 at 475–476, [1963] Ch 88 at 92.)

[28] Whilst not referring to *Alice in Wonderland*, both counsel seem to be agreed that in the same lease, indeed in the same clause of the lease, the word
j 'premises' may bear one meaning at one time and another at another time. In our judgment it is clear that 'premises' is a chameleon-like word which takes its meaning from its context. Since it can mean almost anything the task of the court is to give the word the meaning which it most naturally bears in its context and as reasonably understood by the commercial men who entered into the agreement.

Conclusions as to the meaning of the words 'the said premises'

[29] The first step is to examine how the words are used in the lease. Where appropriate we have added the emphasis. Since the habendum is so obviously important, we start there. It begins in standard form with the words: 'All that piece or parcel of ground with the messuage or dwelling house and all other erections thereupon built situate ...' That would include not only the buildings but the land upon which they are actually built and the basement areas, all of which were created by the work of construction and development of the site and form part of the 'erections thereupon built'. Then the habendum continues: '... which *said* premises are known as St Andrews National Schools and with the dimensions and abuttals thereof are more particularly delineated and described in the Plan ...' Because the plan, if one looks at it carefully, seems to concentrate on giving the precise dimensions in feet and inches of the actual building, then one is inclined to think that the premises known as the St Andrews National Schools with the precise measurements given on the plan must be a reference to the school building alone. Moreover the building is described on the plan as 'business *premises'*. If the clause had been introduced by 'which premises' then one would have been more easily able to adopt (and perhaps adapt) the colloquial meaning and say that 'St Andrews National Schools' was the erection on the land which the draftsman had in mind as the premises because it is that building which is particularly delineated in the plan in feet and inches. The problem with that construction is that the words do not begin 'which premises' but 'which *said* premises'. By use of the word 'said' we are referred back to the preceding words and they cover the whole of the demise. The judge considered that a distinction could be drawn between the building and all else because the habendum continued 'together with all yards areas vaults ways lights easements watercourses and appurtenances to the said premises belonging'. There is force in that view. On closer analysis, however, it is far less clear. The areas and vaults could indeed be said to 'belong' to the building, but they also belong to the whole and certainly the easements more naturally belong to the whole of the premises which are the subject of the demise. That seems made clear by the exception of 'the free passage of water and soil from other premises of the Trustee or the Lessor ... through the channels and drains appertaining to the *said premises hereby demised'*. That would suggest that 'the said premises' which are referred to are 'the said premises' which are the subject of the demise. Then the habendum concludes: 'To hold *the said demised premises* unto the said Lessees ...' The result of this analysis is that one finds in the habendum, which in conveyancing practice is the important starting point of the deed, three phrases, 'the said premises', 'the said premises hereby demised' and 'the said demised premises'. In our judgment the natural meaning to be given to the habendum is that the draftsman was intending to refer to the same thing when using the three different expressions and in this context it should be the whole subject of the demise and we cannot agree with the judge that there is at this stage a coherent distinction between the building and the whole subject matter of the demise. It is not a model of clarity, and, being cautious, we should treat this clause as too opaque to throw illuminating light on cl II(9).

[30] It is next necessary to see how these phrases are used throughout the rest of the lease. We begin with the subparagraphs of cl II. In sub-cl (1) the lessee is to pay the rates payable in respect of 'the said demised premises'. Clearly this is a reference to the whole of the premises demised.

[31] Subclause (2) imposes a repairing covenant in respect of 'all present and future buildings *upon* the said premises'. There is a clear and telling distinction drawn between the buildings themselves and 'the said premises' upon which they are or will be erected. In this clause 'the said premises' must refer to the whole of the demise. Then clarity is blurred by the clause going on to require the lessee to paint 'all the outside wood and ironwork and other outside parts usually painted of the same premises'. When one thinks of painting, one usually thinks of painting the building but the reference to 'ironwork' is perfectly capable of referring to the railings which almost certainly marked the boundary of the whole of the demised premises. We are far from convinced that painting 'the said premises' is limited to painting the building alone.

[32] Subclause (3) requires the lessee to yield up to the lessor 'the said premises so painted ... with all additional erections ... upon the said premises ...'. The lessor has to yield up the whole and there is again the reference to the erections *upon* the said premises.

[33] Subclause (4) requires the lessee to indemnify the lessor for party wall works in respect of 'the premises hereby demised'. Although party wall works obviously affect the building alone, there is also reference to drainage and sewerage and the reference to the premises hereby demised suggests that the whole of the demise is thereby affected.

[34] Subclause (5) requires the lessee to contribute to the repair of sewers etc. used in common 'by the occupiers of the said premises' and the occupiers of other premises contiguous thereto. This is again a reference to the whole.

[35] Subclause (6) gives the trustee and lessor the power to enter 'upon the said premises and examine the state thereof' and to leave notice of any defects 'upon the said demised premises'. This may be a little equivocal but since one cannot enter the building without entering the stairs over the basement areas shown outside the building, on balance it seems to refer to the whole.

[36] Subclause (7) may be more significant. It requires the lessee to insure 'all buildings for the time being in the said demised premises'. Here is again a recognition that the buildings are only part of or, in the language of the clause, are 'in' the said demised premises. We note that whereas in sub-cl (2) there had been reference to 'buildings upon the said premises' here is a reference to 'buildings ... in the said *demised* premises'.

[37] Subclause (8) is the user clause restraining the carrying on without permission or the exercise 'in or upon any part of the said premises the trade business or calling' then listed. If 'the said premises' was confined to the building itself, then the clause would not bite on the sub-basement areas or the covered areas which have replaced them. That seems an unlikely intention to impute to the parties. For the moment we pass over sub-cl (9).

[38] Subclause (10) is more equivocal. It provides that without the lessor's consent—

> 'no building or erection shall at any time be built or placed on the said *demised* premises and no addition or alteration affecting the elevation external structure or stability of the said premises or any parts thereof shall at any time be made to any building or erection for the time being on the said demised premises and that no machinery shall at any time be erected or affixed to the said demised premises ...'

As in sub-cl (7) there is reference to buildings being placed on the said *demised* premises. So the distinction is again drawn between the building and the whole

of the demised premises upon which it is erected. Then the clause continues that
'no addition or alteration affecting the elevation external structure or stability of
the said premises' shall be made 'to any building on the said demised premises'.
Although 'elevation' of 'the said premises' more naturally refers to the building
elevations, 'stability of the said premises' could be a reference to the stability of
the whole including the walls down from the pavement to the basement. What
must not be affected is 'the said premises' that is to say the whole of the demise
and the manner in which it is not to be affected is by alterations made to any
building on (and now making assurance double sure) 'the said demised premises'
ie again the whole. One makes of this what one will.

[39] The judge referred expressly to sub-cl (11) which provided that without
consent 'the ground floor of the said premises shall not at any time be divided into
or used as more than three shops warehouses or offices' with specified
dimensions 'but this restriction is not to prevent the use of a separate door and
passage leading to those portions of the said demised premises other than the
front of the ground floor thereof'. As the premises then stood the only part which
constituted the ground floor of the said premises was the ground floor of the
building so that there the said premises must refer to the building itself. The
proviso allows a separate door to portions of the 'said demised premises other
than the front of the ground floor *thereof*', in other words the ground floor of the
demised premises. That would suggest that the ground floor of the building is
being treated as the ground floor of the whole. This subclause shows, as well as
any, the inconsistent drafting.

[40] Subclause (12) prevents anything done upon or in connection 'with the
said demised premises' which would be an annoyance or nuisance, whereas
when it comes to waste, sub-cl (13) prohibits that being done 'upon the said
premises'. The draftsman can hardly have intended nuisance to extend to the
whole of the demise but waste only to the buildings.

[41] Subclause (14) allows the landlord to erect buildings adjoining or near to
'the said demised premises' and sub-cl (15) deals with the assignment of 'the
demised premises'.

[42] The re-entry clause in cl III gives the right to re-enter upon 'the said
premises' and the covenant for quiet enjoyment in cl IV is again for the
enjoyment of 'the said premises'. There 'said premises' must refer to the whole
of the subject matter of the demise.

[43] The result of this trawl through the lease suggests to us that, with one or
two exceptions where there is some equivocal or ambiguous drafting, the
overwhelming preponderance of reference in this lease to 'the said premises' is a
reference to the whole of the demise.

[44] At last we turn the microscope on cl II(9). It seems to be in two parts, the
second being the final clause beginning 'And' with a capital 'A'.

[45] The first part seems clearly to be concerned with the external appearance
of the property. It prohibits the exhibition of any placard, advertisement or
announcement 'on the outside of the said premises'. 'On the outside of the said
premises' does more naturally refer to the exterior of the building itself because
it would be on the walls that the advertisement would be painted or pasted or
fixed. The landlord contends that this meaning should be given to 'the said
premises' throughout the subclause. It is, therefore, necessary to test whether
that natural meaning in this early part of the clause is the intended meaning. It
does produce anomalies. If, as seems to be common ground, at least this first part
of sub-cl (9) is concerned with the external appearance of the property (using a

a
neutral word) then that purpose is defeated by narrowly confining 'the said premises' to the building itself. If it is so confined, there is nothing to stop the tenant hanging his advertisements on the outside of the railings to the property. He could erect structures in the basement area on which to place his placards. The parties can hardly have intended that. It suggests that the words must have a wider meaning than a reference to the building only. There is, however,

b
another anomaly. If the words 'on the outside of the said premises' are to be literally construed to refer only to the outside perimeter of the demised premises so that 'the said premises' refers only to the whole demise, then again the subclause would not work. It seems to us that a purposive construction would be that no placard, advertisement or announcement should be placed on any external part of the premises.

c
[46] That prohibition is subject to exceptions. The first is to permit the placard, advertisement or announcement to be exhibited 'in the windows of the ground floor of the said *demised* premises' (note, not simply 'the said premises'), provided it related to the goods actually dealt in by and in the ordinary course of the business or occupation of the occupant or occupants 'of the said premises'.

d
One has to read that to mean that the placard may be exhibited in the windows of the ground floor of the building on the demised premises and that it should relate to the goods which the occupant deals with in the ordinary course of his business or occupation of not just part of the demised premises, the building alone, but of the whole of it including the basement area. The phrases 'the said demised premises' and 'the said premises' are here used interchangeably. The

e
second exception is to permit to be placed 'on the outside of the said ground floor by means of a suitable fascia board permanently fixed either above the windows and door or on the window sill an inscription showing the name or names or business or occupation or businesses or occupations of the said occupant or occupants'. The place at which this inscription is to be fixed makes it clear that

f
the draftsman had the building itself in mind. On the other hand, 'the *said* ground floor' is a reference back to the 'ground floor of the said *demised* premises'. And so once again should be read to mean the ground floor of the building on the demised premises.

g
[47] The analysis so far leads us to conclude that there is no consistent or coherent meaning being given to these interchangeable phrases which are being used without any apparent discrimination. It follows that 'the said premises' cannot with certainty be taken to refer to the building. There is much to suggest it is not so confined.

h
[48] So we come finally to the concluding and material part of sub-cl (9). Mr Walker submits that this part of the clause has merely been tacked onto the clause as a whole and is concerned with the different subject matter of preventing street trading in the public thoroughfare rather than with what goes on within the boundary of the demise itself. There is some force perhaps in the thought that the phrase beginning 'And that no goods' may not in its origin have been an integral part of cl II(9) and the use of the capital letter 'A' may suggest that the

j
draftsman was turning to a different subject matter regulating the use of the premises. We are not persuaded that we can treat this as a free-standing subclause standing apart from what precedes it. That is not how it is drafted. Even if it were completely separate, it would still have to be read in the context of the whole.

[49] Taking the words as they stand, they give the lessor power to forbid goods being or remaining in place 'outside the said premises' and there is no hint in the language whether the draftsman was intending to refer to the building or

to the whole of the premises which form the subject of the demise. It seems to us impossible to find the answer from the language itself. *a*

[50] Even if a colloquial meaning is to be given then, as Viscount Hailsham accepted as rightly conceded in *Whitley v Stumbles* [1930] AC 544, the word does not mean only the buildings but the land immediately surrounding the buildings. Given the integrated construction of the building above ground and below ground level, can one confidently say the basement is not part of the building? *b* Would goods on the roof be placed outside the premises?

[51] We have to see whether there was some clear purpose and whether or not one meaning or the other has to yield to business common sense. The lessor's overall case is that throughout the whole of sub-cl (9) the phrase is primarily concerned with anything which may affect the appearance of the exterior of the premises. That does make sense though it can equally be said that *c* his estate may be somewhat blighted if unacceptable goods or piles of rotting rubbish were left on the pavement outside his premises. The lessee's overall case is that this covenant was intended to prohibit the conduct of business outside the property by trading on the pavement. The lessee also submits that the lessor would wish to prevent activity like the regular dumping of unsightly refuse on *d* the pavement which could harm the value of the property. There is some force in each of these contentions. There are perhaps greater difficulties in the lessee's way. Applying his construction to the particular problem that has arisen in this case, it would mean that the lessor could not object to the motor cars being parked on the pavement lights but could seek to ban motor cars being parked in the roadway outside (assuming for the purpose of this argument that the *e* occupants could lawfully park outside). That does seem odd. In the area of the pavement and roadway the lessee is neither the lessee nor the lessor the lessor. Within the area of the demise the relationship of landlord and tenant exists and the lessor may wish to exercise control whereas beyond that area public rights and obligations would seem to take precedence. Had the matter rested there we *f* might have been inclined to accept the lessor's case. However, Mr Hodge could not challenge Mr Walker's submission that it was sometimes a recognised practice in old leases of this kind for the lessor to seek to control what the lessee was doing even outside the boundaries of the demised premises and to control what the lessee was placing in the public highway. If that could have been the purpose, then we cannot confidently assert that it was not the purpose. One has *g* to be sure that it is the purpose of both parties and not just one before one can safely embark on a purposive construction.

[52] If that tool of construction is too blunt, where do we find the meaning of this phrase? In the context of the lease as a whole the words tend almost invariably to mean the whole of the demised premises. In the context of the *h* preceding parts of sub-cl (9) their natural reference to the building is displaced by the lack of consistency and there is much uncertainty as to that meaning. We are driven reluctantly to conclude that the uncertainty pervades the meaning of the clause we have to construe. We are left in real doubt as to what was intended. It follows that the expression is ambiguous and, very much as the last resort, we are *j* driven to construe the clause against the grantor. 'Outside the said premises' means outside the boundaries of the premises the subject of the demise.

The result of the appeal and cross-appeal

[53] Although the appellant was successful in persuading us that the judge attributed the wrong meaning to the word 'goods', the respondent by his

a cross-appeal has also persuaded us that the judge was wrong in his interpretation of 'outside the said premises'. In the result the declaration stands and the appeal must, therefore, be dismissed. We confess that we do not find that result unsatisfactory. This was a 999-year lease which one would hope would leave the lessee as nearly free as a freeholder could be. Cars have been parked here for years without objection and whilst that does not prevent the lessor exercising his

b right, if he has one, there is a sense of opportunism about the lessor's case and it may be thought unfortunate were the lessee to have to pay a considerable annual licence fee for a fortuitous benefit that arose from an alteration of the premises to which the lessor gave approval many years ago.

Appeal dismissed. Permission to appeal refused.

Kate O'Hanlon   Barrister.

Factortame Ltd and others v Secretary of State for the Environment, Transport and the Regions

[2002] EWCA Civ 22

COURT OF APPEAL, CIVIL DIVISION

SIMON BROWN, WALLER AND SEDLEY LJJ

14 DECEMBER 2001, 28 JANUARY 2002

Costs – Payment into court – Costs after payment in – Defendant making payment in – Claimants failing to accept payment in within time limit – Defendant making amendment to case at trial on basis of information in his possession at date of payment in – Claimants accepting payment in immediately after amendment – Whether claimant to be treated as successful party when making late acceptance of payment in following amendment to defendant's case – CPR Pt 36.

Following a decision that the government was liable to compensate the claimants, the assessment of damages was put in the hands of the Technology and Construction Court. In that court, certain claimants became fast-track claimants, and some of those became known as the EC claimants. On 17 December 1999 payments in were made under CPR Pt 36. Those payments were substantially less than the sums claimed. The EC claimants failed to accept the offer within the 21-day time limit prescribed by Pt 36. Before the date of the Pt 36 payments, the government had material in its control from which it was possible to make calculations that would have reduced the damages recoverable by the EC claimants in respect of certain claims (the period 2 claims). However, the research on the material was not carried out until after 17 December 1999. The relevant figures were available by 28 February 2000, but due to a mistake on the government's part the figures were not handed over to the EC claimants until 5 April 2000, a month after the start of the trial. On 13 April, the judge ruled that those figures were admissible in evidence, and on 17 April, at the very end of the trial, the government permitted the EC claimants to accept the Pt 36 offer, subject to the court ruling on costs. On that issue, the EC claimants contended that a material change in the government's case, brought about by a mistake on its part, should entitle them to reassess the Pt 36 payment, and allow them to take the payment out with an order for costs right up to the date of ultimate acceptance. In response, the government contended that the delay in providing the figures had made no difference to the way in which the EC claimants had conducted the case, and that the change in the government's case had simply provided an excuse to take the money out having regard to the way in which the case had gone at trial. The judge held that, in view of the complexities of the litigation, 21 days was insufficient time in which to assess the Pt 36 payment; that instead 7 February 2000 was the date on which the fast-track claimants should have accepted the offer; that it was impossible for him to determine what had influenced the EC claimants to settle the period 2 claims; that the EC claimants would nevertheless be allowed their costs of those claims until 14 February to take account of the chance that the government's calculations might have affected their decision as regards the offer; but that thereafter they were liable for the government's costs in relation to those issues. The EC claimants appealed, *a*   contending that, as a matter of principle, they were to be regarded as the successful party.

Held – Where (i) a defendant made a payment under CPR Pt 36 which the claimant did not accept, (ii) the defendant then made a significant amendment to his case on the basis of information which had always been available to him, and
b   (iii) the claimant then promptly accepted the Pt 36 payment, there was no principle or rule that the claimant should be taken to be the successful party. Rather, each case would turn on its own circumstances, although it was the prima facie rule that a failure to beat a payment in resulted in the claimant being treated as the unsuccessful party as from the date when the payment should have been accepted. So far as possible, the judge should try to assess who in reality was the
c   unsuccessful party and who had been responsible for the fact that costs had been incurred which should not have been. A full-scale trial examining privileged material and listening to ex post facto justification should be avoided. Nor was it right to lay down rules as to where the onus would lie where a defendant was allowed to amend his case. An amendment might be of such a character that a
d   judge would feel that the defendant should have the onus of persuading him that he should continue to apply the prima facie rule. On the other hand, the judge might be quite clear, by reference to his feel of the case, that the amendment was being used as an excuse to take money out of court that should have been accepted when originally made. Some cases would lie between the two extremes, and the judge would have to adjust his assessment to give effect to possibilities
e   which it would be inappropriate to try out and thus by reference to his overall view of the case. In the instant case, the judge had not erred in principle or misdirected himself. He had clearly taken the view that it was doubtful whether the amendments to the figures which he had allowed in April would, if produced in December, have led the EC claimants to accept the payment in, but since he
f   could not be absolutely sure of that, it had been fair to allow the further week. That was an exercise of his discretion with which the Court of Appeal should not even contemplate interfering. Accordingly, the appeal would be dismissed (see [1], [27]–[31], below).

Ford v GKR Construction Ltd [2000] 1 All ER 802 considered.

g   **Notes**

For payments into court generally and the costs consequences where a claimant fails to do better than a Pt 36 payment, see 37 *Halsbury's Laws* (4th edn reissue) paras 807, 825.

h   **Cases referred to in judgments**

Alltrans Express Ltd v CVA Holdings Ltd [1984] 1 All ER 685, [1984] 1 WLR 394, CA.
Findlay v Railway Executive [1950] 2 All ER 969, CA.
Ford v GKR Construction Ltd [2000] 1 All ER 802, [2000] 1 WLR 1397, CA.
Johnsey Estates (1990) Ltd v Secretary of State for the Environment, Transport and the
j   *Regions* [2001] EWCA Civ 535, [2001] L & TR 443.
Jones v Jones [1999] CA Transcript 1701.

Appeal

The claimants (the EC claimants) appealed from that part of the order of Judge Toulmin QC, made in the Technology and Construction Court on 27 July 2000, requiring them to pay, in respect of certain issues in their claims, the costs of the

defendant, the Secretary of State for the Environment, Transport and the
Regions, for the period from 15 February 2000 until 17 April 2000 when they *a*
accepted payments under CPR Pt 36 made on 17 December 1999. The facts are
set out in the judgment of Simon Brown LJ.

Nicholas Strauss QC and *Jonathan Middleburgh* (instructed by *Edwin Coe*) for the EC
  claimants.   *b*
David Friedman QC and *Rachel Ansell* (instructed by the *Treasury Solicitor*) for the
  Secretary of State.

Cur adv vult

28 January 2002. The following judgments were delivered.   *c*

WALLER LJ (giving the first judgment at the invitation of Simon Brown LJ).

Introduction

[1] This is an appeal by certain claimants (the EC claimants) from part of the *d*
order of Judge Toulmin QC dated 27 July 2000 in relation to costs. It is said to
raise a point of principle in relation to the approach of the court to CPR Pt 36
offers. Mr Strauss QC for the EC claimants would suggest that the point of
principle can be expressed in this way:

'Where (a) a defendant makes a Pt 36 payment which the claimant does *e*
not accept, (b) the defendant then makes a significant amendment to his case
on the basis of information which had always been available to him, and
(c) the claimant then promptly accepts the Pt 36 payment which he has
previously refused, in general the answer should be that the claimant is the
successful party.'
                                                                                f
He would suggest that the judge failed to have regard to that principle.
Mr Friedman QC on the other hand would suggest that although it must be a
relevant consideration that a party has amended his case just prior to the
acceptance of a Pt 36 offer, it is for the judge to assess the extent to which that
amendment should dislodge the prima facie position that a person who has failed
to beat the payment in should pay the costs from the date on which the payment *g*
in should have been accepted.

Background

[2] The judge in his judgment set out the full history of what has been termed
the 'Factortame litigation'. Following a decision in the course of that litigation *h*
that the government (the defendants) was liable to compensate the claimants, the
assessment of the damages was put in the hands of the Technology and
Construction Court. In that court certain claimants became fast-track claimants
and others slow-track claimants. Some fast-track claimants were represented by
Thomas Cooper & Stibbard and some by Edwin Coe and as a result became   *j*
known generically as the TCS and EC claimants. All the fast-track claimants
ultimately accepted, or were permitted by the defendants to accept, Pt 36 offers
made by reference to different issues, but they accepted them at different stages
of the litigation. There was no agreement as to the costs implications if
permission was given to accept the offers. That was left to the court. The judge
in his judgment of 27 July 2000 was thus concerned to deal with orders for costs

a in relation to various issues in the context of various Pt 36 offers accepted at various stages of the litigation with the consent of the defendants all outside the 21-day time limit given by Pt 36. The only point live on this appeal relates to the judge's order for costs on one issue—the assessment of damages for what was called period 2. It concerns the EC claimants only. They were permitted by the defendants (subject to the court ruling on costs) to accept on 17 April 2000 a Pt 36

b payment made on 17 December 1999. April 17 2000 was at the very end of the trial. It was also only a day or so after the judge had ruled certain evidence admissible which evidence might have reduced the damages recoverable by the EC claimants for period 2. It was (I should stress) accepted by the defendants that the figures that they were seeking to place in evidence had, through an error on their part, not been supplied to the EC claimants as early as they should have

c been. The figures were calculated from material within the control of the defendants. They thus could have been available even before the dates of the payment in. The defendants carried out the research on the material within their possession only at a stage after 17 December 1999. They actually had the relevant figures by 28 February 2000 which they intended the EC claimants to have at that

d stage. By a mistake for which they were entirely responsible, the figures were not handed over until 5 April 2000.

[3] It will be seen immediately how the battle lines would be likely to be drawn. The EC claimants submitted that a material change in the case of the defendants brought about by a mistake on their part, should entitle them to reassess a Pt 36 payment, and allow them to take the payment out with an order

e for costs right up to the date of the ultimate acceptance. The defendants' submission on the other hand was that it was not the material change in the defendants' case which had made all the difference; that simply provided an excuse to take the money out having regard to the way in which the case had gone at the trial, now nearly completed. Thus the submission was that the EC

f claimants should accept the normal consequences of failing to beat the payment in and pay costs since the date when the payment in should have been accepted.

[4] The judge's ruling I will set out. But to understand it fully I must explain that so far as the TCS claimants were concerned, they had been permitted to accept Pt 36 payments before any amendment in the defendants' case. Their argument had simply been that it would be unfair to take the view that in

g complex litigation such as this 21 days from the date of payment in was a sufficient period in which to consider the offers from the defendants. This argument was also supported as an alternative to their main argument by the EC claimants. On that point the judge had ruled that there was merit in the claimants' point and found that 7 February 2000 was the date on which the payments in

h should have been accepted. On the point relating to the effect of the amendment he ruled as follows:

'The EC claimants have a separate argument on costs. They say that the information on revised catch data mitigating income, which they only

j received on 5 April 2000 (but which they should have received on 28 February 2000) changed fundamentally the nature of the claim, in that it had the effect of reducing significantly the sums which the EC claimants were entitled to receive for period 2 losses. They say that the government should pay all their costs in relation to these issues. They say, as I have already set out, that the fact that this information was decisive in their decision to accept the Pt 36 payments is to be inferred from the fact that they

sought a ruling from me on the admissibility of the evidence on day 22 of the
trial, and that they accepted the payments a few days after I had ruled that *a*
the evidence was admissible. The government says that if one considers the
report of the Edwin Coe fisheries expert, Mr Cox, in November 1999 and his
evidence at trial, it is reasonable to infer that the delay in providing the data
made no difference to the EC claimants' conduct of the case and
consideration of the part 2 offers, since catch data as mitigating income was *b*
only used by Mr Dyson [the claimants' accountancy expert] as a
reasonableness check and not for the purpose of substantive calculations. I
have no means of resolving this conflict. The EC claimants have, as is their
right, chosen not to waive privilege. There is no reason to suggest that they
should have done so. My ruling was given on day 22 of the trial, after much
evidence had been given. I am unable, on the evidence before me, to say or *c*
to infer what influenced the EC claimants to settle their remaining period 2
claims. The furthest I can go on the evidence is to take some account of the
chance that the additional data may have had an effect in relation to the
period 2 claims in influencing the decision of the EC claimants. This can best
be done by extending the period for which the government must pay the *d*
costs in relation to these issues. In relation to these period 2 claims, the EC
claimants are to be entitled to their costs to 14 February 2000. Thereafter
they must pay the government's costs in relation to these issues.'

[5] Complaint is made about the shortage of reasons in the above ruling. But
certain points should be made about that criticism at the outset. First, the judge *e*
had set out the guiding principles applicable at an earlier stage in his judgment
and the real question is whether any complaint can be made about those. Second,
the judge had set out in considerable detail the history of the Factortame
litigation including the history of the assessment of damages aspect. He of course
did so in the context of ruling on various different points, but in his recitation of *f*
the history he pointed up certain factors showing that he was seeking to address
the question as to the extent to which the amendment had provided an excuse to
accept a payment in that should in fact have been accepted earlier. Third,
although the focus of attention of the submissions of the EC claimants, and the
defendants, and thus the judge was on the reasons why the EC claimants
ultimately wished to accept the payments in after the amendments to the *g*
defendants' case, that question is in reality the other side of an equally important
question which is, whether the EC claimants should in fact have accepted the
payment in within the 21-day limit extended by the judge to 7 February 2000, a
question into which the judge in a case where the trial is nearly complete would
have a considerable insight. If the position at the end of the trial was that even *h*
without the new figures the judge felt that it was unlikely that an award would
exceed the payment in, then his conclusion could be that the amendments were
truly being used as an excuse to take money that should have been accepted
much earlier. In that context however he might also feel that if the amended
figures had been available at the time when the original payment in had to be *j*
considered, since those figures might arguably have influenced a decision, some
compensation in costs should be awarded for that factor. This is of course the
exercise that the defendants say the judge can be seen to have done. They say by
ordering the defendants to pay one further week of costs one can see that the
judge had concluded that it was unlikely that the EC claimants would have
beaten the payment in even in the absence of the amendment, but that some

a small adjustment should be made for the lost chance of considering as at 7 February 2000 the defendants' case as it became on 13 April 2000 after his ruling.

Approach of appellate court

[6] Costs are matters within the discretion of the judge. Thus it is that an appellate court should certainly not interfere with the exercise of the discretion

b of the judge merely because it takes the view that it might have exercised that discretion differently. As Chadwick LJ put it in *Johnsey Estates (1990) Ltd v Secretary of State for the Environment, Transport and the Regions* [2001] EWCA Civ 535 at [22], [2001] L & TR 443:

c
'[That] last [principle] requires an appellate court to exercise a degree of self-restraint. It must recognise the advantage which the trial judge enjoys as a result of his "feel" for the case which he has tried. Indeed, as it seems to me, it is not for an appellate court even to consider whether it would have exercised the discretion differently unless it has first reached the conclusion that the judge's exercise of his discretion is flawed. That is to say, that he has erred in principle, taken into account matters which should have been left

d
out of account, left out account matters which should have been taken into account; or reached a conclusion which is so plainly wrong that it can be described as perverse—see *Alltrans Express Ltd v. CVA Holdings Ltd* ([1984] 1 All ER 685 at 690, 692–693, [1984] 1 WLR 394 at 400, 403), *per* Stephenson L.J. and ... Griffiths L.J. ...'

e
[7] In this case the judge had been in charge of interlocutories for a considerable period and had tried the case for 23 days. The trial was almost at an end. No appellate court could conceivably have the same feel for the case that the judge did. The extent of his feel is such that even if I could be persuaded that in some way he misdirected himself or applied a wrong test, it would on any view

f be necessary to send the case back to him to make a reassessment by reference to the right test. This court simply could not be asked to steep itself in the detail to the extent that would be necessary if it was to exercise a discretion afresh.

[8] Two things follow from the above. First, an outline of the history of the litigation is all that is necessary for this court to trace. Second, if the EC claimants are to succeed they must identify a principle to which the judge has not adhered,

g or identify a misdirection, or demonstrate that he was so plainly wrong that his decision can be described as perverse. Mr Strauss has not sought to do other than identify a principle to which he says that the judge did not adhere. He has not suggested that if the judge correctly directed himself then his decision was perverse.

h
The outline

[9] In 1988 by certain regulations the government of the United Kingdom sought to enforce the provisions of the Merchant Shipping Act 1988. The proceedings brought by the claimants alleged incompatibility of the 1988 Act

j and/or the regulations with the Treaty of Rome. It further led to litigation in relation to the question whether interim relief should be granted against the government preventing enforcement of the 1988 Act pending resolution of the question whether that Act was incompatible. The litigation ultimately resulted in the government being found to be in breach of its Community obligations and ultimately led to a finding that the government was bound to compensate the claimants in damages. The claimants claimed loss of profits for two periods.

Period 1 related to the losses between the date when the 1988 Act took effect and
the date when particular vessels resumed fishing, and period 2 losses related to
the period after vessels resumed fishing. The essence of the claim in relation to
period 2 as briefly described to us by Mr Strauss was as follows. The assertion
was that fewer fish were caught on resumption than would have been caught if
vessels had not been kept out of the relevant waters during period 1. One issue
in relation to period 2 was the extent to which the claimants should give credit
for fish that they had caught during period 2. The claimants' case at the outset
was in any event that such fish as were caught during period 2 would have been
caught anyway and thus no credit should be given. The government case was
that allowance should be made for what was described as 'mitigation' by
reference to fish caught during that period.

[10] On 14 May 1999 points of claim setting out the damages claimed for loss
of hake, monk and megrim in period 2 were delivered. A defence was served on
16 July 1999 and further and better particulars of points of claim were delivered
on 23 September 1999.

[11] During September the defendants' experts provided to Mr Dyson, the
claimants' accountancy expert, catch landings data of other species of fish
asserted by the government to have been caught during period 2 and asserted by
the government to be catch which should be taken into account in mitigation
when assessing damages.

[12] In Mr Dyson's reports dated 12 November 1999 the catch data relating to
other species was used to do a 'reasonableness check' ie to check whether having
regard to the total actual and alleged lost volume of fish caught post the 1988 Act,
as compared to the total volume caught pre that Act, credit should be given for
the catch of other species. The conclusion at that stage was that except in the case
of one claimant no credit was appropriate and Mr Dyson and Mr Cox were at one
in taking the view 'that no deduction should be made for any mitigating turnover
... In my view these catches would have been made in any event'.

[13] It was in November 1999 that the defendants' expert discovered that their
records relating to the above catch data might be unreliable. They were however
performing other tasks and did not thus at that stage make any relevant
assessment.

[14] On 17 December 1999 Pt 36 payments were made. Time for acceptance
under Pt 36 would have been 21 days ie 7 January 2000.

[15] On 31 January 2000 the defendants in their expert reports were still using
their previous figures so far as mitigating catch was concerned. In early February
2000 the defendants' experts started to check the figures relating to the catch of
other species. That work was completed by mid-February and it was the
intention of the Treasury Solicitor to provide the EC claimants with the new
figures on 28 February 2000. By an unfortunate error this was not done until
5 April 2000.

[16] The claim being made by the EC claimants for the period 2 losses varied
from £1m to £1·5m, the monetary value of the increase in catch demonstrated by
the new figures varied between £80,500 and £230,000. The payments into court
had varied between £139,010 and £379,220.

[17] On 13 April 2000 after considerable argument the judge ruled that the
new figures of the defendants could be adduced in evidence. On 17 April 2000 the
EC claimants notified the Treasury Solicitor that they wished to accept the Pt 36
payments and it was later agreed that this would be done without prejudice to the
costs issue.

a

[18] As the judge noted:

'The Pt 36 payments ... were very substantially less than the sums claimed originally by the applicants. Apart from one settlement at just over 50% of the sum originally claimed, the other sums which were eventually accepted were a substantially lesser proportion of the sums claimed by the applicants.'

b (The reference to the 50% figure does not relate to any of the Pt 36 offers with which this appeal is concerned.)

[19] It is right just to add to the above that on 11 February 2000 ie prior to receipt of the new figures, Mr Cox, the expert for the EC claimants, had expressed the following view in relation to mitigating catch:

c

'I would agree entirely with Mr Porter that were one able to quantify reliably the amount of additional quantities of non-quota species caught by the applicants' vessels then credit may have to be given. However the answer to Mr Porter's proposition is that I do not see how one can establish what additional quantities if any were caught. There is no legal requirement to record non-quota species in EU log books during the base period ...'

d

That would seem to indicate a slight change of view as to whether the mitigating catch should be taken into account or not.

[20] The trial started on 6 March 2000 and thus had been running for a month before the revised data were sought to be introduced on 5 April 2000. The trial

e ultimately ran for 23 days.

The law relating to costs

[21] The judge directed himself in the following way so far as relevant to the Pt 36 payments with which this appeal is concerned:

f

'The overriding objective in CPR Pt 1 is that the court should deal with cases justly, including a requirement that as far as is practicable the court should ensure that the parties are on an equal footing. The detailed rules are contained in CPR Pt 44 (costs) and Pt 36 (payments into court) and can be summarised as follows. (1) The court has an overall discretion as to whether costs are payable by one party to another, and if payable the amount of those

g costs and when they are to be paid (see r 44.3(1)(a)(b) and (c)). (2) If the court decides to make an order, the general rule is that the unsuccessful party will be ordered to pay the costs of the successful party, but the court may make a different order (see r 44.3(2)(a) and (b)). (3) It is to be inferred from r 36.20 and the case of *Findlay v Railway Executive* [1950] 2 All ER 969 that a

h party which accepts a Pt 36 payment after the expiry of time for accepting such a payment becomes from that date the unsuccessful party when considering the principle in (2) above. (4) In deciding what order to make, the court must have regard to all the circumstances, including (a) the conduct of the parties, (b) whether a party has succeeded on part of his case, even if he has not been wholly successful, and (c) any payment into court or

j admissible offer to settle made by a party (whether or not made in accordance with Pt 36) (see r 44.3(4)). (5) The conduct of the parties includes all conduct, both before and during the proceedings (see r 44.3(5)) ... (7) A Pt 36 offer or payment requires the permission of the court if it is an offer to settle part of the claim or has been accepted more than 21 days after the offer of payment is made, unless the parties have agreed costs. In such cases, the liability for costs shall also be decided by the court (see rr 36.11(3) and 36.15) ... (8) Although it is expressed only to apply at trial, r 36.20 provides guidance where a party accepts a Pt 36 offer or payment after the 21 days. It provides that where at trial a claimant (a) fails to better a Pt 36 payment or (b) fails to obtain a judgment which is more advantageous than a defendant's Pt 36 offer, unless it considers it unjust to do so, the court will order the claimant to pay any costs incurred by the defendant after the latest date on which the payment or offer could have been accepted without needing the permission of the court. In reaching a conclusion on this issue, the court must take into account the consideration set out in r 36.21(5) ... Although a party which fails to accept a Pt 36 payment until after the expiry of time for accepting such a payment is deemed to be the unsuccessful party, this is only a starting point. The court must take into account all the circumstances in which the payment is made, and in particular the circumstances in r 36.21(5) in deciding whether it would be unjust to award the defendant its costs from that date, ie (a) the terms of any Pt 36 offer, (b) the stage at which such Pt 36 payment was made, (c) the information available to the parties at the time when the Pt 36 offer or payment was made, (d) the conduct of the parties with regard to the giving or refusing of information for the purposes of enabling the Pt 36 payment to be evaluated. Although it was decided under the old Rules of the Supreme Court, in *Ford v GKR Construction Ltd* [2000] 1 All ER 802 at 810, [2000] 1 WLR 1397 at 1403, Lord Woolf MR commented in relation to both the old and the new rules that the court has power to make orders other than that costs follow the event where a party fails at the end of the trial to recover a sum larger than the payment into court. He emphasised that the general rule should not apply where it was unjust that it should do so:

> "If a party has not enabled another party to properly assess whether or not to make an offer, or whether or not to accept an offer which is made, because of non-disclosure to the other party of material matters, or if a party comes to a decision which is different from that which would have been reached if there had been proper disclosure, that is a material matter for a court to take into account in considering what orders it should make."

I do not understand Lord Woolf MR to be signalling a change in the law which permits a party to seek to interrogate another party as to its thinking behind the Pt 36 payment; but rather he was emphasising that if the other party was at an unfair disadvantage, because the party had failed to disclose documents or information that it was required to disclose, that was a material matter that the court should take into account. In *Jones v Jones* [1999] CA Transcript 1701, Chadwick LJ made a similar point:

> "The court may also take into account the circumstances which have given rise to a change of mind (whether or not to accept the payment into court). In particular, if the court was satisfied that the change of mind arising from a reassessment of the risk in the light of new material was attributable to the defendant's failure to produce that material at an earlier date (or now in contravention of some protocol), it might take the view that the plaintiff should not be required to bear all or some part of the intervening costs. If the defendant has failed to do what the rules

a   or an order of the court require within the time prescribed, then the price of obtaining the permission of the court to do later what he should have done earlier may be that the plaintiff should have the chance to take the money out of court without penalty. The reason is that the costs which have been thrown away were not incurred by reason of a misreading of the position by the plaintiff on the basis of material which
b   was or should have been available but by reason of the absence of available material which he should have had if the defendant had complied with his obligations."

These two extracts emphasise that in considering whether or not it would be unjust to penalise a party for the late acceptance of a Pt 36 offer, I should take
c   into account any failure by the respondents to provide documents and information which they should have provided under the rules or which was material to the claimant's consideration of the Pt 36 offer. This is a separate issue to the question of whether the government could properly refuse to clarify its Pt 36 offers when it was asked to do so ...'

d
Was the judge right in the way he directed himself?

[22] I can find no fault with the way in which the judge directed himself in relation to Pt 36. One must remember that straightjackets are inapposite for the approach that a judge should take when dealing with costs. The principles are there to guide and the judge clearly set out the relevant guiding factors. The first
e   relevant and important principle is that the unsuccessful party should pay the costs of the successful party. If there has been a payment into court it will follow that the offer contains a further offer that the payer in will meet the costs up to the date when the payment in should have been accepted. So in this case there is no dispute that so far as the costs up to 7 February 2000 are concerned the
f   defendants will, in addition to allowing the payment out, pay the costs.

[23] If a payment in has not been accepted there is a further starting point accepted by the judge and by both sides in this case, that if the claimant fails to beat the payment in, prima facie the claimant will be considered the unsuccessful party as from the date when the payment in should have been accepted. He must pay the costs from that date as a normal rule (see *Findlay v Railway Executive* [1950]
g   2 All ER 969). But that presumption may be dislodged in special circumstances, e g where the judge takes the view that a defendant has withheld material and not allowed a claimant to make a proper appraisal of the defendant's case (see Chadwick LJ in the passage quoted by the judge from *Jones v Jones* [1999] CA Transcript 1701 and Lord Woolf MR in the passage quoted by the judge from
h   *Ford v GKR Construction Ltd* [2000] 1 All ER 802, [2000] 1 WLR 1397).

Submissions of the parties

[24] Mr Strauss sought to persuade the judge and us that there should be a principle that if the defendant amended his case in any material respect and was
j   at fault for failing to do it much earlier and in particular if he was at fault for failing to make the amendment prior to the time of the payment in, that should in effect provide an opportunity for the claimant to reconsider a payment in, and lead thus to the conclusion that if the payment in was accepted immediately following that amendment, the almost inevitable result should be that the claimant received all his costs up to the date of acceptance. His argument in favour of there being such a principle was supported he suggested by the following factors. First, a claimant

was entitled to know what a defendant's case was when considering whether to take out a payment into court. Where material was in the hands of the defendant at the time of the payment in from which the defendant could have made clear his full case when the payment in was originally made, it is the defendant who should be penalised for not having made clear his full case. Second, from an acceptance immediately following an amendment it should be inferred that it was the amendment that was the key influence on the claimants' decision to accept the money in court. Third, it would be invidious to try and establish what in fact influenced the claimant to take the payment in when he did, or not to take the payment in at some earlier stage, both because to try out the point would involve the disclosure of privileged material and because a full-blown trial on issues of costs should be avoided, and the right approach was thus that having regard to the defendant's fault, the claimant should receive the benefit of the doubt.

[25] Mr Friedman submitted that there should be nothing approaching a principle as suggested by Mr Strauss. Mr Strauss characterised Mr Friedman's submission as being that unless the claimant could establish that if the government had correctly stated its case, the claimant would have accepted the payment in, the prima facie rule that a failure to beat the payment in resulted in the claimant being treated as the unsuccessful party should apply. I do not think ultimately his submission went that far. He submitted that the proper approach was as follows. First, the claimant who fails to beat a Pt 36 offer is prima facie the losing party. Where the claimant requires leave to take a payment out of court, the court has a discretion in relation to costs but should have regard to all the circumstances of the case including whether the defendant's conduct has prevented a proper assessment being made by the claimant. When the court concludes that the defendant's culpable conduct did prevent a proper assessment, the court may order the defendant to pay the costs of the claimant (*Ford's* case is an example). What is the proper conclusion to draw will depend on the facts of each case. The fact that a belated acceptance follows disclosure of new information or an amended case is relevant because it may show that the new information prompted a reassessment but it will not necessarily bring about the conclusion that the defendant should pay all the costs up until acceptance of the payment in even if non-disclosure is culpable.

[26] He accepted that there was fault in the instant case though the fault was clearly most serious from 28 February 2000 onwards and more understandable as at the time of the payment in. He further accepted that a full trial of the issue as to precisely what had influenced the decision not to take the payment in as at 7 February 2000 and to take the money out when it was taken out, should be avoided. But his submission was that what the judge should be seeking to establish where a payment in is sought to be accepted so near the end of the trial as was the case in this instance was who in reality was the unsuccessful party. It would be quite wrong, he submitted, if a claimant could simply use an amendment as an excuse to take out a payment in and receive an award of costs if in reality the claimant should have accepted the original payment in.

Conclusion

[27] I would reject any principle or rule of the type suggested by Mr Strauss. Each case will turn on its own circumstances. It seems to me that so far as possible the judge should be trying to assess who in reality is the unsuccessful party and who has been responsible for the fact that costs have been incurred which should not have been. It is plainly right that a full-scale trial examining

a privileged material, and listening to ex post facto justification should be avoided. It furthermore does not seem to me to be right to seek to lay down rules as to where the onus will lie where a defendant is allowed to amend his case. As I have already said straightjackets in this area should be avoided. The starting point is that a claimant who fails to beat a payment in will prima facie be liable for the costs. An amendment may be of such a character that a judge will feel that the *b* onus should be firmly placed on the defendant to persuade him that the prima facie rule should continue to apply; on the other hand the judge may be quite clear by reference to his feel of the case that the amendment is being used as an excuse to take money out of court that should have been accepted when originally made. Some cases will lie between the two extremes, and the judge will have to adjust his assessment to give effect to possibilities which it would be *c* inappropriate to try out and thus by reference to his overall view of the case.

[28] In the instant case the judge correctly identified the starting point. He furthermore correctly identified the possibility that an amendment of the case due to the fault of the defendant might give rise to a dislodging of the prima facie rule and even lead to an award of costs in favour of the claimant (see the two *d* quotations of Chadwick LJ and Lord Woolf MR and the passage of the judgment (at [21], above)). His reasons for concluding that the prima facie rule should continue to apply subject to an award of costs in favour of the EC claimants for the further week between 7 and 14 February 2000 could have been more expansive. However, it seems to me that it cannot be said he erred in principle, nor that he misdirected himself, (nor indeed, if it had been suggested, that his *e* decision was perverse). He had the feel of the case better than anyone. He clearly took the view that it was doubtful whether the amendments to the figures which he allowed in April 2000, if produced in December 1999 would have led the EC claimants to accept the payment in, but since he could not be absolutely sure of that, it was fair to allow the further week. That is an exercise of his discretion *f* with which this court should in my view not even contemplate interfering.

[29] I would dismiss the appeal.

SEDLEY LJ.
[30] I agree.

g **SIMON BROWN LJ.**
[31] I also agree.

Appeal dismissed.

Dilys Tausz   Barrister.

Dunnett v Railtrack plc (in railway administration)

[2002] EWCA Civ 303

COURT OF APPEAL, CIVIL DIVISION

BROOKE, ROBERT WALKER AND SEDLEY LJJ

22 FEBRUARY 2002

Costs – Order for costs – Discretion – Disallowing costs of successful party – Alternative dispute resolution (ADR) – Adverse costs consequences of party rejecting ADR when latter suggested by court – CPR 1.3, 1.4.

A single Lord Justice granted the claimant permission to appeal to the Court of Appeal from the dismissal of her claim for damages against the defendant. He suggested, however, that she ought to explore the possibility of alternative dispute resolution (ADR). That suggestion was in accordance with CPR 1.4[a] which required the court to further the overriding objective of the CPR by active case management, including encouraging the parties to use an ADR procedure if the court considered that appropriate. In response, the claimant indicated that she would be in favour of exploring the possibility of ADR if the defendant was also willing to do so. She referred the suggestion to the defendant, but the latter flatly rejected it, even though CPR 1.3[b] required the parties to help the court to further the overriding objective. Instead, the defendant made offers to pay the claimant a sum in settlement of her claim, but she did not consider the sum offered to be reasonable or fair. Accordingly, the appeal proceeded to a hearing. After the appeal was dismissed, the defendant sought its costs, referring to the offers that it had made. When pressed by the court to explain its unwillingness to contemplate ADR, the defendant stated that that would necessarily have involved the payment of money, which it was not willing to contemplate, over and above the sum that it had already offered.

Held – Having regard to their duties under CPR 1.3, parties and their lawyers might have to face uncomfortable costs consequences if they turned down out of hand the chance of ADR when suggested by the court. Skilled mediators were now able to achieve results satisfactory to both parties in many cases which were quite beyond the power of lawyers and courts to achieve. When the parties were brought together on neutral soil with a skilled mediator to help them resolve their differences, it could very well be that the mediator was able to achieve a result by which the parties shook hands and felt that they had gone away having settled the dispute on terms with which they were happy to live. In the instant case, the defendant appeared to have misunderstood the purpose of ADR. Given its refusal to contemplate ADR at a stage before the costs of the appeal started to flow, it was not appropriate to take into account the offers that had been made.

---

a   Rule 1.4, so far as material, provides: '(1) The court must further the overriding objective by actively managing cases.
    (2) Active case management includes ... (e) encouraging the parties to use an alternative dispute resolution procedure if the court considers that appropriate and facilitating the use of such procedure ...'

b   Rule 1.3 provides: 'The parties are required to help the court to further the overriding objective.'

a Taking into account all the circumstances of the case, the appropriate order on the appeal was no order as to costs (see [13]–[18], below).

Notes

For the overriding objective under the CPR, see 37 *Halsbury's Laws* (4th edn reissue) paras 60–62.

b
Appeal

The claimant, Susan Jane Dunnett, appealed with permission of Schiemann LJ granted on 11 August 2000 from the decision of Judge Graham Jones in the Cardiff County Court on 1 December 1999 dismissing her claim against the defendant, Railtrack plc, for damages for negligence arising out of the death, on *c* 17 July 1996, of three of her horses who had been struck by an express train on the Swansea to London line near Bridgend. The facts are set out in the judgment of Brooke LJ.

Simon Levene (instructed by the *Bar Pro Bono Unit*) for Miss Dunnett.
d *Tim Lord* (instructed by *Beachcroft Wansbroughs*, Bristol) for Railtrack.

The three members of the court delivered judgments dismissing the appeal (see [2002] EWCA Civ 302, [2002] All ER (D) 314 (Feb)). After further argument as to the costs of the appeal, the following judgments were delivered.

e **BROOKE LJ.**
     [1] When the appeal was dismissed, Mr Lord (on behalf of Railtrack plc) asked for his clients' costs. He showed us letters written by his clients' solicitors in relation to this matter. The first was dated 13 March 2001, after Schiemann LJ had given leave to appeal. The letter read:

f   'We refer to recent exchange of e-mails and now have our client's instructions on your suggestion that this action could be compromised. As will appear from the skeleton arguments served with the accompanying letter, our clients are confident that your appeal will fail and that an order for costs of the appeal will be made against you. Nevertheless, they are prepared to offer to you the sum of £2,500 as a lump sum in full and final settlement *g*   of all your claims in this action including interest and costs.'

     [2] Attention was drawn to CPR Pt 36.
     [3] We have also been shown a later exchange of e-mail correspondence this month. It was initiated by Miss Dunnett and followed by an e-mail from Railtrack *h* referring to an offer whereby, if she was to discontinue the appeal, their clients were prepared not to enforce their entitlement as to costs and extending the time in which that offer might be accepted. Miss Dunnett responded that she—

         'would be happy to settle this matter outside of a court action thereby avoiding your clients having the expense of preparing for the court date and *j*   minimising the stress of this matter resulting in another day in court for myself.'

     [4] She asked if Railtrack could be asked 'if they have any offer of a settlement so that this matter may be dispensed with for the benefit of us all'.
     [5] It appears that another offer of £2,500 was made, which Miss Dunnett did not consider to be a reasonable or fair offer.

[6] Throughout this time Miss Dunnett was acting as a litigant in person. It has only been very recently that she has had the good fortune of being assisted by Mr Levene, who has appeared for her as part of the Bar's pro bono scheme.

[7] In the usual way, it would follow that she should pay Railtrack's costs. However, Schiemann LJ, before whom she appeared on 11 August 2000, said in terms in his judgment:

'I have advised her that she ought to explore the possibility of alternative dispute resolution, so as to get shot of this case as soon as possible. She has indicated that she is in favour of doing that, if the other side are also willing to do that. I cannot say any more about that, beyond suggesting that she tries it.'

[8] Miss Dunnett referred this suggestion to Railtrack, who instructed their solicitors to turn it down flat. They were not even willing to consider it. They then instructed their solicitors to oppose Miss Dunnett applying for an extension of time for filing her notice of appeal. She was a little bit out of time.

[9] The matter came back before Schiemann LJ. We have seen the transcript of what he said. He was critical of Railtrack's solicitors in opposing this application. He said:

'I am conscious of the fact that Railtrack say that they have limited funds to deal with a litigant who may well not be able to reimburse them; but they would have been better advised if they had kept those limited funds for fighting the substance of the case rather than taking the point that she is a little out of time in filing a notice of appeal.'

[10] The court has not seen everything which passed between the parties. From something that Mr Lord told us, it appears that passions were running fairly high on Miss Dunnett's side in relation to the death of her horses and the attitude that Railtrack, no doubt on sound legal advice, were adopting. It appears to me that this was a case in which, at any rate before the trial, a real effort should have been made by way of alternative dispute resolution to see if the matter could be satisfactorily resolved by an experienced mediator, without the parties having to incur the no doubt heavy legal costs of contesting the matter at trial. There is no evidence that this was ever suggested by the court. I say nothing more about that except to say that it is understandable, in these circumstances, that passions may have been running fairly high.

[11] However, the time did come when this court in terms suggested that this was a case for alternative dispute resolution. CPR 1.4 reads:

'(1) The court must further the overriding objective by actively managing cases.

(2) Active case management includes ... (e) encouraging the parties to use an alternative dispute resolution procedure if the court considers that appropriate and facilitating the use of such procedure ...'

[12] In the helpful notes to that rule in the Autumn 2001 edition of the White Book (Civil Procedure), the editors write (at para 1.4.11):

'The encouragement and facilitating of ADR [alternative dispute resolution] by the court is an aspect of active case management which in turn is an aspect of achieving the overriding objective. The parties have a duty to help the court in furthering that objective and, therefore, they have a duty to consider seriously the possibility of ADR procedures being utilised for the purpose of resolving their claim or particular issues within it when encouraged by the court to do so. The discharge of the parties' duty in this respect may be relevant to the question of costs because, when exercising its discretion as to costs, the court must have regard to all the circumstances, including the conduct of all the parties (r.44.3(4), see too r.44.5).'

[13] The value of that observation is that it draws attention to the fact that the parties themselves have a duty to further the overriding objective. That is said in terms in CPR 1.3. What is set out in r 1.4 is the duty of the court to further the overriding objective by active case management, which includes the feature to which I have referred.

[14] Mr Lord, when asked by the court why his clients were not willing to contemplate alternative dispute resolution, said that this would necessarily involve the payment of money, which his clients were not willing to contemplate, over and above what they had already offered. This appears to be a misunderstanding of the purpose of alternative dispute resolution. Skilled mediators are now able to achieve results satisfactory to both parties in many cases which are quite beyond the power of lawyers and courts to achieve. This court has knowledge of cases where intense feelings have arisen, for instance in relation to clinical negligence claims. But when the parties are brought together on neutral soil with a skilled mediator to help them resolve their differences, it may very well be that the mediator is able to achieve a result by which the parties shake hands at the end and feel that they have gone away having settled the dispute on terms with which they are happy to live. A mediator may be able to provide solutions which are beyond the powers of the court to provide. Occasions are known to the court in claims against the police, which can give rise to as much passion as a claim of this kind where a claimant's precious horses are killed on a railway line, by which an apology from a very senior police officer is all that the claimant is really seeking and the money side of the matter falls away.

[15] It is to be hoped that any publicity given to this part of the judgment of the court will draw the attention of lawyers to their duties to further the overriding objective in the way that is set out in CPR Pt 1 and to the possibility that, if they turn down out of hand the chance of alternative dispute resolution when suggested by the court, as happened on this occasion, they may have to face uncomfortable costs consequences.

[16] In my judgment, in the particular circumstances of this case, given the refusal of Railtrack to contemplate alternative dispute resolution at a stage before the costs of this appeal started to flow, I do not think that it is appropriate to take into account the offers that were made. In my judgment, taking into account all the circumstances of the case, as we are bound to do under CPR Pt 44, which applies as much to the Court of Appeal as it does to courts at first instance, the appropriate order on the appeal is no order as to costs.

ROBERT WALKER LJ.
[17] I agree.

SEDLEY LJ.
[18] I agree.

Appeal dismissed. No order as to costs of appeal.

James Brooks   Barrister.

L v Director of Public Prosecutions

a

[2001] EWHC Admin 882

QUEEN'S BENCH DIVISION (DIVISIONAL COURT)
PILL LJ AND POOLE J
9 OCTOBER, 8 NOVEMBER 2001

b

Criminal evidence – Burden of proof – Statutory provisions imposing burden of proof on defendant – Statutory provision requiring defendant to prove defence of having good reason for having with him in a public place an article with a blade or sharp point – Whether provision compatible with presumption of innocence under human rights convention – Criminal Justice Act 1988, s 139 – Human Rights Act 1998, Sch 1, Pt I, art 6.

c

A police officer saw the defendant throwing a lock-knife behind a low wall. When interviewed by the police, the defendant accepted that the knife was his and that he had thrown it over the wall. He was charged with having a lock-knife in his possession contrary to s 139[a] of the Criminal Justice Act 1988. Section 139(1) made it an offence for any person to have with him in a public place an article to which s 139 applied, namely an article which had a blade or was sharply pointed. By virtue of s 139(4), it was a defence for a person charged with an offence under s 139 to prove that he had a good reason or lawful authority for having the article with him in a public place. The defendant was convicted, the district judge holding that the probative burden upon a defendant charged under s 139 did not conflict with the presumption of innocence under art 6[b] of the European Convention for the Protection of Human Rights and Fundamental Freedoms 1950 (as set out in Sch 1 to the Human Rights Act 1998). The defendant appealed by way of case stated.

d

e

f

Held – The reverse onus provision in s 139 of the 1988 Act did not conflict with art 6 of the convention. Under the convention, a reverse onus was permissible, but presumptions of fact or law had to be defined within reasonable limits. A fair balance had to be struck, and that fair balance permitted the existence of a reverse onus in the context of s 139. Under that provision, it was for the prosecution to prove that the defendant knowingly had the offending article in his possession. Moreover, there was a strong public interest in bladed articles not being carried in public without good reason. It was not obviously offensive to the rights of the individual that it was for him to prove a good reason on a balance of probabilities. Respect should be given to the way in which a democratically-elected legislature had sought to strike the right balance. Parliament was entitled, without infringing the convention, to deter the carrying of bladed or sharply-pointed articles in public to the extent of placing the burden of proving a good reason on the carrier. Further, the defendant was proving something within his own knowledge. Notwithstanding the adversarial nature of the English proceedings, a defendant was entitled, under art 6 of the convention, to expect the court to scrutinise the evidence with a view to deciding if a good reason existed. That applied whether the defendant gave evidence or not. In the great majority of cases, the fact-finding

g

h

j

a Section 139 is set out at [4], below
b Article 6 is set out at [6], below

a   tribunal would have to make a judgment as to whether there was a good reason
without the decision depending on whether it had to be proved that there was a
good reason or that there was no such reason. The fact-finding tribunal would
need to make a value judgment as to whether, upon all the evidence, the reason
was a good one. Accordingly, the appeal would be dismissed (see [26]–[29], [31],
below).

b   *R v Lambert* [2001] 3 All ER 577 *distinguished.*
Salabiaku v France (1991) 13 EHRR 379 *considered.*

Notes
For the presumption of innocence under the convention, see 8(2) *Halsbury's Laws*
(4th edn reissue) para 142, and for the offence of having an article with a blade or
c   point in a public place, see 11(1) *Halsbury's Laws* (4th edn reissue) para 168.
    For the Criminal Justice Act 1988, s 139, see 12 *Halsbury's Statutes* (4th edn)
(1997 reissue) 1081.
    For the Human Rights Act 1998, Sch 1, Pt 1, art 6, see 7 *Halsbury's Statutes* (4th
edn) (1999 reissue) 523.

d
Cases referred to in judgment
A-G of Hong Kong v Lee Kwong-kut, A-G of Hong Kong v Lo Chak-man [1993] 3 All ER
    939, [1993] AC 951, [1993] 3 WLR 329, PC.
Brown v Stott (Procurator Fiscal, Dunfermline) [2001] 2 All ER 97, [2001] 2 WLR 817,
    PC.
e   *Jayasena v R* [1970] 1 All ER 219, [1970] AC 618, [1970] 2 WLR 448, PC.
R v Chaulk [1990] 3 SCR 1303, Can SC.
R v Downey [1992] 2 SCR 10, Can SC.
R v DPP, ex p Kebeline, R v DPP, ex p Rechachi [1999] 4 All ER 801, [2000] 2 AC 326,
    [1999] 3 WLR 972, HL.
f   *R v Hunt* [1987] 1 All ER 1, [1987] AC 352, [1986] 3 WLR 1115, HL.
R v Lambert [2001] UKHL 37, [2001] 3 All ER 577, [2001] 3 WLR 206; *affg on
    different grounds* [2001] 1 All ER 1014, [2001] 2 WLR 211, CA.
Salabiaku v France (1991) 13 EHRR 379, [1988] ECHR 10589/83, ECt HR.

Case stated
g   The appellant, L, appealed by way of case stated from his conviction at West
London Youth Court on 23 October 2000 of an offence of having in his possession
a lock-knife contrary to s 139 of the Criminal Justice Act 1988. The question for
the opinion of the High Court is set out at [3], below. The facts are set out in the
judgment of Pill LJ.

h
Matthew Ryder (instructed by *Farrell Matthews & Weir*) for the appellant.
David Perry and *Louis Mably* (instructed by the *CPS*) for the Director of Public
    Prosecutions.

Cur adv vult

j
8 November 2001. The following judgments were delivered.

PILL LJ.
    [1] This is an appeal by way of case stated by L against the adjudication of
District Judge Philips sitting at the West London Youth Court on 23 October 2000.
The appellant was found guilty of having in his possession on 30 August 2000 a

lock-knife contrary to s 139 of the Criminal Justice Act 1988. The district judge
found the following facts:

> '(a) On 30 August 2000 at about 22.50 a police officer saw the appellant
> throw an object behind a low wall in Becklow Gardens. (b) That object was
> a lock-knife. (c) When interviewed by the police the appellant said that he
> had brought the knife to show it to friends of his brother. (d) In the
> interview he accepted that the knife was his and that he had thrown it over
> the wall.'

[2] The district judge concluded:

> 'There is a clear social objective in discouraging the carrying of knives. The
> court does not consider the chosen course of the legislator to contravene
> art 6 [of the European Convention for the Protection of Human Rights and
> Fundamental Freedoms 1950 (as set out in Sch 1 to the Human Rights Act
> 1998)] as there is objective justification in the case of knives for the choice,
> and it is not disproportionate.'

[3] The question for the opinion of this court is:

> 'Was I correct in holding that the probative burden upon a defendant
> charged under s 139 of the Criminal Justice Act 1988 does not conflict with
> art 6 of the European Convention on Human Rights or should I have read
> the section under s 3 of the Human Rights Act 1998 to impose but an
> evidential burden upon a defendant?'

[4] The 1988 Act, s 139, as amended by the Offensive Weapons Act 1996,
provides:

> '(1) Subject to subsections (4) and (5) below, any person who has an article
> to which this section applies with him in a public place shall be guilty of an
> offence.
> (2) Subject to subsection (3) below, this section applies to any article
> which has a blade or is sharply pointed except a folding pocketknife.
> (3) This section applies to a folding pocketknife if the cutting edge of its
> blade exceeds 3 inches.
> (4) It shall be a defence for a person charged with an offence under this
> section to prove that he had good reason or lawful authority for having the
> article with him in a public place.
> (5) Without prejudice to the generality of subsection (4) above, it shall be
> a defence for a person charged with an offence under this section to prove
> that he had the article with him—(a) for use at work; (b) for religious
> reasons; or (c) as part of any national costume.
> (6) A person guilty of an offence under subsection (1) above shall be liable
> (a) on summary conviction, to imprisonment for a term not exceeding six
> months, or a fine not exceeding the statutory maximum, or both; (b) on
> conviction on indictment, to imprisonment for a term not exceeding two
> years, or a fine, or both.
> (7) In this section "public place" includes any place to which at the
> material time the public have or are permitted access, whether on payment
> or otherwise.
> (8) This section shall not have effect in relation to anything done before it
> comes into force.'

a [5] I read the specific situations set out in s 139(5) as examples of what are capable of being good reasons and not as meeting a separate standard. No contrary submissions were made.

[6] Article 6 of the convention provides, in so far as is material:

b '1. In the determination of … any criminal charge against him, everyone is entitled to a fair and public hearing within a reasonable time by an independent and impartial tribunal established by law …

2. Everyone charged with a criminal offence shall be presumed innocent until proved guilty according to law.'

c [7] Section 3(1) of the 1998 Act provides: 'So far as it is possible to do so, primary legislation and subordinate legislation must be read and given effect in a way which is compatible with the Convention rights.'

[8] The issue can be stated shortly: is the effect of s 139(1) and (4) of the 1988 Act to place a burden on the prosecution to prove beyond reasonable doubt that the defendant did not have a good reason for having the knife with him in a public place? Reformulated in terms of the duty on the prosecution, that is the second

d question posed by the district judge and the one which has formed the basis for submissions. The two questions posed are not strictly alternatives. Section 139 may conflict with art 6 but remain the law, pending a declaration of incompatibility and action by Parliament. It is first necessary to construe s 139 in the light of s 3 of the 1998 Act. It is submitted on behalf of the appellant that, properly construed, s 139(4) does not impose a probative burden on a defendant. If it does, the issue

e of incompatibility arises. Submissions have been made as to how s 139 should be read in the light of art 6, s 3 and the authorities.

[9] While the issue is not difficult to state, it is one which, in different reverse onus contexts, has attracted very considerable judicial attention in recent years. The volume of analysis and reasoning is such that to attempt fully to summarise

f it, or to analyse the somewhat diverse strands which emerge from it, would make this judgment one of intolerable length and elaboration. I refer to sufficient of the authorities, I hope, to demonstrate the nature of the problem, the guidelines which appear to me to emerge from the cases and the basis for the conclusion I have reached on s 139. Consideration of the issues of statutory construction and of the compatibility of the statute with art 6 are sometimes intertwined in the

g authorities.

[10] The leading case in the European Court of Human Rights is *Salabiaku v France* (1991) 13 EHRR 379. The court stated (at 388 (para 28)):

h 'Presumptions of fact or law operate in every legal system. Clearly, the Convention does not prohibit such presumptions in principle. It does, however, require the Contracting States to remain within certain limits in this respect as regards criminal law … the object and purpose of Article 6, which, by protecting the right to a fair trial and in particular the right to be presumed innocent, is intended to enshrine the fundamental principle of the rule of law. Article 6(2) does not therefore regard presumptions of fact or of

j law provided for in the criminal law with indifference. It requires States to define them within reasonable limits which take into account the importance of what is at stake and maintain the rights of the defence.'

[11] In *A-G of Hong Kong v Lee Kwong-kut, A-G of Hong Kong v Lo Chak-man* [1993] 3 All ER 939, [1993] AC 951 the Judicial Committee of the Privy Council considered whether a reverse onus provision infringed a right in the Hong Kong

Bill of Rights to the same effect as art 6(2). Giving the judgment of the board, Lord Woolf stated the issues involved:

> 'The issues involving the Hong Kong Bill of Rights should be approached with realism and good sense, and kept in proportion. If this is not done the Hong Kong Bill of Rights will become a source of injustice rather than justice and it will be debased in the eyes of the public. In order to maintain the balance between the individual and the society as a whole, rigid and inflexible standards should not be imposed on the legislature's attempts to resolve the difficult and intransigent problems with which society is faced when seeking to deal with serious crime. It must be remembered that questions of policy remain primarily the responsibility of the legislature (see *R v Downey* [1992] 2 SCR 10 at 36, and *R v Chaulk* [1990] 3 SCR 1303 at 1342–1343). It would not assist the individuals who are charged with offences if, because of the approach adopted to "statutory defences" by the courts, the legislature, in order to avoid the risk of legislation being successfully challenged, did not include in the legislation a statutory defence to a charge.' (See [1993] 3 All ER 939 at 954–955, [1993] AC 951 at 975.)

[12] In *Brown v Stott (Procurator Fiscal, Dunfermline)* [2001] 2 All ER 97 at 115, [2001] 2 WLR 817 at 836, Lord Bingham of Cornhill considered statutory provisions alleged to offend against art 6 by removing the privilege against self-incrimination. He stated:

> 'The jurisprudence of the European Court very clearly establishes that while the overall fairness of a criminal trial cannot be compromised, the constituent rights comprised, whether expressly or implicitly, within art 6 are not themselves absolute. Limited qualification of these rights is acceptable if reasonably directed by national authorities towards a clear and proper public objective and if representing no greater qualification than the situation calls for. The general language of the convention could have led to the formulation of hard-edged and inflexible statements of principle from which no departure could be sanctioned whatever the background or the circumstances. But this approach has been consistently eschewed by the court throughout its history.'

[13] In the same case, Lord Hope of Craighead stated the test to be applied when considering whether a statutory provision is incompatible with a right under art 6:

> 'The question whether a legitimate aim is being pursued enables account to be taken of the public interest in the rule of law. The principle of proportionality directs attention to the question whether a fair balance has been struck between the general interest of the community in the realisation of that aim and the protection of the fundamental rights of the individual.' (See [2001] 2 All ER 97 at 130, [2001] 2 WLR 817 at 852.)

[14] In *R v DPP, ex p Kebeline, R v DPP, ex p Rechachi* [1999] 4 All ER 801 at 847, [2000] 2 AC 326 at 384 Lord Hope, by way of comment on *Salabiaku v France*, stated: 'As a matter of general principle therefore a fair balance must be struck between the demands of the general interest of the community and the protection of the fundamental rights of the individual ...' Lord Hope added:

a   '[Counsel for the Director of Public Prosecutions] suggested that in considering where the balance lies it may be useful to consider the following questions. (1) What does the prosecution have to prove in order to transfer the onus to the defence? (2) What is the burden on the accused—does it relate to something which is likely to be difficult for him to prove, or does it relate to something which is likely to be within his knowledge or (I would add) to which

b   he readily has access? (3) What is the nature of the threat faced by society which the provision is designed to combat? It seems to me that these questions provide a convenient way of breaking down the broad issue of balance into its essential components, and I would adopt them for the purpose of pursuing the argument as far as it is proper to go in the present case.' (See [1999] 4 All ER 801 at 848–849, [2000] 2 AC 326 at 386.)

c

[15] R v Lambert [2001] UKHL 37, [2001] 3 All ER 577, [2001] 3 WLR 206, was decided on the question whether the relevant provisions of the 1998 Act were retrospective. Consideration was, however, given to the effect of reverse onus provisions apparently present in ss 28(2) and (3) of the Misuse of Drugs Act 1971.

d   In that context Lord Steyn considered (at [38]) the principle to be applied and the practical effect for a fact-finding tribunal of the decision as to where the onus rests:

'The principle of proportionality requires the House to consider whether there was a pressing necessity to impose a legal rather than an evidential

e   burden on the accused. The effect of s 28 is that in a prosecution for possession of controlled drugs with intent to supply, although the prosecution must establish that prohibited drugs were in the possession of the defendant, and that he or she knew that the package contained something, the accused must prove on a balance of probabilities that he did

f   not know that the package contained controlled drugs. If the jury is in doubt on this issue, they must convict him. This may occur when an accused adduces sufficient evidence to raise a doubt about his guilt but the jury is not convinced on a balance of probabilities that his account is true. *Indeed it obliges the court to convict if the version of the accused is as likely to be true as not.* This is a far reaching consequence: a guilty verdict may be returned in

g   respect of an offence punishable by life imprisonment even though the jury may consider that it is reasonably possible that the accused had been duped. It would be unprincipled to brush aside such possibilities as unlikely to happen in practice. Moreover, as Justice has pointed out in its valuable intervention, there may be real difficulties in determining the real facts upon

h   which the sentencer must act in such cases. In any event, the burden of showing that *only* a reverse legal burden can overcome the difficulties of the prosecution in drugs cases is a heavy one.'

[16] Lord Steyn concluded (at [41]):

j
'In these circumstances I am satisfied that the transfer of the legal burden in s 28 does not satisfy the criterion of proportionality. Viewed in its place in the current legal system s 28 of the 1971 Act is a disproportionate reaction to perceived difficulties facing the prosecution in drugs cases. It would be sufficient to impose an evidential burden on the accused. It follows that s 28 is incompatible with the convention rights.'

[17] Lord Clyde (at [154]) expressed views on reverse onus provisions in the context of certain classes of case:

'A strict responsibility may be acceptable in the case of statutory offences which are concerned to regulate the conduct of some particular activity in the public interest. The requirement to have a licence in order to carry on certain kinds of activity is an obvious example. The promotion of health and safety and the avoidance of pollution are among the purposes to be served by such controls. These kinds of cases may properly be seen as not truly criminal. Many may be relatively trivial and only involve a monetary penalty. Many may carry with them no real social disgrace or infamy.'

[18] However, Lord Clyde stated (at [156]), in the context of s 28 of the 1971 Act, that—

'By imposing a persuasive burden on the accused it would be possible for an accused person to be convicted where the jury believe he might well be innocent but have not been persuaded that he probably did not know the nature of what he possessed.'

[19] Lord Hutton, alone in the House of Lords in R v Lambert, reached a different conclusion upon the effect of s 28(2) and (3). He stated (at [198]):

'Therefore my conclusion is that the difficulty in some cases of convicting those guilty of the crime of possession of a controlled drug with intent to supply, if the burden of proving knowledge beyond a reasonable doubt rests on the prosecution, is not resolved by placing an evidential burden on the defendant, and that it is necessary to impose a persuasive burden as s 28(2) and (3) does. I further consider that the transfer of the onus satisfies the test that it has a legitimate aim in the public interest and that there is a reasonable relationship of proportionality between the means employed and the aim sought to be realised. Accordingly I am of the opinion that s 28(2) and (3) does not violate art 6(2) and I am in full agreement with the Court of Appeal on this issue.'

[20] In the Court of Appeal ([2001] 1 All ER 1014 at 1022, [2001] 2 WLR 211 at 219 (para 16)), Lord Woolf CJ had stated:

'In doing this it is important to start with the structure of the offences. If the defendant is being required to prove an essential element of the offence this will be more difficult to justify. If, however, what the defendant is required to do is establish a special defence or exception this will be less objectionable. The extent of the inroad on the general principle is also important. Here it is important to have in mind that art 6(2) is specifically directed to the application of the presumption of innocence of the "criminal offences" charged. It is also important to have in mind that legislation is passed by a democratically elected Parliament and therefore the courts under the convention are entitled to and should, as a matter of constitutional principle, pay a degree of deference to the view of Parliament as to what is in the interest of the public generally when upholding the rights of the individual under the convention. The courts are required to balance the competing interests involved.'

[21] By reference to Professor Glanville Williams's article on 'The Logic of "Exceptions"' [1988] CLJ 261 at 264–265, Lord Steyn also held that, applying s 3

a of the 1998 Act, it is possible to read s 28 of the 1971 Act in a way which is compatible with convention rights. Both Lord Steyn and Lord Cooke of Thorndon had expressed the same view in *Ex p Kebeline*. Lord Steyn stated that he would read s 28(2) and (3) as creating an evidential burden only, notwithstanding the presence of the words 'it shall be a defence to prove'. He expressed agreement ([2001] 3 All ER 577 at [42]) with these observations of Lord Hope (at [94]):

b   'I would therefore read the words "to prove" in s 28(2) as if the words used in the subsection were "to give sufficient evidence", and I would give the same meaning to the words "if he proves" in s 28(3). The effect which is to be given to this meaning is that the burden of proof remains on the prosecution throughout. If sufficient evidence is adduced to raise the issue, *c*   it will be for the prosecution to show beyond reasonable doubt that the defence is not made out by the evidence.'

[22] On the issue whether a reverse onus provision conflicts with art 6(2) the court has not been invited to depart from the opinions expressed in *R v Lambert* that the words 'for the accused to prove' in s 28(2) of the 1971 Act (or 'for a person *d* charged to prove' under s 139 of the 1988 Act) can be read as covering a situation in which 'sufficient evidence is adduced to raise the issue'. The source of the view expressed in *R v Lambert* is a footnote at pp 265–266 of Professor Glanville Williams's article:

e   'In [*R v Hunt* [1987] 1 All ER 1 at 19, [1987] AC 352 at 385], Lord Ackner objected to this proposal [to leave the burden throughout on the prosecution] on the ground that "the discharge of an evidential burden proves nothing—it merely raises an issue." This is the orthodox view, and I agree that, as a matter of the desirable use of language, it is better not to speak of an evidential burden of proof. But the question now under consideration is not whether a particular use of language is proper or *f*   undesirably lax, but the meaning that our legislators (that is to say, the framers of our legislation) actually intended by the words they used. If, where an evidential burden lies on the defendant, the jury acquit, this is because they feel at least a reasonable doubt whether the defendant is guilty. It does not appear to be wholly discordant with ordinary language to say *g*   that, in such a case, at least a reasonable doubt as to guilt has been established; and if "established" why not "proved"? It may not be the best use of words, but if there is a reasonable possibility that this is how the words "prove" and "proof" have been intended, and if this interpretation diminishes the likelihood of miscarriages of justice, we should accept it.'

h I respectfully agree that it is better not to speak of an evidential burden of proof. It merely raises an issue, as Lord Ackner and Lord Hope have stated. Referring to an evidential burden in *Jayasena v R* [1970] 1 All ER 219 at 221–222, [1970] AC 618 at 624, Lord Devlin stated:

j   'But it is confusing to call it a burden of proof. Further, it is misleading to call it a burden of proof, whether described as legal or evidential or by any other adjective, when it can be discharged by production of evidence that falls short of proof.'

[23] Moreover, the so-called burden may not in substance be a burden on the defendant at all. Evidence raising the issue will often emerge from the evidence, direct and circumstantial, called by the prosecution. A defendant is entitled, if the

hearing is to be a fair hearing under art 6, to have that evidence scrutinised by the court. In a s 139 context, a good reason will often be obvious from the circumstances in which the defendant is found in possession of the article which has a blade or is sharply pointed. The woman with knitting needles in the extreme case mentioned in the course of argument can expect it to emerge, if it be the case, that she is also carrying a ball of wool and is approaching the hall where the weekly knitting guild is being held. Since it is only necessary that an issue be raised, I do most diffidently express the view that to describe it as 'proof' not only is not the 'best use of words' but deprives the word 'proof', as commonly used inside and outside the criminal courts, of any meaning. Better, in my view, to look to incompatibility than to treat the English language in that way. The fact that on the evidence a doubt is present as to whether a proposition is proved does not prove a proposition directly contrary to it.

[24] Assuming that the dissident view I have expressed must be rejected, and that s 3 of the 1998 Act permits the word 'prove' to be construed by the courts in the way stated by Lord Steyn in *R v Lambert*, I still cannot accept that the intention of Parliament in 1988 was to use the word in that way. Parliament intended a reverse onus following a long-standing practice deplored by Professor Glanville Williams. Indeed I do not read the speech of Lord Steyn in *R v Lambert* as requiring the court to construe the word 'prove' in a way which Professor Glanville Williams regarded as 'not the best use of words'. It is necessary to do so to obtain compliance with art 6(2) only if the reverse onus which emerges from the conventional use of the word 'prove' involves a breach of art 6(2). Thus I consider whether art 6(2) permits a reverse onus in present circumstances.

[25] Mr Ryder, for the appellant, submits that the court need look no farther than the opinions of the majority on this issue in *R v Lambert* to decide that a reverse onus breaches art 6(2). In substance the offence under s 139 is not, without good reason, to carry in a public place an article which has a blade or is sharply pointed. The burden of proving each element should be upon the prosecution. Mr Ryder relies upon the widespread carrying in public, for good reasons, of bladed articles and submits that it is oppressive in such circumstances to require a good reason to be proved by a defendant. Moreover, the defence is onerous in that it has a dual requirement, first to establish the facts and then to establish that the facts amount to a good reason. It is also submitted that a reverse burden is more difficult to justify in the case of a young person such as the appellant.

[26] I consider the starting point to be the decision in *Salabiaku v France* (1991) 13 EHRR 379 which permits a reverse onus but requires presumptions of fact or of law to be defined within reasonable limits. As Lord Bingham stated in *Brown v Stott (Procurator Fiscal, Dunfermline)* [2001] 2 All ER 97, [2001] 2 WLR 817, there are no hard-edged and inflexible statements of principle. A fair balance must be struck.

[27] In my judgment, that fair balance permits the existence of a reverse onus in the context of s 139 of the 1988 Act. (1) The section is readily distinguishable, for present purposes, from s 28 of the 1971 Act. As Lord Steyn stated in *R v Lambert* [2001] 3 All ER 577 at [38], s 28 requires the defendant to prove on a balance of probabilities that he did not know that a package proved to be in his possession contained controlled drugs. Under s 139, it is for the prosecution to prove that the defendant knowingly had the offending article in his possession. A defendant is obviously vulnerable in a situation in which a package the contents of which he cannot know is handed to him or the contents of which for a variety

a of reasons he may not know. The present situation is different in that it is for the prosecution to prove that the defendant knows he had the relevant article in his possession. (2) There is a strong public interest in bladed articles not being carried in public without good reason. I do not find it obviously offensive to the rights of the individual that it is for him to prove a good reason on a balance of probabilities. Respect should be given to the way in which a democratically

b elected legislature has sought to strike the right balance, as in my view it has. Parliament is entitled, without infringing the convention, to deter the carrying of bladed or sharply pointed articles in public to the extent of placing the burden of proving a good reason on the carrier. (3) The defendant is proving something within his own knowledge. (4) Notwithstanding the adversarial nature of English proceedings, a defendant is entitled, under art 6, to expect the court to scrutinise

c the evidence with a view to deciding if a good reason exist. That applies whether he gave evidence or not. (5) In the great majority of cases, I would expect the fact-finding tribunal to make a judgment as to whether there was a good reason without the decision depending on whether it has to be proved that there is a good reason or that there is not a good reason. The present case is a good

d illustration. The fact finding tribunal will need to make a value judgment as to whether, upon all the evidence, the reason is a good one. Either there is or there is not a good reason though I accept that there will be cases in which the fact-finding tribunal may attach significance to where the burden of proof rests. (6) In distinguishing *R v Lambert*, I would give some, though limited, weight in striking the balance to the much more restricted power of sentence for this

e offence than for an offence under s 28. A s 139 offence is undoubtedly 'truly criminal' but at least the aggravating feature of a potential life sentence, to which Lord Steyn attached weight in *R v Lambert*, is not present. This factor cannot be decisive, however.

[28] For those reasons, I would answer the latter part of the question for the

f opinion of the court in the negative. I would also hold that s 139 of the 1988 Act does not conflict with art 6 of the convention. I would dismiss the appeal.

POOLE J.

[29] I agree. It is an interesting consequence of the Human Rights legislation that the same word 'prove' must now be taken to mean two wholly different

g things in one and the same subsection, namely s 28(2) of the Misuse of Drugs Act 1971. The common law has traditionally adopted a practical and empirical approach to the questions that come to confront it, and granting the fullest possible weight to the Human Rights Act 1998 and to the convention it enshrines, there is nothing in them that need compel judges to abandon that approach. In

h the course of argument I asked counsel, each of whom (understandably enough) had been prepared to speculate about what the practical effects of our finding this way or that way on the argument would be, whether there was any empirical or even anecdotal evidence that s 139 of the Criminal Justice Act 1988 had worked any verifiable injustice to defendants during the 13 years of its operation by

j reason of the persuasive burden it has imposed on them. In fairness to Mr Ryder, I would not have expected a ready answer from him to the question. It may be in the nature of things that such injustices, if they existed, would remain hidden. But it may be worth recording my instinct that such injustices, if they ever existed at all, would be very hard to find.

[30] There is I think a reason for this, and one that distinguished cases brought under this section from those brought under s 5(3) of the 1971 Act; and it is the

reason noted by Mr Perry both at para 13.3 of his written submissions and again in his argument before us, namely that the essential point is that an accused who *a* carries a knife (or other bladed or sharply pointed article) knows at the time he commits the act in question, that his conduct amounts to a criminal offence unless he can bring himself within the exemption specified within the section: contrast the accused in the prosecution under s 5(3) whose defence is that he did not know he was carrying drugs at all.   *b*

[31] For the rest, I respectfully adopt the reasons of Pill LJ. The social problem at which the section is aimed is only too real, and unhappily it is commonly the case that those who present it are relatively young males. But neither the young apprentice carrying his tools to work, nor the grandmother carrying her knitting needles to her daughter's (both images conjured up in argument) have anything to fear I believe from the reverse onus reading of this section, which I would *c* regard as a proportionate measure, weighed by Parliament, and well within reasonable limits.

Appeal dismissed.

Dilys Tausz   Barrister.

a

R (on the application of Rottman) v Commissioner of Police of the Metropolis

[2002] UKHL 20

b HOUSE OF LORDS

LORD NICHOLLS OF BIRKENHEAD, LORD HOFFMANN, LORD HOPE OF CRAIGHEAD, LORD HUTTON AND LORD RODGER OF EARLSFERRY

13, 14 FEBRUARY, 16 MAY 2002

c *Police – Powers – Right of search and seizure – Extradition – Whether police having common law power of search and seizure in respect of premises where person arrested pursuant to provisional warrant of arrest for extradition crime – Police and Criminal Evidence Act 1984, ss 18, 19 – Extradition Act 1989, s 8 – Criminal Justice (International Co-operation) Act 1990, s 7.*

d Following a request by the German government for the claimant's extradition, the magistrates' court issued a provisional warrant for his arrest under s 8(1)[a] of the Extradition Act 1989. The claimant was arrested in the driveway of his house. The police then searched the house and seized a number of articles. The claimant brought proceedings for judicial review, challenging the lawfulness of the entry and search. The Divisional Court held that the implementation of the Police and
e Criminal Evidence Act 1984 had extinguished the common law power of search and seizure following an arrest; that the relevant provisions in respect of search and seizure under the 1984 Act (ss 18[b] and 19[c]) did not extend to extradition offences; that the police therefore had no power without warrant to search the premises of a person arrested for an extradition crime; and that accordingly the entry and
f search of the claimant's home had been unlawful. In reaching its conclusion, the court relied, inter alia, on s 7(1)[d] of the Criminal Justice (International Co-operation) Act 1990 which permitted a justice of the peace to issue a search warrant in respect of a foreign offence. The police appealed to the House of Lords.

g **Held** – (Lord Hope dissenting) A police officer who had arrested a person in or on his premises pursuant to a warrant of arrest issued under s 8 of the 1989 Act had power to search those premises for, and to seize, any goods or documents which he reasonably believed to be material evidence in relation to the extradition crime in respect of which the warrant had been issued. The police had had such a power before the implementation of the 1984 Act, and it had not been
h extinguished by that Act. It was a well-established principle that a rule of the common law was not extinguished by statute unless the statute made that clear by express provision or by clear implication. Sections 18 and 19 of the 1984 Act were confined to domestic offences, and the Act's provisions did not lead to the conclusion that Parliament had intended to revoke the common law power
j exercisable after the execution of a warrant of arrest for an extradition offence. Although the common law power would not have attached to it any of the disciplines created by s 18 of the 1984 Act, or Code B made pursuant to that Act,

---

a Section 8, so far as material, is set out at [45], below
b Section 18 is set out at [65], below
c Section 19, so far as material, is set out at [65], below
d Section 7(1) is set out at [67], below

that was not a reason for concluding that the existing common law power was extinguished by the Act. The exercise of the common law power had a discipline attached to it in that it could only be exercised after a metropolitan magistrate or justice of the peace was of the opinion from the evidence supplied to him that the alleged conduct of the suspect would constitute an extradition offence and that the issue of a warrant for his arrest would be justified if the conduct had taken place within his jurisdiction. As regards s 7 of the 1990 Act, the fact that Parliament had made provision for a justice of the peace to issue a search warrant in respect of a foreign offence did not point to the conclusion that it was the view of Parliament that there was no common law power to search and seize after an arrest for an extradition offence. The power to seize and search to prevent the disappearance of material evidence was needed where the police, pursuant to a provisional warrant, arrested a suspect whose address in the United Kingdom had been unknown to them until they had located and arrested him and where, prior to finding and arresting the suspect, it was not possible to apply for a search warrant. It followed in the instant case that the police had been entitled to exercise the common law power of search and seizure after the claimant's arrest. Accordingly, the appeal would be allowed (see [1], [2], [62], [63], [66], [67], [75], [77], [78], [81], [82], [84], [106], [110], [111], [113], below).

Ghani v Jones [1969] 3 All ER 1700 and *R v Governor of Pentonville Prison, ex p Osman* [1989] 3 All ER 701 considered.

Notes

For the police's statutory powers of entry and search after arrest and for provisional warrants of arrest for an extradition offence, see respectively 11(1) *Halsbury's Laws* (4th edn reissue) para 684 and 17(2) *Halsbury's Laws* (4th edn reissue) para 1188.

For the Police and Criminal Evidence Act 1984, ss 18, 19, see 12 *Halsbury's Statutes* (4th edn) (1997 reissue) 821, 822.

For the Extradition Act 1989, s 8, see 17 *Halsbury's Statutes* (4th edn) (1999 reissue) 696.

For the Criminal Justice (International Co-operation) Act 1990, s 7, see 12 *Halsbury's Statutes* (4th edn) (1997 reissue) 1236.

Cases referred to in opinions

Adair v McGarry, Byrne v HM Advocate 1933 JC 72.
Air-India v Wiggins [1980] 2 All ER 593, [1980] 1 WLR 815, HL.
Bessell v Wilson (1853) 20 LTOS 233n, 118 ER 518.
Chic Fashions (West Wales) Ltd v Jones [1968] 1 All ER 229, [1968] 2 QB 299, [1968] 2 WLR 201, CA.
de Freitas v Permanent Secretary of Ministry of Agriculture, Fisheries, Lands and Housing [1999] 1 AC 69, [1998] 3 WLR 675, PC.
Dillon v O'Brien and Davis (1887) 16 Cox CC 245.
Elias v Pasmore [1934] 2 KB 164, [1934] All ER Rep 380.
Entick v Carrington (1765) 19 State Tr 1029, [1558–1774] All ER Rep 41, 95 ER 807.
Funke v France (1993) 16 EHRR 297, [1993] ECHR 10828/84, ECt HR.
Ghani v Jones [1969] 3 All ER 1700, [1970] 1 QB 693, [1969] 3 WLR 1158, CA; *affg* [1969] 3 All ER 720.
Jackson v Stevenson (1897) 24 R (J) 38.
Jeffrey v Black [1978] 1 All ER 555, [1978] QB 490, [1977] 3 WLR 895, DC.
Liangsiriprasert v United States Government [1990] 2 All ER 866, [1991] 1 AC 225, [1990] 3 WLR 606, PC.

a   *Macleod v A-G for New South Wales* [1891] AC 455, PC.
     Pringle v Bremner and Stirling (1867) 5 M (HL) 55.
     R v Cox [1961] 3 All ER 1194, [1963] AC 48, [1962] 2 WLR 126, Ct-MAC.
     R v Governor of Brixton Prison, ex p Levin [1997] 3 All ER 289, [1997] AC 741, [1997]
          3 WLR 117, HL.
     R v Governor of Pentonville Prison, ex p Osman [1989] 3 All ER 701, [1990] 1 WLR 277,
b   DC.
     R v Secretary of State for the Home Dept, ex p Daly [2001] UKHL 26, [2001] 3 All ER
          433, [2001] 2 AC 532, [2001] 2 WLR 1622.
     R v Shayler [2002] UKHL 11, [2002] 2 All ER 477, [2002] 2 WLR 754.
     R v Southwark Crown Court and HM Customs and Excise, ex p Sorsky Defries [1996]
          Crim LR 195, DC.
c   *Sunday Times v UK* (1979) 2 EHRR 245, [1979] ECHR 6538/74, ECt HR.

Appeal

The Commissioner of Police of the Metropolis appealed with permission of the
Appeal Committee of the House of Lords given on 1 November 2001 from the
d   order of the Divisional Court (Brooke LJ and Harrison J) on 30 July 2001 ([2001]
EWHC Admin 576, [2001] All ER (D) 315 (Jul)) granting an application by the
respondent, Michael Rottman, for judicial review of a search by the police of his
home, and the seizure of articles found in it, following his arrest under a
provisional warrant issued pursuant to s 8 of the Extradition Act 1989. The
Divisional Court certified that a point of law of general public importance, set out
e   at [42], below, was involved in its decision. The facts are set out in the opinion of
Lord Hutton.

David Perry and *Sarah Whitehouse* (instructed by *Peter Loose*) for the appellant.
Clare Montgomery QC and *Julian Knowles* (instructed by *Christmas & Sheehan*) for
f   the respondent.

Their Lordships took time for consideration.

16 May 2002. The following opinions were delivered.

g   **LORD NICHOLLS OF BIRKENHEAD.**
     [1] My Lords, I have had the advantage of reading in draft the speeches of my
noble and learned friends Lord Hutton and Lord Rodger of Earlsferry. For the
reasons they give, and with which I agree, I would answer the certified question
in the manner Lord Hutton proposes and allow this appeal accordingly.

h   **LORD HOFFMANN.**
     [2] My Lords, I have had the advantage of reading in draft the speeches of my
noble and learned friends Lord Hutton and Lord Rodger of Earlsferry. For the
reasons they give, and with which I agree, I would answer the certified question
in the manner Lord Hutton proposes and allow this appeal accordingly.
j

LORD HOPE OF CRAIGHEAD.
     [3] My Lords, my noble and learned friend, Lord Hutton, whose speech I have
had the advantage of reading in draft, has described the background to this case.
I gratefully adopt his account of it. For the reasons which he has given, and for
the reasons given by my noble and learned friend, Lord Rodger of Earlsferry,
I agree that the powers which are given to the police by ss 18 and 19 of the Police

and Criminal Evidence Act 1984 (PACE) do not apply where a person is arrested under a provisional warrant for an extradition offence. I also agree with Lord *a* Rodger that the power in s 32 of that Act to search premises in which the person was when he was arrested does not apply either as the term 'offence' in sub-s (2)(b) is confined to domestic offences, and that s 17(5) of PACE has nothing to do with the power of the police to search premises once a person has been arrested. I regret however that I am unable to agree with my noble and learned friends' analysis of *b* the powers which are available to a police officer at common law where he is in possession of an arrest warrant.

[4] As Lord Hutton has explained, we are concerned here with a provisional warrant for the arrest of the respondent which was issued under s 8(1) of the Extradition Act 1989. A magistrate has power to issue a warrant of arrest under that section if he is supplied with sufficient evidence to satisfy him that he would *c* be justified in issuing a warrant for the arrest of a person accused of a crime committed within his jurisdiction and that the conduct alleged would constitute an extradition crime (see s 8(3)). The purpose of the arrest, as s 9(1) of the 1989 Act makes clear, is to enable the respondent to be brought before a court of committal as soon as practicable with a view to the commencement of extradition *d* proceedings against him in that court. Section 8(6) provides that, where a warrant is issued under that section for the arrest of a person accused of an offence of stealing or receiving stolen property committed in a designated Commonwealth country or colony, the magistrate shall have the like power to issue a warrant to search for the property as if the offence had been committed within his *e* jurisdiction. But the magistrate did not have power to issue a warrant for search for property in this case, as the alleged offence was one of fraud and it was said to have been committed in Germany. The only power which he had under this statute was to issue a warrant for the respondent's arrest. He had power under s 26(1) of the Theft Act 1968 read with s 24(1) of that Act to issue a warrant to search for and seize stolen goods, but it was not alleged that the respondent had *f* any stolen goods in his custody or possession or on his premises.

[5] Had it not been for the possibility that a police officer executing a warrant of arrest issued under s 8(1) of the 1989 Act has powers of search at common law, therefore, the position in this case would have been quite straightforward. The warrant which was issued to him was a warrant of arrest only. Its sole purpose *g* was to enable the respondent to be taken into custody. It was not a warrant to search. Its purpose was served as soon as the respondent had been arrested in the driveway of his house a few yards from its front door. The decision to search the house was not taken for the purpose of effecting the arrest. It was taken because two German police officers who arrived at the premises afterwards, having *h* spoken to the public prosecutor in Germany, asked for the house to be searched. This was because they suspected that there were computers, computer disks and financial documents which might hold evidence of the offences which the respondent was alleged to have committed or proceeds of those offences. But the officer of the Metropolitan Police to whom that request was made did not have a warrant to search the house. If he had asked for one to be issued to him under *j* s 8(6) of the 1989 Act, it would have been refused. The statutory powers under PACE were not available. In the absence of a relevant common law power, it is plain that the entry and search of the house which the police carried out was unlawful, and that the respondent's rights under art 8 of the European Convention for the Protection of Human Rights and Fundamental Freedoms 1950 (as set out in Sch 1 to the Human Rights Act 1998) were violated.

The common law power

a

[6] There is no doubt that a police officer had power at common law, when executing a warrant for a person's arrest, to search the suspect and to seize any articles which he might find on his person or in his immediate vicinity which might constitute material evidence against him for the purpose of preserving that evidence until trial. The question which is in dispute is whether this common law

b power extended to a search of the premises where the arrest took place for evidence as well as to a search of the person of the suspect. In view of the powers of search upon an arrest which are given to a constable by s 32 of PACE this question is no longer a live issue where the offence for which the person was arrested is a domestic offence. I consider that the authorities as to the state of the common law prior to the coming into force of PACE are at best unclear on the point. Its

c development was not assisted by the fact that the test as to whether evidence obtained in the course of a search is admissible was whether the evidence was relevant and not whether it had been properly obtained (see *Jeffrey v Black* [1978] 1 All ER 555, [1978] QB 490). In that context there was no need to address the question whether the search was lawful. In the present case it is directly relevant.

d In my opinion the better view is that the constable had no common law power to carry out a search of the premises for evidence unless he had the person's consent or the authority of a search warrant.

[7] In *Chic Fashions (West Wales) Ltd v Jones* [1968] 1 All ER 229, [1968] 2 QB 299 Lord Denning MR reviewed the cases relating to the power of a constable entering a house in possession of a search warrant to seize goods not covered by

e the warrant but which he reasonably believed to have been stolen and to be material evidence on a charge of stealing or receiving against the person in possession of them. They included the Scottish case of *Pringle v Bremner and Stirling* (1867) 5 M (HL) 55. That was an action of damages in which it was alleged that a constable who was authorised by a search warrant to search a house for

f pieces of wood and pieces of a fuse used to cause an explosion had taken away private books and papers which he had found in the pursuer's repositories. Lord Chelmsford LC recognised (at 60) that it might be said that the constable had no right whatever to go beyond the terms of his warrant and endeavour to find something else that might implicate the pursuer in the charge. But he added this comment in a passage which Lord Denning MR quoted ([1968] 1 All ER 229

g at 235, [1968] 2 QB 299 at 311):

'But supposing that in a search which might have been improper originally, there were matters discovered which showed the complicity of the pursuer in a crime, then I think the officers, I can hardly say would have been

h justified, but would have been excused by the result of their search.'

[8] That was however, as Lord Denning MR observed ([1968] 1 All ER 229 at 235, [1968] 2 QB 299 at 312) a case on a search warrant. He then went on to consider the power of a constable to seize other goods which go to prove guilt where he was executing a warrant of arrest. In *Dillon v O'Brien and Davis* (1887)

j 16 Cox CC 245 it was held that, where a person was arrested on an arrest warrant, a constable was entitled to take from him property found in his possession which was likely to form material evidence in his prosecution for a crime. Palles CB said (at 249) that constables were entitled, upon a lawful arrest of a person charged with treason or felony to take and detain property 'found in his possession' which would form material evidence in his prosecution for crime. I note in passing that he did not go so far as to say that they were entitled to conduct a search of the premises. In *Elias v Pasmore* [1934] 2 KB 164, [1934] All ER Rep 380 it was held that a constable who was arresting a man named Hannington for sedition was entitled to seize documents which were in his possession which would form material evidence against the plaintiff in that action on a charge of inciting Hannington to commit the crime of sedition. Horridge J said ([1934] 2 KB 164 at 173, [1934] All ER Rep 380 at 384) that their seizure, although improper, would be excused because the documents were capable of being used and were used as evidence in the trial.

[9] The conclusion which Lord Denning MR drew from these cases was that, when a constable enters a house by virtue of a search warrant for stolen goods, he may seize not only the goods which he reasonably believes to be covered by the warrant, but also any other goods which he believes on reasonable grounds to have been stolen and to be material evidence on a charge of stealing or receiving against the person in possession of them or anyone associated with him (see [1968] 1 All ER 229 at 236, [1967] 2 QB 299 at 313). He did not discuss the question which arises in this case, which is whether a constable who is lawfully on premises for the execution of an arrest warrant may conduct a search of those premises for evidence without being in possession of a search warrant.

[10] Diplock LJ said:

'... unless forced to do so by recent binding authority, I decline to accept that a police officer who is unquestionably justified at common law in arresting a person whom he has reasonable grounds to believe is guilty of receiving stolen goods, is not likewise justified in the less draconian act of seizing what he, on reasonable grounds, believes to be the stolen goods in that person's possession'. (See [1968] 1 All ER 229 at 238, [1968] 2 QB 299 at 316.)

Salmon LJ enlarged on this point:

'It would be absurd if the police had the power to arrest a man, but, having failed to catch him, had no power to seize the goods in his house which they reasonably believed he had stolen or unlawfully received. There is no doubt that, if they find the goods in his possession when they arrest him, they may seize the goods (see the observations of LORD CAMPBELL, C.J., in the footnote to *Bessell* v. *Wilson* ((1853) 20 LTOS 233n, 118 ER 518); *Dillon* v. *O'Brien and Davis* ((1887) 16 Cox CC 245); and *Elias* v. *Pasmore* ([1934] 2 KB 164, [1934] All ER Rep 380)). Suppose the police, reasonably believing a man has stolen some jewellery, follow him into his house in order to arrest him. As they enter the front door they see him disappearing out of the back door, but there on the table is the jewellery. Surely they may seize it; the fact that he has evaded capture cannot confer any immunity on him in respect of the stolen goods.' (See [1968] 1 All ER 229 at 240, [1968] 2 QB 299 at 319–320.)

But the situations contemplated in these passages, where stolen goods are found in the person's possession when he is arrested or are in plain view as he evades arrest, are not those which are under consideration in this case. What their Lordships had in contemplation was a power to seize stolen goods which they find in his possession or they happen to see while they are attempting to effect the arrest. There is no discussion in these judgments of the question whether the police officer, having effected the arrest, would then be entitled at common law to conduct a search of the premises for evidence.

[11] The only passage in the authorities which may be said to be directed to this precise issue is to be found in the judgment of Lord Denning MR in

a *Ghani v Jones* [1969] 3 All ER 1700, [1970] 1 QB 693. That was a case where police officers who were inquiring into a woman's disappearance searched without warrant the house of the woman's father-in-law. At their request the father-in-law handed over to them various documents which included several passports. The plaintiffs later asked for the documents to be returned to them, but the police refused to do so. It was held that the police had not shown reasonable grounds

b for believing that the documents were material evidence to prove the commission of a murder or that the plaintiffs were in any way implicated in or accessory to a crime, and the police were ordered to return the documents forthwith.

[12] In the course of his judgment in *Ghani v Jones* [1969] 3 All ER 1700 at 1702–1703, [1970] 1 QB 693 at 705–706 Lord Denning MR said:

c
'So we have a case where the police officers, in investigating a murder, have seized property without a warrant and without making an arrest and have retained it without the consent of the party from whom they took it. Their justification is that they believe it to be of "evidential value" on a

d prosecution for murder. Is this a sufficient justification in law? I would start by considering the law where police officers enter a man's house by virtue of a warrant, or arrest a man lawfully, with or without a warrant, for a serious offence. I take it to be settled law, without citing cases, that the officers are entitled to take any goods which they find in his possession or in his house which they reasonably believe to be material evidence in relation to the

e crime for which he is arrested or for which they enter. If *in the course of their search* they come on any other goods which show him to be implicated in some other crime, they may take them provided they act reasonably and detain them no longer than is necessary. Such appears from the speech of LORD CHELMSFORD in *Pringle* v. *Bremner and Stirling* ((1867) 5 M (HL) 55 at 60)

f and *Chic Fashions (West Wales), Ltd* v. *Jones* ([1968] 1 All ER 229, [1968] 2 QB 299).' (My emphasis.)

[13] Were it not for the presence in this passage of the words which I have highlighted, it would not have been possible to say that it added anything to what could be found in the earlier authorities. The earlier authorities were not

g concerned with the question whether a police officer was entitled at common law, when effecting an arrest, also to conduct a search of the premises for evidence. What then are we to make of Lord Denning MR's use of the phrase 'in the course of their search'?

[14] In my opinion the best guide to what Lord Denning MR had in mind is to

h be found in the fact that he said that he was setting out, without citing cases, what he took to be settled law. It was settled law that a police officer seeking to effect an arrest, with or without a warrant, was entitled to search the person of the suspect. It was also settled law that he was entitled to search premises where the suspect might be hiding for the purpose of finding the suspect and effecting the arrest. And it

j was settled law that he was entitled to seize things found in the course of either of these exercises which he reasonably believed to be material evidence in relation to the crime for which the suspect was being arrested or, having entered the premises in possession of a search warrant, he found articles in relation to a crime other than that for which the search warrant was granted. But there was no basis in the authorities for saying that it was settled law that a police officer, having effected an arrest, was then entitled to conduct a search of the premises for evidence without first having obtained a search warrant. I do not detect in

Lord Denning MR's remarks an intention to extend the law to this effect. Nor was
it necessary for him to do so for the decision in that case. The passage which
I have quoted was plainly obiter, as the decision in the case did not turn on
the question whether the police were entitled to take possession of the documents
without a search warrant.

[15] In *Jeffrey v Black* [1978] 1 All ER 555, [1978] QB 490 the police arrested the
defendant for the offence of stealing a sandwich from a public house. They then
searched his home without a search warrant and without his consent. It was held
that their search of his home in these circumstances was unlawful and that the
evidence which the police had obtained during their search of drug offences had
been irregularly obtained. Reference was made to Lord Denning MR's observations
in *Ghani v Jones*. It was not necessary for the court in that case to decide whether
it would have been open to the police to conduct a search of the premises where
the defendant was arrested with a view to finding material evidence of the
crime for which he was arrested. Lord Widgery CJ said ([1978] 1 All ER 555 at
558, [1978] QB 490 at 497) that it might very well be that they might have made
that inspection without further authority. But he went on to say that they did not
have power to inspect his house at another place when the contents of the house,
on the face of it, bore no relation whatever to the offence with which he was
charged. I agree that there is no hint in this passage or in what Forbes J said
([1978] 1 All ER 555 at 560, [1978] QB 490 at 499) of any criticism of Lord
Denning MR's observations. But here again the judges' comments on the issue
that arises in this case were obiter.

[16] The only other case which bears on this issue is *R v Governor of Pentonville
Prison, ex p Osman* [1989] 3 All ER 701, [1990] 1 WLR 277. In that case the police
officers were in possession of a search warrant issued under the Forgery Act 1981
and a provisional warrant issued under s 6 of the Fugitive Offenders Act 1967
(from which s 8(1) of the 1989 Act is derived). They arrested Osman on the
provisional warrant and then carried out a search in the course of which they
removed a large number of documents. Objection was taken to the search on the
ground that there was no common law power to search and seize documents in
relation to a crime alleged to have been committed abroad. It was rejected by the
Divisional Court for the following reasons which were given by Lloyd LJ:

> 'It is beyond dispute that, in relation to a domestic offence, a police officer
> entering a house in pursuance of a warrant of arrest, or otherwise lawfully
> arresting a defendant, is entitled to take any goods or documents which he
> reasonably believes to be material evidence in relation to the crime for which
> the defendant is being arrested: *Ghani v Jones* ([1969] 3 All ER 1700 at 1703,
> [1970] 1 QB 693 at 706). Is there then any difference between a warrant of
> arrest in domestic proceedings and a provisional warrant under section 6 of
> the Fugitive Offenders Act 1967? We can see none. The police powers of
> search and seizure consequent on a lawful arrest ought to be, and in our
> judgment are, the same in both cases.' (See [1990] 1 WLR 277 at 311.)

[17] I agree that in the first sentence of this passage, read in its context,
Lloyd LJ must be taken to have accepted Lord Denning MR's observations in
Ghani v Jones as authority for the proposition that, where a police officer enters a
house and arrests a suspect in pursuance of a warrant of arrest or otherwise
lawfully, he is entitled to search the entire house and seize any articles which he
reasonably believes to be material evidence. But for the reasons which I have
already given I consider, with great respect, that this was a misreading of those

a observations. In any event, if Lord Denning MR's observations are to be read in this way I think that they went further than was justified by the authorities.

[18] I derive support for my approach from the views expressed by Professor David Feldman *The Law Relating to Entry, Search and Seizure* (1986) pp 241–247 (paras 9.36–9.48). In para 9.36 he observes that, when a person is arrested in private premises, police practice prior to PACE was to search the whole of the

b house or flat and remove any evidence they found and that this practice relied for common law authority on the dictum of Lord Denning MR in *Ghani v Jones* [1969] 3 All ER 1700 at 1703, [1970] 1 QB 693 at 706. In para 9.48 he says that PACE did what the Royal Commission on Criminal Procedure had recommended by regularising the existing police practice on search of the premises where the person is arrested. Of particular interest for present purposes is his examination

c of the common law in paras 9.37–9.47. As he points out, police practice is one thing. What the law is on the matter is quite another. Unless authorised by judicial decision or by statute, police practice is no more than that. It is not the law.

[19] In para 9.37 Professor Feldman says that Lord Denning MR's statement went further than was justified by the authorities, perhaps because of the

d confusion caused by treating powers of arrest as if they were the same as powers under a search warrant, and that the assumption that the police had power to search a man's house after his arrest was not supported by either of the cases which Lord Denning MR cited. As he points out later in the same paragraph:

e 'Cases where authority to search is granted by a magistrate on being convinced (at least in theory) that there is reasonable cause to believe that the articles sought are on the premises are in a different category from searches following arrest. In the latter case, the search will not have been subject to prior review, it will be of a speculative nature and the goods sought will be uncertain. The question is, therefore, whether there is any clear authority for the existence of a power to search anything more than the

f arrested person himself.

9.38 There is no English authority either at common law or under statute for searching an area or taking property which is not under the immediate physical control of the person arrested.'

g [20] The powers of entry to and search of premises by the police were considered by the Royal Commission on Criminal Procedure in its report *The Investigation and Prosecution of Criminal Offences in England and Wales: The Law and Procedure* (Cmnd 8092-1 (January 1981)). Its conclusions as to the powers of the police on arrest are stated at p 11 (para 29) of the report as follows:

h 'The law on whether a constable has power to search the premises of an arrested person is not certain. He is empowered to search areas under the immediate control of the prisoner, as the right to search on arrest described in paragraph 27 [the power to search the arrested person] suggests. This certainly covers the room in which he is arrested. Beyond this the law is

j unclear. There does, however, seem to be a right on arrest to search the premises of the arrested person even if the arrest took place elsewhere. But such a search is unlawful if there is no connection between it and the offence for which the prisoner was arrested.'

The authority for the point made in the last sentence is to be found in the judgment of Lord Widgery CJ in *Jeffrey v Black* [1978] 1 All ER 555 at 558, [1978] QB 490 at 497. The fact that the law on whether a constable has power to search the premises of an arrested person was thought in 1981 by the Royal Commission to be uncertain supports the view which I myself have formed as to the state of the law at that time.

[21] The report of an interdepartmental working party, *A Review of the Law and Practice of Extradition in the United Kingdom* (Home Office (May 1982)) contains this observation (at p 65 (para 11.6)):

'Section 6(5) of the Fugitive Offenders Act 1967 provides that "Where a warrant is issued ... for the arrest of a person accused of an offence of stealing or receiving stolen property or any other offence in respect of property, a justice of the peace in any part of the United Kingdom shall have the like power to issue a warrant to search for the property as if the offence had been committed within the jurisdiction of the justice." The absence of any equivalent provision from the Extradition Act 1870 for many years deprived the police officer seeking to execute a warrant of arrest of the reassurance available from being armed at the same time with a search warrant. However the problem is now adequately dealt with by section 26(1) of the Theft Act 1968, read with section 24(1) of the same Act. These would permit a justice of the peace to issue a search warrant in extradition or fugitive offender cases, and we therefore find it unnecessary to provide specific powers of search in a new extradition statute.'

It is of some interest to see that the working party recognised that there might be a problem if the police officer was not armed with a search warrant, and that it had now been adequately dealt with by the power to issue a search warrant which is contained in s 26(1) of the 1968 Act. It was noted at p 64 (para 11.3) of the report that a sizeable proportion of requests made to the United Kingdom relate to offences such as theft and fraud, and that it was not uncommon for property discovered during searches carried out on or after the fugitive's arrest to be exhibited to the court during extradition proceedings and surrendered to the requesting country with the fugitive. The assumption appears however to have been, as the discussion in para 11.6 indicates, that a search of premises for property in extradition cases would require the issue of a search warrant.

Scottish practice

[22] My noble and learned friend, Lord Rodger, has drawn attention to the fact that when a sheriff in Scotland grants a warrant to search for and to arrest an accused he also, as a matter of routine, grants a warrant to search the house or the premises where the accused is found. In *Renton & Brown's Criminal Procedure* (6th edn, 1996) p 47 (para 5.03) it is stated that complaint and petition warrants normally include warrants to arrest and search the person of the suspect, his dwelling-house, repositories and the place where he is found. A helpful discussion of the practice is to be found in Sheriff Charles N Stoddart's book *Criminal Warrants* (2nd edn, 1999) paras 1.09–1.12. In para 1.12 he points out that the sheriff has power in summary cases, on a complaint under the Criminal Procedure (Scotland) Act 1995 being laid before the court, to grant all competent warrants under s 139(1) of that Act. This subsection includes a power 'to grant warrant to search the person, dwelling-house and repositories of the accused and any place where he may be found for any documents, articles, or property likely to afford evidence of his guilt of, or guilty participation in, any offence charged in the complaint, and to take possession of such documents, articles or property' (see s 139(1)(c)).

a
[23] I am inclined to think that these aspects of Scottish practice, founded as they are upon the granting of warrants which give express power to search and on the exercise of powers which are given to the sheriffs by statute, are of little assistance when one is considering the common law of England on the question of the powers of a police officer who is effecting an arrest under an arrest warrant or otherwise lawfully but has no warrant to search. It is perhaps worth noting

b
also that the power of search which the sheriffs give extends not only to the house or premises where the suspect may be found but also to his repositories and domicile or, as s 139(1) of the 1995 Act puts it, to his 'dwelling-house and repositories'. This goes further than Forbes J was willing to accept was the position in England under the common law (see *Jeffrey v Black* [1978] 1 All ER 555 at 560, [1978] QB 490 at 499).

c
[24] As it happens, however, the common law of Scotland is not entirely silent on this issue. It remains relevant where a person is detained by a constable for questioning at a police station under s 14 of the 1995 Act. Section 14(7)(b) provides that in that event a constable may 'exercise the same powers of search as are available following an arrest'.

d
[25] As to what those powers are, reference may be made to *Adair v McGarry, Byrne v HM Advocate* 1933 JC 72, where the question was whether a police constable was entitled, without the warrant of a magistrate, to take the fingerprints of a man whom he had apprehended. Lord Justice General Clyde said (at 78):

e
'It is beyond all doubt that, provided a person has been legally arrested by the police, they may search him for stolen goods, or weapons, or other real evidence connecting him with the crime; and that neither his consent nor a magistrate's warrant is required for that purpose. This applies even to the limited but well-known class of cases in which the police are entitled to make

f
the arrest without a warrant—*Jackson v. Stevenson* ((1897) 24 R (J) 38). It is also beyond all doubt that, provided a person has been legally arrested by the police, they may examine his person and his clothes for bloodstains and the like, or for any mark on his person which, according to their information, was observed on the person of the criminal when the crime was committed— again, without his consent and without any magistrate's warrant.'

g
Similar observations are to be found in the opinions of Lord Justice-Clerk Alness (at 80), Lord Sands (at 88) and Lord Morison (at 89).

[26] Lord Hunter, who dissented in that case, explained his views on this matter in these words (at 85):

h
'It may be that the right to arrest in some cases infers a right to examine the clothing and person, or it may be the property, of the arrested person, and it may be that in the interests of justice this right can be exercised without a warrant. A policeman arresting a man in the act of committing a crime would have the right to examine the clothing and person of the arrested

j
individual so as to preserve evidence of the commission of the crime. That right may even extend in certain cases to the examination of the contents of the premises in which the arrest took place. In the ordinary case, however, such rights cannot be exercised by the police without a magistrate's warrant. Reference may be made to the decision in *Pringle v. Bremner and Stirling* ((1867) 5 M (HL) 55), where, the Court of Session having dismissed an action, the House of Lords reversed, holding that, as the pursuer's averments of

search and imprisonment without warrant disclosed a *prima facie* case of
wrong, the case was relevant.'

[27] The fact that Lord Hunter was willing to acknowledge that the police
would be entitled 'in certain cases' to examine the contents of the premises in
which the arrest took place is of some significance. But this point was not
developed by the other judges in that case. It has not been the subject of later
decision in any Scottish court. No doubt this is because the usual practice of
granting a warrant to search the premises of the suspect when a warrant for his
arrest is granted has made it unnecessary to deal with it. I am not aware of any
case where the reference in s 14(7)(b) of the 1995 Act to 'the same powers of
search as are available following an arrest' has been held to extend to a search of
the premises for evidence. If symmetry between England and Scotland in this
matter is desirable—and I think it is, as the 1989 Act is a United Kingdom statute
and s 8(1) applies to Scotland without modification—it is of some importance to
note that it would be contrary to current practice in Scotland, and to the current
state of the authorities, for a constable who was in possession of a provisional
warrant of arrest issued under that section to carry out a search of premises for
evidence without the person's consent or the authority of a search warrant.

Does the common law power extend to extradition cases?

[28] Lloyd LJ's observation in *R v Governor of Pentonville Prison, ex p Osman*
[1990] 1 WLR 277 at 311 that the police powers of search and seizure consequent
on a lawful arrest ought to be, and are, the same in the case of an arrest under a
provisional warrant and an arrest in a domestic case is attractive at first sight.
There are good reasons on grounds of public policy for the provision of mutual
assistance between states in the detection and punishment of crime. But I do not
agree that the position which applies in domestic law can be equated so readily
with that which applies in extradition cases.

[29] One important difference between domestic cases and extradition cases
lies in the fact that the procedure which applies in extradition cases depends upon
there having first been a request. Section 7(1) of the 1989 Act provides that a
person shall not be dealt with under Pt III of that Act except in pursuance of an
order of the Secretary of State issued in pursuance of a request for the surrender
of a person under the Act. Another important difference is that, except in the
case of a request for the arrest of a person accused of an offence of stealing or
receiving stolen property committed in a designated Commonwealth country or
colony, the 1989 Act is concerned only with the arrest of the person whose
extradition is being sought. Subject to that exception, the Act it is not concerned
with the collection of evidence or property connected with the crime for which
extradition is sought or with its surrender to the requesting country.

[30] The provisions which enable the United Kingdom to co-operate with
other countries in criminal proceedings and investigations are contained in a
separate statute, the Criminal Justice (International Co-operation) Act 1990.
Section 7(1) of that Act provides that Pt II of PACE, in relation to powers of entry,
seizure and search, shall have effect as if references to serious arrestable offences
in s 8 of and Sch 1 to that Act included any conduct which is an offence under the
law of a country or territory outside the United Kingdom and would constitute a
serious arrestable offence if it had occurred in any part of the United Kingdom.
Section 7(2) gives power to a justice of the peace to issue a warrant to a constable
to enter and search premises and to seize any evidence that is found there.

[31] But these provisions are qualified by s 7(4) of the 1990 Act, which provides that no application for a warrant or order shall be made by virtue of sub-ss (1) or (2) except in pursuance of a direction given by the Secretary of State in response to a request received from an overseas court, tribunal or authority, and that any evidence seized by a constable by virtue of that section shall be furnished by him to the Secretary of State for transmission to that court, tribunal or authority. The fact that Parliament has laid down in these specific terms what is to be done by way of mutual assistance, and has provided that any such assistance must be preceded by a request, is important. It provides a strong indication that it is only on those conditions, except in cases covered by ss 24(1) and 26(1) of the 1968 Act, that powers of entry, search and seizure should be exercised in extradition cases for the purpose of seeking out and taking possession of evidence for use by the overseas court.

Conclusions as to the common law

[32] For these reasons I would hold that the common law powers which are available to a police officer when effecting an arrest do not extend to a search of the premises where the person was arrested for the purpose of obtaining evidence. It is perhaps arguable that an exception might be made where there are compelling reasons in the public interest for carrying out a such a search, for example in cases of urgency. But in the present case the decision to search the house for evidence was not taken on grounds of urgency. It was taken because the police officer considered that he had power to conduct such a search under the common law, and also because he considered that PACE was available for the carrying out of a search in extradition matters. In my opinion the search was unlawful because it was undertaken without the respondent's consent and because the police had not obtained a search warrant.

[33] In any event I would hold that any power which the police might have had to conduct a search of the house for evidence at common law did not apply in this case. The arrest was on a provisional warrant for an extradition offence. The sole purpose for which that warrant was granted was to bring the respondent before the court for committal with a view to his extradition to Germany. The police were not entitled, when effecting this arrest, to exercise the powers of search for evidence which would have been available to them had the arrest been for a domestic offence.

The art 8 convention right

[34] This brings me to the question whether what was done in this case constituted a violation of the respondent's rights under art 8 of the convention. It is clear that searches of private premises infringe the art 8(1) right unless the conditions in art 8(2) are satisfied (see *Funke v France* (1993) 16 EHRR 297). The wording of art 8(2) as applied to this case indicates that any interference with a person's right to respect for his private life, his home and his correspondence must satisfy two basic requirements. First, the interference must be 'in accordance with the law'. This means that it must satisfy the principle of legality. Secondly, it must be such as is 'necessary' for the prevention of crime. This raises the question of proportionality.

[35] It is well established that the principle of legality requires the court to address itself to three distinct questions (see *Sunday Times v UK* (1979) 2 EHRR 245 at 271 (para 49), *R v Shayler* [2002] UKHL 11 at [56], [2002] 2 All ER 477 at [56], [2002] 2 WLR 754). The first is whether there is a legal basis in domestic law for the restriction. The second is whether the law or rule in question is sufficiently

accessible to the individual who is affected by the interference, and sufficiently precise to enable him to understand its scope and foresee the consequences of his actions so that he can regulate his conduct without breaking the law. The third is whether, assuming that these two requirements are satisfied, it is nevertheless open to the criticism on the convention ground that it was applied in a way that was arbitrary because, for example, it has been resorted to in bad faith or in a way that is not proportionate.

[36] For the reasons which I have already given, I consider that there was no settled basis in domestic law for the carrying out by the police of a search of the respondent's house for evidence of an extradition crime without his consent and without having first obtained a search warrant. In any event, it seems to me that, if there was an undoubted power of search at common law, the second and third requirements relating to accessibility, precision and lack of arbitrariness were not satisfied. In the absence of a search warrant the police had no clear authority for what they were doing. The power which they were purporting to exercise was unregulated, and it lacked adequate safeguards against abuse. No limits had been set for its exercise, as the purpose of their search had not been subject to prior review by any judicial officer. The absence of regulation was particularly significant in this case as the conduct alleged was not a domestic offence but an extradition crime. There was an obvious risk that items taken in the course of their search might extend beyond what was strictly necessary for the purpose of prosecuting that crime in the overseas court.

[37] Turning to the question of proportionality, there is a general international understanding as to the matters which should be considered where a question is raised as to whether an interference with a fundamental right is proportionate: see *de Freitas v Permanent Secretary of Ministry of Agriculture, Fisheries, Lands and Housing* [1999] 1 AC 69 at 80, [1998] 3 WLR 675 at 684 per Lord Clyde, *R v Secretary of State for the Home Dept, ex p Daly* [2001] UKHL 26 at [27], [2001] 3 All ER 433 at [27], [2001] 2 AC 532 per Lord Steyn, *R v Shayler* [2002] UKHL 11 at [60]–[61], [2002] 2 All ER 477 at [60]–[61], [2002] 2 WLR 754. The first question is whether the objective sought to be achieved—a pressing social need—is sufficiently important to justify limiting the fundamental right. The second is whether the means chosen to limit that right are rational, fair and not arbitrary. The third is whether the means used impair that right as minimally as is reasonably possible.

[38] I am in no doubt that the public interest in the detection and punishment of crime is a pressing social need which justifies some interference in the rights which a suspect has under art 8(1) of the convention. The objective sought to be achieved in this case satisfies this requirement. But the principle of proportionality requires that any such interference must be rational, fair and not arbitrary. There must be adequate guarantees in domestic law to ensure that any such measures of interference will not be abused.

[39] Here again what was done in this case seems to me to be open to criticism. In the absence of prior review by a judicial officer the exercise which the Metropolitan Police were carrying out in this case appears to me indeed to have been arbitrary. They had no need to search the premises for the purposes of the extradition proceedings which were being conducted in this country. It is not a responsibility of the requested state, unless requested to do so by the requesting state, to look for evidence of the commission of the extradition crime. The only reason why the police proceeded to search the premises was because they were asked to do so by the German police officers, having spoken on the telephone to the public prosecutor. We can assume that the officers of the Metropolitan Police by whom the search was conducted were not familiar with

a German criminal law and procedure. Two separate accounts have been given of the events that followed the arrest, and there is no agreement as to what precisely took place. But it seems likely that, when the Metropolitan Police removed the computer equipment, computer disks and other property from the house, they were wholly dependent on the views of the German police officers as to what to look for and what to seize.

b [40] Where warrants to search are granted they are specific as to the purpose and limitations of the search. But in this case, as there was no such warrant, no systems were in place to ensure that the items which the police seized in the course of their search of the premises were confined strictly to those which were relevant to the prosecution of the extradition crime in the overseas court. It has

c not been suggested that it would have been impracticable for the Metropolitan Police to apply for a search warrant in order to clarify the position before they undertook a search of the premises for any such evidence, or that what they did was done on grounds of urgency. As to whether it has been shown that the interference with the respondent's art 8(1) right was the minimum necessary,

d I consider that it must at least be open to question whether less intrusive and less arbitrary means could have been employed to meet the interests of justice in this case. For these various reasons I would hold that the interference with the respondent's convention right was not proportionate.

Conclusion

e [41] I would answer the certified question in the negative and dismiss the appeal.

LORD HUTTON.

f [42] My Lords, the question certified by the Divisional Court for the consideration of the House on this appeal by the Commissioner of Police of the Metropolis is as follows:

'At common law, does a police officer executing a warrant of arrest issued pursuant to section 8 of the Extradition Act 1989 have power to search for and seize any goods or documents which he reasonably believes to be

g material evidence in relation to the extradition crime in respect of which the warrant was issued?'

The background

h [43] The certified question arises from the following circumstances. The respondent, Mr Michael Rottman, is a German businessman. A court in Germany issued a warrant for his arrest on 27 December 1996. The warrant contained an allegation that he and other persons committed offences of fraud in Germany. The allegation arose out of events dating back to 1990 and concerned Mr Rottman's alleged role in the purchase and subsequent asset-stripping of an East German

j power supply company by a Swiss shell company with which he was associated. The respondent left Germany at the end of 1995 and the German authorities believed that he had access to funds stolen from the East German company.

[44] On 13 September 2000 the Metropolitan Police received a request from the German authorities, via Interpol, for the respondent's extradition to Germany. At that time it was known that he was somewhere in the south of England but his precise whereabouts were not known.

[45] On 22 September 2000 a provisional warrant for the respondent's arrest was issued by the Bow Street Magistrates' Court under s 8(1) of the Extradition Act 1989 which provides:

'For the purposes of this Part of this Act a warrant for the arrest of a person may be issued—(a) on receipt of an authority to proceed—(i) by the chief metropolitan stipendiary magistrate or a designated metropolitan magistrate; (ii) by the sheriff of Lothian and Borders; (b) without such an authority—(i) by a metropolitan magistrate; (ii) by a justice of the peace in any part of the United Kingdom; and (iii) in Scotland, by a sheriff, upon information that the said person is or is believed to be in or on his way to the United Kingdom; and any warrant issued by virtue of paragraph (b) above is in this Act referred to as a "provisional warrant" ...

(3) A person empowered to issue warrants of arrest under this section may issue such a warrant if he is supplied with such evidence as would in his opinion justify the issue of a warrant for the arrest of a person accused or, as the case may be, convicted within his jurisdiction and it appears to him that the conduct alleged would constitute an extradition crime.'

The provisional warrant alleged conspiracy to defraud, which is an extradition crime as defined by s 2 of the 1989 Act. The information placed before the magistrates' court would have justified the issue of a warrant for the arrest of a person accused of such an offence in the United Kingdom.

[46] The police carried out a surveillance operation and on 23 September 2000 the respondent was seen in Henley on Thames. The police followed him to his home, which was a large detached house set in its own grounds in Hazlemere, High Wycombe. The respondent was arrested pursuant to the warrant in the driveway of the house a few yards from its front door. It is not in dispute that the police were entitled under s 17 of the Police and Criminal Evidence Act 1984 (PACE) to enter the grounds of the house to arrest the respondent pursuant to the warrant.

[47] The account of the events that followed the arrest given by the three police officers of the Metropolitan Police Extradition Unit who were present differs to some extent from the account given by the respondent. The Divisional Court found it unnecessary to reconcile the differences between the two accounts. However, it appears to be clear that a short time after the respondent had been arrested two German police officers from the German Fugitive Unit arrived at the premises and asked Detective Sergeant Loudon, the senior Metropolitan Police officer present, to search the house. The police then searched the house and seized a number of articles in it which they took away to New Scotland Yard. Detective Sergeant Loudon said in his evidence filed on behalf of the appellant that in making his decision to search the house he considered a number of factors. First, it was the accepted practice of police officers in the Extradition Unit that they were able to use common law powers to search the premises following the arrest of a person on an extradition warrant, although it usually happened that the person had been arrested within the physical structure of the premises in question. In this instance the respondent had been arrested a few yards from his front door, within the boundary of the property and, in his (the detective sergeant's) belief, on the premises. In addition, he had also read from various sources that PACE was available in extradition matters for the purpose of carrying out a search.

a   [48] The respondent brought an application for judicial review against the appellant and the Home Secretary in respect of the decision by the police to enter his home in Hazlemere to search for and seize items.

[49] The Divisional Court ([2001] EWHC Admin 576, [2001] All ER (D) 315 (Jul)) held in favour of the respondent and (1) declared that the entry and search carried out by the police on 23 September 2000 were unlawful; (2) declared that the
b   respondent's rights under art 8 of the European Convention for the Protection of Human Rights and Fundamental Freedoms 1950 (as set out in Sch 1 to the Human Rights Act 1998) had been violated; (3) ordered that there be a mandatory order requiring the police to deliver up to the claimant all the items seized on 23 September 2000; and (4) ordered that the respondent's claim for damages be adjourned for directions and a hearing before a single judge in the Administrative
c   Court.

[50] The certified question relates to the seizure of 'any goods or documents which [the police officer] reasonably believes to be material evidence in relation to the extradition crime in respect of which the warrant was issued'. Accordingly I will consider the issue on the basis that the items seized in the respondent's
d   house were reasonably believed by the police officers to be material evidence in relation to the extradition crime alleged against the respondent. I will also assume that the question relates to search and seizure in the property in which the suspect has been arrested.

[51] The Divisional Court in its judgment delivered by Brooke LJ held that the common law power of search and seizure following an arrest had been
e   extinguished by PACE and that the relevant provisions in respect of search and seizure in PACE related only to domestic offences and did not extend to extradition offences.

The common law power before PACE

f   [52] It was a well-established principle of the common law that on the arrest of a person pursuant to a warrant the police officer effecting the arrest could search that person and seize any articles which he found on him which he reasonably believed to be material evidence against him for the purpose of preserving that evidence until trial. It was clear that this power to seize also extended to articles which were present in the room where the person was
g   arrested and of which he was in possession. In *Dillon v O'Brien and Davis* (1887) 16 Cox CC 245 the plaintiff was arrested pursuant to a warrant in a room of a house and the police officers effecting the arrest seized banknotes and papers in the room for the purpose of producing them as evidence in the prosecution of the plaintiff. The plaintiff sued the police officers for the wrongful seizure and
h   detention of the banknotes and papers, and on a demurrer the Irish Exchequer Division held that the seizure was lawful and Palles CB stated (at 249, 250):

'I, therefore, think that it is clear, and beyond doubt, that, at least in cases of treason and felony, constables (and probably also private persons) are entitled, upon a lawful arrest by them of one charged with treason or felony,
j   to take and detain property found in his possession which will form material evidence in his prosecution for that crime; and I take the only real question upon this defence as being, whether this right extends to cases of misdemeanour ... the interest of the State in the person charged being brought to trial in due course necessarily extends, as well to the preservation of material evidence of his guilt or innocence, as to his custody for the purpose of trial. His custody is of no value if the law is powerless to prevent

the abstraction or destruction of this evidence, without which a trial would
be no more than an empty form. But if there be a right to production or *a*
preservation of this evidence, I cannot see how it can be enforced otherwise
than by capture.'

Palles CB then held that the power of seizure arose on an arrest for a misdemeanour
as well as on an arrest for a felony. *b*

[53] The judgments of the Court of Appeal in *Chic Fashions (West Wales) Ltd v
Jones* [1968] 1 All ER 229, [1968] 2 QB 299 were cited by counsel in their
submissions to the House, although that case related to seizure in execution of a
search warrant and not to search and seizure after execution of a warrant of
arrest. The issue in that case was whether, when police officers entered premises
pursuant to a search warrant to search for specified stolen goods, they were *c*
entitled to seize on the premises goods other than those specified in the warrant
which they believed on reasonable grounds to have been stolen and to be
material evidence on a charge of stealing or receiving against the person in
possession of them. The Court of Appeal held that the police officers acted
lawfully in seizing such goods. *d*

[54] *Ghani v Jones* [1969] 3 All ER 1700, [1970] 1 QB 693 was also a case where
there was no warrant of arrest. In that case the police, who believed that a woman
had been murdered, searched without a warrant the house of her father-in-law
and took certain documents including the passports of the father-in-law and other
members of his family. The father-in-law and his family brought an action for
the return of the documents and the High Court ([1969] 3 All ER 720) ordered *e*
their return and the order was upheld by the Court of Appeal. But in delivering
his judgment in the Court of Appeal, in which Edmund Davies LJ and Sir Gordon
Willmer concurred, Lord Denning MR considered the powers of the police to
search and seize after executing a warrant of arrest and stated ([1969] 3 All ER
1700 at 1703, [1970] 1 QB 693 at 706.): *f*

'I would start by considering the law where police officers enter a man's
house by virtue of a warrant, or arrest a man lawfully, with or without a
warrant, for a serious offence. I take it to be settled law, without citing cases,
that the officers are entitled to take any goods which they find in his
possession or in his house which they reasonably believe to be material *g*
evidence in relation to the crime for which he is arrested or for which they
enter. If in the course of their search they come on any other goods which
show him to be implicated in some other crime, they may take them
provided they act reasonably and detain them no longer than is necessary.
Such appears from the speech of LORD CHELMSFORD in *Pringle* v. *Bremner and* *h*
Stirling ((1867) 5 M (HL) 55 at 60) and *Chic Fashions (West Wales), Ltd* v. *Jones*
([1968] 1 All ER 229, [1968] 2 QB 299).'

[55] In *R v Governor of Pentonville Prison, ex p Osman* [1989] 3 All ER 701, [1990]
1 WLR 277, which was a case where extradition was sought of Osman to Hong
Kong, the police officers entered a house where he was living. They had with *j*
them a search warrant. Once inside the house they arrested Osman on a
provisional warrant issued under s 6 of the Fugitive Offenders Act 1967. They
then searched the house and seized and removed a large number of documents.

[56] Objection was taken that there was no common law power to search and
seize documents in relation to a crime alleged to have been committed abroad.
Lloyd LJ, giving the judgment of the court, first considered the power to search

a and seize when police officers lawfully arrested a person for a domestic crime. He stated ([1990] 1 WLR 277 at 311):

> 'We do not accept Mr Ross-Munro's first objection. It is beyond dispute that, in relation to a domestic offence, a police officer entering a house in pursuance of a warrant of arrest, or otherwise lawfully arresting a defendant, is entitled to take any goods or documents which he reasonably believes to b be material evidence in relation to the crime for which the defendant is being arrested: *Ghani v Jones* ([1969] 3 All ER 1700 at 1703, [1970] 1 QB 693 at 706).'

Thus it is clear that Lloyd LJ considered that where a police officer enters a house and arrests a suspect pursuant to a warrant of arrest he is entitled to search the entire house and seize any articles which provide evidence against the suspect. c Lloyd LJ then held that the power to search and seize after a lawful arrest applied to an extradition crime as well as to a domestic crime and he said:

> 'Is there then any difference between a warrant of arrest in domestic proceedings and a provisional warrant under section 6 of the Fugitive Offenders Act 1967? We can see none. The police powers of search and d seizure consequent on a lawful arrest ought to be, and in our judgment are, the same in both cases.'

[57] Miss Montgomery QC, for the respondent, accepted that under the common law where a suspect had been arrested in his own house pursuant to a warrant for a domestic crime, the police officers effecting the arrest were entitled e to search the person of the suspect for items which might constitute evidence for a prosecution and also to seize such items which were in his possession in the actual room in which he had been arrested. But she submitted that the earlier authorities did not support the opinion of Lord Denning MR in *Ghani v Jones* and the opinion of Lloyd LJ in *Ex p Osman* that the common law power extended to f searching and seizing articles which would be material evidence in the remainder of the house. She cited the observations of Professor Feldman in his work *The Law Relating to Entry, Search and Seizure* (1986) who stated (at pp 241–242) with reference to the passage in Lord Denning MR's judgment in *Ghani v Jones* [1969] 3 All ER 1700 at 1703, [1970] 1 QB 693 at 706:

g > '9.37 As regards arrests this statement goes further than the authorities will justify, perhaps because of the confusion caused by treating powers following arrest as if they were the same as powers under a search warrant. The assumption that the police have power to search a man's house after his arrest, at least when the arrest has taken place in the house, is not supported h by either of the cases cited by Lord Denning MR [*Pringle v Bremner and Stirling*, and the *Chic Fashions* case which related to searches under a search warrant] ... Cases where authority to search is granted by a magistrate on being convinced (at least in theory) that there is reasonable cause to believe that the articles sought are on the premises are in a different category from searches following arrest. In the latter case, the search will not have been j subject to prior review, it will be of a speculative nature and the goods sought will be uncertain. The question is, therefore, whether there is any clear authority for the existence of a power to search anything more than the arrested person himself.

> **9.38** There is no English authority either at common law or under statute for searching an area or taking property which is not under the immediate physical control of the person arrested.'

Therefore Miss Montgomery submitted that the common law power was too
widely stated by Lord Denning MR and that your Lordships should hold that the   *a*
power was confined to seizing articles in the room where the suspect was present
at the time of his arrest.

[58] My Lords, I am unable to accept that submission. The power of the police
to search the person of the suspect when he had been arrested and to seize articles
in the room where he was present was based, as Diplock LJ stated in the *Chic*   *b*
Fashions case [1968] 1 All ER 229 at 239, [1968] 2 QB 299 at 317, on the robust
common sense of the reasoning of Palles CB in *Dillon's* case. I consider that it
would be contrary to common sense to hold that the power to search and seize
after arrest did not extend to searching the remainder of the premises belonging
to the suspect in which or on which he had been arrested. Suppose after an attack
on another person with a knife the police had pursued the attacker, carrying a   *c*
knife, and had seen him enter his house through the front door and run through
the hall into the kitchen, and the police had then entered the kitchen through the
back door of the house and arrested him but found no knife in the kitchen, were
the police acting unlawfully if they then went into the hall and, on finding that
the suspect had put down the knife in the hall, seized it? To hold that the police   *d*
had no power in law to act in this way would, in my opinion, be contrary to good
sense. When the police are not authorised to arrest a man they should only have
power to search his house pursuant to a search warrant or under statutory
authority. But the position is different when the police are entitled to arrest him.
In the *Chic Fashions* case after referring to the power of a police officer to arrest a
suspect Salmon LJ stated: *e*

    'If the man's person is not sacrosanct in the eyes of the law, how can the
    goods which he is reasonably suspected of having stolen or received be
    sacrosanct? Only if the law regards property as more important than liberty;
    and I do not accept that it does so. It would be absurd if the police had the   *f*
    power to arrest a man, but, having failed to catch him, had no power to seize
    the goods in his house which they reasonably believed he had stolen or
    unlawfully received.' (See [1968] 1 All ER 229 at 240, [1968] 2 QB 299 at 319.)

This reasoning applies with even greater force when the suspect has been
arrested.   *g*

[59] To the argument that after the arrest of a suspect in his house pursuant to
a warrant the police should not be entitled to search the remainder of the house
because they had not been authorised to carry out such a search by a magistrate,
I consider that the answer is that a magistrate had considered it proper to
authorise the arrest of the suspect. The arrest and the taking into custody of a   *h*
person and the entry into his home to effect the arrest is a much greater intrusion
into his home, his liberty and his privacy than the search of his home and seizure
of articles subsequent on his arrest. As such search and seizure will often be
necessary to prevent the disappearance of material evidence before the police
have time to obtain a search warrant, I consider that this action should be
permitted by the law. Therefore I am of opinion that the common law power   *j*
was correctly stated by Lord Denning MR and Lloyd LJ and was a legitimate
extension of the previous case law.

[60] Miss Montgomery submitted that having arrested the respondent, not in
his house, but outside it in the grounds of his property, the police were not
entitled to enter the house to search it. I would not accept this argument because
the house and the grounds surrounding it comprised the premises of the

a respondent and I think that it would be artificial to draw a distinction between a house and its grounds in relation to the power to search following an arrest of a suspect on his premises.

[61] It was further submitted on behalf of the respondent that even if the common law had permitted police officers, after they had arrested a person in his house, to search the house and seize articles in it, the power should have been
b restricted to domestic offences and should not have been extended to extradition offences. Miss Montgomery argued that in the *Chic Fashions* case and in *Ghani v Jones* the Court of Appeal was influenced, not by the need to combat foreign crime, but by the need to combat domestic crime, and she relied on the observation of Lord Denning MR in the former case ([1968] 1 All ER 229 at 236, [1968] 2 QB 299 at 313) that in these times, 'with the ever-increasing wickedness
c there is about', honest citizens must help the police and not hinder them in their efforts to track down criminals, on a similar observation by him in the latter case ([1969] 3 All ER 1700 at 1705, [1970] 1 QB 693 at 708), and on the statement by Salmon LJ in the *Chic Fashions* case ([1968] 1 All ER 229 at 240, [1968] 2 QB 299 at 319), that there had never been a time when the incidence of crime was higher or
d the need for prevention of crime greater.

[62] My Lords, I reject this submission. The effective combating of international crime is as important as the effective combating of domestic crime. As Lord Griffiths said in *Liangsiriprasert v United States Government* [1990] 2 All ER 866 at 878, [1991] 1 AC 225 at 251: 'Unfortunately in this century crime has ceased to be largely local in origin and effect. Crime is now established on an international
e scale and the common law must face this new reality.' If, prior to PACE, the police had power under the common law, after an arrest for a domestic crime, to search the suspect's house and seize articles which would constitute material evidence against him at a subsequent trial, I consider that the common law gave a similar power when an arrest had been made for an extradition crime, and that
f Lloyd LJ was right to hold in *Ex p Osman* that in relation to the power to search and seize there is no difference between a warrant of arrest in domestic proceedings and a warrant of arrest in extradition proceedings. If material evidence in the house of the suspect is not seized by the police at the time of his arrest, the risk of it disappearing soon after the arrest exists whether the arrest is for an extradition crime or for a domestic crime.

g [63] Therefore before PACE came into operation I am of opinion that the police had power under the common law, after arresting a person in his house or in the grounds of his house pursuant to s 8(1)(b) of the 1989 Act, to search the house and seize articles which they reasonably believed to be material evidence in relation to the crime for which they had arrested that person. I am further of
h opinion that this power was one that served a valuable purpose because it ensured that what appeared to be material evidence in the house of the suspect would not disappear after his arrest and before the police had had time to obtain a search warrant.

j *The provisions of PACE*

[64] PACE was enacted on 31 October 1984 and Pt II which contains the relevant sections came into operation on 1 January 1986. Section 17 provides:

'(1) Subject to the following provisions of this section, and without prejudice to any other enactment, a constable may enter and search any premises for the purpose—(a) of executing—(i) a warrant of arrest issued in connection with or arising out of criminal proceedings ...

(2) Except for the purpose specified in paragraph (e) of subsection (1) above, the powers of entry and search conferred by this section—(a) are only exercisable if the constable has reasonable grounds for believing that the person whom he is seeking is on the premises ...

(4) The power of search conferred by this section is only a power to search to the extent that is reasonably required for the purpose for which the power of entry is exercised.

(5) Subject to subsection (6) below, all the rules of common law under which a constable has power to enter premises without a warrant are hereby abolished.

(6) Nothing in subsection (5) above affects any power of entry to deal with or prevent a breach of the peace.'

Section 23 defines 'premises' as including 'any place'. Extradition proceedings are criminal proceedings (see *R v Governor of Brixton Prison, ex p Levin* [1997] 3 All ER 289, [1997] AC 741). Therefore the warrant of arrest issued in this case under s 8(1)(b) of the 1989 Act was a warrant of arrest within the meaning of s 17(1)(a)(i). Accordingly the police had power under s 17(1)(a)(i) to enter the respondent's premises for the purpose of executing the warrant of arrest but, by reason of s 17(4), the police, having arrested the respondent, had no power to search his house.

[65] Section 18 provides:

'(1) Subject to the following provisions of this section, a constable may enter and search any premises occupied or controlled by a person who is under arrest for an arrestable offence, if he has reasonable grounds for suspecting that there is on the premises evidence, other than items subject to legal privilege, that relates—(a) to that offence; or (b) to some other arrestable offence which is connected with or similar to that offence.

(2) A constable may seize and retain anything for which he may search under subsection (1) above.

(3) The power to search conferred by subsection (1) above is only a power to search to the extent that is reasonably required for the purpose of discovering such evidence.'

Section 18 then sets out certain procedures to be observed:

'(4) Subject to subsection (5) below, the powers conferred by this section may not be exercised unless an officer of the rank of inspector or above has authorised them in writing.

(5) A constable may conduct a search under subsection (1) above—(a) before taking the person to a police station; and (b) without obtaining an authorisation under subsection (4) above, if the presence of that person at a place other than a police station is necessary for the effective investigation of the offence.

(6) If a constable conducts a search by virtue of subsection (5) above, he shall inform an officer of the rank of inspector or above that he has made the search as soon as practicable after he has made it.

(7) An officer who—(a) authorises a search; or (b) is informed of a search under subsection (6) above, shall make a record in writing—(i) of the grounds for the search; and (ii) of the nature of the evidence that was sought.

a   (8) If the person who was in occupation or control of the premises at the time of the search is in police detention at the time the record is to be made, the officer shall make the record as part of his custody record.'

Section 19 provides:

b   '(1) The powers conferred by subsections (2), (3) and (4) below are exercisable by a constable who is lawfully on any premises ...
(3) The constable may seize anything which is on the premises if he has reasonable grounds for believing—(a) that it is evidence in relation to an offence which he is investigating or any other offence; and (b) that it is necessary to seize it in order to prevent the evidence being concealed, lost,
c   altered or destroyed ... (5) The powers conferred by this section are in addition to any power otherwise conferred.'

[66] The principal argument advanced by Mr Perry, on behalf of the appellant, was that having lawfully arrested the respondent pursuant to the warrant, the
d   police officers had power under common law to search his house and seize the articles which they considered to be material evidence in relation to the crime, and that this power had not been extinguished by PACE. Mr Perry also submitted that in addition to this common law power the police had power under both ss 18 and 19 to search the respondent's house and to seize the articles. I would reject, as did the Divisional Court, the argument that the police had such a power under
e   either section. Section 18 only applies to the premises of a person who is under arrest for an 'arrestable offence'. An 'arrestable offence' is defined in s 24(1) as an offence for which the sentence is fixed by law, an offence for which a person of 21 years or over (not previously convicted) may be sentenced to imprisonment for a term of five years (or might be so sentenced but for the restrictions imposed
f   by s 33 of the Magistrates' Courts Act 1980) or a long list of domestic offences created by United Kingdom statutes. Therefore it is clear, in my opinion, that an 'arrestable offence' is a domestic offence and the extradition crime alleged to have been committed by the respondent in Germany cannot be regarded as an 'arrestable offence' within the meaning of s 24(1).

[67] Nor, in my opinion, can the appellant rely on s 19(3)(a). That section only
g   applies to the seizure of evidence in relation to 'an offence which [the police officer] is investigating or any other offence'. In R v Southwark Crown Court and HM Customs and Excise, ex p Sorsky Defries [1996] Crim LR 195 (and transcript 6 July 1995) the Divisional Court held that the words in s 19(3)(a), 'any other offence', were confined to domestic offences because (following R v Cox [1961]
h   3 All ER 1194, [1963] AC 48, Air-India v Wiggins [1980] 2 All ER 593, [1980] 1 WLR 815 and Macleod v A-G for New South Wales [1891] AC 455 at 458) in the absence of an express provision to the contrary the word 'offence' in a statute meant a domestic offence. In coming to this conclusion the Divisional Court also took into account s 8(1)(a) of PACE and s 7(1) of the Criminal Justice (International
j   Co-operation) Act 1990. Section 8(1)(a) gives power to a justice of the peace to issue a search warrant if he was satisfied on reasonable grounds that a 'serious arrestable offence' had been committed. Section 7 of the 1990 Act provides:

'(1) Part II of the Police and Criminal Evidence Act 1984 (powers of entry, search and seizure) shall have effect as if references to serious arrestable offences in section 8 of and Schedule 1 to that Act included any conduct which is an offence under the law of a country or territory outside the United

Kingdom and would constitute a serious arrestable offence if it had occurred
in any part of the United Kingdom.'   *a*

Referring to s 7(1), McCowan LJ stated: 'That very provision militates against a
construction that allows "offence" elsewhere in Pt II of PACE to include a foreign
offence.' I consider that the word 'offence' in the phrase 'an offence which he is
investigating' should not be given a wider meaning than the same word
subsequently appearing in sub-cl (a) and is also confined to a domestic offence. In   *b*
this case the police were not investigating a domestic offence and are not entitled
to claim a power to seize under s 19(3)(a).

[68] Section 32(2)(b) gives a police officer power 'to enter and search any
premises in which [an arrested person] was when arrested or immediately before
he was arrested for evidence relating to the offence for which he has been   *c*
arrested', but the appellant cannot rely on this subsection because, for the reasons
which I have given in relation to s 19(3)(a), the term 'offence' is confined to a domestic
offence and does not extend to an extradition offence.

[69] Therefore I turn to consider the question whether the common law
power of search and seizure after an arrest on a warrant issued pursuant to
s 18(1)(b) of the 1989 Act was extinguished by PACE. The reasoning of the   *d*
Divisional Court ([2001] All ER (D) 315 (Jul)) on this question is contained in its
judgment (at [46]–[53]). Brooke LJ stated:

'[46] I turn now to the question whether we should now hold that
whatever the position might have been before PACE came into force, this
common law power must be taken to have been extinguished. It is at once   *e*
noticeable that *Ex p Osman* was decided in the interval between PACE's
appearance on the statute book on 31 October 1984 and the date when Pt II
of PACE came into force. Parliament would therefore have been unaware
of this latest extension of the police's common law powers when it was
considering the bill which became PACE.   *f*

[47] I find it quite impossible to interpret Pt II of PACE as providing any
saving for the common law power identified by Lloyd LJ in *Ex p Osman*.
While it is true that s 18 contains no provision comparable to s 17(5) ('... all
the rules of common law under which a constable has power to enter
premises without a warrant are hereby abolished'), it appears to me that   *g*
Parliament intended s 18 to provide in codified form for the full extent of a
constable's power to enter and search premises after an arrest (for the
purposes identified in that section), and intended it to be limited to police
inquiries into domestic offences.'

[70] Brooke LJ noted (at [48]) that when Parliament enacted PACE on 31 October   *h*
1984 the government was already engaged in a long drawn-out review of
extradition law and practice and he referred to the publication by the government
in February 1985 of a Green Paper entitled *Extradition* (Cmnd 9421) (the Green
Paper) which stated that it was unnecessary to make specific provision in an
extradition statute to allow property connected with an alleged offence to be
seized and surrendered to the requesting state. Brooke LJ then observed that   *j*
there was no hint in this material of any need to extend the powers of search and
seizure contained in the new domestic legislation so as to make them available in
an extradition context.

[71] He stated (at [49]) that it was not until the enactment of the 1990 Act that
Parliament produced a modern code for mutual assistance in criminal
proceedings and investigations and he stated that s 7 of that Act created

a arrangements for the issue of search warrants of varying gravity, which
dovetailed with the language used by PACE in relation to domestic procedure.

[72] He stated (at [50]) that the enactment of the 1990 Act gave Parliament the
opportunity to decide whether it wished to give the police a power to search the
premises of an arrested person without a warrant such as was enacted in a
domestic context in s 18 of PACE, and he observed that Parliament decided not
b to take that opportunity. Instead the 1990 Act obliged the police to obtain a
warrant before entering premises occupied and controlled by the person in
question for the purpose of searching them and seizing relevant evidence found
there.

[73] Brooke LJ then stated (at [51]):

c   'If Mr Perry was correct, then an unnoticed common law power of search
would have survived the coming into force of PACE but would not have
attached to it any of the disciplines created by s 18 of PACE or PACE Code
of Practice B (see para 1.3 for the searches to which that code applies) ...'

[74] He then stated:
d
      '[52] For these reasons, I am satisfied that the common law power of search
which was identified by this court in Ex p Osman was extinguished when Pt II
of PACE came into force. I am also satisfied—and indeed the contrary was
not argued—that the police possessed no statutory power of entry and
e   search without a warrant outside the four corners of PACE, and PACE gave
them no such power in an extradition context. Given that Parliament has
decided to set out the extent of police powers of entry and search without a
warrant, I do not consider that it would be appropriate for us to create new
common law powers today. I do not need to repeat in this judgment the
submissions we received from Miss Montgomery on the ECHR requirements
f   of clarity and accessibility in the context of a potential violation of art 8(1) of
the convention. Where Parliament has legislated in fine detail in relation to
the exercise of powers of entry and search without a warrant in a domestic
context, judges should not act as substitute lawmakers in order to identify
similar powers in an extradition context to which no such fine detail by
necessity could be attached. Because there was no lawful justification for the
g   search without a warrant, Mr Rottman's art 8(1) rights were violated.

      [53] I must make it clear that nothing in this judgment must be taken as
negativing any power of the police to seize articles found in the possession
of the person they are arresting. What the police needed in this case was (i) a
power to enter the dwelling house (which Mr Rottman cannot be taken to
h   have given them voluntarily for the purpose of searching it) and (ii) a power
to search it. In the absence of a warrant from a court they possessed neither
of these powers. In the interests of completeness I would add that if the
search was otherwise lawful, I do not consider that the involvement of the
two German police officers, even on Mr Rottman's account of the matter,
j   would have rendered it unlawful.'

[75] In my opinion the common law power of search and seizure was not
extinguished by PACE and I consider, with respect, that the Divisional Court fell
into error when Brooke LJ stated (at [47]): 'I find it quite impossible to interpret
Pt II of PACE as providing any saving for the common law power identified by
Lloyd LJ in Ex p Osman.' But the question is not whether PACE saved the
common law power—rather the question is whether PACE extinguished it, as

Brooke LJ had recognised in the preceding paragraph. It is a well-established
principle that a rule of the common law is not extinguished by a statute unless the
statute makes this clear by express provision or by clear implication. The
common law power was a valuable one in respect of an extradition offence
because, just as in respect of a domestic offence, it guarded against the risk of the
disappearance from the suspect's house of material evidence after his arrest and
before the police had time to obtain a search warrant. Sections 18 and 19 of
PACE are confined to domestic offences and I do not consider that the provisions
of that Act lead to the conclusion that Parliament intended to revoke the
common law power exercisable after the execution of a warrant of arrest for an
extradition offence; and it is relevant to note that s 19(5) expressly preserved any
power otherwise conferred.

[76] Annex B of the Green Paper set out recommendations of the working
party on extradition accepted in principle and para 22 stated:

'It is unnecessary to make specific provision in an extradition statute to
allow property connected with an alleged offence to be seized and
surrendered to the requesting State (Rec 48).'

I consider that Mr Perry was correct in his submission that this recommendation
meant that the government accepted that there was a common law power to
seize property connected with an alleged extradition offence and considered that
therefore there was no need for an express statutory provision. In my opinion it
did not mean, as the Divisional Court suggests, that the government considered
that there was no need to extend the powers of search and seizure in PACE so as
to make them available in an extradition context.

[77] I also consider that the fact that Parliament made provision in s 7 of the
1990 Act for a justice of the peace to issue a search warrant in respect of a foreign
offence does not point to the conclusion that it was the view of Parliament that
there was no common law power to search and seize after an arrest for an
extradition offence. The issuing of a search warrant in relation to a foreign
offence by a justice of the peace can only take place if particular premises are
specified to the justice of the peace by the police and if a direction to apply for a
search warrant has been given by the Secretary of State after he has received a
request from a foreign court or authority (see s 7(4)). But the power to seize and
search to prevent the disappearance of material evidence is needed where the
police pursuant to a provisional warrant arrest a suspect whose address in this
country had been unknown to them until they located and arrested him (which
appears to have been the position in this case) and where, prior to finding and
arresting the suspect, it was not possible to apply for a search warrant.

[78] Nor do I consider that the fact that the common law power would not
have attached to it any of the disciplines created by s 18 of PACE or PACE Code
of Practice B is a reason for concluding that the existing common law power was
extinguished by PACE. I am of this opinion because the exercise of the power
does have the discipline attached to it that it can only be exercised after a
metropolitan magistrate or a justice of the peace is of the opinion from evidence
supplied to him that the alleged conduct of the suspect would constitute an
extradition offence and that the issue of a warrant for his arrest would be justified
if the conduct had taken place within his jurisdiction.

[79] In its judgment ([2001] All ER (D) 315 (Jul) at [53]) the Divisional Court
states that nothing in its judgment must be taken as negativing any power of the
police to seize articles found in the possession of the person they are arresting. But

a as I have observed, if the police have power at common law to search the person of the individual whom they have arrested under a warrant issued pursuant to s 8(1)(b), it seems contrary to common sense to hold that they do not have power to seize material evidence present in the room where he is arrested and also to search other rooms in his house and seize material evidence found in them. Accordingly I would hold that the common law power of search and seizure after *b* the execution of a warrant of arrest issued pursuant to s 8(1)(b) was not extinguished by PACE and that the police officers were entitled to exercise that power after the arrest of the respondent.

[80] Article 8 of the European Convention for the Protection of Human Rights and Fundamental Freedoms 1950 (as set out in Sch 1 to the Human Rights Act 1998) provides:

c
'1. Everyone has the right to respect for his private and family life, his home and his correspondence.
2. There shall be no interference by a public authority with the exercise of this right except such as is in accordance with the law and is necessary in a democratic society in the interests of national security, public safety or the *d* economic well-being of the country, for the prevention of disorder or crime, for the protection of health or morals, or for the protection of the rights and freedoms of others.'

I am unable to accept the respondent's submission that the common law power of search and seizure after arrest constitutes a violation of his rights under art 8. *e* The search and seizure was in accordance with the law which was clearly stated by Lloyd LJ in *R v Governor of Pentonville Prison, ex p Osman* [1989] 3 All ER 701, [1990] 1 WLR 277. The law was also clearly set out at p 175 of the well-known textbook on extradition published in 1995 by Mr Alun Jones QC (*Jones on Extradition*). The power has the legitimate aim in a democratic society of *f* preventing crime, and is necessary in order to prevent the disappearance of material evidence after the arrest of a suspect. The power is proportionate to that aim because it is subject to the safeguards that it can only be exercised after a warrant of arrest has been issued by a magistrate or a justice of the peace in respect of an extradition crime and where the evidence placed before him would, in his opinion, justify the issue of a warrant for the arrest of a person accused of a *g* similar domestic offence.

[81] Accordingly I would answer the certified question:

'Yes, a police officer who has arrested a person in or on his premises pursuant to a warrant of arrest issued under s 8 of the 1989 Act has power to search those premises for, and to seize, any goods or documents which he *h* reasonably believes to be material evidence in relation to the extradition crime in respect of which the warrant was issued.'

I would allow the appeal and would set aside the order of the Divisional Court.

LORD RODGER OF EARLSFERRY.
j [82] My Lords, I have had the advantage of considering the speech of my noble and learned friend, Lord Hutton, in draft. I agree with it and would accordingly allow the appeal. In view of the careful submissions of counsel, and because my noble and learned friend, Lord Hope of Craighead, is dissenting on certain points, I add some observations of my own.

[83] The provisional warrant for the respondent's arrest was addressed to each and all of the constables of the Metropolitan Police Force. It required them 'to

arrest the defendant and bring the defendant' before the court. In its terms the *a* warrant did not give the officers express authority either to enter premises and search for the respondent in order to arrest him, or to enter premises and search for items which might be material evidence relating to the extradition offence for which he was to be arrested. But, in the light of the observations of my noble and learned friend, Lord Hoffmann, giving the unanimous views of the House in *R v Governor of Brixton Prison, ex p Levin* [1997] 3 All ER 289 at 293–294, [1997] AC 741 *b* at 746–747, it was common ground that the officers executing the warrant for the respondent's arrest in connection with the extradition proceedings were indeed executing a warrant of arrest in connection with 'criminal proceedings' in terms of s 17(1)(a)(i) of the Police and Criminal Evidence Act 1984 (PACE). They accordingly had power under that provision to enter and search the respondent's premises for the purpose of executing the warrant by arresting the respondent. *c*

[84] On behalf of the Crown, Mr Perry submitted that not only did PACE give the officers executing the warrant this power, but it also gave them powers under ss 18 and 19, after arresting the respondent on the driveway of his house, to enter the house and search for and seize items of various kinds, especially those which they had reasonable grounds for believing were evidence in relation to the *d* extradition offence. For the reasons given by Lord Hutton I consider that these statutory powers do not apply where someone is arrested under a warrant for an extradition offence. That, in a sense, is all that needs to be decided. Nevertheless, despite the submissions of both counsel that ss 18 and 19 were the appropriate ones to consider and despite the decision of the Divisional Court on the point, I am far from satisfied that this is in fact correct. The problem is that their *e* approach does not have sufficient regard to the structure of the Act and places an unduly narrow construction on s 32.

[85] Pt I of PACE deals with 'Powers to Stop and Search' and is not relevant for present purposes. Pt II, comprising ss 8 to 23, is entitled 'Powers of Entry, Search and Seizure' and contains a wide range of provisions giving the police *f* powers to enter premises and to search them. These powers include the power to enter for the purposes of arresting someone (see s 17), and the power 'after arrest' to enter and search premises 'occupied or controlled by a person who is under arrest for an arrestable offence' (see s 18). This is, of course, the power which Mr Perry sought to invoke on behalf of the Crown in this case. Section 19 contains a general power for a constable 'who is lawfully on any premises' to *g* seize various items and to require the production of information in a computer (see s 20), the power being in addition to any power otherwise conferred (see s 19(5)). Section 22 allows items seized under ss 19 and 20 to be retained as long as is necessary in all the circumstances.

[86] Then comes Pt III which is headed 'Arrest' and which runs from ss 24 to *h* 33. These sections contain wide-ranging provisions dealing with what is to happen when—if need be, after a search under s 17—the individual is arrested. Among these provisions is s 32, with the side-note title 'Search upon arrest'. Section 32(1) gives a constable power to search an arrested person who 'has been arrested at a place other than a police station' and sub-ss (8) and (9) provide for the seizure and detention of items found during the course of that kind of search. *j* Subsection (2)(b), which also applies when someone has been arrested other than at a police station, gives a police officer power 'to enter and search any premises in which he was when arrested or immediately before he was arrested for evidence relating to the offence for which he has been arrested'. Section 32 contains no provisions dealing with the seizure and detention of any property which may be found during such a search, the reason plainly being that the

a necessary authority for seizure is to be found in ss 19 and 20, while s 22 gives
   the necessary power to retain items. By contrast, since these sections deal only
   with searches of premises and not with searches of the person, it was necessary
   to include sub-ss (8) and (9) giving the specific powers of seizure and retention of
   property found during the search of the arrested person.

   [87] My Lords, but for counsel's insistence that s 32 had no bearing on this
b case, I should readily have concluded from its terms that it was indeed the section
   which dealt with any situation where the police arrested someone away from a
   police station, whether the arrest took place at the person's home or elsewhere.
   In that situation s 32 would give the police officers power to search his person (see
   sub-s (1)) and power to enter and search any premises where he was when he was
   arrested or in which he had been immediately before his arrest (see sub-s (2)(b)).
c These are powers which a constable can use in all such cases without any
   particular authorisation. Miss Montgomery QC argued strenuously, however,
   that where, as here, someone was arrested at his home, s 18 rather than s 32
   applied since the police would be entering and searching premises 'occupied or
   controlled by a person who is under arrest for an arrestable offence' (my
d emphasis). But, in truth, s 18 appears to be dealing, primarily at least, with a
   situation where the person is under arrest for an arrestable offence at a police
   station and the police wish to search premises to look for evidence. In these
   circumstances s 18(1) gives a power to enter and search premises occupied or
   controlled by the person who is under arrest and sub-s (2) gives power to seize
   and retain what is found. Significantly, however, these powers to enter and
e search under sub-s (1) are subject to certain safeguards, as envisaged in the
   recommendations of the Royal Commission on Criminal Procedure referred to
   in [98], below. In addition the powers cannot usually be exercised unless an
   officer of the rank of inspector or above has authorised them (see sub-s (4)). This
   is similar to the requirement that applied under s 42 of the Larceny Act 1916 and
f s 26 of the Theft Act 1968. These safeguards and limitations are consistent with
   the greater caution that the law has tended to show with regard to searches of
   premises other than those where the person was arrested (see *Jeffrey v Black* [1978]
   1 All ER 555, [1978] QB 490).

   [88] Had it been necessary to decide the point, I should therefore have been
   inclined to hold that the powers of a constable to enter and search the premises
g where someone was arrested, or where he had been immediately before his
   arrest, were to be found in s 32, even though the premises in question were the
   person's home. In other words, if the respondent had been arrested in relation to
   domestic proceedings, I should have held that the police officers' powers to
   search for evidence were to be found in s 32 rather than in s 18 and that their
h powers of seizure and retention of any items were to be found in ss 19, 20 and 22
   rather than in ss 18(2) and 20. It is, however, unnecessary to decide the point in
   this case since the power in s 32(2)(b) is to enter and search for evidence relating
   to 'the offence' for which the person has been arrested. For the reasons given by
   Lord Hutton in relation to s 19(3)(a), I am satisfied that in s 32(2)(b) the term
   'offence' is confined to domestic offences and that the provision does not,
j accordingly, cover the situation where the respondent was being arrested in
   connection with offences under German law.

   [89] Since, then, PACE does not provide the authority for the search for
   evidence that the officers carried out in this case, two questions remain to be
   decided: first, whether before the enactment of PACE police officers would have
   had a common law power to search the respondent's premises when arresting
   him for an extradition crime under a warrant from the chief metropolitan

stipendiary magistrate; and, secondly, whether any such common law power of search had in any event been extinguished by the enactment of PACE.

[90] So far as the first question is concerned, Mr Perry submitted that authority for the existence of such a power of search in domestic cases was to be found in the opinion of Lord Denning MR in *Ghani v Jones* [1969] 3 All ER 1700 at 1703, [1970] 1 QB 693 at 706:

'I would start by considering the law where police officers enter a man's house by virtue of a warrant, or arrest a man lawfully, with or without a warrant, for a serious offence. I take it to be settled law, without citing cases, that the officers are entitled to take any goods which they find in his possession or in his house which they reasonably believe to be material evidence in relation to the crime for which he is arrested or for which they enter. If in the course of their search they come upon any other goods which show him to be implicated in some other crime, they may take them provided they act reasonably and detain them no longer than is necessary. Such appears from the speech of LORD CHELMSFORD, in *Pringle* v. *Bremner and Stirling* ((1867) 5 M (HL) 55 at 60) and *Chic Fashions (West Wales), Ltd.* v. *Jones* ([1968] 1 All ER 229, [1968] 2 QB 299).'

As the opening words of the third sentence show, in the previous sentence Lord Denning MR was holding that police officers arresting an individual have a power to search for goods in his possession or in his house and not merely a power to seize those which they happen to come across. It is this proposition of settled law that is of importance for present purposes.

[91] Mr Perry went on to point out that in *R v Governor of Pentonville Prison, ex p Osman* [1990] 1 WLR 277 at 311, Lloyd LJ, giving the judgment of the Divisional Court, held that a police officer executing a provisional warrant under s 6 of the Fugitive Offenders Act 1967 enjoyed the same common law powers of search and seizure as in the case of domestic proceedings. That approach should, Mr Perry submitted, be applied to police officers executing an arrest warrant under s 8 of the Extradition Act 1989.

[92] On the other hand Miss Montgomery argued that the House should not endorse Lord Denning MR's statement of the common law: it contained an unduly expansive version of a police officer's powers of search. In particular, the statement of the law was not supported by the authorities which Lord Denning MR cited. In making this submission she was in effect adopting the criticism made by Professor David Feldman in *The Law Relating to Entry, Search and Seizure* (1986) pp 241–242 (para 9.37). In any event, she argued, Lloyd LJ had been wrong in *Ex p Osman* to hold that the same common law powers would apply to a constable executing an arrest warrant for an extradition offence: with a few exceptions, the common law was concerned only with crimes committed in England and Wales and it could not be used to give police officers acting in extradition proceedings a power that Parliament had not seen fit to bestow on them.

[93] Not the least remarkable feature of the common law on powers of search is the relative paucity of authority. At the beginning stands the constitutional rock of *Entick v Carrington* (1765) 19 State Tr 1029, [1558–1774] All ER Rep 41 but then almost 90 years go by before Lord Campbell CJ's footnote in *Bessell v Wilson* (1853) 20 LTOS 233n, 118 ER 518. Thirty years later there is *Dillon v O'Brien and Davis* (1887) 16 Cox CC 245 but little of importance thereafter until *Elias v Pasmore* [1934] 2 KB 164, [1934] All ER Rep 380. Finally, come *Chic Fashions (West*

Wales) Ltd v Jones [1968] 1 All ER 229, [1968] 2 QB 299 and *Ghani v Jones*. The
decisions are not only few in number: for the most part, the reasoning of the
judges in the older cases is limited to the particular facts and illuminates only a
small part of the landscape, so leaving the reader uncertain how the law applies
just outside that area. In practice, of course, police officers and those advising
them had to decide what their lawful powers were, even in situations where the
courts had not given guidance. By 1929 and the report of the Royal Commission
on Police Powers and Procedure chaired by Viscount Lee of Fareham (Cmnd 3297)
(Ch II (para 33)), it had long been the practice of the police—

> 'to search the dwelling of a person for whose arrest a warrant has been
> issued, and, in cases of arrest without warrant, to search premises as well as
> the arrested person, in cases of serious crime whenever it seems likely that
> any material evidence can be obtained. In normal cases, the Police obtain the
> consent of the occupiers before carrying out a search in such circumstances.
> But it appears that, in the event of a refusal to consent, the Police, if they
> proceed with the search, may be faced with the risk of a subsequent action
> for trespass. This is a risk which is commonly taken by the Police and the
> practice seems to have had the tacit approval of the Courts for so long that,
> in the opinion of the Home Office, it has become part of the common law.'

The matter is restated in Ch IV (para 120) where the Commission repeat the
Home Office view that the police practice 'had, by long use, become part of the
common law'. The Royal Commission were themselves satisfied (at para 121)
that—

> 'the existing practice of the Police as to the search of premises is, in the
> main, necessary and proper in the interests of justice and cannot be regarded
> as in any way an undue infringement of the rights and liberties of the
> subject.'

The Royal Commission accordingly recommended that the existing police
practice should be put on a statutory basis, 'authorising them to search without a
warrant the premises of persons who have been arrested'. See also Ch XII
(para 301 (xxx)).

[94] The practice of police officers searching for material evidence in the
home of a person for whom an arrest warrant had been issued was thus well
established more than 70 years ago—despite there being no case in which the
point had needed to be decided. Moreover, the Royal Commission found the
power to be acceptable and not to be in any way an undue infringement of the
rights and liberties of the subject.

[95] Of course, police practice does not make law, even when it is known to
the courts. None the less, in the absence of any challenge to that practice over
many years, it is hardly surprising that in *Ghani v Jones* 'without citing cases' Lord
Denning MR could regard it as settled law that the police could carry out a search
of this kind. Starting from there he went on to deal with a different point: if, in
the course of the lawful search, the police officers came across items which
showed that the arrested person was implicated in some other crime, they were
entitled to take these items too, provided that they acted reasonably and detained
them no longer than was necessary. Lord Denning MR cited *Pringle v Bremner and
Stirling* (1867) 5 M (HL) 55 and the *Chic Fashions* case as authority for this second
proposition. There is no reason to suppose that he proceeded under some

misapprehension as to the relevance of these cases to the proposition of settled
law that he had already stated.   *a*

[96] Subsequent events have only served to confirm that the proposition itself
was sound. In *Jeffrey v Black* [1978] 1 All ER 555 at 558, 560, [1978] QB 490 at
496–497, 499 both Lord Widgery CJ and Forbes J appear to have proceeded on
the basis that, so far as affirming a right to search the premises where an accused
was arrested, Lord Denning MR's formulation of the law was not open to   *b*
question. Similarly, when it had stood for a further eleven years, in *R v Governor
of Pentonville Prison, ex p Osman* [1989] 3 All ER 701, [1990] 1 WLR 277 Lloyd LJ
regarded the point as being 'beyond dispute'.

[97] The line of cases stops here. To judge from them, until the present
proceedings the power of a police officer to search the house of someone arrested
under a warrant had never been challenged in the courts since the days of   *c*
crinolines and Palles B.

[98] The scope of the power of police officers to search people whom they
have arrested also came under the notice of the Royal Commission on Criminal
Procedure chaired by Sir Cyril Philips. Their report was published in two
volumes in 1981: *Report* (Cmnd 8092) and *The Investigation and Prosecution of*   *d*
Criminal Offences in England and Wales: The Law and Procedure (Cmnd 8092-1). In
The Investigation (p 12 (para 34)) the Commission accepted as accurate the
statement of the law in *Archbold Pleading, Evidence and Practice in Criminal Cases*
(40th edn, 1979), para 1410, which was based, almost word for word, on the
passage in Lord Denning MR's judgment in *Ghani v Jones* [1969] 3 All ER 1700,
[1970] 1 QB 693. The Commission noted (*Report*, p 62 (para 3.119)) that the police   *e*
had power to search the arrested person's 'immediate surroundings' but that
there was doubt about whether the power extended to the premises of a person
arrested elsewhere. They therefore recommended that a statutory power with
suitable safeguards should be introduced (paras 3.120–122). There was, however,
no suggestion that the accepted common law powers of search on arrest should   *f*
be abridged.

[99] Miss Montgomery may well be right, of course, to say that Lord
Denning MR formulated the common law powers of search on arrest more
widely than had been done in earlier cases. What was novel, however, was not
the understanding of the law as such but the fact that it had finally been stated by
a court. As the *Chic Fashions* case [1968] 1 All ER 229 at 236, [1968] 2 QB 299 at   *g*
312–313 shows, Lord Denning MR had been concerned to draw together the
earlier sparse authorities and to restate the law in a more systematic way, that
took account of the circumstances of the day. *Ghani v Jones* is an example of the
same approach. The real question for your Lordships in the present case,
accordingly, is not whether in 1969 the pre-existing authorities technically   *h*
justified Lord Denning MR's statement of the law in this passage in *Ghani v Jones*
but whether the common law today should be regarded as conferring on police
officers executing a warrant for the arrest of an individual such powers to search
for evidence as Lord Denning MR described. I am satisfied that it should.

[100] To insist on a narrow interpretation of the earlier scattered case law and
to confine the police officers' power to searching the accused's person and seizing   *j*
articles in the room where he happens to be when arrested would make it a
matter of chance whether potentially important evidence was recovered or lost.
By contrast, Lord Denning MR's (by no means expansive) rationalisation of the
law at one and the same time removes the element of chance and confirms the
legality of what had been, to the knowledge of the courts, the practice of the
police for decades.

a [101] Moreover, whether one has regard to ss 32 or 18 of PACE, along with
ss 19, 20 and 22, their effect is to give police officers powers that are certainly
subjected to certain refinements, particularly in relation to legal professional
privilege, but that do not otherwise differ greatly in scope from the common law
powers as stated by Lord Denning MR. By enacting these provisions, Parliament
followed the course recommended by the two Royal Commissions and clarified
b the law. In doing so Parliament broadly endorsed the well-established policy
enshrined in Lord Denning MR's statement that police officers should be entitled
to search the home of someone arrested by virtue of a warrant.

[102] I note, moreover, that the practical effect of Lord Denning MR's
approach is to produce a situation which corresponds broadly to that in Scotland
where a sheriff grants a warrant for someone's arrest on a serious charge. In that
c jurisdiction the modern case law contains no equivalent of the debate in England
about the powers of search of police officers executing an arrest warrant. This is
because of the practice of the sheriff court when granting such warrants. The
procurator fiscal asks for a warrant not simply to apprehend the accused person
but 'to *search for* and apprehend' him (my emphasis). So the police officers
d executing the warrant are given express authority from the court to search for the
person in order to arrest him. More importantly for present purposes, the
procurator fiscal's petition always goes on to ask the sheriff—

e
'to grant warrant to search the person, repositories, and domicile of said
accused, and the house or premises in which he may be found, and to secure
for the purpose of precognition and evidence all writs, evidents, and articles
found otherwise tending to establish guilt or participation in the crime
foresaid, and for that purpose to make patent all shut and lockfast places.'

(See the petition set out in form 1 in App I to *Renton and Brown's Criminal
Procedure* (3rd edn, 1956) p 455, unfortunately omitted from later editions.)
f Therefore, when the sheriff grants a warrant to search for, and to arrest, the
accused, as a matter of routine he also grants a warrant to search for evidence
relating to the crime, including the warrant to search the house or premises
where the accused is found. The result is that, when a person is arrested at his
home under a search warrant, the officers carrying out the arrest are authorised
g to search his home—just as Lord Denning MR held that they could under English
law. The fact that sheriffs in Scotland regularly grant this (not dissimilar, though
rather wider) power of search when they grant an arrest warrant tends to confirm
that Lord Denning MR's view of the policy underpinning the English common
law was sound and not unduly generous to the police. The House should not
h now question that view or this aspect of the common law as he stated it.

[103] In *Ghani v Jones* Lord Denning MR was not dealing with arrest warrants
in extradition proceedings. For the reasons given by Lord Hutton, however, I am
satisfied that there is no reason to criticise the Divisional Court's decision in *Ex p
Osman* that police officers should have the same common law powers when
executing an arrest warrant relating to extradition proceedings. As the court
j recognised, the same considerations as make those powers appropriate in a
domestic case make them appropriate in an extradition case. The recognition
that those powers are available in extradition proceedings does not contradict or
cut across any provision of the extradition legislation; rather it supports the policy
of that legislation. The days are long gone when the common law could be blind
to everything occurring outside the realm. Where Parliament has enacted
extradition legislation with a view to assisting the forces of justice, law and order

in certain other countries, there can be no legitimate objection in principle to the common law developing in a manner that promotes rather than hinders that objective.

[104] My noble and learned friend, Lord Hope, concludes from the absence of specific powers of search in the 1989 Act that Parliament did not intend police officers executing an arrest warrant in extradition proceedings to have such powers. Like Lord Hutton I would not share that conclusion. Again, the evidence of practice is of some significance. The report of the inter-departmental working party, *A Review of the Law and Practice of Extradition in the United Kingdom*, was published in 1982, before PACE. Chapter 11 deals with the seizure and surrender of property. The working party had in mind both property that might serve as proof of the extradition offence and property that was in the possession of the person being extradited and might have been acquired by him in connection with the offence. They note that a sizeable proportion of extradition requests relate to offences such as theft and fraud and that, before s 26(1) of the Theft Act 1968 came into force, there was no provision in the Extradition Act 1870 for the issuing of search warrants where someone was arrested for such an offence. In Commonwealth cases there was a specific power to grant search warrants in such cases under s 6(5) of the Fugitive Offenders Act 1967 but—

'[t]he absence of any equivalent provision from the Extradition Act 1870 for many years deprived the police officer seeking to execute a warrant of arrest of the reassurance available from being armed at the same time with a search warrant.'

This passage from para 11.6 suggests that, even though the comfort of a search warrant could not be obtained, in practice police officers did carry out searches when executing arrest warrants—although, as in domestic cases, there was no decision of the courts to say that such searches were lawful. Again, the absence of authority one way or the other must be because the lawfulness of such searches had never been tested in the courts. When it was eventually tested before the Divisional Court in *Ex p Osman*, the challenge was rejected and the court declared that police officers did indeed enjoy the same common law powers of search on arrest under an extradition warrant as on arrest under a domestic warrant.

[105] The working party suggested that s 26(1) of the 1968 Act made s 6(5) of the 1967 Act unnecessary. For some reason, however, Parliament chose to re-enact s 6(5) in s 8(6) of the 1989 Act. That provision covers only a limited range of cases. Whatever may have been the reason for retaining that specific provision, it does not in my view justify the conclusion that Parliament intended to abolish, without replacing, any common law power of search that was available in other cases. Nor did counsel point to any other provision that would have that effect.

[106] I would therefore hold that at common law, before PACE was enacted, police officers arresting someone in the respondent's position in the driveway of his house would have had the power to search his house for evidence relating to the extradition offence. The 1989 Act did not abolish that power.

[107] The second question for decision arises, however, because the Divisional Court ([2001] EWHC Admin 576, [2001] All ER (D) 315 (Jul)) held that, even if the police officers would once have had that common law power to search the respondent's house, it no longer existed, having been extinguished by PACE five years before the 1989 Act was passed. In concluding that any such power had been extinguished in this way, Brooke LJ (at [47]) said that he found it 'quite impossible to interpret Part II of PACE as providing any saving for the common

a law power identified by Lloyd LJ in *Osman*'. As Lord Hutton has noted, and as indeed Brooke LJ had himself noticed in the preceding paragraph of his judgment, the true question is not whether Pt II of PACE saved the common law power but whether it extinguished or abolished that power. In argument before the House Miss Montgomery accepted this and accepted also that she had to identify a provision or provisions in the legislation which had expressly or *b* impliedly abolished the common law power. She pointed to only one provision, s 17(5), as having this effect:

> 'Subject to subsection (6) below, all the rules of common law under which a constable has power to enter premises without a warrant are hereby abolished.'

c   [108] In fact, s 17(5) has nothing whatever to do with the power of police officers to search premises for evidence once a person has been arrested. As I have already noted, in English law arrest warrants do not contain a warrant to search for the individual concerned. If arrests are to be carried out, however, it is obviously necessary that police officers should have the requisite power to search *d* for the individual who is to be arrested. The common law made provision for this, as did various statutes dealing with particular situations. But in 1984 Parliament decided to regulate the power of police officers to enter premises to make arrests by replacing these common law and particular statutory powers with the more specific code of powers set out in s 17 of PACE. The new statutory powers for police officers were intended to be comprehensive and to replace the *e* existing law except in the situation where the police enter premises to deal with, or to prevent, a breach of the peace. Therefore sub-s (5) abolished all the police officers' common law powers of entry for the purpose of arresting persons, except in the case of breach of the peace (see sub-s (6)).

      [109] Since s 17(5) occurs within this very particular context, it is plain that it *f* was intended to abolish only the common law powers relating to entry for the purpose of arrest. The subsection was not intended to affect the common law relating to searches for evidence carried out when someone has been arrested. Indeed Parliament only turns to deal with these kinds of search in s 18 ('Entry and search after arrest') and, as I have discussed, comes back to the topic in s 32 ('Search upon arrest'). As Miss Montgomery readily acknowledged, neither of *g* these sections, nor indeed s 19, contains any provision to abolish the pre-existing common law on such searches. The contrast with s 17(5), abolishing the common law rules on entry and search 'for purpose of arrest', points up the significance of the absence of any equivalent provision abolishing the common law rules in the case of search 'after' or 'upon' arrest.

h   [110] Since neither s 17(5) nor any other provision abolishes the common law powers of search on or after arrest, Miss Montgomery's argument must fail. These common law powers remain available in cases, such as extradition cases, where the new statutory powers do not apply.

      [111] Brooke LJ ([2001] All ER (D) 315 (Jul) at [51]) was concerned that, if this *j* were the position—

> 'then an unnoticed common law power of search would have survived the coming into force of PACE but would not have attached to it any of the disciplines created by section 18 of PACE or PACE Code of Practice B...'

It is not entirely clear to me why the common law power that Parliament has chosen not to abolish should be described as 'unnoticed'. But, in any event, concern about the continued existence of this common law power would be justified only if in enacting PACE Parliament had intended to make a general statement of the law relating to search which was to be applied whenever an arrest was carried out in England or Wales. There is no reason to suppose Parliament had any such intention. The Green Paper *Extradition* (Cmnd 9421 (February 1985)) presented to Parliament by the Home Secretary after the enactment of PACE certainly gave no hint that the responsible minister thought that the Act had in any way changed the law in relation to searches on arrests by virtue of an extradition warrant. Moreover, the respondent's own argument that ss 18 and 19 do not apply to such arrests—which the Divisional Court rightly accepted—shows that Parliament entertained no such far-reaching ambition. Parliament's aim was more modest: it was concerned to regulate such matters in relation to offences that were likely to be tried in England and Wales.

[112] Consistently with that approach, a few years later Parliament enacted the Criminal Justice and Public Order Act 1994, Pt X of which dealt with cross-border enforcement of police powers. Under s 136(2)(a) of the 1994 Act, an arrest warrant issued in Scotland can be executed in England or Wales either by a local constable or by a constable from a Scottish force. In either event, the constable executing the warrant has the same powers and duties, and the arrested person has the same rights, as they would have had if the warrant had been executed by a constable from a Scottish force in Scotland (see sub-s (5)(b)). In other words the constable will have the powers of search routinely granted by Scottish sheriffs when granting an arrest warrant. By contrast, where an English arrest warrant is executed in Scotland or Northern Ireland, the arresting officer has powers of search under s 139 which are similar to those conferred by PACE. Clearly, Parliament accepted that, where the trial is likely to be in Scotland, someone can be arrested in England on a Scottish warrant and subjected to a search which has none of the safeguards of PACE or of the PACE codes of conduct but only the safeguards of the common law of Scotland. There is no reason to believe that Parliament would not also have accepted that, where the offence was likely to be tried abroad, someone could be arrested in England and, in the matter of search, enjoy not the safeguards of PACE and of the PACE codes of conduct but only the safeguards of the common law of England.

[113] In enacting PACE Parliament refrained from abolishing the common law powers of search of police officers executing an arrest warrant. Parliament thus, quite deliberately, left them with those common law powers and left arrested persons with the corresponding common law safeguards. When the police officers in this case arrested the respondent, they were entitled to exercise those common law powers and, equally, the respondent enjoyed the safeguards afforded by the common law. The search of his house was accordingly lawful.

Appeal allowed.

Dilys Tausz   Barrister.

R (on the application of W) v Lambeth London Borough Council

[2002] EWCA Civ 613

COURT OF APPEAL, CIVIL DIVISION

BROOKE, LAWS AND KEENE LJJ

10, 11 APRIL, 3 MAY 2002

Local authority – Statutory powers – Children – Provision of services for children in need – Whether local social services authority having power to provide accommodation for families with dependent children – Children Act 1989, s 17.

The claimant, who was separated from her husband, had the care of two children. In February 2001 she was evicted from her home due to rent arrears. She applied to the defendant local authority for housing assistance as a homeless person. The authority, in its capacity as the local housing authority, provided the claimant with temporary accommodation pending a decision, but subsequently notified her that she had become intentionally homeless. The family was evicted from the temporary accommodation in August 2001, and found other temporary accommodation with a relative. The claimant then asked the authority, in its capacity as the local social services authority, to consider her children's needs under powers conferred on it by Pt III of the Children Act 1989. Part III included s 17[a] which dealt with the provision of services for children in need and their families. In January 2002 the authority's social services department carried out assessments of the children's needs pursuant to s 17, but declined to assist. The claimant sought to challenge that decision in judicial review proceedings, but the judge refused permission to apply, holding that he was bound to do so by a recent Court of Appeal decision (the previous Court of Appeal decision) which had held, inter alia, that s 17 did not empower a local authority to provide accommodation. However, the claimant, who was by then living with her family in bed and breakfast accommodation paid for by the authority, was granted permission to apply by the Court of Appeal which directed that it would hear the substantive application. Subsequently, the authority reassessed the needs of the claimant's children on the assumption that it did have power to assist the family with its accommodation needs under s 17 of the 1989 Act. Once again, however, the authority declined to help, stating that it expected the claimant's extended family to assist her, that it would be obliged to provide accommodation for all intentionally homeless families if it provided accommodation for the claimant and her children, and that that would divert resources from others. It was the lawfulness of that decision which was in issue when the substantive application was heard. At the hearing, the authority sought to rely on the previous Court of Appeal decision, while the claimant contended that that decision was per incuriam since it had been made in ignorance of s 122[b] of the Immigration and Asylum Act 1999 and s 17A[c] of the 1989 Act (inserted by the Carers and Disabled Children Act 2000), both of which assumed that local social services authorities had power under s 17 of the 1989 Act to provide accommodation for homeless

---

a   Section 17, so far as material, is set out at [6], below

b   Section 122 is set out at [68], below

c   Section 17A, so far as material, is set out at [6], below

families with dependent children in circumstances where the housing authority had no duty or power to assist. The claimant therefore argued that the court was entitled to revisit the question of the interpretation of s 17 unfettered by binding authority.

Held – In cases where a family with dependent children was not entitled to help from the local housing authority, s 17 of the 1989 Act gave the local social services authority a power to assist the family with the provision of accommodation, but the exercise of that power was a matter of discretion for the authority, and the latter could, if it saw fit, reserve it to extreme cases. Such a conclusion was not precluded by the previous Court of Appeal decision since that decision had been made per incuriam. If the court in that case had had its attention drawn to the provisions of s 122 of the 1999 Act and s 17A of the 1989 Act, and had appreciated that the housing allocation arrangements in 1989 were not as detailed and comprehensive as they had later become, it would have been bound to have decided the case differently. It would have realised that Parliament had not intended that the assistance a local authority had power to make under Pt III of the 1989 Act should be divided into watertight compartments. The later statutory provisions would be quite unworkable if that were the case. It followed in the instant case that the local authority did have power under s 17 of the 1989 Act to assist the claimant and her family if it saw fit to use it. The authority had, however, given intelligible and adequate reasons why it was not willing to exercise its power, given all the other pressures on its resources. The claimant's case had not yet become an extreme case. Accordingly, there were no sufficient grounds to interfere with the authority's decision, and its assessments would not be quashed (see [52], [57], [60], [73], [76], [83], [84], [87], below).

A-G (*ex rel Tilley*) v *Wandsworth London BC* [1981] 1 All ER 1162 and *R v Tower Hamlets London Borough, ex p Monaf* (1988) 20 HLR 529 applied.

A v *Lambeth London BC* [2001] 3 FCR 673 disapproved in part.

Notes

For a local authority's duty to provide for children in need in general, see 5(3) *Halsbury's Laws* (4th edn reissue) para 1301.

For the Children Act 1989, s 17, see 6 *Halsbury's Statutes* (4th edn) (1999 reissue) 394.

Cases referred to in judgment

A v *Lambeth London BC* [2001] EWCA Civ 1624, [2001] 3 FCR 673; *affg* [2001] LGR 513.

A-G (*ex rel Tilley*) v *Wandsworth London BC* [1981] 1 All ER 1162, [1981] 1 WLR 854, CA.

Barras v Aberdeen Steam Trawling and Fishing Co Ltd [1933] AC 402, [1933] All ER Rep 52, HL.

Birmingham City Corp v West Midland Baptist (Trust) Association (Inc) [1969] 3 All ER 172, [1970] AC 874, [1969] 3 WLR 389, HL.

Duke v Reliance Systems Ltd [1988] 1 All ER 626, [1988] AC 618, [1988] 2 WLR 359, HL; *affg* [1987] 2 All ER 858, [1988] QB 108, [1987] 2 WLR 1225, CA.

IRC v Dowdall O'Mahoney & Co Ltd [1952] 1 All ER 531, [1952] AC 401, HL.

Morelle Ltd v Wakeling [1955] 1 All ER 708, [1955] 2 QB 379, [1955] 2 WLR 672, CA.

R (on the application of G) v Barnet London BC [2001] EWCA Civ 540, [2001] 2 FCR 193.

R (on the application of J) v Enfield London BC [2002] EWHC 432 (Admin), [2002] All ER (D) 209 (Mar).

R v Chard [1983] 3 All ER 637, [1984] AC 279, [1983] 3 WLR 835, HL.

R v Tower Hamlets London Borough, ex p Monaf (1988) 20 HLR 529, CA; *rvsg in part* (1987) 19 HLR 577, DC.

a   *R v Wigan MBC, ex p Tammadge* (1998) 1 CCLR 581.
   Rickards v Rickards [1989] 3 All ER 193, [1990] Fam 194, [1989] 3 WLR 748, CA.
   Williams v Fawcett [1985] 1 All ER 787, [1986] QB 604, [1985] 1 WLR 787, CA.
   Young v Bristol Aeroplane Co Ltd [1944] 2 All ER 293, [1944] KB 718, CA; *affd* [1946]
     1 All ER 98, [1946] AC 163, HL.

b **Application for judicial review**
   The claimant, W, applied for judicial review of the decision of the defendant,
   Lambeth London Borough Council, on 9 April 2002 declining to assist her family
   with the provision of accommodation on an assessment of her children's needs
   under s 17 of the Children Act 1989. On 24 January 2002 Maurice Kay J had
   refused the claimant permission to apply for judicial review of an earlier decision
c   by the council to the same effect, but the Court of Appeal granted permission on
   8 March 2002 and directed that it would hear the substantive application. The
   facts are set out in the judgment of the court.

   John Howell QC and *Stephen Knafler* (instructed by *Flack & Co*) for W.
d *James Goudie QC* and *Charles Béar* (instructed by *Sternberg, Read, Taylor & Gill*) for
   the council.

                                                       Cur adv vult

   3 May 2002. The following judgment of the court was delivered.

e
                        INDEX

BROOKE LJ.

a

(1) *Introduction*

[1] This is an application by the claimant (whom we will call 'W'), a homeless person, for judicial review of decisions by the London Borough of Lambeth (the council) which have the effect of denying her any assistance in meeting the housing needs of her two children. On 24 January 2002 Maurice Kay J refused her *b* permission to apply for judicial review, but on 8 March another division of this court granted such permission and directed that the substantive hearing of this application be heard by this court as soon as possible after 22 March. Since that time the council has made another decision denying her help. It was common ground that it is the lawfulness of this later decision which is now in *c* issue in this case.

(2) *The facts: a brief summary*

[2] W separated from her husband 18 months ago, and has the care of two children, who are now aged 15 and four. She is unemployed and dependent on income support. On 19 February 2001 she was evicted from her home and applied *d* to the council for housing assistance as a homeless person. The council, in its capacity as the local housing authority, provided the family with temporary accommodation pending its decision on this application. On 8 August, however, it notified her, following a review of an earlier decision to the same effect, that she had become intentionally homeless. She had been evicted due to rent arrears. Her present advisors maintain that there would have been grounds for challenging *e* the council's decision in the county court if the necessary application had been made in time.

[3] The family was evicted from their temporary accommodation on 29 August, but were able to find a home on a temporary basis with W's niece. She was living with her two children in a two-bedroomed flat, but this could not be a long-term *f* solution as she was expecting her third child, and in due course she required W and her children to leave. W was unable to obtain private sector accommodation because a minimum payment of £2,000 was usually required, which was quite beyond her means. A further problem was that appropriate private sector accommodation was in short supply. W went to consult a solicitor about her difficulties on 20 December. A full description of W's history may be found in *g* App 1.

(3) *No relief for W under housing legislation*

[4] In order to understand the subsequent history of events and the issues we have to decide in this case, it is necessary to say something about recent *h* developments in the law. The council was both the local housing authority and the local social services authority in W's case. As the local housing authority there was little prospect of it being able to help her with accommodation once her application under Pt VII of the Housing Act 1996 had been rejected. It is obliged to comply with the provisions of Pt VI of that Act in allocating accommodation, but although its allocation scheme has to be framed so as to secure that *j* reasonable preference is given to families with dependent children, or households including someone with a particular need for settled accommodation on welfare grounds, there would be little prospect of W, as a new applicant, achieving any priority treatment once her application for such treatment as a homeless person was dismissed. Relevant statutory provisions are contained in ss 159(1) and (2), 161(1) and 167(1), (2) and (8) of the 1996 Act.

(4) The Children Act 1989

a   [5] In those circumstances W's solicitor considered that it would be more appropriate to invite the council as the local social services authority to consider her children's needs under its powers in Pt III of the Children Act 1989. This part of the Act is entitled 'Local Authority Support for Children and Families'. It has now been quite extensively amended and enlarged by the Carers and Disabled

b Children Act 2000 and the Child (Leaving Care) Act 2001. It is divided up by the following sub-headings. Provision of services for children and their families (ss 17–19). Provision of accommodation for children (ss 20–21). Duties of local authorities in relation to children looked after by them (ss 22–23). Advice and assistance for certain children (s 24). Secure accommodation (s 25). Supplemental (ss 26–30). Sections 17(2), 23(9) and 29(6) also provide links with Sch 2 of the Act,

c and the provisions of para 7 of Pt I of that Schedule featured in the argument before us.

      [6] It is convenient to set out now the provisions of Pt III which featured most prominently in the argument and in the cases we had to consider:

d   '17. *Provision of services for children in need, their families and others.*—(1) It shall be the general duty of every local authority (in addition to the other duties imposed on them by this Part)—(a) to safeguard and promote the welfare of children within their area who are in need; and (b) so far as is consistent with that duty, to promote the upbringing of such children by their families, by providing a range and level of services appropriate to those

e children's needs.

      (2) For the purpose principally of facilitating the discharge of their general duty under this section, every local authority shall have the specific duties and powers set out in Part I of Schedule 2.

      (3) Any service provided by an authority in the exercise of functions conferred on them by this section may be provided for the family of a

f particular child in need ... if it is provided with a view to safeguarding or promoting the child's welfare ...

      (5) Every local authority—(a) shall facilitate the provision by others (including in particular voluntary organisations) of services which the authority have power to provide by virtue of this section, or sections 18, 20,

g 23, 23B to 23D, 24A or 24B ...

      (6) The services provided by a local authority in the exercise of functions conferred on them by this section may include giving assistance in kind or, in exceptional circumstances, in cash.

      (7) Assistance may be unconditional or subject to conditions as to the

h repayment of the assistance or its value (in whole or in part) ...

      (9) No person shall be liable to make any repayment of assistance or of its value at any time when he is in receipt of income support ...

      (10) For the purposes of this Part a child shall be taken to be in need if—(a) he is unlikely to achieve or maintain, or to have the opportunity of achieving or maintaining, a reasonable standard of health or development

j without the provision for him of services by a local authority under this Part ... and "family", in relation to such a child, includes any person who has parental responsibility for the child ...

      17A. *Direct payments.*—(1) Instead of providing services in the exercise of functions conferred on them by section 17, a local authority may make to a person falling within subsection (2) (if he consents) a payment of such amount as, subject to subsections (5) and (6), they think fit in respect of his securing the provision of any of the services which the local authority would otherwise have provided.

(2) The following fall within this subsection—(a) a person with parental responsibility for a disabled child; (b) a disabled child aged 16 or 17 ...

(4) The Secretary of State may by regulations provide that the power conferred by subsection (1) is not to be exercisable in relation to the provision of residential accommodation for any person for a period exceeding a prescribed period ...

20. *Provision of accommodation for children: general.*—(1) Every local authority shall provide accommodation for any child in need within their area who appears to them to require accommodation as a result of ... (c) the person who has been caring for him being prevented (whether or not permanently, and for whatever reason) from providing him with suitable accommodation or care ...

22. *General duty of local authority in relation to children looked after by them.*—(1) In this Act, any reference to a child who is looked after by a local authority is a reference to a child who is—(a) in their care; or (b) provided with accommodation by the authority in the exercise of any functions (in particular those under this Act) which stand referred to their social services committee under the Local Authority Social Services Act 1970 ...

23. *Provision of accommodation and maintenance by local authority for children whom they are looking after.*—(1) It shall be the duty of any local authority looking after a child—(a) when he is in their care, to provide accommodation for him; and (b) to maintain him in other respects apart from providing accommodation for him ...

(6) Subject to any regulations made by the Secretary of State for the purposes of this subsection, any local authority looking after a child shall make arrangements to enable him to live with—(a) [the parent of that child] unless that would not be reasonably practicable or consistent with his welfare.

27. *Co-operation between authorities.*—(1) Where it appears to a local authority that any authority mentioned in subsection (3) could, by taking any specified action, help in the exercise of any of their functions under this Part, they may request the help of that other authority, specifying the action in question.

(2) An authority whose help is so requested shall comply with the request if it is compatible with their own statutory or other duties and obligations and does not unduly prejudice the discharge of any of their functions.

(3) The [authorities] are ... (c) any local housing authority ...

30. *Miscellaneous.*—(1) Nothing in this Part shall affect any duty imposed on a local authority by or under any enactment.'

It should also be noted that s 24B(4), which has been inserted by s 4(1) of the Children (Leaving Care) Act 2001 into that part of Pt III which is concerned with 'advice and assistance', places a duty on a local authority to provide a 'qualifying' person under the age of 24 who is in full-time further or higher education with suitable accommodation during the vacation (or a payment to enable him to secure such accommodation himself) if his term-time accommodation is not available to him then. We mention this to show that provisions expressly dealing with accommodation are not confined to ss 20–23 of the Act.

(5) Three recent cases: G, A and J

a   **[7]** In *R (on the application of G) v Barnet London BC* [2001] EWCA Civ 540, [2001] 2 FCR 193 this court held that the duty under s 20 was a duty to provide accommodation for the child, not for the parent and the child. Section 23 set out the range of choice open to the relevant authority for the performance of this duty but it did not convert it into a duty to house both mother and child.

b   Section 23(6) made no reference to the accommodation in which a child was to live with its mother and it did not import a duty to provide accommodation for the mother where she herself cannot provide it. Ward LJ said in this context:

c   '[Counsel] places s 23(6) at the forefront of his case. In his submission s 23(6) means that the only lawful step for a local authority in circumstances like these is to offer accommodation to mother and child. If he is right, such a far reaching duty which would leave the social services department with practically no discretion, would impose considerable strain on their stretched resources, and would render Pt VII of the Housing Act 1996 virtually irrelevant where the intentionally homeless person is a parent with young children. I would be astonished to find that such a hugely important

d   social provision should be hidden away in the sixth subsection of the seventh section in Pt III of the 1989 Act. The 1989 Act was indeed a great reforming statute but I would have expected that if the reforms went that far then they would find a more prominent place in the statutory framework and be spelt out in clearer language than is urged upon us.' (See [2001] 2 FCR 193 at [29].)

e   **[8]** In *A v Lambeth London BC* [2001] EWCA Civ 1624, [2001] 3 FCR 673 another division of this court was concerned with the question whether s 17 of the 1989 Act might provide a route whereby a social services authority might provide accommodation for the family of a child in need. The appellant had three children, two of whom were autistic and required constant supervision. Her own

f   health had started to deteriorate. The respondent authority assessed the children under s 17 as needing re-housing to appropriate accommodation because their current accommodation severely impaired their health and well-being. Although the family were on the waiting list for a transfer, there seemed little prospect of a transfer occurring.

g   **[9]** This court upheld the decision of Scott Baker J at the first instance (see the report at [2001] LGR 513) and unanimously rejected the appellant's contention that an assessment under s 17 gave rise to an enforceable *duty* to meet the need identified in the assessment. Its members were divided, however, on the question whether s 17 *empowered* the authority to provide accommodation in these

h   circumstances. It will be remembered that sub-s (6) explains that the range of services appropriate to the needs of children in need in their area may include 'giving assistance in kind or, in exceptional circumstances, in cash'.

     [10] Chadwick LJ gave the leading judgment for the majority. He was influenced by the consideration that the 1989 Act marked a change from the earlier statutory scheme for providing residential accommodation for people in

j   need. Section 21 of the National Assistance Act 1948, as amended, had embraced both adults and children in need. Now Pt III of the 1989 Act constituted the statutory vehicle for providing accommodation for people in need, so far as children were concerned. Chadwick LJ summarised the effect of ss 20–23 of that Act. He observed ([2001] 3 FCR 673 at [52]) that a common feature of these provisions was that the obligation of a local authority to provide residential accommodation was confined to circumstances in which the child was not living in a family unit, or where his welfare required that he should not continue to live in a family unit.

[11] It was with those considerations in mind that he was led to the conclusion that s 17 of the 1989 Act was not itself directed to the provision of accommodation. He was not persuaded that Parliament intended that an authority could be required under that section to provide residential accommodation in circumstances in which they would not otherwise be required to do so, either under the subsequent provisions of Pt III of the 1989 Act itself, or (more generally) under the provisions of the Housing Acts.

[12] He observed (at [55]) that in carrying out their functions under the housing legislation a local authority might be expected to have regard to the needs of families with children who were themselves 'in need', but those needs could and should be taken into account in the framing of the housing authority's allocation scheme, in the formulation of its policy in relation to transfers, or in recognising a 'priority need' under s 189(1)(c) of the 1996 Act. He said:

'In my view it would be an extraordinary result—and one which, in the absence of clear words, I cannot hold to reflect the intention of Parliament— if the carefully structured provisions of the housing legislation, which are plainly intended to provide a fair allocation of resources amongst those with housing needs, were to be overridden, in specific cases, by recourse to s 17(1) of the 1989 Act.'

[13] He ended his judgment by saying that the appellant was seeking, in effect, to circumvent the housing transfer scheme by invoking the 1989 Act. He said that in his view this was not an available route to the desired goal of obtaining a transfer to alternative accommodation. It should be noted that the appellant in that case, who already had the benefit of council housing, was seeking a mandatory order requiring the council to provide an alternative suitable property from its own housing stock, to nominate the appellant and her family for re-housing by those associations which owed the council nomination rights, or to buy or lease suitable property for her for occupation with her family.

[14] Sir Philip Otton also declined to interpret s 17 so as to include the provision of accommodation within its scope. He believed that the 1989 Act should not be considered in isolation, but in the context of the whole of the social legislation which existed to protect all the vulnerable and disadvantaged members of society, and that the 1996 Act was another integral part of this all-embracing body of legislation. He said (at [46]):

'It would be wholly impractical for a local authority such as Lambeth to have to decide whether a duty to provide accommodation under s 17 of the 1989 Act in such a case as this family should override or take precedence over an established need within the 1996 Act.'

[15] Laws LJ accepted (at [40]) that there was a respectable argument to the effect that s 17 was not concerned with the provision of accommodation at all. He noted, however, the defendant council's anxiety that there should not be an authoritative finding in this court to the effect that the provision of accommodation would be outwith its s 17 powers, because it might in some unforeseen set of circumstances wish to have recourse to this section, if necessary accommodation could not be provided under any of its other powers. He was influenced by the decision of this court in *A-G (ex rel Tilley) v Wandsworth London BC* [1981] 1 All ER 1162, [1981] 1 WLR 854 (for which see [47]–[49] below), and by

a two more recent decisions of judges at first instance, to conclude that s 17 empowered the provision of accommodation. He thought that this was 'probably the better view, not least given the reference in s 17(6) to assistance in kind'.

[16] The judgments in *A*'s case were delivered on 5 November 2001. W first consulted her present solicitor on 20 December (see [3], above, and App 1, [104], below). When the council's social worker, Mr Bielby, first assessed the children's

b needs in January 2002 (see [110], below), he did so in the belief, fostered by the majority decision in *A*'s case, that the social services department had no power to assist with the accommodation needs of a family who had been found to be intentionally homeless.

[17] It is fair to say that the majority judgments in *A*'s case caused a considerable stir among those concerned with the needs of children whose

c families (not only the 'intentionally homeless') have no home and do not qualify for assistance by a local authority housing department. We have summarised the evidence of Mr Flack, the senior partner in the firm of solicitors who act for W, in App 2 of this judgment, together with the council's response to his evidence. In short, Mr Flack says that in his experience where such a family is unable to stay

d with family or friends, the outcome can be catastrophic. He has known of families with young children under one year old who have been reduced to sleeping in a car, a park or a bus shelter when evicted from their temporary local authority accommodation.

[18] The effect of the decision in *A*'s case was debated in each House of Parliament as early as 12 and 21 November 2001. We have been shown s 12 of

e the Homelessness Act 2002 (which was enacted on 26 February 2002 and is not yet in force). This represents an early statutory attempt to ameliorate the difficulties caused by the majority judgments in *A*'s case. We have also been shown the terms of a suggested new clause in the Adoption and Children Bill, now currently before Parliament. A petition by the appellants in *A*'s case for

f leave to appeal from this court is now before the House of Lords.

[19] However all this may be (and we are concerned with the law as it is, and not what it may one day become), a further element in the equation was introduced on 4 March 2002 by the judgment of Elias J in *R (on the application of J) v Enfield London BC* [2002] EWHC 432 (Admin), [2002] All ER (D) 209 (Mar). That

g judge was concerned with the plight of a Ghanaian overstayer and her two-year-old child who would have nowhere to go when they had to leave the private accommodation the mother had been occupying for the last seven years. After setting out the history and the material provisions of s 17 of the 1989 Act, Elias J said ([2002] All ER (D) 209 (Mar) at [18]):

h 'It is not disputed that the child is a child in need. Moreover, until the decision of the Court of Appeal [in *A*'s case], it was assumed that the local authority could provide accommodation for a child under this provision, and house her family at the same time under s 17(3). Indeed, I am informed that intentionally homeless families were regularly housed under this provision,

j thereby avoiding a break-up of the family and saving the authority the cost of taking the child into care. The claimant accepts that this is no longer possible, at least absent a claim that her human rights have been adversely affected.'

[20] Elias J held that in the light of the majority decision in *A*'s case the defendant council had no power under s 17 to provide J and her daughter with financial assistance to help them to procure a roof over their heads. He accepted

(at [44]) a submission by the council that it was not open to him to ignore the
clear rationale of the decision in A's case 'even if the court were of the view that
it does not sit happily with the earlier authority'. He was then confronted with
an argument that this interpretation of s 17 was incompatible with the European
Convention for the Protection of Human Rights and Fundamental Freedoms
1950 (as set out in Sch 1 to the Human Rights Act 1998) because it involved an
unjustifiable violation of the art 8(1) rights of the claimant and her daughter.
Counsel for the Secretary of State, however, directed his attention to s 2 of the
Local Government Act 2000 (LGA 2000). For reasons which he set out in his
judgment (at [50]–[59]), Elias J concluded that that section was wide enough to
enable the council to provide this family with the financial assistance it sought.
He added, obiter, that but for the power which was capable of being exercised
under that section he would have found that s 17 of the 1989 Act could, pursuant
to s 3 of the Human Rights Act 1998, be construed so as to provide the assistance
the claimant was seeking.

(6) *The arguments on the appeal*

[21] Against this confused background the council wisely re-assessed the
needs of W's children in April 2002 on the supposition that it did have power to
assist the family with their accommodation needs under both s 17 of the 1989 Act
and under s 2 of the LGA 2000. Mr Goudie QC, who appeared for the council on
this appeal, as he had on the earlier case of A, argued before us, however, that:
(i) the case of J was wrongly decided, and s 2 of the LGA 2000 gives the council
no power to assist; (ii) A's case was not decided per incuriam, and only the House
of Lords had the authority to overrule it, if it saw fit; and (iii) arguments founded
on the art 8(1) rights of W and her children could not avail them, notwithstanding
Elias J's obiter observations to contrary effect.

[22] Mr Howell QC, who appeared for W, contended on the other hand that:
(i) A's case was decided per incuriam, and that this court was therefore entitled to
revisit the question of the interpretation of s 17 unfettered by binding authority.
If it did so it should hold that this section did give the council the power to assist
this family; (ii) J's case was correctly decided, so that in any event the council had
power to help the family under s 2 of the LGA 2000; (iii) if both his earlier
contentions were wrong, then the court should interpret s 17 in the manner now
permitted by s 3 of the 1998 Act in order to avoid a violation of the art 8(1) rights
of W and her children. (There was no application for a declaration of convention
incompatibility in this case.) Even if he succeeded in his contention that the
council had the power to help this family, Mr Howell faced the further hurdle of
showing that the council's act of declining help in the exercise of the powers it
assumed that it possessed was unlawful, such that this court could interfere with
the outcome of the s 17 reassessment.

(7) *The pressures besetting Lambeth*

[23] It might be thought that the council, which had fought to retain the full
width of its s 17 powers in the case of A (see [15], above), was now being
inconsistent in its contention that it did not possess any power to help this family
(whether under s 2 of the LGA 2000 or on any permissible interpretation of s 17).
We have therefore, included in App 3 to this judgment a description of the
financial pressures which now beset it, with particular reference to the
contemporary pressures on the families and children division of its social services
department.

a [24] This appendix is based on the evidence contained in two witness statements by Mark Rapley, a former manager in that department who is now employed by the council as an independent consultant. The accuracy of Mr Rapley's evidence has been endorsed by the council's present head of children's services. In short, the council takes the view that child protection, and the need to ensure that the children in their care are appropriately looked after, are the core activities b to which they must now give priority. The council has learned from experience that most potentially homeless families in W's position find accommodation for themselves by one means or another, and the diversion of financial and staff resources to the accommodation needs of all these families can only serve to prejudice the performance of its principal obligations towards children in need in the borough.

c
(8) *Was A's case decided per incuriam?*

[25] In these circumstances it is best to address Mr Howell's contentions in the order set out in [22], above. If, as he urges us, it is open to us to revisit s 17 unshackled by binding authority, and to interpret it as giving the council the d power to help families like W's if it sees fit, then it will not be necessary to dwell for long on his other two arguments. It is first necessary, however, to say a little more about the circumstances in which A's case was argued in this court, and then to recall the principles on which the Court of Appeal is entitled to depart from one of its earlier decisions, which would ordinarily be regarded as having binding effect at this level of the court hierarchy.

e [26] In A's case, the claimant appealed to this court against the decision of Scott Baker J (see [9], above) to the effect that there was no duty on the council, enforceable by the claimant, to accommodate her children in accordance with their special needs (as identified by their assessment under s 17). The claimant was seeking a mandatory order, compared by her advocate with the mandatory f order upheld by this court in *R v Wigan MBC, ex p Tammadge* (1998) 1 CCLR 581 in a case concerned with s 21 of the National Assistance Act 1948. This order would have the effect of requiring the council's social services department to provide better accommodation for the family than the accommodation currently provided to them by the housing department.

[27] This court unanimously upheld Scott Baker J's decision that there was no g such enforceable duty. This ruling would have sufficed for the appeal to be decided in the council's favour. Neither party originally sought to argue that the council had no power under s 17 to provide accommodation for families, or financial help towards their accommodation. There was no mention of the point in the notice of appeal or in the written skeleton arguments prepared for the court h in advance of the hearing. Neither side in these circumstances had prepared any argument on the point. Chadwick LJ, however, took the point of his own motion for the first time at the hearing. It is hardly surprising in these unpropitious circumstances that we enjoyed the benefit of much fuller argument than was available to that court.

j [28] It is impossible, however, to conclude with any certainty that their decision on this point did not form part of the decisive reasoning of the majority in A's case. Chadwick LJ made clear (see [2001] 3 FCR 673 at [57]) that it did for the purposes of his judgment. With Sir Philip Otton's judgment the position is less clear, but since he felt bound to express his own opinion because of what he described as the significance divergence of view of the other two members of the court, it is probably safe to conclude that he, too, would regard his decision on this point as part of his decisive reasoning. Everything else being equal, therefore, we would be bound to follow the majority in *A*'s case, even if the facts (and the relief sought) in that case are far removed from the facts (and the relief sought) in the present appeal.

(9) The principles to apply

[29] There have been two quite recent decisions of this court which define the very rare circumstances in which this court is at liberty to decline to follow one of its earlier decisions. In *Rickards v Rickards* [1989] 3 All ER 193, [1990] Fam 194 the court was confronted by one of its earlier decisions to the effect that it had no jurisdiction to entertain an appeal from a decision by what we would now describe as a first appeal court refusing to extend the time for appealing to itself. The case was unusual, because if the court followed the earlier decision there would be no possibility of an appeal to the House of Lords, since it would not be deciding the appeal: it would be holding that it had no jurisdiction to hear it at all. Lord Donaldson of Lymington MR emphasised the importance of the court following its own earlier decisions (and the limited exceptions to the general rule) in these terms:

'The importance of the rule of *stare decisis* in relation to the Court of Appeal's own decisions can hardly be overstated. We now sometimes sit in eight divisions and, in the absence of such a rule, the law would quickly become wholly uncertain. However, the rule is not without exceptions, albeit very limited. These exceptions were considered in *Young v Bristol Aeroplane Co Ltd* [1944] 2 All ER 293, [1944] KB 718, *Morelle Ltd v Wakeling* [1955] 1 All ER 708, [1955] 2 QB 379 and, more recently, in *Williams v Fawcett* [1985] 1 All ER 787 at 794–795, [1986] QB 604 at 615–616, where relevant extracts from the two earlier decisions are set out. These decisions show that this court is justified in refusing to follow one of its own previous decisions not only where that decision is given in ignorance or forgetfulness of some inconsistent statutory provision or some authority binding on it, but also, in rare and exceptional cases, if it is satisfied that the decision involved a manifest slip or error.' (See [1989] 3 All ER 193 at 198–199, [1990] Fam 194 at 203.)

[30] The court considered that *Rickards* fell into the category of 'rare and exceptional cases' for the reasons given by Lord Donaldson ([1989] 3 All ER 193 at 199, [1990] Fam 194 at 204). In the earlier case of *Duke v Reliance Systems Ltd* [1987] 2 All ER 858, [1988] QB 108 the same judge (with whom Ralph Gibson and Bingham LJJ agreed) had identified the occasions on which this court is entitled to apply the doctrine of per incuriam and decline to follow one of its earlier decisions, which would otherwise be binding. He said:

'I have always understood that the doctrine of per incuriam only applies where another division of this court has reached a decision in the absence of knowledge of a decision binding on it or a statute, and that in either case it has to be shown that, had the court had this material, it must have reached a contrary decision. That is per incuriam. I do not understand the doctrine to extend to a case where, if different arguments had been placed before it or if different material had been placed before it, it might have reached a different conclusion. That appears to me to be the position at which we have arrived today.' (See [1987] 2 All ER 858 at 860, [1988] QB 108 at 113.)

(10) *Mr Howell's arguments*

[31] Mr Howell argued that the present case fell within the first category of cases identified by the court in *Rickards v Rickards*, where the earlier decision was given in ignorance of some inconsistent statutory provision. He accepted that although Chadwick LJ and Sir Philip Otton did not refer to any case law in their judgments at all, all the relevant cases were cited to them, and it would be impossible for him to succeed below the level of the House of Lords on any argument founded on a contention that they were ignorant or forgetful of case law binding on them. On the other hand, he submitted that, no doubt because of the unsatisfactory way in which the critical point first arose in the course of the hearing, it was decided in ignorance of inconsistent statutory provisions.

[32] For this purpose he identified s 122 of the Immigration and Asylum Act 1999, s 17A of the 1989 Act itself (inserted as it was by s 7 of the Carers and Disabled Children Act 2000) and, to a lesser extent, s 22 of the Housing Act 1985 (see [59], below: reference to this section shows that the arrangements for the allocation of council housing in 1989 were far less detailed and comprehensive than those to which Chadwick LJ referred in *A v Lambeth London BC* [2001] 3 FCR 673 at [54]).

[33] Mr Howell also bolstered his argument by reference to other provisions of the 1989 Act itself, such as ss 27 and 30, which show that a housing authority would be entitled to refuse a request for help from a social services authority if to comply with this request would affect its duty to allocate housing in accordance with its allocation scheme. These sections were, however, before the court in *A*'s case, and we think that Mr Howell appreciated in the end that this court could not free itself from the shackles of *A*'s case (supposing it desired to do so) by this route.

[34] It follows from all this that we would only be able to depart from *A*'s case if we were satisfied that if the court in *A*'s case had considered the statutory material identified in [32], above it must have reached a different decision.

(11) *Two other rules of statutory interpretation*

[35] There are two other rules of statutory interpretation to which we must refer at this stage. The first arises in this way. There is no difficulty about s 17A of the 1989 Act (for its terms, see [6], above), because it formed part of the Act which the court in *A*'s case ought to have taken into account, if it had been aware of it, when it was interpreting s 17 in the context of Pt III of the 1989 Act as a whole. Section 122 of the 1999 Act (for its terms, see [68], below) gives rise to different problems. In that section it is clear that Parliament shared the common belief as to the width of s 17 which existed until the judgments in *A*'s case were given, as we explain in [69], below.

[36] The general rule about a 'mistake by Parliament' is expressed in Bennion *Statutory Interpretation* (3rd edn, 1997) in these terms (at p 542):

'Where it appears that an enactment proceeds upon a mistaken view of earlier law, the question may arise whether this effects a change in that law (apart from any amendment directly made by the enactment). Here it is necessary to remember that, except when legislating, Parliament has no power authoritatively to interpret the law. That function belongs to the judiciary alone ... A mere inference that Parliament has mistaken the nature or effect of some legal rule does not in itself amount to a declaration that the rule is other than what it is. However, the view taken by Parliament as to the legal meaning of a doubtful enactment may be treated as of persuasive, though not binding, authority.'

[37] The leading authority in this corner of the law appears in Lord Reid's speech in *IRC v Dowdall O'Mahoney & Co Ltd* [1952] 1 All ER 531, [1952] AC 401. In that case an Irish company with two branches in the United Kingdom complained that it had been subjected to double taxation. The House of Lords held on the proper construction of the relevant provisions of the Income Tax Act 1918 that the proportion of the taxes it paid in Eire in respect of profits of its trade arising in this country were not deductible in arriving at its profits assessable to United Kingdom excess profits tax. It was argued, however, that in enacting later legislation in 1939 and 1940 Parliament must have assumed that there was a pre-existing right to make such deductions on income tax principle, and that this consideration served to alter the meaning of the provisions in the 1918 Act.

[38] Lord Reid accepted ([1952] 1 All ER 531 at 541, [1952] AC 401 at 420) that the terms of the later legislation did indicate a Parliamentary belief that some such right already existed, even though that belief was erroneous. He continued:

'So the question is whether the terms of those paragraphs are such as merely to indicate a belief or whether they can be interpreted as enacting by implication that which Parliament, having its erroneous belief, did not find it necessary to enact expressly. In such circumstances I would not be averse from holding that there was an enactment by implication, but first I must be able to discover precisely what Parliament's belief was. The Finance Act, 1940, s 30, may well contain such an enactment. It is there made clear that Parliament believed that there was already a right to a certain deduction and the scheme of the section will not work unless there is such a right, so it is not difficult to imply the enactment of that right. But the whole section is limited to cases which are covered by an Order in Council, and it is not possible to imply any enactment which goes beyond the scope of the section. There has been no Order in Council which could apply to the present case; and, therefore, in my judgment, even if s 30 were held to contain by implication an enactment authorising deductions such as those claimed by the respondents, that would not help them as they are outside the scope of the section.'

[39] He went on to consider the argument that an enactment allowing the deduction ought to be implied, because without it there would be great injustice. He thought that the question was a difficult one, but he had come to the opinion that it did not, saying ([1952] 1 All ER 531 at 541, [1952] AC 401 at 421):

'[The relevant paragraph in the schedule to the 1939 Act] is very misleading, but to mislead a taxpayer is not the same thing as to entitle him to relief. It may well be that these paragraphs show that Parliament was under a misapprehension as to the existing law at the time, but it does not necessarily follow that if Parliament had been correctly informed it would have altered the law. It is one thing to leave an old deduction untouched, and quite another thing to enact for the first time a new deduction of a new kind.'

[40] Lord Reid revisited this topic in *Birmingham City Corp v West Midland Baptist (Trust) Association (Inc)* [1969] 3 All ER 172 at 179–180, [1970] AC 874 at 898. That case turned on the proper interpretation of a provision of an Act passed in 1919, and the appellants argued that they were entitled to rely on the fact that

a in three recent statutes Parliament had legislated on the assumption that the meaning of the 1919 Act was that for which they contended. Lord Reid, applying *IRC v Dowdall*, said that the mere fact that an enactment showed that Parliament must have thought that the law was one thing did not preclude the courts from deciding that it was in fact something different. All that could be said in the present case was that the later enactments would have a narrower scope if the b law was found to be that for which the respondents contended. But he added, obiter: 'No doubt the position would be different if the provisions of the [later] enactment were such that they would only be workable if the law was as Parliament supposed it to be.'

[41] In our judgment, the effect of these dicta is that we should not pay any particular attention to any difficulties that might be thrown up by s 122 of the c 1999 Act unless part of the scheme contained in that section is found to be unworkable if the interpretation of s 17 by the majority of this court in *A* is adopted. If it is indeed unworkable, we should be willing to look for an alternative meaning which would make it work. We will discuss this question in [69] and [73], below.

d [42] The other rule of statutory interpretation which we have mentioned is often known as 'the Barras principle'. It is taken from the speech of Viscount Buckmaster in *Barras v Aberdeen Steam Trawling and Fishing Co Ltd* [1933] AC 402 at 411, [1933] All ER Rep 52 at 55:

e 'It has long been a well established principle to be applied in the consideration of Acts of Parliament that where a word of doubtful meaning has received a clear judicial interpretation, the subsequent statute which incorporates the same word or the same phrase in a similar context, must be construed so that the word or phrase is interpreted according to the meaning that has previously been assigned to it.'

f [43] Lord Russell of Killowen ([1933] AC 402 at 442, [1933] All ER Rep 52 at 70) treated this 'principle' as a presumption, and Lord Warrington of Clyffe ([1933] AC 402 at 438, [1933] All ER Rep 52 at 68) adopted Viscount Buckmaster's approach. Lord Blanesburgh ([1933] AC 402 at 432–434, [1933] All ER Rep 52 at 65–66) was more cautious, and Lord Macmillan ([1933] AC 402 at 446, [1933] All ER Rep 52 at 72) refused to regard the rule as a 'canon of construction of g absolute obligation'. In this regard his approach was vindicated just over 50 years later by all the members of the House of Lords in *R v Chard* [1983] 3 All ER 637, [1984] AC 279.

[44] In the present context, however, it would have been difficult to apply Viscount Buckmaster's principle slavishly in any event. While it is true that in the h cases to which we will now turn this court twice regarded the predecessor sections to s 17 of the 1989 Act as having a wider compass than that which found favour with the majority of this court in *A*'s case, the language of the 1989 Act is not identical. It is sufficient, perhaps, to say that when the court has earlier favoured a wide interpretation of statutory language concerned with provision for children who are about to be made homeless, one should construe a later j statute, into which the earlier provisions have been subsumed, with great care before concluding that a more restrictive approach should be adopted in the interpretative process.

(12) The earlier case law: Tilley and Monaf

[45] We turn then to the earlier case law to which we have just referred. One of the strands of earlier statute law which was developed in the rather wider

provisions of Pt III of the 1989 Act originated in s 1 of the Children and Young
Persons Act 1963, which was later re-enacted in s 1 of the Child Care Act 1980.　*a*
The relevant parts of these sections are in these terms (and we quote from the
1963 Act for this purpose):

> '**1.**—(1) It shall be the duty of every local authority to make available such
> advice, guidance and assistance as may promote the welfare of children by
> diminishing the need to receive children into or keep them in care under the　*b*
> Children Act 1948, the principal Act or the principal Scottish Act or to bring
> children before a juvenile court; and any provisions made by a local
> authority under this subsection may, if the local authority think fit, include
> provision for giving assistance in kind or, in exceptional circumstances, in
> cash …　　　　　　　　　　　　　　　　　　　　　　　　　　　　　　　　*c*
> (3) Where any provision which may be made by a local authority under
> subsection (1) of this section is made (whether by that or any other authority)
> under any other enactment the local authority shall not be required to make
> the provision under this section but shall have power to do so.'

The language of the similar provision of the 1980 Act is identical, with the single　*d*
exception that the words 'under this Act' replace the rather longer provisions in
sub-s (1) of the 1963 Act.

[46] We will refer in [61]–[63], below to the fate of these provisions when they
were absorbed into the 1989 Act. At present we are concerned to consider how
the courts interpreted these statutory provisions before the 1989 Act came into
force. It will be noted that they imposed on local authorities certain duties to give　*e*
assistance which might promote the welfare of children over and above the
duties imposed on central government through the former statutory schemes for
national assistance and supplementary benefit.

[47] In *Tilley's* case a successful challenge was made to a resolution by the
defendant council to the effect that assistance with alternative housing should not　*f*
be provided under the 1963 Act to a family with young children who were found
to be intentionally homeless. The council's resolution permitted consideration to
be given to the reception into care of the children on their own should their
circumstances warrant it.

[48] Templeman LJ ([1981] 1 All ER 1162 at 1170, [1981] 1 WLR 854 at 857),
with whom the two other members of the court agreed, reminded himself that　*g*
under the Children Act 1948 a child might be taken into care where it appeared
to a local authority that his parents were prevented, through incapacity or any
other circumstances, from providing for his proper accommodation, maintenance
and upbringing. This step would involve the child being removed from his
parents and put with foster parents or in a home. The 1963 Act now imposed on　*h*
the council a duty to see, if possible, that the child could stay with his parents (or,
perhaps, with some other relations), by giving such advice, guidance and
assistance as the council might think appropriate.

[49] In argument, counsel had contended that the final words of s 1(1)
(provision for giving assistance in kind or, in exceptional circumstances, in cash)　*j*
were not apt to cover the provision of accommodation. Templeman LJ commented
on this argument in these terms:

> 'But, in my judgment, that is a misconstruction of the 1963 Act. The Act is
> dealing with children who are taken into care under the Children Act 1948.
> That can happen, as I have already indicated, if the parents are unable to
> provide accommodation for the child, and the 1963 Act provides that if there

a is lack of accommodation the local authority must try and deal with the situation by some other method than by taking the child into care. To my mind the word "assistance" in s 1(1) of the 1963 Act clearly includes the provision of accommodation and then provides that the general powers of the local authority shall include specific powers. The specific powers do not cut down the general powers of the local authority in the way which counsel

b for the local authority argues and which would prevent that authority from diminishing the need to receive children into care by providing them with accommodation or by paying for accommodation.' (See [1981] 1 All ER 1162 at 1170, [1981] 1 WLR 854 at 857.)

[50] The nature of a local authority's duties or powers under these statutory

c provisions was revisited six years later in *R v Tower Hamlets London Borough, ex p Monaf* (1987) 19 HLR 577 (Div Ct), (1988) 20 HLR 529 (CA). This litigation was concerned with families from Bangladesh who were found to be intentionally homeless, and were then refused assistance under s 1 of the 1980 Act, being the statute then in force. In the Divisional Court it was conceded that the local authority was not obliged to provide permanent housing under s 1 of the 1980

d Act. Lloyd LJ commented ((1987) 19 HLR 577 at 590):

'It would indeed be a startling result if they were, since it would seem to make nonsense of Part III of the Housing Act 1985. But once that concession is made, then the extent of the assistance to be provided under section 1, and the manner in which the assistance is to be provided, must be for the local

e authority to decide.'

[51] Stuart-Smith J, for his part, made it clear that he was troubled by the decision of this court in *Tilley*'s case. Section 2(1)(b) of the 1980 Act gave a local authority the duty to receive a child into care if the child's parents were

f prevented, for various specified reasons, from providing for his proper accommodation, maintenance and upbringing, and s 1(1) was concerned to diminish the need to receive children into care 'under this Act'. In those circumstances Stuart-Smith J commented ((1987) 19 HLR 577 at 589–590):

'It might be thought at first sight that in so far as these applicants were

g intentionally homeless (and the point only arises if they were) then they had not been prevented from providing accommodation within the meaning of section 2(1)(b) of the 1980 Act. It might also be thought at first sight that section 1 of the Act has nothing whatever to do with the provision of housing even on a temporary basis. But the Court of Appeal has decided otherwise

h in the case of *Att.-Gen. ex rel Tilley* v. *Wandsworth London Borough Council.*'

[52] Having expressed these misgivings, he then loyally followed the decision in *Tilley*'s case and concluded (at 593):

'On the basis that the children of intentionally homeless persons do fall within section 1 of the Act, it seems to me that that section has to be

j considered in two parts: the first part imposing a duty; the second, a power and a discretion. But I do not accept that the first part imposes a duty to provide accommodation or cash in lieu. The proper way to read the section so as to relate the two parts is, in my view, as follows: "It shall be the duty of every local authority to make available such advice, guidance and assistance (which may, if the local authority think fit, include provision for giving assistance in kind or in exceptional circumstances in cash) as may promote

the welfare," etc. If this is how the section is to be read, then both the
question whether to provide accommodation or cash in lieu and the extent   *a*
of any such provision is a matter for the discretion of the authority and its
provision is not a matter of duty.'

[53] On the appeal to this court Purchas LJ, who had the benefit of eight years'
experience in the Family Division, gave the judgment of a court which also
included Mustill and Mann LJJ. The relevant part of his judgment is reported in   *b*
(1988) 20 HLR 529 at 547–553. He explained (at 547) that this appeared to have
been the first occasion on which the interaction of the statutory duties and
powers in relation to the care and welfare of children arising under the housing
and the child care legislation had come under focus in such a dramatic way.

[54] So far as the legislative history of these provisions was concerned, he   *c*
recalled how s 1 of the Children Act 1948 was the origin of the process later
known as voluntary care. Section 1(3) of this Act gave strong support to the
desirability of a child remaining with one or other or both of his parents (but that
Act did not empower a local authority to give assistance, whether in cash, kind or
otherwise, to bring about this happy outcome). Part III of the National Assistance
Act 1948, on the other hand, imposed a duty on every local authority to provide   *d*
residential accommodation for adults or children in need of care and attention,
including temporary accommodation in cases of urgent need.

[55] Purchas LJ discussed the purpose of the 1963 Act by reference to a
contemporary Home Office circular which 'provided some background context'.
After reciting five paragraphs of the circular in whole or in part, he said (at 549):   *e*

'The approach in 1963 as appears from the Circular would, therefore, be:
(a) that there should be co-operation between the housing and welfare
departments subject to the obvious difficulties where two different
authorities are involved; (b) that assistance should be given in the short term
to the housing department, where such assistance will avoid the reception   *f*
into care of children affected by homelessness; (c) that the welfare services
have no duty to take over the long term functions of the housing
departments; (d) that section 1 of the 1963 Act applies equally to children
being taken into voluntary care, or under the jurisdiction of the juvenile
court; (e) that in the normal case, the welfare of the children will be served if
the family unit is preserved and that this must be an argument for providing   *g*
accommodation, at least in the short term.'

[56] He then turned to the relationship between this new statutory provision
and the homelessness legislation first introduced in 1977. He said that the
question raised in the appeal was whether the 1980 Act created any obligation   *h*
to provide accommodation for children beyond the obligation to secure
accommodation imposed by what was then s 65(3)(a) of the Housing Act 1985.
The Housing (Homeless Persons) Act 1977 had been enacted to replace the
limited duty of local social services authorities to provide temporary accommodation
for those in urgent need imposed by s 21(1)(b) of the National Assistance Act
1948. He said that the 1977 Act imposed wider duties to provide, secure or help   *j*
secure accommodation for homeless persons and those threatened with
homelessness, and the relevant sections of the 1985 Act were in substantially
equivalent terms. For the first time these sections introduced as an element in
their own right the presence of 'dependent children who are residing with the
homeless person'. He noted, however, that no reference was made in the 1977
Act to any section of the Children Act 1948.

a [57] These considerations led him to observe (at 550) that there was no statutory history to make any connection between s 1 of the 1980 Act and the provision of the 1977 Act which was in force when the 1980 Act was enacted. He concluded in these circumstances that in 1980 Parliament intended to extend or qualify the duties imposed on a local authority under the 1977 homelessness legislation:

b 'By the same token, in passing the 1985 Act with its special provision relating to homeless persons having a priority need because, *inter alia*, of dependent children, if the boundaries of this duty were to be affected by the then existing duties imposed upon the local authority by section 1 of the 1980 Act, reference might be expected to have been made by Parliament to that *c* Act. It is clear from the papers before us that the interaction of these two lines of statutory power and duty has caused considerable anxiety in those responsible for administering these parts of the statutory code. The 1977 Act deals with the provision of "bricks and mortar" in the form of a home in certain circumstances. In the case of those with a priority need, the provision of a home is promoted above those who are achieving normal priority on the *d* housing list. This acts prejudicially to the ordinary inhabitants and ratepayers of the area and is justified as a matter of hardship and emergency in line with the considerations based on section 21(1)(b) of the National Assistance Act 1948 as developed through the subsequent legislation. However, where a family is intentionally homeless, the long term provision as a matter of *e* priority of accommodation for the purposes of establishing a home is withdrawn. If it were not to be withdrawn on this ground where the welfare of the children was involved, the intentionally homeless provisions would not have been applied to that particular category of applicant. It was clearly the intention of Parliament in 1977 that this should be so; families with dependent children should be classified as having a priority need, but that *f* those who were intentionally homeless should not receive special treatment beyond that provided in section 65(3) of the 1985 Act. *This does not deprive the children, however, of receiving under section 1 of the 1980 Act such assistance, where appropriate, in the form of accommodation as emergency short term relief to prevent the necessity to take them into care.'* (My emphasis.)

g [58] It is unnecessary for present purposes to read into this judgment the remainder of Purchas LJ's judgment in *Monaf's* case. After considering possible solutions which might keep a family home in place, he said (at 551) that ultimately what steps should be taken must be a decision taken by the social services department of the authority concerned in the unfettered exercise of their *h* discretion under ss 1 and 2 of the 1980 Act. It is noteworthy, however, that he commended as 'eminently sensible' an extract from a report of the director of social services of the respondent authority in that case which addressed the issues facing the officers of her authority when a family with dependent children were declared to be intentionally homeless. The author of this report said:

j 'Local authorities therefore have a duty to consider each case on its merits to decide whether it is appropriate to give assistance (including provision of accommodation) to diminish the need for reception orders into care … The Director of Social Services must accordingly examine each case where reception into care is likely and decide whether by providing temporary accommodation the welfare of children in the family would be promoted by diminishing the need for their reception into care. If he considers that this would be the case then the Council's duty is to make such provisions … It will be evident that there is often an over-lap between the duties of a local authority under the provisions of Part 3 of the Housing Act 1985 to provide temporary accommodation and those contained in section 1 of the Child Care Act 1980. The provisions in the latter Act are not however concerned with such questions as to whether the family are intentionally homeless and perhaps at the end of the day the same Council would foot the bill irrespective of the Department involved.'

[59] That, then, was the state of the law when the 1989 Act was enacted. It should also be noted that in 1989 the arrangements for the allocation of housing to local authority tenants were less prescriptive than they later became. There was at that time no statutory requirement imposed on a local housing authority to allocate housing accommodation (however defined) only to certain categories of 'qualifying persons', or only in accordance with the authority's own rules. Section 22 of the 1985 Act imposed on a local housing authority a duty to secure that in the selection of their tenants a reasonable preference was given to four categories of persons, who included 'persons having large families' and '[persons found to be homeless]'. The authority was also obliged (see s 106 of that Act) to maintain and publish rules for maintaining priority as between applicants in the allocation of its housing accommodation, and governing cases where secure tenants wished to move to other dwelling houses let under secure tenancies by that authority or another body. Section 22 of the 1985 Act did not, however, relate to nominations made by a local housing authority to accommodation let by others. Nor did s 106 (except, as we have observed, in the case of transfers).

[60] In *Monaf*'s case this court explained in clear terms the effect of the separate and independent responsibilities of a local housing authority and a social services authority when questions arose about the housing of homeless families. It was the duty of the housing authority to provide temporary accommodation for these families while the merits of their case were being considered (1985 Act, s 68(1)), and permanent accommodation if they were found eligible and in priority need, and the authority were not satisfied that the applicant became homeless intentionally (see s 65(2)). If they were so satisfied, they were under the limited obligation to provide short-term accommodation, advice and assistance described in s 65(3). The social services authority, on the other hand, had a power (but not a duty) to act as a safety net when the duty imposed on the housing authority came to an end.

(13) *The policy of Pt III of the 1989 Act*

[61] The 1989 Act appears, on the face of it, to have continued the practice of separate and independent existence which Purchas LJ noticed in the context of the interface between the earlier housing and social welfare legislation. No express reference is made to the provisions of the 1985 Act either in Pt III of the 1989 Act or in Sch 2, which puts flesh on some of the provisions of Pt III. It is well known that the philosophy of the Act was to promote the welfare of children, and we are bound to say that we would have found it surprising if Parliament had intended to alter the law set out in the judgment in *Monaf*'s case so as to remove the possibility of the social services authority performing a safety net function if it felt able and if it saw fit to do so.

[62] Four things are at once apparent on a careful study of the provisions of Pt III and Sch 2 of the 1989 Act. (1) That Parliament decided to widen the powers of local authorities to safeguard and promote the children in need in their areas

a and to promote the upbringing of such children by their families by imposing on them a much more widely embracing 'target duty' than that contained in s 1 of the 1980 Act which the 1989 Act replaced (see the broad terms of s 17). (2) That the range and level of services appropriate to such children's needs which local authorities were now under a duty to provide might include giving assistance in kind, or in exceptional circumstances in cash (s 17(6)), but these words on the face

b of them do not confine the power of a local authority, if they think fit, to provide temporary accommodation for an intentionally homeless family (in order to prevent the break-up of that family and the potential damage to the children involved) any more than the presence of the same words did in *Tilley's* case (see [49], above). (3) That the word 'services' which appears in s 17(1) is capable of encompassing the provision of accommodation is made quite clear in s 17(5)(a),

c which makes it clear that this expression encompasses not only day care (see s 18) and advice and assistance (see s 24) but also the provision of accommodation (see ss 20, 23 and 24B). The same wide meaning of the word 'services' is also apparent in Pt I of Sch 2 of the Act. (4) That in relation to the accommodation of children in need (as opposed to their families), Parliament decided to remove them from

d the category of persons for whom provision was made in s 21(1)(a) of the National Assistance Act 1948 (1989 Act, Sch 13, para 11(1)) and to make the more detailed provision contained in s 20 of the 1989 Act.

[63] The second of these propositions requires a little elaboration. In *Tilley's* case Templeman LJ fastened on the wide words 'such ... assistance as may promote the welfare of children by diminishing the need to receive [them] ... into

e care' as encompassing a power to provide them with accommodation, even though the provision of accommodation would not naturally be considered to be 'assistance in kind, or in exceptional circumstances, in cash'. The comparable language of the 1989 Act appears to be wider still. Local authorities were now to be under a general target duty to perform the obligations identified in s 17(1) by

f providing a range and level of services appropriate to the needs of children in their area who are in need. For the purpose of facilitating the performance of this general duty, s 17(2) provided that they were to have the specific duties and powers set out in Pt I of Sch 2. These include a duty (see Sch 2, para 7) to take reasonable steps designed to reduce the need to bring proceedings for care orders

g with respect to children in their area. If it is reasonable to secure that an intentionally homeless family is temporarily housed together (after the obligations of the housing authority are at an end) in order to avoid damage to the children if they have to be separated, then this would be a reasonable step for a local authority to take if it wishes to do so.

h (14) *The Immigration and Asylum Act 1999*

[64] Perusal of s 122 of the 1999 Act shows that in that year Parliament believed that local social services authorities still possessed under the 1989 Act the 'safety net' powers which existed under its predecessor legislation, as described by Purchas LJ in *Monaf's* case. Families who are intentionally homeless are not

j the only persons to whom a local housing authority owes no duty. Mr Howell provided us with a helpful note identifying the people who are not eligible for assistance at all under what are now the homelessness provisions contained in Pt VII of the Housing Act 1996. Such people fall into two categories: those who are subject to immigration control under the Asylum and Immigration Act 1996 (unless they fall into a prescribed class) (see s 185(2) of that Act), and other persons provided for in regulations who are to be treated for this purpose as

persons from abroad who are ineligible for housing assistance (see s 185(3) of that
Act and reg 4 of the Homelessness (England) Regulations 2000, SI 2000/701).   *a*

[65] After describing the effect of relevant provisions of recent immigration
and/or asylum legislation, and regs 2, 3 and 4 of the homelessness regulations,
Mr Howell concluded, and we accept, that:

> 'Those who are ineligible for any assistance under the homelessness
> legislation are thus primarily: (i) those who are not British citizens or   *b*
> nationals of an EEA state (a) who require leave to enter or remain in the
> United Kingdom but do not have it (including asylum seekers); (b) who have
> leave to enter or remain but whose leave is subject to a condition that they
> do not have recourse to public funds; (c) who have such leave given as a
> result of a maintenance undertaking, and (ii) those who are not yet   *c*
> habitually resident in the Common Travel Area unless they have certain
> community and European Economic Area rights to reside here.'

[66] Part VI of the 1999 Act introduced an entirely new statutory scheme of
support for asylum seekers. The essence of this scheme was that a 'person subject
to immigration control' was now to be excluded from mainstream social security,   *d*
housing and other assistance. Instead, an alternative system of support was to be
provided by the Secretary of State, either directly or through arrangements with
local authorities and others. The details of the scheme do not matter. Some of
the provisions of ss 95 and 122 are all that need to be considered for present
purposes.

[67] The broad effect of s 95 is that the Secretary of State is empowered to   *e*
provide support, or arrange for the provision of support, for asylum seekers or
dependants of asylum seekers who appear to him to be destitute or likely to
become destitute within a prescribed period (s 95(1)). For this purpose, a person
is destitute if he does not have adequate accommodation or any means of
obtaining it (whether or not his other essential living needs are met) (s 95(3)(a)).   *f*

[68] Section 122 is entitled 'Support for children'. It needs to be read in full:

> '(1) In this section "eligible person" means a person who appears to the
> Secretary of State to be a person for whom support may be provided under
> section 95.
>
> (2) Subsections (3) and (4) apply if an application for support under   *g*
> section 95 has been made by an eligible person whose household includes a
> dependant under the age of 18 ("the child").
>
> (3) If it appears to the Secretary of State that adequate accommodation is
> not being provided for the child, he must exercise his powers under section 95
> by offering, and if his offer is accepted by providing or arranging for the   *h*
> provision of, adequate accommodation for the child as part of the eligible
> person's household.
>
> (4) If it appears to the Secretary of State that essential living needs of the
> child are not being met, he must exercise his powers under section 95 by
> offering, and if his offer is accepted by providing or arranging for the
> provision of, essential living needs for the child as part of the eligible person's   *j*
> household.
>
> (5) No local authority may provide assistance under any of the child
> welfare provisions in respect of a dependant under the age of 18, or any
> member of his family, at any time when—(a) the Secretary of State is
> complying with this section in relation to him; or (b) there are reasonable
> grounds for believing that—(i) the person concerned is a person for whom

a support may be provided under section 95; and (ii) the Secretary of State would be required to comply with this section if that person had made an application under section 95.

(6) "Assistance" means the provision of accommodation or of any essential living needs.

b (7) "The child welfare provisions" means—(a) section 17 of the Children Act 1989 (local authority support for children and their families); (b) section 22 of the Children (Scotland) Act 1995 (equivalent provision for Scotland); and (c) Article 18 of the Children (Northern Ireland) Order 1995 (equivalent provision for Northern Ireland).

(8) Subsection (9) applies if accommodation provided in the discharge of the duty imposed by subsection (3) has been withdrawn.

c (9) Only the relevant authority may provide assistance under any of the child welfare provisions in respect of the child concerned.

(10) "Relevant authority" means—(a) in relation to Northern Ireland, the authority within whose area the withdrawn accommodation was provided; (b) in any other case, the local authority within whose area the withdrawn

d accommodation was provided.

(11) In such circumstances as may be prescribed, subsection (5) does not apply.'

[69] The effect of this section is that when either of the conditions set out in sub-s (5) are fulfilled, a local authority in England and Wales is not permitted to
e provide assistance under s 17 of the 1989 Act in respect of a dependant under the age of 18 or any member of his family. If, on the other hand, accommodation provided by the Secretary of State in the discharge of his duty under sub-s (3) has been withdrawn, the local authority within whose area the withdrawn accommodation was provided, is to have power under s 17 (not s 20) of the 1989
f Act to provide assistance in respect of the child concerned. This assistance is described in sub-s (7)(a) as 'local authority support'. Given that only s 17 is mentioned, it appears to us inconceivable that Parliament should have thought that the support which the local authority could provide in those circumstances should fall short of the provision of accommodation for the child and such members of his family as seemed appropriate. If Parliament had intended to
g separate such children from their parents by insisting that accommodation could only be provided by a local authority for the children under s 20, it could easily have said so.

(15) Section 17A of the 1989 Act

h [70] The following year Parliament again legislated on the basis of the common understanding of the meaning and effect of s 17 of the 1989 Act, in relation to the ability of social service departments to help homeless families with dependent children to acquire accommodation without breaking up the family in circumstances where the relevant housing authority had no duty or power to assist. This was the occasion when amendments were made to the 1989 Act by
j s 7 of the Carers and Disabled Children Act 2000 by the insertion of ss 17A and 17B. Section 17A enables a local authority to make direct payments to the person who has parental responsibility for a disabled child, in the place of services provided under the 1989 Act. Its terms, so far as material, are set out in [6], above.

[71] The Disabled Children (Direct Payments) (England) Regulations 2001, SI 2001/442 made under the powers created by s 17A(4), now specify the maximum periods of residential accommodation which may be secured by

means of direct payment to a person with parental responsibility for a disabled
child (or to the child itself, if aged 16 or 17), namely periods of 28 days at a time, *a*
and not more than 120 days in total in any period of 12 months.

[72] These provisions, which formed part of the statutory scheme of the 1989
Act at the time *A*'s case was decided by this court, make no sense at all if the
'services which the local authority would otherwise have provided' 'in the
exercise of functions conferred on them by section 17' (see the language of *b*
s 17A(1)) could not as a matter of law include the provision of residential
accommodation.

(16) A must have been decided differently on fuller statutory citation

[73] In our judgment, if the court in *A*'s case had had its attention drawn to the
provisions of s 122 of the 1999 Act and s 17A of the 1989 Act, and had appreciated *c*
that the housing allocation arrangements in 1989 were not as detailed and
comprehensive as they later became, it must have decided that case differently.
It must have realised that Parliament did not intend the assistance a local
authority had power to make under Pt III should be divided into watertight
compartments, as suggested in the judgment of Chadwick LJ in *A*'s case. The *d*
later statutory provisions would be quite unworkable if this were the case. If s 17
is interpreted in the same way as its predecessors (as explained in *Tilley*'s case and
Monaf's case) these difficulties fall away.

(17) Section 2 of the LGA 2000

[74] In these circumstances it is not necessary to say very much about the *e*
decision of Elias J in J (see [19], [20], above) or to seek some other way of
interpreting s 17 of the 1989 Act with the benefit of s 3(1) of the Human Rights
Act 1998. In deference to Mr Goudie's arguments, however, we must deal with
one argument he raised. Part I of the LGA 2000 is principally concerned with the
'community strategy' every local authority must now prepare (see s 4(1)) for *f*
promoting or improving, among other things, the economic or social well-being
of their area. They are given power by s 2(1) to do anything which they consider
is likely to achieve either of these objects, and these powers include power to give
financial assistance to any person or to provide accommodation to any person
(see s 2(4)(b) and (f)).

[75] Because of the view we take of the meaning of s 17 of the 1989 Act it is *g*
unnecessary for us to consider, as Elias J felt obliged to, the appropriateness of s 2
as a vehicle for the powers W seeks to invoke, particularly where a local authority
like Lambeth has not yet finalised their community strategy. Mr Goudie argued,
however, that the power under s 2(1) would not be available to his clients
because they would be unable to provide accommodation to W and her family *h*
because of the 'prohibition, restriction or limitation on their powers' (see s 3(1)),
which is contained in ss 190(3) and 185 of the Housing Act 1996. The language of
those provisions is, however, strikingly different from the language of s 122(5) of
the 1999 Act (see [68], above). Section 190(3), for example, merely provides that
a local housing authority has a more limited duty in cases where an applicant is
not found to have a priority need. It does not constitute a prohibition, restriction *j*
or limitation on their powers. In any event, even if a local housing authority's
powers were indeed limited in the ways suggested by Mr Goudie, these
provisions say nothing about the powers of social service authorities, and we can
see nothing in s 3(1) to preclude a social service authority from providing
financial help, or temporary accommodation, to the family of a child in need if
they think fit.

(18) Mr Bielby's second assessment

[76] Since we have held that s 17 of the 1989 Act does give the council the power to help W and their family if it sees fit to use it, we turn finally to the council's decision not to provide such help. This is now to be found in the assessment of each child which was conducted by Mr Bielby and countersigned by his manager on 9 April 2002. Except that the descriptions of the children's development needs are different, the two assessments are in identical terms. Much of the family history recorded in these assessments is set out in App 1 to this judgment, and we will not repeat it here.

[77] Mr Bielby describes how in his first assessment, carried out three months earlier, he had formed the view that W would have to call on her family and friends to support her in providing temporary accommodation whilst she sought alternative accommodation. Because she said she had a very close supportive family and friends, Mr Bielby thought this was not an unreasonable suggestion, although he did not put it to her directly.

[78] During the new assessment process, Mr Bielby first ascertained W's present circumstances, and then asked her what she would do if social services did not provide her with a deposit for a flat. She replied that she had not really thought about this. She gave a similar answer when she was asked what she would do if she were to lose her current bed and breakfast accommodation. She then described why her family could not help (a matter which her mother also confirmed to Mr Bielby direct), and how the social fund had been unable to help her with a budgeting loan. Mr Bielby's assessment continued in these terms:

'Section 17(6) requires exceptional circumstances for the local authority to provide financial assistance. [W] currently finds herself homeless and without the means to secure suitable accommodation, having been evicted from her previous flat due to a failure to pay rent. I do not consider these circumstances to be exceptional. Regrettably many families find themselves in this situation. [W] is not exceptional by the way of being a single parent caring for two children. This would not be considered exceptional. Neither would being evicted for rent arrears constitute exceptional circumstances in this particular case. The arrears accrued whilst [W] was gainfully employed, which would appear to be exceptional through being in a position to have begun the process of clearing the arrears. However, [W] did say that she did set up a direct debit with the housing association, but they still went ahead with the eviction.'

[79] He then identified the children's only need as being a need for accommodation. This apart, they were very well cared for and appeared to be developing appropriately for their ages. Accommodation, he said, was dealt with under s 20 of the 1989 Act. In accordance with good practice under that Act it would be appropriate for the local authority to explore placing them with extended family members who might be able to provide accommodation for them as a short-term measure, whilst their mother sought alternative accommodation. He concluded that there was provision within the 1989 Act under s 20 to assist these children should the need arise.

[80] Because W had not really thought about what would happen if the council did not help, Mr Bielby said that this implied that the likelihood of her children and her being on the streets would not occur. He expected that her family would assist, as they had done so in the past, not necessarily providing for them as a family unit together. He believed, controversially, that it was

reasonable that W's two children should take precedence, as a temporary arrangement, over her mother's two adult sons in her mother's home.

[81] He ended his assessment by saying that it was reasonable for Lambeth not to assist W and her children for these reasons:

'(A) [W] is typical of somebody who has been found intentionally homeless. Indeed she has something of an advantage compared to some other families ie [W] has a close and extended family with the locality. [W] is a warm and capable mother who has up until recently had a work history. Therefore, the Local Authority would take the view that to provide accommodation for [W] and children would mean in effect having to do so for all of the families that have been found intentionally homeless. This would lead to assessments under the housing legislation being redundant. It would also divert resources from other service users.

(B) The cost of providing accommodation under section 20 varies according to who the children are placed with and the length of the placement. At some point it would become more expensive to use section 20 than to provide financial assistance to enable [W] to obtain accommodation in the private sector (eg by provision of a deposit and payment of the first months rent). However, the cost of providing such assistance in all cases where the presenting problem is one of homelessness would be much greater than the cost of providing Section 20 accommodation in this case.'

(19) *Further evidence by W and her mother*

[82] After these assessments were disclosed, W and her mother made further statements to the court. It appears that Mr Bielby may have misunderstood the position at her mother's home, where one of her adult sons already provides a home for his two children on a fairly regular basis, and the other is a deaf mute who has always lived with his mother, on whom he relies heavily to communicate with the outside world. It also appears that there may have been a misunderstanding when W admittedly gave her answer 'I have not really thought about it' in reply to one of Mr Bielby's questions. W is very concerned that her children's welfare would suffer if they were placed in care away from her family (who cannot help) while she locates suitable accommodation, because they have never lived anywhere without her and they are a very close family. She does not believe that any such measure would be only short term, because she thinks that even if she did obtain a job immediately, it would take her at least 12 months to save £2,000, the sum she would need in order to secure private accommodation. It also appears that she would challenge Mr Bielby's account of the reasons for her original homelessness, even though she is out of time for appealing.

(20) *Our conclusion*

[83] Even allowing all these matters in W's favour—and the council will no doubt reconsider them all carefully when this judgment is delivered—there are no sufficient grounds for this court to interfere with the council's decision. Mr Howell did not seek to reopen the argument fought and lost in *A*'s case last year. He accepted that the council had no duty to help W and her children—and in this case he did not have a favourable assessment to support such an argument. It is true that s 17 imposes on a council what has been called a target duty, but in relation to individual children it only has a power, and it has given intelligible and adequate reasons why it is not willing to exercise its power in this case, given all the other pressures on its resources. It is understandable, in the light of the

a evidence it has furnished, why it is reluctant to continue a 'safety net' policy in respect of all families who cannot receive Pt VII help and who may, in theory at least, one day be on the streets. Experience has shown, it says, that in practice these families do not subsequently present themselves as needing s 20 help. This judgment has shown that in an extreme case, where all else has failed, the council does have power to help under s 17, but it is entitled, if it sees fit, to reserve this
b power to cope with extreme cases, which W's has not yet become.

[84] When we asked Mr Goudie whether, if his submissions were correct, his clients' social services department had no power to help a mother in W's position to find accommodation with her child even though it was clear that that separation would represent a catastrophe for the particular child, he was constrained to say that this would indeed be the position. The council's children and families
c division will no doubt be pleased to know that his submissions were not correct, and that it does indeed have the requisite power. How and when it exercises it is in the first place, at any rate, a matter for it to decide.

[85] We do not consider that the art 8(1) rights of W and her two children affect the position. It is well recognised now that that article does not afford a
d right to a home, but only a right to respect for a home.

[86] In the provision of resources for accommodation at public expense a modern state, and a modern local authority, is subject to many competing pressures. All the vulnerable children for whom Lambeth has recently been found to have made inadequate provision (see App 3, [126], below) have a right to respect for their home and their private and family life. Although art 8 imposes
e positive obligations on public authorities, 'the economic well-being of the country', 'the protection of health or morals' and 'the protection of the rights and freedoms of others' are values which art 8(2) entitles Lambeth (and the government) to take into account when deciding how public resources should be allocated in a situation like the one with which this case is concerned.

f [87] For these reasons, while we would hope that Lambeth's children and families division will reconsider the position of W and her family carefully in the light of the facts set out in this judgment, we would refuse to quash the assessments made by Lambeth on 9 April 2002. Unless agreement can be reached we will hear counsel as to the form of order we should make when this judgment
g is handed down.

Appendix 1

W and her history

h [88] W came from Barbados to live in this country 30 years ago when she was nine years old. Her father died earlier this year. Her mother lives with her stepfather and two of her grown-up brothers. In all, she had five brothers, one sister and a stepsister. We will refer to the brothers not by name but as brothers 1 to 5, as the case may be.

j [89] Her son M was born in January 1987. W says that his father is now unemployed, and M has had no contact with his father for a while. In November 1990 W obtained an assured tenancy of a flat in her own name from a housing association. It appears that until C's father came on the scene there were no significant problems with the rent. In 1996 she obtained a budgeting loan from the Department of Social Security (DSS). Nearly four hundred pounds are still outstanding on this loan, and this sum is being paid off slowly by deductions from her benefits.

[90] Her daughter C was born in May 1998, and she married C's father later
that year. It appears to have been an unhappy marriage, although W was later to
tell a solicitor that her husband was never violent to her while she was living with
him. At the end of September 2000, however, he assaulted her stepfather, and he
also threatened to stab her. She was so frightened that she left home with the
children, and her husband changed the locks. In due course she consulted a
solicitor who managed to persuade her husband to move out without the
necessity for court proceedings. She then went back to her home with the
children just before Christmas 2000.

[91] Unhappily this period of cohabitation, followed by the period when she
was away from her home, wreaked havoc with her rent account. It appears that
as early as September 1998 a council housing officer gave her advice about
clearing the arrears that had accrued, and various letters were then sent to her
warning her of the consequences of not paying the rent. At some stage her
landlords obtained a suspended possession order.

[92] Her plight was aggravated, it is said, by failings on the part of the company
employed by Lambeth to handle housing benefit assessments. Between 1998 and
the end of 1999 her rent arrears increased from £78 to over £2,500. At the end of
this period she was paid £920 housing benefit. In January 2000 she had to make a
new claim for housing benefit. Although she seems to have lodged the necessary
forms on 11 January, and in May the housing benefits office undertook to 'action'
her claim as soon as possible, she had not received an assessment or any payment
of housing benefit by the time she was evicted in February 2001.

[93] Although the details of the history are not completely clear from the
papers, it appears that although she had a two-year-old child W was in employment
during 2000, earning a net monthly salary of £700. In September 2000 she
succeeded in staving off the execution of a warrant for possession by agreeing to
pay the arrears by agreed monthly instalments, and she set up a standing order
with her bank for this purpose. Payments under this standing order were duly
made in September and October 2000, and in November 2000 the court made an
order suspending the execution of the warrant provided that she paid the current
rent and £22 per month off the arrears.

[94] She was unable to make these payments. Everything was by now too
much for her. She had had to flee from her home, and she was worrying about
how to return. Her housing benefit still had not been assessed for the year 2000,
and in any event it did not cover the whole amount of the rent. She became
depressed, and was unable to resume her job. Her employers eventually
terminated her services in March 2001.

[95] By the time the warrant for possession was executed in February 2001,
the arrears had spiralled to £4,400. Once she was evicted, she went to the
Lambeth Homeless Persons Unit. They provided the family with temporary
accommodation in a hostel while they processed her application under Pt VII of
the 1996 Act.

[96] On 4 April 2001 a Lambeth housing officer dismissed her application on
the grounds that she was intentionally homeless. Reference was made to the long
history of arrears on her rent account, and the advice she had received from time
to time about the consequences of non-payment. In these circumstances, it was
said, non-payment of rent should be regarded as an intentional act. An officer at
the housing department advised her to contact the social services department for
help, and was very surprised to be later told that when W followed her advice, a
receptionist at the social services department told her that there was nothing they
could do to help.

[97] She received help from the Brixton Advice Centre, however, and the family's temporary accommodation was continued while a review of the original decision was being carried out. The centre observed to Lambeth that there had been little or no arrears of rent until September 1998, and that the problems had begun with her marriage to her violent and abusive husband. These representations were supported by a letter from her general practitioner, who had treated her for

her recent depression.

[98] On 6 August 2001 the reviewing officer confirmed the original decision. He produced figures which purported to show that W had a net monthly income of £1,180 and outgoings of £730. He set out the history of the arrears, and said that she was in employment, earning enough to pay the rent, but did not do so. There had been no diagnosis of clinical depression. A solicitor advised her that

she did not have a strong enough case to appeal to the county court against this decision.

[99] When she received the decision, she was again advised by the housing department to go to the social services department, where a receptionist again told her that there was nothing they could do for her. It was her fault she had lost

her home, and her children were not at risk. She therefore faced eviction from the hostel, and had nowhere to go.

[100] None of her immediate family could help her. Brother 1 lived with his girlfriend in his girlfriend's mother's home. He had a job as a courier. They were trying to find accommodation themselves, and had no resources to help. Brother 2

lived with his girlfriend and four children in a two-bedroomed property. He was unemployed and they had no resources. Brother 5 lived in Wales and was out of touch with her. Her older sister lived in temporary accommodation herself. Her stepsister, who was younger than her, was unemployed and lived with her mother in Northampton.

[101] Her mother and stepfather were living with brothers 3 and 4 in a

three-bedroomed property. Her 60-year-old mother was disabled and could not work. She had no savings. Her stepfather had a job as a security guard, but any spare money went to help her mother, who received disability benefit. Brother 3 was at one time unemployed. He then got a job at a low wage. He had two children of his own. They came to stay with him, sleeping in the same bed,

during most weekends and the school holidays, because their mother was not available to look after them all the time. He had nowhere else to live. Brother 4 is unemployed and a deaf mute. He receives income support and disability benefit. He has always lived with his mother, and is dependent on her. She would never ask him to leave.

[102] The attitude of W's mother in these circumstances has always been that she is able to provide emotional support for her daughter and her two children, and that if she could have helped with accommodation, she would have. As it is, however desperate the situation, she is quite unable to help. She has high blood pressure and has difficulty in coping with M for any length of time. She can only look after C for a few hours at a time.

[103] The only member of her family who was able to help W with accommodation when she was evicted in August 2001 was her niece. She was an unemployed single mother, living with children aged two and one in a two-bedroomed flat. She allowed W and her children to occupy the other room in her flat for a short while, but the flat was severely overcrowded. In October she insisted that they should leave. W went to her mother, who told her that if the worst came to the worst she could stay with her for one or two nights, but no

longer. When she returned to her niece's home, she found that they were locked out. She had to spend that night sleeping in her car with the children.

[104] The next day she went to the housing department and the social services department who were both unable to help. In those circumstances her niece allowed them to return, but in December she said that she was expecting another baby shortly and that they could not possibly stay with her after the baby was born. It was at that juncture that W obtained an appointment with her present solicitors.

[105] She has described in graphic detail the herculean efforts she has made to find accommodation for herself. Most of the many agencies she approached told her that their clients would not accept tenants on housing benefit. Those private landlords who did not maintain this policy required a deposit of £1,000 and the monthly rent of £1,000 in advance, making £2,000 in all. The DSS refused to give her a crisis loan. It also refused to make a budgeting loan because the 1996 loan was not yet paid off. One agency was willing to help her with an advance of up to £500 for the deposit. Their representative told her solicitor that in the past he would have expected the social services department to complement their help, so that a homeless family could find a home. In short, she has been quite unable to find accommodation anywhere, as a single homeless mother with two dependent children, living on income support.

[106] When C was younger, W said that it was almost impossible for her to find work that would pay her a high enough wage to be able to finance child care for her children whilst she was at work. After she lost her job in March 2001, she tried to find a job. In the next five months she had four interviews and one final interview, but she still did not get a job. She thinks that if she did find work, her net monthly salary would be £700. She believes that because of her other debts it would then take her a year to save enough to pay a deposit of £2,000.

[107] Her present solicitor, who has great experience in homelessness cases, believes that there were so many inaccuracies about the review decision on her Pt VII application that it could have been challenged successfully in the county court. Her husband's marital status was wrong. His alleged job was wrong. The figure for rent was wrong. The figure for food bills was wrong. There were a number of other monthly outgoings, amounting to nearly £600, which were not recorded. And no account was taken of the fact that her plight was accentuated by the failure to assess or pay her entitlement to housing benefit from January 2000 onwards. However, although W had been trying to secure this firm's services from June 2001 onwards, because they have a fine reputation in this field, they had been unable to take on any new clients when she first approached them, and by the time she first consulted them in December 2001, the three-week period allowed for a county court appeal under s 204(2) of the 1996 Act had long since expired.

[108] Since January of this year W and her children have been living in bed and breakfast accommodation paid for by Lambeth at a cost of £455 per week, pursuant to orders for temporary accommodation made by the court in these proceedings. W alleged that on 21 January 2001, the first day that one of these orders took effect, Lambeth were so slow in complying with it that they did not actually tell her where to go until after midnight that night. She was sitting all evening in a friend's house. If help had not arrived, she would have had to spend another night in her car with the children, because her friend would not let them stay. There was simply no room. Lambeth disputed that they took so long to tell her where she was being accommodated.

[109] There are no kitchen facilities or cooking facilities available for them to use where they are now living, so that she has been taking the children to her mother nearly every day to cook food for them and eat it there. The position is very unsatisfactory.

[110] It was against this background that Mr Bielby, a social worker employed by the council conducted an assessment of W's children's needs in January 2002. It is unnecessary to refer in any detail to this assessment, because following criticism of the council's handling of the case Mr Bielby conducted a further assessment of the children shortly before this hearing started. It is sufficient to say that he found nothing exceptional in the case. He explained to her that the council's social services department did not provide accommodation for families.

[111] This refusal of assistance led to the initiation of these proceedings on 18 January 2002. Maurice Kay J refused permission to apply for judicial review on the ground that he was bound by the decision of this court in A's case. In due course Mr Bielby made the further assessments which are now at the centre of this case. Their effect is set out in [78]–[81], above.

Appendix 2

Help for homeless families from the social services department: competing views

[112] W's solicitor Mr Flack (see [16], above) has specialised in housing law since 1994, and has considerable practical experience of the role played by the social services departments in assisting homeless families who find themselves outside the protection of what is now Pt VII of the 1996 Act. In [64], [65], above the different types of family who may be affected in this way are identified. Mr Flack maintains that the shortage of housing stock available to housing authorities, coupled with different forms of financial constraint, have required those authorities to impose stringent rationing on the provision of longer term accommodation, and to make increasingly tough decisions in Pt VII cases.

[113] In his view, the complexity of the law under Pt VII, the strict time limit for appealing to the county court, and the increasing scarcity of publicly-funded advice and assistance available for challenges to such decisions, have had the result that many families with good cases have been unable to appeal. His evidence did not take into account the effect of recent case law on the approach which should now be adopted by a county court on an appeal against the decision of a local authority reviewing officer under s 202(4) of the Act. Whether such decisions may be more often overturned in future remains to be seen. The strict time limit for an appeal remains unchanged.

[114] Mr Flack's evidence about the potentially catastrophic consequences of a family's inability to challenge a negative Pt VII decision is summarised in [17], above. He said that the other categories of people denied access to assistance through Pt VII of the 1996 Acts have been similarly affected. In those circumstances the provision of accommodation under s 17 of the 1989 Act has, in his view, performed a vital safety net function for them for many years.

[115] He observes that although families who have become intentionally homeless may be open to criticism for the decisions they made which led them to this state, it is almost never suggested that they are bad parents and that it would be in their children's interests to be separated from them. He says that this fact, together with concerns about the objectivity of housing authorities' decisions in this area, have led local authorities to be willing to help such families under s 17 of the 1989 Act to enable them to find housing together. This

approach, he says, is in keeping with the main principles of that Act to keep families together, unless there are child protection issues at stake. He says that this is hardly ever a feature of these cases.

[116] In para 7 of his statement he describes the different ways in which social services staff have helped such families in the past. This help has included assistance with locating private sector accommodation, and help with raising the advance rent and/or the deposits required by private sector landlords. Given the existence of such help, and the provision of the expertise of these staff, often working in conjunction with housing department staff, almost all intentionally homeless families, in his experience, are able to locate private sector accommodation at an early stage. In this way the burden on the housing department is alleviated.

[117] He quoted recent research which showed that 9,000 families were deemed to have found themselves to be intentionally homeless in 2001. He said that most of them fend for themselves somehow, but a significant minority are unable to do so. He believed that if local authorities could not assist such families at all, then they would have to take significant numbers of children into voluntary care if they were to avoid physical homelessness with their parents. He added:

'Placing children in voluntary care is always traumatic and can cause irreversible damage to the children and the families involved. Perversely, the consequences in the long term can mean that the children involved are more likely to end up on the streets in later life. Between one-quarter and one-third of people sleeping rough were taken into local authority care as children. When families are torn apart and children taken into care, the child's life is severely disrupted. Moving schools during such a traumatic time can severely affect their education and prospects in the long term.'

[118] He expressed a deep concern that if children were to be placed in voluntary care as a result of their families being unable, through poverty and destitution, to obtain suitable accommodation without local authority help, there was a very strong risk that such families would go into hiding from local authorities rather than seeking help from them. He said that his concern was shared by large numbers of practitioners in this field, whether they act for homeless persons or local authorities.

[119] He believed that W's circumstances were 'exceptional' in that she is homeless (like a very small percentage of the population), intentionally homeless (a smaller sub-group), and not able to fend for herself (an even smaller sub-sub-group).

[120] Lambeth's response to this evidence is to be found in paras 21–23 of Mr Rapley's first witness statement. He accepts that in the field of social policy different views can be taken on what is reasonable and in the best interests of the community overall. He believes that Parliament is the appropriate forum to consider the issues Mr Flack raises. If Parliament decides to impose further duties or powers on local authorities, it can also consider whether to allocate them with additional resources for this purpose.

[121] He did not accept the suggestion that social services departments have recognised shortcomings in the application of housing legislation by themselves making accommodation available. In his experience, the provision of accommodation to families by local authorities under s 17 varied from authority to authority. He believed that many, if not all, such authorities did so largely because of a belief, shown to be wrong by both Scott Baker J and the Court of

a Appeal in A's case, that s 17 imposed a legally enforceable duty on them to meet the needs identified in the specific assessments of individual children and their families. In fact, from early 2001 onwards Lambeth had embarked on a policy of ceasing to provide accommodation for the great majority of families who were being accommodated pursuant to s 17, even before the judgments in A's case were delivered.

b [122] As an experienced social worker he strongly disagreed with the passage in Mr Flack's evidence quoted at [117], above. He said that there were many reasons why a local authority should offer to accommodate a child of a family into care under s 20 of the 1989 Act without the family being 'torn apart'. These reasons might include respite care, looking after a child during a parent's illness, or providing a much-needed short-term breathing space for the parent(s), thereby c giving them an opportunity to organise their lives and perhaps accumulate the resources to find private accommodation. In practice, he said, these steps allowed for internal pressures within the family to be relieved.

[123] He did not consider W's case to be an exceptional one, or one that could be regarded as more serious than the great majority of applications to the social d services department from homeless families.

Appendix 3

Lambeth, its financial difficulties and competing pressures

e [124] The territory embraced by the London Borough of Lambeth includes many deprived inner city areas. The borough is at the top of many of the national indices of social deprivation used by the Social Services Inspectorate (SSI). In common with many other urban areas, Lambeth suffers from a considerable shortage of social housing, and the council's waiting lists of people seeking such housing are extremely long.

f [125] Under pressure from the Audit Commission, Lambeth is now taking steps to bring its finances under control. The commission's annual audit letter for 2000–2001, issued in January 2002, states that the council continues to be one of the lowest performing boroughs. Its 1999–2000 statements of account were found to contain significant errors, and on p 5 of this audit letter there is a table g which sets out the significant changes which converted what appeared to be a general fund surplus of £0·4m to a deficit of £1·5m. For 2000–2001 the draft figures for the general fund showed a £5·8m overspend against budget and a cumulative deficit of £3·8m on the general fund. The auditors said that it was important that the council should continue to maintain its efforts to improve the h timeliness and robustness of its financial monitoring processes, and to take corrective action where appropriate.

[126] These financial pressures impinged on the work of the social services department. A further external pressure on the way in which that department allocated its resources came in the form of a direction by the Secretary of State in November 2000 pursuant to s 7A of the Local Authority Social Services Act 1970. j A SSI inspection and an independent inquiry had raised a number of very serious concerns about the quality of Lambeth's children's services. The essence of these complaints was that the children and families division was not adequately performing their statutory duties towards children with disabilities, children who were 'looked after' by the council, and children in need of protection. These core activities of the division involved its referral and assessment teams in dealing with major problems, such as suggested sexual and other child abuse, and abandoned

and neglected children. The need to give priority to this work within a finite budget necessarily involved a switch of resources from a regime in which 30% of *a* the time of those teams had been taken up with families where the children's only need was a housing need.

[127] The housing and social services departments significantly failed to meet their budget targets in 2001–2002, with the result that a substantial increase in the level of council tax, the first for several years, failed to bring the council's finances *b* into equilibrium. So far as the social services department was concerned, it had been spending approximately £1m per month over its budget in March 2000, mainly due to the pressures in the children and families division. A containment strategy was introduced for 2000–2001 which aimed to reduce expenditure for the year by £5·9m, but this policy still involved drawing £6·1m from the council's reserves. The financial pressures resulting from the policy of providing *c* temporary accommodation to homeless families played a significant part in the department's overspend. The direct costs (excluding staff time) of providing such accommodation were running at a rate of £900,000 per year in April 2001.

[128] In August 2001, in order to reduce its expenditure in this area, the council decided to put into effect a new policy in relation to homeless families. *d* Members were advised that the council had previously believed that it had a duty to accommodate children and parents whom the housing department could not help. The true legal position, they were now told, was that while the social services department had the power to assist families in a variety of ways in exceptional circumstances, it did not have a duty to provide housing or to accommodate children. This advice followed the judgment of Scott Baker J at *e* first instance in *A v Lambeth London BC* [2001] LGR 513, delivered on 25 May 2001.

[129] The implementation of this new policy led to a marked reduction in expenditure by the children and families division on families' housing needs. In 2000–2001 the total net cost of providing bed and breakfast or hostel accommodation for families with children (after crediting housing benefit *f* receipts) was £802,000, at a suggested net cost of £180 per family per week, for the 137 families who were supported during the year. In 2001–2002 only 65 families received support of this kind, at a total net cost of £168,000 and an average weekly net cost of £106 per family. The drop in numbers enabled the council to use lower cost accommodation and to place families in local accommodation which *g* was more appropriately sized.

[130] In early March of this year the current forecast for 2001–2002 was for a net departmental overspend of £694,000 on a total budget of £106m. The forecast overspend for the children and families division was £2m. Given the Audit Commission's concerns about overspending and the level of Lambeth's general *h* reserves, this level of overspend was continuing to cause concern. For 2002–2003 the division is budgeting for expenditure of £27m, as against a budget figure of £32·5m for 2001–2002 and a forecast actual expenditure for that year of £34·5m. The total budget available to the department as a whole is being reduced from £106m to £103m.

[131] Against this background Lambeth believes that it must continue to *j* divert resources within the division from providing for families' accommodation needs (even if it had power to provide for them) to addressing its core activities, which are centred around giving support to abandoned and neglected children, and to children who are suspected victims of sexual or other abuse. At present it estimates that an average of ten families a week apply to the department in relation to homelessness problems of one kind or another. If it provided each of

a them with financial assistance of the kind sought by W (£1,000 deposit plus £1,000 rent in advance) this would be likely to cost about £1m in a full year.

[132] It takes comfort from the fact that although it is now refusing assistance to homeless families, it has not had to provide accommodation under s 20 of the 1989 Act to any child from the 200 families who applied in the five months prior to March 2002 and whose only identified need was the lack of a home. Its officers

b believe that this represents the reality. Parents are able to find accommodation from other sources. Help from other members of the family, budget loans or crisis loans from the DSS, charitable grants, going out to work, and further support from a child's absent father were among the palliatives mentioned in the evidence.

c [133] In addition to resource considerations, Lambeth believes that it would not be in the best interest of all the children and families in its area to adopt a policy under which the general outcome for cases of intentional homelessness was the provision by the local authority of accommodation (or payment for accommodation). Because demand for accommodation within its council housing

d stock greatly exceeds demand, any such accommodation would be likely to be in hostels or bed and breakfast accommodation, and Lambeth believes that this form of life is highly detrimental to children. It also believes that a 'safety net' policy would tend to act as a disincentive to responsible parenting. The number of families who are classified as intentionally homeless for failure to pay the rent might well grow if they felt they were guaranteed an alternative home even if they did not pay the rent.

Application dismissed. Permission to appeal refused.

Kate O'Hanlon   Barrister.

R (on the application of Heather and others) v Leonard Cheshire Foundation and another

[2002] EWCA Civ 366

COURT OF APPEAL, CIVIL DIVISION

LORD WOOLF CJ, LAWS AND DYSON LJJ

25, 26 FEBRUARY, 21 MARCH 2002

Human rights – Public authority – Private person performing functions of a public nature – Local authority having duty to provide accommodation for claimants – Local authority arranging for accommodation to be provided by charitable foundation – Whether foundation exercising functions of a public nature in providing accommodation – National Assistance Act 1948, ss 21, 26 – Human Rights Act 1998, s 6(3)(b).

The claimants were persons to whom the local authority owed a duty to provide accommodation under s 21[a] of the National Assistance Act 1948. The authority made arrangements pursuant to s 26[b] of the 1948 Act for that accommodation to be provided, at public expense, by the defendant charitable foundation, and for over 17 years the claimants had been patients in a home which was owned and run by the foundation. The latter decided to cease to operate the home in its present form. The residents, who would no longer be able to be accommodated at the home, were to be relocated in community-based units. The claimants applied for judicial review of the foundation's decision to close the home. They contended that, in providing them with accommodation, the foundation was exercising functions of a 'public nature' within the meaning of s 6(3)(b)[c] of the Human Rights Act 1998 and so, as a public authority, was required not to act in a way which was incompatible with their right to respect for their home under art 8 of the European Convention for the Protection of Human Rights and Fundamental Freedoms 1950 (as set out in Sch 1 to the 1998 Act). The judge dismissed the application, holding that the foundation was not a public authority within the meaning of s 6(3). On their appeal, the claimants challenged that conclusion, relying, inter alia, on the fact that it would preclude them from relying on art 8 against the foundation. A further issue arose as to whether, if the foundation had not been performing a public function, it had been appropriate to bring the proceedings by way of judicial review.

Held – The role that the foundation was performing manifestly did not involve the performance of public functions. The fact that it was a large and flourishing organisation did not change the nature of its activities from private to public. While the degree of public funding of the activities of an otherwise private body was relevant to the nature of the functions performed, it was not by itself determinative of whether the functions were public or private. The foundation was not standing in the shoes of the local authority. Section 26 of the 1948 Act provided statutory authority for the actions of the local authority, but provided

---

a   Section 21, so far as material, is set out at [11], [12], below
b   Section 26, so far as material, is set out at [13], [14], below
c   Section 6, so far as material, is set out at [15], [16], below

a the foundation with no powers. The foundation was not exercising statutory powers in performing functions for the claimants. The fact that, if the foundation were not performing a public function, the claimants would not be able to rely on art 8 as against it could not change the appropriate classification of the foundation's function. Accordingly, the appeal would be dismissed, although it had been appropriate to bring to the court by way of judicial review the question whether

b the foundation was performing a public function (see [35], [38], [39], below).
  Poplar Housing and Regeneration Community Association Ltd v Donoghue [2001] 4 All ER 604 distinguished.

Notes
For the duty of local authorities to provide accommodation and the provision of
c accommodation in premises maintained by voluntary organisations, see 44(2) *Halsbury's Laws* (4th edn reissue) paras 1029, 1033.
  For the National Assistance Act 1948, ss 21, 26, see 40 *Halsbury's Statutes* (4th edn) (2001 reissue) 22, 29.
  For the Human Rights Act 1998, s 6, see 7 *Halsbury's Statutes* (4th edn) (1999
d reissue) 504.

Cases referred to in judgment
Poplar Housing and Regeneration Community Association Ltd v Donoghue [2001] EWCA Civ 595, [2001] 4 All ER 604, [2002] QB 48, [2001] 3 WLR 183.
R v Disciplinary Committee of the Jockey Club, ex p Aga Khan [1993] 2 All ER 853,
e [1993] 1 WLR 909, CA.
R (on the application of the University of Cambridge) v HM Treasury Case C-380/98 [2000] All ER (EC) 920, sub nom *R v HM Treasury, ex p University of Cambridge* [2000] 1 WLR 2514, ECJ.
R v Muntham House School, ex p R [2000] LGR 255.
f *R v Servite Houses, ex p Goldsmith* [2001] LGR 55.

Appeal
The appellants, Elizabeth Heather and Hilary Callin, appealed with permission of the Court of Appeal (Schiemann and Waller LJJ) granted on 15 October 2001 from the decision of Stanley Burnton J on 15 June 2001 ([2001] All ER (D) 156
g (Jun)) dismissing, after a preliminary hearing, their applications for judicial review of the decision of the first respondent, the Leonard Cheshire Foundation (LCF), on 27 September 2000 to close the home in which they were long-stay patients. The Attorney General was the second respondent. Written submissions were made by JUSTICE. The facts are set out in the judgment of the court.

h *Richard Gordon QC* and *Ian Wise* (instructed by *Coningsbys*) for the appellants.
James Goudie QC and *Dinah Rose* (instructed by *Trowers & Hamlins*) for LCF.
William Henderson (instructed by the *Treasury Solicitor*) for the Attorney General.

The appeal was dismissed for reasons to be given later.

j 21 March 2002. The following judgment of the court was delivered.

LORD WOOLF CJ.

Introduction
  [1] This appeal is by two appellants, Elizabeth Heather and Hilary Callin, from a decision of Stanley Burnton J dated 15 June 2001 ([2001] All ER (D) 156 (Jun)).

At the time of the hearing before Stanley Burnton J there were three claimants
but the second claimant has since withdrawn his appeal. The respondents to the   *a*
appeal are the Leonard Cheshire Foundation (LCF) and the Attorney General.
The appellants are long-stay patients in a home called Le Court which is owned
and run by LCF. The appeal is against the dismissal of their application for
judicial review of LCF's decision to close the home in the way in which it is run
at present. The application was dismissed after a preliminary hearing as a result   *b*
of which Stanley Burnton J held that LCF is not a 'public authority' within the
meaning of that term in s 6 of the Human Rights Act 1998. It is the correctness
of this conclusion which is the subject of this appeal.

[2] The Attorney General was a party to the appeal because of the responsibilities
that he has for charities. He was represented by Mr William Henderson. In the
court below, a further issue arose as to whether or not the proceedings   *c*
constituted 'charity proceedings' within the meaning of s 33 of the Charities Act
1993. If they were charity proceedings their commencement required the
authority of the Charity Commissioners or a Chancery judge. After the
proceedings had started in the court below this issue became academic once the
claimants obtained the necessary authority. Permission to appeal this issue was   *d*
therefore not granted.

[3] Le Court is LCF's first and largest home. It is situated at Greatham, near
Lis, in Hampshire. At the time of the decision in the court below it had 42
long-stay residents. They included the then three claimants, who had all lived
there for periods of more than 17 years.

[4] LCF is the United Kingdom's leading voluntary sector provider of care and   *e*
support services for the disabled. The majority of the residents at the home,
including the appellants, had been placed there by the social services departments
of their local authority or by their health authority. In making the placements
and providing the funding which the placements required, the authorities were
exercising statutory powers.   *f*

[5] It was on 27 September 2000 that the trustees of LCF decided to cease to
operate Le Court in its present form. They approved the development of three
or four smaller, community-based homes to be located in the surrounding towns
and the establishment at Le Court itself of a 16-bed, high-dependency unit. The
residents, who would no longer be able to be accommodated at Le Court, were
to be relocated into the community-based units. That decision was reconsidered   *g*
by the trustees on 7 February 2001 and affirmed.

[6] In the proceedings for judicial review the claimants contended that in
making these decisions LCF was exercising functions of a public nature within the
meaning of s 6(3)(b) of the 1998 Act and so, as a public authority, was required
not to act in a way which was incompatible with art 8 of the European   *h*
Convention for the Protection of Human Rights and Fundamental Freedoms
1950 (as set out in Sch 1 to the 1998 Act). It was argued that instead the trustees
had contravened art 8 by not respecting the claimants' right to a home and failing
to take into account, inter alia, promises made to them that Le Court would be
their 'home for life'. In addition it was alleged that LCF had not obtained   *j*
individual assessments of the claimants' needs and had failed to take into account,
or ignored, LCF's own policy of providing for their residents a 'home for life'.

[7] In the court below Stanley Burnton J reserved his judgment. After he had
prepared a draft of his judgment and had sent it to the parties, but before it could
be delivered, this court handed down its decision in *Poplar Housing and
Regeneration Community Association Ltd v Donoghue* [2001] EWCA Civ 595,

a [2001] 4 All ER 604, [2002] QB 48. Stanley Burnton J recognised that the judgment in *Donoghue*'s case was of obvious relevance to his decision in this case. He therefore invited the parties to make written submissions to him as to the effect of the decision in *Donoghue*'s case on his draft judgment. Stanley Burnton J then re-drafted his judgment, and as he explains ([2001] All ER (D) 156 (Jun)) at [12]):

b '... having considered the judgment of the Court of Appeal in *Donoghue*'s case and the parties' written submissions, I have concluded that my original decision was correct. Rather then rewrite my judgment in the light of that decision, I have retained most of the text of my draft judgment and made reference to the judgment of the Court of Appeal where appropriate. This has the disadvantage that my judgment is now unnecessarily long, and c even longer than it was originally. However, if I had started afresh my original reasoning would have been lost. I hope that in general it will be obvious which parts of my judgment are new.'

[8] The course adopted by Stanley Burnton J has meant that this court has had the benefit of his own analysis and conclusions on the issues which he had to d decide.

[9] Because we appreciated it was very much in the interest of the appellants and LCF that they knew the result as soon as possible, at the end of the hearing we announced to the parties that we had decided to dismiss the appeal. These are our reasons for doing so; they are not identical to those of Stanley Burnton J, but none the less we acknowledge the obvious care and skill with which he has e examined the issues.

[10] JUSTICE attached considerable importance to the outcome of this appeal which they regard as being of general public importance. JUSTICE therefore sought permission which was granted to deliver written submissions in support of the appeal. Those submissions were prepared by Mr Philip Havers QC and f Mr Thomas de la Mare. We have found them of considerable value.

The statutory framework

[11] The National Assistance Act 1948 places a duty on the relevant local authorities to provide accommodation for the claimants. Section 21(1) of the g 1948 Act, as amended, provides:

'*Duty of local authorities to provide accommodation.*—(1) Subject to and in accordance with the provisions of this Part of this Act, a local authority may with the approval of the Secretary of State, and to such extent as he may direct shall, make arrangements for providing—(a) residential accommodation h for persons aged eighteen or over who by reason of age, illness, disability or any other circumstances are in need of care and attention which is not otherwise available to them; and (aa) residential accommodation for expectant and nursing mothers who are in need of care and attention which is not otherwise available to them.'

j [12] The accommodation, which the authorities arrange, may be provided by the authority itself or by another authority. As s 21(4) and (5) of the 1948 Act, as amended, state:

'(4) Subject to the provisions of section 26 of this Act, Accommodation provided by a local authority in the exercise of their functions under this section shall be provided in premises managed by the authority or, to such

extent as may be determined in accordance with the arrangements under
this section, in such premises managed by another local authority as may be
agreed between the two authorities and on such terms, including terms as to
the reimbursement of expenditure incurred by the said other authority, as
may be so agreed.

(5) References in this Act to accommodation provided under this Part
thereof shall be construed as references to accommodation provided in
accordance with this and the five next following sections, and as including
references to board and other services, amenities and requisites provided in
connection with the accommodation except where in the opinion of the
authority managing the premises their provision is unnecessary.'

[13] Under the 1948 Act the authority may also make arrangements for the
accommodation to be provided by third parties under s 26(1) which provides:

'*Provision of accommodation in premises maintained by voluntary organisations.*—
(1) Subject to subsections (1A) and (1B) below, arrangements under section 21
of this Act may include arrangements made with a voluntary organisation or
with any other person who is not a local authority where—(a) that
organisation or person manages premises which provide for reward
accommodation falling within subsection (1)(a) or (aa) of that section, and
(b) the arrangements are for the provision of such accommodation in those
premises.'

This is how the claimants came to be at Le Court.

[14] Section 26(2), as amended, is also relevant since it deals with payment for
the accommodation and is in these terms:

'Any arrangements made by virtue of ... this section shall provide for the
making by the local authority to the other party thereto of payments in
respect of the accommodation provided at such rates as may be determined
by or under the arrangements and subject to subsection (3A) below the local
authority shall recover from each person for whom accommodation is
provided under the arrangements the amount of the refund which he is liable
to make in accordance with the following provisions of this section.'

[15] If the authority itself provides accommodation, it is performing a public
function. It is also performing a public function if it makes arrangements for the
accommodation to be provided by LCF. However, if a body which is a charity,
like LCF, provides accommodation to those to whom the authority owes a duty
under s 21 in accordance with an arrangement under s 26, it does not follow that
the charity is performing a public function. Before the 1998 Act came into force,
we doubt whether it would have even been contemplated that LCF in providing
care homes for people in the position of the appellants would be performing a
public function. Whether under the 1998 Act, LCF are performing a public
function, is critical to this appeal because s 6(1) of the 1998 Act makes it unlawful
for a public authority to act in a way which is incompatible with a convention
right and s 6(3) of the 1998 Act defines who is a public authority for the purpose
of s 6 in these terms: 'In this section "public authority" includes ... (b) any person
certain of whose functions are functions of a public nature ...'

[16] It is to be noted that s 6(3) is not exhaustive as to who is a public authority,
but LCF could only be a public authority under s 6(3). A public authority can be
a hybrid body. That is, a public authority in relation to some of its functions and

a a private body in relation to others. This is the combined consequence of s 6(3) and (5). Section 6(5) states: 'In relation to a particular act, a person is not a public authority by virtue only of subsection (3)(b) if the nature of the act is private.'

[17] The issue here can therefore be refined by asking, is LCF, in providing accommodation for the claimants, performing a public function?

[18] The facts of *Donoghue*'s case [2001] 4 All ER 604 have similarities to those
b in this case. In that case it was stated that the definition of who was a public authority, and what was a public function for the purposes of s 6 should be given a generous interpretation. The court went on, however, to indicate:

'[58] ... The fact that a body performs an activity which otherwise a public body would be under a duty to perform cannot mean that such performance
c is necessarily a public function. A public body in order to perform its public duties can use the services of a private body. Section 6 should not be applied so that if a private body provides such services, the nature of the functions are inevitably public. If this were to be the position, then when a small hotel provides bed and breakfast accommodation as a temporary measure, at the request of a housing authority that is under a duty to provide that
d accommodation, the small hotel would be performing public functions and required to comply with the 1998 Act. This is not what the 1998 Act intended. The consequence would be the same where a hospital uses a private company to carry out specialist services, such as analysing blood samples. The position under the 1998 Act is necessarily more complex ...
e Section 6(3) means that hybrid bodies, who have functions of a public and private nature are public authorities, but *not* in relation to acts which are of a private nature. The renting out of accommodation can certainly be of a private nature. The fact that through the act of renting by a private body a public authority may be fulfilling its public duty, does not automatically change into a public act what would otherwise be a private act. See, by
f analogy, *R v Muntham House School, ex p R* [2000] LGR 255.

[59] The purpose of s 6(3)(b) is to deal with hybrid bodies which have both public and private functions. It is not to make a body, which does not have responsibilities to the public, a public body merely because it performs acts on behalf of a public body which would constitute public functions were
g such acts to be performed by the public body itself. An act can remain of a private nature even though it is performed because another body is under a public duty to ensure that that act is performed.'

[19] The court in *Donoghue*'s case also referred (at [60]) to the fact that if a local authority, in order to fulfil its duty, sent a child to a private school—
h
'the fact that it did this would not mean that the private school was performing public functions. The school would not be a hybrid body. It would remain a private body. The local authority would, however, not escape its duties by delegating the performance to the private school. If there were a breach of the convention, then the responsibility would be that of the
j local authority and not that of the school.'

[20] The court in *Donoghue*'s case came to the conclusion that the housing association there being considered was performing a public function looking at the situation as a whole. The court did so because the role of the housing association was 'so closely assimilated' to that of the local housing authority. The court did, however, identify (at [65]) various features to which they attached

particular importance for coming to the decision. Among those the following
factors have relevance here:

> '... (iii) The act of providing accommodation to rent is not, without more,
> a public function for the purposes of s 6 of the 1998 Act. Furthermore, that
> is true irrespective of the section of society for whom the accommodation is
> provided. (iv) The fact that a body is a charity or is conducted not for profit
> means that it is likely to be motivated in performing its activities by what it
> perceives to be the public interest. However, this does not point to the body
> being a public authority. In addition, even if such a body performs functions
> that would be considered to be of a public nature if performed by a public
> body, nevertheless such acts may remain of a private nature for the purpose
> of s 6(3)(b) and (5). (v) What can make an act, which would otherwise be
> private, public, is a feature or a combination of features which impose a
> public character or stamp on the act. Statutory authority for what is done
> can at least help to mark the act as being public; so can the extent of control
> over the function exercised by another body which is a public authority. The
> more closely the acts that could be of a private nature are enmeshed in the
> activities of a public body, the more likely they are to be public. However,
> the fact that the acts are supervised by a public regulatory body does not
> necessarily indicate that they are of a public nature. This is analogous to the
> position in judicial review, where a regulatory body may be deemed public
> but the activities of the body which is regulated may be categorised private.
> (vi) The closeness of the relationship which exists between Tower Hamlets
> and Poplar. Poplar was created by Tower Hamlets to take a transfer of local
> authority housing stock; five of its board members are also members of
> Tower Hamlets; Poplar is subject to the guidance of Tower Hamlets as to
> the manner in which it acts towards the defendant. (vii) The defendant, at
> the time of transfer, was a sitting tenant of Poplar and it was intended that
> she would be treated no better and no worse than if she remained a tenant
> of Tower Hamlets. While she remained a tenant, Poplar therefore stood in
> relation to her in very much the position previously occupied by Tower
> Hamlets.'

[21] These factors provide little assistance for the claimants' case that in
providing accommodation for the claimants LCF is performing a public function.
All they can point to is that the activity of LCF is regulated (see *Donoghue*'s case
at [65](v)) which can be an indicator that a function is public.

[22] In developing his carefully structured argument in support of the
approach for the appellants, Mr Richard Gordon QC submits:

> '(i) The test of whether a particular function is or is not a "public function"
> so as to create, in that respect, a "hybrid" authority depends neither in whole
> nor in part on being able to ascribe a legislative source for the exercise of
> power although the presence of such a source is likely to be determinative.
> (ii) Essentially, the question that has to be asked in respect of the function in
> question is whether the authority is standing in the shoes of the state when
> exercising that function. If it is, then the function in question is a public
> function. (iii) In determining whether an authority is standing in the shoes
> of the state one very important principle will be whether the authority is the
> means by which the state achieves the exercise of its responsibilities towards
> individuals in a way which leaves the authority both: (i) in a position to

violate convention rights that the individual would, otherwise, have against the state, and (ii) in a position to determine the "fair balance" that is required to be struck by the state when interfering with those convention rights ("the principle").'

[23] In support of his contentions he relies upon the following facts which he contends provided the proximity which is required if LCF's activities are to be categorised as public rather than private:

'(a) Thirty-eight of the forty-three residents at the residential care home known as Le Court are funded by purchasing statutory authorities. Nationally, only 14% of LCF's places are privately funded although there is—even in the case of publicly funded placements—a "top up" element from LCF's own funds derived from voluntary income. (b) A1 and A3's placements (Ms Heather/Callin) are funded by their welfare benefits and by social care funding by Surrey County Council pursuant to a statutory arrangement between Surrey County Council and LCF for which they are eligible by reason of their vulnerability. (c) Such placements are required, by directions issued by the Secretary of State, to be made in respect of persons aged 18 or over who *"by reason of age, illness, disability or any other circumstances are in need of care and attention which is not otherwise available to them"* either directly by the local authority social services department under s 21 of the 1948 Act or (as here) by virtue of arrangements with a private provider under s 26 of the 1948 Act. (d) Where an arrangement is—as here—made with a "private" provider, such as LCF, the residential care home (the subject of the arrangement) is (materially) made subject to statutory regulation under s 26(1A) of the 1948 Act. (e) A2's placement (Mr Ward) is funded by South West Hampshire Health Authority who could have, but did not, purchase the same health care for A2 from an NHS trust under a statutory arrangement pursuant to s 5 of the National Health Service and Community Care Act 1990 and entered into an arrangement with LCF for the self-same purpose, namely to provide NHS services to Mr Ward. (f) So far as funded residents at Le Court are concerned there is a triangular relationship between LCF, the placing/funding authority and the resident whereby the authority pays direct to LCF and LCF enters into a licence agreement with the resident in question: the relationship between the placing/funding authority and the resident is governed entirely by public law. (g) There is no express provision in the licensing agreements between LCF and the residents permitting LCF to re-develop and/or to terminate the agreement in its general discretion or otherwise than for specific identified reason—on the face of the licence the resident is entitled to stay in the home *"for as long as the Resident wishes"*: neither of the placing/funding authorities has challenged the decision of LCF to re-develop.'

[24] Mr Gordon then accepts that the presence of these factors is not necessarily the end of the story. He accepts that there must be a further factor that identifies a 'material relationship' between the function being assumed and a potential clash with convention rights which would otherwise be enforceable against the state. Here it is argued that the clash is created by the claimants' inability otherwise to rely on art 8 as against LCF.

[25] In his reply Mr Gordon also attempted to find a way of avoiding the difficulties which in practice would arise if a lodging house or a small private

nursing home were to become a public body, for the purposes of the 1998 Act, merely because they provided a home for someone in relation to whom a public body undoubtedly is under a public duty to provide accommodation. Mr Gordon was not in fact able to provide a satisfactory solution to this dilemma.

[26] In support of his contentions, Mr Gordon relies upon the comments of Moses J in *R v Servite Houses, ex p Goldsmith* [2001] LGR 55. That was a case which was decided shortly before the 1998 Act came into force. Moses J decided that the housing association was not performing a public function and was not under any public law obligation to the applicants. As to the power of Wandsworth London Borough Council to delegate its responsibility for providing accommodation, Moses J said (at 85):

'I cannot conclude this matter without expressing my sympathy for the applicants. This case represents more than tension between public law and private law rights, but a collision. If I am right in my reasoning, it demonstrates an inadequacy of response to the plight of these applicants now that Parliament has permitted public law obligations to be discharged by entering into private law arrangements. Whether the solution lies in imposing public law standards on private bodies whose powers stem from contract or in imposing greater control over public authorities at the time they first make contractual arrangements may be for others to determine.'

[27] In his judgment, Moses J made it clear that he did not consider it was necessary for him to consider the effect of art 8 of the convention. However, Moses J's judgment provides a convenient introduction to what is perhaps Mr Gordon's strongest argument, namely that for practical purposes if LCF are not at least a hybrid authority, the appellants lose the benefit of art 8 as against LCF. The fact that they may have continuing rights under art 8 as against their local authorities, Mr Gordon contends, does not alleviate their position. This is because their objective is to avoid having to leave Le Court and while their local authorities would then be under an obligation to provide an alternative home for them, this is not what they want. Mr Gordon therefore submits that, while he accepts that the local authorities cannot avoid the duty which they owe to their 'service users' because of both s 6 of the 1998 Act and s 21 of the 1948 Act, the fact remains that effective protection of convention rights is lost as a result of the local authorities' delegating their responsibilities by relying upon s 26 of the 1948 Act. Mr Gordon adopts an observation of Laws LJ in argument that the arrangements under s 26 are but a subset of the s 21 arrangements. He contends they therefore are not intended to operate differently and this is what changes the nature of the function performed by LCF from a private to a public function. This avoids one group of 'service users', namely those for whom provision is made under s 26, being the poor relations of another group who receive direct provision under s 21 when both groups belong to the same class.

[28] Mr Gordon acknowledges that if LCF are subject to art 8, they would, like any other public authority, be entitled to rely upon art 8(2) to establish that the interference with the appellants' art 8 rights by LCF is justified.

[29] In its written submissions, JUSTICE draws attention to parliamentary material and in particular to statements of the Lord Chancellor and the Home Secretary during the passage of the 1998 Act which indicate that s 6(3)(b) should be given a generous application. Perhaps the most persuasive citation is that of the Lord Chancellor when he stated: 'Doctors in general practice would be public authorities in relation to their National Health Service functions, but not in

a relation to their private patients' (see 583 HL Official Report (5th Series) col 811, 24 November 1997). JUSTICE contends this approach reflects the need for there to be 'a broad and protective definition of what constitutes public authority, designed to discharge the United Kingdom's obligations under arts 1 and 13 of the convention'. In JUSTICE's view, 'if it is or would be a public function when discharged by a pure public authority, it is no less a public function when discharged
b by a contractual third party'.

[30] In addition, JUSTICE drew attention to comparative material reflecting the approach in other jurisdictions. However, while comparative material can be very valuable in construing the obligations under the convention, that assistance is limited where as here what is at issue is the proper interpretation of the provisions of domestic legislation, namely s 6 of the 1998 Act.

c [31] Mr James Goudie QC on behalf of LCF, in fairness to his clients, draws attention to the fact that, although the court is not concerned with the merits of the appellants' case, the proposed development of Le Court is to be an evolutionary process with at present no fixed timescale. During this process there will be continuing consultation with the residents and their relatives. LCF stresses that
d before any decision is taken as to the future provision of care for an individual resident, that resident will have a full and thorough assessment of his or her needs and in conjunction with the local authority will be offered an alternative placement which is appropriate to their needs. This is a situation where this is ample protection for the appellants and there is no black hole into which they would sink if they failed on this appeal. In the unlikely event of LCF acting
e inappropriately, there would still be, as Mr Gordon accepts, the appellant's rights against the local authority under s 21 of the 1948 Act. In addition, if any promises were made to the appellants as to a home for life, that could be contractually binding on LCF or create an estoppel. Finally, here, as pointed out by Mr Henderson on behalf of the Attorney General, there is power in charity
f proceedings to prevent trustees acting in a wholly unreasonable manner.

[32] Mr Goudie also submits that LCF's decision to redevelop Le Court was not amenable to judicial review at common law. Both in regard to s 6(3)(b) of the 1998 Act and judicial review, LCF was not a public authority. He, in particular, relies on *R v Disciplinary Committee of the Jockey Club, ex p Aga Khan* [1993] 2 All ER 853, [1993] 1 WLR 909.

g
Conclusions

[33] If this were a situation where a local authority could divest itself of its art 8 obligations by contracting out to a voluntary sector provider its obligations under s 21 of the 1948 Act, then there would be a responsibility on the court to approach
h the interpretation of s 6(3)(b) in a way which ensures, so far as this is possible, that the rights under art 8 of persons in the position of the appellants are protected. This is not, however, the situation. The local authority remains under an obligation under s 21 of the 1948 Act and retains an obligation under art 8 to the appellants even though it has used its powers under s 26 to use LCF as a provider.
j In addition the appellants have their contractual rights against LCF in any event. There is also the possible protection which can be provided by the Attorney General's role but this is not a significant factor.

[34] If the arrangements which the local authorities made with LCF had been made after the 1998 Act came into force, then it would arguably be possible for a resident to require the local authority to enter into a contract with its provider which fully protected the residents' art 8 rights and if this was done, this would

provide additional protection. Local authorities who rely on s 26 to make new arrangements should bear this in mind in the contract which they make with the providers. Then not only could the local authority rely on the contract, but possibly the resident could do so also as a person for whose benefit the contract was made. Here this was not a possibility because the appellants' residence at Le Court began long before the 1998 Act came into force and one feature of a case such as this is that the local authority did not when it entered into the arrangement with LCF intend that LCF should perform on its behalf its art 8 responsibilities, nor did LCF accept any such obligation. It is not without relevance that here, if the appellants are right, the result would be that the function which would previously have been a private function has become a public function in consequence of the 1998 Act coming into force and imposing retrospectively upon LCF additional responsibilities enforceable by law.

[35] The matters already referred to, can however, be put aside. In our judgment the role that LCF was performing manifestly did not involve the performance of public functions. The fact that LCF is a large and flourishing organisation does not change the nature of its activities from private to public. (i) It is not in issue that it is possible for LCF to perform some public functions and some private functions. In this case it is contended that this was what has been happening in regard to those residents who are privately funded and those residents who are publicly funded. But in this case except for the resources needed to fund the residents of the different occupants of Le Court, there is no material distinction between the nature of the services LCF has provided for residents funded by a local authority and those provided to residents funded privately. While the degree of public funding of the activities of an otherwise private body is certainly relevant as to the nature of the functions performed, by itself it is not determinative of whether the functions are public or private. Here we found the case of *R (on the application of the University of Cambridge) v HM Treasury* Case C-380/98 [2000] All ER (EC) 920 at 930, 940–942, sub nom *R v HM Treasury, ex p University of Cambridge* [2000] 1 WLR 2514 at 2523, 2534–2535, relied on by Mr Henderson, an interesting illustration in relation to European Union legislation in different terms to s 6. (ii) There is no other evidence of there being a public flavour to the functions of LCF or LCF itself. LCF is not standing in the shoes of the local authorities. Section 26 of the 1948 Act provides statutory authority for the actions of the local authorities but it provides LCF with no powers. LCF is not exercising statutory powers in performing functions for the appellants. (iii) In truth, all that Mr Gordon can rely upon is the fact that if LCF is not performing a public function the appellants would not be able to rely upon art 8 as against LCF. However, this is a circular argument. If LCF was performing a public function, that would mean that the appellants could rely in relation to that function on art 8, but, if the situation is otherwise, art 8 cannot change the appropriate classification of the function. On the approach adopted in *Poplar Housing and Regeneration Community Association Ltd v Donoghue* [2001] 4 All ER 604, [2002] QB 48, it can be said that LCF is clearly not performing any public function. Stanley Burnton J's conclusion as to this was correct.

The procedure adopted by the claimants

[36] This conclusion is of relevance as to the remedies which can be granted on judicial review but is not conclusive as to the scope of judicial review. As is appropriately set out in Grosz, Beatson, Duffy *Human Rights: The 1998 Act and the*

a *European Convention* (2000) p 61, as to the relationship between the scope of the
1998 Act and the scope of judicial review:

'**4–04** The law on the scope of judicial review cannot, however, be
determinative. First, it will be necessary for the English courts to take into
account the Strasbourg jurisprudence which identifies the bodies whose
actions engage the responsibility of the state for the purpose of the
b Convention, which, as we shall see, differs from the judicial review criteria
in material respects. That jurisprudence also makes clear that the Convention's
reach is determined by reference to "autonomous" concepts of Convention
law and not by the manner in which national law classifies bodies or their
acts. Secondly, notwithstanding the Home Secretary's statement that "the
concepts are reasonably clear", the way English courts have drawn the
c distinction between "public" and "private" for the purpose of judicial review
produced a complicated and not altogether consistent body of cases, using a
variety of tests. Thirdly, as will be seen, not all the acts of "obvious" public
authorities are treated as "public" for the purposes of judicial review. In
contrast, the [Human Rights Act 1998] will apply to *all* their acts.
d Nevertheless, the case law on the judicial review jurisdiction is instructive.'

[**37**] To the points made in *Human Rights,* there is to be added the distinction
between the approach of RSC Ord 53 and CPR Pt 54. RSC Ord 53, r 1, in
identifying cases which were appropriate for an application for judicial review,
focused on the nature of the application. Was it an application for an order of
e mandamus, prohibition or certiorari or an application for a declaration or an
injunction which could be granted on an application for judicial review, if having
regard to the nature and matters in respect of which relief may be granted by way
of one of the prerogative remedies, it would be just and convenient for the
declaration or injunction to be granted on an application for judicial review? CPR
54.1 has changed the focus of the test so that it is also partly functions based. Now
f the relevant provisions of CPR Pt 54 provide:

'**54.1 Scope and Interpretation**
(1) This Part contains rules about judicial review.
(2) In this Part—(a) a "claim for judicial review" means a claim to review
the lawfulness of—(i) an enactment; or (ii) a decision, action or failure to act
g in relation to the exercise of a public function …

54.2 When This Part Must Be Used
The judicial review procedure must be used in a claim for judicial review
where the claimant is seeking—(a) a mandatory order; (b) a prohibiting
h order; (c) a quashing order; or (d) an injunction under section 30 of the
Supreme Court Act 1981 (restraining a person from acting in any office in
which he is not entitled to act) …

54.20 Transfer
The court may (a) order a claim to continue as if it had not been started
j under this Part; and (b) where it does so, give directions about the future
management of the claim.

(Part 30 (transfer) applies to transfers to and from the Administrative
Court)'

[**38**] These changes have not been reflected in any complementary change to
s 31 of the Supreme Court Act 1981, which still is in virtually the same language

as RSC Ord 53. None the less, there was clearly set out in Mr Goudie's skeleton
argument and reflected in the decision of the court below ([2001] All ER (D) 156   *a*
(Jun) at [104]) with its reference to 'A gap in judicial review', an idea that if LCF
was not forming a public function, proceedings by way of judicial review were
wrong. This is an echo of the old demarcation disputes as to when judicial review
was or was not appropriate under RSC Ord 53. CPR Pt 54 is intended to avoid
any such disputes which are wholly unproductive. In a case such as the present   *b*
where a bona fide contention is being advanced (although incorrect) that LCF
was performing a public function, that is an appropriate issue to be brought to the
court by way of judicial review. Because LCF is a charity further procedural
requirements may be involved. We express no view as to this and we heard no
argument on this subject unlike Stanley Burnton J.

[**39**] We wish to make clear that the CPR provide a framework which is   *c*
sufficiently flexible to enable all the issues between the parties to be determined.
Issues, if any, as to the private law rights of the claimants have not been
determined. A decision had to be reached as to what happened to these
proceedings. In view of the decisions of Stanley Burnton J and this court the
claimants have no public law rights. Stanley Burnton J dismissed the proceedings   *d*
having given judgment. In view of a possibility of a misunderstanding as to the
scope of judicial review we draw attention to this and the powers of transfer
under CPR Pt 54. Subject to this we dismiss this appeal.

Appeal dismissed. Permission to appeal refused.

                                                        Kate O'Hanlon   Barrister.

a
On Demand Information plc (in administrative receivership) and another v Michael Gerson (Finance) plc and another

b
[2002] UKHL 13

HOUSE OF LORDS

LORD NICHOLLS OF BIRKENHEAD, LORD BROWNE-WILKINSON, LORD HOBHOUSE OF WOODBOROUGH, LORD MILLETT AND LORD SCOTT OF FOSCOTE

c 18–19 FEBRUARY, 18 APRIL 2002

Contract – Finance lease – Relief from forfeiture – Claimants leasing equipment from defendants – Defendants having right to terminate leases if claimants went into receivership – Claimants going into receivership and defendants terminating leases –
d *Claimants selling leased equipment and applying for relief from forfeiture – Whether sale defeating claim for relief from forfeiture.*

The claimant companies leased video and editing equipment from the defendants under four finance leases. The defendants had the right to treat the leases as repudiated if, inter alia, the claimants went into receivership. The claimants could
e terminate the leases after 36 months (the primary period) by giving a valid notice, failing which the leases continued for further periods of 12 months (the secondary periods) until terminated by the claimants giving notice. If the claimants terminated the leases at the end of the primary period or any secondary period, they were entitled to sell the equipment as the defendants' agents, subject to
f certain conditions. On exercising that power, the claimants would be entitled to a rental rebate equivalent to 95% of the sale price. In February 1998 the claimants went into administrative receivership and the defendants duly treated that event as a repudiatory breach of each of the leases. The receivers wanted to sell one of the businesses operated by the second claimant together with the leased equipment, but could not rely on the contractual power of sale since the claimants had not
g served notices terminating the leases. Instead, they sought and obtained the court's leave to sell the equipment, and the sale proceeds were paid into an escrow account. The claimants subsequently applied for relief from forfeiture on terms that the defendants should be paid only the sum which they would have received if the claimants had exercised the power of sale. The defendants
h contended that the court had no jurisdiction to grant relief from forfeiture of a finance lease, and that accordingly they were entitled to receive the full proceeds of the sale of the equipment. The judge ruled that the court had jurisdiction to grant relief from forfeiture of a finance lease, but held that the sale defeated the claim for relief from forfeiture. Both sides appealed. The Court of Appeal unanimously upheld the judge's ruling that the criteria for the exercise of the
j equitable jurisdiction were present at the date of the application. They rejected the defendants' objection that the leases were purely contractual in nature, and that the jurisdiction to grant relief from forfeiture was restricted to cases where the forfeiture of proprietary rights strictly so-called was in question. The majority nevertheless also upheld the judge's ruling on the effect of the sale. The claimants appealed on the question of the effect of the sale upon their claim for relief from forfeiture.

Held – It was self-evident that the court could not make an an order granting
relief from forfeiture of a lease after the lease had been determined otherwise
than by the forfeiture in question, and the sale in the instant case had brought the
leases to an end independently of the antecedent forfeiture against which relief
was sought. However, the fact that by the time the case was heard the court
could no longer give the claimant the relief claimed in the writ did not mean that
the court was bound to dismiss the claim. If the claimant would have been
entitled to the relief claimed in the writ immediately before the sale and the only
reason that the court could not grant the relief was that the equipment had since
been sold pursuant to an order of the court which was not intended to affect the
parties' rights, then the court should give effect to those rights by making
whatever order in relation to the proceeds of sale best reflected those rights. That
was not to ignore the fact that the equipment had been sold or to grant relief as
if it had not been sold, but was to recognise that the sale was not to affect the
parties' substantive rights and that substantive rights could be given effect in
more than one way. Had it been possible to grant relief from forfeiture
immediately before the equipment had been sold, it would have been on terms
that all outstanding rentals were paid and that the administrative receivers should
guarantee payment of future rentals. No sale could have taken place until the
leases were brought to an end by notice, and accordingly some further secondary
rentals would inevitably have become payable. The equipment would have had to
have been sold at the best available price. Those were all matters which should be
taken into account in deciding the proportions in which the parties were entitled to
the moneys in the escrow account failing agreement between the parties.
Accordingly, the appeal would be allowed and the case remitted to the Chancery
Division (see [1], [2], [9], [38], [39], [41], [42], [52], below).

Decision of the Court of Appeal [2000] 4 All ER 734 reversed in part.

Notes

For relief against forfeiture, see 27(1) *Halsbury's Laws* (4th edn reissue) paras
513–523.

Case referred to in opinions

Shiloh Spinners Ltd v Harding [1973] 1 All ER 90, [1973] AC 691, [1973] 2 WLR 28, HL.

Appeal

The appellant claimants, On Demand Information plc (in administrative receivership)
and On Demand Information International plc (in administrative receivership),
appealed with permission of the Appeal Committee of the House of Lords given
on 11 June 2001 from the order of the Court of Appeal (Pill and Robert Walker LJJ,
Sir Murray Stuart-Smith dissenting) on 31 July 2000 ([2000] 4 All ER 734) dismissing
their appeal from the decision of George Laurence QC ([1999] 2 All ER 811),
sitting as a deputy judge of the High Court on 5 March 1999, dismissing their
application for relief from forfeiture by the defendants, Michael Gerson (Finance)
plc and Michael Gerson (Investments) plc, of certain equipment leases. The facts
are set out in the opinion of Lord Millett.

Dr Fidelis Oditah (instructed by *Walker Morris*, Leeds) for the appellants.
Sir Roy Goode QC and *Hugh Tomlinson* (instructed by *Royds Treadwell*) for the
    respondents.

a Their Lordships took time for consideration.

18 April 2002. The following opinions were delivered.

LORD NICHOLLS OF BIRKENHEAD.

b [1] My Lords, I have had the advantage of reading in draft the speeches of my noble and learned friends, Lord Hobhouse of Woodborough, Lord Millett and Lord Scott of Foscote. For the reasons they give, and with which I agree, I would allow this appeal.

LORD BROWNE-WILKINSON.

c [2] My Lords, I have read the speeches of my noble and learned friends, Lord Millett and Lord Scott of Foscote. For the reasons which they give I would allow the appeal and make the order which Lord Millett proposes.

LORD HOBHOUSE OF WOODBOROUGH.

d [3] My Lords, this dispute has arisen from the special facts of this case, the making of an order for the sale of goods pendente lite which were the subject of financing agreements which had been contractually terminated by the goods owner.

[4] There is no problem about the financing agreements themselves. The appellants needed to obtain computer systems in order to operate their business.
e They did not wish (and maybe were not able) to finance the transaction themselves. They accordingly entered into finance agreements with the respondents. They were elaborate agreements structured so as to keep the cost to the appellants as low as possible. They took the form of hire agreements. The title to the goods remained throughout with the respondents and was not at any time nor in any
f circumstances to pass to the appellants or any company associated with them. The appellants had the possession of the goods but no power to sell or otherwise deal with them either during the currency of the agreements nor afterwards. This structure reflected the fact that one of the important features of the agreements was the inclusion of provisions to enable the respondents to obtain the maximum tax advantages. The appellants had a contractual right to require the respondents
g to sell the goods at the end of the 'primary' contract period but the appellants could only act as the negotiating agent of the respondents in relation to the sale and the sale must be at a price approved by the respondents prior to the sale. Further, this right could only be exercised if the appellants had fully performed all their contractual obligations to the respondents. The benefit to the appellants was
h that the appellants were then entitled to receive a sum equivalent to 95% of the proceeds of sale by way of a rebate on hire previously paid. There were also default provisions of a familiar kind which gave the respondents the right to bring the agreements to an end at any stage if the appellants failed to perform their obligations. These were the forfeiture rights which the respondents exercised and from which the appellants claimed relief in the action. The purpose of
j claiming relief was so that the appellants could take advantage of the provisions for the sale of the goods and enjoy the benefit of the rebate.

[5] There is now no dispute that the agreements were of a character susceptible to relief against forfeiture; they were financing agreements and possession of the goods was given to the debtor. (See *Shiloh Spinners Ltd v Harding* [1973] 1 All ER 90, [1973] AC 691.) Similarly, it is not in dispute that the appellants needed to obtain an order for such relief if they were to be enabled to exercise their

contractual right to require the sale of the goods and obtain the 95% rebate. The
complication which has given rise to these appeals is that, when the appellants'
business collapsed, the receivers wanted to mitigate their loss by selling the
business as a going concern which meant, in commercial terms, that they must
find a way of procuring the sale of both the appellants' goodwill and the
respondents' computer systems together to the same purchaser. They started
their action claiming (inter alia) relief against forfeiture. But they would not be
able to obtain an order sufficiently quickly to enable the combined sale they
needed to go ahead within a time scale acceptable to a purchaser of the business.
They therefore struck upon the idea of applying to the court for an order for the
sale of the goods under RSC Ord 29, r 4. Fortunately for them the response of the
respondents was very helpful. On 2 March 1998, Mr Gerson wrote:

> 'I confirm our conversation of this morning when I put forward the
> suggestion that Without Prejudice to the terms and conditions of our four
> leases and the rights existing under those leases, that in order to enable the
> best realisable price to be negotiated, in the interest of saving jobs at the
> Company, and to preserve any goodwill, you should negotiate a sale to any
> interested party with which we will co-operate as owner ... subject to
> agreement on price with our valuer and that the proceeds of sale be paid into
> an escrow account ...'

In an affidavit dated 5 March, he said that, without accepting that the appellants
had any right to relief against forfeiture but accepting that they had an arguable
case:

> 'I understand that the receivers wish to sell the plaintiffs' business as a
> matter of extreme urgency and that they believe that the equipment is a vital
> part of that sale. In these circumstances, the [respondents] are prepared to
> consent to an order for sale of the equipment and will agree that good title
> shall pass to the purchaser. In order to hold the position pending a full
> hearing of the motion, the proceeds of sale should be paid into an escrow
> account as contemplated by the notice of motion.'

He reserved the respondents' rights in relation to the sales and their contention
that they were entitled to the full value of the goods at the date of sale. He
concluded:

> 'In summary, therefore, the [respondents] are prepared to consent to an
> order which does not prejudice their rights to raise arguments as to the true
> value of the Equipment in due course. The sum which is, in fact, achieved on
> the sale of the Property should be paid into an account in the joint names of the
> parties' solicitors pending the determination of the substantive motion.'

At the hearing of the motion, counsel for the respondents, having made similar
reservations, did not oppose the making of the order for sale.

[6] Whether or not the order for the sale of the computer systems should have
been made under this rule had the respondents opposed it is something about
which we need express no opinion; the purpose of the appellants' application was
collaterally to assist the receivers to realise the best possible value from the sale
of the goodwill and sell the business as a going concern. However, what is clear
is that the order made was of the character of an order made pendente lite
without prejudice to the rights of the parties in the pending litigation. In an ideal
world there would be no need for such orders; the parties' rights would be

a decided then and there. But that is not the real world. The ascertainment of the parties' rights takes some time and there will be a lapse of time before a determination can be arrived at. The mechanism used by the courts to accommodate this fact is to convert the relevant property into money and to treat that money as if it was the property. The task of the court remains the same as before—to ascertain what were the rights of parties in respect of the property and then to give effect to those rights by
b making appropriate orders as to the application of the money.

[7] In the present case, once the question of whether the appellants would have been granted relief against forfeiture (and its terms) and the value to be attributed to the goods at the time of sale had been decided, the questions debated upon this appeal have ceased to exist. An order for a sale pendente lite does not deprive parties of their rights. It simply, for purely practical reasons,
c provides a mechanism for allowing the parties' rights as they existed immediately before the making of the order to be ascertained without in the meantime damaging the value of whatever those rights were. Thus perishable goods may be ordered by a master of the Queen's Bench to be sold and the proceeds paid into court or a ship or cargo under arrest may be ordered to be sold by the Admiralty
d judge or registrar without affecting what were the rights of the parties and other potential claimants over the property sold. The sale is free of encumbrances. There is no longer any lien or mortgage over the property yet a lien holder's or a mortgagee's rights continue to be recognised by the court and are given effect to by making orders in relation to the money now under the control of the court.

[8] There are two main reasons why the decision of the majority of the Court
e of Appeal (see [2000] 4 All ER 734, [2001] 1 WLR 155) was wrong. First, it was implicit in the order made by Harman J that the order was without prejudice to the rights of the parties in the action. The Court of Appeal construed the order as destroying the rights of one of the parties in the action. Secondly, the majority failed to carry out the task of ascertaining what relief the appellants were entitled
f to immediately before the order for sale was made. They treated the necessity of taking time to have a trial and determine what the rights of the parties were as depriving the appellants of their rights. It is true that there has been no relief against forfeiture until a court has made an order granting that relief and that the contractual or proprietary rights do not consequentially revive until the relief has been granted. But that is not relevant here. The court had to put itself back in
g the position Harman J would have been in if he had been able to decide the whole dispute on the day the matter was before him. The majority gave the interim order a substantive effect which it did not have. They failed to recognise its character as an order pendente lite.

[9] For these reasons as well as those to be given by my noble and learned
h friends Lord Millett and Lord Scott of Foscote, whose opinions I have read in draft, I too would allow the appeal and make the order proposed by Lord Millett.

LORD MILLETT.
[10] My Lords, between 5 September 1994 and 17 May 1995 the respondents or one of them (the lessor) granted to the appellants or one of them (the lessee)
j four finance leases of equipment for the making and editing of videos. In all respects material to the question to be decided in the present appeal the four leases were in similar terms.

[11] Each lease was for an initial period (described as the primary period) of 36 months. During this period the lessee was liable to pay a substantial rental (described as the primary rental) which was designed to recoup the lessor by the end of the primary period for the cost of the equipment with interest together

with other costs and profit. The primary rental was payable monthly with an
initial payment of three months' rent at the outset, so that in effect the rent was	*a*
paid three months in advance.

[12] On the expiry of the primary period, the lessee was entitled to continue
the lease indefinitely for successive periods of 12 months (the secondary period)
for a nominal annual rental payable on the first day of each secondary period.

[13] Each lease provided: that the equipment was to be located at the lessee's	*b*
premises (by cl 4A); that it was to remain at all times the sole and exclusive
property of the lessor (by cl 5A); and that the lessee was not to sub-lease, sell,
charge, pledge, mortgage or otherwise dispose of or part with possession of any
of the equipment (by cl 5B).

[14] Each lease provided that it could be determined by the lessee giving a
60-day notice to expire on the last day of the primary period or any secondary	*c*
period. It also provided (by cl 9(B)(iv)) that the appointment of a receiver over all
or any part of the lessee's undertaking or assets should constitute a repudiatory
breach of each of the leases and entitle the lessor to terminate all or any of them
and claim payment of a termination sum from the lessee. The termination sum
was equal to the sum of: (a) all accrued but unpaid rentals with interest at 2% per	*d*
month; (b) the balance of primary rental at the date of repudiation discounted for
accelerated receipt; and (c) all costs incurred in repossessing the equipment or
collecting payments, less the open market value of the equipment at the date of
repudiation.

[15] Each lease also provided (by cl 12) that, subject to the lessee having
performed all its obligations under all the leases, then upon termination of the	*e*
lease at the end of the primary period or at any time thereafter by notice in
accordance with the terms of the lease, the lessee could sell the equipment to an
unconnected third party at the best price available. The price was to be approved
by the lessor prior to the sale and the sale was to be made by the lessee as the
lessor's agent. The lessee was entitled to retain out of the proceeds of sale by way	*f*
of a rebate of rentals a sum equal to 95% of the sale proceeds.

[16] On 12 February 1998 the lessee went into administrative receivership.
One week later the lessor terminated all four leases. Two of the leases were then
in their secondary period and nothing was outstanding by way of rental under
either of them. The primary period under the third lease was due to expire on
30 March 1998 and all the primary rentals had been paid in full. It was too late to	*g*
serve a 60-day notice to bring the lease to an end before the commencement of
the secondary period, but the termination sum did not include secondary rental
which had not accrued due at the date of termination. The primary period under
the fourth lease was due to expire in May 1998. Only the last instalment of
primary rental (£3,887·43) together with interest (£5·11) making a total of £3,892·54	*h*
was outstanding. The last payment of primary rental fell due during the first
week of the receivership.

[17] Following their appointment the administrative receivers took steps to
realise the lessee's assets as best they could. The business was organised in two
divisions: the creative convergence division, which used the leased equipment,
and the new media publishing division. The new media publishing division was	*j*
sold on 20 February. The creative convergence division had 78 employees, was
reliant on them and their contacts, and had little value except as a going concern.
There was a heavy and continuing liability for salaries and wages. Unless the
business could be sold quickly, it would almost certainly have to be closed down.

[18] Despite extensive marketing only one serious offer was received for the
business. This was from the division's management and was for a sale of the

business together with the leased equipment. The lessor also wished to achieve a sale of the equipment and had been attempting to sell it to the lessee or the management, but without success. The receivers had offered the lessor £30,000 in full and final settlement if it consented to a sale of the equipment as part of a sale of the lessee's business as a going concern. This sum was far in excess of 5% of the value of the equipment, but the lessor had refused.

[19] On 4 March 1998 the lessee issued a writ claiming relief from forfeiture and other relief. Relief from forfeiture was needed in order to enable the administrative receivers to sell the equipment pursuant to cl 12 of the leases. As a term of obtaining relief they would, of course, be required to pay the arrears of primary rental and interest; and in order to sell the equipment pursuant to cl 12 they would have to terminate the leases by giving the appropriate notices of termination and paying any secondary rental due in the meantime; but subject thereto they would be entitled to recover a rebate equal to 95% of the sale proceeds.

[20] Unhappily the parties were unable to agree on the proposed sale. There were two points of disagreement. First, the lessor did not accept that the lessee was entitled to relief from forfeiture, though it conceded that this was arguable. Secondly, it did not accept that the price at which the receivers were proposing to sell the equipment was, as cl 12 required, the best price available. The receivers were advised that the equipment was worth £273,000 if sold for use in situ, £178,000 if sold as individual items for removal from the premises at the purchaser's expense, and only £112,000 if sold separately. The lessor was advised that it was worth £251,295 if sold in situ and £134,030 if sold separately. Thus it was in the interests of both parties that the equipment be sold as part of the business; but they were unable to agree whether the lessee was entitled to a rebate of rentals following a sale at the best price available, which depended on whether the lessee was entitled to relief from forfeiture, or on the amount which the equipment should fetch.

[21] In the ordinary way, the receivers would have waited to obtain relief from forfeiture before selling the equipment. But the sale would not wait. Unless the business was sold quickly it would not be sold at all. Accordingly on 4 March they issued two notices of motion for interim relief. One was a notice inter partes which sought relief from forfeiture of each of the four leases. The other was ex parte and sought an interim order for sale of the equipment pursuant to RSC Ord 29, r 4. This provides:

'**Sale of Perishable property, etc.**

4.—(1) The Court may, on the application of any party to a cause or matter, make an order for the sale by such person, in such manner and on such terms (if any) as may be specified in the order of any property (other than land) which is the subject-matter of the cause or matter or as to which any question arises therein and which is of a perishable nature or likely to deteriorate if kept or which for any other good reason it is desirable to sell forthwith.'

[22] The ex parte application came before Harman J on 5 March 1998. The lessor had been notified of the hearing and was present by counsel. The receivers asked for an order that the lessee be at liberty to sell the equipment, give a good title to the purchaser and retain the proceeds of sale in an escrow account pending the hearing of the inter partes motion.

[23] The lessor filed an affidavit in which it stated that it did not accept that the lessee had any right to relief from forfeiture but conceded that this was arguable. *a* It said that it understood that the receivers wished to sell the business as a matter of extreme urgency and that they believed that the equipment was a vital part of the sale. In those circumstances, the lessor was prepared to consent to an order for sale of the equipment and would agree that the purchaser should obtain a good title, and asked that 'in order to hold the position pending a full hearing of *b* the motion' the proceeds of sale should be paid into an escrow account. The lessor expressly reserved its rights in relation to the sale, and asked that it be made clear on the face of the order that it was made without prejudice to the lessor's contention that it was entitled to the full value of the equipment at the date of sale. It also wished to reserve the right to argue that the price at which the receivers proposed to sell the equipment did not represent its full value. *c*

[24] Harman J made an order for the sale of the equipment. It was a term of the order that the net proceeds of sale should be held in an escrow account pending the hearing of the inter partes motion for relief from forfeiture, and it contained a proviso that the lessor should be at liberty to contend that the break-up value of the equipment was more than £130,500. *d*

[25] The business together with the equipment was sold on the following day, and the receivers paid the sum of £132,839·96 into an escrow account as representing the proportion of the gross proceeds of sale which had been allocated to the equipment as between the lessee and the purchaser.

[26] Although the order did not contain a proviso to the effect that the sale was without prejudice to the lessee's application for relief from forfeiture, no one *e* contemplated that it would be automatically defeated by the sale which the judge had ordered. In the course of the hearing Harman J expressed the view that 'relief from forfeiture is obviously available', and the terms of his order, which in this respect reflected those of the lessor's affidavit, clearly contemplated that the parties' respective rights to the proceeds of sale would depend on the outcome of *f* the inter partes motion. There could be no other reason for requiring the proceeds to be paid into an escrow account.

[27] The inter partes motion was heard by Mr George Laurence QC sitting as a deputy judge of the Chancery Division (see [1999] 2 All ER 811) at the end of November 1998 and was by consent treated as the trial of the action. For the purposes of the hearing the lessee agreed that certain factual issues should be *g* assumed in favour of the lessor. For present purposes the material concessions were: (i) that the lessee did not sell the equipment for the best price available; (ii) that the best price available was £251,617; (iii) that the lessor would not have approved a sale of the equipment at less than its written-down value of £251,617, (since this would have had adverse consequences on the lessor's tax position); *h* (iv) that the lessor would have approved a sale of the equipment at £251,617; and (v) that but for the appointment of administrative receivers, the lessee would not have served notice of termination. It was common ground that, if the equipment had been sold pursuant to cl 12 of the leases for £251,617, the lessee would have been entitled to a retain a sum equal to 95% of the net proceeds of sale.

[28] The deputy judge dismissed the action, with the result that the money in *j* the escrow account was payable to the lessor. He held that the criteria for the jurisdiction to grant relief would have been satisfied at the date of the application, since (i) the primary object of the bargain was to secure a stated result, namely the payment of the rentals in full and on time; (ii) at that date that result could effectively be attained when the matter came before the court; and (iii) the forfeiture provision was a security for the production of that result. But he held

a that the court no longer had power to grant relief from forfeiture since the equipment was no longer in the lessee's possession so that it was impossible to restore the status quo. As the deputy judge put it, relief from forfeiture would not make sense: first, a lease of equipment cannot meaningfully be restored if the equipment is gone; and secondly, possession of the equipment cannot be restored to the lessee if there is no longer any equipment to possess. Restoration of the

b status quo, he said, includes restoration of a state of affairs whereby the lessee must either (i) pay the secondary rentals and abide by the other terms of the leases if it wished to continue to possess and use the equipment; or (ii) comply strictly with the 60-day notice requirement and the terms of cl 12 if it wished to sell the equipment and become entitled to the 95% rebate. Neither of those possibilities would exist if the court purported to grant relief from forfeiture after the equipment

c had been sold, and it followed that there was no jurisdiction to grant it.

[29] The Court of Appeal (Pill and Robert Walker LJJ, Sir Murray Stuart-Smith dissenting) dismissed the lessee's appeal (see [2000] 4 All ER 734, [2001] 1 WLR 155). The court unanimously upheld the deputy judge's ruling that the criteria for the exercise of the equitable jurisdiction were present at the date of the

d application. They rejected the lessor's objection that the leases were purely contractual in nature, and that the jurisdiction to grant relief from forfeiture was restricted to cases where the forfeiture of proprietary rights strictly so called was in question. As Robert Walker LJ put it, contractual rights which entitle the hirer to indefinite possession of chattels so long as the hire payments are duly made, and which qualify and limit the owner's general property in the chattels, cannot

e aptly be described as purely contractual rights. For my own part, I regard this conclusion as in accordance with principle; any other would restrict the exercise of a beneficent jurisdiction without any rational justification.

[30] The majority of the Court of Appeal also upheld the deputy judge's ruling on the effect of the sale, substantially for the reasons he had given. Robert

f Walker LJ was prepared to accept that the money in the escrow account might be regarded as a clean substitution for the equipment, but he could not see how the court could grant relief from forfeiture in relation to a sum of money once the equipment had gone. Pill LJ did not doubt the court's power to make the interim order for sale, but considered that its exercise did not affect the question whether

g the parties were thereafter to be treated as if their relationship was the same as had existed at the date of the interim order and as if the order had not been made. Sir Murray Stuart-Smith, who dissented on this part of the case, considered the true question to be whether the sale of the equipment pursuant to the order of the court defeated the lessee's claim to relief from forfeiture because it could not

h be restored to the position before the leases were terminated. He held that it was implicit in the order that the parties' substantive rights were not to be affected by the sale which it authorised.

[31] The lessor has not cross-appealed against the first ground of the Court of Appeal's judgment, nor has it ever appealed from the order of Harman J.

j Accordingly, it must be taken to be settled that the court would have had jurisdiction to grant relief from forfeiture in respect of all four leases on suitable terms at the date of the application for such relief and at all times until the actual sale of the equipment pursuant to Harman J's order, which must be taken to have been properly made. No reason has been advanced before your Lordships why, if the jurisdiction existed, it should not have been exercised, and I would assume that, had the equipment not been sold, the lessee would have obtained relief from forfeiture and sold the equipment pursuant to cl 12 of the leases in due course.

[32] Accordingly, the sole question is that identified by Sir Murray Stuart-Smith, viz, what was the effect of the sale upon the lessee's claim for relief from forfeiture?

[33] My Lords, RSC Ord 29, r 4 gave the court power to make an interim order for the sale of any property (other than land) which is of a perishable nature or likely to deteriorate if kept or which for any other reason it is desirable to sell forthwith. The order does not give the court power to make a free-standing order for sale as a form of independent relief. The property in question must either form the subject matter of the proceedings in which the order is made or be property as to which a question arises in those proceedings. It is the existence of the proceedings or question which gives rise to the difficulty and makes it necessary to invoke the assistance of the court. The paradigm case is where the ownership of the goods is in dispute, so that they cannot be sold except by agreement between the parties or order of the court. The purpose of the court in exercising the power to order a sale is to avoid the injustice that would otherwise result by the property becoming worthless or significantly reduced in value during the interval between the application for sale and the determination of the proceedings or question.

[34] In the present case the leased equipment was not perishable or likely to deteriorate, but there was good reason why it should be sold forthwith before the lessee's claim for relief from forfeiture could be determined. The parties had been unable to agree upon a sale, and neither party could sell without the consent of the other or an order of the court. The lessee could not sell unless and until it obtained relief from forfeiture and brought the leases to an end by the appropriate notices; and the lessor could not sell while the lessee's claim for relief from forfeiture remained outstanding. There was an impasse, which was resolved by the order for sale. Your Lordships are not called upon to consider whether it was properly made, given that the lessee's power of sale had not yet arisen.

[35] The order was not, or not expressly, made by consent, but it bound the lessor as fully as if it had consented to it. Accordingly, the lessor cannot complain that the lessee was in breach of the terms of the leases because the sale was not made pursuant to cl 12 of the leases, or that it constituted a breach of other provisions in the leases, or that it had the effect of bringing the leases to an end without prior notice. They had been determined by a sale of the equipment which was not wrongful.

[36] Given the purpose of Ord 29, r 4, it is clear that the conversion of the property into money effected by the sale is not intended to prejudice the parties' rights. The whole purpose of the sale is to preserve the value of their rights and particularly the rights of the party which is eventually successful in the proceedings.

[37] But while the proceeds of sale are merely a substitute for the property in question, the sale inevitably affects the nature of the remedy which the court can grant. The subject matter of the proceedings, and therefore of the order which the court will ultimately make at trial, is no longer property but money. In the paradigm case, where the ownership of the property is in dispute, the court can no longer make a declaration of title, or order the party in possession to give possession to the other, or give specific relief in relation to the property. After the property has been sold no such relief is possible. Instead, orders which the court would otherwise have made are replaced by orders for payment out of the money (if in court) or declarations of entitlement to give a good receipt for the money (if in an escrow account).

[38] It is self-evident that the court cannot make an order granting relief from forfeiture of a lease after the lease has been determined otherwise than by the forfeiture in question. Harman J's order did not in itself make it impossible for the court to grant relief from forfeiture; this remained possible until the moment the equipment was sold. But the sale brought the leases to an end independently of the antecedent forfeiture against which relief was sought.

[39] But the fact that by the time the case was heard the court could no longer give the lessee the particular relief claimed in the writ does not mean that it was bound to dismiss its claim. If (i) the lessee would have been entitled to the relief claimed in the writ immediately before the sale, and (ii) the only reason that the court could not grant that relief was that the equipment had since been sold pursuant to an order of the court which was not intended to affect the parties' rights, then it should give effect to those rights by making whatever order in relation to the proceeds of sale best reflects them. This is not to ignore the fact that the equipment had been sold or to grant relief as if it had not been sold, but to recognise that the sale was not to affect the parties' substantive rights, and that substantive rights can be given effect in more than one way.

[40] The error in the approach of the deputy judge and the majority of the Court of Appeal, if I may say so, lies in the description of the lessee's right as a right to relief from forfeiture. But that was merely a means to an end. It was the remedy, appropriate in the circumstances obtaining at the date of the writ, which the lessee sought in order to secure commercially valuable rights. Those rights included the right to retain 95% of the proceeds of a sale made under cl 12 of the leases, that is to say a sale made after bringing the leases to an end by notice. It was no longer an appropriate or possible remedy when the case came before the court. The reason it was no longer appropriate or possible was that the equipment had been sold, not pursuant to cl 12 but to an order of the court which was intended so far as possible to preserve the parties' rights. The question was how to give effect to those rights, once they had been determined, by an order in relation to the proceeds of sale. The sale brought an end to the lessee's claim to a particular remedy, viz, relief from forfeiture, but not to the rights to which such a remedy would have responded, and substituted a claim to payment out of the fund.

[41] I do not think there is any real difficulty in formulating an appropriate order in this case. Had it been possible to grant relief from forfeiture immediately before the equipment was sold, it would have been on terms that all outstanding rentals were paid and that the administrative receivers should guarantee payment of future rentals. No sale could have taken place until the leases were brought to an end by notice, and accordingly some further secondary rentals would inevitably have become payable. The equipment would have to be sold at the best available price, now agreed to have been £251,617. These are all matters which should be taken into account in deciding the proportions in which the parties are entitled to the moneys in the escrow account.

[42] I would allow the appeal and, failing agreement between the parties, remit the case to the Chancery Division to make such orders as may be necessary to give effect to the judgment of the House.

LORD SCOTT OF FOSCOTE.

[43] My Lords, I have had the advantage of reading in draft the opinion of my noble and learned friend, Lord Millett, and gratefully adopt his summary of the facts of the case and its history in the courts below.

[44] It was accepted both at first instance ([1999] 2 All ER 811) and in the Court of Appeal ([2000] 4 All ER 734, [2001] 1 WLR 155) that immediately before the sale

of the video and editing equipment pursuant to the order of Harman J on 5 March 1998, or perhaps immediately before the order was made, the court had jurisdiction to grant the appellants relief from the forfeiture of the finance leases that had been brought about by the entry of the appellants into administrative receivership. I have no doubt that it was rightly so accepted. It was accepted before your Lordships by Sir Roy Goode QC, counsel for the respondents, that if there had been no sale the appellants would have succeeded in obtaining relief from forfeiture on terms that would have included the payment of all arrears of rentals. Sir Murray Stuart-Smith was, therefore, right in identifying the question whether the sale of the equipment pursuant to the court's order defeated the appellants' claim to relief from forfeiture as the critical question.

[45] Harman J's order was made in exercise of the power conferred by RSC Ord 29, r 4. Order 29 has been replaced by Pt 25 of the CPR 1998. Rule 25.1(c)(v), in particular, replaces r 4 of Ord 29 and applies to any property, including land, 'which is the subject of a claim or as to which any question may arise on a claim' (see CPR 25.1(2)).

[46] The effect of an interim order for sale, whether made under Ord 29, r 4 or, now, under CPR 25.1(c)(v), is that once the sale pursuant to the order has taken place the proceeds of sale stand in the place of the property sold for the purpose of giving effect, so far as practicable, to the rights claimed by the parties to the litigation in the property sold.

[47] In the present case the rights claimed by the appellants in the equipment were the right to relief from forfeiture and, subject to relief being granted, the right to possess and use the equipment in specie and the right to take 95% of the net proceeds of a sale of the equipment under cl 12 of the leases.

[48] Harman J's order was not intended to prejudice these rights. In particular it was not intended to prejudice the appellants' claim to relief from forfeiture.

[49] If an order for relief from forfeiture were now made it could not revive the contractual rights enjoyed by the appellants under the finance leases. The equipment has been sold. The procedure envisaged by cl 12 can no longer be complied with. None the less the proceeds of sale of the equipment now stand in the place of the equipment.

[50] In these circumstances, and the court being satisfied that an order for relief from forfeiture would have been made if there had been no sale pursuant to Harman J's order, the respective rights that the appellants and the respondents would have had in the proceeds of a cl 12 sale should be given effect to by treating the proceeds of the sale under Harman J's order as the proceeds of a cl 12 sale.

[51] The parties have, very sensibly, agreed that the best price for which the equipment might have been sold under cl 12 should be taken to be £251,617 and that the respondents would have been entitled to 5% of that sum. It seems to me easy to conclude that, subject to account being taken of whatever financial conditions for relief from forfeiture would have been imposed by the court (such as payment of any rental arrears and payment of the costs of the application for relief), the respondents should receive 5% of £251,617 out of the sum in court with the balance going to the respondents.

[52] Accordingly, in agreement with Lord Millett and with his reasons for allowing the appeal, I too would allow the appeal and make the order that he proposes.

Appeal allowed.

Dilys Tausz   Barrister.

a Heaton and others v Axa Equity and Law Life Assurance Society plc and others

[2002] UKHL 15

b HOUSE OF LORDS

LORD BINGHAM OF CORNHILL, LORD MACKAY OF CLASHFERN, LORD STEYN, LORD HOPE
OF CRAIGHEAD AND LORD RODGER OF EARLSFERRY

11–13 MARCH, 25 APRIL 2002

Practice – Compromise of action – Linked actions – Whether agreement settling action
c against one party precluding claimants from bringing fresh but related action against
another party.

The claimants were the shareholders and directors of a company which was
engaged in the sale of investment products to the public as agent or
d representative of T Ltd. After the purchase of T Ltd's sales and marketing division
by the first defendant, the company entered into an agreement with the
defendants (the E&L agreement), by which it was appointed their representative
with a view to selling their financial products to the public. On the same day, the
company entered into an agreement with T Ltd (the T Ltd agreement) with a
view to enabling its representatives to continue to service T Ltd's clients.
e Subsequently, T Ltd summarily terminated that agreement, purportedly acting in
accordance with a term that permitted such termination if the representative
engaged in conduct prejudicial to T Ltd's business, and relying on alleged
misconduct by the company. A few days later, the defendants terminated the
E&L agreement, relying on the equivalent term in that agreement. The
f company brought proceedings for breach of contract against T Ltd, but not
against the defendants. The company later went into liquidation, and its rights of
action against both T Ltd and the defendants were assigned to the shareholders
who proceeded with the claim against T Ltd. In that action, the company
eventually alleged, inter alia, that the termination of the T Ltd agreement had
caused the termination of the E&L agreement, and sought damages for the loss
g of the value of its business, including the loss resulting from the termination of
the E&L agreement. T Ltd denied that it was responsible for the termination of that
agreement. Subsequently, it withdrew the allegations of misconduct and
conceded liability, but without withdrawing its denial of the allegation in respect
of the termination of the E&L agreement. The claim against T Ltd was settled
h by an agreement between the company, the shareholders and the successor to
T Ltd's business. The defendants were not parties to the agreement. Clause 2 of
the agreement provided that it was in full and final settlement of all claims and
potential claims which the parties might have against each other arising from, or
in connection with, the matters set out in cl 2.1. Those matters included the
termination of the E&L agreement. Under cl 5, the parties released and
j discharged each other from all claims in relation to the matters specified in cl 2.1.
The agreement contained no reference to any claims against the defendants.
Subsequently, the shareholders brought an action against the defendants,
claiming, inter alia, damages for breach of the E&L agreement and for negligence
in publishing unfair, inaccurate and untrue reports. The alleged loss and damage
included both the company's loss and that sustained by the shareholders in their
personal capacity, though with credit to be given for the sums recovered from

T Ltd under the settlement agreement. In their defence, the defendants relied, inter alia, on allegations of misconduct similar to those that had been made, and then withdrawn, by T Ltd. On the determination of a preliminary issue, the judge held that the settlement agreement precluded the shareholders from continuing the proceedings and he duly dismissed them. That decision was reversed by the Court of Appeal. On the defendants' appeal to the House of Lords, their Lordships considered the principles applicable in such a case.

Held – (1) In considering whether a sum accepted under a compromise agreement should be taken to fix the full measure of A's loss, so as to preclude action against C in tort in respect of the same damage, and so as to restrict any action against C in contract in respect of the same damage to a claim for nominal damages, the terms of the settlement agreement between A and B had to be the primary focus of attention, and the agreement had to be construed in its appropriate factual context. In construing it, various significant points had to be borne in mind. First, the release of one concurrent tortfeasor did not have the effect in law of releasing another concurrent tortfeasor and the release of one contract-breaker did not have the effect in law of releasing a successive contract-breaker. Secondly, an agreement made between A and B would not affect A's rights against C unless either A agreed to forgo or waive rights that he would otherwise enjoy against C, in which case his agreement was enforceable by B, or the agreement fell within the limited class of contracts that was enforceable by C as a third party. Thirdly, the use of clear and comprehensive language to preclude the pursuit of claims and cross-claims as between A and B had little bearing on the question whether the agreement represented the full measure of A's loss. The more inadequate the compensation agreed to be paid by B, the greater the need for B to protect himself against any possibility of further action by A to obtain a full measure of redress. Fourthly, while an express reservation by A of his right to sue C would fortify the inference that A was not treating the sum recovered from B as representing the full measure of his loss, the absence of such a reservation was of lesser and perhaps of no significance, since there was no need for A to reserve a right to do that which he was in the ordinary way fully entitled to do without any such reservation (see [9], [41], [56], [57], [69], [79], below).

(2) In the instant case, the settlement did not preclude the shareholders from pursuing their action against the defendants. The damage for which the defendants were responsible to the shareholders was the damage caused to them by the termination of the E&L agreement and the defendants' maintenance of their position with regard to the allegations on which the termination had been based. The claim against T Ltd had been in respect of its conduct and damage caused to the shareholders by that conduct. Although the contractual damages claimed in respect of the E&L agreement were wholly encompassed within the damages claimed in respect of the T Ltd agreement, the damage claimed against the defendants was not coincident with the damage claimed against T Ltd and there was nothing in the settlement to show the extent to which T Ltd accepted responsibility for the principal item of claim, namely the destruction of the company's business. It followed that the compromise agreement had not extinguished or exhausted the claims that the shareholders were entitled to pursue against the defendants. Accordingly, the appeal would be dismissed (see [10], [46]–[51], [55]–[57], [86], [87], below); *Jameson (exors of Jameson (decd)) v Central Electricity Generating Board (Babcock Energy Ltd, third party)* [1999] 1 All ER 193 explained and distinguished..

Decision of the Court of Appeal [2000] 4 All ER 673 affirmed.

a **Notes**

For the settlement or compromise of proceedings, see 37 *Halsbury's Laws* (4th edn reissue) para 902.

Cases referred to in opinions

Allison v KPMG Peat Marwick [2000] 1 NZLR 560, NZ CA.

b *Balfour v Archibald Baird & Sons Ltd* 1959 SC 64, Ct of Sess.

Balfour v William Beardmore & Co Ltd 1956 SLT 205, Ct of Sess.

Bank of Credit and Commerce International SA (in liq) v Ali [2001] UKHL 8, [2001] 1 All ER 961, [2001] 2 WLR 735.

Bryce v Swan Hunter Group plc [1988] 1 All ER 659.

Cape & Dalgleish (a firm) v Fitzgerald [2002] UKHL 16, [2002] All ER (D) 231 (Apr).

c *Crawford v Springfield Steel Co Ltd* (18 July 1958, unreported), Ct of Sess.

Crawford v William Beardmore & Co Ltd (30 April 1956, unreported).

Jameson (exors of Jameson (decd)) v Central Electricity Generating Board (Babcock Energy Ltd, third party) [1999] 1 All ER 193, [2000] 1 AC 455, [1999] 2 WLR 141, HL; *rvsg* [1997] 4 All ER 38, [1998] QB 323, [1997] 3 WLR 151, CA.

d *Steven v Broady Norman & Co Ltd* 1928 SC 351, Ct of Sess.

Tang Man Sit (decd) (personal representative) v Capacious Investments Ltd [1996] 1 All ER 193, [1996] AC 514, [1996] 2 WLR 192, PC.

Appeal

e The appellants, Axa Equity & Law Life Assurance Society plc and Axa Equity & Law Unit Trust Managers Ltd, appealed with permission of the Appeal Committee of the House of Lords given on 14 December 2000 from the order of the Court of Appeal (Beldam, Chadwick and Robert Walker LJJ) on 19 May 2000 ([2000] 4 All ER 673, [2001] Ch 173) allowing an appeal by the respondents, David Edgar Heaton, Robert Cheetham and Jack Taylor, from the order of Laddie J on 8 July f 1999 dismissing, on the determination of a preliminary issue, their proceedings against the appellants on the ground that they were precluded by an agreement settling a previous action to which the appellants had not been parties. The facts are set out in the opinion of Lord Mackay of Clashfern.

g *Jonathan Hirst QC* and *Neil Calver* (instructed by *Pinsent Curtis Biddle*, Birmingham) for the appellants.

Leslie Kosmin QC and *Andrew Tabachnik* (instructed by *M&S Solicitors Ltd*, Leicester) for the respondents.

h Their Lordships took time for consideration.

25 April 2002. The following opinions were delivered.

LORD BINGHAM OF CORNHILL.

j [1] My Lords, the issue in this appeal may be expressed in this way: if A, having sued B for damages for breach of contract, enters into a settlement with B expressed to be in full and final settlement of all its claims against B, is A thereafter precluded from pursuing against C a claim for damages for breach of another contract to the extent that this claim is for damages which formed part of A's claim against B? Expressed in another way, the issue is whether the majority decision of the House in *Jameson (exors of Jameson (decd)) v Central Electricity Generating Board (Babcock Energy Ltd, third party)* [1999] 1 All ER 193, [2000] 1 AC

455, properly understood, laid down any rule of law and, if so, whether that rule applies to successive contract-breakers as well as concurrent tortfeasors.

[2] The facts giving rise to these issues have been very fully recorded in the judgment of Chadwick LJ in the decision of the Court of Appeal ([2000] 4 All ER 673 at 676–684, [2001] Ch 173 at 180–188 (paras 3–27)), and are summarised in the opinion of my noble and learned friend Lord Mackay of Clashfern, whose summary I gratefully adopt and need not repeat. The issues in the appeal can, I think, be illuminated by resort to schematic examples.

[3] A brings an action against B claiming damages for negligence in tort. The claim goes to trial, and judgment is given for A for £x. There is no appeal and the judgment sum is paid by B to A. £x will thereafter be taken, in the ordinary way, to represent the full value of A's claim against B. A cannot thereafter maintain an action for damages for negligence in tort against C as a concurrent tortfeasor liable in respect of the same damage for two reasons: first, such a claim will amount to a collateral attack on the judgment already given; and secondly, A will be unable to allege or prove any damage, and damage is a necessary ingredient for a cause of action based on tortious negligence. A cannot maintain an action against C in contract either, in respect of the same damage, for the first reason which bars his tortious claim. There is however no reason of principle, in either case, on the assumptions made in this example, why B should not recover a contribution from C under the Civil Liability (Contribution) Act 1978 as a party liable with him for the same damage suffered by A.

[4] In a second example the facts are varied. A brings an action against B claiming damages for negligence in tort. The action does not proceed to judgment because B compromises A's claim by an agreement providing that he will pay A damages of £x, which he duly does. If £x is agreed or taken to represent the full value of A's claim against B, A cannot thereafter maintain an action against C in tort in respect of the same damage for the second reason given in the last paragraph, and although he is not precluded from pursuing a claim against C in contract in respect of the same damage he cannot claim or recover more than nominal damages. There is again, in the ordinary way, no reason of principle in either case, on the assumptions made in this example, why B should not recover a contribution from C under the 1978 Act as a party liable with him for the damage suffered by A.

[5] There is, however, an obvious difference between the action which culminates in judgment and the action which culminates in compromise: that whereas, save in an exceptional case (such as *Crawford v Springfield Steel Co Ltd* (18 July 1958, unreported) Lord Cameron), a judgment will conclusively decide the full measure of damage for which B is liable to A, a sum agreed to be paid under a compromise may or may not represent the full measure of B's liability to A. Where a sum is agreed which makes a discount for the risk of failure or for a possible finding of contributory negligence or for any other hazard of litigation, the compromise sum may nevertheless be regarded as the full measure of B's liability. But A may agree to settle with B for £x not because either party regards that sum as the full measure of A's loss but for many other reasons: it may be known that B is uninsured and £x represents the limit of his ability to pay; or A may wish to pocket a small sum in order to finance litigation against other parties; or it may be that A is old and ill and prefers to accept a small sum now rather than a larger sum years later; or it may be that there is a contractual or other limitation on B's liability to A. While it is just that A should be precluded from recovering substantial damages against C in a case where he has accepted a sum representing

a the full measure of his estimated loss, it is unjust that A should be so precluded where he has not.

[6] The majority decision of the House in *Jameson*'s case appears to have been understood by some as laying down a rule of law that A, having accepted and received a sum from B in full and final settlement of his claims against B in tort, is thereafter precluded from pursuing against C any claim which formed part of
b his claim against B. I do not think that my noble and learned friend Lord Hope of Craighead, in giving the opinion of the majority of the House, is to be so understood.

[7] Mr Jameson (A) had contracted lung cancer as a result of exposure to asbestos dust during his employment by B. He brought an action in negligence against B claiming damages. Very shortly before his death the claim was settled
c for £80,000, which was paid just after his death. It was appreciated that his claim on a full valuation was worth £130,000 but also that the outcome of the litigation was uncertain. About a year after his death, a claim on behalf of his widow was brought under the Fatal Accidents Act 1976 for damages for her loss of dependency. This second action was brought against C, in whose premises A had
d worked during some of the time when he had been exposed to asbestos dust during his employment by B. Section 4 of the 1976 Act, as substituted by s 3(1) of the Administration of Justice Act 1982, had the effect that the widow did not have, in estimating the value of her dependency, to give credit for the damages of £80,000 which she had inherited from A on his death. Thus, if the claim was maintainable, C would be potentially liable to the widow for a substantial sum
e and could look to B for contribution under the 1978 Act, and B would be potentially liable to contribute without any requirement that credit should be given for the £80,000 it had already paid. The widow could only maintain her claim against C if A, had he lived, would have been able to do so and it was held that A could not have done so because, by accepting £80,000 from B in full and final
f settlement of his claim, he had extinguished it and so had no claim which he could have pursued against C.

[8] This conclusion was reached by a number of steps which included the following. (1) Proof of damage is an essential step in establishing a claim in tortious negligence ([1999] 1 All ER 193 at 202, [2000] 1 AC 455 at 472). (2) Such a claim is a claim for unliquidated damages ([1999] 1 All ER 193 at 203, [2000] 1 AC
g 455 at 473, 474). (3) Such a claim is liquidated when either judgment is given for a specific sum or a specific sum is accepted in a compromise agreement ([1999] 1 All ER 193 at 203, 204, [2000] 1 AC 455 at 473, 474). (4) A judgment on such a claim will ordinarily be taken to fix the full measure of a claimant's loss ([1999] 1 All ER 193 at 203, 204 [2000] 1 AC 455 at 473, 474). (5) A sum accepted in
h settlement of such a claim may also fix the full measure of a claimant's loss ([1999] 1 All ER 193 at 203, 204, [2000] 1 AC 455 at 473, 474): whether it does so or not depends on the proper construction of the compromise agreement in its context ([1999] 1 All ER 193 at 203, 204, 206, [2000] 1 AC 455 at 473, 474, 476). (6) On the facts of A's case, the sum accepted from B in settlement was to be taken as representing the full measure of A's loss: it followed that A's claim in tortious
j negligence was extinguished and he had no claim which could be pursued against C ([1999] 1 All ER 193 at 206, [2000] 1 AC 455 at 476). I do not think the first four of these steps are controversial. The fifth proposition may perhaps have been stated a little too absolutely in *Jameson*'s case, but as expressed above I do not think it can be challenged. There was clearly room for more than one view, as the division of judicial opinion in *Jameson*'s case showed, whether the sum accepted in settlement by A was to be taken as representing the full measure of his loss, but

if it did the conclusion followed: A could not have proved damage, an essential
ingredient, in his action against C, and that was fatal to the widow's Fatal   *a*
Accidents Act claim against C.

[9] In considering whether a sum accepted under a compromise agreement
should be taken to fix the full measure of A's loss, so as to preclude action against
C in tort in respect of the same damage, and so as to restrict any action against C in
contract in respect of the same damage to a claim for nominal damages, the terms   *b*
of the settlement agreement between A and B must be the primary focus of
attention, and the agreement must be construed in its appropriate factual context.
In construing it various significant points must in my opinion be borne clearly in
mind. (1) The release of one concurrent tortfeasor does not have the effect in law
of releasing another concurrent tortfeasor and the release of one contract-breaker
does not have the effect in law of releasing a successive contract-breaker. (2) An   *c*
agreement made between A and B will not affect A's rights against C unless either
(a) A agrees to forgo or waive rights which he would otherwise enjoy against C,
in which case his agreement is enforceable by B, or (b) the agreement falls within
that limited class of contracts which either at common law or by virtue of the
Contracts (Rights of Third Parties) Act 1999 is enforceable by C as a third party.   *d*
(3) The use of clear and comprehensive language to preclude the pursuit of
claims and cross-claims as between A and B has little bearing on the question
whether the agreement represents the full measure of A's loss. The more
inadequate the compensation agreed to be paid by B, the greater the need for B
to protect himself against any possibility of further action by A to obtain a full
measure of redress. (4) While an express reservation by A of his right to sue C   *e*
will fortify the inference that A is not treating the sum recovered from B as
representing the full measure of his loss, the absence of such a reservation is of
lesser and perhaps of no significance, since there is no need for A to reserve a right
to do that which A is in the ordinary way fully entitled to do without any such
reservation. (5) If B, on compromising A's claim, wishes to protect himself   *f*
against any claim against him by C claiming contribution, he may achieve that
end either (a) by obtaining an enforceable undertaking by A not to pursue any
claim against C relating to the subject matter of the compromise, or (b) by
obtaining an indemnity from A against any liability to which B may become
subject relating to the subject matter of the compromise. In my consideration of
this matter I have gained much assistance from the clear and illuminating   *g*
judgments of the New Zealand Court of Appeal in *Allison v KPMG Peat Marwick*
[2000] 1 NZLR 560 and from the perceptive critique of *Jameson's* case in Foskett
The Law and Practice of Compromise (5th edn, 2002) pp 119–125, paras 6-42–6-57.

[10] For reasons given by my noble and learned friend Lord Mackay of
Clashfern I do not conclude, on construing the compromise agreement made in   *h*
this case, that it is to be taken as representing the full measure of the respondents'
loss agreed between the parties to the compromise. The liquidator of Inter City
had assigned to the respondents Inter City's claims against Equity & Law as well
as against Target, but on terms that Inter City's creditors and the liquidator's
costs were to be paid out of any sums recovered in preference to the respondents'
claims. Target never withdrew its denial that it was responsible for loss caused   *j*
by termination of the Equity & Law agreement. When the compromise
agreement was made, Equity & Law was not a party to it and did not contribute
to the £10m paid in settlement, and no reference to the respondents' claims
against it was made in the compromise agreement although the Equity & Law
agreement (dealing with new business) was much more significant than the
Target agreement. The respondents had notified Equity & Law of their intention

a to plead claims for damages for wrongful termination of the Equity & Law agreement in the action commenced by Equity & Law, and it cannot have been thought that they intended to leave themselves defenceless in that action. Equity & Law had never accepted that its summary termination of the Equity & Law agreement had been unjustified: it must have been apparent that the rehabilitation in business of the respondents depended on their showing or securing agreement *b* that it had. There was nothing in the terms of the compromise agreement or in the relevant surrounding circumstances to suggest that the respondents entered into that agreement in full and final satisfaction of all their claims not only against Target but against Equity & Law as well. It follows that the compromise agreement did not extinguish or exhaust the claims which the respondents were entitled to pursue against Equity & Law. I agree with my noble and learned *c* friend Lord Mackay that for the reasons he gives, with which I fully agree, and also for the short reasons given above, this appeal should be dismissed.

LORD MACKAY OF CLASHFERN.

[11] My Lords, this is an appeal against the decision of the Court of Appeal *d* dated 19 May 2000 allowing the respondents' appeal against the decision of Laddie J on 8 July 1999 dismissing, on a trial of a preliminary issue, the respondents' action against the appellants.

[12] The respondents are the shareholders, and were formerly the directors, of Glyne Investments Ltd, which traded under the name of 'Inter City'. Inter City was engaged in the sale of investment products to members of the public as agent *e* or representative for Target Life Assurance Co Ltd (Target) and Target's associated company National Financial Management Corp plc (NFMC).

[13] By agreement dated 25 April 1991 the first appellant purchased the sales and marketing division of Target and NFMC. Pursuant to that agreement, and by special arrangement with Lautro (the Life Assurance and Unit Trust *f* Regulatory Organisation) the appellants established a joint marketing group with Target and NFNC (the marketing group).

[14] Following Lautro's approval of the joint marketing group, Target and NMFC closed to new business on 30 June 1991 and on 4 July 1991 Inter City entered into appointed representative agreements with Target (the Target agreement) and with the appellants (the Equity & Law agreement).

g [15] Under the Equity & Law agreement, Inter City was made an appointed representative of the appellants with a view to selling the appellants' financial products to members of the public. Under the Target agreement, Inter City was made an appointed representative of Target and NFMC with a view to enabling its representatives to continue to service Target/NFMC clients (since Target and *h* NFMC had closed to new business there were no further Target/NFMC financial products to sell). The Target agreement, which referred to the fact that the appellants, Target and NFMC were members of the joint marketing group, incorporated the terms of the Equity & Law agreement, save in relation to three specified matters which are not relevant to the present appeal. Also on 4 July 1991 the respondents were each appointed by the appellants, Target and NFMC *j* to be company representatives of the appellants, Target and NFMC for the purposes of the Lautro rules, and were separately appointed as company representatives by Inter City.

[16] On 29 January 1993 Target (incorporating NFMC) gave notice to Inter City terminating the Target agreement with immediate effect under cl 8.1.2, which permitted summary termination if the appointed representative or a company representative engaged in conduct which in the absolute opinion of

Target/NFMC was or was likely to be prejudicial to the business of Target/NFMC. As a result of this termination, Inter City lost its status as an appointed representative of Target/NFMC, and the respondents lost their status as company representatives of these companies. Target sought to justify this summary termination on the grounds that Inter City had been 'churning' business. The letter of termination alleged that Inter City had 'consistently failed to comply with Lautro regulations and have used sales techniques which in our opinion bring into disrepute the name of and the goodwill of Target'. Notice of the termination of the Target agreement was given to Lautro and to the appellants. 'Churning' is a description of a technique by which clients are persuaded to terminate an existing financial product and replace it with a new product as a result of which the person who made this arrangement on behalf of the seller of the financial product receives higher commission than he would do if the existing financial product had been continued.

[17] By letter dated 8 February 1993, the appellants summarily terminated the Equity & Law agreement under cl 8.1.2 of the Equity & Law agreement. The letter did not identify any particular provision under cl 8.1.2 or give any reason for the termination. As a result of this termination, Inter City lost its status as an appointed representative of the appellants and the respondents lost their status as company representatives of the appellants.

[18] By writ issued on 1 March 1993 Inter City sued Target for a declaration that Target remained liable to Inter City for commission under the Target agreement notwithstanding the purported termination of the Target agreement. The appellants were never made parties to the Target proceedings.

[19] On 8 April 1993 Target served a defence and counterclaim in the Target proceedings alleging that Inter City had been caught 'churning' business. Target purported to justify the summary termination of the Target agreement on the grounds of Inter City's alleged churning, and Target counterclaimed £3,330,000 (later reduced to about £1,765,000) which it said it would be required by Lautro to offer as compensation to those investors who had been subjected to 'churning' by Inter City.

[20] On 20 February 1996 the court ordered the trial of preliminary issues in the Target proceedings. The preliminary issues ordered to be tried were: (1) whether Target's termination of the Target agreement was unlawful; (2) whether Target's refusal thereafter to pay renewal commissions earned by Inter City was unlawful; and (3) whether Inter City was liable in damages to Target for breach of the Target agreement. The central question for purposes of determining these preliminary issues was whether Inter City and the respondents had engaged in churning as alleged by Target.

[21] Before the hearing of the preliminary issue in the Target proceedings, Inter City had on 18 July 1996 commenced a creditors' voluntary winding up on the basis that by reason of its liabilities it was insolvent and unable to pay its debts. Inter City was unable to continue trading because its income from renewal commissions had been withheld and serious allegations of misselling were being pursued against it and its company representatives.

[22] Also on 18 July 1996 Inter City, acting by its liquidator, assigned to the respondents (who were its directors and shareholders) the full and exclusive benefit of all Inter City's rights of action against Target arising out of or in connection with the termination of the Target agreement, and against the appellants arising out of or in connection with the termination of the Equity & Law agreement. The assignment was made on terms that any monies received by the respondents in pursuance of their rights under the assignment should first

a be applied in full satisfaction of Inter City's creditors and the liquidator's costs, with the balance being available to the respondents for their own benefit. On 29 July 1996 the respondents were substituted for Inter City as plaintiffs in the Target proceedings. The respondents were granted legal aid to pursue the Target proceedings.

b [23] The trial of the preliminary issues in the Target proceedings came before Moses J in June 1997. On the tenth day of the hearing, Target unreservedly withdrew all of its allegations of churning and serious misconduct and conceded liability. In his judgment Moses J was highly critical of Target and observed that the result of Target's allegations and the termination of the Target agreement was that Inter City had gone into liquidation, that many dependent on Inter City had lost their jobs and that the respondents were placed in great personal c difficulties as well as having difficulties in finding further work. Moses J ordered that the preliminary issues be determined in the respondents' favour and that Target's counterclaim be dismissed and that Target should pay the respondents' costs of the Target proceedings on an indemnity basis.

d [24] On 29 September 1997 Target (by then known as Hill Samuel Life Assurance Ltd) wrote to the Personal Investment Authority (the PIA) to notify the PIA of the outcome of the trial of the preliminary issues and to withdraw unreservedly all allegations which had been made by Target against Inter City.

[25] Meanwhile on 8 September 1997 the respondents had amended the reamended statement of claim in the Target proceedings to include claims under e the heading 'Destruction of the Plaintiff's Business'. They pleaded that Target's unlawful termination of the Target agreement was the 'effective and dominant' cause of, amongst other things, the termination of the Equity & Law agreement by the appellants and their refusal to pay any further commissions to Inter City. This was denied by Target who contended that the appellants had 'conducted their own investigation' and had 'exercised an independent judgment in deciding f to terminate the Equity & Law agreement'. The respondents set out the losses said to have been suffered by Inter City as a result of the unlawful termination of the Target agreement. The losses pleaded included the loss of the value of the business of Inter City as a going concern, which included the loss of the commissions which had been withheld by the appellants consequent upon the g termination of the Equity & Law agreement.

[26] With a view to identifying the whole of the claim with which Target was faced, the respondents prepared a draft statement of claim in a further proposed action against Target which they sent to Target's solicitors on 3 February 1998. This statement contained claims by the respondents acting both in their own h right and as assignees of Inter City's rights for damages in tort and for breach of contract in connection with the preparation and publication by Target of reports and references concerning Inter City and the respondents after the termination of the Target agreement. In that draft statement it was further alleged that it was foreseeable, by reason of the publication by Target of untrue references and reports, that amongst other things (1) the respondents would be unable to obtain j employment in the financial services industry or elsewhere in responsible management positions and (2) Equity & Law would terminate the Equity & Law agreement. In para 37 it was alleged that these things in fact occurred, and in para 38 it was alleged that by reason of the termination of the Target agreement and the Equity & Law agreement and the provision of untrue and inaccurate references, the respondents each suffered substantial personal losses and damages.

[27] By written agreement dated 23 April 1998 which was incorporated as a
schedule to a consent order in the Target proceedings staying the Target
proceedings, the respondents and Inter City acting by its liquidator agreed terms
of settlement with Target, which had by then become Abbey Life Assurance Co Ltd
(the settlement agreement). The appellants were not parties to the settlement
agreement. The terms of this agreement are crucial to the decision of the issue
between the parties in this appeal.

[28] On 4 November 1993 and consequent upon the termination of the Equity &
Law agreement on 8 February 1993, the first appellant commenced High Court
proceedings against Inter City and the respondents for the repayment of advance
commissions in the sum of £25,012.02 (plus interest) which had been paid
pursuant to the Equity & Law agreement.

[29] In a letter dated 2 November 1993 the respondents' solicitors had said that
whether or not the advance commissions were repayable, Inter City and the
respondents had a substantial set-off and counterclaim against the appellants for
the wrongful termination of the Equity & Law agreement, with the result that
Inter City and the respondents denied liability to the first appellant in the 1993
action.

[30] On 22 December 1993 the first appellant erroneously obtained judgment
in default against Inter City and the respondents in that action and this
judgment was set aside by consent on 1 September 1997. No defence and
counterclaim was served in this action and it became dormant. Nevertheless, the
first appellant made a claim in Inter City's liquidation based on the judgment debt
(since set aside), and the first appellant's claim for repayment of the advance
commissions is, as confirmed by the liquidator, still a contingent claim in Inter
City's liquidation. The claim for repayment advanced in the 1993 action which
with interest now totals over £32,000 was incorporated into the appellants'
counterclaim in the present proceedings. The appellants have confirmed that if
the respondents are not entitled to pursue the present proceedings the appellants
will not pursue the 1993 action nor their counterclaim in these proceedings, and
the appellants will not seek to prove or continue to prove in Inter City's
liquidation.

[31] Following inconclusive correspondence the present proceedings were
commenced by writ issued on 23 November 1998. The respondents claim on
their own behalves and as assignees of Inter City. The validity of the assignment
was challenged by the appellants, with the result that a protective writ in the
name of Inter City was issued on 3 February 1999. By order dated 26 April 1999
the two sets of proceedings were consolidated.

[32] The claims against the appellants in the writs are for (1) damages for
breach of the Equity & Law agreement, (2) damages for negligence in publishing
from and after 8 February 1993 unfair, inaccurate and untrue reports and
references in respect of Inter City / the respondents, (3) in the alternative damages
for breach of contract in respect of the same publications, (4) an order that the
appellants supply the respondents with a list identifying to whom they had
published reports / references, (5) an order that the appellants issue a corrective
statement retracting the errors and inaccuracies in the reports or references
published, and (6) a declaration that the appellants remain liable to pay Inter City
commissions on investment contracts introduced by Inter City, notwithstanding
the termination of the Equity & Law agreement, and an order for payment of
these commissions.

[33] The statement of claim sets out loss and damage claimed as a result of
the appellants not paying the commissions said to be owed to Inter City and the

a respondents, the loss and damage suffered by Inter City as a result of the appellants' alleged unlawful conduct, and the loss and damage claimed by the respondents in their personal capacities as a consequence of the appellants' alleged unlawful conduct. The respondents say that they will give the appellants appropriate credit for the sums recovered by the respondents from Target. The total sum recovered by the respondents from Target was £10m. The balance of the respondents'

b claim which is now being pursued by them in these proceedings is said by the respondents to be worth at least £8m.

[34] The appellants, in their defence and counterclaim served on 1 February 1999, alleged that their termination of the Equity & Law agreement was lawful on the grounds that Inter City had been engaged in the improper conduct of churning Target investment policies into Equity & Law investment policies. By

c a letter dated 22 February 1999 the appellants refused to withdraw their allegation of churning at this stage and observed that if the allegations are proved, then it may be right that they should affect the respondents' reputation and integrity. The appellants have continued at all times thereafter to maintain their allegation of churning against the respondents and did so particularly in the

d hearing before the Court of Appeal. They declined to alter this position at the hearing before your Lordships. Although the appellants' position is that no further reports or references were given by them in respect of Inter City or the respondents after 1994 by letter dated 29 July 1999, the second respondent's application to become an appointed representative introducer of Allied Dunbar Financial Advisers Ltd was refused on the ground that—

e

'the outstanding and to date, unresolved, issues with your previous financial services host company need to be resolved and finalised in order to meet the referencing requirements we undertake prior to issuing introducer contracts.'

f The unresolved issues referred to are with the appellants.

[35] On 27 January 1999 the appellants commenced third party proceedings against Target. These proceedings have not got beyond the issuing of a third party notice and have been stayed by consent pending the resolution of the preliminary issue in the main proceedings.

g [36] The preliminary issue ordered to be tried is in these terms:

'What is the consequence for the plaintiffs' claims in these proceedings of the settlement contained within the order dated 23 April 1998 in the High Court Queen's Bench Division ... made between the plaintiffs and Abbey Life Assurance Co Ltd and satisfied by the payment of £10m paid hereunder.'

h [37] The preliminary issue was tried before Laddie J, who on 8 July 1999 declared that the consequence for the respondents' claims in these proceedings of the settlement agreement was that the respondents were precluded from continuing the proceedings, and ordered that the proceedings be dismissed. Laddie J gave permission to the respondents to appeal.

j [38] On 19 May 2000 the Court of Appeal ([2000] 4 All ER 673, [2001] Ch 173) unanimously allowed the respondents' appeal, the consequence of the Court of Appeal's order being that the settlement agreement does not inhibit the respondents from pursuing their claims in these proceedings against the appellants (save to the extent acknowledged in para 80 of the statement of claim that appropriate credit is to be given to the appellants for the recoveries made from Target).

[39] At first sight it would appear that the respondents are entitled to sue the appellants for any damage that they have suffered as a result of what they allege is the unlawful termination of the Equity & Law agreement on 8 February 1993. That agreement was a separate agreement from the target agreement. It was founded on allegations of improper dealings by the respondents which allegations have been adhered to up until the present time although Target has unreservedly withdrawn the allegations that Target had made to a similar effect in support of their termination of the Target agreement. The appellants were not parties to the settlement agreement between Target and the respondents. The submission that the settlement agreement precludes the respondents carrying on the present proceedings is based on the decision of your Lordships' House in *Jameson (exors of Jameson (decd))* v *Central Electricity Generating Board (Babcock Energy Ltd, third party)* [1999] 1 All ER 193, [2000] 1 AC 455.

[40] That case concerned Mr Jameson who a few days before his death had agreed to accept £80,000 from his former employer Babcock Energy Ltd 'in full and final settlement and satisfaction of all the causes of action in respect of which the plaintiff claimed in the statement of claim'. These were for negligence and/or breach of statutory duty in causing the disease of malignant mesothelioma from which he died by exposing him to asbestos at various premises at which he had been employed, including those of the defendant, for whom his employer had undertaken work. The fatal disease might have been caused by the negligence or breach of statutory duty of either or both of the employer and the defendant. If the employer was liable for causing the disease he was liable for the full extent of the damage which Mr Jameson suffered.

[41] If the defendant was liable the damage caused by its negligence or breach of statutory duty would be included in the damage for which the employer was liable as the exposure at the defendant's premises was included in the exposure which Mr Jameson had suffered in his employment. The £80,000 was significantly less than the full liability value of the claim and in argument it was pointed out that the difficulties of establishing liability in negligence or breach of statutory duty against an employer for exposure to asbestos going back to the 1950s giving rise to mesothelioma were illustrated in a case such as *Bryce* v *Swan Hunter Group plc* [1988] 1 All ER 659. The House by majority held that Mr Jameson's agreement in the settlement to which I have referred precluded a claim by him against the defendant. Lord Browne-Wilkinson and Lord Hoffmann agreed with Lord Hope of Craighead whose detailed speech supported that result. Lord Clyde also delivered a detailed speech supporting the result but on somewhat different grounds and Lord Lloyd of Berwick dissented. I read the majority decision as authority for the proposition that where an action is founded on specified damage suffered by the claimant and the existence of that damage is essential to the success of the action, if the claimant has entered into an agreement under which he accepts a sum as full compensation for that damage, the action cannot proceed. Whether a particular agreement has that effect is a question of construction of the words, in the light of all the relevant facts surrounding it.

[42] The argument for the appellants before your Lordships is substantially that the decision in *Jameson's* case precludes the present action against them just as the settlement in Mr Jameson's case precluded an action by him against the CEGB. The principal clause of the agreement by which the Target proceedings was settled is so far as material in these terms:

'This agreement is in full and final settlement of all claims and potential claims of whatsoever nature and kind (including interest and costs) which the parties have or may have against each other under or in respect of or arising out of or in connection with, whether directly or indirectly:

(1) the termination on 29 January 1993 of the Target agreement ...

(2) the termination on 8 February 1993 of the Equity & Law agreement ...

(3) the personal references, reports and statements made to third parties that were provided in respect of any of the claimants following the termination of any of the Target agreement and the Equity & Law agreement (or either of them);

(4) the matters at issue in action number 1993-G-No.-610 [that is an action about commissions];

(5) any claims or matters identified in the draft statement of claim provided by the plaintiffs' solicitors to the defendants' solicitors under cover of a letter sent on or about 3 February 1998; and without prejudice to the generality of the foregoing, the parties hereto agree not to commence or prosecute any proceedings against one another arising out of or in connection with such matters.'

[43] Clause 3 is a confidentiality clause which does not provide for disclosure of the settlement agreement to the appellants. Clause 5 is in these terms:

'Each of the parties hereto hereby unconditionally and irrevocably releases and discharges each other, and their respective directors, officers and employees from all or any liabilities, actions, causes of action, suits, demands of whatever nature ... in relation to or in any way connected with the matters specified in clause 2.1 above.'

[44] The agreement contains no reference to any claims against the appellants.

[45] The contractual damages for the destruction of Inter City's business claimed in the Equity & Law action in respect of the termination of the Equity & Law agreement are wholly encompassed within the damages claimed in respect of the termination of the Target agreement. Indeed the Target claim was more extensive than the Equity & Law claim but it included all items of loss which are now claimed against Equity & Law under this general head. There are minor differences between the parallel claims made in this action and those in the Target action referred to by Chadwick LJ in the Court of Appeal. At the hearing before your Lordships, counsel for the respondents was content to accept that the claims for money in respect of those matters in both actions were the same. There are claims in the Equity & Law action which were not made against Target. These are the claims in respect of Equity & Law's refusal to withdraw or correct what was said to be the unfair and untrue allegations of churning and other serious misconduct. It has not been suggested that the appellants here were responsible for any damage caused by the termination of the Target agreement but it was alleged against Target that if the Target agreement was terminated Target should have had in contemplation that the Equity & Law agreement would be terminated in consequence.

[46] In my opinion the damage on which the present action against the appellants is based is damage following on their termination of the Equity & Law agreement and the position which they have taken up and maintained in respect of allegations of churning and other serious misconduct. Similar allegations by Target made at an earlier stage were as I have said withdrawn unreservedly before the Target settlement was made.

[47] In my opinion the damage for which Equity & Law are responsible to the respondents is the damage caused to them by the termination of the Equity &

Law agreement and Equity & Law's maintenance of their position with regard to the allegations on which that termination was based to which they have adhered up until the present time. The claim against Target which has been settled was in respect of Target's conduct and the damage occasioned to the respondents by that. I cannot see that the decision of this House in *Jameson's* case provides any basis for saying that the action against the present appellants should not proceed. It is true that the contractual damages claimed in respect of the termination of the Equity & Law agreement are wholly encompassed within the damages claimed in respect of the termination of the Target agreement. The respondents here accept as I have already mentioned that they must give credit for sums paid by Target in respect of matters covered in the claims against the present appellants.

[48] In respect of the claim for destruction of Inter City's business I do not find it possible to extract from the agreement with Target the inference that Target were necessarily accepting the full responsibility for that destruction and it is perfectly possible to read the settlement as a settlement of the claim for Target's part in that destruction not necessarily amounting to the full responsibility for that destruction.

[49] The claim that Target is responsible in damages for the consequences of the termination of the Equity & Law agreement was denied in their defences by Target. That denial was not withdrawn as part of the settlement. The claims against the appellants were the subject of a separate head in the assignation of Inter City's claims to the respondents. There was a separate action in court at the instance of the appellants against the respondents. The appellants had a contingent claim in the liquidation of Inter City. Although there is a provision in the settlement agreement protecting directors and employees of Target, there is no mention whatever of the appellants, and it appears that these appellants made no contribution whatever to the funds required to be paid by Target under the settlement.

[50] In *Jameson's* case, if his employer had responsibility for the damage caused to him by exposure to asbestos the employer was responsible for the whole of that damage and that damage was the sole basis of the claim. Here, as I have said, the damage claimed against the appellants is not coincident with the damage claimed against Target which was the subject of the settlement and there is nothing in the Target settlement to show the extent to which Target accepted responsibility for the principal item of claim, namely the destruction of the Inter City business.

[51] For these reasons I conclude that the Target settlement does not preclude the present action against the appellants.

[52] I consider that the action should proceed and in the ordinary way an assessment should be made of the various claims and a value put upon them at the trial. If the total amount awarded in respect of the heads of damage that are dealt with in the Target settlement exceed the amount of approximately £5m appropriated to them in the Target settlement the award to the respondents would be the difference allocated between Inter City and the individual respondents in proportion to their claims. If the amount awarded is less than £5m this case will have been shown to be unnecessary so far as these heads of claim are concerned and no doubt this would be appropriately reflected in the awards of costs.

[53] In this action, the respondents claim:

'An order that the defendants issue a corrective statement forthwith retracting any and all errors and inaccuracies in such reports or references in

a
such terms as are approved by the plaintiffs (such approval not to be unnecessarily withheld), and that the defendants do thereafter, at their own expense, supply such corrective statement to each of the parties listed pursuant to [the previous paragraph in the statement of claim which referred to a list of those to whom the defendants made these reports or references].'

b
[54] Apart from provisions in the statutory scheme for settlement of a defamation action into which a defendant enters voluntarily, this claim is without precedent. It was supported by counsel for the respondents on the basis that the court should fashion a remedy for breach of contract suitable to the circumstances. He accepted that a declaration could serve the purpose required. In my opinion, that is the appropriate remedy, if the relevant claims of fact in the action are proved. Even if the court so holds, the appellants might still genuinely

c
believe the contrary and the court has no power to order a party to make a statement which he does not accept as true, however unreasonable the court may hold his non-acceptance to be. I would make it a condition of further progress if this claim is to be pursued that it be framed as a claim for an appropriate declaration.

d
[55] For these reasons I am of opinion that this appeal should be dismissed.

LORD STEYN.

[56] My Lords, I have read the opinions of my noble and learned friends Lord Bingham of Cornhill and Lord Mackay of Clashfern. I agree that this appeal

e
should be dismissed for the reasons they have given.

LORD HOPE OF CRAIGHEAD.

[57] My Lords, I have had the advantage of reading in draft the speeches of my noble and learned friends Lord Bingham of Cornhill, Lord Mackay of Clashfern and Lord Rodger of Earlsferry. I agree that the appeal should be

f
dismissed for the reasons which they have given.

LORD RODGER OF EARLSFERRY.

[58] My Lords, I gratefully adopt the account of the facts given by my noble and learned friend Lord Mackay of Clashfern. In light of it I can summarise the

g
main points.

[59] The respondents claim damages from AXA Equity & Law Life Assurance Society plc (Equity & Law) for loss which they allege was caused by Equity & Law's breach of contract and negligence. The respondents sue both as individuals and as the assignees of Glyne Investments Ltd which traded under the name Inter

h
City (Inter City). In connection with the same events Inter City had previously sued the Target Life Assurance Co Ltd (Target) for damages for breach of contract. Inter City's rights in that action were assigned to the respondents and it proceeded in their name. In April 1998 the action was settled by a compromise agreement and subsequent Tomlin order. In terms of the settlement Target paid the respondents £10m. The respondents did not, as individuals, raise proceedings

j
against Target but, when the settlement of Inter City's claim against Target was being negotiated, a draft statement was drawn up setting out this aspect of the respondents' claim. It is common ground that, when the settlement was reached, it took account of the claims of both Inter City and the individual respondents. As counsel for Equity & Law put it, the statement of claim in the present action is, in effect, an amalgamation of the amended statement of claim for Inter City against Target and the draft statement of claim for the respondents as

individuals against Target. In that situation Equity & Law argue, on the basis of *Jameson (exors of Jameson (decd)) v Central Electricity Generating Board (Babcock Energy Ltd, third party)* [1999] 1 All ER 193, [2000] 1 AC 455, that the settlement with Target precludes the respondents from pursuing their claims in the present proceedings against Equity & Law.

[60] In *Jameson's* case Mr Jameson had been employed by Babcock Energy Ltd (Babcock) between October 1953 and 1958. During that time he had worked at various places, including two power stations owned and occupied by the Central Electricity Generating Board (CEGB). In the course of his work on the CEGB sites and elsewhere Mr Jameson was exposed to asbestos for relatively short periods. In 1987 he was diagnosed as suffering from malignant mesothelioma. He raised proceedings against Babcock in tort for damages for causing his illness. The defendants paid £75,000 into court and, soon after, just before Mr Jameson died, the proceedings were settled for the sum of £80,000 plus costs. The balance of the sum and costs due under the settlement was paid to Mr Jameson's solicitors five days after his death when the court pronounced a Tomlin order giving effect to the settlement. At the time of the settlement between Mr Jameson and Babcock 'the view of both parties' advisors was that the claim, including that for future loss of income, was worth about £130,000 if it were to succeed on liability, a valuation which the judge [in the proceedings against CEGB] said was reasonable'. On the other hand, both advisors took the view that there were weaknesses in the claim, mainly because of the short periods of exposure to asbestos and because of doubts as to whether the dangers of exposure to asbestos had been sufficiently widely known at the time (see [1997] 4 All ER 38 at 44, [1998] QB 323 at 332 per Auld LJ). In due course Mr Jameson's executors raised proceedings against CEGB under the Fatal Accidents Act 1976 for his widow's loss of dependency. In terms of s 1(1) as amended they could do so only if CEGB were a person who 'would have been liable' to an action of damages for negligence and breach of statutory duty at the instance of Mr Jameson 'if death had not ensued'. By a majority, your Lordships' House held that CEGB would not have been liable to an action of damages at the instance of Mr Jameson since the effect of the settlement, when it had been implemented in full by Babcock, was to discharge the claim of damages against 'the other concurrent tortfeasors' (see [1999] 1 All ER 193 at 207, [2000] 1 AC 455 at 478). They accordingly allowed the appeal and held that the executors' claim against CEGB was barred by Mr Jameson's settlement with Babock.

[61] As that brief summary shows, the issue in *Jameson's* case was whether, having settled proceedings against one tortfeasor for less than the value of the claim if liability had been established, Mr Jameson could have sued another tortfeasor for damages on the ground that the tort of the second tortfeasor was also a cause of his mesothelioma. Here, by contrast, the question is whether the respondents, having settled proceedings for their loss caused by Target's breach of contract, can sue Equity & Law for part of that loss, on the basis that the alleged breach of contract by Equity & Law was also a cause of that part of their loss. In *Jameson's* case the two sets of proceedings would have been against separate but concurrent tortfeasors for causing the mesothelioma; here the two sets of proceedings are against companies who are alleged to have committed separate and overlapping breaches of contract which caused the part of the respondents' loss claimed in the proceedings against Equity & Law. As I explain in more detail below, the respondents' position in the action against Target was that their breach of contract had led to Equity & Law's breach of contract in terminating the Equity & Law agreement.

a   [62] In *Jameson's* case there was a finding as to the value of Mr Jameson's claim for damages if Babcock had been found liable. In the present case, however, there is no similar finding as to the full value of the respondents' claim against Target: the respondents simply contend that their overall loss from the breaches of contract by Target and Equity & Law is £18m.

    [63] The decision in *Jameson's* case has been criticised—for example, in *Foskett,*
b   *The Law and Practice of Compromise* (5th edn, 2002) p 122, para 6-49 and by the New Zealand Court of Appeal in *Allison v KPMG Peat Marwick* [2000] 1 NZLR 560. The respondents' written case foreshadowed a possible challenge to *Jameson's* case on the basis of these criticisms. In the event, however, counsel did not argue that it had been wrongly decided. Both sides proceeded on the basis that *Jameson's* case was correctly decided: inevitably, however, each had a different view as to its
c   effect in the present circumstances. In particular, as part of his argument, counsel for the respondents contended that the decision in *Jameson's* case applied only to concurrent tortfeasors and should not be extended so as to apply in the case of concurrent or overlapping contract-breakers causing the same loss.

    [64] In giving the decision of the majority in *Jameson's* case my noble and
d   learned friend Lord Hope of Craighead started from the statement of Lord Nicholls of Birkenhead in *Tang Man Sit (decd) (personal representative) v Capacious Investments Ltd* [1996] 1 All ER 193 at 199, [1996] AC 514 at 522. Discussing the limitations on a plaintiff's freedom to sue successively two or more persons who are liable to him concurrently, Lord Nicholls said:

e   'A third limitation is that a plaintiff cannot recover in the aggregate from one or more defendants an amount in excess of his loss. Part satisfaction of a judgment against one person does not operate as a bar to the plaintiff thereafter bringing an action against another who is also liable, but it does operate to reduce the amount recoverable in the second action. However, once a plaintiff has fully recouped his loss, of necessity he cannot thereafter
f   pursue any other remedy he might have and which he might have pursued earlier. Having recouped the whole of his loss, any further proceedings would lack a subject matter. This principle of full satisfaction prevents double recovery.'

g   Statements of the law to the same effect are to be found in Erskine's *Institute of the Law of Scotland* III.1.15, *Steven v Broady Norman & Co Ltd* 1928 SC 351 and *Balfour v Archibald Baird & Sons Ltd* 1959 SC 64. As Lord Justice-Clerk Thomson observed in *Balfour's* case (at 73) if the pursuer—

        'has invited a competent court to give him full satisfaction for the loss
h   sustained by him and if he is awarded damages on that footing that is an end of it. He has got all he is entitled to.'

    [65] It is not only a judgment that can have the effect of extinguishing the relevant loss: if one tortfeasor settles the victim's claim by paying him a sum which fully satisfies his right to damages for loss and injury, the victim cannot
j   then sue any concurrent tortfeasor for damages for the same loss and injury. In *Allison v KPMG Peat Marwick* [2000] 1 NZLR 560 at 589 (para 134) Thomas J put the point in this way:

        'Satisfaction discharges the loss. It is in the nature of an executed judgment in its effect. The loss no longer exists. There is nothing left for anyone to sue on; the injury or loss has been satisfied. As between the parties there is no problem. Where the co-defendants are concurrent tortfeasors, however,

concurrently liable on a different cause of action, the satisfaction of one
obligation cannot in itself discharge the other obligation. The concurrent *a*
tortfeasor will be released only if the satisfaction satisfies the injury or loss
which flows from his or her separate cause of action. Its extinction is then
independent of the agreement between the plaintiff and the defendant.
Simply put, no injury or loss exists on which to sue.'

[66] In *Jameson's* case [1999] 1 All ER 193 at 202, [2000] 1 AC 455 at 472 *b*
Lord Hope stated the main issue in the case in these terms:

'So the first question which arises on the facts of this case is whether
satisfaction for this purpose is achieved where the plaintiff agrees to accept a
sum from one of the alleged concurrent tortfeasors which is expressed to be
in full and final settlement of his claim against that tortfeasor, if that sum is *c*
less than the amount which a judge would have held to be the amount of the
damages which were due to him if the case had gone to trial and the
defendant had been found liable.'

He answered this question by holding that a settlement, even though for less than
the amount that a judge would have awarded on full liability, could constitute *d*
satisfaction of a plaintiff's claim with the effect of preventing him from suing any
other tortfeasor for the same loss and injury. The significance of the agreement
would be found in the effect which the parties intended to give it. The meaning
which was to be given to the agreement would determine its effect (see [1999]
1 All ER 193 at 203, [2000] 1 AC 455 at 473). In deciding whether any particular *e*
settlement did indeed have this effect, the question was, said Lord Hope ([1999]
1 All ER 193 at 206, [2000] 1 AC 455 at 476)—

'not whether the plaintiff has received the full value of his claim but
whether the sum which he has received in settlement of it was intended to
be in full satisfaction of the tort.' *f*

[67] Two points emerge clearly from these passages from Lord Hope's
speech.

[68] First, the reasoning proceeds on the basis that, in certain cases, a
settlement between a claimant and one tortfeasor, even though for a lesser sum
than would have been awarded on full liability, can have the same effect as a *g*
judgment between the claimant and the same tortfeasor in preventing the
claimant from suing another tortfeasor for the same injury. Just as the claimant
who has been paid the sum of damages awarded by the court for his injuries has
everything which he is entitled to and can ask for no more, so, the House held, a
claimant who has been paid a sum which was intended to be in full satisfaction of *h*
his claim is to be treated as having got everything he is entitled to and cannot ask
for any more.

[69] Secondly, the effect of any particular settlement agreement depends on
what the parties intended. Since that can be determined only by interpreting the
agreement in question, in the end the whole issue turns on the interpretation of
the agreement in question. That approach is consistent with the wider picture. *j*

[70] As the authorities make clear, where his claim has been satisfied, the
limitation on a claimant's right to bring successive proceedings follows simply
from the nature of actions for the recovery of damages in compensation of a
claimant's loss. If he has been paid full compensation, he no longer has any loss
that he can seek to recover. The rule does not, therefore, depend on estoppel by
record, on res judicata or on any similar technical doctrine. The second tortfeasor

a who relies on an earlier judgment to stop the action against himself will not have been a party to the earlier proceedings. Frequently, of course, the judge will have said nothing at all about the part played by the second tortfeasor. But if in giving judgment the judge has had occasion to say anything about the actings of the second tortfeasor, his conclusions will not be binding on the second tortfeasor. Similarly, if the second tortfeasor relies on a settlement agreement between the b victim and another tortfeasor, which has in fact given the victim full satisfaction, the agreement will usually not even have mentioned him and, in any event, the second tortfeasor will not have been a party to that agreement.

[71] Whether a prior judgment has the effect of precluding subsequent proceedings depends on what it decides. For instance, the earlier judgment may have been for only a proportion of the claimant's loss. In which case he is not c prevented from seeking the balance of his loss from another tortfeasor. Lord Hope made this point in *Jameson*'s case under reference to the decision of Lord Cameron in *Crawford v Springfield Steel Co Ltd* (18 July 1958, unreported). It is worth exploring the basis of that decision and the relationship between *Crawford*'s case and *Balfour v Archibald Baird & Sons Ltd* 1959 SC 64.

d [72] In both cases the pursuers were steelworkers who were diagnosed as having pneumoconiosis after a mobile X-ray unit carried out an examination of employees of William Beardmore & Co at their foundry at Parkhead Forge in Glasgow in April 1950. Along with ten other workers, Mr Balfour and Mr Crawford raised actions in the Court of Session for damages against William Beardmore & Co. Lord Strachan heard the 12 actions together and in April 1956 e he gave judgment in all of them. The parts of his opinion dealing with liability and with the award of damages to Mr Balfour and another employee, but not with the damages for Mr Crawford, are reported as *Balfour v William Beardmore & Co Ltd* 1956 SLT 205.

[73] It appears that the pursuers' advisors concentrated their fire on William f Beardmore & Co partly, at least, because of uncertainties as to when, exactly, it had become known that inhalation of dust in steel foundries might cause lung disease. The company defended the actions on a number of grounds, one of which was that the various pursuers had worked with other companies and that it could not be said whether they had contracted their illness as a result of their exposure to dust while working with the defenders or while working with g someone else. Expert evidence was led in respect of all the pursuers and Lord Strachan dealt with each of them separately.

[74] Mr Balfour had worked with William Beardmore & Co from April 1943 until June 1950. In his case Lord Strachan concluded that his disease was contracted only after he had been in the defenders' employment for about three h years and that they alone were responsible for Mr Balfour's illness. He therefore awarded him full damages against the defenders for loss of earnings both in the past and in the future, for solatium and for loss of expectation of life. Subsequently, however, the same senior counsel and solicitors raised fresh proceedings in his name, claiming damages for the same disease, against another steel company, Archibald Baird & Sons. That company had employed Mr Balfour from 1927 until j April 1943. It was in these circumstances that Lord Cameron and, on appeal, the Second Division of the Court of Session held that payment of the damages awarded by Lord Strachan in the first action precluded Mr Balfour from pursuing proceedings for damages against Archibald Baird & Sons: *Balfour v Archibald Baird & Sons Ltd* 1959 SC 64.

[75] Mr Crawford, on the other hand, had worked with William Beardmore & Co from May 1947 until June 1950. Before that, with a gap of one year, he had

worked with the Springfield Steel Co from 1928 until 1947. He sued William
Beardmore & Co for solatium and loss of expectation of life only. In his case Lord
Strachan decided that he had very probably contracted pneumoconiosis before
he entered the employment of William Beardmore & Co in May 1947 but that his
exposure to dust while employed with them had caused an aggravation of his
condition which the judge assessed at 10%. Therefore, on the basis of an
approach which he explained in dealing with one of the other employees (1956
SLT 205 at 216), Lord Strachan first assessed what the full value of Mr Crawford's
claim for solatium and loss of expectation of life due to pneumoconiosis would
have been and then awarded him 10% of that amount: *Crawford v William
Beardmore & Co Ltd* (30 April 1956, unreported).

[76] Mr Crawford next raised proceedings for damages against the Springfield
Steel Co on the basis that he had contracted the illness due to exposure to dust
while working in their premises in the years before 1947. In this action he claimed
damages for loss of earnings, both past and prospective, for prejudice to his
earning capacity and for solatium, including loss of expectation of life. The
company defended the action on the basis that, having chosen to sue William
Beardmore & Co and having been paid the damages awarded against them,
Mr Crawford could not now proceed against the Springfield Steel Co. In these
circumstances Lord Cameron repelled certain of the defenders' preliminary pleas
in law and held that the action could proceed, even though some of the heads of
damages had been claimed in the earlier action. While indicating a tentative view
that Lord Strachan's calculation of solatium would not be binding on the judge
assessing damages in the second proceedings, Lord Cameron reserved his
opinion on the point and simply allowed a proof before answer in respect of the
remaining pleas in law: *Crawford v Springfield Steel Co Ltd*. Although the defenders
reclaimed, the action was settled before the Inner House could hear the
reclaiming motion.

[77] For present purposes the important thing to notice is that in the original
action, *Crawford v William Beardmore & Co Ltd*, the court was able to divide up the
harm and to say that the main part had been caused by earlier events and that
only the relatively small aggravation had been due to the fault of the defenders.
The court then awarded damages for that small aggravation only. The clear
inference was that Mr Crawford's exposure to dust in his previous employment
with the Springfield Steel Co had caused the rest of his loss and injury. In his first
action therefore he had not been awarded any damages for what was in effect the
main part of his loss and injury. Not surprisingly, Lord Cameron took the view
that Mr Crawford could proceed with his action against the Springfield Steel Co
to recover damages for that loss and injury. In that situation there was, of course,
no question of double recovery. Cases where the harm can be divided up in this
way and attributed to separate and non-contemporaneous wrongdoers raise
significantly different issues from cases, such as *Balfour's* case, where the pursuer
or claimant in the second action would simply be trying to recover damages for
the same loss and injury as had been covered by the decree in the first action.
I refer to the valuable discussion in Hart and Honoré *Causation in the Law* (2nd
edn, 1985) pp 225–235.

[78] In *Jameson* the case seems to have proceeded on the basis that, on the
available evidence, it would not have been possible to divide up the harm suffered
by Mr Jameson as a result of the fault of Babcock, on the one hand, and of CEGB
on the other, even though it is clear that Mr Jameson spent only part of his time
while employed with Babcock working on sites occupied by CEGB. On the other
hand, at first sight, the present case appears to be one where the harm suffered by

a the respondents can be divided up, at least to a certain extent. In particular, the breach of contract by Target in terminating their agreement occurred over a week before any breach of contract by Equity & Law in terminating the Equity & Law agreement. Any loss and damage caused to the respondents during that intervening period could not, of course, be the result of the alleged breach of contract by Equity & Law and the respondents make no claim for it in the present

b action. But in the proceedings against Target the respondents adopted the position that in fact Target were responsible for any loss and damage due to the wrongful termination of the Equity & Law agreement since that had come about as a result of the termination of the Target agreement. In effect, it was said, Target's allegations of impropriety led Equity & Law to terminate their agreement with the respondents. The respondents' claim for damages against

c Target therefore included a claim for this important element of their loss. In their defence to the action against them Target denied that they were responsible for Equity & Law terminating their agreement with the respondents. At the time of the settlement a trial of that issue was pending. None the less Equity & Law submit that, if the settlement agreement is properly to be interpreted as having

d been intended as full satisfaction of all the respondents' loss and damage flowing from Target's breach of contract, then it must be interpreted as encompassing full satisfaction of their claim for any loss and damage that the respondents suffered as a result of the termination of the Equity & Law agreement. It is as if the respondents had succeeded on this point in their action against Target, had established the necessary causal connection and had recovered damages for their

e loss as a result of the termination of the Equity & Law agreement. On that analysis the case resembles *Balfour's* case rather than *Crawford's* case and, Equity & Law contend, the respondents should therefore not be allowed to seek what would amount to double recovery for this part of their loss.

[79] In *Jameson's* case, the House proceeded on the analogy of a judgment in

f the *Balfour* kind of situation since in any second action Mr Jameson would simply have been trying to recover damages on the basis that, along with Babcock, CEGB had been responsible for his condition as a whole. The House held that the particular settlement was like a judgment giving damages for Mr Jameson's mesothelioma as a whole and that, accordingly, to allow him to recover damages against CEGB would have been to allow double recovery of damages for the

g same loss. But just as the effect of any prior judgment depends on what its scope actually was, so also the effect of any prior settlement must equally depend on what its scope actually was. As your Lordships have observed, whether a sum accepted in settlement of a claim is intended to fix the full measure of a claimant's loss so as to preclude any further proceedings depends on the proper construction of the

h particular compromise agreement in the light of all the relevant facts surrounding it.

[80] Some at least of the arguments for the parties in the present appeal appeared to me to proceed as if *Jameson's* case had been based on a quite different approach. In particular, counsel for the respondents was anxious to demonstrate, from the terms of the agreement, that the parties to it had not intended to

j discharge the respondents' rights against Equity & Law—and hence that their rights were intact. In developing this argument counsel relied, for instance, on a passage from the judgment of Beldam LJ in the Court of Appeal where he said ([2000] 4 All ER 673 at 703, [2001] Ch 173 at 208 (para 81)):

'In my view the terms of the settlement are clear and unequivocal and do not support the argument that the agreement was intended to release the respondents from liability. The parties to the agreement are defined and the subject matter is "the claims which the parties have or may have against each other"; the parties agreed "not to commence or prosecute any proceedings against one other" and by cl 5 they agreed to release and discharge *each other and their respective directors officers and employees.* In my view these express references exclude the implication that it was the parties' intention to confer similar benefits on the respondents.' (Beldam LJ's emphasis.)

In my respectful view, this passage reflects a misunderstanding of the approach of the majority in *Jameson's* case, as I have analysed it. They did not hold that Mr Jameson and Babcock had intended to confer a benefit on CEGB by somehow releasing and discharging Mr Jameson's rights against CEGB. Rather, they held that, because the settlement had been intended to be in full satisfaction of the harm due to his mesothelioma, it had extinguished his loss and, with it, any claim for damages against CEGB. Therefore before his death Mr Jameson could not have sued CEGB. So his executors could not do so either.

[81] In considering whether a settlement agreement has this effect, the proper question is whether, when construed against the appropriate matrix of fact, the terms of the settlement show that the parties intended that the agreed sum should be in full satisfaction of the wrong done to the claimant. In that connection, an indication in the agreement—whether express or implied—that the claimant envisages the possibility of further proceedings against another wrongdoer may, of course, be of significance—but only as a pointer to the conclusion that the parties did not intend that the agreed sum should be in full satisfaction of the harm suffered by the claimant. Equally an indication in the agreement to the opposite effect will be a pointer that the parties intended that the agreed sum should constitute full satisfaction. In either event, the court will draw the appropriate conclusion as to the effect of the agreement on any claims against another wrongdoer.

[82] In arguing that the terms of the settlement agreement in this case showed that the parties intended that the sum of £10m should be in full satisfaction of all the loss set out in the original statement of claim and in the draft statement of claim, counsel for Equity & Life made much of what he saw as the sweeping terms used in the settlement. He stressed that the payment of the sum was to be 'in *full and final* settlement of *all* claims and potential claims of *whatsoever nature and kind'*. On the other hand, counsel for the respondents emphasised that, by contrast with *Jameson's* case, the settlement was not said to be in full and final 'satisfaction' of the claims. While the language used by the parties must always be carefully analysed for any light that it throws on their intention, the language of a settlement agreement will only rarely be entirely fresh, with every word selected for the particular proceedings. More often, such an agreement will incorporate language derived from a form of settlement used on previous occasions by the advisors of one or other of the parties. In *Bank of Credit and Commerce International SA (in liq) v Ali* [2001] UKHL 8 at [38], [2001] 1 All ER 961 at [38], [2001] 2 WLR 735 Lord Hoffmann alluded to the variety of possible formulae, of greater or lesser complexity and prolixity, which are to be found in such agreements. Since the defendant's advisors will wish to do everything to eliminate the risk of any further proceedings against their client and since the plaintiff will not usually be contemplating any further proceedings against that defendant, the language chosen to express the finality of the settlement between the parties will often be fairly comprehensive, as in the present case. Moreover, a settlement agreement is likely to contain much the same kind of language irrespective of whether or not the settlement is, objectively, favourable to the

a   defendant or to the claimant. Indeed, the worse the settlement from the
    claimant's point of view, the more the defendant may feel the need to use
    sweeping language to protect himself against possible future proceedings. For
    these reasons, the background matrix of fact may often be particularly important
    when interpreting a compromise agreement and deciding whether the parties
    intended the agreed sum to be in full satisfaction of the damage to the claimant.
b   The present case and *Cape & Dalgleish (a firm) v Fitzgerald* [2002] UKHL 16, [2002]
    All ER (D) 231 (Apr) illustrate the point.
        [83] Despite the respondents' argument to the contrary, I detect no reason in
    principle why the approach adopted in *Jameson's* case should not be applied in a
    case, such as the present, where the two claims are for breach of contract.
    Settlement of the first claim cannot, of course, prevent a claimant from bringing
c   an action for nominal damages for breach of the second contract. But, if the
    settlement of the first action is to be interpreted as constituting full satisfaction of
    the loss and injury which the claimant suffered as a result of both breaches of
    contract, then it must follow, on the *Jameson* approach, that he has no right to
    recover substantial damages against the second contract-breaker.
d   [84] Counsel for Equity & Law argued that the aim of the settlement
    agreement between Target and the respondents had been to achieve finality, at
    least so far as Target were concerned. Having paid the agreed sum, they were to
    be free from being troubled by any further proceedings relating to the matter. If,
    however, the respondents were allowed to proceed with their action against
    Equity & Law, Equity & Law would inevitably seek a contribution from Target.
e   Indeed they had already served a third party notice on Target for this purpose.
    Target would therefore be left vulnerable, when they should have been made
    secure by the compromise settlement. To avoid this, as a matter of policy, the
    settlement with Target should discharge Equity & Law and thereby remove the
    basis on which they would seek a contribution from Target. In advancing this
f   submission, counsel relied on the comments of Lord Clyde in *Jameson's* case
    [1999] 1 All ER 193 at 211, [2000] 1 AC 455 at 482–483. As he duly recognised, only
    Lord Clyde adopted this particular line of reasoning.
        [85] For my part, I would reject that argument. The problem identified by
    counsel is simply one example of a kind of legal eternal triangle that was already
    familiar to classical Roman lawyers. A not dissimilar example, from about the
g   end of the second century AD, is to be found in D.2.14.32, Paul 3 ad Plautium:
    where a creditor had agreed not to sue the debtor, should the creditor be able to
    sue a surety for the debt if this meant that the surety would seek to recover from
    the debtor? As Lord Clyde expressly acknowledged, the key to solving such
    problems lies not in legal logic but in legal policy. Different legal systems resolve
h   the policy issues in different ways. A succinct account of the issues and of some
    of the solutions is to be found in Mr Tony Weir's chapter on 'Complex Liabilities'
    in the *International Encyclopaedia of Comparative Law* (1976) vol XI-12, pp 69–70,
    para 12-126. By enacting s 1(3) of the Civil Liability (Contribution) Act 1978,
    however, Parliament has resolved the policy issue for English law in cases of tort
j   and breach of contract by coming down in favour of allowing contribution
    proceedings to be taken against a party who has settled and has therefore 'ceased
    to be liable in respect of the damage in question since the time when the damage
    occurred'. That being so, the mere fact that Target may in due course be faced
    with a demand for contribution from Equity & Law is not a reason for holding
    that the respondents should be prevented from suing Equity & Law. It should
    not be forgotten that—as my noble and learned friend Lord Bingham has
    indicated—a party paying a sum to settle proceedings can protect himself against

the risk of contribution proceedings, either by taking an indemnity from the
other party or by obtaining an enforceable undertaking from him not to sue *a*
anyone else for the same damage.

[86] At the end of the hearing of the appeal I was inclined to think
that—particularly having regard to the large amount of money paid to the
respondents—the proper interpretation of the compromise agreement in this
case was that the parties had intended that the sum should be in full satisfaction *b*
of the respondents' claim for loss and damage following on Target's breach of
contract. This would have included the loss which the respondents suffered as a
result of the termination of the Equity & Law agreement. But I have also taken
into account the relevant circumstances surrounding the agreement that Lord
Bingham and Lord Mackay have identified. Having regard to them, I would not
wish to dissent from the view which commends itself to your Lordships, that the *c*
settlement with Target should not be interpreted as having been intended to be
in full satisfaction of the respondents' loss and damage. On that view, the
settlement does not preclude the respondents from proceeding with the present
action in the manner envisaged by Lord Mackay.

[87] For these reasons I agree that the appeal should be dismissed.

Appeal dismissed.

Celia Fox   Barrister.

a **Gough and another v Chief Constable of the Derbyshire Constabulary**

[2002] EWCA Civ 351

COURT OF APPEAL, CIVIL DIVISION
b LORD PHILLIPS OF WORTH MATRAVERS MR, JUDGE AND CARNWATH LJJ
25, 26 FEBRUARY, 20 MARCH 2002

Public order – Football – Football banning order – Whether scheme for imposition of football banning order contravening Community law on freedom of movement – Whether scheme contravening right to fair trial – Football Spectators Act 1989, s 14B – Human Rights Act 1998, Sch 1, Pt I, art 6 – Council Directive (EEC) 73/148, art 2.

The respondent chief constable preferred complaints to the magistrates' court against the appellants, seeking the imposition of football banning orders under s 14B[a] of the Football Spectators Act 1989. By virtue of s 14B(4), the court was *d* required to make such an order if (a) it was proved that the person against whom the order was sought had at any time caused or contributed to any violence or disorder in the United Kingdom or elsewhere, and (b) the court was satisfied that there were reasonable grounds to believe that making a banning order would help to prevent violence or disorder at or in connection with any regulated football matches. The enforcement of such an order was the responsibility of *e* the Football Banning Orders Authority (FBOA) which had the power, in respect of any match, to exempt a person from the requirements imposed under a banning order where it was satisfied that that was justified by 'special circumstances' and that, because of those circumstances, the person would not attend the match if exempted. At the hearing, the deputy district judge held that *f* the proceedings were civil proceedings attracting civil rules of evidence, including the civil standard of proof, and concluded that the matters set out in s 14B(4) had been established. He therefore proceeded to make banning orders for two years against the appellants, preventing them from attending certain football matches in England and Wales and also preventing them from leaving the country when certain matches were taking place outside England and Wales. *g* The appellants appealed unsuccessfully by way of case stated. On their further appeal to the Court of Appeal, the appellants contended, inter alia, that banning orders necessarily involved derogations from the right, conferred on nationals of European Community member states by art 2[b] of Council Directive (EEC) 73/148, to leave the territory of a member state; that such derogations were *h* unlawful unless they could be justified on public policy grounds; and that it was contrary to the Community law principle of proportionality to bar an individual, on the basis of the criteria laid down in s 14B(4) of the 1989 Act, from travelling anywhere within the European Community in order to reduce the risk of trouble at a football match or tournament taking place outside the United Kingdom, *j* particularly where that match was not taking place within the Community. They further contended that the notice of application for a banning order was a 'criminal charge' within the meaning of art 6(1)[c] of the European Convention for

---

a   Section 14B is set out in the Annexe to the judgment
b   Article 2 is set out at [39], below
c   Article 6, so far as material, provides: '1. In the determination ... of any criminal charge against him, everyone is entitled to a fair and public hearing ... '

the Protection of Human Rights and Fundamental Freedoms 1950 (as set out in
Sch 1 to the Human Rights Act 1998); that the procedural guarantees, required by
art 6 of the convention in relation to criminal charges, were not provided for
either in the legislation or in practice; and that the standard of proof under
s 14B(4)(b) was so low that a fair trial was precluded.

Held – (1) Restraints on persons leaving the United Kingdom, imposed under
s 14B(4) of the 1989 Act, were not in themselves unlawful under Community law.
Preventing football hooligans from taking part in violence and disorder in foreign
countries was an imperative reason of public interest which was capable of
justifying restrictions on their freedom of movement. Whilst it was true that the
statutory provisions, if given their natural meaning, were capable of being
applied in a manner that was harsh and disproportionate, the scheme itself, if
properly operated, would satisfy the requirements of proportionality. It was
essential, however, that the appropriate standard of proof at both the first and last
stage of the scheme was appreciated and applied since compliance with the
principles of Community law and the convention depended upon that (see [62],
[84], [86], [88], below).

(2) Although proceedings under s 14B of the 1989 Act were civil proceedings
rather than criminal proceedings, banning orders imposed serious restraints on
freedoms that the citizen normally enjoyed, and magistrates should therefore
apply an exacting standard of proof that would, in practice, be hard to distinguish
from the criminal standard. Thus the necessity in the individual case to impose a
restriction upon a fundamental freedom had to be strictly demonstrated.
Moreover, the manner in which applications for permission to go abroad were
treated was of critical importance. Provided that the reason for going abroad was
other than attendance at the prescribed match, there could be no justification for
refusing permission. When considering whether there were 'special circumstances',
the FBOA or, on appeal, the magistrates, should do no more than satisfy
themselves that that was the true position. The approach of the FBOA to 'special
circumstances' applications appeared to accord with what was appropriate, the
operation of the scheme as a whole was compliant with Community law and the
statutory scheme was not contrary to art 6 of the convention. In the instant case,
it appeared that the deputy district judge had not appreciated that the case for
making a banning order had to be proved to the strict standard set out above.
The evidence, however, would have justified the making of a banning order if the
strict standard had been applied. Accordingly, the banning orders had been
lawfully made, and the appeal would therefore be dismissed (see [89]–[91], [94],
[98], [101], [103], below).

Decision of the Divisional Court [2001] 4 All ER 289 affirmed.

Notes
For football banning orders, see Supp to 45(2) *Halsbury's Laws* (4th edn reissue)
paras 121–125.

For the Human Rights Act 1998, Sch 1, Pt 1, art 6, see 7 *Halsbury's Statutes* (4th
edn) (1999 reissue) 523.

Cases referred to in judgment
Alpine Investments BV v Minister van Financiën Case C-384/93 [1995] All ER (EC)
543, [1995] ECR I-1141, ECJ.

B v B (injunction: restraint on leaving jurisdiction) [1997] 3 All ER 258, [1998] 1 WLR 329.

a   *B v Chief Constable of the Avon and Somerset Constabulary* [2001] 1 All ER 562, [2001]
        1 WLR 340, DC.
     Brown v Stott (Procurator Fiscal, Dunfermline) [2001] 2 All ER 97, [2001] 2 WLR 817, PC.
     Calfa, Criminal proceedings against Case C-348/96 [1999] All ER (EC) 850, [1999]
        ECR I-11, ECJ.
     De Freitas v Permanent Secretary of Ministry of Agriculture, Fisheries, Lands and
b   *Housing* [1999] 1 AC 69, [1998] 3 WLR 675, PC.
     R (on the application of McCann) v Crown Court at Manchester [2001] EWCA Civ 281,
        [2001] 4 All ER 264, [2001] 1 WLR 1084.
     R v A [2001] UKHL 25, [2001] 3 All ER 1, [2002] 1 AC 45, [2001] 2 WLR 1546.
     R v Bouchereau [1981] 2 All ER 924n, [1978] QB 732, [1978] 2 WLR 250, [1977] ECR
        1999, ECJ.
c   *R v Ministry of Agriculture, Fisheries and Food, ex p Hedley Lomas (Ireland) Ltd* Case
        C-5/94 [1996] All ER (EC) 493, [1997] QB 139, [1996] 3 WLR 787, [1996] ECR
        I-2553, ECJ.
     R v Secretary of State for the Home Dept, ex p Daly [2001] UKHL 26, [2001] 3 All ER
        433, [2001] 2 WLR 1622.

d   **Appeal**

The appellants, Carl Gough and Gary Smith, appealed with permission of
Keene LJ from the decision of the Divisional Court (Laws LJ and Poole J) on
13 July 2001 ([2001] EWHC Admin 554, [2001] 4 All ER 289, [2001] 3 WLR 1392)
dismissing their appeal by way of case stated from football banning orders of two
e   years imposed on them, under s 14B of the Football Spectators Act 1989, by
Deputy District Judge Aujla at Derby Magistrates' Court on 2 October 2000 on
the application of the respondent, the Chief Constable of the Derbyshire
Constabulary. The Secretary of State for the Home Department intervened in the
proceedings. The facts are set out in the judgment of the court.

f
Rhodri Thompson and *Arnondo Chakrabarti* (instructed by *Timms*) for the
appellants.
Philip Havers QC and *Simon Davenport* (instructed by *Weightmans*, Leicester) for
the respondent.
David Pannick QC and *Mark Hoskins* (instructed by the *Treasury Solicitor*) for the
g   Secretary of State.

Cur adv vult

20 March 2002. The following judgment of the court was delivered.

h   **LORD PHILLIPS OF WORTH MATRAVERS MR.**

Introduction

[1] The appellants, Carl Gough and Gary Smith, have run foul of the statutory
scheme that has been put in place to combat football hooligans. On 2 October 2000
j   Deputy District Judge Aujla (the judge) made a banning order against each
appellant under the Football Spectators Act 1989 as amended by the Football
(Disorder) Act 2000. The banning orders prevent the appellants from attending
certain football matches in England and Wales. They also prevent the appellants
from leaving the country when certain football matches are taking place outside
England and Wales. The appellants contend that it is not lawful to impose the
latter restrictions upon them. They say that the statutory provisions under which

they are imposed violate Community law in a manner which renders void those provisions. They further contend that the statutory provisions in question violate certain articles of the European Convention for the Protection of Human Rights and Fundamental Freedoms 1950 (as set out in Sch 1 to the Human Rights Act 1998), so that the statutes are incompatible with the convention.

[2] At the request of the appellants, the judge stated a case for the Divisional Court which raised the question of whether the appellants' challenge to the legality of the legislation was well-founded. On 13 July 2001 the Divisional Court roundly rejected the appellants' challenge ([2001] EWHC Admin 554, [2001] 4 All ER 289, [2001] 3 WLR 1392). In the leading judgment, Laws LJ held that compliance with European Community law was 'acte clair' and that there was no conflict with the convention. The appellants now appeal against the decision of the Divisional Court with the permission of Keene LJ, who rightly observed that the grounds of appeal raise issues of some importance.

Football hooliganism

[3] At the beginning of his judgment Laws LJ spoke of the 'shame and menace of football hooliganism'. As questions of proportionality are an important feature of this appeal, we propose to say a little about this phenomenon at the outset.

[4] Football started life as an amateur sport, but professional football is now very big business. Following professional football is an activity pursued with passion by large sections of the populace in this country and abroad.

[5] Over the last 40 years the adversarial encounter on the football pitch has, in this country, been increasingly accompanied by a degree of physical conflict between certain elements of the supporters of at least some of the football clubs. For this reason, rival supporters are now segregated within the grounds. In the vicinity of the grounds where matches are played disorder has now, unhappily, become commonplace.

[6] There is a small minority for whom the attraction of football matches is not the game itself, but the warfare that they intend shall accompany the game. To describe what takes place by the word 'warfare' is hardly too strong. To quote from the witness statement in these proceedings of Supt John Wright:

'It has become common for groups of males to associate themselves with football clubs as a vehicle for them to become involved in violence and disorder. This has developed to the stage where this has become extremely organised. These groups will often make use of mobile phones and the Internet to arrange fights with other like-minded individuals. These fights often involve the use of weapons, eg, knives, bottles, and CS gas. They usually occur away from football grounds at railway stations or in or around city centre public houses.'

[7] The behaviour of a lawless minority at matches within England and Wales has been mirrored by lawlessness on the part of a small minority of those who follow English teams in competitions abroad. Mr David Bohannan, who heads the Home Office section responsible for tackling football-related disorder, provided the court with the following summary of this phenomenon:

'Disorderliness has been associated with football since the end of the nineteenth century when it became a mass spectator sport. However, it only became recognised as a major social problem in the 1960s when domestic football grounds regularly provided a venue for fights and other kinds of disorder involving many hundreds of young males. Since 1977, attention has a also focussed on the behaviour of English football fans when overseas. There has been a catalogue of incidents involving English supporters, including serious outbursts of violence and disorder in Luxembourg (1977), Turin (1980), Basle (1981), Oslo (1981), Paris (1984), West Germany (1988), Italy (1990), Sweden (1992), Amsterdam (1993), Rotterdam (1993), Dublin (1995), Rome (1997), Marseilles (1998), Glasgow (1999), Copenhagen (2000),

b Brussels (2000) and Charleroi (2000). These incidents have mainly taken place in connection with matches played by the English national team. However, serious problems have also arisen in relation to matches played by English club sides, eg the UEFA Cup Final in Copenhagen in 2000 between Arsenal and Galatasaray. In most cases, the disorder has occurred in streets and bars rather than in the grounds and often during the period leading up

c to match day. Each incident has brought shame on our national reputation and also resulted in very many arrests and expulsions of English supporters by host nations. Acts of disorder by English supporters receive wide media coverage both in the United Kingdom and abroad.'

d *The legislation*

[8] The history of legislative measures introduced to address the problem of football hooliganism, together with a summary of the relevant measures, is set out in Laws LJ's judgment ([2001] 4 All ER 289 at [3]–[10]). What this history demonstrates is that, over the years, the legislation has not achieved the intended result of putting an end to football hooliganism and that Parliament's response

e has been progressively to make more stringent the circumstances in which restraints can and will be imposed on those who are believed to be liable to indulge in such behaviour. We shall annexe Laws LJ's helpful summary to this judgment and attempt, in broad and necessarily imprecise detail, to identify the significant changes that have been made to the legislation in question.

f [9] Under Pt IV of the Public Order Act 1986, where a court convicted a defendant of an offence of violence or drunkenness committed in connection with attendance at a football match, it was empowered to make an order excluding the defendant from attending certain prescribed football matches in this country, subject to this proviso in s 30(2):

g 'No exclusion order may be made unless the court is satisfied that making such an order in relation to the accused would help to prevent violence or disorder at or in connection with prescribed football matches.'

[10] The Football Spectators Act 1989 provided that, in similar circumstances to those covered by the 1986 Act and subject to the same proviso, the court could

h place a restriction order on a defendant whereby he would be required to report to a police station during the period within which certain designated football matches were being played abroad. The object of this was to prevent the defendant from travelling to those matches.

[11] The Football (Offences and Disorder) Act 1999 amended the relevant

j provisions of the earlier two Acts. Restriction orders were redefined as 'football banning orders', but the most significant change was in the wording of the proviso. That was, in each Act, amended to read as follows:

'It shall be the duty of the court to make a … football banning order in relation to the accused if it is satisfied that there are reasonable grounds to believe that making the order would help to prevent violence or disorder at or in connection with prescribed [*designated*] football matches.'

[12] The 2000 Act has amended the 1989 Act in such a way as to combine the relevant provisions of that Act and the 1986 Act. It makes provision for the making of a single banning order in relation to 'regulated football matches' (ie prescribed matches) whether in England and Wales or elsewhere.

[13] The amended Act, which we shall from now on describe simply as the 1989 Act, provides for the making of a banning order in two different circumstances. The first, under s 14A, is when a court convicts a defendant of one of the scheduled offences—ie football-related violence. The second, under s 14B, is new, and much more far reaching. The order is made on a complaint to a magistrates' court by the chief officer of police of the area in which the respondent resides. It must appear to the chief officer and he must prove to the court that the respondent has, within the last ten years, 'at any time caused or contributed to any violence or disorder in the United Kingdom or elsewhere'.

[14] By whichever of the two routes the matter comes before the court, the court must make a banning order—

> 'if the court is satisfied that there are reasonable grounds to believe that making a banning order would help to prevent violence or disorder at or in connection with any regulated football matches.'

An appeal lies to the Crown Court against the imposition of a banning order.

[15] Under s 14C, violence is defined as meaning 'violence against persons or property and includes threatening violence', and disorder has a lengthy definition which includes 'using threatening, abusive, or insulting words or behaviour or disorderly behaviour'. There is no requirement for the violence or disorder to be football related.

[16] The same section specifies a number of matters that the court can take into account when considering whether to make a banning order under s 14B. These include 'conduct recorded on video or by other means'.

[17] Regulated football matches taking place outside England and Wales are prescribed by order of the Secretary of State having regard to the risk that they will be an occasion for violence and disorder on the part of English supporters. Under the current order these are matches involving the English or Welsh national teams or clubs which are members of the Football League or the Football Association Premier League.

[18] A person subject to a banning order is not automatically affected by that order in respect of every prescribed overseas game. The Act provides for an 'enforcing authority'—a police authority prescribed by the Secretary of State—whose duties include tailoring the requirements of a banning order to fit the particulars of the individual subject to the order. This is the Football Banning Orders Authority (FBOA). Its functions include issuing individual notices to those made subject to banning orders. These set out the appropriate conditions and reporting restrictions which apply to each individual having regard to the degree of risk associated with the individual person for the individual match.

[19] Section 19(2A) provides that the FBOA must issue a notice if it 'is of the opinion that requiring any person subject to a banning order to report is necessary or expedient in order to reduce the likelihood of violence or disorder at or in connection with the match'. Section 19(2B) provides that the notice must require the person to report at a police station and surrender his passport. The surrender will normally be for a control period which runs from five days before the match to the time that the match finishes.

a [20] Section 19(2D) provides that the FBOA may establish criteria for determining whether such a requirement should be imposed on any person or any class of person.

[21] Mr Jaglall, one of the FBOA officers, described in a witness statement how the FBOA performs this duty in practice:

b 'Notices are sent to all subjects prior to the control period for an England international match played overseas and, where appropriate, prior to the control period for an international club match involving the club that the subject supports. Each club match is looked at individually with a risk assessment made at that particular time. The risk of disorder at some club matches abroad is considered minimal and no reporting requirements are

c imposed. Exceptionally, where intelligence is received that attaches a greater degree of risk to a particular match, notices may be sent to subjects who do not have an allegiance to that club.'

[22] The FBOA has power under s 20(4) to exempt a person from the requirements imposed under a banning order in respect of any match or matches

d where satisfied that this is justified by special circumstances and that, because of these circumstances, that person would not attend the match or matches if so exempted. An appeal lies to the magistrates' court against a refusal to grant an exemption.

[23] The amendments made by the 2000 Act include important provisions, with which we are not concerned, empowering the police, in defined circumstances,

e to prevent from leaving the country individuals on the point of embarking for a football match abroad.

[24] The circumstances that led to the passing of the 2000 Act, and the reasoning behind its provisions, are not in dispute. They were explained to Parliament by the Home Secretary, Mr Jack Straw, in the course of the second

f reading of the Bill on 13 July 2000. They are relevant, not by way of interpretation of the Act, but to inform the debate on proportionality that arises on this appeal.

[25] The 2000 Act was a response to 'appalling scenes' of disorder at Brussels and Charleroi during the Euro 2000 tournament. In the course of that tournament 965 English citizens were arrested by the Belgian police. The English National Criminal Intelligence Service (NCIS) is an agency which dedicates a

g significant proportion of its time and expertise to monitoring the activities of football hooligans. Only 30 of those arrested were known to the NCIS. Only one of the total of 454 individuals who were subject to domestic, but not international, banning orders was among them. Mr Straw summarised the position by stating that the disorder was 'prompted not by a small core of known

h football hooligans, but by xenophobic, racist and offensive behaviour of a significant number of drunken, white males, typically aged between 20 and 35'.

[26] The NCIS carried out an analysis of those arrested. Three hundred and ninety-one—about 40%—had previous convictions: 133 for violence, 200 for disorder, 38 for possession of an offensive weapon and 122 for criminal damage.

j Plainly many of these had convictions for more than one of these offences. The convictions were not, in the main, football related.

The facts

[27] The following account of the facts is an adaptation of a portion of the judgment of Laws LJ. We do not believe that it is controversial.

[28] On 18 September 2000 the Chief Constable of the Derbyshire Constabulary preferred complaints against Mr Gough and Mr Smith (and nine others) under

s 14B(3) with a view to seeking orders under s 14B(4) in the magistrates' court. *a*
The complaints alleged in each case that the condition stipulated in s 14B(2)
—that 'the respondent has at any time caused or contributed to any violence or
disorder in the United Kingdom or elsewhere'—was fulfilled: in Mr Gough's case
specifically by violence resulting in a conviction on 17 March 1998 for common
assault and in Mr Smith's case specifically by violence resulting in a conviction on
26 November 1990 for assault with intent to resist arrest. However, it is plain *b*
from the terms of the case stated that the court attached greater importance to
the 'profile' prepared by the police in respect of each man and it is necessary to
explain what these are and how they come into existence. The football club with
which each appellant is associated is Derby County. As regards Derby County
matches, Supt Wright stated:

c
    'There is currently a group of males that can number between 40 and 60
    for high profile games who come under the banner of the media term
    "football hooligans". The policing term for these people is "football
    prominents". In the Derby group they are males from 18 to 40. The group
    is commonly referred to by the public and themselves as the DLF (Derby
    Lunatic Fringe).' *d*

[29] The tactics of the police have had to respond to this developing
phenomenon. There is a football intelligence system co-ordinated by the NCIS.
Each club has a football intelligence officer, who is known to the prominents as
they are known to him. In relation to each match—certainly as regards Derby *e*
County, for it is what was done in these cases—information is collected by police
'spotters' who watch the prominents. The information is collated in an
information/intelligence report. The profiles are prepared in reliance on the
contents of such reports, and consist in short notes, each giving an outline
description of the particular prominent's involvement in actual or threatened
trouble in relation to any given match. *f*

[30] Fifteen profiles for Mr Gough were put before the magistrates' court,
describing incidents from 14 September 1996 to 29 April 2000; 21 for Mr Smith
from 14 September 1996 to 17 June 2000. Within these there appear to be eight
incidents in which both appellants participated. The following convey the
flavour of the profiles. '8/3/97. Derby v Middlesbrough, 70 of the Derby *g*
prominent group were involved in disturbances with Middlesbrough prominents
both before and after this game. Mr Gough was part of the Derby group.' There
is an identical profile for Mr Smith, referring to the same occasion. There are two
profiles which make no reference to disorder or to prominents: '7/8/99. Leeds v
Derby, Gough seen leaving stadium with three other males' and '11/12/99. *h*
Smith seen sitting in the south-east corner of the ground during the Derby v
Burnley FA Cup game.'

[31] The judge in the magistrates' court referred to this profile in particular:

    '29/4/00. Tottenham v Derby, Gough attended London on this day on a
    rogue coach with 40 other Derby prominents. This coach was stopped and *j*
    searched and was found to contain DLF calling cards, drugs and tickets for
    the game, all had been secreted on the coach. The group were allowed by
    police to walk into central London where they later became involved in
    slight disorder with West Brom prominents.'

[32] Again there is an identical profile for Smith. The expression 'rogue' coach
calls for an explanation. A system exists by which coach trips to away matches

a   are notified to the police. A coach not so notified is a 'rogue' coach. However, the police have no powers to prevent a rogue coach from travelling, nor indeed to require the notification procedure to be followed.

[33] One profile is particularly relevant:

b   '17/6/00. England v Germany Euro 2000 Championships. Smith was seen in the square in Charleroi after the disorder had occurred corralled by the Belgian riot police with around 15 other Derby prominents and 1,500 other England supporters.'

[34] At the hearing Mr Gough, then aged 36, gave unchallenged evidence that he suffered from a brain tumour; that his last football-related conviction had been 18 years previously; that he had never been to a football match outside the United
c   Kingdom; and that he regularly took his children to the Derby town centre for shopping as well as football matches. Mr Smith was 38. He had had no convictions of any kind since November 1990. He said that his last 'football-related incident' had happened nearly 15 years previously.

[35] The appellants gave oral evidence in the magistrates' court and challenged
d   the accuracy of some of the profiles. The judge did not find their evidence credible. He found that their evidence was 'of little assistance to the court'. He concluded as regards each appellant that the matters set out in s 14B(4)(a) and (b) were established and so proceeded to make banning orders, for two years in each case. That was the minimum period permitted by the statute: s 14F(5). The orders as made curtailed the appellants' freedom of movement to a lesser extent
e   than had been sought by the police. As the judge made clear by reference to a map before him, there was no restriction placed upon their going into the city of Derby within the inner ring road.

Judge Aujla's decision
f   [36] The judge held that the chief constable had satisfied the obligation to prove that each appellant had 'caused or contributed to violence or disorder'. Thus the first pre-condition to his obligation to make a banning order was satisfied. As to the second, when dealing with all 11 cases before him, he said this in the case stated:

g   'The other condition is s 14B(4): whether or not I am satisfied that there are reasonable grounds to believe that making a banning order would help to prevent violence or disorder at or in connection with any regulated football matches. I read this section to mean that I have to have reasonable grounds. I only have to have reasonable grounds to believe and, given the nature of
h   the antecedents of all 11 and the matters that I have referred to earlier, I have no choice but to make banning orders on the basis that there are reasonable grounds to believe that they would help to prevent violence or disorder in the future.'

j   [37] Accordingly, the judge imposed banning orders for a period of two years—the minimum period required under s 14B. So far as domestic matches were concerned the order specified a geographical area radiating from the football stadium as the exclusion zone in relation to matches in which Derby County was playing. In relation to international matches, he ordered the appellants to report, within five days, to a local police station for further information. In due course they received the relevant directions from FBOA as to restrictions relating to international travel. The effect of these for the season

2000/2001 was that each was subjected to restrictions preventing travel abroad for three periods: 6–11 October 2000, 10–15 November 2000 and 23–28 March 2001.

The appellants' contentions

[38] Before us the appellants have, to a degree, reformulated the case advanced before the Divisional Court, although not in a manner which involves inconsistency. We propose to proceed directly to the points argued before us, indicating, where appropriate, the manner in which these arguments were dealt with by the court below.

[39] The appellants' case is founded on positive rights conferred on them by arts 1 and 2 of Council Directive (EEC) 73/148 of 21 May 1973 (the 1973 directive), which, so far as material, provide:

'*Article 1*

1. The Member States shall, acting as provided in this Directive, abolish restrictions on the movement and residence of: (a) nationals of a Member State who are established or who wish to establish themselves in another Member State in order to pursue activities as self-employed persons, or who wish to provide services in that State; (b) nationals of Member States wishing to go to another Member State as recipients of services ...

Article 2

1. Member States shall grant the persons referred to in Article 1 the right to leave their territory. Such right shall be exercised simply on production of a valid identity card or passport. Members of the family shall enjoy the same right as the national on whom they are dependent.

2. Member States shall, acting in accordance with their laws, issue to their nationals, or renew, an identity card or passport, which shall state in particular the holder's nationality.

3. The passport must be valid at least for all Member States and for countries through which the holder must pass when travelling between Member States. Where a passport is the only document on which the holder may lawfully leave the country, its period of validity shall be not less than five years.

4. Member States may not demand from the persons referred to in Article 1 any exit visa or any equivalent requirement.'

[40] The following important matters are common ground. (i) The 1973 directive has direct effect in English law. (ii) To the extent that the primary legislation in play in this case is incompatible with the 1973 directive, it is thereby rendered void and this court can and should so declare. (iii) By way of elaboration on the previous point, incompatibility with Community law cannot be amended by severance, with the consequence that if s 14B is incompatible with the 1973 directive, it must be struck down in its entirety.

[41] On behalf of the appellants Mr Rhodri Thompson and Mr Arnondo Chakrabarti have provided the court with lengthy written outline submissions. At the outset they summarise the four broad grounds of appeal as follows:

'(1) Banning orders necessarily involve derogations from the rights conferred on individuals by art 2 of [the 1973 directive]. Such derogations are rendered unlawful by art 8 of [the 1973 directive] unless they can be justified on public policy grounds. [The 1973 directive] has not been implemented in this respect into English law. Articles 2 and 8 are therefore directly enforceable in the English courts and as against United Kingdom public bodies. Thus, independently of the proper interpretation of the 1989 Act, banning orders are unlawful unless the derogations from the rights conferred on the appellants by [the 1973 directive], imposed by the banning orders made in this case, can be justified on public grounds. The applications made by the chief constable and the judgments both of District Judge Aujla and of the Divisional Court are vitiated by failure to consider this issue. Further, there was manifestly no evidence on the basis of which orders could lawfully have been made if that issue had been considered. (2) The United Kingdom legislative regime introduced in 2000 is contrary to Community law and therefore inapplicable in so far as it imposes mandatory restrictions on free movement within the Community on the basis of criteria that are not provided for or permitted by binding Community legislation. (3) It is contrary to the Community law principle of proportionality to prevent an individual made subject to a banning order on the basis of the criteria laid down in s 14B(4) of the 1989 Act from travelling anywhere within the European Community, in order to reduce the risk of trouble at a football match or tournament taking place outside the United Kingdom, particularly where that match or tournament is not to take place within the European Community. (4) As a matter of fundamental rights protected by Community law, the procedures for the imposition of banning orders under s 14B(4) are unfair, in contravention of art 6 of the European Convention on Human Rights: (a) The standard of proof under s 14B(4)(b) is so low that a fair hearing is precluded. (b) A notice of application for banning orders pursuant to s 14B(2) is a "criminal charge" within the meaning of art 6(1) of the convention but the procedural guarantees provided for in art 6(3) are not provided for in the legislation or in practice. Given the broad criteria for the making of such orders and their disproportionate geographical scope, they are also unjustified infringements of art 8 of the convention.'

[42] Article 8 of the 1973 directive provides: 'Member States shall not derogate from the provisions of this Directive save on grounds of public policy, public security or public health.'

[43] The four broad grounds of appeal appear to accept that the 1973 directive leaves it open to the United Kingdom to restrict the freedom of movement conferred by arts 1 and 2 where this can be shown to be necessary on grounds of public policy. It is, indeed, the appellants' primary case that the provisions of the amended 1989 Act which are in play are unlawful in that they manifestly exceed any legitimate requirement of public policy. However, the appellants have a fall back case, should this submission not succeed. They contend that it is uncertain whether a member state has any general power to prevent a national of a member of the European Union from leaving that state to go to another member state for reasons of public policy. Should this question become critical they submit that it should be referred to the European Court. It seems to us that this is a seminal issue which should logically be addressed at the outset.

Is there a public policy exception to art 2 of the 1973 directive?

[44] Mr Thompson's argument runs as follows. (i) Article 8 of the 1973 directive is prohibitive, not permissive. It does not confer a public policy exception to the requirements of art 2 but simply recognises the possibility that one may exist. One must look elsewhere to see the extent to which any public policy exception exists. (ii) The 1973 directive states that it is directed to 'the abolition of restrictions on movement and residence within the Community for nationals

of Member States with regard to establishment and the provision of services'. As such, the directive is aimed at the implementation of Chs 2 and 3 of the EC Treaty. Chapter 3 deals with services and, in that chapter, art 49 provides:

'Within the framework of the provisions set out below, restrictions on freedom to provide services within the Community shall be prohibited in respect of nationals of member states who are established in a state of the Community other than that of the person for whom the services are intended.'

(iii) Article 55 provides that art 49 is subject to art 46. This article is in Ch 2, which deals with establishment. It provides:

'1. The provisions of this Chapter and measures taken in pursuance thereof shall not prejudice the applicability of provisions laid down by law, regulation or administrative action providing for special treatment for foreign nationals on grounds of public policy, public security or public health.'

(iv) The forerunner of the 1973 directive was Council Directive (EEC) 64/220. That directive had an art 8 in identical terms to that in the 1973 directive. One of the recitals to the directive provided, however, that 'co-ordination of measures justified on grounds of public policy, public security or public health' would be dealt with in a separate directive. (v) The separate directive is Council Directive (EEC) 64/221 (the 1964 directive). That directive includes a recital in the following terms:

'Article 1
1. The provisions of this Directive shall apply to any national of a member state who resides in or travels to another member state of the Community, either in order to pursue an activity as an employed or self-employed person, or as a recipient of services ...

Article 2
1. This Directive relates to all measures concerning entry into their territory, issue or renewal of residence permits, or expulsion from their territory, taken by member states on grounds of public policy, public security or public health ...

Article 3
1. Measures taken on grounds of public policy or public security shall be based exclusively on the personal conduct of the individual concerned.
2. Previous criminal convictions shall not in themselves constitute grounds for the taking of such measures ...'

(vi) The last recital to the 1973 directive refers expressly to the 1964 directive. (vii) Thus, all the provisions dealing with restrictions on movement on grounds of public policy refer to restrictions affecting foreign nationals. Nowhere is there any provision which recognises that it is, or could be, lawful for a member state to impose restrictions on movement on its own nationals on grounds of public policy. In the absence of such a provision, no derogation on grounds of public policy could be imposed in respect of the freedom granted to citizens of the United Kingdom to travel to another member state under the 1973 directive.

[45] Mr Thompson put these submissions at the forefront of the argument that he addressed to the Divisional Court. Laws LJ described his submissions as a 'heroic labour'. He rejected them, holding that they were founded on an

a interpretation of art 46 of the EC Treaty which was over literal and would lead to an absurdity. We agree with this conclusion.

[46] Mr Thompson's submissions have the result that the only derogations from the provisions of Chs 2 and 3 permitted by art 46 are those which discriminate against foreign nationals. Restrictions on freedom of establishment or the provision of services imposed on grounds of public policy, public security b or public health, which a member state applied to both foreign nationals and to its own nationals without distinction, would be unlawful. This would patently be an absurd result.

[47] We think that it is understandable why those who agreed the EC Treaty made specific provision in art 46 for derogation in respect of provisions that provided for special treatment for foreign nationals. Chapter 2 deals with c freedom of establishment. Article 43 provides:

'Within the framework of the provisions set out below, restrictions on the freedom of establishment of nationals of a Member State in the territory of another Member State shall be prohibited. Such prohibition shall also apply d to restrictions on the setting up of agencies, branches or subsidiaries by nationals of any Member State established in the territory of any Member State. Freedom of establishment shall include the right to take up and pursue activities as self-employed persons and to set up and manage undertakings, in particular companies or firms within the meaning of the second paragraph of Article 48, under the conditions laid down for its own nationals by the law of e the country where such establishment is effected, subject to the provisions of the Chapter relating to capital.'

[48] Thus Ch 2 is concerned with ensuring that foreign nationals established in a member state enjoy equality of treatment with nationals of that state. The derogation permitted by art 46 naturally relates to discriminatory treatment, for f it is such treatment that Ch 2, in general, prohibits.

[49] Chapter 3 deals with freedom to provide services. More particularly, it provides for the liberalisation of the provision of services. Article 54 provides:

'As long as freedom to provide services has not been abolished, each Member State shall apply such restrictions without distinction on grounds of g nationality or residence to all persons providing services within the meaning of the first paragraph of Article 49.'

[50] Once again one can readily understand why it should be appropriate to apply the provisions of art 46 to this Chapter.

h [51] As Advocate General Jacobs remarked in *Alpine Investments BV v Minister van Financiën* Case C-384/93 [1995] All ER (EC) 543 at 557, [1995] ECR I-1141 at 1159:

'With regard to restrictions on the freedom to provide services imposed by the member state of destination, the case law of the court draws a distinction j between restrictions which are discriminatory and those which are non-discriminatory.

64. Restrictions which are discriminatory are compatible with the Treaty only if they fall within the scope of an express derogation, such as that contained in art 56 ... Restrictions which are non-discriminatory may be compatible with the Treaty even if they do not benefit from an express derogation.'

[**52**] In our judgment the express derogation in art 46 in respect of provisions
for special treatment for foreign nationals does not implicitly preclude the right
of a member state to impose restrictions which are not discriminatory on
grounds of public policy, public security or public health.

[**53**] Mr Thompson accepted that there were certain circumstances under
which the English court exercised a power to prevent a person leaving the
jurisdiction. The writ ne exeat regno was one example, albeit archaic. More
germane is the inherent jurisdiction exercised in the Family Division to restrain a
party from leaving the jurisdiction and to require the surrender of his or her
passport where this is necessary to prevent the proceedings in that court from
being rendered nugatory—see *B v B* (*injunction: restraint on leaving jurisdiction*)
[1997] 3 All ER 258 at 264–265, [1998] 1 WLR 329 at 334. These are examples of
restraints on freedom of movement imposed in this country, without discrimination
between nationals and non-nationals, which can be justified on the grounds of
public policy. We are in no doubt that other member states assert both similar
and dissimilar powers to restrict freedom of movement on grounds of public
policy. It would be startling if provisions of the EC Treaty had been agreed which
rendered the exercise of such powers unlawful.

[**54**] Finally on this topic, we should draw attention to the Council Resolution
of 6 December 2001 dealing with measures to prevent and control violence and
disturbances in connection with football matches with an international
dimension, in which at least one member state is involved. Chapter 3 contains
the following exhortation:

> 'Countries which have the legal possibility to prevent risk fans from
> travelling abroad should take all the necessary measures to achieve this
> objective effectively and should inform the organising country accordingly.
> Each country should take all possible measures to prevent its own citizens
> from participating in and / or organising public order disturbances in another
> country.'

It would be, to say the least, surprising if the Council were urging measures
which were outlawed by Community law.

[**55**] For the reasons that we have given, we are satisfied that Community law
does not outlaw restraints on persons leaving this country if these can be justified
on the grounds of public policy. Article 8 of the 1973 directive recognises that this
is so. Whether public policy justifies the restraints must, of course, be considered
having regard to the established principles of Community law.

Public policy and proportionality

[**56**] The primary case advanced by Mr Thompson accepted, for purposes of
argument and contrary to the submission considered above, that derogation on
grounds of public policy from the obligations imposed by the 1973 directive was
permitted by Community law. On that premise, he submitted that s 14B of the
2000 Act was none the less unlawful under Community law in that it offended
against the doctrine of proportionality.

The ban on leaving the country

[**57**] Mr Thompson accepted that the prevention of football hooliganism was
a legitimate aim of public policy, but submitted that this aim could not justify
prohibiting nationals from leaving the country. Such a step was disproportionate.
He drew attention to the very limited circumstances in which the law of this
country has hitherto prevented persons from leaving the country, as identified by

a Wilson J in *B v B*. He pointed out that there are classes of persons capable of doing much more damage than football hooligans who are free, under domestic law, to leave the country, including drug dealers and paedophiles. The Home Secretary had confirmed in his evidence to the Parliamentary Joint Committee on Human Rights on 14 November 2000 that persons suspected of being, or having links with, international terrorists would be free to leave the country. How then could
b it be proportionate to prevent football hooligans from leaving the country?

[58] Mr Thompson submitted that European law did not normally recognise that public policy permitted one state to restrict Community rights in order to protect its neighbours. The proportionate approach was that each state should give effect to the requirements of public policy within its own boundaries. He suggested that support for this principle could be derived from the decision of the
c European Court of Justice in *R v Ministry of Agriculture, Fisheries and Food, ex p Hedley Lomas (Ireland) Ltd* Case C-5/94 [1996] All ER (EC) 493, [1997] QB 139. In that case the United Kingdom sought to justify the refusal of a licence to export sheep to Spain by relying on art 36 of the EC Treaty. This permitted derogation from the art 34 prohibition of restrictions on exports on the grounds of 'the
d protection of health and life ... of animals'. The licence had been refused on the ground that Spain had not implemented directives on the protection of animals during international transport and on pre-slaughter stunning. Mr Thompson drew our attention to the following statement in the opinion of Advocate General Leger ([1996] All ER (EC) 493 at 502, [1997] QB 139 at 161): 'a member state can rely on art 36 only in order to ensure protection of an interest
e safeguarded by that article *within its own national territory.*'

[59] We do not consider that this case affords any guidance on the question of whether public policy can justify a member state in imposing a restriction of movement that is designed to benefit another member state. The principle to be derived from the case is to be found in the following passage from the judgment
f of the court ([1996] All ER (EC) 493 at 538, [1997] QB 139 at 203): 'A member state may not unilaterally adopt, on its own authority, corrective or protective measures designed to obviate any breach by another member state of rules of Community law ...'

[60] More in point is the decision of the European Court in *Alpine Investments BV v Minister van Financiën* Case C-384/93 [1995] All ER (EC) 543, [1995] ECR
g I-1141. That case concerned the freedom to provide services under art 59 of the EC Treaty. Alpine Investments was a Dutch company, which specialised in selling commodity futures. It challenged a prohibition imposed by the Dutch minister of finance on companies that indulged in such business 'cold calling' potential clients. The court held that this prohibition, in so far as it concerned potential clients
h established in other member states, constituted a restriction on the freedom to provide services under art 59. The question then arose of whether the restriction could be justified. The test to be applied was whether 'imperative reasons of public interest' justified the prohibition on cold calling. As to this the Netherlands argued that the prohibition was justified in that it sought both to safeguard the
j reputation of the Netherlands financial markets and to protect the investing public.

[61] The court held ([1995] All ER (EC) 543 at 566, [1995] ECR I-1141 at 1179):

'43. Although the protection of consumers in the other member states is not, as such, a matter for the Netherlands authorities, the nature and extent of that protection does none the less have a direct effect on the good reputation of Netherlands financial services.

44. Maintaining the good reputation of the national financial sector may therefore constitute an imperative reason of public interest capable of justifying restrictions on the freedom to provide financial services.'

[62] The facts of the *Alpine* case are remote from those of the present case. Indeed the phenomenon of cross-border football hooliganism happily has no parallel. None the less the approach of the court in the *Alpine* case supports the conclusion that we would, in any event, have reached. That conclusion is that preventing football hooligans from taking part in violence and disorder in foreign countries is an imperative reason of public interest which is capable of justifying restrictions on their freedom of movement. Our reasons are as follows. (i) Other member states have requested this country to help in preventing our football hooligans from creating disorder at matches in their countries. This country should, as a matter of international comity, do its best to comply with such requests. (ii) Hooliganism by English and Welsh supporters abroad tarnishes the reputation of this country. (iii) Such hooliganism can lead to the banning of English and Welsh clubs from international competitions. Such a ban will have serious financial implications for the clubs that are banned and for businesses associated with professional football, quite apart from depriving law-abiding football supporters of legitimate pleasure.

The test of proportionality

[63] Mr Thompson submitted that the test of proportionality to be applied in this case was that identified by Lord Clyde in *De Freitas v Permanent Secretary of Ministry of Agriculture, Fisheries, Lands and Housing* [1999] 1 AC 69 at 80, [1998] 3 WLR 675 at 684:

'... whether: (i) the legislative objective is sufficiently important to justify limiting a fundamental right; (ii) the measures designed to meet the legislative objective are rationally connected to it; and (iii) the means used to impair the right or freedom are no more than is necessary to accomplish the objective.'

[64] That was a decision of the Privy Council, but it was cited with approval by Lord Steyn in *R v Secretary of State for the Home Dept, ex p Daly* [2001] UKHL 26 at [27], [2001] 3 All ER 433 at [27], [2001] 2 WLR 1622.

[65] We accept that Lord Clyde's test should be applied. We are in no doubt, for the reasons that we have already given, that the legislative objective is sufficiently important to justify limiting the right of freedom of movement. Mr Thompson submitted, however, that the measures that have been adopted by the legislation lack rational connection to the legislative objective. This was allied to the submission that the means used by the legislature went far beyond what was necessary to accomplish the objective. We are about to turn to consider these submissions. Before doing so, however, we should record some further submissions made by Mr Thompson as to the test to be applied.

[66] Article 3 of the 1964 directive provides:

'1. Measures taken on grounds of public policy or of public security shall be based exclusively on the personal conduct of the individual concerned.
2. Previous criminal convictions shall not in themselves constitute grounds for the taking of such measures.'

[67] The European Court has emphasised, in the context of deportation, that if a derogation from the right of establishment is to be justified, an appraisal of the

a individual who is to be deported must be carried out to make sure that the deportation is necessary in order to achieve the requirements of public policy. A criminal conviction is not, of itself, enough in the absence of a finding that the individual has a propensity to act in the same way in the future: *R v Bouchereau* [1981] 2 All ER 924n at 940, [1978] QB 732 at 759 (para 28); *Criminal proceedings against Calfa* Case C-348/96 [1999] All ER (EC) 850 at 863, [1999] ECR I-11 at 30

b (para 24). Mr Thompson argued that the same principles should be applied to the decision to prevent an individual from leaving a member state.

[68] Once again, we accept Mr Thompson's submission. It seems to us that the principles that he invokes should, in logic, apply as much to a derogation from freedom of movement as they do to the derogation from freedom of establishment. Thus, if the restrictions imposed on the appellants are to be justified: (i) they must

c have been imposed after giving individual consideration to each appellant; (ii) they cannot have been based simply upon the criminal record of each appellant; (iii) they must be rationally connected to the objective of preventing English football hooliganism abroad; (iv) they must be no more than was necessary to achieve that objective.

d
The significance of a criminal record

[69] There is no question in the case of either appellant of the banning order having been made simply on the basis that he had a criminal conviction. Under s 14B of the 1989 Act, a criminal conviction is not even a condition precedent to the making of the order. It so happened that each of the appellants had been

e convicted of offences involving violence or disorder, but it is plain that it was the involvement of each in incidents of football-related disorder that led the deputy district judge to conclude that it was necessary to make a banning order.

Individual consideration

f [70] The scheme of the 1989 Act requires consideration to be given at three different stages as to whether a restraint should be imposed on an individual leaving the country. The first is when the magistrates' court makes the banning order. Individual consideration has to be given to each person at that stage. The court has to be satisfied both that the individual has, in the past, caused or contributed to violence or disorder and that there are reasonable grounds to

g believe that making the order will help to prevent violence or disorder in connection with football matches in the future. This latter requirement also necessarily involves considering the circumstances of the individual who is to be subjected to the order.

[71] The second stage is that at which the FBOA considers whether to issue a

h notice to a person subject to a banning order imposing conditions and restrictions in relation to overseas matches. The wording of s 19(2A) indicates that individual consideration must be given to each person subject to an order. Section 19(2D) detracts from this to the extent that it permits the FBOA to impose conditions and restrictions on a class basis. As Mr Jagllall has made plain, the approach of the

j FBOA is to impose restrictions on all who are subject to banning orders during those periods when England is playing abroad. When individual clubs are playing abroad, restrictions will normally be placed on those who are subject to banning orders who support those clubs.

[72] The third stage at which restrictions are considered arises only where the individual subject to the banning order wishes to go abroad during a period during which he has been placed under restrictions. In order to do so he has to

seek an exemption under s 20(4). When he does so his case will receive individual consideration.

[73] The effect of this rather complex scheme can be summarised as follows. (i) Anyone who is subject to a banning order who would have wished to go to a prescribed match abroad is likely to be prohibited from doing so. The ground on which he will be prevented will be that, on the basis of individual consideration of his circumstances, he has been identified by the magistrates' court as a person likely to become involved in violence or disorder if permitted to go to prescribed football matches. The ban on going to the match abroad will be based on individual consideration of the person subject to the ban. (ii) Anyone who is subject to a banning order who wishes to go abroad during the period of a prescribed overseas match for a purpose other than going to, or near, the match will receive individual consideration. (iii) During the period of a prescribed overseas match, there will be a significant cohort of individuals who would not have wished to go to the match and who do not wish to go abroad for any other reason. They will be subject to the restrictions involving reporting and passport surrender. They will be subject to these restrictions on the basis that they are necessary to ensure that they do not go to the overseas game *should they wish to do so*. Once again the restrictions will be based on the individual consideration by the magistrates court which led to the conclusion that each individual was a person likely to get involved in violence or disorder should he go to or near a prescribed match.

[74] For these reasons we do not consider that the scheme of the 1989 Act is open to attack on the ground that restrictions are imposed without individual consideration of each person who is subjected to the restrictions. If the scheme is vulnerable, this must be because the restrictions that follow from the individual consideration are not rationally connected to the objective or go beyond what is necessary to achieve that objective. Mr Thompson's most vigorous submissions were directed to the contention that this was precisely the position.

Rationality and the scope of the restrictions

[75] The starting point of Mr Thompson's argument was that many who were subjected to banning orders were so subjected solely on the basis that their presence at *domestic* matches would carry the risk of involvement in violence or disorder. Their history might show that they had never been to an overseas match and they might have no wish ever to do so. To ban them from going anywhere abroad at times when prescribed matches were about to be played was irrational and went far beyond any measures that were necessary to achieve the object of preventing football hooliganism at overseas matches.

[76] There were some who were subject to a banning order who would, if not prevented, go to overseas matches and become involved in violence or disorder. There was, so Mr Thompson submitted no reason, let alone necessity, that justified preventing them from travelling *anywhere* in the world in order to be sure that they did not travel to a prescribed match. Less radical solutions were available. Under German law temporal or geographical restrictions would be placed on the validity of a passport where this would suffice to meet the aims of public policy.

[77] For the Secretary of State Mr Pannick QC informed us that such measures had been considered but that it had been concluded that they would be more draconian in effect than the scheme embodied in the 1989 Act. An endorsement on a passport of the nature suggested is likely to produce far-reaching consequences. It is liable to give a signal to the immigration authorities of any

a country that the passport holder is a potential troublemaker and thus lead to a refusal of entry and even the entry of the passport holder on a black list that will bar entry in the future.

Conclusions

b [**78**] At first blush there appears to be force in Mr Thompson's submissions. To forbid all foreign travel during the period that a prescribed match is being played abroad seems irrational and disproportionate if the person subject to the ban has never attended an overseas match and shows no inclination to do so. If a prescribed match is being played in Japan, how can it be rational or necessary to prevent someone who is subject to a banning order from travelling to France? On reflection, however, we have concluded, for the reasons that follow, that this first c blush reaction is unsound.

[**79**] The starting point is that a banning order will normally be made because the past conduct of the individual concerned gives rise to the likelihood that he will get involved in violence or disorder if he goes to certain domestic matches. We are satisfied that the evidence justifies the conclusion that if such a person d chooses to go to a prescribed overseas match, it is just as likely, if not more likely that he will get involved in violence or disorder. Superintendent Wright explained that, in the case of international matches, those who are prominent in scenes of disorder at domestic matches 'are still very prominent around any seat of disorder', but that, in addition, those who would not indulge in disorderly behaviour at home become, often fuelled by drink, 'involved in the national spirit e of disorder'. Thus there is justification for a scheme that is designed to ensure that those subject to banning orders are prevented from attending prescribed overseas matches.

[**80**] The manner in which the scheme sets out to achieve this is first to identify those overseas matches which the individual subject to the banning order might f wish to attend. Restrictions are then imposed which prevent that person from leaving the country during the periods of such matches unless he first obtains permission. In order to obtain permission he must satisfy the FBOA that the reason that he wishes to go abroad is not in order to attend the prescribed match or matches. The critical issue is whether the restrictions involved in this scheme are the minimum necessary if its object is to be achieved and, even then, whether g they are proportionate to the evil that they seek to avoid. Mr Thompson submitted that they were not, but that the 1989 Act was a classic example of 'legislative overkill'—c f *R v A* [2001] UKHL 25 at [43], [2001] 3 All ER 1 at [43], [2002] 1 AC 45 per Lord Steyn.

[**81**] Laws LJ applied a broad brush when rejecting these submissions. After a h wide-ranging review of the principle of proportionality, he concluded:

'The state was entitled to conclude that very firm measures were justified to confront the various sickening ills of football violence. The principle and the requirement which must be respected and followed have clearly been so: the progressive nature of the succeeding measures from 1986 onwards, and the j safeguards clearly established in the 1989 Act, demonstrate as much. In short the terms of s 14B(4)(b) are amply justified in light of [the 1964 directive], the *Calfa* jurisprudence, and the general law relating to proportionality.' (See [2001] 4 All ER 289 at [81], [2001] 3 WLR 1392.)

[**82**] We have found the issue less easy to resolve than did Laws LJ. The fact that previous measures had not prevented football hooliganism by English fans abroad does not demonstrate that the more radical measures introduced by the

banning order, he is likely to contribute to football violence or disorder in the
future. The past conduct may or may not consist of or include the causing or
contributing to violence or disorder that has to be proved under s 14B(4)(a), for
that violence or disorder is not required to be football related. It must, however,
be proved to the same strict standard of proof. Furthermore it must be conduct
that gives rise to the likelihood that, if the respondent is not banned from
attending prescribed football matches, he will attend such matches, or the
environs of them, and take part in violence or disorder.

[93] These matters are not readily susceptible of proof. We can well understand
the practice that is evidenced by this case of using a football intelligence service
to build up profiles of 'football prominents'. Such a practice may well be the only
way of assembling evidence sufficiently cogent to satisfy the requirements of
s 14B(4)(b). Those requirements, if properly applied in the manner described
above, will provide a satisfactory threshold for the making of a banning order.
The banning order, in its turn, will be a satisfactory basis for the conclusion that
the individual subject to it should not be permitted to go to prescribed overseas
matches.

[94] The designation by notice issued by the FBOA of the prescribed overseas
matches in respect of which restrictions will apply to the individual who is subject
to a banning order is a sensible and logical way of limiting the ambit of the
restrictions. It is not, however, of paramount significance in the scheme. It
merely identifies those periods in respect of which the individual must obtain
permission to go abroad. The manner in which applications for such permission
are treated is, however, of critical importance.

[95] We have drawn attention above to the requirement of 'special circumstances'
as a precondition to granting an applicant permission to go abroad during a
prescribed period. This is not a helpful phrase. Were it to be interpreted so that
permission was only granted in extraordinary circumstances, it would not satisfy
the Community requirement of necessity. Individuals subject to banning orders
may have reasons for going abroad during prescribed periods that are perfectly
ordinary and cannot naturally be described as 'special circumstances'. Provided
that the reason for going abroad is other than attendance at the prescribed match,
there can be no justification for refusing permission. When considering whether
there are 'special circumstances' the FBOA, or on appeal the magistrates, should
do no more than satisfy themselves on balance of probabilities that this is the true
position. This should not be something that is difficult to prove, for the bona fide
prospective traveller is like to be in a position to produce some evidence of the
proposed trip.

[96] Happily, the approach of the FBOA to 'special circumstances' applications
appears to accord with that which we have outlined as appropriate. We were
informed by those representing the Secretary of State that there have been about
80 such applications and that all of them were granted. Mr Gough himself
applied for and was granted permission to go abroad on holiday during the period
of a prescribed match. There is thus no evidence to suggest that the scheme is
operating in such a way that those who wish to go abroad for reasons other than
attendance at prescribed matches are being prevented from doing so.

[97] Mr Thompson submitted that it was not legitimate to look to the
provisions for administrative operation of the scheme by the FBOA as providing
justification for it. We do not agree. Both the 1964 directive and the 1973
directive recognise expressly that administrative action can derogate from
Community rights. The operation of the scheme has to be considered as a whole

a in order to evaluate whether it is compliant with Community law.   For the reasons that we have given we are satisfied that it is.

Article 6 of the convention
[98] Mr Thompson's contention that the statutory scheme infringed art 6 of the convention was advanced on the premise that the proceedings that led to the
b banning orders were criminal in nature and that the standard of proof was set below the civil standard of balance of probabilities. We have explained why we consider that these were false premises. The allegation that the statutory scheme is contrary to art 6 is not made out.

Article 8
c [99] Mr Thompson also submitted that art 8 of the convention was engaged. It was conceded by the Secretary of State that a banning order might result in interference with the right to respect for private or family life. Whether it did would depend upon the particular facts and it certainly did not do so in the case of Mr Gough or Mr Smith. We agree with the judge. We would add that if a
d banning order, properly made, interferes with the right to respect for private or family life, the interference is likely to prove justified under art 8(2) on the grounds that it is necessary for the prevention of disorder.

Were the orders justified on the facts?
[100] Mr Thompson submitted that neither the chief constable nor the district
e judge addressed the question of whether the banning orders would be compatible with Community law, and that this fact alone invalidated the orders. We do not agree. Both the chief constable and the district judge acted in accordance with the provisions of the 1989 Act. We have held that Act compliant with the convention. The fact that the chief constable or the district judge may not have
f addressed the question of whether they were acting in accordance with Community law is immaterial.
[101] There was more force in Mr Thompson's complaint that the judge failed to apply the appropriate standard of proof. The judge's ruling that the civil standard of proof applied coupled with the observations that we have set out in [36], above, suggest that he did not appreciate that the case for making a banning
g order had to be proved to the strict standard that we have held should be applied. This is not surprising as the only argument before him was whether the criminal or the civil standard applied and he did not have the assistance of *McCann*'s case, which had yet to be decided. In any event we are in no doubt that the 'profile' of each appellant would have justified the making of a banning order had that strict
h standard been applied.   In each case the cumulative effect of the individual observations pointed unequivocally to the appellant being one of the Derby County football 'prominents'.
[102] Mr Thompson complained that the appellants had not had the opportunity of cross-examining those who had prepared the profiles. Mr Pannick riposted that they had not sought to do so. Had they given notice that they
j wished to cross-examine, the witnesses could have been made available. We do not need to consider the accuracy of that last contention, nor are we in a position to do so. Cross-examination would have been likely to be an arid exercise. The witnesses responsible for preparing the profiles could not have been expected to retain a clear recollection of the individual events that they had recorded. The appellants gave evidence challenging some of the inferences that the chief constable suggested should be drawn from the evidence. This seems to us to

have been the sensible way to challenge the profiles. It was much more likely to
be effective than cross-examination. It placed the judge in a position to form a   *a*
reliable conclusion about whether or not the profiles were accurate. In the event
the judge was not impressed by the appellants' evidence.

[103] For the reasons that we have given, we have concluded that the banning
order was lawfully made in the case of each appellant. This appeal will be
dismissed.   *b*

Appeal dismissed. Permission to appeal refused.

Kate O'Hanlon   Barrister.

                                                                                     c

ANNEXE

Summary of the relevant legislation prepared by Laws LJ (see [2001] 4 All ER 289,
[2001] 3 WLR 1392):

'[3] ... The starting point is to be found in Pt IV of the Public Order Act 1986.
This was the first measure taken by the legislature specifically to address the   *d*
evils of hooliganism at football matches. Section 30(1) empowered a court "by
or before which a person is convicted of an offence to which s 31 applies" to
make an "exclusion order", that is an order "prohibiting him from entering
any premises for the purpose of attending any prescribed football match
there". I will not take time with the meaning of "prescribed football match":   *e*
it is enough to say that it did not include any matches played abroad.
Section 30(2) provided:

> "No exclusion order may be made unless the court is satisfied that
> making such an order in relation to the accused would help to prevent
> violence or disorder at or in connection with prescribed football   *f*
> matches."

Section 31 applied to any offence which fulfilled one or more of three
conditions set out in s 31(2)–(4). I will summarise them briefly, omitting
some of the detail. The first was that the offence was committed within a
defined period of time starting not long before and ending not long after the   *g*
match, and while the accused was at or entering or leaving the football
ground concerned. The second was (essentially) that the offence involved
violence or the threat of violence on the way to or from the match. The third
was that the offence was one committed in breach of other statutory
measures designed to control the consumption of alcohol on the way to or   *h*
from football matches. Section 32(2) provided that the duration of an
exclusion order should be not less than three months. Section 33(1) enabled
a person in relation to whom an exclusion order had been made to apply to
the court to terminate it.

[4] Next in time comes the 1989 Act, as originally enacted. Section 14(1)   *j*
provided in part: "This Part of this Act applies in relation to football matches
in any country outside England and Wales which are designated football
matches ..." Here, then, is the first statutory measure to regulate attendance
at matches abroad; and this Act, in its original form, dealt only with matches
played abroad. Section 14(4) defines a "restriction order" as "an order of a
court under ss 15 or 22 below requiring the person to whom the order

applies to report to a police station on the occasion of designated football matches". Section 15 provided in part:

"(1) A court by or before which a person is convicted of a relevant offence ... may make a restriction order in relation to him.

(2) No restriction order may be made unless the court is satisfied that making such an order in relation to the accused would help to prevent violence or disorder at or in connection with designated football matches. [Effectively the same language as that of s 30(2) of the Act of 1986.]

(3) A restriction order may only be made—(a) in addition to a sentence imposed in respect of the offence of which the accused is (or was) convicted; or (b) in addition to a probation order ...

16.—(1) ... the period for which a restriction order has effect in relation to a person convicted of a relevant offence is—(a) in a case where he was sentenced in respect of that offence to a period of imprisonment taking immediate effect, five years, and (b) in any other case, two years, beginning with the date of the making of the order."

A failure without reasonable excuse to comply with the duty to report to a police station imposed by a restriction order is made a summary criminal offence (s 16(4) and (5)). Section 17 allows a person "in relation to whom a restriction order has had effect for at least one year" to apply to the court to terminate it. "Relevant offence" is defined in great detail in Sch 1. I may deal with it very broadly: it covers a whole series of statutory offences involving violence or the threat of violence, or drunkenness at, near, or on the way to or from a designated football match. Section 22 made provision for offences under the law of countries outside England and Wales to be treated as if they were Sch 1 offences ...

[5] Here, then, were two statutory regimes, respectively constituted by the 1986 and 1989 Acts, made by Parliament to respond to what was plainly an increasing barbarism. The later Act recognised the particular evil of violence and drunkenness by British fans abroad.

[6] The Football (Offences and Disorder) Act 1999 amended both the 1986 Act and the 1989 Act. The 1986 Act was amended by ss 6–8. A "domestic football banning order" was substituted for an exclusion order. A new s 30(2) was enacted as follows:

"Subject to subsection (4), it shall be the duty of the court to make a domestic football banning order in relation to the accused if it is satisfied that there are reasonable grounds to believe that making the order would help to prevent violence or disorder at or in connection with prescribed football matches."

Section 30(4) as substituted provided:

"A domestic football banning order may only be made—(a) in addition to a sentence imposed in respect of the offence of which the accused is (or was) convicted; or (b) in addition to an order discharging him absolutely or conditionally."

Section 32(2) as substituted provided that the duration of a domestic football banning order should be not less than one year and not more than three years.

[7] The 1989 Act was amended so that the following substitute provisions were made in s 15:

a

"(1) Subject to subsection (3) below—(a) a court by or before which a person is convicted of a relevant offence, or (b) [the Crown Court where the person has been committed there] shall have the power to make an international football banning order in relation to him.

b

(2) Subject to subsection (3) below, it shall be the duty of the court to make an international football banning order in relation to the accused if it is satisfied that there are reasonable grounds to believe that making the order would help to prevent violence or disorder at or in connection with designated football matches." [Effectively the same language as is used in the new s 30(2) of the 1986 Act.]

c

The new s 15(3) replicates precisely the new s 30(4) of the 1986 Act.

[8] Now I may come to the 1989 Act (that is, the 1989 Act as amended by the Football (Disorder) Act 2000). It will be clearest if I set out the relevant provisions in full, though there is some replication of what has gone before ...

[10] ... the relevant provisions in the body of the statute are as follows.

d

"**14** ... (2) 'Regulated football match' means an association football match (whether in England and Wales or elsewhere) which is a prescribed match or a match of a prescribed description.

(3) 'External tournament' means a football competition which includes regulated football matches outside England and Wales.

e

(4) 'Banning order' means an order made by the court under this Part which—(a) in relation to regulated football matches in England and Wales, prohibits the person who is subject to the order from entering any premises for the purpose of attending such matches, and (b) in relation to regulated football matches outside England and Wales, requires that person to report at a police station in accordance with this Part.

f

(5) 'Control period', in relation to a regulated football match outside England and Wales, means the period—(a) beginning five days before the day of the match, and (b) ending when the match is finished or cancelled.

(6) 'Control period', in relation to an external tournament, means any period described in an order made by the Secretary of State—(a) beginning five days before the day of the first football match outside England and Wales which is included in the tournament, and (b) ending when the last football match outside England and Wales which is included in the tournament is finished or cancelled, but, for the purposes of paragraph (a), any football match included in the qualifying or pre-qualifying stages of the tournament is to be left out of account ...

g

h

(8) 'Relevant offence' means an offence to which Schedule 1 to this Act applies.

14A.—(1) This section applies where a person (the 'offender') is convicted of a relevant offence.

j

(2) If the court is satisfied that there are reasonable grounds to believe that making a banning order would help to prevent violence or disorder at or in connection with any regulated football matches, it must make such an order in respect of the offender.

(3) If the court is not so satisfied, it must in open court state that fact and give its reasons.

(4) A banning order may only be made under this section—(a) in addition to a sentence imposed in respect of the relevant offence, or (b) in addition to an order discharging him conditionally ...

(6) In this section, 'the court' in relation to an offender means—(a) the court by or before which he is convicted of the relevant offence, or (b) if he is committed to the Crown Court to be dealt with for that offence, the Crown Court.

14B.—(1) An application for a banning order in respect of any person may be made by the chief officer of police for the area in which the person resides or appears to reside, if it appears to the officer that the condition in subsection (2) below is met.

(2) That condition is that the respondent has at any time caused or contributed to any violence or disorder in the United Kingdom or elsewhere.

(3) The application is to be made by complaint to a magistrates' court.

(4) If—(a) it is proved on the application that the condition in subsection (2) above is met, and (b) the court is satisfied that there are reasonable grounds to believe that making a banning order would help to prevent violence or disorder at or in connection with any regulated football matches, the court must make a banning order in respect of the respondent.

14C.—(1) In this Part, 'violence' means violence against persons or property and includes threatening violence and doing anything which endangers the life of any person.

(2) In this Part, 'disorder' includes—(a) stirring up hatred against a group of persons defined by reference to colour, race, nationality (including citizenship) or ethnic or national origins, or against an individual as a member of such a group, (b) using threatening, abusive or insulting words or behaviour or disorderly behaviour, (c) displaying any writing or other thing which is threatening, abusive or insulting.

(3) In this Part, 'violence' and 'disorder' are not limited to violence or disorder in connection with football.

(4) The magistrates' court may take into account the following matters (among others), so far as they consider it appropriate to do so, in determining whether to make an order under section 14B above—(a) any decision of a court or tribunal outside the United Kingdom, (b) deportation or exclusion from a country outside the United Kingdom, (c) removal or exclusion from premises used for playing football matches, whether in the United Kingdom or elsewhere, (d) conduct recorded on video or by any other means.

(5) In determining whether to make such an order—(a) the magistrates' court may not take into account anything done by the respondent before the beginning of the period of ten years ending with the application under section 14B(1) above, except circumstances ancillary to a conviction ...

14D.—(1) An appeal lies to the Crown Court against the making by a magistrates' court of a banning order under section 14B above ...

14E.—(1) On making a banning order, a court must in ordinary language explain its effect to the person subject to the order.

(2) A banning order must require the person subject to the order to report initially at a police station in England and Wales specified in the order within the period of five days beginning with the day on which the order is made.

section 19 above ... and it shall be the duty of the enforcing authority to comply with the regulations.

　　21A.—(1) This section and section 21B below apply during any control period in relation to a regulated football match outside England and Wales or an external tournament if a constable in uniform—(a) has reasonable grounds for suspecting that the condition in section 14B(2) above is met in the case of a person present before him, and (b) has reasonable grounds to believe that making a banning order in his case would help to prevent violence or disorder at or in connection with any regulated football matches.

　　(2) The constable may detain the person in his custody (whether there or elsewhere) until he has decided whether or not to issue a notice under section 21B below, and shall give the person his reasons for detaining him in writing ...

　　21B.—(1) A constable in uniform may exercise the power in subsection (2) below if authorised to do so by an officer of at least the rank of inspector.

　　(2) The constable may give the person a notice in writing requiring him—(a) to appear before a magistrates' court at a time, or between the times, specified in the notice, (b) not to leave England and Wales before that time (or the later of those times), and (c) if the control period relates to a regulated football match outside the United Kingdom or to an external tournament which includes such matches, to surrender his passport to the constable, and stating the grounds referred to in section 21A(1) above ...

　　(4) For the purposes of section 14B above, the notice is to be treated as an application for a banning order made by complaint by the constable to the court in question and subsection (1) of that section is to have effect as if the references to the chief officer of police for the area in which the person resides or appears to reside were references to that constable.

　　21C.—(1) The powers conferred by sections 21A and 21B above may only be exercised in relation to a person who is a British citizen.

　　(2) A person who fails to comply with a notice given to him under section 21B above is guilty of an offence ...

　　21D.—(1) Where a person to whom a notice has been given under section 21B above appears before a magistrates' court and the court refuses the application for a banning order in respect of him, it may order compensation to be paid to him out of central funds if it is satisfied—(a) that the notice should not have been given, (b) that he has suffered loss as a result of the giving of the notice, and (c) that, having regard to all the circumstances, it is appropriate to order the payment of compensation in respect of that loss.

　　(2) An appeal lies to the Crown Court against any refusal by a magistrates' court to order the payment of compensation under subsection (1) above.

　　(3) The compensation to be paid by order of the magistrates' court under subsection (1) above or by order of the Crown Court on an appeal under subsection (2) above shall not exceed £5,000 (but no appeal may be made under subsection (2) in respect of the amount of compensation awarded)."

Schedule 1 ("relevant offences") lists a large number of statutory offences. I do not think it necessary to set them all out. They replicate and update the list contained in Sch 1 to the 1989 Act in its original form.'

a

O'Connor and others v Old Etonian Housing Association Ltd

[2002] EWCA Civ 150

b

COURT OF APPEAL, CIVIL DIVISION

LORD PHILLIPS OF WORTH MATRAVERS MR, WALLER AND BUXTON LJJ

22 JANUARY, 20 FEBRUARY 2002

c

Landlord and tenant – Covenant – Proper working order – Installation for supply of gas, water and electricity – Covenant to keep in proper working order installation for supply of gas, water and electricity – Test of proper working order – Landlord and Tenant Act 1985, s 11(1)(b).

The respondents were the tenants of four flats on the top floor of a block. Their tenancy agreements contained a covenant by the appellant landlord which was in

d the same terms as the covenant implied into certain leases by s 11(1)(b)ᵃ of the Landlord and Tenant Act 1985. Under that provision, a lessor was obliged, inter alia, to keep in 'proper working order' the installations in the dwelling house for the supply of water, gas and electricity. On the determination of preliminary issues in proceedings between the parties, the county court judge held, on the basis of assumed facts, that there had been no breach of the landlord's obligation

e to keep water pipes in proper working order. His decision was reversed on appeal by a High Court judge, again on the basis of the assumed facts. On the landlord's second-tier appeal, the Court of Appeal considered (i) whether the requirement to keep an installation for the supply of water, gas or electricity in 'proper working order' required the landlord to ensure that the installation was so designed and constructed as to be capable of performing its function at the

f commencement of the tenancy; (ii) the extent to which the installation had to be designed and constructed in a manner that would cater for variations in the quantity or character of the water, gas or electricity supplied; and (iii) if, because of some unanticipated change in the quantity or character of the supply, the installation was no longer capable of performing its function, whether the

g landlord was obliged to adapt the installation in order to accommodate the change.

Held – (1) The requirement to keep an installation for the supply of water, gas or electricity in 'proper working order' required the landlord to ensure that the

h installation was so designed and constructed as to be capable of performing its function at the commencement of the tenancy. An installation could not be said to be in proper working order if, by reason of a defect in construction or design, it was incapable of working properly (see [15], [16], below).

(2) Installations for the supply of gas, water and electricity would be in proper

j working order if they were able to function under those conditions of supply that it was reasonable to anticipate would prevail. In relation to installations for the supply of water, statutory obligations on water undertakers as to the minimum pressure at which water had to be supplied, and statutory provisions under which byelaws could be made imposing obligations on property owners as to the design

---

a   Section 11, so far as material, is set out at [7], below

of installations which were to make use of the water supplied, might be relevant. Thus the answer to the second issue was likely to depend on the extent to which supply variations should reasonably be anticipated and provided for, and that would depend upon the particular facts (see [28], [29], below).

(3) An unanticipated change in the nature of the supply of a utility might occur in a variety of circumstances. If the change were imposed deliberately because of some technical or scientific advance, it was likely to be introduced in a manner and subject to conditions under which it was reasonable to expect customers to modify their installations in order to accommodate the change. In such circumstances, business efficacy would suggest that the landlord's duty to keep installations in proper working order had to involve the obligation to make the modifications necessary to enable the installations in question to continue to function. In other circumstances, the change might be forced on the undertaker by some unforeseen event, and if the change were likely to be short-lived, the cost of modifying installations in order to accommodate it might be disproportionate. Where the changed circumstances were likely to persist for a long period, it might seem wholly unreasonable for a landlord to leave his tenants deprived of a satisfactory supply for want of relatively modest expenditure on modifications. How the test of proper working order was to be applied in such circumstances was a question of great difficulty. In the instant case, the assumed facts did not enable the issues to be answered. The appeal would be allowed because the High Court judge could not have reached the answer he had on the assumed facts, but the same was also true of the decision reached by the county court judge (see [30]–[32], [34], below).

Notes

For the landlord's covenant to keep in proper working order the installations in the dwelling house for the supply of water, gas and electricity, see 27(1) *Halsbury's Laws* (4th edn reissue) para 331.

For the Landlord and Tenant Act 1985, s 11, see 23 *Halsbury's Statutes* (4th edn) (1997 reissue) 355.

Cases referred to in judgment

Campden Hill Towers Ltd v Gardner [1977] 1 All ER 739, [1977] QB 823, [1977] 2 WLR 159, CA.

Lee v Leeds CC, Ratcliffe v Sandwell MBC [2002] EWCA Civ 06, [2002] HLR 17, CA.

Liverpool City Council v Irwin [1976] 2 All ER 39, [1977] AC 239, [1976] 2 WLR 562, HL.

Post Office v Aquarius Properties Ltd [1987] 1 All ER 1055, CA.

Proudfoot v Hart (1890) 25 QB 42, [1886–90] All ER Rep 782, CA.

Quick v Taff-Ely BC [1985] 3 All ER 321, [1986] QB 809, [1985] 3 WLR 981, CA.

Smith v A Davies & Co (Shopfitters) Ltd (1968) 5 KIR 320.

Southwark LBC v Mills, Baxter v Camden LBC [1999] 4 All ER 449, [2001] 1 AC 1, [1999] 3 WLR 939, HL.

Wycombe Health Authority v Barnett (1982) 47 P&CR 394, CA.

Cases also cited or referred to in skeleton arguments

Bank of Credit and Commerce International SA v Ali (No 4) (1999) NLJ 1734.

Scholes Windows Ltd v Magnet Ltd (No 2) [2000] ECDR 266.

Stovin v Wise (Norfolk CC, third party) [1996] 3 All ER 801, [1996] AC 923, [1996] 3 WLR 388, HL.

a

Appeal

Old Etonian Housing Association Ltd, the landlord of a block of flats known as Eton House, Leigh Road, London, N5 1SR, appealed with permission of Arden LJ granted on 28 June 2001 from the decision of Blackburne J on 9 February 2001 ([2001] All ER (D) 118 (Feb)) allowing an appeal by the respondent tenants from the decision of Judge Marr-Johnson in the Mayor's and City of London Court on

b

22 August 2000 whereby, on the basis of assumed facts on the determination of preliminary issues, he held that the landlord had not breached its obligation to keep water pipes in the block in proper working order. The facts are set out in the judgment of the court.

c

Ranjit Bhose (instructed by *Prince Evans*) for landlord.
Paul Staddon (instructed by *Wilson Howard*) for the tenants.

Cur adv vult

20 February 2002. The following judgment of the court was delivered.

d

LORD PHILLIPS OF WORTH MATRAVERS MR.

Introduction

e

[1] This appeal raises a point on the construction of s 11(1)(b) of the Landlord and Tenant Act 1985. It raises a similar point on the construction of cl 2(5) of certain tenancy agreements. The question to which the parties would like an answer is what is involved in the obligation to keep pipes carrying water in 'proper working order'. The tenancies with which this appeal is concerned are of four flats on the top floor of Eton House in Leigh Road, north London. The tenancies commenced on various dates between September 1991 and June 1994.

f

The facts as assumed by the judge are appended hereto. The key points assumed are (i) prior to any of the tenancies commencing in 1986/1987 the landlords refurbished Eton House and replaced the water pipework with pipework of a smaller bore; (ii) those smaller pipes carried water successfully to the top floors of the relevant premises for some years; (iii) from the summer of 1992 onwards the smaller pipes did not do so, the water pressure having fallen; (iv) the previous

g

pipes would have carried water to the third floor successfully during that period; (v) the landlord could have installed a pump to make the smaller pipes carry the water to the third floor; (vi) from 1998, once the water authority had constructed a new pumping station, the water was carried successfully to the third floor flats by the smaller pipes.

h

[2] On 22 August 2000 Judge Marr-Johnson in the Mayor's and City of London Court held, on the facts as assumed, that there was no breach of the obligation to keep pipes in proper working order. His reasoning in essence was that since the smaller pipes worked perfectly successfully for a period of years, and since nothing had altered except the water pressure, there was no failure to keep in proper working order.

j

[3] On appeal to Blackburne J, however, by a judgment dated 9 February 2001 ([2001] All ER (D) 118), the judge, again on the assumed facts, allowed the appeal. He held that the obligation to keep in proper working order was an obligation 'to ensure that the [pipes were] physically or ... mechanically capable of supplying water to the flats' and he held that on the assumed facts the landlord could have so ensured but did not.

[4] This is thus a second-tier appeal brought with leave of Arden LJ. She gave leave on the grounds that there was a real prospect of success on the issue of statutory construction whether a breach of the obligation imposed by s 11(1)(b) of the 1985 Act can arise where an installation is in mechanical order but fails to carry out its function due to some matter for which responsibility cannot be attributed to the landlord. She also identified a point of principle—an opportunity for the court to consider its decision in *Campden Hill Towers Ltd v Gardner* [1977] 1 All ER 739, [1977] QB 823 in relation to what was held by the House of Lords in *Liverpool City Council v Irwin* [1976] 2 All ER 39, [1977] AC 239.

[5] Although there is no doubt that the question of statutory construction and the point of principle do arise in the litigation between the tenants and the landlord, the method chosen for deciding the points has not proved satisfactory for two reasons.

[6] In the first place the assumed facts were agreed for the purpose only of the determination of preliminary issues. Thus, although Blackburne J ruled in favour of the tenants on the agreed facts, this did not rule out the need for a trial in order to determine what the facts actually were. This was not a satisfactory result. More fundamentally, however, we have concluded that, even if the facts are proved as agreed, they will not be adequate to found a decision on liability. In explaining why this is so we shall, however, cast some light on the important issue of construction that arises in this case.

The issues ordered to be tried

[7] Section 11(1)(b) of the 1985 Act provides as follows:

'(1) In a lease to which this section applies ... there is implied a covenant by the lessor ... (b) to keep in repair and proper working order the installations in the dwelling-house for the supply of water, gas and electricity and for sanitation (including basins, sinks, baths and sanitary conveniences, but not other fixtures, fittings and appliances for making use of the supply of water, gas or electricity) ...'

[8] It is unnecessary to set out cl 2(5) of each tenancy agreement. It is sufficient to say that the language is the same as that of the statute, in that it obliges the landlord to 'keep in repair and proper working order any installations'.

[9] Issues were ordered to be tried in relation to the construction of both s 11(1)(b) and cl 2(5) but it is only necessary to set out one such issue, the language of both being the same. The issue ordered by the district judge was as follows:

'Whether, on the proper construction of s 11(1)(b) of the Landlord and Tenant Act 1985, and on the assumption, for current purposes only, that the supply of water to the premises referred to in the particulars of claim was intermittent and inadequate, the defendant can be liable in law for breach of the implied covenant by reason only of the fact that the pipes supplying the water to the premises are of one-inch diameter as opposed to one-and-a-quarter-inch diameter and/or that no booster pump was installed at Eton House.'

A re-formulation of the issues

[10] The issue as formulated does not adequately accommodate the peculiar features of a case such as this. It seems to us that three issues can be identified, although these issues overlap to a considerable extent: (i) Does the requirement

a to keep an installation for the supply of water, gas or electricity 'in proper working order' require the landlord to ensure that the installation is so designed and constructed as to be capable of performing its function at the commencement of the tenancy? (ii) To what extent must the installation be designed and constructed in a manner that will cater for variations in the quantity or character of the water, gas or electricity supplied? (iii) If, because of some change in the
b quantity or character of the supply, the installation is no longer capable of performing its function, is the landlord obliged to adapt the installation in order to accommodate the change?

The first issue

c [11] For the tenants, Mr Staddon argued that the landlord's duty at the commencement of the tenancy was to provide installations for the supply of water, gas and electricity that were capable of performing their function of conveying the water, gas and electricity received from the undertaker to the appliances which used them in each tenant's flat. In so submitting, he relied principally upon the decision of the House of Lords in *Liverpool City Council v*
d *Irwin* [1976] 2 All ER 39, [1977] AC 239, which dealt with the predecessor to s 11 (s 32 of the Housing Act 1961). The relevant issue was whether lavatory cisterns, which, because of a design defect were liable to overflow, constituted a breach of the landlord's duty to keep the installations in proper working order. As to this, Lord Edmund-Davies commented:

e   'It is clear that s 32(1)(b) of the Housing Act 1961 imposes an *absolute* duty on the landlord "to keep in repair and proper working order the installations in the dwelling-house ..." It could be said that the opening words ("to keep ...") apparently limit the landlord's obligation to preserving the *existing* plant in its original state and create no obligation to improve plant which was, by its
f   very design, at all times defective and inefficient. But the phrase has to be read as a whole and, as I think, it presupposes that at the inception of the letting the installation was "in proper working order", and that if its design was such that it did not work "properly" the landlord is in breach. Bathroom equipment which floods when it ought merely to flush is clearly not in "working order", leave alone "proper" working order (if, indeed, the adjective
g   adds anything). To say that such whimsical behaviour is attributable solely to faulty design is to advance an explanation that affords no excuse for the clear failure "to keep ... in proper working order". Just as badly designed apparatus has been held not of "good construction" (*Smith v A Davies & Co (Shopfitters) Ltd* per Cooke J ((1968) 5 KIR 320 at 327)), so in my judgment the
h   corporation here was in breach of s 32(1)(b) by supplying bathroom equipment which, due to bad design, throughout behaved as badly as did the appellants' cistern. I do not, however, find established any of the other statutory breaches alleged.' (See [1976] 2 All ER 39 at 56–57, [1977] AC 239 at 269–270.)

j [12] Implicit in this passage are two principles which bear on the first issue. First, something which is not working because it is badly designed is not 'in proper working order'. Second, if there is an obligation to 'keep' in 'proper working order' there must by inference be an obligation to supply at the commencement of the tenancy the installation in proper working order. It is implicit in the speeches of Lord Cross of Chelsea, Lord Salmon and Lord Fraser of Tullybelton ([1976] 2 All ER 39 at 46, 52, 57, [1977] AC 239 at 257, 264, 270 *a* respectively) that they agreed with Lord Edmund-Davies.

[13] Mr Staddon suggested that the approach of Lord Edmund-Davies was supported by a dictum of Lord Esher MR in *Proudfoot v Hart* (1890) 25 QB 42 at 50, [1886–90] All ER Rep 782 at 784 where Lord Esher said:

> 'But it has been decided—and, I think, rightly decided—that, where the *b* premises are not in repair when the tenant takes them, he must put them into repair in order to discharge his obligation under a contract to keep and deliver them up in repair. If the premises are out of repair at any time during the tenancy the landlord is entitled to say to the tenant, "you have now broken your contract to keep them in repair;" ...'

[14] *Proudfoot's* case involved consideration of a tenant's duty to 'keep and *c* deliver up the premises in good tenantable repair'. For the landlord, Mr Bhose referred us to a number of authorities which establish that the obligation to keep in repair, whether it falls on the landlord or the tenant, does not of itself require the obligee to remedy defects of design or construction, even if their consequence is that the premises are not reasonably habitable. The duty is to prevent the *d* physical condition of the ill-designed premises from deterioration (see *Quick v Taff-Ely BC* [1985] 3 All ER 321, [1986] QB 809; *Post Office v Aquarius Properties Ltd* [1987] 1 All ER 1055; *Southwark LBC v Mills, Baxter v Camden LBC* [1999] 4 All ER 449, [2001] 1 AC 1; *Lee v Leeds CC, Ratcliffe v Sandwell MBC* [2002] EWCA Civ 06, [2002] HLR 17).

[15] We do not consider that these cases are in point. There is an obvious *e* distinction between the duty to keep 'in repair' and the duty to keep 'in proper working order'. We are concerned with the latter duty. An installation cannot be said to be in proper working order if, by reason of a defect in construction or design, it is incapable of working properly.

[16] Accordingly we have no difficulty in resolving the first issue. At the *f* commencement of the tenancy the installations for the supply of water, gas and electricity must be so designed and constructed as to be capable of performing their functions. The assumed facts of this case demonstrate, however, that the question of whether installations for the supply of water, gas or electricity are capable of performing their function can raise a difficult question as to how this is to be judged. This brings us to the second issue. *g*

The second issue

[17] The function of water pipes within a building is to convey within the building the water that is supplied to the building. The assumed facts demonstrate that whether the pipes with which this action is concerned will perform this *h* function to all parts of the building depends upon the pressure under which the statutory undertaker supplies the water to the building. To what extent must the pipes supplied by the landlord be designed and constructed in a manner which will ensure that they perform their function, despite variations in water pressure?

[18] Mr Bhose submitted that if, at the time of installation, the pipes conveyed *j* water to all parts of the building, this demonstrated that they were in proper working order. If at a later date they ceased to do so because of a drop in water pressure, this did not and could not mean that they had ceased to be in proper working order. The fact that they were no longer working properly was attributable, not to any shortcoming in the pipes, but to a shortcoming in the supply, for which the landlord was not responsible.

a

[19] In support of this submission, Mr Bhose relied upon a passage in the judgment of Megaw LJ in *Campden Hill Towers Ltd v Gardner* [1977] 1 All ER 739, [1977] QB 823, dealing with the proper construction of s 32(1)(b) of the 1961 Act. That, as we have said, was the predecessor of s 11 of the 1985 Act with which this case is concerned. But it should be emphasised that the main point in the case related to the physical area in which the installations had to be situated, if they

b

were to be covered by the landlord's obligations. The *Campden Hill* case decided that on the proper construction of s 32(1) the installations had to be 'in' the dwelling house and it was to reverse that decision that sub-ss (1A) and (1B) of s 11 were inserted into s 11 of the 1985 Act by the Housing Act 1988. In that context Megaw LJ by reference to s 32(1) said:

c

'The lessees contend that, despite the words of the paragraph "installations *in* the dwelling-house", [in para (b) of s 32(1)] the paragraph applies to anything outside the flat, the proper functioning of which is required in order to enable the installation within the flat to function as it is intended to do. If it were not for the words "proper working order" in para (b), it would, we

d

think, be difficult to find any support for the lessees' contention. But the inclusion of those words does provide some possible support. It would, however, produce very odd results if that were so. First, there is nothing in s 32 which requires a lessor to provide such installations. Any such obligation would have to be derived from either non-statutory terms of the lease itself, which would be a matter of contractual negotiation, or from

e

some other statute. Secondly, if "proper working order" did include, for example, the necessity of a supply of hot water to a radiator, or water to a cistern there would be imposed by statute an absolute obligation, with no qualifications, which in some respects would be quite outside the lessors' control. For example, the central heating boiler in the basement may be

f

operated by gas. The gas supply is cut off by the Gas Board for some reason outside the control of the lessors; or the water supply is cut off, or limited to certain times of the day, by the water authority. The hot water radiator, or the water cistern, while in perfectly good repair and perfectly good "working order", cannot perform their function. If the covenant has the meaning suggested by the lessees, the lessors are liable for breach of the implied

g

covenant. In our judgment, the meaning of para (b) is as is contended for by the lessors. The installations in the physical confines of the flat must be kept in repair and capable, so far as their own structural and mechanical condition is concerned, of working properly. But no more than that. The lessors may be under additional obligations but, if so, they do not arise from this statute.'

h

(See [1977] 1 All ER 739 at 745–746, [1977] QB 823 at 835.)

[20] Mr Bhose sought, as we understood him, to draw from the above proposition that whether an installation conveying water, gas or electricity is in good working order falls to be determined without reference to the particular

j

characteristics of the supply, at least if it worked properly having regard to the prevailing characteristics at the time that it was installed.

[21] We do not consider that this proposition can be drawn from the *Campden Hill* case. The examples given by Megaw LJ were of temporary and untoward interruptions to the normal supply. Plainly installations deprived of supply in such circumstances could not be said to be out of proper working order. Those examples afford no assistance in answering the question of the extent to which

installations must be able to accommodate alterations in the characteristics of the supply.

[22] Mr Staddon submitted that the duty to keep the pipes 'in proper working order' required the landlord to provide pipes that could perform their function of conveying water to the individual tenants' flats at the pressure at which the undertaker supplied the water from time to time. In support of this submission he referred us to a passage in the judgment of May LJ in *Wycombe Health Authority v Barnett* (1982) 47 P&CR 394 at 401:

'I do not think that a water installation in a cottage ceases to be in proper working order within the statutory provision just because the water in one of the pipes freezes ... In my opinion the phrase "proper working order" in its context relates to the physical or mechanical condition of the installation as such and involves that it shall be capable of working properly as an installation.'

[23] Here again we do not think that the passage affords any assistance in answering the second issue. The requirement that the pipes should be 'capable of working properly as an installation' merely begs the question.

[24] We have concluded that there is no authority which bears on the second issue. This may explain why the two judges who have so far considered this case came to firm conclusions which were diametrically opposed. In accepting Mr Rundell's submissions (who then appeared for the landlord), Judge Marr-Johnson held:

'In my judgment, the proper analysis in this case is that the physical condition of the installation was such that it was perfectly capable of working properly as an installation, provided only that water was supplied by the statutory undertaker at a sufficient pressure. I conclude, therefore, that on the agreed facts the claimants are unable to show that these defendants have at any time failed to keep in proper working order the installations for the supply of water at the affected premises, either within the meaning of s 11(1)(b) of the 1985 Act, or pursuant to the express terms of the tenancy agreement applicable in each case.'

[25] In reversing this decision, and preferring the argument of Mr Staddon, Blackburne J held:

'Putting the matter in my own words, the landlord's obligation under s 11, in so far as it relates to keeping in proper working order the installation for the supply of water, is to ensure that the installations in each flat, and also in the remainder of Eton House so far as they serve directly or indirectly the flats in question, are physically or, if one likes, mechanically capable of supplying water to the flats. That does not merely mean that they should be so capable, given certain minimum water pressures; nor does it mean that the obligation is absolute and unqualified such that the landlord will be in breach even if there is an interruption in water supply for which the landlord is not responsible. It merely means, in my judgment, in so far as there is a supply of water to Eton House, that the installations in the building for the supply of water to each flat must be physically capable of ensuring that a supply of water is maintained.'

[26] We have concluded that there is no easy test which answers the second issue. The characteristics of the supply of water, gas and electricity are all capable of

a varying, whether by accident or design. An obligation which required the landlord to provide installations which would function regardless of the vagaries of supply would be manifestly unreasonable. Equally unreasonable would be an obligation which enabled the landlord to supply installations which would accommodate no changes in the character of supply after the date of installation, even though some variations were reasonably to be anticipated.

b [27] Our conclusion is that, in so far as installations for the supply of water, gas and electricity are concerned an installation will be in proper working order if it is able to function under those conditions of supply that it is reasonable to anticipate will prevail. While the test as formulated may appear to involve uncertainty, we suspect that if the evidence relevant to the test is considered, it may be easier to apply in practice.

c [28] In so far as installations for the supply of water are concerned, we raised before the hearing the possibility that statutory obligations on water undertakers as to the minimum pressure at which water must be supplied might have some bearing on the issue in this case. There are indeed such obligations, but counsel did not find them easy to assemble or to digest. There are also statutory

d provisions under which byelaws can be made imposing obligations on property owners as to the design of installations which are to make use of the water supplied. These also might be of relevance.

[29] Thus it seems to us that the answer to the second issue is likely to depend upon the extent to which supply variations should reasonably be anticipated and

e provided for. This will depend upon the particular facts. We turn to the third issue.

The third issue

[30] If, after a tenancy has commenced, a variation occurs to the supply which

f could not reasonably have been anticipated but which requires some alteration to the installation if the installation is to continue to function properly, is the landlord obliged to make that change or modification? Here again we do not think that it is possible to give a categoric answer. An unanticipated change in the nature of the supply of a utility may occur in a variety of circumstances. Sometimes the change is imposed deliberately because of some scientific or

g technical advance—a change in the voltage of electrical supply, or the change from coal gas to natural gas are examples. In such circumstances the change is likely to be introduced in a manner and subject to conditions under which it is reasonable to expect customers to modify their installations in order to accommodate the change. In such circumstances, business efficacy would

h suggest that the landlord's duty to keep installations in proper working order must involve the obligation to make the modifications necessary to enable the installations in question to continue to function.

[31] In other circumstances the change may be forced on the undertaker by some unforeseen event—the collapse of a reservoir or a drought, resulting in a

j drop in water pressure. If the change is likely to be short-lived, the cost of modifying installations in order to accommodate it may be disproportionate. Where the changed circumstances are likely to persist for a lengthy period, it may seem wholly unreasonable for a landlord to leave his tenants deprived of satisfactory supply for want of relatively modest expenditure on modifications.

[32] How the test of proper working order is to be applied in such circumstances is a question of great difficulty. We have in this judgment sought

to illuminate the issues and to explain why it is that we do not believe that the
assumed facts enable them to be answered.

[33] A case such as this cries out for compromise—the more so because the
attempt to resolve the issue on the basis of assumed facts has failed.   If
compromise cannot be reached, then the difficult issues raised must be resolved
in the light of findings, or binding agreement, of the material facts,

[34] The appeal must be allowed, because Blackburne J could not have
reached the answer that he did on the assumed facts. But the same is true of the
decision reached by Judge Marr-Johnson. We shall hear counsel as to the
appropriate order if this cannot be agreed.

Appeal allowed.

Kate O'Hanlon   Barrister.

APPENDIX

'Drinking water is supplied to Eton House by the statutory undertaker and
thence into the pipework in the common parts provided by the defendant [that
is the landlord] which pipework is described in the statement of facts as the
communal pipework. Water is then carried through the common parts in the
communal pipework and into individual flats. The communal pipework was
replaced by the defendant in 1986/1987 and one-inch pipes were installed in
place of pipes with a wider bore. No works of repair or improvement or
alteration have been done to the communal pipework since then. Prior to the
replacement, the existing wider pipes had provided an adequate supply of
water to the flats and had no serious defects. From the summer of 1992
onwards and on intermittent but regular and lengthy occasions, there has been
an inadequate supply of water to the pipes in the individual flats. At all material
times the communal pipework has been in repair in the sense of not having
deteriorated from any earlier state. It has, however, not been in repair in the
sense of carrying out its function of supplying an adequate water supply. (The
use of "repair" in this paragraph is descriptive only and no legal significance is
intended to be attached to its use.) If the communal pipework had been of
one-and-a-quarter-inch bore rather than one-inch bore, at all material times the
pipes in the individual flats would have received an adequate supply of water.
Further, if, on notice of the problem, the defendant had installed a booster
pump and break tanks at the block, an adequate supply would have been
achieved. The inadequate supply of water to the pipes in the individual flats
was caused by the fact of demand in the surrounding areas for water
increasing, having a negative effect on the water pressure at which the
statutory undertaker supplied water into the communal pipework. This state
of affairs ceased once a new pumping station at Maiden Lane Reservoir was
built and in service in about 1998. The provision of one-and-a-quarter-inch
pipes and/or a booster pump and break tanks would have effected an adequate
supply from 1992 to 1998. Since about 1998 none of the claimants [the tenants]
have suffered any inadequate water supply on any occasion to any of their
individual flats. Provision of a booster pump and break tanks would have cost
in the region of £8,750 plus value added tax.'